KT-199-483

REFERENCE
ONLY

THE UNIVERSITY OF LAW
Manchester
Library

HALSBURY'S
Laws of England

FIFTH EDITION
2016

Volume 14

This is volume 14 of the Fifth Edition of Halsbury's Laws of England, containing the first part of the title COMPANIES.

The title COMPANIES replaces the COMPANIES title contained in volumes 14 (2009) and 15 (2009). Volumes 14 (2009) and 15 (2009) may now be archived.

For a full list of volumes comprised in a current set of Halsbury's Laws of England please see overleaf.

Fifth Edition volumes:

1 (2008), 2 (2008), 3 (2011), 4 (2011), 5 (2013), 6 (2011), 7 (2015), 8 (2015), 9 (2012), 10 (2012), 11 (2015), 12 (2015), 12A (2015), 13 (2009), 14 (2016), 15 (2016), 15A (2016), 16 (2011), 17 (2011), 18 (2009), 19 (2011), 20 (2014), 21 (2016), 22 (2012), 23 (2013), 24 (2010), 25 (2016), 26 (2016), 27 (2015), 28 (2015), 29 (2014), 30 (2012), 31 (2012), 32 (2012), 33 (2013), 34 (2011), 35 (2015), 36 (2015), 37 (2013), 38 (2013), 38A (2013), 39 (2014), 40 (2014), 41 (2014), 41A (2014), 42 (2011), 43 (2011), 44 (2011), 45 (2010), 46 (2010), 47 (2014), 47A (2014), 48 (2015), 49 (2015), 50 (2016), 50A (2016), 51 (2013), 52 (2014), 53 (2014), 54 (2008), 55 (2012), 56 (2011), 57 (2012), 58 (2014), 58A (2014), 59 (2014), 59A (2014), 60 (2011), 61 (2010), 62 (2012), 63 (2012), 64 (2012), 65 (2015), 66 (2015), 67 (2008), 68 (2008), 69 (2009), 70 (2012), 71 (2013), 72 (2015), 73 (2015), 74 (2011), 75 (2013), 76 (2013), 77 (2016), 78 (2010), 79 (2014), 80 (2013), 81 (2010), 82 (2010), 83 (2010), 84 (2013), 84A (2013), 85 (2012), 86 (2013), 87 (2012), 88 (2012), 88A (2013), 89 (2011), 90 (2011), 91 (2012), 92 (2015), 93 (2008), 94 (2008), 95 (2013), 96 (2012), 97 (2015), 97A (2014), 98 (2013), 99 (2012), 100 (2009), 101 (2009), 102 (2010), 103 (2010), 104 (2014)

Consolidated Index and Tables:

2016 Consolidated Index (A–E), 2016 Consolidated Index (F–O), 2016 Consolidated Index (P–Z), 2016 Consolidated Table of Statutes, 2016 Consolidated Table of Statutory Instruments, etc, 2016 Consolidated Table of Cases (A–G), 2016 Consolidated Table of Cases (H–Q), 2016 Consolidated Table of Cases (R–Z, ECJ Cases)

Updating and ancillary materials:

2016 Annual Cumulative Supplement; Monthly Current Service; Annual Abridgments 1974–2015

July 2016

HALSBURY'S Laws of England

Volume 14

2016

Members of the LexisNexis Group worldwide

United Kingdom	RELX (UK) Ltd, trading as LexisNexis, 1–3 Strand, London WC2N 5JR and 9–10 St Andrew Square, Edinburgh EH2 2AF
Australia	Reed International Books Australia Pty Ltd trading as LexisNexis, Chatswood, New South Wales
Austria	LexisNexis Verlag ARD Orac GmbH & Co KG, Vienna
Benelux	LexisNexis Benelux, Amsterdam
Canada	LexisNexis Canada, Markham, Ontario
China	LexisNexis China, Beijing and Shanghai
France	LexisNexis SA, Paris
Germany	LexisNexis GmbH, Dusseldorf
Hong Kong	LexisNexis Hong Kong, Hong Kong
India	LexisNexis India, New Delhi
Italy	Giuffrè Editore, Milan
Japan	LexisNexis Japan, Tokyo
Malaysia	Malayan Law Journal Sdn Bhd, Kuala Lumpur
New Zealand	LexisNexis New Zealand Ltd, Wellington
Singapore	LexisNexis Singapore, Singapore
South Africa	LexisNexis, Durban
USA	LexisNexis, Dayton, Ohio

FIRST EDITION	*Published in 31 volumes between 1907 and 1917*
SECOND EDITION	*Published in 37 volumes between 1931 and 1942*
THIRD EDITION	*Published in 43 volumes between 1952 and 1964*
FOURTH EDITION	*Published in 56 volumes between 1973 and 1987, with reissues between 1988 and 2008*
FIFTH EDITION	*Published between 2008 and 2014, with reissues from 2014*

A CIP Catalogue record for this book is available from the British Library.

ISBN 978-1-4743-0168-8

9 781474 301688

ISBN for the set: 9781405734394

ISBN for this volume: 9781474301688

Typeset by LexisNexis
Printed and bound by CPI Group (UK) Ltd, Croydon, CR0 4YY

Visit LexisNexis at www.lexisnexis.co.uk

HALSBURY ADVISORY BOARD

EDITORS OF THIS VOLUME

RICHARD DEY, BA, LLB, LLM

CAROL MARSH, LLB, MA

and

MOHINI TULLOCH, LLM

COMMISSIONING EDITOR

CLAIRE TURPIN, LLB, MSc

MANAGING EDITOR

HELEN HALVEY, LLB

COMPANIES

Consultant Editor

ARAD REISBERG, LLB (cum laude), LLM, DPhil (Oxon),
Professor of Corporate Law,
Head of Brunel Law School,
Brunel University London

The law stated in this volume is in general that in force on 1 June 2016, although subsequent changes have been included wherever possible.

Any future updating material will be found in the Current Service and annual Cumulative Supplement to Halsbury's Laws of England.

TABLE OF CONTENTS

HOW TO USE HALSBURY'S LAWS OF ENGLAND

Volumes

Each text volume of Halsbury's Laws of England contains the law on the titles contained in it as at a date stated at the front of the volume (the operative date).

Information contained in Halsbury's Laws of England may be accessed in several ways.

First, by using the tables of contents.

Each volume contains both a general Table of Contents, and a specific Table of Contents for each title contained in it. From these tables you will be directed to the relevant part of the work.

Readers should note that the current arrangement of titles can be found in the Current Service.

Secondly, by using tables of statutes, statutory instruments, cases or other materials.

If you know the name of the Act, statutory instrument or case with which your research is concerned, you should consult the Consolidated Tables of statutes, cases and so on (published as separate volumes) which will direct you to the relevant volume and paragraph.

(Each individual text volume also includes tables of those materials used as authority in that volume.)

Thirdly, by using the indexes.

If you are uncertain of the general subject area of your research, you should go to the Consolidated Index (published as separate volumes) for reference to the relevant volume(s) and paragraph(s).

(Each individual text volume also includes an index to the material contained therein.)

Updating publications

The text volumes of Halsbury's Laws should be used in conjunction with the annual Cumulative Supplement and the monthly Noter-Up.

The annual Cumulative Supplement

The Supplement gives details of all changes between the operative date of the text volume and the operative date of the Supplement. It is arranged in the same volume, title and paragraph order as the text volumes. Developments affecting particular points of law are noted to the relevant paragraph(s) of the text volumes.

For narrative treatment of material noted in the Cumulative Supplement, go to the Annual Abridgment volume for the relevant year.

Destination Tables

In certain titles in the annual *Cumulative Supplement*, reference is made to Destination Tables showing the destination of consolidated legislation. Those Destination Tables are to be found either at the end of the titles within the annual *Cumulative Supplement*, or in a separate *Destination Tables* booklet provided from time to time with the *Cumulative Supplement.*

The Noter-Up

The Noter-Up is contained in the Current Service Noter-Up booklet, issued monthly and noting changes since the publication of the annual Cumulative Supplement. Also arranged in the same volume, title and paragraph order as the text volumes, the Noter-Up follows the style of the Cumulative Supplement.

For narrative treatment of material noted in the Noter-Up, go to the relevant Monthly Review.

REFERENCES AND ABBREVIATIONS

ACT	Australian Capital Territory
A-G	Attorney General
Admin	Administrative Court
Admlty	Admiralty Court
Adv-Gen	Advocate General
affd	affirmed
affg	affirming
Alta	Alberta
App	Appendix
art	article
Aust	Australia
B	Baron
BC	British Columbia
C	Command Paper (of a series published before 1900)
c	chapter number of an Act
CA	Court of Appeal
CAC	Central Arbitration Committee
CA in Ch	Court of Appeal in Chancery
CB	Chief Baron
CCA	Court of Criminal Appeal
CCR	County Court Rules 1981 (as subsequently amended)
CCR	Court for Crown Cases Reserved
CJEU	Court of Justice of the European Union
C-MAC	Courts-Martial Appeal Court
CO	Crown Office
COD	Crown Office Digest
CPR	Civil Procedure Rules
Can	Canada
Cd	Command Paper (of the series published 1900–18)
Cf	compare
Ch	Chancery Division
ch	chapter
cl	clause
Cm	Command Paper (of the series published 1986 to date)
Cmd	Command Paper (of the series published 1919–56)
Cmnd	Command Paper (of the series published 1956–86)
Comm	Commercial Court

Comr .... Commissioner
Court Forms (2nd Edn) .... Atkin's Encyclopaedia of Court Forms in Civil Proceedings, 2nd Edn. See note 2 post.
CrimPR .... Criminal Procedure Rules
DC............................ Divisional Court
DPP........................... Director of Public Prosecutions
EAT........................... Employment Appeal Tribunal
EC .... European Community
ECJ .... Court of Justice of the European Community (before the Treaty of Lisbon (OJ C306, 17.12.2007, p 1) came into force on 1 December 2009); European Court of Justice (after the Treaty of Lisbon (OJ C306, 17.12.2007, p 1) came into force on 1 December 2009)
EComHR .... European Commission of Human Rights
ECSC.......................... European Coal and Steel Community
ECtHR Rules of Court ..... Rules of Court of the European Court of Human Rights
EEC........................... European Economic Community
EFTA .... European Free Trade Association
EGC .... European General Court
EWCA Civ .... Official neutral citation for judgments of the Court of Appeal (Civil Division)
EWCA Crim .... Official neutral citation for judgments of the Court of Appeal (Criminal Division)
EWHC .... Official neutral citation for judgments of the High Court
Edn .... Edition
Euratom...................... European Atomic Energy Community
EU .... European Union
Ex Ch .... Court of Exchequer Chamber
ex p........................... ex parte
Fam........................... Family Division
Fed............................ Federal
Forms & Precedents (5th Edn) .... Encyclopaedia of Forms and Precedents other than Court Forms, 5th Edn. See note 2 post
GLC .... Greater London Council
HC............................ High Court
HC............................ House of Commons
HK............................ Hong Kong
HL .... House of Lords
IAT .... Immigration Appeal Tribunal
ILM........................... International Legal Materials
INLR .... Immigration and Nationality Law Reports

IRC .... Inland Revenue Commissioners
Ind .... India
Int Rels .... International Relations
Ir .... Ireland
J .... Justice
JA .... Judge of Appeal
Kan .... Kansas
LA .... Lord Advocate
LC .... Lord Chancellor
LCC .... London County Council
LCJ .... Lord Chief Justice
LJ .... Lord Justice of Appeal
LoN .... League of Nations
MR .... Master of the Rolls
Man .... Manitoba
n .... note
NB .... New Brunswick
NI .... Northern Ireland
NS .... Nova Scotia
NSW .... New South Wales
NY .... New York
NZ .... New Zealand
OHIM .... Office for Harmonisation in the Internal Market
OJ .... The Official Journal of the European Union published by the Publications Office of the European Union
Ont .... Ontario
P .... President
PC .... Judicial Committee of the Privy Council
PEI .... Prince Edward Island
Pat .... Patents Court
q .... question
QB .... Queen's Bench Division
QBD .... Queen's Bench Division of the High Court
Qld .... Queensland
Que .... Quebec
r .... rule
RDC .... Rural District Council
RPC .... Restrictive Practices Court
RSC .... Rules of the Supreme Court 1965 (as subsequently amended)
reg .... regulation
Res .... Resolution
revsd .... reversed

Rly	Railway
s	section
SA	South Africa
S Aust	South Australia
SC	Supreme Court
SI	Statutory Instruments published by authority
SR & O	Statutory Rules and Orders published by authority
SR & O Rev 1904	Revised Edition comprising all Public and General Statutory Rules and Orders in force on 31 December 1903
SR & O Rev 1948	Revised Edition comprising all Public and General Statutory Rules and Orders and Statutory Instruments in force on 31 December 1948
SRNI	Statutory Rules of Northern Ireland
STI	Simon's Tax Intelligence (1973–1995); Simon's Weekly Tax Intelligence (1996-current)
Sask	Saskatchewan
Sch	Schedule
Sess	Session
Sing	Singapore
TCC	Technology and Construction Court
TS	Treaty Series
Tanz	Tanzania
Tas	Tasmania
UDC	Urban District Council
UKHL	Official neutral citation for judgments of the House of Lords
UKPC	Official neutral citation for judgments of the Privy Council
UN	United Nations
V-C	Vice-Chancellor
Vict	Victoria
W Aust	Western Australia
Zimb	Zimbabwe

NOTE 1. A general list of the abbreviations of law reports and other sources used in this work can be found at the beginning of the Consolidated Table of Cases.

NOTE 2. Where references are made to other publications, the volume number precedes and the page number follows the name of the publication; eg the reference '12 Forms & Precedents (5th Edn) 44' refers to volume 12 of the Encyclopaedia of Forms and Precedents, page 44.

NOTE 3. An English statute is cited by short title or, where there is no short title, by regnal year and chapter number together with the name by which it is commonly known or a description of its subject matter and date. In the case of a foreign statute, the mode of citation generally follows the style of citation in use in the country concerned with the addition, where necessary, of the name of the country in parentheses.

NOTE 4. A statutory instrument is cited by short title, if any, followed by the year and number, or, if unnumbered, the date.

TABLE OF STATUTES

TABLE OF STATUTORY INSTRUMENTS

PARA

Register of People with Significant Control Regulations 2016, SI 2016/339—*continued*
reg 36 (1)–(6) ... 504
37 (1)–(6) ... 505
38 (1)–(6) ... 506
39 (1) ... 504–506
(2) ... 504–506
(d) ... 510
(e) ... 507
(f) ... 508
(3), (4) ... 504–506
40 (1)–(4) ... 504–506
41 (1)–(6) ... 510
42 (1)–(3) ... 509
43 (1), (2) ... 507
44 (1)–(6) ... 508
45 (1)–(4) ... 511
46 (1)–(6) ... 509
47 ... 469
Sch 1 ... 466–467
2 Pt 1 (para 1–3) ... 469
2 (para 4–6) ... 469
3 (para 7) ... 469
4 (para 8) ... 469
5 (para 9–16) ... 469
6 (para 17–24) ... 469
para 25 ... 469
3 ... 493, 539
4 para 1–5 ... 493
6–12 ... 494
13 (a)–(d) ... 493

Registrar of Companies and Applications for Striking Off (Amendment) Regulations 2016, SI 2016/441
reg 3 ... 159

Registrar of Companies and Applications for Striking Off Regulations 2009, SI 2009/1803 ... 164
reg 1 (1) ... 1525
(2) ... 159
2 (1), (2) ... 1707
3 ... 143
4 (1A) ... 159
(5)–(9) ... 159
5 (1)–(15) ... 159
6 ... 165
7, 8 ... 164
Schedule ... 164

Registrar of Companies (Fees) (Companies, Overseas Companies and Limited Liability Partnerships) Regulations 2012, SI 2012/1907
reg 2 ... 130
3 ... 167–173, 175–179, 181–182, 218, 1381, 1390, 2015, 2019–2020
4, 5 ... 133, 145, 163
Sch 1 ... 30
3, 4 ... 1594, 1598, 2019–2020
8 (a) ... 104
(c) ... 167–173, 175–179, 181–182
(d) ... 1381
(e) ... 1390

PARA

Registrar of Companies (Fees) (Companies, Overseas Companies and Limited Liability Partnerships) Regulations 2012, SI 2012/1907—*continued*
Sch 1 para 8 (f) ... 1594, 1598
(g) ... 218
(h) ... 1463
(i) ... 1707
11 (a), (b) ... 2015
(d) ... 2019–2020
2 para 7, 8 ... 133, 145, 163
9 ... 133, 145, 163
(1) ... 218
(2) ... 217
10–12 ... 133, 145, 163
3 ... 148–149, 493–494, 539–541

Registrar of Companies (Fees) (European Economic Interest Grouping and European Public Limited-Liability Company) Regulations 2012, SI 2012/1908 ... 1829, 1831
reg 4–8 ... 1824
13–16 ... 1824
18–20 ... 1824
Sch 4 ... 1824

Reports on Payments to Governments Regulations 2014, SI 2014/3209
reg 2 (1)–(4) ... 774
3 (1), (2) ... 774
4–7 ... 774
8 (1), (2) ... 774
9 ... 774
10 (1)–(5) ... 774
11 (1), (2) ... 774
12, 13 ... 774
14 (1), (2) ... 774
(3) ... 136, 774
15 (1), (2) ... 774
(3) ... 136, 774
16 (1)–(6) ... 774
17 (1)–(6) ... 774
(7)(a)–(k) ... 774
(8)–(14) ... 774
18 (1)–(11) ... 774
19 ... 774

Secretary of State for Business, Innovation and Skills Order 2009, SI 2009/2748
art 1 ... 6
3, 4 ... 6
6, 7 ... 6

Small Business, Enterprise and Employment Act 2015 (Commencement No 1) Regulations 2015, SI 2015/1329
reg 3 (a) ... 466
(c) ... 1785

Small Business, Enterprise and Employment Act 2015 (Commencement No 2 and Transitional Provisions) Regulations 2015, SI 2015/1689
reg 4 (b) ... 553
Schedule para 1 ... 1773, 1788
2 ... 1769
3 ... 1783
4 ... 1809

PARA

Solicitors' Recognised Bodies Order 1991, SI 1991/2684
art 2 (1) 1728
3 1728
4 (a) 1728
Sch 1 1728

Statutory Auditors (Amendment of Companies Act 2006 and Delegation of Functions etc) Order 2012, SI 2012/1741
art 2 .... 770, 1021, 1046, 1129, 1139, 1145, 1154, 1175
7 (1) 1067
(2) 1067
(a) 1060, 1131
(b) 1088
(c), (d) 1147
(e) 1152
(f) 1159
(g) 1164
(h) 1059
(i) 1142
(3) 1067
(b) 1157
(c) 1155
(d) 1165
(e) 1141
(4) 1067
(a), (b) 1126
(c) 1166
(5), (6) 1067
8 1046
9 1068
10, 11 1067
12 (1), (2) 1129, 1164
(3) 1164
13 1139
14 1175
15 1021
18 1145
19 1147
20 (1), (2) 1145
23 770

Statutory Auditors and Third Country Auditors Regulations 2013, SI 2013/1672
reg 5 1160
6 (1)–(7) 1160
7 (1)–(6) 1161
8 1161
9 (1)–(3) 1162
10 1162
11 1163

Statutory Auditors and Third Country Auditors Regulations 2016, SI 2016/649
reg 1 (1) (a) 1058
(3) 1078
(4) (a) 1011
(5) 1071–1077
(7) 1078–1080
(8) 1078, 1104, 1107
(9) 1078
(10) 982, 1078
(11) 771, 1078
3 (1)–13) 1069
4 (1)–(4) 1034
5 (1)–(11) 1078

PARA

Statutory Auditors and Third Country Auditors Regulations 2016, SI 2016/649—*continued*
reg 6 (1)–(5) 1079
7–8 1080
9 (1)–(11) 1081
11 (1)–(8) 1082
12 (1)–(3) 1091
13 (1)–(3) 1005
21 (1)–(3) 1153
22 (2) (b) 1169
24 (1)–(6) 1058
Sch 1 para 1–8 1070
9 (1)–(5) 1071
(6) 1070
10 1072
11 1073
12 1074
13, 14 1075
15 1076
16 1077
2 para 1–3 1083
4 1084
5 1085

Stock Transfer (Addition and Substitution of Forms) Order 1996, SI 1996/1571 411

Stock Transfer (Addition of Forms) Order 1979, SI 1979/277
art 3 (1), (2) 411
4 411

Stock Transfer (Amendment of Forms) Order 1974, SI 1974/1214 411

Stock Transfer (Gilt-edged Securities) (CGO Service) (Amendment) Regulations 1999, SI 1999/1208 441

Stock Transfer (Recognised Stock Exchanges) Order 1973, SI 1973/536 411

Stock Transfer (Substitution of Forms) Order 1990, SI 1990/18
art 4 411

Supervision of Accounts and Reports (Prescribed Body) and Companies (Defective Accounts and Directors' Reports) (Authorised Person) Order 2012, SI 2012/1439
art 1 (3) 980
3 771
4 .... 771, 980

Supply of Services (Exclusion of Implied Terms) Order 1982, SI 1982/1771
art 2 (2) 588

Transfer of Functions (Financial Services) Order 1992, SI 1992/1315
art 5 1752
Sch 3 para 3 1752

Uncertificated Securities Regulations 2001, SI 2001/3755
reg 2 (1) 431–432
(2) 431
3 (2) 432

TABLE OF PROCEDURE

Civil Procedure

Civil Procedure Rules 1998, SI 1998/3132 (CPR)

Practice Directions relating to Civil Procedure

TABLE OF EUROPEAN UNION LEGISLATION

Primary Legislation

PARA

Treaty on the Functioning of the European Union (Rome, 25 March 1957; TS 1 (1973); Cmnd 5179)
art 19 17
50 para 2 (g) 20
51 para 1 20
54, 55 16
63 para 1, 2 18
65 para 1–3 18
288 .... 19–20, 1823–1825
352 1822

Secondary Legislation

Decisions

PARA

Commission Decision (EU) 2011/30 (OJ L15, 20.1.2011, p 12) 20, 1058

Directives

PARA

Commission Directive (EC) 2007/14 (OJ L69, 9.3.2007, p 27) 20
Council Directive (EC) 2001/23 (OJ L82, 22.3.2001, p 16) 20
Council Directive (EC) 2001/86 (OJ L294, 10.11.2001, p 22) 1825
Council Directive (EC) 2003/72 (OJ L207, 18.8.2003, p 25) 19
Council Directive (EC) 2004/25 (OJ L142, 30.4.2004, p 12 20
Council Directive (EEC) 82/891 (OJ L378, 31.12.82, p 47) 20
Council Directive (EEC) 86/635 (OJ L372, 31.12.1986, p 1) 20
Council Directive (EEC) 89/666 (OJ L395, 30.12.89, p 36) 20
Council Directive (EEC) 91/674 (OJ L374, 31.12.1991, p 7)
art 2 767
European Parliament and Council Directive (EC) 2001/34 (OJ L184, 6.7.2001, p 1) 20
European Parliament and Council Directive (EC) 2002/14 (OJ L80, 23.2.2002, p 29) 20
European Parliament and Council Directive (EC) 2003/71 (OJ L345, 31.12.2003, p 64) 20
art 2 (1)(f) 994
(t) 1000
European Parliament and Council Directive (EC) 2004/25 (OJ L142, 30.4.2004, p 12)
art 1 (1) 1663
European Parliament and Council Directive (EC) 2004/39 (OJ L145, 30.4.2004, p 1)
art 4.1 (14) 335, 1153

Regulations

TABLE OF CASES

PARA

PARA

PARA

PARA

Greenwood v Humber & Co (Portugal) Ltd (1898) 6 Mans 42 1270
Greenwood v Leather Shod Wheel Co [1900] 1 Ch 421, 69 LJ Ch 131, 7 Mans 210, 44 Sol Jo 156, 81 LT 595, 16 TLR 117, CA 1262
Gresham House Estate Co v Rossa Grande Gold Mining Co [1870] WN 119 704
Gresham Life Assurance Society, Re, ex p Penney (1872) 8 Ch App 446, [1861–73] All ER Rep 903, 42 LJ Ch 183, 21 WR 186, 28 LT 150, CA in Ch 354, 404, 583
Greymouth-Point Elizabeth Rly and Coal Co Ltd, Re, Yuill v Greymouth-Point Elizabeth Rly and Coal Co Ltd [1904] 1 Ch 32, 73 LJ Ch 92, 11 Mans 85 .... 267, 569, 1969
Greythorn Ltd, Re [2002] 1 BCLC 437, [2001] All ER (D) 284 (Dec) 1697
Grierson, Oldham and Adams Ltd, Re [1968] Ch 17, [1967] 1 All ER 192, [1967] 1 WLR 385, 110 Sol Jo 887 1701
Griffin Hotel Co Ltd, Re, Joshua Tetley & Son Ltd v Griffin Hotel Co Ltd [1941] Ch 129, [1940] 4 All ER 324, 110 LJ Ch 51, [1940–1941] B & CR 38, 84 Sol Jo 695, 165 LT 57, 57 TLR 123 1516
Griffith, Re, Carr v Griffith (1879) 12 Ch D 655, 28 WR 28, 41 LT 540 .... 2, 1581
Griffith v Paget (1877) 5 Ch D 894, 46 LJ Ch 493, 25 WR 523 .... 234, 654
Griffith v Paget (1877) 6 Ch D 511, 25 WR 821, 37 LT 141 .... 54, 247, 265, 1623
Griffith v Tower Publishing Co Ltd and Moncrieff [1897] 1 Ch 21, [1895–9] All ER Rep 323, 66 LJ Ch 12, 45 WR 73, 41 Sol Jo 29, 75 LT 330, 13 TLR 9 1531
Griffiths v Secretary of State for Social Services [1974] QB 468, [1973] 3 All ER 1184, [1973] 3 WLR 831, 117 Sol Jo 873 1523
Griffiths Cycle Corpn Ltd, Re, Dunlop Pneumatic Tyre Co Ltd v John Griffiths Cycle Corpn Ltd (1902) 46 Sol Jo 229, 85 LT 776, CA 1551
Grigson (or Gregson) v Taplin & Co (1915) 85 LJ Ch 75, [1915] HBR 226, 59 Sol Jo 349, 112 LT 985 .... 1458, 1543
Grimwade v BPS Syndicate Ltd (1915) 31 TLR 531 583
Grimwade v Mutual Society (1884) 52 LT 409, 1 TLR 115 588
Grosvenor and West End Rly Terminus Hotel Co Ltd, Re (1897) 76 LT 337, [1895–9] All ER Rep Ext 1836, 41 Sol Jo 365, 13 TLR 309, CA 1725
Grosvenor Press plc, Re [1985] 1 WLR 980, [1985] BCLC 286, 1 BCC 412, [1985] PCC 260, 129 Sol Jo 541, [1985] LS Gaz R 2817 .... 1368, 1370, 1379
Grove v Advantage Healthcare (T10) Ltd [2000] 1 BCLC 661, [1999] All ER (D) 1294 1474
Grundt v Great Boulder Pty Gold Mines Ltd [1948] Ch 145, [1948] 1 All ER 21, [1948] LJR 1100, 92 Sol Jo 71, CA 242, 555, 581, 708, 1958
Grundy v Briggs [1910] 1 Ch 444, 79 LJ Ch 244, 17 Mans 30, 54 Sol Jo 163, 101 LT 901 .... 410, 531, 533
Grupo Torras SA and Torras Hostench London Ltd v Sheikh Fahad Mohammed Al-Sabah [1996] 1 Lloyd's Rep 7, CA 2030
Guardian Assurance Co, Re [1917] 1 Ch 431, 86 LJ Ch 214, [1917] HBR 113, 61 Sol Jo 232, 116 LT 193, 33 TLR 169, CA 1605, 1612
Guest v Worcester, Bromyard and Leominster Rly Co (1868) LR 4 CP 9, 38 LJCP 23 .... 1901, 1904
Guidezone Ltd, Re [2000] 2 BCLC 321 .... 659–660, 668
Guinness v Land Corpn of Ireland Ltd (1882) 22 Ch D 349, 52 LJ Ch 177, 31 WR 341, 47 LT 517, CA 227, 259, 305, 1248, 1585
Guinness & Co's Trade Mark, Re (1888) 5 RPC 316 198
Guinness plc v Saunders [1988] 2 All ER 940, [1988] 1 WLR 863, [1988] BCLC 607, 4 BCC 377, 132 Sol Jo 820, [1988] NLJR 142, CA; on appeal [1990] 2 AC 663, [1990] 1 All ER 652, [1990] 2 WLR 324, [1990] BCLC 402, 134 Sol Jo 457, [1990] 9 LS Gaz R 42, HL 558–559, 562, 590, 600
Gunn's Case. See Universal Banking Corpn, Re, Gunn's Case
Gurney v Rawlins (1836) 6 LJ Ex 7, 2 Gale 235, 2 M & W 87 59

PARA

I

PARA

PARA

Keenan Bros Ltd, Re [1986] BCLC 242, 2 BCC 98, 970, [1985] IR 401, Ir SC 1455–1456

Keighley, Maxsted & Co v Durant [1901] AC 240, [1900–3] All ER Rep 40, 70 LJKB 662, 45 Sol Jo 536, 84 LT 777, 17 TLR 527, HL 277, 1274

Keith Prowse & Co Ltd, Re [1918] 1 Ch 487, [1918–19] All ER Rep 946, 87 LJ Ch 290, 118 LT 591, 34 TLR 283 354

Kelk's Case. See Cobre Copper Mine Co, Re, Kelk's Case

Kellock v Enthoven (1874) LR 9 QB 241, 43 LJQB 90, 22 WR 322, 30 LT 68, Ex Ch 402

Kelner v Baxter (1866) LR 2 CP 174, [1861–73] All ER Rep Ext 2009, 36 LJCP 94, 12 Jur NS 1016, 15 WR 278, 15 LT 213 .... 59, 278–279

Kemp v Baerselman [1906] 2 KB 604, 75 LJKB 873, 50 Sol Jo 615, CA 285

Kemp v Courage & Co Ltd (1890) 55 JP 264, 7 TLR 50 297

Kempe v Ambassador Insurance Co [1998] 1 WLR 271, [1998] 1 BCLC 234, [1998] BCC 311, 142 Sol Jo LB 28, PC 1613

Kempf v Offin River Gold Estates Ltd (1908) Times, 10 April 560

Kennedy v North British Wireless Schools Ltd (1916) 53 SLR 543 404

Kensington International Ltd v Republic of Congo [2005] EWHC 2684 (Comm), [2006] 2 BCLC 296, [2005] All ER (D) 370 (Nov) 116

Kensington Station Act, Re (1875) LR 20 Eq 197, 23 WR 463, 32 LT 183, Ct of Ch 1884

Kent v Freehold Land and Brick-Making Co (1867) LR 4 Eq 588; revsd (1868) 3 Ch App 493, 32 JP 742, 37 LJ Ch 653, 16 WR 990 1262–1263

Kent and Sussex Sawmills Ltd, Re [1947] Ch 177, [1946] 2 All ER 638, [1947] LJR 534, 91 Sol Jo 12, 176 LT 167, 62 TLR 747 1474

Kent's Case. See Land Development Association, Re, Kent's Case

Kent Coal Exploration Co Ltd v Martin (1900) 16 TLR 486, CA 1270

Kent Coalfields Syndicate, Re [1898] 1 QB 754, 67 LJQB 500, 5 Mans 88, 46 WR 453, 42 Sol Jo 363, 78 LT 443, 14 TLR 305, CA 125, 350, 748, 1505

Kent Collieries Ltd, Re, Day v Kent Collieries Ltd (1907) 51 Sol Jo 498, 23 TLR 559, CA 1501

Kent County Gas Light and Coke Co Ltd, Re [1913] 1 Ch 92, 82 LJ Ch 28, 19 Mans 358, 57 Sol Jo 112, 107 LT 641 62

Kent County Gas Light and Coke Co Ltd, Re, ex p Brown (1906) 95 LT 756 1262

Kent Tramways Co, Re (1879) 12 Ch D 312, 28 WR 158, CA 1884, 1980

Kent Waterworks (Company of Proprietors) v Lamplough. See Lamplough v Kent Waterworks (Company of Proprietors)

Kenyon (Donald) Ltd, Re [1956] 3 All ER 596, [1956] 1 WLR 1397, 100 Sol Jo 818 1721

Kenyon Swansea Ltd, Re [1987] BCLC 514, 3 BCC 259 .... 657, 659, 661, 665

Kernaghan v Dublin Trunk Connecting Rly Co, James Case (1867) LR 3 QB 47, 8 B & S 773, 37 LJQB 50, 16 WR 107 1905

Kernaghan v Williams (1868) LR 6 Eq 228 .... 252, 576

Kerr v John Mottram Ltd [1940] Ch 657, [1940] 2 All ER 629, 109 LJ Ch 243, 84 Sol Jo 358, 163 LT 222, 56 TLR 711 740

Kerr v Marine Products Ltd (1928) 44 TLR 292 558

Kerr v Walker 1933 SC 458, Ct of Sess 578

Kerry v Maori Dream Gold Mines Ltd (1898) 14 TLR 402, CA 584

Kettle v Dunster and Wakefield (1927) 138 LT 158, 43 TLR 770 .... 294, 1551

Key (W) & Son Ltd, Re [1902] 1 Ch 467, 71 LJ Ch 254, 9 Mans 181, 50 WR 234, 46 Sol Jo 231, 86 LT 374, 18 TLR 263 .... 336, 353, 397, 407

Key Homes Bradford Ltd v Patel [2015] 1 BCLC 402, [2014] All ER (D) 69 (Jan) 744

Keynsham Blue Lias Lime Co Ltd v Baker (1863) 2 H & C 729, 33 LJ Ex 41, 9 Jur NS 1346, 12 WR 156, 9 LT 418 117

PARA

PARA

Leeds Banking Co, Re, Fearnside and Dean's Case (1866) 1 Ch App 231, 35 LJ Ch 307, 12 Jur NS 60, 14 WR 255, 13 LT 694 .... 375, 445
Leeds Banking Co, Re, Howard's Case (1866) 1 Ch App 561, 36 LJ Ch 42, 12 Jur NS 655, 14 WR 942, 14 LT 747 .... 577, 1278, 1323
Leeds Banking Co, Re, ex p Barrett (1865) 2 Drew & Sm 415, 11 Jur NS 234 328
Leeds Estate, Building and Investment Co v Shepherd (1887) 36 Ch D 787, 57 LJ Ch 46, 36 WR 322, 57 LT 684, 3 TLR 841 .... 558, 631, 679, 682, 1004
Leeds United Holdings plc, Re [1996] 2 BCLC 545, [1997] BCC 131 659
Leeke's Case. See Empire Assurance Corpn, Re, Leeke's Case
Lees v Tod (1882) 9 R 807, 19 SLR 513 1272
Lees Brook Spinning Co, Re [1906] 2 Ch 394, 75 LJ Ch 565, 13 Mans 262, 54 WR 563, 95 LT 54, 22 TLR 629 1372
Legal Costs Negotiators Ltd, Re [1999] 2 BCLC 171, [1999] All ER (D) 166, CA 657, 659
Legg v Mathieson (1860) 2 Giff 71, 29 LJ Ch 385, 5 Jur NS 1010, 2 LT 112 1861
Lehman Brothers International (Europe) (in admin), Re [2012] EWHC 2997 (Ch), [2014] 2 BCLC 295, [2012] All ER (D) 32 (Nov) 1455
Lehman Brothers International (Europe) (in admin) (No 2), Re [2009] EWCA Civ 1161, [2010] Bus LR 489, [2010] 1 BCLC 496, [2010] BCC 272, (2009) Times, 12 November, [2009] All ER (D) 83 (Nov) 1607, 1612
Leicester Club and County Racecourse Co, Re, ex p Cannon (1885) 30 Ch D 629, 55 LJ Ch 206, 34 WR 14, 53 LT 340, 1 TLR 658 561
Leicester Mortgage Co Ltd, Re [1894] WN 108, 38 Sol Jo 531, 606 570
Leinster Contract Corpn, Re [1902] 1 IR 349 1302
Leitch (William C) Bros Ltd, Re [1932] 2 Ch 71, [1932] All ER Rep 892, 101 LJ Ch 380, 148 LT 106 317
Lemon v Austin Friars Investment Trust Ltd [1926] Ch 1, [1925] All ER Rep 255, 95 LJ Ch 97, 69 Sol Jo 762, 133 LT 790, 41 TLR 629, CA 1482, 1505
Lennard's Carrying Co Ltd v Asiatic Petroleum Co Ltd [1915] AC 705, [1914–15] All ER Rep 280, 84 LJKB 1281, 13 Asp MLC 81, 20 Com Cas 283, 59 Sol Jo 411, 113 LT 195, 31 TLR 294, HL 313
Lennox Publishing Co Ltd, Re, ex p Storey (1890) 2 Meg 266, 62 LT 791, 6 TLR 357 1263
Leominster Canal Navigation Co v Shrewsbury and Hereford Rly Co (1857) 3 K & J 654, 26 LJ Ch 764, 3 Jur NS 930, 5 WR 868, 29 LTOS 342 1967
Lethbridge v Adams, ex p International Life Assurance Society (Liquidator) (1872) LR 13 Eq 547, 41 LJ Ch 710, 20 WR 352, 26 LT 147 37
Letheby and Christopher Ltd, Re [1904] 1 Ch 815, 73 LJ Ch 509, 11 Mans 209, 52 WR 460, 48 Sol Jo 416, 90 LT 774 410
Lever v Land Securities Co Ltd (1891) 8 TLR 94 1586–1587
Lever Bros Ltd v IRC [1938] 2 KB 518, [1938] 2 All ER 808, 107 LJKB 669, 82 Sol Jo 452, 159 LT 136, 54 TLR 892, CA 1615
Levi v Ayers (1878) 3 App Cas 842, 47 LJPC 83, 27 WR 79, 38 LT 725, PC 414
Levita's Case. See International Contract Co, Re, Levita's Case
Levy v Abercorris Slate and Slab Co (1887) 37 Ch D 260, [1886–90] All ER Rep 509, 57 LJ Ch 202, 36 WR 411, 58 LT 218, 4 TLR 34 .... 1281, 1482
Levy v Langridge (1838) 7 LJ Ex 387, [1835–42] All ER Rep 586, 1 Horn & H 325, 4 M & W 337, sub nom Langridge v Levy Ex Ch 1273
Lewis, Re, Lewis v Lewis (1910) 103 LT 495, [1908–10] All ER Rep 281, 55 Sol Jo 29, [1910] WN 217 558
Lewis v Daily Telegraph Ltd (No 2) [1964] 2 QB 601, [1964] 1 All ER 705, [1964] 2 WLR 736, 108 Sol Jo 94, CA 301
Lewis v Daily Telegraph Ltd. See Rubber Improvement Ltd v Daily Telegraph Ltd
Lewis v IRC [2001] 3 All ER 499, [2001] 2 BCLC 392, (2000) Times, 15 November, (2000) Independent, 18 December, [2000] All ER (D) 1641, CA 1460
Lewis v Secretary of State for Trade and Industry [2001] 2 BCLC 597, [2003] BCC 567, (2001) Times, 16 August, [2001] All ER (D) 254 (Jul) 1800

M

PARA

PARA

PARA

PARA

P

PARA

PARA

Prince v Prince (1866) LR 1 Eq 490, 35 Beav 386, 35 LJ Ch 290, 12 Jur NS 221, 14 WR 383, 14 LT 43 14

Prince of Wales Assurance Co v Harding (1858) EB & E 183, 27 LJQB 297, 4 Jur NS 851, sub nom Prince of Wales Assurance Society v Athenaeum Assurance Society 3 CBNS 756n, 31 LTOS 149 266

Pringle v Callard [2007] EWCA Civ 1075, [2008] 2 BCLC 505, [2007] All ER (D) 91 (Aug) 663, 668

Printing Telegraph and Construction Co of Agence Havas v Drucker [1894] 2 QB 801, 64 LJQB 58, 9 R 677, 42 WR 674, 38 Sol Jo 661, 71 LT 172, 10 TLR 641, CA 637

Printing Telegraph and Construction Co of the Agence Havas Re, ex p Cammell [1894] 1 Ch 528; affd [1894] 2 Ch 392, 63 LJ Ch 536, 1 Mans 274, 7 R 191, 38 Sol Jo 437, 70 LT 705, 10 TLR 441, CA 244, 336, 346, 353, 532, 589

Pro4Sport Ltd (in liq), Re [2015] EWHC 2540 (Ch), [2016] 1 BCLC 257, subnom Hedger (Liquidator of Pro4Sport Ltd) v Adams [2015] All ER (D) 12 (Sep) 585, 588

Probe Data Systems Ltd, Re [1989] BCLC 561, 5 BCC 384 1787

Probe Data Systems Ltd (No 3), Re [1992] BCLC 405, [1992] BCC 110, CA 1787

Produce Marketing Consortium Ltd, Re [1989] 3 All ER 1, [1989] 1 WLR 745, [1989] BCLC 513, 5 BCC 569, 133 Sol Jo 945 645

Profinance Trust SA v Gladstone [2001] EWCA Civ 1031, [2002] 1 WLR 1024, [2002] 1 BCLC 141, [2001] 30 LS Gaz R 37, (2001) Times, 7 August, [2001] All ER (D) 08 (Jul) 666–667

Progress Property Co Ltd v Moorgrath Group Ltd; sub nom Progress Property Co Ltd v Moore [2009] EWCA Civ 629, [2009] All ER (D) 294 (Jun) 1562

Promwalk Services Ltd, Re, Frewen v Secretary of State for Trade and Industry [2002] EWHC 2688 (Ch), [2003] 2 BCLC 305, [2002] All ER (D) 134 (Dec) 1769, 1784

Property Discount Corpn Ltd v Lyon Group Ltd [1981] 1 All ER 379, [1981] 1 WLR 300, 125 Sol Jo 185, CA 1458, 1474

Provincial Motor Cab Co Ltd v Dunning [1909] 2 KB 599, 7 LGR 765, 73 JP 387, 78 LJKB 822, 22 Cox CC 159, 101 LT 231, 25 TLR 646, DC 312

Prudential Assurance Co Ltd v Chatterley-Whitfield Collieries Ltd. See Chatterley-Whitfield Collieries Ltd, Re

Prudential Assurance Co Ltd v Newman Industries Ltd (No 2) [1982] Ch 204, [1982] 1 All ER 354, [1982] 2 WLR 31, 126 Sol Jo 32, CA 383, 654

Puddephatt v Leith [1916] 1 Ch 200, [1914–15] All ER Rep 260, 85 LJ Ch 185, 60 Sol Jo 210, 114 LT 454, 32 TLR 228 .... 250, 724

Pugh and Sharman's Case. See Hercules Insurance Co, Re, Pugh and Sharman's Case

Pulbrook v Richmond Consolidated Mining Co (1878) 9 Ch D 610, 48 LJ Ch 65, 27 WR 377 .... 353, 383, 533, 583

Punt v Symons & Co Ltd [1903] 2 Ch 506, [1900–3] All ER Rep Ext 1040, 72 LJ Ch 768, 10 Mans 415, 52 WR 41, 47 Sol Jo 619, 89 LT 525 .... 234, 583, 654–655

Pure Spirit Co v Fowler (1890) 25 QBD 235, 59 LJQB 537, 38 WR 686, 63 LT 559, 6 TLR 390 309

Purnchard's Will Trusts, Re, Public Trustee v Pelly [1948] Ch 312, [1948] 1 All ER 790, [1948] LJR 1274, 92 Sol Jo 245 1491

Pybus v Gibb (1856) 6 E & B 902, 26 LJQB 41, 3 Jur NS 315, Saund & M 160, 5 WR 44, 28 LTOS 81 1977

Pyle Works, Re (1890) 44 Ch D 534, [1886–90] All ER Rep Ext 1286, 59 LJ Ch 489, 2 Meg 83, 38 WR 674, 62 LT 887, 6 TLR 268, CA 229, 1451–1452, 1933

Pyle Works (No 2), Re [1891] 1 Ch 173, 60 LJ Ch 114, 2 Meg 327, 39 WR 235, 63 LT 628, 6 TLR 142 .... 570, 575–576, 1444, 1451

Q

Qayoumi v Oakhouse Property Holdings plc [2002] EWHC 2547 (Ch), [2003] 1 BCLC 352, [2003] BPIR 1, [2002] All ER (D) 469 (Jul) 652

PARA

Railway Sleepers Supply Co, Re (1885) 29 Ch D 204, 54 LJ Ch 720, 33 WR 595, 52 LT 731, 1 TLR 399 704
Railway Time Tables Publishing Co, Re, ex p Sandys (1889) 42 Ch D 98, [1886–90] All ER Rep Ext 1375, 58 LJ Ch 504, 1 Meg 208, 37 WR 531, 61 LT 94, 5 TLR 397, CA 327, 333, 352, 398, 1279
Rainbow Syndicate Ltd, Re, Owen v Rainbow Syndicate Ltd [1916] WN 178 1508
Rainford v Keith and Blackman Co Ltd [1905] 1 Ch 296, 74 LJ Ch 156, 12 Mans 162, 92 LT 49, 21 TLR 160; revsd [1905] 2 Ch 147, 74 LJ Ch 531, 12 Mans 278, 54 WR 189, 49 Sol Jo 551, 92 LT 786, 21 TLR 582, CA 399, 588, 1894
Rainham Chemical Works Ltd v Belvedere Fish Guano Co [1921] 2 AC 465, [1921] All ER Rep 48, 19 LGR 657, 90 LJKB 1252, 66 Sol Jo 7, 126 LT 70, 37 TLR 973, HL 115–116, 633
Rakusens Ltd v Baser Ambalaj Plastik Sanayi Ticaret AS [2001] EWCA Civ 1820, [2002] 1 BCLC 104, [2001] 42 LS Gaz R 37, (2001) Times, 9 November, 145 Sol Jo LB 237, [2001] All ER (D) 199 (Oct) 2025
Rama Corpn Ltd v Proved Tin and General Investments Ltd [1952] 2 QB 147, [1952] 1 All ER 554, 96 Sol Jo 197, [1952] 1 TLR 709 .... 265, 271
Ramsgate Victoria Hotel Co v Montefiore (1866) LR 1 Exch 109, [1861–73] All ER Rep Ext 2232, 4 H & C 164, 35 LJ Ex 90, 12 Jur NS 455, 14 WR 335, 13 LT 715 .... 328, 1277
Ramskill v Edwards (1885) 31 Ch D 100, 55 LJ Ch 81, 34 WR 96, 53 LT 949, 2 TLR 37 .... 589, 631, 637
Rance's Case. See County Marine Insurance Co, Re, Rance's Case
Randall (H E) Ltd v British and American Shoe Co Ltd [1902] 2 Ch 354, 71 LJ Ch 683, 10 Mans 109, 19 RPC 393, 50 WR 697, 87 LT 442, 18 TLR 611 .... 198, 220
Randt Gold Mining Co, Re [1904] 2 Ch 468, 73 LJ Ch 598, 12 Mans 93, 53 WR 90, 91 LT 174, 20 TLR 619 1330
Randt Gold Mining Co Ltd v Wainwright [1901] 1 Ch 184, 70 LJ Ch 90, 8 Mans 61, 45 Sol Jo 60, 84 LT 348, 17 TLR 29 .... 724, 1406
Ranger v Great Western Rly Co (1854) 5 HL Cas 72, [1843–60] All ER Rep 321, 18 Jur 795, 24 LTOS 22, HL 297
Rankin and Blackmore Ltd, Re 1950 SC 218, 1950 SLT 160, Ct of Sess 1609
Ransomes plc, Re [1999] 2 BCLC 591, [1999] All ER (D) 712, CA 1379
Rapid Road Transit Co, Re [1909] 1 Ch 96, 78 LJ Ch 132, 16 Mans 289, 53 Sol Jo 83, 99 LT 774 683
Rashdall v Ford (1866) LR 2 Eq 750, 35 LJ Ch 769, 14 WR 950, 14 LT 790 635
Rastrick v Derbyshire, Staffordshire and Worcestershire Junction Rly Co (1853) 7 Ry & Can Cas 799, 23 LJ Ex 2, 9 Exch 149, 17 Jur 977, 2 WR 14, 22 LTOS 79 1903–1904
Ratford v Northavon District Council [1987] QB 357, [1986] 3 All ER 193, [1986] 3 WLR 770, 85 LGR 443, [1986] RA 137, 150 JP 605, [1986] BCLC 397, 2 BCC 99, 242, 130 Sol Jo 786, CA 1524
Rathbone Brothers Plc v Novae Corporate Underwriting [2014] EWCA Civ 1464, [2015] Lloyd's Rep IR 95, [2015] WTLR 301, [2014] All ER (D) 172 (Nov) 242
Ratners Group plc, Re [1988] BCLC 685, 4 BCC 293 .... 1360, 1371
Ravenhart Service (Holdings) Ltd, Re, Reiner v Gershinson [2004] EWHC 76 (Ch), [2004] 2 BCLC 376, [2004] All ER (D) 68 (Jan) 659, 663
Rayfield v Hands [1960] Ch 1, [1958] 2 All ER 194, [1958] 2 WLR 851, 102 Sol Jo 348 .... 245, 326, 405
Rayner (J H) (Mincing Lane) Ltd v Department of Trade and Industry [1990] 2 AC 418, [1989] 3 WLR 969, 5 BCC 872, 133 Sol Jo 1485, sub nom Maclaine Watson & Co Ltd v Department of Trade and Industry [1989] 3 All ER 523, HL 115–116
Read v Astoria Garage (Streatham) Ltd [1952] Ch 637, [1952] 2 All ER 292, [1952] 2 TLR 130, CA 557, 578
Rearden v Provincial Bank of Ireland [1896] 1 IR 532, 30 ILT 117 .... 344, 1395

PARA

Rover International Ltd v Cannon Film Sales Ltd (No 3) [1987] BCLC 540; revsd [1989] 3 All ER 423, [1989] 1 WLR 912, [1988] BCLC 710n, CA 59
Rowe, Re, ex p West Coast Gold Fields Ltd [1904] 2 KB 489, 73 LJKB 852, 11 Mans 272, 52 WR 608, 48 Sol Jo 545, 91 LT 101 .... 1333, 1393
Rowell v John Rowell & Sons Ltd [1912] 2 Ch 609, 81 LJ Ch 759, 19 Mans 371, 56 Sol Jo 704, 107 LT 374 .... 305, 1407
Rowland and Marwood's Steamship Co Ltd and Reduced, Re (1906) 51 Sol Jo 131 1370
Rowley v Desborough (1916) 60 Sol Jo 429 1545
Roxburghe Press, Re, Spiers and Bevan's Case [1899] 1 Ch 210, 68 LJ Ch 111, 6 Mans 57, 47 WR 281, 80 LT 280, 15 TLR 132 1299
Royal Bank of Australia, Re, Meux's Executors' Case (1852) 2 De GM & G 522, 20 LTOS 11 274
Royal Bank of Australia, Re, Robinson's Executor's Case (1856) 6 De GM & G 572, 26 LJ Ch 95, 2 Jur NS 1173, 5 WR 126, 28 LTOS 167 373
Royal Bank of India's Case. See Asiatic Banking Corpn, Re, Royal Bank of India's Case
Royal Bank of Scotland plc v Bannerman Johnstone Maclay (a firm) (2002) Times, 1 August, 2003 SC 125, 2003 SLT 181, OH; affd 2005 SLT 579 1029
Royal Bank of Scotland plc v Sandstone Properties Ltd [1998] 2 BCLC 429 .... 391, 442
Royal British Bank, Re, Mixer's Case (1859) 4 De G & J 575, 28 LJ Ch 879, 7 WR 677, 1 LT 19 1260
Royal British Bank, Re, Nicol's Case (1859) 3 De G & J 387, 28 LJ Ch 257, 5 Jur NS 205, 7 WR 217, 33 LTOS 14 .... 403, 1260, 1273
Royal British Bank, Re, ex p Walton, ex p Hue (1857) 26 LJ Ch 545, 3 Jur NS 853, 5 WR 637, 29 LTOS 322 403
Royal British Bank v Turquand (1856) 6 E & B 327, [1843–60] All ER Rep 435, 25 LJQB 317, 2 Jur NS 663, 119 ER 886, Ex Ch 262, 266, 297, 571, 1448, 1966
Royal Brunei Airlines Sdn Bhd v Tan [1995] 2 AC 378, [1995] 3 All ER 97, [1995] 3 WLR 64, [1995] BCC 899, [1995] 27 LS Gaz R 33, [1995] NLJR 888, PC 632
Royal College of Music v Westminster Vestry [1898] 1 QB 809, 62 JP 357, 67 LJQB 540, 78 LT 441, 14 TLR 351, CA 1581
Royal Copper Mines of Cobre Co, Re, Kelk's Case, Pahlen's Case. See Cobre Copper Mine Co, Re, Kelk's Case
Royal Naval School, Re, Seymour v Royal Naval School [1910] 1 Ch 806, 79 LJ Ch 366, 54 Sol Jo 407, 102 LT 490, 26 TLR 382 1899
Royal Trust Bank v National Westminster Bank plc [1996] 2 BCLC 699, [1996] BCC 613, CA 1455
Royal Westminster Investments SA v Varma [2012] EWHC 3439 (Ch), [2012] All ER (D) 370 (Nov) 383
Royscot Trust Ltd v Rogerson [1991] 2 QB 297, [1991] 3 All ER 294, [1991] 3 WLR 57, 135 Sol Jo 444, [1991] NLJR 493, CA 1276
Rubber Improvement Ltd v Daily Telegraph Ltd [1964] AC 234, [1963] 2 WLR 1063, 107 Sol Jo 356, sub nom Lewis v Daily Telegraph Ltd [1963] 2 All ER 151, HL 301
Ruben v Great Fingall Consolidated [1906] AC 439, [1904–7] All ER Rep 460, 75 LJKB 843, 13 Mans 248, 95 LT 214, 22 TLR 712, HL 122, 267, 276, 286, 398
Ruby Consolidated Mining Co, Re, Askew's Case (1874) 9 Ch App 664, 43 LJ Ch 633, 22 WR 833, 31 LT 55 354
Rudolph v Inns of Court Hotel Co. See R v Inns of Court Hotel Co Ltd, ex p Rudolf
Rudow v Great Britain Mutual Life Assurance Society (1881) 17 Ch D 600, [1881–5] All ER Rep 1124, 50 LJ Ch 504, 29 WR 585, 44 LT 688, CA 1270
Rule v Jewell (1881) 18 Ch D 660, 29 WR 755 1403
Runciman v Walter Runciman plc [1992] BCLC 1084, [1993] BCC 223 .... 567, 584, 600
Russell v East Anglian Rly Co (1850) 6 Ry & Can Cas 501, 572, 20 LJ Ch 257, 14 Jur 1033, 15 Jur 935, 3 Mac & G 104, 125, 16 LTOS 317, 17 LTOS 298 .... 1550, 1932, 1934, 1938, 1941

PARA

T

V

PARA

West Jewell Tin Mining Co, Re, Weston's Case (1879) 10 Ch D 579, 48 LJ Ch 425, 27 WR 310, 40 LT 43, CA 58

West London Commercial Bank Ltd v Kitson (1884) 13 QBD 360, 53 LJQB 345, 32 WR 757, 50 LT 656, CA 276, 294, 635, 1261

West London Rly Co v Bernard (1843) 3 QB 873, 3 Ry & Can Cas 649, 13 LJQB 68, 1 Dav & Mer 397, 8 Jur 144, 2 LTOS 187 1971

West Mercia Safetywear Ltd v Dodd [1988] BCLC 250, 4 BCC 30, CA 585, 638

West of England Bank, Re, ex p Booker (1880) 14 Ch D 317, 49 LJ Ch 400, 28 WR 809, 42 LT 619 259–260

West Somerset Mineral Rly Co v Robinson (1917) 62 Sol Jo 175, 34 TLR 132 1974

West Yorkshire Darracq Agency Ltd v Coleridge [1911] 2 KB 326, 80 LJKB 1122, 18 Mans 307, 105 LT 215 558

Westburn Sugar Refineries Ltd, ex p [1951] AC 625, [1951] 1 All ER 881, 95 Sol Jo 317, [1951] 1 TLR 728, HL 1368, 1372

Western Bank of Scotland v Addie (1867) LR 1 Sc & Div 145, HL 297, 325, 1260, 1270, 1273

Western Bank of Scotland v Bairds' Trustees (1872) 11 M 96 520

Western Counties Steam Bakeries and Milling Co, Re [1897] 1 Ch 617, 66 LJ Ch 354, 45 WR 418, 41 Sol Jo 365, 76 LT 239, 13 TLR 276, CA 520, 679, 682, 1004

Western Finance Co Ltd v Tasker Enterprises Ltd (1979) 106 DLR (3d) 81, Man CA 583

Western of Canada Oil, Lands and Works Co, Re [1874] WN 148 1612

Western of Canada Oil, Lands and Works Co, Re, Carling, Hespeler and Walsh's Cases (1875) 1 Ch D 115, 45 LJ Ch 5, 24 WR 165, 33 LT 645, CA 47, 533

Western of Canada Oil, Lands and Works Co v Walker (1875) 10 Ch App 628, 45 LJ Ch 165, 23 WR 738, CA in Ch 309

WestLB AG v Nomura Bank International plc [2010] EWHC 2863 (Comm), [2010] All ER (D) 136 (Nov); affd [2012] EWCA Civ 495, [2012] All ER (D) 116 (Apr) 65

Westmaze Ltd, Re [1999] BCC 441, (1998) Times, 15 July 1455

Westmid Packaging Services Ltd, Re, Secretary of State for Trade and Industry v Griffiths [1995] BCC 203 1787

Westmid Packing Services Ltd, Re, Secretary of State for Trade and Industry v Griffiths [1998] 2 All ER 124, [1998] 2 BCLC 646, [1998] BCC 836, CA 577, 579, 589, 1802

Westminster City Council v Treby [1936] 2 All ER 21, 80 Sol Jo 465 1516

Westminster Corpn v Haste [1950] Ch 442, [1950] 2 All ER 65, 49 LGR 67, 114 JP 340, 66 (pt 1) TLR 1083 1516

Westminster Motor Garage Co, Re, Boyers v Westminster Motor Garage Co (1914) 84 LJ Ch 753, 112 LT 393 1551

Westminster Property Group plc, Re [1985] 2 All ER 426, [1985] 1 WLR 676, [1985] BCLC 188, [1985] PCC 176, 129 Sol Jo 115, [1985] LS Gaz R 1085, CA 1734

Westminster Property Management Ltd, Re, Official Receiver v Stern. See Official Receiver v Stern

Westminster Syndicate Ltd, Re [1908] WN 236, 99 LT 924, 25 TLR 95 ..... 1452, 1550

Westmoreland Green and Blue Slate Co, Re, Bland's Case [1893] 2 Ch 612, 62 LJ Ch 975, 2 R 509, 69 LT 700, CA 54–55, 58

Westmoreland Green and Blue Slate Co v Feilden [1891] 3 Ch 15, 60 LJ Ch 680, 40 WR 23, 65 LT 428, 7 TLR 585, CA 1331

Weston v New Guston Co (1889) 1 Meg 225, 62 LT 275, CA; affd (1891) 64 LT 815, HL 1620

Weston's Case. See Cobre Copper Mining Co, Re, Weston's Case

Weston's Case. See West Jewell Tin Mining Co, Re, Weston's Case

Wetherspoon (J D) plc v Van de Berg & Co Ltd [2007] EWHC 1044 (Ch), [2007] All ER (D) 82 (May) 574

X

Decisions of the European Court of Justice are listed below numerically. These decisions are also included in the preceding alphabetical list.

COMPANIES

Volume 14

Volume 15A

1. COMPANY LAW: INTRODUCTION

(1) COMPANIES AND OTHER BUSINESS STRUCTURES: IN GENERAL

1. General meaning of 'company'. The general sense of the word 'company' denotes an association of individuals formed together for some common purpose[1]. The word is defined for the strict purposes of the Companies Act 2006 to mean a company that has been formed and registered under that Act (and, accordingly, is governed by its provisions)[2], although it may include companies formed and registered under earlier enactments[3].

Company law has developed in such a way that it recognises an incorporated company to be an entity with a personality that is distinct from the members (or, where the company has a share capital, the shareholders) who collectively constitute the company[4].

There are many other bodies corporate[5] which, although they may largely or partially engage in trading or comparable activities, are not commonly described as companies. These fall broadly into two categories:

(1) those incorporated pursuant to some general Act of Parliament permitting incorporation to be effected by any body of persons which fulfils specified conditions: of these the chief examples are building societies[6] and industrial and provident societies, co-operative societies and community benefit societies[7]; and

(2) those known as public corporations: these are created to fulfil in each case some special social or economic purpose, and are created either by royal charter[8] or, more commonly, by statute[9] which defines the objects, constitution and powers of the corporation: examples include the British Broadcasting Corporation[10]; the Office of Communications ('OFCOM')[11]; Transport for London[12]; the Independent Police Complaints Commission[13]; and the Office of Rail and Road[14].

1 For present needs, there is an implication in the word 'company' that the purpose for which the individuals have joined together is of a more or less permanent character. Companies, particularly those formed under the Companies Acts, typically provide for investment in trade with a view to generating profits in order to benefit their proprietors: see eg *Re a Company (No 00709 of 1992), O'Neill v Phillips* [1999] 2 All ER 961 at 966, [1999] 1 WLR 1092 at 1098, HL, per Lord Hoffmann ('a company is an association of persons for an economic purpose, usually entered into with legal advice and some degree of formality'). Contrast with the legal definition of a club as a society of persons associated together, not for the principal purposes of trade, but for social reasons, the promotion of politics, sport, art, science or literature, or for any other lawful purpose: see CLUBS vol 13 (2009) PARA 201.

In a legal context, it has been said that the word 'company', while having no strictly technical meaning, involves two ideas (*Re Stanley, Tennant v Stanley* [1906] 1 Ch 131 at 134 per Buckley J), namely:

(1) that the members of the association are so numerous that it cannot aptly be described as a firm or partnership; and

(2) that a member may transfer his interest in the association without the consent of all the other members.

As to the meanings of 'firm' and 'partnership' see PARTNERSHIP vol 79 (2014) PARA 1; and see *Smith v Anderson* (1880) 15 ChD 247 at 273, CA, per James LJ (discussing ordinary partnerships). However, in contrast to what is stated in head (1) above, a company formed and registered under the Companies Act 2006 may legally consist of only one person (see s 7; and PARA 95); and, in contrast to what is stated in head (2) above, the typical modern form of company is a private company limited by shares where restrictions on the transfer of the member's shares in the company are commonplace (see PARA 403 et seq). Note also that, while companies limited by shares typically are formed for the purposes of trade and profit, many companies limited by guarantee operate on a not-for-profit basis and in the community interest. Community interest companies (which are governed by the provisions of the Companies Acts, subject to the Companies (Audit, Investigations and Community Enterprise) Act 2004 Pt 2 (ss 26–63): see the Companies Act 2006 s 6; and PARA 75) also constitute a form of registered corporate vehicle whose activities are intended to be carried on for the benefit of the community rather than its members. As to the meaning of the 'Companies Acts' see PARA 13; and as to the meanings of 'company limited by shares', 'company limited by guarantee' and 'private company' see PARA 95. As to community interest companies see PARA 75 et seq.

There is no definitive authority for what constitutes 'trade'. The balance of authority indicates that 'trade' is a wider term than 'business' (see eg *Re a Debtor (No 3 of 1926)* [1927] 1 Ch 97, [1926] All ER Rep 337, CA; *Re a Debtor, ex p Debtor (No 490 of 1935)* [1936] Ch 237, CA), although it has been equated with 'business' (see *Grainger & Son v Gough* [1896] AC 325 at 343, HL, per Lord Morris). 'Business' is an occupation or duty which requires attention (*Rolls v Miller* (1884) 27 ChD 71 at 88, CA, per Lindley LJ) whether or not this involves economic activity or any profit or gain (*Rael-Brook Ltd v Minister of Housing and Local Government* [1967] 2 QB 65, [1967] 1 All ER 262). 'Gain' is not limited to pecuniary gain or confined to commercial profits only; and a company is formed for the acquisition of gain if it is formed to acquire something, as distinguished from a company formed for spending something: *Re Arthur Average Association for British, Foreign and Colonial Ships, ex p Hargrove & Co* (28 April 1875, unreported) per Jessel MR, cited in *Re Arthur Average Association for British, Foreign and Colonial Ships, ex p Hargrove & Co* (1875) 10 Ch App 542 at 546n, 547n. Business is 'carried on' only where there is a joint relation of persons for the common purpose of performing jointly a succession of acts, and not where the relation exists for a purpose which is to be completed by the performance of one act: *Smith v Anderson* (1880) 15 ChD 247, CA (overruling *Sykes v Beadon* (1879) 11 ChD 170); *Dominion Iron and Steel Co Ltd v Invernairn* [1927] WN 277. See also *IRC v Marine Steam Turbine Co Ltd* [1920] 1 KB 193, 12 TC 174 ('carrying on' business is not merely a question of whether there is business involved in what people are doing; the word 'business' means an active occupation or profession continually carried on). Business can be carried on where a company is still continuing to solicit for a particular type of work and retains the capacity to resume work of that kind were it given the opportunity so to do, even though that type of work is not presently being carried out: *Pamment v Sutton* (1998) Times, 15 December.

A single individual may, if he wishes, carry on business under the style of 'Such and such Company', but he does not thereby become a 'company'. The use of other stylings, which include the forms 'plc' or 'limited' as the last word, is prohibited unless certain conditions are met: see PARA 224. As to structures that might be used as an alternative to the registered company for the conduct of business see PARA 4.

2 As to the meaning of 'company' for the purposes of the Companies Acts see PARA 21. As to companies formed and registered under the Companies Act 2006, and the different forms that a company may take, see PARA 65 et seq. It is possible for a company, whether registered under the Companies Acts or not, to be illegally formed, in which case its existence is not recognised in law: see PARA 99 et seq.

3 The long title of the Companies Act 2006 states that it is an 'Act to reform company law and restate the greater part of the enactments relating to companies'. It is the successor to various earlier statutes which from time to time made general provision for companies to be established with a legal status and personality of their own ('incorporation') by means of registration with the registrar of companies: see PARA 10. As to the meaning of 'registrar of companies' see PARA 126 note 2. Increasingly, incorporation by registration replaced the previous practice which had required the obtaining of a special Act of Parliament or a royal charter (see head (2) in the text): see PARA 10 note 1. As to the development of companies legislation leading up to the Companies Act 1985, and the review of company law which led to the Companies Act 2006 as enacted, see PARAS 11–13.

4 See PARAS 2, 116. The directors owe any fiduciary duties to the company, not to its members (whether treated as individuals or as a class or as a body): see PARA 572 et seq. Statute also imposes a duty on directors to have regard to the interests of the company's employees: see PARA 584.

5 For the purposes of the Companies Acts, 'body corporate' and 'corporation' include a body incorporated outside the United Kingdom, but do not include a corporation sole, or a partnership that, whether or not a legal person, is not regarded as a body corporate under the law by which it is governed: Companies Act 2006 s 1173(1). As to corporations sole see CORPORATIONS vol 24 (2010) PARAS 314–315. As to the legal personality of a partnership or firm generally see PARTNERSHIP vol 79 (2014) PARA 2. As to companies and corporations see further PARA 2.

In any Act, unless the contrary intention appears, 'United Kingdom' means Great Britain and Northern Ireland: Interpretation Act 1978 s 5, Sch 1. Neither the Isle of Man nor the Channel Islands are within the United Kingdom: see CONSTITUTIONAL AND ADMINISTRATIVE LAW vol 20 (2014) PARA 3. 'Great Britain' means England, Scotland and Wales: Union with Scotland

Act 1706, preamble art I; Interpretation Act 1978 s 22(1), Sch 2 para 5(a). 'England' means, subject to any alteration of the boundaries of local government areas, the areas consisting of the counties established by the Local Government Act 1972 s 1 (see LOCAL GOVERNMENT vol 69 (2009) PARAS 5, 24), and Greater London and the Isles of Scilly: see the Interpretation Act 1978 s 5, Sch 1. As to local government areas in England see LOCAL GOVERNMENT vol 69 (2009) PARA 22 et seq; and as to boundary changes see LOCAL GOVERNMENT vol 69 (2009) PARA 54 et seq. As to Greater London see LONDON GOVERNMENT vol 71 (2013) PARA 14 et seq. 'Wales' means the combined areas of the counties created by the Local Government Act 1972 s 20 (as originally enacted) (see LOCAL GOVERNMENT vol 69 (2009) PARAS 5, 37), but subject to any alteration made under s 73 (consequential alteration of boundary following alteration of watercourse: see LOCAL GOVERNMENT vol 69 (2009) PARA 90): see the Interpretation Act 1978 Sch 1 (definition substituted by the Local Government (Wales) Act 1994 s 1(3), Sch 2 para 9). See further CONSTITUTIONAL AND ADMINISTRATIVE LAW vol 20 (2014) PARAS 3, 75.

6 As to the general nature of building societies see FINANCIAL INSTITUTIONS vol 48 (2015) PARA 330.

7 As to the nature of industrial and provident societies and co-operative and community benefit societies see FINANCIAL INSTITUTIONS vol 48 (2015) PARA 880. Such societies are normally described as 'limited': see the Co-operative and Community Benefits Societies Act 2014 s 10(2); and FINANCIAL INSTITUTIONS vol 48 (2015) PARA 927.

8 Companies created by royal charter fall within the provisions of the Companies Act 2006 that apply to 'unregistered companies': see s 1043; and PARA 1353. See also PARA 3.

9 When a corporation has been incorporated by an Act of Parliament, the Act becomes the charter of the corporation, declaring its rights and powers and prescribing its duties and obligations: see CORPORATIONS vol 24 (2010) PARA 346. Incorporation by special Act of Parliament was formerly much used, particularly where the company was intended to provide services of a quasi-public nature. (Most such corporations were dissolved in consequence of the nationalisation of their undertakings, eg by the Transport Act 1947 in the case of railway and canal companies, although some still survive). This method of incorporation is now rare: see CORPORATIONS vol 24 (2010) PARA 344 et seq; and see PARA 2 note 9. Companies created by special Act of Parliament are regulated by the Companies Clauses Acts (see PARAS 1858–2012) rather than by the Companies Acts.

10 The British Broadcasting Corporation is a body incorporated by royal charter: see BROADCASTING vol 4 (2011) PARA 603.

11 See the Office of Communications Act 2002 s 1; and TELECOMMUNICATIONS vol 97 (2015) PARA 2.

12 See the Greater London Authority Act 1999 s 154; and LONDON GOVERNMENT vol 71 (2013) PARA 163 et seq.

13 See the Police Reform Act 2002 s 9; and POLICE AND INVESTIGATORY POWERS vol 84 (2013) PARA 287 et seq.

14 See the Railways and Transport Safety Act 2003 ss 15(1), 15A; and RAILWAYS AND TRAMWAYS vol 86 (2013) PARA 49 et seq.

2. Companies and corporations. A company may be either incorporated (that is, a body corporate with perpetual succession[1]) or unincorporated[2]. An incorporated company is recognised by the law as having a personality which is distinct from the separate personalities of the members of the company in question[3]. An unincorporated company has no such separate existence and it is not in law an entity distinguishable from its members[4].

Corporations may be classified according to their method of creation or by their nature and purpose[5]. By number, most corporations are formed for the purpose of securing a profit for their members, either by trading or by the holding of investments or other property, and are incorporated under the Companies Acts or one of the other statutes authorising the creation of corporate status by registration[6]. Although there are still a few privately owned trading corporations incorporated by royal charter[7], and a number of such corporations incorporated by special Act of Parliament[8], corporations formed for the profit of their members are no longer formed by these methods[9]. Corporations formed for public purposes are usually incorporated by public general Act of Parliament[10]. Incorporation by royal charter is now in practice limited to institutions such as universities and the principal scientific, cultural, professional or charitable organisations. Other organisations of these kinds are incorporated under the Companies Acts if they desire to have corporate status.

1 As to the meaning of 'body corporate' under the Companies Acts see PARA 1 note 5; and as to the meaning of the 'Companies Acts' see PARA 13. As to the creation of corporations generally see CORPORATIONS vol 24 (2010) PARA 329 et seq.
2 *Re St James' Club* (1852) 2 De GM & G 383 at 389; *Re Griffith, Carr v Griffith* (1879) 12 ChD 655. However, see PARA 3.
3 See the Companies Act 2006 s 16(2), (3); and PARA 115.
4 A company which is neither a corporation nor a partnership is a thing unknown to the common law: see *Macintyre v Connell* (1851) 1 Sim NS 225 at 233. As to unincorporated companies see PARA 3.
5 See CORPORATIONS vol 24 (2010) PARA 301 et seq.
6 See PARA 1; and CORPORATIONS vol 24 (2010) PARA 344.
7 See PARA 1; and CORPORATIONS vol 24 (2010) PARA 331.
8 See PARA 1 note 9.
9 A private Act of Parliament may sometimes be obtained to facilitate the merger of existing corporations by constituting one corporation the 'universal successor' (ie successor to the liabilities as well as the assets) of one or more other corporations: see eg the National Westminster Bank Act 1969, passed in connection with the merger of the National Provincial Bank Ltd and the Westminster Bank Ltd into the National Westminster Bank Ltd (which had itself been incorporated under the Companies Act 1948).
10 See PARA 1. In a few cases corporations having public functions of a local nature may be incorporated by local Act of Parliament: see eg the Chichester Harbour Conservancy, incorporated by the Chichester Harbour Conservancy Act 1971.

3. Unincorporated companies and companies formed by royal charter. Despite having origins which predate all the Companies Acts legislation, unincorporated companies and companies formed by royal charter remain as lawful company associations.

Notwithstanding the repeal of the Chartered Companies Act 1837 and the Chartered Companies Act 1884[1], the power of Her Majesty to grant a charter of incorporation of limited duration or to extend or renew such a charter or privileges of such a charter is not affected[2].

However, few, if any, unincorporated companies that were in existence before 2 November 1862[3] now remain[4].

1 Ie the Chartered Companies Act 1837 and the Chartered Companies Act 1884 (both repealed by the Statute Law (Repeals) Act 1993 s 1(1), Sch 1 Pt V).
2 See the Statute Law (Repeals) Act 1993 s 1(2), Sch 2 para 11.
3 Ie the date when the Companies Act 1862 (see PARA 10) came into full operation: see s 2 (repealed).
4 Unincorporated companies were usually formed under deeds of settlement setting out the company's objects and constitution. The question sometimes arose as to whether such companies had power to transfer the whole of their undertaking to new companies: see *Re Era Assurance Co, Williams' Case, Anchor Case* (1860) 30 LJ Ch 137; *Kearns v Leaf* (1864) 1 Hem & M 681; *Re European Assurance Society Arbitration Acts, Doman's Case* (1876) 3 ChD 21, CA; *Re Argus Life Assurance Co* (1888) 39 ChD 571.

4. Alternative structures to the registered company. The structure of a company registered under the Companies Acts[1] may not be appropriate for the conduct of a particular business[2]. Alternative structures for a business include:

(1) a sole trader[3];
(2) a firm or partnership[4];
(3) a limited partnership[5]; and
(4) a limited liability partnership[6].

One significant difference between a partnership and a company is that, in general, apart from the exceptions listed under heads (3) and (4) above, a partnership does not confer limited liability on the partners[7].

1 As to the meaning of the 'Companies Acts' see PARA 13. As to companies formed and registered under the Companies Acts see PARA 95 et seq.
2 As to the legal effect on a company of incorporation under the Companies Acts see PARA 115.
3 Ie an individual who is carrying on business and is not in partnership with any other person. As to the meaning of 'carry on business' generally see PARA 1 note 1. The stated policy objectives for the review of company law that led to the passing of the Companies Act 2006 included making the administrative burden for small private companies, which constituted the bulk of the number of companies formed and registered in the United Kingdom, lighter and more appropriate to their needs (the 'Think Small First' approach): see HM Government's White Paper *Modernising Company Law* (Cm 5553) (2002); and White Paper *Company Law Reform* (Cm 6456) (2005). Accordingly, the requirement for private companies to have a company secretary is abolished (see the Companies Act 2006 s 270; and PARA 669) and private companies may take decisions by means of written resolution, the need for Annual General Meetings (AGMs) having become optional (see s 288; and PARA 695). The Companies Act 2006 also provides for a single person to form a public company: see s 7; and PARA 95. As to the meanings of 'public company' and 'private company' see PARA 95.
4 As to the meanings of 'firm' and 'partnership' see PARTNERSHIP vol 79 (2014) PARA 1; and as to the legal personality of a partnership or firm generally see PARTNERSHIP vol 79 (2014) PARA 2.
5 Ie a partnership formed under the Limited Partnerships Act 1907 which allows a limited partner's liability to the creditors of the firm to be strictly limited: see PARTNERSHIP vol 79 (2014) PARA 217 et seq. See also the Legislative Reform (Limited Partnerships) Order 2009, SI 2009/1940, which clarifies some uncertainties about the application of the Limited Partnerships Act 1907, principally regarding the process for registration of limited partnerships by the registrar of companies.
6 Ie a body corporate, with legal personality separate from that of its members, which is governed primarily by the Limited Liability Partnerships Act 2000, the Limited Liability Partnerships Regulations 2001, SI 2001/1090, and the Limited Liability Partnerships (Application of Companies Act 2006) Regulations 2009, SI 2009/1804: see PARTNERSHIP vol 79 (2014) PARA 233 et seq. As to the application of certain company law provisions to limited liability partnerships see PARA 27.
7 See PARTNERSHIP vol 79 (2014) PARA 3.

5. European companies: in general. A small number of European Union ('EU') Regulations provide for new forms of trading entity to be formed whose legal personality is recognised by all member states[1]. For the purposes of making further provision in relation to those EU Regulations, Parliament makes secondary legislation, some of whose provisions typically apply relevant sections of the Companies Acts[2] to these structures, notably in relation to their formation and registration, but also in relation to other subjects for which provision is required under the parent EU Regulation[3]. The following structures have been provided for under EU Regulations:

(1) European Economic Interest Grouping[4];
(2) European Company ('Societas Europaea')[5].

There is also a more recent proposal for a new EU Directive under which single-member private limited liability companies formed and operating in compliance with its provisions would add to their names a common, easily identifiable abbreviation 'SUP' ('Societas Unius Personae')[6].

1 As to EU Regulations that have relevance to company law generally see PARA 19.
2 As to the meaning of the 'Companies Acts' see PARA 13.
3 Subjects such as accounts or employee participation are sometimes specifically provided for in the parent EU Regulation. As to formation and registration under the Companies Acts see PARA 95 et seq.
4 See Council Regulation (EEC) 2137/85 of 25 July 1985 (OJ L199, 31.07.1985, p 1) on the European Economic Interest Grouping ('EEIG'); and PARA 1823. The EEIG provides a vehicle for smaller commercial undertakings to co-operate with others from different member states in the European Union, and to provide common support activities for members with unlimited liability, by pooling resources or skills to the benefit of the group, and by allowing for the development of

academic or technical advancements that would not have been achievable by individual concerns acting alone. For the purposes of making further provision in relation to this Regulation, the European Economic Interest Grouping Regulations 1989, SI 1989/638, and the Registrar of Companies (Fees) (European Economic Interest Grouping and European Public Limited-Liability Company) Regulations 2012, SI 2012/1908, have been made: see PARA 1824. From the date of registration of an EEIG in the United Kingdom, an EEIG is a body corporate: see the European Economic Interest Grouping Regulations 1989, SI 1989/638, reg 3; and PARA 1824. As to the meaning of 'United Kingdom' see PARA 1 note 5.

5 See Council Regulation (EC) 2157/2001 (OJ L294, 10.11.2001, p 1) on the Statute for a European Company; and PARA 1825 et seq. See also Council Directive (EC) 2001/86 (OJ L294, 10.11.2001, p 22) supplementing the Statute for a European Company with regard to the involvement of employees. For the purposes of implementing that Directive, and for making further provision in relation to the Regulation, the European Public Limited-Liability Company Regulations 2004, SI 2004/2326, the European Public Limited-Liability Company (Employee Involvement) (Great Britain) Regulations 2009, SI 2009/2401, and the Registrar of Companies (Fees) (European Economic Interest Grouping and European Public Limited-Liability Company) Regulations 2012, SI 2012/1908, have been made: see PARAS 1829, 1831. A European Company is a form of public limited-liability company and it has legal personality: see Council Regulation (EC) 2157/2001 (OJ L294, 10.11.2001, p 1) art 1; and PARA 1825.

6 See PARA 20 note 18.

(2) SECRETARY OF STATE'S FUNCTIONS IN RELATION TO COMPANIES

6. Meaning of 'Secretary of State'; Secretary of State with responsibility for companies matters. In any enactment, 'Secretary of State' means one of Her Majesty's principal Secretaries of State[1]. The office of Secretary of State is a unified office, and in law each Secretary of State is capable of performing the functions of all or any of them[2].

For the purposes of the Companies Acts[3], the powers of the Secretary of State are exercised in practice by the Secretary of State for Business, Innovation and Skills[4]. However, provision is made for certain statutory functions of the Secretary of State to be contracted out or formally delegated and this power has been exercised by the Secretary of State in relation to certain of his powers under the Companies Acts[5].

Except as otherwise provided, or as the context otherwise requires, the provisions of the Companies Act 2006 extend to the whole of the United Kingdom[6].

1 See the Interpretation Act 1978 s 5, Sch 1.

2 See CONSTITUTIONAL AND ADMINISTRATIVE LAW vol 20 (2014) PARA 153.

3 As to the meaning of the 'Companies Acts' see PARA 13.

4 The Secretary of State for Business, Innovation and Skills is often known as the 'Business Secretary' and is also the President of the Board of Trade. The Secretary of State for Business, Innovation and Skills Order 2009, SI 2009/2748, came into force on 13 November 2009 (see art 1); and provided for the functions of the Secretary of State for Business, Enterprise and Regulatory Reform, and for the functions of the Secretary of State for Innovation, Universities and Skills, to be transferred to the Secretary of State for Business, Innovation and Skills (see art 4). As to the corresponding transfers of property, rights and liabilities see art 5; as to the incorporation of the Secretary of State for Business, Innovation and Skills see art 3; and as to other supplemental provision see arts 6, 7. The responsibilities entrusted to the Secretary of State for Business, Innovation and Skills were described in a press notice issued by the Prime Minister's Office on 5 June 2009, which was referred to in the Prime Minister's written statement to Parliament: see 494 HC Official Report (6th series), 18 June 2009, written ministerial statements col 452W.

5 See PARA 7.

6 See the Companies Act 2006 s 1299; and PARA 26.

7. Company law functions of the Secretary of State subject to contracting out and delegation. The numerous functions of the Secretary of State[1] in relation to the formation and supervision of companies are considered elsewhere in this title[2].

Any function of the Secretary of State which is conferred by or under any enactment and which, by virtue of any enactment or rule of law, may be exercised by an officer of his and which is not otherwise excluded[3] may, if the Secretary of State by order so provides, be exercised by, or by employees of, such person, if any, as may be authorised in that behalf by the Secretary of State[4].

Such an order may provide that any function to which it applies may be exercised, and an authorisation given by virtue of such an order may, subject to the provisions of the order, authorise the exercise of such a function[5]:

(1) either wholly or to such extent as may be specified in the order or authorisation[6];

(2) either generally or in such cases or areas as may be so specified[7]; and

(3) either unconditionally or subject to the fulfilment of such conditions as may be so specified[8].

An authorisation given by virtue of such an order:

(a) must be for such period, not exceeding ten years, as is specified in the authorisation[9];

(b) may be revoked at any time by the Secretary of State[10]; and

(c) must not prevent the Secretary of State or any other person from exercising the function to which the authorisation relates[11].

Where by virtue of such an order a person is authorised to exercise any function of the Secretary of State[12], anything done or omitted to be done by or in relation to the authorised person, or an employee of his, in, or in connection with, the exercise or purported exercise of the function is to be treated for all purposes as done or omitted to be done[13] by or in relation to the Secretary of State in his capacity as such[14]. However, this provision does not apply[15]:

(i) for the purposes of so much of any contract made between an authorised person and the Secretary of State as relates to the exercise of the function[16]; or

(ii) for the purposes of any criminal proceedings brought in respect of anything done or omitted to be done by the authorised person (or any employee of his)[17].

Where by virtue of such an order a person is authorised to exercise any function of the Secretary of State[18] and the order or authorisation is revoked at a time when a relevant contract[19] is subsisting[20], the authorised person is entitled to treat the relevant contract as repudiated by the Secretary of State, and not as frustrated by reason of the revocation[21].

1 As to the Secretary of State generally see PARA 6.

2 See PARA 21 et seq.

3 Deregulation and Contracting Out Act 1994 s 69(1). The text refers to any function which is not otherwise excluded from s 69 by s 71: see s 69(1). A function is excluded by s 69 if:

(1) its exercise would constitute the exercise of jurisdiction of any court or of any tribunal which exercises the judicial power of the state (s 71(1)(a)); or

(2) its exercise, or a failure to exercise it, would necessarily interfere with or otherwise affect the liberty of any individual (s 71(1)(b)); or

(3) it is a power or right of entry, search or seizure into or of any property (s 71(1)(c)); or

(4) it is a power or duty to make subordinate legislation (s 71(1)(d)).

The provisions of s 71(1)(b), (c) (see heads (2)–(3) above) do not exclude any function of the official receiver attached to any court: s 71(2). As to the official receiver see COMPANY AND PARTNERSHIP INSOLVENCY vol 16 (2011) PARA 453 et seq.

4 Deregulation and Contracting Out Act 1994 s 69(2). In exercise of the powers so conferred the Secretary of State has made the Contracting Out (Functions in relation to the Registration of Companies) Order 1995, SI 1995/1013, art 5, Sch 3: see PARA 8. As to contracting out the

functions of the registrar of companies see PARAS 128–129. As to the power to contract out functions of the official receiver see COMPANY AND PARTNERSHIP INSOLVENCY vol 16 (2011) PARAS 455–456.
5 Deregulation and Contracting Out Act 1994 s 69(4).
6 Deregulation and Contracting Out Act 1994 s 69(4)(a).
7 Deregulation and Contracting Out Act 1994 s 69(4)(b).
8 Deregulation and Contracting Out Act 1994 s 69(4)(c).
9 Deregulation and Contracting Out Act 1994 s 69(5)(a).
10 Deregulation and Contracting Out Act 1994 s 69(5)(b).
11 Deregulation and Contracting Out Act 1994 s 69(5)(c).
12 Deregulation and Contracting Out Act 1994 s 72(1).
13 Deregulation and Contracting Out Act 1994 s 72(2).
14 Deregulation and Contracting Out Act 1994 s 72(2)(a).
15 Deregulation and Contracting Out Act 1994 s 72(3).
16 Deregulation and Contracting Out Act 1994 s 72(3)(a).
17 Deregulation and Contracting Out Act 1994 s 72(3)(b).
18 Deregulation and Contracting Out Act 1994 s 73(1)(a).
19 For these purposes, 'relevant contract' means so much of any contract made between the authorised person and the Secretary of State as relates to the exercise of the function: Deregulation and Contracting Out Act 1994 s 73(3).
20 Deregulation and Contracting Out Act 1994 s 73(1)(b).
21 Deregulation and Contracting Out Act 1994 s 73(2).

8. Contracted out and delegated company law functions of the Secretary of State. Any function of the Secretary of State[1] which is listed in any of heads (1) to (3) below may be exercised by, or by employees of, such person, if any, as may be authorised in that behalf by the Secretary of State[2]:

(1) functions conferred by or under the following provisions of the Companies Acts:
   (a) those[3] relating to the prohibition on registration of certain names except with the approval of the Secretary of State[4];
   (b) those[5] relating to the extension by the Secretary of State of the period allowed for laying and delivering accounts and reports[6];
   (c) those[7] relating to the extension of the period for delivering accounts and reports of an overseas company[8];
(2) functions conferred[9] relating to the prohibition of use of certain business names[10];
(3) functions as conferred under head (2) above[11] but as applied[12] to European Economic Interest Groupings[13].

In addition, the Financial Reporting Council Limited is designated for the purpose of enabling it to exercise certain functions of the Secretary of State relating to statutory auditors under Part 42[14] of the Companies Act 2006[15].

1 As to the Secretary of State generally see PARA 6.
2 See the Contracting Out (Functions in relation to the Registration of Companies) Order 1995, SI 1995/1013, art 5.
3 Ie the Companies Act 2006 ss 54(1)–(3), 55(1) (formerly the Companies Act 1985 s 26(2)) (see PARA 195): see the Contracting Out (Functions in relation to the Registration of Companies) Order 1995, SI 1995/1013, art 5, Sch 3 para 1(a); and the Interpretation Act 1978 s 17(2)(b).
4 Contracting Out (Functions in relation to the Registration of Companies) Order 1995, SI 1995/1013, Sch 3 para 1(a).
5 Ie the Companies Act 2006 s 442(5) (formerly the Companies Act 1985 s 244(5)) (see PARA 951): see the Contracting Out (Functions in relation to the Registration of Companies) Order 1995, SI 1995/1013, Sch 3 para 1(b); and the Interpretation Act 1978 s 17(2)(b).
6 Contracting Out (Functions in relation to the Registration of Companies) Order 1995, SI 1995/1013, Sch 3 para 1(b).
7 Ie the Overseas Companies Regulations 2009, SI 2009/1801, reg 40, made under the Companies Act 2006 s 1049 (see PARA 2019): see the Contracting Out (Functions in relation to the Registration of Companies) Order 1995, SI 1995/1013, Sch 3 para 1(c); and the Interpretation Act 1978 s 17(2)(b).

8 Contracting Out (Functions in relation to the Registration of Companies) Order 1995, SI 1995/1013, Sch 3 para 1(c). As to the meaning of 'overseas company' see PARA 2013.
9 Ie by or under the Companies Act 2006 ss 1193, 1194 (formerly the Business Names Act 1985 s 2) (see PARA 223): see the Contracting Out (Functions in relation to the Registration of Companies) Order 1995, SI 1995/1013, Sch 3 para 2; and the Interpretation Act 1978 s 17(2)(b).
10 Contracting Out (Functions in relation to the Registration of Companies) Order 1995, SI 1995/1013, Sch 3 para 2.
11 Ie by or under the Companies Act 2006 ss 1193, 1194 (formerly the Business Names Act 1985 s 2) (see PARA 223): see the Contracting Out (Functions in relation to the Registration of Companies) Order 1995, SI 1995/1013, Sch 3 para 3; and the Interpretation Act 1978 s 17(2)(b).
12 Ie by the European Economic Interest Groupings Regulations 1989, SI 1989/638, reg 17 (revoked): see the Contracting Out (Functions in relation to the Registration of Companies) Order 1995, SI 1995/1013, Sch 3 para 3.
13 Contracting Out (Functions in relation to the Registration of Companies) Order 1995, SI 1995/1013, Sch 3 para 3. For these purposes, 'European Economic Interest Grouping' means a European Economic Interest Grouping being a grouping formed in pursuance of Council Regulation (EC) 2137/85 of 25 July 1985 (OJ L199, 31.07.1985, p 1) art 1 (see PARA 1823): European Economic Interest Grouping Regulations 1989, SI 1989/638, reg 2(1) (definition applied by the Contracting Out (Functions in relation to the Registration of Companies) Order 1995, SI 1995/1013, art 2(1)).
14 Ie the Companies Act 2006 Pt 42 (ss 1209–1264) (see PARA 1059 et seq).
15 See the Statutory Auditors (Amendment of Companies Act 2006 and Delegation of Functions etc) Order 2012, SI 2012/1741, arts 6–16; and PARA 1067 et seq.

(3) OUTLINE OF COMPANIES LEGISLATION

(i) Domestic Legislation relating to Companies

9. Companies: the statutory framework. The main piece of legislation currently governing company law is the Companies Act 2006[1]. Although some statutes were repealed as a consequence of this Act, and although most of the provisions of the predecessor Companies Act 1985 are restated therein, the 2006 Act itself was not considered to be properly a consolidating measure[2], and provision continues to be made under earlier Acts in relation to certain discrete areas of the law, such as company investigations[3], orders imposing restrictions on shares following an investigation[4], and community interest companies[5]. Other measures which are not considered to fall within the strict purview of company law also continue to be relevant and are discussed in this title, most pertinently those surviving provisions of the Companies Act 1989 which confer powers to require information and documents to assist overseas regulatory authorities[6], and those provisions of the Companies (Audit, Investigations and Community Enterprise) Act 2004 which govern the supervision of accounts and reports[7] and bodies concerned with professional accounting standards[8].

Other notable pieces of legislation related to company law which are discussed in this title concern the disqualification of persons from being directors of companies or otherwise concerned with a company's affairs[9], the criminal offence of insider dealing[10], and insolvency matters[11].

Since 1986, there has been a growing body of primary and secondary legislation, supplemented by significant non-statutory rules, governing financial markets and securities regulation[12]. These matters had previously been dealt with primarily under companies legislation but they now constitute a separate, albeit still related, area of law, which develops along its own path, with boundaries between the two areas continuing to shift[13].

1 See PARA 21 et seq. As to legislation that applies when a company is not registered under the Companies Act 2006 see PARA 1. The statutory scheme based upon the Companies Act 2006

relies to a certain extent on HM Government's definition of what is and what is not a 'company law' provision: see PARA 13. Only the Companies Act 2006 Pts 1–39 (ss 1–1181), and Pts 45–47 (ss 1284–1300) so far as they apply for the purposes of Pts 1–39, are 'company law' provisions according to this definition. (See also the definition of the 'Companies Acts' in the Companies Act 2006 s 2 (cited in PARA 13)). It follows that Pts 40–44 (ss 1182–1283) do not constitute 'company law' provisions in these terms, despite lying within the 2006 Act. Parts 40–44 make provision in the following areas:

(1) company directors subject to foreign disqualification (see Pt 40 (ss 1182–1191); and PARAS 1811–1815);
(2) business names (see Pt 41 (ss 1192–1208); and PARAS 222–225);
(3) statutory auditors (see Pt 42 (ss 1209–1264); and PARA 1059 et seq);
(4) transparency obligations (see Pt 43 (ss 1265–1273); PARA 20; and FINANCIAL SERVICES REGULATION vol 50A (2016) PARA 623 et seq); and
(5) miscellaneous matters (see Pt 44 (ss 1274–1283), mostly amending provisions).

Conversely, although the provisions mentioned in the text and notes 3–5 lie outside the Companies Act 2006, they continue to constitute 'company law' provisions under the current statutory scheme. Further to head (1) above, the equivalent domestic provisions are contained in the Company Directors Disqualification Act 1986 (see the text and note 9; and PARA 1762 et seq).

2 The long title of the Companies Act 2006 states that it is an 'Act to reform company law and restate the greater part of the enactments relating to companies'. See also PARA 13.

3 Ie the Companies Act 1985 Pt XIV (ss 431–453D): see PARA 1725 et seq. Although these provisions can apply to bodies other than companies, they are still regarded as company law provisions under the statutory scheme mentioned in note 1. As to the meaning of 'company law provisions' for these purposes see PARA 13 note 6.

4 Ie the Companies Act 1985 Pt XV (ss 454–457): see PARAS 1732–1734. The Companies Act 2006 ss 797–802 impose similar restrictions to those set out in the Companies Act 1985 ss 454–457: see PARAS 457–460.

5 Ie the Companies (Audit, Investigations and Community Enterprise) Act 2004 Pt 2 (ss 26–63): see PARA 75 et seq. Note that, although the provisions which govern community interest companies are still regarded as company law provisions under the statutory scheme mentioned in note 1, they are, however, regarded under that scheme as forming a distinct body of regulation which is additional to, and sits alongside, company law rather than forming part of it. The provisions of the Companies Acts, apart from the Companies Act 2006 s 6 (see PARA 75), have effect subject to the Companies (Audit Investigations and Community Enterprise) Act 2004 Pt 2: see the Companies Act 2006 s 6(2); and PARA 75.

6 Ie the Companies Act 1989 Pt III (ss 55–91) (overseas regulation): see PARA 1752 et seq. The provisions contained in Pt VII (ss 154–191) (financial markets and insolvency) also are not regarded as company law provisions under the statutory scheme mentioned in note 1 and have not been repealed by the Companies Act 2006: see FINANCIAL SERVICES REGULATION vol 50A (2016) PARA 728 et seq.

7 Ie the Companies (Audit, Investigations and Community Enterprise) Act 2004 ss 14, 15–15E (see PARA 771), which allow for the appointment of a body, the conduct committee established under the articles of the Financial Reporting Council Limited, to review the accounts of all listed companies, whether Companies Act companies or otherwise, and to review compliance with the accounting requirements of the Listing Rules. These provisions are considered to relate more to financial services law than to company law under the statutory scheme mentioned in note 1. As to the Financial Conduct Authority's Listing Rules ('Part 6 rules') see FINANCIAL SERVICES REGULATION vol 50A (2016) PARA 584.

8 Ie the Companies (Audit, Investigations and Community Enterprise) Act 2004 ss 16, 17: see PARA 772. Because these provisions govern such matters as the operation and funding of certain financial reporting and accounting bodies, rather than the conduct of companies generally, they are not regarded as company law provisions under the statutory scheme mentioned in note 1.

9 Ie the Company Directors Disqualification Act 1986: see PARA 1762 et seq.

10 Ie the Criminal Justice Act 1993 Pt V (ss 52–64): see FINANCIAL SERVICES REGULATION vol 50A (2016) PARA 793 et seq.

11 Ie matters governed by the Insolvency Act 1986: see COMPANY AND PARTNERSHIP INSOLVENCY vol 16 (2011) PARA 1 et seq.

12 The parallel development of financial markets and securities law led to the enactment of the Financial Services Act 1986 (repealed) (see now the Financial Services and Markets Act 2000, especially Pt VI (ss 73A–103) (official listing); and FINANCIAL SERVICES REGULATION vol 50A (2016) PARA 584 et seq).

13 See PARA 1255 et seq. The provisions about the Financial Reporting Council Limited (see the text and notes 7–8) are regarded as relating more to financial services law than to company law under the statutory scheme mentioned in note 1 but are discussed in this title. Many developments in

company law and in financial services and securities regulation have their origin in European Union legislative programmes: see PARA 16 et seq.

10. Companies legislation prior to 1985. Such of the earlier statutes as were then in force were repealed by the Companies Act 1862[1], but this repeal did not affect the incorporation of any company registered under any Act so repealed[2]. The Companies Act 1862 governed all companies registered after 2 November 1862[3], until 1 April 1909[4], and its provisions (except Table A) also applied to companies formed and registered, or registered but not formed, under the Joint Stock Companies Acts[5], or any of them, as if they had been formed and registered under that Act (as companies limited by shares or unlimited as the case might be) with the necessary qualifications as to reference to the date of registration, and as to the power of altering Table B of the Joint Stock Companies Act 1856[6]. The Companies Act 1862 permitted registration under the Act of every then existing company (including those registered under the Joint Stock Companies Acts) consisting of seven or more members, and any company thereafter formed in pursuance of any Act (except the Companies Act 1862) or letters patent, or being a company working mines within and subject to the stannaries jurisdiction, or being otherwise duly constituted by law, and consisting of seven or more members[7]. The registration might be with unlimited liability, or with liability limited by shares or by guarantee; and the registration might take place with a view to the company being wound up[8]. This enactment was subject to certain exceptions and regulations[9] practically identical with the exceptions and regulations in regard to the power for existing companies to register under the Companies Act 2006[10].

Restrictions on the formation of new companies, associations or partnerships for the purpose of carrying on business for gain without being registered under the Act were imposed by the Companies Act 1862[11]. Similar provisions imposed by the Companies Act 1985 have since been repealed[12].

The Companies Act 1862 was amended by subsequent statutes, and was, with those statutes, repealed by the Companies (Consolidation) Act 1908, which incorporated most of their provisions. That Act was amended by the Companies Act 1913, the Companies (Particulars as to Directors) Act 1917 and the Companies Act 1928, and on 1 November 1929 those Acts were in their turn repealed and consolidated, together with certain other enactments, by the Companies Act 1929. The Companies Act 1929, and all subsequent companies legislation until the advent of the Companies Act 2006, extended to Great Britain only[13].

The provisions of various enactments, including the Companies Act 1929, were later consolidated by the Companies Act 1948[14]. The Companies Act 1948 was substantially amended by Part I of the Companies Act 1967[15], which came into force at various dates between 27 October 1967 and 27 July 1968[16].

The European Communities Act 1972[17] contained provisions implementing the First Council Directive on company law[18]. The Stock Exchange (Completion of Bargains) Act 1976, which was passed mainly to facilitate the adoption of a computerised settlement and stock transfer system, affected the procedures relating to the issue of certificates and the maintenance of registers and other records. The Insolvency Act 1976 provided for the disqualification of directors in certain circumstances from the management of companies[19]. The general law of companies was again amended, principally in relation to accounts, disclosure of interests in shares and disqualification orders, by the Companies Act 1976 which came into force at various dates between 24 January 1977 and 1 January 1985[20].

The Companies Act 1980 was intended mainly to implement the Second Council Directive on company law[21], in so far as not previously enacted. The 1980 Act regulated the formation of public companies, and provided for the maintenance of their capitals. It also dealt with the duties of directors and conflicts of interest, and made insider dealing a criminal offence. It came into force at various dates between 23 June 1980 and 1 October 1983[22].

The Companies Act 1981 was intended mainly to implement the Fourth Council Directive on company law[23]. It dealt with the form and content of company accounts. It also dealt with company and business names, share capital and the disclosure of interests in voting shares in public companies. It came into force at various dates between 1 January 1984 and 1 January 1985[24]. With a view to facilitating the consolidation of the Companies Acts, the Companies Act 1981[25] contained novel provisions offering an alternative to the normal parliamentary procedure applicable to consolidation bills[26].

The Stock Transfer Act 1982 contained minor amendments of the Companies Act 1948 relating to transfers[27]; and the Employment Act 1982 amended the Companies Act 1967[28] in relation to the contents of the directors' report concerning the involvement of employees in the affairs of the company[29].

The Companies (Beneficial Interests) Act 1983, which came into force on 26 July 1983[30], dealt with the beneficial interest of companies in shares[31].

1 See the Companies Act 1862 s 205, Sch 3 (repealed). Other statutes (collectively referred to as the Companies Clauses Acts) contain provisions that remain generally applicable to companies incorporated by special statutes for public purposes and these are considered in PARA 1858 et seq.
2 Companies Act 1862 s 206 (repealed).
3 Companies Act 1862 s 2 (repealed).
4 Companies (Consolidation) Act 1908 s 296 (repealed).
5 As to the meaning of the 'Joint Stock Companies Acts' in the Companies Act 1862 see s 175 (repealed).
6 See the Companies Act 1862 ss 176, 177 (repealed).
7 Companies Act 1862 s 180 (repealed).
8 Companies Act 1862 s 180 (repealed).
9 See the Companies Act 1862 s 179 (repealed).
10 See PARA 21 et seq. As to the meanings of 'carry on', 'business' and 'gain' generally see PARA 1 note 1.
11 See the Companies Act 1862 s 4 (repealed).
12 Ie the Companies Act 1985 ss 716, 717 (repealed).
13 As to the geographical extent of the Companies Acts see PARA 26. As to the meaning of 'Great Britain' see PARA 1 note 5.
14 The Companies Act 1948 came into force on 1 July 1948, almost wholly repealing and replacing the Companies Act 1947, which had come into force on the same day: see the Companies Act 1947 (Commencement) Order 1948, SI 1948/439, art 1 (revoked); and the Companies Act 1948 ss 459(1), 462(2), Sch 17 (repealed).
15 Ie the Companies Act 1967 Pt I (ss 1–57) (now repealed).
16 The Companies Act 1967 ss 25–34 (all now repealed) came into force on 27 October 1967 (three months after the Act was passed); ss 2–16, 18–24 and Schs 1 and 2 (all now repealed) came into force on 27 January 1968 (six months after the Act was passed); and s 27 (now repealed) came into force on 27 July 1968 (12 months after the Act was passed): s 57(1) (repealed).

Meanwhile, the concept of a floating charge was for the first time introduced into the law of Scotland by the Companies (Floating Charges) (Scotland) Act 1961 (repealed). The 1948 and 1961 Acts and Part I of and Schedules 1 to 4 to the 1967 Act were collectively referred to as the Companies Acts 1948 to 1967: see the Companies Act 1967 s 130(2) (repealed).
17 Ie the European Communities Act 1972 s 9 (repealed).
18 Ie Council Directive (EEC) 68/151 (OJ L65, 14.03.68, p 8) (now repealed and replaced: see PARA 20 note 14).
19 See the Insolvency Act 1976 s 9 (repealed).
20 See the Companies Act 1976 s 45(3) (repealed), and the various commencement orders made under it. The Companies Act 1948, Parts I and III of the Companies Act 1967, the Companies (Floating Charges and Receivers) (Scotland) Act 1972, the European Communities Act 1972,

the Stock Exchange (Completion of Bargains) Act 1976 ss 1–4 (repealed), the Insolvency Act 1976, and the Companies Act 1976 were collectively referred to as the Companies Acts 1948 to 1976: see the Companies Act 1976 s 45(2) (repealed).

21 Ie Council Directive (EEC) 77/91 (OJ L26, 31.01.77, p 1) (repealed). See now European Parliament and Council Directive (EU) 2012/30 (OJ L315, 14.11.2012, p 74); and PARA 20 head (5).

22 See the Companies Act 1980 s 90(3) (repealed), and the various commencement orders made under it. The Companies Acts 1948 to 1980 comprised the Acts cited as the Companies Acts 1948 to 1976 together with the 1980 Act: see the Companies Act 1980 s 90(2) (repealed).

23 Ie Council Directive (EEC) 78/660 (OJ L222, 14.8.78, p 11) relating to annual accounts of certain types of companies (repealed and replaced by European Parliament and Council Directive (EU) 2013/34 (OJ L 182, 29.6.2013, p 19): see PARA 20 head (g)).

24 See the Companies Act 1981 s 119(3) (repealed), and the various commencement orders made under it. The Acts cited as the Companies Acts 1948 to 1980 together with the 1981 Act (except for the Companies Act 1981 ss 28, 29 (repealed)) were known as the Companies Acts 1948 to 1981: see the Companies Act 1981 s 119(2) (repealed).

25 Ie the Companies Act 1981 s 116 (repealed).

26 As to the normal parliamentary procedure applicable to consolidation bills see STATUTES AND LEGISLATIVE PROCESS vol 96 (2012) PARA 884.

It was provided that Her Majesty might, by Order in Council, make such amendments of the Companies Acts (ie the Companies Acts 1948 to 1981 and any enactments passed after the Companies Act 1981 for the citation of which together with those Acts provision was made by any enactment so passed: see the Companies Act 1981 s 116(4) (repealed)) and of any other enactment relating to companies, whenever passed, as might be jointly recommended by the Law Commission and the Scottish Law Commission as desirable to enable a satisfactory consolidation of the whole or the greater part of the Companies Acts to be produced: see the Companies Act 1981 s 116(1) (repealed). In exercise of this power, the following Orders were made: the Companies Acts (Pre-Consolidation Amendments) Order 1984, SI 1984/134; and the Companies Acts (Pre-Consolidation Amendments) (No 2) Order 1984, SI 1984/1169 (both now lapsed). Such an Order in Council could not be made unless a draft of the Order had been laid before and approved by a resolution of each House of Parliament (Companies Act 1981 s 116(2)(a) (repealed)); nor would it come into force unless there was passed either a single Act consolidating the whole or the greater part of the Companies Acts (with or without other enactments relating to companies) or a group of two or more Acts which between them consolidated the whole or the greater part of those Acts (with or without other enactments so relating) (Companies Act 1981 s 116(2)(b) (repealed)). If such an Act or group of Acts was passed, the Order would come into force on the day on which that Act or group of Acts came into force (Companies Act 1981 s 116(2)(c) (repealed)). The date is 1 July 1985 (ie the date on which the consolidating legislation of 1985 came into force: see the Companies Act 1985 s 746 (prospectively repealed by the Companies Act 2006 Sch 16)). No Order in Council might be made subsequently: Companies Act 1981 s 116(3) (repealed). Pursuant to the consolidation provisions, two Orders in Council were made (the Companies Acts (Pre-Consolidation Amendments) Order 1984, SI 1984/134; and the Companies Acts (Pre-Consolidation Amendments) (No 2) Order 1984, SI 1984/1169 (both now lapsed)) amending the Companies Acts 1948 to 1983 (as to which see note 31), thus paving the way for their consolidation.

27 See the Stock Transfer Act 1982 Sch 2 (now largely repealed).

28 Ie the Companies Act 1967 s 16 (repealed).

29 See the Employment Act 1982 s 1 (repealed).

30 Ie the date of the Royal Assent.

31 That Act, and the Companies Acts 1948 to 1981, were cited together as the Companies Acts 1948 to 1983: Companies (Beneficial Interests) Act 1983 s 7(2) (repealed).

11. The consolidating companies legislation of 1985. The consolidating legislation of 1985[1] consisted of four Acts, which all came into force on 1 July 1985[2]:

(1) the Companies Act 1985, which consolidated the main provisions of earlier companies legislation[3];

(2) the Company Securities (Insider Dealing) Act 1985[4];

(3) the Business Names Act 1985[5]; and

(4) the Companies Consolidation (Consequential Provisions) Act 1985[6], which made provision for transitional matters and savings, repeals (including, in accordance with the recommendations of the Law Commission[7], the repeal of certain provisions of the Companies Act 1948 which were no longer of practical utility)[8] and consequential amendment of other Acts.

No repeal brought about by this consolidation affected the incorporation of any company registered or re-registered under the former Companies Acts[9]. Most such companies, as well as any company formed and registered under the Companies Act 2006, are now regulated by the 2006 Act[10].

1 As to preparations made for the consolidation of the Companies Acts see PARA 10.
2 See the Companies Act 1985 s 746 (prospectively repealed); the Company Securities (Insider Dealing) Act 1985 s 18 (repealed) (see note 4); the Business Names Act 1985 s 10 (repealed) (see note 5); and the Companies Consolidation (Consequential Provisions) Act 1985 s 34 (repealed).
3 The Companies Act 1985 was passed to consolidate the Companies Acts 1948 to 1983 (see PARA 10) other than the provisions dealing with insider dealing (see head (2) in the text) and business names (see head (3) in the text). As to the effect of the consolidation on the incorporation of any company registered or re-registered under any repealed enactment see the text and notes 8–9. As to the Acts which may be cited as the 'Companies Acts 1948 to 1983' see PARA 10 note 31.
4 The Company Securities (Insider Dealing) Act 1985 has been repealed and replaced by the Criminal Justice Act 1993 Pt V (ss 52–64) (see PARA 12; and see FINANCIAL SERVICES REGULATION vol 50A (2016) PARA 793 et seq): see the Criminal Justice Act 1993 s 79(14), Sch 6 Pt I.
5 Ie the Business Names Act 1985 (repealed): see now the Companies Act 2006 Pt 5 (ss 53–85), Pt 41 (ss 1192–1208); and PARA 195 et seq.
6 The Companies Consolidation (Consequential Provisions) Act 1985 was repealed on 20 May 2011 subject to savings: see the Companies Act 2006 (Consequential Amendments and Transitional Provisions) Order 2011, SI 2011/1265.
7 See *Statute Law Revision: Eleventh Report: Obsolete Provisions in the Companies Act 1948* (Law Com no 135) (Cm 9236) (1984).
8 See the Companies Consolidation (Consequential Provisions) Act 1985 ss 28, 29, Sch 1 (repealed). So much of the Companies Act 1967 Pt II (ss 58–108) (insurance companies) as was then unrepealed was left outstanding: see the Companies Consolidation (Consequential Provisions) Act 1985 Sch 1 (repealed). See also note 6.
9 See the Companies Consolidation (Consequential Provisions) Act 1985 s 31(8)(a) (repealed). For these purposes, the 'former Companies Acts' means the Joint Stock Companies Acts, the Companies Act 1862, the Companies (Consolidation) Act 1908, the Companies Act 1929 and the Companies Acts 1948 to 1983: see the Companies Act 1985 s 735(1)(c) (repealed); the Companies Consolidation (Consequential Provisions) Act 1985 s 32 (repealed). 'Joint Stock Companies Acts' means the Joint Stock Companies Act 1856, the Joint Stock Companies Acts 1856, 1857, the Joint Stock Banking Companies Act 1857 and the Act to enable Joint Stock Banking Companies to be formed on the principle of limited liability, or any one or more of those Acts (as the case may require), but does not include the Joint Stock Companies Act 1844: Companies Act 1985 s 735(3) (repealed).
10 See the Companies Act 2006 s 1; and PARA 21. See also the Companies Consolidation (Consequential Provisions) Act 1985 s 31 (repealed).

12. Legislation subsequent to the 1985 consolidation and prior to the Companies Act 2006. Subsequent to the consolidation of company law effected in 1985[1], there was much further legislation of major importance in company law.

The Insolvency Act 1985 was passed on 30 October 1985. Part II of that Act dealt with company insolvency, and substantially altered the provisions of the Companies Act 1985 in relation to winding up, besides introducing an entirely new procedure in the shape of the making of an administration order[2], and facilitating the making of voluntary arrangements[3]. It also altered the law relating to receivers, whether appointed in or out of court[4], and introduced the new concept of an 'administrative receiver'[5]. The Act was directed to be brought into force on such a day as the Secretary of State might, by order made by statutory instrument, appoint, with power for different days to be appointed for different purposes and for different provisions[6]. It was itself largely repealed by the Insolvency Act 1986[7], which consolidated the winding-up provisions of the Companies Act 1985 and of the Insolvency Act 1985, and related matters. The Insolvency Act 1986 was directed to come into force on the day appointed for the coming into force of Part III of the Insolvency Act 1985, immediately after that Part of that Act came into force for England and Wales, which proved to be 29 December 1986[8]. The remainder of the Insolvency Act 1985, in so far as it dealt with companies, was concerned with the disqualification of company directors, and the provisions for this were consolidated with the like provisions of the Companies Act 1985 by the Company Directors Disqualification Act 1986, which was directed to come into force simultaneously with the Insolvency Act 1986[9].

The Financial Services Act 1986, whose main concern is indicated in its title[10], had considerable effect in relation to prospectuses[11], takeover offers[12], and insider dealing[13]. The Act was brought into effect piecemeal from 15 November 1986[14]. It has been wholly repealed and replaced by the Financial Services and Markets Act 2000[15], which shares the same focus as its predecessor while introducing some new elements; the provisions most of note for present purposes being those dealing with the official listing of companies[16], the powers to impose penalties for market abuse[17] and powers of enforcement and investigation[18]. While some provisions of this Act came into force immediately[19], it was provided that the rest should come into force on such day as the Treasury might by order appoint, and that different days might be appointed for different purposes[20].

The Companies Act 1989 was passed to amend, among other matters, the law relating to company accounts; to make new provision with respect to the persons eligible for appointment as company auditors; to amend the provisions of the Companies Act 1985 and certain other enactments with respect to investigations and powers to obtain information and to confer new powers exercisable to assist overseas regulatory authorities; and to make new provision with respect to the registration of company charges (although these latter provisions were never brought into force)[21]. The Act was brought into effect piecemeal from 16 November 1989[22].

The Foreign Corporations Act 1991 was passed to make provision about the status in the United Kingdom of bodies incorporated or formerly incorporated under the laws of certain territories outside the United Kingdom[23], and came into force on 25 September 1991[24]; and the Oversea Companies and Credit and Financial Institutions (Branch Disclosure) Regulations 1992[25] introduced new provisions relating to the disclosure requirements in respect of branches opened by certain companies in a member state and the publication of annual accounting documents by credit and financial institutions with effect from 1 January 1993[26].

Part V of the Criminal Justice Act 1993[27] repealed the Company Securities (Insider Dealing) Act 1985 and introduced new provisions relating to insider dealing with effect from 1 March 1994[28].

The Insolvency Act 1994 was passed to amend the law relating to contracts of employment adopted by administrators, administrative receivers and certain other receivers[29] in respect of contracts of employment adopted on or after 15 March 1994[30]; and the Insolvency (No 2) Act 1994 was passed to amend the law relating to corporate insolvency and winding up, so far as it concerns the adjustment of certain prior transactions[31], with effect from 26 July 1994[32].

The Deregulation and Contracting Out Act 1994 contains, among other matters, provisions to reduce certain of the burdens affecting the Secretary of State, the registrar of companies and the official receiver[33].

The Political Parties, Elections and Referendums Act 2000 made provision for the control of political donations made by companies and for the disclosure of political donations and expenditure in directors' reports[34] with effect from 16 February 2001[35].

The Insolvency Act 2000 introduced the concept of a company voluntary arrangement with a moratorium[36]; and it also amended the Company Directors Disqualification Act 1986 in order to allow the Secretary of State to accept disqualification undertakings[37]. Most of the provisions of this Act were brought into effect piecemeal from 2 April 2001[38].

The Enterprise Act 2002 introduced a new regime for administration (replacing Part II of the Insolvency Act 1986[39]) as well as making provision in relation to preferential debts and unsecured creditors[40]. Most of the provisions of this Act were brought into effect piecemeal from 18 March 2003[41].

1 As to which see PARA 11.
2 See the Insolvency Act 1985 ss 27–44 (repealed).
3 See the Insolvency Act 1985 ss 20–26 (repealed).
4 See the Insolvency Act 1985 ss 45–55 (repealed); and see PARA 1542 et seq.
5 See the Insolvency Act 1985 ss 48–54 (repealed).
6 See the Insolvency Act 1985 s 236(2) (repealed). As to the Secretary of State see PARA 6. The Act was brought into effect piecemeal between 1 February and 29 December 1986: see the various commencement orders made under the Insolvency Act 1985 s 236(2), the last of which still left two provisions of the Insolvency Act 1985 not yet brought into force, namely Sch 6 para 45 (subsequently repealed by the Companies Act 1989 s 212, Sch 24) (extension of the period from two to 12 years from dissolution during which the court might declare such dissolution void), and the Insolvency Act 1985 Sch 10 (subsequently repealed by the Insolvency Act 1986 s 438, Sch 12) in so far as it provided for the repeal of the Companies Act 1985 s 467(3)–(5) (relating to the disqualifications for appointment of a person as a receiver in Scotland): see the Insolvency Act 1985 (Commencement No 5) Order 1986, SI 1986/1924, art 4.
7 See the Insolvency Act 1986 s 438, Sch 12.
8 See the Insolvency Act 1986 s 443; and the Insolvency Act 1985 (Commencement No 5) Order 1986, SI 1986/1924. As to the meanings of 'England' and 'Wales' see PARA 1 note 5.
9 See the Company Directors Disqualification Act 1986 s 25.
10 See the Financial Services Act 1986 preamble (repealed).
11 See the Financial Services Act 1986 Pt IV (ss 142–156B) (repealed), Pt V (ss 158–171) (repealed). As to the requirement for a prospectus see now the Financial Services and Markets Act 2000 s 85; and FINANCIAL SERVICES REGULATION vol 50A (2016) PARA 603.
12 See the Financial Services Act 1986 Pt VI (s 172), Sch 12 (repealed).
13 See the Financial Services Act 1986 Pt VII (ss 173–178) (repealed).
14 See the various commencement orders made under the Financial Services Act 1986 s 211(1) (repealed).
15 See the Financial Services and Markets Act 2000 (Consequential Amendments and Repeals) Order 2001, SI 2001/3649 (now revoked).
16 See the Financial Services and Markets Act 2000 Pt VI (ss 73A–103); and FINANCIAL SERVICES REGULATION vol 50A (2016) PARA 584 et seq.
17 See the Financial Services and Markets Act 2000 Pt VIII (ss 118–131A); and FINANCIAL SERVICES REGULATION vol 50A (2016) PARA 648 et seq. These powers supplement the provisions relating to insider dealing: see the Criminal Justice Act 1993 Pt V (ss 52–64); and see FINANCIAL SERVICES REGULATION vol 50A (2016) PARA 793 et seq.
18 See eg the Financial Services and Markets Act 2000 Pt XI (ss 165–177); and FINANCIAL SERVICES REGULATION vol 50A (2016) PARA 658 et seq.
19 See the Financial Services and Markets Act 2000 s 431(1). The Act received Royal Assent on 14 June 2000.
20 See the Financial Services and Markets Act 2000 s 431(2). As to the Treasury see CONSTITUTIONAL AND ADMINISTRATIVE LAW vol 20 (2014) PARA 262 et seq. The Act was brought into effect piecemeal from 25 February 2001: see the various commencement orders made under the Financial Services and Markets Act 2000 s 431(2).
21 See the Companies Act 1989 preamble.

22 See the Companies Act 1989 s 215(1), and the various commencement orders made under s 215(2), (3).
23 See the Foreign Corporations Act 1991 preamble; and PARA 2030. As to the meaning of 'United Kingdom' see PARA 1 note 5.
24 See the Foreign Corporations Act 1991 s 2(3).
25 Ie the Oversea Companies and Credit and Financial Institutions (Branch Disclosure) Regulations 1992, SI 1992/3179 (revoked and replaced by the Overseas Companies Regulations 2009, SI 2009/1801: see PARA 2013 et seq). These regulations implement Council Directive (EEC) 89/666 (OJ L395, 30.12.89, p 36) of 21 December 1989, concerning disclosure requirements in respect of branches opened in a member state by certain types of company governed by the law of another state (the 'Eleventh Company Law Directive'): see PARA 20 head (2).
26 See the Oversea Companies and Credit and Financial Institutions (Branch Disclosure) Regulations 1992, SI 1992/3179, reg 1(3) (revoked).
27 Ie the Criminal Justice Act 1993 Pt V (ss 52–64): see FINANCIAL SERVICES REGULATION vol 50A (2016) PARA 793 et seq.
28 See the Criminal Justice Act 1993 (Commencement No 5) Order 1994, SI 1994/242, art 2, Schedule.
29 See the Insolvency Act 1994 preamble.
30 See the Insolvency Act 1994 s 1(7).
31 See the Insolvency (No 2) Act 1994 preamble.
32 See the Insolvency (No 2) Act 1994 s 6(2).
33 See the Deregulation and Contracting Out Act 1994 preamble; and see PARA 7.
34 The Political Parties, Elections and Referendums Act 2000 added new provisions to the Companies Act 1985 (see ss 347A–347K (repealed)). See now the Companies Act 2006 Pt 14 (ss 362–379); and PARAS 760–764).
35 See the Political Parties, Elections and Referendums Act 2000 (Commencement No 1 and Transitional Provisions) Order 2001, SI 2001/222, made under the Political Parties, Elections and Referendums Act 2000 s 163(2).
36 See the Insolvency Act 2000 s 1, Sch 1.
37 See the Insolvency Act 2000 ss 5, 6.
38 See the Insolvency Act 2000 s 16, and the various commencement orders made thereunder.
39 See the Enterprise Act 2002 s 248.
40 See the Enterprise Act 2002 ss 251, 252.
41 See the Enterprise Act 2002 s 279, and the various commencement orders made thereunder.

13. The Company Law Review and the Companies Act 2006. Much of the policy that informed what became the Companies Act 2006 had its origins in the Company Law Review, a fundamental review of domestic company law which was conducted under the auspices of the then Department of Trade and Industry between 1998 and 2001[1]. Subsequently, proposals for reform were set out in two white papers[2]. The Bill that was introduced in late 2005 to effect these reforms was originally cast as an amending provision[3]. However, the huge scope of the proposed legislation tested the usual legislative procedures to breaking point and the Companies Act 2006 emerged as a comprehensive (albeit not a definitive) restatement of company law[4]. Although the 2006 Act is not properly a consolidating measure, some statutes are repealed as a consequence and most of the provisions that were previously contained in the Companies Act 1985 are restated in the 2006 Act[5]. Accordingly, for the purposes of the Companies Act 2006, the 'Companies Acts' means:

(1) the company law provisions of that Act[6];
(2) Part 2 of the Companies (Audit, Investigations and Community Enterprise) Act 2004[7]; and
(3) the provisions of the Companies Act 1985 that remain in force[8].

The Companies Act 2006 also made statutory provision for the first time in some new areas:

(a) it codifies directors' duties (many of which were previously contained in diffuse case law)[9] and also provides a statutory basis for derivative claims in some areas[10];

(b) it allows auditors to limit their liability[11];
(c) it introduced new reporting requirements to be included in the business review in annual reports[12];
(d) it recalibrates criminal liability (primarily in respect of how such liability may fall with regard to the company and its officers) and brings in protections for directors and auditors[13]; and
(e) it facilitates where possible the use of electronic communications[14].

Subject to any specific transitional provision or saving contained in the Companies Act 2006[15], where any provision of that Act re-enacts (with or without modification) an enactment repealed by that Act[16], the repeal and re-enactment does not affect the continuity of the law[17]. Anything done (including subordinate legislation made), or having effect as if done, under or for the purposes of the repealed provision that could have been done under or for the purposes of the corresponding provision of the Companies Act 2006, if in force or effective immediately before the commencement of that corresponding provision, has effect thereafter as if done under or for the purposes of that corresponding provision[18].

Any reference (express or implied) in the Companies Act 2006 or any other enactment, instrument or document to a provision of the Companies Act 2006 must be construed (so far as the context permits) as including, as respects times, circumstances or purposes in relation to which the corresponding repealed provision had effect, a reference to that corresponding provision[19]. Any reference (express or implied) in any enactment, instrument or document to a repealed provision must be construed (so far as the context permits), as respects times, circumstances and purposes in relation to which the corresponding provision of the Companies Act 2006 has effect, as being or (according to the context) including a reference to the corresponding provision of the Companies Act 2006[20].

1 The starting point of the Company Law Review ('CLR') was the publication of a Consultation Paper called *Modern Company Law for a Competitive Economy* (March 1998). Its stated aim was to modernise company law in order to provide a simple, efficient and cost-effective framework for British business: see paras 1.1–1.6. The CLR was conducted by a Steering Group ('CLRSG') comprising an independent group of experts and practitioners from business, law, commerce, accountancy and academia, with the support of a broadly based Consultative Group. The CLRSG issued various interim recommendations and consultation documents (each covering particular areas of interest) and presented its Final Report on 26 July 2001 (see *Modern Company Law: For A Competitive Economy—Final Report* (2001) (URN 01/943)).

2 See HM Government's White Paper *Modernising Company Law* (Cm 5553) (2002), which formed the government's response to the recommendations of the CLRSG (see note 1); and White Paper *Company Law Reform* (Cm 6456) (2005). Further consultations followed the publication of each of these papers. Some of the Review's recommendations were given legislative effect in the meantime by the Companies (Audit, Investigations and Community Enterprise) Act 2004 which sought not only to establish a new business form (the community interest company) but also to re-establish confidence in corporate governance and the auditing process in the wake of contemporary corporate scandals (see PARA 75 et seq).

3 The Bill had a remarkable legislative history, starting in the House of Lords, where alone there were over 1,400 amendments in Committee and nearly 500 on Report.

4 The long title of the Companies Act 2006 states that it is an 'Act to reform company law and restate the greater part of the enactments relating to companies'.

5 The revised statutory scheme relies to a certain extent on HMG's definition of what is and what is not a pure 'company law' provision. See 686 HL Official Report (5th series), 2 November 2006, col 431 per Lord Sainsbury ('All the company law provisions of the 1985, 1989 and 2004 Acts have been brought into the Bill, other than the self-standing provisions on community enterprise companies and the provisions on investigations which go wider than companies'). As to the general statutory scheme which is set up thereby see PARA 9. As to the provisions of earlier enactments that are still regarded as company law provisions under this statutory scheme and which have not been

repealed see the Companies Act 1985 Pt XIV (ss 431–453D) (cited in PARA 1725 et seq); Pt XV (ss 454–457) (cited in PARAS 1732–1734); and the Companies (Audit, Investigations and Community Enterprise) Act 2004 Pt 2 (ss 26–63) (cited in PARA 75 et seq), although it should be noted that those provisions of the 2004 Act are regarded as forming a distinct body of regulation which is additional to, and sits alongside, company law rather than forming part of it. The following provisions are not regarded as company law provisions under the statutory scheme and have not been repealed by the Companies Act 2006: the Companies Act 1989 Pt III (ss 55–91) (overseas regulation) (see PARA 1752 et seq); Pt VII (ss 154–191) (Financial Markets and Insolvency) (see FINANCIAL SERVICES REGULATION vol 50A (2016) PARA 728 et seq); and the Companies (Audit, Investigations and Community Enterprise) Act 2004 ss 14–17 (cited in PARA 771 et seq). As to the continuity of the law following the enactment of the Companies Act 2006 see PARA 13.

6 Companies Act 2006 s 2(1)(a). The company law provisions of the Companies Act 2006 are the provisions of Pts 1–39 (ss 1–1181), and the provisions of Pts 45–47 (ss 1284–1300) so far as they apply for the purposes of Pts 1–39: s 2(2). See also PARA 9.

7 Companies Act 2006 s 2(1)(b). The text refers to the provisions of the Companies (Audit, Investigations and Community Enterprise) Act 2004 Pt 2 (ss 26–63) (cited in PARA 75 et seq); and see note 5.

8 Companies Act 2006 s 2(1)(c). The text refers to the provisions of the Companies Act 1985 Pt XIV (ss 431–453D) (cited in PARA 1725 et seq), Pt XV (ss 454–457) (cited in PARAS 1732–1734). The Companies Act 2006 s 2(1)(c) also refers to the provisions of the Companies Consolidation (Consequential Provisions) Act 1985 that remain in force, but that Act is now repealed by the Companies Act 2006 (Consequential Amendments and Transitional Provisions) Order 2011, SI 2011/1265, art 2, although art 5(1), Sch 1 preserve the effect of the provisions of the Companies Consolidation (Consequential Provisions) Act 1985 relating to old public companies (see PARA 183 et seq), and the Companies Act 2006 (Consequential Amendments and Transitional Provisions) Order 2011, SI 2011/1265, art 5(2) contains other transitional savings.

9 See PARA 572 et seq.

10 See PARA 646 et seq.

11 See PARA 1052 et seq.

12 See PARA 1594 et seq. These requirements are, however, replaced by a duty to deliver annual confirmation statements, introduced by the Small Business, Enterprise and Employment Act 2015: see PARAS 15, 1590 et seq.

13 See PARA 1816 et seq. The general principle adopted as to whether a company should be liable for a breach of requirements of the Companies Acts is that where the only victims of the offence are the company or its members, the company should not be liable for the offence; on the other hand, where other persons may be victims of the offence, then the company should be potentially liable for a breach, whether or not the offence may also harm the company or its members: see PARA 316.

14 See eg PARAS 751, 754.

15 See the Companies Act 2006 s 1297(6). References in s 1297 to the Companies Act 2006 include subordinate legislation made under that Act: s 1297(7). For these purposes, 'subordinate legislation' has the same meaning as in the Interpretation Act 1978 (see STATUTES AND LEGISLATIVE PROCESS vol 96 (2012) PARA 608): Companies Act 2006 s 1297(8).

Although certain provisions of the Companies Act 2006 came into force on 8 November 2006 (ie the day the Act was passed), most of its provisions came into force on such days as could be appointed by order of the Secretary of State or the Treasury: see s 1300. The Secretary of State or the Treasury may by order make such transitional provision and savings as they consider necessary or expedient in connection with the commencement of any provision made by or under the Companies Act 2006: s 1296(1). Such orders are subject to negative resolution procedure (ie the statutory instrument containing the order is subject to annulment in pursuance of a resolution of either House of Parliament): ss 1289, 1296(4). As to the making of orders under the 2006 Act generally see ss 1288–1292. An order may, in particular, make such adaptations of provisions brought into force as appear to be necessary or expedient in consequence of other provisions of that Act not yet having come into force: s 1296(2). Transitional provision and savings that are so made are additional, and without prejudice, to those made by or under any other provision of the 2006 Act: s 1296(3). Among the orders made under the powers so conferred are the Companies Act 2006 (Commencement No 1, Transitional Provisions and Savings) Order 2006, SI 2006/3428; the Companies Act 2006 (Commencement No 2, Consequential Amendments, Transitional Provisions and Savings) Order 2007, SI 2007/1093; the Companies Act 2006 (Commencement No 3, Consequential Amendments, Transitional Provisions and Savings) Order 2007, SI 2007/2194; the Companies Act 2006 (Commencement No 4 and Commencement No 3 (Amendment) Order 2007, SI 2007/2607; the Companies Act 2006 (Commencement No 5, Transitional Provisions and Savings) Order 2007, SI 2007/3495; the Companies Act 2006 (Commencement No 6, Saving and Commencement Nos 3 and 5 (Amendment)) Order 2008, SI 2008/674; the Companies Act 2006 (Consequential Amendments etc) Order 2008, SI 2008/948; the Companies Act 2006 (Consequential Amendments) (Taxes and National Insurance) Order 2008, SI 2008/954; the Companies Act 2006 (Commencement No 7, Transitional Provisions and Savings) Order 2008, SI 2008/1886; the Companies Act 2006 (Commencement No 8, Transitional Provisions and Savings) Order 2008, SI 2008/2860; the Companies Act 2006 (Part 35) (Consequential Amendments, Transitional Provisions and Savings) Order 2009, SI 2009/1802; and the Companies Act 2006 (Consequential Amendments and Transitional Provisions) Order 2011, SI 2011/1265.

Accordingly, all the provisions of the Companies Act 2006 that affect the law in England and Wales had come into force by 1 October 2009, and four provisions not commenced (namely: s 327(2)(c) and s 330(6)(c); s 1175 as it applies in Northern Ireland; and s 1175, Sch 9 Pt 2 (relating to the Companies (Northern Ireland) Order 1986, SI 1986/1032 (NI 6))) were repealed by the Deregulation Act 2015. Where transitional provisions that are contained in the orders still have effect at the date at which this volume states the law, those provisions are mentioned in the text where they so have effect. As to the Secretary of State see PARA 6. As to the Treasury see CONSTITUTIONAL AND ADMINISTRATIVE LAW vol 20 (2014) PARA 262 et seq.

16 See the Companies Act 2006 s 1297(1). As to repeals made by the Companies Act 2006 see s 1295, Sch 16. In the Companies Act 2006, unless the context otherwise requires, 'enactment' includes an enactment contained in subordinate legislation within the meaning of the Interpretation Act 1978 (see STATUTES AND LEGISLATIVE PROCESS vol 96 (2012) PARA 609), an enactment contained in, or in an instrument made under, a Measure or Act of the National Assembly for Wales, an enactment contained in, or in an instrument made under, an Act of the Scottish Parliament, and an enactment contained in, or in an instrument made under, Northern Ireland legislation within the meaning of the Interpretation Act 1978: Companies Act 2006 s 1293 (amended by the Small Business, Enterprise and Employment Act 2015 s 90(4)).

17 See the Companies Act 2006 s 1297(2). Without prejudice to s 1297(2), where a provision creating an offence is repealed and re-enacted without modification by or under the Companies Act 2006, an offence committed before the commencement of the new law is to be charged under the old law; an offence committed after the commencement of the new law is to be charged under the new law; and an offence committed partly before and partly after the commencement of the new law is to be charged under the new law and not under the old: see the Companies Act 2006 (Commencement No 8, Transitional Provisions and Savings) Order 2008, SI 2008/2860, art 7(1), (4). For this purpose, an offence is committed partly before and partly after the commencement of the new law if a relevant event occurs before commencement and another relevant event occurs after commencement, where 'relevant event' means an act, omission or other event (including any result of one or more acts or omissions) proof of which is required for conviction of the offence: art 7(2), (3).

18 Companies Act 2006 s 1297(3). This provision applies:

(1) in relation to a company to which the Companies Act 1985 s 675(1) (repealed) (companies formed and registered under earlier companies legislation) applied as if the company had been formed and registered under Pt 1 (ss 1–42) (repealed) (Companies Act 2006 (Commencement No 8, Transitional Provisions and Savings) Order 2008, SI 2008/2860, art 5, Sch 2 para 1(2)(a));

(2) in relation to a company to which the Companies Act 1985 s 676(1) (repealed) (companies registered but not formed under earlier companies legislation) applied as if the company had been registered under Pt 22 Ch 2 (ss 680–690) (repealed) (Companies Act 2006 (Commencement No 8, Transitional Provisions and Savings) Order 2008, SI 2008/2860, Sch 2 para 1(2)(b));

(3) in relation to a company to which the Companies Act 1985 s 677(1) (repealed) (companies re-registered under earlier companies legislation) applied as if the company had been re-registered under Pt 2 (ss 43–55) (repealed) (Companies Act 2006 (Commencement No 8, Transitional Provisions and Savings) Order 2008, SI 2008/2860, Sch 2 para 1(2)(c)).

A reference in any enactment to a company formed and registered under the Companies Act 2006, to a company registered but not formed under that Act, or to a company re-registered under that Act, includes a company treated as so formed and registered, registered or re-registered by virtue of s 1297(3), including that provision as applied by the Companies Act 2006 (Commencement No 8, Transitional Provisions and Savings) Order 2008, SI 2008/2860, art 5, Sch 2 para 1(2): see the Companies Act 2006 (Consequential Amendments, Transitional Provisions and Savings) Order 2009, SI 2009/1941, art 3.

Nothing in the Companies Act 2006 (Commencement No 8, Transitional Provisions and Savings) Order 2008, SI 2008/2860, Sch 2 para 1 or in the Companies Act 2006 s 1297(3) is to be read as affecting any reference to the date on which a company was registered or re-registered: Companies Act 2006 (Commencement No 8, Transitional Provisions and Savings) Order 2008, SI 2008/2860, Sch 2 para 1(3). For the purposes of the Companies Act 2006 s 1297(3) as it applies to treat a company formed and registered under the Companies Act 1985 Pt 1 (see head (1) above) as if formed and registered under the corresponding provisions of the Companies Act 2006, the registration of a company on an application to which the Companies Act 2006 (Commencement No 8, Transitional Provisions and Savings) Order 2008, SI 2008/2860, Sch 2 para 2(3) applies (see PARA 21) is to be regarded as in force and effective immediately before the commencement of the Companies Act 2006 Pt 1 (ss 1–6): Companies Act 2006 (Commencement No 8, Transitional Provisions and Savings) Order 2008, SI 2008/2860, Sch 2 para 2(5). For the purposes of the Companies Act 2006 s 1297(3) as it applies to treat the registration of a company under the Companies Act 1985 Pt 22 Ch 2 (see head (2) above) as if done under the corresponding provisions of the Companies Act 2006, the registration of a company on an application to which the Companies Act 1985 Pt 22 Ch 2 continues to apply is to be regarded as in force and effective immediately before the commencement of the Companies Act 2006 Pt 33 Ch 1 (ss 1040–1042): see the Companies Act 2006 (Commencement No 8, Transitional Provisions and Savings) Order 2008, SI 2008/2860, Sch 2 para 93(6). For the purposes of the Companies Act 2006 s 1297(3) as it applies to treat a company re-registered under the Companies Act 1985 (see head (3) above) as if re-registered under the corresponding provisions of the Companies Act 2006, the re-registration of a company on an application to which the Companies Act 2006 (Commencement No 8, Transitional Provisions and Savings) Order 2008, SI 2008/2860, Sch 2 para 22(3) applies is to be regarded as in force and effective immediately before the commencement of the Companies Act 2006 Pt 7 (ss 89–111): Companies Act 2006 (Commencement No 8, Transitional Provisions and Savings) Order 2008, SI 2008/2860, Sch 2 para 22(6). A company that is formed and registered, or re-registered, under the Companies Act 1985 on or after 1 October 2009 by virtue of the Companies Act 2006 (Commencement No 8, Transitional Provisions and Savings) Order 2008, SI 2008/2860, Sch 2 para 2(3) or Sch 2 para 22(3) is known as a 'transitional company': see art 2. See also PARA 14.

19 Companies Act 2006 s 1297(4).

20 Companies Act 2006 s 1297(5).

14. General savings for existing companies under the Companies Act 2006. Nothing in the Companies Act 2006 affects:

(1) the registration or re-registration of a company under the former Companies Acts, or the continued existence of a company by virtue of such registration or re-registration[1]; or

(2) the application in relation to an existing company of[2]:

  (a) Table B in the Joint Stock Companies Act 1856[3]; or

  (b) Table A in the former Companies Acts[4];

  (c) the Companies (Tables A to F) Regulations 1985[5].

In relation to companies registered on or after 1 October 2009, new model articles have been made in place of those tables mentioned under head (2) above[6].

1 Companies Act 2006 (Commencement No 8, Transitional Provisions and Savings) Order 2008, SI 2008/2860, art 5, Sch 2 para 1(1)(a). Nothing in Sch 2 para 1 or in the Companies Act 2006 s 1297(3) (see PARA 13) is to be read as affecting any reference to the date on which a company was registered or re-registered: Companies Act 2006 (Commencement No 8, Transitional Provisions and Savings) Order 2008, SI 2008/2860, Sch 2 para 1(3).

In the Companies Acts, the 'former Companies Acts' means the Joint Stock Companies Acts, the Companies Act 1862, the Companies (Consolidation) Act 1908, the Companies Act 1929, the Companies Acts 1948 to 1983, and the provisions of the Companies Act 1985 and the Companies Consolidation (Consequential Provisions) Act 1985 that are no longer in force: see the Companies Act 2006 s 1171. It should be noted that the Companies Consolidation (Consequential Provisions) Act 1985 (see above) was repealed on 20 May 2011 subject to savings: see the Companies Act 2006 (Consequential Amendments and Transitional Provisions) Order 2011, SI 2011/1265; and generally PARAS 183–189. The 'Joint Stock Companies Acts' means the Joint Stock Companies Act 1856, the Joint Stock Companies Acts 1856, 1857, the Joint Stock Banking Companies Act 1857, and the Act to enable Joint Stock Banking Companies to be formed on the principle of limited liability (1858), but does not include the Joint Stock Companies Act 1844: see the Companies Act 2006 s 1171. As to the meaning of the 'Companies Acts' see PARA 13. As to the Acts which may be cited as the 'Companies Acts 1948 to 1983' see PARA 10 note 31; and as to the provisions of the Companies Act 1985 and the Companies Consolidation (Consequential Provisions) Act 1985 that are no longer in force see PARA 13.

2 Companies Act 2006 (Commencement No 8, Transitional Provisions and Savings) Order 2008, SI 2008/2860, Sch 2 para 1(1)(b). For these purposes, 'existing company' means a company that

immediately before 1 October 2009 was formed and registered under the Companies Act 1985 or was an existing company for the purposes of that Act (as to which see PARA 21 note 5): Companies Act 2006 (Commencement No 8, Transitional Provisions and Savings) Order 2008, SI 2008/2860, art 2.

3 Companies Act 2006 (Commencement No 8, Transitional Provisions and Savings) Order 2008, SI 2008/2860, Sch 2 para 1(1)(b)(i). As to the preservation of such a company's power under the Joint Stock Companies Act 1856 to make contracts in writing signed by its agents see *Prince v Prince* (1866) LR 1 Eq 490.

4 Companies Act 2006 (Commencement No 8, Transitional Provisions and Savings) Order 2008, SI 2008/2860, Sch 2 para 1(1)(b)(ii). The Companies Act 1948 Sch 1, Table A was divided into two parts, Part II applying to private companies as then defined. Part II was repealed by the Companies Act 1980 s 88, Sch 4, which also made minor changes in various articles in Table A Part 1. A new Table A intended to come into force 'on the day on which there comes into force an Act to consolidate the greater part of the Companies Acts' was proposed to be introduced by the Companies (Alteration of Table A etc) Regulations 1984, SI 1984/1717, but those regulations were revoked before they could come into effect by the Companies (Tables A to F) Regulations 1985, SI 1985/805, made on 22 May 1985. These latter regulations themselves came into effect on 1 July 1985: Companies (Tables A to F) Regulations 1985, SI 1985/805, reg 1. As they were made before 1 July 1985 (ie the date on which the Companies Act 1985 came into force), they were made in exercise of the powers conferred on the Secretary of State by the Companies Act 1948 s 454(2) (repealed), as well as under the powers conferred by the Companies Act 1985 s 3 (repealed) and s 8 (repealed). As to the effect of this see PARA 13. As to the treatment under the Companies Act 2006 of articles made pursuant to the Companies (Tables A to F) Regulations 1985, SI 1985/805, see PARA 229.

5 Ie the Companies (Tables A to F) Regulations 1985, SI 1985/805 (see note 4): Companies Act 2006 (Commencement No 8, Transitional Provisions and Savings) Order 2008, SI 2008/2860, Sch 2 para 1(1)(b)(iii).

6 See the Companies (Model Articles) Regulations 2008, SI 2008/3229, which came into force on 1 October 2009 (see reg 1); and see PARAS 227–229.

15. Revision of the Companies Act 2006. The Companies Act 2006[1], like most major legislation, has continued to be revised and amended in response to ongoing developments. While all relevant amendments are covered in this title as appropriate, some areas of significant change are highlighted below.

The Companies Act 2006 (Amendment of Part 25) Regulations 2013[2] introduce a new system for the registration of company charges created on or after 6 April 2013[3].

The Enterprise and Regulatory Reform Act 2013 introduces new provisions in the Companies Act 2006 as from 1 October 2013[4] regarding remuneration payments to directors of quoted companies[5].

The Small Business, Enterprise and Employment Act 2015 makes a number of amendments to the Companies Act 2006, not all of which were in force at the date at which this title states the law. Among those changes are the following:

(1) partly as from 6 April 2016 and mainly as from 30 June 2016, there are new provisions with regard to information about people with significant control over a company[6];

(2) as from 30 June 2016[7], private companies[8] may keep certain information on the register kept by the registrar of companies[9] instead of entering it in their register of members[10] and the Secretary of State[11] may by regulations[12] amend the Companies Act 2006 to extend this ability to public companies[13] or public companies of a class specified in the regulations, and make such other amendments as he thinks fit in consequence of that extension[14];

(3) as from a day to be appointed[15], the requirement for at least one director to be a natural person[16] will be replaced by a prohibition, subject to some limited exceptions, on appointing any directors who are not natural persons[17];

(4) as from 30 June 2016[18], provisions of the Companies Act 2006 allow for an alternative method of record-keeping for directors' details in the case of private companies[19], and there are corresponding provisions in regard to company secretaries' details[20];

(5) partly as from 1 May 2016 and mainly as from 30 June 2016[21], there are new provisions in the Companies Act 2006 relating to the annual confirmation of the accuracy of the information on the register[22].

With effect from 1 October 2015[23], the Deregulation Act 2015 makes new provision with regard to the removal, resignation etc of company auditors[24]. That Act also makes minor changes with regard to proxy voting at company meetings[25].

1 As to the Companies Act 2006 generally, the Company Law Review and the continuity of the law see PARA 13. As to general savings for existing companies under the Companies Act 2006 see PARA 14.

2 Ie the Companies Act 2006 (Amendment of Part 25) Regulations 2013, SI 2013/600, art 2, Sch 1. For transitional provisions see art 6.

3 See the Companies Act 2006 Pt 25 Ch A1 (ss 859A–859Q) (added by SI 2013/600); and PARA 1462 et seq. The Companies Act 2006 ss 860–892 (relating to charges created before 6 April 2013) were repealed with savings by SI 2013/600: see PARA 1473 et seq.

4 See the Enterprise and Regulatory Reform Act 2013 ss 79–82; and the Enterprise and Regulatory Reform Act 2013 (Commencement No 3, Transitional Provisions and Savings) Order 2013, SI 2013/2227, art 2(h).

5 See the Companies Act 2005 Pt 10 Ch 4A (ss 226A–226F); and PARAS 604, 605.

6 See the Companies Act 2006 Pt 21A (ss 790A–790ZG) (added by the Small Business, Enterprise and Employment Act 2015 Sch 3 para 1); and PARA 466 et seq. As to the commencement dates see the Small Business, Enterprise and Employment Act 2015 (Commencement No 3) Regulations 2015, SI 2015/2029, arts 4, 5.

7 See the Small Business, Enterprise and Employment Act 2015 (Commencement No 4, Transitional and Savings Provisions) Regulations 2016, SI 2016/321, reg 6(c).

8 As to the meaning of 'private company' see PARA 95.

9 As to the meaning of 'registrar of companies' see PARA 126 note 2. As to the meaning of 'company' under the Companies Acts see PARA 21; and as to the central register see PARA 142 et seq.

10 See the Companies Act 2006 Pt 8 Ch 2A (ss 128A–128K) (added by the Small Business, Enterprise and Employment Act 2015 Sch 5 Pt 1 paras 1, 3); and PARA 363 et seq.

11 As to the Secretary of State see PARA 6.

12 Regulations so made are subject to affirmative resolution procedure: see the Companies Act 2006 ss 128K(2), 1290; and PARA 363.

13 As to the meaning of 'public company' see PARA 95.

14 See the Companies Act 2006 s 128K(2); and PARA 363.

15 Ie as from a day to be appointed under the Small Business, Enterprise and Employment Act 2015 s 164(1). At the date at which this volume states the law, no such order had been made.

16 See the Companies Act 2006 s 155 (prospectively repealed); and PARA 525.

17 See the Companies Act 2006 ss 156A–156C (prospectively added by the Small Business, Enterprise and Employment Act 2015 s 87(1), (4); not yet in force); and PARA 526. As to relevant directions see PARA 527.

18 See note 7.

19 Ie the Companies Act 2006 ss 161A (alternative method of record-keeping), ss 167A–167E (option to keep information on central register) (added by the Small Business, Enterprise and Employment Act 2015 Sch 5 paras 5, 6, 7): see PARA 551 et seq. As to the company's general duty to notify changes to directors and particulars see PARA 153. As to the power to extend the alternative method of record-keeping to public companies see the Companies Act 2006 s 167F; and PARA 551. As to the meanings of 'private company' and 'public company' see PARA 95.

20 Ie the Companies Act 2006 s 274A (alternative method of record-keeping), ss 279A–279F (option to keep information on the central register) (added by the Small Business, Enterprise and Employment Act 2015 Sch 5 paras 8, 9, 10): see PARA 673, 675 et seq. As to the power to extend the alternative method of record-keeping to public companies see the Companies Act 2006 s 279F; and PARA 675.

21 See the Small Business, Enterprise and Employment Act 2015 (Commencement No 4, Transitional and Savings Provisions) Regulations 2016, SI 2016/321, regs 5, 6(a).

22 See the Companies Act 2006 Pt 24 (ss 853A–853L) (added by the Small Business, Enterprise and Employment Act 2015 s 92); and PARA 1598 et seq. As to the replaced provisions see the Companies Act 2006 ss 854–858; and PARAS 1594–1597.
23 See the Deregulation Act 2015 (Commencement No 3 and Transitional and Saving Provisions) Order 2015, SI 2015/1732, art 2(d).
24 See PARA 1037 et seq.
25 See PARAS 736–737.

(ii) European Union Legislation relating to Companies

A. EU TREATY REQUIREMENTS REGARDING COMPANIES

16. Treatment of companies under the Treaty on the Functioning of the European Union: in general. Companies or firms[1] formed in accordance with the law of a member state of the European Union (the 'EU')[2] and having their registered office, central administration or principal place of business within the EU must, for the purpose of applying the provisions of the Treaty on the Functioning of the European Union (the 'TFEU') dealing with the right of establishment[3], be treated in the same way as natural persons who are nationals of the member states[4].

Member states must accord nationals of other member states the same treatment as their own nationals as regards participation in the capital of companies or firms[5].

1 For these purposes, 'companies or firms' means companies or firms constituted under civil or commercial law, including co-operative societies and other legal persons governed by public or private law, save for those which are not profit-making: Treaty on the Functioning of the European Union (Rome, 25 March 1957; TS 1 (1973); Cmnd 5179) ('TFEU') art 54. The TFEU was formerly known as the Treaty Establishing the European Community (often abbreviated to TEC and also known as the 'EC Treaty' or the Treaty of Rome) and was renamed by the Treaty of Lisbon Amending the Treaty Establishing the European Union and the Treaty Establishing the European Community (Lisbon, 13 December 2007, ECS 13 (2007); Cm 7294) (often referred to as the 'Lisbon Treaty') which came into force on 1 December 2009: see CONSTITUTIONAL AND ADMINISTRATIVE LAW vol 20 (2014) PARA 25 et seq; EUROPEAN UNION vol 47A (2014) PARA 6. The provisions of the TEC were renumbered by virtue of the Treaty of Amsterdam (see *Treaty Citation (No 2) (Note)* [1999] All ER (EC) 646, ECJ) and renumbered again by the Lisbon Treaty. The TFEU is cited throughout this title in the 2012 consolidated version (OJ C326, 26.10.2012, p 47). See also EUROPEAN UNION vol 47A (2014) PARA 6.
2 As to the European Union see EUROPEAN UNION vol 47A (2014) PARA 1 et seq.
3 Ie the TFEU Title IV Ch 2 (arts 49–55). As to the right of establishment see also PARA 17.
4 TFEU art 54.
5 TFEU art 55. This is without prejudice to the application of the other provisions of the Treaties: TFEU art 55. See also PARA 18.

17. Freedom of establishment under the Treaty on the Functioning of the European Union. The Treaty on the Functioning of the European Union (the 'TFEU')[1] prohibits restrictions on the freedom of establishment of nationals of a member state of the European Union (the 'EU') in the territory of another member state[2]. This prohibition also applies to restrictions on the setting up of agencies, branches or subsidiaries by nationals of any member state established in the territory of any member state[3]. Freedom of establishment includes the right to take up and pursue activities as self-employed persons and to set up and manage undertakings, in particular companies or firms[4], under the conditions laid down for its own nationals by the law of the country where such establishment is effected[5].

However, the problems associated with transferring a company's registered office, central administration or principal place of business from one member state to another, whilst retaining their status as companies incorporated under the law of the first member state, are not resolved by the Treaty provisions governing freedom of establishment[6].

1 As to the TFEU and its citation see PARA 16 note 1.

2 TFEU art 49. The prohibition mentioned in the text applies within the framework of the provisions set out in the TFEU Title IV Ch 2 (arts 49–55): art 49. See also PARA 16.

A company may exercise its right of establishment where national legislation, under which the company is incorporated, hinders its establishment in another member state: Case C-200/98 *X AB and Y v Riksskatteverket* [2000] 3 CMLR 1337, [1999] ECR I-8261, ECJ. The same principle applies where a member state hinders the establishment in another member state of one of its own nationals: Case C-251/98 *Baars v Inspecteur der Balstingdienst Particulieren/Ondernemingen (Gorinchem)* [2000] ECR I-2787, [2002] 1 CMLR 1437, ECJ (freedom of establishment includes the right of individuals to set up and manage companies in another member state). See also Case C-168/01 *Bosal Holdings BV v Staatssecretaris van Financien* [2003] All ER (EC) 959, [2003] 3 CMLR 674, ECJ (deductibility of costs arising from a parent company's holding in the capital of a subsidiary established in another member state).

What is now the TFEU art 49, read in conjunction with art 54 (see PARA 16), does not preclude legislation of member state under which a resident company is taxed in respect of an unusual or gratuitous advantage where such advantage has been granted to a company established in another member state with which it has a relationship of interdependence, whereas the resident company cannot be taxed on such advantage where the advantage has been granted to another resident company with which it has such a relationship: Case C-311/08 *Société de Gestion Industrielle SA (SGI) v Etat Belge* [2010] ECR I-487, [2010] 2 CMLR 1017, [2010] All ER (D) 151 (Feb), ECJ. The TFEU art 49 precludes legislation of a member state that allows a parent company to set off against an advance payment of corporation tax for which it is liable when it redistributes dividends paid by its subsidiaries the tax credit applied to the distribution of those dividends if they originate from a subsidiary in that member state, but does not offer that option if the dividends originate from a subsidiary in another member state: Case C-310/09 *Ministre du Budget, des Comptes publics et de la Fonction publique v Accor* [2011] ECR I-8115, [2012] STC 438, ECJ. The TFEU art 49 precludes legislation of a member state which makes the grant of a reduction in capital tax conditional on remaining liable to the tax for the next five years: Case C-380/11 *DI VI Finanziaria di Diego della Valle & C SapA v Administration des contributions en matiere d'impots* [2013] 1 CMLR 75, [2012] All ER (D) 81 (Sep), ECJ. See also Case C-378/10 *Re Vale Epitesi KFT* [2013] 1 WLR 294, [2012] 3 CMLR 959, ECJ; Case C-498/10 *X NV v Staatssecretaris van Financien* [2013] 1 CMLR 982, [2012] All ER (D) 14 (Nov), ECJ; Case C-18/11 *Revenue and Customs Comrs v Philips Electronics UK Ltd* [2013] 1 CMLR 210, [2013] STC 41, ECJ; Case C-591/13 *European Commission v Germany* ECLI:EU:C:2015:230, [2015] 3 CMLR 676, [2015] All ER (D) 127 (Apr), ECJ.

The TFEU art 49 does not, however, preclude a member state's tax regime under which, in the event of transfer by a resident company to a non-resident company within the same group of a permanent establishment situated in another member state, the losses previously deducted in respect of the establishment transferred were reincorporated into the taxable profit of the transferring company where, under a double taxation convention, the income of such a permanent establishment was exempt from tax in the member state in which the company to which that establishment belonged had its seat: Case C-388/14 *Timac Agro Deutschland GmbH v Finanzamt Sankt Augustin* ECLI:EU:C:2015:829, [2016] All ER (D) 106 (Jan), ECJ.

3 TFEU art 49.

In addition to setting up agencies, branches, or subsidiaries, a company may also exercise its right of establishment by taking part in the incorporation of a company in another member state: see Case 81/87 *R v HM Treasury, ex p Daily Mail and General Trust plc* [1989] QB 446, [1989] 1 All ER 328, ECJ.

4 Ie companies or firms within TFEU art 54: see PARA 16.

5 TFEU art 49; Case 81/87 *R v HM Treasury, ex p Daily Mail and General Trust plc* [1989] QB 446, [1989] 1 All ER 328, ECJ. The right of establishment is subject to the provisions of the TFEU Title IV Ch 2 relating to capital (ie art 55: see PARA 16): 56–60): art 49.

The right of establishment cannot be interpreted as conferring on companies incorporated under a law of a member state the right to transfer their central management and control and their central administration to another member state while retaining their status as companies incorporated under the legislation of the first member state: *R v HM Treasury, ex p Daily Mail and General Trust plc* [1989] QB 446, [1989] 1 All ER 328, ECJ. In Case C-208/00 *Uberseering BV v Nordic Construction Co Baumanagement GmbH* [2002] ECR I-9919, [2005] 1 WLR 315, ECJ, it was inferred that the question whether a company formed in accordance with the legislation of one member state could transfer its registered office or de facto centre of administration to another member state without losing its personality under the law of the member state of incorporation, and in some circumstances the rules relating to that transfer, were determined by the national law in accordance with which the company was incorporated. Accordingly, a member state is able, in the case of a company incorporated under its national law, to make the company's right to retain its legal personality under that law subject to restrictions on the transfer to a foreign country of the country's actual centre of administration: Case C-208/00 *Uberseering BV v Nordic Construction Co Baumanagement GmbH* [2002] ECR I-9919, [2005] 1 WLR 315, ECJ.

See also Case C-371/10 *National Grid Indus BV v Inspecteur van de Belastingdienst Rijnmond/Kantoor Rotterdam* [2011] ECR I-12273, [2012] All ER (EC) 883, ECJ (company incorporated under the law of a member state that transferred its place of effective management to another member state, without the transfer affecting the company's status as a company of the former member state, might rely on the TFEU art 49 for the purpose of challenging the lawfulness of tax imposed on it by the former member state on transfer); Case C-31/11 *Scheunemann v Finanzamt Bremerhaven* [2012] 3 CMLR 1228 at para 35, [2012] All ER (D) 268 (Jul), ECJ (TFEU art 49 et seq not intended to apply to a situation concerning a shareholding held in a company which has its registered office in a third country); Case E-15/11 *Arcade Drilling AS v Norwegian State* [2013] 1 CMLR 416, 15 ITLR 405, EFTA.

6 Case 81/87 *R v HM Treasury, ex p Daily Mail and General Trust plc* [1989] QB 446, [1989] 1 All ER 328, ECJ; Case C-208/00 *Uberseering BV v Nordic Construction Co Baumanagement GmbH* [2002] ECR I-9919, [2005] 1 WLR 315, ECJ.

In Case C-210/06 *Cartesio Oktató és Szolgáltató bt* [2009] All ER (EC) 269, [2009] 1 CMLR 1394, ECJ, it was confirmed that a member state had the power to define both the connecting factor required of a company if it was to be regarded as incorporated under the law of that state (and, as such, capable of enjoying the right of establishment) and the connecting factor required if the company was to be able subsequently to maintain that status (eg following a cross-border merger); accordingly, as what is now EU law stood, what is now TFEU art 49 was to be interpreted as not precluding legislation of a member state under which a company incorporated under the law of that member state might not transfer its seat to another member state whilst retaining its status as a company governed by the law of the member state of incorporation. See also Case C-212/97 *Centros Ltd v Erhverys-og Selskabsstyrelsen* [2000] Ch 446, [1999] ECR I-1459, ECJ (the fact that a company was formed in a particular member state for the sole purpose of enjoying more favourable legislation did not in itself constitute an abuse, even if that company conducted its activities entirely or mainly in a second state); and Case C-167/01 *Kamer van Koophandel en Fabrieken voor Amsterdam v Inspire Art Ltd* [2003] ECR I-10155, ECJ. The issue raised in Case C-411/03 *Re SEVIC Systems AG* [2006] All ER (EC) 363, [2005] ECR I-10805, [2006] 2 BCLC 510, ECJ (national law which refuses registration of a merger proposed across member states constitutes a restriction within the meaning of what is now the TFEU art 49 if a merger within the member state would be registered) has been resolved by European Parliament and Council Directive (EC) 2005/56 (OJ L310, 25.11.2005, p 1) on cross-border mergers of limited liability companies (see PARA 20).

18. Free movement of capital under the Treaty on the Functioning of the European Union. The Treaty on the Functioning of the European Union (the 'TFEU')[1] prohibits all restrictions on the movement of capital between member states and between member states and third countries[2]. All restrictions on payments between member states and between member states and third countries are also prohibited[3].

These provisions are without prejudice to the right of member states[4]:

(1) to apply the relevant provisions of their tax law which distinguish between taxpayers who are not in the same situation with regard to their place of residence or with regard to the place where their capital is invested[5];

(2) to take all requisite measures to prevent infringements of national law and regulations, in particular in the field of taxation and the prudential supervision of financial institutions, or to lay down procedures for the declaration of capital movements for purposes of administrative or statistical information, or to take measures which are justified on grounds of public policy or public security[6].

The provisions relating to capital and payments[7] are without prejudice to the applicability of restrictions on the right of establishment[8] which are compatible with the EU Treaties[9]. Such measures and procedures[10] must not constitute a means of arbitrary discrimination or a disguised restriction on the free movement of capital and payments[11].

1 As to the TFEU and its citation see PARA 16 note 1.

2 See the TFEU art 63 para 1. The prohibition mentioned in the text applies within the framework of the provisions set out in the TFEU Title IV Ch 4 (arts 63–66): art 63 para 1. The provisions of what is now the TFEU art 63 have direct effect: Cases C-163/94, 165/94, 250/94 *Criminal Proceedings against Locas Emilio Sanz de Lera* [1995] ECR I-4821, [1996] 1 CMLR 631, ECJ. See also Case C-233/09 *Dijkman v Belgium* ECLI:EU:C:2010:397, [2011] 1 CMLR 161, ECJ; Case C-284/09 *Re Taxation of Dividends: European Commission v Germany* [2011] ECR I-9879, [2012] 1 CMLR 1207, ECJ; Case C-417/10 *Ministero Dell'Economia E Delle Finanze v 3M Italia SpA* [2012] 2 CMLR 945, [2012] STC 1495, ECJ. As to what constitutes a movement of capital see also Case C-450/09 *Schroder v Finanzamt Hameln* [2011] ECR I-2497, [2011] STC 1248, ECJ.

The TFEU does not preclude legislation which excludes a reduction in the value of shares as a result of a distribution of dividends where the reduction would have reduced the acquirer's basis of assessment: Case C-182/08 *Glaxo Wellcome GmbH & Co KG v Finanzamt Munchen II* [2010] STC 244, [2010] 1 CMLR 459, ECJ. Legislation of a member state that allows a parent company to set off against an advance payment of corporation tax for which it is liable when it redistributes dividends paid by its subsidiaries the tax credit applied to the distribution of those dividends if they originate from a subsidiary in that member state, but does not offer that option if the dividends originate from a subsidiary in another member state is not precluded by the TFEU: Case C-310/09 *Ministre du Budget, des Comptes publics et de la Fonction publique v Accor* [2011] ECR I-8115,[2012] STC 438, ECJ. See also Case C-387/11 *European Commission v Belgium* [2013] 1 CMLR 1223, [2013] STC 587, ECJ.

3 See the TFEU art 63 para 2. The prohibition mentioned in the text applies within the framework of the provisions set out in the TFEU Title IV Ch 4 arts 63–66: see the TFEU art 63 para 2. See also Case C-233/09 *Dijkman v Belgium* ECLI:EU:C:2010:397, [2011] 1 CMLR 161, ECJ; Case C-284/09 *Re Taxation of Dividends: European Commission v Germany* [2011] ECR I-9879, [2012] 1 CMLR 1207, ECJ; Case C-417/10 *Ministero Dell'Economia E Delle Finanze v 3M Italia SpA* [2012] 2 CMLR 945, [2012] STC 1495, ECJ.

4 TFEU art 65 para 1.

5 TFEU art 65 para 1(a). A bilateral tax Convention, under which dividends distributed by a company established in one member state to a shareholder residing in another are liable to be taxed in both member states, is not precluded by the TFEU: Case C-128/08 *Damseaux v Etat Belge* [2009] ECR I-6823, [2009] 3 CMLR 1447, ECJ. National law can preclude a taxpayer who disposes of property at a loss in an overseas member state from setting off the loss against taxable profits in a home member state: Case C-322/11 *Re K* [2013] All ER (D) 123 (Nov), ECJ.

6 TFEU art 65 para 1(b). The retention of a degree of influence within privatised undertakings (by the use of 'golden shares') by the governments of member states has been declared liable to impede the acquisition of shares in those undertakings and to dissuade investors in other member states from investing in their capital so as to constitute a restriction on the freedom of movement of capital. Such a restriction may be implemented only by national rules justified by reasons referred to in the TFEU art 65 para 1 or by overriding requirements of the general interest and, in order to be so justified, the national legislation must accord with the principle of proportionality: see Case C-367/98 *EC Commission v Portugal*, Case C-483/99 *EC Commission v France*, Case C-503/99 *EC Commission v Belgium* [2003] QB 233, [2002] ECR I-4731, ECJ (national measures granted the state prerogatives ('golden shares') to intervene in the share structure and management of privatised undertakings in strategically important areas of the economy); Case C-463/00 *EC Commission v Spain* [2003] ECR I-4581, [2003] All ER (EC) 878, ECJ (disposal of certain shareholdings in some strategically important industries subject to a system of prior administrative approval); Case C-98/01 *EC Commission v United Kingdom* [2003] ECR I-4641, [2003] All ER (EC) 878, ECJ (special share held by the United Kingdom government made some of the company's operations subject to prior administrative approval and prevented the substantial acquisition of the voting capital by any person); Cases C-463/04 and C-464/04 *Federconsumatori v Comune di Milano* [2007] ECR I-10419, [2008] 1 CMLR 1187, ECJ (by giving public shareholders an instrument enabling them to restrict the possibility of the other shareholders participating in the company with a view to establishing or maintaining lasting and direct economic links with it such as to enable them to participate effectively in the management of that company or in its control, a national provision such as the one at issue was liable to deter direct investors from other member states from investing in the company's capital).

7 Ie the provisions set out in the TFEU Title IV Ch 4 arts 63–66.

8 See PARAS 16–17.
9 TFEU art 65 para 2. As to the EU Treaties see EUROPEAN UNION vol 47A (2014) PARA 6.
10 Ie the measures and procedures referred to in the TFEU art 65 paras 1–2 (see the text and notes 4–9).
11 TFEU art 65 para 3.

B. EU REGULATIONS AND DIRECTIVES RELATING TO COMPANY LAW

19. EU Regulations relating to company law. European Union ('EU') Regulations are of general application and are binding in their entirety and directly applicable in all member states[1]. The following Regulations make significant provision with regard to company law:

(1) the Regulation on the application of international accounting standards[2], which:
   (a) has as its objective the adoption and use of international accounting standards[3] in the EU with a view to harmonising the financial information presented by publicly traded companies[4] in order to ensure a high degree of transparency and comparability of financial statements and hence an efficient functioning of the EU capital market and of the internal market[5];
   (b) provides that the European Commission ('the Commission')[6] is to decide on the applicability within the EU of international accounting standards and sets out the procedure for their adoption[7];
   (c) provides that the consolidated accounts of publicly traded companies must be prepared in accordance with international accounting standards[8] and that member states may permit or require the annual accounts of such companies, and the consolidated and/or annual accounts of other companies, to be prepared in accordance with those standards[9];

(2) the Regulation providing for certain types of cross-border insolvency proceedings[10];

(3) the Regulation on specific requirements regarding the statutory audit of public interest entities[11], which:
   (a) sets out conditions for carrying out the statutory audit[12] of public interest entities[13];
   (b) makes provision with regard to the appointment of statutory auditors[14] or audit firms[15] by public interest entities[16]; and
   (c) makes provision for the surveillance of the activities of statutory auditors and audit firms carrying out statutory audit of public interest entities[17];

(4) the Regulation on the European Economic Interest Grouping ('EEIG')[18] which creates a legal framework to enable natural persons, companies, firms and other legal bodies to form groupings so as to co-operate effectively across frontiers for the purpose of facilitating the adaptation of their activities to the economic conditions of what is now the European Union[19];

(5) the Regulation on the Statute for a European Company (Societas Europaea or 'SE')[20] which makes provision, in the context of the completion of the internal market and for the purpose of enabling companies whose business is not limited to satisfying purely local needs to be able to plan and carry out the reorganisation of their business on

an EU scale, for the creation and management of companies with a European dimension free from the obstacles arising from the disparity and the limited territorial application of national company law[21].

In addition to the new forms of trading entity described in heads (4) and (5) above, other forms of less significance for the United Kingdom have also been provided for by means of Regulations[22].

EU Regulations that are more closely related to the regulation of financial markets and securities have some relevance to company law[23], in particular the Regulation on markets in financial instruments[24] and the Market Abuse Regulation[25].

1 See the TFEU art 288; and EUROPEAN UNION vol 47A (2014) PARA 92. As to the TFEU and its citation see PARA 16 note 1.

2 Ie European Parliament and Council Regulation (EC) 1606/2002 (OJ L243, 11.9.2002, p 1) on the application of international accounting standards. See also Commission Regulation (EC) 1126/2008 (OJ L320, 29.11.2008, p 1) which sets out the international accounting standards to be adopted: see art 1, Annex (which has been extensively amended). See also PARA 765 et seq.

3 For these purposes, 'international accounting standards' means International Accounting Standards ('IAS'), International Financial Reporting Standards ('IFRS') and related Interpretations ('SIC-IFRIC interpretations'), subsequent amendments to those standards and related interpretations, future standards and related interpretations issued or adopted by the International Accounting Standards Board ('IASB'): European Parliament and Council Regulation (EC) 1606/2002 (OJ L243, 11.9.2002, p 1) art 2.

4 As to such companies see European Parliament and Council Regulation (EC) 1606/2002 (OJ L243, 11.9.2002, p 1) art 4.

5 European Parliament and Council Regulation (EC) 1606/2002 (OJ L243, 11.9.2002, p 1) art 1.

6 As to the Commission see EUROPEAN UNION vol 47A (2014) PARA 48.

7 See European Parliament and Council Regulation (EC) 1606/2002 (OJ L243, 11.9.2002, p 1) art 3 (amended by European Parliament and Council Regulation (EC) 297/2008 (OJ L97, 9.4.2008, p 62)). See also Commission Regulation (EC) 1126/2008 (OJ L320, 29.11.2008, p 1) which sets out the international accounting standards to be adopted: see art 1, Annex (which has been extensively amended).

The Commission is to be assisted by an accounting regulatory committee: see European Parliament and Council Regulation (EC) 1606/2002 (OJ L243, 11.9.2002, p 1) art 6 (amended by European Parliament and Council Regulation (EC) 297/2008 (OJ L97, 9.4.2008, p 62). The Commission must liaise on a regular basis with the Committee about the status of active IASB projects and any related documents issued by the IASB in order to co-ordinate positions and to facilitate discussions concerning the adoption of standards that might result from these projects and documents: European Parliament and Council Regulation (EC) 1606/2002 (OJ L243, 11.9.2002, p 1) art 7(1). The Commission must duly report to the Committee in a timely manner if it intends not to propose the adoption of a standard: art 7(2).

8 See European Parliament and Council Regulation (EC) 1606/2002 (OJ L243, 11.9.2002, p 1) art 4.

9 See European Parliament and Council Regulation (EC) 1606/2002 (OJ L243, 11.9.2002, p 1) art 5. Where member states take measures by virtue of art 5, they must immediately communicate these to the Commission and to other member states: art 8.

10 Ie Council Regulation (EC) 1346/2000 (OJ L160, 30.6.2000, p 1) on insolvency proceedings (extensively amended; repealed and replaced subject to transitional provisions) which continues to apply to insolvency proceedings which have been opened before 26 June 2017 and which fall within its scope: see European Parliament and Council Regulation (EU) 2015/848 (OJ L 141, 5.6.2015, p 19) art 84(2), which applies only to insolvency proceedings opened after 26 June 2017 (art 84(1)). See further COMPANY AND PARTNERSHIP INSOLVENCY vol 16 (2011) PARA 58 et seq.

11 Ie European Parliament and Council Regulation (EU) 537/2014 (OJ L158, 27.5.2014, p 77). With the exception of art 16(6), which applies from 17 June 2017, the Regulation applies from 17 June 2016: art 44. The member states must adopt appropriate provisions to ensure its effective application: art 42. The Statutory Auditors and Third Country Auditors Regulations 2016, SI 2016/649 (see PARAS 1005, 1034, 1069 et seq, 1091), are partly made for this purpose.

'Public interest entities' means the following (European Parliament and Council Directive (EC) 2006/43 (OJ L157, 9.6.2006, p 87) art 2(13) (amended by European Parliament and Council Directive (EU) 2014/56 (OJ L158, 27.5.2014, p 196)); definitions in European Parliament and Council Directive (EC) 2006/43 (OJ L157, 9.6.2006, p 87) art 2 applied for these purposes by European Parliament and Council Regulation (EU) 537/2014 (OJ L158, 27.5.2014, p 77) art 3)), ie:

(1) entities governed by the law of a member state whose transferable securities are admitted to trading on a regulated market of any member state within the meaning of European Parliament and Council Directive (EC) 2004/39 (OJ L 145, 30.4.2004, p 1) art 4(1) point (14);

(2) credit institutions as defined in European Parliament and Council Directive (EU) 2013/36 (OJ L176, 27.6.2013, p 338) art 3(2) point (1), other than those referred to in art 2;

(3) insurance undertakings within the meaning of Council Directive (EEC) 91/674 ((OJ L374, 31.12.1991, p 7) art 2(1); or

(4) entities designated by member states as public interest entities, for instance undertakings that are of significant public relevance because of the nature of their business, their size or the number of their employees.

12 'Statutory audit' means an audit of annual financial statements or consolidated financial statements in so far as required by EU law, required by national law as regards small undertakings, or voluntarily carried out at the request of small undertakings which meets national legal requirements that are equivalent to those for an audit required by national law as regards small undertakings, where national legislation defines such audits as statutory audits: see European Parliament and Council Directive (EC) 2006/43 (OJ L157, 9.6.2006, p 87) art 2(1) (as amended and applied: see note 11).

13 See European Parliament and Council Regulation (EU) 537/2014 (OJ L158, 27.5.2014, p 77) Title II (arts 4–15).

14 'Statutory auditor' means a natural person who is approved in accordance with European Parliament and Council Directive (EC) 2006/43 (OJ L157, 9.6.2006, p 87) by the competent authorities of a member state to carry out statutory audits: art 2(2) (as applied: see note 11).

15 'Audit firm' means a legal person or any other entity, regardless of its legal form, that is approved in accordance with European Parliament and Council Directive (EC) 2006/43 (OJ L157, 9.6.2006, p 87) by the competent authorities of a member state to carry out statutory audits: art 2(3) (as applied: see note 11).

16 See European Parliament and Council Regulation (EU) 537/2014 (OJ L158, 27.5.2014, p 77) Title III (arts 16–19).

17 See European Parliament and Council Regulation (EU) 537/2014 (OJ L158, 27.5.2014, p 77) Title IV (arts 20–44).

18 Ie Council Regulation (EEC) 2137/85 (OJ L199, 31.07.1985, p 1) on the European Economic Interest Grouping ('EEIG'); and see PARA 1823.

19 See Council Regulation (EEC) 2137/85 (OJ L199, 31.07.1985, p 1) on the European Economic Interest Grouping ('EEIG') preamble. See further PARA 1823.

For the purposes of making further provision in relation to this regulation, the European Economic Interest Grouping Regulations 1989, SI 1989/638, and the Registrar of Companies (Fees) (European Economic Interest Grouping and European Public Limited-Liability Company) Regulations 2012, SI 2012/1908, have been made: see PARA 1824. From the date of registration of an EEIG in the United Kingdom, an EEIG is a body corporate: see the European Economic Interest Grouping Regulations 1989, SI 1989/638, reg 3; and PARA 1824. As to the meaning of 'United Kingdom' see PARA 1 note 5.

20 Ie Council Regulation (EC) 2157/2001 (OJ L294, 10.11.2001, p 1) on the Statute for a European Company (Societas Europaea) ('SE'). See also Council Directive (EC) 2001/86 (OJ L294, 10.11.2001, p 22) supplementing the Statute for a European Company with regard to the involvement of employees; and PARA 1825 et seq. For the purposes of implementing the Directive, and for making further provision in relation to the Regulation, the European Public Limited-Liability Company Regulations 2004, SI 2004/2326, the European Public Limited-Liability Company (Employee Involvement) (Great Britain) Regulations 2009, SI 2009/2401, and the Registrar of Companies (Fees) (European Economic Interest Grouping and European Public Limited-Liability Company) Regulations 2012, SI 2012/1908, have been made: see PARAS 1829, 1831. A European Company is a form of public limited-liability company and it has legal personality: see Council Regulation (EC) 2157/2001 (OJ L294, 10.11.2001, p 1) art 1; and PARA 1825.

21 See Council Regulation (EC) 2157/2001 (OJ L294, 10.11.2001, p 1) preamble. See further PARA 1825 et seq.

22 See Council Regulation (EC) 1435/2003 (OJ L207, 18.8.2003, p 1) on the Statute for a European Co-operative Society ('SCE') (corrected in OJ L49, 17.2.2007, p 35). For the purposes of making further provision in relation to that Regulation, the European Co-operative Society

Regulations 2006, SI 2006/2078, have been made. The rules on the involvement of employees in such a society are laid down in Council Directive (EC) 2003/72 (OJ L207, 18.8.2003, p 25); and for the purposes of implementing this Directive, the European Co-operative Society (Involvement of Employees) Regulations 2006, SI 2006/2059, have been made. See also European Parliament and Council Regulation (EC) 1082/2006 (OJ L210, 31.7.2006, p 19) on a European grouping of territorial co-operation ('EGTC') (amended by European Parliament and Council Regulation (EU) 1302/2013 (OJ L347, 0.12.2013, p 303)) in relation to the implementation of which the European Grouping of Territorial Co-operation Regulations 2015, SI 2015/1493, have been made.

23 Although public issues and offers of securities used to be governed domestically by company law legislation (see PARA 9), EU law has had an impact that has seen the development of financial markets and securities regulation as a separate (albeit related) strand of law: see PARA 20 note 21.

24 Ie European Parliament and Council Regulation (EU) 600/2014 (OJ L173, 12.6.2014, p 84) on markets in financial instruments (with application in part from 4 June 2014, in part from 3 January 2017, and in part from 3 January 2019: see art 55).

25 Ie European Parliament and Council Regulation (EU) 596/2014 (OJ L173, 12.6.2014, p 1) on market abuse (with application in part on 2 July 2014 and in part from 3 July 2016: see art 39(2)).

20. EU Directives relating to company law. In order to attain freedom of establishment[1] as regards a particular activity, the European Parliament and the Council, acting in accordance with the ordinary legislative procedure[2] and after consulting the Economic and Social Committee[3], must act by means of Directives[4]. They must carry out the duties so devolving upon them by, in particular and among other matters, co-ordinating to the necessary extent the safeguards which, for the protection of the interests of members and others, are required by member states of companies or firms[5] with a view to making such safeguards equivalent throughout the European Union (the 'EU')[6]. A Directive is binding, as to the result to be achieved, upon each member state to which it is addressed, but leaves to the national authorities the choice of form and methods[7].

In December 2015, the European Commission published a proposal for a Directive repealing and codifying the following company law Directives[8]:

(1) the Sixth Company Law Directive of 17 December 1982, relating to the division of public limited liability companies[9];

(2) the Eleventh Company Law Directive of 21 December 1989, concerning disclosure requirements in respect of branches opened in a member state by certain types of company governed by the law of another state[10];

(3) a Company Law Directive of 26 October 2005 on cross-border mergers of limited liability companies (commonly referred to as the 'Tenth Company Law Directive')[11];

(4) the Directive concerning mergers of public limited liability companies[12]; and

(5) the Directive concerning the formation of public limited liability companies and the maintenance and alteration of their capital[13].

There are many other company law Directives which the Commission does not propose to include in that codification. These include:

(a) a Directive governing the co-ordination of national provisions concerning disclosure of basic documents and other information, the validity of obligations entered into by limited liability companies, and the 'nullity' of such companies[14];

(b) a Directive on the annual accounts and consolidated accounts of banks and other financial institutions[15];

(c) the Thirteenth Company Law Directive of 21 April 2004, on takeover bids (the 'Takeovers Directive')[16];

(d) the Audit Directive[17];

(e) a Directive on single-member private limited liability companies[18];

(f) the Shareholders' Rights Directive[19]; and

(g) a Directive on the annual financial statements, consolidated financial statements and related reports of certain types of undertakings ('the New Accounting Directive')[20].

A number of other Directives that are more closely related to the regulation of financial markets and securities have some relevance to company law[21]. Among the latter category are those Directives which govern:

(i) the admission of securities to official stock exchange listing and on information to be published on those securities (the 'Consolidated Admissions and Reporting Directive' or 'CARD')[22];

(ii) the prospectus to be published when transferable securities are offered to the public or admitted to trading[23];

(iii) the harmonisation of transparency requirements with regard to information about issuers whose securities are admitted to trading on a regulated market (the 'Transparency Directive')[24]; and

(iv) criminal sanctions for market abuse[25].

Other Directives of note in a more general context are those which govern the safeguarding of employees' rights in the event of transfers of undertakings or businesses or parts of them (the 'Acquired Rights Directive')[26], and the establishment of a general framework for informing and consulting employees in the European Union[27].

1 As to freedom of establishment see PARA 17.

2 As to the ordinary legislative procedure see EUROPEAN UNION vol 47A (2014) PARA 99. As to the European Parliament see EUROPEAN UNION vol 47A (2014) PARAS 40–41; and as to the Council see EUROPEAN UNION vol 47A (2014) PARAS 44–47.

3 As to the Economic and Social Committee see EUROPEAN UNION vol 47A (2014) PARA 76.

4 TFEU art 51 para 1. As to TFEU and its citation see PARA 16 note 1.

5 Ie companies or firms within the meaning of the TFEU art 54: see PARA 16 note 1.

6 TFEU art 50 para 2(g).

7 See the TFEU art 288; and EUROPEAN UNION vol 47A (2014) PARA 92. As to the effect of such Directives in English law see CONSTITUTIONAL AND ADMINISTRATIVE LAW vol 20 (2014) PARA 28.

8 See Proposal for a Directive of the European Parliament and of the Council relating to certain aspects of company law (codification) COM/2015/0616 final.

9 Ie Council Directive (EEC) 82/891 (OJ L378, 31.12.82, p 47) (amended by European Parliament and Council Directive (EC) 2007/63 (OJ L300, 17.11.2007, p 47); European Parliament and Council Directive (EC) 2009/109 (OJ L259, 2.10.2009, p 14); European Parliament and Council Directive (EU) 2014/59 (OJ L173, 12.6.2014, p 190)). See the Companies Act 2006 Pt 27 (ss 902–941) (mergers and divisions of public companies); and PARA 1629 et seq. See also PARA 139.

10 Ie Council Directive (EEC) 89/666 (OJ L395, 30.12.89, p 36) (amended by European Parliament and Council Directive (EU) 2012/17 (OJ L156, 16.6.2012, p 1)). The Overseas Companies Regulations 2009, SI 2009/1801, have been made for the purpose of implementing that Directive: see PARA 2013 et seq.

11 Ie European Parliament and Council Directive (EC) 2005/56 (OJ L310, 25.11.2005, p 1) on cross-border mergers of limited liability companies (commonly referred to as the 'Tenth Company Law Directive') (amended by European Parliament and Council Directive (EC) 2009/109 (OJ L259, 2.10.2009, p 14); European Parliament and Council Directive (EU) 2012/17 (OJ L156, 16.6.2012, p 1); European Parliament and Council Directive (EU) 2014/59 (OJ L173, 12.6.2014, p 190)). For the purposes of implementing the Tenth Company Law Directive, the Companies (Cross-Border Mergers) Regulations 2007, SI 2007/2974, have been made: see PARA 1631.

12 Ie European Parliament and Council Directive (EU) 2011/35 (OJ L110, 29.4.2011, p 1) (amended by Council Directive (EU) 2013/24 (OJ L158, 10.6.2013, p 365); European Parliament and Council Directive (EU) 2014/59 (OJ L173, 12.6.2014, p 190)), which repeals and replaces the Directive known as the 'Third Company Law Directive' (ie Council Directive (EC) 78/855 (OJ L295, 20.10.78, p 36)). See the Companies Act 2006 Pt 27 (ss 902–941); and PARA 1629 et seq.

13 Ie European Parliament and Council Directive (EU) 2012/30 (OJ L315, 14.11.2012, p 74) (amended by Council Directive (EU) 2013/24 (OJ L158, 10.6.2013, p 365; European Parliament and Council Directive (EU) 2014/59 (OJ L173, 12.6.2014) p 190)). That Directive is concerned

with the co-ordination of safeguards which, for the protection of the interests of members and others, are required by member states of companies within the meaning of the TFEU art 54 (see PARA 16), in respect of the formation of public limited liability companies and the maintenance and alteration of their capital, with a view to making such safeguards equivalent. As to such safeguards see the Companies Act 2006 ss 724–732 (treasury shares); and PARA 1437 et seq.

14 Ie European Parliament and Council Directive (EC) 2009/101 (OJ L258, 1.10.2009, p 11) (amended by European Parliament and Council Directive (EU) 2012/17 (OJ L156, 16.6.2012, p 1; Council Directive (EU) 2013/24 (OJ L158, 10.6.2013, p 365)). This repeals and replaces the 'First Company Directive' (ie Council Directive (EEC) 68/151 (OJ L65, 14.3.68, p 8). See the Companies Act 2006 ss 40–42; and PARA 262; Pt 35 (ss 1059A–1133); and PARA 126 et seq. See also the Companies Act 2006 (Interconnection of Registers) Order 2014, SI 2014/1557, which amends the Companies Act 2006 s 1059A(3) (see PARA 126), s 1078(1) (see PARA 139) and adds s 1079A (see PARA 126). It was held that the First Company Directive (now repealed) protected innocent parties dealing with the company and did not prevent national laws being applied in relation to conflicts of interests, etc: Case C-104/96 *Co-öperatieve Rabobank 'Vecht en Plassengebied' BA v Minderhoud* [1998] 1 WLR 1025, [1998] 2 BCLC 507, ECJ.

Technical specifications and procedures required for the system of interconnection of registers established by European Parliament and Council Directive (EC) 2009/101 (OJ L258, 1.10.2009, p 11) are established by Commission Implementing Regulation (EU) 2015/884 (OJ L144, 10.6.2015, p 1).

15 Ie Council Directive (EEC) 86/635 (OJ L 372, 31.12.1986, p 1) (amended by European Parliament and Council Directive (EC) 2001/65 (OJ L283, 27.10.2001, p 28); European Parliament and Council Directive (EC) 2003/51 (OJ L178, 17.7.2003, p 16); European Parliament and Council Directive (EC) 2006/46 (OJ L224, 16.8.2006, p 1)).

16 Ie Council Directive (EC) 2004/25 (OJ L142, 30.4.2004, p 12) (amended by European Parliament and Council Regulation (EC) 219/2009 (OJ L87, 31.3.2009, p 109); European Parliament and Council Directive (EU) 2014/59 (OJ L173, 12.6.2014, p 190)). For the purposes of implementing Council Directive (EC) 2004/25 (OJ L142, 30.4.2004, p 12), the Companies Act 2006 Pt 28 (ss 942–992) has been made: see PARA 1662 et seq.

17 Ie European Parliament and Council Directive (EC) 2006/43 (OJ L157, 09.06.2006, p 87) on statutory audits of annual accounts and consolidated accounts (the 'Audit Directive') (amended by European Parliament and Council Directive (EC) 2008/30 (OJ L81, 20.03.2008, p 53); European Parliament and Council Directive (EU) 2013/34 (OJ L182, 29.6.2013, p 19); European Parliament and Council Directive (EU) 2014/56 (OJ L158, 27.5.2014, p 196)). See also Commission Decision (EU) 2011/30 (OJ L15, 20.1.2011, p 12) on the equivalence of certain third country public oversight, quality assurance, investigation and penalty systems for auditors and audit entities and a transitional period for audit activities of certain third country auditors and audit entities in the European Union (amended by Commission Regulation (EU) 519/2013 (OJ L158, 10.6.2013, p 74); Commission Implementing Decision (EU) 2013/288 (OJ L163, 15.6.2013, p 26)). As to the implementation of the Audit Directive see PARA 1058.

18 Ie European Parliament and Council Directive (EC) 2009/102 (OJ L258, 1.10.2009, p 20) (amended by Council Directive (EU) 2013/24 (OJ L158, 10.6.2013, p 365)). Accordingly, a company is formed under the Companies Act 2006 by one or more persons: see s 7; and PARA 95. Note that the European Commission has proposed the repeal of European Parliament and Council Directive (EC) 2009/102 (OJ L258, 1.10.2009, p 20) within 24 months of the coming into force of a new proposed Directive on single-member companies. Under that proposed Directive, single-member private limited liability companies formed and operating in compliance with its provisions would add to their names a common, easily identifiable abbreviation 'SUP' (Societas Unius Personae): see Proposal for a Directive of the European Parliament and of the Council on single-member private limited liability companies 2014/0120 (COD).

19 Ie European Parliament and Council Directive (EC) 2007/36 (OJ L184, 14.07.2007, p 17) on the exercise of certain rights of shareholders in listed companies (amended by European Parliament and Council Directive (EU) 2014/59 (OJ L173, 12.6.2014, p 190)). For the purposes of implementing that Directive, the Companies (Shareholders' Rights) Regulations 2009, SI 2009/1632, have been made, amending the Companies Act 2006 Pt 13 (ss 281–361) (see PARA 689 et seq).

20 Ie European Parliament and Council Directive (EU) 2013/34 (OJ L 182, 29.6.2013, p 19) (amended by European Parliament and Council Directive (EU) 2014/95 (OJ L330, 15.11.2014, p 1) ('the Non-Financial Reporting Directive', which must be transposed into domestic law by 6 December 2016, so as to apply for the financial year starting on 1 January 2017 or during the calendar year 2017; see art 4(1)); and by Council Directive (EU) 2014/102 (OJ L334, 21.11.2014, p 86)). The Small Companies (Micro-Entities' Accounts) Regulations 2013, SI 2013/3008 (see PARA 766 et seq), the Reports on Payments to Governments Regulations 2014, SI 2014/3209 (see

PARA 774), and the Companies, Partnerships and Groups (Accounts and Reports) Regulations 2015, SI 2015/980 (see PARA 766 et seq), have been made in order to implement the New Accounting Directive.

21 Although public issues and offers of securities used to be governed domestically by company law legislation (see PARA 9), EU law has had an impact that has seen the development of financial markets and securities regulation as a separate (albeit related) strand of law (see Council Directive (EEC) 79/279 of 5 March 1979 (OJ L66, 16.03.1979, p 21) co-ordinating the conditions for the admission of securities to official stock exchange listing (repealed); Council Directive (EEC) 80/390 of 17 March 1980 (OJ L100, 17.04.1980, p 1) co-ordinating the requirements for the drawing up, scrutiny and distribution of the listing particulars to be published for the admission of securities to official stock exchange listing (repealed); and Council Directive (EEC) 82/121 of 15 February 1982 (OJ L48, 20.02.1982, p 26) on information to be published on a regular basis by companies the shares of which have been admitted to official stock-exchange listing (repealed); and see now European Parliament and Council Directive (EC) 2001/34 (OJ L184, 6.7.2001, p 1) on the admission of securities to official stock exchange listing and on information to be published on those securities (the 'Consolidated Admissions and Reporting Directive') (cited in the text and note 22). The pre-eminent principle of current EU regulation of the public issue of securities is to ensure that disclosures are made regarding the issuing company and the shares on offer: see eg European Parliament and Council Directive (EC) 2003/71 (OJ L345, 31.12.2003, p 64) on the prospectus to be published when securities are offered to the public or admitted to trading (cited in the text and note 24). The concept of regulated markets has also overtaken 'official listing' as one of the guiding principles: see European Parliament and Council Directive (EC) 2004/39 (OJ L145, 30.04.2004, p 1) on markets in financial instruments (with subsequent amendments); and FINANCIAL SERVICES REGULATION vol 50A (2016) PARA 584 et seq); European Parliament and Council Directive (EC) 2004/109 (OJ L390, 31.12.2004, p 38) on the harmonisation of transparency requirements in relation to information about issuers whose securities are admitted to trading on a regulated market (cited in the text and note 24); European Parliament and Council Directive (EU) 2014/57 (OJ L173, 12.6.2014, p 179) on criminal sanctions for market abuse; and European Parliament and Council Directive (EU) 2014/59 (OJ L173, 12.6.2014, p 190) establishing a framework for the recovery and resolution of credit institutions and investment firms.

22 Ie European Parliament and Council Directive (EC) 2001/34 (OJ L184, 6.7.2001, p 1) on the admission of securities to official stock exchange listing and on information to be published on those securities (amended by European Parliament and Council Directive (EC) 2003/6 (OJ L96, 12.4.2003 p16); European Parliament and Council Directive (EC) 2003/71 (OJ L345, 31.12.2003, p 64); European Parliament and Council Directive (EC) 2004/109 (OJ L390, 31.12.2004, p 38); European Parliament and Council Directive (EC) 2005/1 (OJ L79, 24.03.2005, p 9)). Provision has also been made by way of amendment to the Financial Services and Markets Act 2000 and the Financial Services Authority's Listing Rules (see PARA 1255 et seq) for the purposes of implementing European Parliament and Council Directive (EC) 2001/34: see FINANCIAL SERVICES REGULATION vol 50A (2016) PARA 597 et seq.

23 Ie European Parliament and Council Directive (EC) 2003/71 (OJ L345, 31.12.2003, p 64) on the prospectus to be published when securities are offered to the public or admitted to trading (amended by European Parliament and Council Directive (EC) 2008/11 (OJ L76, 19.3.2008, p 37; European Parliament and Council Directive (EU) 2010/73 (OJ L327, 11.12.2010, p 1), European Parliament and Council Directive (EU) 2010/78 (OJ L331, 15.12.2010, p 120), European Parliament and Council Directive (EU) 2013/50 (OJ L294, 6.11.2013, p 13), European Parliament and Council Directive (EU) 2014/51 (OJ L153, 22.5.2014, p 1); and see also Commission Regulation (EC) 809/2004 (OJ L 149, 30.4.2004, p 1) and Commission Delegated Regulation (EU) 2016/301 (OJ L 58, 4.3.2016, p 13), respectively implementing and supplementing that Directive. For the purposes of implementing that Directive in domestic law, the Prospectus Regulations 2005, SI 2005/1433 (which substitute the Financial Services and Markets Act 2000 ss 84–87 and add ss 84–87R) have been made: see FINANCIAL SERVICES REGULATION vol 50A (2016) PARA 601 et seq.

In November 2015, however, the European Commission published a proposal to replace that Directive with an EU Regulation, as part of its Capital Markets Union action plan: see European Commission Press Release, Brussels, 30 November 2015, IP/15/6196.

24 Ie European Parliament and Council Directive (EC) 2004/109 2004 (OJ L390, 31.12.2004, p 38) on the harmonisation of transparency requirements in relation to information about issuers whose securities are admitted to trading on a regulated market (amended by European Parliament and Council Directive (EC) 2008/22 (OJ L76, 19.03.2008, p 50); European Parliament and Council Directive (EU) 2010/73 (OJ L327, 11.12.2010, p 1), European Parliament and Council Directive (EU) 2010/78 (OJ L331, 15.12.2010, p 120), European Parliament and Council Directive (EU) 2013/50 (OJ L294, 6.11.2013, p 13)). See also the related Commission Directive (EC) 2007/14 (OJ L69, 09.03.2007, p 27) (amended by European Parliament

and Council Directive (EU) 2013/50 (OJ L294, 6.11.2013, p 13)) laying down detailed rules for the implementation of certain provisions of European Parliament and Council Directive (EC) 2004/109.

For the purposes of implementing these measures, the Companies Act 2006 Pt 43 (ss 1265–1273) has been made, largely by means of making amendments to the Financial Services and Markets Act 2000 (see FINANCIAL SERVICES REGULATION vol 50A (2016) PARA 623 et seq) and by making provision in the Financial Services Authority's Disclosure and Transparency Rules using powers under the Financial Services and Markets Act 2000: see FINANCIAL SERVICES REGULATION vol 50A (2016) PARA 623 et seq. In addition the Secretary of State has power under the Companies Act 2006 s 1273 to make regulations for the purpose of implementing, enabling the implementation of or dealing with matters arising out of or related to, any EU obligation relating to the corporate governance of issuers who have requested or approved admission of their securities to trading on a regulated market, and about corporate governance in relation to such issuers for the purpose of implementing, or dealing with matters arising out of or related to, any EU obligation: see s 1273(1) (amended by SI 2011/1043). As to the Secretary of State see PARA 6. For these purposes, 'corporate governance', in relation to an issuer, includes the following (Companies Act 2006 s 1273(2)), ie:

(1) the nature, constitution or functions of the organs of the issuer;
(2) the manner in which organs of the issuer conduct themselves;
(3) the requirements imposed on organs of the issuer;
(4) the relationship between different organs of the issuer;
(5) the relationship between the organs of the issuer and the members of the issuer or holders of the issuer's securities

For these purposes, 'issuer', 'securities' and 'regulated market' have the same meaning as in the Financial Services and Markets Act 2000 Pt VI (ss 73A–103) (official listing) (see FINANCIAL SERVICES REGULATION vol 50A (2016) PARA 593 et seq): Companies Act 2006 s 1273(6). The regulations may make provision by reference to any specified code on corporate governance that may be issued from time to time by a specified body, may create new criminal offences (subject to s 1273(4)) and may make provision excluding liability in damages in respect of things done or omitted for the purposes of, or in connection with, the carrying on, or purported carrying on, of any specified activities: s 1273(3). For these purposes, 'specified' means specified in the regulations: s 1273(3). The regulations may not create a criminal offence punishable by a greater penalty than (on indictment) a fine or (on summary conviction) a fine not exceeding the statutory maximum or (if calculated on a daily basis) £100 a day: s 1273(4). By virtue of the Legal Aid, Sentencing and Punishment of Offenders Act 2012 s 85, however, where the offence is committed on or after 12 March 2015, it is punishable by a fine of an unlimited amount. As to the powers of magistrates' courts to issue fines on summary conviction see SENTENCING vol 92 (2015) PARA 176. Regulations under the Companies Act 2006 s 1273 are subject to negative resolution procedure (ie the statutory instrument containing the regulations is subject to annulment in pursuance of a resolution of either House of Parliament): ss 1273(5), 1289. As to the making of regulations under the Companies Act 2006 generally see ss 1288–1292. At the date at which this volume states the law, no regulations have been made in exercise of the power conferred by s 1273.

25 Ie European Parliament and Council Directive (EU) 2014/57 (OJ L173, 12.6.2014, p 179). Market abuse itself, which was formerly the subject of Directives, is now dealt with by means of an EU Regulation: see PARA 19.

26 Ie Council Directive (EC) 2001/23 (OJ L82, 22.3.2001, p 16) on the approximation of the laws of the member states relating to the safeguarding of employees' rights in the event of transfers of undertakings, businesses or parts of undertakings or businesses (amended by European Parliament and Council Directive (EU) 2015/1794 (OJ L263, 8.10.2015, p 1)). For the purpose of implementing that Directive the Transfer of Undertakings (Protection of Employment) Regulations 2006, SI 2006/246, have been made (see EMPLOYMENT vol 39 (2014) PARA 136 et seq).

27 Ie European Parliament and Council Directive (EC) 2002/14 (OJ L80, 23.2.2002, p 29) (amended by European Parliament and Council Directive (EU) 2015/1794 (OJ L263, 8.10.2015, p 1)). For the purpose of implementing that Directive, the Information and Consultation of Employees Regulations 2004, SI 2004/3426, have been made (see EMPLOYMENT vol 41A (2014) PARA 1289 et seq).

See also European Parliament and Council Directive (EC) 2009/38 (OJ L122, 16.5.2009, p 28) on the establishment of a European Works Council or a procedure in Community-scale undertakings and Community-scale groups of undertakings for the purposes of informing and consulting employees (amended by European Parliament and Council Directive (EU) 2015/1794 (OJ L263, 8.10.2015, p 1)). For the purposes of implementing that Directive, the Transnational Information and Consultation of Employees (Amendment) Regulations 2010, SI 2010/1088, have been made (see EMPLOYMENT vol 41A (2014) PARA 1237 et seq).

2. COMPANIES REGISTERED UNDER THE COMPANIES ACTS

(1) APPLICATION OF THE COMPANIES ACTS: IN GENERAL

21. Meanings of 'company' and 'UK-registered company' in the Companies Acts. In the Companies Acts[1], unless the context otherwise requires, 'company' means a company formed and registered under the Companies Act 2006[2], that is:

(1) a company so formed and registered after the commencement of Part 1 of the 2006 Act[3]; or

(2) a company that, immediately before the commencement of Part 1 of the 2006 Act, either was formed and registered under the Companies Act 1985[4] or was an existing company for the purposes of the 1985 Act[5], which is to be treated on commencement as if formed and registered under the Companies Act 2006[6].

In the Companies Acts, 'UK-registered company' means a company registered under the Companies Act 2006, but does not include an overseas company[7] that has complied with the statutory duty to register particulars in specified circumstances[8].

1 As to the meaning of the 'Companies Acts' for these purposes see PARA 13.

2 Companies Act 2006 s 1(1). As to company formation and registration under the Companies Act 2006, and the different forms that such a company may take, see PARA 65 et seq. As to companies not registered, or registered but not formed, under the Companies Act 2006, and as to overseas companies, see PARA 29. As to the meaning of 'company' more generally see PARA 1.

3 Companies Act 2006 s 1(1)(a). The date of commencement for the majority of Pt 1 (ss 1, 3–6) was 1 October 2009: see the Companies Act 2006 (Commencement No 8, Transitional Provisions and Savings) Order 2008, SI 2008/2860, art 3(a). The dates of commencement for the Companies Act 2006 s 2 were 1 January 2007 and 20 January 2007 for certain purposes (see the Companies Act 2006 (Commencement No 1, Transitional Provisions and Savings) Order 2006, SI 2006/3428, arts 2(2)(a), 3(2)(a)) and 6 April 2007 for remaining purposes (see the Companies Act 2006 (Commencement No 2, Consequential Amendments, Transitional Provisions and Savings) Order 2007, SI 2007/1093, art 2(1)(a)).

In the definition of 'company' in the Companies Act 2006 s 1, the reference to a company formed and registered after the commencement of Pt 1 (ss 1–6) must be read as a reference to a company formed and registered on an application received by the registrar on or after 1 October 2009 and made in accordance with ss 7–16 (see PARA 95 et seq): see the Companies Act 2006 (Commencement No 8, Transitional Provisions and Savings) Order 2008, SI 2008/2860, art 5, Sch 2 para 2(1), (6)(a).

4 Companies Act 2006 s 1(1)(b)(i). This applies equally to a company that was formed and registered under the Companies (Northern Ireland) Order 1986, SI 1986/1032 (NI 6): see the Companies Act 2006 s 1(1)(b)(i).

In the definition of 'company' in s 1, the reference to a company formed and registered under the Companies Act 1985 immediately before the commencement of the Companies Act 2006 Pt 1 includes a company formed and registered on an application for registration if it was received by the registrar, and if the requirements as to registration that are set out in the corresponding provisions of the Companies Act 1985 were met in relation to it, before 1 October 2009: see the Companies Act 2006 (Commencement No 8, Transitional Provisions and Savings) Order 2008, SI 2008/2860, Sch 2 para 2(3), (6)(b).

5 Companies Act 2006 s 1(1)(b)(ii). This applies equally to a company that was an existing company for the purposes of the Companies (Northern Ireland) Order 1986, SI 1986/1032 (NI 6): see the Companies Act 2006 s 1(1)(b)(ii). As to general savings for existing companies etc under the Companies Act 2006 see PARA 14.

For the purposes of the Companies Act 1985, 'existing company' was defined as a company formed and registered under the former Companies Acts, but did not include a company registered under the Joint Stock Companies Acts, the Companies Act 1862 or the Companies (Consolidation) Act 1908 in what was then Ireland: Companies Act 1985 s 735(1)(b) (repealed). The 'former Companies Acts' were defined as the Joint Stock Companies Acts, the Companies Act 1862, the Companies (Consolidation) Act 1908, the Companies Act 1929 and the Companies Acts

1948 to 1983: Companies Act 1985 s 735(1)(c) (repealed). The 'Joint Stock Companies Acts' were defined as the Joint Stock Companies Act 1856, the Joint Stock Companies Acts 1856, 1857, the Joint Stock Banking Companies Act 1857 and the Act to enable Joint Stock Banking Companies to be formed on the principle of limited liability, or any one or more of those Acts (as the case may require), but did not include the Joint Stock Companies Act 1844: Companies Act 1985 s 735(3) (repealed). As to the meaning of the 'former Companies Acts' for the purposes of the Companies Acts, which restates the definition of the 'Joint Stock Companies Acts' given above, see PARA 14 note 1. As to the Acts which may be cited as 'the Companies Acts 1948 to 1983' see PARA 10 note 31.

6 Companies Act 2006 s 1(1)(b).

7 As to the meaning of 'overseas company' see PARA 2013.

8 Companies Act 2006 s 1158. The text refers to an overseas company that has registered particulars under s 1046 (see PARA 2015): see s 1158.

22. Meanings of 'subsidiary', 'holding company' and 'wholly-owned subsidiary'. A company[1] is a 'subsidiary' of another company, its 'holding company', if that other company:

(1) holds a majority of the voting rights in it[2]; or
(2) is a member of it and has the right to appoint or remove a majority of its board of directors[3]; or
(3) is a member of it and controls alone, pursuant to an agreement with other members, a majority of the voting rights in it[4],

or if it is a subsidiary of a company which is itself a subsidiary of that other company[5].

A company is a 'wholly-owned subsidiary' of another company if it has no members except that other and that other's wholly-owned subsidiaries or persons acting on behalf of that other or its wholly-owned subsidiaries[6].

Rights which are exercisable only in certain circumstances are taken into account only when the circumstances have arisen, and for so long as they continue to obtain, or when the circumstances are within the control of the person having the rights[7]. Rights which are normally exercisable but are temporarily incapable of exercise must continue to be taken into account[8].

Rights held by a person[9] in a fiduciary capacity are treated as not held by him[10].

Rights held by a person as nominee for another are treated as held by the other[11].

Rights attached to shares held by way of security are treated as held by the person providing the security[12]:

(a) where apart from the right to exercise them for the purpose of preserving the value of the security, or of realising it, the rights are exercisable only in accordance with his instructions[13]; and
(b) where the shares are held in connection with the granting of loans as part of normal business activities and apart from the right to exercise them for the purpose of preserving the value of the security, or of realising it, the rights are exercisable only in his interests[14].

Rights are treated as held by a company if they are held by any of its subsidiary companies[15]. However, nothing in the provisions relating to rights held by one person as nominee for another[16], or in the provisions relating to rights attached to shares held by way of security[17] is to be construed as requiring rights held by a company to be treated as held by any of its subsidiaries[18].

The voting rights in a company are to be reduced by any rights held by the company itself[19].

The Secretary of State[20] may by regulations[21] amend the provisions which relate to the meanings of 'subsidiary', 'holding company' and 'wholly-owned subsidiary'[22] so as to alter the meanings of those expressions[23].

1 For the purposes of the Companies Act 2006 s 1159 and Sch 6, 'company' includes any body corporate: s 1159(4). As to the meaning of 'body corporate' for the purposes of the Companies Acts see PARA 1 note 5; and as to the meaning of 'company' under the Companies Acts see PARA 21. As to the meaning of the 'Companies Acts' for these purposes see PARA 13.

2 Companies Act 2006 s 1159(1)(a). For the purposes of s 1159(1)(a), (c) (see heads (1), (3) in the text), the references to the voting rights in a company are references to the rights conferred on shareholders in respect of their shares or, in the case of a company not having a share capital, on members, to vote at general meetings of the company on all, or substantially all, matters: Sch 6 paras 1, 2. As to the meaning of 'member' see PARA 323; and as to the meaning of 'share' and 'company having a share capital' see PARA 1231. As to share capital, including the allotment of shares, see PARA 1231 et seq; and as to shareholders and membership of companies generally see PARA 323 et seq. As to company meetings see PARA 701 et seq.

3 Companies Act 2006 s 1159(1)(b). For the purposes of s 1159(1)(b), the reference to the right to appoint or remove a majority of the board of directors is a reference to the right to appoint or remove directors holding a majority of the voting rights at meetings of the board on all, or substantially all, matters: Sch 6 paras 1, 3(1). For these purposes a company is treated as having the right to appoint to a directorship if a person's appointment to it follows necessarily from his appointment as director of the company or if the directorship is held by the company itself (Sch 6 paras 1, 3(2)); and a right to appoint or remove which is exercisable only with the consent or concurrence of another person must be left out of account unless no other person has a right to appoint or, as the case may be, remove in relation to that directorship (Sch 6 paras 1, 3(3)). As to the meaning of 'director' see PARA 512. As to meetings of directors, and the rights of appointment etc, see PARA 568 et seq.

4 Companies Act 2006 s 1159(1)(c). See also note 2.

5 Companies Act 2006 s 1159(1). See *Farstad Supply A/S v Enviroco Ltd, The Far Service* [2011] UKSC 16, [2011] 3 All ER 451, [2011] 1 WLR 921 (meaning of 'subsidiary' in context of charterparty whose wording used cross-reference to statutory definition).

6 Companies Act 2006 s 1159(2).

7 Companies Act 2006 Sch 6 paras 1, 4(1).

8 Companies Act 2006 Sch 6 paras 1, 4(2).

9 For these purposes, references in any provision of the Companies Act 2006 Sch 6 paras 5–9 (see the text and notes 10–19) to rights held by a person include rights falling to be treated as held by him by virtue of any other provision of Sch 6 paras 5–9 but not rights which by virtue of any such provision are to be treated as not held by him: Sch 6 paras 1, 10.

10 Companies Act 2006 Sch 6 paras 1, 5. For these purposes, where a registered shareholder is the vendor under an uncompleted but specifically enforceable contract for the sale of his shares, he acts as a fiduciary: *Michaels v Harley House (Marylebone) Ltd* [2000] Ch 104, [1999] 1 All ER 356, CA.

11 Companies Act 2006 Sch 6 paras 1, 6(1). Rights are regarded as held as nominee for another if they are exercisable only on his instructions or with his consent or concurrence: Sch 6 paras 1, 6(2). See also note 9.

12 Companies Act 2006 Sch 6 paras 1, 7. See also note 9.

13 Companies Act 2006 Sch 6 paras 1, 7(a). For these purposes, rights are treated as being exercisable in accordance with the instructions or in the interests of a company if they are exercisable in accordance with the instructions of or, as the case may be, in the interests of any subsidiary or holding company of that company or any subsidiary of a holding company of that company: Sch 6 paras 1, 8(3).

14 Companies Act 2006 Sch 6 paras 1, 7(b).

15 Companies Act 2006 Sch 6 paras 1, 8(1). See also note 9.

16 Ie the Companies Act 2006 Sch 6 paras 1, 6 (see the text and note 11): see Sch 6 paras 1, 8(2).

17 Ie the Companies Act 2006 Sch 6 paras 1, 7 (see the text and notes 12–14): see Sch 6 paras 1, 8(2).

18 Companies Act 2006 Sch 6 paras 1, 8(2). See also note 9.

19 Companies Act 2006 Sch 6 paras 1, 9. See also note 9.

20 As to the Secretary of State see PARA 6.

21 As to the making of regulations under the Companies Act 2006 generally see ss 1288–1292.

22 Ie the Companies Act 2006 s 1159 and Sch 6 (see the text and notes 1–19): see s 1160(1).

23 See the Companies Act 2006 s 1160(1). Such regulations are subject to negative resolution procedure (ie the statutory instrument containing the regulations is subject to annulment in pursuance of a resolution of either House of Parliament): ss 1160(2), 1289. At the date at which

this volume states the law, no such regulations have been made in exercise of the power conferred by s 1160. Any amendment made by such regulations does not apply for the purposes of enactments outside the Companies Acts unless the regulations so provide: Companies Act 2006 s 1160(3). So much of the Interpretation Act 1978 s 23(3) as applies s 17(2)(a) (effect of repeal and re-enactment) (see STATUTES AND LEGISLATIVE PROCESS vol 96 (2012) PARA 702) to deeds, instruments and documents other than enactments does not apply in relation to any repeal and re-enactment effected by regulations under the Companies Act 2006 s 1160: s 1160(4). As to the meaning of 'enactment' see PARA 13 note 16.

23. Meanings of 'parent undertaking', 'subsidiary undertaking' etc in the Companies Acts. For the purposes of the Companies Acts[1], the expressions 'parent undertaking' and 'subsidiary undertaking' are to be construed as follows[2].

An undertaking is a 'parent undertaking' in relation to another undertaking, a 'subsidiary undertaking', if:

(1) it holds a majority of the voting rights[3] in the undertaking[4];

(2) it is a member of the undertaking and has the right to appoint or remove a majority of its board of directors[5];

(3) it has the right to exercise a dominant influence over the undertaking[6] by virtue of provisions contained in the undertaking's articles[7] or by virtue of a control contract[8]; or

(4) it is a member of the undertaking and controls alone, pursuant to an agreement with other shareholders or members, a majority of the voting rights[9] in the undertaking[10].

For these purposes, an undertaking is treated as a member of another undertaking if any of its subsidiary undertakings is a member of that undertaking or if any shares in that other undertaking are held by a person acting on behalf of the undertaking or any of its subsidiary undertakings[11].

An undertaking is also a parent undertaking in relation to another undertaking, a 'subsidiary undertaking', if it has the power to exercise, or actually exercises, dominant influence[12] or control over it[13], or if it and the subsidiary undertaking are managed on a unified basis[14].

A parent undertaking is treated as the parent undertaking of undertakings in relation to which any of its subsidiary undertakings are, or are to be treated as, parent undertakings; and references to its subsidiary undertakings must be construed accordingly[15].

References in the Companies Acts to 'fellow subsidiary undertakings' are to undertakings which are subsidiary undertakings of the same parent undertaking but are not parent undertakings or subsidiary undertakings of each other[16].

1 As to the meaning of the 'Companies Acts' see PARA 13.

2 Companies Act 2006 s 1162(1). The expressions 'parent undertaking' and 'subsidiary undertaking' are defined by s 1162 and s 1162(6), Sch 7 for the purposes mentioned in the text: see s 1162(1). See also PARA 24. In the Companies Acts, 'undertaking' means either a body corporate or partnership, or an unincorporated association carrying on a trade or business, with or without a view to profit (s 1161(1)); and 'parent company' means a company that is a parent undertaking (as defined by s 1162, Sch 7) (s 1173(1)). Other expressions appropriate to companies are to be construed, in relation to an undertaking which is not a company, as references to the corresponding persons, officers, documents or organs, as the case may be, appropriate to undertakings of that description: s 1161(3). This is subject to provision in any specific context providing for the translation of such expressions: s 1161(3). As to the meanings of 'carry on', 'business' and 'gain' generally see PARA 1 note 1. As to the meaning of 'body corporate' for the purposes of the Companies Acts see PARA 1 note 5; and as to the meaning of 'company' under the Companies Acts see PARA 21. As to the meaning of 'officer' generally under the Companies Act 2006 see PARA 679. As to companies and corporations and partnerships etc see PARAS 2–4.

3 For the purposes of the Companies Act 2006 s 1162(2)(a), (d) (see heads (1), (4) in the text), the references to the voting rights in an undertaking are references to the rights conferred on shareholders in respect of their shares or, in the case of an undertaking not having a share capital, on members, to vote at general meetings of the undertaking on all, or substantially all, matters:

Sch 7 paras 1, 2(1). In relation to an undertaking which does not have general meetings at which matters are decided by the exercise of voting rights, the references to the holding of a majority of the voting rights in the undertaking are to be construed as references to having the right under the constitution of the undertaking to direct the overall policy of the undertaking or to alter the terms of its constitution: Sch 7 paras 1, 2(2). As to the meaning of 'member' see PARA 323; and as to the meanings of 'share' and 'company having a share capital' see PARA 1231. As to share capital, including the allotment of shares, see PARA 1231 et seq; and as to shareholders and membership of companies generally see PARA 323 et seq. As to company meetings see PARA 701 et seq.

In s 1162 and Sch 7, references to shares, in relation to an undertaking, are to allotted shares: s 1162(7). In the Companies Acts, references to shares:

(1) in relation to an undertaking with capital but no share capital, are references to rights to share in the capital of the undertaking (Companies Act 2006 s 1161(2)(a)); and
(2) in relation to an undertaking without capital, are references to interests conferring any right to share in the profits or liability to contribute to the losses of the undertaking, or to interests giving rise to an obligation to contribute to the debts or expenses of the undertaking in the event of a winding up (s 1161(2)(b)).

As to winding up in general see COMPANY AND PARTNERSHIP INSOLVENCY vol 16 (2011) PARA 380 et seq.

4 Companies Act 2006 s 1162(2)(a).
5 Companies Act 2006 s 1162(2)(b). For these purposes, the reference to the right to appoint or remove a majority of the board of directors is a reference to the right to appoint or remove directors holding a majority of the voting rights at meetings of the board on all, or substantially all, matters: Sch 7 paras 1, 3(1). An undertaking is treated as having the right to appoint to a directorship if a person's appointment to it follows necessarily from his appointment as director of the undertaking, or if the directorship is held by the undertaking itself: Sch 7 paras 1, 3(2). A right to appoint or remove which is exercisable only with the consent or concurrence of another person must be left out of account unless no other person has a right to appoint or, as the case may be, remove in relation to that directorship: Sch 7 paras 1, 3(3). As to the meaning of 'director' see PARA 512. As to meetings of directors, and the rights of appointment etc, see PARA 568 et seq.
6 For these purposes, an undertaking is not to be regarded as having the right to exercise a dominant influence over another undertaking unless it has a right to give directions with respect to the operating and financial policies of that other undertaking which its directors are obliged to comply with whether or not they are for the benefit of that other undertaking: Companies Act 2006 Sch 7 paras 1, 4(1). However, Sch 7 para 4 is not to be read as affecting the construction of the expression 'actually exercises a dominant influence' in s 1162(4)(a) (see the text and notes 12–13): Sch 7 paras 1, 4(3).
7 As to the meaning of references to a company's 'articles' see PARA 227 note 2. As to a company's articles of association generally see PARA 227 et seq.
8 Companies Act 2006 s 1162(2)(c). For these purposes, a 'control contract' means a contract in writing conferring such a right which is of a kind authorised by the articles of the undertaking in relation to which the right is exercisable, and which is permitted by the law under which that undertaking is established: Sch 7 paras 1, 4(2). See also note 6.
9 See note 3.
10 Companies Act 2006 s 1162(2)(d).
11 Companies Act 2006 s 1162(3).
12 See note 6.
13 Companies Act 2006 s 1162(4)(a).
14 Companies Act 2006 s 1162(4)(b).
15 Companies Act 2006 s 1162(5).
16 Companies Act 2006 s 1161(4).

24. Rights in relation to parent and subsidiary undertakings. In relation to parent and subsidiary undertakings[1], rights which are exercisable only in certain circumstances are to be taken into account only when the circumstances have arisen (and only for so long as they continue to obtain), or when the circumstances are within the control of the person having the rights[2]. Rights which are normally exercisable but are temporarily incapable of exercise must continue to be taken into account[3].

Rights held by a person[4] in a fiduciary capacity are to be treated as not held by him[5].

Rights held by a person as nominee for another are to be treated as held by the other[6].

Rights attached to shares[7] held by way of security are to be treated as held by the person providing the security[8]:

(1) where, apart from the right to exercise them for the purpose of preserving the value of the security, or of realising it, the rights are exercisable only in accordance with his instructions[9]; and

(2) where the shares are held in connection with the granting of loans as part of normal business activities and apart from the right to exercise them for the purpose of preserving the value of the security, or of realising it, the rights are exercisable only in his interests[10].

Rights are to be treated as held by a parent undertaking if they are held by any of its subsidiary undertakings[11]. However, nothing in the provisions relating to rights held by a person as nominee for another[12], or in the provisions relating to rights attached to shares held by way of security[13] is to be construed as requiring rights held by a parent undertaking to be treated as held by any of its subsidiary undertakings[14].

The voting rights in an undertaking must be reduced by any rights held by the undertaking itself[15].

1 As to the meanings of 'parent undertaking' and 'subsidiary undertaking' in the Companies Acts see PARA 23.
2 Companies Act 2006 s 1162(6), Sch 7 paras 1, 5(1).
3 Companies Act 2006 Sch 7 paras 1, 5(2).
4 References in any provision of the Companies Act 2006 Sch 7 paras 6–10 (see the text and notes 5–15) to rights held by a person include rights falling to be treated as held by him by virtue of any other provision of Sch 7 paras 6–10 but not rights which by virtue of any such provision are to be treated as not held by him: Sch 7 paras 1, 11.
5 Companies Act 2006 Sch 7 paras 1, 6. See also note 4. See *Michaels v Harley House (Marylebone) Ltd* [2000] Ch 104, [1999] 1 All ER 356, CA.
6 Companies Act 2006 Sch 7 paras 1, 7(1). Rights are to be regarded as held by a nominee for another if they are exercisable only on his instructions or with his consent or concurrence: Sch 7 paras 1, 7(2). See also note 4.
7 As to the meaning of 'shares' for these purposes see PARA 23 note 3.
8 Companies Act 2006 Sch 7 paras 1, 8. See also note 4.
9 Companies Act 2006 Sch 7 paras 1, 8(a). For these purposes, rights are to be treated as being exercisable in accordance with the instructions or in the interests of an undertaking if they are exercisable in accordance with the instructions of or, as the case may be, in the interests of any group undertaking: Sch 7 paras 1, 9(3). In the Companies Acts, 'group undertaking', in relation to an undertaking, means an undertaking which is either a parent undertaking or subsidiary undertaking of that undertaking, or a subsidiary undertaking of any parent undertaking of that undertaking: s 1161(5).
10 Companies Act 2006 Sch 7 paras 1, 8(b). See also note 9.
11 Companies Act 2006 Sch 7 paras 1, 9(1). See also note 4.
12 Ie the Companies Act 2006 Sch 7 paras 1, 7 (see the text and note 6): see Sch 7 paras 1, 9(2).
13 Ie the Companies Act 2006 Sch 7 paras 1, 8 (see the text and notes 7–10): see Sch 7 paras 1, 9(2).
14 Companies Act 2006 Sch 7 paras 1, 9(2). See also note 4.
15 Companies Act 2006 Sch 7 paras 1, 10. See also note 4.

25. Meaning of 'dormant company'. For the purposes of the Companies Acts[1], a company[2] is 'dormant' during any period in which it has no significant accounting transaction[3].

In determining whether or when a company is dormant, there must be disregarded[4]:

(1) any transaction arising from the taking of shares[5] in the company by a subscriber to the memorandum[6] as a result of an undertaking of his in connection with the formation of the company[7];

(2) any transaction consisting of the payment of:

(a) a fee to the registrar[8] on a change of the company's name[9];
(b) a fee to the registrar on the re-registration of the company[10];
(c) a penalty[11] for failure to file accounts[12]; or
(d) a fee to the registrar for the registration of a confirmation statement[13].

Any reference in the Companies Acts to a body corporate[14] other than a company being dormant has a corresponding meaning[15].

1 As to the meaning of the 'Companies Acts' see PARA 13.
2 As to the meaning of 'company' under the Companies Acts see PARA 21.
3 Companies Act 2006 s 1169(1). For these purposes, a 'significant accounting transaction' means a transaction that is required by s 386 (see PARA 782) to be entered in the company's accounting records: s 1169(2).
4 Companies Act 2006 s 1169(3).
5 As to the meaning of 'share' see PARA 1231. As to share capital generally see PARA 1231 et seq.
6 As to subscribers to the memorandum see PARA 97.
7 Companies Act 2006 s 1169(3)(a). As to company formation under the Companies Act 2006 see PARA 95 et seq.
8 As to the meaning of 'registrar of companies' see PARA 126 note 2.
9 Companies Act 2006 s 1169(3)(b)(i). As to change of a company's name see PARAS 216–218.
10 Companies Act 2006 s 1169(3)(b)(ii). As to re-registration and its effects see PARA 167 et seq.
11 Ie a civil penalty under the Companies Act 2006 s 453 (see PARA 962): see the Companies Act 2006 s 1169(3)(b)(iii).
12 Companies Act 2006 s 1169(3)(b)(iii).
13 Companies Act 2006 s 1169(3)(b)(iv) (amended by the Small Business, Enterprise and Employment Act 2015 s 93(1), (6)). As to the registration of a confirmation statement see PARA 1598. Confirmation statements replace annual returns; as to registration of an annual return under the previous law see PARAS 1594–1597.
14 As to the meaning of 'body corporate' for the purposes of the Companies Acts see PARA 1 note 5.
15 Companies Act 2006 s 1169(4).

26. Geographical extent of the Companies Acts. Except as otherwise provided (or the context otherwise requires), the provisions of the Companies Act 2006 extend to the whole of the United Kingdom[1].

Specific provision is made also to extend the Companies Acts[2] and related legislation to Northern Ireland[3].

In the Companies Acts, 'EEA company' and 'EEA undertaking' mean a company[4] or undertaking governed by the law of an EEA state[5].

1 Companies Act 2006 s 1299. Since 1929, and before the advent of the Companies Act 2006, Companies Acts legislation had extended to Great Britain only: see PARA 10. As to the meanings of 'Great Britain' and 'United Kingdom' see PARA 1 note 5. One of the main aims of the Company Law Review Steering Group (CLRSG) (as to which see PARA 13 note 1) was to make company law a less devolved matter than previously: see *Modern Company Law: For A Competitive Economy—Final Report* (2001) (URN 01/943) paras 11.21–11.33. Nevertheless, certain provisions of the Companies Act 2006 do not extend to Scotland (see eg s 42 (constitutional limitations: companies that are charities) (see PARA 264); s 45 (common seal) (see PARA 282); s 49(3) (the official seal when duly affixed to a document has the same effect as the company's common seal) (see PARA 289); s 181 (modification of provisions in relation to charitable companies) (see PARA 573); s 508 (guidance for regulatory and prosecuting authorities: England, Wales and Northern Ireland) (see PARA 1022); s 1084 (records relating to companies that have been dissolved etc) (see PARA 142)); and other provisions of the 2006 Act either have particular application to Scotland or form part of the law of Scotland only (see eg s 48 (formalities of doing business under the law of Scotland); Pt 11 Ch 2 (ss 265–269) (derivative proceedings in Scotland); s 483 (Scottish public sector companies: audit by Auditor General for Scotland); s 509 (guidance for regulatory authorities: Scotland); s 742 (debentures to bearer (Scotland)); s 781 (offences in connection with share warrants (Scotland)); and ss 1020–1022 (effect of Crown disclaimer: Scotland)).

Despite the main geographical extent of the Companies Act 2006, registration must remain separate for England and Wales, for Scotland and for Northern Ireland due to differences in other aspects of the law that affect companies; also, language provisions may allow a company to elect to locate its registered office in Wales: see PARAS 124–125.
2 As to the meaning of the 'Companies Acts' see PARA 13.

3 See the Companies Act 2006 Pt 45 (ss 1284–1287). This extension may have definitional consequences because, under the Companies Act 2006, companies fall under the umbrella of 'UK companies' rather than 'GB companies' or 'Northern Ireland companies': see PARA 21. However, this extension does not affect the legislative competence of Northern Ireland: formally, company law remains a transferred matter (see CONSTITUTIONAL AND ADMINISTRATIVE LAW vol 20 (2014) PARA 85), and a future Northern Ireland Assembly could separately amend or repeal the Companies Act 2006 in Northern Ireland if that were so desired: see Explanatory Notes to the Companies Act 2006 paras 12, 1706.

4 As to the meaning of 'company' under the Companies Acts see PARA 21.

5 Companies Act 2006 s 1170. For these purposes, 'EEA state', in relation to any time, means a state which at that time is a member state or any other state which at that time is a party to the EEA Agreement, where 'EEA Agreement' means the Agreement on the European Economic Area (Oporto, 2 May 1992; EC 7 (1992); Cm 2183) as adjusted by the Protocol (Brussels, 17 March 1993; EC 2 (1993); Cm 2183), as modified or supplemented from time to time: see the Interpretation Act 1978 s 5, Sch 1 (definitions added by the Legislative and Regulatory Reform Act 2006 s 26(1); definition of 'EEA state' applied by the Companies Act 2006 s 1170 (definition substituted by SI 2007/732)). 'Member' in the expression 'member state' refers to membership of the European Union (the 'EU'): see the European Communities Act 1972 Sch 1 Pt II and the Interpretation Act 1978 Sch 1 (both amended by the European Union (Amendment) Act 2008 s 3(3), Schedule).

27. Application of the companies legislation to other forms of business organisation. Certain provisions of the existing statute law which relate to companies are applied with modifications to limited liability partnerships[1] and to open-ended investment companies[2].

The application of the existing statute law to various forms of European Company is discussed elsewhere in this title[3].

1 See the Limited Liability Partnerships Regulations 2001, SI 2001/1090; the Limited Liability Partnerships (Application of Companies Act 2006) Regulations 2009, SI 2009/1804; and PARTNERSHIP vol 79 (2014) PARA 243 et seq. As to limited liability partnerships generally see PARTNERSHIP vol 79 (2014) PARA 233 et seq.

See also the Limited Liability Partnerships (Accounts and Audit) (Application of Companies Act 2006) Regulations 2008, SI 2008/1911; the Small Limited Liability Partnerships (Accounts) Regulations 2008, SI 2008/1912; and the Large and Medium-sized Limited Liability Partnerships (Accounts) Regulations 2008, SI 2008/1913 (all made under the Limited Liability Partnerships Act 2000), which apply provisions of the Companies Act 2006 Pts 15, 16 (ss 380–539) (accounts and audit) (see PARA 765 et seq) to limited liability partnerships; and the Limited Liability Partnerships (Register of People with Significant Control) Regulations 2016, SI 2016/340, which apply provisions of the Companies Act 2006 Pt 21A (ss 790A–790ZG) (see PARA 466 et seq) to limited liability partnerships.

2 See the Open-Ended Investment Companies Regulations 2001, SI 2001/1228 (made under the Financial Services and Markets Act 2000 s 262); and FINANCIAL SERVICES REGULATION vol 50A (2016) PARA 873 et seq.

3 See PARA 5.

28. Companies and associations incapable of registration. The companies or associations which may not be registered under the Companies Act 2006 are:

(1) trade unions and other organisations of workers[1];

(2) one or more persons associated together for any unlawful purpose[2]; and

(3) companies not formed under the companies legislation and prohibited in express terms by the Companies Act 2006 from registering thereunder[3].

1 A trade union, other than a special register body, may not be registered as a company under the Companies Act 2006; and any such registration of a trade union, whenever effected, is void: see the Trade Union and Labour Relations (Consolidation) Act 1992 ss 10(3)(a), 117(3)(a)(ii); and EMPLOYMENT vol 41 (2014) PARA 897. As to the meaning of 'special register body' for these purposes see EMPLOYMENT vol 41 (2014) PARA 899.

2 See the Companies Act 2006 s 7(1), (2), which specifies that a company duly formed under the Act by one or more persons may not be so formed for an unlawful purpose; and see PARAS 95, 99.

3 See the Companies Act 2006 s 1040; and PARA 30.

29. Companies not registered, or registered but not formed, under the Companies Act 2006; overseas companies. Certain specified provisions of the Companies Acts[1] apply to:

(1) companies[2] registered, but not formed, under the Companies Act 2006[3];

(2) bodies incorporated in the United Kingdom[4] but not registered under the 2006 Act[5];

(3) companies incorporated outside the United Kingdom ('overseas companies')[6].

1 As to the meaning of the 'Companies Acts' for these purposes see PARA 13.

2 As to the meaning of 'company' under the Companies Acts see PARA 21.

3 Companies Act 2006 s 1(2)(a). See further Pt 33 Ch 1 (ss 1040–1042), and the regulations made thereunder (cited in PARAS 28, 30 et seq).

4 As to the meaning of 'United Kingdom' see PARA 1 note 5.

5 Companies Act 2006 s 1(2)(b). See further Pt 33 Ch 2 (s 1043), and the regulations made thereunder (cited in PARA 1856 et seq).

6 Companies Act 2006 s 1(3). See further Pt 34 (ss 1044–1059), and the regulations made thereunder (cited in PARA 2013 et seq). As to the meaning of 'overseas company' see PARA 2013.

(2) COMPANIES NOT FORMED UNDER COMPANIES LEGISLATION BUT AUTHORISED TO REGISTER

(i) Classes of Company Authorised to Register

30. Classes of company not formed under companies legislation but authorised to register. Any of the following companies[1] may on making application register[2] under the Companies Act 2006[3]:

(1) any company that was in existence on 2 November 1862[4], including any company registered under the Joint Stock Companies Acts[5];

(2) any company formed after 2 November 1862, whether before or after 1 October 2009[6], either in pursuance of an Act of Parliament (other than the Companies Act 2006 or any of the former Companies Acts)[7] or in pursuance of letters patent[8], or any such company that is otherwise duly constituted according to law[9].

Such a company may[10] register as an unlimited company[11], as a company limited by shares[12], or as a company limited by guarantee[13].

However, a company having the liability of its members[14] limited by Act of Parliament or letters patent:

(a) may not so register[15] unless it is a joint stock company[16]; and

(b) may not so register[17] as an unlimited company or a company limited by guarantee[18].

A company that is not a joint stock company may not so register[19] as a company limited by shares[20].

The registration of a company in this way[21] is not invalid by reason that it has taken place with a view to the company being wound up[22]. However, registration after the commencement of a winding up is a nullity[23].

A company governed by a deed of settlement may register under the Companies Acts with a view to going into voluntary liquidation, and then selling its assets to another company under the statutory provisions relating to winding up[24]. However, by registering in this way, a company may lose powers which it possessed under its former constitution[25].

The Secretary of State[26] may make provision by regulations[27]:

(i) for and in connection with the registration of companies so authorised to register[28] under the Companies Act 2006[29]; and
(ii) as to the application to companies so registered of the provisions of the Companies Acts[30].

Without prejudice to the generality of that power, such regulations may make provision corresponding to any provision formerly made by those sections of the Companies Act 1985[31] that governed companies not formed under companies legislation but authorised to register[32].

Accordingly, provisions have been made in regulations[33] which apply in relation to the registration of a company[34] under the Companies Act 2006[35] in cases where companies have not been formed under companies legislation but are authorised to register thereunder[36].

1 As to the meaning of 'company' under the Companies Acts see PARA 21; and as to the meaning of the 'Companies Acts' see PARA 13.

2 As to the provision that may be made for registration see the text and notes 26–32. As to registration under the Companies Act 2006 generally see PARA 104 et seq.

3 Companies Act 2006 s 1040(2). As to fees payable for the registration of a company under Pt 33 Ch 1 (ss 1040–1042) see the Registrar of Companies (Fees) (Companies, Overseas Companies and Limited Liability Partnerships) Regulations 2012, SI 2012/1907, Sch 1 (amended, with effect from 30 June 2016, by SI 2016/621). Industrial and provident societies and friendly societies are by other statutes empowered to register as companies under the Companies Acts: see FINANCIAL INSTITUTIONS vol 48 (2015) PARAS 696, 835, 1056.

4 Ie the date on which the Companies Act 1862 came into force: see PARA 10.

5 Companies Act 2006 s 1040(1)(a). As to the meaning of the 'Joint Stock Companies Acts' under the Companies Acts see PARA 14 note 1.

6 Ie the date by which all the provisions of the Companies Act 2006 that affect the law in England and Wales had come into force: see PARA 13 note 15.

7 Companies Act 2006 s 1040(1)(b)(i). As to the meaning of the 'former Companies Acts' see PARA 14 note 1.

8 Companies Act 2006 s 1040(1)(b)(ii).

9 Companies Act 2006 s 1040(1)(b)(iii). A company duly constituted according to law is one which is constituted by registration under some Act of Parliament or in pursuance of an Act of Parliament (eg a company incorporated by a special Act: see PARAS 1, 1858 et seq) or under letters patent or under some constitution ejusdem generis: *Re Cussons Ltd* (1904) 73 LJ Ch 296.

10 Ie subject to the Companies Act 2006 s 1040(4)–(6) (see the text and notes 14–22): see the Companies Act 2006 s 1040(3).

11 As to the meaning of 'unlimited company' see PARA 95. See also PARA 74. As to the re-registration of an unlimited company as limited under the Companies Act 2006 see PARAS 168–175. As to the meaning of 'limited company' see PARA 95.

12 As to the meaning of 'company limited by shares' see PARA 95. See also PARA 71 et seq. As to the meaning of 'share' see PARA 1231. As to share capital generally see PARA 1231 et seq.

13 Companies Act 2006 s 1040(3). As to the meaning of 'company limited by guarantee' see PARA 95. See also PARA 72.

14 As to the meaning of 'member' see PARA 323. As to shareholders and the membership of companies generally see PARA 323 et seq.

15 Ie under the Companies Act 2006 s 1040 (see the text and notes 1–13, 21–22): see the Companies Act 2006 s 1040(4)(a).

16 Companies Act 2006 s 1040(4)(a). For these purposes, 'joint stock company' means a company:
(1) having a permanent paid-up or nominal share capital of fixed amount divided into shares, also of fixed amount, or held and transferable as stock, or divided and held partly in one way and partly in the other (s 1041(1)(a)); and
(2) formed on the principle of having for its members the holders of those shares or that stock, and no other persons (s 1041(1)(b)).

Such a company when registered with limited liability under the Companies Act 2006 is deemed a company limited by shares: s 1041(2). As to classes of share capital see PARA 1231 et seq. As to the registration of a joint stock company not formed (but authorised to register) under the Companies Acts see PARA 31. As to an application for a joint stock company to be registered as a public company when applying to be registered as a company limited by shares see PARA 32.

17 Ie under the Companies Act 2006 s 1040 (see the text and notes 1–13, 21–22): see the Companies Act 2006 s 1040(4)(b).

18 Companies Act 2006 s 1040(4)(b).
19 Ie under the Companies Act 2006 s 1040 (see the text and notes 1–13, 21–22): see the Companies Act 2006 s 1040(5).
20 Companies Act 2006 s 1040(5).
21 Ie under the Companies Act 2006 s 1040 (see the text and notes 1–13, 22): see the Companies Act 2006 s 1040(6).
22 Companies Act 2006 s 1040(6). As to the liability of contributories of companies that have been registered, but not formed, under the Companies Act 2006 and are being wound up, in respect of the company's debts and liabilities contracted before registration, see PARA 40. As to winding up in general see COMPANY AND PARTNERSHIP INSOLVENCY vol 16 (2011) PARA 380 et seq.
23 *Re Hercules Insurance Co* (1871) LR 11 Eq 321 at 323. As to the effect of commencement of winding up generally see COMPANY AND PARTNERSHIP INSOLVENCY vol 16 (2011) PARAS 439–440.
24 *Southall v British Mutual Life Assurance Society* (1871) 6 Ch App 614.
25 *Droitwich Patent Salt Co Ltd v Curzon* (1867) LR 3 Exch 35.
26 As to the Secretary of State see PARA 6.
27 Companies Act 2006 s 1042(1). Regulations under s 1042 are subject to negative resolution procedure (ie the statutory instrument containing the regulations is subject to annulment in pursuance of a resolution of either House of Parliament): ss 1042(3), 1289. As to the making of regulations under the Companies Act 2006 generally see ss 1288–1292. Partly in exercise of the powers conferred by s 1042, the Secretary of State has made the Companies (Companies Authorised to Register) Regulations 2009, SI 2009/2437 (see PARAS 31–39).
28 Ie for and in connection with registration under the Companies Act 2006 s 1040 (see the text and notes 1–13, 20–21): see the Companies Act 2006 s 1042(1)(a).
29 Companies Act 2006 s 1042(1)(a).
30 Companies Act 2006 s 1042(1)(b).
31 Ie the Companies Act 1985 Pt XXII Ch II (ss 680–690) (repealed): see the Companies Act 2006 s 1042(2).
32 Companies Act 2006 s 1042(2). The Companies (Companies Authorised to Register) Regulations 2009, SI 2009/2437 (see note 27) replace the provision formerly made by the Companies Act 1985 ss 681–682, 684–690, Sch 21 (repealed).
33 Ie the Companies (Companies Authorised to Register) Regulations 2009, SI 2009/2437, Pt 2 (regs 2–12) (see also PARAS 31–34, 36): see reg 2(1). The Companies (Companies Authorised to Register) Regulations 2009, SI 2009/2437, have been made by the Secretary of State in exercise of the powers conferred by the European Communities Act 1972 s 2(2) and by the Companies Act 2006 s 1042 (as to which see the text and notes 26–32).
34 In the Companies (Companies Authorised to Register) Regulations 2009, SI 2009/2437, Pt 2 (see also PARAS 31–34, 36), references to a company are to a company authorised to register under the Companies Act 2006 s 1040 (see s 1040(1), (4), (5); and the text and notes 1–9, 14–20); and references to registration are to registration under s 1040: Companies (Companies Authorised to Register) Regulations 2009, SI 2009/2437, reg 2(2).
35 Ie in pursuance of the Companies Act 2006 s 1040 (the text and notes 1–22): see the Companies (Companies Authorised to Register) Regulations 2009, SI 2009/2437, reg 2(1).
36 Companies (Companies Authorised to Register) Regulations 2009, SI 2009/2437, reg 2(1).

(ii) Requirements for Registration of Companies not formed under Companies Legislation

31. Requirement for assent before registration of companies authorised to register. A company must not register[1] without the assent of a majority of such of its members[2] as are present in person or by proxy (in cases where proxies are allowed) at a general meeting summoned for the purpose[3]. Where a company not having the liability of its members limited by an enactment or letters patent wishes to register as a limited company[4], the majority required to assent that is required[5] is not less than 75 per cent of the members present in person or by proxy at the meeting[6].

1 Ie in pursuance of the Companies Act 2006 s 1040 (see PARA 30). The provisions of the Companies (Companies Authorised to Register) Regulations 2009, SI 2009/2437, Pt 2 (regs 2–12) (see also PARAS 32–34, 36) apply in relation to the registration of a company under the Companies Act 2006 in pursuance of the Companies Act 2006 s 1040 (companies not formed

under companies legislation but authorised to register): see the Companies (Companies Authorised to Register) Regulations 2009, SI 2009/2437, reg 2(1); and PARA 30. As to the meaning of references to a company and to registration for these purposes see PARA 30 note 34.
2 As to membership of companies generally see PARA 323 et seq.
3 Companies (Companies Authorised to Register) Regulations 2009, SI 2009/2437, reg 3(1). Where the company proposes to register as a company limited by guarantee, the members' assent to its being registered must be accompanied by a resolution containing a statement of guarantee: see reg 6(1); and PARA 32. As to company meetings see PARA 701 et seq. As to the meanings of 'company limited by shares', 'company limited by guarantee' and 'limited company' see PARA 95.
4 As to the meaning of 'limited company' under the Companies Acts see PARA 95.
5 Ie as required by the Companies (Companies Authorised to Register) Regulations 2009, SI 2009/2437, reg 3(1) (see the text and notes 1–3): see reg 3(2).
6 Companies (Companies Authorised to Register) Regulations 2009, SI 2009/2437, reg 3(2). In computing any majority under reg 3 when a poll is demanded, regard is to be had to the number of votes to which each member is entitled according to the company's regulations: reg 3(3).

32. Application for registration where a company is authorised to register. An application for the registration of a company which has been authorised to register under the Companies Act 2006[1] must be delivered to the registrar of companies together with the documents that are required[2] and a statement of compliance[3]. The application for registration must state:

(1) the name with which the company is proposed to be registered[4];
(2) whether the company's registered office[5] is to be situated in England and Wales[6] (or in Wales), in Scotland or in Northern Ireland[7];
(3) whether the liability of the members of the company is to be limited, and if so whether it is to be limited by shares or by guarantee[8]; and
(4) whether the company is to be a private or a public company[9].

The application must contain (in the case of a joint stock company[10]) a statement of capital and initial shareholdings[11], (in the case of a company that is to be limited by guarantee) a statement of guarantee[12], and a statement of the company's proposed officers[13]. The application also must contain a statement of the intended address of the company's registered office[14], and a copy of any enactment, royal charter, letters patent, deed of settlement, contract of partnership or other instrument constituting or regulating the company[15]. The application must be delivered to the registrar of companies for England and Wales, if the registered office of the company is to be situated in England and Wales (or in Wales)[16].

1 Ie in pursuance of the Companies Act 2006 s 1040 (see PARA 30). The provisions of the Companies (Companies Authorised to Register) Regulations 2009, SI 2009/2437, Pt 2 (regs 2–12) (see also PARAS 30–31, 33–34, 36) apply in relation to the registration of a company under the Companies Act 2006 in pursuance of the Companies Act 2006 s 1040 (companies not formed under companies legislation but authorised to register): see the Companies (Companies Authorised to Register) Regulations 2009, SI 2009/2437, reg 2(1); and PARA 30. As to the meaning of references to a company and to registration for these purposes see PARA 30 note 34.
2 Ie required by the Companies (Companies Authorised to Register) Regulations 2009, SI 2009/2437, reg 4 (see the text and notes 10–16): see reg 4(1).
3 Companies (Companies Authorised to Register) Regulations 2009, SI 2009/2437, reg 4(1). The statement of compliance required to be delivered to the registrar is a statement that the requirements of Pt 2 as to registration have been complied with: reg 8(1). The registrar may accept the statement of compliance as sufficient evidence of compliance: reg 8(2). As to the registrar of companies see PARA 126 et seq. As to the delivery of documents to the registrar see PARA 136; and as to the requirements generally for the proper delivery of documents to the registrar see PARA 137.
4 Companies (Companies Authorised to Register) Regulations 2009, SI 2009/2437, reg 4(2)(a). As to the company's name see PARA 34. As to restrictions on the use of company names and trading names generally see PARA 195 et seq.
5 As to the company's registered office see PARA 124.
6 As to the meanings of 'England' and 'Wales' see PARA 1 note 5.
7 Companies (Companies Authorised to Register) Regulations 2009, SI 2009/2437, reg 4(2)(b).

8 Companies (Companies Authorised to Register) Regulations 2009, SI 2009/2437, reg 4(2)(c). As to the meanings of 'company limited by shares', 'company limited by guarantee' and 'limited company' under the Companies Acts see PARA 95. As to membership of companies generally see PARA 323 et seq.

9 Companies (Companies Authorised to Register) Regulations 2009, SI 2009/2437, reg 4(2)(d). As to the meanings of 'private company' and 'public company' see PARA 95.

10 As to the meaning of 'joint stock company' for these purposes see PARA 30 note 16.

11 Companies (Companies Authorised to Register) Regulations 2009, SI 2009/2437, reg 4(3)(a). As to the statement of capital and initial shareholdings required in the case of a joint stock company see reg 5: reg 4(3)(a). Accordingly, the statement of capital and initial shareholdings that is required to be delivered in the case of a joint stock company must comply with reg 5: reg 5(1). It must state:

(1) the total number of shares of the company that on a date specified in the statement (the 'reference date') are held by members of the company (reg 5(2)(a));
(2) the aggregate nominal value of those shares (reg 5(2)(b));
(3) the aggregate amount (if any) unpaid on those shares (whether on account of their nominal value or by way of premium) (reg 5(2)(ba) (added by SI 2016/599));
(4) for each class of shares:
  (a) the particulars specified in heads (i)–(iv) below of the rights attached to the shares (Companies (Companies Authorised to Register) Regulations 2009, SI 2009/2437, reg 5(2)(c)(i));
  (b) the total number of shares of that class (reg 5(2)(c)(ii)); and
  (c) the aggregate nominal value of shares of that class (reg 5(2)(c)(iii)).

For these purposes, the reference date must be not more than 28 days before the date of the application for registration: reg 5(3). The particulars referred to in head (4)(a) above are:

(i) particulars of any voting rights attached to the shares, including rights that arise only in certain circumstances (reg 5(4)(a));
(ii) particulars of any rights attached to the shares, as respects dividends, to participate in a distribution (reg 5(4)(b));
(iii) particulars of any rights attached to the shares, as respects capital, to participate in a distribution (including on winding up) (reg 5(4)(c)); and
(iv) whether the shares are to be redeemed or are liable to be redeemed at the option of the company or the shareholder (reg 5(4)(d)).

As to the nominal value of shares, and as to paid up and unpaid shares, see PARA 1231 et seq. As to classes of shares, and rights attached to classes of shares generally, see PARA 1246 et seq; as to redeemable shares see PARAS 1241, 1416 et seq; and as to distributions and dividends see PARA 1562 et seq. As to winding up in general see COMPANY AND PARTNERSHIP INSOLVENCY vol 16 (2011) PARA 380 et seq.

The statement of capital and initial shareholdings must also state the names and service addresses of all persons who on the reference date were members of the company (reg 5(5)(a)), and, with respect to each member of the company, the number, nominal value (of each share) and class of shares held by that member on that date (reg 5(5)(b)(i)), and the amount to be paid up and the amount (if any) to be unpaid on each share (whether on account of the nominal value of the share or by way of premium) (reg 5(5)(b)(ii)). For the purposes of reg 5(5)(a), a person's 'name' means his Christian name (or other forename) and surname, except that in the case of a peer, or an individual usually known by a title, the title may be stated instead of his Christian name (or other forename) and surname or in addition to either or both of them: reg 5(6). Where a member of the company holds shares of more than one class, the information required under reg 5(5)(b)(i) is required for each class: reg 5(7).

12 Companies (Companies Authorised to Register) Regulations 2009, SI 2009/2437, reg 4(3)(b). As to the statement of guarantee required in the case of a company that is to be limited by guarantee see reg 6: see reg 4(3)(b). Where the company proposes to register as a company limited by guarantee, the members' assent to its being registered (see reg 3; and PARA 31) must be accompanied by a resolution containing a statement of guarantee: reg 6(1). The statement of guarantee required is a statement that each member undertakes that, if the company is wound up while he is a member, or within one year after he ceases to be a member, he will contribute to the assets of the company such amount as may be required for the following, not exceeding a specified amount (reg 6(2)):

(1) payment of the debts and liabilities of the company contracted before he ceases to be a member (reg 6(2)(a));
(2) payment of the costs, charges and expenses of winding up (reg 6(2)(b)); and
(3) adjustment of the rights of the contributories among themselves (reg 6(2)(c)),

The statement of guarantee required to be delivered to the registrar in the case of a company that is to be limited by guarantee is a copy of the resolution containing the statement of guarantee: reg 6(3).

13 Companies (Companies Authorised to Register) Regulations 2009, SI 2009/2437, reg 4(3)(c). The text refers to the statement of the company's proposed officers whose required particulars are specified in reg 7: see reg 4(3)(c). Accordingly, the statement of the company's proposed officers required to be delivered to the registrar must contain the required particulars of:

(1) the person who is, or persons who are, to be the first director or directors of the company on registration (reg 7(1)(a));

(2) in the case of a company that is to be a private company, any person who is (or any persons who are) to be the first secretary (or joint secretaries) of the company on registration (reg 7(1)(b));

(3) in the case of a company that is to be a public company, the person who is (or the persons who are) to be the first secretary (or joint secretaries) of the company on registration (reg 7(1)(c)).

The statement under reg 7(1) must be accompanied by a statement by the company that each person named as a director, as secretary or as one of joint secretaries has consented to act in the relevant capacity: reg 7(2A) (added by SI 2015/1695).

The required particulars are the particulars that will be required to be stated:

(a) in the case of a director, in the company's register of directors and register of directors' residential addresses (see the Companies Act 2006 ss 162–165; and PARAS 535–536) (Companies (Companies Authorised to Register) Regulations 2009, SI 2009/2437, reg 7(2)(a));

(b) in the case of a secretary, in the company's register of secretaries (see the Companies Act 2006 ss 277–279; and PARA 673) (Companies (Companies Authorised to Register) Regulations 2009, SI 2009/2437, reg 7(2)(b)).

As to a company's directors see PARA 517 et seq; and as to the company secretary see PARA 669 et seq.

The Companies (Disclosure of Address) Regulations 2009, SI 2009/214, reg 7 (application on behalf of proposed directors to withhold protected information) (see PARA 544) applies as if references to a subscriber to the memorandum of association were to any member of the company, and as if references to the proposed company were to the company proposing to register: Companies (Companies Authorised to Register) Regulations 2009, SI 2009/2437, reg 7(3).

14 Companies (Companies Authorised to Register) Regulations 2009, SI 2009/2437, reg 4(4)(a).

15 Companies (Companies Authorised to Register) Regulations 2009, SI 2009/2437, reg 4(4)(b). As to companies formed under any other enactment, royal charter, letters patent etc see further PARA 1.

16 Companies (Companies Authorised to Register) Regulations 2009, SI 2009/2437, reg 4(5)(a). As to where the registered office of the company is to be situated in Scotland or in Northern Ireland see reg 4(5)(b), (c).

33. Registration of a joint stock company as a public company. A joint stock company[1] may be registered[2] as a public company limited by shares[3] if[4]:

(1) the following conditions are met[5], namely:

(a) that the requirements of the Companies Act 2006[6] are met as regards its share capital[7];

(b) the requirements of the Companies Act 2006[8] are met as regards its net assets[9]; and

(c) if the provisions of the Companies Act 2006 governing the recent allotment of shares for non-cash consideration apply[10], that the requirements of those provisions are met[11]; and

(2) the application for registration is accompanied by the documents specified as follows[12], namely:

(a) a copy of the resolution that the company be a public company[13];

(b) a copy of the balance sheet[14] prepared as at a date not more than seven months before the date on which the application to re-register is delivered to the registrar of companies[15], an unqualified report[16] by the company's auditor on that balance sheet[17], and a written statement by the company's auditor that in his opinion at the balance sheet date the amount of the company's net assets was not less than the aggregate of its called-up share capital and undistributable reserves[18]; and

(c) if the provisions of the Companies Act 2006 governing the recent allotment of shares for non-cash consideration apply[19], a copy of the valuation report[20] (if any)[21].

The statement of compliance required to be delivered with the application is a statement that the requirements as to registration[22] as a public company have been complied with[23]. The registrar may accept the statement of compliance as sufficient evidence that the company is entitled to be registered as a public company[24].

1 As to the meaning of 'joint stock company' for these purposes see PARA 30 note 16.

2 Ie in pursuance of the Companies Act 2006 s 1040 (see PARA 30). The provisions of the Companies (Companies Authorised to Register) Regulations 2009, SI 2009/2437, Pt 2 (regs 2–12) (see also PARAS 30–32, 34, 36) apply in relation to the registration of a company under the Companies Act 2006 in pursuance of the Companies Act 2006 s 1040 (companies not formed under companies legislation but authorised to register): see the Companies (Companies Authorised to Register) Regulations 2009, SI 2009/2437, reg 2(1); and PARA 30. As to the meaning of references to a company and to registration for these purposes see PARA 30 note 34.

3 As to the meanings of 'company limited by shares' and 'public company' under the Companies Acts see PARA 95.

4 Companies (Companies Authorised to Register) Regulations 2009, SI 2009/2437, reg 9(1).

5 Companies (Companies Authorised to Register) Regulations 2009, SI 2009/2437, reg 9(1)(a).

6 Ie the requirements of the Companies Act 2006 s 91 (see PARA 169): see the Companies (Companies Authorised to Register) Regulations 2009, SI 2009/2437, reg 9(2)(a). The Companies Act 2006 ss 91–93 (see PARAS 169–171) apply for this purpose as in the case of a private company applying to be re-registered under s 90 (re-registration of private company as public) (see PARA 168), but as if any reference to the special resolution required by s 90 were to the joint stock company's resolution that it be a public company: Companies (Companies Authorised to Register) Regulations 2009, SI 2009/2437, reg 9(3). As to the meaning of 'private company' see PARA 95. As to the meaning of 'joint stock company' for these purposes see PARA 30 note 16. As to special resolutions see PARA 686.

7 Companies (Companies Authorised to Register) Regulations 2009, SI 2009/2437, reg 9(2)(a). As to the meanings of 'share' and 'share capital' see PARA 1231.

8 Ie the requirements of the Companies Act 2006 s 92 (see PARA 170): see the Companies (Companies Authorised to Register) Regulations 2009, SI 2009/2437, reg 9(2)(b). See also note 6.

9 Companies (Companies Authorised to Register) Regulations 2009, SI 2009/2437, reg 9(2)(b). As to the meaning of 'net assets' for these purposes see PARA 170 note 5.

10 Ie if the Companies Act 2006 s 93 (see PARA 171) applies: see the Companies (Companies Authorised to Register) Regulations 2009, SI 2009/2437, reg 9(2)(c). See also note 6. As to the meanings of 'allotted', 'cash' and consideration 'other than cash' in relation to the allotment or payment up of shares in a company see PARA 1280.

11 Companies (Companies Authorised to Register) Regulations 2009, SI 2009/2437, reg 9(2)(c).

12 Companies (Companies Authorised to Register) Regulations 2009, SI 2009/2437, reg 9(1)(b). The documents specified in heads (2)(a)–(2)(c) in the text must be delivered to the registrar with the application for registration as well as those required by reg 4 (see PARA 32): reg 9(4). As to the registrar of companies see PARA 126 et seq. As to the delivery of documents to the registrar see PARA 136; and as to the requirements generally for the proper delivery of documents to the registrar see PARA 137.

13 Companies (Companies Authorised to Register) Regulations 2009, SI 2009/2437, reg 9(4)(a).

14 Head (2)(b) in the text refers to the balance sheet and other documents referred to in the Companies Act 2006 s 92(1) (see PARA 170): see the Companies (Companies Authorised to Register) Regulations 2009, SI 2009/2437, reg 9(4)(b). See also note 6.

15 See the Companies Act 2006 s 92(1)(a); the Companies (Companies Authorised to Register) Regulations 2009, SI 2009/2437, reg 9(4)(b). See also note 6.

16 As to the meaning of 'unqualified report' for these purposes see PARA 170 note 5.

17 See the Companies Act 2006 s 92(1)(b); Companies (Companies Authorised to Register) Regulations 2009, SI 2009/2437, reg 9(4)(b). See also note 6. As to eligibility for appointment as a company's auditor see PARA 1060 et seq.

18 See the Companies Act 2006 s 92(1)(c); Companies (Companies Authorised to Register) Regulations 2009, SI 2009/2437, reg 9(4)(b). See also note 6. As to the meaning of 'undistributable reserves' for these purposes see PARA 170 note 5. As to the meaning of 'called-up share capital' see PARA 1237.
19 Ie if the Companies Act 2006 s 93 (see PARA 171) applies: see the Companies (Companies Authorised to Register) Regulations 2009, SI 2009/2437, reg 9(4)(c).
20 Ie under the Companies Act 2006 s 93(2)(a) (see PARA 171): see the Companies (Companies Authorised to Register) Regulations 2009, SI 2009/2437, reg 9(4)(c).
21 Companies (Companies Authorised to Register) Regulations 2009, SI 2009/2437, reg 9(4)(c).
22 Ie the requirements of the Companies (Companies Authorised to Register) Regulations 2009, SI 2009/2437, Pt 2: see the Companies (Companies Authorised to Register) Regulations 2009, SI 2009/2437, reg 9(5).
23 Companies (Companies Authorised to Register) Regulations 2009, SI 2009/2437, reg 9(5).
24 Companies (Companies Authorised to Register) Regulations 2009, SI 2009/2437, reg 9(6).

34. Name of company not formed under companies legislation on registration. Where the name of a company, which has been authorised to register under the Companies Act 2006 and is seeking registration[1], is a name by which it is precluded from being registered by any provision of the Companies Acts[2], either:

(1) because it is directly prohibited from being registered with that name[3]; or

(2) because the Secretary of State[4] would not approve the company being registered with that name[5],

the company may change its name with effect from the date on which it is registered[6].

Any such change of name[7] requires the like assent of the company's members as is required[8] for registration[9].

1 Ie in pursuance of the Companies Act 2006 s 1040 (see PARA 30). The provisions of the Companies (Companies Authorised to Register) Regulations 2009, SI 2009/2437, Pt 2 (regs 2–12) (see also PARAS 30–33, 36) apply in relation to the registration of a company under the Companies Act 2006 in pursuance of the Companies Act 2006 s 1040 (companies not formed under companies legislation but authorised to register): see the Companies (Companies Authorised to Register) Regulations 2009, SI 2009/2437, reg 2(1); and PARA 30. As to the meaning of references to a company and to registration for these purposes see PARA 30 note 34.
2 Companies (Companies Authorised to Register) Regulations 2009, SI 2009/2437, reg 10(1). As to the meaning of the 'Companies Acts' generally see PARA 13. As to the naming of a company and changes of name generally see PARA 199 et seq.
3 Companies (Companies Authorised to Register) Regulations 2009, SI 2009/2437, reg 10(1)(a).
4 As to the Secretary of State see PARA 6 et seq.
5 Companies (Companies Authorised to Register) Regulations 2009, SI 2009/2437, reg 10(1)(b).
6 Companies (Companies Authorised to Register) Regulations 2009, SI 2009/2437, reg 10(1).
7 Ie under the Companies (Companies Authorised to Register) Regulations 2009, SI 2009/2437, reg 10: see reg 10(2).
8 Ie by the Companies (Companies Authorised to Register) Regulations 2009, SI 2009/2437, reg 3 (see PARA 31): see reg 10(2). As to membership of a company see PARA 323 et seq.
9 Companies (Companies Authorised to Register) Regulations 2009, SI 2009/2437, reg 10(2).

(iii) Registration of Companies not formed under Companies Legislation and its Effect

35. Application of the Companies Acts to company not formed under companies legislation but authorised to register. The provisions of the Companies Acts[1] apply to a registered company[2], and to its members[3] and contributories[4], in the same manner as if it had been formed and registered under the Companies Act 2006[5].

The model articles of association[6] do not apply to such a company unless adopted by special resolution[7].

The provisions relating to the numbering of shares[8] do not apply to any joint stock company[9] whose shares are not numbered[10].

1 References in the Companies (Companies Authorised to Register) Regulations 2009, SI 2009/2437, regs 18–22 (see also PARAS 38–39) to the Companies Acts include the Companies (Cross-Border Mergers) Regulations 2007, SI 2007/2974 (see PARA 1631), and do not include the Companies (Audit, Investigations and Community Enterprise) Act 2004 Pt 2 (ss 26–63) (see PARA 75 et seq): Companies (Companies Authorised to Register) Regulations 2009, SI 2009/2437, reg 18(2). As to the meaning of the 'Companies Acts' generally see PARA 13.

2 Ie a company registered in pursuance of the Companies Act 2006 s 1040 (see PARA 30). In the Companies (Companies Authorised to Register) Regulations 2009, SI 2009/2437, Pt 3 (regs 13–23) (see also PARA 37 et seq), 'registration' means registration under the Companies Act 2006 in pursuance of s 1040: Companies (Companies Authorised to Register) Regulations 2009, SI 2009/2437, reg 13.

3 As to membership of a company generally see PARA 323 et seq.

4 As to the meaning of 'contributory' see COMPANY AND PARTNERSHIP INSOLVENCY vol 17 (2011) PARA 661. As to the meaning of 'contributory' under the Companies Acts see PARA 109 note 10.

5 Companies (Companies Authorised to Register) Regulations 2009, SI 2009/2437, reg 18(1). This is subject to regs 19–22 (see PARAS 35, 38–39): see reg 18(1). As to formation and registration under the Companies Act 2006 see PARA 95 et seq.

6 Ie the model articles of association prescribed by the Secretary of State under the Companies Act 2006 s 19 (see PARA 227): see the Companies (Companies Authorised to Register) Regulations 2009, SI 2009/2437, reg 19(1). As to the Secretary of State see PARA 6 et seq.

7 Companies (Companies Authorised to Register) Regulations 2009, SI 2009/2437, reg 19(1). As to special resolutions see PARA 686.

8 See PARA 1239.

9 As to the meaning of 'joint stock company' for these purposes see PARA 30 note 16.

10 Companies (Companies Authorised to Register) Regulations 2009, SI 2009/2437, reg 19(2).

36. Formal registration of company not formed under companies legislation; issue of the certificate of registration. If the registrar of companies[1] is satisfied that the statutory requirements as to registration[2] are complied with, he must register the documents delivered to him[3].

On the registration of a company, the registrar must give a certificate that the company is incorporated[4]. The certificate must state:

(1) the name and registered number of the company[5];
(2) the date of its incorporation[6];
(3) whether it is a limited or unlimited company[7], and if it is limited whether it is limited by shares or limited by guarantee[8];
(4) whether it is a private or a public company[9]; and
(5) whether the company's registered office[10] is situated in England and Wales[11] (or in Wales), in Scotland or in Northern Ireland[12].

The certificate must be signed by the registrar or authenticated by the registrar's official seal[13]. It is conclusive evidence that the requirements[14] as to registration have been complied with and that the company is duly registered under the Companies Act 2006[15].

The registrar is also required to cause notice of the issue of the certificate to be published[16].

1 As to the registrar of companies see PARA 126 et seq.

2 Ie the requirements of the Companies (Companies Authorised to Register) Regulations 2009, SI 2009/2437, Pt 2 (regs 2–12) (see also PARAS 30–34): see reg 11. The provisions of Pt 2 apply in relation to the registration of a company under the Companies Act 2006 in pursuance of the Companies Act 2006 s 1040 (companies not formed under companies legislation but authorised to register): see the Companies (Companies Authorised to Register) Regulations 2009, SI 2009/2437, reg 2(1); and PARA 30. As to the meaning of references to a company and to registration for these purposes see PARA 30 note 34.

3 Companies (Companies Authorised to Register) Regulations 2009, SI 2009/2437, reg 11. As to the documents that are required as mentioned in the text see PARAS 31–33. As to the delivery of

documents to the registrar see PARA 136; and as to the requirements generally for the proper delivery of documents to the registrar see PARA 137.

4 Companies (Companies Authorised to Register) Regulations 2009, SI 2009/2437, reg 12(1).

5 Companies (Companies Authorised to Register) Regulations 2009, SI 2009/2437, reg 12(2)(a). As to company names and trading names generally see PARA 195 et seq. As to a company's registered number see PARAS 134–135.

6 Companies (Companies Authorised to Register) Regulations 2009, SI 2009/2437, reg 12(2)(b). The company is incorporated from the beginning of the date mentioned in the certificate of incorporation: see PARA 114 note 7.

7 As to the meanings of 'limited company' and 'unlimited company' see PARA 95.

8 Companies (Companies Authorised to Register) Regulations 2009, SI 2009/2437, reg 12(2)(c). As to the meanings of 'company limited by shares' and 'company limited by guarantee' see PARA 95.

9 Companies (Companies Authorised to Register) Regulations 2009, SI 2009/2437, reg 12(2)(d). As to the meanings of 'private company' and 'public company' see PARA 95.

10 As to the company's registered office see PARA 124.

11 As to the meanings of 'England' and 'Wales' see PARA 1 note 5.

12 Companies (Companies Authorised to Register) Regulations 2009, SI 2009/2437, reg 12(2)(e).

13 Companies (Companies Authorised to Register) Regulations 2009, SI 2009/2437, reg 12(3). As to the registrar's official seal see PARA 126.

14 Ie the requirements of the Companies (Companies Authorised to Register) Regulations 2009, SI 2009/2437, Pt 2: see reg 12(4).

15 Companies (Companies Authorised to Register) Regulations 2009, SI 2009/2437, reg 12(4).

16 The Companies Act 2006 s 1064 (public notice of certificate of incorporation) (see PARA 133) applies to a certificate of incorporation issued under the Companies (Companies Authorised to Register) Regulations 2009, SI 2009/2437, reg 12: reg 12(5).

37. Vesting of property on registration of company not formed under companies legislation; liabilities and legal proceedings. All property belonging to or vested in a company[1] at the date of its registration[2] passes to and vests in the company on registration for all the estate and interest of the company in the property[3].

Registration does not affect the company's rights or liabilities in respect of any debt or obligation incurred, or contract entered into, by, to, with or on behalf of the company before registration[4].

If an unregistered company[5] registers with unlimited liability[6], the shareholders are, in a winding up[7], liable beyond the amount unpaid on their shares[8] for the expenses of the winding up, but not beyond that amount for any breach of contract under the terms of which there was only a limited liability[9].

Where a member of an unregistered company who is personally liable to be sued for the debts of the company has parted with his shares before registration, and so has not become a member of the registered company, he is not, by reason only of the registration, released from his pre-existing liability[10].

All actions and other legal proceedings which at the time of a company's registration are pending by or against a company, or the public officer or any member[11] of it, may be continued in the same manner as if registration had not taken place[12]. However, execution of any judgment, decree or order obtained in such an action or proceeding must not issue against the effects of any individual member of the company[16]; but, in the event of the property and effects of the company being insufficient to satisfy the judgment, decree or order, an order may be obtained for winding up the company[17].

1 Ie a company registered in pursuance of the Companies Act 2006 s 1040 (see PARA 30).

2 As to the meaning of 'registration' for these purposes see PARA 35 note 2. As to formal registration and issue of the certificate of registration for these purposes see PARA 36.

3 Companies (Companies Authorised to Register) Regulations 2009, SI 2009/2437, reg 14(1). As to whether the property of partners so passes to the company where the partnership is wrongfully registered see *Re Cussons Ltd* (1904) 73 LJ Ch 296; *Hammond v Prentice Bros Ltd* [1920] 1 Ch 201.

4 Companies (Companies Authorised to Register) Regulations 2009, SI 2009/2437, reg 14(2).

5 As to the meaning of 'unregistered company' see PARA 1857 note 10.

6 As to the meaning of 'unlimited company' see PARA 95.
7 As to winding up in general see COMPANY AND PARTNERSHIP INSOLVENCY vol 16 (2011) PARA 380 et seq.
8 As to shares generally see PARA 1244.
9 *Lethbridge v Adams, ex p Liquidator of the International Life Assurance Society* (1872) LR 13 Eq 547.
10 *Lanyon v Smith* (1863) 3 B & S 938; *Harvey v Clough* (1863) 8 LT 324.
11 As to membership of a company see PARA 323 et seq.
12 Companies (Companies Authorised to Register) Regulations 2009, SI 2009/2437, reg 15(1).
16 Companies (Companies Authorised to Register) Regulations 2009, SI 2009/2437, reg 15(2).
17 Companies (Companies Authorised to Register) Regulations 2009, SI 2009/2437, reg 15(2).

38. Certain provisions to have continuing effect on registration of company not formed under companies legislation. All provisions contained in any enactment or other instrument[1] constituting or regulating the company[2] are deemed to be conditions and regulations of the company, in the same manner and with the same incidents as if so much of them as would, if the company had been formed and registered under the Companies Act 2006[3], be contained in registered articles of association[4]. The provisions so brought in[5] include, in the case of a company registered as a company limited by guarantee[6], those of the resolution declaring the amount of the guarantee[7].

The provisions with respect to:

(1) the re-registration of an unlimited company as limited[8];
(2) the powers of an unlimited company on re-registration as a limited company to provide that a portion of its share capital is not capable of being called up except in the event of winding up[9]; and
(3) the power of a limited company to determine that a portion of its share capital is not capable of being called up except in that event[10],

apply notwithstanding any provisions contained in any enactment, royal charter or other instrument constituting or regulating the company[11].

1 In the Companies (Companies Authorised to Register) Regulations 2009, SI 2009/2437, Pt 3 (regs 13–23) (see also PARAS 35, 37, 39), 'instrument' includes a deed of settlement, a contract of partnership or letters patent: reg 13.
2 Ie a company registered in pursuance of the Companies Act 2006 s 1040 (see PARA 30). See also PARA 35 note 2.
3 As to formation and registration under the Companies Act 2006 see PARA 95 et seq.
4 Companies (Companies Authorised to Register) Regulations 2009, SI 2009/2437, reg 16(1). As to a company's articles of association generally see PARA 227 et seq.
5 Ie by the Companies (Companies Authorised to Register) Regulations 2009, SI 2009/2437, reg 16(1): see reg 16(2).
6 As to the meanings of 'company limited by guarantee' and 'limited company' see PARA 95.
7 Companies (Companies Authorised to Register) Regulations 2009, SI 2009/2437, reg 16(2).
8 Companies (Companies Authorised to Register) Regulations 2009, SI 2009/2437, reg 21(a). As to the re-registration of an unlimited company as limited under the Companies Act 2006 see PARAS 178–180. As to the meanings of 'limited company' and 'unlimited company' see PARA 95.
9 Companies (Companies Authorised to Register) Regulations 2009, SI 2009/2437, reg 21(b). As to the meaning of 'called up share capital' see PARA 1237. As to winding up in general see COMPANY AND PARTNERSHIP INSOLVENCY vol 16 (2011) PARA 380 et seq.
10 Companies (Companies Authorised to Register) Regulations 2009, SI 2009/2437, reg 21(c).
11 Companies (Companies Authorised to Register) Regulations 2009, SI 2009/2437, reg 21.

39. Power to alter constitution of company not formed under companies legislation and to substitute articles of association. Except for the power of court to regulate the conduct of the company's affairs[1], none of the statutory companies provisions[2] affects any power of altering the company's constitution[3] or regulations vested in the company by virtue of any enactment or other instrument[4] constituting or regulating it[5].

However, subject to the provisions which govern the effect of registration[6], the company does not have power to alter any provision contained in an enactment relating to the company[7] or, without the consent of the Secretary of State[8], to alter any provision contained in letters patent relating to the company[9]. Nor does the company have power to alter any provision contained in a royal charter or letters patent with respect to the company's objects[10]. Where, in this way[11], a company does not have power to alter a provision, it does not have power to ratify acts of the directors in contravention of the provision[12].

A registered company[13] may by special resolution[14] alter the form of its constitution by substituting articles of association[15] for any instrument constituting or regulating the company, other than an enactment, a royal charter or letters patent[16].

1 The Companies (Companies Authorised to Register) Regulations 2009, SI 2009/2437, reg 22(1) does not apply to the power of the court under the Companies Act 2006 s 996(2) (protection of members against unfair prejudice) (see PARA 666): Companies (Companies Authorised to Register) Regulations 2009, SI 2009/2437, reg 22(2).

2 Ie none of the provisions of the Companies (Companies Authorised to Register) Regulations 2009, SI 2009/2437, Pt 3 (regs 13–23) (see also PARA 35 et seq) or of the Companies Acts: see reg 22(1). As to the meaning of references to the 'Companies Acts' for these purposes see PARA 35 note 1.

3 As to the meaning of references to a company's constitution under the Companies Act 2006 see PARA 226. The text refers to a company registered in pursuance of the Companies Act 2006 s 1040 (see PARA 30). See also PARA 35 note 2.

4 As to the meaning of 'instrument' for these purposes see PARA 38 note 1.

5 Companies (Companies Authorised to Register) Regulations 2009, SI 2009/2437, reg 22(1). See *Droitwich Patent Salt Co v Curzon* (1867) LR 3 Exch 35; *Holmes v Newcastle-upon-Tyne Freehold Abattoir Co* (1875) 1 ChD 682.

6 Ie subject to the provisions of the Companies (Companies Authorised to Register) Regulations 2009, SI 2009/2437, Pt 3: see the Companies (Companies Authorised to Register) Regulations 2009, SI 2009/2437, reg 20(1).

7 Companies (Companies Authorised to Register) Regulations 2009, SI 2009/2437, reg 20(1)(a). See also *Re Salisbury Railway and Market House Co Ltd* [1969] 1 Ch 349, [1967] 1 All ER 813.

8 As to the Secretary of State see PARA 6 et seq.

9 Companies (Companies Authorised to Register) Regulations 2009, SI 2009/2437, reg 20(1)(b).

10 See the Companies (Companies Authorised to Register) Regulations 2009, SI 2009/2437, reg 20(2). As to the statement of a company's objects see PARA 239.

11 Ie by virtue of the Companies (Companies Authorised to Register) Regulations 2009, SI 2009/2437, reg 20(1), (2) (see the text and notes 6–10): see reg 20(3).

12 Companies (Companies Authorised to Register) Regulations 2009, SI 2009/2437, reg 20(3). As to the ratification by a company of conduct by a director amounting to negligence, default, breach of duty or breach of trust in relation to the company, see the Companies Act 2006 s 239; and PARA 638.

13 Ie a company registered in pursuance of the Companies Act 2006 s 1040 (see PARA 30). See also PARA 35 note 2.

14 As to special resolutions see PARA 686.

15 As to a company's articles of association generally see PARA 227 et seq.

16 Companies (Companies Authorised to Register) Regulations 2009, SI 2009/2437, reg 17. See further PARA 1.

40. Liability of contributories of companies not formed, but authorised to register, under the Companies Act 2006. In the event of a company being wound up[1] which has been registered, but not formed[2], under the Companies Act 2006[3], every person is a contributory[4], in respect of the company's debts and liabilities contracted before registration, who is liable[5]:

(1) to pay, or contribute to the payment of, any debt or liability so contracted[6]; or

(2) to pay, or contribute to the payment of, any sum for the adjustment of the rights of the members among themselves in respect of any such debt or liability[7]; or

(3) to pay, or contribute to the amount of, the expenses of winding up the company, so far as relates to the debts or liabilities mentioned above[8].

Every such contributory is liable to contribute to the assets of the company, in the course of the winding up, all sums due from him in respect of any such liability[9].

1 As to winding up in general see COMPANY AND PARTNERSHIP INSOLVENCY vol 16 (2011) PARA 380 et seq.

2 As to registration under the Companies Act 2006 generally see PARA 104 et seq. As to companies formed under previous legislation see PARA 10 et seq.

3 See the Insolvency Act 1986 s 83(1); and COMPANY AND PARTNERSHIP INSOLVENCY vol 17 (2011) PARA 672.

4 As to the meaning of 'contributory' see COMPANY AND PARTNERSHIP INSOLVENCY vol 17 (2011) PARA 661. As to the meaning of 'contributory' under the Companies Acts see PARA 109 note 10.

5 See the Insolvency Act 1986 s 83(2); and COMPANY AND PARTNERSHIP INSOLVENCY vol 17 (2011) PARA 672.

6 See the Insolvency Act 1986 s 83(2)(a); and COMPANY AND PARTNERSHIP INSOLVENCY vol 17 (2011) PARA 672.

7 See the Insolvency Act 1986 s 83(2)(b); and COMPANY AND PARTNERSHIP INSOLVENCY vol 17 (2011) PARA 672.

8 See the Insolvency Act 1986 s 83(2)(c); and COMPANY AND PARTNERSHIP INSOLVENCY vol 17 (2011) PARA 672.

9 See the Insolvency Act 1986 s 83(3); and COMPANY AND PARTNERSHIP INSOLVENCY vol 17 (2011) PARA 672. In the event of the death, bankruptcy or insolvency of any such contributory, the provisions of the Insolvency Act 1986 with respect to the personal representatives of deceased contributories (see COMPANY AND PARTNERSHIP INSOLVENCY vol 17 (2011) PARA 699) and to the trustees of bankrupt or insolvent contributories (see COMPANY AND PARTNERSHIP INSOLVENCY vol 17 (2011) PARA 667) apply: see s 83(4); and COMPANY AND PARTNERSHIP INSOLVENCY vol 17 (2011) PARA 672. As to the meaning of 'personal representative' see WILLS AND INTESTACY vol 103 (2010) PARA 608.

41. Winding up of companies not formed, but authorised to register, under the Companies Act 2006; stay of proceedings. The provisions of the Insolvency Act 1986 with respect to staying and restraining actions or proceedings against a company at any time after the presentation of a winding-up petition and before the making of a winding-up order[1], where the application to stay or restrain is by a creditor, extend to actions or proceedings against any contributory[2] of a company which has been registered but not formed[3] under the Companies Act 2006[4].

When an order has been made for winding up a company registered but not formed under the Companies Act 2006, no action or proceeding may be commenced or proceeded with against the company or its property or any contributory of the company, in respect of any debt of the company, except with the permission of the court, and subject to such terms as the court may impose[5].

1 Ie the provisions of the Insolvency Act 1986 s 126(1) (see COMPANY AND PARTNERSHIP INSOLVENCY vol 17 (2011) PARA 845): see the Insolvency Act 1986 s 126(2). As to winding up in general see COMPANY AND PARTNERSHIP INSOLVENCY vol 16 (2011) PARA 380 et seq.

2 As to the meaning of 'contributory' see COMPANY AND PARTNERSHIP INSOLVENCY vol 17 (2011) PARA 661. As to the meaning of 'contributory' under the Companies Acts see PARA 109 note 10.

3 As to registration under the Companies Act 2006 generally see PARA 104 et seq. As to companies formed under previous legislation see PARA 10 et seq.

4 Insolvency Act 1986 s 126(2) (amended by SI 2009/1941).

5 Insolvency Act 1986 s 130(3) (amended by SI 2009/1941). See COMPANY AND PARTNERSHIP INSOLVENCY vol 17 (2011) PARA 851.

(3) PROMOTION OF COMPANIES

(i) Nature of Promoters of Companies

42. Meaning of 'promoter'. The term 'promoter' is not now defined by statute[1]. The meaning of the term has, however, been dealt with in numerous cases[2].

The term 'promoter' is not a term of law, but of business[3]. It is a short and convenient way of designating those who set in motion the machinery by which companies legislation enables them to create an incorporated company[4]. It involves the idea of exertion for the purpose of getting up and starting a company[5], and also the idea of some duty towards the company imposed by, or arising from, the position which the so-called promoter assumes towards it[6].

The question whether a person is or is not a promoter is a question of fact depending upon what the so-called promoter really did[7], and a judge in summing up to a jury is not bound to define the term[8].

A person who as principal procures or aids in procuring the incorporation of a company is generally a promoter of it, and he does not escape from liability by acting through agents[9]. However, persons who act in a promotion only in a professionally capacity (such as counsel, solicitors, accountants, printers of offer documents, and the like) are not promoters[10].

1 In the Joint Stock Companies Act 1844 s 3 (repealed), the term was defined as meaning 'every person acting by whatever name in the forming and establishing of a company at any period prior to the company obtaining complete registration'. 'Promoter' was later defined, in connection with liability for statements in a prospectus or offer for sale, to mean a promoter who was a party to the prospectus or offer for sale, or the portion of it containing the untrue statement, other than a person acting in a professional capacity: see the Companies Act 1948 s 43(5); and the Companies Act 1985 s 67(3) (both repealed). References to promoters of companies occur in the Companies Act 2006 s 553 (permitted commission) (see PARA 1340) and s 762 (procedure for public company obtaining trading certificate) (see PARA 67).

2 See the text and notes 3–10; and PARA 43 et seq.

3 *Whaley Bridge Calico Printing Co v Green* (1879) 5 QBD 109 at 111 per Bowen J. As to the meaning of 'business' generally see PARA 1 note 1.

4 *Erlanger v New Sombrero Phosphate Co* (1879) 3 App Cas 1218 at 1268, HL, per Lord Blackburn. See *Twycross v Grant* (1877) 2 CPD 469 at 541, CA, per Cockburn CJ. Persons working together to form a company are not necessarily to be regarded as partners: *Keith Spicer Ltd v Mansell* [1970] 1 All ER 462, [1970] 1 WLR 333, CA.

5 *Official Receiver and Liquidator of Jubilee Cotton Mills Ltd v Lewis* [1924] AC 958 at 968, HL, per Lord Dunedin.

6 *Emma Silver Mining Co v Lewis & Son* (1879) 4 CPD 396 at 407 per Lindley J; *Re Great Wheal Polgooth Co Ltd* (1883) 53 LJ Ch 42.

7 *Lydney and Wigpool Iron Ore Co v Bird* (1886) 33 ChD 85 at 93, CA, per Lindley LJ; *Twycross v Grant* (1877) 2 CPD 469 at 476, CA, per Lord Coleridge CJ, and at 541 per Lindley J; *Emma Silver Mining Co v Lewis & Son* (1879) 4 CPD 396.

8 *Emma Silver Mining Co v Lewis & Son* (1879) 4 CPD 396 at 407 per Lindley J.

9 *Phosphate Sewage Co v Hartmont* (1877) 5 ChD 394, CA; *Official Receiver and Liquidator of Jubilee Cotton Mills Ltd v Lewis* [1924] AC 958, HL.

10 See *Re Great Wheal Polgooth Co Ltd* (1883) 53 LJ Ch 42 (solicitors).

43. Examples showing persons found to be promoters. Where a person wishing to sell property agrees with others that they are to form a company, and that he is to sell the property to it, the others receiving part of the purchase money, then, when the agreement is performed, the others are promoters[1]; and the owner of the property is also a promoter[2]. A person who joins with other persons in agreeing to purchase property with the view of selling it to a company which they intend to form, and subsequently do form, is a promoter[3]. Where a person takes in hand the formation of a company to buy the property of a third person, he is a promoter; and he incurs the liabilities of a promoter, even though the company is substantially different in character from the one he had anticipated, if he stands by and allows his agent to alter the plan of promotion[4].

Where the owner of a concession agrees with a financial agent that the concession is to be sold to contractors with a view to its being sold by them to a company to be formed forthwith for the purpose, the contractors finding funds necessary for such formation, the owner, the agent and the contractors are all promoters[5]. Similarly, where the agent of a syndicate, or trustee for a company, purchases property and sells it to a new company formed forthwith by the syndicate or company for the purpose, the members of the syndicate (or the company, as the case may be) are promoters[6].

Where the owners of property agree with two persons that they are to form a company to purchase it, and one of such persons agrees with a third person to carry out the scheme, and all three take part in procuring a board for the company, and in the preparation and issue of a prospectus, all three are promoters[7]. Brokers who, in consideration of being paid part of the purchase money, assist a person in selling property to a proposed company and allow their names to appear on the company's prospectus as being ready to answer any inquiries relating to the property, and answer such inquiries, are promoters[8].

Where a person purchases property with the view of selling it to a company which he subsequently forms, and another person enters into a sham contract with him for the purchase of the property, to be used in negotiating the sale to the company, and the company subsequently buys on terms which give a profit, they are both promoters[9]. Where a person agrees with the owners of property to form a company to purchase it at cost price, the company agreeing to pay a commission to him, and he thereupon forms the company, and is a party to the preparation and issue of the prospectus and the procuring of a board of directors, he is a promoter[10].

Directors of a promoting company are promoters where the promoting company is an alias for themselves, they being the only directors and entitled to share all the profits[11].

1 *Hichens v Congreve* (1831) 4 Sim 420.
2 *Beck v Kantorowicz* (1857) 3 K & J 230; *Bagnall v Carlton* (1877) 6 ChD 371 at 382, CA, per Bacon V-C.
3 *Lindsay Petroleum Co v Hurd* (1874) LR 5 PC 221; *Gluckstein v Barnes* [1900] AC 240, HL.
4 See *Official Receiver and Liquidator of Jubilee Cotton Mills Ltd v Lewis* [1924] AC 958 at 965, HL, per Viscount Finlay (where the defendant had intended the company to be a private company having as its shareholders only two others who knew the facts of the promotion).
5 *Twycross v Grant* (1877) 2 CPD 469, CA.
6 *Erlanger v New Sombrero Phosphate Co* (1878) 3 App Cas 1218, HL.
7 *Bagnall v Carlton* (1877) 6 ChD 371, CA. Cf *Re Leeds and Hanley Theatres of Varieties Ltd* [1902] 2 Ch 809, CA (where a company was held to be a promoter).
8 *Emma Silver Mining Co v Lewis & Son* (1879) 4 CPD 396.
9 *Whaley Bridge Calico Printing Co v Green* (1879) 5 QBD 109.
10 *Emma Silver Mining Co v Grant* (1879) 11 ChD 918.
11 *Re Darby, ex p Brougham* [1911] 1 KB 95.

44. When persons are not promoters. Persons do not become promoters on purchasing a property and shortly afterwards selling it at a profit to a company subsequently formed to buy it, if at the time of the contract they have taken no step to form the company[1], and even though the price is agreed to be paid partly in shares of a company which the purchasers propose to form[2]. If, however, the whole essence of the scheme from the first is that a number of persons are to purchase property and form a company to purchase it from them, they must disclose to the company, when formed, the whole of the profits made by them on the transaction[3].

1 *Ladywell Mining Co v Brookes* (1887) 35 ChD 400 at 409, CA, per Cotton LJ; *Re Cape Breton Co* (1885) 29 ChD 795, CA (affd sub nom *Cavendish Bentinck v Fenn* (1887) 12 App Cas 652, HL); *Gluckstein v Barnes* [1900] AC 240, HL; *Re Lady Forrest (Murchison) Gold Mine Ltd* [1901] 1 Ch 582.

2 *Re Coal Economising Gas Co, Gover's Case* (1875) 1 ChD 182, CA.

3 *Gluckstein v Barnes* [1900] AC 240, HL.

45. When promotion begins and ends. It is a question of fact in each case at what time a person begins[1] or ceases to be a promoter of a company.

A person may become a promoter of a company either before or after its incorporation[2]. A person, although not a director, may be a promoter of a company which is already incorporated but the capital of which has not been taken up, and which is not yet in a position to perform the obligations imposed upon it by its creators[3].

A promoter does not cease to be such by reason only of the formation of the company and the appointment of its directors, but only when the directors take into their own hands what remains to be done in the way of forming the company[4], and when there is no question open between the promoter and the company[5].

1 *Ladywell Mining Co v Brookes* (1887) 35 ChD 400, CA; *Re Olympia Ltd* [1898] 2 Ch 153 at 181–182, CA, per Collins LJ (affd sub nom *Gluckstein v Barnes* [1900] AC 240, HL); *Tyrrell v Bank of London* (1862) 10 HL Cas 26 at 40, HL, per Lord Westbury LC (disapproved in *FHR European Ventures LLP v Mankarious* [2014] UKSC 45, [2015] AC 250, [2014] 4 All ER 79); *Albion Steel and Wire Co v Martin* (1875) 1 ChD 580.

2 *Twycross v Grant* (1877) 2 CPD 469 at 503, CA, per Bramwell LJ. See also *Lagunas Nitrate Co v Lagunas Syndicate* [1899] 2 Ch 392 at 428, CA, per Lindley MR.

3 *Emma Silver Mining Co v Lewis & Son* (1879) 4 CPD 396 at 407 per Lindley J.

4 *Twycross v Grant* (1877) 2 CPD 469 at 541, CA, per Lindley J.

5 *Eden v Ridsdales Rly Lamp and Lighting Co Ltd* (1889) 23 QBD 368, CA.

(ii) Fiduciary Relation of Promoters to the Company

46. Promoter not trustee or agent of company. A promoter stands in a fiduciary position with respect to the company which he promotes from the time when he first becomes until he ceases to be a promoter of it[1]; but his relation to the company is not that of trustee and beneficiary, or agent and principal[2]. A promoter may acquire assets as a trustee for a company. Whether he does so or not is a question of fact and, where the plan of promotion is that he should sell assets to an intended company at a profit, the presumption is that as regards those assets he is not a trustee in the ordinary sense, but may, as vendor or agent to the vendors, make a profit on the sale to the company, even if he is also its director or one of its directors, provided that he makes full disclosure to the company[3]. The onus, however, lies upon the promoter to prove that he has made full disclosure[4].

1 *Twycross v Grant* (1877) 2 CPD 469 at 538, CA, per Cockburn CJ; *Erlanger v New Sombrero Phosphate Co* (1878) 3 App Cas 1218 at 1236, HL, per Lord Cairns LC, and at 1269 per Lord Blackburn; *Lagunas Nitrate Co v Lagunas Syndicate* [1899] 2 Ch 392 at 422, CA, per Lindley MR; *Gluckstein v Barnes* [1900] AC 240, HL.

2 *Lydney and Wigpool Iron Ore Co v Bird* (1886) 33 ChD 85, CA; *Lagunas Nitrate Co v Lagunas Syndicate* [1899] 2 Ch 392 at 426, CA, per Lindley MR. A promoter was held not to be a 'trustee or person acting in a fiduciary capacity' within the meaning of the Debtors Act 1869 s 4(3): see *Phosphate Sewage Co v Hartmont* (1877) 25 WR 743.

3 *Erlanger v New Sombrero Phosphate Co* (1878) 3 App Cas 1218 at 1236, HL, per Lord Cairns LC; *Salomon v A Salomon & Co Ltd* [1897] AC 22 at 33, HL, per Lord Halsbury LC; *Lagunas Nitrate Co v Lagunas Syndicate* [1899] 2 Ch 392 at 422, CA, per Lindley MR; *A-G for Canada v Standard Trust Co of New York* [1911] AC 498, PC; *Omnium Electric Palaces Ltd v Baines* [1914] 1 Ch 332 at 347 per Sargant J. See also *Jacobus Marler Estates Ltd v Marler* (1913) 85 LJPC 167n. As a director with an interest in a proposed transaction with the company, the director must comply with the Companies Act 2006 s 177 (duty to declare interest in proposed transaction or arrangement with the company) (see PARA 595) and such other of the general duties, especially s 171(b) (director of company must only exercise powers for the purposes for which they are conferred) (see PARA 580) and s 172 (duty to promote the success of the company) (see PARA 584), as are applicable (see s 179 (except as otherwise provided, more than one of the general duties may apply in any given case); and PARA 572).

In the limited circumstances prescribed by the Companies Act 2006 s 598 (agreement for transfer to public company of non-cash asset in initial period by a person who is a subscriber to the company's memorandum), independent valuation and approval of the transfer by members are both required: see PARA 1314. In the event of a contravention, any consideration given by the company under the agreement, or an amount equal to the value of the consideration at the time of the agreement, is recoverable; and the agreement, so far as it is not carried out, is void: see s 604(2); and PARA 1318.

4 *Cavendish Bentinck v Fenn* (1887) 12 App Cas 652 at 661, HL, per Lord Herschell; *Re Darby, ex p Brougham* [1911] 1 KB 95; *Re Jubilee Cotton Mills Ltd* [1922] 1 Ch 100 at 117 per Astbury J (revsd [1923] 1 Ch 1, CA; revsd sub nom *Official Receiver and Liquidator of Jubilee Cotton Mills Ltd v Lewis* [1924] AC 958, HL). See also *Bristol and West Building Society v Mothew (t/a Stapley & Co)* [1998] Ch 1 at 18, [1996] 4 All ER 698 at 712 per Millett LJ. See further PARAS 53–54.

47. Claiming account of secret profits made by promoter. A promoter may not, without full disclosure, retain any profit made out of a transaction to which the company is a party[1]. Where disclosure has not been made, the company may affirm the contract and sue him for an account and payment of profits[2]. The claim of the company may also be enforced by proceedings for misfeasance in the winding up of the company[3], and is provable in bankruptcy[4].

Interest may be recovered as from the time when the promoter received the profits[5]. The burden of proving that profit has in fact been made by a promoter lies on the company[6].

If the vendors to a company are the same persons as its shareholders, and the consideration is shares of the company, the profit (if any) is not secret and the company cannot recover it[7].

1 See PARAS 53–54.

2 *Lydney and Wigpool Iron Ore Co v Bird* (1886) 33 ChD 85, CA; *Beck v Kantorowicz* (1857) 3 K & J 230; *Hitchens v Congreve* (1831) 4 Sim 420; *Fawcett v Whitehouse* (1829) 1 Russ & M 132; *Whaley Bridge Calico Printing Co v Green* (1879) 5 QBD 109; *Bagnall v Carlton* (1877) 6 ChD 371, CA; *Emma Silver Mining Co v Grant* (1879) 11 ChD 918; *Mann and Beattie v Edinburgh Northern Tramways Co* [1893] AC 69, HL; *Gluckstein v Barnes* [1900] AC 240. See also *Re Sale Hotel and Botanical Gardens Co Ltd, ex p Hesketh* (1898) 78 LT 368, CA.

3 *Re Caerphilly Colliery Co, Pearson's Case* (1877) 5 ChD 336, CA; *Nant-y-Glo and Blaina Ironworks Co v Grave* (1878) 12 ChD 738; *Official Receiver and Liquidator of Jubilee Cotton Mills Ltd v Lewis* [1924] AC 958, HL; *Gluckstein v Barnes* [1900] AC 240, HL. The promoters taking fully paid up shares, although they may have to pay the nominal value of them, are not contributories in respect of them: *Re Western of Canada Oil, Lands and Works Co, Carling, Hespeler, and Walsh's Cases* (1875) 1 ChD 115, CA; *Re British Provident Life and Guarantee Association, De Ruvigne's Case* (1877) 5 ChD 306, CA. See COMPANY AND PARTNERSHIP INSOLVENCY vol 17 (2011) PARA 690. As to proceedings for misfeasance see COMPANY AND PARTNERSHIP INSOLVENCY vol 17 (2011) PARA 646 et seq.

4 See PARA 62; and the cases cited there.

5 *Gluckstein v Barnes* [1900] AC 240 at 255, HL, per Lord Macnaghten; *Nant-y-Glo and Blaina Ironworks Co v Grave* (1878) 12 ChD 738.

6 *Cavendish Bentinck v Fenn* (1887) 12 App Cas 652 at 659, HL, per Lord Herschell.

7 *Re Ambrose Lake Tin and Copper Mining Co, ex p Taylor, ex p Moss* (1880) 14 ChD 390, CA.

48. Amount of secret profit for which promoter is liable. In estimating the amount of secret profit for which a promoter is liable, deductions are made for legitimate expenses incurred in forming and bringing out the company (such as fees for reports of surveyors, charges of solicitors and brokers, sums expended in good faith in securing the services of directors, and payments to officers of the company and the press in relation to the company)[1]. However, deductions cannot be claimed for sums paid to the company by the vendors to compromise the company's proceedings against them to rescind the purchase[2], nor for the difference (arranged under a compromise to which the company is not a party) between what was to be paid by the promoter to the agent of the company and what was actually paid[3], nor for the value of the services in respect of which the profit is paid to him[4]. Deductions have been disallowed in the case of sums paid in obtaining from another person a guarantee for the taking of shares[5].

1 *Emma Silver Mining Co v Grant* (1879) 11 ChD 918; *Bagnall v Carlton* (1877) 6 ChD 371, CA; *Lydney and Wigpool Iron Ore Co v Bird* (1886) 33 ChD 85, CA; *Benson v Heathorn* (1842) 1 Y & C Ch Cas 326 at 340 per Shadwell V-C; *Re Darby, ex p Brougham* [1911] 1 KB 95 at 101 per Phillimore J; *Official Receiver and Liquidator of Jubilee Cotton Mills Ltd v Lewis* [1924] AC 958, HL.

2 *Bagnall v Carlton* (1877) 6 ChD 371, CA.

3 *Grant v Gold Exploration and Development Syndicate Ltd* [1900] 1 QB 233, CA.

4 *Re Sale Hotel and Botanical Gardens Co Ltd, Hesketh's Case* (1897) 77 LT 681 at 682 per Wright J (revsd on other grounds (1898) 78 LT 368, CA).

5 *Lydney and Wigpool Iron Ore Co v Bird* (1886) 33 ChD 85, CA. It would appear that the ground for the decision in that case was that the whole transaction was improper and not that the payment of such a sum would in itself have been illegal even if made by the company: see *Metropolitan Coal Consumers' Association v Scrimgeour* [1895] 2 QB 604 at 607–608, CA, per Lindley LJ. The latter question cannot now arise: see PARA 1339 et seq.

49. Joint and several liability of promoters in respect of secret profits. Promoters are jointly and severally liable in respect of secret profits, and, if one pays the whole of the joint liability, he may recover the proper proportion from his co-promoters[1].

1 *Gluckstein v Barnes* [1900] AC 240 at 247, 255, HL, per Lord Macnaghten. See also *Gerson v Simpson* [1903] 2 KB 197, CA.

50. Rescission of contract in place of claiming account of secret profits. Instead of claiming an account of the secret profits, the company may bring a claim for rescission of the contract for sale and return of the consideration and payment of dividends and interest paid on shares and debentures forming part of the consideration; and, if the shares have been sold, the company may claim payment of the proceeds with interest[1]. Where part of the consideration is exchanged for shares in another company, the amount repayable is the actual value of those shares and not the value for purposes of the exchange[2]. As a general rule, rescission of a voidable contract may be obtained against a vendor only where the property can be restored to him; but this rule has no application where the property has been reduced by his fault, and, moreover, if compensation can be made for any deterioration, rescission with compensation may be awarded[3]. A company cannot be deprived of its remedy of rescission or other remedies by any provisions in its articles[4].

The remedy by rescission may be the only remedy where the promoter has bought and paid for the property before he sells it to the company, and was not at the time of his purchase in a fiduciary relation to the company[5].

1 This is implied in the judgments in *Erlanger v New Sombrero Phosphate Co* (1878) 3 App Cas 1218, HL; *Phosphate Sewage Co v Hartmont* (1877) 5 ChD 394, CA; *Lagunas Nitrate Co v*

Lagunas Syndicate [1899] 2 Ch 392, CA; *Official Receiver and Liquidator of Jubilee Cotton Mills Ltd v Lewis* [1924] AC 958, HL.

2 *Official Receiver and Liquidator of Jubilee Cotton Mills Ltd v Lewis* [1924] AC 958 at 967, HL, per Viscount Finlay.

3 *Lagunas Nitrate Co v Lagunas Syndicate* [1899] 2 Ch 392 at 456, CA, per Rigby LJ. As to the remedy of rescission see CONTRACT vol 22 (2012) PARA 577 et seq; MISREPRESENTATION vol 76 (2013) PARA 811 et seq.

4 *Omnium Electric Palaces Ltd v Baines* [1914] 1 Ch 332 at 347, CA, per Sargant J. As to a company's articles of association see PARA 227 et seq.

5 *Ladywell Mining Co v Brookes* (1887) 35 ChD 400, CA; *Re Cape Breton Co* (1885) 29 ChD 795, CA (affd sub nom *Cavendish Bentinck v Fenn* (1887) 12 App Cas 652, HL); *Burland v Earle* [1902] AC 83, PC.

51. Other remedies of company for breach of duty by promoter. If the remedy by rescission is not open, or if the company elects to affirm the contract, the company may have a good cause of action for deceit or fraud, negligent misrepresentation[1] or breach of duty[2]. Where there has been a breach of duty, nominal damages, or if the breach has resulted in loss to the funds and assets of the company, substantial damages, may be recovered[3]. The liability for breach of duty cannot be enforced by a contributory in a winding up by means of proceedings for misfeasance unless the breach of duty has resulted in a loss to the assets of the company[4]. Where a vendor has agreed to give to a promoter a profit undisclosed by the promoter, the company may recover from the vendor any part of such profit which has not been paid over[5].

1 Ie under the Misrepresentation Act 1967 s 2 (see MISREPRESENTATION vol 76 (2013) PARA 762).

2 See eg *Ellis v Colman, Bates and Husler* (1858) 25 Beav 662 (specific performance of ultra vires contract refused on the ground that the court could neither enforce the contract nor compel the defendants to make good their representations; the remedy of the plaintiffs lay in action at law for damages); and see MISREPRESENTATION vol 76 (2013) PARA 701 et seq; SPECIFIC PERFORMANCE vol 95 (2013) PARA 313 et seq.

3 *Cavendish Bentinck v Fenn* (1887) 12 App Cas 652 at 658, 662, 664, HL, per Lord Herschell; *Re Leeds and Hanley Theatres of Varieties Ltd* [1902] 2 Ch 809 at 826, CA, per Vaughan Williams LJ, and at 830 per Romer LJ. See also *Jacobus Marler Estates Ltd v Marler* (1913) 85 LJPC 167n.

4 *Cavendish Bentinck v Fenn* (1887) 12 App Cas 652, HL (affg *Re Cape Breton Co* (1885) 29 ChD 795, CA). As to proceedings for misfeasance see COMPANY AND PARTNERSHIP INSOLVENCY vol 17 (2011) PARA 646 et seq.

5 *Whaley Bridge Calico Printing Co v Green* (1879) 5 QBD 109. Cf *Grant v Gold Exploration and Development Syndicate* [1900] 1 QB 233, CA.

52. Remedies of shareholders and debenture holders against promoter. Where a shareholder or debenture or debenture stock holder who has been injured makes a claim, a promoter may be liable in respect of a false or misleading prospectus or listing particulars either for compensation under the statutory liability[1] or for damages for deceit[2] or for misrepresentation[3].

1 See PARA 1259 et seq.

2 See PARA 1270 et seq. As to criminal liability of a promoter generally see PARA 63.

3 See PARA 1276.

(iii) Disclosure by Promoters

53. Promoter's duty of full disclosure. In order to be in a position to retain any profit made by him, or to resist a claim for rescission or damages, a promoter, before completion of the transaction out of which the profit is made, must have made full disclosure to the company of the fact that he is interested in the transaction, of the nature of his interest, and of all other material facts[1].

It is not clear whether the exact amount of profit is required to be stated[2]. However, in making an application for a trading certificate[3], without which a public company[4] cannot do business[5] or exercise any borrowing powers[6], the company must specify any amount or benefit paid or given (or intended to be paid or given) to any promoter of the company, and the consideration for the payment or benefit[7].

1 *Re Darby, ex p Brougham* [1911] 1 KB 95; *A-G for Canada v Standard Trust Co of New York* [1911] AC 498, PC. See also the cases cited in PARA 48 note 1.

2 See *Chesterfield and Boythorpe Colliery Co v Black* (1877) 37 LT 740; *Re Lady Forrest (Murchison) Gold Mine Ltd* [1901] 1 Ch 582; *Lagunas Nitrate Co v Lagunas Syndicate* [1899] 2 Ch 392, CA; *Gluckstein v Barnes* [1900] AC 240 at 258, HL, per Lord Robertson. Cf *Gwembe Valley Development Co Ltd (in receivership) v Koshy (No 3)* [2003] EWCA Civ 1048 at [64]–[68], [2004] 1 BCLC 131 (director had not proved full disclosure to all of the other directors and shareholders of either his intended personal interest in a company that was involved in the transactions at issue or the source and scale of his intended profit).

A person may buy a property at one price and sell it to a company at a higher price without disclosing even the fact that he is getting a profit, provided that he is not a promoter: *Re Coal Economising Gas Co, Gover's Case* (1875) 1 ChD 182, CA.

3 A 'trading certificate' is a certificate issued by the registrar of companies under the Companies Act 2006 s 761; and an application for such a certificate must be made in accordance with s 762: see PARA 67.

4 Ie a company that is registered as a public company on its original incorporation rather than by virtue of its re-registration as a public company: see the Companies Act 2006 s 761(1); and PARA 67. As to the meanings of 'private company' and 'public company' see PARA 95.

5 As to the meaning of 'business' generally see PARA 1 note 1.

6 As to a company's borrowing powers see PARA 1442 et seq.

7 See the Companies Act 2006 ss 761, 762; and PARA 67.

54. What amounts to disclosure by promoter. Disclosure may be made in any one of several ways, as, for example, by the articles of association of the company[1], or by communication to such shareholders of the company as become such by applying for shares on the footing of a prospectus or an offer for sale which makes due disclosure[2], or by communication to a board of directors of the company which is independent of the promoters[3], or by communication in any way to the original shareholders, at any rate if no future shareholders are contemplated[4].

Even if disclosure is made to the original shareholders or if for other reasons they cannot complain of the want of it, there may, in some cases, exist a fiduciary relation between the promoters and future shareholders if the admission of the latter to membership of the company formed part of the plan of promotion[5].

1 *Re British Seamless Paper Box Co* (1881) 17 ChD 467 at 475, CA, per Jessel MR. Disclosure is made in this way because of the notice which every member and outsider dealing with the company has of the contents of the articles (see *Re Bank of Hindustan, China and Japan, Campbell's Case, Hippisley's Case, Alison's Case* (1873) 9 Ch App 1 at 22 per Lord Selborne LC; *Griffith v Paget* (1877) 6 ChD 511 at 517 per Jessel MR; *Mahony v East Holyford Mining Co* (1875) LR 7 HL 869 at 893 per Lord Hatherley; and PARA 247), and possibly because of the statutory effect of the articles (see the Companies Act 2006 s 33; *Lagunas Nitrate Co v Lagunas Syndicate* [1899] 2 Ch 392 at 424, CA, per Lindley MR; and PARA 242). See, however, *Gluckstein v Barnes* [1900] AC 240, HL.

2 *Lagunas Nitrate Co v Lagunas Syndicate* [1899] 2 Ch 392 at 428, CA, per Lindley MR; *Gluckstein v Barnes* [1900] AC 240 at 249, HL, per Lord Macnaghten; *Omnium Electric Palaces Ltd v Baines* [1914] 1 Ch 332 at 347, CA, per Sargant J, and at 351 per Cozens-Hardy MR.

3 *Erlanger v New Sombrero Phosphate Co* (1878) 3 App Cas 1218 at 1236, HL, per Lord Cairns LC; *Re Fitzroy Bessemer Steel Co Ltd* (1884) 50 LT 144; *Gluckstein v Barnes* [1900] AC 240, HL. See further PARA 55.

4 *Salomon v A Salomon & Co Ltd* [1897] AC 22, HL. See also *Re Ambrose Lake Tin and Copper Mining Co, ex p Taylor, ex p Moss* (1880) 14 ChD 390, CA; *Re British Seamless Paper Box Co* (1881) 17 ChD 467, CA; *A-G for Canada v Standard Trust Co of New York* [1911] AC 498, PC.

5 See *Re British Seamless Paper Box Co* (1881) 17 ChD 467, CA; *Re Postage Stamp Automatic Delivery Co* [1892] 3 Ch 566; *Re Westmoreland Green and Blue Slate Co, Bland's Case* [1893] 2 Ch 612, CA; *Lagunas Nitrate Co v Lagunas Syndicate* [1899] 2 Ch 392 at 428, CA, per Lindley MR; *Re Leeds and Hanley Theatres of Varieties Ltd* [1902] 2 Ch 809 at 827, CA, per Vaughan Williams LJ; *Re Darby, ex p Brougham* [1911] 1 KB 95.

55. What is an independent executive. A board of directors, whether provided by the promoters or otherwise, is an independent executive when its members are aware that the property which the company is asked to buy is the property of the promoters, and when they are competent and intelligent judges as to whether the purchase ought or ought not to be made, and capable of exercising an intelligent, independent and impartial judgment on the transaction[1]. Directors appointed by the vendors do not generally constitute an independent board; in such a case the only effective way of making disclosure by a promoter is by the articles, and, if a prospectus is issued, in the prospectus also[2]. Where promoters appoint themselves, or some of their number, to be sole guardians and protectors of their creature, the company, they are not an independent board, and the fact that the articles purport to protect them from the liability to account as persons standing in a fiduciary relation to the company will not help them[3]. If a company is avowedly formed with a board of directors who are not independent, but who are stated to be the intended vendors of property to the company, or their agents, the company cannot set aside the purchase agreement merely on the ground that the directors are not independent[4].

Where a company is one which does not invite the public to subscribe for its shares (and every shareholder is aware of all the circumstances attending the formation of the company), the absence of an independent board of directors is immaterial[5].

1 *Erlanger v New Sombrero Phosphate Co* (1878) 3 App Cas 1218, HL.

2 *Re Olympia Ltd* [1898] 2 Ch 153, CA; affd sub nom *Gluckstein v Barnes* [1900] AC 240, HL. See also *Selangor United Rubber Estates Ltd v Cradock (No 3)* [1968] 2 All ER 1073, [1968] 1 WLR 1555 (persons nominated as directors to do what they are told by an outsider are fixed with his knowledge).

3 *Gluckstein v Barnes* [1900] AC 240 at 248, HL, per Lord Macnaghten; *Re Westmoreland Green and Blue Slate Co, Bland's Case* [1893] 2 Ch 612, CA.

4 *Lagunas Nitrate Co v Lagunas Syndicate* [1899] 2 Ch 392 at 425, CA, per Lindley MR. Cf *Re Olympia Ltd* [1898] 2 Ch 153 at 168, CA, per Lindley MR; affd sub nom *Gluckstein v Barnes* [1900] AC 240, HL (where a clause in the articles, declaring that the validity of the agreement for sale should not be impeached on the ground that the vendors as promoters or otherwise stood in a fiduciary relation to the company, was held nugatory).

Directors in this situation remain subject to the general duties imposed by the Companies Act 2006 Pt 10 Ch 2 (ss 170–181) (see PARA 572 et seq), whose effect is cumulative (see s 179 (except as otherwise provided, more than one of the general duties may apply in any given case); and PARA 572).

5 *Salomon v A Salomon & Co Ltd* [1897] AC 22 at 36, HL, per Lord Watson, and at 57 per Lord Davey; *Larocque v Beauchemin* [1897] AC 358 at 364, PC; *Felix Hadley & Co Ltd v Hadley* (1897) 77 LT 131; *Re Innes & Co Ltd* [1903] 2 Ch 254 at 260, CA, per Vaughan Williams LJ.

(iv) Payment by Company of Promoter's Expenses

56. Company's liability to promoter. A promoter has no right of indemnity against the company which he promotes in respect of any obligation undertaken on its behalf before its incorporation[1], and may not sue it upon a contract, made by him with an agent or trustee on its behalf before its incorporation, stipulating that it shall pay the promoters a certain sum for preliminary expenses, even where the articles of association provide that the company shall defray the preliminary expenses[2]. Thus, in spite of such a provision, the solicitor who prepares the memorandum and articles cannot sue the company for his costs of doing so, and the promoter, or his solicitor, who has paid the fees on registering the company, cannot recover them from the company[3]; nor is the promoter, or a person employed by him, entitled to sue the company in respect of any payment for services rendered or expenses incurred before its incorporation in promoting it, unless after its incorporation it expressly agrees with him to make such payment, or, from other facts, the court can infer a new contract to reimburse him[4]. The company cannot ratify an agreement purporting to be made on its behalf before its incorporation[5]; and its acts cannot be evidence of a new agreement to reimburse the promoter if they can be shown to have been made with reference to the obligations of the company to indemnify a third person[6]. A company is not bound in equity to pay the preliminary expenses because it has adopted and derived benefit from services performed before its incorporation[7]. Where a promoter procures a company to be formed by fraudulent means and by fraud induces shareholders to join it, he cannot recover expenses which he otherwise might have recovered[8].

Whether there is a fresh contract between the company and the promoters after incorporation is a question of fact[9].

1 *Melhado v Porto Alegre Rly Co* (1874) LR 9 CP 503. As to pre-incorporation contracts see also PARA 279.
2 *Melhado v Porto Alegre Rly Co* (1874) LR 9 CP 503. As to the personal liability of a person purporting to contract on behalf of a company at a time when the company is not formed see PARA 59. As to a company's articles of association see PARA 227 et seq.
3 See PARA 278 note 1.
4 See the cases cited in PARA 279 notes 1–2.
5 See the cases cited in PARA 278 note 2.
6 *Re Rotherham Alum and Chemical Co* (1883) 25 ChD 103, CA.
7 *Re English and Colonial Produce Co Ltd* [1906] 2 Ch 435, CA, overruling the dictum in *Re Hereford and South Wales Waggon and Engineering Co* (1876) 2 ChD 621 at 624, CA, per Mellish LJ (which had been cited as authority for the proposition that a company, because it has taken the benefit of work done under a contract entered into before the formation of the company, can be made liable in equity under that contract), and probably some similar observations in *Re Empress Engineering Co* (1880) 16 ChD 125, CA. See also *Re National Motor Mail-Coach Co Ltd, Clinton's Claim* [1908] 2 Ch 515, CA.
8 *Re Hereford and South Wales Waggon and Engineering Co* (1876) 2 ChD 621, CA.
9 *Browning v Great Central Mining Co* (1860) 5 H & N 856; *Howard v Patent Ivory Manufacturing Co, Re Patent Ivory Manufacturing Co* (1888) 38 ChD 156 at 165 per Kay J. Cf *Re English and Colonial Produce Co Ltd* [1906] 2 Ch 435, CA.

57. Power of company to pay registration etc expenses to promoters. Generally, a company, and its directors by its articles of association[1], are expressly empowered to pay all expenses of and incidental to its incorporation and flotation[2]. Even where there is express general power to pay preliminary expenses to a promoter, payment should not be made without vouchers or investigation[3]; but, if the directors are empowered without further authority to pay a specific sum for the costs and expenses of promoters, payment may be made without a bill of costs being required[4]. The expenses which may be properly paid include registration fees, a sum charged for a report on the value of property to be purchased by it, legal costs, advertisements, printing and brokers' fees[5]. Directors may be made personally liable for sums improperly paid to promoters[6]. Where the articles state the amounts to be paid to promoters for procuring concessions and for preliminary expenses, shareholders may not complain that the amounts are excessive[7] unless the promoter has acted fraudulently[8]. If, however, the money is paid and proceedings to recover it are compromised with knowledge of the facts, the money cannot afterwards be recovered[9].

1 As to a company's articles of association see PARA 227 et seq.
2 The Companies (Model Articles) Regulations 2008, SI 2008/3229, Sch 3 Pt 4 art 44 expressly provides for a public company to pay any person a commission in consideration for that person subscribing, or agreeing to subscribe, for shares, or procuring, or agreeing to procure, subscriptions for shares: see PARA 1340. See also the Companies Act 2006 s 553 (permitted commission) (see PARA 1340); and note the requirement, where a public company applies for a trading certificate, without which it cannot do business or exercise any borrowing powers, for the company to specify, in making such an application, the amount, or estimated amount, of the company's preliminary expenses (see s 762; and PARA 67). No express provision for the payment of commission appears in the model articles of association provided for use by a private company, which merely provide that the directors may exercise all the powers of the company: see the Companies (Model Articles) Regulations 2008, SI 2008/3229, Sch 1 Pt 2 arts 3, 4 (private company limited by shares); the Companies (Tables A to F) Regulations 1985, SI 1985/805, Schedule Table A art 70; and PARA 581. As to the model articles and Table A generally see PARAS 228–229.
3 *Re Englefield Colliery Co* (1878) 8 ChD 388 at 401, CA, per Baggallay LJ (where directors' calls were paid out of payments to promoters).
4 *Croskey v Bank of Wales* (1863) 4 Giff 314 at 332 per Sir John Stuart V-C.
5 *Lydney and Wigpool Iron Ore Co v Bird* (1886) 33 ChD 85, CA. See also PARA 48. Reasonable sums may be paid to brokers for placing a company's shares: see *Metropolitan Coal Consumers' Association v Scrimgeour* [1895] 2 QB 604, CA, distinguishing *Re Faure Electric Accumulator Co* (1888) 40 ChD 141, and overruling that case in so far as it held that payment of brokerage by a company was in itself illegal. See also the Companies Act 2006 s 552(3); and PARA 1339; and see PARA 1346.
6 *Re Anglo-French Co-operative Society, ex p Pelly* (1882) 21 ChD 492, CA; *Re London and Provincial Starch Co* (1869) 20 LT 390; *Re Brighton Brewery Co, Hunt's Case* (1868) 37 LJ Ch 278.
7 *Re Anglo-Greek Steam Co* (1866) LR 2 Eq 1.
8 *Re Madrid Bank, ex p Williams* (1866) LR 2 Eq 216.
9 *Re General Exchange Bank, ex p Preston* (1868) 37 LJ Ch 618.

58. Acceptance of presents from promoters. Directors or other officers of the company or its agents at the time of promotion accepting gifts from promoters are liable to account to the company for the money or shares or other property received[1], and, in the case of fully paid shares which have diminished in value, the nominal amount of the shares must be accounted for[2]. An article authorising a promoter to give shares to the directors has been rejected as fraudulent[3], but full disclosure may prevent liability[4]. Where several directors receive presents with mutual knowledge, they are jointly and severally liable for the whole amount[5].

The acceptance of gifts by an agent of the company is a ground for the company rescinding the purchase contract[6] if the transaction is not revealed to the company[7], whether or not the gift influences the conduct of the agent[8]. If the promised gift is not handed over, the agent cannot recover it[9].

1 *Re Caerphilly Colliery Co, Pearson's Case* (1877) 5 ChD 336, CA; *Re British Provident Life and Guarantee Association, De Ruvigne's Case* (1877) 5 ChD 306, CA; *Nant-y-Glo and Blaina Ironworks Co v Grave* (1878) 12 ChD 738; *Re Diamond Fuel Co, Mitcalfe's Case* (1879) 13 ChD 169, CA; *Re Carriage Co-operative Supply Association* (1884) 27 ChD 322; *Eden v Ridsdales Rly Lamp and Lighting Co Ltd* (1889) 23 QBD 368, CA; *Re Morvah Consols Tin Mining Co, McKay's Case* (1875) 2 ChD 1, CA; *Re Howatson Patent Furnace Co* (1887) 4 TLR 152; *Re North Australian Territory Co, Archer's Case* [1892] 1 Ch 322, CA (agreement by promoters to buy directors' shares at par); *Re London and South Western Canal Ltd* [1911] 1 Ch 346 (directors had promoters' shares transferred to them as their qualification and held them on trust for the promoters). See further COMPANY AND PARTNERSHIP INSOLVENCY vol 17 (2011) PARA 652.

A director, and any person who ceases to be a director, continues to be subject to the duty not to accept a benefit from a third party conferred by reason of either his being a director, or his doing (or not doing) anything as director: see the Companies Act 2006 s 170 (see PARA 573), s 176 (see PARA 593).

2 See the cases cited in note 1; and see *Re Canadian Oil Works Corpn, Hay's Case* (1875) 10 Ch App 593; *Weston's Case* (1879) 10 ChD 579, CA; *Re Westmoreland Green and Blue Slate Co, Bland's Case* [1893] 2 Ch 612, CA (directors inaccurately stated in the contract with the company to be part vendors).

3 *Re Eskern and Slate Slab Quarries Co Ltd, Clarke and Helden's Cases* (1877) 37 LT 222. Cf *Re Australian Direct Steam Navigation Co, Miller's Case* (1877) 5 ChD 70, CA.

4 *Re Postage Stamp Automatic Delivery Co* [1892] 3 Ch 566 (disclosure in a contract registered with the registrar); *Re Olympia Ltd* [1898] 2 Ch 153 at 169, CA, per Lindley MR, and at 174 per Collins LJ (affd sub nom *Gluckstein v Barnes* [1900] AC 240, HL); *Re Innes & Co Ltd* [1903] 2 Ch 254 at 265–266, CA, per Cozens-Hardy LJ. As to the law relating to disclosure by promoters see PARAS 53–55.

5 *Re Carriage Co-operative Supply Association* (1884) 27 ChD 322.

6 *Panama and South Pacific Telegraph Co v India Rubber, Gutta Percha, and Telegraph Works Co* (1875) 10 Ch App 515, CA; *Smith v Sorby* (1875) 3 QBD 552n.

7 *Panama and South Pacific Telegraph Co v India Rubber, Gutta Percha, and Telegraph Works Co* (1875) 10 Ch App 515, CA; *Smith v Sorby* (1875) 3 QBD 552n.

8 *Industries and General Mortgage Co Ltd v Lewis* [1949] 2 All ER 573. See also AGENCY vol 1 (2008) PARA 93.

9 *Harrington v Victoria Graving Dock Co* (1878) 3 QBD 549.

(v) Promoter's Liability

59. Promoter's liability under contract that purports to be made by or on behalf of unformed company. Under the Companies Act 2006, a contract that purports to be made by or on behalf of a company[1] at a time when the company has not been formed[2] has effect, subject to any agreement to the contrary, as one made with the person purporting to act for the company or as agent for it[3], and he is personally liable on the contract accordingly[4]. The person purporting to act for, or as agent of, the unformed company is also entitled to enforce the contract against the other party unless such enforcement is otherwise precluded by the ordinary common law principles governing contractual arrangements[5]. No exclusion of personal liability will be implied merely by the manner of signature of the contract[6]. Personal liability under the contract comes to an end once it has been performed, or rescinded by either party under some power in the contract, or by consent of all parties, or when the company has, with the consent of the other contracting party, undertaken the liability of the promoter under the contract[7]. Where, however, there is a contract to pay out of a specific fund, the personal liability exists only to the extent of the fund, if any[8].

1 As to the meaning of 'company' under the Companies Acts see PARA 21; and as to the meaning of the 'Companies Acts' see PARA 13.

2 This does not cover the situation where a company has been formed but changes its name; contracts made at that time are not pre-incorporation contracts since a change of name is not a re-formation or re-incorporation of the company (*Oshkosh B'Gosh Inc v Dan Marbel Inc Ltd* [1989] 1 CMLR 94, [1989] BCLC 507, CA); nor does it cover contracts entered into by a company which has been formed but which was trading under an incorrect name (*Badgerhill Properties Ltd v Cottrell* [1991] BCLC 805, CA). As to pre-incorporation contracts see also PARAS 278–279.

3 For these purposes, a contract can purport to be made on behalf of a company or by a company even though both parties know that the company is not formed and that it is only about to be formed: *Phonogram Ltd v Lane* [1982] QB 938 at 943, [1981] 3 All ER 182 at 186, CA, per Lord Denning MR. A contract cannot, however, purport to be made on behalf of a company not yet formed if no one had thought of the new company at the time of contracting: *Cotronic (UK) Ltd v Dezonie* [1991] BCLC 721, CA (parties contracted with first company which in fact had been struck off the register and dissolved; when this was discovered years later, a second company was incorporated; it was impossible to say that the contract purported to be made by or on behalf of the second company).

4 Companies Act 2006 s 51(1). This provision applies to the making of a deed under the law of England and Wales as it applies to the making of a contract: s 51(2). As to the meanings of 'England' and 'Wales' see PARA 1 note 5. The provisions of s 51 apply to unregistered companies

by virtue of the Unregistered Companies Regulations 2009, SI 2009/2436, Sch 1 para 3(g): see PARA 1857. As to the meaning of 'unregistered company' see PARA 1856. The Secretary of State has made provision by regulations (see the Companies Act 2006 s 1045; and PARA 2014) applying s 51 also to overseas companies, but with modifications: see the Overseas Companies (Execution of Documents and Registration of Charges) Regulations 2009, SI 2009/1917, reg 6. As to the meaning of 'overseas company' see PARA 2013.

The Companies Act 2006 s 51(1) re-enacts the Companies Act 1985 s 36C(1) (itself re-enacting in substantially the same terms the Companies Act 1985 s 36(4) (as originally enacted), which re-enacted the European Communities Act 1972 s 9(2), (9) (repealed)), and negatives the decisions in *Hollman v Pullin* (1884) Cab & El 254 and *Newborne v Sensolid (Great Britain) Ltd* [1954] 1 QB 45, [1953] 1 All ER 708, CA. For the law prior to this provision see *Nockels v Crosby* (1825) 3 B & C 814; *Re Rotherham Alum and Chemical Co* (1883) 25 ChD 103, CA; *Mant v Smith* (1859) 4 H & N 324; *Lake v Duke of Argyll* (1844) 6 QB 477. See further PARA 278. See also *Rover International Ltd v Cannon Film Sales Ltd* [1987] BCLC 540; revsd on other grounds sub nom *Rover International Ltd v Cannon Film Sales Ltd (No 3)* [1989] 3 All ER 423, [1989] 1 WLR 912, CA.

5 *Braymist Ltd v Wise Finance Co Ltd* [2002] EWCA Civ 127, [2002] Ch 273, [2002] 2 All ER 333.

6 *Phonogram Ltd v Lane* [1982] QB 938, [1981] 3 All ER 182, CA. Much had seemed to turn in the older cases on the manner in which contracts had been signed, although they might more accurately have been stated as turning on issues of the parties' intentions: *Phonogram Ltd v Lane* [1982] QB 938 at 945, [1981] 3 All ER 182 at 188, CA per Oliver LJ. It was argued in *Phonogram Ltd v Lane* [1982] QB 938, [1981] 3 All ER 182, CA, that questions as to the manner of signature were still relevant to what is now the Companies Act 2006 s 51 (see the text and notes 1–5) in view of the words 'subject to any agreement to the contrary'. This view was rejected, since to interpret the statutory provision in that way would defeat the whole purpose of that provision: *Phonogram Ltd v Lane* [1982] QB 938 at 946, [1981] 3 All ER 182 at 188, CA per Oliver LJ. Unless there is a clear exclusion of personal liability, the promoter is personally liable however he expresses his signature: *Phonogram Ltd v Lane* [1982] QB 938 at 944, [1981] 3 All ER 182 at 187, CA per Lord Denning MR.

7 *Re English and Colonial Produce Co Ltd* [1906] 2 Ch 435, CA; *Kelner v Baxter* (1866) LR 2 CP 174; *Re Northumberland Avenue Hotel Co* (1886) 33 ChD 16, CA; *Scott v Lord Ebury* (1867) LR 2 CP 255. A company cannot adopt or ratify a pre-incorporation contract but must contract again on identical terms: *Natal Land and Colonization Co Ltd v Pauline Colliery and Development Syndicate Ltd* [1904] AC 120, PC. See also PARAS 278–279. The issue is not addressed by the statutory provisions.

8 *Giles v Smith* (1847) 11 Jur 334; *Andrews v Ellison* (1821) 6 Moore CP 199; *Gurney v Rawlins* (1836) 2 M & W 87 at 90; *Re Athenaeum Society and Prince of Wales Society, Durham's Case* (1858) 4 K & J 517.

60. Promoters as partners. Promoters associated only to form a company are not in partnership[1]. However, where they incur joint liability, each is liable to make contribution to the extent of his share[2]; and they may be partners if they join together in buying property in order to sell it at a profit to a company which they form to purchase it[3].

1 *Wood v Duke of Argyll* (1844) 6 Man & G 928; *Bright v Hutton, Hutton v Bright* (1852) 3 HL Cas 341 at 368; *Keith Spicer Ltd v Mansell* [1970] 1 All ER 462, [1970] 1 WLR 333, CA. As to the essential characteristics of a partnership see PARTNERSHIP vol 79 (2014) PARA 1 et seq.

2 *Boulter v Peplow* (1850) 9 CB 493; *Batard v Hawes* (1853) 2 E & B 287 at 290 (provisional committee members of projected company are not partners, but liable to contribute as co-contractors); *Edger v Knapp* (1843) 5 Man & G 753 (joint contractors; one having paid debt was entitled to contribution from others; contractors had acted as directors of proposed company); *Mant v Smith* (1859) 4 H & N 324 (taxation by one partner of the bill of a solicitor employed by the partnership).

3 Ie if they carry on the business of acquiring the property and reselling it with a view of profit: see the Partnership Act 1890 s 1; and PARTNERSHIP vol 79 (2014) PARA 1.

61. Liability of several promoters to and for each other. In the absence of an express contract, one of several promoters may not sue another for remuneration for services in connection with the promotion[1]; but a person assisting promoters may sue for remuneration for his services if there is a contract express or implied to pay for them[2].

Promoters are not as such agents for each other, or liable for the other's acts; but an authority to act for each other may be inferred from the terms of a public prospectus or from conduct[3].

1 *Holmes v Higgins* (1822) 1 B & C 74.
2 *Mant v Smith* (1859) 4 H & N 324; *Lucas v Beach* (1840) 1 Man & G 417.
3 *Reynell v Lewis, Wyld v Hopkins* (1846) 15 M & W 517; *McEwan v Campbell* (1857) 2 Macq 499, HL.

62. Circumstances in which promoter's liability terminated. After the dissolution of the company no proceedings may be taken against the promoter on behalf of the company unless the dissolution is set aside[1].

Where a promoter is adjudged bankrupt, a company may prove in his bankruptcy for any secret profits obtained by him[2]. Under the Insolvency Act 1986, his order of discharge releases him from any debt or liability to the company which is provable in the bankruptcy, unless it was a debt he incurred in respect of, or forbearance in respect of which was secured by means of, any fraud or fraudulent breach of trust to which he was a party[3].

Where a promoter has received a secret profit, he cannot, in proceedings by the company or its liquidator to recover the profit, set up the provisions of the Limitation Act 1980 by way of defence[4].

In general, the liability of a promoter has always been enforceable against his estate after his death[5]; since 25 July 1934 all causes of action subsisting against a deceased at his death, except causes of action for defamation, survive against his estate[6].

1 See *Coxon v Gorst* [1891] 2 Ch 73. See also COMPANY AND PARTNERSHIP INSOLVENCY vol 17 (2011) PARA 891.
2 *Re Darby, ex p Brougham* [1911] 1 KB 95. See further *Re Kent County Gas Light and Coke Co Ltd* [1913] 1 Ch 92 (where it was held that the liquidator of a company having proved in the bankruptcy of a promoter for a sum as damages for breach of trust in relation to the company could not, after so electing to prove against the promoter, prove against the joint estate of a firm of which that promoter and another promoter were the partners).
3 See the Insolvency Act 1986 s 281(3); and BANKRUPTCY AND INDIVIDUAL INSOLVENCY vol 5 (2013) PARA 650.
4 See the Limitation Act 1980 s 32(1) (period of limitation postponed in relation to claim by a beneficiary under a trust in respect of any fraud or fraudulent breach of trust to which the trustee was a party or privy or to recover from the trustee trust property or its proceeds in his possession or previously received by him and converted to his use); and LIMITATION PERIODS vol 68 (2008) PARA 1220 et seq. See also *Re Sale Hotel and Botanical Gardens Co Ltd, Hesketh's Case* (1897) 77 LT 681 (revsd on other grounds (1898) 78 LT 368, CA); *Re Sharpe, Re Bennett, Masonic and General Life Assurance Co v Sharpe* [1892] 1 Ch 154 at 172, CA, per Fry LJ. Cf *Tintin Exploration Syndicate Ltd v Sandys* (1947) 177 LT 412.
As to defences founded on unconscionable delay ('laches') see *Lindsay Petroleum Co v Hurd* (1874) LR 5 PC 221 at 239; *Erlanger v New Sombrero Phosphate Co* (1878) 3 App Cas 1218, HL; *Re Sharpe, Re Bennett, Masonic and General Life Assurance Co v Sharpe* [1892] 1 Ch 154 at 168, CA per Lindley LJ; *Concha v Murrieta* (1889) 40 ChD 543 at 553, CA per Cotton LJ (varied on the facts [1892] AC 670, HL).
5 For analogous cases against directors see PARA 631 note 18.
6 See the Law Reform (Miscellaneous Provisions) Act 1934 s 1(1); and WILLS AND INTESTACY vol 103 (2010) PARA 1280.

63. Criminal liability of promoters. Promoters of a company may incur criminal liability in connection with:

(1) an offer to the public of certain transferable securities unless an approved prospectus has been made available to the public before the offer is made[1];

(2) a request to admit certain transferable securities to trading on a regulated market unless an approved prospectus has been made available to the public before the request is made[2]; or

(3) misleading statements or practices with regard to investments[3].

In certain cases, promoters may be indicted for conspiracy[4].

1 See the Financial Services and Markets Act 2000 s 85; and FINANCIAL SERVICES REGULATION vol 50A (2016) PARA 603.

2 See the Financial Services and Markets Act 2000 s 85; and FINANCIAL SERVICES REGULATION vol 50A (2016) PARA 603.

3 See the Financial Services Act 2012 Pt 7 (ss 89–95); and FINANCIAL SERVICES REGULATION vol 50A (2016) PARA 788.

4 *R v Aspinall* (1876) 2 QBD 48, CA.

64. Disqualification of promoters from managing companies. The court[1] may make a disqualification order[2] against a person where he is convicted of an indictable offence (whether on indictment or summarily) in connection with the promotion, formation, management, liquidation or striking off of a company[3], with the receivership of a company's property, or with his being an administrative receiver of a company[4].

The maximum period of disqualification which may be imposed for these purposes is five years (where the disqualification order is made by a court of summary jurisdiction) or (in any other case) 15 years[5].

An application for such an order may be made by the Secretary of State[6], the official receiver or the liquidator or any past or present member or creditor of the company in relation to which the person in question has committed or is alleged to have committed an offence or other default[7].

1 As to the meaning of 'court' for these purposes see PARA 1764 note 1.

2 As to the meaning of 'disqualification order' see PARA 1762.

3 For these purposes, unless the context otherwise requires, 'company' means a company registered under the Companies Act 2006 in Great Britain, or a company that may be wound up under the Insolvency Act 1986 Pt V (ss 220–229) (see COMPANY AND PARTNERSHIP INSOLVENCY vol 17 (2011) PARA 1109 et seq): Company Directors Disqualification Act 1986 s 22(1), (2) (s 22(2) substituted by SI 2009/1941). As to the meaning of 'Great Britain' see PARA 1 note 5. As to registration under the Companies Act 2006 see PARA 104 et seq. As to the appointment of a liquidator see COMPANY AND PARTNERSHIP INSOLVENCY vol 16 (2011) PARA 909.

4 See the Company Directors Disqualification Act 1986 s 2(1); and PARA 1764. As to administrative receivers see COMPANY AND PARTNERSHIP INSOLVENCY vol 16 (2011) PARA 329 et seq.

5 See the Company Directors Disqualification Act 1986 s 2(3); and PARA 1764.

6 As to the Secretary of State see PARA 6.

7 See the Company Directors Disqualification Act 1986 s 16(2); and PARA 1790.

(4) COMPANY FORMATION AND REGISTRATION

(i) Categories of Company

A. PRIVATE COMPANY

65. Private companies and the restrictions on their powers. A 'private company' within the meaning of the Companies Act 2006 is a company[1] that is not a public company[2].

Under the Companies Act 2006, a private company that is limited by shares[3], or is limited by guarantee and having a share capital[4], is prohibited both from making any offer to the public[5] of any securities[6] of the company, and from allotting (or agreeing to allot) any securities of the company with a view to their being offered to the public[7]. Any contravention, or proposed contravention, of this prohibition may be remedied by order[8].

1 As to the meaning of 'company' under the Companies Acts see PARA 21; and as to the meaning of the 'Companies Acts' see PARA 13.
2 See the Companies Act 2006 s 4(1); and PARA 95. For the two major differences between private and public companies see Pt 20 Ch 1 (ss 755–760) (prohibition of public offers by private companies) (see PARA 1255) and Pt 20 Ch 2 (ss 761–767) (minimum share requirement for public companies) (see PARA 67 et seq): see s 4(4); and PARA 95. As to the meaning of 'public company' see PARA 95. As to the required indications in the name of a private limited company see PARA 199 et seq.
3 As to the meanings of 'company limited by shares' and 'private company' see PARA 95; and as to the meaning of 'share' see PARA 1231. See also PARA 71. As to the valuation of shares in an investment fund repackaged as financial instruments see *WestLB AG v Nomura Bank International plc* [2010] EWHC 2863 (Comm), [2010] All ER (D) 136 (Nov); affd [2012] EWCA Civ 495, [2012] All ER (D) 116 (Apr).
4 As to the meaning of 'company limited by guarantee' see PARA 95; and as to the meanings of 'company having a share capital' and 'share capital' see PARA 1231. See also PARA 72.
5 As to the meaning of 'offer to the public' for these purposes see the Companies Act 2006 s 756; and PARA 1255.
6 For these purposes, 'securities' means shares or debentures: see the Companies Act 2006 s 755(5); and PARA 1255. As to the meaning of 'debenture' see PARA 1482.
7 See the Companies Act 2006 ss 755, 760; and PARA 1255.
8 See the Companies Act 2006 ss 757–759; and PARA 1255.

B. PUBLIC COMPANY

(A) Nature and Powers of Public Company

66. Nature and powers of public company: in general. A 'public company' within the meaning of the Companies Act 2006 is a company[1] limited by shares[2], or limited by guarantee and having a share capital[3], being a company[4]:

(1) whose certificate of incorporation[5] states that it is a public company[6]; and
(2) in relation to which the requirements of the Companies Act 2006[7], or the former Companies Acts[8], as to the registration[9] or re-registration of a company as a public company[10] have been complied with on or after 22 December 1980[11].

With effect from 22 December 1980[12], a public company limited by guarantee may not be formed[13].

A company that is registered as a public company on its original incorporation[14] may not do business or exercise any borrowing powers unless the registrar of companies[15] has issued it with a certificate (a 'trading certificate')[16] indicating that he is satisfied that the nominal value[17] of the company's allotted share capital[18] is not less than the authorised minimum[19]. Such a certificate is conclusive evidence that the company is entitled to do business and exercise any borrowing powers[20].

1 As to the meaning of 'company' under the Companies Acts see PARA 21; and as to the meaning of the 'Companies Acts' see PARA 13.
2 As to the meaning of 'company limited by shares' see PARA 95; and as to the meaning of 'share' see PARA 1231. See also see PARA 71.
3 As to the meaning of 'company limited by guarantee' see PARA 95; and as to the meanings of 'company having a share capital' and 'share capital' see PARA 1231. See also PARA 72.
4 See the Companies Act 2006 s 4(2); and PARA 95. For the two major differences between private and public companies see Pt 20 Ch 1 (ss 755–760) (prohibition of public offers by private companies) (see PARA 1255) and Pt 20 Ch 2 (ss 761–767) (minimum share requirement for public companies) (see PARA 67 et seq): see s 4(4); and PARA 95. As to the meaning of 'private company' see PARA 95.
5 As to a company's certificate of incorporation see PARA 114.

6 See the Companies Act 2006 s 4(2)(a); and PARA 95. As to the required indications in the name of a public limited company see PARA 199.
7 References in the company law provisions of the Companies Act 2006 to the requirements of that Act include the requirements of regulations and orders made under it: s 1172. As to the meaning of the 'company law provisions' of the Companies Act 2006 see PARA 13 note 6.
8 As to the meaning of the 'former Companies Acts' see PARA 14 note 1.
9 As to the requirements for company registration under the Companies Act 2006 see PARA 104 et seq.
10 As to the re-registration of a private company as a public company under the Companies Act 2006 see PARAS 168–172.
11 See the Companies Act 2006 s 4(2)(b), (3); and PARA 95. The date of 22 December 1980 referred to in the text is the date on which the corresponding provisions of the Companies Act 1980 (now repealed) came into force. As to the Companies Act 1980 generally see PARA 10.
12 See note 11.
13 This is the effect of the Companies Act 2006 s 5(1), (2) (see PARAS 72, 95) when combined with the definition of a public company as having a share capital: see s 4(2); and PARA 95.
14 Ie registered in accordance with the Companies Act 2006 s 9: see PARA 104.
15 As to the meaning of 'registrar of companies' see PARA 126 note 2.
16 See the Companies Act 2006 s 761(1); and PARA 67.
17 As to the nominal value of shares see PARA 1233.
18 As to the meaning of 'allotted share capital' see PARA 1234.
19 See the Companies Act 2006 s 761(1)–(3); and PARA 67. As to the meaning of 'authorised minimum' see PARA 68.
20 See the Companies Act 2006 s 761(4); and PARA 67.

(B) Share Capital Requirements for Public Companies

67. Minimum share capital requirement for public companies. A company[1] that is a public company[2] must not do business[3] or exercise any borrowing powers[4] unless the registrar of companies[5] has issued it with a certificate (a 'trading certificate')[6]. The registrar must issue a trading certificate if, on an application made to him in accordance with the statutory requirements[7], he is satisfied that the nominal value of the company's allotted share capital[8] is not less than the authorised minimum[9]. An application for such a certificate must:

(1) state that the nominal value of the company's allotted share capital is not less than the authorised minimum[10];
(2) specify the amount, or estimated amount, of the company's preliminary expenses[11];
(3) specify any amount or benefit paid or given, or intended to be paid or given, to any promoter[12] of the company, and the consideration for the payment or benefit[13];
(4) be accompanied by a statement of compliance[14], being a statement that the company meets the requirements for the issue of a trading certificate[15]; and
(5) as from 30 June 2016[16], be accompanied by a statement of the aggregate amount paid up on the shares of the company on account of their nominal value[17].

The registrar may accept the statutory statement of compliance as sufficient evidence of the matters stated in it[18].

A trading certificate has effect from the date on which it is issued and is conclusive evidence that the company is entitled to do business and exercise any borrowing powers[19]. Evidence cannot be received to show that the facts did not warrant the issuing of the certificate[20].

If a company does business or exercises borrowing powers in contravention of the prohibition on doing so without a trading certificate[21], an offence is committed by the company, and by any officer of it who is in default[22].

1 As to the meaning of 'company' under the Companies Acts see PARA 21; and as to the meaning of the 'Companies Acts' see PARA 13.
2 Ie a company that is registered as a public company on its original incorporation rather than by virtue of its re-registration as a public company: see the Companies Act 2006 s 761(1). As to incorporation by registration under the Companies Act 2006 see PARA 104 et seq; and as to the re-registration of a private company as a public company under the Companies Act 2006 see PARAS 168–172. As to the meanings of 'private company' and 'public company' see PARA 95. See also PARAS 65–66.
3 As to the meaning of 'business' generally see PARA 1 note 1.
4 As to a company's borrowing powers see PARA 1442 et seq.
5 As to the meaning of 'registrar of companies' see PARA 126 note 2.
6 Companies Act 2006 s 761(1). A 'trading certificate' is a certificate issued by the registrar of companies under s 761: see s 761(1).
7 Ie in accordance with the Companies Act 2006 s 762 (see the text and notes 10–18): see s 761(2).
8 As to the meaning of 'allotted share capital' see PARA 1234. As to the meaning of 'allotted' see PARA 1280; and as to the meaning of 'share capital' see PARA 1231. A share allotted in pursuance of an employees' share scheme may not be taken into account for these purposes (ie in determining the nominal value of the company's allotted share capital) unless it is paid up as to at least one-quarter of the nominal value of the share, and as to the whole of any premium on the share: Companies Act 2006 s 761(3). As to the meaning of 'share' see PARA 1231. As to the meaning of 'employees' share scheme' see PARA 169 note 20. As to the meaning of 'premium' see PARA 1335. As to the nominal value of shares, and as to paid up shares, see PARA 1233 et seq.
9 Companies Act 2006 s 761(2). As to the 'authorised minimum' in relation to the nominal value of a public company's allotted share capital see PARA 68. At the time that a special resolution is passed, that a private company should be re-registered as a public company, the nominal value of the company's allotted share capital also must be not less than the authorised minimum: see s 91(1)(a); and PARA 169. As to the procedure on application to re-register a private company as a public company see PARA 168.
10 Companies Act 2006 s 762(1)(a).
11 Companies Act 2006 s 762(1)(b).
12 As to promoters see PARA 42 et seq.
13 Companies Act 2006 s 762(1)(c) (amended by the Small Business, Enterprise and Employment Act 2015 s 98(1), (3)(a)).
14 Companies Act 2006 s 762(1)(d). A statement of compliance delivered under s 762 is subject to the disclosure requirements in s 1078: see s 1078(3); and PARA 139.
15 Companies Act 2006 s 762(2).
16 See the Small Business, Enterprise and Employment Act 2015 (Commencement No 4, Transitional and Savings Provisions) Regulations 2016, SI 2016/321, reg 6(f).
17 Companies Act 2006 s 762(1)(e) (added by the Small Business, Enterprise and Employment Act 2015 s 98(1), (3)(b)). See also note 16.
18 Companies Act 2006 s 762(3).
19 Companies Act 2006 s 761(4). As to the conclusiveness of the registrar's certificate see *Re Yolland, Husson and Birkett Ltd, Leicester v Yolland, Husson and Birkett Ltd* [1908] 1 Ch 152, CA. As to the validity of transactions entered into before a company is entitled to commence business or exercise borrowing powers see PARA 69.
20 *Re Yolland, Husson & Birkitt Ltd, Leicester v Yolland, Husson & Birkitt Ltd* [1908] 1 Ch 152, CA.
21 Ie in contravention of the Companies Act 2006 s 761 (see the text and notes 1–9,19): see s 767(1).
22 Companies Act 2006 s 767(1). As to the meaning of 'officer' generally under the Companies Act 2006 see PARA 679; and as to the meaning of 'officer in default' see PARA 316. and every person guilty of such an offence is liable, whether on conviction on indictment or on summary conviction, to a fine: see s 767(2). In the case of liability on summary conviction the fine is one not exceeding the statutory maximum: see s 767(2). By virtue of the Legal Aid, Sentencing and Punishment of Offenders Act 2012 s 85, however, where the offence is committed on or after 12 March 2015, it is punishable by a fine of an unlimited amount. As to the statutory maximum and the powers of magistrates' courts to issue fines on summary conviction see SENTENCING vol 92 (2015) PARA 176.

68. The 'authorised minimum' in relation to the nominal value of a public company's allotted share capital. Subject to any exercise of the power to alter the authorised minimum[1], the 'authorised minimum', in relation to the nominal value of a public company's allotted share capital[2], is £50,000 or the prescribed euro equivalent[3]. The Secretary of State may by order[4] alter the sterling amount of the authorised minimum, and make a corresponding alteration of the prescribed euro equivalent[5].

The initial requirement for a public company to have allotted share capital of a nominal value not less than the authorised minimum[6] must be met either by reference to allotted share capital denominated in sterling or by reference to allotted share capital denominated in euros (but not partly in one and partly in the other)[7]. Whether the requirement is met is determined in the first case by reference to the sterling amount and in the second case by reference to the prescribed euro equivalent[8]. No account is to be taken of any allotted share capital of the company denominated in a currency other than sterling or, as the case may be, euros[9]. If the company could meet the requirement either by reference to share capital denominated in sterling or by reference to share capital denominated in euros, it must elect in its application for a trading certificate or, as the case may be, for re-registration as a public company which is to be the currency by reference to which the matter is determined[10].

The Secretary of State may make provision by regulations as to the application of the authorised minimum in relation to a public company[11] that has shares denominated in more than one currency or in a currency other than sterling or euros[12], that redenominates the whole or part of its allotted share capital[13], or allots new shares[14].

1 Ie subject to any exercise of the power conferred by the Companies Act 2006 s 764 (see the text and notes 4–5): see s 763(6).

2 As to the nominal value of shares see PARA 1233. As to the meaning of 'allotted share capital' see PARA 1234. As to the meaning of 'allotted' see PARA 1280; and as to the meaning of 'share capital' see PARA 1231. See also PARA 67 note 8. As to the meaning of 'public company' see PARA 95; as to the meaning of 'company' under the Companies Acts see PARA 21; and as to the meaning of the 'Companies Acts' see PARA 13. As to public companies see also PARA 66.

3 Companies Act 2006 s 763(1). The Secretary of State may by order, subject to negative resolution procedure (ie the statutory instrument containing the order being subject to annulment in pursuance of a resolution of either House of Parliament), prescribe the amount in euros that is for the time being to be treated as equivalent to the sterling amount of the authorised minimum: see ss 763(2), (5), 1289. This power may be exercised from time to time as appears to the Secretary of State to be appropriate: s 763(3). The amount prescribed is to be determined by applying an appropriate spot rate of exchange to the sterling amount and rounding to the nearest 100 euros: s 763(4). In the Companies Acts, 'prescribed' means prescribed (by order or by regulations) by the Secretary of State: Companies Act 2006 s 1167. As to the making of orders and regulations under the Companies Act 2006 generally see ss 1288–1292. As to the Secretary of State see PARA 6. Partly in exercise of the powers conferred by s 763(2), the Secretary of State has made the Companies (Authorised Minimum) Regulations 2009, SI 2009/2425. Accordingly, for the purposes of the definition of the 'authorised minimum' in the Companies Act 2006 s 763(1), the amount in euros that is to be treated as equivalent to the sterling amount is €57,100: Companies (Authorised Minimum) Regulations 2009, SI 2009/2425, reg 2. This is subject to the transitional provisions and savings in reg 9: see reg 2.

4 Such an order is subject to affirmative resolution procedure (ie the order must not be made unless a draft of the statutory instrument containing it has been laid before Parliament and approved by a resolution of each House of Parliament): see the Companies Act 2006 ss 764(4), 1290.

5 Companies Act 2006 s 764(1). The amount of the prescribed euro equivalent is to be determined by applying an appropriate spot rate of exchange to the sterling amount and rounding to the nearest 100 euros: s 764(2). Such an order that increases the authorised minimum may:

(1) require a public company having an allotted share capital of which the nominal value is less than the amount specified in the order to increase that value to not less than that amount, or to re-register as a private company (s 764(3)(a));

(2) make provision in connection with any such requirement for any of the matters for which provision is made by the Companies Act 2006 relating to a company's registration, re-registration or change of name, to payment for shares

comprised in a company's share capital, and to offers to the public of shares in or debentures of a company, including provision as to the consequences (in criminal law or otherwise) of a failure to comply with any requirement of the order (s 764(3)(b));
(3) provide for any provision of the order to come into force on different days for different purposes (s 764(3)(c)).

As to the meaning of 'debenture' see PARA 1482; as to the meaning of 'private company' see PARA 95; and as to the meaning of 'share' see PARA 1231. As to the requirements for company registration under the Companies Act 2006 see PARA 104 et seq; as to re-registration as a private company under the Companies Act 2006 see PARA 173 et seq; and as to re-registration and its effects generally see PARA 167 et seq. As to change of a company's name see PARAS 216–218. As to payment for shares comprised in a company's share capital see PARA 1302 et seq. As to public offers of a company's securities see PARA 1255 et seq.

6 Ie the requirement in the Companies Act 2006 s 761(2) (see PARA 67) for the issue of a trading certificate, or the requirement in s 91(1)(a) (see PARA 169) for re-registration as a public company: see s 765(1). As to the meaning of 'trading certificate' see PARA 67.
7 Companies Act 2006 s 765(1).
8 Companies Act 2006 s 765(2).
9 Companies Act 2006 s 765(3). See *Re Scandinavian Bank Group plc* [1988] Ch 87 at 104, [1987] 2 All ER 70 at 77 per Harman J (company must have an authorised minimum in prescribed currencies [in 1987, sterling; now, sterling or euros] whatever other capital it may have in other currencies).
10 Companies Act 2006 s 765(4).
11 Companies Act 2006 s 766(1). The regulations may make provision as to the currencies, exchange rates and dates by reference to which it is to be determined whether the nominal value of the company's allotted share capital is less than the authorised minimum: s 766(2). Any regulations made under s 766 are subject to negative resolution procedure (ie the statutory instrument containing the regulations is subject to annulment in pursuance of a resolution of either House of Parliament): ss 766(6), 1289. Any such regulations have effect subject to s 765 (see the text and notes 6–10): s 766(5). In exercise of the powers conferred by s 766(1)(a) (see the text and note 12) and by s 766(2), the Secretary of State has made the Companies (Authorised Minimum) Regulations 2009, SI 2009/2425: see regs 3–7, providing for the application of the authorised minimum requirement for the purposes of the Companies Act 2006 s 650 (see PARA 1381), s 662(2) (see PARA 1387), s 667 (see PARA 1391), ss 757, 758 (see PARA 1255), and Pt 30 (ss 994–999) (protection of members against unfair prejudice) (see PARA 657 et seq). See also the Companies (Authorised Minimum) Regulations 2008, SI 2008/729: see regs 3–5, 7, providing for the application of the authorised minimum requirement for the purposes of the Companies Act 1985 ss 137–139, 146, 147(3), (4), 149(2) (all now repealed).
12 Companies Act 2006 s 766(1)(a) (substituted by SI 2011/1265).
13 Companies Act 2006 s 766(1)(b). The regulations may provide that, where a company has redenominated the whole or part of its allotted share capital, and the effect of the redenomination is that the nominal value of the company's allotted share capital is less than the authorised minimum, the company must re-register as a private company: s 766(3). Regulations under s 766(3) may make provision corresponding to any provision made by ss 664–667 (re-registration as private company in consequence of cancellation of shares) (see PARAS 1390–1391): s 766(4). As to the redenomination of share capital see PARA 1354 et seq.
14 Companies Act 2006 s 766(1)(c).

69. Transactions entered into without a trading certificate. If a company[1] does business[2] or exercises borrowing powers[3] in contravention of the prohibition on doing so without a trading certificate[4], any such contravention does not affect the validity of a transaction entered into by the company[5]. However, if a company:

(1) enters into a transaction in contravention of that prohibition[6]; and
(2) fails to comply with its obligations in connection with the transaction within 21 days from being called on to do so[7],

the directors of the company[8] are jointly and severally liable to indemnify any other party to the transaction in respect of any loss or damage suffered by him by reason of the company's failure to comply with its obligations[9].

1 Ie a company that is registered as a public company on its original incorporation rather than by virtue of its re-registration as a public company: see the Companies Act 2006 s 761(1); and PARA 67. As to the meaning of 'company' under the Companies Acts see PARA 21; and as to the meaning of the 'Companies Acts' see PARA 13. As to incorporation by registration under

the Companies Act 2006 see PARA 104 et seq; and as to the re-registration of a private company as a public company under the Companies Act 2006 see PARAS 168–172. As to the meanings of 'private company' and 'public company' see PARA 95. See also PARAS 65–66.
2 As to the meaning of 'business' generally see PARA 1 note 1.
3 As to a company's borrowing powers see PARA 1442 et seq.
4 Ie in contravention of the Companies Act 2006 s 761 (see PARA 67): see s 767(1), (3); and PARA 67. As to the meaning of 'trading certificate' see PARA 67.
5 See the Companies Act 2006 s 767(3).
6 Companies Act 2006 s 767(3)(a). Head (1) in the text refers to a transaction entered into in contravention of s 761 (see PARA 67): see s 767(3)(a).
7 Companies Act 2006 s 767(3)(b).
8 As to the meaning of 'director' see PARA 512.
9 Companies Act 2006 s 767(3). The directors who are so liable are those who were directors at the time the company entered into the transaction: s 767(4).

(C) Quoted, Unquoted and Traded Companies

70. Meanings of 'quoted company', 'unquoted company' and 'traded company' in the Companies Act 2006. The terms 'quoted company' and 'unquoted company' are defined in the Companies Act 2006 for the purposes of the provisions relating to accounts and reports[1]; and the term 'quoted company', as so defined, is applied for the purposes of the provisions relating to resolutions and meetings of the company[2] and the provisions relating to certain transactions with directors of quoted companies which require the approval of members of the company[3].

Accordingly, a 'quoted company' means a company[4] whose equity share capital[5] either has been included in the official list in accordance with the provisions of Part VI of the Financial Services and Markets Act 2000[6] or is officially listed in an EEA state[7], or is admitted to dealing on either the New York Stock Exchange or the exchange known as Nasdaq[8].

An 'unquoted company' means a company that is not a quoted company[9].

If a company is to obtain admission to the official list, it must undertake to observe certain obligations once its securities have been admitted to listing[10].

For the purposes of the provisions of the Companies Act 2006 which govern resolutions and meetings of the company[11], a 'traded company' is defined to mean a company any shares of which carry rights to vote at general meetings and are admitted to trading on a regulated market in an EEA state by or with the consent of the company[12].

1 Ie by virtue of the Companies Act 2006 s 385, which defines 'quoted company' and 'unquoted company' for the purposes of Pt 15 (ss 380–474) (see PARA 765 et seq): see PARA 770.
2 Ie by virtue of the Companies Act 2006 s 361, which applies the meaning of 'quoted company' in Pt 15 for the purposes of Pt 13 (ss 281–361) (see PARA 689 et seq).
3 Ie by virtue of the Companies Act 2006 s 226A(1), which applies the meaning of 'quoted company' in Pt 15 for the purposes of Pt 10 Ch 4A (ss 226A–226F) (see PARA 601 et seq).
4 As to the meaning of 'company' under the Companies Acts see PARA 21; and as to the meaning of the 'Companies Acts' see PARA 13.
5 As to the meaning of 'equity share capital' see PARA 1236.
6 Ie in accordance with the Financial Services and Markets Act 2000 Pt VI (ss 73A–103) (official listing): see FINANCIAL SERVICES REGULATION vol 50A (2016) PARA 593 et seq. For these purposes, 'official list' has the meaning given by the Financial Services and Markets Act 2000 s 103(1) (see FINANCIAL SERVICES REGULATION vol 50A (2016) PARA 593): see the Companies Act 2006 s 385(2); and PARA 769. As to the meaning of the 'official list' also see PARA 1258 note 6; and FINANCIAL SERVICES REGULATION vol 50A (2016) PARA 593 et seq.
7 As to the meaning of 'EEA state' see PARA 26 note 5.
8 See the Companies Act 2006 s 385(2); and PARA 769.
9 See the Companies Act 2006 s 385(3); and PARA 769.
10 See PARA 1255 et seq.
11 Ie in the Companies Act 2006 Pt 13 (see PARA 689 et seq).

12 See the Companies Act 2006 s 360C; and PARA 702. As to the meaning of 'share' see PARA 1231; as to the meaning of 'regulated market' see PARA 335 note 11; and as to rights attached to classes of shares generally see PARA 1246 et seq.

C. COMPANY LIMITED BY SHARES

71. Meaning of a company limited by shares. A company[1] is a 'limited company' if the liability of its members[2] is limited by its constitution[3].

The memorandum of association[4] of a company limited by shares[5] is a memorandum stating that the subscribers[6] wish to form a company under the Companies Act 2006, and that they agree to become members of the company and to take at least one share each[7].

The memorandum must be authenticated by each subscriber and must be in the prescribed form[8].

There is no provision in the Companies Act 2006 for the memorandum of association to be amended[9].

1 As to the meaning of 'company' under the Companies Acts see PARA 21; and as to the meaning of the 'Companies Acts' see PARA 13.

2 As to the meaning of 'member' see PARA 323. As to membership of a company generally see PARA 323 et seq.

3 See the Companies Act 2006 s 3(1); and PARA 95. As to the meaning of references to a company's constitution see PARA 226.

4 As to the meaning of 'memorandum of association' see PARA 97.

5 Ie being a company that is to have a share capital: see the Companies Act 2006 s 8(1); and PARA 97. As to the meaning of 'company limited by shares' see PARA 95; and as to the meanings of 'company having a share capital', 'share capital' and 'share' see PARA 1231. As to the required indications in the name of a limited company see PARA 199 et seq.

6 As to subscribers to the memorandum see PARA 97.

7 See the Companies Act 2006 s 8(1); and PARA 97. As to shareholders generally see PARA 323 et seq. If no number is written after his name, a subscriber is liable to pay for one share at least: *Portal v Emmens* (1876) 1 CPD 664 at 667, CA, per Jessel MR. As to the other requirements that must be met before a company is duly formed (including delivery of the memorandum) see PARA 95 et seq.

8 See the Companies Act 2006 s 8(2); and PARA 97. In relation to the authentication of a document under the Companies Act 2006 see s 1146; and PARA 750 et seq.

In the Companies Acts, 'prescribed' means prescribed (by order or by regulations) by the Secretary of State: Companies Act 2006 s 1167. As to the making of orders and regulations under the Companies Act 2006 generally see ss 1288–1292. As to the Secretary of State see PARA 6. Partly in exercise of the powers conferred by s 8(2), the Secretary of State has made the Companies (Registration) Regulations 2008, SI 2008/3014. Accordingly, for the purposes of the Companies Act 2006 s 8, the memorandum of association of a company having a share capital must be in the form set out in the Companies (Registration) Regulations 2008, SI 2008/3014, reg 2(a), Sch 1. For existing companies (see PARA 229), the prescribed form of memorandum for a company limited by shares is given in the Companies (Tables A to F) Regulations 1985, SI 1985/805, reg 2, Schedule Table B (private company limited by shares) and in Schedule Table F (public company limited by shares). As to the meanings of 'private company' and 'public company' see PARA 95.

9 Cf the articles of association which can be so amended: see PARA 231 et seq. The effect of this is that the memorandum of association becomes an historical document and all provisions concerning the day-to-day management of the company come to be included in the articles of association.

D. COMPANY LIMITED BY GUARANTEE

72. Meaning of a company limited by guarantee. A company[1] is a 'limited company' if the liability of its members[2] is limited by its constitution[3].

The memorandum of association[4] of a company limited by guarantee[5] is a memorandum stating that the subscribers[6] wish to form a company under the Companies Act 2006, and that they agree to become members of the company[7].

The memorandum must be authenticated by each subscriber and must be in the prescribed form[8]. There is no provision in the Companies Act 2006 for the memorandum of association to be amended[9].

With effect from 22 December 1980[10], a company cannot be formed as, or become, a company limited by guarantee with a share capital[11]. Nor may a public company limited by guarantee be formed as from that date[12].

Under the Companies Act 2006, a private company that is limited by guarantee and having a share capital is prohibited both from making any offer to the public[13] of any securities of the company, and from allotting (or agreeing to allot) any securities of the company with a view to their being offered to the public[14].

1 As to the meaning of 'company' under the Companies Acts see PARA 21; and as to the meaning of the 'Companies Acts' see PARA 13.

2 As to the meaning of 'member' see PARA 323. As to membership of a company generally see PARA 323 et seq.

3 See the Companies Act 2006 s 3(1); and PARA 95. As to the meaning of references to a company's constitution see PARA 226.

4 As to the meaning of 'memorandum of association' see PARA 97.

5 As to the meaning of 'company limited by guarantee' see PARA 95.

6 As to subscribers to the memorandum see PARA 97.

7 See the Companies Act 2006 s 8(1); and PARA 97. As to the other requirements that must be met before a company is duly formed (including delivery of the memorandum) see PARA 95 et seq. As to shareholders generally see PARA 323 et seq. Companies that are limited by guarantee and have a share capital are historical entities (see the text and notes 10–11) and accordingly the requirements of s 8 regarding companies having a share capital have no application to companies limited by guarantee that are formed under the Companies Act 2006. Previously, under the Companies Act 1948 s 2(4) (repealed), if the company had a share capital, the memorandum had also to state the amount of the share capital with which the company proposed to be registered and the division thereof into shares of a fixed amount, and each subscriber had to write opposite his name the number of shares he took, not being less than one share. As to the meanings of 'company having a share capital', 'share capital' and 'share' see PARA 1231.

A 'commonhold association' is a private company limited by guarantee the memorandum of which states that an object of the company is to exercise the functions of a commonhold association in relation to specified commonhold land: see COMMONHOLD vol 13 (2009) PARA 305.

8 See the Companies Act 2006 s 8(2); and PARA 97. In relation to the authentication of a document under the Companies Act 2006 see s 1146; and PARA 750 et seq.

In the Companies Acts, 'prescribed' means prescribed (by order or by regulations) by the Secretary of State: Companies Act 2006 s 1167. As to the making of orders and regulations under the Companies Act 2006 generally see ss 1288–1292. As to the Secretary of State see PARA 6. Partly in exercise of the powers conferred by s 8(2), the Secretary of State has made the Companies (Registration) Regulations 2008, SI 2008/3014. Accordingly, for the purposes of the Companies Act 2006 s 8, the memorandum of association of a company not having a share capital must be in the form set out in the Companies (Registration) Regulations 2008, SI 2008/3014, reg 2(b), Sch 2. For existing companies (see PARA 229), the prescribed form of memorandum for a company limited by guarantee is given in the Companies (Tables A to F) Regulations 1985, SI 1985/805, reg 2, Schedule Table C (company limited by guarantee and not having a share capital), in Schedule Table D Pt I (public company limited by guarantee and having a share capital) and in Schedule Table D Pt II (private company limited by guarantee and having a share capital). As to the meanings of 'private company' and 'public company' see PARA 95.

9 Cf the articles of association which can be so amended: see PARA 231 et seq. The effect of this is that the memorandum of association becomes an historical document and all provisions concerning the day-to-day management of the company come to be included in the articles of association.

10 Ie the date on which the corresponding provisions of the Companies Act 1980 (now repealed) came into force. As to the Companies Act 1980 generally see PARA 10.

11 Companies Act 2006 s 5(1), (2)(a).

12 This is the effect of the Companies Act 2006 s 5(1), (2) when combined with the definition of a public company as having a share capital: see s 4(2); and PARA 66.

13 As to the meaning of 'offer to the public' for these purposes see the Companies Act 2006 s 756; and PARA 1255.

14 See the Companies Act 2006 ss 755, 760; and PARA 1255.

73. Effect of dividing undertaking of company limited by guarantee into shares or interests. For the purpose of the provisions of the Companies Act 2006 relating to a company limited by guarantee[1] that has been registered on or after 1 January 1901[2], any provision in the constitution[3] of such a company that purports to divide the undertaking of the company into shares[4] or interests is to be treated as a provision for a share capital[5], and this applies whether or not the nominal value[6] or number of the shares or interests is specified by the provision[7].

1 As to the meaning of 'company' under the Companies Acts see PARA 21; and as to the meaning of the 'Companies Acts' see PARA 13. As to the meaning of 'company limited by guarantee' see PARA 95. See also PARA 72.
2 Ie the date on which the Companies Act 1900 (repealed) came into force. See further note 7.
3 As to the meaning of references to a company's constitution see PARA 226.
4 As to the meaning of 'share' see PARA 1231.
5 As to the meaning of 'share capital' see PARA 1231.
6 As to the nominal value of shares see PARA 1233.
7 See the Companies Act 2006 s 5(3). A company limited by guarantee and not having a share capital, registered before 1 January 1901, could, by special resolution, divide its undertaking into a specified number of shares or interests of no defined or fixed monetary amount, each share or interest being merely a certain proportion of the whole undertaking: *Malleson v General Mineral Patents Syndicate Ltd* [1894] 3 Ch 538.

E. UNLIMITED COMPANY

74. Meaning of 'unlimited company'. A company[1] is an 'unlimited company' if there is no limit on the liability of its members[2].

The memorandum of association[3] of an unlimited company is a memorandum stating that the subscribers[4] wish to form a company under the Companies Act 2006, that they agree to become members of the company and, in the case of a company that is to have a share capital[5], that they agree to take at least one share each[6].

The memorandum must be authenticated by each subscriber and must be in the prescribed form[7].

There is no provision in the Companies Act 2006 for the memorandum of association to be amended[8].

1 As to the meaning of 'company' under the Companies Acts see PARA 21; and as to the meaning of the 'Companies Acts' see PARA 13.
2 See the Companies Act 2006 s 3(4); and PARA 95. As to the meaning of 'member' see PARA 323. As to membership of a company generally see PARA 323 et seq.
3 As to the meaning of 'memorandum of association' see PARA 97.
4 As to subscribers to the memorandum see PARA 97.
5 As to the meanings of 'company having a share capital', 'share capital' and 'share' see PARA 1231.
6 See the Companies Act 2006 s 8(1); and PARA 97. As to the other requirements that must be met before a company is duly formed (including delivery of the memorandum) see PARA 95 et seq.
7 See the Companies Act 2006 s 8(2); and PARA 97. In relation to the authentication of a document under the Companies Act 2006 see s 1146; and PARA 750 et seq.

In the Companies Acts, 'prescribed' means prescribed (by order or by regulations) by the Secretary of State: Companies Act 2006 s 1167. As to the making of orders and regulations under the Companies Act 2006 generally see ss 1288–1292. As to the Secretary of State see PARA 6. Partly in exercise of the powers conferred by s 8(2), the Secretary of State has made the Companies (Registration) Regulations 2008, SI 2008/3014. Accordingly, for the purposes of the Companies Act 2006 s 8, the memorandum of association of a company having a share capital must be in the form set out in the Companies (Registration) Regulations 2008, SI 2008/3014, reg 2(a), Sch 1, and the memorandum of association of a company not having a share capital must be in the form set out in reg 2(b), Sch 2. For existing companies (see PARA 229), the prescribed form of memorandum for an unlimited company having a share capital is given in the Companies (Tables A to F) Regulations 1985, SI 1985/805, reg 2, Schedule Table E (an unlimited company having a share capital).

8 Cf the articles of association which can be so amended: see PARA 231 et seq. The effect of this is that the memorandum of association becomes an historical document and all provisions concerning the day-to-day management of the company come to be included in the articles of association.

F. COMMUNITY INTEREST COMPANIES

(A) Community Interest Companies: Introduction

75. Becoming a community interest company. In accordance with Part 2 of the Companies (Audit, Investigations and Community Enterprise) Act 2004[1]:

(1) a company limited by shares[2] or a company limited by guarantee and not having a share capital[3] may be formed as or become a community interest company[4]; and

(2) a company limited by guarantee and having a share capital may become a community interest company[5].

However, a community interest company established for charitable purposes is to be treated as not being so established[6].

The other provisions of the Companies Acts[7] have effect subject to Part 2 of the 2004 Act[8].

1 Ie in accordance with the Companies (Audit, Investigations and Community Enterprise) Act 2004 Pt 2 (ss 26–63) (community interest companies): see s 26(2); and the Companies Act 2006 s 6(1).
2 As to the meaning of 'company' under the Companies Acts see PARA 21; and as to the meaning of the 'Companies Acts' see PARA 13. As to the meaning of 'company limited by shares' see PARA 95; and as to the meaning of 'share' see PARA 1231. See also PARA 71.
3 As to the meaning of 'company limited by guarantee' see PARA 95; and as to the meanings of 'company having a share capital' and 'share capital' see PARA 1231. See also PARA 72.
4 Companies (Audit, Investigations and Community Enterprise) Act 2004 s 26(2)(a); Companies Act 2006 s 6(1)(a). The community interest company was a new type of company introduced by the Companies (Audit, Investigations and Community Enterprise) Act 2004: see s 26(1).
5 Companies (Audit, Investigations and Community Enterprise) Act 2004 s 26(2)(b); Companies Act 2006 s 6(1)(b).
6 Companies (Audit, Investigations and Community Enterprise) Act 2004 s 26(3). Accordingly, such a company is not an English charity: s 26(3)(a) (amended by SI 2007/1093). For these purposes, 'English charity' means a charity as defined by the Charities Act 2011 s 1(1) (see CHARITIES vol 8 (2015) PARA 1): see the Companies (Audit, Investigations and Community Enterprise) Act 2004 s 63(1) (definition added by SI 2007/1093; amended by the Charities Act 2011 Sch 7 Pt 2 para 99).
7 Ie apart from the Companies Act 2006 s 6: see s 6(2).
8 Companies Act 2006 s 6(2).

76. Regulator of Community Interest Companies. The Secretary of State[1] must appoint a person to be the Regulator[2], who has such functions relating to community interest companies as are conferred or imposed by or by virtue of the Companies (Audit, Investigations and Community Enterprise) Act 2004 or any other enactment[3].

The Regulator must adopt an approach to the discharge of those functions which is based on good regulatory practice[4], that is an approach adopted having regard to:

(1) the likely impact on those who may be affected by the discharge of those functions[5];

(2) the outcome of consultations with, and with organisations representing, community interest companies and others with relevant experience[6]; and

(3) the desirability of using the Regulator's resources in the most efficient and economic way[7].

The Regulator may issue guidance, or otherwise provide assistance, about any matter relating to community interest companies[8]; and the Secretary of State may require the Regulator to issue guidance or otherwise provide assistance about any matter relating to community interest companies which is specified by the Secretary of State[9]. Any guidance so issued must be such that it is readily accessible to, and capable of being easily understood by, those at whom it is aimed[10]; and any other assistance so provided must be provided in the manner which the Regulator considers is most likely to be helpful to those to whom it is provided[11].

A public authority[12] may disclose to the Regulator, for any purpose connected with the exercise of the Regulator's functions, information received by the authority in connection with its functions[13]; and the Regulator may disclose to a public authority any information received by the Regulator in connection with the functions of the Regulator, either for a purpose connected with the exercise of those functions[14], or for a purpose connected with the exercise by the authority of its functions[15]. In deciding whether to disclose information to a public authority in a country or territory outside the United Kingdom[16], the Regulator must have regard to the considerations listed in the Enterprise Act 2002[17] regarding overseas disclosures[18].

The powers to disclose information conferred in this way on a public authority[19] and on the Regulator[20] are subject to any restriction on disclosure imposed by or by virtue of an enactment[21], and any express restriction on disclosure subject to which information was supplied[22]. Information also may be disclosed in this way[23] subject to a restriction on its further disclosure[24]. A person who discloses information in contravention of any restriction so imposed[25] is guilty of an offence[26], and liable on summary conviction to a fine not exceeding level 3 on the standard scale[27]. However, a prosecution for such an offence may be instituted in England and Wales[28] only with the consent of the Regulator or the Director of Public Prosecutions[29]. If any relevant offence under the Companies (Audit, Investigations and Community Enterprise) Act 2004[30] committed by a body corporate is proved[31] either to have been committed with the consent or connivance of an officer[32], or to be attributable to any neglect on the part of an officer[33], the officer as well as the body corporate is guilty of the offence and liable to be proceeded against and punished accordingly[34].

1 As to the Secretary of State see PARA 6.

2 Companies (Audit, Investigations and Community Enterprise) Act 2004 s 27(2). The officer known as the Regulator of Community Interest Companies is referred to in Pt 2 (ss 26–63) as the 'Regulator': see ss 27(1), 63(1). Further provision about the Regulator is made (see s 27(8)) in relation to:
   (1) the Regulator's terms of appointment (Sch 3 para 1);
   (2) remuneration and pensions (Sch 3 para 2);
   (3) staff (Sch 3 paras 3–4 (Sch 3 para 4 substituted by the Charities Act 2011 Sch 7 Pt 2 para 100));
   (4) delegation of functions (Companies (Audit, Investigations and Community Enterprise) Act 2004 Sch 3 para 5);
   (5) finance (Sch 3 para 6); and
   (6) reports and other information (Sch 3 para 7).

3 Companies (Audit, Investigations and Community Enterprise) Act 2004 s 27(3). As to community interest companies see PARA 75.

4 Companies (Audit, Investigations and Community Enterprise) Act 2004 s 27(4).

5 Companies (Audit, Investigations and Community Enterprise) Act 2004 s 27(4)(a).

6 Companies (Audit, Investigations and Community Enterprise) Act 2004 s 27(4)(b).

7 Companies (Audit, Investigations and Community Enterprise) Act 2004 s 27(4)(c).

8 Companies (Audit, Investigations and Community Enterprise) Act 2004 s 27(5).

9 Companies (Audit, Investigations and Community Enterprise) Act 2004 s 27(6).

10 Companies (Audit, Investigations and Community Enterprise) Act 2004 s 27(7).

11 Companies (Audit, Investigations and Community Enterprise) Act 2004 s 27(7).

12 For these purposes, 'public authority' means a person or body having functions of a public nature: Companies (Audit, Investigations and Community Enterprise) Act 2004 s 59(11).
13 Companies (Audit, Investigations and Community Enterprise) Act 2004 s 59(4).
14 Companies (Audit, Investigations and Community Enterprise) Act 2004 s 59(5)(a).
15 Companies (Audit, Investigations and Community Enterprise) Act 2004 s 59(5)(b).
16 As to the meaning of 'United Kingdom' see PARA 1 note 5.
17 Ie in the Enterprise Act 2002 s 243(6) (see COMPETITION vol 18 (2009) PARA 333), but as if the reference to information of a kind to which s 237 of that Act applies were to information of the kind the Regulator is considering disclosing: see the Companies (Audit, Investigations and Community Enterprise) Act 2004 s 59(6).
18 Companies (Audit, Investigations and Community Enterprise) Act 2004 s 59(6).
19 Ie in the Companies (Audit, Investigations and Community Enterprise) Act 2004 s 59(4) (see the text and notes 12–13): see s 59(7).
20 Ie in the Companies (Audit, Investigations and Community Enterprise) Act 2004 s 59(5) (see the text and notes 14–15): see s 59(7).
21 Companies (Audit, Investigations and Community Enterprise) Act 2004 s 59(7)(a).
22 Companies (Audit, Investigations and Community Enterprise) Act 2004 s 59(7)(b).
23 Ie under the Companies (Audit, Investigations and Community Enterprise) Act 2004 s 59(4), (5) (see the text and notes 12–15): see s 59(8).
24 Companies (Audit, Investigations and Community Enterprise) Act 2004 s 59(8).
25 Ie imposed under the Companies (Audit, Investigations and Community Enterprise) Act 2004 s 59(8) (see the text and notes 23–24): see s 59(9).
26 Companies (Audit, Investigations and Community Enterprise) Act 2004 s 59(9).
27 Companies (Audit, Investigations and Community Enterprise) Act 2004 s 59(10). As to the standard scale and the powers of magistrates' courts to issue fines on summary conviction see SENTENCING vol 92 (2015) PARA 176.
28 As to the meanings of 'England' and 'Wales' see PARA 1 note 5.
29 Companies (Audit, Investigations and Community Enterprise) Act 2004 s 59(9)(a) (substituted by SI 2007/1093). As to the Director of Public Prosecutions see CRIMINAL PROCEDURE vol 27 (2015) PARAS 25, 30 et seq.
30 Ie an offence under the Companies (Audit, Investigations and Community Enterprise) Act 2004 s 48 (see PARA 91), s 59 (see the text and notes 12–29) or s 42(3), Sch 7 para 5 (see PARA 85): see s 60(1) (amended by SI 2009/1941).
31 Companies (Audit, Investigations and Community Enterprise) Act 2004 s 60(1) (as amended: see note 30).
32 Companies (Audit, Investigations and Community Enterprise) Act 2004 s 60(1)(a). For these purposes, 'officer' means a director, manager, secretary or other similar officer of the body corporate, or a person purporting to act in any such capacity (s 60(2)); and 'director' includes a shadow director and, if the affairs of a body corporate are managed by its members, means a member of the body (s 60(3)). As to shadow directors see PARA 513.
33 Companies (Audit, Investigations and Community Enterprise) Act 2004 s 60(1)(b).
34 Companies (Audit, Investigations and Community Enterprise) Act 2004 s 60(1).

77. Appeal Officer for community interest companies. The Secretary of State[1] must appoint a person to be the Appeal Officer[2], who has the function of determining appeals against decisions and orders of the Regulator[3] which under or by virtue of the Companies (Audit, Investigations and Community Enterprise) Act 2004 or any other enactment lie to the Appeal Officer[4].

An appeal to the Appeal Officer against a decision or order of the Regulator may be brought on the ground that the Regulator made a material error of law or fact[5].

On such an appeal, the Appeal Officer must dismiss the appeal[6], allow the appeal[7], or remit the case to the Regulator[8].

Where a case is remitted, the Regulator must reconsider it in accordance with any rulings of law and findings of fact made by the Appeal Officer[9].

1 As to the Secretary of State see PARA 6.
2 Companies (Audit, Investigations and Community Enterprise) Act 2004 s 28(2). The officer known as the Appeal Officer for Community Interest Companies is referred to in Pt 2 (ss 26–63) as the 'Appeal Officer': see ss 28(1), 63(1). Further provision about the Appeal Officer is made (see s 28(7)) in relation to:
  (1) the Appeal Officer's terms of appointment (Sch 4 para 1);

(2) remuneration and pensions (Sch 4 para 2); and
(3) finance (Sch 4 para 3).

Regulations may make provision about the practice and procedure to be followed by the Appeal Officer; and such regulations may in particular impose time limits for bringing appeals: Sch 4 para 4. In exercise of the powers conferred by Sch 4 para 4, the Secretary of State has made the Community Interest Company Regulations 2005, SI 2005/1788, Pt 11 (regs 37–42) (reg 38 amended by SI 2007/1093). Provision is made in relation to:

(a) time limits for appeals (see the Community Interest Company Regulations 2005, SI 2005/1788,reg 37);
(b) the notice of appeal (see reg 38 (as so amended));
(c) appeal procedure etc (see reg 39);
(d) determination of the appeal (see reg 40);
(e) dismissal of an appeal (see reg 41); and
(f) the Appeal Officer's duty to give reasons (see reg 42).

3 As to the Regulator see PARA 76.
4 Companies (Audit, Investigations and Community Enterprise) Act 2004 s 28(3).
5 Companies (Audit, Investigations and Community Enterprise) Act 2004 s 28(4). See also note 2 heads (a)–(d).
6 Companies (Audit, Investigations and Community Enterprise) Act 2004 s 28(5)(a). See also note 2 heads (e), (f).
7 Companies (Audit, Investigations and Community Enterprise) Act 2004 s 28(5)(b). See also note 2 head (f).
8 Companies (Audit, Investigations and Community Enterprise) Act 2004 s 28(5)(c). See also note 2 head (f).
9 Companies (Audit, Investigations and Community Enterprise) Act 2004 s 28(6).

78. Official Property Holder for community interest companies. The Regulator[1] must appoint a member of his staff[2] to be the Official Property Holder[3], who has such functions relating to property of community interest companies[4] as are conferred or imposed by or by virtue of the Companies (Audit, Investigations and Community Enterprise) Act 2004 or any other enactment[5].

1 As to the Regulator see PARA 76.
2 As to the Regulator's staff see the Companies (Audit, Investigations and Community Enterprise) Act 2004 Sch 3 paras 3–4; and PARA 76.
3 Companies (Audit, Investigations and Community Enterprise) Act 2004 s 29(2). The officer known as the Official Property Holder for Community Interest Companies is referred to in Pt 2 (ss 26–63) as the 'Official Property Holder': see ss 29(1), 63(1). Further provision about the Official Property Holder is made (see s 29(4)) in relation to:

(1) status (Sch 5 para 1);
(2) relationship with the Regulator (Sch 5 para 2);
(3) the effect of a vacancy (Sch 5 para 3);
(4) property (Sch 5 para 4);
(5) finance (Sch 5 para 5); and
(6) reports (Sch 5 para 6).

4 As to community interest companies see PARA 75.
5 Companies (Audit, Investigations and Community Enterprise) Act 2004 s 29(3).

(B) *Statutory Requirements for Community Interest Companies*

79. Eligibility to form a community interest company. A company is eligible to be formed as a community interest company[1] if:

(1) its articles[2] comply with the statutory requirements that are so imposed[3];
(2) its proposed name complies with the relevant statutory requirements[4]; and
(3) the Regulator[5], having regard to the application and accompanying documents and any other relevant considerations, considers that the company will satisfy the community interest test and is not an excluded company[6].

1 As to community interest companies see PARA 75.

2 As to a community interest company's articles of association see PARA 98; and as to a company's articles of association generally see PARA 227 et seq.
3 Companies (Audit, Investigations and Community Enterprise) Act 2004 s 36A(2)(a) (s 36A added by SI 2009/1941). Head (1) in the text refers to the requirements imposed by and by virtue of the Companies (Audit, Investigations and Community Enterprise) Act 2004 s 32 (see PARA 98): see s 36A(2)(a) (as so added).
4 Companies (Audit, Investigations and Community Enterprise) Act 2004 s 36A(2)(b) (as added: see note 3). Head (2) in the text refers to the requirements of s 33 (see PARA 202): see s 36A(2)(b) (as so added).
5 As to the Regulator see PARA 76.
6 Companies (Audit, Investigations and Community Enterprise) Act 2004 s 36A(2)(c) (as added: see note 3). As to the community interest test and excluded companies see PARA 80.

80. Community interest test and excluded companies. For the purposes of the statutory provisions which govern community interest companies[1], a company satisfies the community interest test if a reasonable person might consider that its activities are being carried on for the benefit of the community[2]. An object stated in the articles of association[3] of the company is a community interest object of the company if a reasonable person might consider that the carrying on of activities by the company in furtherance of the object is for the benefit of the community[4].

Regulations may provide that activities of a description prescribed by the regulations are to be treated as being, or as not being, activities which a reasonable person might consider are activities carried on for the benefit of the community[5].

A company is an excluded company if it is a company of a description prescribed by regulations[6].

1 Ie for the purposes of the Companies (Audit, Investigations and Community Enterprise) Act 2004 Pt 2 (ss 26–63) (community interest companies): see s 35(1). As to community interest companies see PARA 75.
2 Companies (Audit, Investigations and Community Enterprise) Act 2004 s 35(1), (2). Accordingly, the term 'community interest test' is to be construed in accordance with s 35(2): see s 63(1).

For these purposes, 'community' includes a section of the community (whether in the United Kingdom or anywhere else); and regulations may make provision about what does, does not or may constitute a section of the community: s 35(5) (amended by SI 2007/1093). As to the making of regulations under the Companies (Audit, Investigations and Community Enterprise) Act 2004 generally see s 62 (amended by SI 2009/1941). In exercise of the powers conferred by s 35(4)–(6), the Secretary of State has made the Community Interest Company Regulations 2005, SI 2005/1788, Pt 2 (regs 3-5) (reg 3 amended by SI 2007/1093; the Community Interest Company Regulations 2005, SI 2005/1788, reg 5 substituted by SI 2009/1942). Provision is made in relation to:

(1) political activities which are not to be treated as being carried on for the benefit of the community (Community Interest Company Regulations 2005, SI 2005/1788, reg 3 (as so amended));
(2) other activities which are not to be treated as being carried on for the benefit of the community (reg 4); and
(3) groups of individuals who may constitute a section of the community for the purposes of the community interest test (reg 5) (as so substituted).

See also note 6. As to the Secretary of State see PARA 6. As to the meaning of 'United Kingdom' see PARA 1 note 5.
3 As to a community interest company's articles of association see PARA 98; and as to a company's articles of association generally see PARA 227 et seq.
4 Companies (Audit, Investigations and Community Enterprise) Act 2004 s 35(3) (amended by SI 2009/1941). Accordingly, the term 'community interest object' is to be construed in accordance with the Companies (Audit, Investigations and Community Enterprise) Act 2004 s 35(3): see s 63(1).
5 Companies (Audit, Investigations and Community Enterprise) Act 2004 s 35(4). See note 2 heads (1)–(2).
6 Companies (Audit, Investigations and Community Enterprise) Act 2004 s 35(6). Accordingly, the term 'excluded company' is to be construed in accordance with s 35(6): see s 63(1). For the purposes of s 35(6), the following are excluded companies:

(1) a company which is (or when formed would be) a political party (Community Interest Company Regulations 2005, SI 2005/1788, reg 6(a));
(2) a company which is (or when formed would be) a political campaigning organisation (reg 6(b)); or
(3) a company which is (or when formed would be) a subsidiary of a political party or of a political campaigning organisation (reg 6(c)).

81. Cap on distributions and payment of interest by community interest companies. Community interest companies[1] must not distribute assets to their members unless regulations make provision authorising them to do so[2]; and if regulations authorise community interest companies to distribute assets to their members, the regulations may impose limits on the extent to which they may do so[3]. Regulations also may impose limits on the payment of interest on debentures issued by, or debts of, community interest companies[4].

Such regulations may make provision for limits to be set by the Regulator[5], and he may:

(1) set a limit by reference to a rate determined by any other person (as it has effect from time to time)[6]; and
(2) set different limits for different descriptions of community interest companies[7].

However, the Regulator must[8]:

(a) undertake appropriate consultation before setting a limit[9]; and
(b) in setting a limit, have regard to its likely impact on community interest companies[10].

Such regulations may include power for the Secretary of State to require the Regulator to review a limit or limits[11].

Where the Regulator sets a limit, he must publish notice of it in the Gazette[12].

1 As to community interest companies see PARA 75.
2 Companies (Audit, Investigations and Community Enterprise) Act 2004 s 30(1). As to the making of regulations under the Companies (Audit, Investigations and Community Enterprise) Act 2004 generally see s 62 (amended by SI 2009/1941). In exercise of the powers conferred by the Companies (Audit, Investigations and Community Enterprise) Act 2004 s 30(1)–(4), (7), the Secretary of State has made the Community Interest Company Regulations 2005, SI 2005/1788, regs 17–22, 24–25, Sch 4) (reg 17 amended by SI 2009/1942; SI 2014/2483; the Community Interest Company Regulations 2005, SI 2005/1788, regs 18, 21 amended by SI 2007/1093; the Community Interest Company Regulations 2005, SI 2005/1788, reg 22 amended by SI 2014/2483). As to the Secretary of State see PARA 6.
Provision is made in relation to:
(1) declaration of dividends (Community Interest Company Regulations 2005, SI 2005/1788, reg 17 (as so amended));
(2) the maximum aggregate dividend for a financial year (reg 19);
(3) the interest rate cap on debentures issued by, and debts of, a community interest company in respect of which a performance-related rate of interest is payable and the agreement to pay interest at a performance-related rate was entered into by the company on or after the date on which it became a community interest company (reg 21);
(4) the initial level and subsequent variation of the dividend cap and interest cap (reg 22, Sch 4 (reg 22 as so amended));
(5) the redemption and purchase of shares (reg 24); and
(6) the reduction of share capital (reg 25).
3 Companies (Audit, Investigations and Community Enterprise) Act 2004 s 30(2). See note 2.
4 Companies (Audit, Investigations and Community Enterprise) Act 2004 s 30(3). See note 2.
5 Companies (Audit, Investigations and Community Enterprise) Act 2004 s 30(4). See note 2. As to the Regulator see PARA 76.
6 Companies (Audit, Investigations and Community Enterprise) Act 2004 s 30(5)(a).
7 Companies (Audit, Investigations and Community Enterprise) Act 2004 s 30(5)(b).
8 Ie in accordance with the Companies (Audit, Investigations and Community Enterprise) Act 2004 s 27 (see PARA 76): see s 30(6).
9 Companies (Audit, Investigations and Community Enterprise) Act 2004 s 30(6)(a).

10 Companies (Audit, Investigations and Community Enterprise) Act 2004 s 30(6)(b).
11 Companies (Audit, Investigations and Community Enterprise) Act 2004 s 30(7). See note 2.
12 Companies (Audit, Investigations and Community Enterprise) Act 2004 s 30(8).

82. Distribution of assets on winding up of community interest company. Regulations may make provision for and in connection with the distribution, on the winding up of a community interest company[1], of any assets of the company which remain after satisfaction of the company's liabilities[2]. Such regulations may, in particular, amend or modify the operation of any enactment or instrument[3].

1 As to community interest companies see PARA 75.
2 Companies (Audit, Investigations and Community Enterprise) Act 2004 s 31(1). As to the making of regulations under the Companies (Audit, Investigations and Community Enterprise) Act 2004 generally see s 62 (amended by SI 2009/1941). In exercise of the powers conferred by the Companies (Audit, Investigations and Community Enterprise) Act 2004 s 31, the Secretary of State has made the Community Interest Company Regulations 2005, SI 2005/1788, reg 23 (amended by SI 2007/1093; SI 2009/1942; SI 2010/671). As to the Secretary of State see PARA 6.
3 Companies (Audit, Investigations and Community Enterprise) Act 2004 s 31(2). See note 2.

83. Community interest company reports. The directors of a community interest company[1] must prepare in respect of each financial year a report about the company's activities during the financial year (a 'community interest company report')[2]; and regulations must make provision requiring the directors of a community interest company to deliver to the registrar of companies[3] a copy of the community interest company report[4].

Regulations also:

(1) must make provision requiring community interest company reports to include information about the remuneration of directors[5];
(2) may make provision as to the form of, and other information to be included in, community interest company reports[6]; and
(3) may apply provisions of the Companies Act 2006 relating to directors' reports to community interest company reports (with any appropriate modifications)[7].

The registrar of companies must forward to the Regulator[8] a copy of each community interest company report so delivered[9] to the registrar[10].

1 As to community interest companies see PARA 75.
2 Companies (Audit, Investigations and Community Enterprise) Act 2004 s 34(1).
3 As to the registrar of companies see PARA 126 et seq. As to the delivery of documents to the registrar see PARA 136; and as to the requirements generally for the proper delivery of documents to the registrar see PARA 137.
4 Companies (Audit, Investigations and Community Enterprise) Act 2004 s 34(2) (amended by SI 2008/948). As to the making of regulations under the Companies (Audit, Investigations and Community Enterprise) Act 2004 generally see s 62 (amended by SI 2009/1941). In exercise of the powers conferred by the Companies (Audit, Investigations and Community Enterprise) Act 2004 s 34(2), the Secretary of State has made the Community Interest Company Regulations 2005, SI 2005/1788, reg 29A (added by SI 2012/2335). As to the Secretary of State see PARA 6.

The directors of a community interest company must deliver to the registrar of companies for each financial year a copy of the community interest company report: Community Interest Company Regulations 2005, SI 2005/1788, reg 29A(1) (as so added). For these purposes, the Companies Act 2006 ss 441–443 (see PARAS 950–951), s 445(1), (5) (see PARA 954), s 446(1), (3) (see PARA 955), s 447(1), (3) (see PARA 956) and ss 451–453 (see PARAS 960–962) apply to a community interest company report as they apply to a directors' report; and s 444(1), (6) (see PARA 952), s 444A(1), (3) (see PARA 953) apply to a community interest company report as they apply to a directors' report with prescribed modifications: see the Community Interest Company Regulations 2005, SI 2005/1788, reg 29A(2), (3) (as so added).
5 Companies (Audit, Investigations and Community Enterprise) Act 2004 s 34(3)(a). In exercise of the powers conferred by s 34(3), the Secretary of State has made the Community Interest Company Regulations 2005, SI 2005/1788, regs 26–29 (reg 26 amended by SI 2007/1093; SI 2008/948; SI 2009/1942; the Community Interest Company Regulations 2005, SI 2005/1788, reg 27 substituted

by SI 2014/2483; the Community Interest Company Regulations 2005, SI 2005/1788, reg 29 substituted by SI 2008/948; amended by SI 2012/2335). As to the Secretary of State see PARA 6.
Provision is made in relation to:
(1) the general contents of a report (Community Interest Company Regulations 2005, SI 2005/1788, reg 26 (as so amended));
(2) information about dividends (reg 27 (as so substituted));
(3) information about debts or debentures on which a performance-related rate is payable (reg 28); and
(4) the application of certain provisions of the Companies Act 2006 relating to directors' reports (ie s 419 (approval and signing: see PARA 906), ss 423–425, 430–433, 436 (publication: see PARA 935 et seq), ss 437, 438 (public companies: laying before general meeting: see PARA 946) and s 454 (voluntary revision: see PARA 963) (reg 29 (as so substituted and amended)).

6 Companies (Audit, Investigations and Community Enterprise) Act 2004 s 34(3)(b). See also note 5.
7 Companies (Audit, Investigations and Community Enterprise) Act 2004 s 34(3)(c) (amended by SI 2008/948). See also note 5.
8 As to the Regulator see PARA 76.
9 Ie by virtue of the Companies (Audit, Investigations and Community Enterprise) Act 2004 s 34: see s 34(4).
10 Companies (Audit, Investigations and Community Enterprise) Act 2004 s 34(4).

(C) *Supervision of Community Interest Companies by Regulator*

84. Conditions for exercise of Regulator's supervisory powers. In deciding whether and how to exercise his supervisory powers[1], the Regulator[2] must adopt an approach which is based on the principle that those powers should be exercised only to the extent necessary to maintain confidence in community interest companies[3].

No power so conferred on the Regulator in relation to the appointment of a director[4], the removal of a director[5], the appointment of a manager[6], or dealing with property[7], is exercisable in relation to a community interest company unless the company default condition is satisfied in relation to the power and the company[8]. The company default condition is satisfied in relation to a power and a company if it appears to the Regulator necessary to exercise the power in relation to the company because[9]:
(1) there has been misconduct or mismanagement in the administration of the company[10];
(2) there is a need to protect the company's property or to secure the proper application of that property[11];
(3) the company is not satisfying the community interest test[12]; or
(4) if the company has community interest objects[13], the company is not carrying on any activities in pursuit of those objects[14].

The power conferred on the Regulator in relation to the transfer of shares etc[15] is not exercisable in relation to a community interest company unless it appears to the Regulator that the company is an excluded company[16].

1 Ie the powers conferred by the Companies (Audit, Investigations and Community Enterprise) Act 2004 ss 42–51 (see PARA 85 et seq): see s 41(1).
2 As to the Regulator see PARA 76.
3 Companies (Audit, Investigations and Community Enterprise) Act 2004 s 41(1). As to community interest companies see PARA 75.
4 Companies (Audit, Investigations and Community Enterprise) Act 2004 s 41(2)(a). The text refers to the power conferred by s 45 (see PARA 88): see s 41(2)(a).
5 Companies (Audit, Investigations and Community Enterprise) Act 2004 s 41(2)(b). The text refers to the power conferred by s 46 (see PARA 89): see s 41(2)(b).
6 Companies (Audit, Investigations and Community Enterprise) Act 2004 s 41(2)(c). The text refers to the power conferred by s 47 (see PARA 90): see s 41(2)(c).

7 Companies (Audit, Investigations and Community Enterprise) Act 2004 s 41(2)(d). The text refers to the power conferred by s 48 (see PARA 91): see s 41(2)(d).
8 Companies (Audit, Investigations and Community Enterprise) Act 2004 s 41(2).
9 Companies (Audit, Investigations and Community Enterprise) Act 2004 s 41(3).
10 Companies (Audit, Investigations and Community Enterprise) Act 2004 s 41(3)(a).
11 Companies (Audit, Investigations and Community Enterprise) Act 2004 s 41(3)(b).
12 Companies (Audit, Investigations and Community Enterprise) Act 2004 s 41(3)(c). As to the community interest test see PARA 80.
13 As to community interest objects see the Companies (Audit, Investigations and Community Enterprise) Act 2004 s 35(3); and PARA 80.
14 Companies (Audit, Investigations and Community Enterprise) Act 2004 s 41(3)(d).
15 Ie the power conferred by the Companies (Audit, Investigations and Community Enterprise) Act 2004 s 49 (see PARA 92): see s 41(4).
16 Companies (Audit, Investigations and Community Enterprise) Act 2004 s 41(4). As to excluded companies see PARA 80.

85. Investigation of community interest company by or on behalf of Regulator. The Regulator[1] may either investigate the affairs of a community interest company[2] or appoint any person, other than a member of the Regulator's staff[3], to investigate the affairs of a community interest company on behalf of the Regulator[4].

The investigator of a community interest company[5] may require the company or any other person to produce such documents[6], or documents of such description, as the investigator may specify[7], and to provide such information, or information of such description, as the investigator may specify[8]. Such a requirement must be complied with at such time and place as may be specified by the investigator[9]; but a person on whom such a requirement is imposed may require the investigator to produce evidence of his authority[10]. The production of a document in pursuance of this power does not affect any lien which a person has on the document[11]; but the investigator may take copies of or extracts from a document so produced[12]. The power to require the production of documents and the provision of information does not, however, require[13]:

(1) a person to produce a document or provide information in respect of which a claim could be maintained, in an action in the High Court, to legal professional privilege[14], although a person who is a lawyer may be required to provide the name and address of his client[15]; or
(2) a person carrying on the business of banking to produce a document, or provide information, relating to the affairs of a customer unless a requirement to produce the document, or provide the information, has been so imposed[16] on the customer[17].

A statement made by a person in compliance with a requirement so imposed to provide information[18] may be used in evidence against the person[19]; but, in criminal proceedings, no evidence relating to the statement may be adduced by or on behalf of the prosecution[20], and no question relating to it may be asked by or on behalf of the prosecution[21], unless evidence relating to it is adduced or a question relating to it is asked in the proceedings by or on behalf of that person[22].

If a person fails to comply with a requirement so imposed to produce documents or to provide information[23], the investigator may certify that fact in writing to the court[24]; and, if, after hearing any witnesses who may be produced against or on behalf of the alleged offender[25], and any statement which may be offered in defence[26], the court is satisfied that the offender failed without reasonable excuse to comply with the requirement, it may deal with him as if he had been guilty of contempt of the court[27].

A person commits an offence if, in purported compliance with a requirement so imposed to provide information[28], the person provides information which the person knows to be false in a material particular, or recklessly provides information which is false in a material particular[29]. A prosecution for such an offence may be instituted in England and Wales[30] only with the consent of the Director of Public Prosecutions[31].

1 As to the Regulator see PARA 76; and as to the conditions he must observe in the exercise of his supervisory powers see PARA 84.
2 Companies (Audit, Investigations and Community Enterprise) Act 2004 s 42(1)(a). As to community interest companies see PARA 75.
3 As to the Regulator's staff see the Companies (Audit, Investigations and Community Enterprise) Act 2004 s 27(8), Sch 3 paras 3–4; and PARA 76.
4 Companies (Audit, Investigations and Community Enterprise) Act 2004 s 42(1)(b). This power described in the text to this note is in addition to Sch 3 para 5 (powers of Regulator exercisable by authorised members of staff) (see PARA 76) and does not affect the application of Sch 3 para 5 to the Regulator's power under s 42(1)(a) (see head (1) in the text): s 42(2).
5 For these purposes, the 'investigator of a community interest company' means a person investigating the company's affairs under the Companies (Audit, Investigations and Community Enterprise) Act 2004 s 42 (see the text and notes 1–4): see Sch 7 para 1(7).
6 For these purposes, 'document' includes information recorded in any form: see the Companies (Audit, Investigations and Community Enterprise) Act 2004 Sch 7 para 1(7). In relation to information recorded otherwise than in legible form, the power to require production of it includes power to require the production of a copy of it in legible form or in a form from which it can readily be produced in visible and legible form: Sch 7 para 1(6).
7 Companies (Audit, Investigations and Community Enterprise) Act 2004 Sch 7 para 1(1)(a). See also note 6.
8 Companies (Audit, Investigations and Community Enterprise) Act 2004 Sch 7 para 1(1)(b). See also note 6.
9 Companies (Audit, Investigations and Community Enterprise) Act 2004 Sch 7 para 1(3).
10 Companies (Audit, Investigations and Community Enterprise) Act 2004 Sch 7 para 1(2).
11 Companies (Audit, Investigations and Community Enterprise) Act 2004 Sch 7 para 1(4).
12 Companies (Audit, Investigations and Community Enterprise) Act 2004 Sch 7 para 1(5).
13 Ie nothing in the Companies (Audit, Investigations and Community Enterprise) Act 2004 Sch 7 para 1 (see the text and notes 5–12) requires the actions set out in heads (1)–(2) in the text: see Sch 7 para 2(1), (2).
14 Companies (Audit, Investigations and Community Enterprise) Act 2004 Sch 7 para 2(1)(a). As to legal professional privilege see LEGAL PROFESSIONS vol 65 (2015) PARAS 351, 538; LEGAL PROFESSIONS vol 66 (2015) PARA 877.
15 Companies (Audit, Investigations and Community Enterprise) Act 2004 Sch 7 para 2(1).
16 Ie under the Companies (Audit, Investigations and Community Enterprise) Act 2004 Sch 7 para 1 (see the text and notes 5–12): see Sch 7 para 2(2).
17 Companies (Audit, Investigations and Community Enterprise) Act 2004 Sch 7 para 2(2).
18 Ie under the Companies (Audit, Investigations and Community Enterprise) Act 2004 Sch 7 para 1 (see the text and notes 5–12): see Sch 7 para 3(1).
19 Companies (Audit, Investigations and Community Enterprise) Act 2004 Sch 7 para 3(1).
20 Companies (Audit, Investigations and Community Enterprise) Act 2004 Sch 7 para 3(2)(a).
21 Companies (Audit, Investigations and Community Enterprise) Act 2004 Sch 7 para 3(2)(b).
22 Companies (Audit, Investigations and Community Enterprise) Act 2004 Sch 7 para 3(2). However, Sch 7 para 3(2) does not apply to proceedings in which a person is charged either with an offence under Sch 7 para 5 (false information) (see the text and notes 28–33), or with an offence under the Perjury Act 1911 s 5 (false statutory declarations and other false statements without oath) (see CRIMINAL LAW vol 26 (2016) PARA 782): Companies (Audit, Investigations and Community Enterprise) Act 2004 Sch 7 para 3(3) (amended by SI 2007/1093).
23 Ie under the Companies (Audit, Investigations and Community Enterprise) Act 2004 Sch 7 para 1 (see the text and notes 5–12): see Sch 7 para 4(1).
24 Companies (Audit, Investigations and Community Enterprise) Act 2004 Sch 7 para 4(1), (2).
25 Companies (Audit, Investigations and Community Enterprise) Act 2004 Sch 7 para 4(1), (3)(a).
26 Companies (Audit, Investigations and Community Enterprise) Act 2004 Sch 7 para 4(1), (3)(b).
27 Companies (Audit, Investigations and Community Enterprise) Act 2004 Sch 7 para 4(1), (3).
28 Ie under the Companies (Audit, Investigations and Community Enterprise) Act 2004 Sch 7 para 1 (see the text and notes 5–12): see Sch 7 para 5(1) (amended by SI 2007/1093).
29 Companies (Audit, Investigations and Community Enterprise) Act 2004 Sch 7 para 5(1) (as amended: see note 28). As to the liability of directors and other officers of a body corporate for

offences committed under the Companies (Audit, Investigations and Community Enterprise) Act 2004 Pt 2 (ss 26–63) see PARA 76. A person guilty of such an offence is liable on conviction on indictment to imprisonment for a term not exceeding two years or a fine, or to both, and on summary conviction to imprisonment for a term not exceeding 12 months or a fine, or to both: see the Companies (Audit, Investigations and Community Enterprise) Act 2004 Sch 7 para 5(2). In the case of liability on summary conviction the fine is one not exceeding the statutory maximum: see Sch 7 para 5(2). By virtue of the Legal Aid, Sentencing and Punishment of Offenders Act 2012 s 85, however, where the offence is committed on or after 12 March 2015, it is punishable by a fine of an unlimited amount. As to the statutory maximum and the powers of magistrates' courts to issue fines on summary conviction see SENTENCING vol 92 (2015) PARA 176. In relation to an offence committed after the commencement of the Companies Act 2006 s 1131 (summary proceedings) (see PARA 1818), but before a day is appointed in relation to the commencement of the Criminal Justice Act 2003 s 154(1) (general limit on magistrates' courts' power to impose imprisonment), the reference in the Companies (Audit, Investigations and Community Enterprise) Act 2004 Sch 7 para 5(2) to '12 months' must be read as a reference to 'six months': see the Companies (Audit, Investigations and Community Enterprise) Act 2004 Sch 7 para 5(3); the Companies Act 2006 ss 1131, 1133; and see PARA 1818.

30 As to the meanings of 'England' and 'Wales' see PARA 1 note 5.

31 Companies (Audit, Investigations and Community Enterprise) Act 2004 Sch 7 para 5(1A) (added by SI 2007/1093). As to the Director of Public Prosecutions see CRIMINAL PROCEDURE vol 27 (2015) PARAS 25, 30 et seq.

86. Audit of community interest company's accounts ordered by Regulator. The Regulator[1] may by order[2] require a community interest company[3] to allow the annual accounts of the company to be audited by a qualified auditor appointed by the Regulator[4]. The provisions which govern the auditor's rights to information under the Companies Act 2006[5] apply in relation to an auditor so appointed[6].

An audit ordered by the Regulator in this way[7] is in addition to, and does not affect, any audit required by or by virtue of any other enactment[8].

On completion of the audit, the auditor must make a report to the Regulator on such matters and in such form as the Regulator specifies[9].

The expenses of the audit, including the remuneration of the auditor, are to be paid by the Regulator[10].

1 As to the Regulator see PARA 76; and as to the conditions he must observe in the exercise of his supervisory powers see PARA 84.

2 As to orders made by the Regulator under the Companies (Audit, Investigations and Community Enterprise) Act 2004 Pt 2 (ss 26–63) (community interest companies) see s 61.

3 As to community interest companies see PARA 75.

4 Companies (Audit, Investigations and Community Enterprise) Act 2004 s 43(1). For these purposes, a person is a qualified auditor if he is eligible for appointment as a statutory auditor under the Companies Act 2006 Pt 42 (ss 1209–1264) (see PARA 1143 et seq): Companies (Audit, Investigations and Community Enterprise) Act 2004 s 43(2) (amended by SI 2008/948).

5 Ie the Companies Act 2006 ss 499–501 (see PARA 1030): see the Companies (Audit, Investigations and Community Enterprise) Act 2004 s 43(3) (amended by SI 2007/2194; SI 2008/948).

6 Companies (Audit, Investigations and Community Enterprise) Act 2004 s 43(3) (as amended: see note 5).

7 Ie under the Companies (Audit, Investigations and Community Enterprise) Act 2004 s 43: see s 43(6).

8 Companies (Audit, Investigations and Community Enterprise) Act 2004 s 43(6). As to the general requirement for company accounts to be audited see PARA 983 et seq.

9 Companies (Audit, Investigations and Community Enterprise) Act 2004 s 43(4).

10 Companies (Audit, Investigations and Community Enterprise) Act 2004 s 43(5).

87. Institution of civil proceedings by Regulator. The Regulator[1] may bring civil proceedings in the name and on behalf of a community interest company[2]. Before instituting such proceedings, the Regulator must give written notice to the company[3], stating the cause of action[4], the remedy sought[5] and a summary of the facts on which the proceedings are to be based[6]. Any director of the company may apply to the court for an order:

(1) that proposed proceedings are not to be instituted in this way[7]; or

(2) that proceedings instituted in this way are to be discontinued[8].

On such an application, the court may make such order as it thinks fit[9]; and, in particular, the court may, as an alternative to making an order to the effect of head (1) or head (2) above, order[10]:

(a) that the proposed proceedings may be instituted[11], or the proceedings that have been instituted[12] may be continued, on such terms and conditions as the court thinks fit[13];

(b) that any proceedings instituted by the company are to be discontinued[14]; or

(c) that any proceedings instituted by the company may be continued on such terms and conditions as the court thinks fit[15].

The Regulator must indemnify the company against any costs incurred by it in connection with proceedings so brought by him[16]. Any costs either awarded to the company in connection with such proceedings[17], or incurred by the company in connection with the proceedings and which it is agreed should be paid by a defendant[18], are to be paid to the Regulator[19].

1 As to the Regulator see PARA 76; and as to the conditions he must observe in the exercise of his supervisory powers see PARA 84.
2 Companies (Audit, Investigations and Community Enterprise) Act 2004 s 44(1). As to community interest companies see PARA 75.
3 Companies (Audit, Investigations and Community Enterprise) Act 2004 s 44(2).
4 Companies (Audit, Investigations and Community Enterprise) Act 2004 s 44(2)(a).
5 Companies (Audit, Investigations and Community Enterprise) Act 2004 s 44(2)(b).
6 Companies (Audit, Investigations and Community Enterprise) Act 2004 s 44(2)(c).
7 Companies (Audit, Investigations and Community Enterprise) Act 2004 s 44(3)(a).
8 Companies (Audit, Investigations and Community Enterprise) Act 2004 s 44(3)(b).
9 Companies (Audit, Investigations and Community Enterprise) Act 2004 s 44(4).
10 Companies (Audit, Investigations and Community Enterprise) Act 2004 s 44(5).
11 Ie under the Companies (Audit, Investigations and Community Enterprise) Act 2004 s 44: see s 44(5)(a).
12 See note 11.
13 Companies (Audit, Investigations and Community Enterprise) Act 2004 s 44(5)(a).
14 Companies (Audit, Investigations and Community Enterprise) Act 2004 s 44(5)(b).
15 Companies (Audit, Investigations and Community Enterprise) Act 2004 s 44(5)(c).
16 Companies (Audit, Investigations and Community Enterprise) Act 2004 s 44(6).
17 Companies (Audit, Investigations and Community Enterprise) Act 2004 s 44(7)(a).
18 Companies (Audit, Investigations and Community Enterprise) Act 2004 s 44(7)(b).
19 Companies (Audit, Investigations and Community Enterprise) Act 2004 s 44(7).

88. Appointment of director of community interest company by Regulator. The Regulator[1] may by order[2] appoint a director of a community interest company[3].

The person appointed may be anyone whom the Regulator thinks appropriate, other than a member of the Regulator's staff[4], and a person may be so appointed whether or not the person is a member of the company[5], and irrespective of any provision made by the articles of the company[6] or a resolution of the company[7].

An order appointing a person to be a director of a company in this way must specify the terms on which the director is to hold office[8]. Those terms have effect as if contained in a contract between the director and the company[9]; and the terms specified must include the period for which the director is to hold office, and may include terms as to the remuneration of the director by the company[10].

A director so appointed[11] has all the powers of the directors appointed by the company (including powers exercisable only by a particular director or class of directors)[12]; and such a director may not be removed by the company, although he may be removed by the Regulator at any time[13].

Where a person is appointed to be a director of the company in this way, or where a person so appointed ceases to be a director of the company, the obligation which would otherwise be imposed on the company[14] to notify any change among directors to the registrar[15] is instead an obligation of the Regulator[16]. Where a person appointed to be a director of the company under these provisions[17] ceases to be a director of the company[18], the company must give notification of that fact to the Regulator in a form approved by the Regulator before the end of the period of 14 days beginning with the date on which the person ceases to be a director[19]. If default is made in complying with this requirement to notify[20], an offence is committed by the company and by every officer of the company who is in default[21].

The company may appeal to the Appeal Officer[22] against an order made by the Regulator appointing a director of a community interest company[23].

1 As to the Regulator see PARA 76; and as to the conditions he must observe in the exercise of his supervisory powers see PARA 84.
2 As to orders made by the Regulator under the Companies (Audit, Investigations and Community Enterprise) Act 2004 Pt 2 (ss 26–63) (community interest companies) see s 61.
3 Companies (Audit, Investigations and Community Enterprise) Act 2004 s 45(1). As to community interest companies see PARA 75.
4 Companies (Audit, Investigations and Community Enterprise) Act 2004 s 45(2). As to the Regulator's staff see s 27(8), Sch 3 paras 3–4; and PARA 76.
5 Companies (Audit, Investigations and Community Enterprise) Act 2004 s 45(3)(a). As to membership of companies generally see PARA 323 et seq.
6 As to a community interest company's articles of association see PARA 98; and as to a company's articles of association generally see PARA 227 et seq.
7 Companies (Audit, Investigations and Community Enterprise) Act 2004 s 45(3)(b) (amended by SI 2008/948; SI 2009/1941). As to company resolutions generally see PARA 684 et seq.
8 Companies (Audit, Investigations and Community Enterprise) Act 2004 s 45(4).
9 See note 8.
10 Companies (Audit, Investigations and Community Enterprise) Act 2004 s 45(5).
11 Ie under the Companies (Audit, Investigations and Community Enterprise) Act 2004 s 45: see s 45(6).
12 Companies (Audit, Investigations and Community Enterprise) Act 2004 s 45(6).
13 Companies (Audit, Investigations and Community Enterprise) Act 2004 s 45(7).
14 Ie under the Companies Act 2006 s 167(1)(a) (see PARA 550): see the Companies (Audit, Investigations and Community Enterprise) Act 2004 s 45(8) (amended by SI 2009/1941).
15 As to the registrar of companies see PARA 126 et seq. As to the delivery of documents to the registrar see PARA 136; and as to the requirements generally for the proper delivery of documents to the registrar see PARA 137.
16 Companies (Audit, Investigations and Community Enterprise) Act 2004 s 45(8) (as amended: see note 14).
17 Ie under the Companies (Audit, Investigations and Community Enterprise) Act 2004 s 45: see s 45(10).
18 Ie otherwise than by removal under the Companies (Audit, Investigations and Community Enterprise) Act 2004 s 45(7) (see the text and note 13): see s 45(10). As to removal of a director by the Regulator generally see PARA 89.
19 Companies (Audit, Investigations and Community Enterprise) Act 2004 s 45(10). If s 45(10) applies, the Companies Act 2006 s 167(1)(a) (see PARA 550) applies as if the period within which the Regulator must send a notification to the registrar of companies is 14 days from the date on which the Regulator receives notification under the Companies (Audit, Investigations and Community Enterprise) Act 2004 s 45(10): s 45(9) (amended by SI 2009/1941).
20 Ie in complying with the Companies (Audit, Investigations and Community Enterprise) Act 2004 s 45(10) (see the text and notes 17–19): see s 45(11) (s 45(11), (12) substituted by SI 2009/1941).
21 Companies (Audit, Investigations and Community Enterprise) Act 2004 s 45(11) (as substituted: see note 20). For these purposes, a shadow director is treated as an officer of the company: s 45(11) (as so substituted). As to shadow directors see PARA 513. As to the liability of directors and other officers of a body corporate for offences committed under the Companies (Audit, Investigations and Community Enterprise) Act 2004 Pt 2 see PARA 76.

A person guilty of such an offence is liable on summary conviction to a fine, and for continued contravention to a daily default fine not to exceed one-tenth of the greater of £5,000 or level 4 on the standard scale: see s 45(12) (as so substituted; amended by SI 2015/664). As to the meaning of 'daily default fine' see PARA 1816. In the case of liability on summary conviction the fine is one not exceeding the statutory maximum: see the Companies (Audit, Investigations and Community Enterprise) Act 2004 s 45(12) (as so substituted). By virtue of the Legal Aid, Sentencing and

Punishment of Offenders Act 2012 s 85, however, where the offence is committed on or after 12 March 2015, it is punishable by a fine of an unlimited amount. As to the statutory maximum and the powers of magistrates' courts to issue fines on summary conviction see SENTENCING vol 92 (2015) PARA 176.

22 As to the Appeal Officer for community interest companies see PARA 77.

23 Companies (Audit, Investigations and Community Enterprise) Act 2004 s 45(13).

89. Removal or suspension of director of community interest company by Regulator. The Regulator[1] may by order[2]:

(1) remove a director of a community interest company[3]; or

(2) suspend a director of the company pending a decision whether to remove him[4], up to a maximum period of one year[5].

Before making an order under either head (1) or head (2) above in relation to a director, the Regulator must give at least 14 days' notice to the director, and to the company[6]; and, where an order is made in relation to a director under either head (1) or head (2) above, the director may appeal against the order to the High Court[7].

If a person has been removed under head (1) above, the company may not subsequently appoint him a director of the company[8], and any assignment to the person of the office of director of the company is of no effect, even if approved by special resolution of the company[9].

If the Regulator suspends a director under head (2) above, the Regulator may give directions in relation to the performance of the director's functions[10].

The Regulator may discharge an order made under head (1) above[11], but such a discharge does not reinstate the person removed by the order as a director of the company[12].

The Regulator must also from time to time review any order made under head (2) above and, if it is appropriate to do so, discharge the order[13].

The Regulator must, before the end of the period of 14 days beginning with the date on which:

(a) an order under head (1) above is made or discharged[14]; or

(b) an order under head (2) above is made or discharged or expires[15]; or

(c) an order under head (1) or head (2) above is quashed on appeal[16],

give notification of that event to the registrar of companies[17] in a form approved by the registrar[18].

1 As to the Regulator see PARA 76; and as to the conditions he must observe in the exercise of his supervisory powers see PARA 84.

2 As to orders made by the Regulator under the Companies (Audit, Investigations and Community Enterprise) Act 2004 Pt 2 (ss 26–63) (community interest companies) see s 61.

3 Companies (Audit, Investigations and Community Enterprise) Act 2004 s 46(1). As to community interest companies see PARA 75.

4 Companies (Audit, Investigations and Community Enterprise) Act 2004 s 46(3).

5 Companies (Audit, Investigations and Community Enterprise) Act 2004 s 46(4).

6 Companies (Audit, Investigations and Community Enterprise) Act 2004 s 46(9).

7 Companies (Audit, Investigations and Community Enterprise) Act 2004 s 46(10).

8 Companies (Audit, Investigations and Community Enterprise) Act 2004 s 46(2)(a).

9 Companies (Audit, Investigations and Community Enterprise) Act 2004 s 46(2)(b). As to special resolutions see PARA 686.

10 Companies (Audit, Investigations and Community Enterprise) Act 2004 s 46(5).

11 Companies (Audit, Investigations and Community Enterprise) Act 2004 s 46(6).

12 Companies (Audit, Investigations and Community Enterprise) Act 2004 s 46(7). Rather, on the discharge of the order under head (1) in the text, s 46(2) (see the text and notes 8–9) ceases to apply to the person: see s 46(7).

13 Companies (Audit, Investigations and Community Enterprise) Act 2004 s 46(8).

14 Companies (Audit, Investigations and Community Enterprise) Act 2004 s 46(11)(a).

15 Companies (Audit, Investigations and Community Enterprise) Act 2004 s 46(11)(b).

16 Companies (Audit, Investigations and Community Enterprise) Act 2004 s 46(11)(c).

17 As to the registrar of companies see PARA 126 et seq. As to the delivery of documents to the registrar see PARA 136; and as to the requirements generally for the proper delivery of documents to the registrar see PARA 137.

18 Companies (Audit, Investigations and Community Enterprise) Act 2004 s 46(11). However, where s 45(11) imposes an obligation to notify the registrar of companies of an event, the Companies Act 2006 s 167(1)(a) (requirement that company notify change among directors to registrar) (see PARA 550) does not apply in respect of the event: Companies (Audit, Investigations and Community Enterprise) Act 2004 s 46(12) (amended by SI 2009/1941).

90. Appointment of manager by Regulator. The Regulator[1] may by order[2] appoint a manager in respect of the property and affairs of a community interest company[3]. The person appointed may be anyone whom the Regulator thinks appropriate, other than a member of the Regulator's staff[4].

Such an order of appointment[5] may make provision as to the functions to be exercised by, and the powers of, the manager[6]; and such an order may in particular provide for the manager to have such of the functions of the company's directors as are specified in the order[7], and for the company's directors to be prevented from exercising any of those functions[8].

In carrying out his functions, the manager acts as the company's agent[9]; and a person dealing with the manager in good faith and for value need not inquire whether the manager is acting within his powers[10].

The appointment of the manager does not affect any right of any person to appoint a receiver or manager of the company's property[11], or the rights of a receiver or manager appointed by a person other than the Regulator[12].

The manager's functions are to be discharged by him under the supervision of the Regulator[13]; and the Regulator must from time to time review the order by which the manager is appointed and, if it is appropriate to do so, discharge it in whole or in part[14]. In particular, the Regulator must discharge the order on the appointment of a person to act as administrative receiver, administrator, provisional liquidator or liquidator of the company[15].

The Regulator may apply to the court for directions in relation to any matter arising in connection with the manager's functions or powers[16]; and on such an application the court may give such directions or make such orders as it thinks fit[17].

Regulations[18] may authorise the Regulator to require a manager to make reports[19], to require a manager to give security for the due exercise of the manager's functions[20], and to remove a manager in circumstances prescribed by the regulations[21]. Regulations also may provide for a manager's remuneration to be payable from the property of the company[22], and may authorise the Regulator to determine the amount of a manager's remuneration and to disallow any amount of remuneration in circumstances prescribed by the regulations[23].

The company may appeal to the Appeal Officer[24] against an order of the Regulator appointing a manager in respect of the property and affairs of a community interest company[25].

1 As to the Regulator see PARA 76; and as to the conditions he must observe in the exercise of his supervisory powers see PARA 84.

2 As to orders made by the Regulator under the Companies (Audit, Investigations and Community Enterprise) Act 2004 Pt 2 (ss 26–63) (community interest companies) see s 61.

3 Companies (Audit, Investigations and Community Enterprise) Act 2004 s 47(1). As to community interest companies see PARA 75.

Notice must be given to the registrar of companies of the appointment in relation to a company of a manager appointed under the Companies (Audit, Investigations and Community Enterprise) Act 2004 s 47: Companies Act 2006 s 1154(1)(c). Such notice must be given by the Regulator of Community Interest Companies (s 1154(2)(c)); and it must specify an address at which service of documents (including legal process) may be effected on the person appointed (s 1154(3)). Notice of a change in the address for service may be given to the registrar by the person appointed: s 1154(3). Where notice has been given under s 1154 of the appointment of a person, notice must also be given by the Regulator to the registrar of the termination of the appointment: s 1154(2)(c), (4). As to the registrar of companies see PARA 126 et seq. As to the delivery of documents to the registrar see PARA 136; and as to the requirements generally for the proper delivery of documents to the registrar see PARA 137.

4 Companies (Audit, Investigations and Community Enterprise) Act 2004 s 47(2). As to the Regulator's staff see s 27(8), Sch 3 paras 3–4; and PARA 76.

5 Ie under the Companies (Audit, Investigations and Community Enterprise) Act 2004 s 47(1) (see the text and notes 1–3): see s 47(3).

6 Companies (Audit, Investigations and Community Enterprise) Act 2004 s 47(3).

7 Companies (Audit, Investigations and Community Enterprise) Act 2004 s 47(4)(a).

8 Companies (Audit, Investigations and Community Enterprise) Act 2004 s 47(4)(b).

9 Companies (Audit, Investigations and Community Enterprise) Act 2004 s 47(5).

10 See note 9.

11 Companies (Audit, Investigations and Community Enterprise) Act 2004 s 47(6)(a).

12 Companies (Audit, Investigations and Community Enterprise) Act 2004 s 47(6)(b).

13 Companies (Audit, Investigations and Community Enterprise) Act 2004 s 47(7).

14 See note 13.

15 Companies (Audit, Investigations and Community Enterprise) Act 2004 s 47(8). As to administrators see COMPANY AND PARTNERSHIP INSOLVENCY vol 16 (2011) PARA 158 et seq; as to administrative receivers see COMPANY AND PARTNERSHIP INSOLVENCY vol 16 (2011) PARA 329 et seq; and as to the appointment of a liquidator see COMPANY AND PARTNERSHIP INSOLVENCY vol 17 (2011) PARA 909.

16 Companies (Audit, Investigations and Community Enterprise) Act 2004 s 47(9). The costs of any application under s 47(9) are to be paid by the company: s 47(11).

17 Companies (Audit, Investigations and Community Enterprise) Act 2004 s 47(10).

18 As to the making of regulations under the Companies (Audit, Investigations and Community Enterprise) Act 2004 generally see s 62 (amended by SI 2009/1941). In exercise of the powers conferred by the Companies (Audit, Investigations and Community Enterprise) Act 2004 s 47(12), (13) (see the text and notes 19–23), the Secretary of State has made the Community Interest Company Regulations 2005, SI 2005/1788, regs 30–33. As to the Secretary of State see PARA 6.

Provision is made with regard to:

(1) a manager's remuneration (see reg 30);

(2) security to be given by the manager (see reg 31);

(3) failure by a manager to give security or discharge any function, and his removal by the Regulator (see reg 32); and

(4) reports by the manager (see reg 33).

19 Companies (Audit, Investigations and Community Enterprise) Act 2004 s 47(12)(a). See note 18 head (4).

20 Companies (Audit, Investigations and Community Enterprise) Act 2004 s 47(12)(b). See note 18 head (2).

21 Companies (Audit, Investigations and Community Enterprise) Act 2004 s 47(12)(c). See note 18 head (3).

22 Companies (Audit, Investigations and Community Enterprise) Act 2004 s 47(13)(a). See note 18 head (1).

23 Companies (Audit, Investigations and Community Enterprise) Act 2004 s 47(13)(b). See note 18 head (1).

24 As to the Appeal Officer for community interest companies see PARA 77.

25 Companies (Audit, Investigations and Community Enterprise) Act 2004 s 47(14).

91. Regulator's power to deal in community interest company property. The Regulator[1] may by order[2]:

(1) vest in the Official Property Holder[3] any property held by or in trust for a community interest company[4]; or

(2) require persons in whom such property is vested to transfer it to the Official Property Holder[5].

The Regulator may order:

(a) a person who holds property on behalf of a community interest company, or on behalf of a trustee of a community interest company, not to part with the property without the Regulator's consent[6]; and

(b) any debtor of a community interest company not to make any payment in respect of the debtor's liability to the company without the Regulator's consent[7].

The Regulator may by order restrict:

(i) the transactions which may be entered into by a community interest company[8]; or

(ii) the nature or amount of the payments that a community interest company may make[9],

and the order may in particular provide that transactions may not be entered into or payments made without the Regulator's consent[10].

The Regulator must from time to time review any such order[11] and, if it is appropriate to do so, discharge the order in whole or in part[12]. On discharging such an order, the Regulator may make any order as to the vesting or transfer of the property, and give any directions, which he considers appropriate[13].

If a person fails to comply with an order under head (2) above, the Regulator may certify that fact in writing to the court[14]. If, after hearing any witnesses who may be produced against or on behalf of the alleged offender[15], and any statement which may be offered in defence[16], the court is satisfied that the offender failed without reasonable excuse to comply with the order, it may deal with him as if he had been guilty of contempt of the court[17].

A person who contravenes an order under head (a), head (b), head (i) or head (ii) above commits an offence[18]. A prosecution for such an offence may be instituted, in England and Wales[19], only with the consent of the Regulator or of the Director of Public Prosecutions[20]. These provisions regarding criminal offences[21] do not prevent the bringing of civil proceedings in respect of a contravention of an order under head (2) above, or under head (a), head (b), head (i) or head (ii) above[22].

The company and any person to whom the order is directed may appeal to the Appeal Officer[23] against an order under head (1), head (2), head (a) or head (b) above[24]; and the company may appeal to the Appeal Officer against an order under head (i) or head (ii) above[25].

1 As to the Regulator see PARA 76; and as to the conditions he must observe in the exercise of his supervisory powers see PARA 84.

2 As to orders made by the Regulator under the Companies (Audit, Investigations and Community Enterprise) Act 2004 Pt 2 (ss 26–63) (community interest companies) see s 61.

3 As to the Official Property Holder for community interest companies see PARA 78.

4 Companies (Audit, Investigations and Community Enterprise) Act 2004 s 48(1)(a). As to community interest companies see PARA 75. The vesting of property under the Companies (Audit, Investigations and Community Enterprise) Act 2004 s 48(1) does not constitute a breach of a covenant or condition against alienation, and no right listed in heads (1)–(7) below operates or becomes exercisable as a result of the vesting (s 48(4)), namely:

(1) a right of reverter (s 48(5)(a));
(2) a right of pre-emption (s 48(5)(b));
(3) a right of forfeiture (s 48(5)(c));
(4) a right of re-entry (s 48(5)(d));
(5) (in Scotland) a right of irritancy (s 48(5)(e));
(6) an option (s 48(5)(f)); and
(7) any right similar to those listed in heads (1)–(6) above (s 48(5)(g)).

5 Companies (Audit, Investigations and Community Enterprise) Act 2004 s 48(1)(b). The transfer of property under the Companies (Audit, Investigations and Community Enterprise) Act 2004 s 48(1) does not constitute a breach of a covenant or condition against alienation, and no right listed in note 4 heads (1) to (7) operates or becomes exercisable as a result of the transfer: see s 48(4), (5).

6 Companies (Audit, Investigations and Community Enterprise) Act 2004 s 48(2)(a).

7 Companies (Audit, Investigations and Community Enterprise) Act 2004 s 48(2)(b).
8 Companies (Audit, Investigations and Community Enterprise) Act 2004 s 48(3)(a).
9 Companies (Audit, Investigations and Community Enterprise) Act 2004 s 48(3)(b).
10 Companies (Audit, Investigations and Community Enterprise) Act 2004 s 48(3).
11 Ie any order under the Companies (Audit, Investigations and Community Enterprise) Act 2004 s 48: s 48(6).
12 Companies (Audit, Investigations and Community Enterprise) Act 2004 s 48(6).
13 Companies (Audit, Investigations and Community Enterprise) Act 2004 s 48(7).
14 Companies (Audit, Investigations and Community Enterprise) Act 2004 s 48(8).
15 Companies (Audit, Investigations and Community Enterprise) Act 2004 s 48(9)(a).
16 Companies (Audit, Investigations and Community Enterprise) Act 2004 s 48(9)(b).
17 Companies (Audit, Investigations and Community Enterprise) Act 2004 s 48(9).
18 Companies (Audit, Investigations and Community Enterprise) Act 2004 s 48(10). As to the liability of directors and other officers of a body corporate for offences committed under the Companies (Audit, Investigations and Community Enterprise) Act 2004 Pt 2 see PARA 76. A person guilty of such an offence is liable on summary conviction to a fine: see s 48(11). The fine is one not exceeding level 5 on the standard scale: see s 48(11). By virtue of the Legal Aid, Sentencing and Punishment of Offenders Act 2012 s 85, however, where the offence is committed on or after 12 March 2015, it is punishable by a fine of an unlimited amount. As to the standard scale and the powers of magistrates' courts to issue fines on summary conviction see SENTENCING vol 92 (2015) PARA 176.
19 As to the meanings of 'England' and 'Wales' see PARA 1 note 5.
20 Companies (Audit, Investigations and Community Enterprise) Act 2004 s 48(10)(a) (substituted by SI 2007/1093). As to the Director of Public Prosecutions see CRIMINAL PROCEDURE vol 27 (2015) PARA 25.
21 Ie the Companies (Audit, Investigations and Community Enterprise) Act 2004 s 48(8)–(10) (see the text and notes 14–18, 19–20): see s 48(12).
22 Companies (Audit, Investigations and Community Enterprise) Act 2004 s 48(12).
23 As to the Appeal Officer for community interest companies see PARA 77.
24 Companies (Audit, Investigations and Community Enterprise) Act 2004 s 48(13).
25 Companies (Audit, Investigations and Community Enterprise) Act 2004 s 48(14).

92. Regulator's power to transfer shares etc in community interest company. If a community interest company[1] has a share capital[2], the Regulator[3] may by order[4] transfer specified shares in the company to specified persons[5]. However, such an order may not transfer any shares in respect of which a dividend may be paid[6], or in respect of which a distribution of the company's assets may be made if the company is wound up[7].

If a community interest company is a company limited by guarantee[8], the Regulator may by order extinguish the interests in the company of specified members of the company, otherwise than as shareholders[9], and appoint a new member in place of each member whose interest has been extinguished[10].

Any order made pursuant to the power to transfer shares or to replace members[11] in relation to a company may only transfer shares to, and appoint as new members, persons who have consented to the transfer or appointment[12], and may be made irrespective of any provision made by the articles of the company[13] or a resolution of the company[14].

The company and any person from whom shares are transferred by an order[15] may appeal to the Appeal Officer[16] against the order[17]; and the company and any person whose interest is extinguished by the order[18] may appeal to the Appeal Officer against that order[19].

1 As to community interest companies see PARA 75.
2 As to share capital and shares generally see PARA 1231 et seq.
3 As to the Regulator see PARA 76; and as to the conditions he must observe in the exercise of his supervisory powers see PARA 84.
4 As to orders made by the Regulator under the Companies (Audit, Investigations and Community Enterprise) Act 2004 Pt 2 (ss 26–63) (community interest companies) see s 61.
5 Companies (Audit, Investigations and Community Enterprise) Act 2004 s 49(1). For these purposes, 'specified', in relation to an order, means specified in the order: s 49(7).

6 Companies (Audit, Investigations and Community Enterprise) Act 2004 s 49(3)(a). As to the declaration and payment of dividends see PARA 1581 et seq.
7 Companies (Audit, Investigations and Community Enterprise) Act 2004 s 49(3)(b). As to the Regulator's power to petition for the winding up of a community interest company see PARA 93. As to winding up in general see COMPANY AND PARTNERSHIP INSOLVENCY vol 16 (2011) PARA 380 et seq.
8 As to companies limited by guarantee see PARAS 72, 95.
9 Companies (Audit, Investigations and Community Enterprise) Act 2004 s 49(2)(a). As to shareholders and the membership of companies generally see PARA 323 et seq.
10 Companies (Audit, Investigations and Community Enterprise) Act 2004 s 49(2)(b).
11 Ie an order under the Companies (Audit, Investigations and Community Enterprise) Act 2004 s 49: see s 49(4).
12 Companies (Audit, Investigations and Community Enterprise) Act 2004 s 49(4)(a).
13 As to a community interest company's articles of association see PARA 98; and as to a company's articles of association generally see PARA 227 et seq.
14 Companies (Audit, Investigations and Community Enterprise) Act 2004 s 49(4)(b) (amended by SI 2009/1941). As to resolutions of the company see PARA 684 et seq.
15 Ie under the Companies (Audit, Investigations and Community Enterprise) Act 2004 s 49(1) (see the text and notes 1–5): see s 49(5).
16 As to the Appeal Officer for community interest companies see PARA 77.
17 Companies (Audit, Investigations and Community Enterprise) Act 2004 s 49(5).
18 Ie under the Companies (Audit, Investigations and Community Enterprise) Act 2004 s 49(1) (see the text and notes 1–5): see s 49(6).
19 Companies (Audit, Investigations and Community Enterprise) Act 2004 s 49(6).

93. Petition for winding up of community interest company; dissolution and striking off. The Regulator[1] may present a petition for a community interest company[2] to be wound up[3] if the court is of the opinion that it is just and equitable that the company should be wound up[4]. However, this provision does not apply if the company is already being wound up by the court[5].

If a community interest company has been dissolved[6], or has been struck off the register either as a defunct company[7] or because the company is in liquidation[8], the Regulator may apply to the court[9] for an order restoring the company's name to the register[10].

If an application[11] by a company to strike itself off the register is made on behalf of a community interest company, the provisions governing the persons to be notified of such an application[12] are to be treated as also requiring a copy of the application to be given to the Regulator[13].

1 As to the Regulator see PARA 76; and as to the conditions he must observe in the exercise of his supervisory powers see PARA 84.
2 As to community interest companies see PARA 75.
3 As to winding up in general see COMPANY AND PARTNERSHIP INSOLVENCY vol 16 (2011) PARA 380 et seq.
4 Companies (Audit, Investigations and Community Enterprise) Act 2004 s 50(1).
5 Companies (Audit, Investigations and Community Enterprise) Act 2004 s 50(2).
6 As to the dissolution of a company generally see PARA 1703 et seq.
7 Ie under the Companies Act 2006 s 1000 (see PARA 1703): see the Companies (Audit, Investigations and Community Enterprise) Act 2004 s 51(1): see the text and note 10.
8 Ie under the Companies Act 2006 s 1001 (see PARA 1704): see the Companies (Audit, Investigations and Community Enterprise) Act 2004 s 51(1) (as substituted: see note 10).
9 Ie under the Companies Act 2006 s 1029 (see PARA 1718): see the Companies (Audit, Investigations and Community Enterprise) Act 2004 s 51(1) (as substituted: see note 10).
10 Companies (Audit, Investigations and Community Enterprise) Act 2004 s 51(1) (substituted by SI 2009/1941).
11 Ie under the Companies Act 2006 s 1003 (striking off on application by company) (see PARA 1707): see the Companies (Audit, Investigations and Community Enterprise) Act 2004 s 51(3) (as amended: see note 13).
12 Ie the Companies Act 2006 s 1006 (see PARA 1710): see the Companies (Audit, Investigations and Community Enterprise) Act 2004 s 51(3) (as amended: see note 13).
13 Companies (Audit, Investigations and Community Enterprise) Act 2004 s 51(3) (amended by SI 2009/1941).

(D) *Fees Payable in relation to Community Interest Companies*

94. Fees payable to the Regulator etc. Regulations made under the Companies (Audit, Investigations and Community Enterprise) Act 2004[1] may require the payment of such fees in connection with the Regulator's functions[2] as may be specified in the regulations[3]. However, the regulations may provide for fees to be paid to the registrar of companies[4] rather than to the Regulator[5].

The Regulator may charge a fee for any service which is provided otherwise than in pursuance of an obligation imposed by law, other than the provision of guidance which the Regulator considers to be of general interest[6].

Fees paid in this way[7] are to be paid into the Consolidated Fund[8].

1 As to the making of regulations under the Companies (Audit, Investigations and Community Enterprise) Act 2004 generally see s 62 (amended by SI 2009/1941). In exercise of the powers conferred by the Companies (Audit, Investigations and Community Enterprise) Act 2004 s 57(1), (2) (see the text and notes 2–5), the Secretary of State has made the Community Interest Company Regulations 2005, SI 2005/1788, reg 36, Sch 5 (Sch 5 substituted by SI 2009/1942). As to the Secretary of State see PARA 6.

2 As to the Regulator and his functions see PARA 76.

3 Companies (Audit, Investigations and Community Enterprise) Act 2004 s 57(1). See note 1.

4 As to the registrar of companies see PARA 126 et seq.

5 Companies (Audit, Investigations and Community Enterprise) Act 2004 s 57(2). The Community Interest Company Regulations 2005, SI 2005/1788, Sch 5 so provides.

6 Companies (Audit, Investigations and Community Enterprise) Act 2004 s 57(3).

7 Ie by virtue of the Companies (Audit, Investigations and Community Enterprise) Act 2004 s 57: see s 57(4).

8 Companies (Audit, Investigations and Community Enterprise) Act 2004 s 57(4). As to the Consolidated Fund see CONSTITUTIONAL AND ADMINISTRATIVE LAW vol 20 (2014) PARA 480 et seq; PARLIAMENT vol 78 (2010) PARAS 1028–1031.

(ii) Formation of Companies

A. FORMATION OF COMPANY: IN GENERAL

95. Formation of new company under the Companies Act 2006. A company[1] is formed under the Companies Act 2006 by one or more persons[2]: subscribing their names to a memorandum of association[3] and complying with the requirements of the Companies Act 2006 as to registration[4]. A company may not be so formed for an unlawful purpose[5].

A company is a 'limited company' if the liability of its members is limited by its constitution[6]. It may be limited by shares[7] or limited by guarantee[8]: if the liability of its members is limited to the amount, if any, unpaid on the shares held by them, the company is 'limited by shares'[9]; if their liability is limited to such amount as the members undertake to contribute to the assets of the company in the event of its being wound up[10], the company is 'limited by guarantee'[11]. If there is no limit on the liability of its members, the company is an 'unlimited company'[12].

A 'public company' within the meaning of the Companies Act 2006 is a company limited by shares, or limited by guarantee and having a share capital[13], being a company[14]:

(1) whose certificate of incorporation[15] states that it is a public company[16]; and

(2) in relation to which the requirements of the Companies Act 2006, or the former Companies Acts[17], as to the registration or re-registration of a company as a public company[18] have been complied with on or after 22 December 1980[19].

A 'private company' within the meaning of the Companies Act 2006 is a company that is not a public company[20].

With effect from 22 December 1980[21], a company cannot be formed as, or become, a company limited by guarantee with a share capital[22]. Nor may a public company limited by guarantee and not having a share capital be formed as from that date[23].

Any contract, so far as it relates to the formation of a company[24] or to its constitution, or the rights or obligations of its corporators or members, is exempt from the prohibitions on the exclusion of liability imposed[25] by the Unfair Contract Terms Act 1977[26].

1 As to the meaning of 'company' under the Companies Acts see PARA 21; and as to the meaning of the 'Companies Acts' see PARA 13.

2 As to the meaning of 'person' for these purposes see PARA 96; and as to the meaning of 'person' generally see PARA 312 note 2. Any enactment or rule of law applicable to companies formed by two or more persons or having two or more members applies with any necessary modification in relation to a company formed by one person or having only one person as a member: Companies Act 2006 s 38. This provision is made in order to implement Council Directive (EC) 89/667 (OJ L395, 30.12.89, p 40) (the 'Twelfth Company Law Directive') on single-member private limited liability companies (now repealed and replaced by European Parliament and Council Directive (EC) 2009/102 (OJ L258, 1.10.2009, p 20): see PARA 20. As to the meaning of 'enactment' see PARA 13 note 16. As to the meaning of 'member' see PARA 323. As to membership of a company generally see PARA 323 et seq.

3 Companies Act 2006 s 7(1)(a). As to the meaning of 'memorandum of association' see PARA 97. As to subscribers to the memorandum of association see s 8; and PARA 97. As to subscribers as members of the company see PARA 323; and as to restrictions on agreements for the transfer to subscribers of non-cash assets in the 'initial period' see PARA 1314.

4 Companies Act 2006 s 7(1)(b). References in the company law provisions of the Companies Act 2006 to the requirements of that Act include the requirements of regulations and orders made under it: s 1172. As to the meaning of the 'company law provisions' of the Companies Act 2006 see PARA 13 note 6. As to the registration requirements mentioned in the text see ss 9–13; and PARA 104 (application to registrar for registration), PARA 105 (requisite particulars of directors and secretaries), PARA 106 (statement of initial significant control), PARA 107 (statement of capital and initial shareholdings required in the case of a company limited by shares), PARA 109 (statement of guarantee required in the case of a company that is to be limited by guarantee).

As to the registration requirements for companies formed under the Companies (Audit, Investigations and Community Enterprise) Act 2004 see PARA 112. The provisions which govern community interest companies (ie the Companies (Audit, Investigations and Community Enterprise) Act 2004 Pt 2 (ss 26–63): see PARA 75 et seq) are still regarded as company law provisions under the statutory framework established by the Companies Act 2006, but they are regarded as forming a distinct body of regulation which is additional to, and sits alongside, company law rather than forming part of it. The provisions of the Companies Acts, apart from the Companies Act 2006 s 6 (see PARA 75), have effect subject to the Companies (Audit, Investigations and Community Enterprise) Act 2004 Pt 2: see the Companies Act 2006 s 6(2); and PARA 75.

5 Companies Act 2006 s 7(2). The registrar of companies has a duty not to register an unlawful association: *R v Registrar of Companies, ex p Bowen* [1914] 3 KB 1161 at 1167. See also *R v Registrar of Companies, ex p A-G* [1991] BCLC 476 (where the registration of a company whose main object was the organising of the services of a prostitute was quashed as the purpose was contrary to public policy and unlawful). As to companies which are formed for an illegal purpose see PARA 99 et seq. As to the registrar of companies see PARA 126 et seq.

6 Companies Act 2006 s 3(1). As to the meaning of references to a company's constitution see PARA 226.

7 As to companies limited by shares see also PARA 71.

8 Companies Act 2006 s 3(1). As to companies limited by guarantee see also PARA 72.

9 Companies Act 2006 s 3(2).

10 As to winding up in general see COMPANY AND PARTNERSHIP INSOLVENCY vol 16 (2011) PARA 380 et seq.

11 Companies Act 2006 s 3(3).

12 Companies Act 2006 s 3(4). As to unlimited companies see PARA 74.

13 As to the meanings of 'company having a share capital' and 'share capital' see PARA 1231. With the coming into effect of the Companies Act 1980 (repealed), and in accordance with all

subsequent Companies Acts, it has not been possible to form a company which is limited by guarantee and having a share capital, although such companies that had existed up to that point have not been extinguished by any act of law and they may continue to exist, legally, as historical entities: see the text and notes 22–23.

14 Companies Act 2006 s 4(2). As to public companies and their powers generally see PARA 66. As to the share capital requirements that are imposed on public companies see PARA 67 et seq. In the case of an unregistered company (see PARA 1856 et seq), any reference to a public company must be read as referring to a company that has power under its constitution to offer its shares or debentures to the public: see the Unregistered Companies Regulations 2009, SI 2009/2436, reg 5(1)(a); and PARA 1857. As to the meaning of 'unregistered company' see PARA 1856.

Before the enactment of the Companies Act 1907 (repealed), the term 'public company' was understood to mean a company which invited the public to subscribe for its shares, and companies which did not do so were often called private companies and are so described in many judgments (see *Re British Seamless Paper Box Co* (1881) 17 ChD 467 at 473, CA; *Re George Newman & Co* [1895] 1 Ch 674 at 685, CA; *Salomon v A Salomon & Co Ltd* [1897] AC 22 at 43, HL; *Re Wragg Ltd* [1897] 1 Ch 796 at 807, CA), although the legal status of such a company is that of a public company (*Re Sharp, Rickett v Sharp* (1890) 45 ChD 286 at 290, CA; *Re Lysaght, Lysaght v Lysaght* [1898] 1 Ch 115 at 122, CA; *Trevor v Whitworth* (1887) 12 App Cas 409 at 434, HL). Thereafter the term 'public company', which was not defined, was used in contradistinction to 'private company', which was defined as a company which by its articles restricted the right to transfer its shares, limited the number of its members (excluding persons in or formerly in the employment of the company) to 50, and prohibited any invitation to the public to subscribe for its shares and debentures: see the Companies Act 1948 ss 28, 455(1) (repealed). In other Acts, the term 'public company', although not expressly defined, may include a private company: see eg *Re White, Theobald v White* [1913] 1 Ch 231 at 238 (decided under the Apportionment Act 1870). As to private companies under the Companies Act 2006 see the text and note 22; and see PARA 65.

15 As to a company's certificate of incorporation see PARA 114.

16 Companies Act 2006 s 4(2)(a). As to the required indications in the name of a public limited company see PARA 199 et seq.

17 As to the meaning of the 'former Companies Acts' see PARA 14 note 1.

18 As to the re-registration of a private company as a public company under the Companies Act 2006 see PARAS 168–172.

19 Companies Act 2006 s 4(2)(b), (3)(a). The date of 22 December 1980 referred to in the text is the date on which the corresponding provisions of the Companies Act 1980 (now repealed) came into force: see the Companies Act 1980 (Commencement No 2) Order 1980, SI 1980/1785. As to the Companies Act 1980 generally see PARA 10.

20 Companies Act 2006 s 4(1). For the two major differences between private and public companies see Pt 20 Ch 1 (ss 755–760) (prohibition of public offers by private companies) (as to which see PARA 1255) and Pt 20 Ch 2 (ss 761–767) (minimum share requirement for public companies) (as to which see PARA 67 et seq): s 4(4). See also note 14. As to private companies and the restrictions on their powers see also PARA 65.

In the case of an unregistered company (see PARA 1856 et seq), any reference to a private company must be read as referring to a company that does not have power to offer its shares or debentures to the public: see the Unregistered Companies Regulations 2009, SI 2009/2436, reg 5(1)(b); and PARA 1857.

21 See note 19.

22 See the Companies Act 2006 s 5(1), (2)(a); and PARA 72.

23 This is the effect of the Companies Act 2006 s 5(1), (2) (see the text and note 22) when combined with the definition of a public company given in s 4(2) (see the text and note 14).

24 For these purposes, 'company' means any body corporate or unincorporated association and includes a partnership: Unfair Contract Terms Act 1977 Sch 1 para 1(d). As to the meaning of 'body corporate' see PARA 1 note 5. As to the meaning of 'partnership' see PARA 4.

25 Ie such a contract is exempt from the operation of the Unfair Contract Terms Act 1977 ss 3, 7: see s 1(2) (amended by the Consumer Rights Act 2015 Sch 4 paras 2, 3).

26 Unfair Contract Terms Act 1977 Sch 1 para 1(d). As to the exemptions from liability arising in contract referred to in the text generally see CONTRACT vol 22 (2012) PARA 416.

96. Meaning of 'person' as subscriber to the memorandum of association. For the purpose of subscribing to the memorandum of association[1], 'person' includes a foreigner although residing abroad[2], a person who is a trustee for another subscriber[3], and a person who signs by an agent, although only orally appointed[4]. It also includes a corporation and limited company[5], and it may perhaps also include a minor[6].

If a firm name is, with the authority of the firm, subscribed to a memorandum, the partners are joint holders of the shares subscribed for[7]. If an individual subscribes in his own name as agent for a firm, and the firm takes up the shares subscribed for, he is absolved from liability[8].

1 As to a company's memorandum of association see PARA 97 et seq.
2 *Princess Reuss v Bos* (1871) LR 5 HL 176.
3 *Salomon v A Salomon & Co Ltd* [1897] AC 22 at 46, HL, per Lord Herschell.
4 *Re Whitley Partners Ltd* (1886) 32 ChD 337, CA.
5 See the Interpretation Act 1978 ss 5, 22(1), 23(1), Sch 1, Sch 2 para 4(1)(a) (meaning of 'person') (see STATUTES AND LEGISLATIVE PROCESS vol 96 (2012) PARA 1214); and the Companies Act 2006 s 323 (see PARA 733). See also PARA 312 note 2. See also *Re Barned's Banking Co, ex p Contract Corpn* (1867) 3 Ch App 105; *Pharmaceutical Society v London and Provincial Supply Association* (1880) 5 App Cas 857, HL; *Union Steamship Co of New Zealand Ltd v Melbourne Harbour Trust Comrs* (1884) 9 App Cas 365, PC.
6 See *Re Laxon & Co (No 2)* [1892] 3 Ch 555; *Re Nassau Phosphate Co* (1876) 2 ChD 610. On attaining full age a minor may repudiate the contract which arises on his signature (*Re Hertfordshire Brewery Co* (1874) 43 LJ Ch 358; *Re Laxon & Co (No 2)* at 561–562 per Vaughan Williams J); but such repudiation does not invalidate the incorporation of the company (*Re Hertfordshire Brewery Co*). See also PARA 332.
7 *Re Land Credit Co of Ireland, Weikersheim's Case* (1873) 8 Ch App 831. See also *Niemann v Niemann* (1889) 43 ChD 198, CA. As to the meaning of 'share' generally see PARA 1231.
8 *Re Glory Paper Mills Co, Dunster's Case* [1894] 3 Ch 473, CA.

97. Requirements of memorandum under the Companies Act 2006. A 'memorandum of association' is a memorandum stating that the subscribers[1]:

(1) wish to form a company[2] under the Companies Act 2006[3]; and
(2) agree to become members of the company[4] and, in the case of a company that is to have a share capital[5], to take at least one share each[6].

The memorandum must be in the prescribed form[7] and must be authenticated by each subscriber[8].

A company must have articles of association[9] prescribing regulations for the company[10].

1 Companies Act 2006 s 8(1). As to subscribers of the memorandum see also PARA 323 et seq.
2 As to the meaning of 'company' under the Companies Acts see PARA 21; and as to the meaning of the 'Companies Acts' see PARA 13.
3 Companies Act 2006 s 8(1)(a). As to formation of a company under the Companies Act 2006 see PARA 95. As to restrictions on agreements for the transfer by subscribers to the company of non-cash assets in the 'initial period' see PARA 1314. As to the memorandum and articles of association of a community interest company see PARA 98.
4 As to the meaning of 'member' see PARA 323. As to membership of a company see PARA 323 et seq.
5 As to the meanings of 'company having a share capital' and 'share capital' see PARA 1231.
6 Companies Act 2006 s 8(1)(b). As to the meaning of 'share' see PARA 1231.
7 In the Companies Acts, 'prescribed' means prescribed (by order or by regulations) by the Secretary of State: Companies Act 2006 s 1167. As to the making of orders and regulations under the Companies Act 2006 generally see ss 1288–1292. As to the Secretary of State see PARA 6. Partly in exercise of the powers conferred by s 8(2), the Secretary of State has made the Companies (Registration) Regulations 2008, SI 2008/3014. Accordingly, for the purposes of the Companies Act 2006 s 8, the memorandum of association of a company having a share capital must be in the form set out in the Companies (Registration) Regulations 2008, SI 2008/3014, reg 2(a), Sch 1 (see PARAS 71 note 8, 74 note 7); and the memorandum of association of a company not having a share capital must be in the form set out in reg 2(b), Sch 2 (see PARAS 72 note 8, 74 note 7).

For existing companies (see PARA 229), the prescribed form of memorandum for a company limited by shares is given in the Companies (Tables A to F) Regulations 1985, SI 1985/805, reg 2, Schedule Table B (private company limited by shares) and in Schedule Table F (public company limited by shares) (see PARA 71 note 8); the prescribed form of memorandum for a company limited by guarantee is given in Schedule Table C (company limited by guarantee and not having a share capital), in Schedule Table D Pt I (public company limited by guarantee and having a share capital) and in Schedule Table D Pt II (private company limited by guarantee and having a share capital) (see PARA 72 note 8); and the prescribed form of memorandum for an unlimited company having a share capital is given in the Companies (Tables A to F) Regulations 1985, SI 1985/805, reg 2, Schedule Table E (an unlimited company having a share capital) (see PARA 74 note 7). As to the meanings of 'company limited by shares', 'company limited by guarantee', 'limited company', 'private company', 'public company' and 'unlimited company' see PARA 95.

Provisions that immediately before 1 October 2009 were contained in a company's memorandum but are not provisions of the kind mentioned in the Companies Act 2006 s 8 are to be treated after that date as provisions of the company's articles: see s 28(1); and PARA 227. 1 October 2009 is the date by which s 8 had come fully into force: see the Companies Act 2006 (Commencement No 8, Transitional Provisions and Savings) Order 2008, SI 2008/2860, art 3(b).

8 Companies Act 2006 s 8(2). In relation to the authentication of a document under the Companies Act 2006 see s 1146; and PARAS 750–751. As to the requirement to deliver the memorandum to the registrar of companies see PARA 104. A company's memorandum is subject to the disclosure requirements in s 1078: see s 1078(2); and PARA 139.

9 As to the meaning of references to a company's 'articles' see PARA 227 note 2. As to a company's articles of association generally see PARA 227 et seq. See also note 7.

10 See the Companies Act 2006 s 18; and PARA 227.

98. Requirements relating to a community interest company. The articles of association[1] of a community interest company[2] must state that the company is to be a community interest company[3].

The articles of a community interest company of any description[4]:

(1) must at all times include such provisions as regulations require to be included in the articles of every community interest company or a community interest company of that description[5]; and

(2) must not include such provisions as regulations require not to be so included[6].

The articles of a community interest company are of no effect to the extent that they[7]:

(a) are inconsistent with provisions required[8] to be included in the articles of the company[9]; or

(b) include provisions required[10] not to be included[11].

Regulations may make provision for and in connection with restricting the ability of a community interest company to amend its articles so as to add, remove or alter a statement of the company's objects[12].

1 As to a company's articles of association generally see PARA 227 et seq.

2 As to community interest companies see PARA 75 et seq. As to a community interest company's articles of association see the text and notes 3–12.

3 Companies (Audit, Investigations and Community Enterprise) Act 2004 s 32(1) (amended by SI 2009/1941).

4 Companies (Audit, Investigations and Community Enterprise) Act 2004 s 32(3) (amended by SI 2009/1941).

5 Companies (Audit, Investigations and Community Enterprise) Act 2004 s 32(3)(a) (amended by SI 2009/1941). The provisions required by regulations under the Companies (Audit, Investigations and Community Enterprise) Act 2004 s 32(3)(a) to be included in the articles of a community interest company may (in particular) include the following (s 32(4) (amended by SI 2009/1941)):

(1) provisions about the transfer and distribution of the company's assets (including their distribution on a winding up) (Companies (Audit, Investigations and Community Enterprise) Act 2004 s 32(4)(a));

(2) provisions about the payment of interest on debentures issued by the company or debts of the company (s 32(4)(b));

(3) provisions about membership of the company (s 32(4)(c));

(4) provisions about the voting rights of members of the company (s 32(4)(d));

(5) provisions about the appointment and removal of directors of the company (s 32(4)(e)); and

(6) provisions about voting at meetings of directors of the company (s 32(4)(f)).

As to the making of regulations under the Companies (Audit, Investigations and Community Enterprise) Act 2004 generally see s 62 (amended by SI 2009/1941). In exercise of the powers conferred by the Companies (Audit, Investigations and Community Enterprise) Act 2004 s 32(3), (4), (6), the Secretary of State has made the Community Interest Company Regulations 2005, SI 2005/1788, regs 7–10, 13–16, Sch 1–3 (regs 7, 8 substituted by, and regs 10, 13–16 amended by,

SI 2009/1942; the Community Interest Company Regulations 2005, SI 2005/1788, regs 9, 15–16 amended by SI 2007/1093; the Community Interest Company Regulations 2005, SI 2005/1788, Schs 1–3 amended by SI 2007/1093; SI 2008/948; SI 2009/1942; SI 2014/1815). As to the Secretary of State see PARA 6. As to meetings of directors see PARA 567 et seq.

Provision is made with regard to:

(a) requirements for a company without share capital (see the Community Interest Company Regulations 2005, SI 2005/1788, reg 7 (as so substituted), Sch 1 (as so amended));

(b) requirements for a company with share capital (see reg 8 (as so substituted), Schs 2, 3 (as so amended));

(c) alternative wording which may be used in certain of the provisions prescribed by Schs 1–3 (see reg 9 (as so amended));

(d) declaration of dividends (see reg 10 (as so amended));

(e) alteration of the company's objects (see regs 13–16 (as so amended)).

6 Companies (Audit, Investigations and Community Enterprise) Act 2004 s 32(3)(b). See also note 5.

7 Companies (Audit, Investigations and Community Enterprise) Act 2004 s 32(5) (amended by SI 2009/1941).

8 Ie by regulations under the Companies (Audit, Investigations and Community Enterprise) Act 2004 s 32(3)(a) (see head (1) in the text): see s 32(5)(a) (as amended: see note 9).

9 Companies (Audit, Investigations and Community Enterprise) Act 2004 s 32(5)(a) (amended by SI 2009/1941).

10 Ie by regulations under the Companies (Audit, Investigations and Community Enterprise) Act 2004 s 32(3)(b) (see head (2) in the text): see s 32(5)(b).

11 Companies (Audit, Investigations and Community Enterprise) Act 2004 s 32(5)(b).

12 Companies (Audit, Investigations and Community Enterprise) Act 2004 s 32(6) (amended by SI 2009/1941). See also note 5.

99. Companies formed for an illegal purpose. A company of a dangerous and mischievous character or formed for a fraudulent purpose is probably illegal at common law[1]; and a company, the proposed constitution of which involves an offence against the general law, cannot properly be registered[2]. In the event of such a company being registered[3], that act in itself would not render its objects legal[4]. Thus a company formed to set up a commercial lottery in England[5], other than a company authorised by licence to run or promote lotteries[6], or to sell tickets in England in a lottery in a foreign state where lotteries are legal, would, if registered under the Companies Act 2006, be an illegal company[7]; but a company formed to set up a lottery in a foreign state where such lotteries are legal would not be illegal[8].

The fact that some only of the provisions of a company's constitution are illegal does not necessarily make the company an illegal one, or prevent the court from giving effect to such of the rules as are legal[9]; but, where the objects of a company include an illegal object, and other objects of the company, although in themselves legal, are mere applications of the governing principle stated in the illegal object, the company is an illegal company[10]. If a company is formed for legal purposes, the commission by it of illegal acts does not make it an illegal company[11].

1 An Act of 1719 (6 Geo 1 c 18) ss 18, 19 (repealed; popularly known as the 'Bubble Act') declared to be illegal and void dangerous and mischievous undertakings and attempts tending to the common grievance, prejudice and inconvenience of the King's subjects, or great numbers of them, and more particularly by unincorporated companies presuming to act as if they were corporate bodies, and pretending to make their shares or stocks transferable, without any legal authority by Act of Parliament or charter; but, even before that Act was repealed, there were conflicting decisions as to whether acting, by an unincorporated company, as a corporation, without the authority of a statute or charter, and pretending to be possessed of transferable stock, was illegal: *Duvergier v Fellows* (1828) 5 Bing 248 at 267; *Blundell v Winsor* (1837) 8 Sim 601; *Walburn v Ingilby* (1883) 1 My & K 61 at 76. After that Act had been partly repealed in 1825 (by 6 Geo 4 c 91), notwithstanding the recital in the repealing Act that the several undertakings, attempts, practices, acts, matters and things referred to in the repealed Act should be adjudged and dealt with in like manner as they might have been adjudged and dealt with 'according to the common law,

notwithstanding the Act', the mere raising and transfer of stock in an unincorporated company was not an offence at common law: *Garrard v Hardey* (1843) 5 Man & G 471; *Harrison v Heathorn* (1843) 6 Man & G 81.

2 *R v Registrar of Joint Stock Companies, ex p More* [1931] 2 KB 197 at 201, CA; *R v Registrar of Companies, ex p Bowen* [1914] 3 KB 1161; *Bowman v Secular Society Ltd* [1917] AC 406, HL. As to registration under the Companies Act 2006 see PARA 104.

3 Because the Companies Act 2006 is not expressed to bind the Crown, it would appear that, in the event of such a company being incorporated by registration under that Act (see PARA 114), the Attorney General could institute proceedings by way of a quashing order to cancel the registration: *Bowman v Secular Society Ltd* [1917] AC 406 at 439–440, HL, per Lord Parker of Waddington; and see the cases cited in note 2. As to quashing orders see JUDICIAL REVIEW vol 61 (2010) PARA 693. In practice, the registrar can be relied upon to refuse to register such a company, and consequently the question of what is the status of such a company has never been decided: see PARA 114. As to the meaning of 'registrar' see PARA 126 note 2.

4 However, the effect of the Companies Act 2006 s 15(4) (conclusiveness of the certificate of incorporation: see PARA 114) appears to be that the courts will recognise the corporate existence of a company all of whose objects are transparently illegal, while the certificate remains unrevoked: *Bowman v Secular Society Ltd* [1917] AC 406 at 439, HL, per Lord Parker of Waddington.

5 As to lotteries see LICENSING AND GAMBLING vol 68 (2008) PARA 686 et seq. As to the meaning of 'England' see PARA 1 note 5.

6 See the National Lottery etc Act 1993 ss 5(1), 6(1); and LICENSING AND GAMBLING vol 68 (2008) PARAS 691–692.

7 *R v Registrar of Joint Stock Companies, ex p More* [1931] 2 KB 197, CA. A company (not being an unregistered company) carrying on an illegal business may be wound up in the public interest on a petition by the Secretary of State under the Insolvency Act 1986 s 124A: see COMPANY AND PARTNERSHIP INSOLVENCY vol 16 (2011) PARA 392. See also *Re Alpha Club (UK) Ltd* [2002] EWHC 884 (Ch), [2002] 2 BCLC 612; *Re Delfin International SA Ltd, Re Delfin Marketing (UK) Ltd* [2000] 1 BCLC 71 (both cases involving illegal lottery and trading schemes); *Re Millennium Advanced Technology Ltd* [2004] EWHC 711 (Ch), [2004] 4 All ER 465, [2004] 1 WLR 2177; *Re UK-Euro Group plc* [2006] EWHC 2102 (Ch), [2007] 1 BCLC 812. Cf *Re Portfolios of Distinction Ltd* [2006] EWHC 782 (Ch), [2006] 2 BCLC 261. See also *Re Inertia Partnership LLP* [2007] EWHC 539 (Ch), [2007] 1 BCLC 739. As to the grounds on which an unregistered company may be wound up see COMPANY AND PARTNERSHIP INSOLVENCY vol 17 (2011) PARA 1113.

8 *Macnee v Persian Investment Corpn* (1890) 44 ChD 306 (company held not to be an illegal company in the proper sense of the term, as no illegality was shown in the memorandum of association of the company). See also note 11. Provisions that immediately before 1 October 2009 were contained in a company's memorandum but are not provisions of the kind mentioned in the Companies Act 2006 s 8 (which substantially altered the purpose of the memorandum of association) (see PARA 97) are to be treated after that date as provisions of the company's articles: see s 28(1); and PARA 227. Under the Companies Act 2006, unless a company's articles of association specifically restrict the objects of the company, its objects are unrestricted: see PARA 239.

9 *Strick v Swansea Tin-Plate Co* (1887) 36 ChD 558; *Swaine v Wilson* (1889) 24 QBD 252, CA. See also *Re General Co for the Promotion of Land Credit* (1870) 5 Ch App 363 (affd sub nom *Princess Reuss v Bos* (1871) LR 5 HL 176); *McGlade v Royal London Mutual Insurance Society Ltd* [1910] 2 Ch 169, CA.

10 *Bowman v Secular Society Ltd* [1917] AC 406 at 421, HL.

11 *Macnee v Persian Investment Corpn* (1890) 44 ChD 306 at 311. Thus it would appear that a money-lending company which failed to comply with the then statutory requirements as to moneylenders was not an illegal company but was merely liable to the penalties imposed by those requirements: see further *Lodge v National Union Investment Co Ltd* [1907] 1 Ch 300. The same would appear to apply to a company which carries on the business of dentistry without complying with the requirements of the Dentists Act 1984 s 43 (see MEDICAL PROFESSIONS vol 74 (2011) PARA 427), or which carries on business under the style or title of 'architect' without complying with the requirements of the Architects Act 1997 s 20(1) (see BUILDING CONTRACTS vol 6 (2011) PARA 428).

100. Proceedings by or against illegal companies. An illegal company (that is, one formed for an illegal purpose) cannot sustain a claim to recover a debt incurred for money lent, either to members or outsiders[1], or on any contract made directly for the purpose of carrying on its business[2]. A trustee for the illegal company is in no better position[3].

Money lent to an illegal company for the purpose of carrying out its objects cannot be recovered[4], and persons making other contracts with an illegal company may not be able to enforce them against it[5]. Persons subscribing to the formation of a company, the agreement to form which is illegal, may, however, recover the money before it is actually applied to the illegal purpose[6], and the court will order any persons who have received the money subscribed to render an account[7]; but the question, even now, seems open whether the courts will assist members of illegal companies to recover their subscriptions from the persons who have been the recipients of them, and, if so, by what means[8].

The members of an illegal company may be beneficial owners of property, and, if an officer of the company steals funds entrusted to him, he may be indicted for theft[9].

1 *Jennings v Hammond* (1882) 9 QBD 225.

2 *Jennings v Hammond* (1882) 9 QBD 225. See, however, *Hill v Secretary of State for the Environment, Food and Rural Affairs* [2005] EWHC 696 (Ch), [2006] 1 BCLC 601 (claimant company formed to carry on farming business for the benefit of person disqualified under the Company Directors Disqualification Act 1986 s 11 (see PARA 1780) could enforce contracts entered into by it in the course of its being unlawfully managed; defence of illegality rejected on public policy grounds). As to void and illegal contracts see generally CONTRACT vol 22 (2012) PARA 424 et seq.

3 *Shaw v Benson* (1883) 11 QBD 563, CA.

4 *Phillips v Davies* (1888) 5 TLR 98.

5 *Re Padstow Total Loss and Collision Assurance Association* (1882) 20 ChD 137, CA.

6 *Strachan v Universal Stock Exchange (No 2)* [1895] 2 QB 697, CA; *Burge v Ashley and Smith Ltd* [1900] 1 QB 744, CA. As to the formation of a company under the Companies Act 2006 see PARA 95 et seq.

7 *Greenberg v Cooperstein* [1926] Ch 657.

8 See *Greenberg v Cooperstein* [1926] Ch 657 at 666 per Tomlin J, *Hume v Record Reign Jubilee Syndicate* (1899) 80 LT 404; *Sheppard v Oxenford* (1855) 1 K & J 491; *Marrs v Thompson* (1902) 86 LT 759, DC; *Re One and All Sickness and Accident Assurance Association* (1909) 25 TLR 674.

9 *R v Tankard* [1894] 1 QB 548; *R v Stainer* (1870) LR 1 CCR 230.

As to the offence of theft see the Theft Act 1968; and CRIMINAL LAW vol 25 (2016) PARA 315 et seq. See also the Fraud Act 2006 s 4 (fraud by abuse of position); and CRIMINAL LAW vol 25 (2016) PARA 346.

101. Winding up of illegal company. An illegal company cannot be wound up by the court under the Insolvency Act 1986 on its own petition or that of a member[1], or on the petition of a creditor, at any rate if the petitioner had notice of the illegality[2]. If a winding-up order is made, it is effective unless and until discharged on appeal and, while it exists, the illegality of the company is not a bar to proceedings in the winding up[3].

1 *Re Mexican and South American Mining Co, Barclay's Case* (1858) 26 Beav 177 at 179–180 (court will not sanction or notice an illegal association nor exercise its powers in favour of it); *Re London and Eastern Banking Corpn, Longworth's Case* (1859) 1 De GF & J 17 at 30–31, CA. As to winding up in general see COMPANY AND PARTNERSHIP INSOLVENCY vol 16 (2011) PARA 380 et seq.

2 *Re Padstow Total Loss and Collision Assurance Association* (1882) 20 ChD 137, CA; *Re South Wales Atlantic Steamship Co* (1876) 2 ChD 763, CA; *Re Arthur Average Association for British, Foreign and Colonial Ships, ex p Hargrove & Co* (1875) 10 Ch App 542 at 545n; *Re Building Society* [1901] 1 Ch 102. The court may, however, administer a trust where the beneficiaries exceed 20, even though the trust involves the carrying on of some business, provided the business is carried on by trustees who are less than 20 in number: *Smith v Anderson* (1880) 15 ChD 247, CA.

3 *Re Padstow Total Loss and Collision Assurance Association* (1882) 20 ChD 137, CA; *Re Arthur Average Association for British, Foreign and Colonial Ships, ex p Hargrove & Co* (1875) 10 Ch App 542; *Re Arthur Average Association* (1876) 3 ChD 522; *Re Queen's Average Association, ex p Lynes* (1878) 38 LT 90; *Re London Marine Insurance Association, Andrews and*

Alexander's Case, Chatt's Case, Cook's Case, Crew's Case (1869) LR 8 Eq 176. See also COMPANY AND PARTNERSHIP INSOLVENCY vol 16 (2011) PARA 391.

102. Company's right to set up illegality in proceedings against it. An illegal company may set up its own illegality in answer to proceedings against it[1]; but, where effect is given to that defence, the company may not be allowed costs[2].

1 *Phillips v Davies* (1888) 5 TLR 98; *Re Ilfracombe Permanent Mutual Benefit Building Society* [1901] 1 Ch 102. Cf *Re Padstow Total Loss and Collision Assurance Association* (1882) 20 ChD 137, CA; *Doolan v Midland Rly Co* (1877) 2 App Cas 792 at 806, HL.

2 *Phillips v Davies* (1888) 5 TLR 98; *Re Ilfracombe Permanent Mutual Benefit Building Society* [1901] 1 Ch 102.

103. Sale of shares in an illegal company. The sale of shares or scrip in an illegal company or intended company is illegal[1]; and a broker who is employed to sell or purchase them cannot recover from his principal any commission or any sums expended on his behalf [2]. The buyer cannot recover any purchase money paid to the broker[3].

1 *Josephs v Pebrer* (1825) 3 B & C 639; *Buck v Buck* (1808) 1 Camp 547.

2 *Josephs v Pebrer* (1825) 3 B & C 639. Cf *Re Edmond, ex p Neilson* (1863) 3 De GM & G 556.

3 *Buck v Buck* (1808) 1 Camp 547.

B. COMPANY REGISTRATION REQUIREMENTS

104. Application to registrar for registration of company. The memorandum of association[1] must be delivered to the registrar[2] together with an application for registration of the company[3], the other documents required[4] for registration and a statement of compliance[5].

The application for registration must state[6]:

(1) the company's proposed name[7];

(2) whether the company's registered office is to be situated in England and Wales (or in Wales), in Scotland or in Northern Ireland[8];

(3) whether the liability of the members of the company[9] is to be limited, and if so whether it is to be limited by shares[10] or by guarantee[11]; and

(4) whether the company is to be a private[12] or a public company[13].

The application must contain[14]:

(a) in the case of a company that is to have a share capital[15], a statement of capital and initial shareholdings[16];

(b) in the case of a company that is to be limited by guarantee, a statement of guarantee[17];

(c) a statement of the company's proposed officers[18];

(d) as from 6 April 2016[19], a statement of initial significant control[20].

and the application must also contain:

(i) a statement of the intended address of the company's registered office[21];

(ii) and a copy of any proposed articles of association[22], to the extent that these are not supplied by the default application of model articles[23]; and

(iii) as from 30 June 2016[24], a statement of the type of company it is to be[25] and its intended principal business activities[26,26].

The statement of compliance required to be delivered to the registrar is a statement that the requirements of the Companies Act 2006 as to registration have been complied with[26,26]. The registrar may accept the statement of compliance as sufficient evidence of compliance[27].

If the registrar is satisfied that the requirements of the Companies Act 2006 as to registration are complied with, he must register the documents delivered to him[28]. The duty of the registrar as to registration has never been purely ministerial[29]. He should consider whether the requirements of the Companies Acts have been complied with and refuse registration if he conceives that they have not[30]. The court will not interfere[31] with the decision of the registrar unless it is shown that the registrar had not in fact exercised his discretion, or that he had exercised it upon some wrong principle of law, or that he had been influenced by extraneous considerations which he ought not to have taken into account[32].

1 As to the meaning of 'memorandum of association' see PARA 97.
2 Ie to the registrar of companies for England and Wales, if the registered office of the company is to be situated in England and Wales (or in Wales): Companies Act 2006 s 9(6)(a). As to where the registered office of the company is to be situated in Scotland or in Northern Ireland see s 9(6)(b), (c). As to the meaning of 'registrar of companies' see PARA 126 note 2; and as to the meanings of 'England' and 'Wales' see PARA 1 note 5. As to the delivery of documents to the registrar see PARA 136; and as to the requirements generally for the proper delivery of documents to the registrar see PARA 137. As to the company's registered office see PARA 124.
3 If the application is delivered by a person as agent for the subscribers to the memorandum of association, it must state his name and address: Companies Act 2006 s 9(3). Any obligation under the Companies Acts to give a person's address is, unless otherwise expressly provided, to give a service address for that person: Companies Act 2006 s 1142. As to service of documents on a company generally see PARA 743. As to the meaning of 'company' under the Companies Acts see PARA 21; and as to the meaning of the 'Companies Acts' see PARA 13. As to subscribers to the memorandum see PARA 97.
4 Ie required by the Companies Act 2006 s 9: see s 9(1).
5 Companies Act 2006 s 9(1). As to the statement of compliance see the text and notes 26–27.
6 Companies Act 2006 s 9(2).
7 Companies Act 2006 s 9(2)(a). As to restrictions on the use of company names and trading names generally see PARA 195 et seq.
8 Companies Act 2006 s 9(2)(b). See also note 2.
9 As to the meaning of 'member' see PARA 323. As to membership of a company generally see PARA 323 et seq.
10 As to the meaning of 'company limited by shares' see PARA 95; and as to the meaning of 'share' see PARA 1231. See also PARA 71.
11 Companies Act 2006 s 9(2)(c). As to the meaning of 'company limited by guarantee' see PARA 95. See also PARA 72.
12 As to the meaning of 'private company' see PARA 95.
13 Companies Act 2006 s 9(2)(d). As to the meaning of 'public company' see PARA 95.
14 Companies Act 2006 s 9(4).
15 As to the meanings of 'company having a share capital' and 'share capital' see PARA 1231.
16 Companies Act 2006 s 9(4)(a). As to the statement of capital and initial shareholdings required in the case of a company limited by shares see s 10; and PARA 107.
17 Companies Act 2006 s 9(4)(b). As to the statement of guarantee required in the case of a company that is to be limited by guarantee see s 11; and PARA 109.
18 Companies Act 2006 s 9(4)(c). As to the meaning of 'officer' generally under the Companies Act 2006 see PARA 679. As to the statement of the company's proposed officers see s 12; and PARA 105.
19 See the Small Business, Enterprise and Employment Act 2015 (Commencement No 3) Regulations 2015, SI 2015/2029, reg 4.
20 Companies Act 2006 s 9(4)(d) (added by the Small Business, Enterprise and Employment Act 2015 Sch 3 Pt 2 paras 3, 4). As to the statement of initial significant control see the Companies Act 2006 s 12A; and PARA 106.
21 Companies Act 2006 s 9(5)(a).
22 As to the meaning of references to a company's 'articles' see PARA 227 note 2. As to a company's articles of association generally see PARA 227 et seq.
23 Companies Act 2006 s 9(5)(b). A limited company need not register its articles: see PARA 97. As to the default application of the model articles see s 20; and PARA 227.
24 See the Small Business, Enterprise and Employment Act 2015 (Commencement No 4, Transitional and Savings Provisions) Regulations 2016, SI 2016/321, reg 6(b).
25 The information as to the company's type must be given by reference to the classification scheme prescribed for these purposes: Companies Act 2006 s 9(5A) (s 9(5A), (5B) added by the Small Business, Enterprise and Employment Act 2015 s 93(1), (3)). In the Companies Acts, 'prescribed' means prescribed (by order or by regulations) by the Secretary of State: Companies Act 2006 s 1167. For the classification scheme prescribed for the purposes of s 9(5A) see the Companies and

Limited Liability Partnerships (Filing Requirements) Regulations 2016, SI 2016/599, reg 6, Sch 4. As to the meaning of the 'Companies Acts' see PARA 13. As to the making of orders and regulations under the Companies Act 2006 generally see ss 1288–1292. As to the Secretary of State see PARA 6.

26 Companies Act 2006 s 9(5)(c) (added by the Small Business, Enterprise and Employment Act 2015 s 93(1), (2)). The information as to the company's intended principal business activities may be given by reference to one or more categories of any prescribed system of classifying business activities: Companies Act 2006 s 9(5B) (as added: see note 25). The Standard Industrial Classification 2007 is prescribed for the purposes of s 9(5B), with the addition of the codes and designations in the table in the Companies and Limited Liability Partnerships (Filing Requirements) Regulations 2016, SI 2016/599, Sch 5, where the code set out in column 1 of the table represents the designation opposite it in column 2 of the table: reg 7(1). For these purposes, 'Standard Industrial Classification 2007' means the UK Standard Industrial Classification of Economic Activities 2007, prepared by the Office for National Statistics and published by Palgrave MacMillan with the permission of the Office of Public Sector Information (OPSI) with ISBN number 978-0-230-21012-7: Companies and Limited Liability Partnerships (Filing Requirements) Regulations 2016, SI 2016/599, reg 7(2).

26 Companies Act 2006 s 13(1). The statement of compliance need not be witnessed. References in the company law provisions of the Companies Act 2006 to the requirements of that Act include the requirements of regulations and orders made under it: s 1172. As to the meaning of the 'company law provisions' of the Companies Act 2006 see PARA 13 note 6.

26 Companies Act 2006 s 9(5)(c) (added by the Small Business, Enterprise and Employment Act 2015 s 93(1), (2)). The information as to the company's intended principal business activities may be given by reference to one or more categories of any prescribed system of classifying business activities: Companies Act 2006 s 9(5B) (as added: see note 25). The Standard Industrial Classification 2007 is prescribed for the purposes of s 9(5B), with the addition of the codes and designations in the table in the Companies and Limited Liability Partnerships (Filing Requirements) Regulations 2016, SI 2016/599, Sch 5, where the code set out in column 1 of the table represents the designation opposite it in column 2 of the table: reg 7(1). For these purposes, 'Standard Industrial Classification 2007' means the UK Standard Industrial Classification of Economic Activities 2007, prepared by the Office for National Statistics and published by Palgrave MacMillan with the permission of the Office of Public Sector Information (OPSI) with ISBN number 978-0-230-21012-7: Companies and Limited Liability Partnerships (Filing Requirements) Regulations 2016, SI 2016/599, reg 7(2).

26 Companies Act 2006 s 13(1). The statement of compliance need not be witnessed. References in the company law provisions of the Companies Act 2006 to the requirements of that Act include the requirements of regulations and orders made under it: s 1172. As to the meaning of the 'company law provisions' of the Companies Act 2006 see PARA 13 note 6.

27 Companies Act 2006 s 13(2).

28 Companies Act 2006 s 14. As to fees payable under s 14 see the Registrar of Companies (Fees) (Companies, Overseas Companies and Limited Liability Partnerships) Regulations 2012, SI 2012/1907, Sch 1 para 8(a) (amended with effect from 30 June 2016 by SI 2016/621). As to incorporation and its effects see PARA 114 et seq.

29 *R v Registrar of Companies* [1912] 3 KB 23 at 34, DC, per Avery J; *Bowman v Secular Society Ltd* [1917] AC 406 at 439, HL, per Lord Parker of Waddington.

30 *Codman v Brougham* [1918] AC 514 at 523, HL, per Lord Wrenbury; *R v Registrar of Joint Stock Companies, ex p More* [1931] 2 KB 197, CA (refusal to register company with unlawful objects). As to the refusal of registration where the name of the company is undesirable see PARA 195.

31 Ie by way of a mandatory order (formerly an order of mandamus). As to mandatory orders see JUDICIAL REVIEW vol 61 (2010) PARA 703 et seq.

32 *R v Registrar of Companies* [1912] 3 KB 23 at 34, DC, per Avery J. See also *R v Registrar of Companies, ex p Bowen* [1914] 3 KB 1161; *R v Registrar of Companies, ex p A-G* [1991] BCLC 476; and see the cases cited in PARA 114 note 27.

105. Statement of proposed officers of the company. The statement of proposed officers[1] required to be delivered[2] to the registrar of companies[3] must contain the required particulars of[4]:

(1) the person who is, or persons who are, to be the first director or directors of the company[5];

(2) in the case of a company that is to be a private company[6], any person who is, or any persons who are, to be the first secretary, or joint secretaries, of the company[7];

(3) in the case of a company that is to be a public company[8], the person who is, or the persons who are, to be the first secretary, or joint secretaries, of the company[9].

The required particulars are the particulars that will or would[10] be required to be stated[11]:

(a) in the case of a director, in the company's register of directors[12] and register of directors' residential addresses[13];

(b) in the case of a secretary, in the company's register of secretaries[14].

The statement must also include a statement by the subscribers to the memorandum of association that each of the persons named as a director, as secretary or as one of the joint secretaries has consented to act in the relevant capacity[15].

Whenever the registrar registers the statement of proposed officers required on formation of a company, as soon as reasonably practicable after registering the document, he must notify the person or each person named in the statement as a director of the company[16]. The notice must state that the person is named in the document as a director of the company, and include such information relating to the office and duties of a director, or such details of where information of that sort can be found, as the Secretary of State may from time to time direct the registrar to include[17].

1 As to the meaning of 'officer' generally under the Companies Act 2006 see PARA 679. As to the company secretary and other officers see PARA 671.

2 Ie in accordance with the Companies Act 2006 s 9(1), (4): see PARA 104. Such a statement is subject to the disclosure requirements in s 1078: see s 1078(2); and PARA 139. As to the effect of the statement of proposed officers upon the registration of a company under the Companies Act 2006 see s 16(1), (6); and PARA 115.

The Secretary of State may make provision by regulations requiring a statement sent under s 12 that relates (wholly or partly) to a person who is a person disqualified under Pt 40 (ss 1182–1191) (foreign disqualification etc: see PARA 1811 et seq), or is subject to a disqualification order or disqualification undertaking under the Company Directors Disqualification Act 1986, to be accompanied by an additional statement: see s 1189; and PARA 1815. As to the Secretary of State see PARA 6.

3 Ie to the registrar of companies for England and Wales, if the registered office of the company is to be situated in England and Wales (or in Wales): see the Companies Act 2006 s 9(6)(a); and PARA 104. As to where the registered office of the company is to be situated in Scotland or in Northern Ireland see s 9(6)(b), (c); and PARA 104. As to the meaning of 'company' under the Companies Acts see PARA 21; as to the meaning of the 'Companies Acts' see PARA 13; as to the meaning of 'registrar of companies' see PARA 126 note 2; and as to the meanings of 'England' and 'Wales' see PARA 1 note 5. As to the delivery of documents to the registrar see PARA 136; and as to the requirements generally for the proper delivery of documents to the registrar see PARA 137. As to the company's registered office see PARA 124.

4 Companies Act 2006 s 12(1).

5 Companies Act 2006 s 12(1)(a). As to the meaning of 'director' see PARA 512.

6 As to the meaning of 'private company' see PARA 95.

7 Companies Act 2006 s 12(1)(b). Private companies are not required to have a secretary: see PARA 669.

8 As to the meaning of 'public company' see PARA 95.

9 Companies Act 2006 s 12(1)(c).

10 Ie the particulars that would be required to be stated in the absence of an election under the Companies Act 2006 s 167A or s 279A: see PARAS 551, 675.

11 Companies Act 2006 s 12(2) (amended by the Small Business, Enterprise and Employment Act 2015 Sch 5 Pt 2 paras 11, 12).

12 As to the register of directors see the Companies Act 2006 ss 162–164, 166; and PARA 535; and as to the option to keep directors' information on the central register see PARA 551 et seq.

13 Companies Act 2006 s 12(2)(a). As to the register of directors' residential addresses see ss 165–166; and PARA 536; and as to the option to keep directors' information on the central register see PARA 551 et seq.

14 Companies Act 2006 s 12(2)(b). As to the register of secretaries see ss 277–279; and PARA 673; and as to the option to keep secretaries' information on the central register see PARA 675 et seq.

15 Companies Act 2006 s 12(3) (amended by the Small Business, Enterprise and Employment Act 2015 s 100(1), (2)). For transitional provisions see s 100(6). If all the partners in a firm are to be joint secretaries, consent may be given by one partner on behalf of all of them: Companies Act 2006 s 12(3). In the Companies Acts, 'firm' means any entity, whether or not a legal person, that is not an individual and includes a body corporate, a corporation sole and a partnership or other unincorporated association: s 1173(1). As to firms and partnerships generally see PARTNERSHIP vol 79 (2014) PARA 1. As to corporations sole see CORPORATIONS vol 24 (2010) PARAS 314–315.

16 Companies Act 2006 s 1079B(1)(a), (2)(a) (s 1079B added by the Small Business, Enterprise and Employment Act 2015 s 101(1)). For transitional provisions see s 101(2). The notice may be sent in hard copy or electronic form to any address for the person that the registrar has received from either the subscribers or the company: Companies Act 2006 s 1079B(4) (as so added).

Section 1079B applies to unregistered companies in cases where the document registered by the registrar is a notice under s 167 (see PARA 550) of a person having become a director of a company, by virtue of the Unregistered Companies Regulations 2009, SI 2009/2436, Sch 1 para 19A (added by SI 2015/1695) (see PARA 1857). As to the meaning of 'unregistered company' see PARA 1856.

17 Companies Act 2006 s 1079B(3) (as added: see note 16).

106. Statement of initial significant control of the company. The statement of initial significant control required to be delivered[1] to the registrar of companies[2] must:

(1) state whether, on incorporation[3], there will be anyone who will count for the purposes of the statutory provision regarding the register of people with significant control over a company[4] as either a registrable person[5] or a registrable relevant legal entity[6] in relation to the company[7];

(2) include the required particulars[8] of anyone who will count as such[9]; and

(3) include any other matters that on incorporation will be required (or, in the absence of an election to keep particulars of people with significant control on the central register[10], would be required) to be entered[11] in the company's PSC register[12].

If the statement includes required particulars of an individual, it must also contain a statement that those particulars are included with the knowledge of that individual[13].

1 Ie in accordance with the Companies Act 2006 s 9(1), (4): see PARA 104. Such a statement is subject to the disclosure requirements in s 1078: see s 1078(3); and PARA 139.

2 Ie to the registrar of companies for England and Wales, if the registered office of the company is to be situated in England and Wales (or in Wales): see the Companies Act 2006 s 9(6)(a); and PARA 104. As to where the registered office of the company is to be situated in Scotland or in Northern Ireland see s 9(6)(b), (c); and PARA 104. As to the meaning of 'company' under the Companies Acts see PARA 21; as to the meaning of the 'Companies Acts' see PARA 13; as to the meaning of 'registrar of companies' see PARA 126 note 2; and as to the meanings of 'England' and 'Wales' see PARA 1 note 5. As to the delivery of documents to the registrar see PARA 136; and as to the requirements generally for the proper delivery of documents to the registrar see PARA 137. As to the company's registered office see PARA 124.

3 As to the incorporation of a company see PARA 114 et seq. The Companies Act 2006 s 12A (see the text and notes 1–2, 4–13) is modified in its application to SEs so that the references to 'incorporation' are read as 'registration': European Public Limited-Liability Company (Register of People with Significant Control) Regulations 2016, SI 2016/375, reg 4. For these purposes, 'SE' means a European public limited-liability company (or Societas Europaea) within the meaning of Council Regulation (EC) 2157/2001 (OJ L 294, 10.11.2001, p 1) of 8 October 2001 on the Statute for a European Company which is to be, or is, registered in the United Kingdom: European Public Limited-Liability Company (Register of People with Significant Control) Regulations 2016, SI 2016/375, reg 2. As to such companies see PARA 1825 et seq.

4 Ie for the purposes of the Companies Act 2006 s 790M: see PARA 480.

5 As to the meaning of 'registrable person' see PARA 467 text and note 22 (definition applied by the Companies Act 2006 s 12A(4) (s 12A added by the Small Business, Enterprise and Employment Act 2015 Sch 3 Pt 2 paras 3, 5, with effect from 6 April 2016: see the Small Business, Enterprise and Employment Act 2015 (Commencement No 3) Regulations 2015, SI 2015/2029, reg 4).

6 As to the meaning of 'registrable relevant legal entity' see PARA 467 text and note 26 (definition as applied: see note 5).

7 Companies Act 2006 s 12A(1)(1)(a) (as added: see note 5).

8 As to the meaning of 'required particulars' see PARA 469 (definition as applied: see note 5).

9 Companies Act 2006 s 12A(1)(1)(b) (as added: see note 5). It is not necessary to include under s 12A(1)(b) the date on which someone becomes a registrable person or a registrable relevant legal entity in relation to the company: s 12A(2) (as so added).

10 Ie an election under the Companies Act 2006 s 790X: see PARA 485.

11 Ie by virtue of the Companies Act 2006 s 790M: see PARA 480.

12 Companies Act 2006 s 12A(1)(1)(c) (as added: see note 5). As to the meaning of 'company's PSC register' see PARA 470 note 5; and as to that register see PARA 480.

13 Companies Act 2006 s 12A(3) (as added: see note 5).

107. Statement of capital and initial shareholdings. The statement of capital and initial shareholdings that is required to be delivered[1] in the case of a company limited by shares[2] must comply with the following provisions[3], namely:

(1) it must state:
   (a) the total number of shares of the company to be taken on formation by the subscribers to the memorandum of association[4];
   (b) the aggregate nominal value of those shares[5];
   (c) either, before 30 June 2016, the amount to be paid up and the amount, if any, to be unpaid on each share, whether on account of the nominal value of the share or by way of premium[6], or, on or after that date[7], the aggregate amount, if any, to be unpaid on those shares, whether on account of their nominal value or by way of premium[8];
   (d) for each class of shares[9] prescribed particulars of the rights attached to the shares[10], the total number of shares of that class[11] and the aggregate nominal value of shares of that class[12];

(2) it must contain such information as may be prescribed for the purpose of identifying the subscribers to the memorandum of association[13]; and

(3) it must state, with respect to each subscriber to the memorandum:
   (a) the number, nominal value (of each share) and class of shares to be taken by him on formation[14]; and
   (b) the amount to be paid up and the amount (if any) to be unpaid on each share (whether on account of the nominal value of the share or by way of premium)[15].

1 Ie in accordance with the Companies Act 2006 s 9(1), (4): see PARA 104. Such a statement is subject to the disclosure requirements in s 1078: see s 1078(3); and PARA 139.

2 Ie being a company that is to have a share capital: see the Companies Act 2006 s 10(1). As to the meaning of 'company' under the Companies Acts see PARA 21; and as to the meaning of the 'Companies Acts' see PARA 13. As to the meaning of 'company limited by shares' see PARA 95; and as to the meanings of 'company having a share capital', 'share capital' and 'share' see PARA 1231. As to the requirements that must be met before a company is duly formed see PARA 95 et seq; and as to the required indications in the name of a limited company see PARA 199 et seq.

3 Companies Act 2006 s 10(1).

4 Companies Act 2006 s 10(2)(a). As to the meaning of 'memorandum of association' see PARA 97. As to the memorandum of association of a company limited by shares see PARA 71; and as to subscribers to a company's memorandum of association see PARA 97.

5 Companies Act 2006 s 10(2)(b). As to the nominal value of shares see PARA 1233.

6 Companies Act 2006 s 10(2)(d) (repealed by the Small Business, Enterprise and Employment Act 2015 Sch 6 paras 1, 2(b)). See also note 7. As to paid up and unpaid shares see PARA 1231 et seq.
7 See the Small Business, Enterprise and Employment Act 2015 (Commencement No 4, Transitional and Savings Provisions) Regulations 2016, SI 2016/321, reg 6(e).
8 Companies Act 2006 s 10(2)(ba) (added by the Small Business, Enterprise and Employment Act 2015 Sch 6 paras 1, 2(a)).
9 Companies Act 2006 s 10(2)(c). As to classes of shares generally see PARA 1246 et seq.
10 Companies Act 2006 s 10(2)(c)(i). In the Companies Acts, 'prescribed' means prescribed (by order or by regulations) by the Secretary of State: Companies Act 2006 s 1167. As to the meaning of the 'Companies Acts' see PARA 13. As to the making of orders and regulations under the Companies Act 2006 generally see ss 1288–1292. As to the Secretary of State see PARA 6. Partly in exercise of the powers conferred by s 10(2)(c)(i), the Secretary of State has made the Companies (Shares and Share Capital) Order 2009, SI 2009/388. Accordingly, the following particulars of the rights attached to shares are prescribed for the purposes of the Companies Act 2006 s 10(2)(c)(i) (see the Companies (Shares and Share Capital) Order 2009, SI 2009/388, art 2(1), (2)(a)):
(1) particulars of any voting rights attached to the shares, including rights that arise only in certain circumstances (art 2(3)(a));
(2) particulars of any rights attached to the shares, as respects dividends, to participate in a distribution (art 2(3)(b));
(3) particulars of any rights attached to the shares, as respects capital, to participate in a distribution (including on winding up) (art 2(3)(c)); and
(4) whether the shares are to be redeemed or are liable to be redeemed at the option of the company or the shareholder (art 2(3)(d)).

As to rights attached to classes of shares generally see PARA 1246 et seq; as to redeemable shares see PARAS 1241, 1416 et seq; and as to distributions and dividends see PARA 1562 et seq. As to winding up in general see COMPANY AND PARTNERSHIP INSOLVENCY vol 16 (2011) PARA 380 et seq.
11 Companies Act 2006 s 10(2)(c)(ii).
12 Companies Act 2006 s 10(2)(c)(iii).
13 Companies Act 2006 s 10(3). Partly in exercise of the powers conferred by s 10(3), the Secretary of State has made the Companies (Registration) Regulations 2008, SI 2008/3014. Accordingly, for the purposes of the Companies Act 2006 s 10(3), the statement of capital and initial shareholdings must contain the name and address of each subscriber to the memorandum of association: Companies (Registration) Regulations 2008, SI 2008/3014, reg 3. Any obligation under the Companies Acts to give a person's address is, unless otherwise expressly provided, to give a service address for that person: Companies Act 2006 s 1142.
14 Companies Act 2006 s 10(4)(a). Where a subscriber to the memorandum is to take shares of more than one class, the information required under s (4)(a) is required for each class: s 10(5).
15 Companies Act 2006 s 10(4)(b).

108. Articles of association of a company limited by shares. A company limited by shares[1] need not register its articles of association[2].

However, on the formation of a limited company[3]:

(1) if articles of association are not registered[4]; or
(2) if articles are registered (in so far as they do not exclude or modify the model articles[5] prescribed for a company of that description as in force at the date on which the company is registered)[6],

the model articles, so far as applicable, form part of the company's articles in the same manner and to the same extent as if articles in the form of those articles had been duly registered[7].

1 Ie a company that is to have a share capital. As to the meaning of 'company' under the Companies Acts see PARA 21; and as to the meaning of the 'Companies Acts' see PARA 13. As to the meaning of 'company limited by shares' see PARA 95; and as to the meanings of 'company having a share capital', 'share capital' and 'share' see PARA 1231. See also PARA 71. As to the required indications in the name of a limited company see PARA 199 et seq.
2 See the Companies Act 2006 ss 18(1), (2), 20; and PARA 227. As to the meaning of references to a company's 'articles' see PARA 227 note 2. As to a company's articles of association generally see PARA 227 et seq.
3 As to the meaning of 'limited company' see PARA 95. As to the requirements that must be met before a company is duly formed see PARA 95 et seq.
4 See the Companies Act 2006 s 20(1)(a); and PARA 227.

5 As to the power to prescribe model articles, and their application, see PARA 227. As to the model articles, and the legacy articles that still may have application, see PARAS 228, 229. Provided that he follows the general form of the relevant model articles, the draftsman is free to add, subtract or vary the articles as circumstances require: *Gaiman v National Association for Mental Health* [1971] Ch 317, [1970] 2 All ER 362.
6 See the Companies Act 2006 s 20(1)(b), (2); and PARA 227. As to the importance of using words clearly excluding the default articles see *Fisher v Black and White Publishing Co* [1901] 1 Ch 174, CA.
7 See the Companies Act 2006 s 20(1); and PARA 227.

109. Statement of guarantee required to be delivered on application for registration. The statement of guarantee required to be delivered[1] in the case of a company that is to be limited by guarantee[2] must comply with the following requirements[3], namely:

(1) it must contain such information as may be prescribed for the purpose of identifying the subscribers to the memorandum of association[4];
(2) it must state that each member[5] undertakes that, if the company is wound up[6] while he is a member, or within one year after he ceases to be a member, he will contribute to the assets of the company such amount as may be required for:
  (a) payment of the debts and liabilities of the company contracted before he ceases to be a member[7];
  (b) payment of the costs, charges and expenses of winding up[8]; and
  (c) adjustment of the rights of the contributories among themselves[9],

not exceeding a specified amount[10].

1 Ie in accordance with the Companies Act 2006 s 9(1), (4): see PARA 104.
2 As to the meaning of 'company' under the Companies Acts see PARA 21; and as to the meaning of the 'Companies Acts' see PARA 13. As to the meaning of 'company limited by guarantee' see PARA 95. See also PARA 72. As to the requirements that must be met before a company is duly formed see PARA 95 et seq.
3 Companies Act 2006 s 11(1).
4 Companies Act 2006 s 11(2). In the Companies Acts, 'prescribed' means prescribed (by order or by regulations) by the Secretary of State: s 1167. As to the making of orders and regulations under the Companies Act 2006 generally see ss 1288–1292. As to the Secretary of State see PARA 6. Partly in exercise of the powers conferred by s 11(2), the Secretary of State has made the Companies (Registration) Regulations 2008, SI 2008/3014. Accordingly, for the purposes of the Companies Act 2006 s 11(2), the statement of guarantee must contain the name and address of each subscriber to the memorandum of association: Companies (Registration) Regulations 2008, SI 2008/3014, reg 4. As to the meaning of 'memorandum of association' see PARA 97. As to the memorandum of association of a company limited by guarantee see PARA 72; and as to subscribers to a company's memorandum of association see PARA 97.
5 As to the meaning of 'member' see PARA 323. As to membership of a company generally see PARA 323 et seq.
6 As to winding up in general see COMPANY AND PARTNERSHIP INSOLVENCY vol 16 (2011) PARA 380 et seq.
7 Companies Act 2006 s 11(3)(a).
8 Companies Act 2006 s 11(3)(b).
9 Companies Act 2006 s 11(3)(c).
10 Companies Act 2006 s 11(3). In the Companies Acts, 'contributory' means every person liable to contribute to the assets of a company in the event of its being wound up: s 1170B(1) (s 1170B added by SI 2009/1941). For the purposes of all proceedings for determining, and all proceedings prior to the final determination of, the persons who are to be deemed contributories, the expression includes any person alleged to be a contributory: Companies Act 2006 s 1170B(2) (as so added). The reference in s 1170B(1) to persons liable to contribute to the assets does not include a person so liable by virtue of a declaration by the court under the Insolvency Act 1986 s 213 (fraudulent trading) (see COMPANY AND PARTNERSHIP INSOLVENCY vol 17 (2011) PARA 869) or under s 214 (wrongful trading) (see COMPANY AND PARTNERSHIP INSOLVENCY vol 17 (2011) PARA 872): Companies Act 2006 s 1170B(3) (as so added).

110. Articles of association of a company limited by guarantee. A company limited by guarantee[1] need not register[2] its articles of association[3].

However, on the formation of a limited company[4]:

(1) if articles of association are not registered[5]; or

(2) if articles are registered (in so far as they do not exclude or modify the model articles[6] prescribed for a company of that description as in force at the date on which the company is registered)[7],

the model articles (so far as applicable) form part of the company's articles in the same manner and to the same extent as if articles in the form of those articles had been duly registered[8].

In the case of a company that is limited by guarantee and has no share capital[9], and is registered on or after 1 January 1901[10], any provision in the company's articles, or in any resolution of the company[11], purporting to give any person[12] a right to participate in the divisible profits of the company, otherwise than as a member[13], is void[14].

1 As to the meaning of 'company' under the Companies Acts see PARA 21; and as to the meaning of the 'Companies Acts' see PARA 13. As to the meaning of 'company limited by guarantee' see PARA 95. See also PARA 72.
2 Ie in accordance with the Companies Act 2006 s 9(1), (4): see PARA 104.
3 See the Companies Act 2006 ss 18(1), (2), 20; and PARA 227. As to the meaning of references to a company's 'articles' see PARA 227 note 2. As to a company's articles of association generally see PARA 227 et seq.
4 As to the meaning of 'limited company' see PARA 95. As to the requirements that must be met before a company is duly formed see PARA 95 et seq.
5 See the Companies Act 2006 s 20(1)(a); and PARA 227.
6 As to the power to prescribe model articles, and their application, see PARA 227. As to the model articles, and the legacy articles that still may have application, see PARAS 228, 229. Provided that he follows the general form of the relevant model articles, the draftsman is free to add, subtract or vary the articles as circumstances require: *Gaiman v National Association for Mental Health* [1971] Ch 317, [1970] 2 All ER 362.
7 See the Companies Act 2006 s 20(1)(b), (2); and PARA 227. As to the importance of using words clearly excluding the default articles see *Fisher v Black and White Publishing Co* [1901] 1 Ch 174, CA.
8 See the Companies Act 2006 s 20(1); and PARA 227.
9 As to the meanings of 'company having a share capital' and 'share capital' see PARA 1231.
10 Ie the date on which the Companies Act 1900 (repealed) came into force.
11 As to company resolutions generally see PARA 684 et seq.
12 As to the meaning of 'person' see PARA 96.
13 As to the meaning of 'member' see PARA 323. As to membership of a company generally see PARA 323 et seq.
14 See the Companies Act 2006 s 37. This provision prevents a person from sharing in the profits of a guarantee company registered on or after 1 January 1901, unless he is a member, and as such is under a liability to contribute to the assets of the company in the event of its being wound up (see PARA 109).

111. Articles of association of an unlimited company. In the case of an unlimited company[1], there must be registered[2] with the memorandum[3], articles of association[4] prescribing regulations for the company[5]. These articles may adopt all or any of the model articles that have been prescribed[6].

A company registered as unlimited may re-register itself as a limited company[7].

1 As to the meaning of 'company' under the Companies Acts see PARA 21; and as to the meaning of the 'Companies Acts' see PARA 13. As to the meaning of 'unlimited company' see PARA 95.
2 Ie in accordance with the Companies Act 2006 s 9(1), (4): see PARA 104.
3 As to the meaning of 'memorandum of association' see PARA 97. As to the memorandum of association of an unlimited company see PARA 74.
4 As to the meaning of references to a company's 'articles' see PARA 227 note 2. As to a company's articles of association generally see PARA 227 et seq.
5 See the Companies Act 2006 ss 18(1), (2), 20; and PARA 227.

6 See the Companies Act 2006 s 19; and PARA 227. As to the power to prescribe model articles, and their application, see PARA 227. As to the model articles, and the legacy articles that still may have application, see PARAS 228, 229.
7 See PARAS 178–180.

112. Registration of new company formed as a community interest company. If a company is to be formed as a community interest company[1], the documents delivered to the registrar of companies[2] must be accompanied by the prescribed formation documents[3].

On receiving the documents so delivered and the prescribed formation documents, the registrar of companies must, instead of registering the documents, forward a copy of each of the documents to the Regulator[4], and retain the documents pending the Regulator's decision[5].

The Regulator must decide whether the company is eligible to be formed as a community interest company[6]. A company is eligible to be formed as a community interest company if:

(1) its articles[7] comply with the statutory requirements that are so imposed[8];
(2) its proposed name complies with the relevant statutory requirements[9]; and
(3) the Regulator, having regard to the application and accompanying documents and any other relevant considerations, considers that the company will satisfy the community interest test and is not an excluded company[10].

The Regulator must give notice of the decision to the registrar of companies, but the registrar is not required to record it[11].

If the Regulator decides that the company is eligible to be formed as a community interest company, the registrar of companies must proceed in accordance with the statutory requirements which govern the registration of the documents delivered to him[12] and the issue of certificates of incorporation[13]; and if the company is entered on the register[14], he must also retain and record the prescribed formation documents[15].

The certificate of incorporation must state that the company is a community interest company[16]; and the fact that the certificate of incorporation contains such a statement is conclusive evidence that the company is a community interest company[17].

If the Regulator decides that the company is not eligible to be formed as a community interest company, any subscriber to the memorandum of association[18] may appeal to the Appeal Officer[19] against the decision[20].

1 As to community interest companies see PARA 75.
2 Ie under the Companies Act 2006 s 9 (registration documents) (see PARA 104): see the Companies (Audit, Investigations and Community Enterprise) Act 2004 s 36(1) (s 36 substituted by SI 2009/1941). As to the registrar of companies see PARA 126 et seq.
3 Companies (Audit, Investigations and Community Enterprise) Act 2004 s 36(1) (as substituted: see note 2). For these purposes, the 'prescribed formation documents' means such declarations or statements as are required by regulations to accompany the application, in such form as may be approved in accordance with the regulations: s 36(2) (as so substituted). As to the making of regulations under the Companies (Audit, Investigations and Community Enterprise) Act 2004 generally see s 62 (amended by SI 2009/1941). In exercise of the powers conferred by the Companies (Audit, Investigations and Community Enterprise) Act 2004 s 36(2), the Secretary of State has made the Community Interest Company Regulations 2005, SI 2005/1788, reg 11. As to the Secretary of State see PARA 6.

The prescribed formation documents are a community interest statement signed by each person who is to be a first director of the company and a declaration that the company, when formed, will not be an excluded company: reg 11(1). That declaration must be in a form approved by the

Regulator and must be made by each person who is to be a first director of the company: reg 11(2). As to the meaning of 'excluded company' see PARA 80 note 6; and as to the Regulator see PARA 76.

4 Companies (Audit, Investigations and Community Enterprise) Act 2004 s 36(3)(a) (as substituted: see note 2).

5 Companies (Audit, Investigations and Community Enterprise) Act 2004 s 36(3)(b) (as substituted: see note 2). The material so retained is not available for public inspection: see the Companies Act 2006 s 1087(1)(j); and PARA 146.

6 Companies (Audit, Investigations and Community Enterprise) Act 2004 s 36A(1) (s 36A added by SI 2009/1941).

7 As to a community interest company's articles of association see PARA 98; and as to a company's articles of association generally see PARA 227 et seq.

8 See the Companies (Audit, Investigations and Community Enterprise) Act 2004 s 36A(2)(a) (as added: see note 6). Head (1) in the text refers to the requirements imposed by and by virtue of s 32 (see PARA 98): see s 36A(2)(a) (as so added).

9 Companies (Audit, Investigations and Community Enterprise) Act 2004 s 36A(2)(b) (as added: see note 6). Head (2) in the text refers to the requirements of s 33 (see PARA 202): see s 36A(2)(b); and PARA 112.

10 Companies (Audit, Investigations and Community Enterprise) Act 2004 s 36A(2)(c) (as added: see note 6). As to the community interest test see PARA 80.

11 Companies (Audit, Investigations and Community Enterprise) Act 2004 s 36A(3) (as added: see note 6).

12 Ie he must proceed in accordance with the Companies Act 2006 s 14 (see PARA 104): see the Companies (Audit, Investigations and Community Enterprise) Act 2004 s 36B(1)(a) (s 36B added by SI 2009/1941).

13 Companies (Audit, Investigations and Community Enterprise) Act 2004 s 36B(1)(a) (as added: see note 12). The text refers to the requirement that the registrar proceed in accordance with the Companies Act 2006 s 15 (see PARA 114): see the Companies (Audit, Investigations and Community Enterprise) Act 2004 s 36B(1)(a) (as so added).

14 As to the register see PARA 142.

15 Companies (Audit, Investigations and Community Enterprise) Act 2004 s 36B(1)(b) (as added: see note 12).

16 Companies (Audit, Investigations and Community Enterprise) Act 2004 s 36B(2) (as added: see note 12).

17 See the Companies (Audit, Investigations and Community Enterprise) Act 2004 s 36B(2) (as added: see note 12).

18 As to subscribers to the memorandum see PARA 97.

19 As to the Appeal Officer for community interest companies see PARA 77.

20 Companies (Audit, Investigations and Community Enterprise) Act 2004 s 36B(3) (as added: see note 12).

C. INTRODUCTION OF STREAMLINED REGISTRATION

113. Streamlined company registration. The Secretary of State[1] must secure that, by no later than 31 May 2017, a system for streamlined company registration is in place[2]. For these purposes, a system for streamlined company registration is a system which enables all of the registration information[3] to be delivered by or on behalf of a person who wishes to form a company after 31 May 2017 on a single occasion to a single recipient, and by electronic means[4].

The Secretary of State must prepare a report before the end of each reporting period[5] about the progress that has been made during that period towards putting in place a system for streamlined company registration[6]. The first report must set out the steps which the Secretary of State expects will be taken during the next reporting period towards putting the system in place[7]. The second report must include an assessment of what steps, if any, the Secretary of State expects to take to put in place a system for the streamlining of other information delivery processes relating to businesses[8]. Both reports must include the Secretary of State's assessment as to when the system for streamlined company registration will be in place[9]. The Secretary of State must publish each report and lay each report before Parliament[10].

1 As to the Secretary of State see PARA 6.
2 Small Business, Enterprise and Employment Act 2015 s 15(1).
3 'Registration information' means:
   (1) the documents which must be delivered to the registrar under the Companies Act 2006 s 9 (registration documents: see PARA 104) in respect of the formation of a company (Small Business, Enterprise and Employment Act 2015 s 15(3)(a));
   (2) the documents or other information which must or may be delivered to Her Majesty's Revenue and Customs in respect of registration of a company for purposes connected with VAT, corporation tax and PAYE (Small Business, Enterprise and Employment Act 2015 s 15(3)(b)).

   'VAT' means value added tax charged in accordance with the Value Added Tax Act 1994: Small Business, Enterprise and Employment Act 2015 s 15(4). As to the meaning of 'company' see PARA 21; as to the meaning of 'electronic means' see PARA 751 note 3; and as to the meaning of 'the registrar' see PARA 126 note 2 (definitions applied by s 15(4)).
4 Small Business, Enterprise and Employment Act 2015 s 15(2).
5 The following are reporting periods (Small Business, Enterprise and Employment Act 2015 s 16(2)):
   (1) the period beginning with 26 May 2015 (ie the day on which s 16 came into force: see s 164(3)(b)(i)) and ending on 31 March 2016;
   (2) the subsequent period of 12 months ending on 31 March 2017.
6 Small Business, Enterprise and Employment Act 2015 s 16(1).
7 Small Business, Enterprise and Employment Act 2015 s 16(3).
8 Small Business, Enterprise and Employment Act 2015 s 16(5).
9 Small Business, Enterprise and Employment Act 2015 s 16(4).
10 Small Business, Enterprise and Employment Act 2015 s 16(6).

D. INCORPORATION AND ITS EFFECTS

114. Certificate of incorporation. On the registration of a company[1], the registrar of companies[2] must give a certificate that the company is incorporated[3]. The certificate must state[4]:

(1) the name[5] and registered number of the company[6];
(2) the date of its incorporation[7];
(3) whether it is a limited[8] or unlimited company[9], and if it is limited whether it is limited by shares[10] or limited by guarantee[11];
(4) whether it is a private[12] or a public company[13];
(5) whether the company is a community interest company[14];
(6) whether the company's registered office[15] is situated in England and Wales[16] (or in Wales), in Scotland or in Northern Ireland[17].

The certificate must be signed by the registrar or authenticated by the registrar's official seal[18]. The registrar's duty to certify may be enforced by a mandatory order[19]. The registrar is also required to cause notice of the issue of the certificate to be published[20].

The certificate is conclusive evidence that the requirements of the Companies Act 2006[21] as to registration have been complied with and that the company is duly registered under that Act[22].

If a company is registered with illegal objects[23], the existence of a certificate precludes its corporate status being challenged without, however, making those objects legal[24]; but the registration provision[25] is not expressed to bind the Crown, and the Attorney General, on behalf of the Crown, may institute proceedings by way of a quashing order[26] to cancel a registration improperly or erroneously allowed[27].

A copy of the certificate certified in writing by the registrar is admissible in evidence in legal proceedings[28], and, as against the company itself, registration may be evidenced by other means, for example by producing its sealed share certificate[29].

1 As to the meaning of 'company' under the Companies Acts see PARA 21; and as to the meaning of the 'Companies Acts' see PARA 13. As to company registration see PARA 104 et seq.
2 As to the meaning of 'registrar of companies' see PARA 126 note 2.
3 Companies Act 2006 s 15(1). As to the effect of incorporation see PARA 115.
4 Companies Act 2006 s 15(2).
5 As to company names and trading names generally see PARA 195 et seq.
6 Companies Act 2006 s 15(2)(a). As to a company's registered number see ss 1066, 1067; and PARAS 134–135.
7 Companies Act 2006 s 15(2)(b). The company is incorporated from the beginning of the date mentioned in the certificate of incorporation: *Official Receiver and Liquidator of Jubilee Cotton Mills Ltd v Lewis* [1924] AC 958, HL. The statute does not authorise the day to be ante-dated: *Official Receiver and Liquidator of Jubilee Cotton Mills Ltd v Lewis* at 974.
8 As to the meaning of 'limited company' see PARA 95.
9 As to the meaning of 'unlimited company' see PARA 95.
10 As to the meaning of 'company limited by shares' see PARA 95; and as to the meaning of 'share' see PARA 1231.
11 Companies Act 2006 s 15(2)(c). As to the meaning of 'company limited by guarantee' see PARA 95. See also PARA 72.
12 As to the meaning of 'private company' see PARA 95.
13 Companies Act 2006 s 15(2)(d). As to the meaning of 'public company' see PARA 95.
14 See the Companies (Audit, Investigations and Community Enterprise) Act 2004 s 36B(2); and PARA 112. As to community interest companies see PARA 75.
15 As to the company's registered office see PARA 124.
16 As to the meanings of 'England' and 'Wales' see PARA 1 note 5.
17 Companies Act 2006 s 15(2)(e).
18 Companies Act 2006 s 15(3). As to the registrar's official seal see PARA 126.
19 This was the procedure adopted in *R v Whitmarsh* (1850) 15 QB 600; *R v Registrar of Joint Stock Companies* (1847) 10 QB 839. As to mandatory orders see JUDICIAL REVIEW vol 61 (2010) PARA 703 et seq.
20 As to public notice of the issue of certificates of incorporation see the Companies Act 2006 s 1064; and PARA 133.
21 References in the company law provisions of the Companies Act 2006 to the requirements of that Act include the requirements of regulations and orders made under it: s 1172. As to the meaning of the 'company law provisions' of the Companies Act 2006 see PARA 13 note 6.
22 Companies Act 2006 s 15(4). Before the Companies Act 1900 (repealed), there was some doubt as to the meaning of 'conclusive': see *Re National Debenture and Assets Corpn* [1891] 2 Ch 505, CA. See also *Ladies' Dress Association Ltd v Pulbrook* [1900] 2 QB 376, CA. The extended wording of the Companies Act 1900 s 1 (repealed) (see now the Companies Act 2006 s 15) shows that 'conclusive' means what it says: *Hammond v Prentice Bros Ltd* [1920] 1 Ch 201. As to the possibility of proceedings in the nature of a scire facias see *Salomon v A Salomon & Co Ltd* [1897] AC 22 at 30, HL. As to scire facias see CONSTITUTIONAL AND ADMINISTRATIVE LAW vol 20 (2014) PARA 661; and see also CORPORATIONS vol 24 (2010) PARA 503; CROWN AND CROWN PROCEEDINGS vol 29 (2014) PARA 90.
23 As to companies formed for an illegal purpose see PARA 99.
24 *Bowman v Secular Society Ltd* [1917] AC 406 at 438–439, HL, per Lord Parker of Waddington.
25 Ie the Companies Act 2006 s 15 (see the text and notes 1–20).
26 As to quashing orders see JUDICIAL REVIEW vol 61 (2010) PARA 693.
27 *Bowman v Secular Society Ltd* [1917] AC 406 at 439–440, HL, per Lord Parker of Waddington. See also *Cotman v Brougham* [1918] AC 514 at 519, HL, per Lord Parker of Waddington. Cf *R v Registrar of Joint Stock Companies, ex p More* [1931] 2 KB 197, CA (refusal of the registrar to register a company formed to deal in tickets in the Irish Hospitals Sweepstake upheld). See also note 19.

   Since the Companies Act 2006 is not expressed to bind the Crown, the issue of a certificate of incorporation may be challenged by the Attorney General (but by nobody else) by way of judicial review: see *R v Registrar of Companies, ex p Central Bank of India* [1986] QB 1114 at 1169–1171, [1986] 1 All ER 105 at 117–118, CA, per Lawton LJ, at 1175–1178 and 122–124 per Slade LJ, and at 1178–1180, 1182–1183 and 124–125, 127–128 per Dillon LJ; *R v Registrar of Companies, ex p A-G* [1991] BCLC 476.
28 See the Companies Act 2006 ss 1086, 1091(3); and PARA 145.
29 *Mostyn v Calcott Hall Mining Co* (1858) 1 F & F 334.

115. Effect of incorporation. As from the date of incorporation[1], the subscribers of the memorandum of association[2], together with such other persons as may from time to time become members of the company[3], are a body corporate[4] by the name stated in the certificate of incorporation[5]. That body corporate is then capable forthwith of exercising all the functions of an incorporated company[6], except that, if the company is registered as a public company[7], it must not do business[8] or exercise any borrowing power[9] unless the registrar[10] has issued it with a further certificate (a 'trading certificate')[11] to the effect that he is satisfied that its allotted share capital[12] is not less than the authorised minimum[13]. In the case of a company having a share capital[14], the subscribers to the memorandum become holders of the shares specified in the statement of capital and initial shareholdings[15].

The body corporate, as a legal entity, is separate from, and distinct from, the individual members of the company[16]. Its status and registered office[17] are as stated in, or in connection with, the application for registration[18].

The persons named in the statement of proposed officers[19] as director[20], or as secretary[21] or joint secretary of the company, are, as from the date of the company's incorporation, deemed to have been appointed to that office[22].

1 Ie the date mentioned in the certificate of incorporation, following the registration of a company: see PARA 114 note 7. As to the meaning of 'company' under the Companies Acts see PARA 21; and as to the meaning of the 'Companies Acts' see PARA 13. As to incorporation by registration under the Companies Act 2006 see PARA 104 et seq.

2 As to the meaning of 'memorandum of association' see PARA 97. As to subscribers of the memorandum see PARA 97.

3 As to the meaning of 'member' see PARA 323. As to membership of a company generally see PARA 323 et seq.

4 As to the meaning of 'body corporate' see PARA 1 note 5.

5 Companies Act 2006 s 16(1), (2). As to the company's name see PARA 199 et seq. A company or other corporation may be represented at trial by an employee if the employee has been authorised by the company or corporation to appear at trial on its behalf, and if the court gives permission: see CPR 39.6; and CIVIL PROCEDURE vol 12 (2015) PARA 1066. Permission is not normally granted in jury trials or in contempt proceedings: see CPR PD 39A—*Miscellaneous Provisions relating to Hearings* para 5.6; and CIVIL PROCEDURE vol 12 (2015) PARA 1066. In relation to the small-claims track, a corporate party may be represented by any of its officers or employees: see CPR PD 27—*Small Claims Track* para 3.2(4); and CIVIL PROCEDURE vol 11 (2015) PARA 219. See also PARA 307.

6 Companies Act 2006 s 16(1), (3). As to the capacity of a company that is incorporated by registration see PARA 251 et seq.

7 Ie a company that is registered as a public company on its original incorporation rather than by virtue of its re-registration as a public company: see the Companies Act 2006 s 761(1); and PARA 67. As to the meanings of 'private company' and 'public company' see PARA 95. As to the re-registration of a private company as a public company under the Companies Act 2006 see PARA 168 et seq.

8 As to the meaning of 'business' generally see PARA 1 note 1.

9 As to a company's borrowing powers see PARA 1442 et seq.

10 As to the meaning of 'registrar of companies' see PARA 126 note 2.

11 Ie in accordance with the Companies Act 2006 s 762 (see PARA 67): see s 761(2); and PARA 67. A 'trading certificate' is a certificate issued by the registrar of companies under s 761: see PARA 67.

12 As to the meaning of 'allotted share capital' see PARA 1234. As to the meaning of 'allotted' see PARA 1280; and as to the meanings of 'share' and 'share capital' see PARA 1231.

13 See the Companies Act 2006 s 761; and PARA 67. As to the 'authorised minimum' in relation to the nominal value of a public company's allotted share capital see PARA 68.

14 As to the meaning of 'company having a share capital' see PARA 1231.

15 Companies Act 2006 s 16(1), (5). As to the statement of capital and initial shareholdings required in the case of a company limited by shares see s 10; and PARA 107. As to the meaning of 'company limited by shares' see PARA 95; and as to the meaning of 'share' see PARA 1231.

16 See PARA 116; and see *John Foster & Sons v IRC* [1894] 1 QB 516 at 528, CA, per Lindley LJ, and at 530 per Kay LJ; *Salomon v A Salomon & Co Ltd* [1897] AC 22 at 42, HL, per Lord Herschell, and at 51 per Lord Macnaughten; *Booth v Helliwell* [1914] 3 KB 252; *R v Grubb*

[1915] 2 KB 683, CCA; *IRC v Sansom* [1921] 2 KB 492, CA; *Rainham Chemical Works Ltd (in liquidation) v Belvedere Fish Guano Co* [1921] 2 AC 465 at 475, HL, per Lord Buckmaster; *Re Fasey, ex p Trustees* [1923] 2 Ch 1 at 18, CA, per Atkin LJ; *Gramophone and Typewriter Ltd v Stanley* [1908] 2 KB 89 at 99, CA, per Fletcher Moulton LJ; *Ebbw Vale UDC v South Wales Traffic Area Licensing Authority* [1951] 2 KB 366 (sub nom *R v South Wales Traffic Licensing Authority, ex p Ebbw Vale UDC* [1951] 1 All ER 806); *Lee v Lee's Air Farming Ltd* [1961] AC 12, [1960] 3 All ER 420, PC; *Tunstall v Steigmann* [1962] 2 QB 593, [1962] 2 All ER 417, CA; *JH Rayner (Mincing Lane) Ltd v Department of Trade and Industry* [1990] 2 AC 418 at 482, HL, per Lord Templeman (sub nom *Maclaine Watson & Co Ltd v Department of Trade and Industry* [1989] 3 All ER 523 at 531, HL, per Lord Templeman, and at 505–506 and 549 per Lord Oliver of Aylmerton). See also *Coleg Elidyr (Camphill Communities Wales) Ltd v Koeller* [2005] EWCA Civ 856, [2005] 2 BCLC 379 (company formed to establish and maintain centres for the development of working communities for handicapped persons was an entirely separate entity from the communities themselves, which were not legal entities).

The principle that a company is a legal entity separate from, and distinct from, its members has the consequence that even if one shareholder controls a company through his shareholding, the court may still apply that principle so that he is treated as an employee for certain purposes, so long as the facts of the case can establish an employer-employee relationship: see *Lee's v Lee's Air Farming Ltd* [1961] AC 12, [1960] 3 All ER 420, PC (widow of the controlling shareholder and governing director of a company qualified for payments under worker's compensation legislation); *Secretary of State for Trade and Industry v Bottrill* [2000] 1 All ER 915, [1999] ICR 592, CA (facts of the case allowed the managing director and sole shareholder of a company to claim redundancy payments, pursuant to statute) (cf *Buchan v Secretary of State for Employment, Ivey v Secretary of State for Employment* [1997] IRLR 80, EAT (a person who, by reason of a controlling interest in the shares of the company, is able to prevent his own dismissal from his position in the company is outside the class of persons intended to be protected by employment protection legislation), which was not followed in *Secretary of State for Trade and Industry v Bottrill*); *Ultraframe (UK) Ltd v Fielding* [2003] EWCA Civ 1805, [2004] RPC 479, [2003] All ER (D) 232 (Dec) (ownership of design rights); *Clark v Clark Construction Initiatives* [2008] ICR 635, [2008] IRLR 364, EAT (contract of employment not found where the controlling shareholder of a company was dismissed from that company following the transfer of his shareholding to a third party). *Clark v Clark Construction Initiatives* [2008] ICR 635 at [61]–[98], [2008] IRLR 364 reviewed the authorities on this point and the EAT in that case suggested principles for determining the circumstances where it may be legitimate not to give effect to what is alleged to be a binding contract of employment, and the factors that a tribunal should consider in deciding whether effect should be given to a contract of employment between a controlling shareholder and his company. This guidance was approved on appeal (where the decision was upheld on other grounds) ([2008] EWCA Civ 1446, [2009] ICR 718, [2008] All ER (D) 191 (Dec)) and has been further approved (and expanded upon) in *Neufeld v Secretary of State for Business, Enterprise and Regulatory Reform* [2009] EWCA Civ 280 at [79]–[90], [2009] 3 All ER 790. See further EMPLOYMENT vol 39 (2014) PARA 8.

As to the circumstances in which an individual or individuals may be considered the directing mind of the company see PARA 313.

17 As to the company's registered office see PARA 124.

18 Companies Act 2006 s 16(1), (4). As to the application for registration see PARA 104.

19 As to the statement of proposed officers see PARA 105. As to the meaning of 'officer' generally under the Companies Act 2006 see PARA 679.

20 As to the meaning of 'director' see PARA 512.

21 As to the company secretary and other officers see PARA 671.

22 Companies Act 2006 s 16(1), (6).

116. Piercing the corporate veil. A company is a legal entity that is separate from, and distinct from, the individual members of the company[1]. This is also the position within a group of companies where the fundamental principle is that each company in a group (a relatively modern concept) is a separate legal entity possessed of separate legal rights and liabilities[2]. There may, however, be cases where the wording of a particular statute[3] or contract justifies the treatment of parent and subsidiary as one company, at least for some purposes[4]; or where the court will 'pierce' (or 'lift') 'the corporate veil'. The doctrine of piercing the corporate veil should only be invoked where a person is under an existing legal obligation or liability or subject to an existing legal restriction which he deliberately evades or whose enforcement he deliberately frustrates by interposing a company under his control[5].

The court will go behind the status of the company as a separate legal entity distinct from its shareholders, and will consider who are the persons, as shareholders or even as agents, directing and controlling the activities of the company[6]. The device of a corporate structure will often have been used to evade limitations imposed on conduct by law[7] and rights of relief which third parties already possess[8] against a defendant[9], so justifying the court's 'piercing' (or 'lifting') the veil.

Where, however, this is not the position, even though an individual's connection with a company may cause a transaction with that company to be subjected to strict scrutiny, the corporate veil will not be pierced[10]. Nor is the court entitled to lift the veil as against a company which is a member of a corporate group merely because the corporate structure has been used so as to ensure that the legal liability, if any, in respect of particular future activities of the company will fall on another member of the group rather than the defendant company[11].

It may be that liabilities or obligations will arise without piercing the corporate veil because there is an agency relationship between a parent company and a subsidiary[12], or between a company and its shareholders[13], but this may not be inferred merely from control of the company or ownership of its shares[14] or from the level of paid up capital[15]. It will depend on an investigation of all aspects of the relationship between the parties and there is no presumption of such agency[16].

For the purpose of taxation, there are numerous statutory provisions which in effect require the corporate veil to be pierced[17]; and the courts have shown a tendency for such purposes to look at the economic consequences of transactions rather than their strict format, thus in effect bypassing the question of corporate identity[18].

1 Having chosen to incorporate, the court will be reluctant to allow an individual to claim that he, rather than the company, should be treated as the party to a transaction or dealing, as the case may be: see *JP Morgan Chase Bank v Pollux Holding Ltd, Diamantides v JP Morgan Chase Bank* [2005] EWCA Civ 1612, [2005] All ER (D) 323 (Dec) (affg *Diamantides v JP Morgan Chase Bank* [2005] EWHC 263 (Comm), [2005] All ER (D) 404 (Feb)) (any advisory duties owed by the bank were owed to company rather than to the claimant); cf *Conway v Ratiu* [2005] EWCA Civ 1302 at [78], [2006] 1 All ER 571n at [78], [2006] 1 EGLR 125 per Auld LJ (where it was accepted that, in some circumstances where a third party owes a fiduciary duty to the company, that fiduciary duty may extend to persons in or behind the company).

If a company is so under the unfettered control of one particular individual as to be in effect his alter ego, it may be concluded that documents belonging to the company are within the 'power' of the individual for the purpose of disclosure: *Dallas v Dallas* (1960) 24 DLR (2d) 746, BC CA. Cf *B v B* [1978] Fam 181, [1979] 1 All ER 801; but compare with *Re Tecnion Investments Ltd* [1985] BCLC 434, CA (where a contrary conclusion was reached).

2 *Albacruz v Albazero, The Albazero* [1977] AC 774 at 807, [1975] 3 All ER 21 at 28, CA, per Roskill LJ; *Bank of Tokyo Ltd v Karoon* [1987] AC 45n at 64n, [1986] 3 All ER 468 at 486, CA, per Goff LJ; *Adams v Cape Industries plc* [1990] Ch 433 at 532, [1991] 1 All ER 929 at 1016, CA, per Slade LJ; *Acatos & Hutcheson plc v Watson* [1995] 1 BCLC 218; *Ord v Belhaven Pubs Ltd* [1998] 2 BCLC 447 at 458, [1998] BCC 607 at 615, CA, per Hobhouse LJ. Dicta by Lord Denning MR to the effect that the courts should look at the whole group of companies as an economic entity (see *Littlewoods Mail Order Stores Ltd v McGregor (Inspector of Taxes), Littlewoods Mail Order Stores Ltd v IRC* [1969] 3 All ER 855 at 860, [1969] 1 WLR 1241 at 1254, CA; *Wallersteiner v Moir* [1974] 3 All ER 217 at 238, [1974] 1 WLR 991 at 1013, CA; *DHN Food Distributors Ltd v London Borough of Tower Hamlets* [1976] 3 All ER 462, sub nom *DHN Food Distributors Ltd v Tower Hamlets London Borough Council* [1976] 1 WLR 852, CA) have been disapproved subsequently: *Woolfson v Strathclyde Regional Council* 1978 SLT 159, HL. See also *Bank of Tokyo v Karoon* [1987] AC 45n at 64, [1986] 3 All ER 468 at 485, CA, per

Goff LJ (distinction between parent and subsidiary company a matter of law not economics); *Ord v Belhaven Pubs Ltd* at 457 and 614 per Hobhouse LJ; *Adams v Cape Industries plc*; *Re Polly Peck International (No 3)* [1996] 2 All ER 433 at 448, [1996] 1 BCLC 428 at 444 per Robert Walker J (it was not open to the court to disregard the principle of separate corporate personality and to treat a closely-integrated group of companies as a single economic unit on the basis merely of perceived injustice). For certain purposes, statute may address the relationship between individual companies in a group: see eg the Companies Act 2006 s 192 (transactions with directors requiring members' approval) (see PARAS 606–607), s 399 (duty to prepare group accounts) (see PARA 853), s 679 (public company giving financial assistance for acquisition of shares in a private holding company) (see PARA 1412) and ss 1159–1162 (meaning of 'subsidiary', 'undertaking' and related expressions) (see PARAS 22–23).

3 In *Dimbleby & Sons Ltd v National Union of Journalists* [1984] 1 All ER 751 at 758, [1984] 1 WLR 427 at 435, HL, Lord Diplock noted that, if the veil is to be pierced by a statutory provision, one would expect that parliamentary intention to be expressed in clear and unequivocal language. See also note 2.

4 *Adams v Cape Industries plc* [1990] Ch 433 at 536, [1991] 1 All ER 929 at 1019, CA, per Slade LJ, where the Court of Appeal would have categorised the following cases in this way: *Harold Holdsworth & Co (Wakefield) Ltd v Caddies* [1955] 1 All ER 725, [1955] 1 WLR 352 (contract governing management obligations of director of parent company could make provision for management of subsidiary); *Scottish Co-operative Wholesale Society Ltd v Meyer* [1959] AC 324, [1958] 3 All ER 66, HL (parent company activities inseparable from those of subsidiary for the purposes of the Companies Act 1948 s 210 (repealed: minority remedy in case of oppression) (and see *Nicholas v Soundcraft Electronics Ltd* [1993] BCLC 360, CA, on similar facts); *DHN Food Distributors Ltd v London Borough of Tower Hamlets* [1976] 3 All ER 462, sub nom *DHN Food Distributors Ltd v Tower Hamlets London Borough Council* [1976] 1 WLR 852, CA (companies without separate business activities treated as one for the purposes of a statute governing compensation payable for compulsory purchase order made by local council); *Revlon Inc v Cripps and Lee Ltd* [1980] FSR 85, CA (companies in a group treated as one for the purposes of the meaning of 'proprietor' of a trade mark in the Trade Marks Act 1938 (repealed)); Cases 6–7/73 *Instituto Chemioterapico Italiano SpA andCommercial Solvents Corpn v EC Commission* [1974] ECR 223, [1974] 1 CMLR 309, ECJ (parent and subsidiary to be treated as one undertaking for the purposes of EU competition law). See also Case C-73/95P *Viho Europe BV v EC Commission (supported by Parker Pen Ltd, intervener)* [1996] ECR I-5457, [1997] 4 CMLR 419, ECJ (where subsidiaries had no freedom to act independently, the parent company and its subsidiaries constituted one economic unit, and a distribution policy pursued by a single economic unit fell outside what is now the TFEU art 101). Cf *Adams v Cape Industries plc* [1990] Ch 433 at 536, [1991] 1 All ER 929 at 1019, CA, per Slade LJ. As to the TFEU and its citation see PARA 16 note 1.

5 *Prest v Petrodel Resources Ltd* [2013] UKSC 34 at [35], [81], [2013] 2 AC 415, [2013] 4 All ER 673.

6 See *Merchandise Transport Ltd v British Transport Commission* [1962] 2 QB 173 at 206–207, [1961] 3 All ER 495 at 517–518, CA, per Danckwerts LJ.

7 *Re Darby, ex p Brougham* [1911] 1 KB 95 (company formed by fraudulent company promoters treated as a mere alias for them); *Daimler Co Ltd v Continental Tyre and Rubber Co (Great Britain) Ltd* [1916] 2 AC 307, HL (company formed in England but controlled by German shareholders regarded as an enemy alien); *Jones v Lipman* [1962] 1 All ER 442, [1962] 1 WLR 832 (specific performance ordered against company to which defendant had transferred property to avoid such an action against himself; the company was a device and a sham); *Gilford Motor Co Ltd v Horne* [1933] Ch 935 (company used deliberately as a vehicle for conduct of activities which it was unlawful for the defendant to conduct); *Re Bugle Press Ltd, Re Houses and Estates Ltd* [1961] Ch 270, [1960] 3 All ER 791, CA (company incorporated to facilitate the expropriation of minority shareholders in another company by majority); *Aveling Barford Ltd v Perion Ltd* [1989] BCLC 626 (sale of assets at gross undervalue by company to another controlled by the same shareholder in an attempt to disguise an unauthorised return of capital to that shareholder); *Re H* [1996] 2 All ER 391, [1996] 2 BCLC 500, CA; *Gencor ACP Ltd v Dalby* [2000] 2 BCLC 734, [2000] All ER (D) 1067. There is a degree of overlap between this category of cases and the cases cited in note 8.

8 *Re a Company* [1985] BCLC 333, CA (chain of companies used to dispose of assets otherwise susceptible to a Mareva injunction (so called following *Mareva Cia Naviera SA v International Bulkcarriers SA, The Mareva* [1980] 1 All ER 213n, CA; now known as an asset-freezing order) treated in same way as owner would have been); *Bank of Credit and Commerce International SA v BRS Kumar Bros Ltd* [1994] 1 BCLC 211 (company shifted assets to another company to avoid reach of charges granted to creditors of first company; receiver appointed over assets of second

company); *Trustor AB v Smallbone (No 2)* [2001] 1 WLR 1177, [2001] 2 BCLC 436. See also *Ord v Belhaven Pubs Ltd* [1998] 2 BCLC 447, CA (restructuring of company explained as a response to prevailing market conditions rather than as an attempt to evade liability). See also *Kensington International Ltd v Republic of* [2005] EWHC 2684 (Comm), [2006] 2 BCLC 296.

9 See *Adams v Cape Industries plc* [1990] Ch 433 at 544, [1991] 1 All ER 929 at 1026, CA, per Slade LJ; and the text and note 11.

10 See *Farrar v Farrars Ltd* (1888) 40 ChD 395 at 406, CA, per Chitty J (sale by mortgagee to company in which he held shares). 'A sale by a person to a corporation of which he is a member is not, either in form or in substance, a sale by a person to himself': *Farrar v Farrars Ltd* (1888) 40 ChD 395 at 409 per Lindley LJ. See also *Salomon v A Salomon & Co Ltd* [1897] AC 22, HL. In matrimonial proceedings, piercing the corporate veil cannot be justified by reference to any general principle of law and it is impossible to say that a special and wider principle applies by virtue of the Matrimonial Causes Act 1973 s 24(1)(a): *Prest v Petrodel Resources Ltd* [2013] UKSC 34, [2013] 2 AC 415, [2013] 4 All ER 673 (the husband was beneficial owner of properties held by companies on resultant trust for him: this was the only basis on which the companies could be ordered to convey the relevant properties to the wife). See also *Mubarak v Mubarak* [2001] 1 FLR 673 (court can only make orders directly or indirectly regarding company's assets where a spouse is the owner and controller of the company concerned and there are no adverse third parties whose position or interests are likely to be prejudiced).

11 *Adams v Cape Industries plc* [1990] Ch 433 at 544, [1991] 1 All ER 929 at 1026, CA, per Slade LJ.

12 *Firestone Tyre and Rubber Co Ltd v Llewellin (Inspector of Taxes)* [1957] 1 All ER 561, [1957] 1 WLR 464, HL (an assessment of tax upheld where the business of both the parent company and the subsidiary were carried on by the subsidiary as agent for the parent company); *Smith, Stone and Knight Ltd v Birmingham Corpn* [1939] 4 All ER 116 (compensation for compulsory purchase payable by local authority where subsidiary carried on business as agent for the parent company); *Re FG (Films) Ltd* [1953] 1 All ER 615, [1953] 1 WLR 483 (British subsidiary brought into existence for sole purpose of obtaining British classification for film made in reality by American parent company).

13 *Rainham Chemical Works Ltd (in liquidation) v Belvedere Fish Guano Co Ltd* [1921] 2 AC 465, HL.

14 *Salomon v A Salomon & Co Ltd* [1897] AC 22, HL, *JH Rayner (Mincing Lane) Ltd v Department of Trade and Industry* [1989] Ch 72 at 188, sub nom *Maclaine Watson & Co Ltd v Department of Trade and Industry* [1988] 3 All ER 257 at 310, CA, per Kerr LJ. As to the meaning of 'share' see PARA 1231.

15 *Re Polly Peck International (No 3)* [1996] 2 All ER 433 at 445, [1996] 1 BCLC 428 at 441 per Robert Walker J (subsidiary company had small paid up capital because it existed solely as the vehicle for a particular financing transaction). As to paid up capital see PARA 1237.

16 *Adams v Cape Industries plc* [1990] Ch 433 at 536, [1991] 1 All ER 929 at 1020, CA, per Slade LJ.

17 See eg the Inheritance Tax Act 1984 s 94 (see INHERITANCE TAXATION vol 59A (2014) PARA 35 et seq); the Corporation Tax Act 2010 s 460 (see INCOME TAXATION vol 59 (2014) PARA 1822); the Taxation of Chargeable Gains Act 1992 ss 29, 30 (see CAPITAL GAINS TAXATION vol 6 (2011) PARAS 623, 635).

18 See eg *Furniss (Inspector of Taxes) v Dawson* [1984] AC 474, [1984] 1 All ER 530, HL; *Craven (Inspector of Taxes) v White* [1989] AC 398, [1988] 3 All ER 495, HL; *Fitzwilliam v IRC* [1993] 3 All ER 184, [1993] 1 WLR 1189, HL. The Commissioners for Revenue and Customs will look at the real transaction carried out by the taxpayer: see INCOME TAXATION vol 58 (2014) PARA 25. As to tax avoidance see INCOME TAXATION vol 59 (2014) PARA 2129 et seq.See also *Re H (restraint order: realisable property)* [1996] 2 All ER 391, [1996] 2 BCLC 500, CA (although the court had no jurisdiction to appoint a receiver to sell the realisable property of companies that were owned by defendants in criminal proceedings where the companies themselves had not been charged with any offences, the corporate veil could be lifted where the defendants controlled companies that were seemingly cloaks for fraudulent activity, so that the assets of the companies could be treated as being held for the defendants).

117. Nationality, domicile and residence of company. When incorporated, the company is a legal entity or persona distinct from its members[1], and its property is not the property of the members[2]. The nationality[3] and domicile[4] of a company are determined by its place of registration. A company incorporated in the United Kingdom[5] will normally have both British nationality and English or Scottish domicile, depending upon its place of registration, and it will be unable to change that domicile[6]. A company incorporated in the United Kingdom will nevertheless be regarded as having an enemy character if the persons in de facto control of its affairs are resident in an enemy country, or, wherever resident, are adhering to the enemy or taking instructions from or acting under the control of enemies[7].

The residence of a company is of great importance in revenue law[8], and at common law the test of company residence is where its real business is carried on, that is to say where its central control and management is located[9]. A company which is incorporated in the United Kingdom is, however, regarded for the purposes of the Taxes Acts as resident there and, accordingly, if a different place of residence is given by any rule of law, that place is no longer to be taken into account for those purposes[10]. A company incorporated outside the United Kingdom is resident in the United Kingdom if its central management and control is in the United Kingdom[11]. It follows that, if such central control is divided, the company, provided that it is not incorporated in the United Kingdom, may have more than one residence[12].

The centre of a company's main interest is of increasing significance in the context of insolvency, especially where the Council Regulation on insolvency proceedings[13] applies; that Council Regulation sets up, in the case of companies and legal persons, a rebuttable presumption that the centre of a debtor's main interests is the place of the registered office[14].

Issues as to title to shares[15] in a company are to be decided by the law of the place where the shares are situated, the lex situs, which in the ordinary way will be the law of the place where the company is incorporated[16]. The head office of a company is not necessarily the registered office of the company, but is the place where the substantial business of the company is carried on and its negotiations conducted[17]. Like an individual or a firm, a company may, for the purposes of civil procedure rules, carry on business in more places than one[18].

1 See PARA 115.

2 *Re George Newman & Co* [1895] 1 Ch 674 at 685, CA.

3 *Janson v Driefontein Consolidated Mines Ltd* [1902] AC 484, HL.

4 *Gasque v IRC* [1940] 2 KB 80.

5 As to the meaning of 'United Kingdom' see PARA 1 note 5.

6 *Gasque v IRC* [1940] 2 KB 80. As to company registration see PARA 104 et seq.

7 *Daimler Co Ltd v Continental Tyre Rubber Co (Great Britain) Ltd* [1916] 2 AC 307, HL. Such a company is still an English, or Scottish, company and subject to the common law prohibition against trading with the enemy: *Kuenigl v Donnersmarck* [1955] 1 QB 515, [1955] 1 All ER 46. As to the meaning of 'enemy' see ARMED CONFLICT AND EMERGENCY vol 3 (2011) PARA 198. As to incorporation by registration under the Companies Act 2006 see PARA 114 et seq.

8 As to residence for the purposes of corporation tax see INCOME TAXATION vol 59 (2014) PARA 1843. As to the locality of assets for the purposes of inheritance tax see INHERITANCE TAXATION vol 59A (2014) PARA 214 et seq. As to service on foreign companies, for which purpose considerations of residence are relevant, see the Companies Act 2006 s 1056; the Overseas Companies Regulations 2009, SI 2009/1801, regs 6, 75; and PARAS 744, 2015 et seq.

9 See *De Beers Consolidated Mines Ltd v Howe* [1906] AC 455, HL; *Egyptian Delta Land and Investment Co Ltd v Todd (Inspector of Taxes)* [1929] AC 1, 14 TC 119, HL; *Unit Construction Co Ltd v Bullock (Inspector of Taxes)* [1960] AC 351, [1959] 3 All ER 831, HL. As to the meaning of 'carry on business' generally see PARA 1 note 1. In determining whether a company is ordinarily resident out of the jurisdiction for the purpose of making an order for security for costs against a company, the test is that applied in tax cases for assessing a company's place of residence (ie where the central control and management of the company actually abides): *Re Little Olympian Each Ways Ltd (No 2)* [1994] 4 All ER 561, [1995] 1 BCLC 48.

10 See the Corporation Tax Act 2009 s 14; and INCOME TAXATION vol 59 (2014) PARA 1779. A company which would otherwise be resident in the United Kingdom for these purposes may be treated as resident outside the United Kingdom as a result of an arrangement for double taxation relief: see INCOME TAXATION vol 58A (2014) PARA 1326 et seq.

11 See the cases cited in note 9. See also *Swedish Central Rly Co Ltd v Thompson* [1925] AC 495, HL. Cf *The Polzeath* [1916] P 241, CA; *Re Hilton, Gibbes v Hale-Hinton* [1909] 2 Ch 548. In seeking to determine where 'central management and control' of a company incorporated outside the United Kingdom lay, it is essential to recognise the distinction between cases where management and control of the company were exercised through its own constitutional organs (the board of directors or the general meeting) and cases where the functions of those constitutional organs were 'usurped', in the sense that management and control were exercised independently of, or without regard to, those constitutional organs; and, in cases which fell within the former class, it is essential to recognise the distinction (in concept, at least) between the role of an 'outsider' in proposing, advising and influencing the decisions which the constitutional organs took in fulfilling their functions and the role of an outsider who dictated the decisions which were to be taken: *Wood v Holden (Inspector of Taxes)* [2006] EWCA Civ 26, [2006] 1 WLR 1393, [2006] 2 BCLC 210. As to companies incorporated outside the United Kingdom ('overseas companies') see PARA 2013 et seq.

12 *Union Corpn Ltd v IRC* [1952] 1 All ER 646, CA; affd without reference to this point [1953] AC 482, [1953] 1 All ER 729, HL. See further CORPORATIONS vol 24 (2010) PARA 326.

13 Ie Council Regulation (EC) 1346/2000 (OJ L160, 30.6.2000, p 1) on insolvency proceedings (see COMPANY AND PARTNERSHIP INSOLVENCY vol 16 (2011) PARA 58 et seq). Note that Council Regulation (EC) 1346/2000 (OJ L160, 30.6.2000, p 1) is repealed as from 26 June 2017, except in relation to insolvency proceedings which fall within its scope and have been opened at that date, and replaced by European Parliament and Council Regulation (EU) 2015/848 (OJ L141, 5.6.2015, p 19) on insolvency proceedings: see art 91. References to the 2000 Regulation are to be construed, from that date, as references to European Parliament and Council Regulation (EU) 2015/848 (OJ L141, 5.6.2015, p 19) and are to be read in accordance with the correlation table set out in Annex D thereto: art 91.

14 See Council Regulation (EC) 1346/2000 (OJ L160, 30.6.2000, p 1) art 3; and COMPANY AND PARTNERSHIP INSOLVENCY vol 16 (2011) PARA 60. See also note 13.

15 As to the meaning of 'share' see PARA 1231.

16 *Macmillan Inc v Bishopsgate Investment Trust plc (No 3)* [1996] 1 All ER 585, [1996] 1 WLR 387, CA. As to the lex situs generally see CONFLICT OF LAWS vol 19 (2011) PARA 676. As to the assignment of negotiable instruments and documents of title see CONFLICT OF LAWS vol 19 (2011) PARA 705. The locality of the shares of a company is that of the register of shares which is usually, but not always, kept in the country of incorporation: *Baelz v Public Trustee* [1926] Ch 863; *A-G v Higgins* (1857) 2 H & N 339; *Brassard v Smith* [1925] AC 371, PC; *Erie Beach Co Ltd v A-G for Ontario* [1930] AC 161, PC; *International Credit and Investment Co (Overseas) Ltd v Adham* [1994] 1 BCLC 66.

17 *Keynsham Blue Lias Lime Co Ltd v Baker* (1863) 2 H & C 729; and see *Aberystwyth Promenade Pier Co Ltd v Cooper* (1865) 35 LJQB 44 (a pier erected and maintained by the company was at Aberystwyth but the registered office was at Westminster, where the company's business was carried on and service should be effected). As to the company's registered office see PARA 124.

18 *Davies v British Geon Ltd* [1957] 1 QB 1, [1956] 3 All ER 389, CA.

118. Change of company's residence. There is no longer any requirement for a company to obtain Treasury consent where that company wishes to transfer its residence from the United Kingdom[1]. Certain bodies corporate are, however, required to report certain matters in relation to the international movement of capital to an officer of Revenue and Customs[2].

1 The Income and Corporation Taxes Act 1988 ss 765(1)–767 were repealed in their entirety by the Finance Act 2009 s 37, Sch 17 para 1. As to the meaning of 'United Kingdom' see PARA 1 note 5. As to the Treasury see CONSTITUTIONAL AND ADMINISTRATIVE LAW vol 20 (2014) PARA 262 et seq.

2 See the Finance Act 2009 Sch 17 Pt 2 (paras 4–12); and INCOME TAXATION vol 59 (2014) PARA 1776.

119. Company trading in more than one state. The domicile of a trading company is not changed by its doing business in another country; but, if it carries on business[1] in several states, it resides, for the purposes of legal proceedings, in as many places as it carries on business[2].

A company may have localised its obligation to a creditor by the course of its business[3], or by the terms of the contract as to where the debt should be recoverable[4].

1 As to the meaning of 'to carry on business' generally see PARA 1 note 1.
2 *Carron Iron Co v Maclaren* (1855) 5 HL Cas 416 at 450 per Lord St Leonards; *New York Life Insurance Co v Public Trustee* [1924] 2 Ch 101 at 120, CA, per Atkin LJ. Cf PARA 117.
3 *R v Lovitt* [1912] AC 212, PC.
4 *New York Life Insurance Co v Public Trustee* [1924] 2 Ch 101, CA. See further CONFLICT OF LAWS vol 19 (2011) PARA 682.

120. Powers of the company. As from the date of a company's incorporation by registration under the Companies Acts, it becomes a statutory corporation[1], and therefore does not have, as a corporation at common law has, prima facie the power to deal with its property and to bind itself by contract as freely as an ordinary individual[2]. The statute must not be taken to have created a corporation at common law and then scrutinised to see how far any of the incidents of a corporation at common law have been thereby excluded. The statute or the constitution of the company is, as it were, its charter, and defines its powers[3]. The company has no powers other than those which are expressly conferred upon it by the statute or by its constitution or are incidental to the objects therein defined or enumerated[4]; but this restriction is of less significance now in view of the statutory protection given to third parties dealing with a company against limitations arising under the company's constitution[5].

A company, if it is registered as a public company[6], cannot exercise all its functions immediately upon incorporation, in as much as it has to comply with certain statutory requirements before it can commence business or exercise its borrowing powers[7].

1 See PARA 115; and see *Ashbury Railway Carriage and Iron Co v Riche* (1875) LR 7 HL 653 at 693 per Lord Selborne.
2 *Baroness Wenlock v River Dee Co* (1883) 36 ChD 675n at 685n, CA, per Bowen LJ (affd (1885) 10 App Cas 354, HL); and see CORPORATIONS vol 24 (2010) PARA 431. As to the capacity generally of a company that is incorporated by registration see PARA 251 et seq.
3 *Ashbury Railway Carriage and Iron Co v Riche* (1875) LR 7 HL 653 at 667–668 per Lord Cairns LC. As to a company's memorandum of association generally see PARA 97 et seq.
4 *Ashbury Railway Carriage and Iron Co v Riche* (1875) LR 7 HL 653; and see *Blackburn Building Society v Cunliffe, Brooks & Co* (1882) 22 ChD 61 at 70, CA, per Lord Selborne LC (affd sub nom *Cunliffe, Brooks & Co v Blackburn and District Benefit Building Society* (1884) 9 App Cas 857, HL); *Cotman v Brougham* [1918] AC 514, HL. Under the Companies Act 2006, unless a company's articles of association specifically restrict the objects of the company, its objects are unrestricted: see PARA 239.
5 See the Companies Act 2006 ss 39–42; and PARAS 262–264.
6 As to the meaning of 'public company' see PARA 95.
7 See PARAS 67 et seq, 115.

121. Companies subject to constructive notice rule. A company is subject to the rule that, where the conduct of a party charged with notice shows that he had suspicions of a state of facts the knowledge of which would affect his legal rights, but that he deliberately refrained from making inquiries, he will be treated as having had notice[1], though he is not entitled to claim for his own advantage to be treated as having knowledge of the facts which inquiry would have disclosed[2].

1 *Jones v Smith* (1841) 1 Hare 43. As to the application of this doctrine to allow notice of a company's constitution to be assumed see PARA 265.
2 *Houghton & Co v Nothard, Lowe and Wills Ltd* [1927] 1 KB 246, CA; affd [1928] AC 1, HL.

122. Notice to company officers. In order that notice to a company may be effectual it should either be given to the company through its proper officers[1] or received by it in the course of its business[2]. Notice to a director or other officer of the company in that character is sufficient[3], but not a notice received by him in the course of a transaction in which he is not concerned as such director or officer[4] or as a director of another company[5], or if it relates to a matter which he is not bound to[6], and does not[7], disclose, or in which he is acting fraudulently or, possibly[8], in breach of duty falling short of fraud[9]. Oral notice to a sitting board will suffice[10].

An oral notice given to a clerk of the company at its registered office, in office hours, and during the absence of the secretary[11], is good notice to the company itself[12], as is an oral notice given to a managing director or the secretary in the course of his duties as such[13].

The notice which a company receives through its officers or other agents is not properly called constructive notice, but is actual notice[14].

Notice or knowledge of facts possessed by an agent of a company does not of necessity preclude the recovery by the company of money paid under a mistake of fact, where the agent had no idea that the matter to which his knowledge was relevant was being acted upon[15].

1 *Re Eyles, ex p Stright* (1832) Mont 502; *Alletson v Chichester* (1875) LR 10 CP 319.

2 As to notice of assignments see CHOSES IN ACTION vol 13 (2009) PARA 72. As to the meaning of 'business' generally see PARA 1 note 1.

3 *Re Carew's Estate Act (No 2)* (1862) 31 Beav 39 at 46 per Romilly MR; *Gale v Lewis* (1846) 9 QB 730; *Bank of Ireland v Cogry Spinning Co* [1900] 1 IR 219; *Re European Bank, ex p Oriental Commercial Bank* (1870) 5 Ch App 358.

4 *SociétéGénérale de Paris v Tramways Union Co* (1884) 14 QBD 424, CA (affd sub nom *SociétéGénérale de Paris v Walker* (1885) 11 App Cas 20, HL, where it was suggested that a director might be personally liable in disregarding a notice); *Peruvian Rlys Co v Thames and Mersey Marine Insurance Co, Re Peruvian Rlys Co* (1867) 2 Ch App 617; *North British Insurance Co v Hallett* (1861) 7 Jur NS 1263; *Powles v Page* (1846) 3 CB 16.

5 *Re Marseilles Extension Rly Co, ex p Crédit Foncier and Mobilier of England* (1871) 7 Ch App 161.

6 *Re David Payne & Co Ltd, Young v David Payne & Co Ltd* [1904] 2 Ch 608, CA (where the same person was director of both contracting companies); *Re Fenwick Stobart & Co, Deep Sea Fishery Co's (Ltd) Claim* [1902] 1 Ch 507; *Re Hampshire Land Co* [1896] 2 Ch 743.

7 *Lagunas Nitrate Co v Lagunas Syndicate* [1899] 2 Ch 392 at 431–432, CA, per Lindley MR.

8 See *Stone & Rolls Ltd (in liquidation) v Moore Stephens (a firm)* [2009] UKHL 39 at [198], [2009] AC 1391 at [198], [2009] 4 All ER 431 per Lord Brown.

9 *Re Hampshire Land Co* [1896] 2 Ch 743. The application of the principle in *Re Hampshire Land Co* [1896] 2 Ch 743, otherwise described as the adverse interest rule, was considered in *Stone & Rolls Ltd (in liquidation) v Moore Stephens (a firm)* [2009] UKHL 39, [2009] AC 1391, [2009] 4 All ER 431. By a 3-2 majority (Lords Scott and Mance dissenting), their Lordships ruled that the adverse interest rule had no application where the director and sole shareholder of the company was one and the same person, whose knowledge was logically that of the company. However, the 'extreme' facts of this case were acknowledged: see *Stone & Rolls Ltd (in liquidation) v Moore Stephens (a firm)* [2009] UKHL 39 at [18], [2009] AC 1391 at [18], [2009] 4 All ER 431 per Lord Phillips.

See also *Re European Bank, ex p Oriental Commercial Bank* (1870) 5 Ch App 358; *Re Hirth, ex p Trustee* [1899] 1 QB 612 at 625, CA, per Vaughan Williams LJ. Cf *Cave v Cave* (1880) 15 ChD 639; *Ruben v Great Fingall Consolidated* [1906] AC 439, HL; *Gluckstein v Barnes* [1900] AC 240 at 247, HL, per Halsbury LC; *Houghton & Co v Nothard, Lowe and Wills Ltd* [1928] AC 1, HL; *Kwei Tek Chao (t/a Zung Fu Co) v British Traders and Shippers Ltd* [1954] 2 QB 459, [1954] 1 All ER 779; *Belmont Finance Corpn Ltd v Williams Furniture Ltd* [1979] Ch 250, [1979] 1 All ER 118, CA.

10 *Re Worcester, ex p Agra Bank* (1868) 3 Ch App 555.

11 As to the company secretary see PARA 669.

12 *Re Brewery Assets Corpn, Truman's Case* [1894] 3 Ch 272. See also *Re Natal Investment Co Ltd, Wilson's Case* (1869) 20 LT 962.

13 *Jaeger's Sanitary Woollen System Co Ltd v Walker & Sons* (1897) 77 LT 180, CA; *Alletson v Chichester* (1875) LR 10 CP 319.

14 *Espin v Pemberton* (1859) 3 De G & J 547. As to constructive notice see PARA 121.

15 *Anglo-Scottish Beet Sugar Corpn Ltd v Spalding UDC* [1937] 2 KB 607, [1937] 3 All ER 335; *Turvey v Dentons (1923) Ltd* [1953] 1 QB 218, [1952] 1 All ER 1025. As to when notice to an agent is regarded also as notice to his principal see AGENCY vol 1 (2008) PARA 137. As to mistake of fact see MISTAKE vol 77 (2016) PARA 12 et seq.

123. Examples of statutory duties placed on companies. A company[1] has certain statutory duties, attaching to it from the time of its incorporation under the Companies Acts[2], for example[3]:

(1) to have a registered office[4] and to give notice of any change in its situation to the registrar of companies[5];
(2) to disclose its name in specified locations, in specified documents and on request to those it deals with in the course of business[6];
(3) if it has a common seal[7], to have its name engraved in legible characters on the seal[8];
(4) to keep, and to allow the inspection of, such registers as are required by the Companies Act 2006[9];
(5) to issue, on request by any member[10], an up-to-date copy of the company's articles[11], a copy of any document, resolution or agreement which affects a company's constitution[12], a copy of any court order sanctioning a compromise or arrangement or facilitating a reconstruction or amalgamation[13], a copy of any court order that alters the company's constitution and is issued under the court's powers to protect members against unfair prejudice[14], a copy of the company's current certificate of incorporation (and of any past certificates of incorporation)[15], a current statement of capital (if applicable)[16] and a copy of the statement of guarantee (if applicable)[17];
(6) to issue share certificates[18] and debentures[19] within the statutory period[20];
(7) to register transfers of shares on request by the transferor in the same manner and subject to the same conditions as if the request were made by the transferee, and to provide the transferee with such further information about the reasons for any refusal as the transferee may reasonably request[21];
(8) to make the required returns of allotments[22] and annual returns[23];
(9) to keep proper accounting records[24] and (if a public company) to lay before the members in general meeting copies of the company's annual accounts and reports[25];
(10) (if a public company) to hold the annual general meetings required by the Companies Act 2006[26].

1 As to the meaning of 'company' under the Companies Acts see PARA 21; and as to the meaning of the 'Companies Acts' see PARA 13.
2 As to the time and effect of incorporation by registration under the Companies Act 2006 see PARA 115.
3 The list given here is not exhaustive.
4 As to a company's registered office see PARA 124.
5 See the Companies Act 2006 ss 86, 87; and PARA 124. As to the meaning of 'registrar of companies' see PARA 126 note 2. As to the delivery of documents to the registrar see PARA 136; and as to the requirements generally for the proper delivery of documents to the registrar see PARA 137. As to the meanings of 'document' and of references to delivering a document for these purposes see PARA 136 note 2.
6 See the Companies Act 2006 s 82; and PARAS 219–220. As to the meanings of 'business' and related expressions generally see PARA 1 note 1.
7 A company may have a common seal, but need not have one: see the Companies Act 2006 s 45; and PARA 282.
8 See the Companies Act 2006 s 45; and PARA 282.

9 As to the registers etc to be kept at a company's registered office subject to inspection see PARA 125.
10 As to membership of companies generally see PARA 323 et seq. As to the provision made for the sending or supplying of documents or information to or from a company (the 'company communications provisions') see PARA 750 et seq.
11 See the Companies Act 2006 s 32(1)(a); and PARA 241. As to the meaning of references to a company's 'articles' see PARA 227 note 2. As to a company's articles of association generally see PARA 227 et seq.
12 See the Companies Act 2006 s 32(1)(b), (c); and PARA 241. As to resolutions and agreements of the company to which Pt 3 Ch 3 (ss 29–30) applies (resolutions and agreements affecting a company's constitution) see PARA 230. As to the notices required to be sent to the registrar where a company's constitution has been altered by enactment or by order of court or other authority see PARA 235. As to the meaning of references to a company's constitution see PARA 226.
13 See the Companies Act 2006 s 32(1)(d); and PARA 241. As to court orders sanctioning a compromise or arrangement see PARA 1611; and as to court orders facilitating a reconstruction or amalgamation see PARA 1614.
14 See the Companies Act 2006 s 32(1)(e); and PARA 241. As to the court's powers to protect members against unfair prejudice see PARA 666.
15 See the Companies Act 2006 s 32(1)(f); and PARA 241. As to the issue of a company's certificate of incorporation upon successful completion of registration see PARA 114; and as to certificates issued by the registrar after a company's status has been altered following re-registration see PARA 167 et seq.
16 See the Companies Act 2006 s 32(1)(g); and PARA 241. As to the statement of capital required by s 32(1)(g) see PARA 241 note 18. As to the initial statement of capital and initial shareholdings required in the case of a company limited by shares see PARA 107. As to the meaning of 'company limited by shares' see PARA 95.
17 See the Companies Act 2006 s 32(1)(h); and PARA 241. As to the statement of guarantee required of a company limited by guarantee see PARA 109. As to the meaning of 'company limited by guarantee' see PARA 95.
18 As to the issue of share certificates see PARA 394 et seq.
19 As to the meaning of 'debenture' see PARA 1482.
20 See the Companies Act 2006 s 769; and PARAS 394, 421.
21 See the Companies Act 2006 ss 771, 772; and PARAS 404, 410, 425–426.
22 See the Companies Act 2006 s 555(2); and PARA 1297.
23 See the Companies Act 2006 s 855; and PARA 1594 et seq.
24 See the Companies Act 2006 s 386; and PARA 782.
25 See the Companies Act 2006 s 437; and PARA 946. A private company must send a copy of its annual accounts and reports for each financial year to every member: see s 423; and PARA 935.
26 See the Companies Act 2006 s 336; and PARA 702.

E. COMPANY'S REGISTERED OFFICE

124. A company's registered office. A company[1] must at all times have a registered office to which all communications and notices may be addressed[2]. The intended address of the company's registered office must be stated in the application for registration delivered to the registrar of companies[3] and, upon the company's incorporation[4], the registered office becomes as stated in, or in connection with, that application[5]. The address of the registered office fixes the domicile of the company[6].

A company may, however, change the address of its registered office by giving notice to the registrar[7]. The change takes effect upon the notice being registered by the registrar[8]; but, until the end of the period of 14 days beginning with the date on which it is registered, a person may validly serve any document on the company at the address previously registered[9].

For the purpose of any duty of a company[10]:

(1) to keep available for inspection at its registered office any register, index or other document[11]; or

(2) to mention the address of its registered office in any document[12],

a company that has given notice to the registrar of a change in the address of its registered office may act on the change as from such date, not more than 14 days after the notice is given, as it may determine[13]. Where a company unavoidably ceases to perform at its registered office any such duty as is mentioned in head (1) above in circumstances in which it was not practicable to give prior notice to the registrar of a change in the address of its registered office[14], but:

(a) resumes performance of that duty at other premises as soon as practicable[15]; and

(b) gives notice accordingly to the registrar of a change in the situation of its registered office within 14 days of doing so[16],

it is not to be treated as having failed to comply with that duty[17].

The problems associated with transferring a company's registered office (or central administration or principal place of business) from one member state to another, whilst remaining incorporated in the first member state, are not resolved by the European Union provisions governing the right of establishment[18].

1 As to the meaning of 'company' under the Companies Acts see PARA 21; and as to the meaning of the 'Companies Acts' see PARA 13.

2 Companies Act 2006 s 86. As to the service of documents on a company generally see PARA 743 et seq; and as to the provision made for the sending or supplying of documents or information to or from a company (the 'company communications provisions') see PARA 750 et seq.

The provisions of the Companies Act 2006 ss 86, 87 apply to unregistered companies by virtue of the Unregistered Companies Regulations 2009, SI 2009/2436, reg 3, Sch 1 para 5, but as modified thereby: see PARA 1857. As to the meaning of 'unregistered company' see PARA 1856.

3 Ie in accordance with the Companies Act 2006 s 9: see PARA 104. As to the meaning of 'registrar of companies' see PARA 126 note 2. As to the delivery of documents to the registrar see PARA 136; and as to the requirements generally for the proper delivery of documents to the registrar see PARA 137. A company registered in England and Wales ought never to have a registered office in Scotland: *Re Baby Moon (UK) Ltd* (1985) 1 BCC 99, 298.

A company whose registered office is in Wales, and as to which it is stated in the register that its registered office is to be situated in England and Wales, may by special resolution require the register to be amended so that it states that the company's registered office is to be situated in Wales: Companies Act 2006 s 88(2). Similarly, a company whose registered office is in Wales, and as to which it is stated in the register that its registered office is to be situated in Wales, may by special resolution require the register to be amended so that it states that the company's registered office is to be situated in England and Wales: s 88(3). Where a company passes a resolution under s 88 it must give notice to the registrar, who must amend the register accordingly, and issue a new certificate of incorporation altered to meet the circumstances of the case: s 88(4). In the Companies Acts, a 'Welsh company' means a company as to which it is stated in the register that its registered office is to be situated in Wales: s 88(1). As to the meanings of 'England' and 'Wales' see PARA 1 note 5; and as to the meaning of 'special resolution' see PARA 686. As to the register generally see PARA 142. As to a company's certificate of incorporation issued on its formation see PARA 114. As to the possible effect on the company's name if the registered office is situated in Wales see PARA 199; and as to documents relating to Welsh companies see PARA 165.

4 As to incorporation by registration under the Companies Act 2006 see PARA 104 et seq.

5 See the Companies Act 2006 s 16(1), (4); and PARA 115. As to the requirement to disclose specified company details in specified locations see PARA 219.

6 *Gasque v IRC* [1940] 2 KB 80. See also PARA 117.

7 Companies Act 2006 s 87(1). Notification of any change of the company's registered office is subject to the disclosure requirements in s 1078: see s 1078(2); and PARA 139.

On receipt of a notice from a company under s 87 to change the address of the company's registered office from a default address, the registrar may require the company to provide evidence, or descriptions of evidence, listed in the Companies (Address of Registered Office) Regulations 2016, SI 2016/423, Schedule, or any other information or documents that show the company is authorised to use a proposed address as its registered office: reg 18. As to the meaning of 'default address' see PARA 160 note 33.

8 Companies Act 2006 s 87(2). This ensures that the situation of the registered office is always as indicated by the registrar of companies and resolves earlier confusion as to the date on which the change of situation takes effect: see eg *Re Garton (Western) Ltd* [1989] BCLC 304 (where the date of the passing of the resolution to change the registered office was suggested as the effective date).

9 Companies Act 2006 s 87(2).

10 Companies Act 2006 s 87(3).

11 Companies Act 2006 s 87(3)(a). As to the registers etc to be kept at a company's registered office see PARA 125.
12 Companies Act 2006 s 87(3)(b).
13 Companies Act 2006 s 87(3).
14 See the Companies Act 2006 s 87(4).
15 Companies Act 2006 s 87(4)(a).
16 Companies Act 2006 s 87(4)(b).
17 Companies Act 2006 s 87(4).
18 See PARAS 16, 17, 20.

125. Registers etc to be kept at registered office. A company[1] has a duty to keep the following at its registered office[2] or at another specified place:

(1) the register of members[3] and the register of debenture[4] holders[5];
(2) the index of members' names[6] (unless the register of members is in such a form as to constitute in itself an index) and the overseas branch register[7], or a duplicate of it, which must be kept at the place where the register of members is kept available for inspection[8];
(3) the register of people with significant control over the company[9];
(4) the register of directors[10] and the register of secretaries[11], the register of charges of a limited company[12] and a copy of every instrument creating or amending a charge requiring registration[13], but in the case of a series of uniform debentures a copy of one debenture of the series is sufficient[14];
(5) a record of all directors' service contracts (or, if the contract is not in writing, a written memorandum setting out its terms)[15] and a copy of any qualifying indemnity provision made for a director (or, if the provision is not in writing, a written memorandum setting out its terms)[16];
(6) the register of directors' interests in shares in the company or associated companies[17];
(7) records comprising copies of all resolutions of members passed otherwise than at general meetings, minutes of all proceedings of general meetings, and details provided to the company regarding the decisions of a sole member[18].

The duty of a company to keep its registers at the registered office ceases when the company is in liquidation and possession of the registers has been taken by the liquidator[19].

1 As to the meaning of 'company' under the Companies Acts see PARA 21; and as to the meaning of the 'Companies Acts' see PARA 13.
2 As to a company's registered office see PARA 124.
3 See the Companies Act 2006 s 114; and PARA 348. As to the register of members see PARA 336 et seq; and as to the option to keep membership information on the central register see PARA 363 et seq.
4 As to the meaning of 'debenture' see PARA 1482.
5 See the Companies Act 2006 s 743; and PARA 1504.
6 As to the index of members' names see PARA 340; and as to the option to keep membership information on the central register see PARA 363 et seq.
7 As to how the overseas branch register is kept see PARA 360.
8 See the Companies Act 2006 ss 115(1), (4), 132(1); and PARAS 340, 360.
9 See the Companies Act 2006 s 790M; and PARA 480. As to the option to keep information about people with significant control on the central register see PARA 484 et seq.
10 See the Companies Act 2006 s 162; and PARA 535; and as to the option to keep directors' information on the central register see PARA 551 et seq. As to the meaning of 'director' see PARA 512.
11 See the Companies Act 2006 s 275; and PARA 673; and as to the option to keep secretaries' information on the central register see PARA 675 et seq. As to the company secretary see PARA 669 et seq.

12 As to the registration of charges see PARA 1468 et seq. As to the Secretary of State's power to make provision for the effect of registration of charges in a special register, other than the central register, see PARA 1480.
13 See PARA 1472.
14 See PARA 1472 text and notes 5–6.
15 See the Companies Act 2006 s 228; and PARA 565.
16 See the Companies Act 2006 s 237; and PARA 643.
17 See the Companies Act 2006 s 809; and PARA 464.
18 See the Companies Act 2006 ss 355, 358; and PARAS 740–741.
19 *Re Kent Coalfields Syndicate* [1898] 1 QB 754, CA; and see COMPANY AND PARTNERSHIP INSOLVENCY vol 16 (2011) PARA 519.

(iii) The Registrar of Companies

A. THE REGISTRAR OF COMPANIES: IN GENERAL

126. Appointment and functions of registrar of companies. For the purposes of the registration of companies under the Companies Acts[1], there is a registrar of companies for England and Wales[2], who is appointed by the Secretary of State[3].

The registrar must perform the functions conferred on the registrar by or under the Companies Acts or any other enactment[4], and must perform such functions on behalf of the Secretary of State, in relation to the registration of companies or other matters, as the Secretary of State may from time to time direct[5].

The registrar must have an official seal for the authentication of documents in connection with the performance of the registrar's functions[6].

The registrar must provide the required information[7] for publication on the European e-Justice portal[8] in accordance with the portal's rules and technical requirements[9].

In so far as the registrar of companies does not already have power to do so, he may authorise an officer of his to exercise any function of his which is conferred by or under any enactment[10]. Anything done or omitted to be done by an officer so authorised in, or in connection with, the exercise or purported exercise of the function is to be treated for all purposes as done or omitted to be done by the registrar of companies in his capacity as such[11], although this provision does not apply for the purposes of any criminal proceedings brought in respect of anything so done or omitted to be so done[12].

Where, by virtue of an order made under the Deregulation and Contracting Out Act 1994[13], a person is authorised by the registrar of companies to accept delivery of any class of documents that are under any enactment to be delivered to the registrar[14], then:

(1) the registrar may direct that documents of that class are to be delivered to a specified address of the authorised person; and
(2) any such direction must be printed and made available to the public (with or without payment)[15].

Any document of that class which is delivered to an address other than the specified address is treated for these purposes as not having been delivered[16].

1 As to the meaning of 'company' under the Companies Acts see PARA 21; and as to the meaning of the 'Companies Acts' see PARA 13.

The scheme of the Companies Act 2006 Pt 35 (ss 1059A–1119) (see also PARA 130 et seq) is as follows (s 1059A(1) (s 1059A added by SI 2009/1802)):

(1) the following provisions apply generally (to the registrar, to any functions of the registrar, or to documents delivered to or issued by the registrar under any enactment, as the case may be): the Companies Act 2006 s 1060(1), (2) (see the text and notes 2, 3), ss 1061–1063 (see the text and notes 4–6; and PARA 130), ss 1068–1071 (see PARA 136), ss 1072–1076 (see PARAS 137–138), s 1080(1), (4), (5) (see PARA 142),

s 1083 (see PARA 142), s 1084A (see PARA 141), s 1092 (see PARA 145), ss 1108–1110 (see PARA 164), s 1111 (see PARA 136) and s 1114 (interpretation), s 1115 (see PARA 131), s 1116 (see PARA 133), s 1117 (see PARA 131), s 1118 (see PARA 130), s 1119 (see PARAS 126, 128) (s 1059A(2) (as so added; amended by the Small Business, Enterprise and Employment Act 2015 s 95(2));

(2) the following provisions apply in relation to companies (to companies or for the purposes of the Companies Acts, as the case may be): the Companies Act 2006 s 1060(3), (4) (see note 2), ss 1064, 1065 (see PARA 133), s 1066 (see PARA 134), ss 1077–1079A (see PARAS 126, 139–140), s 1080(2), (3) (see PARA 142), s 1081 (see PARA 143), s 1082 (see PARA 144) and s 1084 (see PARA 142), ss 1085, 1086 (see PARA 145), s 1087 (see PARA 146), s 1088 (see PARA 150), ss 1089–1091 (see PARA 145), ss 1093, 1094 (see PARA 157), s 1095 (see PARA 158), ss 1096, 1097 (see PARA 161), s 1098 (see PARA 162), s 1106 (see PARA 164), s 1112 (see PARA 132) and s 1113 (see PARA 166) (s 1059A(3) (as so added; amended by SI 2014/1557);

(3) the following provisions apply as indicated in the provisions concerned: the Companies Act 2006 s 1067 (see PARA 135), ss 1099–1101 (see PARA 163), ss 1102, 1103 (see PARA 164), s 1104 (see PARA 165), s 1105 (see PARA 164) and s 1107 (see PARA 164) (s 1059A(4) (as so added)); and

(4) unless the context otherwise requires, the provisions of Pt 35 apply to an overseas company as they apply to a company as defined in s 1 (see PARA 21) (s 1059A(5) (as so added)).

As to the meaning of 'overseas company' see PARA 2013. As to incorporation by registration under the Companies Act 2006 see PARA 104 et seq. As to the application of provisions of the Companies Act 2006 to unregistered companies see the Unregistered Companies Regulations 2009, SI 2009/2436; and PARA 1857. See also notes 2, 11. As to the meaning of 'unregistered company' see PARA 1856.

2 Companies Act 2006 s 1060(1)(a). As to Scotland and Northern Ireland see s 1060(1)(b), (c). In the Companies Acts, the 'registrar of companies' and the 'registrar' mean the registrar of companies for England and Wales, Scotland or Northern Ireland, as the case may require (s 1060(3)); and references in the Companies Acts to registration in a particular part of the United Kingdom are to registration by the registrar for that part of the United Kingdom (s 1060(4)). As to the meanings of 'England', 'Wales' and 'United Kingdom' see PARA 1 note 5. The local situation of the registered office (ie whether the company's registered office is to be situated in England and Wales (or in Wales), in Scotland or in Northern Ireland) must be stated in the company's application for registration: see PARA 104.

Currently, the registrar of companies for England and Wales is the chief executive of Companies House, an executive agency sponsored by the Department for Business, Innovation and Skills. As to the Companies House trading fund see the Companies House Trading Fund Order 1991, SI 1991/1795. The operations so funded include operations of the registrar of companies for Northern Ireland: see the Companies House Trading Fund (Amendment) Order 2009, SI 2009/2622, art 2.

All the regulatory functions of the registrar of companies for England and Wales and the registrar of companies for Northern Ireland are functions to which the Legislative and Regulatory Reform Act 2006 ss 21, 22 apply: Legislative and Regulatory Reform (Regulatory Functions) Order 2007, SI 2007/3544, art 2, Schedule Pt 1. This is subject to arts 3, 4, which exclude any regulatory function exercisable by Order in Council, order, rules, regulations, scheme, warrant, byelaw or other subordinate instrument under a public general Act or local Act (art 3), any function, so far as exercisable in Northern Ireland, if or to the extent that the function relates to matters which are transferred matters (art 4(b)) or any function exercisable only in or as regards Wales (art 4(c)). Any person exercising a regulatory function to which the Legislative and Regulatory Reform Act 2006 s 21 applies must have regard to the principles in s 21(2) in the exercise of the function: s 21(1). Those principles are that regulatory activities should be carried out in a way which is transparent, accountable, proportionate and consistent and should be targeted only at cases in which action is needed: s 21(2). The duty in s 21(1) is subject to any other requirement affecting the exercise of the regulatory function: s 21(3). A Minister of the Crown may issue and from time to time revise a code of practice in relation to the exercise of regulatory functions: s 22(1). Any person exercising a regulatory function to which s 22 applies must, except in a case where s 22(3) applies, have regard to the code in determining any general policy or principles by reference to which the person exercises the function: s 22(2). Any person exercising a regulatory function to which s 22 applies which is a function of setting standards or giving guidance generally in relation to the exercise of other regulatory functions must have regard to the code in the exercise of the function: s 22(3). The duties in s 22(2), (3) are subject to any other requirement affecting the exercise of the regulatory function: s 22(4).

The provisions of the Companies Act 2006 ss 1060(1), (2), 1061, 1062 apply to unregistered companies by virtue of the Unregistered Companies Regulations 2009, SI 2009/2436, Sch 1 para 17(1), (2)(a): see PARA 1857.

3 Companies Act 2006 s 1060(2). As to the Secretary of State see PARA 6 et seq.

4 Companies Act 2006 s 1061(1)(a) (substituted by SI 2009/1802). As to the meaning of 'enactment' see PARA 13 note 16. References in the Companies Act 2006 to the functions of the registrar are to functions within s 1061(1)(a) or s 1061(1)(b): s 1061(3).

5 Companies Act 2006 s 1061(1)(b). See also note 4.

6 Companies Act 2006 s 1062. As to the meaning of 'document' for these purposes see PARA 136 note 2. A document that is required to be authenticated by the registrar's seal must, if sent by electronic means, be authenticated in such manner as may be specified by registrar's rules: see PARA 133. As to the authentication of documents by the registrar generally see PARA 145.

7 Ie the information required by European Parliament and Council Directive (EC) 2009/101 (OJ L258, 1.10.2009, p 11) art 3a(1) (added by European Parliament and Council Directive (EU) 2012/17 (OJ L156, 16.6.2012, p1) (up to date information explaining the provisions of national law according to which third parties can rely on particulars and each type of document referred to in European Parliament and Council Directive (EC) 2009/101 (OJ L258, 1.10.2009, p 11) art 2). References for these purposes to that 2009 Directive and to art 3a of that Directive are to that Directive, and that provision, as amended from time to time: Companies Act 2006 s 1079A(3) (s 1079A added by SI 2014/1557).

8 For these purposes, 'the European e-Justice portal' means the single European electronic access point for legal information, judicial and administrative institutions, registers, databases and other services referred to in European Parliament and Council Directive (EC) 2009/101 (OJ L258, 1.10.2009, p 11): Companies Act 2006 s 1079A(2) (as added: see note 7).

9 Companies Act 2006 s 1079A(1) (as added: see note 7).

10 Deregulation and Contracting Out Act 1994 s 74(1), (4)(a) (s 74(4)(a) amended by SI 2009/1941). As to the delegation of the registrar's functions see also PARA 128.

11 Deregulation and Contracting Out Act 1994 s 74(2), (4)(a) (s 74(4)(a) as amended: see note 10).

12 Deregulation and Contracting Out Act 1994 s 74(3), (4)(a) (s 74(4)(a) as amended: see note 10).

13 Ie under the Deregulation and Contracting Out Act 1994 s 69 (see PARA 128): see the Companies Act 2006 s 1119(1).

14 Companies Act 2006 s 1119(1). As to the meaning of references to delivering a document for these purposes see PARA 136 note 2.

The provisions of the Companies Act 2006 s 1119 apply to unregistered companies by virtue of the Unregistered Companies Regulations 2009, SI 2009/2436, Sch 1 para 17(1), (2)(g): see PARA 1857. As to the meaning of 'unregistered company' see PARA 1856.

15 Companies Act 2006 s 1119(1).

16 Companies Act 2006 s 1119(2).

127. Provision for liaison between the registrar and the Regulator of Community Interest Companies. Regulations[1] may require the registrar of companies[2] to notify the Regulator of Community Interest Companies[3] of matters specified in the regulations[4], and to provide the Regulator with copies of documents specified in the regulations[5].

1 As to the making of regulations under the Companies (Audit, Investigations and Community Enterprise) Act 2004 generally see s 62 (amended by SI 2009/1941). See also note 5.

2 As to the registrar of companies see PARAS 126, 128 et seq.

3 As to the Regulator see PARA 76.

4 Companies (Audit, Investigations and Community Enterprise) Act 2004 s 59(1)(a).

5 Companies (Audit, Investigations and Community Enterprise) Act 2004 s 59(1)(b). In exercise of the powers conferred by s 59(1), the Secretary of State has made the Community Interest Company Regulations 2005, SI 2005/1788, regs 34, 35 (reg 34 amended by SI 2007/1093; SI 2009/1942; the Community Interest Company Regulations 2005, SI 2005/1788, reg 35 amended by SI 2007/1093). By virtue of the Community Interest Company Regulations 2005, SI 2005/1788, reg 35, the registrar of companies must, on receiving any notice under the Insolvency Act 1986 s 109(1) (notice by liquidator of his appointment: see COMPANY AND PARTNERSHIP INSOLVENCY vol 17 (2011) PARA 916) in relation to a community interest company, provide a copy of that notice to the Regulator: Community Interest Company Regulations 2005, SI 2005/1788, reg 35(1) (as so amended). The registrar of companies must also, on receiving any copy of a winding-up order forwarded under the Insolvency Act 1986 s 130(1) (consequences of a winding-up order: see COMPANY AND PARTNERSHIP INSOLVENCY vol 16 (2011) PARA 436) in relation to a community interest company, provide the Regulator with a copy of that

winding-up order: Community Interest Company Regulations 2005, SI 2005/1788, reg 35(2) (as so amended). As to reg 34 (notice published of documents received) see also PARA 139.

128. Functions of the registrar of companies subject to contracting out. Any function of the registrar of companies[1] which is conferred by or under any enactment and which, by virtue of any enactment or rule of law, may be exercised by an officer of his and which is not otherwise excluded[2] may be exercised, if the Secretary of State by order so provides[3], by, or by employees of, such person, if any, as may be authorised in that behalf by the registrar[4].

Such an order may provide that any function to which it applies may be exercised, and an authorisation given by virtue of such an order may, subject to the provisions of the order, authorise the exercise of such a function[5]:

(1) either wholly or to such extent as may be specified in the order or authorisation[6];
(2) either generally or in such cases or areas as may be so specified[7]; and
(3) either unconditionally or subject to the fulfilment of such conditions as may be so specified[8].

An authorisation given by virtue of such an order:

(a) must be for such period, not exceeding ten years, as is specified in the authorisation[9];
(b) may be revoked at any time by the registrar[10]; and
(c) must not prevent the registrar or any other person from exercising the function to which the authorisation relates[11].

Where by virtue of such an order a person is authorised to exercise any function of the registrar[12], anything done or omitted to be done by or in relation to the authorised person (or an employee of his) in, or in connection with, the exercise or purported exercise of the function is to be treated for all purposes as done or omitted to be done[13] by or in relation to the registrar in his capacity as such[14]. However, this provision does not apply[15]:

(i) for the purposes of so much of any contract made between an authorised person and the registrar as relates to the exercise of the function[16]; or
(ii) for the purposes of any criminal proceedings brought in respect of anything done or omitted to be done by the authorised person, or any employee of his[17].

Where by virtue of such an order a person is authorised to exercise any function of the registrar[18] and the order or authorisation is revoked at a time when a relevant contract[19] is subsisting[20], the authorised person is entitled to treat the relevant contract as repudiated by the registrar, and not as frustrated by reason of the revocation[21].

1 As to the registrar of companies, and his functions generally, see PARA 126.
2 Deregulation and Contracting Out Act 1994 ss 69(1), 79(1) (definition of 'office-holder for these purposes in s 79(1) substituted by SI 2009/1941).

The text refers to any function which is not otherwise excluded from the Deregulation and Contracting Out Act 1994 s 69 by s 71: see s 69(1). A function is excluded by s 69 if:

(1) its exercise would constitute the exercise of jurisdiction of any court or of any tribunal which exercises the judicial power of the state (s 71(1)(a)); or
(2) its exercise, or a failure to exercise it, would necessarily interfere with or otherwise affect the liberty of any individual (s 71(1)(b)); or
(3) it is a power or right of entry, search or seizure into or of any property (s 71(1)(c)); or
(4) it is a power or duty to make subordinate legislation (s 71(1)(d)).

The provisions of s 71(1)(b), (c) (see heads (2)–(3) above) do not exclude any function of the official receiver attached to any court (s 71(2)); and registrar's rules made under the Companies Act 2006 (see s 1117; and PARA 131) are not subordinate legislation for the purposes of the Deregulation and Contracting Out Act 1994 s 71 (see head (4) above) (Companies Act 2006 s 1119(3)). See also PARA 126 note 14. As to the official receiver see COMPANY AND PARTNERSHIP INSOLVENCY vol 16 (2011) PARA 453 et seq. As to the power to contract out functions of the official receiver see COMPANY AND PARTNERSHIP INSOLVENCY vol 16 (2011) PARAS 455–456.

3 The Secretary of State may not make such an order in relation to the registrar of companies without first consulting the registrar: Deregulation and Contracting Out Act 1994 ss 69(3), 79(1). As to the Secretary of State see PARA 6 et seq. As to the order that has been made see the Contracting Out (Functions in relation to the Registration of Companies) Order 1995, SI 1995/1013, art 3, Sch 1; and PARA 129.

4 Deregulation and Contracting Out Act 1994 s 69(2).

5 Deregulation and Contracting Out Act 1994 s 69(4).

6 Deregulation and Contracting Out Act 1994 s 69(4)(a).

7 Deregulation and Contracting Out Act 1994 s 69(4)(b).

8 Deregulation and Contracting Out Act 1994 s 69(4)(c).

9 Deregulation and Contracting Out Act 1994 s 69(5)(a).

10 Deregulation and Contracting Out Act 1994 ss 69(5)(b), 79(1).

11 Deregulation and Contracting Out Act 1994 ss 69(5)(c), 79(1).

12 Deregulation and Contracting Out Act 1994 ss 72(1), 79(1).

13 Deregulation and Contracting Out Act 1994 s 72(2).

14 Deregulation and Contracting Out Act 1994 ss 72(2)(a), 79(1).

15 Deregulation and Contracting Out Act 1994 s 72(3).

16 Deregulation and Contracting Out Act 1994 ss 72(3)(a), 79(1).

17 Deregulation and Contracting Out Act 1994 s 72(3)(b).

18 Deregulation and Contracting Out Act 1994 ss 73(1)(a), 79(1).

19 For these purposes, 'relevant contract' means so much of any contract made between the authorised person and the registrar of companies as relates to the exercise of the function: Deregulation and Contracting Out Act 1994 ss 73(3), 79(1).

20 Deregulation and Contracting Out Act 1994 ss 73(1)(b), 79(1).

21 Deregulation and Contracting Out Act 1994 ss 73(2), 79(1).

129. Contracted out functions of the registrar of companies. Any function of the registrar of companies for England and Wales[1] which is listed in heads (1) to (7) below may be exercised by, or by employees of, such person (if any) as may be authorised in that behalf by the registrar[2], namely:

(1) any function of receiving any return, account or other document required to be filed with, delivered or sent to the registrar[3], or receiving notice of any matter required to be given to him, which is conferred by or under any enactment[4];

(2) any functions in relation to:

(a) the incorporation of companies[5] and the change of name of companies[6];

(b) the re-registration and change of status of companies[7], the registration of an order and statement of reduction of share capital[8], and the re-registration of public companies[9] on reduction of capital[10];

(3) functions conferred by or under the following provisions of the Companies Act 2006:

(a) those relating to companies' registered numbers[11] and the registration of branches of overseas companies[12], except in so far as they relate respectively to the determination of the form of companies' registered numbers and branches' registered numbers[13];

(b) those relating to the delivery to the registrar of documents in legible form[14], except in so far as they relate to specification of requirements for the purpose of enabling the copying of documents delivered to the registrar[15];

(c) those relating to the delivery to the registrar of documents other than in legible form[16], except in so far as they relate to the approval of the non-legible form in which information may be conveyed to the registrar[17];

(d) those relating to inspection etc of records kept by the registrar[18], except in so far as they relate to the determination of the means of facilitating the exercise of the right of persons to inspect records kept by the registrar, or the form in which copies of the information contained in those records may be made available[19];

(e) those relating to certificates of incorporation[20];

(f) those relating to the provision and authentication by the registrar of documents in non-legible form[21], except in so far as they relate to the approval of the means of communication to the registrar of information in non-legible form[22];

(4) functions conferred by or under the Limited Partnerships Act 1907[23] relating to the inspection of documents registered[24];

(5) functions conferred by or under the European Economic Interest Grouping Regulations 1989[25] relating to the inspection of documents[26];

(6) functions conferred by or under any provision of the Companies Act 2006 listed in heads (2) and (3) above (to the extent specified in heads (2) and (3) above) where any such provision is applied[27] to European Economic Interest Groupings[28].

1 As to the registrar of companies, and his functions generally, see PARA 126. As to the meanings of 'England' and 'Wales' see PARA 1 note 5.
2 Contracting Out (Functions in relation to the Registration of Companies) Order 1995, SI 1995/1013, art 3. As to the contracting out of functions of the registrar of companies for Scotland see art 4, Sch 2.
3 As to delivery to the registrar of documents see PARA 136 et seq.
4 Contracting Out (Functions in relation to the Registration of Companies) Order 1995, SI 1995/1013, Sch 1 para 1.
5 Ie by or under the Companies Act 2006 Pt 2 (ss 7–16): see PARA 95 et seq.
6 Contracting Out (Functions in relation to the Registration of Companies) Order 1995, SI 1995/1013, Sch 1 para 2(a); Interpretation Act 1978 s 17(2)(b). Companies change their names under the Companies Act 2006 Pt 5 Ch 5 (ss 77–81): see PARAS 216–218.
7 Ie by or under the Companies Act 2006 Pt 7 (ss 89–111): see PARA 167 et seq.
8 Ie by or under the Companies Act 2006 s 649: see PARA 1380. As to the meaning of 'share capital' see PARA 1231.
9 Ie by or under the Companies Act 2006 s 650 (see PARA 1381) or s 664 (see PARA 1390).
10 Contracting Out (Functions in relation to the Registration of Companies) Order 1995, SI 1995/1013, Sch 1 para 2(b); Interpretation Act 1978 s 17(2)(b).
11 Ie the Companies Act 2006 s 1066 (formerly the Companies Act 1985 s 705): see PARA 134.
12 Ie the Companies Act 2006 s 1067 (formerly the Companies Act 1985 s 705A): see PARA 135. As to the meaning of 'overseas company' see PARA 2013.
13 Contracting Out (Functions in relation to the Registration of Companies) Order 1995, SI 1995/1013, Sch 1 para 3(a); Interpretation Act 1978 s 17(2)(b).
14 Ie the Companies Act 1985 s 706 (repealed).
15 Contracting Out (Functions in relation to the Registration of Companies) Order 1995, SI 1995/1013, Sch 1 para 3(b).
16 Contracting Out (Functions in relation to the Registration of Companies) Order 1995, SI 1995/1013, Sch 1 para 3(c) refers to the Companies Act 1985 s 707 (repealed), but as to delivery to the registrar using electronic communications see s 707B (repealed).
17 Contracting Out (Functions in relation to the Registration of Companies) Order 1995, SI 1995/1013, Sch 1 para 3(c).
18 Ie the Companies Act 2006 s 1085: see PARA 145.
19 Contracting Out (Functions in relation to the Registration of Companies) Order 1995, SI 1995/1013, Sch 1 para 3(d); Interpretation Act 1978 s 17(2)(b).

20 Contracting Out (Functions in relation to the Registration of Companies) Order 1995, SI 1995/1013, Sch 1 para 3(e). See PARA 133.
21 Ie the Companies Act 2006 s 1115: see PARA 131.
22 Contracting Out (Functions in relation to the Registration of Companies) Order 1995, SI 1995/1013, Sch 1 para 3(f); Interpretation Act 1978 s 17(2)(b).
23 Ie by or under the Limited Partnerships Act 1907 s 16 (see PARTNERSHIP vol 79 (2014) PARA 220).
24 Contracting Out (Functions in relation to the Registration of Companies) Order 1995, SI 1995/1013, Sch 1 para 5.
25 Ie by or under the European Economic Interest Grouping Regulations 1989, SI 1989/638, reg 14 (see PARA 1824).
26 Contracting Out (Functions in relation to the Registration of Companies) Order 1995, SI 1995/1013, art 2(1), Sch 1 para 7.
27 Ie by the European Economic Interest Grouping Regulations 1989, SI 1989/638, reg 18 (see PARA 1824).
28 Contracting Out (Functions in relation to the Registration of Companies) Order 1995, SI 1995/1013, Sch 1 para 8. As to the meaning of 'European Economic Interest Grouping' (EEIG') see PARA 1824 note 6 (definition applied by the Contracting Out (Functions in relation to the Registration of Companies) Order 1995, SI 1995/1013, art 2(1)).

130. Fees payable to registrar of companies. The Secretary of State[1] may make provision by regulations[2] requiring the payment to the registrar of companies[3] of fees in respect of:

(1) the performance of any of the registrar's functions[4]; or
(2) the provision by the registrar of services or facilities for purposes incidental to, or otherwise connected with, the performance of any of the registrar's functions[5].

The matters for which fees may be charged include:

(a) the performance of a duty imposed on the registrar or the Secretary of State[6];
(b) the receipt of documents delivered to the registrar[7]; and
(c) the inspection, or provision of copies, of documents kept by the registrar[8].

The regulations may:

(i) provide for the amount of the fees to be fixed by or determined under the regulations[9];
(ii) provide for different fees to be payable in respect of the same matter in different circumstances[10];
(iii) specify the person by whom any fee payable under the regulations is to be paid[11];
(iv) specify when and how fees are to be paid[12].

In respect of the performance of functions or the provision of services or facilities:

(A) for which fees are not provided for by regulations[13]; or
(B) in circumstances other than those for which fees are provided for by regulations[14],

the registrar may determine from time to time what fees (if any) are chargeable[15].

Fees received by the registrar are to be paid into the Consolidated Fund[16].

1 As to the Secretary of State see PARA 6 et seq.
2 As to the making of regulations under the Companies Act 2006 generally see ss 1288–1292. Regulations under s 1063 are subject to negative resolution procedure (ie the statutory instrument containing the regulations is subject to annulment in pursuance of a resolution of either House of Parliament): see ss 1063(4), 1289. The provisions of s 1063 apply to unregistered companies by virtue of the Unregistered Companies Regulations 2009, SI 2009/2436, Sch 1 para 17(1), (2)(a): see PARA 1857. As to the meaning of 'unregistered company' see PARA 1856.

Partly in exercise of the powers conferred by the Companies Act 2006 s 1063(1)–(3), the Secretary of State has made the Registrar of Companies (Fees) (Companies, Overseas Companies and Limited Liability Partnerships) Regulations 2012, SI 2012/1907. In those regulations, 'company' includes, where appropriate, a reference to a company to which the Companies Act 2006 s 1040 (see PARA 30) or s 1043 (see PARAS 1856–1857) applies: Registrar of Companies (Fees) (Companies, Overseas Companies and Limited Liability Partnerships) Regulations 2012, SI 2012/1907, reg 2. See also PARTNERSHIP vol 79 (2014) PARAS 234, 236, 245. Any regulations made under the Companies Act 1985 s 708 (repealed) that were in force immediately before 1 October 2009 have effect on or after that date as if made under the Companies Act 2006 s 1063: see the Companies Act 2006 (Commencement No 8, Transitional Provisions and Savings) Order 2008, SI 2008/2860, art 5, Sch 2 para 94. Accordingly, the following regulations have effect as if made under the Companies Act 2006 s 1063: the Open-Ended Investment Companies (Investment Companies with Variable Capital) (Fees) Regulations 1998, SI 1998/3087 (amended by SI 2000/3324).

3 As to the meaning of 'registrar of companies' see PARA 126 note 2. As to the meaning of 'company' under the Companies Acts see PARA 21; and as to the meaning of the 'Companies Acts' see PARA 13.

Regulations made under the Companies (Audit, Investigations and Community Enterprise) Act 2004 may require the payment of such fees as are payable in connection with the Regulator's functions to be paid to the registrar of companies rather than to the Regulator: see the Companies (Audit, Investigations and Community Enterprise) Act 2004 s 57; and PARA 94. As to Community Interest Companies generally see PARA 75 et seq; and as to the Regulator and his functions see PARA 76.

4 Companies Act 2006 s 1063(1)(a). See also note 2. As to the registrar's functions generally see PARA 126; and as to the application of Pt 35 (ss 1059A–1119) (see also PARAS 126, 131 et seq) see PARA 126 note 1.

5 Companies Act 2006 s 1063(1)(b). See also note 2.

6 Companies Act 2006 s 1063(2)(a). See also note 2.

7 Companies Act 2006 s 1063(2)(b). See also note 2. As to the meanings of 'document' and of references to delivering a document for these purposes see PARA 136 note 2. Where, in relation to any matter in respect of which a fee is payable under the Registrar of Companies (Fees) (Companies, Overseas Companies and Limited Liability Partnerships) Regulations 2012, SI 2012/1907, Sch 1:

(1) the means of delivery to the registrar of the documents required to be delivered in relation to that matter, or the form of those documents are not specified, that fee is payable only in respect of documents that are delivered in hard copy form (Sch 1 para 6);

(2) no provision is made for same day registration of the documents required to be delivered to the registrar in relation to that matter, that fee is only payable in respect of the delivery of documents other than for same day registration (Sch 1 para 7).

For these purposes, documents are delivered for 'same day registration' if:

(a) a request for same day registration and all documents required to be delivered to the registrar in connection with that registration are received by the registrar before 3.00 pm on the day in question (Sch 1 para 5(a)); and

(b) the registration is completed on that day (Sch 1 para 5(b)).

As to documents or information sent or supplied in hard copy form see PARA 750.

8 Companies Act 2006 s 1063(2)(c). See also note 2.

9 Companies Act 2006 s 1063(3)(a). See also note 2.

10 Companies Act 2006 s 1063(3)(b). See also note 2.

11 Companies Act 2006 s 1063(3)(c). See also note 2.

12 Companies Act 2006 s 1063(3)(d). See also note 2.

13 Companies Act 2006 s 1063(5)(a).

14 Companies Act 2006 s 1063(5)(b).

15 Companies Act 2006 s 1063(5).

16 Companies Act 2006 s 1063(6). All fees payable to the registrar of companies in his capacity as registrar of companies (except fees in respect of proceedings in the winding-up of companies the method of collection of which is directed by the Companies (Board of Trade) Fees Order 1929, SR & O 1929/831 (revoked), or any Order amending or replacing the same), and all fees payable to the registrar of companies under the Limited Partnerships Act 1907 (see PARTNERSHIP vol 79 (2014) PARA 220) must be collected in money: Companies Registration Office (Fees) Order 1963, SI 1963/511, arts 1–2; Companies Registration Office (Fees) (No 2) Order 1963, SI 1963/596, art 1.

Nothing in the Companies Acts or any other enactment as to the payment of receipts into the Consolidated Fund is to be read as affecting the operation in relation to the registrar of the Government Trading Funds Act 1973 s 3(1) (see CONSTITUTIONAL AND ADMINISTRATIVE LAW vol 20 (2014) PARA 521): Companies Act 2006 s 1118. As to the meaning of 'enactment' see PARA 13 note 16. As to the Consolidated Fund see CONSTITUTIONAL AND ADMINISTRATIVE LAW vol 20 (2014) PARA 480 et seq; PARLIAMENT vol 78 (2010) PARAS 1028–1031. The provisions of the Companies Act 2006 s 1118 apply to unregistered companies by virtue of the Unregistered Companies Regulations 2009, SI 2009/2436, Sch 1 para 17(g): see PARA 1857. As to the meaning of 'unregistered company' see PARA 1856.

131. Rules made by registrar of companies ('registrar's rules'). Where any provision of Part 35 of the Companies Act 2006[1] enables the registrar of companies[2] to make provision, or impose requirements, as to any matter, the registrar may make such provision or impose such requirements by means of rules ('registrar's rules')[3]. This is without prejudice to the making of such provision or the imposing of such requirements by other means[4].

Registrar's rules may require a company, or other body, to give any necessary consents to the use of electronic means for communications by the registrar to the company, or other body, as a condition of making use of any facility to deliver material to the registrar by electronic means[5]; and a document[6] that is required to be signed by the registrar or authenticated by the registrar's seal[7] must, if sent by electronic means, be authenticated in such manner as may be specified by registrar's rules[8].

The registrar must both publicise the rules in a manner appropriate to bring them to the notice of persons affected by them[9], and make copies of the rules available to the public in hard copy or electronic form[10].

1 Ie any provision of the Companies Act 2006 Pt 35 (ss 1059A–1119) (registrar of companies) (see PARAS 126, 130, 132 et seq): see s 1117(1). As to the application of Pt 35 see PARA 126 note 1.

2 As to the meaning of 'registrar of companies' see PARA 126 note 2. As to the meaning of 'company' under the Companies Acts see PARA 21; and as to the meaning of the 'Companies Acts' see PARA 13.

3 Companies Act 2006 s 1117(1). The text refers to rules ('registrar's rules') made under s 1117: see s 1117(1). Because such rules are not made under statutory instrument they are not recorded in this work. The current rules were accessible, at the date at which this volume states the law, on the Companies House website. Registrar's rules may make different provision for different cases, and may allow the registrar to disapply or modify any of the rules: Companies Act 2006 s 1117(2). Such rules made under s 1117 are not subordinate legislation for the purposes of the Deregulation and Contracting Out Act 1994 s 71: see the Companies Act 2006 s 1119(3); and PARA 128.

The provisions of the Companies Act 2006 ss 1115, 1117 apply to unregistered companies by virtue of the Unregistered Companies Regulations 2009, SI 2009/2436, Sch 1 para 17(1), (2)(g): see PARA 1857. As to the meaning of 'unregistered company' see PARA 1856.

4 Companies Act 2006 s 1117(1).

5 Companies Act 2006 s 1115(1) (amended by SI 2009/1802). As to the meaning of references to sending documents by electronic means see PARA 751 note 3.

6 As to the meaning of 'document' for these purposes see PARA 136 note 2.

7 As to the registrar's official seal see PARA 126.

8 Companies Act 2006 s 1115(2).

9 Companies Act 2006 s 1117(3)(a).

10 Companies Act 2006 s 1117(3)(b). As to documents or information sent or supplied in hard copy form under the Companies Acts see PARA 750 note 4; and as to documents or information sent or supplied in electronic form see PARA 751 note 3.

132. Offence of making false statements to registrar of companies. It is an offence for a person knowingly or recklessly:

(1) to deliver or cause to be delivered to the registrar of companies[1], for any purpose of the Companies Acts, a document[2]; or

(2) to make to the registrar, for any such purpose, a statement[3],

that is misleading, false or deceptive in a material particular[4].

1 As to the meaning of 'registrar of companies' see PARA 126 note 2. As to the meaning of 'company' under the Companies Acts see PARA 21; and as to the meaning of the 'Companies Acts' see PARA 13.

2 Companies Act 2006 s 1112(1)(a). As to the meaning of 'document', and as to the meaning of references to delivering a document, for these purposes see PARA 136 note 2. As to the application of Pt 35 (ss 1059A–1119) (see also PARAS 126, 130–131, 133 et seq) see PARA 126 note 1.

3 Companies Act 2006 s 1112(1)(b).

4 Companies Act 2006 s 1112(1). A person guilty of such an offence is liable on conviction on indictment to imprisonment for a term not exceeding two years or a fine, or to both, or on summary conviction to imprisonment for a term not exceeding 12 months or a fine, or to both: see s 1112(2). In the case of liability on summary conviction the fine is one not exceeding statutory maximum: see s 1112(2). By virtue of the Legal Aid, Sentencing and Punishment of Offenders Act 2012 s 85, however, where the offence is committed on or after 12 March 2015, it is punishable by a fine of an unlimited amount. As to the statutory maximum and the powers of magistrates' courts to issue fines on summary conviction see SENTENCING vol 92 (2015) PARA 176. In relation to an offence committed before the coming into force of the Criminal Justice Act 2003 s 154(1) (not yet in force), the maximum term of imprisonment on summary conviction is six months: see the Companies Act 2006 s 1131; and PARA 1818.

B. PUBLIC NOTICE OF ISSUE OF CERTIFICATES OF INCORPORATION

133. Public notice of issue of certificates of incorporation. The registrar of companies[1] must cause to be published in the Gazette[2], or in accordance with the provisions governing alternative means of giving public notice[3], notice of the issue by the registrar of any certificate of incorporation of a company[4]. The notice must state the name[5] and registered number[6] of the company and the date of issue of the certificate[7].

Notices that would otherwise need to be published by the registrar in the Gazette may instead be published by such means as may from time to time be approved by the registrar in accordance with regulations made by the Secretary of State[8]. The Secretary of State may make provision by regulations as to what alternative means may be approved[9]. The regulations may, in particular:

(1) require the use of electronic means[10];

(2) require the same means to be used for all notices or for all notices of specified descriptions, and whether the company or other body to which the notice relates is registered in England and Wales, Scotland or Northern Ireland[11]; and

(3) impose conditions as to the manner in which access to the notices is to be made available[12].

Before starting to publish notices by means approved in this way[13] the registrar must publish at least one notice to that effect in the Gazette[14]. However, nothing[15] prevents the registrar from giving public notice both in the Gazette and by any alternative means that have been so approved[16].

Any person may require the registrar to provide him with a copy of any certificate of incorporation of a company, either signed by the registrar or authenticated by the registrar's seal[17].

1 As to the meaning of 'registrar of companies' see PARA 126 note 2. As to the meaning of 'company' under the Companies Acts see PARA 21; and as to the meaning of the 'Companies Acts' see PARA 13.

2 Companies Act 2006 s 1064(1)(a). In the Companies Acts, the 'Gazette' means, as respects companies registered in England and Wales, the London Gazette: s 1173(1). As to the meanings of 'England' and 'Wales' see PARA 1 note 5. As to the registration of companies under the Companies Act 2006 see PARA 104 et seq. As to the application of Pt 35 (ss 1059A–1119) (see also PARAS 126, 130 et seq, 134 et seq) see PARA 126 note 1.

3 Companies Act 2006 s 1064(1)(b). The text refers to the giving of public notice in accordance with the alternative means provided by s 1116 (see the text and notes 8–16): see s 1064(1)(b).

4 Companies Act 2006 s 1064(1). The provisions of s 1064 apply to a certificate of incorporation issued under s 80 (change of name) (see PARA 218), s 88 (Welsh companies) (see PARA 124), or any provision of Pt 7 (ss 89–111) (re-registration) (see PARA 167 et seq), as well as to the certificate issued on a company's formation: s 1064(3). The provisions of s 1064 apply equally to

certificates of incorporation issued under the Companies Act 2006, and to certificates of incorporation issued under the Companies Act 1985 on or after 1 October 2009: see the Companies Act 2006 (Commencement No 8, Transitional Provisions and Savings) Order 2008, SI 2008/2860, art 5, Sch 2 para 95. 1 October 2009 is the date by which all the provisions of the Companies Act 2006 that affect the law in England and Wales had come into force: see PARA 13 note 15. As to a company's certificate of incorporation issued on its formation see PARA 114. As to the Companies Act 1985, and the provision that has been made generally for continuity in the law, see PARAS 11–13.

5 As to the company's name see PARA 199 et seq.

6 As to a company's registered number see the Companies Act 2006 ss 1066, 1067; and PARAS 134, 135.

7 Companies Act 2006 s 1064(2). A company is incorporated from the beginning of the date mentioned in the certificate of incorporation: see PARA 114.

8 Companies Act 2006 s 1116(1). As to the making of regulations under the Companies Act 2006 generally see ss 1288–1292. As to the Secretary of State see PARA 6 et seq. Regulations under s 1116 are subject to negative resolution procedure (ie the statutory instrument containing the regulations is subject to annulment in pursuance of a resolution of either House of Parliament): see ss 1116(4), 1289. At the date at which this volume states the law, no such regulations have been made.

The provisions of the Companies Act 2006 s 1116 apply to unregistered companies by virtue of the Unregistered Companies Regulations 2009, SI 2009/2436, Sch 1 para 17(g): see PARA 1857. As to the meaning of 'unregistered company' see PARA 1856.

9 Companies Act 2006 s 1116(2). See also note 8.

10 Companies Act 2006 s 1116(3)(a). As to the meaning of references to electronic means in the Companies Acts see PARA 751 note 3.

11 Companies Act 2006 s 1116(3)(b) (amended by SI 2009/1802).

12 Companies Act 2006 s 1116(3)(c).

13 Ie approved under the Companies Act 2006 s 1116: see s 1116(5).

14 Companies Act 2006 s 1116(5).

15 Ie nothing in the Companies Act 2006 s 1116: see s 1116(6).

16 Companies Act 2006 s 1116(6). In the case mentioned in the text, the requirement of public notice is met when notice is first given by either means: see s 1116(6).

17 Companies Act 2006 s 1065. The provisions of s 1065 apply to certificates of incorporation whenever issued: see the Companies Act 2006 (Commencement No 8, Transitional Provisions and Savings) Order 2008, SI 2008/2860, Sch 2 para 96. As to the registrar's official seal see PARA 126; and as to the authentication of documents by the registrar generally see PARA 145.

As to fees payable in respect of the performance of the registrar's functions in relation to the provision of a copy certificate of incorporation under the Companies Act 2006 s 1065 see the Registrar of Companies (Fees) (Companies, Overseas Companies and Limited Liability Partnerships) Regulations 2012, SI 2012/1907, reg 4, Sch 2 Pt 2 (paras 7–12) (amended with effect from 30 June 2016 by SI 2016/621). The fees prescribed in relation to see the Registrar of Companies (Fees) (Companies, Overseas Companies and Limited Liability Partnerships) Regulations 2012, SI 2012/1907, Sch 2 paras 7(a), 8(a) and 10(a) are not payable in respect of any month for which the applicant pays a fee to the registrar for subscription to Companies House Direct, Extranet or XML (those terms are defined in Sch 2 para 1) under regulations providing for the payment of fees in respect of the functions of the registrar in relation to the inspection, or provision of copies, of documents kept by the registrar relating to European Economic Interest Groupings and limited partnerships: reg 5.

C. COMPANIES' REGISTERED NUMBERS

134. Companies' registered numbers. The registrar of companies[1] must allocate to every company[2] a number, which is to be known as the company's registered number[3]. Companies' registered numbers must be in such form, consisting of one or more sequences of figures or letters, as the registrar may from time to time determine[4]; and, upon adopting a new form of registered number, the registrar may make such changes of existing registered numbers as appear necessary[5].

A change of a company's registered number has effect from the date on which the company is notified by the registrar of the change[6]. However, for a period of three years beginning with the date on which such notification is sent by the registrar, any requirement to disclose the company's registered number that is imposed by regulations[7] is satisfied by the use of either the old number or the new[8].

1 As to the meaning of 'registrar of companies' see PARA 126 note 2. Any function of the registrar of companies for England and Wales conferred by or under the Companies Act 2006 s 1066 (formerly the Companies Act 1985 s 705) may be exercised by, or by employees of, such person, if any, as may be authorised in that behalf by the registrar of companies for England and Wales, except in so far as it relates to the determination of the form of companies' registered numbers: see the Contracting Out (Functions in relation to the Registration of Companies) Order 1995, SI 1995/1013, Sch 1 para 3(a); the Interpretation Act 1978 s 17(2)(b); and PARAS 128–129. As to the application of Pt 35 (ss 1059A–1119) (see also PARAS 126, 130 et seq, 135 et seq) see PARA 126 note 1.

2 For these purposes, 'company' includes an overseas company whose particulars have been registered under the Companies Act 2006 s 1046 (see PARA 2015), other than a company that appears to the registrar not to be required to register particulars under that provision: s 1066(6). As to the meaning of 'company' under the Companies Acts generally see PARA 21; and as to the meaning of the 'Companies Acts' see PARA 13. As to the meaning of 'overseas company' see PARA 2013. As to the registered numbers of UK establishments of an overseas company see PARA 135.

The provisions of the Companies Act 2006 s 1066 apply to unregistered companies by virtue of the Unregistered Companies Regulations 2009, SI 2009/2436, Sch 1 para 18, but with the modifications as specified thereby: see PARA 1857. As to the meaning of 'unregistered company' see PARA 1856.

3 Companies Act 2006 s 1066(1). See also note 1.

4 Companies Act 2006 s 1066(2). See also note 1.

5 Companies Act 2006 s 1066(3). See also note 1.

6 Companies Act 2006 s 1066(4). See also note 1.

7 Ie under the Companies Act 2006 s 82 (see PARA 219): see s 1066(5).

8 Companies Act 2006 s 1066(5). See also note 1.

135. Registered numbers of UK establishments of overseas company. The registrar of companies[1] must allocate to every UK establishment of an overseas company[2] whose particulars are registered[3] a number, which is to be known as the UK establishment's registered number[4].

The registered numbers of UK establishments of overseas companies must be in such form, consisting of one or more sequences of figures or letters, as the registrar may determine[5]; and, upon adopting a new form of registered number, the registrar may make such changes of existing registered numbers as appear necessary[6].

A change of the registered number of a UK establishment has effect from the date on which the company is notified by the registrar of the change[7]. However, for a period of three years beginning with the date on which such notification is sent by the registrar, any requirement to disclose the UK establishment's registered number that is imposed by regulations[8] is satisfied by the use of either the old number or the new[9].

1 As to the meaning of 'registrar of companies' see PARA 126 note 2. As to the meaning of 'company' under the Companies Acts see PARA 21; and as to the meaning of the 'Companies Acts' see PARA 13. Any function of the registrar of companies for England and Wales conferred by or under the Companies Act 2006 s 1067 (formerly the Companies Act 1985 s 705A) may be exercised by, or by employees of, such person (if any) as may be authorised in that behalf by the registrar of companies for England and Wales, except in so far as it relates to the determination of the form of companies' registered numbers: see the Contracting Out (Functions in relation to the Registration of Companies) Order 1995, SI 1995/1013, Sch 1 para 3(a); the Interpretation Act 1978 s 17(2)(b); and PARAS 128–129. As to the application of the Companies Act 2006 Pt 35 (ss 1059A–1119) (see also PARAS 126, 130 et seq, 136 et seq) see PARA 126 note 1.

2 In the Companies Act 2006 Pt 35, 'establishment', in relation to an overseas company, means a branch within the meaning of the Eleventh Company Law Directive (ie Council Directive (EC) 89/666 (OJ L395, 30.12.89, p 36) of 21 December 1989, concerning disclosure requirements in respect of branches opened in a member state by certain types of company governed by the law of another state), or a place of business that is not such a branch; and 'UK establishment' means

an establishment in the United Kingdom: Companies Act 2006 s 1067(6) (added by SI 2009/1802). As to the meaning of 'overseas company' see PARA 2013. As to the meaning of 'United Kingdom' see PARA 1 note 5. As to the Eleventh Company Law Directive see PARA 20.

3 Ie registered under the Companies Act 2006 s 1046 (see PARA 2015): see s 1067(1) (as amended: see note 4).

4 Companies Act 2006 s 1067(1) (amended by SI 2009/1802). See also note 1. As to the registered numbers of an overseas company see PARA 134.

5 Companies Act 2006 s 1067(2) (amended by SI 2009/1802). See also note 1.

6 Companies Act 2006 s 1067(3). See also note 1.

7 Companies Act 2006 s 1067(4) (amended by SI 2009/1802). See also note 1.

8 Ie under the Companies Act 2006 s 1051 (see PARA 2021): see s 1067(5) (as amended: see note 9).

9 Companies Act 2006 s 1067(5) (amended by SI 2009/1802). See also note 1.

D. DELIVERY OF DOCUMENTS TO THE REGISTRAR OF COMPANIES

136. Delivery of documents to the registrar of companies: in general. The registrar of companies[1] may impose requirements as to the form, authentication and manner of delivery of documents[2] required or authorised to be delivered to the registrar under any enactment[3].

As regards the form of the document, the registrar may require the contents of the document to be in a standard form[4], and he may impose requirements for the purpose of enabling the document to be scanned or copied[5].

As regards authentication, the registrar may:

(1) require the document to be authenticated by a particular person or a person of a particular description[6];

(2) specify the means of authentication[7];

(3) require the document to contain or be accompanied by the name[8] or registered number[9], or both, of the company or other body to which it relates[10].

As regards the manner of delivery, the registrar may specify requirements as to:

(a) the physical form of the document, for example, hard copy or electronic form[11];

(b) the means to be used for delivering the document, for example, by post or electronic means[12];

(c) the address to which the document is to be sent[13];

(d) in the case of a document to be delivered by electronic means, the hardware and software to be used, and technical specifications, for example, matters relating to protocol, security, anti-virus protection or encryption[14].

The registrar must secure that[15] all documents subject to the Directive disclosure requirements[16] may be delivered to the registrar by electronic means[17].

However, the requirements imposed in this way in relation to form, authentication and manner of delivery[18] must not be inconsistent with requirements imposed by any enactment with respect to the form, authentication or manner of delivery of the document concerned[19].

Where a document required or authorised to be delivered to the registrar under any enactment is required[20] to be certified as an accurate translation or transliteration[21], or to be certified as a correct copy or verified[22], the registrar may impose requirements as to the person, or description of person, by whom the certificate or verification is to be given[23]. The power conferred in relation to the registrar's requirements as to form, authentication and manner of delivery[24] is exercisable in relation to the certificate or verification as if it were a separate document[25]. However, the requirements imposed in relation to certification or verification[26] must not be inconsistent with requirements imposed by any enactment with respect to the certification or verification of the document concerned[27].

A document is not delivered to the registrar until it is received by the registrar[28]; and provision may be made by registrar's rules as to when a document is to be regarded as received[29].

1 As to the meaning of 'registrar of companies' see PARA 126 note 2. As to the meaning of 'company' under the Companies Acts see PARA 21; and as to the meaning of the 'Companies Acts' see PARA 13.

2 For the purposes of the Companies Act 2006 Pt 35 (ss 1059A–1119) (registrar of companies) (see PARAS 126, 130 et seq, 137 et seq), 'document' means information recorded in any form (s 1114(1)(a)); and references to delivering a document include forwarding, lodging, registering, sending, producing or submitting it or (in the case of a notice) giving it (s 1114(1)(b)). Except as otherwise provided, Pt 35 applies in relation to the supply to the registrar of information otherwise than in documentary form as it applies in relation to the delivery of a document: s 1114(2). As to the application of Pt 35 see PARA 126 note 1.

3 Companies Act 2006 s 1068(1). As to the meaning of 'enactment' see PARA 13 note 16.

The provisions of the Companies Act 2006 ss 1068–1071, 1111, 1114 apply to unregistered companies by virtue of the Unregistered Companies Regulations 2009, SI 2009/2436, Sch 1 para 17(1), (2)(b), (g): see PARA 1857. As to the meaning of 'unregistered company' see PARA 1856.

4 Companies Act 2006 s 1068(2)(a).

5 Companies Act 2006 s 1068(2)(b).

6 Companies Act 2006 s 1068(3)(a).

7 Companies Act 2006 s 1068(3)(b).

8 As to company names generally see PARA 195 et seq.

9 As to a company's registered number see PARAS 134, 135.

10 Companies Act 2006 s 1068(3)(c) (substituted by SI 2009/1802).

11 Companies Act 2006 s 1068(4)(a). As to documents or information sent or supplied in hard copy form see PARA 750; and as to documents or information sent or supplied in electronic form see PARA 751.

The power conferred by s 1068 does not authorise the registrar to require documents to be delivered by electronic means: s 1068(6). That power does, however, authorise the registrar to require any document permitted or required to be delivered to the registrar under the Companies Act 2006 Pt 8 Ch 2A (ss 128A–128K) (option to keep membership information on central register: see PARA 363 et seq) or Pt 21A Ch 4 (ss 790W–790ZE) (option to keep PSC information on central register: see PARA 484 et seq) to be delivered by electronic means: s 1068(6A) (added by the Small Business, Enterprise and Employment Act 2015 Sch 5 Pt 2 paras 11, 30; amended by Sch 3 Pt 2 paras 3, 7).

The Secretary of State may make regulations requiring documents that are authorised or required to be delivered to the registrar to be delivered by electronic means: Companies Act 2006 s 1069(1). Such regulations are subject to affirmative resolution procedure (ie the regulations must not be made unless a draft of the statutory instrument containing them has been laid before Parliament and approved by a resolution of each House of Parliament): see ss 1069(3), 1290. Any such requirement to deliver documents by electronic means is effective only if registrar's rules have been published with respect to the detailed requirements for such delivery: s 1069(2). As to the Secretary of State see PARA 6 et seq; and as to the making of regulations under the Companies Act 2006 generally see ss 1288–1292. Partly in the exercise of this power the Secretary of State has made the Reports on Payments to Governments Regulations 2014, SI 2014/3209. A report or consolidated report delivered under reg 14 or information delivered under reg 15 (see para 774) must be delivered to the registrar by electronic means: regs 14(3), 15(3). As to the meaning of 'registrar's rules' see PARA 131. As to the meaning of references to documents or information sent or supplied by electronic means see PARA 751 note 3. Registrar's rules may require a company to give any necessary consents to the use of electronic means for communications by the registrar to the company as a condition of making use of any facility to deliver material to the registrar by electronic means: see the Companies Act 2006 s 1115; and PARA 131.

Notwithstanding the Secretary of State's power to make regulations under s 1069, the registrar may agree with a company or other body that documents relating to the company or other body that are required or authorised to be delivered to the registrar (s 1070(1) (amended by SI 2009/1802)):

(1) will be delivered by electronic means, except as provided for in the agreement (Companies Act 2006 s 1070(1)(a)); and

(2) will conform to such requirements as may be specified in the agreement or specified by the registrar in accordance with the agreement (s 1070(1)(b)).

An agreement under s 1070 may relate to all or any description of documents to be delivered to the registrar (s 1070(2)); and documents in relation to which an agreement is in force under s 1070 must be delivered in accordance with the agreement (s 1070(3)).

12 Companies Act 2006 s 1068(4)(b).
13 Companies Act 2006 s 1068(4)(c).
14 Companies Act 2006 s 1068(4)(d).
15 Ie as from 1 January 2007: see the Companies Act 2006 s 1068(5).
16 As to documents subject to the Directive disclosure requirements see the Companies Act 2006 s 1078; and PARA 139. The requirements are those referred to in European Parliament and Council Directive (EC) 2009/101 (OJ L258, 1.10.2009, p 11) art 3, which, among other matters, requires member states to ensure that the filing by companies, as well as by other persons and bodies required to make or assist in making notifications, of all documents and particulars which must be disclosed pursuant to art 2 is possible by electronic means: see art 3(3); and PARA 139.
17 Companies Act 2006 s 1068(5).
18 Ie the requirements imposed under the Companies Act 2006 s 1068: see s 1068(7).
19 Companies Act 2006 s 1068(7).
20 Companies Act 2006 s 1111(1).
21 Companies Act 2006 s 1111(1)(a). As to language requirements in relation to documents that are required to be delivered to the registrar see PARAS 164–165.
22 Companies Act 2006 s 1111(1)(b).
23 Companies Act 2006 s 1111(1).
24 Ie under the Companies Act 2006 s 1068 (see the text and notes 1–19): see s 1111(2).
25 Companies Act 2006 s 1111(2).
26 Ie under the Companies Act 2006 s 1111: see s 1111(3).
27 Companies Act 2006 s 1111(3).
28 Companies Act 2006 s 1071(1).
29 Companies Act 2006 s 1071(2).

137. Requirements for proper delivery to the registrar of companies. A document[1] delivered to the registrar of companies[2] is not properly delivered unless all the following requirements are met[3], namely:

(1) the requirements of the provision under which the document is to be delivered to the registrar as regards both the contents of the document[4], and its form, authentication and manner of delivery[5];
(2) any applicable requirements under the provisions which govern the registrar's requirements as to form, authentication and manner of delivery[6], the Secretary of State's[7] power to require delivery by electronic means[8], or agreements between the registrar and a company for delivery by electronic means[9];
(3) any requirements of Part 35 of the Companies Act 2006[10] as to the language in which the document is drawn up and delivered or as to its being accompanied on delivery by a certified translation into English[11];
(4) in so far as it consists of or includes names and addresses, any requirements of Part 35 of the Companies Act 2006 as to permitted characters, letters or symbols or as to its being accompanied on delivery by a certificate as to the transliteration of any element[12];
(5) any applicable requirements under the provisions that govern the registrar's requirements as to certification or verification[13];
(6) any requirement of regulations under the provisions that govern the use of unique identifiers[14];
(7) any requirements as regards payment of a fee in respect of its receipt by the registrar[15].

A document that is not properly delivered is treated for the purposes of the provision requiring or authorising it to be delivered as not having been delivered, subject to the registrar's power to accept documents not meeting requirements for proper delivery[16].

1 As to the meaning of 'document' for these purposes see PARA 136 note 2.
2 As to the meaning of 'registrar of companies' see PARA 126 note 2. As to the meaning of 'company' under the Companies Acts see PARA 21; and as to the meaning of the 'Companies Acts' see PARA 13. As to the meaning of references to delivering a document for these purposes see PARA 136 note 2. As to the application of the Companies Act 2006 Pt 35 (ss 1059A–1119) (see also PARAS 126, 130 et seq, 138 et seq) see PARA 126 note 1.
3 Companies Act 2006 s 1072(1).
The provisions of the Companies Act 2006 s 1072 apply to unregistered companies by virtue of the Unregistered Companies Regulations 2009, SI 2009/2436, Sch 1 para 17(c): see PARA 1857. As to the meaning of 'unregistered company' see PARA 1856.
4 Companies Act 2006 s 1072(1)(a)(i). If unnecessary material cannot readily be separated from the rest of the document, the document is treated as not meeting the requirements for proper delivery: see s 1074(4); and PARA 138.
5 Companies Act 2006 s 1072(1)(a)(ii). As to the power of the registrar of companies to impose requirements as to the form, authentication and manner of delivery of documents that are required or authorised to be delivered to him under any enactment see PARA 136.
6 Ie under the Companies Act 2006 s 1068 (see PARA 136): see s 1072(1)(b).
7 As to the Secretary of State see PARA 6 et seq.
8 Ie under the Companies Act 2006 s 1069 (see PARA 136): see s 1072(1)(b). As to the meaning of references to sending documents by electronic means see PARA 751 note 3.
9 Companies Act 2006 s 1072(1)(b). The text refers to the provisions governing agreements between the registrar and a company for delivery by electronic means under s 1070 (see PARA 136): see s 1072(1)(b).
10 Ie the Companies Act 2006 Pt 35 (registrar of companies) (see PARAS 126, 130 et seq, 138 et seq): see s 1072(1)(c).
11 Companies Act 2006 s 1072(1)(c). As to the meaning of 'certified translation' see PARA 164 note 8. As to language requirements in relation to documents that are required to be delivered to the registrar see PARAS 164–165.
12 Companies Act 2006 s 1072(1)(d). As to permitted characters etc in relation to documents that are required to be delivered to the registrar see PARA 164.
13 Companies Act 2006 s 1072(1)(e). The text refers to the provisions governing the registrar's requirements as to certification or verification under s 1111 (see PARA 136): see s 1072(1)(e).
14 Companies Act 2006 s 1072(1)(f). The text refers to the provisions governing the use of unique identifiers under s 1082 (see PARA 144): see s 1072(1)(f).
15 Companies Act 2006 s 1072(1)(g). As to provision made for fees to be payable to the registrar see PARA 130.
16 Companies Act 2006 s 1072(2). The text refers to the registrar's power to accept documents not meeting requirements for proper delivery that is contained in s 1073 (see PARA 138): see s 1072(2). In the case of a document that by virtue of s 1072(2) is treated as not having been delivered, the registrar is not required to annotate the register: see s 1081(3); and PARA 143.

138. Documents not meeting requirements for proper delivery to the registrar of companies. The registrar of companies[1] may accept and register a document[2] that does not comply with the requirements for proper delivery[3]. A document accepted by the registrar in this way[4] is treated as received by the registrar for the purpose of the provisions that require him to give public notice of the receipt of certain documents[5].

No objection may be taken to the legal consequences of a document's being accepted or registered by the registrar in this way[6] on the ground that the requirements for proper delivery were not met[7]. The acceptance of a document by the registrar in this way[8] does not affect[9]:

(1) the continuing obligation to comply with the requirements for proper delivery[10]; or
(2) any liability for failure to comply with those requirements[11].

Head (2) above is subject to the proviso that, for the purposes of the provisions that impose a civil penalty for a failure to file accounts and reports[12], and for the purposes of any enactment[13] imposing a daily default fine[14] for failure to deliver the document[15], the period after the document is accepted does not count as a period during which there is default in complying with the requirements for proper delivery[16]. However, if, subsequently, the registrar issues a notice of administrative removal from the register[17] in respect of the document[18], and the requirements for proper delivery are not complied with before the end of the period of 14 days after the issue of that notice[19], any subsequent period of default does count for the purposes of those provisions[20].

Where a document delivered to the registrar contains unnecessary material[21], and if the unnecessary material cannot readily be separated from the rest of the document, the document is treated as not meeting the requirements for proper delivery[22]. However, if the unnecessary material can readily be separated from the rest of the document, the registrar may register the document either with the omission of the unnecessary material, or as delivered[23].

The registrar may accept a replacement for a document previously delivered[24] that either did not comply with the requirements for proper delivery[25], or contained unnecessary material[26]. However, a replacement document must not be accepted unless the registrar is satisfied that it is delivered by either the person by whom the original document was delivered[27], or the company (or other body) to which the original document relates[28], and that it complies with the requirements for proper delivery[29]. The power of the registrar to impose requirements as to the form and manner of delivery[30] includes power to impose requirements as to the identification of the original document and the delivery of the replacement in a form and manner enabling it to be associated with the original[31].

A document delivered to the registrar[32] may be corrected by the registrar if it appears to the registrar to be incomplete or internally inconsistent[33]. However, this power is exercisable only on instructions[34], and only if the company or other body to which the document relates has given and has not withdrawn its consent to such instructions being given[35]. A document that is corrected in this way[36] is treated, for the purposes of any enactment relating to its delivery, as having been delivered when the correction is made[37].

1 As to the meaning of 'registrar of companies' see PARA 126 note 2. As to the meaning of 'company' under the Companies Acts see PARA 21; and as to the meaning of the 'Companies Acts' see PARA 13. As to the application of the Companies Act 2006 Pt 35 (ss 1059A–1119) (see also PARAS 126, 130 et seq, 139 et seq) see PARA 126 note 1.

2 As to the meaning of 'document' for these purposes see PARA 136 note 2.

3 Companies Act 2006 s 1073(1). See also note 33. As to the requirements for the proper delivery of documents to the registrar see PARA 137. As to the meaning of references to delivering a document for these purposes see PARA 136 note 2.

The provisions of the Companies Act 2006 ss 1073–1076 apply to unregistered companies by virtue of the Unregistered Companies Regulations 2009, SI 2009/2436, Sch 1 para 17(1), (2)(c): see PARA 1857. As to the meaning of 'unregistered company' see PARA 1856.

4 Ie under the Companies Act 2006 s 1073: see s 1073(2).

5 Companies Act 2006 s 1073(2). The text refers to the provisions that govern the registrar's duty to give public notice of the receipt of certain documents under s 1077 (see PARA 139): see s 1073(2).

6 Ie under the Companies Act 2006 s 1073: see s 1073(3).

7 Companies Act 2006 s 1073(3).

8 Ie under the Companies Act 2006 s 1073: see s 1073(4).

9 Companies Act 2006 s 1073(4).

10 Companies Act 2006 s 1073(4)(a).

11 Companies Act 2006 s 1073(4)(b). Head (2) in the text is subject to s 1073(5), (6) (see the text and notes 12–20): see s 1073(4)(b).

12 Companies Act 2006 s 1073(5)(a). The text refers to the purposes of s 453 (see PARA 962): see s 1073(5)(a).

13 As to the meaning of 'enactment' see PARA 13 note 16.
14 As to the meaning of 'daily default fine' see PARA 1816.
15 Companies Act 2006 s 1073(5)(b).
16 Companies Act 2006 s 1073(5).
17 Ie under the Companies Act 2006 s 1094(4) (see PARA 157): see s 1073(6)(a).
18 Companies Act 2006 s 1073(6)(a).
19 Companies Act 2006 s 1073(6)(b).
20 Companies Act 2006 s 1073(6).
21 Companies Act 2006 s 1074(1). For these purposes, 'unnecessary material' means material that is not necessary in order to comply with an obligation under any enactment, and is not specifically authorised to be delivered to the registrar: s 1074(2). For this purpose, an obligation to deliver a document of a particular description, or conforming to certain requirements, is regarded as not extending to anything that is not needed for a document of that description or, as the case may be, conforming to those requirements: s 1074(3). As to the delivery of optional information to the registrar see, however, s 1084A; and PARA 141.
22 Companies Act 2006 s 1074(4). As to other requirements for proper delivery to the registrar see PARA 137.
23 Companies Act 2006 s 1074(5).
24 The Companies Act 2006 s 1076 does not apply where the original document was delivered under Pt 25 (company charges) (see PARA 1462 et seq) (but see s 859M (rectification of register); and PARA 1470): s 1076(4) (amended by SI 2013/600). The Companies Act 2006 s 1076 applies to documents to which s 1072 (see PARA 137), ss 1073–1074 (see the text and notes 1–23) apply: see the Companies Act 2006 (Commencement No 8, Transitional Provisions and Savings) Order 2008, SI 2008/2860, art 5, Sch 2 para 102 (substituted by SI 2009/1802).
25 Companies Act 2006 s 1076(1)(a).
26 Companies Act 2006 s 1076(1)(b). The text refers to unnecessary material within the meaning of s 1074 (see note 21): see s 1076(1)(b).
27 Companies Act 2006 s 1076(2)(a).
28 Companies Act 2006 s 1076(2)(b) (amended by SI 2009/1802).
29 Companies Act 2006 s 1076(2).
30 As to the power of the registrar of companies to impose requirements as to the form, authentication and manner of delivery of documents that are required or authorised to be delivered to him under any enactment see PARA 136.
31 Companies Act 2006 s 1076(3).
32 The Companies Act 2006 s 1075 applies in relation to documents delivered under Pt 25 (ss 859A–894) (company charges) (see PARA 1462 et seq) by a person other than the company or other body as if the references to the company or other body were to the company or other body or the person by whom the document was delivered: s 1075(5) (amended by SI 2009/1802).
33 Companies Act 2006 s 1075(1). However, the power conferred by s 1075 is not exercisable if the document has been registered under s 1073 (power to accept documents not meeting requirements for proper delivery) (see the text and notes 1–20): s 1075(7).
34 Companies Act 2006 s 1075(2)(a). The following requirements must be met as regards the instructions:
   (1) the instructions must be given in response to an inquiry by the registrar (s 1075(3)(a));
   (2) the registrar must be satisfied that the person giving the instructions is authorised to do so either by the person by whom the document was delivered, or by the company (or other body) to which the document relates (s 1075(3)(b) (amended by SI 2009/1802));
   (3) the instructions must meet any requirements of registrar's rules as to both the form and manner in which they are given, and authentication (Companies Act 2006 s 1075(3)(c)).

   As to the meaning of 'registrar's rules' see PARA 131.
35 Companies Act 2006 s 1075(2)(b) (amended by SI 2009/1802). The consent of the company or other body to instructions being given under the Companies Act 2006 s 1075, and any withdrawal of such consent, may be in hard copy or electronic form, and must be notified to the registrar: s 1075(4) (amended by SI 2009/1802). However, any document received by the registrar in connection with the giving or withdrawal of consent under the Companies Act 2006 s 1075 must not be made available by the registrar for public inspection: see s 1087(1)(d); and PARA 146. As to documents or information sent or supplied in hard copy form see PARA 750; and as to documents or information sent or supplied in electronic form see PARA 751.
36 Ie under the Companies Act 2006 s 1075: see s 1075(6).
37 Companies Act 2006 s 1075(6). A document that has been corrected under s 1075 must have details relating to the nature and date of the correction noted by the registrar in the register: see s 1081(1)(b); and PARA 143.

139. Public notice of receipt of documents subject to the Directive disclosure requirements. The registrar of companies[1] must cause to be published in the Gazette[2], or in accordance with the provisions governing alternative means of giving public notice[3], notice of the receipt by him of any document[4] that, on receipt, is subject to the Directive disclosure requirements[5]. The notice must state the name[6] and registered number[7] of the company, the description of the document and the date of receipt[8].

The documents subject to the 'Directive disclosure requirements' are as follows[9].

In the case of every company, those documents are[10]:

(1) the following constitutional documents[11], being:
 (a) the company's memorandum and articles[12];
 (b) any amendment of the company's articles (including every resolution or agreement required to be embodied in or annexed to copies of the company's articles issued by the company)[13];
 (c) after any amendment of the company's articles, the text of the articles as amended;
 (d) any notice of a change of the company's name[14];

(2) in relation to its directors[15]:
 (a) the statement of proposed officers required on formation of the company[16];
 (b) notification of any change among the company's directors[17];
 (c) notification of any change in the particulars of directors required to be delivered to the registrar[18];

(3) in relation to its accounts and reports etc[19]:
 (a) all documents required to be delivered to the registrar under the provisions that govern the duty to file accounts and reports[20];
 (b) all documents delivered to the registrar under the provisions relating to the conditions for qualifying subsidiary companies' exemption from the audit, preparation and filing of individual accounts[21];
 (c) either, before 30 June 2016, the company's annual return[22] or, as from that date[23], any confirmation statement delivered by the company[24];

(4) in relation to its registered office[25], notification of any change of the company's registered office[26];

(5) in relation to winding up[27]:
 (a) a copy of any winding-up order in respect of the company[28];
 (b) any notice of the appointment of liquidators[29];
 (c) any order for the dissolution of a company on a winding up[30];
 (d) any return by a liquidator of the final meeting of a company on a winding up[31].

In the case of a public company[32], those documents are[33]:

(i) in relation to its share capital[34]:
 (A) any statement of capital and initial shareholdings[35];
 (B) any return of allotments and the statement of capital accompanying it[36];
 (C) a copy of any resolution[37] disapplying pre-emption rights[38];
 (D) a copy of any report as to the value of a non-cash asset[39];
 (E) any statement of capital accompanying notice given[40] of the redenomination of shares;

(F) any statement of capital accompanying notice given[41] of a reduction of capital in connection with the redenomination of shares;

(G) any notice delivered under the provisions governing the requirement to give notice of any new name of a class of shares[42] or under the provisions governing the requirement to give notice of any variation of the rights attached to shares[43];

(H) any statement of capital accompanying a court order delivered under the provisions that allow for a reduction of capital to be confirmed[44];

(I) notification[45] of the redemption of shares and the statement of capital accompanying it;

(J) any statement of capital accompanying a return delivered under the requirement to give notice of the cancellation of shares on the purchase by a company of its own shares[46] or under the requirement to give notice of any cancellation of shares held as treasury shares[47];

(K) any statement of compliance delivered[48] confirming that the company meets the conditions for issue of a trading certificate[49];

(L) as from 30 June 2016[50], any statement of the aggregate amount paid up on shares on account of their nominal value[51];

(ii) in relation to mergers and divisions[52]:

(A) a copy of any draft of the terms of a scheme required to be delivered to the registrar in relation either to a merger[53] or a division[54];

(B) a copy of any order[55] in respect of a compromise or arrangement to which Part 27 of the Companies Act 2006[56] applies.

In the case of an overseas company[57], those documents are such particulars, returns and other documents required to be delivered under Part 34 of the Companies Act 2006[58] as may be specified by the Secretary of State by regulations[59].

As from 30 June 2016[60], in the case of a private company[61] which applies to re-register as a public company, the statement of the aggregate amount paid up on shares on account of their nominal value[62] is subject to the Directive disclosure requirements[63].

Where a private company re-registers as a public company[64], the last statement of capital relating to the company received by the registrar under any provision of the Companies Acts becomes subject to the Directive disclosure requirements[65], and the provisions that require the registrar to give public notice of the receipt of certain documents[66] apply as if the statement had been received by the registrar when the re-registration takes effect[67].

Where a company is required[68] deliver to the registrar a report or consolidated report on payments to governments, that report or consolidated report is subject to the Directive disclosure requirements[69]; and where a company is required[70] to deliver to the registrar information on payments to governments which is contained in a report or consolidated report prepared in accordance with equivalent reporting requirements[71], that information is also subject to the Directive disclosure requirements[72].

1 As to the meaning of 'registrar of companies' see PARA 126 note 2. As to the meaning of 'company' under the Companies Acts see PARA 21; and as to the meaning of the 'Companies Acts'

see PARA 13. As to the application of the Companies Act 2006 Pt 35 (ss 1059A–1119) (see also PARAS 126, 130 et seq, 140 et seq) see PARA 126 note 1.

2 As to the meaning of the 'Gazette' see PARA 133 note 2.

3 Ie in accordance with the alternative means provided by the Companies Act 2006 s 1116 (see PARA 133): see s 1077(1).

4 As to the meanings of 'document' and of references to the delivery of documents for these purposes see PARA 136 note 2. As to the delivery of documents to the registrar see PARA 136; and as to the requirements for the proper delivery of documents to the registrar see PARA 137. A document accepted by the registrar under the Companies Act 2006 s 1073, despite not meeting the requirements for proper delivery to the registrar, is treated as received by him for the purpose of s 1077: see s 1073(2); and PARA 138.

5 Companies Act 2006 s 1077(1). However, the registrar is not required to cause notice of the receipt of a document to be published before the date of incorporation of the company to which the document relates: s 1077(3). The date of incorporation of a company is the date mentioned in the company's certificate of incorporation: see PARA 114 note 7. As to the Directive disclosure requirements see the text and notes 9–72. As to the effect of a failure to give the required public notice of the receipt of documents see PARA 140. The registrar of companies must not cause to be published in the Gazette notice pursuant to s 1077 of the receipt of documents under the Companies (Audit, Investigations and Community Enterprise) Act 2004 s 37C(3) (see PARA 190) or s 54C(4) (see PARA 193) unless the registrar records those documents pursuant to s 38A(1)(b) (see PARA 190) or s 55A(1)(b) (see PARA 193) respectively: Community Interest Company Regulations 2005, SI 2005/1788, reg 34(1) (substituted by SI 2009/1942).

The provisions of the Companies Act 2006 ss 1077, 1078 apply to unregistered companies by virtue of the Unregistered Companies Regulations 2009, SI 2009/2436, Sch 1 para 19 (amended by SI 2012/2301; SI 2016/599) but with the modifications as specified thereby: see PARA 1857. As to the meaning of 'unregistered company' see PARA 1856.

6 As to company names generally see PARA 195 et seq.

7 As to a company's registered number see PARAS 134, 135.

8 Companies Act 2006 s 1077(2).

9 Companies Act 2006 s 1078(1). The requirements referred to are those of European Parliament and Council Directive (EC) 2009/101 (OJ L258, 1.10.2009, p 11) art 3, as amended, extended and applied: see the Companies Act 2006 s 1078(1) (amended by SI 2014/1557). As to that Directive see PARA 20; and see PARA 136 note 16.

10 Companies Act 2006 s 1078(2) (amended by the Small Business, Enterprise and Employment Act 2015 s 93(1), (5); and by SI 2012/2301).

11 As to the meaning of references to a company's constitution see PARA 226.

12 As to the meaning of 'memorandum of association' see PARA 97. As to the meaning of references to a company's 'articles' see PARA 227 note 2. As to a company's articles of association generally see PARA 227 et seq.

13 As to the amendment of articles of association see PARA 231 et seq. As to company resolutions generally see PARA 684 et seq.

14 As to the change of a company's name see PARAS 217–218.

15 As to the meaning of 'director' see PARA 512.

16 As to the meaning of 'officer' generally under the Companies Act 2006 see PARA 679. As to the statement of the company's proposed officers see s 12; and PARA 105.

17 As to notification of a change among the directors see PARA 550.

18 As to the requisite particulars of directors see PARA 105.

19 Until 30 June 2016, this heading in the Companies Act 2006 s 1078(2) reads 'Accounts, Reports and Returns'.

20 Ie documents required to be delivered to the registrar under the Companies Act 2006 s 441 (see PARA 950).

21 Ie all documents delivered to the registrar under the Companies Act 2006 s 394A(2)(e) (see PARA 791), s 448A(2)(e) (see PARA 957) and s 479A(2)(e) (see PARA 988).

22 As to the duty on a company to deliver annual returns see PARA 1594 et seq.

23 See the Small Business, Enterprise and Employment Act 2015 (Commencement No 4, Transitional and Savings Provisions) Regulations 2016, SI 2016/321, reg 6(b).

24 Ie any confirmation statement delivered by the company under the Companies Act 2006 s 853A: see PARA 1598.

25 As to the registered office of a company see PARA 124.

26 As to changes in the situation of a company's registered office see PARA 124.

27 As to winding up in general see COMPANY AND PARTNERSHIP INSOLVENCY vol 16 (2011) PARA 380 et seq.

28 A copy of a winding-up order is forwarded under the Insolvency Act 1986 s 130(1): see COMPANY AND PARTNERSHIP INSOLVENCY vol 16 (2011) PARA 436.
29 As to the appointment of a liquidator see COMPANY AND PARTNERSHIP INSOLVENCY vol 17 (2011) PARA 909.
30 As to the power of the court to make a winding-up order see COMPANY AND PARTNERSHIP INSOLVENCY vol 17 (2011) PARA 1320.
31 Companies Act 2006 s 1078(2) (amended by the Small Business, Enterprise and Employment Act 2015 s 93(1), (5)). At the date at which this volume states the law, a return by a liquidator of the final meeting is made under the Insolvency Act 1986 s 94(3) (as originally enacted), and is sent together with a copy of the account of the winding up made by the liquidator: see COMPANY AND PARTNERSHIP INSOLVENCY vol 17 (2011) PARA 983. As from a day to be appointed, however, s 94(3) is substituted by the Small Business, Enterprise and Employment Act 2015 Sch 9 Pt 1 paras 1, 18 and no longer refers to a return of the final meeting but only to sending a copy of the account of the winding up.
32 As to the meaning of 'public company' see PARA 95.
33 Companies Act 2006 s 1078(3) (amended by the Small Business, Enterprise and Employment Act 2015 s 98(1), (4)(a)).
34 As to the meanings of 'share' and 'share capital' see PARA 1231.
35 As to the statement of capital and initial shareholdings required in the case of a company limited by shares see PARA 107. As to the meaning of 'company limited by shares' see PARA 95.
36 As to the return of allotments etc to the registrar see PARA 1297.
37 Ie under the Companies Act 2006 s 570 or s 571 (see PARA 1292).
38 As to the disapplication of pre-emption rights by special resolution see PARA 1290 et seq.
39 Ie any report under the Companies Act 2006 s 593 (see PARA 1309) or s 599 (see PARA 1314).
40 Ie under the Companies Act 2006 s 625 (see PARA 1356).
41 Ie under the Companies Act 2006 s 627 (see PARA 1358).
42 Ie under the Companies Act 2006 s 636 (see PARA 1253).
43 Ie under the Companies Act 2006 s 637 (see PARA 1253).
44 Ie any statement of capital accompanying an order delivered under the Companies Act 2006 s 649 (see PARA 1380).
45 Ie under the Companies Act 2006 s 689 (see PARA 1420).
46 Ie under the Companies Act 2006 s 708 (notice of cancellation of shares on purchase of own shares) (see PARA 1426).
47 Ie under the Companies Act 2006 s 730 (see PARA 1439). As to the meaning of 'treasury share' see PARA 1437.
48 Ie under the Companies Act 2006 s 762 (see PARA 67).
49 As to the meaning of 'trading certificate' see PARA 67.
50 See the Small Business, Enterprise and Employment Act 2015 (Commencement No 4, Transitional and Savings Provisions) Regulations 2016, SI 2016/321, reg 6(f).
51 Ie any statement delivered under the Companies Act 2006 s 762(1)(e) (see PARA 67).
52 As to mergers and divisions of public companies see PARA 1629 et seq.
53 Ie a copy of any draft of the terms of a scheme required to be delivered to the registrar under the Companies Act 2006 s 906 (see PARA 1633).
54 Ie a copy of any draft of the terms of a scheme of division required to be delivered to the registrar under s 921 (see PARA 1647).
55 Ie a copy of any order under the Companies Act 2006 s 899 (see PARA 1613) (order sanctioning scheme of arrangement) or s 900 (see PARA 1614) (making of order to facilitate reconstruction and amalgamation) in respect of a compromise or arrangement to which Pt 27 (ss 902–941) (mergers and divisions of public companies) (see PARA 1629 et seq) applies.
56 Ie the Companies Act 2006 Pt 27 (see PARA 1629 et seq).
57 As to the meaning of 'overseas company' see PARA 2013.
58 Ie the Companies Act 2006 Pt 34 (ss 1044–1059) (see PARA 2013 et seq): see s 1078(5).
59 Companies Act 2006 s 1078(5). Regulations made under s 1078(5) are subject to negative resolution procedure (ie the statutory instrument containing the regulations is subject to annulment in pursuance of a resolution of either House of Parliament): ss 1078(6), 1289. As to the making of regulations under the Companies Act 2006 generally see ss 1288–1292. As to the Secretary of State see PARA 6. Partly in exercise of the power conferred under s 1078(5), the Secretary of State has made the Overseas Companies Regulations 2009, SI 2009/1801. Accordingly, the particulars, returns and other documents specified for the purposes of the Companies Act 2006 s 1078(5) (overseas companies: documents subject to Directive disclosure requirements) are any return or document delivered under the Overseas Companies Regulations 2009, SI 2009/1801, Pt 2 (regs 3–11) (initial registration of particulars) (see PARA 2015); any return or document delivered under Pt 3 (regs 12–17) (alterations in registered

particulars) (see PARA 2015); any document delivered under Pt 5 (regs 30–42) (delivery of accounting documents: general) (see PARA 2019); any document delivered under Pt 6 (regs 43–57) (delivery of accounting documents: credit or financial institutions) (see PARA 2020); any return delivered under reg 69 (return in case of winding up) or reg 70 (returns to be made by liquidator) (see PARA 2023); and any notice under reg 77 (duty to give notice of closure of UK establishment) (see PARA 2018): see reg 76.

60 See the Small Business, Enterprise and Employment Act 2015 (Commencement No 4, Transitional and Savings Provisions) Regulations 2016, SI 2016/321, reg 6(f).
61 As to the meaning of 'private company' see PARA 95.
62 Ie the statement delivered under the Companies Act 2006 s 94(2)(e) (see PARA 168).
63 See the Companies Act 2006 s 1078(3A) (added by the Small Business, Enterprise and Employment Act 2015 s 98(1), (4)(b)).
64 Ie under the Companies Act 2006 s 96 (see PARA 172): see s 1078(4).
65 Companies Act 2006 s 1078(4)(a).
66 Ie the Companies Act 2006 s 1077 (see the text and notes 1–8): see s 1078(4)(b).
67 Companies Act 2006 s 1078(4)(b).
68 Ie by the Reports on Payments to Governments Regulations 2014, SI 2014/3209, reg 14 (see PARA 774).
69 See the Companies Act 2006 s 1078(4A) (s 1078(4A), (4B) added by SI 2014/3209).
70 Ie by the Reports on Payments to Governments Regulations 2014, SI 2014/3209, reg 15 (see PARA 774).
71 Ie within the meaning of the Reports on Payments to Governments Regulations 2014, SI 2014/3209 (see PARA 774 note 27).
72 See the Companies Act 2006 s 1078(4B) (as added: see note 69).

140. Effect of failure by registrar of companies to give public notice of receipt of certain documents. The purpose of the statutory provisions which require the registrar of companies[1] to give public notice of the receipt of certain documents[2] is not to ensure constructive notice of the relevant events to persons dealing with the company[3], but rather to ensure that such persons have an opportunity, if they wish to avail themselves of it, to find out information about these events[4]. Further, a company is not entitled to rely against other persons on the happening of any of the following events[5], namely:

(1) an amendment of the company's articles of association[6]; or
(2) a change among the company's directors[7]; or
(3) as regards service of any document on the company[8], a change of the company's registered office[9],
(4) the making of a winding-up order in respect of the company[10]; or
(5) the appointment of a liquidator in a voluntary winding up of the company[11],

unless the event has been officially notified[12] at the material time[13], or unless the company shows that the person concerned knew of the event at the material time[14]. If the material time falls on or before the fifteenth day after the date of official notification[15] (or, where the fifteenth day was not a working day[16], on or before the next day that was)[17] the company is not entitled to rely on the happening of the event as against a person who shows that he was unavoidably prevented from knowing of the event at that time[18].

1 As to the meaning of 'registrar of companies' see PARA 126 note 2. As to the meaning of 'company' under the Companies Acts see PARA 21; and as to the meaning of the 'Companies Acts' see PARA 13. As to the application of the Companies Act 2006 Pt 35 (ss 1059A–1120) (see also PARAS 126, 130 et seq, 142 et seq) see PARA 126 note 1.
2 Ie the Companies Act 2006 s 1077: see PARA 139. As to the meanings of 'document' and of references to delivering a document for these purposes see PARA 136 note 2. As to the delivery of documents to the registrar see PARA 136; and as to the requirements for the proper delivery of documents to the registrar see PARA 137.
3 As to notice of the constitution of a company see PARA 265.
4 *Official Custodian of Charities v Parway Estates Developments Ltd* [1985] Ch 151, [1984] 3 All ER 679, CA.

5 Companies Act 2006 s 1079(1).
The provisions of the Companies Act 2006 s 1079 apply to unregistered companies by virtue of the Unregistered Companies Regulations 2009, SI 2009/2436, Sch 1 para 19, but with the modifications as specified thereby: see PARA 1857. As to the meaning of 'unregistered company' see PARA 1856.
6 Companies Act 2006 s 1079(2)(a). As to the meaning of references to a company's 'articles' see PARA 227 note 2. As to a company's articles of association generally see PARA 227 et seq; and as to the amendment of articles of association see PARA 231 et seq.
7 Companies Act 2006 s 1079(2)(b). As to the meaning of 'director' see PARA 512. As to notification of a change among the directors see PARAS 550, 553.
8 As to the service of documents on a company generally see PARA 743 et seq; and as to the provision made for the sending or supplying of documents or information to or from a company (the 'company communications provisions') see PARA 749 et seq.
9 Companies Act 2006 s 1079(2)(c). As to changes in the situation of a company's registered office see PARA 124.
10 Companies Act 2006 s 1079(2)(d). See *Re Peek, Winch and Tod Ltd* (1979) 130 NLJ 116, CA. As to winding up in general see COMPANY AND PARTNERSHIP INSOLVENCY vol 16 (2011) PARA 380 et seq. As to the power of the court to make a winding-up order see COMPANY AND PARTNERSHIP INSOLVENCY vol 17 (2011) PARA 1320.
11 Companies Act 2006 s 1079(2)(e). See *Re Peek, Winch and Tod Ltd* (1979) 130 NLJ 116, CA. As to the appointment of a liquidator where a company goes into voluntary liquidation see COMPANY AND PARTNERSHIP INSOLVENCY vol 17 (2011) PARA 909.
12 For these purposes, 'official notification' means:
(1) in relation to an amendment of the company's articles, notification in accordance with the Companies Act 2006 s 1077 (public notice of receipt by registrar of certain documents) (see PARA 139) of the amendment and the amended text of the articles (s 1079(4)(a));
(2) in relation to anything else stated in a document subject to the Directive disclosure requirements (see PARA 139), notification of that document in accordance with s 1077 (s 1079(4)(b));
(3) in relation to the appointment of a liquidator in a voluntary winding up, notification of that event in accordance with the Insolvency Act 1986 s 109 (see COMPANY AND PARTNERSHIP INSOLVENCY vol 17 (2011) PARA 916) (Companies Act 2006 s 1079(4)(c)).
13 Companies Act 2006 s 1079(1)(a).
14 Companies Act 2006 s 1079(1)(b).
15 Companies Act 2006 s 1079(3)(a).
16 In the Companies Acts, 'working day', in relation to a company, means a day that is not a Saturday or Sunday, Christmas Day, Good Friday and any day that is a bank holiday under the Banking and Financial Dealings Act 1971 (see TIME vol 97 (2015) PARA 321) in the part of United Kingdom where the company is registered: Companies Act 2006 s 1173(1). As to the meaning of 'United Kingdom' see PARA 1 note 5. As to company registration under the Companies Act 2006 see PARA 104 et seq.
17 Companies Act 2006 s 1079(3)(b).
18 Companies Act 2006 s 1079(3).

141. Delivery of optional information to the registrar of companies. The Secretary of State[1] may make provision by regulations[2] authorising a company[3] or other body to deliver optional information[4] of a prescribed description[5] to the registrar of companies[6]. The regulations may, in particular, include provision:
(1) imposing requirements on a company or other body in relation to keeping any of its optional information recorded on the register[7] up to date;
(2) about the consequences of a company or other body failing to do so[8].

1 As to the Secretary of State see PARA 6.
2 As to the making of regulations under the Companies Act 2006 generally see ss 1288–1292. Regulations under s 1084A are subject to affirmative resolution procedure: s 1084A(4) (s 1084A added by the Small Business, Enterprise and Employment Act 2015 s 95(1)). As to the application of the Companies Act 2006 Pt 35 (ss 1059A–1119) (see also PARAS 126, 130 et seq, 139 et seq) see PARA 126 note 1.
3 As to the meaning of 'company' under the Companies Acts see PARA 21; and as to the meaning of the 'Companies Acts' see PARA 13.

4 For these purposes, 'optional information', in relation to a company or other body, means information about the company or body which, but for the regulations, the company or body would not be obliged or authorised under any enactment to deliver to the registrar: Companies Act 2006 s 1084A(2) (as added: see note 2). As to the meaning of 'registrar of companies' see PARA 126 note 2.
5 In the Companies Acts, 'prescribed' means prescribed (by order or by regulations) by the Secretary of State: Companies Act 2006 s 1167.
6 Companies Act 2006 s 1084A(1) (as added: see note 2). At the date at which this volume states the law, no such regulations had been made.
7 As to the meaning of the 'register' see PARA 142.
8 Companies Act 2006 s 1084A(3) (as added: see note 2).

E. THE REGISTER

(A) Records kept by the Registrar of Companies

142. Keeping of company records (the 'register') by the registrar. The registrar of companies[1] must keep records of:

(1) the information contained in documents[2] delivered to the registrar[3] under any enactment[4]; and

(2) certificates issued by the registrar under any enactment[5].

The records relating to companies are referred to collectively in the Companies Acts as the 'register'[6], and the records kept by the registrar must be such that information relating to a company or other registered body is associated with that body, in such manner as the registrar may determine, so as to enable all the information relating to the body to be retrieved[7].

Information deriving from documents subject to the Directive disclosure requirements[8] that are delivered to the registrar[9] must be kept by the registrar in electronic form[10]. Subject to that, information contained in documents delivered to the registrar may be recorded and kept by him in any form he thinks fit, provided that it is possible to inspect the information and to produce a copy of it[11]. This is sufficient compliance with any duty of his to keep, file or register the document or to record the information contained in it[12].

The originals of documents delivered to the registrar in hard copy form[13] must be kept for three years after they are received by the registrar, after which they may be destroyed provided the information contained in them has been recorded[14]. However, this is subject to the proviso that material which is not made available by the registrar for public inspection[15] need not be retained by him for longer than appears to him reasonably necessary for the purposes for which the material was delivered to the registrar[16].

Where a company is dissolved[17], or where an overseas company[18] ceases to have any connection with the United Kingdom[19] by virtue of which it is required to register particulars[20], or where a credit institution[21] or financial institution[22] ceases to be required[23] to file accounts with the registrar[24], and, at any time after two years from the date on which it appears to the registrar that such an event has occurred[25], the registrar may direct that any records relating to the company or institution may be removed to the Public Record Office[26]; and records in respect of which such a direction is given must be disposed of under the enactments relating to the Public Record Office and the rules made under them[27].

Where the registrar undertakes to alter the status of a company on the register which it is his duty to keep, in particular by recording a winding-up order against it[28], he assumes a responsibility to that company, but not to anyone else, to take reasonable care to ensure that the winding-up order is not registered against the wrong company, since it is foreseeable that if a company is wrongly said on the register to be in liquidation it will suffer serious harm[29].

1 As to the meaning of 'registrar of companies' see PARA 126 note 2. As to the meaning of 'company' under the Companies Acts see PARA 21; and as to the meaning of the 'Companies Acts' see PARA 13. As to the application of the Companies Act 2006 Pt 35 (ss 1059A–1119) (see also PARAS 126, 130 et seq, 143 et seq) see PARA 126 note 1.

2 As to the meaning of 'document' for these purposes see PARA 136 note 2.

3 As to the meaning of references to delivering a document for these purposes see PARA 136 note 2. As to the delivery of documents to the registrar see PARA 136; and as to the requirements for the proper delivery of documents to the registrar see PARA 137.

4 Companies Act 2006 s 1080(1)(a). As to the meaning of 'enactment' see PARA 13 note 16.

The provisions of the Companies Act 2006 ss 1080(1)–(5), 1083 apply to unregistered companies by virtue of the Unregistered Companies Regulations 2009, SI 2009/2436, Sch 1 paras 17(1), (2)(d), (e), 20(1)(a): see PARA 1857. As to the meaning of 'unregistered company' see PARA 1856.

5 Companies Act 2006 s 1080(1)(b) (substituted by SI 2009/1802). As to the issuing of a company's certificate of incorporation see PARAS 114, 133.

6 Companies Act 2006 s 1080(2). Regulations made under s 1188 or s 1189 (statements relating to company directors who are subject to foreign restrictions) (see PARA 1815) may provide that a statement sent to the registrar of companies under the regulations is to be treated as a record relating to a company for the purposes of s 1080: see s 1190(1); and PARA 1815.

7 Companies Act 2006 s 1080(5) (amended by SI 2009/1802).

8 As to the Directive disclosure requirements see the Companies Act 2006 s 1078; and PARA 139.

9 Ie on or after 1 January 2007: see the Companies Act 2006 s 1080(3).

10 Companies Act 2006 s 1080(3). As to the meaning of references to documents or information sent or supplied in electronic form see PARA 751 note 3.

11 Companies Act 2006 s 1080(4).

12 See note 11.

13 The registrar is under no obligation to keep the originals of documents delivered in electronic form, provided the information contained in them has been recorded: Companies Act 2006 s 1083(2) (amended by SI 2009/1802). As to documents or information sent or supplied in hard copy form see PARA 750.

14 Companies Act 2006 s 1083(1) (amended by SI 2009/1802).

The Companies Act 2006 s 1083 applies to documents held by the registrar on 1 October 2009 (ie when that section came into force: see the Companies Act 2006 (Commencement No 8, Transitional Provisions and Savings) Order 2008, SI 2008/2860, art 3(r)) as well as to documents subsequently received: Companies Act 2006 s 1083(3).

15 Ie under the Companies Act 2006 s 1087 (see PARA 146): see s 1083(1).

16 Companies Act 2006 ss 1083(1), 1087(3). See PARA 146.

17 Companies Act 2006 s 1084(1)(a). In s 1084(1)(a), 'company' includes a company provisionally or completely registered under the Joint Stock Companies Act 1844 (repealed): Companies Act 2006 s 1084(4). As to the dissolution of a company see PARA 1703 et seq.

18 As to the meaning of 'overseas company' see PARA 2013.

19 As to the meaning of 'United Kingdom' see PARA 1 note 5.

20 Companies Act 2006 s 1084(1)(b). The text refers to the requirement placed on an overseas company to register particulars under s 1046 (see PARA 2015): see s 1084(1)(b).

21 In the Companies Acts, 'credit institution' means a credit institution as defined in European Parliament and Council Regulation (EU) 575/2013 (OJ L176, 27.6.2013, p 1) art 4.1(1) (ie an undertaking the business of which is to take deposits or other repayable funds from the public and to grant credits for its own account): see the Companies Act 2006 s 1173(1) (definition substituted by SI 2013/3115).

22 In the Companies Acts, 'financial institution' means a financial institution within the meaning of Council Directive (EEC) 89/117 (OJ L44, 16.2.1989, p 40) on the obligations of branches established in a member state of credit and financial institutions having their head offices outside that member state regarding the publication of annual accounting documents (the 'Bank Branches Directive') art 1.1: Companies Act 2006 s 1173(1).

23 Ie ceases to be within the Companies Act 2006 s 1050 (see PARA 2020): see s 1084(1)(c).

24 Companies Act 2006 s 1084(1)(c).

25 Ie at any time after two years from the date on which it appears to the registrar that:

(1) the company has been dissolved (s 1084(2)(a));

(2) the overseas company has ceased to have any connection with the United Kingdom by virtue of which it is required to register particulars under s 1046 (see PARA 2015) (s 1084(2)(b)); or

(3) the credit or financial institution has ceased to be within s 1050 (see PARA 2020) (s 1084(2)(c)).

26 Companies Act 2006 s 1084(2). As to the Public Record Office see CONSTITUTIONAL AND ADMINISTRATIVE LAW vol 20 (2014) PARA 343 et seq.

27 Companies Act 2006 s 1084(3).

28 As to winding up in general see COMPANY AND PARTNERSHIP INSOLVENCY vol 16 (2011) PARA 380 et seq.

29 See *Sebry v Companies House* [2015] EWHC 115 (QB), [2015] 4 All ER 681, [2015] 1 BCLC 670. There is, however, nothing in the Companies Act 2006 to indicate that there is a cause of action for damages for breach of statutory duty against the registrar in relation to his functions under that Act, as opposed to a cause of action for damages for negligence at common law: *Sebry v Companies House* [2015] EWHC 115 (QB), [2015] 4 All ER 681 [2015] 1 BCLC 670, obiter.

143. Annotation of the register. The registrar of companies[1] must place a note in the register[2] recording:

(1) the date on which a document[3] is delivered to the registrar[4];

(2) if a document is corrected informally by the registrar[5], the nature and date of the correction[6];

(3) if a document is replaced, whether or not material derived from it is removed[7], the fact that it has been replaced and the date of delivery of the replacement[8];

(4) if material is removed[9], what was removed (giving a general description of its contents)[10], under what power[11], and the date on which that was done[12];

(5) if a document is rectified[13], the nature and date of rectification[14];

(6) if a document is replaced[15], the fact that it has been replaced and the date of delivery of the replacement[16].

As from 30 June 2016[17], if the registrar registers a document delivered by a company under the provision imposing a duty on a private company which has elected to keep information about its members on the central register to notify the registrar of any changes[18] and that document does not specify the relevant date[19], the registrar must place a note in the register recording as that date the date on which the document was registered by the registrar[20].

The Secretary of State[21] may make provision by regulations[22] authorising or requiring the registrar to annotate the register in such other circumstances as may be specified in the regulations[23], and as to the contents of any such annotation[24].

Notes placed in the register in this way[25] are part of the register for all purposes of the Companies Acts[26].

A note may be removed if it no longer serves any useful purpose[27]. In any case, any duty or power of the registrar with respect to annotation of the register is subject to the court's power[28] to direct that a note be removed from the register[29] or that no note is to be made of the removal of material that is the subject of the court's order[30].

1 As to the meaning of 'registrar of companies' see PARA 126 note 2. As to the meaning of 'company' under the Companies Acts see PARA 21; and as to the meaning of the 'Companies Acts' see PARA 13. As to the application of the Companies Act 2006 Pt 35 (ss 1059A–1119) (see also PARAS 126, 130 et seq, 144 et seq) see PARA 126 note 1.

2 As to the meaning of the 'register' see PARA 142.

3 As to the meaning of 'document' for these purposes see PARA 136 note 2.

4 Companies Act 2006 s 1081(1)(a). No annotation is required in the case of a document that by virtue of s 1072(2) (documents not meeting requirements for proper delivery) (see PARA 137) is treated as not having been delivered: s 1081(3). As to the meaning of references to delivering a

document for these purposes see PARA 136 note 2. As to the delivery of documents to the registrar see PARA 136; and as to the requirements generally for the proper delivery of documents to the registrar see PARA 137.

5 Ie under the Companies Act 2006 s 1075 (see PARA 138): see s 1081(1)(b). A document delivered to the registrar may be corrected by the registrar, subject to certain conditions, if it appears to the registrar to be incomplete or internally inconsistent: see s 1075; and PARA 138.

6 Companies Act 2006 s 1081(1)(b).

7 The registrar may accept a replacement for a document previously delivered that either did not comply with the requirements for proper delivery, or contained unnecessary material: see the Companies Act 2006 s 1076; and PARA 138. As to the meaning of 'unnecessary material' for these purposes see PARA 138 note 21.

8 Companies Act 2006 s 1081(1)(c).

9 Companies Act 2006 s 1081(1)(d). Regulations made under s 1188 or s 1189 (statements relating to company directors who are subject to foreign restrictions) (see PARA 1815) may provide that s 1081 (note of removal of material from the register) does not apply, or applies with such modifications as may be specified, in the case of material removed from the register under the regulations: see s 1190(4); and PARA 1815.

10 Companies Act 2006 s 1081(1)(d)(i).

11 Companies Act 2006 s 1081(1)(d)(ii).

12 Companies Act 2006 s 1081(1)(d)(iii).

13 Ie under the Companies Act 2006 s 859M: see PARA 1470.

14 Companies Act 2006 s 1081(1)(e) (s 1081(1)(e), (f) added by SI 2013/600).

15 Ie under the Companies Act 2006 s 859N: see PARA 1471.

16 Companies Act 2006 s 1081(1)(f) (as added: see note 14).

17 See the Small Business, Enterprise and Employment Act 2015 (Commencement No 4, Transitional and Savings Provisions) Regulations 2016, SI 2016/321, reg 6(c).

18 Ie a document delivered under the Companies Act 2006 s 128E: see PARA 366.

19 Ie by virtue of the Companies Act 2006 s 128E(3)(a), (b) or (c).

20 See the Companies Act 2006 s 1081(1A) (added by the Small Business, Enterprise and Employment Act 2015 Sch 5 Pt 2 paras 11, 31(1), (2)).

21 As to the Secretary of State see PARA 6.

22 As to the making of regulations under the Companies Act 2006 generally see ss 1288–1292. Regulations made under s 1081 are subject to negative resolution procedure (ie the statutory instrument containing the regulations is subject to annulment in pursuance of a resolution of either House of Parliament): see ss 1081(7), 1289. In exercise of the powers conferred by 1081(2), the Secretary of State has made the Registrar of Companies and Applications for Striking Off Regulations 2009, SI 2009/1803, reg 3. Accordingly, where it appears to the registrar that material on the register is misleading or confusing, the registrar may place a note in the register containing such information as appears to the registrar to be necessary to remedy, as far as possible, the misleading or confusing nature of the material: reg 3.

23 Companies Act 2006 s 1081(2)(a). See also note 22.

24 Companies Act 2006 s 1081(2)(b). See also note 22.

25 Ie in accordance with the Companies Act 2006 s 1081(1) (see the text and notes 1–16) or s 1081(1A) (see the text and notes 17–20), or in pursuance of regulations under s 1081(2) (see the text and notes 21–24): see s 1081(6) (amended by the Small Business, Enterprise and Employment Act 2015 Sch 5 Pt 2 paras 11, 31(1), (3)).

26 Companies Act 2006 s 1081(6) (as amended: see note 25).

27 Companies Act 2006 s 1081(4).

28 Ie under the Companies Act 2006 s 1097 (powers of court on ordering removal of material from the register) (see PARA 161): see s 1081(5).

29 Companies Act 2006 s 1081(5)(a).

30 Companies Act 2006 s 1081(5)(b).

144. Allocation of unique identifiers. The Secretary of State[1] may make provision[2] for the use, in connection with the register[3], of reference numbers ('unique identifiers') to identify each person who[4]:

(1) is a director of a company[5];

(2) is secretary, or a joint secretary, of a company[6]; or

(3) in the case of an overseas company[7] whose particulars are registered[8], holds any such position as may be specified for these purposes by regulations made in relation to overseas companies generally[9].

The regulations may:

(a) provide that a unique identifier may be in such form, consisting of one or more sequences of letters or numbers, as the registrar may from time to time determine[10];
(b) make provision for the allocation of unique identifiers by the registrar[11];
(c) require there to be included, in any specified description of documents delivered to the registrar, as well as a statement of the person's name[12]:
  (i) a statement of the person's unique identifier[13]; or
  (ii) a statement that the person has not been allocated a unique identifier[14];
(d) enable the registrar to take steps, where a person appears to have more than one unique identifier, to discontinue the use of all but one of them[15].

1 As to the Secretary of State see PARA 6.
2 The wording of the Companies Act 2006 s 1082 that follows on from 'provision' suggests that 'provision by regulations' is meant. Regulations made under s 1082 are subject to affirmative resolution procedure (ie the regulations must not be made unless a draft of the statutory instrument containing them has been laid before Parliament and approved by a resolution of each House of Parliament): see ss 1082(5), 1290. As to the making of regulations under the Companies Act 2006 generally see ss 1288–1292. The regulations may make different provision for different descriptions of person and different descriptions of document (s 1082(4)); and the regulations may contain provision for the application of the scheme in relation to persons appointed, and documents registered, before the commencement of the Companies Act 2006 (s 1082(3)). As to the meaning of 'document' for these purposes see PARA 136 note 2. As to the commencement of the Companies Act 2006 see PARA 13. At the date at which this volume states the law, no such regulations have been made. As to the application of the Companies Act 2006 Pt 35 (ss 1059A–1119) (see also PARAS 126, 130 et seq, 145 et seq) see PARA 126 note 1.
3 As to the meaning of the 'register' see PARA 142.
4 Companies Act 2006 s 1082(1).
5 Companies Act 2006 s 1082(1)(a). As to the meaning of 'director' see PARA 512.
6 Companies Act 2006 s 1082(1)(b). As to the company secretary and other officers see PARA 671.
7 As to the meaning of 'overseas company' see PARA 2013.
8 Ie registered under the Companies Act 2006 s 1046 (see PARA 2015): see s 1082(1)(c).
9 Companies Act 2006 s 1082(1)(c). The text refers to any such position as may be specified for the purposes of s 1082 by regulations under s 1046 (see PARA 2015): see s 1082(1)(c). However, at the date at which this volume states the law, the regulations that have been made thereunder, ie the Overseas Companies Regulations 2009, SI 2009/1801, make no such provision.
10 Companies Act 2006 s 1082(2)(a).
11 Companies Act 2006 s 1082(2)(b).
12 Companies Act 2006 s 1082(2)(c).
13 Companies Act 2006 s 1082(2)(c)(i).
14 Companies Act 2006 s 1082(2)(c)(ii).
15 Companies Act 2006 s 1082(2)(d).

(B) Inspection of Records kept by the Registrar of Companies

145. Inspection etc of records kept by the registrar of companies. Subject to the statutory provisions which govern material that is not available for public inspection[1]:

(1) any person may inspect the register[2]; and
(2) any person may require a copy of any material on the register[3].

The right of inspection under head (1) above extends to the originals of documents[4] delivered to the registrar of companies[5] in hard copy form if, and only if, the record kept by the registrar of the contents of the document is illegible or unavailable[6].

The registrar may specify the form and manner in which application is to be made for inspection under head (1) above, or for provision of a copy under head (2) above[7].

As regards the form and manner in which copies are to be provided under head (2) above[8], copies of documents subject to the Directive disclosure requirements must[9] be provided in hard copy or electronic form, as the applicant chooses[10]. This is subject to the proviso that the registrar is not obliged[11] to provide copies in electronic form of a document that was delivered to the registrar in hard copy form[12], if:

(a) the document was delivered to the registrar on or before 31 December 1996[13]; or

(b) the document was delivered to the registrar on or before 31 December 2006 and ten years or more elapsed between the date of delivery and the date of receipt of the first application for a copy on or after 1 January 2007[14].

Subject to these provisions[15], the registrar may determine the form and manner in which copies are to be provided[16].

Copies provided under head (2) above in hard copy form must be certified as true copies unless the applicant dispenses with such certification[17]; and copies so provided in electronic form must not be certified as true copies unless the applicant expressly requests such certification[18]. A copy provided under head (2) above, certified by the registrar (whose official position it is unnecessary to prove) to be an accurate record of the contents of the original document, is in all legal proceedings admissible in evidence[19] as of equal validity with the original document[20] and as evidence of any fact stated in the original document of which direct oral evidence would be admissible[21]. Except in the case of documents that are subject to the Directive disclosure requirements[22], copies provided by the registrar may, instead of being certified in writing to be an accurate record, be sealed with the registrar's official seal[23].

No process for compelling the production of a record kept by the registrar may issue from any court except with the permission of the court[24]; and any such process must bear on it a statement that it is issued with the permission of the court[25].

1 Ie subject to the Companies Act 2006 s 1087 (see PARA 146): see ss 1085(3), 1086(3). As to the application of the Companies Act 2006 Pt 35 (ss 1059A–1119) (see also PARAS 126, 130 et seq, 146 et seq) see PARA 126 note 1.

The provisions of the Companies Act 2006 ss 1085, 1086, 1089–1091 apply to unregistered companies by virtue of the Unregistered Companies Regulations 2009, SI 2009/2436, Sch 1 para 20(1)(b), (d), (e), (4) but with the modifications to the Companies Act 2006 s 1091 specified thereby: see PARA 1857. As to the meaning of 'unregistered company' see PARA 1856.

2 Companies Act 2006 s 1085(1). As to the meaning of the 'register' see PARA 142. As to the categories of material that must not be made available by the registrar of companies for public inspection see PARA 146 et seq.

3 Companies Act 2006 s 1086(1). The fee for any such copy of material derived from a document subject to the Directive disclosure requirements (see s 1078; and PARA 139), whether in hard copy or electronic form, must not exceed the administrative cost of providing it: s 1086(2). As to fees payable to the registrar see PARA 130. As to documents or information sent or supplied in hard copy form see PARA 750; and as to documents or information sent or supplied in electronic form see PARA 751.

4 The period for which such originals are to be kept is limited by the Companies Act 2006 s 1083(1) (see PARA 142): s 1085(2). As to the meaning of 'document' for these purposes see PARA 136 note 2.

5 As to the meaning of 'registrar of companies' see PARA 126 note 2. As to the meaning of 'company' under the Companies Acts see PARA 21; and as to the meaning of the 'Companies Acts' see PARA 13. As to the meaning of references to delivering a document for these purposes see PARA 136 note 2. As to the delivery of documents to the registrar see PARA 136; and as to the requirements for the proper delivery of documents to the registrar see PARA 137.

Any function of the registrar of companies for England and Wales conferred by or under the Companies Act 2006 s 1085 may be exercised by, or by employees of, such person (if any) as may be authorised in that behalf by the registrar of companies for England and Wales, except in so far as it relates to the determination of the means of facilitating the exercise of the right of persons to inspect records kept by the registrar, or the form in which copies of the information contained in those records may be made available: see the Contracting Out (Functions in relation to the Registration of Companies) Order 1995, SI 1995/1013, art 3, Sch 1 para 3(d); the Interpretation Act 1978 s 17(2)(b); and PARA 129. As to the meanings of 'England' and 'Wales' see PARA 1 note 5. As to the contracting out of the registrar of companies' functions generally see PARAS 128–129.

6 Companies Act 2006 s 1085(2).

7 Companies Act 2006 s 1089(1). As from 1 January 2007, applications in respect of documents subject to the Directive disclosure requirements (as to which see PARA 139) may be submitted to the registrar in hard copy or electronic form, as the applicant chooses; this does not affect the registrar's power under s 1089(1) to impose requirements in respect of other matters: s 1089(2).

The provisions of the Companies Act 2006 s 1089 apply to unregistered companies by virtue of the Unregistered Companies Regulations 2009, SI 2009/2436, Sch 1 para 20(1)(d): see PARA 1857. As to the meaning of 'unregistered company' see PARA 1856.

As to fees payable in respect of the performance of the registrar's functions in relation to the inspection of the register and the provision of copies of material on the register see the Registrar of Companies (Fees) (Companies, Overseas Companies and Limited Liability Partnerships) Regulations 2012, SI 2012/1907, reg 4, Sch 2 Pt 2 (paras 7–12) (amended with effect from 30 June 2016 by SI 2016/621). The fees prescribed in relation to Sch 2 paras 7(a), 8(a) and 10(a) are not payable in respect of any month for which the applicant pays a fee to the registrar for subscription to Companies House Direct, Extranet or XML (those terms are defined in the Registrar of Companies (Fees) (Companies, Overseas Companies and Limited Liability Partnerships) Regulations 2012, SI 2012/1907, Sch 2 para 1) under regulations providing for the payment of fees in respect of the functions of the registrar in relation to the inspection, or provision of copies, of documents kept by the registrar relating to European Economic Interest Groupings and limited partnerships: reg 5.

8 Companies Act 2006 s 1090(1). The provisions of the Companies Act 2006 s 1090 apply to unregistered companies by virtue of the Unregistered Companies Regulations 2009, SI 2009/2436, Sch 1 para 20(1)(d): see PARA 1857.

9 Ie as from 1 January 2007: see the Companies Act 2006 s 1090(2).

10 Companies Act 2006 s 1090(2).

11 Ie not obliged by the Companies Act 2006 s 1090(2) (see the text and notes 9–11): see s 1090(3).

12 Companies Act 2006 s 1090(2), (3).

13 Companies Act 2006 s 1090(3)(a).

14 Companies Act 2006 s 1090(3)(b).

15 Ie subject to the Companies Act 2006 s 1090(1)–(3) (see the text and notes 8–14): see s 1090(4).

16 Companies Act 2006 s 1090(4).

17 Companies Act 2006 s 1091(1).

18 Companies Act 2006 s 1091(2). The Secretary of State may make provision by regulations as to the manner in which such a certificate is to be provided in a case where the copy is provided in electronic form: s 1091(4). As to the making of regulations under the Companies Act 2006 generally see ss 1288–1292. As to the Secretary of State see PARA 6. Partly in exercise of the powers conferred by s 1091(4), the Secretary of State has made the Companies (Registrar, Languages and Trading Disclosures) Regulations 2006, SI 2006/3429. Accordingly, where a person requires a copy of material on the register under the Companies Act 2006 s 1086 (see head (2) in the text), and where that person expressly requests that the copy be certified as a true copy, and where the registrar provides the copy in electronic form, then the registrar's certificate that the copy is an accurate record of the contents of the original document must be authenticated by means of an electronic signature that is uniquely linked to the registrar, that indicates that the registrar has caused it to be applied, that is created using means that the registrar can maintain under his sole control, and that is linked both to the certificate and to the copy provided under s 1086, in such a manner that any subsequent change of the data comprised in either is detectable: Companies (Registrar, Languages and Trading Disclosures) Regulations 2006, SI 2006/3429, reg 2(1), (2). For these purposes, an 'electronic signature' means data in electronic form which are attached to or logically associated with other electronic data and which serve as a method of authentication: reg 2(3).

19 Companies Act 2006 s 1091(3).

20 Companies Act 2006 s 1091(3)(a).

21 Companies Act 2006 s 1091(3)(b).

22 As to the Directive disclosure requirements see the Companies Act 2006 s 1078; and PARA 139.

23 Companies Act 2006 s 1091(5). As to the registrar's official seal see PARA 126. A document that is required to be signed by the registrar or authenticated by the registrar's seal must, if sent by electronic means, be authenticated in such manner as may be specified by registrar's rules: see s 1115(2); and PARA 131.

24 Companies Act 2006 s 1092(1).

The provisions of the Companies Act 2006 s 1092 apply to unregistered companies by virtue of the Unregistered Companies Regulations 2009, SI 2009/2436, Sch 1 para 17(1), (2)(d): see PARA 1857. As to the meaning of 'unregistered company' see PARA 1856.

25 Companies Act 2006 s 1092(2).

146. Material not to be made available by the registrar for public inspection. The following material must not be made available by the registrar of companies[1] for public inspection[2]:

(1) the contents of any document[3] sent to the registrar[4] containing views expressed[5] by a specified government department or other body in relation to company names that either suggest some connection with a government or public authority or contain other sensitive words or expressions[6];

(2) protected information within the provision[7] regarding directors' residential addresses or any corresponding provision of the regulations[8] that govern overseas companies[9];

(3) representations received by the registrar in response to a notice under the relevant statutory provision[10] of a proposal to put a director's usual residential address on the public record[11] or under any corresponding provision of the regulations[12] that govern overseas companies[13];

(4) as from 6 April 2016[14], information[15] regarding residential addresses of people with significant control over the company or such information under any corresponding provision of the regulations[16] that govern overseas companies[17];

(5) also as from that date[18], information that, by virtue of regulations[19] the registrar must omit from the material on the register that is available for inspection[20];

(6) any application to the registrar[21] for administrative restoration to the register that has not yet been determined or was not successful[22];

(7) any document received by the registrar in connection with the giving or withdrawal of consent by a company[23] with regard to the registrar's power to make informal corrections to documents received[24];

(8) as from 6 April 2016[25], certain information[26] about a person's date of birth[27];

(9) any application or other document delivered to the registrar[28] under the provisions that allow addresses to be made unavailable for public inspection, and any address in respect of which such an application is successful[29];

(10) any application or other document delivered to the registrar[30] in relation to any rectification of the register[31];

(11) any court order[32] made in relation to any rectification of the register that the court has directed[33] is not to be made available for public inspection[34];

(12) any application or other document delivered to the registrar regarding rectification of the register relating to a company registered office[35] other than an order or direction of the court[36];

(13) any email address, identification code or password deriving from a document delivered for the purpose of authorising or facilitating electronic filing procedures or providing information by telephone[37];

(14) the contents of any documents held by the registrar pending a decision of the Regulator of Community Interest Companies[38] on a company's eligibility for registration as, conversion to, or conversion from, a community interest company[39], and that the registrar is not later required to record[40];

(15) any other material excluded from public inspection by or under any other enactment[41].

A restriction applying by reference to material deriving from a particular description of document does not affect the availability for public inspection of the same information contained in material derived from another description of document in relation to which no such restriction applies[42].

Any such material that is not to be made available by the registrar of companies for public inspection[43] need not be retained by the registrar for longer than appears to him reasonably necessary for the purposes for which the material was delivered to him[44].

1 As to the meaning of 'registrar of companies' see PARA 126 note 2. As to the meaning of 'company' under the Companies Acts see PARA 21; and as to the meaning of the 'Companies Acts' see PARA 13. As to the application of the Companies Act 2006 Pt 35 (ss 1059A–1119) (see also PARAS 126, 130 et seq, 147 et seq) see PARA 126 note 1.

2 Companies Act 2006 s 1087(1). As to the inspection and copying of records kept by the registrar generally see PARA 145.

The provisions of the Companies Act 2006 s 1087 apply to unregistered companies by virtue of the Unregistered Companies Regulations 2009, SI 2009/2436, reg 3, Sch 1 para 20(1)(c), (2) (amended by SI 2015/1689; and by virtue of SI 2016/599) but with the modifications as specified thereby: see PARA 1857. As to the meaning of 'unregistered company' see PARA 1856.

3 As to the meaning of 'document' for these purposes see PARA 136 note 2.

4 As to the delivery of documents to the registrar see PARA 136; and as to the requirements generally for the proper delivery of documents to the registrar see PARA 137. As to the meaning of references to delivering a document for these purposes see PARA 136 note 2.

5 Ie pursuant to the Companies Act 2006 s 56 (see PARA 195): see s 1087(1)(a).

6 Companies Act 2006 s 1087(1)(a).

7 Ie within the Companies Act 2006 s 242(1) (see PARA 538): see s 1087(1)(b).

8 Ie made under the Companies Act 2006 s 1046 (see PARA 2015). See further the Overseas Companies Regulations 2009, SI 2009/1801, Pt 4 (regs 18–29, Schs 1–3); and PARA 2015.

9 Companies Act 2006 s 1087(1)(b). As to the meaning of 'overseas company' see PARA 2013. The Secretary of State may make provision by regulations requiring the registrar, on application, to make any other address on the register unavailable for public inspection: see PARA 150. As to the Secretary of State see PARA 6.

10 Ie under the Companies Act 2006 s 245(2)(a) (see PARA 549): see s 1087(1)(ba)(i) (s 1087(1)(ba) added by SI 2009/1802).

11 Companies Act 2006 s 1087(1)(ba)(i) (as added: see note 10).

12 See note 8.

13 Companies Act 2006 s 1087(1)(ba)(ii) (as added: see note 10).

14 See the Small Business, Enterprise and Employment Act 2015 (Commencement No 3) Regulations 2015, SI 2015/2029, reg 4.

15 Ie information to which the Companies Act 2006 ss 240–244 (see PARAS 537–539, 548) are applied by s 790ZF(1) (see PARA 491): see s 1087(1)(bb) (s 1087(1)(bb), (bc) added by the Small Business, Enterprise and Employment Act 2015 Sch 3 Pt 2 paras 3, 8).

16 See note 8.

17 Companies Act 2006 s 1087(1)(bb) (as added: see note 15).

18 See note 14.

19 Ie regulations under the Companies Act 2006 s 790ZG (see PARA 492) or any corresponding provision of regulations under s 1046 (see PARA 2015): s 1087(1)(bc) (as added: see note 15).

20 Companies Act 2006 s 1087(1)(bc) (as added: see note 15).

21 Ie under the Companies Act 2006 s 1024 (see PARA 1714): see s 1087(1)(c).

22 Companies Act 2006 s 1087(1)(c).

23 Ie under the Companies Act 2006 s 1075 (see PARA 138): see s 1087(1)(d).

24 Companies Act 2006 s 1087(1)(d).

25 See note 14.
26 Ie information falling within the Companies Act 2006 s 1087A(1) (see PARA 147): s 1087(1)(da) (added by the Small Business, Enterprise and Employment Act 2015 s 96(1), (2)).
27 Companies Act 2006 s 1087(1)(da) (as added: see note 26).
28 Ie under the Companies Act 2006 s 1088 (see PARA 150): see s 1087(1)(e).
29 Companies Act 2006 s 1087(1)(e).
30 Ie under the Companies Act 2006 s 1095 (see PARA 158): see s 1087(1)(f).
31 Companies Act 2006 s 1087(1)(f).
32 Ie under the Companies Act 2006 s 1096 (see PARA 161): see s 1087(1)(g).
33 Ie under the Companies Act 2006 s 1097 (powers of court on ordering the removal of material from the register) (see PARA 161): see s 1087(1)(g).
34 Companies Act 2006 s 1087(1)(g).
35 Ie under the Companies Act 2006 s 1097A (see PARA 160): see s 1087(1)(ga) (added by the Small Business, Enterprise and Employment Act 2015 s 99(2)).
36 Companies Act 2006 s 1087(1)(ga) (as added: see note 35).
37 Companies Act 2006 s 1087(1)(i).
38 As to the Regulator of Community Interest Companies see PARA 76.
39 Ie under the Companies (Audit, Investigations and Community Enterprise) Act 2004 s 36A (eligibility for registration as community interest company) (see PARA 112) or under s 38 (eligibility for conversion to community interest company) (see PARA 190) or under s 55 (eligibility for conversion from community interest company to charity) (see PARA 193): see the Companies Act 2006 s 1087(1)(j) (as substituted: see note 40).
40 Companies Act 2006 s 1087(1)(j) (substituted by SI 2009/1941).
41 Companies Act 2006 s 1087(1)(k). As to the meaning of 'enactment' see PARA 13 note 16.
42 Companies Act 2006 s 1087(2).
43 Ie any material to which the Companies Act 2006 s 1087 applies (see the text and notes 1–42): see s 1087(3).
44 Companies Act 2006 s 1087(3). The provisions which govern the retention of original documents by the registrar generally (ie s 1083) are made subject to s 1087(3): see PARA 142.

147. Restrictions on disclosure of date of birth information by the registrar. Partly as from 10 October 2015 and partly as from 30 June 2016[1], the following provisions have effect.

Information is restricted date of birth information ('restricted DOB information')[2] at any time ('the relevant time') if:

(1) it is DOB information[3];
(2) it is contained in a document[4] delivered to the registrar of companies[5] that is protected[6] at the relevant time as regards that information;
(3) the document is one in which such information is required to be stated; and
(4) if the document has more than one part, the part in which the information is contained is a part in which such information is required to be stated[7].

Nothing in heads (1) to (4) above obliges the registrar to check other documents or, as the case may be, other parts of the document to ensure the absence of DOB information[8].

The registrar must not disclose restricted DOB information unless:

(a) the same information about the relevant person, whether in the same or a different capacity, is made available by the registrar for public inspection as a result of being contained in another description of document in relation to which no statutory restriction on disclosure[9] applies[10]; or
(b) disclosure of the information by the registrar is permitted by head (i) or head (ii) below or by another provision of the Companies Act 2006[11].

The registrar may disclose restricted DOB information:

(i) to a public authority specified for these purposes by regulations made by the Secretary of State[12]; or

(ii) to a credit reference agency[13].

The above provisions[14] do not apply to restricted DOB information about a relevant person in his or her capacity as someone whose particulars are stated in the company's register of persons with significant control ('PSC register')[15] if an application under regulations for protecting PSC particulars[16] has been granted with respect to that information and not been revoked[17].

1 The Small Business, Enterprise and Employment Act 2015 s 96(1), (3), which adds the Companies Act 2006 ss 1087A, 1087B (see the text and notes 2–17), came into force on 10 October 2015, with the exception of the addition of ss 1087A(3)(b), 1087A(4)(a), (b), 1087A(5), 1087A(6), 1087A(7) and 1087B(4): see the Small Business, Enterprise and Employment Act 2015 (Commencement No 2 and Transitional Provisions) Regulations 2015, SI 2015/1689, reg 4(a). The remainder of the Small Business, Enterprise and Employment Act 2015 s 96 came into force on 30 June 2016: see the Small Business, Enterprise and Employment Act 2015 (Commencement No 4, Transitional and Savings Provisions) Regulations 2016, SI 2016/321, reg 6(d).

The provisions of the Companies Act 2006 ss 1087A, 1087B apply to unregistered companies by virtue of the Unregistered Companies Regulations 2009, SI 2009/2436, Sch 1 para 20(1)(ca) (added by SI 2015/1695): see PARA 1857. As to the meaning of 'unregistered company' see PARA 1856.

2 'Restricted DOB information' means information falling within the Companies Act 2006 s 1087A(1): s 1087B(5) (ss 1087A, 1087B added by the Small Business, Enterprise and Employment Act 2015 s 96(1), (3)).

3 'DOB information' is information as to the day of the month (but not the month or year) on which a relevant person was born: Companies Act 2006 s 1087A(2) (as added: see note 2). A 'relevant person' is an individual who is a director of a company (s 1087A(3)(a) (as so added)), or an individual whose particulars are stated in a company's PSC register as a registrable person in relation to that company (see Pt 21A (ss 790A–790ZG)); and PARA 466 et seq) (s 1087A(3)(b) (as added: see note 2).

4 As to the meaning of 'document' for these purposes see PARA 136 note 2.

5 As to the delivery of documents to the registrar see PARA 136; and as to the requirements generally for the proper delivery of documents to the registrar see PARA 137. As to the meaning of references to delivering a document for these purposes see PARA 136 note 2. As to the meaning of 'registrar of companies' see PARA 126 note 2. As to the meaning of 'company' under the Companies Acts see PARA 21; and as to the meaning of the 'Companies Acts' see PARA 13. As to the application of the Companies Act 2006 Pt 35 (ss 1059A–1119) (see also PARAS 126, 130 et seq, 150 et seq) see PARA 126 note 1.

6 A document delivered to the registrar is 'protected' at any time unless:

(1) it is an election period document (Companies Act 2006 s 1087A(4)(a) (as added: see note 2));

(2) s 1087A(7) applies to it at the time (s 1087A(4)(b) (as so added);

(3) it was registered before s 1087A comes into force (s 1087A(4)(c) (as so added)).

As regards DOB information about a relevant person in his or her capacity as a director of the company, each of the following is an 'election period document' (s 1087A(5) (as so added), ie:

(a) a statement of the company's proposed officers delivered under s 9 (see PARA 104) in circumstances where the subscribers gave notice of election under s 167A (election to keep information on central register: see PARA 551) in respect of the company's register of directors when the statement was delivered;

(b) a document delivered by the company under s 167D (duty to notify registrar of changes while election in force: see PARA 553).

As regards DOB information about a relevant person in his or her capacity as someone whose particulars are stated in the company's PSC register, each of the following is an 'election period document' (s 1087A(6) (as so added)), ie:

(i) a statement of initial significant control delivered under s 9 in circumstances where the subscribers gave notice of election under s 790X (see PARA 485) in respect of the company when the statement was delivered;

(ii) a document containing a statement or updated statement delivered by the company under s 790X(6)(b) or (7) (statement accompanying notice of election made after incorporation);

(iii) a document delivered by the company under s 790ZA (duty to notify registrar of changes while election in force) (see PARA 487).

Section 1087A(7) applies to a document in the following circumstances (see s 1087A(7) (as so added)), ie if:

(A) the DOB information relates to the relevant person in his or her capacity as a director of the company;
(B) an election under s 167A is or has previously been in force in respect of the company's register of directors;
(C) the document was delivered to the registrar at some point before that election took effect;
(D) the relevant person was a director of the company when that election took effect; and
(E) the document was either a statement of proposed officers delivered under s 9 naming the relevant person as someone who was to be a director of the company, or notice given under s 167 (see PARA 550) of the relevant person having become a director of the company.

7 Companies Act 2006 s 1087A(1) (as added: see note 2). Information about a person does not cease to fall within s 1087A(1) when he or she ceases to be a relevant person and, to that extent, references in s 1087A to a relevant person include someone who used to be a relevant person: s 1087A(8) (as so added).

The provisions of the Companies Act 2006 ss 1087A, 1087B apply to unregistered companies by virtue of the Unregistered Companies Regulations 2009, SI 2009/2436, Sch 1 para 20(1)(ca) (added by SI 2015/1695): see PARA 1857. As to the meaning of 'unregistered company' see PARA 1856.

8 Companies Act 2006 s 1087A(9) (as added: see note 2).
9 Ie no restriction under the Companies Act 2006 s 1087 (see s 1087(2); and PARA 146.
10 Companies Act 2006 s 1087B(1)(a) (as added: see note 2).
11 Companies Act 2006 s 1087B(1)(b) (as added: see note 2).
12 Companies Act 2006 s 1087B(2)(a) (as added: see note 2). See PARA 148. As to the making of orders and regulations under the Companies Act 2006 generally see ss 1288–1292. As to the Secretary of State see PARA 6.

Section 243(3)–(8) (permitted use or disclosure of directors' residential addresses etc by the registrar: see PARA 539) applies for the purposes of s 1087B(2) as for the purposes of s 243 (reading references there to protected information as references to restricted DOB information): s 1087B(3) (as so added). As to the meaning of 'public authority' see PARA 539 note 5 (definition in s 243(7) as so applied).

13 Companies Act 2006 s 1087B(2)(b) (as added: see note 2). See PARA 149. See also note 12. As to the meaning of 'credit reference agency' see PARA 539 note 8 (definition in s 243(7) as applied: see note 12).
14 Ie the Companies Act 2006 s 1087B: see the text and notes 9–13.
15 As to the PSC register see PARA 480.
16 Ie an application under regulations made under the Companies Act 2006 s 790ZG (see PARAS 469, 492).
17 Companies Act 2006 s 1087B(4) (as added: see note 2).

148. Permitted disclosure by registrar to specified public authorities of restricted date of birth information. The registrar of companies[1] may disclose restricted DOB information[2] to a specified public authority[3] where the following conditions[4] are satisfied[5]:

(1) the specified public authority has delivered to the registrar a statement that it intends to use the restricted DOB information only for the purpose of facilitating the carrying out by that specified public authority of a public function[6];
(2) the specified public authority ('the authority') has delivered to the registrar a statement that it will, where it supplies a copy of the restricted DOB information to a processor[7] for the purpose of processing the information for use in respect of facilitating the carrying out of a public function by that authority[8]:
    (a) ensure that the processor is one who carries on business in the European Economic Area[9];
    (b) require that the information is not transmitted outside the European Economic Area by the processor[10]; and
    (c) require that the processor does not disclose the information except to the authority or an employee of the authority[11].

A specified public authority must deliver to the registrar such information or evidence as he may direct for the purpose of enabling him to determine[12] whether to disclose restricted DOB information to a specified public authority[13]; and the registrar may require such information or evidence to be verified in such manner as he may direct[14].

The specified public authority must inform the registrar immediately of any change in respect of any statement so delivered to the registrar[15] or information or evidence provided for the purpose of enabling him to determine whether to disclose restricted DOB information[16].

1 As to the registrar of companies see PARA 126 et seq.
2 As to the meaning of 'restricted DOB information' for the purposes of the Companies Act 2006 s 1087B, under which the Companies (Disclosure of Date of Birth Information) Regulations 2015, SI 2015/1694, have partly been made, see PARA 147.
3 For these purposes, 'specified public authority' means any public authority specified in the Companies (Disclosure of Date of Birth Information) Regulations 2015, SI 2015/1694, Sch 1 (amended by SI 2016/599) which sets out the public authorities that are specified for the purposes of the Companies Act 2006 s 1087B (see PARA 146): Companies (Disclosure of Date of Birth Information) Regulations 2015, SI 2015/1694, regs 1(2), 2(5).
4 Ie the conditions specified in the Companies (Disclosure of Date of Birth Information) Regulations 2015, SI 2015/1694, Sch 2 paras 2, 3 (see heads (1)–(2) in the text): see reg 2(1). Schedule 2 paras 2, 3 set out the conditions specified for the disclosure of restricted DOB information by the registrar to a specified public authority: Sch 2 para 1.
5 Companies (Disclosure of Date of Birth Information) Regulations 2015, SI 2015/1694, reg 2(1). As to the fee payable for an application by a specified public authority under reg 2 see the Registrar of Companies (Fees) (Companies, Overseas Companies and Limited Liability Partnerships) Regulations 2012, SI 2012/1907, Sch 3 (substituted with effect from 30 June 2016 by SI 2016/621).
6 Companies (Disclosure of Date of Birth Information) Regulations 2015, SI 2015/1694, Sch 2 para 2. For these purposes:
   (1) 'public function' includes any function conferred by or in accordance with any provision contained in any enactment, any function conferred by or in accordance with any provision contained in the EU Treaties or any EU instrument, any similar function conferred on persons by or under provisions having effect as part of the law of a country or territory outside the United Kingdom and any function exercisable in relation to the investigation of any criminal offence or for the purpose of any criminal proceedings (see Sch 2 para 11(1));
   (2) any reference to the disclosure for the purpose of facilitating the carrying out of a public function includes disclosure in relation to, and for the purpose of, any proceedings whether civil, criminal or disciplinary in which the specified public authority engages while carrying out its public functions (Sch 2 para 11(2)(b)).
7 For these purposes, 'processor' means any person who provides a service which consists of putting information into data form or processing information in data form and any reference to a processor includes a reference to its employees: Companies (Disclosure of Date of Birth Information) Regulations 2015, SI 2015/1694, Sch 2 para 11(1). In Sch 2, any reference to an employee of any person who has access to restricted DOB information is deemed to include any person working or providing services for the purposes of that person or employed by or on behalf of, or working for, any person who is so working or who is supplying such a service: Sch 2 para 11(2)(a).
8 Companies (Disclosure of Date of Birth Information) Regulations 2015, SI 2015/1694, Sch 2 para 3. The provisions of Sch 2 para 3 are subject to Sch 2 para 4: see Sch 2 para 3. Accordingly, Sch 2 para 3 does not apply where the specified public authority is the National Crime Agency, Secret Intelligence Service, Security Service or Government Communications Headquarters: Sch 2 para 4 (amended by SI 2016/599). As to the Government Communications Headquarters see CONSTITUTIONAL AND ADMINISTRATIVE LAW vol 20 (2014) PARA 245; as to the Secret Intelligence Service see CONSTITUTIONAL AND ADMINISTRATIVE LAW vol 20 (2014) PARA 244; and as to the Security Service see CONSTITUTIONAL AND ADMINISTRATIVE LAW vol 20 (2014) PARA 243.
9 Companies (Disclosure of Date of Birth Information) Regulations 2015, SI 2015/1694, Sch 2 para 3(a). See also note 8.

10 Companies (Disclosure of Date of Birth Information) Regulations 2015, SI 2015/1694, Sch 2 para 3(b). See also note 8.
11 Companies (Disclosure of Date of Birth Information) Regulations 2015, SI 2015/1694, Sch 2 para 3(c). See also note 8.
12 Ie in accordance with the Companies (Disclosure of Date of Birth Information) Regulations 2015, SI 2015/1694: see reg 2(2).
13 Companies (Disclosure of Date of Birth Information) Regulations 2015, SI 2015/1694, reg 2(2).
14 Companies (Disclosure of Date of Birth Information) Regulations 2015, SI 2015/1694, reg 2(3).
15 Ie delivered pursuant to the Companies (Disclosure of Date of Birth Information) Regulations 2015, SI 2015/1694, Sch 2: see the text and notes 4–11.
16 Companies (Disclosure of Date of Birth Information) Regulations 2015, SI 2015/1694, reg 2(4).

149. Permitted disclosure by registrar to credit reference agencies of restricted date of birth information. The registrar of companies[1] may disclose restricted DOB information[2] to a credit reference agency[3] where the following conditions[4] are satisfied[5]:

(1) the credit reference agency:
   (a) is carrying on in the United Kingdom[6] or in another EEA State a business comprising the furnishing of information relevant to the financial standing of individuals, being information collected by the agency for that purpose[7];
   (b) maintains appropriate procedures to ensure that an independent person can investigate and audit the measures maintained by the agency for the purposes of ensuring the security of any restricted DOB information disclosed to that agency[8], and for the purposes of ensuring that it complies with its obligations under the Data Protection Act 1998[9], or, where the agency carries on business in a EEA state other than the United Kingdom, with its obligations under legislation implementing[10] the Data Protection Directive[11];
   (c) has not been found guilty of an offence under the Companies Act 2006 provisions which prohibit the making of false statements to the registrar[12] or under the false representation provisions of the Fraud Act 2006[13] or under the provisions of the Data Protection Act 1998 which govern a failure to comply with an enforcement notice, an information notice or a special information notice[14] in circumstances where it has used the protected information for purposes other than those described in heads (2)(a) to (2)(e) below[15];

(2) the credit reference agency has delivered to the registrar a statement that it intends to use the restricted DOB information only for the purposes of[16];
   (a) providing an assessment of the financial standing of a person[17];
   (b) meeting any obligations contained in money laundering rules[18] or in any legislation of another EEA state implementing[19] the Directive concerning money laundering and terrorist financing[20];
   (c) conducting conflict of interest checks required or made necessary by any enactment[21];
   (d) the provision of restricted DOB information to either a specified public authority[22] or a credit reference agency[23] which has satisfied the relevant requirements[24] necessary before the registrar can disclose restricted DOB information to it[25]; or
   (e) conducting checks for the prevention and detection of crime and fraud[26];

(3) the credit reference agency has delivered to the registrar a statement that it intends to take delivery of and to use the restricted DOB information only in the United Kingdom or in another EEA state[27];

(4) the credit reference agency has delivered to the registrar a statement that it will, where it supplies a copy of the restricted DOB information to a processor[28] for the purpose of processing the information for use in respect of the purposes referred to in head (2) above[29]:

(a) ensure that the processor is one who carries on business in the European Economic Area[30];

(b) require that the information is not transmitted outside the European Economic Area by the processor[31]; and

(c) require that the processor does not disclose the information except to the credit reference agency or an employee of the credit reference agency[32];

(5) the credit reference agency has delivered to the registrar a statement that it meets the conditions in head (1) above[33].

A credit reference agency must[34] deliver to the registrar such information or evidence in addition to the statement required by head (5) above as the registrar may direct for the purpose of enabling him to determine[35] whether to disclose restricted DOB information to a credit reference agency[36]; and the registrar may require such information or evidence to be verified in such manner as he may direct[37].

The credit reference agency must inform the registrar immediately of any change in respect of any statement so delivered to the registrar[38] or information or evidence provided for the purpose of enabling the registrar to determine whether to disclose restricted DOB information[39].

1 As to the registrar of companies see PARA 126 et seq.

2 As to the meaning of 'restricted DOB information' for the purposes of the Companies Act 2006 s 1087B, under which the Companies (Disclosure of Date of Birth Information) Regulations 2015, SI 2015/1694, have partly been made, see PARA 147.

3 As to the meaning of 'credit reference agency see PARA 539 note 8 (definition in the Companies Act 2006 s 243(7) applied for the purposes of s 1087B: see PARA 147 notes 12–13).

4 Ie the conditions specified in the Companies (Disclosure of Date of Birth Information) Regulations 2015, SI 2015/1694, Sch 2 paras 6–10 (see heads (1)–(5) in the text): see reg 3(1). Schedule 2 paras 6–10 set out the conditions specified for the disclosure of restricted DOB information by the registrar to a specified public authority: Sch 2 para 5.

5 Companies (Disclosure of Date of Birth Information) Regulations 2015, SI 2015/1694, reg 3(1). As to the fee payable for an application by a credit reference agency under reg 3 see the Registrar of Companies (Fees) (Companies, Overseas Companies and Limited Liability Partnerships) Regulations 2012, SI 2012/1907, Sch 3 (substituted with effect from 30 June 2016 by SI 2016/621).

6 As to the meaning of 'United Kingdom' see PARA 1 note 5.

7 Companies (Disclosure of Date of Birth Information) Regulations 2015, SI 2015/1694, Sch 2 para 6(a).

8 Companies (Disclosure of Date of Birth Information) Regulations 2015, SI 2015/1694, Sch 2 para 6(b)(i).

9 As to a person's obligations under the Data Protection Act 1998 generally see CONFIDENCE AND INFORMATIONAL PRIVACY vol 19 (2011) PARA 95 et seq.

10 Ie legislation implementing Council Directive (EC) 95/46 (OJ L281, 23.11.95, p 31) on the protection of individuals with regard to the processing of personal data and on the free movement of such data (as to which see CONFIDENCE AND INFORMATIONAL PRIVACY vol 19 (2011) PARA 95 et seq): see the Companies (Disclosure of Date of Birth Information) Regulations 2015, SI 2015/1694, Sch 2 para 6(b)(ii).

11 Companies (Disclosure of Date of Birth Information) Regulations 2015, SI 2015/1694, Sch 2 para 6(b)(ii).

12 Ie the Companies Act 2006 s 1112 (general offence of making false statements to registrar) (see PARA 132): see the Companies (Disclosure of Date of Birth Information) Regulations 2015, SI 2015/1694, Sch 2 para 6(c)(i).
13 Companies (Disclosure of Date of Birth Information) Regulations 2015, SI 2015/1694, Sch 2 para 6(c)(i). The text refers to an offence under the Fraud Act 2006 s 2 (fraud by false representation) (see CRIMINAL LAW vol 25 (2016) PARA 346): see the Companies (Disclosure of Date of Birth Information) Regulations 2015, SI 2015/1694, Sch 2 para 6(c)(i).
14 Ie under the Data Protection Act 1998 s 47 (see CONFIDENCE AND INFORMATIONAL PRIVACY vol 19 (2011) PARA 166): see the Companies (Disclosure of Date of Birth Information) Regulations 2015, SI 2015/1694, Sch 2 para 6(c)(ii). As to enforcement notices see CONFIDENCE AND INFORMATIONAL PRIVACY vol 19 (2011) PARA 152; as to information notices see CONFIDENCE AND INFORMATIONAL PRIVACY vol 19 (2011) PARA 158; and as to special information notices see CONFIDENCE AND INFORMATIONAL PRIVACY vol 19 (2011) PARA 159.
15 Companies (Disclosure of Date of Birth Information) Regulations 2015, SI 2015/1694, Sch 2 para 6(c)(ii).
16 Companies (Disclosure of Date of Birth Information) Regulations 2015, SI 2015/1694, Sch 2 para 7. As to the delivery of documents to the registrar see PARA 136; and as to the requirements generally for the proper delivery of documents to the registrar see PARA 137.
17 Companies (Disclosure of Date of Birth Information) Regulations 2015, SI 2015/1694, Sch 2 para 7(a).
18 Ie obligations contained in the Money Laundering Regulations 2007, SI 2007/2157 (see FINANCIAL SERVICES REGULATION vol 50A (2016) PARA 759 et seq), or any rules made pursuant to the Financial Services and Markets Act 2000 s 137A which relate to the prevention and detection of money laundering in connection with the carrying on of regulated activities by authorised persons (see FINANCIAL SERVICES REGULATION vol 50 (2016) PARA 59): see the Companies (Disclosure of Date of Birth Information) Regulations 2015, SI 2015/1694, Sch 2 para 7(b).
19 Ie legislation implementing European Parliament and Council Directive (EC) 2005/60 (OJ L309, 25.11.2005, p 15) on the prevention of the use of the financial system for the purpose of money laundering and terrorist financing (see FINANCIAL SERVICES REGULATION vol 50A (2016) PARA 759 et seq): see the Companies (Disclosure of Date of Birth Information) Regulations 2015, SI 2015/1694, Sch 2 para 7(b). Note that (European Parliament and Council Directive (EC) 2005/60 (OJ L309, 25.11.2005, p 15) is repealed and replaced by European Parliament and Council Directive (EU) 2015/849 (OJ L141, 5.6.2015, p 73), with effect from 26 June 2017: art 66. As from that date, references to the 2005 Directive are to be construed as references to European Parliament and Council Directive (EU) 2015/849 (OJ L141, 5.6.2015, p 73) Directive and are to be read in accordance with the correlation table set out in Annex IV thereto: art 66. Member states must bring into force the laws, regulations and administrative provisions necessary to comply with European Parliament and Council Directive (EU) 2015/849 (OJ L141, 5.6.2015, p 73) by 26 June 2017: art 67(1).
20 Companies (Disclosure of Date of Birth Information) Regulations 2015, SI 2015/1694, Sch 2 para 7(b).
21 Companies (Disclosure of Date of Birth Information) Regulations 2015, SI 2015/1694, Sch 2 para 7(c).
22 Ie a public authority specified in the Companies (Disclosure of Date of Birth Information) Regulations 2015, SI 2015/1694, Sch 1 (see PARA 148): see the Companies (Disclosure of Date of Birth Information) Regulations 2015, SI 2015/1694, Sch 2 para 7(d)(i).
23 See the Companies (Disclosure of Date of Birth Information) Regulations 2015, SI 2015/1694, Sch 2 para 7(d)(ii).
24 Ie, in relation to a specified public authority, satisfied the requirements of the Companies (Disclosure of Date of Birth Information) Regulations 2015, SI 2015/1694, Sch 2 paras 2, 3 (see PARA 148) and, in relation to a credit reference agency, satisfied the requirements of Sch 2 Pt 2 (paras 5–10) (see the text and notes 4–33): see Sch 2 para 7(d)(i), (ii).
25 Companies (Disclosure of Date of Birth Information) Regulations 2015, SI 2015/1694, Sch 2 para 7(d)(i), (ii).
26 Companies (Disclosure of Date of Birth Information) Regulations 2015, SI 2015/1694, Sch 2 para 7(e).
27 Companies (Disclosure of Date of Birth Information) Regulations 2015, SI 2015/1694, Sch 2 para 8.
28 As to the meaning of 'processor for these purposes see PARA 148 note 7.
29 Companies (Disclosure of Date of Birth Information) Regulations 2015, SI 2015/1694, Sch 2 para 9.

30 Companies (Disclosure of Date of Birth Information) Regulations 2015, SI 2015/1694, Sch 2 para 9(a).
31 Companies (Disclosure of Date of Birth Information) Regulations 2015, SI 2015/1694, Sch 2 para 9(b).
32 Companies (Disclosure of Date of Birth Information) Regulations 2015, SI 2015/1694, Sch 2 para 9(c). As to the meaning of references to 'employee' for these purposes see PARA 148 note 7.
33 Companies (Disclosure of Date of Birth Information) Regulations 2015, SI 2015/1694, Sch 2 para 10. The registrar may rely on a statement so delivered him by a credit reference agency as sufficient evidence of the matters stated in it: reg 3(2).
34 Ie notwithstanding the Companies (Disclosure of Date of Birth Information) Regulations 2015, SI 2015/1694, reg 3(2) (see note 33): see reg 3(3).
35 Ie in accordance with the Companies (Disclosure of Date of Birth Information) Regulations 2015, SI 2015/1694: see reg 3(3).
36 Companies (Disclosure of Date of Birth Information) Regulations 2015, SI 2015/1694, reg 3(3).
37 Companies (Disclosure of Date of Birth Information) Regulations 2015, SI 2015/1694, reg 3(4).
38 Ie delivered pursuant to the Companies (Disclosure of Date of Birth Information) Regulations 2015, SI 2015/1694, Sch 2 (see the text and notes 4–33): see reg 3(5).
39 Companies (Disclosure of Date of Birth Information) Regulations 2015, SI 2015/1694, reg 3(4).

150. Addresses on the register not to be made available by the registrar of companies for public inspection. The Secretary of State[1] may make provision by regulations[2] requiring the registrar of companies[3], on application, to make an address on the register[4] unavailable for public inspection[5]. The regulations may make provision as to:

(1) who may make an application[6];
(2) the grounds on which an application may be made[7];
(3) the information to be included in and documents to accompany an application[8];
(4) the notice to be given of an application and of its outcome[9]; and
(5) how an application is to be determined[10].

An application must specify the address to be removed from the register and indicate where on the register it is[11]. The regulations may provide:

(a) that an address is not to be made unavailable for public inspection in this way[12] unless replaced by a service address[13]; and
(b) that, in such a case, the application must specify a service address[14].

1 As to the Secretary of State see PARA 6.
2 Regulations made under the Companies Act 2006 s 1088 are subject to affirmative resolution procedure (ie the regulations must not be made unless a draft of the statutory instrument containing them has been laid before Parliament and approved by a resolution of each House of Parliament): see ss 1088(6), 1290. As to the making of regulations under the Companies Act 2006 generally see ss 1288–1292. Partly in exercise of the power conferred by s 1088(1), (2), (3) and (5), the Secretary of State has made the Companies (Disclosure of Address) Regulations 2009, SI 2009/214 (as to which see PARA 151 et seq). As to the application of the Companies Act 2006 Pt 35 (ss 1059A–1119) (see also PARAS 126, 130 et seq, 157 et seq) see PARA 126 note 1.
The provisions of the Companies Act 2006 s 1088 apply to unregistered companies by virtue of the Unregistered Companies Regulations 2009, SI 2009/2436, Sch 1 para 20(1)(c), (3), but substituted as specified thereby: see PARA 1857. As to the meaning of 'unregistered company' see PARA 1856.
3 As to the meaning of 'registrar of companies' see PARA 126 note 2. As to the meaning of 'company' under the Companies Acts see PARA 21; and as to the meaning of the 'Companies Acts' see PARA 13.
4 As to the meaning of the 'register' see PARA 142.
5 Companies Act 2006 s 1088(1). See also note 2. As to the inspection and copying of records kept by the registrar generally see PARA 145; and as to the general categories of material that must not be made available by the registrar of companies for public inspection see PARA 146.
6 Companies Act 2006 s 1088(2)(a).
7 Companies Act 2006 s 1088(2)(b).
8 Companies Act 2006 s 1088(2)(c).
9 Companies Act 2006 s 1088(2)(d).

10 Companies Act 2006 s 1088(2)(e). Provision under s 1088(2)(e) may in particular:
(1) confer a discretion on the registrar (s 1088(3)(a)); and
(2) provide for a question to be referred to a person other than the registrar for the purposes of determining the application (s 1088(3)(b)).

11 Companies Act 2006 s 1088(4). Any application or other document delivered to the registrar under s 1088, and any address in respect of which such an application is successful, is not to be made available by the registrar of companies for public inspection: see s 1087(1)(e); and PARA 146.

12 Ie under the Companies Act 2006 s 1088: see s 1088(5)(a).

13 Companies Act 2006 s 1088(5)(a). As to the meaning of 'service address' see PARA 745.

14 Companies Act 2006 s 1088(5)(b).

151. Application by individual to withhold address placed on the register. An application[1] for the purpose of requiring the registrar of companies[2] to make an address on the register[3] unavailable for public inspection (a 'section 1088 application')[4] may be made to the registrar by an individual whose usual residential address was placed on the register[5], in respect of that usual residential address where it was placed on the register on or after 1 January 2003[6]. The grounds on which such an application may be made are that the individual making the application[7]:

(1) considers that there is a serious risk that he, or a person who lives with him, will be subjected to violence or intimidation as a result of the activities of at least one of the companies of which[8]:
  (a) he is, or proposes to become, a director[9];
  (b) he is not a director but of which he has been at any time a director, secretary[10] or permanent representative[11];
  (c) that individual is, or proposes to become, a registrable person[12]; or
  (d) that individual used to be a registrable person[13];
(2) is or has been employed by a relevant organisation[14];
(3) is a 'section 243 beneficiary'[15], being an individual:
  (a) who has made an application[16] for the purpose of requiring the registrar to refrain from disclosing protected information relating to a director to a credit reference agency (a 'section 243 application') in respect of which a determination by the registrar on such an application in favour of the applicant (a 'section 243 decision') has been made[17]; or
  (b) on whose behalf a company or a subscriber to a memorandum of association[18] has made a section 243 application in respect of which a section 243 decision has been made[19]; or
  (c) in relation to whom a confidentiality order[20] was in force immediately before 1 October 2009 and who is treated[21] as having made a section 243 application in respect of which a section 243 decision has been made[22]; or
(4) is the subject of an application to protect usual residential address information[23] which has been determined by the registrar in favour of the applicant and that determination has not ceased[24] to have effect[25].

The application must contain:

(i) a statement of the grounds on which the application is made[26];
(ii) the name and any former name of the applicant[27];
(iii) the usual residential address of the applicant that is to be made unavailable for public inspection[28];
(iv) an address for correspondence in respect of the application[29];

(v) the name and registered number of each company of which the applicant is or has been at any time since 1 January 2003 a director, registrable person, secretary or permanent representative[30];
(vi) the service address which is to replace that usual residential address on the register[31];
(vii) except where the application is delivered to the registrar on the same day as the applicant delivers a section 243 application[32], the date of birth of the applicant[33], the name of each company of which the applicant proposes to become a director or registrable person[34] and, where the registrar has allotted a unique identifier to the applicant, that unique identifier[35];
(viii) where the grounds of the application are those described in head (4) above, the name and registered number of the company in relation to which the determination was made[36].

The application must be accompanied by evidence which:
(A) where the grounds of the application are those described in head (1) above, supports the applicant's assertion that his application falls within the grounds stated in his application[37];
(B) where the grounds of the application are those described in head (2) above, establishes that the applicant is or has been employed by a relevant organisation[38];
(C) where the grounds of the application are those described in head (3) above, establishes that he is a section 243 beneficiary[39].

For these purposes, the registrar may direct that additional information or evidence should be delivered to him, what such information or evidence should be and how it should be verified[40].

The registrar may refer to a relevant body[41] any question relating to an assessment of:
(I) the nature and extent of any risk of violence or intimidation considered by the applicant to arise in relation to himself, or a person who lives with him, as a result of the activities of any company of which he is or proposes to become a director or registrable person or has been at any time a director, registrable person, secretary or permanent representative[42]; or
(II) whether the applicant is or has been employed by a relevant organisation[43].

For the purpose of determining any section 1088 application, the registrar may accept any answer to a question which is referred in this way[44] as providing sufficient evidence (where the grounds of the application are those described in head (1) above) of the nature and extent of any risk relevant to the applicant, or to persons who live with the applicant[45], or as providing sufficient evidence of whether an applicant is or has been employed by a relevant organisation[46].

The registrar must determine the application and send the applicant to the address for correspondence stated in his application, notice of his determination on the section 1088 application within five working days of that determination being made[47].

1 Ie under the Companies Act 2006 s 1088 (application to registrar to make address unavailable for public inspection) (see PARA 150): see the Companies (Disclosure of Address) Regulations 2009, SI 2009/214, reg 1(2).

2 As to the registrar of companies see PARA 126 et seq. As to the delivery of documents to the registrar see PARA 136; and as to the requirements generally for the proper delivery of documents to the registrar see PARA 137.

3 As to the register generally see PARA 142.
4 See the Companies (Disclosure of Address) Regulations 2009, SI 2009/214, reg 1(2).
5 Ie under the Companies Act 1985 s 10 (documents to be sent to registrar) (repealed), s 288 (register of directors and secretaries) (repealed), s 363 (duty to deliver annual returns) (repealed), s 691 (documents to be delivered to registrar by overseas company) (repealed), s 692 (registration of altered particulars by overseas company) (repealed) or s 690A(2), or Sch 21A para 2 (registration of overseas companies with branch in Great Britain) (repealed), as a service address under the European Public Limited-Liability Company Regulations 2004, SI 2004/2326, reg 80C (duty to notify registrar of changes of particulars of members of an SE's supervisory organ) (see PARA 1849), or under reg 79 (as originally enacted), as a service address under the Companies Act 2006 s 12 (statement of proposed officers) (see PARA 105), s 167 (duty to notify registrar of changes of director's particulars) (see PARA 550) or s 855 (contents of annual return) (see PARA 1595), or under regulations made under s 1046 (see PARA 2015), as a service address in a statement of initial significant control delivered to the registrar under s 9 (registration documents: see PARA 104), as a service address included in the required particulars of a registrable person delivered to the registrar to comply with an obligation in Pt 21A (ss 790A–790ZG) (see PARA 466 et seq), as a service address delivered to the registrar at the same time as a confirmation statement under s 853I(a) (duty to deliver information about people with significant control: see PARA 1603), or as a service address delivered to the registrar at the same time as a confirmation statement under s 853G (duty to deliver shareholder information: certain traded companies: see PARA 1602): see the Companies (Disclosure of Address) Regulations 2009, SI 2009/214, reg 9(1) (amended by SI 2009/1941; SI 2009/2400; SI 2016/339; SI 2016/599).
6 Companies (Disclosure of Address) Regulations 2009, SI 2009/214, reg 9(1) (as amended: see note 5).
7 Companies (Disclosure of Address) Regulations 2009, SI 2009/214, reg 9(2).
8 Companies (Disclosure of Address) Regulations 2009, SI 2009/214, reg 9(2)(a).
9 Companies (Disclosure of Address) Regulations 2009, SI 2009/214, reg 9(2)(a)(i). As to the appointment and duties etc of directors see PARA 512 et seq.
10 As to the company secretary and other officers see PARA 671.
11 Companies (Disclosure of Address) Regulations 2009, SI 2009/214, reg 9(2)(a)(ii). For these purposes, 'permanent representative' means an individual who was a permanent representative for the purposes of the Companies Act 1985 s 723B and s 723C (both repealed) (effect of confidentiality orders): see the Companies (Disclosure of Address) Regulations 2009, SI 2009/214, reg 1(2).
12 Companies (Disclosure of Address) Regulations 2009, SI 2009/214, reg 9(2)(a)(iii) (added by SI 2016/339). 'Registrable person' means a registrable person under the Companies Act 2006 Pt 21A (ss 790A–790ZG) (see PARA 466 et seq): Companies (Disclosure of Address) Regulations 2009, SI 2009/214, reg 1(2) (definition added by SI 2016/339).
13 Companies (Disclosure of Address) Regulations 2009, SI 2009/214, reg 9(2)(a)(iv) (added by SI 2016/339).
14 Companies (Disclosure of Address) Regulations 2009, SI 2009/214, reg 9(2)(b). For these purposes, 'relevant organisation' means the Government Communications Headquarters, the Secret Intelligence Service, the Security Service or a police force, where 'police force' means a police force within the meaning of the Police Act 1996 s 101(1) (ie a force maintained by a local policing body) (see POLICE AND INVESTIGATORY POWERS vol 84 (2013) PARA 2), the Police (Scotland) Act 1967 s 50 (meaning of police area, etc) or the Police (Northern Ireland) Act 2000 s 1 (name of the police in Northern Ireland): see the Companies (Disclosure of Address) Regulations 2009, SI 2009/214, reg 1(2). As to the Government Communications Headquarters see CONSTITUTIONAL AND ADMINISTRATIVE LAW vol 20 (2014) PARA 245; as to the Secret Intelligence Service see CONSTITUTIONAL AND ADMINISTRATIVE LAW vol 20 (2014) PARA 244; and as to the Security Service see CONSTITUTIONAL AND ADMINISTRATIVE LAW vol 20 (2014) PARA 243.
15 Companies (Disclosure of Address) Regulations 2009, SI 2009/214, reg 9(2)(c).
16 Ie under the Companies Act 2006 s 243(4) (permitted use or disclosure by the registrar) (see PARA 539): see the Companies (Disclosure of Address) Regulations 2009, SI 2009/214, reg 1(2).
17 See the Companies (Disclosure of Address) Regulations 2009, SI 2009/214, reg 1(2).
18 As to subscribers to a company's memorandum of association see PARA 97.
19 See the Companies (Disclosure of Address) Regulations 2009, SI 2009/214, reg 1(2).
20 For these purposes, 'confidentiality order' means an order under the Companies Act 1985 s 723B (repealed) (confidentiality orders): see the Companies (Disclosure of Address) Regulations 2009, SI 2009/214, reg 1(2).
21 Ie by the Companies Act 2006 (Commencement No 8, Transitional Provisions and Savings) Order 2008, SI 2008/2860, art 5, Sch 2 para 37: see the Companies (Disclosure of Address) Regulations 2009, SI 2009/214, reg 1(2). Accordingly, a director in relation to whom a confidentiality

order under the Companies Act 1985 s 723B (repealed) was in force immediately before 1 October 2009 is treated on and after that date as if they had made an application under the Companies Act 2006 s 243(4) (permitted use or disclosure by the registrar) (see PARA 539), and as if that application had been determined by the registrar in their favour: Companies Act 2006 (Commencement No 8, Transitional Provisions and Savings) Order 2008, SI 2008/2860, Sch 2 para 37(1). The provisions of regulations under the Companies Act 2006 s 243(4) relating to decisions of the registrar in favour of an applicant (in particular, as to the duration and revocation of such a decision) apply accordingly (Companies Act 2006 (Commencement No 8, Transitional Provisions and Savings) Order 2008, SI 2008/2860, Sch 2 para 37(2)); and as those regulations apply in accordance with Sch 2 para 37 any reference to an offence under the Companies Act 2006 s 1112 (false statements made to registrar) (see PARA 132) must be read as a reference to an offence under regulations under the Companies Act 1985 s 723E(1)(a) (repealed) in relation to the application for the confidentiality order (Companies Act 2006 (Commencement No 8, Transitional Provisions and Savings) Order 2008, SI 2008/2860, Sch 2 para 37(3)). The date of 1 October 2009 was the date by which all the provisions of the Companies Act 2006 that affect the law in England and Wales had come into force: see PARA 13 note 16.

22 See the Companies (Disclosure of Address) Regulations 2009, SI 2009/214, reg 1(2).

23 Ie an application made under the Register of People with Significant Control Regulations 2016, SI 2016/339, reg 25 (see PARA 496), reg 26 (see PARA 497) or reg 27 (see PARA 498).

24 Ie under the Register of People with Significant Control Regulations 2016, SI 2016/339, reg 31: see PARA 499.

25 Companies (Disclosure of Address) Regulations 2009, SI 2009/214, reg 9(2)(d) (added by SI 2016/339).

26 Companies (Disclosure of Address) Regulations 2009, SI 2009/214, reg 9(3)(a)(i).

27 Companies (Disclosure of Address) Regulations 2009, SI 2009/214, reg 9(3)(a)(ii). For these purposes, 'name' means a person's Christian name (or other forename) and surname, except that in the case of a peer, or an individual usually known by a title, the title may be stated instead of his Christian name (or other forename) and surname or in addition to either or both of them: Companies (Disclosure of Address) Regulations 2009, SI 2009/214, reg 1(2). 'Former name' means a name by which an individual was formerly known and which has been notified to the registrar under the Companies Act 1985 s 10 (documents to be sent to registrar) (repealed) or s 288 (register of directors and secretaries) (repealed), or under the Companies Act 2006 s 12 (statement of proposed officers) (see PARA 105) or s 167 (duty to notify registrar of changes of director's particulars) (see PARA 550): Companies (Disclosure of Address) Regulations 2009, SI 2009/214, reg 1(2).

28 Companies (Disclosure of Address) Regulations 2009, SI 2009/214, reg 9(3)(a)(iii).

29 Companies (Disclosure of Address) Regulations 2009, SI 2009/214, reg 9(3)(a)(iv).

30 Companies (Disclosure of Address) Regulations 2009, SI 2009/214, reg 9(3)(a)(v) (amended by SI 2016/339). As to company names and trading names generally see PARA 195 et seq. As to a company's registered number see PARAS 134, 135.

31 Companies (Disclosure of Address) Regulations 2009, SI 2009/214, reg 9(3)(a)(vi).

32 Companies (Disclosure of Address) Regulations 2009, SI 2009/214, reg 9(4).

33 Companies (Disclosure of Address) Regulations 2009, SI 2009/214, reg 9(3)(a)(vii)(aa).

34 Companies (Disclosure of Address) Regulations 2009, SI 2009/214, reg 9(3)(a)(vii)(bb) (amended by SI 2016/339).

35 Companies (Disclosure of Address) Regulations 2009, SI 2009/214, reg 9(3)(a)(vii)(cc).

36 Companies (Disclosure of Address) Regulations 2009, SI 2009/214, reg 9(3)(a)(viii) (added by SI 2016/339).

37 Companies (Disclosure of Address) Regulations 2009, SI 2009/214, reg 9(3)(b)(i).

38 Companies (Disclosure of Address) Regulations 2009, SI 2009/214, reg 9(3)(b)(ii).

39 Companies (Disclosure of Address) Regulations 2009, SI 2009/214, reg 9(3)(b)(iii).

40 Companies (Disclosure of Address) Regulations 2009, SI 2009/214, reg 12(1).

41 For these purposes, 'relevant body' means any police force and any other person whom the registrar considers may be able to assist in answering a question referred to that person by the registrar under the Companies (Disclosure of Address) Regulations 2009, SI 2009/214: reg 1(2).

42 Companies (Disclosure of Address) Regulations 2009, SI 2009/214, reg 9(5)(a) (amended by SI 2016/339).

43 Companies (Disclosure of Address) Regulations 2009, SI 2009/214, reg 9(5)(b).

44 Ie referred in accordance with the Companies (Disclosure of Address) Regulations 2009, SI 2009/214, reg 9(5) (see the text and notes 39–42): see reg 12(2).

45 Companies (Disclosure of Address) Regulations 2009, SI 2009/214, reg 12(2)(a).

46 Companies (Disclosure of Address) Regulations 2009, SI 2009/214, reg 12(2)(b).

47 Companies (Disclosure of Address) Regulations 2009, SI 2009/214, reg 9(6). For these purposes, 'working day' means a day that is not a Saturday or Sunday, Christmas Day, Good Friday or any

day that is a bank holiday under the Banking and Financial Dealings Act 1971 (see TIME vol 97 (2015) PARA 321) in England and Wales: reg 1(2). As to the meanings of 'England' and 'Wales' see PARA 1 note 5. As to the effect of a successful application to withhold an address placed on the register see PARA 154; and as to provision made to appeal an unsuccessful application to withhold an address placed on the register see PARA 155.

152. Application by company to withhold address placed on the register. A section 1088 application[1] may be made to the registrar of companies[2] by a company in respect of the addresses of[3]:

(1) all of its members[4] and former members whose addresses were contained in an annual return[5], or in a return of allotment of shares[6], delivered to the registrar on or after 1 January 2003[7]; or

(2) the subscribers to its memorandum of association[8] where that memorandum was delivered to the registrar on or after 1 January 2003[9].

The grounds on which such an application may be made are that the company making the application considers that, as a result of its activities, the availability to members of the public of the addresses described in heads (1) and (2) above creates a serious risk that its members or former members or subscribers, or persons who live at those addresses, will be subjected to violence or intimidation[10].

The application must contain the name of the applicant company and its registered number[11], and a statement of the grounds on which the application is made[12]. The application must be accompanied by evidence which supports the applicant's assertion that its application falls within the grounds stated in its application[13] or, where the court has made an order[14] directing the applicant not to comply with a request[15] for inspection of, or for copies of, the register[16] or the index of members' names[17], a copy of that order[18].

For these purposes, the registrar may direct that additional information or evidence should be delivered to him, what such information or evidence should be and how it should be verified[19].

The registrar may refer to a relevant body[20] any question relating to the assessment of the nature and extent of any risk of violence or intimidation considered by the applicant company to arise in relation to any of its members or former members or subscribers, or persons who live at the addresses described in heads (1) and (2) above, as a result of its activities by virtue of the availability to members of the public of particulars of the addresses of such members or former members or subscribers[21]. For the purpose of determining any section 1088 application, the registrar may accept any answer to a question which is referred in this way[22] as providing sufficient evidence (where the grounds of the application relate to the addresses described in heads (1) and (2) above[23]) of the nature and extent of any risk relevant to the subscribers or members or former members of an applicant company or to persons who live with them or (in the case of members, former members or subscribers) to persons who live at their addresses[24].

The registrar must determine the application and send the applicant company to its registered office notice of his determination on the section 1088 application within five working days of that determination being made[25].

1 As to the meaning of 'section 1088 application' see PARA 151.
2 As to the registrar of companies see PARA 126 et seq. As to the delivery of documents to the registrar see PARA 136; and as to the requirements generally for the proper delivery of documents to the registrar see PARA 137.
3 Companies (Disclosure of Address) Regulations 2009, SI 2009/214, reg 10(1).
4 As to membership of a company generally see PARA 323 et seq.
5 Companies (Disclosure of Address) Regulations 2009, SI 2009/214, reg 10(1)(a)(i). As to the duty on a company to deliver annual returns made up to a return date before 30 June 2016 see

PARA 1594 et seq. The duty to deliver annual returns is replaced, with effect from 30 June 2016 and subject to transitional provisions, by a duty to deliver confirmation statements: see PARA 1598 et seq.

6 Companies (Disclosure of Address) Regulations 2009, SI 2009/214, reg 10(1)(a)(ii). As to a return of allotment of shares see PARA 1297.

7 Companies (Disclosure of Address) Regulations 2009, SI 2009/214, reg 10(1)(a).

8 As to subscribers to a company's memorandum of association see PARA 97.

9 Companies (Disclosure of Address) Regulations 2009, SI 2009/214, reg 10(1)(b).

10 Companies (Disclosure of Address) Regulations 2009, SI 2009/214, reg 10(2).

11 Companies (Disclosure of Address) Regulations 2009, SI 2009/214, reg 10(3)(a)(i). As to company names and trading names generally see PARA 195 et seq. As to a company's registered number see PARAS 134, 135.

12 Companies (Disclosure of Address) Regulations 2009, SI 2009/214, reg 10(3)(a)(ii).

13 Companies (Disclosure of Address) Regulations 2009, SI 2009/214, reg 10(3)(b)(i).

14 Ie under the Companies Act 2006 s 117(3) (register of members: response to request for inspection or copy) (see PARA 350): see the Companies (Disclosure of Address) Regulations 2009, SI 2009/214, reg 10(3)(b)(ii).

15 Ie under the Companies Act 2006 s 116 (rights to inspect and require copies) (see PARA 350): see the Companies (Disclosure of Address) Regulations 2009, SI 2009/214, reg 10(3)(b)(ii).

16 As to the register generally see PARA 142.

17 As to the index of members' names see PARA 340.

18 Companies (Disclosure of Address) Regulations 2009, SI 2009/214, reg 10(3)(b)(ii).

19 Companies (Disclosure of Address) Regulations 2009, SI 2009/214, reg 12(1).

20 As to the meaning of 'relevant body' for these purposes see PARA 151 note 41.

21 Companies (Disclosure of Address) Regulations 2009, SI 2009/214, reg 10(4).

22 Ie referred in accordance with the Companies (Disclosure of Address) Regulations 2009, SI 2009/214, reg 10(4) (see the text and notes 20–21): see reg 12(2).

23 Ie where the grounds of the application are those described in the Companies (Disclosure of Address) Regulations 2009, SI 2009/214, reg 10(2) (see the text and note 10): see reg 12(2).

24 Companies (Disclosure of Address) Regulations 2009, SI 2009/214, reg 12(2)(a).

25 Companies (Disclosure of Address) Regulations 2009, SI 2009/214, reg 10(5). As to the meaning of 'working day' for these purposes see PARA 151 note 47. As to the effect of a successful application to withhold an address placed on the register see PARA 154; and as to provision made to appeal an unsuccessful application to withhold an address placed on the register see PARA 155.

153. Application by person registering a charge to withhold address placed on the register. A section 1088 application[1] may be made to the registrar of companies[2] by a person who has registered a charge[3], and who is not the company which created the charge or acquired the property subject to a charge[4], in respect of his address delivered to the registrar for the purposes of that registration[5].

The grounds on which such an application may be made are that the person making the application considers that there is a serious risk that he (or, if applicable, his employees) or persons who live with him or his employees, will be subjected to violence or intimidation as a result of the activities of the company which is, or was, subject to the charge[6].

The application must contain[7]:

(1) a statement of the grounds on which the application is made[8];
(2) the name of the applicant[9] and, where the applicant is a company, its registered number[10];
(3) the address of the applicant that is to be made unavailable for public inspection[11];
(4) the name and registered number of the company which is or was subject to the charge[12];
(5) an address for correspondence with the registrar in respect of the application[13]; and
(6) where the applicant is the chargee, the service address which is to replace the address of the applicant on the register[14].

The application must be accompanied by evidence which supports the applicant's assertion that there is a serious risk that he (or, if applicable, his employees) or persons who live with him or his employees, will be subjected to violence or intimidation as a result of the activities of the company which is or was subject to the charge[15].

For these purposes, the registrar may direct that additional information or evidence should be delivered to him, what such information or evidence should be and how it should be verified[16].

The registrar may refer to a relevant body[17] any question relating to the assessment of the nature and extent of any risk of violence or intimidation considered by the applicant to arise in relation to himself (or, if applicable, his employees), or persons who live with him or his employees, as a result of the activities of the company which is or was subject to the charge[18]. For the purpose of determining any section 1088 application, the registrar may accept any answer to a question which is referred in this way[19] as providing sufficient evidence (where the grounds of the application relate to the activities of a company which is, or was, subject to a registered charge[20]) of the nature and extent of any risk relevant to (where the applicant is an individual) the applicant, or to any employees of an applicant, or to persons who live with them[21].

The registrar must determine the application and send the applicant to the address stated in the application in accordance with head (5) above notice of his determination on the section 1088 application within five working days of that determination being made[22].

1 As to the meaning of 'section 1088 application' see PARA 151.
2 As to the registrar of companies see PARA 126 et seq. As to the delivery of documents to the registrar see PARA 136; and as to the requirements generally for the proper delivery of documents to the registrar see PARA 137.
3 Ie by a person who has registered a charge, on or after 1 January 2003, under the Companies Act 1985 Pt XII (ss 395–409) (registration of charges (England)) (repealed) or under the Companies Act 2006 Pt 25 (ss 859A–894) (company charges) (see PARA 1462 et seq), or under regulations made under s 1052 (overseas companies) (see PARA 2022): see the Companies (Disclosure of Address) Regulations 2009, SI 2009/214, reg 11(1)(a) (amended by SI 2009/1941).
4 Companies (Disclosure of Address) Regulations 2009, SI 2009/214, reg 11(1)(b).
5 Companies (Disclosure of Address) Regulations 2009, SI 2009/214, reg 11(1).
6 Companies (Disclosure of Address) Regulations 2009, SI 2009/214, reg 11(2).
7 Companies (Disclosure of Address) Regulations 2009, SI 2009/214, reg 11(3)(a).
8 Companies (Disclosure of Address) Regulations 2009, SI 2009/214, reg 11(3)(a)(i).
9 As to the meaning of 'name', in relation to an individual, for these purposes see PARA 151 note 27.
10 Companies (Disclosure of Address) Regulations 2009, SI 2009/214, reg 11(3)(a)(ii). As to company names and trading names generally see PARA 195 et seq. As to a company's registered number see PARAS 134–135.
11 Companies (Disclosure of Address) Regulations 2009, SI 2009/214, reg 11(3)(a)(iii).
12 Companies (Disclosure of Address) Regulations 2009, SI 2009/214, reg 11(3)(a)(iv).
13 Companies (Disclosure of Address) Regulations 2009, SI 2009/214, reg 11(3)(a)(v).
14 Companies (Disclosure of Address) Regulations 2009, SI 2009/214, reg 11(3)(a)(vi).
15 Companies (Disclosure of Address) Regulations 2009, SI 2009/214, reg 11(3)(b).
16 Companies (Disclosure of Address) Regulations 2009, SI 2009/214, reg 12(1).
17 As to the meaning of 'relevant body' for these purposes see PARA 151 note 41.
18 Companies (Disclosure of Address) Regulations 2009, SI 2009/214, reg 11(4).
19 Ie referred in accordance with the Companies (Disclosure of Address) Regulations 2009, SI 2009/214, reg 11(4) (see the text and notes 17–18): see reg 12(2).
20 Ie where the grounds of the application are those described in the Companies (Disclosure of Address) Regulations 2009, SI 2009/214, reg 11(2) (see the text and note 6): see reg 12(2).
21 Companies (Disclosure of Address) Regulations 2009, SI 2009/214, reg 12(2).
22 Companies (Disclosure of Address) Regulations 2009, SI 2009/214, reg 11(5). As to the meaning of 'working day' for these purposes see PARA 151 note 47. As to the effect of a successful

application to withhold an address placed on the register see PARA 154; and as to provision made to appeal an unsuccessful application to withhold an address placed on the register see PARA 155.

154. Effect of successful application to withhold address placed on the register. Where a section 1088 application[1] has been determined in favour of the applicant, the registrar of companies[2] must:

(1) in the case of an application made by an individual[3] or by a person who registers or has registered a charge[4], make the specified address[5] unavailable for public inspection[6];

(2) in the case of an application by a company[7], make all of the addresses of the members[8], former members or subscribers to the memorandum of association[9] unavailable for public inspection[10];

(3) in the case of a director[11] or secretary[12] in relation to whom a confidentiality order[13] was in force immediately before 1 October 2009[14], make unavailable for public inspection any address that immediately before that date was contained in confidential records[15].

A section 1088 decision[16] continues to have effect until the registrar has made a revocation decision[17] in relation to the section 1088 beneficiary[18].

1 As to the meaning of 'section 1088 application' see PARA 151.
2 As to the registrar of companies see PARA 126 et seq.
3 Ie under the Companies (Disclosure of Address) Regulations 2009, SI 2009/214, reg 9(1) (see PARA 151): see reg 13(1)(a).
4 Ie under the Companies (Disclosure of Address) Regulations 2009, SI 2009/214, reg 11(1) (see PARA 153): see reg 13(1)(a).
5 For these purposes, 'specified address' means the address specified in the application as being the one to be made unavailable for public inspection: Companies (Disclosure of Address) Regulations 2009, SI 2009/214, reg 13(2).
6 Companies (Disclosure of Address) Regulations 2009, SI 2009/214, reg 13(1)(a).
7 Ie under the Companies (Disclosure of Address) Regulations 2009, SI 2009/214, reg 10(1) (see PARA 152): see reg 13(1)(b).
8 As to membership of a company generally see PARA 323 et seq.
9 As to subscribers to a company's memorandum of association see PARA 97.
10 Companies (Disclosure of Address) Regulations 2009, SI 2009/214, reg 13(1)(b).
11 As to directors of a company see PARA 512 et seq.
12 As to the company secretary and other officers see PARA 671.
13 As to the meaning of 'confidentiality order' see PARA 151 note 20.
14 Ie in the case of a person to whom the Companies Act 2006 (Commencement No 8, Transitional Provisions and Savings) Order 2008, SI 2008/2860, art 5, Sch 2 para 36 applies: see the Companies (Disclosure of Address) Regulations 2009, SI 2009/214, reg 13(1)(c). Accordingly, a director or secretary in relation to whom a confidentiality order under the Companies Act 1985 s 723B (repealed) was in force immediately before 1 October 2009 is treated on and after that date as if they had made an application under the Companies Act 2006 s 1088 (application to make address unavailable for public inspection) (see PARA 150) in respect of any address that immediately before that date was contained in 'confidential records' as defined in the Companies Act 1985 s 723D(3) (repealed), and as if that application had been determined by the registrar in their favour: Companies Act 2006 (Commencement No 8, Transitional Provisions and Savings) Order 2008, SI 2008/2860, Sch 2 para 36(1). The provisions of regulations under the Companies Act 2006 s 1088 relating to decisions of the registrar in favour of an applicant (in particular, as to the duration and revocation of such a decision) apply accordingly (Companies Act 2006 (Commencement No 8, Transitional Provisions and Savings) Order 2008, SI 2008/2860, Sch 2 para 36(2)); and as those regulations apply in accordance with Sch 2 para 36 any reference to an offence under the Companies Act 2006 s 1112 (false statements made to registrar) (see PARA 132) must be read as a reference to an offence under regulations under the Companies Act 1985 s 723E(1)(a) (repealed) in relation to the application for the confidentiality order (Companies Act 2006 (Commencement No 8, Transitional Provisions and Savings) Order 2008, SI 2008/2860, Sch 2 para 36(3)). The date of 1 October 2009 was the date by which all the provisions of the Companies Act 2006 that affect the law in England and Wales had come into force: see PARA 13 note 16.
15 Companies (Disclosure of Address) Regulations 2009, SI 2009/214, reg 13(1)(c). The text refers to 'confidential records' as defined in the Companies Act 1985 s 723D(3) (repealed) (see note 14):

see the Companies Act 2006 (Commencement No 8, Transitional Provisions and Savings) Order 2008, SI 2008/2860, Sch 2 para 36(1); Companies (Disclosure of Address) Regulations 2009, SI 2009/214, reg 13(1)(c).

16 For these purposes, 'section 1088 decision' means a determination by the registrar on a section 1088 application in favour of the applicant: Companies (Disclosure of Address) Regulations 2009, SI 2009/214, reg 1(2).

17 For these purposes, 'revocation decision' in relation to a section 1088 decision means a determination by the registrar to revoke that decision in accordance with the Companies (Disclosure of Address) Regulations 2009, SI 2009/214, reg 16 (see PARA 156): see reg 15(3).

18 Companies (Disclosure of Address) Regulations 2009, SI 2009/214, reg 15(2). For these purposes, 'section 1088 beneficiary' means a person who has made a section 1088 application in respect of which a section 1088 decision has been made: Companies (Disclosure of Address) Regulations 2009, SI 2009/214, reg 1(2).

155. Appeal against decision that application to withhold address placed on the register has been unsuccessful. An applicant who has received notice[1] that his section 1088 application[2] has been unsuccessful may appeal to the High Court on the grounds that the decision is unlawful[3], is irrational or unreasonable[4], or has been made on the basis of a procedural impropriety or otherwise contravenes the rules of natural justice[5]. No such appeal may be brought, however, unless the permission of the court has been obtained[6]. No application for such permission may be made after 28 days beginning with the date of the notice of determination[7] unless the court is satisfied that there was good reason for the failure of the applicant to seek permission before the end of that period[8]. An applicant who seeks permission to appeal must serve written notice of the application on the registrar within seven days beginning with the date on which the application for permission was issued[9].

The court determining an appeal may either dismiss the appeal[10] or quash the decision[11]. Where the court quashes a decision, it may refer the matter to the registrar of companies[12] with a direction to reconsider it and make a determination in accordance with the findings of the court[13].

1 Ie under the Companies (Disclosure of Address) Regulations 2009, SI 2009/214, reg 9(6) (see PARA 151), reg 10(5) (see PARA 152) or reg 11(5) (see PARA 153): see reg 14(1).

2 As to the meaning of 'section 1088 application' see PARA 151.

3 Companies (Disclosure of Address) Regulations 2009, SI 2009/214, reg 14(1)(a).

4 Companies (Disclosure of Address) Regulations 2009, SI 2009/214, reg 14(1)(b).

5 Companies (Disclosure of Address) Regulations 2009, SI 2009/214, reg 14(1)(c). As to procedural fairness and the rules of natural justice see JUDICIAL REVIEW vol 61 (2010) PARA 625 et seq.

6 Companies (Disclosure of Address) Regulations 2009, SI 2009/214, reg 14(2) (amended by SI 2016/339).

7 Ie the notice under the Companies (Disclosure of Address) Regulations 2009, SI 2009/214, reg 9(6) (see PARA 151), reg 10(5) (see PARA 152) or reg 11(5) (see PARA 153).

8 Companies (Disclosure of Address) Regulations 2009, SI 2009/214, reg 14(3) (substituted by SI 2016/339).

9 Companies (Disclosure of Address) Regulations 2009, SI 2009/214, reg 14(3A) (added by SI 2016/339).

10 Companies (Disclosure of Address) Regulations 2009, SI 2009/214, reg 14(4)(a).

11 Companies (Disclosure of Address) Regulations 2009, SI 2009/214, reg 14(4)(b).

12 As to the registrar of companies see PARA 126 et seq.

13 Companies (Disclosure of Address) Regulations 2009, SI 2009/214, reg 14(4).

156. Revocation of decision to withhold address placed on the register. The registrar of companies[1] may revoke a section 1088 decision[2] at any time if he is satisfied that the section 1088 beneficiary[3] or any other person, in purported compliance with any provision of the Disclosure of Address Regulations[4], is found guilty of an offence of making false statements to the registrar[5] (a 'revocation decision')[6].

If the registrar proposes to make a revocation decision, he must send the beneficiary notice of his intention[7]. The notice must:

(1) inform the beneficiary that he may, within the period of 28 days beginning with the date of the notice, deliver representations in writing to the registrar[8]; and

(2) state that, if representations are not received by the registrar within that period, the revocation decision will be made at the expiry of that period[9].

If, within the period so specified[10], the beneficiary delivers representations as to why the revocation decision should not be made, the registrar must have regard to the representations in determining whether to make the revocation decision, and must, within five working days of making his decision, send notice of it to the beneficiary[11].

Any communication by the registrar in respect of a revocation decision or proposed revocation decision must be sent to the beneficiary[12]:

(a) in the case of an individual, to his usual residential address[13];

(b) in the case of a company, to its registered office[14]; or

(c) in the case of a partnership[15], to the address specified in its section 1088 application[16].

1 As to the registrar of companies see PARA 126 et seq.
2 As to the meaning of 'section 1088 decision' see PARA 154 note 16.
3 As to the meaning of 'section 1088 beneficiary' see PARA 154 note 18.
4 Ie in purported compliance with any provision of the Companies (Disclosure of Address) Regulations 2009, SI 2009/214 (as to which see PARA 151 et seq): see reg 16(1).
5 Ie under the Companies Act 2006 s 1112 (false statements made to registrar) (see PARA 132): see the Companies (Disclosure of Address) Regulations 2009, SI 2009/214, reg 16(1).
6 Companies (Disclosure of Address) Regulations 2009, SI 2009/214, reg 16(1).
7 Companies (Disclosure of Address) Regulations 2009, SI 2009/214, reg 16(2).
8 Companies (Disclosure of Address) Regulations 2009, SI 2009/214, reg 16(3)(a).
9 Companies (Disclosure of Address) Regulations 2009, SI 2009/214, reg 16(3)(b).
10 Ie within the period specified in the Companies (Disclosure of Address) Regulations 2009, SI 2009/214, reg 16(3) (see the text and notes 8–9): see reg 16(4).
11 Companies (Disclosure of Address) Regulations 2009, SI 2009/214, reg 16(4). As to the meaning of 'working day' for these purposes see PARA 151 note 47.
12 Companies (Disclosure of Address) Regulations 2009, SI 2009/214, reg 16(5).
13 Companies (Disclosure of Address) Regulations 2009, SI 2009/214, reg 16(5)(a).
14 Companies (Disclosure of Address) Regulations 2009, SI 2009/214, reg 16(5)(b). As to a company's registered office see PARA 124.
15 For these purposes, 'partnership' includes a limited liability partnership (Companies (Disclosure of Address) Regulations 2009, SI 2009/214, reg 16(6)), where 'limited liability partnership' means a limited liability partnership incorporated under the Limited Liability Partnerships Act 2000 (as to which see PARTNERSHIP vol 79 (2014) PARA 233 et seq) (Companies (Disclosure of Address) Regulations 2009, SI 2009/214, reg 1(2)).
16 Companies (Disclosure of Address) Regulations 2009, SI 2009/214, reg 16(5)(c). As to the meaning of 'section 1088 application' see PARA 151.

F. CORRECTION OF MATERIAL KEPT ON THE REGISTER

157. Removal or rationalisation of material on the register. Where it appears to the registrar of companies[1] that the information contained in a document[2] delivered to the registrar[3] is inconsistent with other information on the register[4], the registrar may give notice to the company to which the document relates[5], stating in what respects the information contained in it appears to be inconsistent with other information on the register[6], and requiring the company to take steps to resolve the inconsistency[7]. The notice must state the date on which it is issued[8], and require the delivery to the registrar, within 14 days after that date, of such replacement or additional documents as may be required to resolve the inconsistency[9]. If the necessary documents are not delivered within the period specified, an offence is committed by the company, and by every officer of the company who is in default[10].

The registrar may remove from the register anything that there was power, but no duty, to include[11]. This power is exercisable, in particular, so as to remove unnecessary material[12], and to remove material derived from a document that has been replaced, either because it did not meet the requirements for proper delivery[13], or pursuant to a notice to remedy an inconsistency on the register[14]. However, this power does not authorise the removal from the register of:

(1) anything whose registration has had legal consequences in relation to the company, as regards:
   (a) its formation[15];
   (b) a change of name[16];
   (c) its re-registration[17];
   (d) its becoming or ceasing to be a community interest company[18];
   (e) a reduction of capital[19];
   (f) a change of registered office[20];
   (g) the registration of a charge[21];
   (h) its dissolution[22]; or
   (i) as from 30 June 2016[23], a change in its membership particulars of which were delivered to the registrar under the statutory duty[24] to notify him of changes while an election to keep information on the central register is in force[25];

(2) an address that is a person's registered address for the purposes of the service of documents on directors, secretaries and others[26].

On or before removing any material in this way[27] (otherwise than at the request of the company) the registrar must give notice[28]:

(i) to the person by whom the material was delivered (if the identity, and name and address of that person are known)[29]; or

(ii) to the company to which the material relates (if notice cannot be given under head (i) above and the identity of that company is known)[30].

The notice must state what material the registrar proposes to remove (or has removed) and on what grounds[31], and it must state the date on which it is issued[32].

1 As to the meaning of 'registrar of companies' see PARA 126 note 2. As to the meaning of 'company' under the Companies Acts see PARA 21; and as to the meaning of the 'Companies Acts' see PARA 13. As to the application of the Companies Act 2006 Pt 35 (ss 1059A–1119) (see also PARAS 126, 130 et seq, 158 et seq) see PARA 126 note 1.

2 As to the meaning of 'document' for these purposes see PARA 136 note 2.

3 As to the delivery of documents to the registrar see PARA 136; and as to the requirements generally for the proper delivery of documents to the registrar see PARA 137. As to the meaning of references to delivering a document for these purposes see PARA 136 note 2.

4 As to the meaning of the 'register' see PARA 142.

5 Companies Act 2006 s 1093(1).

6 Companies Act 2006 s 1093(1)(a).

7 Companies Act 2006 s 1093(1)(b).

8 Companies Act 2006 s 1093(2)(a).

9 Companies Act 2006 s 1093(2)(b).

10 Companies Act 2006 s 1093(3). As to the meaning of 'officer' generally under the Companies Act 2006 see PARA 679; and as to the meaning of 'officer in default' see PARA 316. A person guilty of such an offence is liable on summary conviction to a fine and for continued contravention to a daily default fine not exceeding one-tenth of the greater of £5,000 or level 4 on the standard scale: see s 1093(4) (amended by SI 2015/664). In the case of liability on summary conviction the fine is one not exceeding level 5 on the standard scale: see the Companies Act 2006 s 1093(4) (as so amended). By virtue of the Legal Aid, Sentencing and Punishment of Offenders Act 2012 s 85, however, where the offence is committed on or after 12 March 2015, it is punishable by a fine of

an unlimited amount. As to the standard scale and the powers of magistrates' courts to issue fines on summary conviction see SENTENCING vol 92 (2015) PARA 176. As to the meaning of 'daily default fine' see PARA 1816.

11 Companies Act 2006 s 1094(1). The registrar is required to give public notice of the removal from the register of any document which is subject to the Directive disclosure requirements (as to which see s 1078; and PARA 139) or of any material derived from such a document: see PARA 139.
12 Ie within the meaning of the Companies Act 2006 s 1074 (see PARA 138 note 21): see s 1094(2).
13 Ie under the Companies Act 2006 s 1076 (see PARA 138): see s 1094(2).
14 Companies Act 2006 s 1094(2). The text refers to a notice to remedy an inconsistency on the register under s 1093 (see the text and notes 1–13): see s 1094(2).
15 Companies Act 2006 s 1094(3)(a)(i). As to company formation under the Companies Act 2006 see PARA 95 et seq.
16 Companies Act 2006 s 1094(3)(a)(ii). As to change of a company's name see PARAS 216–218.
17 Companies Act 2006 s 1094(3)(a)(iii). As to company re-registration and its effects generally see PARA 167 et seq.
18 Companies Act 2006 s 1094(3)(a)(iv). As to becoming a community interest company see PARA 75; and as to ceasing to be a community interest company see PARA 192.
19 Companies Act 2006 s 1094(3)(a)(v). As to reduction of share capital generally see PARA 1360 et seq. As to the meaning of 'share capital' see PARA 1231.
20 Companies Act 2006 s 1094(3)(a)(vi). As to changes in the situation of a company's registered office see PARA 124.
21 Companies Act 2006 s 1094(3)(a)(vii). As to the registration of charges see PARA 1474 et seq.
22 Companies Act 2006 s 1094(3)(a)(viii). As to the dissolution of a company see PARA 1703 et seq.
23 See the Small Business, Enterprise and Employment Act 2015 (Commencement No 4, Transitional and Savings Provisions) Regulations 2016, SI 2016/321, reg 6(c).
24 Ie under the Companies Act 2006 s 128E (see PARA 366).
25 Companies Act 2006 s 1094(3)(a)(ix) (added by the Small Business, Enterprise and Employment Act 2015 Sch 5 Pt 2 paras 11, 32).
26 Companies Act 2006 s 1094(3)(b). Head (2) in the text refers to the purposes of s 1140 (see PARA 744): see s 1094(3)(b). As to the meaning of 'director' see PARA 512. As to the company secretary and other officers see PARA 671.
27 Ie under the Companies Act 2006 s 1094: see s 1094(4).
28 Companies Act 2006 s 1094(4).
29 Companies Act 2006 s 1094(4)(a).
30 Companies Act 2006 s 1094(4)(b).
31 Companies Act 2006 s 1094(5)(a).
32 Companies Act 2006 s 1094(5)(b).

158. Provision made for rectification of the register on application to the registrar of companies. The Secretary of State[1] may make provision by regulations[2] requiring the registrar of companies[3], on application, to remove from the register[4] material of a description specified in the regulations that[5]:

(1) derives from anything invalid or ineffective or that was done without the authority of the company[6]; or
(2) is factually inaccurate, or is derived from something that is factually inaccurate or forged[7].

The regulations may make provision as to:

(a) who may make an application[8];
(b) the information to be included in and documents to accompany an application[9];
(c) the notice to be given of an application and of its outcome[10];
(d) a period in which objections to an application may be made[11]; and
(e) how an application is to be determined[12].

An application must specify what is to be removed from the register and indicate where on the register it is[13], and must be accompanied by a statement that the material specified in the application complies with the statutory requirements[14] and with the regulations[15]. If no objections are made to the application, the registrar may accept the statement as sufficient evidence that the material specified in the application should be removed from the register[16]. As from 6 April 2016[17], however, in a case where:

(i) the material specified in the application is material naming a person in a statement of a company's proposed officers as a person who is to be a director of the company, or in a notice given by a company[18] as a person who has become a director of the company; and

(ii) the application is made by or on behalf of the person named and is accompanied by a statement that the person did not consent to act as director of the company[19],

if the company provides the registrar with the necessary evidence[20] within the time required by the regulations, the registrar must not remove the material from the register[21]. If the company does not provide the registrar with the necessary evidence within that time, the material is conclusively presumed for these purposes to be derived from something that is factually inaccurate[22], and the registrar must accept the applicant's statement as sufficient evidence that the material should be removed from the register[23].

Where anything is removed from the register in this way[24], the registration of which has had legal consequences in relation to the company, as regards:

(A) its formation[25];

(B) a change of name[26];

(C) its re-registration[27];

(D) its becoming or ceasing to be a community interest company[28];

(E) a reduction of capital[29];

(F) a change of registered office[30];

(G) the registration of a charge[31];

(H) its dissolution[32]; or

(I) as from 30 June 2016[33], a change in its membership particulars of which were delivered to the registrar under the statutory duty[34] to notify him of changes while an election to keep information on the central register is in force[35],

any person appearing to the court to have a sufficient interest may apply to the court for such consequential orders as appear just with respect to the legal effect, if any, to be accorded to the material by virtue of its having appeared on the register[36].

1 As to the Secretary of State see PARA 6.

2 Regulations made under the Companies Act 2006 s 1095 are subject to affirmative resolution procedure (ie the regulations must not be made unless a draft of the statutory instrument containing them has been laid before Parliament and approved by a resolution of each House of Parliament): see ss 1095(6), 1290. As to the making of regulations under the Companies Act 2006 generally see ss 1288–1292. Partly in exercise of the power conferred by s 1095(1), (2), the Secretary of State has made the Registrar of Companies and Applications for Striking Off Regulations 2009, SI 2009/1803: see regs 4, 5; and PARA 159.

As to the application of the Companies Act 2006 Pt 35 (ss 1059A–1119) (see also PARAS 126, 130 et seq, 161 et seq) see PARA 126 note 1.

3 As to the meaning of 'registrar of companies' see PARA 126 note 2. As to the meaning of 'company' under the Companies Acts see PARA 21; and see PARA 126 note 1. As to the meaning of the 'Companies Acts' see PARA 13.

4 As to the meaning of the 'register' see PARA 142.

5 Companies Act 2006 s 1095(1).

6 Companies Act 2006 s 1095(1)(a).

7 Companies Act 2006 s 1095(1)(b).

8 Companies Act 2006 s 1095(2)(a).

9 Companies Act 2006 s 1095(2)(b). As to the meaning of 'document' for these purposes see PARA 136 note 2.

10 Companies Act 2006 s 1095(2)(c).

11 Companies Act 2006 s 1095(2)(d).
12 Companies Act 2006 s 1095(2)(e).
13 Companies Act 2006 s 1095(3)(a).
14 Ie complies with the Companies Act 2006 s 1095: see s 1095(3)(b).
15 Companies Act 2006 s 1095(3)(b). Any application or other document delivered to the registrar under s 1095 is not to be made available by the registrar of companies for public inspection: see s 1087(1)(f); and PARA 146.
16 Companies Act 2006 s 1095(4). The registrar is required to give public notice of the removal from the register of any document which is subject to the Directive disclosure requirements (as to which see s 1078; and PARA 139) or of any material derived from such a document: see PARA 139.
17 See the Small Business, Enterprise and Employment Act 2015 (Commencement No 4, Transitional and Savings Provisions) Regulations 2016, SI 2016/321, reg 3(a).
18 Ie under the Companies Act 2006 s 167 (see PARA 550) or s 167D (see PARA 553).
19 Companies Act 2006 s 1095(4A) (s 1095(4A)–(4D) added by the Small Business, Enterprise and Employment Act 2015 s 102(1)).
20 'The necessary evidence' is evidence sufficient to satisfy the registrar that the person did consent to act as director of the company, plus a statement by the company that the evidence provided by it is true and is not misleading or deceptive in any material particular: Companies Act 2006 s 1095(4D) (as added: see note 19).
21 Companies Act 2006 s 1095(4B) (as added: see note 19).
22 Companies Act 2006 s 1095(4C)(a) (as added: see note 19).
23 Companies Act 2006 s 1095(4C)(b) (as added: see note 19).
24 Ie under the Companies Act 2006 s 1095: see s 1095(5).
25 Companies Act 2006 ss 1094(3)(a)(i), 1095(5). As to company formation under the Companies Act 2006 see PARA 95 et seq.
26 Companies Act 2006 ss 1094(3)(a)(ii), 1095(5). As to change of a company's name see PARAS 216–218.
27 Companies Act 2006 ss 1094(3)(a)(iii), 1095(5). As to company re-registration and its effects generally see PARA 167 et seq.
28 Companies Act 2006 ss 1094(3)(a)(iv), 1095(5). As to becoming a community interest company see PARA 75; and as to ceasing to be a community interest company see PARA 192.
29 Companies Act 2006 ss 1094(3)(a)(v), 1095(5). As to reduction of share capital generally see PARA 1360 et seq. As to the meaning of 'share capital' see PARA 1231.
30 Companies Act 2006 ss 1094(3)(a)(vi), 1095(5). As to changes in the situation of a company's registered office see PARA 124.
31 Companies Act 2006 ss 1094(3)(a)(vii), 1095(5). As to the registration of charges see PARA 1474 et seq.
32 Companies Act 2006 ss 1094(3)(a)(viii), 1095(5). As to the dissolution of a company see PARA 1703 et seq.
33 See the Small Business, Enterprise and Employment Act 2015 (Commencement No 4, Transitional and Savings Provisions) Regulations 2016, SI 2016/321, reg 6(c).
34 Ie under the Companies Act 2006 s 128E (see PARA 366).
35 Companies Act 2006 ss 1094(3)(a)(ix), 1095(5) (s 1094(3)(a)(ix) added by the Small Business, Enterprise and Employment Act 2015 Sch 5 Pt 2 paras 11, 32).
36 Companies Act 2006 s 1095(5).

159. Rectification of the register on application to the registrar of companies. On application[1], and subject to certain exceptions[2], the registrar of companies must remove from the register any relevant material[3] that either derives from anything invalid or ineffective or that was done without the authority of the company or overseas company to which the material relates[4], or that is factually inaccurate, or is derived from something that is factually inaccurate or forged[5]. An application to the registrar for the removal from the register, on such a ground[6], of:

(1) material that was included in a standard form required for giving notice[7] of a change of address of the registered office, or of material that is derived from material that was included in such a form, may be made by, and only by, the company to which the material relates[8];

(2) material that was included in, or is derived from material that was included in, so much of a standard form required for delivering a return in relation to an overseas company[9] as is required for details of the alteration of particulars[10] may be made by, and only by, the overseas company to which the material relates[11]; and

(3) other relevant material[12] may be made by, and (subject to a prescribed exception[13]) only by, the person by whom the relevant company form or relevant overseas company form, as the case may be, was delivered to the registrar[14], by the company or overseas company to which the material relates[15], or by any other person to whom the material relates[16].

Such an application to the registrar must, in addition to satisfying the relevant requirements of the Companies Act 2006[17]:

(a) state the applicant's name and address[18];

(b) where the application is an application referred to in head (1) or head (2) above, confirm that the applicant is the company or, as the case may be, the overseas company to which the relevant material which is the subject of the application relates[19];

(c) where the applicant is making the application in reliance on the exception to head (3) above[20], confirm that the person named in the relevant material which is the subject of the application has consented to the applicant making the application on that person's behalf, or explain the basis on which the applicant is otherwise entitled to make the application on that person's behalf[21];

(d) in any other case, state whether the applicant is a person by whom the relevant company form or relevant overseas company form, as the case may be, was delivered to the registrar, or is the company or overseas company to which the material relates or is any other person to whom the material relates[22]; and

(e) state whether the relevant material which is the subject of the application derives from anything invalid or ineffective[23], derives from anything that was done without the authority of the company or overseas company to which the material relates[24], is factually inaccurate or is derived from something that is factually inaccurate[25], or is derived from something that is forged[26].

Where the application is an application referred to in head (1) above, the registrar must give notice of the application to the person who delivered the standard form mentioned in that regulation to the registrar (but only if the registrar knows the identity and name and address of that person)[27], to every person who, to the registrar's knowledge, was a director or secretary of the company at the time when the application was delivered to the registrar[28], and to the company at the address of its registered office[29]. Where the material which is the subject of the application relates to a company (rather than an overseas company), but the application is not an application referred to in head (1) above, the registrar must give notice of the application to every person mentioned in head (3) above whose identity and name and address the registrar knows, other than the applicant[30], and every person who, to the registrar's knowledge, was a director or secretary of the company at the time when the application was delivered to the registrar[31].

Where the application is an application referred to in head (2) above, the registrar must give notice of the application to the person who delivered the standard form[32] to the registrar (but only if the registrar knows the identity and name and address of that person)[33], to every person duly registered[34], at the time when the application was delivered to the registrar, as a director or secretary of the overseas company[35], to every person duly registered[36] (at the time when the application was delivered to the registrar) as a person authorised to accept service of documents on behalf of the overseas company in respect of a UK establishment of the company[37], and to every person duly registered[38] (at the time when the application was delivered to the registrar) as a permanent representative of the overseas company in respect of a UK establishment of the company[39], and to the overseas company[40]. Where the material which is the subject of the application relates to an overseas company, but the application is not an application referred to in head (2) above, the registrar must give notice of the application to every person mentioned in head (3) above whose identity and name and address the registrar knows, other than the applicant[41], to every person duly registered[42], at the time when the application was delivered to the registrar, as a director or secretary of the overseas company[43], and to every person duly registered[44] (at the time when the application was delivered to the registrar) as a person authorised to accept service of documents on behalf of the overseas company in respect of a UK establishment of the company[45], and to every person duly registered[46] (at the time when the application was delivered to the registrar) as a permanent representative of the overseas company in respect of a UK establishment of the company[47].

Where the material which is the subject of the application is material that was included in, or is derived from material that was included in, a relevant overseas company form[48], the notice which the registrar is required[49] to give to the overseas company must be given to the company at the address which was, at the time when the application was delivered to the registrar, duly registered[50] as the address of the company's UK establishment to which the material relates, and notice need not be given to the company at any other address[51].

The notice of the application so given by the registrar[52] must:

(i) where the material which is the subject of the application relates to a company (rather than an overseas company), state the name and registered number of the company to which the material relates[53];
(ii) where the material which is the subject of the application relates to an overseas company, state the overseas company's name as duly registered[54] and its registered number as duly allocated[55];
(iii) where the material which is the subject of the application is material that was included in, or is derived from material that was included in, a relevant overseas company form[56] state the registered number duly allocated[57] to the UK establishment to which the material relates[58];
(iv) specify what is to be removed from the register and indicate where on the register it is[59];
(v) state the information provided to the registrar under head (d) above[60];
(vi) state the date on which the notice is issued[61];
(vii) give particulars of the recipient's right to object to the application and the requirements applying to that right[62];
(viii) explain the effect of a valid objection being made[63]; and
(ix) explain the effect of the provisions which govern rectification of the register by the registrar[64].

An objection to an application[65] may be made to the registrar by any person[66]; and such an objection must be made by giving notice in writing to the registrar, and the notice must state the name and address of the person making the objection and identify the application to which the objection relates[67]. A person to whom notice of an application was duly given[68] and who wishes to object to the application must do so before the end of the period of 28 days beginning with the date on which that notice was issued, as stated in the notice[69]. However, the registrar must not take account of an objection made by any other person after the end of the period of 28 days beginning with the date on which the notices[70] were issued[71]. If a valid objection is made to the application, the registrar must reject the application[72]. When a valid objection is made, the registrar must also send an acknowledgment of receipt to the person who made the objection[73], notify the applicant of the fact that an objection has been made[74], and notify every other person to whom the registrar gave due notice[75] (but not the person who made the objection or any other person who has made an objection)[76]. If no valid objection is made, the registrar must notify the applicant of that fact[77].

1 Ie under the Registrar of Companies and Applications for Striking Off Regulations 2009, SI 2009/1803, reg 4: see reg 4(1).

2 The Registrar of Companies and Applications for Striking Off Regulations 2009, SI 2009/1803, reg 4(1) (see the text and notes 3–5) does not apply in the following circumstances (see reg 4(1A) (added by SI 2016/441)), ie:

(1) in a case mentioned in the Companies Act 2006 s 1095(4A) (application for removal from register of material about directors: see PARA 158), if the registrar is required under s 1095(4B) not to remove the material from the register;

(2) in any other case, if there is a valid objection to the application.

For these purposes, a 'valid objection' is either an objection made in accordance with the Registrar of Companies and Applications for Striking Off Regulations 2009, SI 2009/1803, reg 5(10) (see the text and note 67) and reg 5(11) (see the text and notes 68–69) by a person to whom notice of the application was given under reg 5(2), (3), (4) or (5) (see the text and notes 27–47), or an objection made in accordance with reg 5(10) by any other person which is not an objection that the registrar of companies is prevented from taking into account under reg 5(12) (see the text and notes 70–71): regs 1(2), 4(8). As to the meaning of 'registrar of companies' see PARA 126 note 2. As to the Secretary of State's duty to carry out a review of the Registrar of Companies and Applications for Striking Off (Amendment) Regulations 2016, SI 2016/441, see reg 3.

3 For these purposes, 'relevant material' means material on the register that was included in, or is derived from material that was included in, a relevant company form or a relevant overseas company form delivered to the registrar by any person: Registrar of Companies and Applications for Striking Off Regulations 2009, SI 2009/1803, regs 1(2), 4(2). A 'relevant company form' is either a standard form required for giving notice under the Companies Act 2006 s 87 (change of address of registered office) (see PARA 124), s 167 or s 167D (changes relating to directors) (see PARAS 550, 553) or s 276 (changes relating to secretaries) (see PARA 674), or so much of a standard form required for delivering an application under s 9 (application for registration of a company) (see PARA 104) as is required for the statement of a company's proposed officers referred to in s 9(4)(c): Registrar of Companies and Applications for Striking Off Regulations 2009, SI 2009/1803, regs 1(2), 4(3). A 'relevant overseas company form' is either of the following (see regs 1(2), 4(4)), ie:

(1) so much of a standard form required for delivering a return under the Overseas Companies Regulations 2009, SI 2009/1801, reg 4 (see PARA 2015) as is required for the list referred to in reg 6(1)(d) (list of directors and secretary of an overseas company) (see PARA 2015), for the names and service addresses referred to in reg 7(1)(e) (names and service addresses of persons authorised to accept service of documents on behalf of an overseas company in respect of a UK establishment) (see PARA 2015) or for the list referred to in reg 7(1)(f) (list of permanent representatives of an overseas company in respect of a UK establishment) (see PARA 2015); or

(2) so much of a standard form required for delivering a return under reg 13 as is required for details of the alteration of particulars delivered under reg 6(1)(d), reg 7(1)(a) (address of UK establishment) (see PARA 2015), reg 7(1)(e) or reg 7(1)(f).

For these purposes, 'required' means required by rules made by the registrar under the Companies Act 2006 s 1117 (see PARA 131): see the Registrar of Companies and Applications for Striking Off Regulations 2009, SI 2009/1803, reg 4(9). As to the meaning of 'overseas company' see PARA 2013.

4 Registrar of Companies and Applications for Striking Off Regulations 2009, SI 2009/1803, reg 4(1)(a).

5 Registrar of Companies and Applications for Striking Off Regulations 2009, SI 2009/1803, reg 4(1)(b).
6 Ie on the grounds in the Registrar of Companies and Applications for Striking Off Regulations 2009, SI 2009/1803, reg 4(1) (see the text and notes 1–5): see reg 4(5)–(7).
7 Ie under the Companies Act 2006 s 87 (see PARA 124): see the Registrar of Companies and Applications for Striking Off Regulations 2009, SI 2009/1803, reg 4(5).
8 Registrar of Companies and Applications for Striking Off Regulations 2009, SI 2009/1803, reg 4(5).
9 Ie under the Overseas Companies Regulations 2009, SI 2009/1801, reg 13 (see PARA 2015): see the Registrar of Companies and Applications for Striking Off Regulations 2009, SI 2009/1803, reg 4(6).
10 Ie under the Overseas Companies Regulations 2009, SI 2009/1801, reg 7(1)(a) (address of UK establishment) (see PARA 2015): see the Registrar of Companies and Applications for Striking Off Regulations 2009, SI 2009/1803, reg 4(6).
11 Registrar of Companies and Applications for Striking Off Regulations 2009, SI 2009/1803, reg 4(6).
12 Ie relevant material other than material referred to in the Registrar of Companies and Applications for Striking Off Regulations 2009, SI 2009/1803, reg 4(5), (6) (see the text and notes 6–11): see reg 4(7).
13 An application specifying material of the kind mentioned in the Companies Act 2006 s 1095(4A)(a) (material naming a person as a director: see PARA 158), which is accompanied by a statement of the kind mentioned in s 1095(4A)(b), may also be made on behalf of the person named in the material: Registrar of Companies and Applications for Striking Off Regulations 2009, SI 2009/1803, reg 4(7A) (added by SI 2016/441).
14 Registrar of Companies and Applications for Striking Off Regulations 2009, SI 2009/1803, reg 4(7)(a). See also note 13.
15 Registrar of Companies and Applications for Striking Off Regulations 2009, SI 2009/1803, reg 4(7)(b). See also note 13.
16 Registrar of Companies and Applications for Striking Off Regulations 2009, SI 2009/1803, reg 4(7)(c). See also note 13.
17 Ie in addition to satisfying the requirements of the Companies Act 2006 s 1095(3) (see PARA 158): see the Registrar of Companies and Applications for Striking Off Regulations 2009, SI 2009/1803, reg 5(1).
18 Registrar of Companies and Applications for Striking Off Regulations 2009, SI 2009/1803, reg 5(1)(a).
19 Registrar of Companies and Applications for Striking Off Regulations 2009, SI 2009/1803, reg 5(1)(b).
20 Ie in reliance on the Registrar of Companies and Applications for Striking Off Regulations 2009, SI 2009/1803, reg 4(7A): see note 13.
21 Registrar of Companies and Applications for Striking Off Regulations 2009, SI 2009/1803, reg 5(1)(ba) (added by SI 2016/441).
22 Registrar of Companies and Applications for Striking Off Regulations 2009, SI 2009/1803, regs 4(7), 5(1)(c). Head (d) in the text requires the application to state whether the applicant is a person mentioned in reg 4(7)(a) (see the text and note 14), a person mentioned in reg 4(7)(b) (see the text and note 15) or a person mentioned in reg 4(7)(c) (see the text and note 16): see reg 5(1)(c).
23 Registrar of Companies and Applications for Striking Off Regulations 2009, SI 2009/1803, reg 5(1)(d)(i).
24 Registrar of Companies and Applications for Striking Off Regulations 2009, SI 2009/1803, reg 5(1)(d)(ii).
25 Registrar of Companies and Applications for Striking Off Regulations 2009, SI 2009/1803, reg 5(1)(d)(iii).
26 Registrar of Companies and Applications for Striking Off Regulations 2009, SI 2009/1803, reg 5(1)(d)(iv).
27 Registrar of Companies and Applications for Striking Off Regulations 2009, SI 2009/1803, reg 5(2)(a). As to the notice that is required to be so given see the text and notes 52–64.
28 Registrar of Companies and Applications for Striking Off Regulations 2009, SI 2009/1803, reg 5(2)(b). As to the notice that is required to be so given see the text and notes 52–64.
29 Registrar of Companies and Applications for Striking Off Regulations 2009, SI 2009/1803, reg 5(2)(c). As to the notice that is required to be so given see the text and notes 52–64. As to a company's registered office see PARA 124.
30 Registrar of Companies and Applications for Striking Off Regulations 2009, SI 2009/1803, reg 5(3)(a). As to the notice that is required to be so given see the text and notes 52–64.

31 Registrar of Companies and Applications for Striking Off Regulations 2009, SI 2009/1803, reg 5(3)(b). As to the notice that is required to be so given see the text and notes 52–64.
32 Ie the standard form mentioned in the Registrar of Companies and Applications for Striking Off Regulations 2009, SI 2009/1803, reg 4(6) (see the text and notes 9–11): see reg 5(4)(a).
33 Registrar of Companies and Applications for Striking Off Regulations 2009, SI 2009/1803, reg 5(4)(a). As to the notice that is required to be so given see the text and notes 52–64.
34 Ie under the Overseas Companies Regulations 2009, SI 2009/1801, reg 4 or reg 13 (see PARA 2015): see the Registrar of Companies and Applications for Striking Off Regulations 2009, SI 2009/1803, reg 5(4)(b).
35 Registrar of Companies and Applications for Striking Off Regulations 2009, SI 2009/1803, reg 5(4)(b). As to the notice that is required to be so given see the text and notes 52–64.
36 Ie under the Overseas Companies Regulations 2009, SI 2009/1801, reg 4 or reg 13 (see PARA 2015): see the Registrar of Companies and Applications for Striking Off Regulations 2009, SI 2009/1803, reg 5(4)(c), (6)(a).
37 Registrar of Companies and Applications for Striking Off Regulations 2009, SI 2009/1803, reg 5(4)(c), (6)(a). As to the notice that is required to be so given see the text and notes 52–64. For these purposes, 'UK establishment' has the meaning given in the Companies Act 2006 s 1067(6) (see PARA 135): see the Registrar of Companies and Applications for Striking Off Regulations 2009, SI 2009/1803, reg 5(16).
38 Ie under the Overseas Companies Regulations 2009, SI 2009/1801, reg 4 or reg 13 (see PARA 2015): see the Registrar of Companies and Applications for Striking Off Regulations 2009, SI 2009/1803, reg 5(4)(c), (6)(b).
39 Registrar of Companies and Applications for Striking Off Regulations 2009, SI 2009/1803, reg 5(4)(c), (6)(b). As to the notice that is required to be so given see the text and notes 52–64.
40 Registrar of Companies and Applications for Striking Off Regulations 2009, SI 2009/1803, reg 5(4)(d). As to the notice that is required to be so given see the text and notes 52–64.
41 Registrar of Companies and Applications for Striking Off Regulations 2009, SI 2009/1803, reg 5(5)(a). As to the notice that is required to be so given see the text and notes 52–64.
42 Ie under the Overseas Companies Regulations 2009, SI 2009/1801, reg 4 or reg 13 (see PARA 2015): see the Registrar of Companies and Applications for Striking Off Regulations 2009, SI 2009/1803, reg 5(5)(b).
43 Registrar of Companies and Applications for Striking Off Regulations 2009, SI 2009/1803, reg 5(5)(b). As to the notice that is required to be so given see the text and notes 52–64.
44 Ie under the Overseas Companies Regulations 2009, SI 2009/1801, reg 4 or reg 13 (see PARA 2015): see the Registrar of Companies and Applications for Striking Off Regulations 2009, SI 2009/1803, reg 5(5)(c), (6)(a).
45 Registrar of Companies and Applications for Striking Off Regulations 2009, SI 2009/1803, reg 5(5)(c), (6)(a). As to the notice that is required to be so given see the text and notes 52–64.
46 Ie under the Overseas Companies Regulations 2009, SI 2009/1801, reg 4 or reg 13 (see PARA 2015): see the Registrar of Companies and Applications for Striking Off Regulations 2009, SI 2009/1803, reg 5(5)(c), (6)(b).
47 Registrar of Companies and Applications for Striking Off Regulations 2009, SI 2009/1803, reg 5(5)(c), (6)(b). As to the notice that is required to be so given see the text and notes 52–64.
48 Ie as described in the Registrar of Companies and Applications for Striking Off Regulations 2009, SI 2009/1803, reg 4(4), except in relation to references made therein to the list that is referred to in the Overseas Companies Regulations 2009, SI 2009/1801, reg 6(1)(d) (see note 3): see the Registrar of Companies and Applications for Striking Off Regulations 2009, SI 2009/1803, reg 5(7).
49 Ie by the Registrar of Companies and Applications for Striking Off Regulations 2009, SI 2009/1803, reg 5(4) (see the text and notes 32–40) or reg 5(5) (see the text and notes 41–47): see reg 5(7).
50 Ie under the Overseas Companies Regulations 2009, SI 2009/1801, reg 4 or reg 13 (see PARA 2015): see the Registrar of Companies and Applications for Striking Off Regulations 2009, SI 2009/1803, reg 5(7).
51 Registrar of Companies and Applications for Striking Off Regulations 2009, SI 2009/1803, reg 5(7).
52 Ie under the Registrar of Companies and Applications for Striking Off Regulations 2009, SI 2009/1803, reg 5(2) (see the text and notes 27–29), reg 5(3) (see the text and notes 30–31), reg 5(4) (see the text and notes 32–40), or reg 5(5) (see the text and notes 41–47): see reg 5(8).
53 Registrar of Companies and Applications for Striking Off Regulations 2009, SI 2009/1803, reg 5(8)(a).
54 Ie under the Overseas Companies Regulations 2009, SI 2009/1801, reg 4 or reg 13 (see PARA 2015) or under the Companies Act 2006 s 1048 (see PARA 2016): see the Registrar of Companies and Applications for Striking Off Regulations 2009, SI 2009/1803, reg 5(8)(b).

55 Registrar of Companies and Applications for Striking Off Regulations 2009, SI 2009/1803, reg 5(8)(b). The text refers to a registered number allocated under the Companies Act 2006 s 1066 (see PARA 134): see the Registrar of Companies and Applications for Striking Off Regulations 2009, SI 2009/1803, reg 5(8)(b).

56 Ie as described in the Registrar of Companies and Applications for Striking Off Regulations 2009, SI 2009/1803, reg 4(4), except in relation to references made therein to the list that is referred to in the Overseas Companies Regulations 2009, SI 2009/1801, reg 6(1)(d) (see note 3): see reg 5(8)(c).

57 Ie allocated under the Companies Act 2006 s 1067 (see PARA 135): see the Registrar of Companies and Applications for Striking Off Regulations 2009, SI 2009/1803, reg 5(8)(c).

58 Registrar of Companies and Applications for Striking Off Regulations 2009, SI 2009/1803, reg 5(8)(c).

59 Registrar of Companies and Applications for Striking Off Regulations 2009, SI 2009/1803, reg 5(8)(d).

60 Registrar of Companies and Applications for Striking Off Regulations 2009, SI 2009/1803, reg 5(8)(e).

61 Registrar of Companies and Applications for Striking Off Regulations 2009, SI 2009/1803, reg 5(8)(f).

62 Registrar of Companies and Applications for Striking Off Regulations 2009, SI 2009/1803, reg 5(8)(g). Head (vii) in the text refers to the requirements applying to the right to object under reg 5(10) (see the text and note 67) and reg 5(11) (see the text and notes 68–69): see reg 5(8)(g).

Regulation 5(15B)–(15F) applies in a case mentioned in the Companies Act 2006 s 1095(4A) (see PARA 158) (but not in any other case), in place of the Registrar of Companies and Applications for Striking Off Regulations 2009, SI 2009/1803, reg 5(8)(g)–(i), (9)–(15): reg 5(15A) (reg 5(15A)–(15F) added by SI 2016/441). The notice of the application given by the registrar under reg 5(3) must give particulars of the right of the company to which the application relates to provide the registrar with evidence that the person named in the material did consent to act as a director of the company and of the requirements applying to that right under reg 5(15C); and must explain the effect of reg 4(1), (1A)(a), reg 5(15F) and the Companies Act 2006 s 1095(4B), (4C): Registrar of Companies and Applications for Striking Off Regulations 2009, SI 2009/1803, reg 5(15B) (as so added). If the company to which the application relates wishes to provide the registrar with evidence that the person named in the material did consent to act as a director of the company, it must, before the end of the period of 28 days beginning with the date on which the registrar's notice under reg 5(3) was issued (as stated in the notice), provide the registrar with the evidence in writing (and identify the application to which the evidence relates) (reg 5(15C)(a) (as so added)) and provide the registrar with a statement by the company that the evidence provided by it is true and is not misleading or deceptive in any material particular (reg 5(15C)((b) as so added)). If the registrar is provided by the company with evidence and a statement as mentioned in reg 5(15C), the registrar must send an acknowledgement of receipt to the company: reg 5(15D) (as so added). The registrar must notify the applicant and every person to whom a notice was given under reg 5(3) of the outcome of the application: reg 5(15E) (as so added). If the outcome of the application is that the registrar does not remove the material from the register, the notice to the applicant under reg 5(15E) must be accompanied by a copy of the evidence provided by the company to the registrar under reg (15C)(a): reg 5(15F) (as so added).

63 Registrar of Companies and Applications for Striking Off Regulations 2009, SI 2009/1803, reg 5(8)(h). Head (viii) in the text refers to the effect of reg 5(13) (see the text and note 72): see reg 5(8)(h). See also note 62.

64 Registrar of Companies and Applications for Striking Off Regulations 2009, SI 2009/1803, reg 5(8)(i). Head (ix) in the text refers to the effect of reg 4(1), (1A)(b) (see the text and notes 1–5) and the Companies Act 2006 s 1095(4) (see PARA 158): see the Registrar of Companies and Applications for Striking Off Regulations 2009, SI 2009/1803, reg 5(8)(i) (amended by SI 2016/441). See also note 62.

65 Ie under the Registrar of Companies and Applications for Striking Off Regulations 2009, SI 2009/1803, reg 4 (see the text and notes 1–15): see reg 5(9).

66 Registrar of Companies and Applications for Striking Off Regulations 2009, SI 2009/1803, reg 5(9). See also note 62.

67 Registrar of Companies and Applications for Striking Off Regulations 2009, SI 2009/1803, reg 5(10). See also note 62.

68 Ie under the Registrar of Companies and Applications for Striking Off Regulations 2009, SI 2009/1803, reg 5(2) (see the text and notes 27–29), reg 5(3) (see the text and notes 30–31), reg 5(4) (see the text and notes 32–40), or reg 5(5) (see the text and notes 41–47): see reg 5(11).

69 Registrar of Companies and Applications for Striking Off Regulations 2009, SI 2009/1803, reg 5(11). See also note 62.

70 Ie under the Registrar of Companies and Applications for Striking Off Regulations 2009, SI 2009/1803, reg 5(2) (see the text and notes 27–29), reg 5(3) (see the text and notes 30–31), reg 5(4) (see the text and notes 32–40), or reg 5(5) (see the text and notes 41–47): see reg 5(12).
71 Registrar of Companies and Applications for Striking Off Regulations 2009, SI 2009/1803, reg 5(12). See also note 62.
72 Registrar of Companies and Applications for Striking Off Regulations 2009, SI 2009/1803, reg 5(13). See also note 62.
73 Registrar of Companies and Applications for Striking Off Regulations 2009, SI 2009/1803, reg 5(14)(a). See also note 62.
74 Registrar of Companies and Applications for Striking Off Regulations 2009, SI 2009/1803, reg 5(14)(b). See also note 62.
75 Ie under the Registrar of Companies and Applications for Striking Off Regulations 2009, SI 2009/1803, reg 5(2) (see the text and notes 27–29), reg 5(3) (see the text and notes 30–31), reg 5(4) (see the text and notes 32–40), or reg 5(5) (see the text and notes 41–47): see reg 5(14)(c).
76 Registrar of Companies and Applications for Striking Off Regulations 2009, SI 2009/1803, reg 5(14)(c). See also note 62.
77 Registrar of Companies and Applications for Striking Off Regulations 2009, SI 2009/1803, reg 5(15). See also note 62.

160. Rectification of register relating to company registered office. The Secretary of State[1] may make provision by regulations[2] requiring the registrar of companies[3], on application, to change the address of a company's registered office[4] if the registrar is satisfied that the company is not authorised to use the address[5]. The applicant and the company must provide such information as the registrar may require for the purposes of determining such an application[6].

The regulations may make provision as to:

(1) who may make an application[7];
(2) the information to be included in and documents to accompany an application[8];
(3) the notice to be given of an application and of its outcome[9];
(4) the period in which objections to an application may be made[10];
(5) how an application is to be determined, including in particular the evidence, or descriptions of evidence, which the registrar may without further inquiry rely on to be satisfied that the company is authorised to use the address[11];
(6) the referral of the application, or any question relating to the application, by the registrar for determination by the court[12];
(7) the registrar requiring a company to provide an address to be the company's registered office[13];
(8) the nomination by the registrar of an address (a 'default address') to be the company's registered office[14];
(9) the effect of the registration of any change[15].

Provision made by virtue of head (9) above may in particular include provision, in relation to the registration of a default address:

(a) for the suspension, for up to 28 days beginning with the date on which it is registered, of duties of the company under the Companies Act 2006 relating to the inspection of company records or to the provision, disclosure or display of information[16];
(b) that the default address may not be used for the purpose of keeping the company's registers, indexes or other documents[17];
(c) for there to be no requirement that documents delivered to the default address for the company must be opened[18];
(d) for the collection of such documents by the company, or the forwarding of such documents to the company[19];

(e) for the circumstances in which, and the period of time after which, such documents may be destroyed[20];

(f) about evidence, or descriptions of evidence, that the registrar may require a company to provide if giving notice to the registrar to change the address of its registered office from a default address[21].

Subject to further provision which may be made by virtue of head (9) above, the change takes effect upon it being registered by the registrar, but until the end of the period of 14 days beginning with the date on which it is registered a person may validly serve any document on the company at the address previously registered[22].

The applicant or the company may appeal the outcome of an application under these provisions to the court[23]. On an appeal, the court must direct the registrar to register such address as the registered office of the company as the court considers appropriate in all the circumstances of the case[24]. The regulations may make further provision about an appeal and in particular:

(i) provision about the time within which an appeal must be brought and the grounds on which an appeal may be brought[25];

(ii) provision for the suspension, pending the outcome of an appeal, of duties of the company under the Companies Act 2006 relating to the inspection of company records or to the provision, disclosure or display of information[26];

(iii) further provision about directions[27] by the court to the registrar on such an appeal[28].

In the exercise of the above power, the Secretary of State has made the Companies (Address of Registered Office) Regulations 2016[29]. Those regulations make provision:

(A) allowing an application to the registrar to change the address of a company's registered office to be made by any person[30];

(B) for the withdrawal of such an application[31];

(C) as to the procedure to be followed by the registrar following receipt of such an application[32];

(D) requiring the registrar to change the address of a company's registered office to a default address[33] if he is satisfied that the company is not authorised to use the address as its registered office, or if the company does not respond to the registrar within the specified period[34];

(E) requiring the registrar to dismiss an application if neither of the circumstances set out in head (D) above applies, or if the company delivers to the registrar a notice to change the address of the company's registered office[35] within the specified period[36];

(F) as to the manner in which the registrar is to determine an application[37];

(G) for the registrar to give notice of his decision[38];

(H) as to the effect of a change of address[39];

(I) prohibiting the use of the default address for the purpose of keeping, or making available for inspection, the company's registers, indexes or other documents[40];

(J) as to administration of the default address[41];

(K) as to appeals[42]; and

(L) for the Secretary of State to carry out a review of those regulations[43].

1 As to the Secretary of State see PARA 6.

2 Regulations under the Companies Act 2006 s 1097A (see the text and notes 3–28) are subject to affirmative resolution procedure (ie the regulations must not be made unless a draft of the statutory instrument containing them has been laid before Parliament and approved by a resolution of each House of Parliament): see ss 1097A(10), 1290 (s 1097A added by the Small

Business, Enterprise and Employment Act 2015 s 99(1)). As to the making of regulations under the Companies Act 2006 generally see ss 1288–1292.

The regulations may include such provision applying (including applying with modifications), amending or repealing an enactment contained in the Companies Act 2006 as the Secretary of State considers necessary or expedient in consequence of any provision made by the regulations: s 1097A(9) (as so added).

3 As to the meaning of 'registrar of companies' see PARA 126 note 2. As to the meaning of 'company' under the Companies Acts see PARA 21; and as to the meaning of the 'Companies Acts' see PARA 13. As to the application of the Companies Act 2006 Pt 35 (ss 1059A–1119) (see also PARAS 126, 130 et seq, 161 et seq) see PARA 126 note 1.

4 As to a company's registered office see PARA 124.

5 Companies Act 2006 s 1097A(1) (as added: see note 2).

6 Companies Act 2006 s 1097A(2) (as added: see note 2). Any application or other document delivered to the registrar under s 1097A must not be made available by the registrar for public inspection: see s 1087(1)(ga); and PARA 146.

7 Companies Act 2006 s 1097A(3)(a) (as added: see note 2).

8 Companies Act 2006 s 1097A(3)(b) (as added: see note 2). As to the meaning of 'document' for these purposes see PARA 136 note 2.

9 Companies Act 2006 s 1097A(3)(c) (as added: see note 2).

10 Companies Act 2006 s 1097A(3)(d) (as added: see note 2).

11 Companies Act 2006 s 1097A(3)(e) (as added: see note 2).

12 Companies Act 2006 ss 1097A(3)(f) (as added: see note 2). Except as otherwise provided, in the Companies Acts 'the court' means, in England and Wales, the High Court or the County Court: Companies Act 2006 s 1156(1)(a) (amended by the Crime and Courts Act 2013 Sch 9 Pt 2 para 43(a)). The provisions of the Companies Acts conferring jurisdiction on 'the court' as defined above have effect subject to any enactment or rule of law relating to the allocation of jurisdiction or distribution of business between courts in any part of the United Kingdom: Companies Act 2006 s 1156(2). As to the meaning of 'United Kingdom' see PARA 1 note 5.

13 Companies Act 2006 s 1097A(3)(g) (as added: see note 2).

14 Companies Act 2006 s 1097A(3)(h) (as added: see note 2).

15 Companies Act 2006 s 1097A(3)(i) (as added: see note 2).

16 Companies Act 2006 s 1097A(5)(a) (as added: see note 2).

17 Companies Act 2006 s 1097A(5)(b) (as added: see note 2).

18 Companies Act 2006 s 1097A(5)(c) (as added: see note 2).

19 Companies Act 2006 s 1097A(5)(d) (as added: see note 2).

20 Companies Act 2006 s 1097A(5)(e) (as added: see note 2).

21 Companies Act 2006 s 1097A(5)(f) (as added: see note 2).

22 Companies Act 2006 s 1097A(4) (as added: see note 2).

23 Companies Act 2006 s 1097A(6) (as added: see note 2).

24 Companies Act 2006 s 1097A(7) (as added: see note 2).

25 Companies Act 2006 s 1097A(8)(a) (as added: see note 2).

26 Companies Act 2006 s 1097A(8)(b) (as added: see note 2).

27 Ie directions by virtue of the Companies Act 2006 s 1097A(7) (see the text and note 24).

28 See the Companies Act 2006 s 1097A(8)(c) (as added: see note 2).

29 Ie the Companies (Address of Registered Office) Regulations 2016, SI 2016/423, which came into force on 6 April 2016: see reg 1(1).

30 See the Companies (Address of Registered Office) Regulations 2016, SI 2016/423, reg 2. An application to the registrar must state the applicant's name and address, identify the company and the address of its registered office, include a statement explaining the grounds of the application and provide any documents or information which support or supports the application: see reg 3.

31 An application under the Companies (Address of Registered Office) Regulations 2016, SI 2016/423, may be withdrawn by the applicant by written notice to the registrar: reg 4(1). Where an application is withdrawn, the registrar must notify the company of the withdrawal: reg 4(2).

32 Upon receiving an application, the registrar must either:

(1) dismiss the application if the registrar considers there is no reasonable chance of the application succeeding and notify the applicant of the decision under the Companies (Address of Registered Office) Regulations 2016, SI 2016/423, reg 10 (see note 38) (reg 5(1)(a)); or

(2) give notice of the application to the company at the address of its registered office, the service address of every person who (to the registrar's knowledge) is a director or secretary of the company, the residential address of every person who (to the registrar's knowledge) is a director of the company, and an address specified by the

company for communications in electronic form under the Companies Act 2006 Sch 4 para 7 (see PARA 751) (Companies (Address of Registered Office) Regulations 2016, SI 2016/423, reg 5(1)(b)).

As to the notice to be given under head (2) above see further reg 6(1), (2). For these purposes, 'residential address' means the usual residential address of a director of a company stated in the company's register of directors' residential addresses and notified to the registrar under the Companies Act 2006 s 167 (see PARA 550); and 'service address' means an address notified to the registrar under s 167 or s 276 (see PARA 674) respectively, which is one of the following (Companies (Address of Registered Office) Regulations 2016, SI 2016/423, reg 1(2)), ie:

(a) in the case of a director or secretary who is an individual, the address stated in the company's register of directors or register of secretaries respectively;

(b) in the case of a director or secretary who is a body corporate or a firm that is a legal person under the law by which it is governed, the address of its registered or principal office stated in the company's register of directors or register of secretaries respectively.

33 For these purposes, 'default address' means an address nominated by the registrar by virtue of rules made under the Companies Act 2006 s 1117 (see PARA 110): Companies (Address of Registered Office) Regulations 2016, SI 2016/423, reg 1(2).

34 See the Companies (Address of Registered Office) Regulations 2016, SI 2016/423, reg 7. The 'specified period' must be must be at least 28 days beginning on the day after the day on which the notice was sent to the company, and may be extended at the discretion of the registrar at any time before the specified period ends: reg 6(2).

35 Ie under the Companies Act 2006 s 87: see PARA 124.

36 See the Companies (Address of Registered Office) Regulations 2016, SI 2016/423, reg 8.

37 For the purposes of determining the application, the registrar may:

(1) refer the application, or any question relating to the application, for determination by the court (Companies (Address of Registered Office) Regulations 2016, SI 2016/423, reg 9(a));

(2) without further inquiry rely on the evidence, or descriptions of evidence, listed in the Schedule, received in connection with an application under the 2016 Regulations, to be satisfied that the company is authorised to use the address (reg 9(b)); or

(3) consider information and documents received in connection with any previous application made under those regulations that is materially the same as the current application (reg 9(c)).

38 Upon determining an application, the registrar must provide notice of the decision to the applicant and to the company at each of the addresses listed in the Companies (Address of Registered Office) Regulations 2016, SI 2016/423, reg 5 (see note 32): reg 10(1). The notice must state the reasons for making the decision and provide a copy of any evidence upon which the registrar relied: reg 10(2). Where the registrar changes the address of a company's registered office to a default address, the registrar must also provide details of the default address to the company: reg 10(3).

39 Where the registrar changes the address of a company's registered office under the Companies Act 2006 s 1097A(7) (see the text and note 24) or the Companies (Address of Registered Office) Regulations 2016, SI 2016/423, the following duties of the company under the Companies Act 2006 are suspended for a period of 28 days beginning on the day the address was changed (Companies (Address of Registered Office) Regulations 2016, SI 2016/423, reg 11), ie:

(1) the duty under the following provisions of the Companies Act 2006 to make company records available for inspection: s 114 (register of members: see PARA 348); s 162 (register of directors: see PARA 535); s 228 (directors' service contracts or memorandum of terms: see PARA 565); s 237 (directors' indemnities: see PARA 643); s 275 (register of secretaries: see PARA 673); s 358 (records of resolutions etc: see PARA 741); s 388 (accounting records: see PARA 783); s 702 (contracts relating to the purchase of own shares: see PARA 1427); s 720 (documents relating to redemption or purchase of own shares out of capital by a private company: see PARA 1433); s 743 (register of debenture holders: see PARA 1504); s 805 (report to members of outcome of investigation by public company into interests in its shares: see PARA 462); s 809 (register of interests in shares disclosed to public company: see PARA 464); and s 859Q (instruments creating charges: see PARA 1472);

(2) the duty to display a company's registered name at the company's registered office under the Company, Limited Liability Partnership and Business (Names and Trading Disclosures) Regulations 2015, SI 2015/17, reg 21(1)(a) (see PARA 220);

(3) the duty to state information about the company's registered office in descriptions of document or communication specified under reg 25(1) (see PARA 220);

(4) the duty to provide information about a company's registered office on request to those persons the company deals with in the course of business under reg 27(1)(a) (see PARA 220).

40 See the Companies (Address of Registered Office) Regulations 2016, SI 2016/423, reg 12.

41 The registrar will not be required to open any documents delivered to the company at the default address: Companies (Address of Registered Office) Regulations 2016, SI 2016/423, reg 13. The registrar must provide for the collection by the company of any documents delivered to the company at the default address, unless the documents have been destroyed in accordance with reg 14(2): reg 14(1). The registrar may destroy any document not collected by the company 12 months after receipt of the document: reg 14(2). Where the company has changed the address of its registered office from the default address to a new address under the Companies Act 2006 s 87, the registrar may forward the documents to the new address: Companies (Address of Registered Office) Regulations 2016, SI 2016/423, reg 15.

42 An appeal to the court under the Companies Act 2006 s 1097A(6) (see the text and note 23) must be brought within a period of 28 days beginning on the day the address of a company's registered office is changed to a default address, or, where the registrar dismissed the application, the day a notice of the registrar's decision is sent under the Companies (Address of Registered Office) Regulations 2016, SI 2016/423, reg 10 (see note 38): reg 16. Where an appeal is brought before the court by the company, the duty to display a company's registered name at the company's registered office under the Company, Limited Liability Partnership and Business (Names and Trading Disclosures) Regulations 2015, SI 2015/17, reg 21(1)(a) is suspended until 28 days after the appeal is withdrawn or the court makes a decision: Companies (Address of Registered Office) Regulations 2016, SI 2016/423, reg 17.

43 See the Companies (Address of Registered Office) Regulations 2016, SI 2016/423, reg 22.

161. Rectification of the register under court order. The registrar of companies[1] must remove from the register[2] any material[3]:

(1) that derives from anything that the court has declared to be invalid or ineffective, or to have been done without the authority of the company[4]; or

(2) that a court declares to be factually inaccurate, or to be derived from something that is factually inaccurate, or forged[5],

and that the court directs should be removed from the register[6].

The court order must specify what is to be removed from the register and indicate where on the register it is[7]. However, the court must not make an order for the removal from the register of anything the registration of which has had legal consequences in relation to the company[8], as regards:

(a) its formation[9];
(b) a change of name[10];
(c) its re-registration[11];
(d) its becoming or ceasing to be a community interest company[12];
(e) a reduction of capital[13];
(f) a change of registered office[14];
(g) the registration of a charge[15];
(h) its dissolution[16]; or
(i) as from 30 June 2016[17], a change in its membership particulars of which were delivered to the registrar under the statutory duty[18] to notify him of changes while an election to keep information on the central register is in force[19],

unless satisfied[20] both that the presence of the material on the register has caused, or may cause, damage to the company[21], and that the company's interest in removing the material outweighs any interest of other persons in the material continuing to appear on the register[22].

Where in such a case the court does make an order for removal, it may make such consequential orders as appear just with respect to the legal effect, if any, to be accorded to the material by virtue of its having appeared on the register[23]. A copy of the court's order must be sent to the registrar for registration[24].

Where the court makes an order for the removal of anything from the register in this way[25], it may give the following directions[26]:

(i) it may direct that any note on the register[27] that is related to the material that is the subject of the court's order is to be removed from the register[28];
(ii) it may direct that its order must not be available for public inspection as part of the register[29];
(iii) it may direct that no note is to be made on the register as a result of its order[30], or that any such note must be restricted to such matters as may be specified by the court[31].

However, the court must not give any such direction[32] unless it is satisfied[33]:
(A) that either the presence on the register of the note, or, as the case may be, of an unrestricted note[34] or the availability for public inspection of the court's order[35], may cause damage to the company[36]; and
(B) that the company's interest in non-disclosure outweighs any interest of other persons in disclosure[37].

1 As to the meaning of 'registrar of companies' see PARA 126 note 2. As to the meaning of 'company' under the Companies Acts see PARA 21; and as to the meaning of the 'Companies Acts' see PARA 13. As to the application of the Companies Act 2006 Pt 35 (ss 1059A–1119) (see also PARAS 126, 130 et seq, 162 et seq) see PARA 126 note 1.
2 As to the meaning of the 'register' see PARA 142.
3 Companies Act 2006 s 1096(1).
4 Companies Act 2006 s 1096(1)(a). As to the meaning of 'the court' see PARA 160 note 12.
5 Companies Act 2006 s 1096(1)(b).
6 Companies Act 2006 s 1096(1). The provisions of s 1096 do not apply where the court has other, specific, powers to deal with the matter, for example under the provisions of Pt 15 (ss 380–474) (see PARA 765 et seq) relating to the revision of defective accounts and reports (see PARA 963 et seq), or s 859M (rectification of register of charges) (see PARA 1470): s 1096(6) (amended by SI 2013/600). The registrar is required to give public notice of the removal from the register of any document which is subject to the Directive disclosure requirements (as to which see the Companies Act 2006 s 1078; and PARA 139) or of any material derived from such a document: see PARA 139. As to the meaning of 'document' for these purposes see PARA 136 note 2.
7 Companies Act 2006 s 1096(2).
8 Companies Act 2006 s 1096(3).
9 Companies Act 2006 ss 1094(3)(a)(i), 1096(3). As to company formation under the Companies Act 2006 see PARA 95 et seq.
10 Companies Act 2006 ss 1094(3)(a)(ii), 1096(3). As to change of a company's name see PARAS 216–218.
11 Companies Act 2006 ss 1094(3)(a)(iii), 1096(3). As to company re-registration and its effects generally see PARA 167 et seq.
12 Companies Act 2006 ss 1094(3)(a)(iv), 1096(3). As to becoming a community interest company see PARA 75; and as to ceasing to be a community interest company see PARA 192.
13 Companies Act 2006 ss 1094(3)(a)(v), 1096(3). As to reduction of share capital generally see PARA 1360 et seq. As to the meaning of 'share capital' see PARA 1231.
14 Companies Act 2006 ss 1094(3)(a)(vi), 1096(3). As to changes in the situation of a company's registered office see PARA 124.
15 Companies Act 2006 ss 1094(3)(a)(vii), 1096(3). As to the registration of charges see PARA 1474 et seq.
16 Companies Act 2006 ss 1094(3)(a)(viii), 1096(3). As to the dissolution of a company see PARA 1703 et seq.
17 See the Small Business, Enterprise and Employment Act 2015 (Commencement No 4, Transitional and Savings Provisions) Regulations 2016, SI 2016/321, reg 6(c).
18 Ie under the Companies Act 2006 s 128E (see PARA 366).
19 Companies Act 2006 ss 1094(3)(a)(ix), 1096(3) (s 1094(3)(a)(ix) added by the Small Business, Enterprise and Employment Act 2015 Sch 5 Pt 2 paras 11, 32).
20 Companies Act 2006 s 1096(3).
21 Companies Act 2006 s 1096(3)(a).
22 Companies Act 2006 s 1096(3)(b).
23 Companies Act 2006 s 1096(4).
24 Companies Act 2006 s 1096(5).
25 Ie under the Companies Act 2006 s 1096 (see the text and notes 1–8, 20–24): see s 1097(1).

26 Companies Act 2006 s 1097(1). Further to heads (i), (iii) in the text, any general duty or power of the registrar with respect to annotation of the register is subject to the court's power under s 1097 to direct either that a note be removed from the register (ie under head (i) in the text), or that no note is to be made of the removal of material that is the subject of the court's order (ie under head (iii) in the text): see s 1081(5); and PARA 143. Further to head (ii) in the text, any court order made under s 1096 that the court has directed under s 1097 is not to be made available for public inspection must itself not be made available by the registrar of companies for public inspection: see s 1087(1)(g); and PARA 146.

27 As to the provisions that authorise or require the registrar to annotate the register see PARA 143.

28 Companies Act 2006 s 1097(2). See also note 26.

29 Companies Act 2006 s 1097(3). See also note 26. As to the inspection and copying of records kept by the registrar see PARA 145; and as to material that must not be made available by the registrar of companies for public inspection generally see PARA 146 et seq.

30 Companies Act 2006 s 1097(4)(a). See also note 26.

31 Companies Act 2006 s 1097(4)(b). See note 26.

32 Ie under the Companies Act 2006 s 1097 (see the text and notes 25–31): see s 1097(5).

33 Companies Act 2006 s 1097(5).

34 Companies Act 2006 s 1097(5)(a)(i). As to the notes mentioned in head (A) in the text see head (iii) in the text.

35 Companies Act 2006 s 1097(5)(a)(ii).

36 Companies Act 2006 s 1097(5)(a).

37 Companies Act 2006 s 1097(5)(b).

162. Public notice of removal of certain material from the register. The registrar of companies[1] must cause to be published in the Gazette[2], or in accordance with the provisions governing alternative means of giving public notice[3], notice of the removal from the register[4] of any document[5] subject to the Directive disclosure requirements[6] or of any material derived from such a document[7]. The notice must state the name[8] and registered number[9] of the company, the description of document and the date of receipt[10].

1 As to the meaning of 'registrar of companies' see PARA 126 note 2. As to the meaning of 'company' under the Companies Acts see PARA 21; and as to the meaning of the 'Companies Acts' see PARA 13. As to the application of the Companies Act 2006 Pt 35 (ss 1059A–1119) (see also PARAS 126, 130 et seq, 163 et seq) see PARA 126 note 1.

2 As to the meaning of the 'Gazette' see PARA 133 note 2.

3 Ie in accordance with the alternative means provided by the Companies Act 2006 s 1116 (see PARA 133): see s 1098(1).

4 As to the meaning of the 'register' see PARA 142. As to the provisions that authorise or require the registrar to remove material from the register see PARA 146 et seq.

5 As to the meaning of 'document' for these purposes see PARA 136 note 2.

6 As to the Directive disclosure requirements see the Companies Act 2006 s 1078; and PARA 139.

7 Companies Act 2006 s 1098(1).

8 As to company names and trading names generally see PARA 195 et seq.

9 As to a company's registered number see the Companies Act 2006 ss 1066, 1067; and PARAS 134–135.

10 Companies Act 2006 s 1098(2).

G. THE REGISTRAR'S INDEX OF COMPANY NAMES

163. Registrar's index of company names. The registrar of companies[1] must keep an index (called the 'registrar's index of company names') of the names of the following companies and other bodies[2]:

(1) UK-registered companies[3];
(2) any body to which any provision of the Companies Acts applies by virtue of regulations[4] that govern unregistered companies[5]; and
(3) overseas companies[6] that have registered particulars with the registrar[7], other than companies that appear to the registrar not to be required to do so[8];
(4) limited partnerships registered in the United Kingdom[9];
(5) limited liability partnerships incorporated in the United Kingdom[10];

(6) European Economic Interest Groupings registered in the United Kingdom[11];
(7) open-ended investment companies authorised in the United Kingdom[12];
(8) societies registered under the Co-operative and Community Benefit Societies Act 2014 or the Industrial and Provident Societies Act (Northern Ireland) 1969[13].

Any person may inspect the registrar's index of company names[14].

The Secretary of State[15] may by order[16] amend the list at heads (4) to (8) above[17] either by the addition of any description of body, or by the deletion of any description of body[18]; and the Secretary of State may by regulations[19] amend the enactments[20] relating to any description of body for the time being within heads (4) to (8) above[21], so as to[22]:

(a) require the registrar to be provided with information as to the names of bodies registered, incorporated, authorised or otherwise regulated under those enactments[23]; and
(b) make provision in relation to such bodies corresponding to that made by the Companies Act 2006 in relation to company names which are the same as, or similar to, an existing company name[24].

1 As to the meaning of 'registrar of companies' see PARA 126 note 2. As to the meaning of 'company' under the Companies Acts see PARA 21; and as to the meaning of the 'Companies Acts' see PARA 13. As to the application of the Companies Act 2006 Pt 35 (ss 1059A–1119) (see also PARAS 126, 130 et seq, 164 et seq) see PARA 126 note 1.
2 Companies Act 2006 s 1099(1). As to provision made to amend the list in s 1099(3) (see heads (4)–(8) in the text) see the text and notes 15–24.
3 Companies Act 2006 s 1099(2)(a). As to the meaning of 'UK-registered company' see PARA 21.
4 Ie regulations made under the Companies Act 2006 s 1043 (see PARA 1856): see s 1099(2)(b).
5 Companies Act 2006 s 1099(2)(b). As to the meaning of 'unregistered company' see PARA 1856.
6 As to the meaning of 'overseas company' see PARA 2013.
7 Ie under the Companies Act 2006 s 1046 (see PARA 2015): see s 1099(2)(c).
8 Companies Act 2006 s 1099(2)(c).
9 Companies Act 2006 s 1099(3)(a). As to limited partnerships registered in the United Kingdom see PARTNERSHIP vol 79 (2014) PARA 217 et seq. As to the meaning of 'United Kingdom' see PARA 1 note 5.
10 Companies Act 2006 s 1099(3)(b). As to limited liability partnerships incorporated in the United Kingdom see PARTNERSHIP vol 79 (2014) PARA 233 et seq.
11 Companies Act 2006 s 1099(3)(c). As to European Economic Interest Groupings registered in the United Kingdom see PARAS 1823–1824.
12 Companies Act 2006 s 1099(3)(d). As to open-ended investment companies authorised in the United Kingdom see FINANCIAL SERVICES REGULATION vol 50A (2016) PARA 873 et seq.
13 Companies Act 2006 s 1099(3)(e) (amended by the Co-operative and Community Benefit Societies Act 2014 Sch 4 Pt 2 paras 99, 101). As to societies registered under the Co-operative and Community Benefit Societies Act 2014 see FINANCIAL INSTITUTIONS vol 48 (2015) PARA 881 et seq.
14 Companies Act 2006 s 1100.
As to fees payable in respect of the performance of the registrar's functions in relation to the provision of copies of a page of the registrar's index of company names see the Registrar of Companies (Fees) (Companies, Overseas Companies and Limited Liability Partnerships) Regulations 2012, SI 2012/1907, reg 4, Sch 2 Pt 2 (paras 7–12) (amended with effect from 30 June 2016 by SI 2016/621). The fees prescribed in relation to the Registrar of Companies (Fees) (Companies, Overseas Companies and Limited Liability Partnerships) Regulations 2012, SI 2012/1907, Sch 2 paras 7(a), 8(a) and 10(a) are not payable in respect of any month for which the applicant pays a fee to the registrar for subscription to Companies House Direct, Extranet or XML (those terms are defined in Sch 2 para 1) under regulations providing for the payment of fees in respect of the functions of the registrar in relation to the inspection, or provision of copies, of documents kept by the registrar relating to European Economic Interest Groupings and limited partnerships: reg 5.
15 As to the Secretary of State see PARA 6 et seq.

16 Any such order is subject to negative resolution procedure (ie the statutory instrument containing the order is subject to annulment in pursuance of a resolution of either House of Parliament): see the Companies Act 2006 ss 1099(5), 1289. At the date at which this volume states the law, no such order had been made. As to the making of orders under the Companies Act 2006 generally see ss 1288–1292.
17 Ie may amend the Companies Act 2006 s 1099(3) (the list of bodies other than companies whose names are to be entered in the registrar's index) (see heads (4)–(8) in the text): see s 1099(4).
18 Companies Act 2006 s 1099(4).
19 Regulations under the Companies Act 2006 s 1101 are subject to affirmative resolution procedure (ie the regulations must not be made unless a draft of the statutory instrument containing them has been laid before Parliament and approved by a resolution of each House of Parliament): see ss 1101(2), 1290. As to the regulations so made see the Limited Liability Partnerships (Application of Companies Act 2006) Regulations 2009, SI 2009/1804; and PARTNERSHIP vol 79 (2014) PARAS 234, 236–237, 245.
20 As to the meaning of 'enactment' see PARA 13 note 16.
21 Ie within the Companies Act 2006 s 1099(3) (bodies other than companies whose names are to be entered in the registrar's index) (see heads (4)–(8) in the text): see s 1101(1).
22 Companies Act 2006 s 1101(1).
23 Companies Act 2006 s 1101(1)(a).
24 Companies Act 2006 s 1101(1)(b). Head (b) in the text refers specifically to the provisions of s 66 (company name not to be the same as another in the index) (see PARA 204) and ss 67–68 (power to direct change of company name in case of similarity to existing name) (see PARA 204): see s 1101(1)(b). As to restrictions on the use of company names and trading names generally see PARA 195 et seq.

H. LANGUAGE REQUIREMENTS FOR DOCUMENTS DELIVERED TO THE REGISTRAR OF COMPANIES

164. Translation and transliteration requirements relating to documents. In relation to all documents[1] required to be delivered to the registrar of companies[2] under any provision of the Companies Acts, or of the Insolvency Act 1986[3], provision has been made[4] for:

(1) documents to be drawn up and delivered in English[5];
(2) documents relating to Welsh companies[6];
(3) documents that may be drawn up and delivered in other languages[7]; and
(4) certified translations[8].

Accordingly, the general rule is that all documents required to be delivered to the registrar must be drawn up and delivered in English[9]. This is subject to the provisions listed in heads (2) and (3) above[10].

The following documents[11], namely:

(a) agreements required to be forwarded to the registrar[12] because they affect the company's constitution[13];
(b) documents required to be delivered[14] under the provisions relating to companies included in the accounts of a larger group[15];
(c) certified copies required to be delivered[16] under the provisions relating to company charges[17];
(d) documents of any other description specified in regulations made by the Secretary of State[18],

may be drawn up and delivered to the registrar in a language other than English, but when delivered to the registrar they must be accompanied by a certified translation into English[19].

A company may deliver to the registrar one or more certified translations of any document relating to the company that is or has been delivered to the registrar[20]. The Secretary of State may by regulations[21] specify the languages, and the descriptions of document, in relation to which this facility is available[22]. The power of the registrar to impose requirements as to the form and manner of delivery[23] includes power to impose requirements as to the identification of the original document and the delivery of the translation in a form and manner enabling it to be associated with the original[24].

Names and addresses in a document delivered to the registrar must contain only letters, characters and symbols, including accents and other diacritical marks, that are permitted[25]. The Secretary of State may make provision by regulations[26] as to the letters, characters and symbols, including accents and other diacritical marks, that are permitted[27], and permitting or requiring the delivery of documents in which names and addresses have not been transliterated into a permitted form[28].

Where a name or address is or has been delivered to the registrar in a permitted form using other than Roman characters, the company, or other body, to which the document relates may deliver to the registrar a transliteration into Roman characters[29]. The power of the registrar to impose requirements as to the form and manner of delivery[30] includes power to impose requirements as to the identification of the original document and the delivery of the transliteration in a form and manner enabling it to be associated with the original[31].

The Secretary of State may make provision by regulations[32] requiring the certification of transliterations and prescribing the form of certification[33]; and different provision may be made for compulsory and voluntary transliterations[34].

1 As to the meaning of 'document' for these purposes see PARA 136 note 2.

2 As to the meaning of 'registrar of companies' see PARA 126 note 2. As to the meaning of 'company' under the Companies Acts see PARA 21; and as to the meaning of the 'Companies Acts' see PARA 13. As to the delivery of documents to the registrar see PARA 136; and as to the requirements generally for the proper delivery of documents to the registrar see PARA 137. As to the meaning of references to delivering a document for these purposes see PARA 136 note 2. As to the application of the Companies Act 2006 Pt 35 (ss 1059A–1119) (see also PARAS 126, 130 et seq, 165 et seq) see PARA 126 note 1.

3 As to the Insolvency Act 1986 see COMPANY AND PARTNERSHIP INSOLVENCY vol 16 (2011) PARA 1 et seq.

4 Companies Act 2006 s 1102(1). The Secretary of State may make provision by regulations applying all or any of the provisions listed at heads (1)–(4) in the text, with or without modifications, in relation to documents delivered to the registrar under any other enactment: s 1102(2). Regulations made under s 1102 are subject to negative resolution procedure (ie the statutory instrument containing the regulations is subject to annulment in pursuance of a resolution of either House of Parliament): see ss 1102(4), 1289. As to the meaning of 'enactment' see PARA 13 note 16. As to the Secretary of State see PARA 6. As to the making of regulations under the Companies Act 2006 generally see ss 1288–1292. Partly in the exercise of the power under s 1102(2), the Secretary of State has made:

(1) the Companies (Cross-Border Mergers) Regulations 2007, SI 2007/2974 (see further PARA 1631);

(2) the European Public Limited-Liability Company (Amendment) Regulations 2009, SI 2009/2400, which amend the European Public Limited-Liability Company Regulations 2004, SI 2004/2326 (see further PARA 1825 et seq).

5 Companies Act 2006 s 1102(3). Head (1) in the text refers to the provision made by s 1103 (see the text and notes 9–10): see s 1102(3).

6 Companies Act 2006 s 1102(3). Head (2) in the text refers to the provision made by s 1104 (see PARA 165): see s 1102(3). As to the meaning of 'Welsh company' see PARA 124 note 3.

7 Companies Act 2006 s 1102(3). Head (3) in the text refers to the provision made by s 1105 (see the text and notes 11–19): see s 1102(3).

8 Companies Act 2006 s 1102(3). Head (4) in the text refers to the provision made by s 1107: see s 1102(3). For the purposes of Pt 35, a 'certified translation' means a translation certified to be a correct translation: s 1107(1). In the case of any discrepancy between the original language version of a document and a certified translation, the company may not rely on the translation as against a third party, but a third party may rely on the translation unless the company shows that the third party had knowledge of the original: s 1107(2). For these purposes, a 'third party' means a person other than the company or the registrar: s 1107(3).

9 Companies Act 2006 s 1103(1).

10 Companies Act 2006 s 1103(2).

11 Companies Act 2006 s 1105(1).

12 Ie documents required to be delivered under the Companies Act 2006 Pt 3 Ch 3 (ss 29–30) (resolutions and agreements affecting a company's constitution) (see PARA 230): see s 1105(2)(a). As to the meaning of references to a company's constitution see PARA 226.
13 Companies Act 2006 s 1105(2)(a).
14 Ie documents required to be delivered under the Companies Act 2006 s 400(2)(e) (exemption for company included in EEA group accounts of larger group) (see PARA 859) or s 401(2)(f) (exemption for company included in non-EEA group accounts of larger group) (see PARA 860): see s 1105(2)(b).
15 Companies Act 2006 s 1105(2)(b).
16 Ie documents required to be delivered under the Companies Act 2006 Pt 25 (ss 859A–894) (company charges) (see PARA 1462 et seq): see s 1105(2)(c).
17 Companies Act 2006 s 1105(2)(c) (amended by SI 2013/600).
18 Companies Act 2006 s 1105(2)(d). Regulations made under s 1105 are subject to negative resolution procedure (ie the statutory instrument containing the regulations is subject to annulment in pursuance of a resolution of either House of Parliament): see ss 1105(3), 1289. In exercise or partly in exercise of the powers conferred by s 1105(2)(d), the Secretary of State has made:
   (1) the Companies (Registrar, Languages and Trading Disclosures) Regulations 2006, SI 2006/3429, reg 4;
   (2) the Registrar of Companies and Applications for Striking Off Regulations 2009, SI 2009/1803, reg 7, specifying the following documents:
      (a) a memorandum of association;
      (b) a company's articles;
      (c) a valuation report required to be delivered to the registrar under the Companies Act 2006 s 94(2)(d) (see PARA 168);
      (d) any order made by a competent court in the United Kingdom or elsewhere;
      (e) copies of the consolidated accounts, the auditor's report and the consolidated annual report to be delivered to the registrar under s 394A(2)(e) (see PARA 791), s 448A(2)(e) (see PARA 958) or s 479A(2)(e) (see PARA 988) (qualifying subsidiaries: conditions for exemption from the audit, preparation and filing of individual accounts) (Registrar of Companies and Applications for Striking Off Regulations 2009, SI 2009/1803, reg 7(1), (2) (amended by SI 2012/2301);
   (3) the Overseas Companies Regulations 2009, SI 2009/1801, reg 78;
   (4) the Companies (Cross-Border Mergers) Regulations 2007, SI 2007/2974 (as to which see note 4);
   (5) the Companies and Limited Liability Partnerships (Accounts and Audit Exemptions and Change of Accounting Framework) Regulations 2012, SI 2012/2301; and
   (6) the Reports on Payments to Governments Regulations 2014, SI 2014/3209.
19 Companies Act 2006 s 1105(1). However, s 1105 does not apply to a document relating to a Welsh company that is drawn up and delivered in Welsh: see s 1104(5); and PARA 165. See also note 8.
20 Companies Act 2006 s 1106(1). The provisions of s 1106 do not apply where the original document was delivered to the registrar before 1 January 2007 (ie the day on which s 1106 came into force: see the Companies Act 2006 (Commencement No 1, Transitional Provisions and Savings) Order 2006, SI 2006/3428, art 2(1)(g)): Companies Act 2006 s 1106(6). See also note 8.
21 Regulations made under the Companies Act 2006 s 1106 are subject to negative resolution procedure (ie the statutory instrument containing the regulations is subject to annulment in pursuance of a resolution of either House of Parliament): see ss 1106(5), 1289. The regulations must provide that the facility mentioned in s 1106 is available as from 1 January 2007 in relation to all the official languages of the European Union, and in relation to all documents subject to the Directive disclosure requirements (see s 1078; and PARA 139): s 1106(3). In exercise of the powers conferred by s 1106(2), the Secretary of State has made the Companies (Registrar, Languages and Trading Disclosures) Regulations 2006, SI 2006/3429; and see the Companies (Cross-Border Mergers) Regulations 2007, SI 2007/2974 (as to which see note 4). Accordingly, the facility described in the Companies Act 2006 s 1106 is available in relation to all the official languages of the European Union, and all documents subject to the Directive disclosure requirements: Companies (Registrar, Languages and Trading Disclosures) Regulations 2006, SI 2006/3429, reg 5.
22 Companies Act 2006 s 1106(2). As to the regulations so made see note 21.
23 As to this power see PARA 136.
24 Companies Act 2006 s 1106(4).
25 Companies Act 2006 s 1108(1).

The provisions of the Companies Act 2006 ss 1108–1110 apply to unregistered companies by virtue of the Unregistered Companies Regulations 2009, SI 2009/2436, reg 3, Sch 1 para 17(1), (2)(f): see PARA 1857. As to the meaning of 'unregistered company' see PARA 1856.

26 Regulations made under the Companies Act 2006 s 1108 are subject to negative resolution procedure (ie the statutory instrument containing the regulations is subject to annulment in pursuance of a resolution of either House of Parliament): see ss 1108(3), 1289. In exercise of the powers conferred by s 1108(2), the Secretary of State has made the Registrar of Companies and Applications for Striking Off Regulations 2009, SI 2009/1803, reg 8, Schedule (reg 8(2) amended by SI 2009/2399; SI 2009/2400; SI 2012/2301; SI 2013/600; SI 2014/2382; the Registrar of Companies and Applications for Striking Off Regulations 2009, SI 2009/1803, Schedule substituted by SI 2015/17). The specified characters and symbols are those in the Registrar of Companies and Applications for Striking Off Regulations 2009, SI 2009/1803, Schedule, together with full stops, commas, colons, semi-colons and hyphens and the numerals 0–9: reg 8(3). The requirement that names and addresses in documents delivered to the registrar must contain only those characters and symbols does not, however, apply to the following (reg 8(2) (as so amended)), ie:

(1) a memorandum of association;
(2) a company's articles;
(3) an order made by a competent court in the United Kingdom or elsewhere;
(4) an agreement required to be forwarded to the registrar under the Companies Act 2006 Pt 3 Ch 3 (ss 29–30) (agreements affecting a company's constitution: see PARA 230);
(5) a valuation report required to be delivered to the registrar under s 94(2)(d) (see PARA 168);
(6) a document required to be delivered to the registrar under s 400(2)(e) (see PARA 859) or s 401(2)(f) (see PARA 860) (company included in accounts of larger group: required to deliver copy of group accounts);
(7) an instrument or copy instrument delivered to the registrar under Pt 25 (ss 859A–894) (company charges: see PARA 1462 et seq);
(8) a certified copy of the constitution of an overseas company required to be delivered to the registrar under the Overseas Companies Regulations 2009, SI 2009/1801, reg 8, reg 14 or reg 15;
(9) a copy of accounting documents of an overseas company required to be delivered to the registrar under reg 9, reg 32, reg 45 or reg 46;
(10) a copy of the annual accounts of an overseas company, or of a credit or financial institution to which Pt 6 Ch 2 (regs 44–50) applies, required to be delivered to the registrar under the Companies Act 2006 s 441 (see PARA 950);
(11) a contract for the formation of a European Economic Interest Grouping;
(12) an amendment to such a contract;
(13) documents specified in respect of any of the forms mentioned in the European Public Limited-Liability Company Regulations 2004, SI 2004/2326, regs 5–11 (provisions relating to registration etc);
(14) copies of transfer proposals required to be delivered under reg 68(1)(a) of those Regulations (publication of terms of transfer);
(15) copies of draft terms required to be delivered under reg 68(2)(a) or (3)(a) (publication of terms for formation of holding SE or conversion of company into SE);
(16) copies of amendments to statutes required to be delivered under reg 82(1)(a) (notification of amendments to statutes);
(17) documents required to be delivered under reg 85 (registration of a public company by conversion of SE);
(18) copies of draft terms required to be delivered under reg 86 of those Regulations (publication of draft terms of conversion);
(19) copies of the consolidated accounts, the auditor's report and the consolidated annual report to be delivered to the registrar under the Companies Act 2006 s 394A(2)(e) (see PARA 791), s 448A(2)(e) (see PARA 958) or s 479A(2)(e) (see PARA 988) (qualifying subsidiaries: conditions for exemption from the audit, preparation and filing of individual accounts).

27 Companies Act 2006 s 1108(2)(a). See note 26.
28 Companies Act 2006 s 1108(2)(b). See note 26.
29 Companies Act 2006 s 1109(1) (amended by SI 2009/1802).
30 As to this power see PARA 136.
31 Companies Act 2006 s 1109(2).
32 Regulations made under the Companies Act 2006 s 1110 are subject to negative resolution procedure (ie the statutory instrument containing the regulations is subject to annulment in pursuance of a resolution of either House of Parliament): see ss 1110(3), 1289. At the date at which this volume states the law, no such regulations had been made.
33 Companies Act 2006 s 1110(1).
34 Companies Act 2006 s 1110(2).

165. Documents relating to Welsh companies. In relation to all documents[1] required to be delivered to the registrar of companies[2] under any provision of the Companies Acts, or of the Insolvency Act 1986[3], provision has been made[4] to allow for such documents, where they relate to a Welsh company[5], to be drawn up and delivered to the registrar in Welsh[6].

On delivery to the registrar, any such document must be accompanied by a certified translation[7] into English, unless it is:

(1) of a description excepted from that requirement by regulations made by the Secretary of State[8]; or

(2) in a form prescribed[9] in Welsh (or partly in Welsh and partly in English)[10].

Where a document is properly delivered to the registrar in Welsh without a certified translation into English, the registrar must obtain such a translation if the document is to be available for public inspection[11]. The translation is treated as if delivered to the registrar in accordance with the same provision as the original[12].

A Welsh company may deliver to the registrar a certified translation into Welsh of any document in English that relates to the company and is or has been delivered to the registrar[13].

1 As to the meaning of 'document' for these purposes see PARA 136 note 2.

2 As to the meaning of 'registrar of companies' see PARA 126 note 2. As to the meaning of 'company' under the Companies Acts see PARA 21; and as to the meaning of the 'Companies Acts' see PARA 13. As to the delivery of documents to the registrar see PARA 136; and as to the requirements generally for the proper delivery of documents to the registrar see PARA 137. As to the meaning of references to delivering a document for these purposes see PARA 136 note 2. As to the application of the Companies Act 2006 Pt 35 (ss 1059A–1119) (see also PARAS 126, 130 et seq, 166) see PARA 126 note 1.

3 As to the Insolvency Act 1986 see COMPANY AND PARTNERSHIP INSOLVENCY vol 16 (2011) PARA 1 et seq.

4 See the Companies Act 2006 s 1102(1); and PARA 164.

5 As to the meaning of 'Welsh company' see PARA 124 note 3.

6 See the Companies Act 2006 s 1104(1). Accordingly, s 1105 (which requires certified translations into English of documents delivered to the registrar in another language) (see PARA 164) does not apply to a document relating to a Welsh company that is drawn up and delivered in Welsh: s 1104(5).

7 As to the meaning of 'certified translation' see PARA 164 note 8.

8 Companies Act 2006 s 1104(2)(a). As to the making of regulations under the Companies Act 2006 generally see ss 1288–1292. As to the Secretary of State see PARA 6. In exercise of the power conferred by s 1104(2)(a), the Secretary of State has made the Registrar of Companies and Applications for Striking Off Regulations 2009, SI 2009/1803, reg 6 (amended by SI 2012/2301). The following documents are excepted from the requirement that they are accompanied by a certified translation (Registrar of Companies and Applications for Striking Off Regulations 2009, SI 2009/1803, reg 6(1)–(3) (as so amended)), ie:

(1) a non-traded company's memorandum of association;

(2) a non-traded company's articles;

(3) a community interest company report prepared for a non-traded company the Companies (Audit, Investigations and Community Enterprise) Act 2004 s 34 (see PARA 83);

(4) a resolution or agreement which was agreed to by members of a non-traded company and to which the Companies Act 2006 Pt 3 Ch 3 (ss 29–30) (see PARA 230) applies, except for a resolution or agreement listed below, ie:

(a) a special resolution that a private company should be re-registered as a public company, a public company should be re-registered as a private limited company, a private limited company should be re-registered as an unlimited company or an unlimited company should be re-registered as a limited company;

(b) a special resolution agreeing to the change of a company's name;

(c) a special resolution required by the Companies (Audit, Investigations and Community Enterprise) Act 2004 s 37 (requirements for an existing company to become a community interest company: see PARA 190);

(d) a resolution or agreement as altered by an enactment other than an enactment amending the general law, required to be delivered to the registrar under the Companies Act 2006 s 34 (see PARA 237);

(e) a resolution or agreement as altered by an order of a court or other authority, required to be delivered to the registrar under s 35 (see PARA 238) or s 999 (see PARA 666);
(f) a special resolution under s 88(2) (see PARA 124) requiring the register to be amended so that it states that a company's registered office is to be situated in Wales;
(g) a special resolution under s 626 (reduction of capital in connection with redenomination: see PARA 1357);
(h) a special resolution under s 641(1)(a) (resolution for reducing the share capital of a private limited company supported by solvency statement: see PARA 1360);
(i) a resolution under s 664(1) (see PARA 1390) that a public company should be re-registered as a private company to comply with s 662 (see PARA 1387);

(5) annual accounts and reports of a non-traded company required to be delivered to the registrar under the Companies Act 2006 Pt 15 (ss 380–474) (see PARA 765 et seq);
(6) a declaration referred to in the Community Interest Company Regulations 2005, SI 2005/1788, reg 11(1)(b) (see PARA 112) or reg 12(1)(b) or (c) (see PARA 190) which relates to a non-traded company;
(7) revised accounts and any revised report of a non-traded company, and any auditor's report on such revised accounts and reports, required to be delivered to the registrar by the Companies (Revision of Defective Accounts and Reports) Regulations 2008, SI 2008/373 (see PARA 963 et seq);
(8) a document required to be appended to the group accounts of a non-traded company by the Large and Medium-sized Companies and Groups (Accounts and Reports) Regulations 2008, SI 2008/410, Sch 6 para 30(2) (banking groups: information as to undertaking in which shares held as a result of financial assistance operation);
(9) all documents to be delivered to the registrar by a non-traded company under the companies Act 2006 s 394A(2)(e) (see PARA 791), s 448A(2)(e) (see PARA 958) and s 479A(2)(e) (see PARA 988) (qualifying subsidiaries: conditions for exemption from the audit, preparation and filing of individual accounts).

9 Ie by virtue of the Welsh Language Act 1993 s 26 (power to prescribe Welsh version) (see CONSTITUTIONAL AND ADMINISTRATIVE LAW vol 20 (2014) PARA 78): see the Companies Act 2006 s 1104(2)(b). In the Companies Acts, 'prescribed' means prescribed (by order or by regulations) by the Secretary of State: Companies Act 2006 s 1167.
10 Companies Act 2006 s 1104(2)(b).
11 Companies Act 2006 s 1104(3).
12 See note 11.
13 Companies Act 2006 s 1104(4).

I. ENFORCEMENT OF DUTY TO DELIVER DOCUMENTS ETC TO REGISTRAR

166. Enforcement of company's filing obligations. Where a company[1] has made default in complying with any obligation under the Companies Acts either to deliver a document[2] to the registrar of companies[3] or to give notice to him of any matter[4], the registrar, or any member[5] or creditor of the company, may give notice to the company requiring it to comply with the obligation[6].

If the company fails to make good the default within 14 days after the service of a notice requiring it to do so, the registrar, or any member or creditor of the company, may apply to the court[7] for an order directing the company, and any specified officer[8] of it, to make good the default within a specified time[9]. Any such order may provide that all costs of and incidental to the application are to be borne by the company or by any officers of the company responsible for the default[10].

Nothing in these enforcement provisions[11] affects the operation of any enactment making it an offence, or imposing a civil penalty, in respect of any such default[12].

1 As to the meaning of 'company' under the Companies Acts see PARA 21; and as to the meaning of the 'Companies Acts' see PARA 13. As to the application of the Companies Act 2006 Pt 35 (ss 1059A–1120) (see also PARA 126, 135 et seq) see PARA 126 note 1.
2 As to the meaning of 'document' for these purposes see PARA 136 note 2.
3 Companies Act 2006 s 1113(1)(a). As to the meaning of 'registrar of companies' see PARA 126 note 2. As to the delivery of documents to the registrar see PARA 136; and as to the requirements

generally for the proper delivery of documents to the registrar see PARA 137. As to the meaning of references to delivering a document for these purposes see PARA 136 note 2.

4 Companies Act 2006 s 1113(1)(b).

5 As to the meaning of 'member' see PARA 323. As to membership of a company generally see PARA 323 et seq.

6 Companies Act 2006 s 1113(2). As to the service of documents on a company generally see PARA 743 et seq; and as to the provision made for the sending or supplying of documents or information to or from a company (the 'company communications provisions') see PARA 750 et seq.

7 As to applications made under the Companies Act 2006 see generally PARA 306.

8 As to the meaning of 'officer' generally under the Companies Act 2006 see PARA 679.

9 Companies Act 2006 s 1113(3). For a successful application for attachment by the registrar based on failure to comply with such an order see *Re George Dowman Ltd* (1960) Times, 26 July.

10 Companies Act 2006 s 1113(4).

11 Ie nothing in the Companies Act 2006 s 1113: see s 1113(5).

12 Companies Act 2006 s 1113(5). As to the making of disqualification orders under the Company Directors Disqualification Act 1986 s 3 following the making of an order under the Companies Act 2006 s 1113 (formerly the Companies Act 1985 s 713 (repealed)) see PARA 1765. Failure to deliver documents to the registrar of companies as required may give the registrar reasonable cause to believe that the company is defunct, in which case the company may be struck off the register: see PARA 1703 et seq.

(5) RE-REGISTRATION AND ITS EFFECTS

(i) Re-registration of a Company: in general

167. Alteration of company's status by re-registration. A company[1] may, by re-registration under the Companies Act 2006[2], alter its status[3]:

(1) from a private company[4] to a public company[5];
(2) from a public company to a private company[6];
(3) from a private limited company[7] to an unlimited company[8];
(4) from an unlimited private company to a limited company[9];
(5) from a public company to an unlimited private company[10].

In accordance with Part 2 of the Companies (Audit, Investigations and Community Enterprise) Act 2004[11], an existing company may become a community interest company[12] and a community interest company may become a charity[13] or an industrial and provident society[14].

It is not possible for a company limited by shares[15] to alter its status to a company limited by guarantee[16], or vice versa.

1 As to the meaning of 'company' under the Companies Acts see PARA 21; and as to the meaning of the 'Companies Acts' see PARA 13.

2 Ie under the Companies Act 2006 Pt 7 (ss 89–111) (see also PARA 168 et seq): see s 89. As to fees payable under Pt 7 see the Registrar of Companies (Fees) (Companies, Overseas Companies and Limited Liability Partnerships) Regulations 2012, SI 2012/1907, reg 3, Sch 1 para 8(c).

3 Companies Act 2006 s 89.

4 As to the meaning of 'private company' see PARA 95.

5 Companies Act 2006 s 89(a). Head (1) in the text refers to the provisions of ss 90–96 (see PARA 168 et seq): see s 89(a). As to the meaning of 'public company' see PARA 95.

6 Companies Act 2006 s 89(b). Head (2) in the text refers to the provisions of ss 97–101 (see PARA 173 et seq): see s 89(b).

7 As to the meaning of 'limited company' see PARA 95.

8 Companies Act 2006 s 89(c). Head (3) in the text refers to the provisions of ss 102–104 (see PARAS 176–177): see s 89(c). As to the meaning of 'unlimited company' see PARA 95.

9 Companies Act 2006 s 89(d). Head (4) in the text refers to the provisions of ss 105–108 (see PARA 178 et seq): see s 89(d).

10 Companies Act 2006 s 89(e). Head (5) in the text refers to the provisions of ss 109–111 (see PARAS 181–182): see s 89(e).

11 Ie in accordance with the Companies (Audit, Investigations and Community Enterprise) Act 2004 Pt 2 (ss 26–63) (community interest companies): see s 26(2); the Companies Act 2006 s 6(1); and PARA 75 et seq.
12 Ie in accordance with the Companies (Audit, Investigations and Community Enterprise) Act 2004 ss 37, 38: see PARA 190.
13 Ie in accordance with the Companies (Audit, Investigations and Community Enterprise) Act 2004 ss 54, 55: see PARA 193.
14 Ie in accordance with the Companies (Audit, Investigations and Community Enterprise) Act 2004 s 56: see PARA 194.
15 As to the meaning of 'company limited by shares' see PARA 95. See also PARA 71 et seq. As to the meaning of 'share' see PARA 1231. As to share capital generally see PARA 1231 et seq.
16 As to the meaning of 'company limited by guarantee' see PARA 95. See also PARA 72.

(ii) Private Company becoming a Public Company

168. Procedure on application to re-register a private company as a public company. A private company[1], whether limited[2] or unlimited[3], may be re-registered under the Companies Act 2006[4] as a public company limited by shares[5] provided that[6]:

(1) a special resolution[7] that it should be so re-registered is passed[8];
(2) the following conditions are met[9], namely:
    (a) that the company has a share capital[10];
    (b) that the statutory requirements are met[11] as regards its share capital[12];
    (c) that the statutory requirements are met[13] as regards its net assets[14];
    (d) if the provisions regarding the recent allotment[15] of shares for a non-cash consideration apply[16], that the statutory requirements of those provisions are met[17]; and
    (e) that the company has not previously been re-registered as unlimited[18]; and
(3) an application for re-registration is delivered to the registrar of companies[19], together with the other necessary documents[20], and a statement of compliance[21].

An application for re-registration as a public company must contain:

(i) a statement of the company's proposed name on re-registration[22]; and
(ii) in the case of a company without a secretary[23], a statement of the company's proposed secretary[24].

The statement of the company's proposed secretary must contain the required particulars of the person who is or the persons who are to be the secretary or joint secretaries of the company[25]. It must also satisfy the requirements as to consent by the person named as secretary, or each of the persons named as joint secretaries, to act in the relevant capacity[26].

The application must be accompanied by:

(A) a copy of the special resolution[27] that the company should re-register as a public company[28];
(B) a copy of the company's articles of association[29] as proposed to be amended[30];
(C) a copy of the balance sheet and of any other documents that are required[31] regarding the company's net assets[32];
(D) if the provisions regarding the recent allotment of shares for a non-cash consideration apply[33], a copy of the valuation report[34], if any[35]; and

(E) as from 30 June 2016[36], a statement of the aggregate amount paid up on the shares of the company on account of their nominal value[37].

The statement of compliance that is required to be delivered under head (3) above together with the application is a statement that the statutory requirements[38] as to re-registration as a public company have been complied with[39]. The registrar may accept the statement of compliance as sufficient evidence that the company is entitled to be re-registered as a public company[40].

1 As to the meaning of 'company' under the Companies Acts see PARA 21; and as to the meaning of the 'Companies Acts' see PARA 13. As to the meaning of 'private company' see PARA 95.
2 As to the meaning of 'limited company' see PARA 95.
3 As to the meaning of 'unlimited company' see PARA 95.
4 Ie under the Companies Act 2006 Pt 7 (ss 89–111) (see PARAS 167, 169 et seq): see s 89; and PARA 167. As to fees payable under Pt 7 see the Registrar of Companies (Fees) (Companies, Overseas Companies and Limited Liability Partnerships) Regulations 2012, SI 2012/1907, reg 3, Sch 1 para 8(c).
5 As to the meanings of 'public company' and 'company limited by shares' see PARA 95. As to the meaning of 'share' see PARA 1231.
6 Companies Act 2006 s 90(1).
7 As to the meaning of 'special resolution' see PARA 686.
8 Companies Act 2006 s 90(1)(a).
9 Companies Act 2006 s 90(1)(b).
10 Companies Act 2006 s 90(2)(a). As to the meanings of 'company having a share capital' and 'share capital' see PARA 1231.
11 Ie that the requirements of the Companies Act 2006 s 91 (see PARA 169) are met: see s 90(2)(b). References in the company law provisions of the Companies Act 2006 to the requirements of that Act include the requirements of regulations and orders made under it: s 1172. As to the meaning of the 'company law provisions' of the Companies Act 2006 see PARA 13 note 6.
12 Companies Act 2006 s 90(2)(b).
13 Ie that the requirements of the Companies Act 2006 s 92 (see PARA 170) are met: see s 90(2)(c).
14 Companies Act 2006 s 90(2)(c).
15 As to the meaning of 'allotted' shares see PARA 1280.
16 Ie if the Companies Act 2006 s 93 (see PARA 171) applies: see s 90(2)(d). As to non-cash consideration for shares see PARA 1309 et seq.
17 Companies Act 2006 s 90(2)(d).
18 Companies Act 2006 s 90(2)(e).
19 Ie in accordance with the requirements of the Companies Act 2006 s 94 (see the text and notes 22–28): see s 90(1)(c). As to the meaning of 'registrar of companies' see PARA 126 note 2. As to the delivery of documents to the registrar see PARA 136; and as to the requirements generally for the proper delivery of documents to the registrar see PARA 137. As to the meanings of 'document' and of references to delivering a document for these purposes see PARA 136 note 2.
20 Ie the other documents required by the Companies Act 2006 s 94 (see the text and notes 22–24, 28–40): see s 90(1)(c).
21 Companies Act 2006 s 90(1)(c).
22 Companies Act 2006 s 94(1)(a). The company must make such changes in its name as are necessary in connection with its becoming a public company: s 90(3)(a). As to the change of a company's name see PARAS 216–218. As to the required indications in the name of a public limited company see PARA 199 et seq.
23 There is no requirement for a private company to have a company secretary: see PARA 669.
24 Companies Act 2006 s 94(1)(b).
25 Companies Act 2006 s 95(1). The required particulars are the particulars that will be required to be stated in the company's register of secretaries (see ss 277–279; and PARA 673): s 95(2).
26 See the Companies Act 2006 s 95(3). The statement must also include a statement by the company that the person named as secretary, or each of the persons named as joint secretaries, has consented to act in the relevant capacity: s 95(3) (substituted by the Small Business, Enterprise and Employment Act 2015 s 100(1), (3)). For transitional provisions see s 100(6). As to the meaning of 'firm' see PARA 105 note 15.
27 Ie unless a copy has already been forwarded to the registrar under the Companies Act 2006 Pt 3 Ch 3 (ss 29–30) (resolutions and agreements affecting a company's constitution) (see PARA 230): see s 94(2)(a). As to the meaning of references to a company's constitution see PARA 226.
28 Companies Act 2006 s 94(2)(a).

29 As to the meaning of references to a company's 'articles' see PARA 227 note 2. As to a company's articles of association generally see PARA 227 et seq.
30 Companies Act 2006 s 94(2)(b). The company must make such changes in its articles as are necessary in connection with its becoming a public company: s 90(3)(b). If the company is unlimited, it must also make such changes in its articles as are necessary in connection with its becoming a company limited by shares: s 90(4). As to the amendment of articles of association see PARA 231 et seq.
31 Ie the other documents required by the Companies Act 2006 s 92(1) (see PARA 170): see s 94(2)(c).
32 Companies Act 2006 s 94(2)(c).
33 Ie if the Companies Act 2006 s 93 (see PARA 171) applies: see s 94(2)(d).
34 Ie under the Companies Act 2006 s 93(2)(a) (see PARA 171): see s 94(2)(d).
35 Companies Act 2006 s 94(2)(d).
36 See the Small Business, Enterprise and Employment Act 2015 (Commencement No 4, Transitional and Savings Provisions) Regulations 2016, SI 2016/321, reg 6(f).
37 Companies Act 2006 s 94(2)(e) (added by the Small Business, Enterprise and Employment Act 2015 s 98(1), (2)).
38 Ie the requirements of the Companies Act 2006 Pt 7 (see PARAS 167, 169 et seq): see s 94(3).
39 Companies Act 2006 s 94(3).
40 Companies Act 2006 s 94(4).

169. Additional requirements for re-registration as public company which relate to share capital. At the time that the special resolution is passed[1], that a private company[2] should be re-registered as a public company[3], the following requirements with respect to its share capital[4] must be met[5]:

(1) the nominal value[6] of the company's allotted share capital[7] must be not less than the authorised minimum[8];
(2) each of the company's allotted shares must be paid up[9] at least as to one-quarter of the nominal value of that share and the whole of any premium on it[10];
(3) if any shares in the company or any premium on them have been fully or partly paid up by an undertaking given by any person that he or another should do work or perform services, whether for the company or any other person, the undertaking must have been performed or otherwise discharged[11];
(4) if shares have been allotted as fully or partly paid up as to their nominal value or any premium on them otherwise than in cash[12], and the consideration for the allotment consists of or includes an undertaking to the company (other than one to which the condition in head (3) above applies)[13], then either the undertaking must have been performed or otherwise discharged[14], or there must be a contract between the company and some person pursuant to which the undertaking is to be performed within five years from the time the special resolution for re-registration[15] is passed[16].

For the purpose of determining whether the requirements in heads (2), (3) and (4) above are met, the following shares in the company may be disregarded[17]:

(a) shares which were allotted before 22 June 1982[18], in the case of a company then registered in Great Britain[19];
(b) shares which were allotted in pursuance of an employees' share scheme[20] and by reason of which the company would, but for this provision, be precluded under head (2) above, but not otherwise, from being re-registered as a public company[21].

Shares disregarded under head (a) or head (b) above are to be treated as not forming part of the allotted share capital for the purposes of head (1) above[22].

A company must not be re-registered as a public company if it appears to the registrar of companies[23] that[24]:

(i) the company has resolved to reduce its share capital[25];
(ii) the reduction:
 (A) is made under the provisions[26] that allow a limited company to pass a resolution redenominating some or all of its shares (that is, for the purpose of adjusting the nominal values of the redenominated shares and so obtain values that are, in the opinion of the company, more suitable)[27]; or
 (B) is supported by a statutory solvency statement[28]; or
 (C) has been confirmed by an order of the court[29]; and
(iii) the effect of the reduction is, or will be, that the nominal value of the company's allotted share capital is below the authorised minimum[30].

1 Ie the special resolution required by the Companies Act 2006 s 90(1)(a): see PARA 168. As to the meaning of 'special resolution' see PARA 686.
2 As to the meaning of 'company' under the Companies Acts see PARA 21; and as to the meaning of the 'Companies Acts' see PARA 13. As to the meaning of 'private company' see PARA 95.
3 As to the procedure on application to re-register a private company as a public company see PARA 168. As to the meaning of 'public company' see PARA 95.
4 As to the meanings of 'share' and 'share capital' see PARA 1231.
5 Companies Act 2006 s 91(1).
6 As to the nominal value of shares see PARA 1233.
7 As to the meaning of 'allotted share capital' see PARA 1280. Shares disregarded under the Companies Act 2006 s 91(2) (see the text and notes 17–21) are treated as not forming part of the allotted share capital for the purposes of s 91(1)(a): see s 91(4); and the text and note 22.
8 Companies Act 2006 s 91(1)(a). As to the meaning of 'authorised minimum' see PARA 68.
9 As to payments for shares and paid up shares see PARA 1237 et seq. As to the meaning of 'allotted shares' see PARA 1234.
10 Companies Act 2006 s 91(1)(b).
11 Companies Act 2006 s 91(1)(c).
12 As to the meaning of 'cash' see PARA 606 note 7.
13 Companies Act 2006 s 91(1)(d).
14 Companies Act 2006 s 91(1)(d)(i).
15 See note 1.
16 Companies Act 2006 s 91(1)(d)(ii).
17 Companies Act 2006 s 91(2).
18 Ie before the date which marked the end of the transitional period for which provision was made by the Companies Act 1980: see s 87(1) (repealed).
19 Companies Act 2006 s 91(2)(a). As to the meaning of 'Great Britain' see PARA 1 note 5. However, no more than one-tenth of the nominal value of the company's allotted share capital is to be disregarded under s 91(2)(a): s 91(3). For this purpose, the allotted share capital is treated as not including shares disregarded under s 91(2)(b) (see head (b) in the text): s 91(3).
20 For the purposes of the Companies Acts, an 'employees' share scheme' is a scheme for encouraging or facilitating the holding of shares in, or debentures of, a company, either by or for the benefit of the bona fide employees or former employees of the company, of any subsidiary of the company, or of the company's holding company, or any subsidiary of the company's holding company, or by or for the benefit of the spouses, civil partners, surviving spouses, surviving civil partners, or minor children or step-children of such employees or former employees: Companies Act 2006 s 1166. As to the meaning of 'debenture' see PARA 1482; and as to the meanings of 'holding company' and 'subsidiary' see PARA 22.
21 Companies Act 2006 s 91(2)(b).
22 Companies Act 2006 s 91(4).
23 As to the meaning of 'registrar of companies' see PARA 126 note 2. As to fees payable to the registrar under Pt 7 (ss 89–111) (see PARAS 167 et seq, 170 et seq) see the Registrar of Companies (Fees) (Companies, Overseas Companies and Limited Liability Partnerships) Regulations 2012, SI 2012/1907, reg 3, Sch 1 para 8(c).
24 Companies Act 2006 s 91(5).
25 Companies Act 2006 s 91(5)(a).
26 Ie under the Companies Act 2006 s 626 (see PARA 1357): see s 91(5)(b)(i).
27 Companies Act 2006 s 91(5)(b)(i).
28 Companies Act 2006 s 91(5)(b)(ii). The text refers to a solvency statement that is made under s 643 (see PARA 1365): see s 91(5)(b)(ii).

29 Companies Act 2006 s 91(5)(b)(iii). The text refers to an order of the court, confirming a reduction in capital, made under s 648 (see PARA 1379 et seq): see s 91(5)(b)(iii).
30 Companies Act 2006 s 91(5)(c).

170. Additional requirements relating to net assets; meaning of 'unqualified report'. A private company[1] applying to re-register as a public company[2] must obtain[3]:

(1) a balance sheet prepared as at a date not more than seven months before the date on which the application to re-register is delivered to the registrar of companies[4];
(2) an unqualified report[5] by the company's auditor on that balance sheet[6]; and
(3) a written statement by the company's auditor that in his opinion at the balance sheet date the amount of the company's net assets was not less than the aggregate of its called-up share capital and undistributable reserves[7].

Between the balance sheet date and the date on which the application for re-registration is delivered to the registrar, there must be no change in the company's financial position that results in the amount of its net assets becoming less than the aggregate of its called-up share capital and undistributable reserves[8].

1 As to the meaning of 'company' under the Companies Acts see PARA 21; and as to the meaning of the 'Companies Acts' see PARA 13. As to the meaning of 'private company' see PARA 95.
2 As to the meaning of 'public company' see PARA 95. As to the procedure on application to re-register a private company as a public company see PARA 168. As to fees payable to the registrar under the Companies Act 2006 Pt 7 (ss 89–111) (see PARAS 167 et seq, 171 et seq) see the Registrar of Companies (Fees) (Companies, Overseas Companies and Limited Liability Partnerships) Regulations 2012, SI 2012/1907, reg 3, Sch 1 para 8(c).
3 Companies Act 2006 s 92(1).
4 Companies Act 2006 s 92(1)(a). As to the meaning of 'registrar of companies' see PARA 126 note 2. As to the delivery of documents to the registrar see PARA 136; and as to the requirements generally for the proper delivery of documents to the registrar see PARA 137.
5 For these purposes, an 'unqualified report' means:
  (1) if the balance sheet was prepared for a financial year of the company, a report stating without material qualification the auditor's opinion that the balance sheet has been properly prepared in accordance with the requirements of the Companies Act 2006 (s 92(3)(a));
  (2) if the balance sheet was not prepared for a financial year of the company, a report stating without material qualification the auditor's opinion that the balance sheet has been properly prepared in accordance with the provisions of the Companies Act 2006 which would have applied if it had been prepared for a financial year of the company (s 92(3)(b)).

  References in the company law provisions of the Companies Act 2006 to the requirements of that Act include the requirements of regulations and orders made under it: s 1172. As to the meaning of the 'company law provisions' of the Companies Act 2006 see PARA 13 note 6. For the purposes of s 92(3), a qualification is material unless the auditor states in his report that the matter giving rise to the qualification is not material for the purpose of determining (by reference to the company's balance sheet) whether at the balance sheet date the amount of the company's net assets was not less than the aggregate of its called-up share capital and undistributable reserves: s 92(5). In Pt 7, 'net assets' and 'undistributable reserves' have the same meaning as in s 831 (net asset restriction on distributions by public companies) (see PARA 1566): s 92(6). For the purposes of an auditor's report on a balance sheet that was not prepared for a financial year of the company, the provisions of the Companies Act 2006 apply with such modifications as are necessary by reason of that fact: s 92(4). As to the meanings of 'share' and 'share capital' see PARA 1231; and as to the meaning of 'called-up share capital' see PARA 1237. As to the meaning of 'financial year' see PARA 785. As to the meaning of 'balance sheet date' see PARA 793 note 13.
6 Companies Act 2006 s 92(1)(b).
7 Companies Act 2006 s 92(1)(c).
8 Companies Act 2006 s 92(2).

171. Recent allotment of shares for non-cash consideration. If shares[1] have been allotted[2] by the company[3] in the period between the date as at which the required balance sheet[4] is prepared and the passing of the special resolution[5] that the private company[6] in question should re-register as a public company[7], and if those shares were allotted as fully or partly paid up[8] as to their nominal value[9] or any premium on them otherwise than in cash[10], then the registrar of companies[11] must not entertain an application by the company for re-registration as a public company[12] unless[13]:

(1) the consideration for the allotment[14] has been independently valued[15]; and

(2) the valuer's report has been made to the company in accordance with such procedure during the six months immediately preceding the allotment of the shares[16],

or unless the allotment is in connection with either a share exchange[17] or a proposed merger with another company[18].

An allotment is in connection with a share exchange if[19]:

(a) the shares are allotted in connection with an arrangement[20] under which the whole or part of the consideration for the shares allotted is provided by[21]:

  (i) the transfer to the company allotting the shares of shares, or shares of a particular class, in another company[22]; or

  (ii) the cancellation of shares, or shares of a particular class, in another company[23]; and

(b) the allotment is open to all the holders of the shares of the other company in question[24] (or, where the arrangement applies only to shares of a particular class, to all the holders of the company's shares of that class) to take part in the arrangement in connection with which the shares are allotted[25].

It is immaterial, for the purposes of deciding whether an allotment is in connection with a share exchange, whether or not the arrangement in connection with which the shares are allotted involves the issue to the company allotting the shares of shares, or shares of a particular class, in the other company[26].

There is a proposed merger with another company[27] for these purposes if one of the companies concerned proposes to acquire all the assets and liabilities of the other in exchange for the issue of its shares or other securities to shareholders of the other, whether or not accompanied by a cash payment[28].

1 As to the meaning of 'share' see PARA 1231.

2 As to the meanings of 'allotted shares' see PARA 1280. As to allotment generally see PARA 1277 et seq.

3 As to the meaning of 'company' under the Companies Acts see PARA 21; and as to the meaning of the 'Companies Acts' see PARA 13.

4 Ie the balance sheet required by the Companies Act 2006 s 92 (see PARA 170): see s 93(1)(a).

5 Ie the special resolution required by the Companies Act 2006 s 90(1)(a): see PARA 168. As to the meaning of 'special resolution' see PARA 686.

6 As to the meaning of 'private company' see PARA 95.

7 Companies Act 2006 s 93(1)(a). As to the meaning of 'public company' see PARA 95.

8 As to payments for shares and paid up shares see PARA 1237.

9 As to the nominal value of shares see PARA 1233.

10 Companies Act 2006 s 93(1)(b). As to the meaning of 'cash' see PARA 606 note 7.

11 As to the meaning of 'registrar of companies' see PARA 126 note 2.

12 As to the procedure on application to re-register a private company as a public company see PARA 168. As to fees payable to the registrar under the Companies Act 2006 Pt 7 (ss 89–111) (see PARAS 167 et seq, 172 et seq) see the Registrar of Companies (Fees) (Companies, Overseas Companies and Limited Liability Partnerships) Regulations 2012, SI 2012/1907, reg 3, Sch 1 para 8(c).

13 Companies Act 2006 s 93(2).

14 For these purposes, the consideration for an allotment does not include any amount standing to the credit of any of the company's reserve accounts, or of its profit and loss account, that has been applied in paying up (to any extent) any of the shares allotted or any premium on those shares: Companies Act 2006 s 93(7)(a).
15 Companies Act 2006 s 93(2)(a). Head (1) in the text refers to the need for the requirements of s 593(1)(a) (see PARA 1309) to have been complied with: see s 93(2)(a). The provisions of ss 1150–1153 (see PARA 1311) apply to the valuation and report required by s 93: s 1149.
16 Companies Act 2006 s 93(2)(a). Head (2) in the text refers to the need for the requirements of s 593(1)(b) (see PARA 1309) to have been complied with: see s 93(2)(b). See also note 15.
17 Companies Act 2006 s 93(2)(b)(i). As to a share exchange as mentioned in the text see s 93(3)–(5); and the text and notes 19–26.
18 Companies Act 2006 s 93(2)(b)(ii). As to a proposed merger as mentioned in the text see s 93(6); and the text and notes 27–28.
19 Companies Act 2006 s 93(3).
20 For these purposes, 'arrangement' means any agreement, scheme or arrangement, including an arrangement sanctioned in accordance with the Companies Act 2006 Pt 26 (ss 895–901) (arrangements and reconstructions) (see PARA 1605 et seq) or the Insolvency Act 1986 s 110 (liquidator in voluntary winding up accepting shares as consideration for sale of company's property) (see PARA 1618; and COMPANY AND PARTNERSHIP INSOLVENCY vol 17 (2011) PARA 922): Companies Act 2006 s 93(7)(b).
21 Companies Act 2006 s 93(3)(a).
22 Companies Act 2006 s 93(3)(a)(i). As to classes of shares generally see PARA 1246 et seq.
23 Companies Act 2006 s 93(3)(a)(ii).
24 In determining whether a person is a holder of shares for the purposes of the Companies Act 2006 s 93(3), there must be disregarded shares held by (or by a nominee of) the company allotting the shares, and shares held by (or by a nominee of) the holding company of the company allotting the shares, a subsidiary of the company allotting the shares, or a subsidiary of the holding company of the company allotting the shares: s 93(4). As to the meanings of 'holding company' and 'subsidiary' see PARA 22.
25 Companies Act 2006 s 93(3)(b).
26 Companies Act 2006 s 93(5).
27 For these purposes, 'another company' includes any body corporate: Companies Act 2006 s 93(6). As to the meaning of 'body corporate' for the purposes of the Companies Acts see PARA 1 note 5.
28 Companies Act 2006 s 93(6).

172. Issue of certificate of re-registration as a public company. If, on an application for re-registration as a public company[1], the registrar of companies[2] is satisfied that the company is entitled to be so re-registered, the company must be re-registered accordingly[3].

The registrar must issue a certificate of incorporation[4] altered to meet the circumstances of the case[5]; and the certificate must state that it is issued on re-registration and it must state the date on which it is issued[6]. However, the registrar must not issue the certificate if it appears to him that the company has resolved to reduce its share capital[7] under certain specified statutory provisions[8] and that the effect of the reduction is, or will be, that the nominal value[9] of the company's allotted share capital[10] is below the authorised minimum[11].

On the issue to a company of the certificate[12]:

(1) the company, by virtue of the issue of that certificate, becomes a public company[13];
(2) the changes in the company's name and articles take effect[14]; and
(3) where the application contained a statement of the proposed secretary[15], the person or persons named in the statement as secretary or joint secretary of the company are deemed to have been appointed to that office[16].

The certificate is conclusive evidence that the requirements of the Companies Act 2006[17] as to re-registration[18] have been complied with[19].

Where a private company re-registers as a public company, the last statement of capital relating to the company received by the registrar[20] under any provision of the Companies Acts becomes subject to the Directive disclosure requirements[21], and the provisions that require the registrar to give public notice of the receipt of certain documents[22] apply as if the statement had been received by the registrar when the re-registration takes effect[23].

1 As to the meaning of 'public company' see PARA 95. As to the meaning of 'company' under the Companies Acts see PARA 21; and as to the meaning of the 'Companies Acts' see PARA 13. As to the procedure on application to re-register a private company as a public company see PARA 168.
2 As to the meaning of 'registrar of companies' see PARA 126 note 2.
3 Companies Act 2006 s 96(1). The registrar may accept the statement of compliance required by s 90(1)(c) (see PARA 168) as sufficient evidence that the company is entitled to be re-registered as a public company: see s 94(4); and PARA 168. As to fees payable to the registrar under Pt 7 (ss 89–111) (see PARAS 167 et seq, 173 et seq) see the Registrar of Companies (Fees) (Companies, Overseas Companies and Limited Liability Partnerships) Regulations 2012, SI 2012/1907, reg 3, Sch 1 para 8(c).
4 As to a company's certificate of incorporation see PARA 114. As to public notice of the issue of certificates of incorporation see the Companies Act 2006 s 1064; and PARA 133.
5 Companies Act 2006 s 96(2).
6 Companies Act 2006 s 96(3).
7 As to the meanings of 'share' and 'share capital' see PARA 1231.
8 Ie if the reduction is made under the Companies Act 2006 s 626 (see PARA 1357) or is supported by a solvency statement that is made under s 643 (see PARA 1365) or has been confirmed by an order of the court under s 648 (see PARA 1379 et seq): see s 91(5); and PARA 169.
9 As to the nominal value of shares see PARA 1233.
10 As to the meaning of 'allotted share capital' see PARA 1234.
11 See the Companies Act 2006 s 91(5); and PARA 169. As to the meaning of 'authorised minimum' see PARA 68.
12 Companies Act 2006 s 96(4).
13 Companies Act 2006 s 96(4)(a). As to the nature and powers of a public company see PARA 66.
14 Companies Act 2006 s 96(4)(b). An application for re-registration as a public company must contain a statement of the company's proposed name on re-registration and such an application must be accompanied by a copy of the company's articles of association as proposed to be amended: see s 94; and PARA 168. As to the change of a company's name see PARAS 216–218. As to the required indications in the name of a public limited company see PARA 199 et seq. As to the meaning of references to a company's 'articles' see PARA 227 note 2. As to a company's articles of association generally see PARA 227 et seq.
15 As to the statement of the proposed secretary see the Companies Act 2006 ss 94, 95; and PARA 168. There is no requirement for a private company to have a company secretary: see PARA 669.
16 Companies Act 2006 s 96(4)(c).
17 References in the company law provisions of the Companies Act 2006 to the requirements of that Act include the requirements of regulations and orders made under it: s 1172. As to the meaning of the 'company law provisions' of the Companies Act 2006 see PARA 13 note 6.
18 Ie under the Companies Act 2006 Pt 7: see s 89; and PARA 167.
19 Companies Act 2006 s 96(5).
20 As to the statement of capital and initial shareholdings required in the case of a company limited by shares see PARA 107.
21 As to the Directive disclosure requirements see the Companies Act 2006 s 1078; and PARA 139.
22 Ie the Companies Act 2006 s 1077: see PARA 139.
23 See the Companies Act 2006 s 1078(4); and PARA 139.

(iii) Public Company becoming a Private Company

173. Procedure on application to re-register a public company as a private limited company. A public company[1] may be re-registered under the Companies Act 2006[2] as a private limited company[3] if:

(1) a special resolution[4] that it should be so re-registered is passed[5];
(2) the following conditions are met[6], namely:

(a) where no application[7] for cancellation of the resolution has been made[8], that either, having regard to the number of members[9] who consented to or voted in favour of the resolution, no such application may be made[10], or the period within which such an application could be made has expired[11]; or

(b) where such an application has been made[12], that either the application has been withdrawn[13], or an order has been made confirming the resolution and a copy of that order has been delivered to the registrar of companies[14];

(3) an application for re-registration is delivered to the registrar[15], together with the other necessary documents[16], and a statement of compliance[17].

An application for re-registration as a private limited company must contain a statement of the company's proposed name on re-registration[18]; and the application must be accompanied by:

(i) a copy of the special resolution[19] that the company should re-register as a private limited company[20];

(ii) a copy of the company's articles of association[21] as proposed to be amended[22].

The statement of compliance that is required to be delivered under head (3) above together with the application is a statement that the statutory requirements[23] as to re-registration as a private limited company have been complied with[24]. The registrar may accept the statement of compliance as sufficient evidence that the company is entitled to be re-registered as a private limited company[25].

1 As to the meaning of 'company' under the Companies Acts see PARA 21; and as to the meaning of the 'Companies Acts' see PARA 13. As to the meaning of 'public company' see PARA 95.

2 Ie under the Companies Act 2006 Pt 7 (ss 89–111) (see PARAS 167 et seq, 174 et seq): see s 89; and PARA 167. As to fees payable to the registrar under Pt 7 see the Registrar of Companies (Fees) (Companies, Overseas Companies and Limited Liability Partnerships) Regulations 2012, SI 2012/1907, reg 3, Sch 1 para 8(c).

3 As to the meanings of 'private company' and 'limited company' see PARA 95.

4 As to the meaning of 'special resolution' see PARA 686. The court has the power to cancel such a resolution under the Companies Act 2006 s 98 on application by certain specified persons (but not by a person who has consented to or voted in favour of the resolution): see PARA 174.

5 Companies Act 2006 s 97(1)(a). However, where the court makes an order confirming a reduction of a public company's capital which has the effect of bringing the nominal value of its allotted share capital below the authorised minimum, the court may authorise the company to be re-registered as a private company under an expedited procedure which does not require the special resolution as specified in head (1) in the text to be passed: see s 651; and PARA 1381. As to the meaning of 'allotted share capital' see PARA 1234; and as to the meaning of 'authorised minimum' see PARA 68. As to the meaning of 'share' see PARA 1231. As to the nominal value of shares see PARA 1233.

6 Companies Act 2006 s 97(1)(b).

7 Ie under the Companies Act 2006 s 98 (see PARA 174): see s 97(2)(a).

8 Companies Act 2006 s 97(2)(a).

9 As to the meaning of 'member' see PARA 323. As to membership of a company generally see PARA 323 et seq.

10 Companies Act 2006 s 97(2)(a)(i).

11 Companies Act 2006 s 97(2)(a)(ii).

12 Companies Act 2006 s 97(2)(b).

13 Companies Act 2006 s 97(2)(b)(i).

14 Companies Act 2006 s 97(2)(b)(ii). As to the meaning of 'registrar of companies' see PARA 126 note 2. As to the delivery of documents to the registrar see PARA 136; and as to the requirements generally for the proper delivery of documents to the registrar see PARA 137. As to the meanings of 'document' and of references to delivering a document for these purposes see PARA 136 note 2.

15 Ie in accordance with the Companies Act 2006 s 100 (see the text and notes 18–25): see s 97(1)(c).

16 Ie the other documents required by the Companies Act 2006 s 100 (see the text and notes 18–25): see s 97(1)(c).
17 Companies Act 2006 s 97(1)(c).
18 Companies Act 2006 s 100(1). The company must make such changes in its name as are necessary in connection with its becoming a private company limited by shares or, as the case may be, by guarantee: s 97(3)(a). As to the meanings of 'company limited by shares' and 'company limited by guarantee' see PARA 95. As to the change of a company's name see PARAS 216–218. As to the required indications in the name of a private limited company see PARA 199 et seq.
19 Ie unless a copy has already been forwarded to the registrar under the Companies Act 2006 Pt 3 Ch 3 (ss 29–30) (resolutions and agreements affecting a company's constitution) (see PARA 230): see s 100(2)(a). As to the meaning of references to a company's constitution see PARA 226.
20 Companies Act 2006 s 100(2)(a).
21 As to the meaning of references to a company's 'articles' see PARA 227 note 2. As to a company's articles of association generally see PARA 227 et seq.
22 Companies Act 2006 s 100(2)(b). The company must make such changes in its articles as are necessary in connection with its becoming a private company limited by shares or, as the case may be, by guarantee: s 97(3)(b). As to the amendment of articles of association see PARA 231 et seq.
23 Ie the requirements of the Companies Act 2006 Pt 7: see s 100(3). References in the company law provisions of the Companies Act 2006 to the requirements of that Act include the requirements of regulations and orders made under it: s 1172. As to the meaning of the 'company law provisions' of the Companies Act 2006 see PARA 13 note 6.
24 Companies Act 2006 s 100(3).
25 Companies Act 2006 s 100(4).

174. Application to court to cancel resolution to re-register as private limited company. Where a special resolution[1] by a public company[2] to be re-registered as a private limited company[3] has been passed[4], an application to the High Court for the cancellation of that resolution may be made[5]:

(1) by the holders of not less in the aggregate than 5 per cent in nominal value[6] of the company's issued share capital[7] or any class of it[8];
(2) if the company is not limited by shares[9], by not less than 5 per cent of its members[10]; or
(3) by not less than 50 of the company's members[11],

but not by a person who has consented to or voted in favour of the resolution[12].

The application must be made within 28 days after the passing of the resolution and may be made on behalf of the persons entitled to make the application by such one or more of their number as they may appoint for the purpose[13].

On making such an application[14], the applicants, or the person making the application on their behalf, must immediately give notice to the registrar of companies[15]. On being served with notice of any such application, the company must immediately give notice to the registrar[16]; and, if a company fails to comply with this requirement, an offence is committed by the company, and by every officer of the company who is in default[17], and any person guilty of such an offence is liable on summary conviction to a fine not exceeding level 3 on the standard scale[18] and for continued contravention a daily default fine[19] not exceeding one-tenth of level 3 on the standard scale[20].

On the hearing of the application, the court must make an order either cancelling[21] or confirming[22] the resolution[23]; and may:

(a) make that order on such terms and conditions as it thinks fit[24];
(b) adjourn the proceedings, if it thinks fit, in order that an arrangement may be made to the satisfaction of the court for the purchase of the interests of dissentient members[25]; and
(c) give such directions and make such orders as it thinks expedient for facilitating or carrying into effect any such arrangement[26].

The court's order may, if the court thinks fit, provide for the purchase by the company of the shares of any of its members[27] and for the reduction accordingly of the company's capital[28], and may make such alteration in the company's articles[29] as may be required in consequence of that provision[30].

Within 15 days of the making of the court's order on the application, or within such longer period as the court may at any time direct, the company must deliver to the registrar of companies a copy of the order[31]. A company which fails to comply with this requirement, and any officer of it who is in default, commits an offence[32] and any person guilty of such an offence is liable on summary conviction to a fine not exceeding level 3 on the standard scale and for continued contravention a daily default fine not exceeding one-tenth of level 3 on the standard scale[33].

The court's order may, if the court thinks fit, require the company not to make any, or any specified, amendments to its articles without the permission of the court[34].

1 As to the meaning of 'special resolution' see PARA 686.

2 As to the meaning of 'company' under the Companies Acts see PARA 21; and as to the meaning of the 'Companies Acts' see PARA 13. As to the meaning of 'public company' see PARA 95.

3 As to the meanings of 'private company' and 'limited company' see PARA 95.

4 Ie as required by the Companies Act 2006 s 97 (see PARA 173): see s 98(1). As to the procedure on application to re-register a public company as a private limited company under s 97 see PARA 173.

5 Companies Act 2006 s 98(1), (7) (s 98(7) added by SI 2014/821). The application should state why the special resolution is being challenged, and it may be struck out where no proper grounds for complaint have been disclosed by the applicant and the court can, on an application for striking out, consider how appropriate is the remedy sought and how reasonable is the conduct of the petitioner in the light of offers made to him to purchase his shares: *Re a Company (No 005685 of 1988), ex p Schwarcz (No 2)* [1989] BCLC 427. As to shares generally see PARA 1231.

6 As to the nominal value of shares see PARA 1233.

7 As to the meanings of 'company having a share capital', 'share' and 'share capital' see PARA 1231. As to the meaning of 'issued share capital' see PARA 1234.

8 Companies Act 2006 s 98(1)(a). For these purposes, any of the company's issued share capital held as treasury shares must be disregarded: see s 98(1)(a). As to treasury shares see PARA 1437. As to classes of shares generally see PARA 1246 et seq.

Persons holding the ultimate economic interest in shares held in another person's name are not 'holders' of issued share capital for these purposes and have no standing to bring an application under s 98: *Re DNick Holding plc, Eckerle v Wickeder Westfalenstahl GmbH* [2013] EWHC 68 (Ch), [2014] Ch 196, [2013] NLJR 107.

9 As to the meaning of 'company limited by shares' see PARA 95.

10 Companies Act 2006 s 98(1)(b). As to the meaning of 'member' see PARA 323. As to membership of a company generally see PARA 323 et seq.

11 Companies Act 2006 s 98(1)(c).

12 Companies Act 2006 s 98(1).

13 Companies Act 2006 s 98(2).

14 Ie under the Companies Act 2006 s 98 (see the text and notes 1–13): see s 99(1).

15 Companies Act 2006 s 99(1). This requirement is without prejudice to any provision of rules of court as to service of notice of the application: see s 99(1). As to the meaning of 'registrar of companies' see PARA 126 note 2. As to the delivery of documents to the registrar see PARA 136; and as to the requirements generally for the proper delivery of documents to the registrar see PARA 137. As to the meanings of 'document' and of references to delivering a document for these purposes see PARA 136 note 2.

16 Companies Act 2006 s 99(2).

17 Companies Act 2006 s 99(4). As to the meaning of 'officer' generally under the Companies Act 2006 see PARA 679; and as to the meaning of 'officer in default' see PARA 316.

18 As to the standard scale and the powers of magistrates' courts to issue fines on summary conviction see SENTENCING vol 92 (2015) PARA 176.

19 As to the meaning of 'daily default fine' see PARA 1816.

20 Companies Act 2006 s 99(5).

21 The court may be disinclined to cancel the resolution where a very large majority of the shareholders have voted in favour of the resolution: see *Re a Company (No 005685 of 1988), ex p Schwarcz (No 2)* [1989] BCLC 427 (94.5% of the shareholders voted in favour).

22 Little guidance is given to the court as to the exercise of its discretion. It would appear from the Companies Act 2006 s 98(4)(a), (b), (5) (see the text and notes 24–25, 27–30) with its reference to the sale of the dissentient's shares that it was envisaged that it might be appropriate to invoke the court's jurisdiction where a dissentient shareholder finds himself locked into a company whereas previously, when the company was a public limited company, he had been able to transfer his shares more freely: see *Re a Company (No 005685 of 1988), ex p Schwarcz (No 2)* [1989] BCLC 427 at 437. Where the court has confirmed the resolution, the company may be re-registered under the Companies Act 2006 s 97: see s 97(2)(b); and PARA 173.
23 Companies Act 2006 s 98(3).
24 Companies Act 2006 s 98(4)(a).
25 Companies Act 2006 s 98(4)(b).
26 Companies Act 2006 s 98(4)(c).
27 The court may be disinclined to do this if a fair offer to purchase the petitioner's shares has been available but not taken up by the petitioner: *Re a Company (No 005685 of 1988), ex p Schwarcz (No 2)* [1989] BCLC 427.
28 Companies Act 2006 s 98(5)(a).
29 As to the meaning of references to a company's 'articles' see PARA 227 note 2. As to a company's articles of association generally see PARA 227 et seq.
30 Companies Act 2006 s 98(5)(b). As to the amendment of articles of association see PARA 231 et seq.
31 Companies Act 2006 s 99(3).
32 Companies Act 2006 s 99(4).
33 Companies Act 2006 s 99(5).
34 Companies Act 2006 s 98(6).

175. Issue of certificate of re-registration as private limited company. If, on an application for re-registration as a private limited company[1], the registrar of companies[2] is satisfied that the company is entitled to be so re-registered, the company must be re-registered accordingly[3].

The registrar must issue a certificate of incorporation[4] altered to meet the circumstances of the case[5]; and the certificate must state that it is issued on re-registration and it must state the date on which it is issued[6].

On the issue to a company of the certificate:

(1) the company, by virtue of the issue of that certificate, becomes a private limited company[7]; and

(2) the changes in the company's name and articles take effect[8].

The certificate is conclusive evidence that the requirements of the Companies Act 2006[9] as to re-registration[10] have been complied with[11].

1 As to the meaning of 'company' under the Companies Acts see PARA 21; and as to the meaning of the 'Companies Acts' see PARA 13. As to the meanings of 'private company' and 'limited company' see PARA 95. As to the procedure on application to re-register a public company as a private limited company see PARA 173.
2 As to the meaning of 'registrar of companies' see PARA 126 note 2.
3 Companies Act 2006 s 101(1). The registrar may accept the statement of compliance required by s 97(1)(c) (see PARA 173) as sufficient evidence that the company is entitled to be re-registered as a private limited company: see s 100(4); and PARA 173. As to fees payable to the registrar under Pt 7 (ss 89–111) (see PARAS 167 et seq, 176 et seq) see the Registrar of Companies (Fees) (Companies, Overseas Companies and Limited Liability Partnerships) Regulations 2012, SI 2012/1907, reg 3, Sch 1 para 8(c).
4 As to a company's certificate of incorporation see PARA 114. As to public notice of the issue of certificates of incorporation see the Companies Act 2006 s 1064; and PARA 133.
5 Companies Act 2006 s 101(2).
6 Companies Act 2006 s 101(3).
7 Companies Act 2006 s 101(4)(a).
8 Companies Act 2006 s 101(4)(b). An application for re-registration as a private limited company must contain a statement of the company's proposed name on re-registration and such an application must be accompanied by a copy of the company's articles of association as proposed to be amended: see s 99; and PARA 174. As to the change of a company's name see PARAS 216–218. As to the required indications in the name of a private limited company see

PARA 199 et seq. As to the meaning of references to a company's 'articles' see PARA 227 note 2. As to a company's articles of association generally see PARA 227 et seq.

9 References in the company law provisions of the Companies Act 2006 to the requirements of that Act include the requirements of regulations and orders made under it: s 1172. As to the meaning of the 'company law provisions' of the Companies Act 2006 see PARA 13 note 6.

10 Ie under the Companies Act 2006 Pt 7: see s 89; and PARA 167.

11 Companies Act 2006 s 101(5).

(iv) Private Limited Company becoming an Unlimited Company

176. Procedure on application to re-register as unlimited company. A private limited company[1] may be re-registered as an unlimited company[2] if:

(1) all the members of the company[3] have assented to its being so re-registered[4];

(2) the following condition is met[5], namely that the company has not previously been re-registered as limited[6]; and

(3) an application for re-registration is delivered to the registrar of companies[7], together with the other necessary documents[8], and a statement of compliance[9].

An application for re-registration as an unlimited company must contain a statement of the company's proposed name on re-registration[10]; and the application must be accompanied by:

(a) the prescribed form of assent[11] to the company's being registered as an unlimited company, authenticated by or on behalf of all the members of the company[12];

(b) a copy of the company's articles[13] as proposed to be amended[14].

The statement of compliance that is required to be delivered under head (3) above together with the application is a statement that the statutory requirements as to re-registration[15] as an unlimited company have been complied with[16]. The statement must contain a statement by the directors[17] of the company[18]:

(i) that the persons by whom or on whose behalf the form of assent is authenticated constitute the whole membership of the company[19]; and

(ii) if any of the members have not authenticated that form themselves, that the directors have taken all reasonable steps to satisfy themselves that each person who authenticated it on behalf of a member was lawfully empowered to do so[20].

The registrar may accept the statement of compliance as sufficient evidence that the company is entitled to be re-registered as an unlimited company[21].

1 As to the meaning of 'company' under the Companies Acts see PARA 21; and as to the meaning of the 'Companies Acts' see PARA 13. As to the meanings of 'private company' and 'limited company' see PARA 95.

2 Ie under the Companies Act 2006 Pt 7 (ss 89–111) (see PARAS 167 et seq, 177 et seq): see s 89; and PARA 167. As to the meaning of 'unlimited company' see PARA 95. As to fees payable to the registrar under Pt 7 see the Registrar of Companies (Fees) (Companies, Overseas Companies and Limited Liability Partnerships) Regulations 2012, SI 2012/1907, reg 3, Sch 1 para 8(c).

3 As to the meaning of 'member' see PARA 323. As to membership of a company generally see PARA 323 et seq.

4 Companies Act 2006 s 102(1)(a). For these purposes, a trustee in bankruptcy of a member of the company is entitled, to the exclusion of the member, to assent to the company's becoming unlimited (s 102(4)(a)); and the personal representative of a deceased member of the company may assent on behalf of the deceased (s 102(4)(b)). As to the trustee in bankruptcy see BANKRUPTCY AND INDIVIDUAL INSOLVENCY vol 5 (2013) PARA 314 et seq. As to the meaning of 'personal representative' see WILLS AND INTESTACY vol 103 (2010) PARA 608.

5 Companies Act 2006 s 102(1)(b).

6 Companies Act 2006 s 102(2). An unlimited company may have been re-registered as limited under the Companies Act 1967 s 44 (repealed) or the Companies Act 2006 s 105 (see PARA 178).

7 Ie in accordance with the Companies Act 2006 s 103 (see the text and notes 10–21): see s 102(1)(c). As to the meaning of 'registrar of companies' see PARA 126 note 2. As to the delivery of documents to the registrar see PARA 136; and as to the requirements generally for the proper delivery of documents to the registrar see PARA 137. As to the meanings of 'document' and of references to delivering a document for these purposes see PARA 136 note 2.

8 Ie the other documents required by the Companies Act 2006 s 103 (see the text and notes 10–21): see s 102(1)(c).

9 Companies Act 2006 s 102(1)(c).

10 Companies Act 2006 s 103(1). The company must make such changes in its name as are necessary in connection with its becoming an unlimited company, and, if it is to have a share capital, as are necessary in connection with its becoming an unlimited company having a share capital: s 102(3). As to the meanings of 'company having a share capital', 'share' and 'share capital' see PARA 1231. As to the change of a company's name see PARAS 216–218. As to the required indications in the name of an unlimited company see PARA 199 et seq.

11 In the Companies Acts, 'prescribed' means prescribed (by order or by regulations) by the Secretary of State: Companies Act 2006 s 1167. As to the making of orders and regulations under the Companies Act 2006 generally see ss 1288–1292. As to the Secretary of State see PARA 6. Partly in exercise of the powers conferred by s 103(2)(a), the Secretary of State has made the Companies (Registration) Regulations 2008, SI 2008/3014. Accordingly, for the purposes of the Companies Act 2006 s 103(2)(a), the prescribed form is the form set out in the Companies (Registration) Regulations 2008, SI 2008/3014, reg 5, Sch 3.

12 Companies Act 2006 s 103(2)(a). In relation to the authentication of a document under the Companies Act 2006 see s 1146; and PARA 750 et seq.

13 As to the meaning of references to a company's 'articles' see PARA 227 note 2. As to a company's articles of association generally see PARA 227 et seq.

14 Companies Act 2006 s 103(2)(b). The company must make such changes in its articles as are necessary in connection with its becoming an unlimited company, and, if it is to have a share capital, as are necessary in connection with its becoming an unlimited company having a share capital: s 102(3). As to the amendment of articles of association see PARA 231 et seq.

15 Ie the requirements of the Companies Act 2006 Pt 7: see s 103(3). References in the company law provisions of the Companies Act 2006 to the requirements of that Act include the requirements of regulations and orders made under it: s 1172. As to the meaning of the 'company law provisions' of the Companies Act 2006 see PARA 13 note 6.

16 Companies Act 2006 s 103(3).

17 As to the meaning of 'director' see PARA 512.

18 Companies Act 2006 s 103(4).

19 Companies Act 2006 s 103(4)(a).

20 Companies Act 2006 s 103(4)(b).

21 Companies Act 2006 s 103(5).

177. Issue of certificate of re-registration as unlimited company. If, on an application for re-registration of a private limited company[1] as an unlimited company[2], the registrar of companies[3] is satisfied that the company is entitled to be so re-registered, the company must be re-registered accordingly[4].

The registrar must issue a certificate of incorporation[5] altered to meet the circumstances of the case[6]; and the certificate must state that it is issued on re-registration and it must state the date on which it is issued[7].

On the issue to a company of the certificate:

(1) the company, by virtue of the issue of that certificate, becomes an unlimited company[8]; and

(2) the changes in the company's name and articles take effect[9].

The certificate is conclusive evidence that the requirements of the Companies Act 2006[10] as to re-registration[11] have been complied with[12].

1 As to the meaning of 'company' under the Companies Acts see PARA 21; and as to the meaning of the 'Companies Acts' see PARA 13. As to the meanings of 'private company' and 'limited company' see PARA 95.

2 As to the meaning of 'unlimited company' see PARA 95. As to the procedure on application to re-register a private limited company as unlimited see PARA 176.

3 As to the meaning of 'registrar of companies' see PARA 126 note 2.

4 Companies Act 2006 s 104(1). The registrar may accept the statement of compliance required by s 102(1)(c) (see PARA 176) as sufficient evidence that the company is entitled to be re-registered as an unlimited company: see s 103(5); and PARA 176. As to fees payable to the registrar under Pt 7 (ss 89–111) (see PARAS 167 et seq, 178 et seq) see the Registrar of Companies (Fees) (Companies, Overseas Companies and Limited Liability Partnerships) Regulations 2012, SI 2012/1907, reg 3, Sch 1 para 8(c).

5 As to a company's certificate of incorporation see PARA 114. As to public notice of the issue of certificates of incorporation see the Companies Act 2006 s 1064; and PARA 133.

6 Companies Act 2006 s 104(2).

7 Companies Act 2006 s 104(3).

8 Companies Act 2006 s 104(4)(a). As to the nature and powers of an unlimited company see PARA 74.

9 Companies Act 2006 s 104(4)(b). An application for the re-registration of a private limited company as unlimited must contain a statement of the company's proposed name on re-registration and such an application must be accompanied by a copy of the company's articles of association as proposed to be amended: see s 103; and PARA 176. As to the change of a company's name see PARAS 216–218. As to the required indications in the name of an unlimited company see PARA 199 et seq. As to the meaning of references to a company's 'articles' see PARA 227 note 2. As to a company's articles of association generally, including their amendment, see PARA 227 et seq.

10 References in the company law provisions of the Companies Act 2006 to the requirements of that Act include the requirements of regulations and orders made under it: s 1172. As to the meaning of the 'company law provisions' of the Companies Act 2006 see PARA 13 note 6.

11 Ie under the Companies Act 2006 Pt 7: see s 89; and PARA 167.

12 Companies Act 2006 s 104(5).

(v) Unlimited Company becoming a Limited Company

178. Procedure on application to re-register unlimited company as private limited company. An unlimited company[1] may be re-registered as a private limited company[2] if:

(1) a special resolution[3] that it should be so re-registered is passed[4];

(2) the following condition is met[5], namely that the company has not previously been re-registered as unlimited[6]; and

(3) an application for re-registration is delivered to the registrar of companies[7], together with the other necessary documents[8], and a statement of compliance[9].

An application for re-registration as a limited company must contain a statement of the company's proposed name on re-registration[10]; and it must be accompanied by:

(a) a copy of the special resolution[11] that the company should re-register as a private limited company[12];

(b) if the company is to be limited by guarantee, a statement of guarantee[13];

(c) a copy of the company's articles of association[14] as proposed to be amended[15].

The statement of compliance that is required to be delivered under head (3) above together with the application is a statement that the statutory requirements as to re-registration[16] as a limited company have been complied with[17]. The registrar may accept the statement of compliance as sufficient evidence that the company is entitled to be re-registered as a limited company[18].

The statement of guarantee that is required to be delivered under head (b) above in the case of a company that is to be limited by guarantee must state that each member[19] undertakes that, if the company is wound up[20] while he is a member, or within one year after he ceases to be a member, he will contribute to the assets of the company such amount as may be required for[21]:

(i) payment of the debts and liabilities of the company contracted before he ceases to be a member[22];
(ii) payment of the costs, charges and expenses of winding up[23]; and
(iii) adjustment of the rights of the contributories among themselves[24],

not exceeding a specified amount[25].

1 As to the meaning of 'company' under the Companies Acts see PARA 21; and as to the meaning of the 'Companies Acts' see PARA 13. As to the meaning of 'unlimited company' see PARA 95.
2 Ie under the Companies Act 2006 Pt 7 (ss 89–111) (see PARAS 167 et seq, 179 et seq): see s 89; and PARA 167. As to the meanings of 'private company' and 'limited company' see PARA 95. As to fees payable to the registrar under Pt 7 see the Registrar of Companies (Fees) (Companies, Overseas Companies and Limited Liability Partnerships) Regulations 2012, SI 2012/1907, reg 3, Sch 1 para 8(c).
3 As to the meaning of 'special resolution' see PARA 686.
4 Companies Act 2006 s 105(1)(a). The special resolution must state whether the company is to be limited by shares or by guarantee: s 105(3). As to the meanings of 'company limited by shares' and 'company limited by guarantee' see PARA 95. As to the meaning of 'share' see PARA 1231.
5 Companies Act 2006 s 105(1)(b).
6 Companies Act 2006 s 105(2).
7 Ie in accordance with the Companies Act 2006 s 106 (see the text and notes 10–25): see s 105(1)(c). As to the meaning of 'registrar of companies' see PARA 126 note 2. As to the delivery of documents to the registrar see PARA 136; and as to the requirements generally for the proper delivery of documents to the registrar see PARA 137. As to the meanings of 'document' and of references to delivering a document for these purposes see PARA 136 note 2.
8 Ie the other documents required by the Companies Act 2006 s 106 (see the text and notes 10–25): see s 105(1)(c).
9 Companies Act 2006 s 105(1)(c).
10 Companies Act 2006 s 106(1). The company must make such changes in its name as are necessary in connection with its becoming a company limited by shares or, as the case may be, by guarantee: s 105(4). As to the change of a company's name see PARAS 216–218. As to the required indications in the name of a limited company see PARA 199 et seq.
11 Ie unless a copy has already been forwarded to the registrar under the Companies Act 2006 Pt 3 Ch 3 (ss 29–30) (resolutions and agreements affecting a company's constitution) (see PARA 230): see s 106(2)(a). As to the meaning of references to a company's constitution see PARA 226.
12 Companies Act 2006 s 106(2)(a).
13 Companies Act 2006 s 106(2)(b).
14 As to the meaning of references to a company's 'articles' see PARA 227 note 2. As to a company's articles of association generally see PARA 227 et seq.
15 Companies Act 2006 s 106(2)(c). The company must make such changes in its articles as are necessary in connection with its becoming a company limited by shares or, as the case may be, by guarantee: s 105(4). As to the amendment of articles of association see PARA 231 et seq.
16 Ie the requirements of the Companies Act 2006 Pt 7: see s 106(4). References in the company law provisions of the Companies Act 2006 to the requirements of that Act include the requirements of regulations and orders made under it: s 1172. As to the meaning of the 'company law provisions' of the Companies Act 2006 see PARA 13 note 6.
17 Companies Act 2006 s 106(4).
18 Companies Act 2006 s 106(5).
19 As to the meaning of 'member' see PARA 323. As to membership of a company generally see PARA 323 et seq.
20 As to winding up in general see COMPANY AND PARTNERSHIP INSOLVENCY vol 16 (2011) PARA 380 et seq.
21 Companies Act 2006 s 106(3).
22 Companies Act 2006 s 106(3)(a).
23 Companies Act 2006 s 106(3)(b).
24 Companies Act 2006 s 106(3)(c).
25 Companies Act 2006 s 106(3).

179. Issue of certificate of re-registration as private limited company. If, on an application for re-registration of an unlimited company[1] as a limited company[2], the registrar of companies[3] is satisfied that the company is entitled to be so re-registered, the company must be re-registered accordingly[4].

The registrar must issue a certificate of incorporation[5] altered to meet the circumstances of the case[6]; and the certificate must state that it is issued on re-registration and it must state the date on which it is so issued[7].

On the issue to a company of the certificate:

(1) the company, by virtue of the issue of that certificate, becomes a limited company[8]; and

(2) the changes in the company's name and articles take effect[9].

The certificate is conclusive evidence that the requirements of the Companies Act 2006[10] as to re-registration[11] have been complied with[12].

1 As to the meaning of 'company' under the Companies Acts see PARA 21; and as to the meaning of the 'Companies Acts' see PARA 13. As to the meaning of 'unlimited company' see PARA 95.

2 As to the procedure on application to re-register an unlimited company as a private limited company see PARA 178. As to the meanings of 'private company' and 'limited company' see PARA 95.

3 As to the meaning of 'registrar of companies' see PARA 126 note 2.

4 Companies Act 2006 s 107(1). The registrar may accept the statement of compliance required by s 105(1)(c) (see PARA 178) as sufficient evidence that the company is entitled to be re-registered as a limited company: see s 106(5); and PARA 178. As to fees payable to the registrar under Pt 7 (ss 89–111) (see PARAS 167 et seq, 180 et seq) see the Registrar of Companies (Fees) (Companies, Overseas Companies and Limited Liability Partnerships) Regulations 2012, SI 2012/1907, reg 3, Sch 1 para 8(c).

5 As to a company's certificate of incorporation see PARA 114. As to public notice of the issue of certificates of incorporation see the Companies Act 2006 s 1064; and PARA 133.

6 Companies Act 2006 s 107(2).

7 Companies Act 2006 s 107(3).

8 Companies Act 2006 s 107(4)(a).

9 Companies Act 2006 s 107(4)(b). An application for the re-registration of an unlimited company as limited must contain a statement of the company's proposed name on re-registration and such an application must be accompanied by a copy of the company's articles of association as proposed to be amended: see s 106; and PARA 178. As to the change of a company's name see PARAS 216–218. As to the required indications in the name of a limited company see PARA 199 et seq. As to the meaning of references to a company's 'articles' see PARA 227 note 2. As to a company's articles of association generally see PARA 227 et seq.

10 References in the company law provisions of the Companies Act 2006 to the requirements of that Act include the requirements of regulations and orders made under it: s 1172. As to the meaning of the 'company law provisions' of the Companies Act 2006 see PARA 13 note 6.

11 Ie under the Companies Act 2006 Pt 7: see s 89; and PARA 167.

12 Companies Act 2006 s 107(5).

180. Statement of capital required where company already has share capital. An unlimited company[1] which on re-registration as a private limited company[2] already has allotted share capital[3] must, within 15 days after the re-registration, deliver a statement of capital to the registrar of companies[4]. This does not, however, apply if the information which would be included in the statement has already been sent to the registrar[5].

The statement of capital must state with respect to the company's share capital[6] on re-registration[7]:

(1) the total number of shares of the company[8];

(2) the aggregate nominal value of those shares[9];

(3) until 30 June 2016, the amount paid up and the amount, if any, unpaid on each share[10] (whether on account of the nominal value of the share or by way of premium)[11], or, as from that date[12], the aggregate amount, if any, unpaid on those shares (whether on account of their nominal value or by way of premium)[13];

(4) for each class of shares[14]:

(a) prescribed particulars of the rights attached to the shares[15];

(b) the total number of shares of that class[16]; and

(c) the aggregate nominal value of shares of that class[17].

If default is made in complying with these requirements[18], an offence is committed by the company, and by every officer of the company who is in default[19].

1 As to the meaning of 'company' under the Companies Acts see PARA 21; and as to the meaning of the 'Companies Acts' see PARA 13. As to the meaning of 'unlimited company' see PARA 95.

2 Ie under the Companies Act 2006 s 107 (see PARA 179): see s 108(1). As to the meanings of 'private company' and 'limited company' see PARA 95.

3 As to the meaning of 'allotted share capital' see PARA 1234.

4 Companies Act 2006 s 108(1). As to the meaning of 'registrar of companies' see PARA 126 note 2. As to the delivery of documents to the registrar see PARA 136; and as to the requirements generally for the proper delivery of documents to the registrar see PARA 137. As to the meanings of 'document' and of references to delivering a document for these purposes see PARA 136 note 2.

5 See the Companies Act 2006 s 108(2). The information may have been already sent to the registrar:

(1) in a statement of capital and initial shareholdings (see s 10; and PARA 107) (see s 108(2)(a));

(2) before 30 June 2016, in a statement of capital contained in an annual return under s 856(2) (see PARA 1596) (see s 108(2)(b) (as originally enacted)); or

(3) as from that date, the last statement of capital sent by the company (if different) (see the Companies Act 2006 s 108(2)(b) (substituted by the Small Business, Enterprise and Employment Act 2015 s 93(1), (4)); and the Small Business, Enterprise and Employment Act 2015 (Commencement No 4, Transitional and Savings Provisions) Regulations 2016, SI 2016/321, reg 6(b)).

As to the meaning of 'company limited by shares' see PARA 95. As to the meaning of 'share' see PARA 1231.

6 As to the meanings of 'company having a share capital' and 'share capital' see PARA 1231.

7 Companies Act 2006 s 108(3).

8 Companies Act 2006 s 108(3)(a).

9 Companies Act 2006 s 108(3)(b). As to the nominal value of shares see PARA 1233.

10 As to paid up and unpaid shares see PARA 1231 et seq.

11 Companies Act 2006 s 108(3)(d) (repealed by the Small Business, Enterprise and Employment Act 2015 Sch 6 paras 1, 4(b)). See also note 12.

12 See the Small Business, Enterprise and Employment Act 2015 (Commencement No 4, Transitional and Savings Provisions) Regulations 2016, SI 2016/321, reg 6(e).

13 Companies Act 2006 s 108(3)(ba) (added by the Small Business, Enterprise and Employment Act 2015 Sch 6 paras 1, 4(a)).

14 Companies Act 2006 s 108(3)(c). As to classes of shares generally see PARA 1246 et seq.

15 Companies Act 2006 s 108(3)(c)(i). In the Companies Acts, 'prescribed' means prescribed (by order or by regulations) by the Secretary of State: Companies Act 2006 s 1167. As to the meaning of the 'Companies Acts' see PARA 13. As to the making of orders and regulations under the Companies Act 2006 generally see ss 1288–1292. As to the Secretary of State see PARA 6. Partly in exercise of the powers conferred by s 108(3)(c)(i), the Secretary of State has made the Companies (Shares and Share Capital) Order 2009, SI 2009/388. Accordingly, the following particulars of the rights attached to shares are prescribed for the purposes of the Companies Act 2006 s 108(3)(c)(i) (see the Companies (Shares and Share Capital) Order 2009, SI 2009/388, art 2(1), (2)(c)):

(1) particulars of any voting rights attached to the shares, including rights that arise only in certain circumstances (art 2(3)(a));

(2) particulars of any rights attached to the shares, as respects dividends, to participate in a distribution (art 2(3)(b));

(3) particulars of any rights attached to the shares, as respects capital, to participate in a distribution (including on winding up) (art 2(3)(c)); and

(4) whether the shares are to be redeemed or are liable to be redeemed at the option of the company or the shareholder (art 2(3)(d)).

As to rights attached to classes of shares generally see PARA 1246 et seq; as to redeemable shares see PARAS 1241, 1416 et seq; and as to distributions and dividends see PARA 1563 et seq. As to winding up in general see COMPANY AND PARTNERSHIP INSOLVENCY vol 16 (2011) PARA 380 et seq.

16 Companies Act 2006 s 108(3)(c)(ii).

17 Companies Act 2006 s 108(3)(c)(iii).

18 Ie the requirements of the Companies Act 2006 s 108: see s 108(4). References in the company law provisions of the Companies Act 2006 to the requirements of that Act include the requirements

of regulations and orders made under it: s 1172. As to the meaning of the 'company law provisions' of the Companies Act 2006 see PARA 13 note 6.

19 Companies Act 2006 s 108(4). As to the meaning of 'officer' generally under the Companies Act 2006 see PARA 679; and as to the meaning of 'officer in default' see PARA 315.

Any person guilty of such an offence is liable on summary conviction to a fine not exceeding level 3 on the standard scale and for continued contravention to a daily default fine not exceeding one-tenth of level 3 on the standard scale: Companies Act 2006 s 108(5). As to the standard scale and the powers of magistrates' courts to issue fines on summary conviction see SENTENCING vol 92 (2015) PARA 176; and as to the meaning of 'daily default fine' see PARA 1816.

(vi) Public Company becoming Private and Unlimited

181. Procedure on application to re-register public company as a private unlimited company. A public company limited by shares[1] may be re-registered as an unlimited private company with a share capital[2] if:

(1) all the members of the company[3] have assented to its being so re-registered[4];

(2) the following condition is met[5], namely that the company has not previously been re-registered either as limited or as unlimited[6]; and

(3) an application for re-registration is delivered to the registrar of companies[7], together with the other necessary documents[8], and a statement of compliance[9].

An application for the re-registration of a public company as an unlimited private company must contain a statement of the company's proposed name on re-registration[10]; and the application must be accompanied by:

(a) the prescribed form of assent[11] to the company's being registered as an unlimited company, authenticated by or on behalf of all the members of the company[12];

(b) a copy of the company's articles[13] as proposed to be amended[14].

The statement of compliance that is required to be delivered under head (3) above together with the application is a statement that the statutory requirements as to re-registration[15] as an unlimited private company have been complied with[16]. The statement must contain a statement by the directors[17] of the company[18]:

(i) that the persons by whom or on whose behalf the form of assent is authenticated constitute the whole membership of the company[19]; and

(ii) if any of the members have not authenticated that form themselves, that the directors have taken all reasonable steps to satisfy themselves that each person who authenticated it on behalf of a member was lawfully empowered to do so[20].

The registrar may accept the statement of compliance as sufficient evidence that the company is entitled to be re-registered as an unlimited private company[21].

1 As to the meaning of 'company' under the Companies Acts see PARA 21; and as to the meaning of the 'Companies Acts' see PARA 13. As to the meanings of 'public company' and 'company limited by shares' see PARA 95. As to the meaning of 'share' see PARA 1231.

2 Ie under the Companies Act 2006 Pt 7 (ss 89–111) (see PARAS 167 et seq, 182): see s 89; and PARA 167. As to the meanings of 'private company' and 'unlimited company' see PARA 95. As to the meanings of 'company having a share capital' and 'share capital' see PARA 1231. As to fees payable to the registrar under Pt 7 see the Registrar of Companies (Fees) (Companies, Overseas Companies and Limited Liability Partnerships) Regulations 2012, SI 2012/1907, reg 3, Sch 1 para 8(c).

3 As to the meaning of 'member' see PARA 323. As to membership of a company generally see PARA 323 et seq.

4 Companies Act 2006 s 109(1)(a). For these purposes, a trustee in bankruptcy of a member of the company is entitled, to the exclusion of the member, to assent to the company's re-registration as unlimited (s 109(4)(a)); and the personal representative of a deceased member of the company may assent on behalf of the deceased (s 109(4)(b)). As to the trustee in bankruptcy see

BANKRUPTCY AND INDIVIDUAL INSOLVENCY vol 5 (2013) PARA 314 et seq. As to the meaning of 'personal representative' see WILLS AND INTESTACY vol 103 (2010) PARA 608.
5 Companies Act 2006 s 109(1)(b).
6 Companies Act 2006 s 109(2).
7 Ie in accordance with the Companies Act 2006 s 110 (see the text and notes 10–21): see s 109(1)(c). As to the meaning of 'registrar of companies' see PARA 126 note 2. As to the delivery of documents to the registrar see PARA 136; and as to the requirements generally for the proper delivery of documents to the registrar see PARA 137. As to the meanings of 'document' and of references to delivering a document for these purposes see PARA 136 note 2.
8 Ie the other documents required by the Companies Act 2006 s 110 (see the text and notes 10–21): see s 109(1)(c).
9 Companies Act 2006 s 109(1)(c).
10 Companies Act 2006 s 110(1). The company must make such changes in its name as are necessary in connection with its becoming an unlimited private company: s 109(3). As to the change of a company's name see PARAS 216–218. As to the required indications in the name of an unlimited company see PARA 199 et seq.
11 In the Companies Acts, 'prescribed' means prescribed (by order or by regulations) by the Secretary of State: Companies Act 2006 s 1167. As to the making of orders and regulations under the Companies Act 2006 generally see ss 1288–1292. As to the Secretary of State see PARA 6. Partly in exercise of the powers conferred by s 110(2)(a), the Secretary of State has made the Companies (Registration) Regulations 2008, SI 2008/3014. Accordingly, for the purposes of the Companies Act 2006 s 110(2)(a), the prescribed form is the form set out in the Companies (Registration) Regulations 2008, SI 2008/3014, reg 6, Sch 4.
12 Companies Act 2006 s 110(2)(a). In relation to the authentication of a document under the Companies Act 2006 see s 1146; and PARA 750 et seq.
13 As to the meaning of references to a company's 'articles' see PARA 227 note 2. As to a company's articles of association generally see PARA 227 et seq.
14 Companies Act 2006 s 110(2)(b). The company must make such changes in its articles as are necessary in connection with its becoming an unlimited private company: s 109(3). As to the amendment of articles of association see PARA 231 et seq.
15 Ie the requirements of the Companies Act 2006 Pt 7: see s 110(3). References in the company law provisions of the Companies Act 2006 to the requirements of that Act include the requirements of regulations and orders made under it: s 1172. As to the meaning of the 'company law provisions' of the Companies Act 2006 see PARA 13 note 6.
16 Companies Act 2006 s 110(3).
17 As to the meaning of 'director' see PARA 512.
18 Companies Act 2006 s 110(4).
19 Companies Act 2006 s 110(4)(a).
20 Companies Act 2006 s 110(4)(b).
21 Companies Act 2006 s 110(5).

182. Issue of certificate of re-registration as private unlimited company. If, on an application for re-registration of a public company[1] as an unlimited private company[2], the registrar of companies[3] is satisfied that the company is entitled to be so re-registered, the company must be re-registered accordingly[4].

The registrar must issue a certificate of incorporation[5] altered to meet the circumstances of the case[6]; and the certificate must state that it is issued on re-registration and it must state the date on which it is so issued[7].

On the issue to a company of the certificate:

(1) the company, by virtue of the issue of that certificate, becomes an unlimited private company[8]; and
(2) the changes in the company's name and articles take effect[9].

The certificate is conclusive evidence that the requirements of the Companies Act 2006[10] as to re-registration[11] have been complied with[12].

1 As to the meaning of 'company' under the Companies Acts see PARA 21; and as to the meaning of the 'Companies Acts' see PARA 13. As to the meaning of 'public company' see PARA 95.
2 Ie under the Companies Act 2006 Pt 7 (ss 89–111) (see PARA 167 et seq): see s 89; and PARA 167. As to the meanings of 'private company' and 'unlimited company' see PARA 95. As to the procedure on application to re-register a public company as an unlimited private company see

PARA 181. As to fees payable to the registrar under Pt 7 see the Registrar of Companies (Fees) (Companies, Overseas Companies and Limited Liability Partnerships) Regulations 2012, SI 2012/1907, reg 3, Sch 1 para 8(c).

3 As to the meaning of 'registrar of companies' see PARA 126 note 2.

4 Companies Act 2006 s 111(1). The registrar may accept the statement of compliance required by s 109(1)(c) (see PARA 181) as sufficient evidence that the company is entitled to be re-registered as an unlimited private company: see s 110(5); and PARA 181.

5 As to a company's certificate of incorporation see PARA 114. As to public notice of the issue of certificates of incorporation see the Companies Act 2006 s 1064; and PARA 133.

6 Companies Act 2006 s 111(2).

7 Companies Act 2006 s 111(3).

8 Companies Act 2006 s 111(4)(a).

9 Companies Act 2006 s 111(4)(b). An application for the re-registration of a public company as an unlimited private company must contain a statement of the company's proposed name on re-registration and such an application must be accompanied by a copy of the company's articles of association as proposed to be amended: see s 110; and PARA 181. As to the change of a company's name see PARAS 216–218. As to the required indications in the name of an unlimited company see PARA 199 et seq. As to the meaning of references to a company's 'articles' see PARA 227 note 2. As to a company's articles of association generally see PARA 227 et seq.

10 References in the company law provisions of the Companies Act 2006 to the requirements of that Act include the requirements of regulations and orders made under it: s 1172. As to the meaning of the 'company law provisions' of the Companies Act 2006 see PARA 13 note 6.

11 Ie under the Companies Act 2006 Pt 7 (see PARA 167 et seq): see s 89; and PARA 167.

12 Companies Act 2006 s 111(5).

(vii) Old Public Companies

183. Meaning and classification of 'old public company'. An 'old public company' is a company[1] limited by shares[2] or by guarantee[3] and having a share capital[4] in respect of which the following conditions are satisfied[5]:

(1) the company either existed on 22 December 1980[6] or was incorporated after that date pursuant to an application made before that date[7];

(2) on that date or, if later, on the day of the company's incorporation, the company was not or, as the case may be, would not have been a private company within the Companies Act 1948[8]; and

(3) the company has not since that date or the day of the company's incorporation, as the case may be, either been re-registered as a public company[9] or become[10] a private company[11].

With some exceptions[12], references in the Companies Acts to a public company, or a company other than a private company, are to be read as including, unless the context otherwise requires, references to an old public company[13], and references to a private company are to be read accordingly[14].

1 As to the meaning of 'company' under the Companies Acts see PARA 21; and as to the meaning of the 'Companies Acts' see PARA 13.

2 As to the meaning of 'company limited by shares' see PARA 95.

3 As to the meaning of 'company limited by guarantee' see PARA 95.

4 As to the meanings of 'company having a share capital' and 'share capital' see PARA 1231.

5 Companies Act 2006 (Consequential Amendments and Transitional Provisions) Order 2011, SI 2011/1265, Sch 1 para 1.

6 Ie the date on which the corresponding provisions of the Companies Act 1980 (ie s 8) (now repealed) came into force. As to the Companies Act 1980 generally see PARA 10.

7 Companies Act 2006 (Consequential Amendments and Transitional Provisions) Order 2011, SI 2011/1265, Sch 1 para 1(a).

8 Companies Act 2006 (Consequential Amendments and Transitional Provisions) Order 2011, SI 2011/1265, Sch 1 para 1(b). Under the Companies Act 1948 s 28 (repealed), a private company was defined as one which by its articles restricted the right to transfer its shares, limited the number of its members (with certain exceptions) to 50, and prohibited any invitation to the public to subscribe for any shares or debentures of the company.

9 Ie within the meaning of the Companies Act 1985 s 1(3) (repealed) or the Companies Act 2006 s 4(2). As to the meaning of 'public company' see PARA 95.
10 Ie within the meaning of the Companies Act 1985 s 1(3) (repealed) or the Companies Act 2006 s 4(1).
11 Companies Act 2006 (Consequential Amendments and Transitional Provisions) Order 2011, SI 2011/1265, Sch 1 para 1(c). As to the meaning of 'private company' see PARA 95. As to the re-registration of old public companies see PARA 184 et seq.
12 The Companies Act 2006 (Consequential Amendments and Transitional Provisions) Order 2011, SI 2011/1265, Sch 1 para 2(1), (2) (see the text and notes 13–14) does not apply in relation to the Companies Act 2006 Pt 7 (ss 89–111) (re-registration as a means of altering a company's status: see para 167 et seq) and ss 662–669 (treatment of shares held by or for public company: see PARA 1387 et seq) (see the Companies Act 2006 (Consequential Amendments and Transitional Provisions) Order 2011, SI 2011/1265, Sch 1 para 7(1), (2); and para 187): Sch 1 para 2(3)(a). Nor does it restrict the power to make provision by regulations under the Companies Act 2006 s 65 (inappropriate use of indications of company type or legal form: see PARA 203): Companies Act 2006 (Consequential Amendments and Transitional Provisions) Order 2011, SI 2011/1265, Sch 1 para 2(3)(b).
13 Companies Act 2006 (Consequential Amendments and Transitional Provisions) Order 2011, SI 2011/1265, Sch 1 para 2(1).
14 Companies Act 2006 (Consequential Amendments and Transitional Provisions) Order 2011, SI 2011/1265, Sch 1 para 2(2).

184. Re-registration of old public company as public company. The provisions of the Companies Act 2006 regarding re-registration as a public company limited by shares[1] apply to an old public company[2]. As they so apply, references to a private company[3] are to be read as references to an old public company[4] and references to a special resolution of the company are to be read as references to a resolution of the directors[5].

1 Ie the Companies Act 2006 ss 90–96: see PARA 168 et seq. As to the meaning of 'public company' see PARA 95. As to the meaning of 'company' under the Companies Acts see PARA 21; and as to the meaning of the 'Companies Acts' see PARA 13.
2 Companies Act 2006 (Consequential Amendments and Transitional Provisions) Order 2011, SI 2011/1265, Sch 1 para 3(1). References in Sch 1 to re-registration as a public company, in relation to an old public company, are to re-registration by virtue of Sch 1 para 3: Sch 1 para 3(4). As to the meaning of 'old public company' see PARA 183.
3 As to the meaning of 'private company' see PARA 95.
4 Companies Act 2006 (Consequential Amendments and Transitional Provisions) Order 2011, SI 2011/1265, Sch 1 para 3(2)(a).
5 Companies Act 2006 (Consequential Amendments and Transitional Provisions) Order 2011, SI 2011/1265, Sch 1 para 3(2)(b). As to the meaning of 'director' see PARA 512. The Companies Act 2006 Pt 3 Ch 3 (ss 29–30) (resolutions and agreements affecting a company's constitution) (see PARA 230) applies to such a resolution of the directors: Companies Act 2006 (Consequential Amendments and Transitional Provisions) Order 2011, SI 2011/1265, Sch 1 para 3(3).

185. Old public company becoming private. An old public company[1] may pass a special resolution[2] not to be re-registered as a public company[3]. If either:

(1) 28 days from the passing of the resolution elapse without an application being made to the court to cancel the resolution[4]; or

(2) such an application is made and proceedings are concluded on the application without the court making an order for the cancellation of the resolution[5],

the registrar of companies[6] must issue the company with a certificate stating that it is a private company[7]. The company then becomes a private company by virtue of the issue of the certificate[8]. A certificate so issued to a company is conclusive evidence that the above requirements have been complied with and that the company is a private company[9].

If an old public company delivers to the registrar a statutory declaration[10] by a director[11] or secretary of the company[12] that the company does not at the time of the declaration satisfy the conditions for the company to be re-registered as public[13], the registrar must issue the company with a certificate stating that it is a private company[14]. The company then becomes a private company by virtue of the issue of the certificate[15]. A certificate so issued to a company is conclusive evidence that these requirements have been complied with and that the company is a private company[16].

1 As to the meaning of 'old public company' see PARA 183.
2 As to special resolutions generally see PARA 686.
3 Companies Act 2006 (Consequential Amendments and Transitional Provisions) Order 2011, SI 2011/1265, Sch 1 para 4(1). As to the meaning of 'public company' see PARA 95. As to the meaning of 'company' under the Companies Acts see PARA 21; and as to the meaning of the 'Companies Acts' see PARA 13.

The Companies Act 2006 ss 98, 99 (application to court to cancel resolution; notice to registrar of court application or order: see PARA 174) apply to such a resolution as they would apply to a special resolution by a public company to be re-registered as private: Companies Act 2006 (Consequential Amendments and Transitional Provisions) Order 2011, SI 2011/1265, Sch 1 para 4(2).

4 Ie under the Companies Act 2006 s 98 (see PARA 174) as applied (see note 3).
5 For the purposes of the Companies Act 2006 (Consequential Amendments and Transitional Provisions) Order 2011, SI 2011/1265, Sch 1 para 4(3)(b) (see head (2) in the text), proceedings on the application are concluded either when the period mentioned in the Companies Act 2006 s 99(3) (see PARA 174) as applied (see note 3) for delivering a copy of the court's order on the application to the registrar has expired, or when the company has been notified that the application has been withdrawn: Companies Act 2006 (Consequential Amendments and Transitional Provisions) Order 2011, SI 2011/1265, Sch 1 para 4(5).
6 As to the meaning of 'registrar of companies' see PARA 126 note 2. As to the delivery of documents to the registrar see PARA 136; and as to the requirements generally for the proper delivery of documents to the registrar see PARA 137.
7 Companies Act 2006 (Consequential Amendments and Transitional Provisions) Order 2011, SI 2011/1265, Sch 1 para 4(3).
8 Companies Act 2006 (Consequential Amendments and Transitional Provisions) Order 2011, SI 2011/1265, Sch 1 para 4(4).
9 Companies Act 2006 (Consequential Amendments and Transitional Provisions) Order 2011, SI 2011/1265, Sch 1 para 4(6).
10 Statutory declarations are made by virtue of the Statutory Declarations Act 1835: see CIVIL PROCEDURE vol 12 (2015) PARA 827.
11 As to the meaning of 'director' see PARA 512.
12 As to the company secretary see PARA 669 et seq.
13 As to re-registration of an old public company as a public company see PARA 184.
14 Companies Act 2006 (Consequential Amendments and Transitional Provisions) Order 2011, SI 2011/1265, Sch 1 para 5(1).
15 Companies Act 2006 (Consequential Amendments and Transitional Provisions) Order 2011, SI 2011/1265, Sch 1 para 5(2).
16 Companies Act 2006 (Consequential Amendments and Transitional Provisions) Order 2011, SI 2011/1265, Sch 1 para 5(3).

186. Failure by old public company to obtain new classification. If at any time a company which is an old public company[1] has not delivered to the registrar of companies[2] a declaration that the company does not at the time of the declaration satisfy the conditions for the company to be re-registered as public[3], the company and any officer of it who is in default[4] is guilty of an offence unless at the time the company:

(1) has applied to be re-registered as a public company[5], and the application has not been refused or withdrawn; or
(2) has passed a special resolution[6] not to be re-registered as a public company, and the resolution has not been revoked and has not been[7] cancelled[8].

1 As to the meaning of 'old public company' see PARA 183.

2 As to the meaning of 'registrar of companies' see PARA 126 note 2. As to the delivery of documents to the registrar see PARA 136; and as to the requirements generally for the proper delivery of documents to the registrar see PARA 137.
3 Ie a declaration under the Companies Act 2006 (Consequential Amendments and Transitional Provisions) Order 2011, SI 2011/1265, Sch 1 para 5 (see PARA 185): see Sch 1 para 6(1). As to the meaning of 'public company' see PARA 95. As to the meaning of 'company' under the Companies Acts see PARA 21; and as to the meaning of the 'Companies Acts' see PARA 13.
4 As to the meaning of 'officer' generally under the Companies Act 2006 see PARA 679; and as to the meaning of 'officer in default' see PARA 316.
5 As to re-registration of an old public company as a public company see PARA 184.
6 As to special resolutions generally see PARA 686.
7 Ie under the Companies Act 2006 s 98 (see PARA 174) as applied by the Companies Act 2006 (Consequential Amendments and Transitional Provisions) Order 2011, SI 2011/1265, Sch 1 para 5 (see PARA 185).
8 Companies Act 2006 (Consequential Amendments and Transitional Provisions) Order 2011, SI 2011/1265, Sch 1 para 6(1). A person guilty of such an offence is liable on summary conviction to a fine not exceeding level 3 on the standard scale and, for continued contravention, to a daily default fine not exceeding one-tenth of level 3 on the standard scale: Companies Act 2006 (Consequential Amendments and Transitional Provisions) Order 2011, SI 2011/1265, Sch 1 para 6(2). As to the standard scale and the powers of magistrates' courts to issue fines on summary conviction see SENTENCING vol 92 (2015) PARA 176; and as to the meaning of 'daily default fine' see PARA 1816.

187. Shares of old public company held by or charged to itself. In the provisions of the Companies Act 2006 regarding the treatment of shares held by or for a public company[1], references to a public company do not include an old public company[2].

In the case of a company that after 22 March 1982[3] remained an old public company, and did not before that date apply to be re-registered as a public company, any charge on its own shares[4] which was in existence on or immediately before that date is a permitted charge and not void[5] under the Companies Act 2006[6].

1 Ie the Companies Act 2006 ss 662–669 (see PARA 1387 et seq). As to the meaning of 'public company' see PARA 95. As to the meaning of 'company' under the Companies Acts see PARA 21; and as to the meaning of the 'Companies Acts' see PARA 13. As to the meaning of 'share' see PARA 1231
2 Companies Act 2006 (Consequential Amendments and Transitional Provisions) Order 2011, SI 2011/1265, Sch 1 para 7(1). However, the Companies Act 2006 s 668 (application of ss 662–667 to private company re-registering as public company: see PARA 1390) applies to an old public company as to a private company: Companies Act 2006 (Consequential Amendments and Transitional Provisions) Order 2011, SI 2011/1265, Sch 1 para 7(2). As to the meaning of 'old public company' see PARA 183; and as to the meaning of 'private company' see PARA 95.
3 Ie the final date of the re-registration period for the purposes of the Companies Act 1980 s 9(1) (repealed). As to the Companies Act 1980 generally see PARA 10.
4 As to charges of a public company on its own shares generally see PARA 1398.
5 Ie not void under the Companies Act 2006 s 670 (see PARA 1398).
6 Companies Act 2006 (Consequential Amendments and Transitional Provisions) Order 2011, SI 2011/1265, Sch 1 para 7(3).

188. Old public company trading under misleading name. An old public company[1] is guilty of an offence if it carries on any trade[2], profession or business[3] under a name which includes, as its last part, the words 'public limited company' or the Welsh[4] equivalent ('cwmni cyfyngedig cyhoeddus')[5]. Where such an offence is committed by a company, an offence is also committed by every officer of the company who is in default[6].

1 As to the meaning of 'old public company' see PARA 183.
2 As to the meanings of 'carry on' and 'trade' generally see PARA 1 note 1.
3 As to the meaning of 'business' generally see PARA 1 note 1.
4 As to the meaning of 'Wales' see PARA 1 note 5.

5 Companies Act 2006 (Consequential Amendments and Transitional Provisions) Order 2011, SI 2011/1265, Sch 1 para 8(1). As to the penalty for such an offence see note 6. As to the requirements for, and limitations placed on, a company name see PARA 199 et seq.
6 Companies Act 2006 (Consequential Amendments and Transitional Provisions) Order 2011, SI 2011/1265, Sch 1 para 8(2). As to the meaning of 'officer' generally under the Companies Act 2006 see PARA 679; and as to the meaning of 'officer in default' see PARA 316.
A person guilty of such an offence is liable on summary conviction to a fine not exceeding level 3 on the standard scale and for continued contravention to a daily default fine not exceeding one-tenth of level 3 on the standard scale: Companies Act 2006 (Consequential Amendments and Transitional Provisions) Order 2011, SI 2011/1265, Sch 1 para 8(3). As to the standard scale and the powers of magistrates' courts to issue fines on summary conviction see SENTENCING vol 92 (2015) PARA 176; and as to the meaning of 'daily default fine' see PARA 1816.

189. Old public companies: payment for share capital. Certain additional rules in the Companies Act 2006 relating to payment for shares[1] apply to an old public company[2] whose directors[3] have passed and not revoked a resolution to be re-registered as a public company[4], as those provisions apply to a public company[5].

1 Ie the Companies Act 2006 ss 584–587 (see PARAS 1303–1306). As to the meaning of 'share' see PARA 1231.
2 As to the meaning of 'old public company' see PARA 183. As to the meaning of 'company' under the Companies Acts see PARA 21; and as to the meaning of the 'Companies Acts' see PARA 13.
3 As to the meaning of 'director' see PARA 512.
4 As to re-registration as a public company see PARA 184. As to the meaning of 'public company' see PARA 95.
5 Companies Act 2006 (Consequential Amendments and Transitional Provisions) Order 2011, SI 2011/1265, Sch 1 para 9.

(viii) Existing Company becoming Community Interest Company

190. Existing company becoming a community interest company. If a company is to become a community interest company[1]:

(1) the company must by special resolution[2]:
  (a) state that it is to be a community interest company[3];
  (b) make such alterations of its articles of association[4] as it considers necessary to comply with the statutory requirements[5] or otherwise appropriate in connection with becoming a community interest company[6]; and
  (c) change its name to comply with the statutory requirements[7];
(2) the following specified conditions must be met[8], namely that:
  (a) where no application[9] for cancellation of the special resolutions has been made, having regard to the number of members who consented to or voted in favour of the resolutions, no such application may be made[10], or the period within which such an application could be made has expired[11]; or
  (b) where such an application has been made, the application has been withdrawn[12], or an order has been made confirming the resolutions and a copy of that order has been delivered to the registrar of companies[13]; and
(3) an application must be delivered to the registrar of companies[14] together with the other documents that are so required[15].

The statutory duty to forward to the registrar of companies copies of resolutions that affect the company's constitution[16] applies to the special resolutions[17].

Where special resolutions have been passed with a view to the company becoming a community interest company, an application to the court for the cancellation of the resolutions may be made[18]:

(i) by the holders of not less in the aggregate than 15 per cent in nominal value of the company's issued share capital[19] or any class of the company's issued share capital[20] (disregarding any shares held by the company as treasury shares)[21];

(ii) if the company is not limited by shares[22], by not less than 15 per cent of its members[23]; or

(iii) by the holders of not less than 15 per cent of the company's debentures[24] entitling the holders to object to an alteration of its objects[25];

but not by a person who has consented to or voted in favour of the resolutions[26]. The application must be made within 28 days after the date on which the resolutions are passed or made (or, if the resolutions are passed or made on different days, the date on which the last of them is passed or made)[27], and they may be made on behalf of the persons entitled to make it by such one or more of their number as they may appoint for the purpose[28]. On the hearing of the application, the court must make an order either cancelling or confirming the resolutions[29]. The court may make that order on such terms and conditions as it thinks fit[30]; if it thinks fit, the court may adjourn the proceedings in order that an arrangement may be made to the satisfaction of the court for the purchase of the interests of dissentient members[31]; and the court may give such directions, and make such orders, as it thinks expedient for facilitating or carrying into effect any such arrangement[32]. The court's order may, if the court thinks fit, provide for the purchase by the company of the shares of any of its members and for the reduction accordingly of the company's capital[33], and make such alteration in the company's articles as may be required in consequence of that provision[34]. The court's order may, if the court thinks fit, require the company not to make any, or any specified, amendments to its articles without the leave of the court[35].

An application to become a community interest company must be accompanied by a copy of the special resolutions[36], by a copy of the company's articles as proposed to be amended[37], and by the prescribed conversion documents[38].

On receiving an application to become a community interest company together with the other documents required to accompany it, the registrar of companies must, instead of recording the documents and entering a new name on the register[39], forward a copy of each of the documents to the Regulator[40], and retain the documents pending the Regulator's decision[41].

The Regulator must decide whether the company is eligible to become a community interest company[42]. A company is eligible to become a community interest company if:

(A) its articles (as proposed to be amended) comply with the statutory requirements[43];

(B) its proposed name complies with the statutory requirements[44]; and

(C) the Regulator, having regard to the application and accompanying documents and any other relevant considerations, considers that the company will satisfy the community interest test and is not an excluded company[45].

The Regulator must give notice of the decision to the registrar of companies, but the registrar is not required to record it[46].

If the Regulator decides that the company is eligible to be formed as a community interest company, the registrar of companies must proceed in accordance with the statutory requirements which govern registration on a change of name and the issue of a new certificate of incorporation[47]; and, if the registrar enters the new name of the company on the register, he must also retain and record the application to become a community interest company together with the other documents required to accompany it[48]. The new certificate of incorporation must state that it is issued on the company's conversion to a community interest company[49], must state the date on which it is issued[50], and must state that the company is a community interest company[51]. On the issue of the certificate, the company by virtue of the issue of the certificate becomes a community interest company[52], and the changes in the company's name and articles take effect[53]. The certificate is conclusive evidence that the company is a community interest company[54].

If the Regulator decides that the company is not eligible to become a community interest company, the company may appeal to the Appeal Officer[55] against the decision[56].

If a company that is an English charity becomes a community interest company, that does not affect the application of any property acquired under any disposition or agreement previously made otherwise than for full consideration in money or money's worth, or any property representing property so acquired, or the application of any property representing income which has previously accrued, or the application of the income from any such property[57].

1 As to community interest companies see PARA 75.

2 Companies (Audit, Investigations and Community Enterprise) Act 2004 s 37(1)(a) (s 37 substituted by SI 2009/1941). As to special resolutions see PARA 686.

3 Companies (Audit, Investigations and Community Enterprise) Act 2004 s 37(1)(a)(i) (as substituted: see note 2).

4 As to a community interest company's articles of association see PARA 98; and as to a company's articles of association generally see PARA 227 et seq.

5 Ie make alterations by special resolution in order to comply with requirements imposed by and by virtue of the Companies (Audit, Investigations and Community Enterprise) Act 2004 s 32 (see PARA 98): see s 37(1)(a)(ii) (as substituted: see note 2).

6 Companies (Audit, Investigations and Community Enterprise) Act 2004 s 37(1)(a)(ii) (as substituted: see note 2).

7 Companies (Audit, Investigations and Community Enterprise) Act 2004 s 37(1)(a)(iii) (as substituted: see note 2). The text refers to a special resolution to change the name of the company to comply with s 33 (see PARA 202): see s 37(1)(a)(iii) (as so substituted). However, a company that is an English charity may not become a community interest company without the prior written consent of the Charity Commission: s 39(1) (amended by the Charities Act 2006 s 75(1), Sch 8 paras 200, 201; and by SI 2007/1093; SI 2009/1941). If a company that is an English charity contravenes this restriction, the Charity Commission may apply to the High Court for an order quashing any altered certificate of incorporation issued under the Companies (Audit, Investigations and Community Enterprise) Act 2004 s 38A (see the text and notes 47–56): s 39(2) (as amended). As to the meaning of 'English charity' see PARA 75 note 6. As to the Charity Commission see CHARITIES vol 8 (2015) PARA 543 et seq.

8 Companies (Audit, Investigations and Community Enterprise) Act 2004 s 37(1)(b) (as substituted: see note 2).

9 Ie under the Companies (Audit, Investigations and Community Enterprise) Act 2004 s 37A (see the text and notes 18–35): see s 37(2)(a) (as substituted: see note 2).

10 Companies (Audit, Investigations and Community Enterprise) Act 2004 s 37(2)(a)(i) (as substituted: see note 2).

11 Companies (Audit, Investigations and Community Enterprise) Act 2004 s 37(2)(a)(ii) (as substituted: see note 2).

12 Companies (Audit, Investigations and Community Enterprise) Act 2004 s 37(2)(b)(i) (as substituted: see note 2).

13 Companies (Audit, Investigations and Community Enterprise) Act 2004 s 37(2)(b)(ii) (as substituted: see note 2). As to the registrar of companies see PARA 126 et seq.

14 Ie in accordance with the Companies (Audit, Investigations and Community Enterprise) Act 2004 s 37C (see the text and notes 36–41): see s 37(1)(c) (as substituted: see note 2).

15 Companies (Audit, Investigations and Community Enterprise) Act 2004 s 37(1)(c) (as substituted: see note 2). The text refers to the other documents that are required by s 37C (see the text and notes 36–41): see s 37(1)(c) (as so substituted).
16 Ie the duty under the Companies Act 2006 s 30 (see PARA 230): see the Companies (Audit, Investigations and Community Enterprise) Act 2004 s 37(3) (as substituted: see note 2).
17 Companies (Audit, Investigations and Community Enterprise) Act 2004 s 37(3) (as substituted: see note 2). The Companies Act 2006 s 30 (see PARA 230) applies to the special resolutions as follows (Companies (Audit, Investigations and Community Enterprise) Act 2004 s 37(3)(a)–(c) (as so substituted)), ie:
    (1) the Companies Act 2006 s 30 is complied with by forwarding copies of the resolutions together with the application in accordance with the Companies (Audit, Investigations and Community Enterprise) Act 2004 s 37C (see the text and notes 36–41);
    (2) copies of the resolutions must not be so forwarded before the relevant date; and
    (3) the Companies Act 2006 s 30(1) (see PARA 230) has effect in relation to the resolutions as if it referred to 15 days after the relevant date.

    For these purposes, the relevant date is:
    (a) if an application is made under the Companies (Audit, Investigations and Community Enterprise) Act 2004 s 37A (see the text and notes 18–35) for cancellation of the special resolutions, either the date on which the court determines the application (or if there is more than one application, the date on which the last to be determined by the court is determined), or such later date as the court may order (s 37(4)(a) (as so substituted));
    (b) if there is no such application, either, if having regard to the number of members who consented to or voted in favour of the resolutions, no such application may be made, the date on which the resolutions were passed or made (or, if the resolutions were passed or made on different days, the date on which the last of them was passed or made) or, in any other case, the end of the period for making such an application (s 37(4)(b) (as so substituted)).
18 Companies (Audit, Investigations and Community Enterprise) Act 2004 s 37A(1) (ss 37A–37C added by SI 2009/1941). On making an application under the Companies (Audit, Investigations and Community Enterprise) Act 2004 s 37A the applicants, or the person making the application on their behalf (see the text and notes 27–28), must immediately give notice to the registrar of companies: s 37B(1) (as so added). This is without prejudice to any provision of rules of court as to service of notice of the application: s 37B(1) (as so added). On being served with notice of any such application, the company must immediately give notice to the registrar: s 37B(2) (as so added). If a company fails to comply with s 37B(2), an offence is committed by the company, and by every officer of the company who is in default: s 37B(4) (as so added). A person guilty of such an offence is liable (on summary conviction) to a fine not exceeding level 3 on the standard scale and (for continued contravention) a daily default fine not exceeding one-tenth of level 3 on the standard scale: s 37B(5) (as so added). As to the meaning of 'officer who is in default' see PARA 316; and as to the meaning of 'officer' generally see PARA 679. As to the meaning of 'daily default fine' see PARA 1816. As to the standard scale and the powers of magistrates' courts to issue fines on summary conviction see SENTENCING vol 92 (2015) PARA 176.
19 As to the meaning of 'issued share capital' see PARA 1234. As to the meanings of 'company having a share capital', 'share' and 'share capital' see PARA 1231. As to the nominal value of shares see PARA 1233.
20 As to the meaning of classes of share see PARA 1246. As to classes of shares generally see PARA 1246 et seq.
21 Companies (Audit, Investigations and Community Enterprise) Act 2004 s 37A(1)(a) (as added: see note 18). As to treasury shares see PARA 1437.
22 As to the meaning of 'company limited by shares' see PARA 95.
23 Companies (Audit, Investigations and Community Enterprise) Act 2004 s 37A(1)(b) (as added: see note 18). As to membership of a company generally see PARA 323 et seq.
24 As to the meaning of 'debenture' see PARA 1482.
25 Companies (Audit, Investigations and Community Enterprise) Act 2004 s 37A(1)(c) (as added: see note 18). As to a company's objects see PARA 239.
26 Companies (Audit, Investigations and Community Enterprise) Act 2004 s 37A(1) (as added: see note 18).
27 Companies (Audit, Investigations and Community Enterprise) Act 2004 s 37A(2)(a) (as added: see note 18).
28 Companies (Audit, Investigations and Community Enterprise) Act 2004 s 37A(2)(b) (as added: see note 18).
29 Companies (Audit, Investigations and Community Enterprise) Act 2004 s 37A(3) (as added: see note 18). Within 15 days of the making of the court's order on the application, or such longer

period as the court may at any time direct, the company must deliver to the registrar a copy of the order: s 37B(3) (as so added). If a company fails to comply with s 37B(3), an offence is committed by the company, and by every officer of the company who is in default: s 37B(4) (as so added). A person guilty of such an offence is liable (on summary conviction) to a fine not exceeding level 3 on the standard scale and (for continued contravention) a daily default fine not exceeding one-tenth of level 3 on the standard scale: s 37B(5) (as so added).

30 Companies (Audit, Investigations and Community Enterprise) Act 2004 s 37A(4)(a) (as added: see note 18).

31 Companies (Audit, Investigations and Community Enterprise) Act 2004 s 37A(4)(b) (as added: see note 18).

32 Companies (Audit, Investigations and Community Enterprise) Act 2004 s 37A(4)(c) (as added: see note 18).

33 Companies (Audit, Investigations and Community Enterprise) Act 2004 s 37A(5)(a) (as added: see note 18).

34 Companies (Audit, Investigations and Community Enterprise) Act 2004 s 37A(5)(b) (as added: see note 18).

35 Companies (Audit, Investigations and Community Enterprise) Act 2004 s 37A(6) (as added: see note 18).

36 Companies (Audit, Investigations and Community Enterprise) Act 2004 s 37C(1)(a) (as added: see note 18).

37 Companies (Audit, Investigations and Community Enterprise) Act 2004 s 37C(1)(b) (as added: see note 18). As to the procedure for altering a company's constitutional documents generally see PARA 231 et seq.

38 Companies (Audit, Investigations and Community Enterprise) Act 2004 s 37C(1)(c) (as added: see note 18). For these purposes, the 'prescribed conversion documents' means such declarations or statements as are required by regulations to accompany the application, in such form as may be approved in accordance with the regulations: s 37C(2) (as so added). As to the making of regulations under the Companies (Audit, Investigations and Community Enterprise) Act 2004 generally see s 62 (amended by SI 2009/1941). In exercise of the powers conferred by the Companies (Audit, Investigations and Community Enterprise) Act 2004 s 37C(2), the Secretary of State has made the Community Interest Company Regulations 2005, SI 2005/1788, reg 12 (amended by SI 2007/1093; SI 2009/1942). As to the Secretary of State see PARA 6.

39 Companies (Audit, Investigations and Community Enterprise) Act 2004 s 37C(3) (as added: see note 18).

40 Companies (Audit, Investigations and Community Enterprise) Act 2004 s 37C(3)(a) (as added: see note 18). As to the Regulator see PARA 76.

41 Companies (Audit, Investigations and Community Enterprise) Act 2004 s 37C(3)(b) (as added: see note 18). The material so retained is not available for public inspection: see the Companies Act 2006 s 1087(1)(j); and PARA 146. The registrar of companies must not cause to be published in the Gazette notice pursuant to the Companies Act 2006 s 1077 (see PARA 139) of the receipt of documents under the Companies (Audit, Investigations and Community Enterprise) Act 2004 s 37C(3) unless the registrar records those documents pursuant to s 38A(1)(b) (see the text and note 48): see the Community Interest Company Regulations 2005, SI 2005/1788, reg 34(1); and PARA 139.

42 Companies (Audit, Investigations and Community Enterprise) Act 2004 s 38(1) (s 38 substituted by SI 2009/1941).

43 Companies (Audit, Investigations and Community Enterprise) Act 2004 s 38(2)(a) (as substituted: see note 42). The text refers to the requirements imposed by and by virtue of s 32 (see PARA 98): see s 38(2)(a) (as so substituted).

44 Companies (Audit, Investigations and Community Enterprise) Act 2004 s 38(2)(b) (as substituted: see note 42). The text refers to compliance with the requirements of s 33 (see PARA 202): see s 38(2)(b) (as so substituted).

45 Companies (Audit, Investigations and Community Enterprise) Act 2004 s 38(2)(c) (as substituted: see note 42). As to the community interest test and excluded companies see PARA 80.

46 Companies (Audit, Investigations and Community Enterprise) Act 2004 s 38(3) (as substituted: see note 42).

47 Companies (Audit, Investigations and Community Enterprise) Act 2004 s 38A(1)(a) (s 38A added by SI 2009/1941). The text refers to the requirement that the registrar proceed in accordance with the Companies Act 2006 s 80 (see PARA 218): see the Companies (Audit, Investigations and Community Enterprise) Act 2004 s 38A(1)(a) (as so added).

48 Companies (Audit, Investigations and Community Enterprise) Act 2004 s 38A(1)(b) (as added: see note 47). The text refers to the requirement that the registrar retain and record the documents

mentioned in s 37C(3) (see the text and notes 39–41): see s 38A(1)(b) (as so added). See also note 41.
49 Companies (Audit, Investigations and Community Enterprise) Act 2004 s 38A(2)(a) (as added: see note 47).
50 Companies (Audit, Investigations and Community Enterprise) Act 2004 s 38A(2)(b) (as added: see note 47).
51 Companies (Audit, Investigations and Community Enterprise) Act 2004 s 38A(2)(c) (as added: see note 47).
52 Companies (Audit, Investigations and Community Enterprise) Act 2004 s 38A(3)(a) (as added: see note 47).
53 Companies (Audit, Investigations and Community Enterprise) Act 2004 s 38A(3)(b) (as added: see note 47).
54 Companies (Audit, Investigations and Community Enterprise) Act 2004 s 38A(4) (as added: see note 47).
55 As to the Appeal Officer for community interest companies see PARA 77.
56 Companies (Audit, Investigations and Community Enterprise) Act 2004 s 38A(5) (as added: see note 47).
57 Companies (Audit, Investigations and Community Enterprise) Act 2004 s 39(3) (amended by SI 2007/1093).

(ix) Changes of Status affecting Community Interest Companies

191. Limitations on re-registration of community interest company. A community interest company[1] is excluded from re-registering[2] as an unlimited company[3].

If a community interest company which is not a public company[4] re-registers as a public company[5], or if a community interest company which is a public company re-registers as a private company[6], the certificate of incorporation issued in each case[7] must contain a statement that the company is a community interest company[8]. The fact that the certificate of incorporation contains such a statement is conclusive evidence that the company is a community interest company[9].

1 As to community interest companies see PARA 75.
2 Ie under the Companies Act 2006 s 102 (see PARA 176): see the Companies (Audit, Investigations and Community Enterprise) Act 2004 s 52(1) (amended by SI 2009/1941).
3 Companies (Audit, Investigations and Community Enterprise) Act 2004 s 52(1) (as amended: see note 2). As to the meaning of 'unlimited company' see PARA 95.
4 As to the meaning of 'public company' see PARA 95.
5 Ie under the Companies Act 2006 s 90 (see PARA 168): see the Companies (Audit, Investigations and Community Enterprise) Act 2004 s 52(2) (as amended: see note 8).
6 Ie under the Companies Act 2006 s 97 (see PARA 173): see the Companies (Audit, Investigations and Community Enterprise) Act 2004 s 52(2) (as amended: see note 8). As to the meaning of 'private company' see PARA 95.
7 Ie under the Companies Act 2006 s 96(2) (re-registration as a public company) (see PARA 172) or under s 101(2) (re-registration as a private limited company) (see PARA 175): see the Companies (Audit, Investigations and Community Enterprise) Act 2004 s 52(2) (as amended: see note 8). As to a company's certificate of incorporation generally see PARA 114.
8 Companies (Audit, Investigations and Community Enterprise) Act 2004 s 52(2) (amended by SI 2009/1941).
9 Companies (Audit, Investigations and Community Enterprise) Act 2004 s 52(3).

192. Ceasing to be a community interest company: in general. A community interest company[1] may not cease to be a community interest company except by dissolution[2] or by virtue of the provisions which allow for such a company to become a charity[3] or (if regulations are so made[4]) by virtue of regulations that allow for such a company to become a registered society[5].

1 As to community interest companies see PARA 75.
2 As to the dissolution of a company generally see PARA 1703 et seq.
3 Ie as provided by the Companies (Audit, Investigations and Community Enterprise) Act 2004 ss 54–55A (see PARA 193): see s 53(a) (amended by SI 2008/948; SI 2009/1941). For these

purposes, 'charity' means an English charity: Companies (Audit, Investigations and Community Enterprise) Act 2004 s 63(1) (definition substituted by SI 2007/1093). As to the meaning of 'English charity' see PARA 75 note 6. As to provision made for existing charitable companies to become a community interest company see PARA 190.

4 Ie if regulations are made under the Companies (Audit, Investigations and Community Enterprise) Act 2004 s 56 (see PARA 194): see s 53(b) (amended by the Co-operative and Community Benefit Societies Act 2014 Sch 4 Pt 2 paras 87, 89).

5 Companies (Audit, Investigations and Community Enterprise) Act 2004 s 53 (as amended: see notes 3–4). As to registered societies generally see FINANCIAL INSTITUTIONS vol 48 (2015) PARA 555 et seq.

193. Community interest company becoming a charity. If a company is to cease being a community interest company[1] and become a charity[2]:

(1) the company must by special resolution[3]:
  (a) state that it is to cease to be a community interest company[4];
  (b) make such alterations of its articles of association[5] as it considers appropriate[6]; and
  (c) change its name so that it does not comply with the statutory requirements that govern the names that are reserved for community interest companies[7];

(2) the following specified conditions must be met[8], namely that:
  (a) where no application[9] for cancellation of the special resolutions has been made, having regard to the number of members who consented to or voted in favour of the resolutions, no such application may be made[10], or the period within which such an application could be made has expired[11]; or
  (b) where such an application has been made, the application has been withdrawn[12], or an order has been made confirming the resolutions and a copy of that order has been delivered to the registrar of companies[13]; and

(3) an application must be delivered to the registrar of companies[14] together with the other documents that are so required[15].

The statutory duty to forward to the registrar of companies copies of resolutions that affect the company's constitution[16] applies to the special resolutions[17].

Where special resolutions have been passed with a view to a company ceasing to be a community interest company and becoming a charity, an application to the court for the cancellation of the resolutions may be made[18]:

(i) by the holders of not less in the aggregate than 15 per cent in nominal value of the company's issued share capital[19] or any class of the company's issued share capital[20] (disregarding any shares held by the company as treasury shares)[21];
(ii) if the company is not limited by shares[22], by not less than 15 per cent of its members[23]; or
(iii) by the holders of not less than 15 per cent of the company's debentures[24] entitling the holders to object to an alteration of its objects[25];

but not by a person who has consented to or voted in favour of the resolutions[26]. The application must be made within 28 days after the date on which the resolutions were passed or made (or, if the resolutions were passed or made on different days, the date on which the last of them was passed or made)[27], and they may be made on behalf of the persons entitled to make it by such one or more of their number as they may appoint for the purpose[28]. On the hearing of the application, the court must make an order either cancelling or confirming the resolutions[29]. The court may make that order on such terms and conditions as it thinks fit[30]; if it thinks fit, the court may adjourn the proceedings in order that an arrangement may be made to the satisfaction of the court for the purchase of the interests of dissentient members[31]; and the court may give such directions, and make such orders, as it thinks expedient for facilitating or carrying into effect any such arrangement[32]. The court's order may, if the court thinks fit, provide for the purchase by the company of the shares of any of its members and for the reduction accordingly of the company's capital[33], and make such alteration in the company's articles as may be required in consequence of that provision[34]. The court's order may, if the court thinks fit, require the company not to make any, or any specified, amendments to its articles without the leave of the court[35].

An application to cease to be a community interest company and become a charity must be accompanied by a copy of the special resolutions[36], by a copy of the company's articles as proposed to be amended[37], and by the statement that is required[38].

On receiving an application to cease to be a community interest company and become a charity, together with the other documents required to accompany it, the registrar of companies must, instead of recording the documents and entering a new name on the register[39], forward a copy of each of the documents to the Regulator[40], and retain the documents pending the Regulator's decision[41].

The Regulator must decide whether the company is eligible to cease being a community interest company[42]. A company is eligible to cease being a community interest company if it has complied with the provisions above that govern such an application[43] and if none of the following applies[44], namely:

(A) the Regulator has[45] appointed an auditor to audit the company's annual accounts and the audit has not been completed[46];

(B) civil proceedings instituted by the Regulator in the name of the company[47] have not been either determined or discontinued[48];

(C) a director of the company holds office by virtue of an order[49] of the Regulator appointing him as a director of the company[50];

(D) a director of the company is suspended[51] by order of the Regulator pending a decision whether to remove him as director[52];

(E) there is a manager in respect of the property and affairs of the company appointed[53] by order of the Regulator[54];

(F) the Official Property Holder[55] holds property as trustee for the company[56];

(G) the Regulator has ordered[57] a person who holds property on behalf of a community interest company (or on behalf of a trustee of a community interest company) not to part with the property without the Regulator's consent, and ordered any debtor of a community interest company not to make any payment in respect of the debtor's liability to the company without the Regulator's consent, and that order is still in force in relation to the company[58];

(H) the Regulator has by order[59] restricted the transactions which may be entered into by a community interest company, or the nature or amount of the payments that a community interest company may make, and that order is still in force in relation to the company[60];

(I) a petition has been presented for the company to be wound up[61].

The Regulator must give notice of the decision to the registrar of companies, but the registrar is not required to record it[62].

If the Regulator decides that the company is eligible to cease being a community interest company, the registrar of companies must proceed in accordance with the statutory requirements which govern registration on a change of name and the issue of a new certificate of incorporation[63]; and, if the registrar enters the new name of the company on the register, he must also retain and record the application to become a community interest company together with the other documents that are required to accompany it[64]. The new certificate of incorporation must state that it is issued on the company's ceasing to be a community interest company[65], and it must state the date on which it is issued[66]. On the issue of the certificate, the changes in the company's name and articles take effect[67], and the company ceases to be a community interest company[68].

If the Regulator decides that the company is not eligible to cease being a community interest company, the company may appeal to the Appeal Officer[69] against the decision[70].

1 As to community interest companies see PARA 75.
2 Companies (Audit, Investigations and Community Enterprise) Act 2004 s 54(1) (s 54 substituted by SI 2009/1941). As to the meaning of 'charity' for these purposes see PARA 192 note 3.
3 Companies (Audit, Investigations and Community Enterprise) Act 2004 s 54(1)(a) (as substituted: see note 2). As to special resolutions see PARA 686.
4 Companies (Audit, Investigations and Community Enterprise) Act 2004 s 54(1)(a)(i) (as substituted: see note 2).
5 As to a community interest company's articles of association see PARA 98; and as to a company's articles of association generally see PARA 227 et seq.
6 Companies (Audit, Investigations and Community Enterprise) Act 2004 s 54(1)(a)(ii) (as substituted: see note 2).
7 Companies (Audit, Investigations and Community Enterprise) Act 2004 s 54(1)(a)(iii) (as substituted: see note 2). The text refers to a special resolution to change the company's name so that it does not comply with s 33 (see PARA 202): see s 54(1)(a)(iii) (as so substituted).
8 Companies (Audit, Investigations and Community Enterprise) Act 2004 s 54(1)(b) (as substituted: see note 2).
9 Ie under the Companies (Audit, Investigations and Community Enterprise) Act 2004 s 54A (see the text and notes 18–35): see s 54(2)(a) (as substituted: see note 2).
10 Companies (Audit, Investigations and Community Enterprise) Act 2004 s 54(2)(a)(i) (as substituted: see note 2).
11 Companies (Audit, Investigations and Community Enterprise) Act 2004 s 54(2)(a)(ii) (as substituted: see note 2).
12 Companies (Audit, Investigations and Community Enterprise) Act 2004 s 54(2)(b)(i) (as substituted: see note 2).
13 Companies (Audit, Investigations and Community Enterprise) Act 2004 s 54(2)(b)(ii) (as substituted: see note 2). As to the registrar of companies see PARA 126 et seq.
14 Ie in accordance with the Companies (Audit, Investigations and Community Enterprise) Act 2004 s 54C (see the text and notes 36–41): see s 54(1)(c) (as substituted: see note 2).
15 Companies (Audit, Investigations and Community Enterprise) Act 2004 s 54(1)(c) (as substituted: see note 2). The text refers to the other documents that are required by s 54C (see the text and notes 36–41): see s 54(1)(c) (as so substituted).
16 Ie the duty under the Companies Act 2006 s 30 (see PARA 230): see the Companies (Audit, Investigations and Community Enterprise) Act 2004 s 54(3) (as substituted: see note 2).
17 Companies (Audit, Investigations and Community Enterprise) Act 2004 s 54(3) (as substituted: see note 2). The Companies Act 2006 s 30 (see PARA 230) applies to the special resolutions as follows (Companies (Audit, Investigations and Community Enterprise) Act 2004 s 54(3)(a)–(c) (as so substituted)), ie:
  (1) the Companies Act 2006 s 30 is complied with by forwarding copies of the resolutions together with the application in accordance with the Companies (Audit, Investigations and Community Enterprise) Act 2004 s 54C (see the text and notes 36–41);
  (2) copies of the resolutions must not be so forwarded before the relevant date; and
  (3) the Companies Act 2006 s 30(1) (see PARA 230) has effect in relation to the resolutions as if it referred to 15 days after the relevant date.

  For these purposes, the relevant date is:
  (a) if an application is made under the Companies (Audit, Investigations and Community Enterprise) Act 2004 s 54A (see the text and notes 18–35) for cancellation of the special resolutions, either the date on which the court determines the application (or if there is

more than one application, the date on which the last to be determined by the court is determined), or such later date as the court may order (s 54(4)(a) (as so substituted));

(b) if there is no such application, either, if having regard to the number of members who consented to or voted in favour of the resolutions, no such application may be made, the date on which the resolutions were passed or made (or, if the resolutions were passed or made on different days, the date on which the last of them was passed or made) or, in any other case, the end of the period for making such an application (s 54(4)(b) (as so substituted)).

18 Companies (Audit, Investigations and Community Enterprise) Act 2004 s 54A(1) (ss 54A–54C added by SI 2009/1941). On making an application under the Companies (Audit, Investigations and Community Enterprise) Act 2004 s 54A, the applicants, or the person making the application on their behalf (see the text and notes 27–28), must immediately give notice to the registrar of companies: s 54B(1) (as so added). This is without prejudice to any provision of rules of court as to service of notice of the application: s 54B(1) (as so added). On being served with notice of any such application, the company must immediately give notice to the registrar: s 54B(2) (as so added). If a company fails to comply with s 54B(2), an offence is committed by the company, and by every officer of the company who is in default: s 54B(4) (as so added). A person guilty of such an offence is liable on summary conviction to a fine not exceeding level 3 on the standard scale and for continued contravention to a daily default fine not exceeding one-tenth of level 3 on the standard scale: s 54B(5) (as so added). As to the meaning of 'officer who is in default' see PARA 316; and as to the meaning of 'officer' generally see PARA 679. As to the meaning of 'daily default fine' see PARA 1816. As to the standard scale and the powers of magistrates' courts to issue fines on summary conviction see SENTENCING vol 92 (2015) PARA 176.

19 As to the meaning of 'issued share capital' see PARA 1234. As to the meanings of 'company having a share capital', 'share' and 'share capital' see PARA 1231. As to the nominal value of shares see PARA 1233.

20 As to classes of shares generally see PARA 1246 et seq.

21 Companies (Audit, Investigations and Community Enterprise) Act 2004 s 54A(1)(a) (as added: see note 18). As to treasury shares see PARA 1437.

22 As to the meaning of 'company limited by shares' see PARA 95.

23 Companies (Audit, Investigations and Community Enterprise) Act 2004 s 54A(1)(b) (as added: see note 18). As to membership of a company generally see PARA 323 et seq.

24 As to the meaning of 'debenture' see PARA 1482.

25 Companies (Audit, Investigations and Community Enterprise) Act 2004 s 54A(1)(c) (as added: see note 18). As to a company's objects see PARA 239.

26 Companies (Audit, Investigations and Community Enterprise) Act 2004 s 54A(1) (as added: see note 18).

27 Companies (Audit, Investigations and Community Enterprise) Act 2004 s 54A(2)(a) (as added: see note 18).

28 Companies (Audit, Investigations and Community Enterprise) Act 2004 s 54A(2)(b) (as added: see note 18).

29 Companies (Audit, Investigations and Community Enterprise) Act 2004 s 54A(3) (as added: see note 18). Within 15 days of the making of the court's order on the application, or such longer period as the court may at any time direct, the company must deliver to the registrar a copy of the order: s 54B(3) (as so added). If a company fails to comply with s 54B(3), an offence is committed by the company, and by every officer of the company who is in default: s 54B(4) (as so added). A person guilty of such an offence is liable on summary conviction to a fine not exceeding level 3 on the standard scale and for continued contravention to a daily default fine not exceeding one-tenth of level 3 on the standard scale: s 54B(5) (as so added).

30 Companies (Audit, Investigations and Community Enterprise) Act 2004 s 54A(4)(a) (as added: see note 18).

31 Companies (Audit, Investigations and Community Enterprise) Act 2004 s 54A(4)(b) (as added: see note 18).

32 Companies (Audit, Investigations and Community Enterprise) Act 2004 s 54A(4)(c) (as added: see note 18).

33 Companies (Audit, Investigations and Community Enterprise) Act 2004 s 54A(5)(a) (as added: see note 18).

34 Companies (Audit, Investigations and Community Enterprise) Act 2004 s 54A(5)(b) (as added: see note 18).

35 Companies (Audit, Investigations and Community Enterprise) Act 2004 s 54A(6) (as added: see note 18).

36 Companies (Audit, Investigations and Community Enterprise) Act 2004 s 54C(1)(a) (as added: see note 18).

37 Companies (Audit, Investigations and Community Enterprise) Act 2004 s 54C(1)(b) (as added: see note 18). As to the procedure for altering a company's constitutional documents generally see PARA 231 et seq.

38 Companies (Audit, Investigations and Community Enterprise) Act 2004 s 54C(1)(c) (as added: see note 18). For these purposes, the statement required is (where the company is to become an English charity) a statement by the Charity Commission that, in its opinion, if the proposed changes take effect the company will be an English charity and will not be an exempt charity, where 'exempt charity' has the same meaning as in the Charities Act 2011 (see s 22; and CHARITIES vol 8 (2015) PARA 1): Companies (Audit, Investigations and Community Enterprise) Act 2004 s 54C(2)(a), (3) (as so added; s 54C amended by the Charities Act 2011 Sch 7 Pt 2 para 98). As to the meaning of 'English charity' see PARA 75 note 6. As to the Charity Commission see CHARITIES vol 8 (2015) PARA 543 et seq.

39 Companies (Audit, Investigations and Community Enterprise) Act 2004 s 54C(4) (as added: see note 18).

40 Companies (Audit, Investigations and Community Enterprise) Act 2004 s 54C(4)(a) (as added: see note 18). As to the Regulator see PARA 76.

41 Companies (Audit, Investigations and Community Enterprise) Act 2004 s 54C(4)(b) (as added: see note 18). The material so retained is not available for public inspection: see the Companies Act 2006 s 1087(1)(j); and PARA 146. The registrar of companies must not cause to be published in the Gazette notice pursuant to the Companies Act 2006 s 1077 (see PARA 139) of the receipt of documents under the Companies (Audit, Investigations and Community Enterprise) Act 2004 s 54C(4) unless the registrar records those documents pursuant to s 55A(1)(b) (see the text and note 64): see the Community Interest Company Regulations 2005, SI 2005/1788, reg 34(1); and PARA 139.

42 Companies (Audit, Investigations and Community Enterprise) Act 2004 s 55(1) (s 55 substituted by SI 2009/1941).

43 Ie if it has complied with the Companies (Audit, Investigations and Community Enterprise) Act 2004 s 54 (see the text and notes 1–17) and s 54C (see the text and notes 36–41): see s 55(2) (as substituted: see note 42).

44 Companies (Audit, Investigations and Community Enterprise) Act 2004 s 55(2) (as substituted: see note 42).

45 Ie under the Companies (Audit, Investigations and Community Enterprise) Act 2004 s 43 (see PARA 86): see s 55(2)(a) (as substituted: see note 42).

46 Companies (Audit, Investigations and Community Enterprise) Act 2004 s 55(2)(a) (as substituted: see note 42).

47 Ie under the Companies (Audit, Investigations and Community Enterprise) Act 2004 s 44 (see PARA 87): see s 55(2)(b) (as substituted: see note 42).

48 Companies (Audit, Investigations and Community Enterprise) Act 2004 s 55(2)(b) (as substituted: see note 42).

49 Ie under the Companies (Audit, Investigations and Community Enterprise) Act 2004 s 45 (see PARA 88): see s 55(2)(c) (as substituted: see note 42).

50 Companies (Audit, Investigations and Community Enterprise) Act 2004 s 55(2)(c) (as substituted: see note 42).

51 Ie under the Companies (Audit, Investigations and Community Enterprise) Act 2004 s 46(3) (see PARA 89): see s 55(2)(d) (as substituted: see note 42).

52 Companies (Audit, Investigations and Community Enterprise) Act 2004 s 55(2)(d) (as substituted: see note 42).

53 Ie under the Companies (Audit, Investigations and Community Enterprise) Act 2004 s 47 (see PARA 90): see s 55(2)(e) (as substituted: see note 42).

54 Companies (Audit, Investigations and Community Enterprise) Act 2004 s 55(2)(e) (as substituted: see note 42).

55 As to the Official Property Holder for community interest companies see PARA 78.

56 Companies (Audit, Investigations and Community Enterprise) Act 2004 s 55(2)(f) (as substituted: see note 42).

57 Ie under the Companies (Audit, Investigations and Community Enterprise) Act 2004 s 48(2) (see PARA 91): see s 55(2)(g) (as substituted: see note 42).

58 Companies (Audit, Investigations and Community Enterprise) Act 2004 s 55(2)(g) (as substituted: see note 42).

59 Ie under the Companies (Audit, Investigations and Community Enterprise) Act 2004 s 48(3) (see PARA 91): see s 55(2)(g) (as substituted: see note 42).

60 Companies (Audit, Investigations and Community Enterprise) Act 2004 s 55(2)(g) (as substituted: see note 42).

61 Companies (Audit, Investigations and Community Enterprise) Act 2004 s 55(2)(h) (as substituted: see note 42). As to the Regulator's power to petition for a community interest company to be wound up see PARA 93. As to winding up in general see COMPANY AND PARTNERSHIP INSOLVENCY vol 16 (2011) PARA 380 et seq.
62 Companies (Audit, Investigations and Community Enterprise) Act 2004 s 55(3) (as substituted: see note 42).
63 Companies (Audit, Investigations and Community Enterprise) Act 2004 s 55A(1)(a) (s 55A added by SI 2009/1941). The text refers to the requirement that the registrar proceed in accordance with the Companies Act 2006 s 80 (see PARA 218): see the Companies (Audit, Investigations and Community Enterprise) Act 2004 s 55A(1)(a) (as so added).
64 Companies (Audit, Investigations and Community Enterprise) Act 2004 s 55A(1)(b) (as added: see note 63). The text refers to the requirement that the registrar retain and record the documents mentioned in s 54C(4) (see the text and notes 39–41): see s 55A(1)(b) (as so added). See also note 41.
65 Companies (Audit, Investigations and Community Enterprise) Act 2004 s 55A(2)(a) (as added: see note 63).
66 Companies (Audit, Investigations and Community Enterprise) Act 2004 s 55A(2)(b) (as added: see note 63).
67 Companies (Audit, Investigations and Community Enterprise) Act 2004 s 55A(3)(a) (as added: see note 63).
68 Companies (Audit, Investigations and Community Enterprise) Act 2004 s 55A(3)(b) (as added: see note 63).
69 As to the Appeal Officer for community interest companies see PARA 77.
70 Companies (Audit, Investigations and Community Enterprise) Act 2004 s 55A(4) (as added: see note 63).

194. Community interest company becoming a registered society. Unless regulations made under the Companies (Audit, Investigations and Community Enterprise) Act 2004[1] make provision to the contrary[2], a community interest company[3] may not convert itself into a registered society under the Co-operative and Community Benefit Societies Act 2014[4]. However, if regulations do make such provision[5] they may include provision modifying the relevant provisions of the Co-operative and Community Benefit Societies Act 2014[6] in their application by virtue of the regulations[7].

Accordingly[8], a community interest company may convert itself into a permitted society[9] by following the prescribed procedure[10].

1 As to the making of regulations under the Companies (Audit, Investigations and Community Enterprise) Act 2004 generally see s 62 (amended by SI 2009/1941).
2 See the text and notes 8–11.
3 As to community interest companies see PARA 75.
4 Companies (Audit, Investigations and Community Enterprise) Act 2004 s 56(1) (amended by the Co-operative and Community Benefit Societies Act 2014 Sch 4 Pt 2 paras 87, 90). The text refers to conversion into a registered society under the Co-operative and Community Benefit Societies Act 2014 s 115 (see FINANCIAL INSTITUTIONS vol 48 (2015) PARA 905 et seq): see the Companies (Audit, Investigations and Community Enterprise) Act 2004 s 56(1) (as so amended). As to registered societies generally see FINANCIAL INSTITUTIONS vol 48 (2015) PARA 555 et seq.
5 Ie allowing the conversion of community interest companies under the Co-operative and Community Benefit Societies Act 2014 s 115 (see FINANCIAL INSTITUTIONS vol 48 (2015) PARA 905 et seq): see the Companies (Audit, Investigations and Community Enterprise) Act 2004 s 56(2). See the text and notes 8–11.
6 Ie modifying the Co-operative and Community Benefit Societies Act 2014 s 115 (see FINANCIAL INSTITUTIONS vol 48 (2015) PARA 905 et seq): see the Companies (Audit, Investigations and Community Enterprise) Act 2004 s 56(2). See the text and notes 8–11.
7 Companies (Audit, Investigations and Community Enterprise) Act 2004 s 56(2). See the text and notes 8–11.
8 Ie pursuant to the Companies (Audit, Investigations and Community Enterprise) Act 2004 s 56 (see the text and notes 1–7): see the Community Interest Company Regulations 2005, SI 2005/1788, reg 6A (added by SI 2009/1942; amended by SI 2014/1815).

9 'Permitted society' means a registered society which has a restriction on the use of its assets in accordance with the Community Benefit Societies (Restriction on Use of Assets) Regulations 2006, SI 2006/264, reg 4: see the Community Interest Company Regulations 2005, SI 2005/1788, reg 2 (definition substituted by SI 2014/1815).

10 See the Community Interest Company Regulations 2005, SI 2005/1788, reg 6A (as added and amended: see note 8). Regulation 6A substitutes the Industrial and Provident Societies Act 1965 s 53 (now repealed) for these purposes.

(6) COMPANY AND BUSINESS NAMES

(i) General Requirements as to Company Name

195. Prohibition or restriction on registration under certain names. A company[1] must not be registered under the Companies Act 2006[2] by a name[3] if, in the opinion of the Secretary of State[4], its use by the company would constitute a criminal offence[5], or it is offensive[6].

The approval of the Secretary of State[7] is required for a company to be registered under the Companies Act 2006 by a name that:

(1) would be likely to give the impression that the company is connected with Her Majesty's government or the Welsh Assembly Government[8], or with a local authority[9], or with any public authority[10] that is specified for these purposes[11] by regulations made by the Secretary of State[12]; or

(2) includes a word or expression for the time being specified in regulations made by the Secretary of State for these purposes[13].

The Secretary of State may by regulations made under head (1) or under head (2) above require that, in connection with an application for his approval[14], the applicant must seek the view of a specified[15] government department or other body[16]. Where such a requirement applies, the applicant must request the specified department or other body, in writing, to indicate whether, and if so why, it has any objections to the proposed name[17]. Where such a request is made in connection with an application for the registration of a company under the Companies Act 2006, the application must include a statement that such a request has been made[18] and must be accompanied by a copy of any response received[19]. Where such a request is made in connection with a change in a company's name[20], the notice of the change sent to the registrar of companies[21] must be accompanied by a statement by a director[22] or secretary[23] of the company that such a request has been made[24], and a copy of any response received[25].

1 As to the meaning of 'company' under the Companies Acts see PARA 21; and as to the meaning of the 'Companies Acts' see PARA 13.

2 As to company registration under the Companies Act 2006 see PARA 104 et seq. As to companies registered but not formed under the Companies Act 2006, and as to overseas companies, see PARA 29.

3 As to the company name generally see PARA 199 et seq. As to the registered name of an overseas company see PARA 2016.

4 Companies Act 2006 s 53. As to the Secretary of State see PARA 6.

All the regulatory functions of the Secretary of State under Pt 5 (ss 53–85) are functions to which the Legislative and Regulatory Reform Act 2006 ss 21, 22 apply: Legislative and Regulatory Reform (Regulatory Functions) Order 2007, SI 2007/3544, art 2, Schedule Pt 2 (amended by SI 2009/2981). This is subject to arts 3, 4, which exclude any regulatory function exercisable by Order in Council, order, rules, regulations, scheme, warrant, byelaw or other subordinate instrument under a public general Act or local Act (art 3), any function, so far as exercisable in Northern Ireland, if or to the extent that the function relates to matters which are transferred matters (art 4(b)) or any function exercisable only in or as regards Wales (art 4(c)). As to the Legislative and Regulatory Reform Act 2006 ss 21, 22 see PARA 126 note 2.

5 Companies Act 2006 s 53(a).

6 Companies Act 2006 s 53(b).

7 Before determining under the Companies Act 2006 s 55 (see head (2) in the text) whether to approve the registration of a company under a name which includes the expression 'chamber of commerce' or 'siambr fasnach', or any other expression for the time being specified in regulations under s 55 which begins with the words 'chamber of' or 'chambers of' (or the Welsh equivalents), the Secretary of State must consult at least one relevant representative body: Company and Business Names (Chamber of Commerce, etc) Act 1999 s 2(1) (amended by SI 2009/1941). The Secretary of State may publish guidance with respect to factors which may be taken into account in determining whether to approve the registration of a name to which the Company and Business Names (Chamber of Commerce, etc) Act 1999 s 2 applies: s 2(2). The relevant representative bodies for these purposes are the British Chambers of Commerce and the body known as the Scottish Chambers of Commerce (see s 4(1)); but the Secretary of State may by order made by statutory instrument amend s 4(1) by adding or deleting from it the name of any body (whether corporate or unincorporated) (see s 4(2), (3)). At the date at which this volume states the law, no such order had been made.

The functions conferred on the Secretary of State by the Companies Act 2006 s 54 and s 55 (both formerly the Companies Act 1985 s 26(2) (repealed)) may be exercised by, or by employees of, such person (if any) as may be authorised in that behalf by the Secretary of State: see the Contracting Out (Functions in relation to the Registration of Companies) Order 1995, SI 1995/1013, art 5, Sch 3 para 1(a); the Interpretation Act 1978 s 17(2)(b); and PARA 8.

8 Companies Act 2006 s 54(1)(a) (amended by SI 2009/2958). This provision also applies to a name that would be likely to give the impression that the company is connected with any part of the Scottish administration or Her Majesty's Government in Northern Ireland: see the Companies Act 2006 s 54(1)(a) (as so amended).

9 Companies Act 2006 s 54(1)(b). For these purposes, 'local authority' means a local authority within the meaning of the Local Government Act 1972 (see LOCAL GOVERNMENT vol 69 (2009) PARA 23) (or a council constituted under the Local Government etc (Scotland) Act 1994 s 2 or a district council in Northern Ireland), the Common Council of the City of London or the Council of the Isles of Scilly: Companies Act 2006 s 54(2). As to the Common Council of the City of London see LONDON GOVERNMENT vol 71 (2013) PARA 34 et seq. As to the Council of the Isles of Scilly see LOCAL GOVERNMENT vol 69 (2009) PARA 36.

10 For these purposes, 'public authority' includes any person or body having functions of a public nature: Companies Act 2006 s 54(2). As to public bodies and public authorities generally see CONSTITUTIONAL AND ADMINISTRATIVE LAW vol 20 (2014) PARAS 93 et seq (parliament), 126 et seq (the judiciary), 148 et seq (the executive) and 311 et seq (other public bodies).

11 Ie for the purposes of the Companies Act 2006 s 54: see s 54(1)(c).

12 Companies Act 2006 s 54(1)(c). Regulations made under s 54 are subject to affirmative resolution procedure (ie the regulations must not be made unless a draft of the statutory instrument containing them has been laid before Parliament and approved by a resolution of each House of Parliament): see ss 54(3), 1290. As to the making of regulations under the Companies Act 2006 generally see ss 1288–1292. As to the regulations that have been made under s 54 see the Company, Limited Liability Partnership and Business (Names and Trading Disclosures) Regulations 2015, SI 2015/17, reg 9, Sch 4. Each of the persons and bodies set out in Sch 4 col 1(1) is specified for these purposes: reg 9(1).

13 Companies Act 2006 s 55(1). Head (2) in the text refers to regulations made by the Secretary of State under s 55: see s 55(1). Such regulations are subject to approval after being made: s 55(2). Regulations under the Companies Act 2006 that are subject to 'approval after being made' must be laid before Parliament after being made, and they must cease to have effect at the end of 28 days beginning with the day on which they were made unless during that period they are approved by resolution of each House: s 1291(1). In reckoning the period of 28 days, no account is to be taken of any time during which Parliament is dissolved or prorogued or during which both Houses are adjourned for more than four days: s 1291(2). The regulations ceasing to have effect does not affect anything previously done under them or it, or the making of new regulations: s 1291(3). It is the duty of the Secretary of State to secure that the expression 'chamber of commerce' and its Welsh equivalent ('siambr fasnach') is specified in regulations under s 55 (company names requiring approval of Secretary of State), as an expression for the registration of which as or as part of a company's name the approval of the Secretary of State is required: Company and Business Names (Chamber of Commerce, etc) Act 1999 s 1 (amended by SI 2009/1941). Accordingly, as to the words and expressions that are specified for the purposes of the Companies Act 2006 s 55(1) see the Company, Limited Liability Partnership and Business Names (Sensitive Words and Expressions) Regulations 2014, SI 2014/3410, regs 3, 4, Sch 1 Pts 1, 2.

14 Ie under the Companies Act 2006 s 54 (see head (1) in the text) or under s 55 (see head (2) in the text), as the case may be: see s 56(1).

15 For these purposes, 'specified' means specified in the regulations: Companies Act 2006 s 56(5). Accordingly:

(1) in connection with an application for the approval of the Secretary of State under the Companies Act 2006 s 54 in relation to a name that would be likely to give the impression of a connection with a public authority so set out the applicant must seek the view of the government department or other body set out opposite that public authority in the Company, Limited Liability Partnership and Business (Names and Trading Disclosures) Regulations 2015, SI 2015/17, Sch 4 col (2) (reg 9(2));

(2) in connection with an application for the approval of the Secretary of State under the Companies Act 2006 s 55 in relation to a name that includes a word or expression specified in the Company, Limited Liability Partnership and Business Names (Sensitive Words and Expressions) Regulations 2014, SI 2014/3410, Sch 2, where the word or expression is specified in Sch 2 Pt 1 col (1) and the situation of the registered office or principal place of business is irrelevant, the applicant must seek the view of the government department or other body set out opposite that word or expression in Sch 2 Pt 1 col (2) (reg 5); and where the word or expression is specified in Sch 2 Pt 2 col (1) and the situation of the registered office or principal place of business is relevant, the applicant must seek the view of a government department or other body set out opposite that word or expression:

(a) in Sch 2 Pt 2 col (2), in the case of a company or limited liability partnership that has already been registered, whose registered office is situated in England and Wales, a proposed company or limited liability partnership that has not yet been registered under the Companies Act 2006, whose registered office is to be situated in England and Wales, a business, whose principal place of business is or is to be situated in England, and an overseas company (see s 1044; and PARA 2013) (Company, Limited Liability Partnership and Business Names (Sensitive Words and Expressions) Regulations 2014, SI 2014/3410, reg 6(a));

(b) in Sch 2 Pt 2 col (3), in the case of a company or limited liability partnership that has already been registered, that is a Welsh company or Welsh LLP (see the Companies Act 2006 s 88; and PARA 124), a proposed company or limited liability partnership that has not yet been registered, that is to be a Welsh company or Welsh LLP, and a business, whose principal place of business is or is to be situated in Wales (Company, Limited Liability Partnership and Business Names (Sensitive Words and Expressions) Regulations 2014, SI 2014/3410, reg 6(b)).

16 Companies Act 2006 s 56(1).

17 Companies Act 2006 s 56(2). As to the provision made for the sending or supplying of documents or information to or from a company (the 'company communications provisions') see PARA 750 et seq.

18 Companies Act 2006 s 56(3)(a).

19 Companies Act 2006 s 56(3)(b).

20 As to change of a company's name see PARAS 216–218.

21 As to the procedure that must be followed on a change of company name, and the effect of such a change, see PARA 218. As to the methods generally by which a company name may be changed see PARA 216. As to the meaning of 'registrar of companies' see PARA 126 note 2. As to the delivery of documents to the registrar see PARA 136; and as to the requirements for the proper delivery of documents to the registrar see PARA 137.

22 As to the meaning of 'director' see PARA 512.

23 As to the company secretary and other officers see PARA 671.

24 Companies Act 2006 s 56(4)(a).

25 Companies Act 2006 s 56(4)(b). The contents of any document sent to the registrar containing views expressed pursuant to s 56 must not be made available by him for public inspection: see s 1087; and PARA 146.

196. Permitted characters etc in company names. The Secretary of State[1] may make provision by regulations[2]:

(1) as to the letters or other characters, signs or symbols (including accents and other diacritical marks) and punctuation that may be used in the name of a company[3] registered under the Companies Act 2006[4]; and

(2) specifying a standard style or format for the name of a company for the purposes of registration[5].

The regulations may prohibit the use of specified[6] characters, signs or symbols when appearing in a specified position, in particular, at the beginning of a name[7]. A company may not be registered under the Companies Act 2006 by a name that consists of or includes anything that is not permitted in accordance with such regulations[8].

1 As to the Secretary of State see PARA 6 et seq. See also PARA 195 note 4.
2 Companies Act 2006 s 57(1). As to the making of regulations under the Companies Act 2006 generally see ss 1288–1292. Regulations under s 57 are subject to negative resolution procedure (ie the statutory instrument containing the regulations is subject to annulment in pursuance of a resolution of either House of Parliament): see ss 57(4), 1289. Partly in the exercise of the power under s 57, the Secretary of State has made the Company, Limited Liability Partnership and Business (Names and Trading Disclosures) Regulations 2015, SI 2015/17. See notes 4, 7–8.
3 As to the meaning of 'company' under the Companies Acts see PARA 21; and as to the meaning of the 'Companies Acts' see PARA 13.
4 Companies Act 2006 s 57(1)(a). Accordingly, the characters, signs, symbols and punctuation that may be used in any part of the name of a company registered under the Companies Act 2006 (the 'permitted characters') are (as follows (Company, Limited Liability Partnership and Business (Names and Trading Disclosures) Regulations 2015, SI 2015/17, reg 2(1), (2)):
   (1) any character, character with an accent or other diacritical mark, sign or symbol set out in the Company, Limited Liability Partnership and Business (Names and Trading Disclosures) Regulations 2015, SI 2015/17, Sch 1 table 1;
   (2) 0, 1, 2, 3, 4, 5, 6, 7, 8 or 9;
   (3) full stop, comma, colon, semi-colon or hyphen; and
   (4) any other punctuation referred to in Sch 1 table 2 col 1 but only in one of the forms set out opposite that punctuation in Sch 1 table 2.

   As to company registration under the Companies Act 2006 see PARA 104 et seq. As to companies registered but not formed under the Companies Act 2006, and as to overseas companies, see PARA 29.
5 Companies Act 2006 s 57(1)(b).
6 For these purposes, 'specified' means specified in the regulations: Companies Act 2006 s 57(5).
7 Companies Act 2006 s 57(2). Accordingly, the signs and symbols set out in the Company, Limited Liability Partnership and Business (Names and Trading Disclosures) Regulations 2015, SI 2015/17, Sch 1 table 3 are permitted characters that may be used but not as one of the first three permitted characters of the name: reg 2(1), (3).
8 Companies Act 2006 s 57(3). The name must not consist of more than 160 permitted characters: Company, Limited Liability Partnership and Business (Names and Trading Disclosures) Regulations 2015, SI 2015/17, reg 2(1), (4). For the purposes of computing the number of permitted characters in reg 2(4) (but not in reg 2(3)), any blank space between one permitted character and another in the name is to be counted as though it was a permitted character: reg 2(5).

197. Other restrictions on names. A company[1] may not carry on business[2] with a name containing the words 'Red Cross', 'Geneva Cross', 'Red Crescent', 'Red Lion and Sun' or 'Red Crystal' without the authority of the Secretary of State[3]; nor a name closely resembling the name of an association incorporated by royal charter, which has its name protected[4] by Order in Council, without the authority of the association[5]; nor a name containing the word 'Anzac' or any word closely resembling that word without the authority of the Secretary of State given on the request of the government of Australia or New Zealand[6]. In all these cases, the registrar of companies[7] will refuse to register[8] a company unless the relevant authority is produced.

If a company carries on business under a business name which does not consist of its corporate name without any addition, it must comply with the relevant requirements of the Companies Act 2006 which govern business names[9].

The words 'limited' or 'cyfyngedig' may be lawfully used as the last word of a trading name only by a company incorporated with limited liability[10]. However, there is on the one hand no necessity to use the word 'company' as part of the company's name, nor on the other is there any restriction on its use. Subject to the restrictions previously mentioned[11], the subscribers of the memorandum may choose any name they please[12].

In certain circumstances, a director[13] or shadow director[14] of a company may be personally debarred from using the name of that company if it has gone into insolvent liquidation on or after 29 December 1986, or any name so similar as to suggest an association with that company[15].

1 As to the meaning of 'company' generally see PARA 1.
2 As to the meaning of 'carry on business' generally see PARA 1 note 1.
3 See the Geneva Conventions Act 1957 s 6; and TRADE MARKS AND TRADE NAMES vol 97A (2014) PARA 473.
4 Ie under the Chartered Associations (Protection of Names and Uniforms) Act 1926 s 1(1).
5 See the Chartered Associations (Protection of Names and Uniforms) Act 1926 s 1(3); and CORPORATIONS vol 24 (2010) PARA 322.
6 See the 'Anzac' (Restriction on Trade Use of Word) Act 1916 s 1(1); and TRADE MARKS AND TRADE NAMES vol 97A (2014) PARA 474.
7 As to the meaning of 'registrar of companies' see PARA 126 note 2.
8 As to company registration under the Companies Act 2006 see PARA 104 et seq. As to companies registered but not formed under the Companies Act 2006, and as to overseas companies, see PARA 29.
9 See PARA 222 et seq. The text refers to the requirements of the Companies Act 2006 Pt 41 (ss 1192–1208). References in the company law provisions of the Companies Act 2006 to the requirements of that Act include the requirements of regulations and orders made under it: s 1172. As to the meaning of the 'company law provisions' of the Companies Act 2006 see PARA 13 note 6.
10 See PARA 225. The inclusion of the word 'limited' in a corporate name is not, however, restricted to bodies incorporated under the Companies Act 2006.
11 See the text and notes 1–10; and PARAS 195–196.
12 A company cannot, however, monopolise a word in ordinary use in the English language: *Aerators Ltd v Tollitt* [1902] 2 Ch 319. As to liability for passing-off see TRADE MARKS AND TRADE NAMES vol 97A (2014) PARA 287 et seq. As to subscribers of the memorandum see PARAS 97, 323 et seq.
13 As to the meaning of 'director' see PARA 512.
14 As to the meaning of 'shadow director' see PARA 513; and for these purposes see also COMPANY AND PARTNERSHIP INSOLVENCY vol 17 (2011) PARA 863.
15 See the Insolvency Act 1986 s 216; and COMPANY AND PARTNERSHIP INSOLVENCY vol 17 (2011) PARA 874.

198. Name consisting of trade mark. Where a registered trade mark[1] contains, or consists of, the name of a company[2], and the name of the company is subsequently changed, application should be made to the Registrar of Trade Marks[3] to enter the change of name in the register of trade marks[4].

Where the registered proprietors of a mark transfer their business to a company under the same name with the addition of the word 'limited', that word will be allowed to be added to the mark[5], but the word 'limited' must not be abbreviated[6].

A company which has carried on business under another name is entitled to protection for the latter as a trade name, although it has not complied with the statutory requirements[7] as to the use of its name[8].

1 As to registered trade marks see TRADE MARKS AND TRADE NAMES vol 97A (2014) PARA 12.
2 As to company names generally see PARA 195 et seq.
3 As to the Registrar of Trade Marks see TRADE MARKS AND TRADE NAMES vol 97A (2014) PARA 19.
4 See the Trade Marks Act 1994 s 44; and TRADE MARKS AND TRADE NAMES vol 97A (2014) PARA 375. As to the register of trade marks see TRADE MARKS AND TRADE NAMES vol 97A (2014) PARA 21 et seq.
5 *Re Guinness & Co's Trade Mark* (1888) 5 RPC 316. See also TRADE MARKS AND TRADE NAMES vol 97A (2014) PARA 375.

6 *Re Richard Hayward & Sons Ltd's Trade Marks* (1896) 13 RPC 729; *Re Holbrooks Ltd's Registered Trade Marks* (1901) 18 RPC 447. See also TRADE MARKS AND TRADE NAMES vol 97A (2014) PARA 375.
7 As to the statutory requirements mentioned in the text see PARAS 195 et seq, 219 et seq.
8 *HE Randall Ltd v British and American Shoe Co Ltd* [1902] 2 Ch 354; *Pearks, Gunston and Tee Ltd v Thompson, Talmey & Co* (1901) 18 RPC 185, CA; and see *Employers' Liability Assurance Corpn v Sedgwick, Collins & Co* [1927] AC 95 at 119–120, HL, per Lord Blanesburgh.

(ii) Indications of Company Type or Legal Form

A. PUBLIC AND PRIVATE LIMITED COMPANIES GENERALLY

199. Required indications for limited companies. Any application for company registration[1] must state the proposed name of the company[2].

The name of a limited company[3] that is a public company[4] must end with the words 'public limited company' or 'plc'[5]. In the case of a Welsh company[6], its name may instead end with 'cwmni cyfyngedig cyhoeddus' or 'ccc'[7].

The name of a limited company that is a private company[8] must end with 'limited' or 'ltd'[9], although, in the case of a Welsh company, its name may instead end with 'cyfyngedig' or 'cyf'[10]. Certain private companies are exempt from this requirement[11].

Separate provision is made in relation to community interest companies[12].

Under the provisions that govern reductions made in a company's share capital[13], the court may, if for any special reason it thinks proper to do so, make an order directing that the company must, during such period (commencing on or at any time after the date of the order) as is specified in the order, add to its name as its last words the words 'and reduced'[14]. In practice, however, such orders are not made.

1 As to a company's application for registration under the Companies Act 2006 see PARA 104. As to companies registered but not formed under the Companies Act 2006, and as to overseas companies, see PARA 29. As to the meaning of 'company' under the Companies Acts see PARA 21; and as to the meaning of the 'Companies Acts' see PARA 13.
2 See the Companies Act 2006 s 9(2); and PARA 104. As to required disclosures of a company's name see PARA 219 et seq.
3 As to the meaning of 'limited company' see PARA 95.
4 As to the meaning of 'public company' see PARA 95.
5 Companies Act 2006 s 58(1). See also *Banque de l'Indochine et de Suez SA v Euroseas Group Finance Co Ltd* [1981] 3 All ER 198 (whether 'Co' may replace 'Company').
6 As to the meaning of 'Welsh company' see PARA 124 note 3.
7 Companies Act 2006 s 58(2).
8 As to the meaning of 'private company' see PARA 95.
9 Companies Act 2006 s 59(1).
10 Companies Act 2006 s 59(2).
11 Companies Act 2006 s 59(3). The text refers to the exemption from the requirement to use the word 'limited' in a company name that is provided by s 60 (see PARA 200): see s 59(3).
12 The Companies Act 2006 ss 58, 59 (see the text and notes 1–11) do not apply to community interest companies (but see the Companies (Audit, Investigations and Community Enterprise) Act 2004 s 33(1)–(4); and PARA 202): Companies Act 2006 ss 58(3), 59(4). As to community interest companies see PARA 75 et seq.
13 Ie under the Companies Act 2006 Pt 17 Ch 10 (ss 641–653): see PARA 1360 et seq. As to the meanings of 'share capital' and 'company having a share capital' see PARA 1231.
14 See the Companies Act 2006 s 648(4); and PARA 1379. If such an order is made, those words are, until the end of the period specified in the order, deemed to be part of the company's name: see s 648(4); and PARA 1379.

B. EXEMPTION FROM REQUIREMENT TO USE 'LIMITED'

200. Exemption from requirement to use 'limited' as part of name. A private company[1] is exempt from the requirement to have its name end with the word 'limited' or one of the permitted alternatives[2] if:

(1) it is a charity[3];

(2) it is exempted from the requirement[4] by regulations made by the Secretary of State[5]; or

(3) it meets the conditions specified to allow either a private company limited by shares[6], or a private company limited by guarantee[7], as the case may be, to continue an existing exemption[8].

Further to head (3) above, a private company limited by shares that on 25 February 1982[9] was registered in Great Britain[10], and had a name that, by virtue of a licence under the Companies Act 1948[11] (or corresponding earlier legislation[12]), did not include the word 'limited' or any of the permitted alternatives[13], is exempt from the requirement to have a name ending with 'limited' (or a permitted alternative)[14] so long as it does not change its name[15], and so long as it continues to meet the following two conditions[16], namely:

(a) that the objects of the company are the promotion of commerce, art, science, education, religion, charity or any profession, and anything incidental or conducive to any of those objects[17]; and

(b) that the company's articles[18] require its income to be applied in promoting its objects[19], prohibit the payment of dividends, or any return of capital, to its members[20], and require all the assets that would otherwise be available to its members generally to be transferred on its winding up[21] either to another body with objects similar to its own[22], or to another body the objects of which are the promotion of charity and anything incidental or conducive thereto[23], whether or not the body is a member of the company[24].

Also further to head (3) above, a private company limited by guarantee that immediately before 1 October 2009[25] was exempt[26] from the requirement to have a name including the word 'limited' (or a permitted alternative)[27], and had a name that did not include the word 'limited' (or any of the permitted alternatives)[28], is exempt from the requirement to have a name ending with 'limited' (or a permitted alternative)[29] so long as it does not change its name, and so long as it continues to meet the following two conditions[30], namely:

(i) that the objects of the company are the promotion of commerce, art, science, education, religion, charity or any profession, and anything incidental or conducive to any of those objects[31]; and

(ii) that the company's articles require its income to be applied in promoting its objects[32], prohibit the payment of dividends to its members[33], and require all the assets that would otherwise be available to its members generally to be transferred on its winding up[34] either to another body with objects similar to its own[35], or to another body the objects of which are the promotion of charity and anything incidental or conducive thereto[36], whether or not the body is a member of the company[37].

The registrar of companies[38] may refuse to register a private limited company by a name that does not include the word 'limited' (or a permitted alternative) unless a statement has been delivered to him that the company meets the conditions for exemption[39]. The registrar may accept the statement as sufficient evidence of the matters stated in it[40].

1 As to the meaning of 'private company' see PARA 95. As to the meaning of 'company' under the Companies Acts see PARA 21; and as to the meaning of the 'Companies Acts' see PARA 13.

2 Ie exempt from the Companies Act 2006 s 59 (as to which see PARA 199): see s 60(1). A company which ceases to be entitled to exemption may be directed to change its name: see PARA 212.

3 Companies Act 2006 s 60(1)(a). As to the meaning of 'charity' generally see CHARITIES vol 8 (2015) PARA 1 et seq.

4 Ie exempted from the requirement of the Companies Act 2006 s 59 (as to which see PARA 199): see s 60(1)(b).

5 Companies Act 2006 s 60(1)(b). As to the Secretary of State see PARA 6 et seq. See also PARA 195 note 4. Regulations under s 60 are subject to negative resolution procedure (ie the statutory instrument containing the regulations is subject to annulment in pursuance of a resolution of either House of Parliament): see ss 60(4), 1289. Partly in the exercise of the power under s 60, the Secretary of State has made the Company, Limited Liability Partnership and Business (Names and Trading Disclosures) Regulations 2015, SI 2015/17. Accordingly, a private company limited by guarantee is exempt from the requirement of the Companies Act 2006 s 59 (as to which see PARA 199) so long as it meets the following two conditions (Company, Limited Liability Partnership and Business (Names and Trading Disclosures) Regulations 2015, SI 2015/17, reg 3(1)), namely:

(1) that the objects of that company are the promotion or regulation of commerce, art, science, education, religion, charity or any profession, and anything incidental or conducive to any of those objects (reg 3(2));

(2) that the company's articles of association require its income to be applied in promoting its objects (reg 3(3)(a)); prohibit the payment of dividends, or any return of capital, to its members (reg 3(3)(b)); and require all the assets that would otherwise be available to its members generally to be transferred on its winding up either to another body with objects similar to its own, or to another body the objects of which are the promotion of charity and anything incidental or conducive thereto (whether or not the body is a member of the company) (reg 3(3)(c)).

As to the meaning of 'private company limited by guarantee' see PARA 95. As to a company's articles of association see PARA 227 et seq; and as to a company's objects (which are no longer a required part of a company's constitution) see PARA 239. As to the declaration and payment of dividends see PARA 1581 et seq; and as to membership of a company see PARA 323 et seq. As to winding up in general see COMPANY AND PARTNERSHIP INSOLVENCY vol 16 (2011) PARA 380 et seq. As to the power of the Secretary of State to direct a company to change its name if the company exemption ceases see PARA 212.

6 Ie meets the conditions specified in the Companies Act 2006 s 61 (see the text and notes 9–24): see s 60(1)(c). As to the meaning of 'private company limited by shares' see PARA 95. As to the meaning of 'share' see PARA 1231.

7 Ie meets the conditions specified in the Companies Act 2006 s 62 (see the text and notes 25–37): see s 60(1)(c).

8 Companies Act 2006 s 60(1)(c).

9 Ie the day before the coming into force of the Companies Act 1981 s 25 (repealed), which was the predecessor of the Companies Act 2006 s 61.

10 Companies Act 2006 s 61(1)(a)(i). As to the meaning of 'Great Britain' see PARA 1 note 5.

11 Ie the Companies Act 1948 s 19 (repealed): see the Companies Act 2006 s 61(1)(a)(ii).

12 As to the provision that has been made generally for continuity in the law see PARAS 11–13.

13 Companies Act 2006 s 61(1)(a)(ii).

14 Ie is exempt from the Companies Act 2006 s 59 (as to which see PARA 199): see s 61(2). As to restrictions on the amendment of articles imposed on a company which is exempt under s 61 see PARA 201. A company which ceases to be entitled to exemption may be directed to change its name: see PARA 212.

15 Companies Act 2006 s 61(2)(b).

16 Companies Act 2006 s 61(2)(a).

17 Companies Act 2006 s 61(3). 'Science' is not confined to pure or speculative science, or science generally, but includes various branches of science, such as mechanical or engineering science: *IRC v Forrest* (1890) 15 App Cas 334, HL.

18 As to the meaning of references to a company's 'articles' under the Companies Act 2006 see PARA 227 note 2.

19 Companies Act 2006 s 61(4)(a).

20 Companies Act 2006 s 61(4)(b). See also s 63(4); and PARA 201. As to the meaning of 'member' see PARA 323.

21 Companies Act 2006 s 61(4)(c).

22 Companies Act 2006 s 61(4)(c)(i).
23 Companies Act 2006 s 61(4)(c)(ii).
24 Companies Act 2006 s 61(4)(c).
25 Ie immediately before the commencement of the Companies Act 2006 Pt 5 (ss 53–85) (as to which see PARAS 195 et seq, 201 et seq) (see the Companies Act 2006 (Commencement No 8, Transitional Provisions and Savings) Order 2008, SI 2008/2860, art 3(e)): see the Companies Act 2006 s 62(1).
26 Ie by virtue of the Companies Act 1985 s 30 (repealed): see the Companies Act 2006 s 62(1)(a).
27 Companies Act 2006 s 62(1)(a).
28 Companies Act 2006 s 62(1)(b).
29 Ie is exempt from the Companies Act 2006 s 59 (as to which see PARA 199): see s 62(1). As to restrictions on the amendment of articles imposed on a company which is exempt under s 62 see PARA 201. A company which ceases to be entitled to exemption may be directed to change its name: see PARA 212.
30 Companies Act 2006 s 62(1).
31 Companies Act 2006 s 62(2).
32 Companies Act 2006 s 62(3)(a).
33 Companies Act 2006 s 62(3)(b).
34 Companies Act 2006 s 62(3)(c).
35 Companies Act 2006 s 62(3)(c)(i).
36 Companies Act 2006 s 62(3)(c)(ii).
37 Companies Act 2006 s 62(3)(c).
38 As to the meaning of 'registrar of companies' see PARA 126 note 2.
39 Companies Act 2006 s 60(2). As to the delivery of documents to the registrar see PARA 136; and as to the requirements generally for the proper delivery of documents to the registrar see PARA 137.
40 Companies Act 2006 s 60(3).

201. Prohibition on alteration of articles which affect conditions for exemption. A private company[1] that is exempt[2] from the requirement to use 'limited' or a permitted alternative as part of its name[3], and whose name does not include 'limited' or any of the permitted alternatives[4], must not amend its articles[5] so that it ceases to comply with the required conditions for exemption[6]. If this prohibition is contravened, an offence is committed by the company and by every officer of the company who is in default[7].

1 As to the meaning of 'private company' see PARA 95. As to the meaning of 'company' under the Companies Acts see PARA 21; and as to the meaning of the 'Companies Acts' see PARA 13.
2 Ie that is exempt under the Companies Act 2006 s 61 or s 62 (as to which see PARA 200): see s 63(1)(a). A company which ceases to be entitled to exemption may be directed to change its name: see PARA 212.
3 Companies Act 2006 s 63(1)(a). As to the requirement for a company to use 'limited' (or a permitted alternative) as part of its name see s 59; and PARA 199.
4 Companies Act 2006 s 63(1)(b).
5 As to the meaning of references to a company's 'articles' see PARA 227 note 2. As to the amendment of a company's articles see PARA 231.
6 Companies Act 2006 s 63(1). The text refers to the conditions to be met by a private company limited by shares (see s 61; and PARA 200) or by a private company limited by guarantee (see s 62; and PARA 200), so that an existing exemption may continue: see s 63(1). As to the meanings of 'private company limited by shares' and 'private company limited by guarantee' see PARA 95. As to the power of the Secretary of State to direct a company to change its name if the company exemption ceases see PARA 212.

Where, immediately before 1 October 2009 (ie immediately before the commencement of s 63: see the Companies Act 2006 (Commencement No 8, Transitional Provisions and Savings) Order 2008, SI 2008/2860, art 3(e)):

(1) a company was exempt by virtue of the Companies Act 1985 s 30 (repealed) from the requirement to have a name including the word 'limited' (or a permitted alternative) (Companies Act 2006 s 63(4)(a)); and
(2) the company's memorandum or articles contained provision preventing an alteration of them without the approval of either the Board of Trade (or any other department or Minister) or the Charity Commission (s 63(4)(b)),

that provision, and any condition of any such licence as is mentioned in s 61(1)(a)(ii) (ie a licence under the Companies Act 1948 s 19 or corresponding earlier legislation) (see PARA 200) requiring such provision, ceases to have effect (Companies Act 2006 s 63(4)). However, this does not apply if, or to the extent that, the provision is required by or under any other enactment: s 63(4). As to the meaning of 'enactment' see PARA 13 note 16. Provisions that immediately before 1 October 2009 were contained in a company's memorandum but are not provisions of the kind mentioned in s 8 (which substantially altered the purpose of the memorandum of association) (see PARA 97) are to be treated after that date as provisions of the company's articles: see s 28(1); and PARA 227. As to a company's memorandum of association generally see PARA 97 et seq. As to the Charity Commission see CHARITIES vol 8 (2015) PARA 543 et seq.

7 Companies Act 2006 s 63(2). For these purposes, a shadow director is treated as an officer of the company: s 63(2). As to the meaning of 'shadow director' see PARA 513. As to the meaning of 'officer who is in default' see PARA 316. As to the meaning of 'officer' generally see PARA 679.

Any person guilty of such an offence is liable on summary conviction to a fine and for continued contravention to a daily default fine not exceeding one-tenth of the greater of £5,000 or level 4 on the standard scale: s 63(3) (amended by SI 2015/664). As to the meaning of 'daily default fine' see PARA 1816. In the case of liability on summary conviction the fine is one not exceeding level 5 on the standard scale: see the Companies Act 2006 s 63(3) (as so amended). By virtue of the Legal Aid, Sentencing and Punishment of Offenders Act 2012 s 85, however, where the offence is committed on or after 12 March 2015, it is punishable by a fine of an unlimited amount. As to the standard scale and the powers of magistrates' courts to issue fines on summary conviction see SENTENCING vol 92 (2015) PARA 176.

C. NAMES OF COMMUNITY INTEREST COMPANIES

202. Names of a community interest company. The name of a community interest company[1] which is not a public company[2] must end with either 'community interest company', or 'cic'[3]. In the case of a Welsh company[4], its name may instead end with 'cwmni buddiant cymunedol', or 'cbc'[5].

The name of a community interest company which is a public company must end with 'community interest public limited company', or 'community interest plc'[6]. In the case of a Welsh company, its name may instead end with 'cwmni buddiant cymunedol cyhoeddus cyfyngedig', or 'cwmni buddiant cymunedol ccc'[7].

1 As to community interest companies see PARA 75. As to restrictions on the use of company names and trading names generally see PARAS 195 et seq, 203 et seq.
2 As to public companies see PARAS 66, 95.
3 Companies (Audit, Investigations and Community Enterprise) Act 2004 s 33(1).
4 As to the meaning of 'Welsh company' under the Companies Acts see PARA 124 note 3.
5 Companies (Audit, Investigations and Community Enterprise) Act 2004 s 33(2) (amended by SI 2009/1941).
6 Companies (Audit, Investigations and Community Enterprise) Act 2004 s 33(3).
7 Companies (Audit, Investigations and Community Enterprise) Act 2004 s 33(4) (amended by SI 2009/1941).

D. INAPPROPRIATE USE OF INDICATIONS OF COMPANY TYPE OR LEGAL FORM

203. Inappropriate use in name of indications of company type or legal form. The Secretary of State[1] may make provision by regulations[2] prohibiting the use in a company name[3] of specified[4] words, expressions or other indications[5]:

(1) that are associated with a particular type of company or form of organisation[6]; or
(2) that are similar to words, expressions or other indications associated with a particular type of company or form of organisation[7].

The regulations may prohibit the use of words, expressions or other indications either in a specified part, or otherwise than in a specified part, of a company's name[8], or in conjunction with, or otherwise than in conjunction with, such other words, expressions or indications as may be specified[9].

A company must not be registered under the Companies Act 2006[10] by a name that consists of or includes anything prohibited by such regulations[11].

Accordingly, a company must not be so registered by a name that includes:

(a) otherwise than at the end of the name, a specified expression or abbreviation of such an expression[12] (or any expression or abbreviation specified as similar)[13];

(b) in any part of the name a specified expression or abbreviation[14] (or any expression or abbreviation specified as similar) unless that company is a RTE company[15];

(c) in any part of the name a specified expression or abbreviation[16] (or any expression or abbreviation specified as similar) unless that company is a RTM company[17];

(d) in any part of the name a specified expression or abbreviation[18] (or any expression or abbreviation specified as similar)[19];

(e) immediately before a specified expression or abbreviation[20] any of the other specified abbreviations[21] (or any abbreviation specified as similar)[22].

A private company limited by guarantee[23] which is exempt from the requirement to have its name end with the word 'limited' (or one of the permitted alternatives)[24] must not be registered under the Companies Act 2006 by a name that concludes with any of the specified words[25] (or any word specified as similar)[26] or by a name that concludes with a specified expression or abbreviation of such an expression[27] (or any expression or abbreviation specified as similar)[28].

An unlimited company[29] must not be registered under the Companies Act 2006 by a name that concludes with a word or abbreviation specified for these purposes[30] (or any word or abbreviation specified as similar)[31] or by a name that concludes with a specified expression or abbreviation of such an expression[32] (or any expression or abbreviation specified as similar)[33].

1 As to the Secretary of State see PARA 6 et seq. See also PARA 195 note 4.

2 As to the making of regulations under the Companies Act 2006 generally see ss 1288–1292. Regulations under s 65 are subject to negative resolution procedure (ie the statutory instrument containing the regulations is subject to annulment in pursuance of a resolution of either House of Parliament): see ss 65(5), 1289. Partly in exercise of the power under s 65, the Secretary of State made the Company, Limited Liability Partnership and Business (Names and Trading Disclosures) Regulations 2015, SI 2015/17. See the text and notes 12–33.

3 As to restrictions on the use of company names and trading names generally see PARAS 195 et seq, 204 et seq. As to the meaning of 'company' under the Companies Acts see PARA 21; and as to the meaning of the 'Companies Acts' see PARA 13.

4 For these purposes, 'specified' means specified in the regulations: Companies Act 2006 s 65(4).

5 Companies Act 2006 s 65(1).

6 Companies Act 2006 s 65(1)(a).

7 Companies Act 2006 s 65(1)(b).

8 Companies Act 2006 s 65(2)(a).

9 Companies Act 2006 s 65(2)(b).

10 As to company registration under the Companies Act 2006 see PARA 104 et seq. As to companies registered but not formed under the Companies Act 2006, and as to overseas companies, see PARA 29.

11 Companies Act 2006 s 65(3).

12 Ie an expression or abbreviation specified in inverted commas in the Company, Limited Liability Partnership and Business (Names and Trading Disclosures) Regulations 2015, SI 2015/17, Sch 2 para 3(a)–(f): see reg 4(1).

13 Company, Limited Liability Partnership and Business (Names and Trading Disclosures) Regulations 2015, SI 2015/17, reg 4(1). Head (a) in the text is subject to reg 5(b) (see the text and notes 27–28) and reg 6(b) (see the text and notes 32–33): reg 4(6). The expressions and abbreviations specified as similar to the expressions and abbreviations set out in inverted commas in Sch 2 para 3 are any in which one or more permitted characters have been omitted, one or more permitted characters have been added or each of one or more permitted characters has been substituted by one or more other permitted characters, in such a way as to be likely to mislead the

public as to the legal form of a company or business if included in the registered name of the company or in a business name: Sch 2 para 4. See *Cotronic (UK) Ltd v Dezonie* [1991] BCLC 721, CA.

14 Ie an expression or abbreviation specified in inverted commas in the Company, Limited Liability Partnership and Business (Names and Trading Disclosures) Regulations 2015, SI 2015/17, Sch 2 para 3(g), (h): see reg 4(2).

15 Company, Limited Liability Partnership and Business (Names and Trading Disclosures) Regulations 2015, SI 2015/17, reg 4(2). The text refers to a RTE company within the meaning of the Leasehold Reform, Housing and Urban Development Act 1993 s 4A (see LANDLORD AND TENANT vol 64 (2012) PARA 1692). See also note 13.

16 Ie an expression or abbreviation specified in inverted commas in the Company, Limited Liability Partnership and Business (Names and Trading Disclosures) Regulations 2015, SI 2015/17, Sch 2 para 3(i), (j): see reg 4(3).

17 Company, Limited Liability Partnership and Business (Names and Trading Disclosures) Regulations 2015, SI 2015/17, reg 4(3). The text refers to a RTM company within the meaning of the Commonhold and Leasehold Reform Act 2002 s 73 (see LANDLORD AND TENANT vol 62 (2012) PARA 515). See also note 13.

18 Ie an expression or abbreviation specified in inverted commas in the Company, Limited Liability Partnership and Business (Names and Trading Disclosures) Regulations 2015, SI 2015/17, Sch 2 para 3(k)–(x): see reg 4(4).

19 Company, Limited Liability Partnership and Business (Names and Trading Disclosures) Regulations 2015, SI 2015/17, reg 4(4). See also note 13.

20 Ie an expression or abbreviation specified in inverted commas in the Company, Limited Liability Partnership and Business (Names and Trading Disclosures) Regulations 2015, SI 2015/17, Sch 2 para 3(a)–(j): see reg 4(5).

21 Ie an abbreviation specified in inverted commas in the Company, Limited Liability Partnership and Business (Names and Trading Disclosures) Regulations 2015, SI 2015/17, Sch 2 para 3(y): see reg 4(5).

22 Company, Limited Liability Partnership and Business (Names and Trading Disclosures) Regulations 2015, SI 2015/17, reg 4(5). See also note 13.

23 As to the meaning of 'private company' and 'limited by guarantee' see PARA 95.

24 Ie is exempt from the requirement of the Companies Act 2006 s 59 (as to which see PARA 199) under s 60 (as to which see PARA 200): see the Company and Business Names (Miscellaneous Provisions) Regulations 2009, SI 2009/1085, reg 5.

25 Ie a word specified in inverted commas in the Company, Limited Liability Partnership and Business (Names and Trading Disclosures) Regulations 2015, SI 2015/17, Sch 2 para 1(c), (d): see reg 5(a).

26 Company, Limited Liability Partnership and Business (Names and Trading Disclosures) Regulations 2015, SI 2015/17, reg 5(a). For these purposes, the words specified as similar to the words set out in inverted commas in Sch 2 para 1(c), (d) and the words and abbreviations specified as similar to the words and abbreviations set out in inverted commas in Sch 2 para 1(a), (b) (see note 31) are any in which one or more permitted characters have been omitted, one or more permitted characters have been added, or each of one or more permitted characters has been substituted by one or more other permitted characters, in such a way as to be likely to mislead the public as to the legal form of a company or business if included in the registered name of the company or in a business name: Sch 2 para 2.

27 Ie an expression or abbreviation of such an expression specified in inverted commas in the Company, Limited Liability Partnership and Business (Names and Trading Disclosures) Regulations 2015, SI 2015/17, Sch 2 para 3(a)–(f), or (y): see reg 5(b).

28 Company, Limited Liability Partnership and Business (Names and Trading Disclosures) Regulations 2015, SI 2015/17, reg 5(b). See note 13.

29 As to the meaning of 'unlimited company' see PARA 95.

30 Ie a word or abbreviation specified in inverted commas in the Company, Limited Liability Partnership and Business (Names and Trading Disclosures) Regulations 2015, SI 2015/17, Sch 2 para 1(a), (b): see reg 6(a).

31 Company, Limited Liability Partnership and Business (Names and Trading Disclosures) Regulations 2015, SI 2015/17, reg 6(a). See note 26.

32 Ie an expression or abbreviation of such an expression specified in inverted commas in the Company, Limited Liability Partnership and Business (Names and Trading Disclosures) Regulations 2015, SI 2015/17, Sch 2 para 3(a)–(f) or (y): see reg 6(b).

33 Company, Limited Liability Partnership and Business (Names and Trading Disclosures) Regulations 2015, SI 2015/17, reg 6(b). See note 13.

(iii) Procedure where Company Names are Similar

A. SIMILARITY TO OTHER NAME ON REGISTRAR'S INDEX

204. Name that is the same as or similar to an existing name. A company[1] must not be registered under the Companies Act 2006[2] by a name that is the same as another name appearing in the index of company names[3] which is kept by the registrar of companies[4].

The Secretary of State[5] may make provision by regulations[6] supplementing this prohibition[7]. Such regulations may make provision as to matters that are to be disregarded[8], and as to words, expressions, signs or symbols that are, or are not, to be regarded as the same[9], for these purposes[10]; and such regulations may provide:

(1) that registration by a name that would otherwise be so prohibited[11] is permitted either in specified circumstances[12], or with specified consent[13]; and

(2) that if those circumstances obtain or that consent is given at the time a company is registered by a name, a subsequent change of circumstances or withdrawal of consent does not affect the registration[14].

Accordingly, a company may be registered under the Companies Act 2006 by a proposed same name[15] if the following conditions are met[16], namely:

(a) that the company or other body whose name already appears in the registrar's index of company names ('Body X') consents to the proposed same name being the name of a company ('Company Y')[17];

(b) that Company Y forms, or is to form, part of the same group as Body X[18]; and

(c) that Company Y provides to the registrar a copy of a statement made by Body X indicating[19] the consent of Body X as referred to in head (a) above[20] and that Company Y forms, or is to form, part of the same group as Body X[21].

The registrar may accept the statement referred to in head (c) above as sufficient evidence that the conditions referred to in head (a) and head (b) above have been met[22].

If the written consent referred to in head (a) above is given by Body X, a subsequent withdrawal of that consent does not affect the registration of Company Y by that proposed same name[23].

1 As to the meaning of 'company' under the Companies Acts see PARA 21; and as to the meaning of the 'Companies Acts' see PARA 13.

2 As to company registration under the Companies Act 2006 see PARA 104 et seq. As to companies registered but not formed under the Companies Act 2006, and as to overseas companies, see PARA 29.

3 As to the index of company names see PARA 163. As to restrictions on the use of company names and trading names generally see PARAS 195 et seq, 204 et seq.

4 Companies Act 2006 s 66(1). As to the meaning of 'registrar of companies' see PARA 126 note 2.

5 As to the Secretary of State see PARA 6 et seq. See also PARA 195 note 4.

6 As to the making of regulations under the Companies Act 2006 generally see ss 1288–1292. Regulations under s 66 are subject to negative resolution procedure (ie the statutory instrument containing the regulations is subject to annulment in pursuance of a resolution of either House of Parliament): see ss 66(5), 1289. Partly in exercise of the power under s 66, the Secretary of State made the Company, Limited Liability Partnership and Business (Names and Trading Disclosures) Regulations 2015, SI 2015/17. See notes 8–9; and the text and notes 15–21.

7 Companies Act 2006 s 66(2).

8 Companies Act 2006 s 66(3)(a). For these purposes, the Company, Limited Liability Partnership and Business (Names and Trading Disclosures) Regulations 2015, SI 2015/17, Sch 3 has effect for setting out the matters to be disregarded: reg 7(a).

9 Companies Act 2006 s 66(3)(b). For these purposes, the Company, Limited Liability Partnership and Business (Names and Trading Disclosures) Regulations 2015, SI 2015/17, Sch 3 has effect for setting out the words, expressions, signs and symbols that are to be regarded as the same: reg 7(b).

10 Companies Act 2006 s 66(3).

11 Ie prohibited under the Companies Act 2006 s 66: see s 66(4)(a).

12 Companies Act 2006 s 66(4)(a)(i). For these purposes, 'specified' means specified in the regulations: s 66(6).

13 Companies Act 2006 s 66(4)(a)(ii).

14 Companies Act 2006 s 66(4)(b).

15 For these purposes, 'proposed same name' means a name which is, due to the application of the Company, Limited Liability Partnership and Business (Names and Trading Disclosures) Regulations 2015, SI 2015/17, reg 8 and Sch 3, considered the same as a name appearing in the registrar's index of company names and differs from that name appearing in the index only by one of the matters set out in inverted commas in Sch 3 para 5: reg 8(6)(b).

16 Company, Limited Liability Partnership and Business (Names and Trading Disclosures) Regulations 2015, SI 2015/17, reg 8(1). See note 19.

17 Company, Limited Liability Partnership and Business (Names and Trading Disclosures) Regulations 2015, SI 2015/17, reg 8(2)(a).

18 Company, Limited Liability Partnership and Business (Names and Trading Disclosures) Regulations 2015, SI 2015/17, reg 8(2)(b). For these purposes, 'group' means a parent undertaking and its subsidiary undertakings: Companies Act 2006 s 474(1) (definition applied by the Company, Limited Liability Partnership and Business (Names and Trading Disclosures) Regulations 2015, SI 2015/17, reg 8(6)(a)). As to the meanings of 'parent undertaking' and 'subsidiary undertaking' in the Companies Acts see PARA 23.

19 Company, Limited Liability Partnership and Business (Names and Trading Disclosures) Regulations 2015, SI 2015/17, reg 8(2)(c). If the proposed same name is to be taken by a company which has not yet been incorporated, the copy of such statement must be provided to the registrar instead by the person who delivers to the registrar the application for registration of the company (and the reference in reg 8(1) to the conditions in reg 8(2) must be read accordingly): reg 8(3).

20 Company, Limited Liability Partnership and Business (Names and Trading Disclosures) Regulations 2015, SI 2015/17, reg 8(2)(c)(i).

21 Company, Limited Liability Partnership and Business (Names and Trading Disclosures) Regulations 2015, SI 2015/17, reg 8(2)(c)(ii).

22 Company, Limited Liability Partnership and Business (Names and Trading Disclosures) Regulations 2015, SI 2015/17, reg 8(4).

23 Company, Limited Liability Partnership and Business (Names and Trading Disclosures) Regulations 2015, SI 2015/17, reg 8(5).

B. SIMILARITY TO OTHER NAME IN WHICH PERSON HAS GOODWILL

(A) Company Names Adjudicators and Rules of Procedure

205. Appointment of company names adjudicators. The Secretary of State[1] must appoint persons to be company names adjudicators[2].

The persons appointed must have such legal or other experience as, in the Secretary of State's opinion, makes them suitable for appointment[3].

An adjudicator:

(1) holds office in accordance with the terms of his appointment[4];
(2) is eligible for re-appointment when his term of office ends[5];
(3) may resign at any time by notice in writing given to the Secretary of State[6]; and
(4) may be dismissed by the Secretary of State on the ground of incapacity or misconduct[7].

One of the adjudicators must be appointed Chief Adjudicator[8], who performs such functions as the Secretary of State may assign to him[9]. The other adjudicators are to undertake such duties as the Chief Adjudicator may determine[10].

The Secretary of State also may:

(a) appoint staff for the adjudicators[11];
(b) pay remuneration and expenses to the adjudicators and their staff[12];

(c) defray other costs arising in relation to the performance by the adjudicators of their functions[13];
(d) compensate persons for ceasing to be adjudicators[14].

1 As to the Secretary of State see PARA 6. See also PARA 195 note 4.
2 Companies Act 2006 s 70(1).
3 Companies Act 2006 s 70(2).
4 Companies Act 2006 s 70(3)(a).
5 Companies Act 2006 s 70(3)(b).
6 Companies Act 2006 s 70(3)(c).
7 Companies Act 2006 s 70(3)(d).
8 Companies Act 2006 s 70(4).
9 Companies Act 2006 s 70(4).
10 Companies Act 2006 s 70(5).
11 Companies Act 2006 s 70(6)(a).
12 Companies Act 2006 s 70(6)(b).
13 Companies Act 2006 s 70(6)(c).
14 Companies Act 2006 s 70(6)(d).

206. Rules of procedure before company names adjudicator. The Secretary of State[1] may make rules[2] about proceedings before a company names adjudicator[3]. The rules may, in particular, make provision:

(1) as to how an application is to be made and the form and content of an application or other documents[4];
(2) for fees to be charged[5];
(3) about the service of documents and the consequences of failure to serve them[6];
(4) as to the form and manner in which evidence is to be given[7];
(5) for circumstances in which hearings are required and those in which they are not[8];
(6) for cases to be heard by more than one adjudicator[9];
(7) setting time limits for anything required to be done in connection with the proceedings (and allowing for such limits to be extended, even if they have expired)[10];
(8) enabling the adjudicator to strike out an application, or any defence, in whole or in part, either on the ground that it is vexatious, has no reasonable prospect of success or is otherwise misconceived[11], or for failure to comply with the requirements of the rules[12];
(9) conferring power to order security for costs[13];
(10) as to how far proceedings are to be held in public[14];
(11) requiring one party to bear the costs of another and as to assessing the amount of such costs[15].

The rules may confer on the Chief Adjudicator[16] power to determine any matter that could be the subject of provision in the rules[17].

1 As to the Secretary of State see PARA 6. See also PARA 195 note 4.
2 Rules under the Companies Act 2006 s 71 must be made by statutory instrument which is subject to annulment in pursuance of a resolution of either House of Parliament: s 71(4). As to the rules so made see the Company Names Adjudicator Rules 2008, SI 2008/1738; and PARA 207 et seq.
3 Companies Act 2006 s 71(1). As to company names adjudicators see s 70; and PARA 205. As to proceedings before a company names adjudicator see PARA 207 et seq.
4 Companies Act 2006 s 71(2)(a).
5 Companies Act 2006 s 71(2)(b).
6 Companies Act 2006 s 71(2)(c).
7 Companies Act 2006 s 71(2)(d).
8 Companies Act 2006 s 71(2)(e).
9 Companies Act 2006 s 71(2)(f).
10 Companies Act 2006 s 71(2)(g).

11 Companies Act 2006 s 71(2)(h)(i).
12 Companies Act 2006 s 71(2)(h)(ii).
13 Companies Act 2006 s 71(2)(i).
14 Companies Act 2006 s 71(2)(j).
15 Companies Act 2006 s 71(2)(k).
16 As to the Chief Adjudicator see PARA 205.
17 Companies Act 2006 s 71(3).

(B) Objection to Company's Registered Name

207. Application objecting to a company's registered name. A person (the 'applicant') may object to a company's registered name[1] on the ground[2]:

(1) that it is the same as a name associated with the applicant in which he has goodwill[3]; or

(2) that it is sufficiently similar to such a name that its use in the United Kingdom[4] would be likely to mislead by suggesting a connection between the company and the applicant[5].

The objection must be made by application to a company names adjudicator[6]; and such an application must:

(a) be made on the appropriate form[7];

(b) include a concise statement of the grounds on which the application is made[8];

(c) include an address for service in the United Kingdom[9]; and

(d) be filed at the Office[10].

The company concerned is the primary respondent to the application[11]; but any of its members[12] or directors[13] may be joined as respondents[14].

The adjudicator must send a copy of the appropriate form to the primary respondent[15]; and he must specify a period within which the primary respondent must file its defence[16]. The primary respondent, before the end of that period, must file a counter-statement on the appropriate form[17], otherwise the adjudicator may treat it as not opposing the application and may make an order[18] as he would if an application were upheld[19]. In its counter-statement, the primary respondent must:

(i) include an address for service in the United Kingdom[20];

(ii) include a concise statement of the grounds on which it relies[21];

(iii) state which of the allegations in the statement of grounds of the applicant it admits and which it denies[22]; and

(iv) state which of the allegations it is unable to admit or deny, but which it requires the applicant to prove[23].

When the specified period[24] within which the primary respondent must file its defence has expired, the adjudicator must specify the periods within which evidence may be filed by the parties[25]. All evidence must be accompanied by the appropriate form, and must be copied to all other parties in the proceedings[26]. Where the applicant files no evidence in support of its application, the adjudicator may treat it as having withdrawn its application[27]. The adjudicator also may strike out the application or any defence in whole or in part if it is vexatious, has no reasonable prospect of success or is otherwise misconceived[28].

1 As to the company name generally see PARA 199 et seq. As to the meaning of 'company' under the Companies Acts see PARA 21; and as to the meaning of the 'Companies Acts' see PARA 13. As to company registration under the Companies Act 2006 see PARA 104 et seq. As to companies registered but not formed under the Companies Act 2006, and as to overseas companies, see PARA 29. As to the registered name of an overseas company see PARA 2016.
2 Companies Act 2006 s 69(1).
3 Companies Act 2006 s 69(1)(a). For these purposes, 'goodwill' includes reputation of any description: s 69(7).

4 As to the meaning of 'United Kingdom' see PARA 1 note 5.
5 Companies Act 2006 s 69(1)(b).
6 Companies Act 2006 s 69(2). As to company names adjudicators see s 70; and PARA 205. As to the rules of procedure that apply before a company names adjudicator see PARA 206; and as to the procedure in hearings before a company names adjudicator see PARA 208.
7 Company Names Adjudicator Rules 2008, SI 2008/1738, r 3(1)(a). For these purposes, the 'appropriate form' means the form determined by the Chief Adjudicator in relation to a particular matter: r 1(2). The Chief Adjudicator has the power to determine the form and content of any form required to be used by the Company Names Adjudicator Rules 2008, SI 2008/1738: r 2(1). Where a form is so required to be used, that form must be accompanied by the fee, if any, specified in r 2(2), Schedule in respect of that matter: r 2(2). Accordingly, a fee is specified in respect of the form required by r 3(1): Schedule. As to the Chief Adjudicator see PARA 205.
8 Company Names Adjudicator Rules 2008, SI 2008/1738, r 3(1)(b).
9 Company Names Adjudicator Rules 2008, SI 2008/1738, r 3(1)(c). Where a person has provided an address for service in the United Kingdom under r 3, he may substitute a new address for service in the United Kingdom by notifying the adjudicator on the appropriate form: r 13(1). As to the appropriate form see note 7. Where the primary respondent has a registered office in the United Kingdom, the adjudicator may treat this as the address for service in the United Kingdom unless and until an alternative address is provided: r 13(2). As to a company's registered office see PARA 124.
10 Company Names Adjudicator Rules 2008, SI 2008/1738, r 3(1)(d). For these purposes, the 'Office' means the office of the company names adjudicator at the Intellectual Property Office, Concept House, Cardiff Road, Newport, South Wales NP10 8QQ: r 1(2). For the transaction of relevant business by the public under the Companies Act 2006, the Office must be open on Monday to Friday between 9 am and midnight, and on Saturday between 9 am and 1 pm, unless the day is an excluded day: Company Names Adjudicator Rules 2008, SI 2008/1738, r 14(1). For the transaction of all other business by the public under the Companies Act 2006, the Office must be open on Monday to Friday between 9 am and 5 pm unless the day is an excluded day: Company Names Adjudicator Rules 2008, SI 2008/1738, r 14(2). The following are excluded days for the transaction of any business by the public under the Companies Act 2006: a Sunday; Good Friday; Christmas Day; a day which is specified or proclaimed to be a bank holiday by or under the Banking and Financial Dealings Act 1971 s 1 (see TIME vol 97 (2015) PARA 321); or a Saturday where the previous Friday and the following Monday are both excluded days: Company Names Adjudicator Rules 2008, SI 2008/1738, r 15(1). Any application or document received on an excluded day must be treated as having been filed on the next day on which the Office is open for relevant business: r 15(2). Where any period for filing any document ends on an excluded day that period must be extended to the next day on which the Office is open for relevant business: r 15(3). For the purposes of rr 14, 15 'relevant business' means the filing of any application or other document: r 14(3).
11 Companies Act 2006 s 69(3).
12 As to the meaning of 'member' see PARA 323.
13 As to the meaning of 'director' see PARA 512.
14 Companies Act 2006 s 69(3). Any member or director of the primary respondent who is joined as a respondent to the application must be joined before the end of a period specified by the adjudicator: Company Names Adjudicator Rules 2008, SI 2008/1738, r 3(6).
15 Company Names Adjudicator Rules 2008, SI 2008/1738, r 3(2).
16 Company Names Adjudicator Rules 2008, SI 2008/1738, r 3(3).
17 Company Names Adjudicator Rules 2008, SI 2008/1738, r 3(4). A fee is specified in respect of the form required by r 3(4): Schedule. The adjudicator must send a copy of the appropriate form referred to in r 3(4) to the applicant: r 3(7).
18 Ie under the Companies Act 2006 s 73(1) (see PARA 210): see the Company Names Adjudicator Rules 2008, SI 2008/1738, r 3(4).
19 Company Names Adjudicator Rules 2008, SI 2008/1738, r 3(4).
20 Company Names Adjudicator Rules 2008, SI 2008/1738, r 3(5)(a).
21 Company Names Adjudicator Rules 2008, SI 2008/1738, r 3(5)(b).
22 Company Names Adjudicator Rules 2008, SI 2008/1738, r 3(5)(c).
23 Company Names Adjudicator Rules 2008, SI 2008/1738, r 3(5)(d).
24 Ie the period specified under the Company Names Adjudicator Rules 2008, SI 2008/1738, r 3(3) (see the text and note 16): see r 4(1).
25 Company Names Adjudicator Rules 2008, SI 2008/1738, r 4(1).
26 Company Names Adjudicator Rules 2008, SI 2008/1738, r 4(2). As to the 'appropriate form' see note 7. A fee is specified in respect of the form required by r 4(2): Schedule.
27 Company Names Adjudicator Rules 2008, SI 2008/1738, r 5(1).
28 Company Names Adjudicator Rules 2008, SI 2008/1738, r 5(2).

(C) Procedure before Company Names Adjudicator; Decisions and Orders

208. Procedure in hearings before company names adjudicator. Any party to an application which has been made objecting to a company's registered name[1] may, by filing the appropriate form[2], request to be heard in person before a decision is made by the company names adjudicator[3] under the Companies Act 2006 or under the company names adjudicator rules[4]. Following such a request, the adjudicator must decide whether a decision can be made without an oral hearing in circumstances where[5]:

(1) the primary respondent[6] files no evidence[7]; or
(2) the applicant files no evidence in reply to the respondent's evidence[8]; or
(3) the decision will not terminate the proceedings[9].

Where the adjudicator decides that a decision can be made without an oral hearing, the adjudicator will specify a period for the parties to submit written submissions before making a decision[10]. Where the adjudicator decides that a hearing is necessary, he must require the parties or their legal representatives to attend a hearing and he must give the parties at least 14 days' notice of the hearing[11].

At any stage of proceedings before him, the adjudicator may direct that the parties to the proceedings attend a case management conference or pre-hearing review[12]. The adjudicator may give such directions as to the management of the proceedings as he thinks fit, and in particular he may[13]:

(a) direct a document to be filed or to be copied to a party to proceedings within a specified period[14];
(b) allow for the electronic filing and sending of documents[15];
(c) direct how documents filed or sent electronically are to be authenticated[16];
(d) direct that a document shall not be available for public inspection[17];
(e) require a translation of any document[18];
(f) direct that a witness be cross-examined[19];
(g) consolidate proceedings[20];
(h) direct that proceedings are to be heard by more than one adjudicator[21];
(i) direct that part of any proceedings be dealt with as separate proceedings[22]; or
(j) suspend or stay proceedings[23].

The adjudicator may control the evidence by giving directions as to the issues on which he requires evidence[24], the nature of the evidence which he requires to decide those issues[25], and the way in which the evidence is to be placed before him[26]; and the adjudicator may use this power to exclude evidence which would otherwise be admissible[27]. Subject to this rule, evidence that is filed[28] may be given by witness statement[29], affidavit[30] or statutory declaration[31], or in any other form which would be admissible as evidence in proceedings before the court[32]. A witness statement may only be given in evidence if it includes a statement of truth[33], being, for these purposes, a statement that the person making the statement believes that the facts stated in a particular document are true[34]. Such a statement must be dated and signed by the maker of the statement[35].

The adjudicator may extend, or further extend, any period which has been specified under the company names adjudicator rules[36] even if the period has expired[37]; and any party can request an extension of any such time period[38]. Any request for a retrospective extension must be filed before the end of the period of two months beginning with the date the time period in question expired[39].

Any hearing before the adjudicator of proceedings relating to an application[40] must be held in public[41], although any party to the proceedings may apply to the adjudicator for the hearing to be held in private[42]. However, the adjudicator may only grant such an application[43] where it is in the interests of justice for the hearing to be in held in private[44], and where all the parties to the proceedings have had an opportunity to be heard on the matter[45]. Where the application is granted, the hearing must be held in private[46].

All documents connected to proceedings are available for public inspection unless the adjudicator directs otherwise[47].

Any irregularity in procedure may be rectified on such terms as the adjudicator may direct[48].

The adjudicator may, at any stage in any proceedings before him under the Companies Act 2006, award to any party by order such costs as he considers reasonable, and direct how and by what parties they are to be paid[49]. An application for security for costs must be made on the appropriate form[50]. The adjudicator may require a person to give security for costs if he is satisfied, having regard to all the circumstances of the case, that it is just to require such security[51].

1 As to applications made objecting to a company's registered name see PARA 207. As to the company name generally see PARA 199 et seq. As to company registration under the Companies Act 2006 see PARA 104 et seq. As to companies registered but not formed under the Companies Act 2006, and as to overseas companies, see PARA 29. As to the registered name of an overseas company see PARA 2016.
2 As to the 'appropriate form' see PARA 207 note 7. A fee is specified in respect of the form required by the Company Names Adjudicator Rules 2008, SI 2008/1738, r 5(3): r 2(2), Schedule.
3 As to company names adjudicators see the Companies Act 2006 s 70; and PARA 205. As to the rules of procedure that apply before a company names adjudicator see PARA 206.
4 Company Names Adjudicator Rules 2008, SI 2008/1738, r 5(3). The company names adjudicator rules are those rules made under the Companies Act 2006 and contained in the Company Names Adjudicator Rules 2008, SI 2008/1738: see the Companies Act 2006 s 71; and PARA 206.
5 Company Names Adjudicator Rules 2008, SI 2008/1738, r 5(4).
6 The company whose registered name is concerned in the proceedings is the primary respondent to the application, although any of its members or directors may be joined as respondents: see the Companies Act 2006 s 69(3); and PARA 207.
7 Company Names Adjudicator Rules 2008, SI 2008/1738, r 5(4)(a). As to provision made for the filing of evidence see PARA 207.
8 Company Names Adjudicator Rules 2008, SI 2008/1738, r 5(4)(b).
9 Company Names Adjudicator Rules 2008, SI 2008/1738, r 5(4)(c).
10 Company Names Adjudicator Rules 2008, SI 2008/1738, r 5(5).
11 Company Names Adjudicator Rules 2008, SI 2008/1738, r 5(6).
12 Company Names Adjudicator Rules 2008, SI 2008/1738, r 6(1).
13 Company Names Adjudicator Rules 2008, SI 2008/1738, r 6(2).
14 Company Names Adjudicator Rules 2008, SI 2008/1738, r 6(2)(a).
15 Company Names Adjudicator Rules 2008, SI 2008/1738, r 6(2)(b).
16 Company Names Adjudicator Rules 2008, SI 2008/1738, r 6(2)(c).
17 Company Names Adjudicator Rules 2008, SI 2008/1738, r 6(2)(d).
18 Company Names Adjudicator Rules 2008, SI 2008/1738, r 6(2)(e).
19 Company Names Adjudicator Rules 2008, SI 2008/1738, r 6(2)(f).
20 Company Names Adjudicator Rules 2008, SI 2008/1738, r 6(2)(g).
21 Company Names Adjudicator Rules 2008, SI 2008/1738, r 6(2)(h).
22 Company Names Adjudicator Rules 2008, SI 2008/1738, r 6(2)(i).
23 Company Names Adjudicator Rules 2008, SI 2008/1738, r 6(2)(j).
24 Company Names Adjudicator Rules 2008, SI 2008/1738, r 6(3)(a).
25 Company Names Adjudicator Rules 2008, SI 2008/1738, r 6(3)(b).
26 Company Names Adjudicator Rules 2008, SI 2008/1738, r 6(3)(c).
27 Company Names Adjudicator Rules 2008, SI 2008/1738, r 6(3).
28 Ie under any provision of the Company Names Adjudicator Rules 2008, SI 2008/1738: see r 9(1).

29 In the Company Names Adjudicator Rules 2008, SI 2008/1738, a witness statement is a written statement signed by a person that contains the evidence which that person would be allowed to give orally: r 9(3). As to witness statements generally see CIVIL PROCEDURE vol 12 (2015) PARA 771 et seq.
30 As to affidavits see CIVIL PROCEDURE vol 12 (2015) PARA 779 et seq.
31 Company Names Adjudicator Rules 2008, SI 2008/1738, r 9(1)(a). Statutory declarations are made by virtue of the Statutory Declarations Act 1835: see CIVIL PROCEDURE vol 12 (2015) PARA 827.
32 Company Names Adjudicator Rules 2008, SI 2008/1738, r 9(1)(b).
33 Company Names Adjudicator Rules 2008, SI 2008/1738, r 9(1).
34 Company Names Adjudicator Rules 2008, SI 2008/1738, r 9(2)(a).
35 Company Names Adjudicator Rules 2008, SI 2008/1738, r 9(2)(b).
36 Ie specified under any provision of the Company Names Adjudicator Rules 2008, SI 2008/1738: see r 7(1).
37 Company Names Adjudicator Rules 2008, SI 2008/1738, r 7(1).
38 Company Names Adjudicator Rules 2008, SI 2008/1738, r 7(2). The text refers to an extension of any time period specified under any provision of the Company Names Adjudicator Rules 2008, SI 2008/1738: see r 7(2). Any request made under r 7(2) must be made on the appropriate form and must include reasons why the extra time is required: r 7(4). As to the 'appropriate form' see PARA 207 note 7. A fee is specified in respect of the form required by r 7(4): Schedule.
39 Company Names Adjudicator Rules 2008, SI 2008/1738, r 7(3). A request for a retrospective extension must also include reasons why the request is being made out of time: r 7(4).
40 Ie under the Companies Act 2006 s 69(2) (see PARA 207): see the Company Names Adjudicator Rules 2008, SI 2008/1738, r 8(1). For these purposes, a reference to a hearing includes any part of a hearing: r 8(5).
41 Company Names Adjudicator Rules 2008, SI 2008/1738, r 8(1). This provision is subject to r 8(3), (4) (see the text and notes 43–46): see r 8(1).
42 Company Names Adjudicator Rules 2008, SI 2008/1738, r 8(2).
43 Ie an application under the Company Names Adjudicator Rules 2008, SI 2008/1738, r 8(2) (see the text and note 42): see r 8(3). Any hearing of an application under r 8(2) itself must be held in private: r 8(4).
44 Company Names Adjudicator Rules 2008, SI 2008/1738, r 8(3)(a).
45 Company Names Adjudicator Rules 2008, SI 2008/1738, r 8(3)(b).
46 Company Names Adjudicator Rules 2008, SI 2008/1738, r 8(3).
47 Company Names Adjudicator Rules 2008, SI 2008/1738, r 8(7).
48 Company Names Adjudicator Rules 2008, SI 2008/1738, r 10(1). Where rectification includes the amendment of a document by the adjudicator the parties will be given notice of this amendment: r 10(2).
49 Company Names Adjudicator Rules 2008, SI 2008/1738, r 11.
50 Company Names Adjudicator Rules 2008, SI 2008/1738, r 12. As to the 'appropriate form' see PARA 207 note 7. A fee is specified in respect of the form required by r 12: Schedule.
51 Company Names Adjudicator Rules 2008, SI 2008/1738, r 12.

209. Decisions in hearings before company names adjudicator. If either ground upon which a person (the 'applicant') may object to a company's registered name[1], that is to say:

(1) that it is the same as a name associated with the applicant in which he has goodwill[2]; or

(2) that it is sufficiently similar to such a name that its use in the United Kingdom[3] would be likely to mislead by suggesting a connection between the company and the applicant[4],

is established upon an application making objection to such a name, it is for the respondents[5] to show[6]:

(a) that the name was registered before the commencement of the activities on which the applicant relies to show goodwill[7]; or

(b) that the company is operating under the name[8], or is proposing to do so and has incurred substantial start-up costs in preparation[9], or was formerly operating under the name and is now dormant[10]; or

(c) that the name was registered in the ordinary course of a company formation business and the company is available for sale to the applicant on the standard terms of that business[11]; or

(d) that the name was adopted in good faith[12]; or

(e) that the interests of the applicant are not adversely affected to any significant extent[13].

If none of those is shown, the objection must be upheld[14]. If the facts mentioned in head (a), head (b) or head (c) above are established, the objection must nevertheless be upheld if the applicant shows that the main purpose of the respondents, or any of them, in registering the name was to obtain money or other consideration from the applicant or prevent him from registering the name[15]. If the objection is not upheld under either such provision[16], it must be dismissed[17].

When the adjudicator has made a decision on the application[18], he must send to the parties written notice of it, stating the reasons for his decision[19]; and, within 90 days of determining such an application[20], he must make his decision and his reasons for it available to the public[21].

1 As to applications made objecting to a company's registered name, and as to applicants, see PARA 207. As to the company name generally see PARA 199 et seq. As to the meaning of 'company' under the Companies Acts see PARA 21; and as to the meaning of the 'Companies Acts' see PARA 13. As to company registration under the Companies Act 2006 see PARA 104 et seq. As to companies registered but not formed under the Companies Act 2006, and as to overseas companies, see PARA 29. As to the registered name of an overseas company see PARA 2016.

2 Ie the ground specified in the Companies Act 2006 s 69(1)(a) (see PARA 207): see s 69(4). As to the meaning of 'goodwill' for these purposes see PARA 207 note 3.

3 As to the meaning of 'United Kingdom' see PARA 1 note 5.

4 Ie the ground specified in the Companies Act 2006 s 69(1)(b) (see PARA 207): see s 69(4).

5 The company whose registered name is concerned in the proceedings is the primary respondent to the application, although any of its members or directors may be joined as respondents: see the Companies Act 2006 s 69(3); and PARA 207.

6 Companies Act 2006 s 69(4). As to the rules of procedure that apply before a company names adjudicator see PARA 206; and as to the procedure in hearings before a company names adjudicator see PARA 208. As to company names adjudicators see PARA 205.

7 Companies Act 2006 s 69(4)(a).

8 Companies Act 2006 s 69(4)(b)(i).

9 Companies Act 2006 s 69(4)(b)(ii).

10 Companies Act 2006 s 69(4)(b)(iii). As to the meaning of a company that is 'dormant' see PARA 25.

11 Companies Act 2006 s 69(4)(c).

12 Companies Act 2006 s 69(4)(d).

13 Companies Act 2006 s 69(4)(e).

14 Companies Act 2006 s 69(4). As to hearings before, and decisions of, company names adjudicators see PARA 208.

15 Companies Act 2006 s 69(5).

16 Ie under either the Companies Act 2006 s 69(4) (see the text and notes 1–14) or s 69(5) (see the text and note 15): see s 69(6).

17 Companies Act 2006 s 69(6).

18 Ie the application under the Companies Act 2006 s 69(2) (see PARA 207): see the Company Names Adjudicator Rules 2008, SI 2008/1738, r 5(7).

19 Company Names Adjudicator Rules 2008, SI 2008/1738, r 5(7). The date on which the decision was sent to the parties is taken to be the date of the decision for the purposes of any appeal: r 5(8). As to appeals from the adjudicator's decision see PARA 211.

20 Ie an application under the Companies Act 2006 s 69 (see PARA 207): see s 72(1).

21 Companies Act 2006 s 72(1). The adjudicator may make his decision and his reasons for it available to the public by means of a website or by such other means as appear to him to be appropriate: s 72(2).

210. Orders following decision by company names adjudicator. If an application made objecting to a company's registered name[1] is upheld[2], the company names adjudicator must make an order[3]:

(1) requiring the respondent company[4] to change its name to one that is not an offending name[5]; and

(2) requiring all the respondents to take all such steps as are within their power to make, or facilitate the making, of that change[6], and not to cause or permit any steps to be taken calculated to result in another company being registered with a name that is an offending name[7].

The order must specify a date by which the respondent company's name is to be changed[8] and may be enforced in the same way as an order of the High Court[9].

If the respondent company's name is not changed in accordance with the order by the specified date, the adjudicator may determine a new name for the company[10]. If the adjudicator determines a new name for the respondent company, he must give notice of his determination to the applicant[11], to the respondents[12], and to the registrar of companies[13].

1 Ie an application under the Companies Act 2006 s 69 (see PARA 207): see s 73(1). As to the company name generally see PARA 199 et seq. As to the meaning of 'company' under the Companies Acts see PARA 21; and as to the meaning of the 'Companies Acts' see PARA 13. As to company registration under the Companies Act 2006 see PARA 104 et seq. As to companies registered but not formed under the Companies Act 2006, and as to overseas companies, see PARA 29. As to the registered name of an overseas company see PARA 2016.

2 As to decisions in hearings before a company names adjudicator see PARA 209. As to the rules of procedure that apply before a company names adjudicator see PARA 206; and as to the procedure in hearings before a company names adjudicator see PARA 208. As to company names adjudicators see PARA 205.

3 Companies Act 2006 s 73(1).

4 The company whose registered name is concerned in the proceedings is the primary respondent to the application, although any of its members or directors may be joined as respondents: see the Companies Act 2006 s 69(3); and PARA 207.

5 Companies Act 2006 s 73(1)(a). For these purposes, an 'offending name' means a name that, by reason of its similarity to the name associated with the applicant under s 69 (see PARA 207) in which he claims goodwill, would be likely either to be the subject of a direction under s 67 (power of Secretary of State to direct change of name: see PARA 213), or to give rise to a further application under s 69: s 73(2). As to the meaning of 'goodwill' for these purposes see PARA 207 note 3.

6 Companies Act 2006 s 73(1)(b)(i).

7 Companies Act 2006 s 73(1)(b)(ii).

8 For these purposes, a company's name is changed when the change takes effect in accordance with the Companies Act 2006 s 81(1) (on the issue of the new certification of incorporation) (see PARA 218): s 73(6). As to the issue of a new certificate on a change of name see PARA 218.

9 Companies Act 2006 s 73(3).

10 Companies Act 2006 s 73(4). The practice is to alter the company's name to its registered number.

11 Companies Act 2006 s 73(5)(a). As to the applicant see PARA 207.

12 Companies Act 2006 s 73(5)(b).

13 Companies Act 2006 s 73(5)(c). Any notice of a change of the company's name is subject to the disclosure requirements in s 1078: see PARA 139. As to the meaning of 'registrar of companies' see PARA 126 note 2. As to the procedure that must be followed on a change of company name, and the effect of such a change, see PARA 218. As to the methods generally by which a company name may be changed see PARA 216.

211. Appeal from company names adjudicator's decision. An appeal lies to the court[1] from any decision of a company names adjudicator[2] to uphold or dismiss an application made[3] objecting to a company's registered name[4].

Notice of appeal against a decision upholding an application must be given before the date specified in the adjudicator's order by which the respondent company's name is to be changed[5]. If notice of appeal is given against a decision upholding an application, the effect of the adjudicator's order is suspended[6].

If on appeal the court either affirms the decision of the adjudicator to uphold the application[7], or reverses the decision of the adjudicator to dismiss the application[8], the court may, as the case may require, specify the date by which the adjudicator's order is to be complied with, remit the matter to the adjudicator or make any order or determination that the adjudicator might have made[9].

If the court determines a new name for the company it must give notice of the determination both to the parties to the appeal[10], and to the registrar of companies[11].

1 As to the meaning of 'the court' see PARA 160 note 12.
2 As to decisions in hearings before a company names adjudicator see PARA 209. As to the rules of procedure that apply before a company names adjudicator see PARA 206; and as to the procedure in hearings before a company names adjudicator see PARA 208. As to company names adjudicators see PARA 205.
3 Ie under the Companies Act 2006 s 69 (see PARA 207): see s 74(1).
4 Companies Act 2006 s 74(1). As to the company name generally see PARA 199 et seq. As to the meaning of 'company' under the Companies Acts see PARA 21; and as to the meaning of the 'Companies Acts' see PARA 13. As to company registration under the Companies Act 2006 see PARA 104 et seq. As to companies registered but not formed under the Companies Act 2006, and as to overseas companies, see PARA 29. As to the registered name of an overseas company see PARA 2016.
5 Companies Act 2006 s 74(2). As to orders made following a decision by a company names adjudicator see PARA 210.
6 Companies Act 2006 s 74(3).
7 Companies Act 2006 s 74(4)(a).
8 Companies Act 2006 s 74(4)(b).
9 Companies Act 2006 s 74(4).
10 Companies Act 2006 s 74(5)(a).
11 Companies Act 2006 s 74(5)(b). Any notice of a change of the company's name is subject to the disclosure requirements in s 1078: see PARA 139. As to the meaning of 'registrar of companies' see PARA 126 note 2. As to the procedure that must be followed on a change of company name, and the effect of such a change, see PARA 218. As to the methods generally by which a company name may be changed see PARA 216.

(iv) Secretary of State's Powers to Direct Change of Name

212. Power to direct change of name where company exemption ceases. If it appears to the Secretary of State[1] that a company[2] whose name does not include 'limited' (or any of the permitted alternatives)[3]:

(1) has ceased to be entitled to exemption under the protections afforded charities[4] or companies that fall within regulations made for the purpose[5] by the Secretary of State[6]; or
(2) has carried on any business other than the promotion of any of the objects allowed under the conditions[7] which provide for existing exemptions to continue[8]; or
(3) has allowed its income to be applied otherwise than in promoting such objects[9]; or
(4) has paid a dividend to its members[10] or (in the case of a private company limited by shares only) made any return of capital to its members[11],

he may direct the company to change its name[12] so that its name ends with 'limited' (or one of the permitted alternatives)[13]. The direction must be in writing and must specify the period within which the company is to change its name[14].

If the company fails to comply with such a direction, an offence is committed by the company and by every officer of the company who is in default[15].

A company that has been directed to change its name in this way[16] may not, without the approval of the Secretary of State, subsequently change its name so that it does not include 'limited' (or one of the permitted alternatives)[17].

1 As to the Secretary of State see PARA 6. See also PARA 195 note 4.

2 As to the meaning of 'company' under the Companies Acts see PARA 21; and as to the meaning of the 'Companies Acts' see PARA 13.
3 Companies Act 2006 s 64(1). As to the requirement for a company to use 'limited' (or a permitted alternative) as part of its name see s 59; and PARA 199. As to the meaning of 'limited company' see PARA 95.
4 Ie has ceased to be entitled to exemption under the Companies Act 2006 s 60(1)(a) (see PARA 200): see s 64(1)(a).
5 Ie has ceased to be entitled to exemption under the Companies Act 2006 s 60(1)(b) (see PARA 200): see s 64(1)(a). As to the conditions for such exemption see the Company, Limited Liability Partnership and Business (Names and Trading Disclosures) Regulations 2015, SI 2015/17, reg 3; and PARA 200.
6 Companies Act 2006 s 64(1)(a).
7 Ie the conditions to be met by a private company limited by shares under the Companies Act 2006 s 61(3) (see PARA 200) or by a private company limited by guarantee under s 62(2) (see PARA 200): see s 64(1)(b)(i). As to the meanings of 'private company', 'limited by shares' and 'limited by guarantee' see PARA 95. As to the meanings of 'share, 'company having a share capital' and 'share capital' see PARA 1231.
8 Companies Act 2006 s 64(1)(b)(i). Heads (2)–(4) in the text apply in the case of a company within s 61 or s 62 (see PARA 200), which impose conditions as to the objects and articles of the company: s 64(1)(b). As to the meaning of references to a company's 'articles' under the Companies Act 2006 see PARA 227 note 2. As to a company's articles of association see PARA 227 et seq; and as to a company's objects (which are no longer a required part of a company's constitution) see PARA 239.
9 Companies Act 2006 s 64(1)(b)(ii). Head (3) in the text refers to a company that has acted inconsistently with the provision required, in relation to a private company limited by shares, by s 61(4)(a) (see PARA 200) or, in relation to a private company limited by guarantee, by s 62(3)(a) (see PARA 200): see s 64(1)(b)(ii). See also note 8.
10 As to membership of a company see PARA 323 et seq.
11 Companies Act 2006 s 64(1)(b)(ii). Head (4) in the text refers to a company that has acted inconsistently with the provision required, in relation to a private company limited by shares, by s 61(4)(b) (see PARA 200) or, in relation to a private company limited by guarantee, by s 62(3)(b) (see PARA 200): see s 64(1)(b)(ii). See also note 8.
12 A change of name in order to comply with a direction under the Companies Act 2006 s 64 may be made by resolution of the directors: s 64(3). This is without prejudice to any other method of changing the company's name (as to which see PARA 216): see s 64(3). Where a resolution of the directors is passed in accordance with s 64(3), the company must give notice to the registrar of companies of the change; and ss 80, 81 (procedure on, and effect of, change of company's name) (see PARA 218) apply as regards the registration and effect of the change: s 64(4). As to the meaning of 'director' see PARA 512; and as to the meaning of 'registrar of companies' see PARA 126 note 2. As to the delivery of documents to the registrar see PARA 136; and as to the requirements generally for the proper delivery of documents to the registrar see PARA 137. As to meetings of directors and the taking of resolutions see PARA 568 et seq. As to change of a company's name generally see PARAS 216–218. Any notice of a change of the company's name is subject to the disclosure requirements in s 1078: see PARA 139.
13 Companies Act 2006 s 64(1).
14 Companies Act 2006 s 64(2).
15 Companies Act 2006 s 64(5). As to the meaning of 'officer who is in default' see PARA 316. As to the meaning of 'officer' generally see PARA 679.

Any person guilty of such an offence is liable on summary conviction to a fine and for continued contravention to a daily default fine not exceeding one-tenth of the greater of £5,000 or level 4 on the standard scale: see s 64(6) (amended by SI 2015/664). As to the meaning of 'daily default fine' see PARA 1816. In the case of liability on summary conviction the fine is one not exceeding level 5 on the standard scale: see the Companies Act 2006 s 64(6) (as so amended). By virtue of the Legal Aid, Sentencing and Punishment of Offenders Act 2012 s 85, however, where the offence is committed on or after 12 March 2015, it is punishable by a fine of an unlimited amount. As to the standard scale and the powers of magistrates' courts to issue fines on summary conviction see SENTENCING vol 92 (2015) PARA 176.
16 Ie under the Companies Act 2006 s 64: see s 64(7).
17 Companies Act 2006 s 64(7). This does not apply to a change of name on re-registration or on conversion to a community interest company: s 64(7). As to a change of name when a company alters it status by means of re-registration see PARA 167 et seq; and as to conversion to a community interest company see PARA 190 et seq.

213. Direction to change company name that is the same as or similar to an existing name. The Secretary of State[1] may direct a company[2] to change its name if it has been registered in a name[3] that is the same as or, in the opinion of the Secretary of State, too like a name appearing at the time of the registration in the index of company names[4] which is kept by the registrar of companies[5], or a name that should have appeared in that index at that time[6].

Any such direction must be given within 12 months of the company's registration by the name in question[7], and must specify the period within which the company is to change its name[8], although the Secretary of State may by a further direction extend that period[9].

If a company fails to comply with such a direction, an offence is committed by the company and by every officer of the company who is in default[10]; and any person guilty of such an offence is liable on summary conviction to a fine not exceeding level 3 on the standard scale[11] and for continued contravention to a daily default fine[12] not exceeding one-tenth of level 3 on the standard scale[13].

The Secretary of State may make provision by regulations[14] supplementing his power to direct a change of name[15]. Such regulations may make provision as to matters that are to be disregarded[16], and as to words, expressions, signs or symbols that are, or are not, to be regarded as the same[17], for these purposes[18]; and such regulations may provide:

(1) that no such direction is to be given in respect of a name in specified circumstances[19], or if specified consent is given[20]; and
(2) that a subsequent change of circumstances or withdrawal of consent does not give rise to grounds for such a direction[21].

Except in the circumstances mentioned above, a company registered under the Companies Acts is not entitled to carry on its business[22] in such a way, or under such a name, as to represent that its business is the business of any other company or firm or person; and the absence of fraud is immaterial[23]. In such cases, the old company or firm may apply to the court for an injunction, and the principles then apply which apply to individuals trading under identical or similar names[24]. This remedy is equally available to companies registered under the Companies Acts.

In some cases the court will grant an injunction before the new company has been registered[25], and will protect a foreign trader who has a market in England[26] from having the benefit of his trade name annexed by a trader in England through registration under the Companies Act 2006 of a company which assumes the name without justification[27].

1 As to the Secretary of State see PARA 6. See also PARA 195 note 4.
2 As to the meaning of 'company' under the Companies Acts see PARA 21; and as to the meaning of the 'Companies Acts' see PARA 13.
3 As to company registration under the Companies Act 2006 see PARA 104 et seq. As to companies registered but not formed under the Companies Act 2006, and as to overseas companies, see PARA 29. As to restrictions on the use of company names and trading names generally see PARAS 195 et seq, 214 et seq.
4 As to the index of company names see PARA 163.
5 Companies Act 2006 s 67(1)(a). As to the meaning of 'registrar of companies' see PARA 126 note 2.
6 Companies Act 2006 s 67(1)(b).
7 Companies Act 2006 s 68(2)(a). A direction under s 67 (see the text and notes 1–6) must be in writing: s 68(4). The provisions of s 68 have effect in relation to a direction under s 67: s 68(1).
8 Companies Act 2006 s 68(2)(b). See also note 7. As to the procedure that must be followed on a change of company name, and the effect of such a change, see PARA 218. As to the methods generally by which a company name may be changed see PARA 216. Any notice of a change of the company's name is subject to the disclosure requirements in s 1078: see PARA 139.

9 Companies Act 2006 s 68(3). Any such direction must be given before the end of the period for the time being specified: s 68(3). See also note 7.
10 Companies Act 2006 s 68(5). For these purposes, a shadow director is treated as an officer of the company: s 68(5). See also note 7. As to the meaning of 'shadow director' see PARA 513. As to the meaning of 'officer who is in default' see PARA 316. As to the meaning of 'officer' generally see PARA 679.
11 As to the standard scale and the powers of magistrates' courts to issue fines on summary conviction see SENTENCING vol 92 (2015) PARA 176.
12 As to the meaning of 'daily default fine' see PARA 1816.
13 Companies Act 2006 s 68(6). See also note 7.
14 As to the making of regulations under the Companies Act 2006 generally see ss 1288–1292. Regulations under s 67 are subject to negative resolution procedure (ie the statutory instrument containing the regulations is subject to annulment in pursuance of a resolution of either House of Parliament): see ss 67(5), 1289. At the date at which this volume states the law, no such regulations had been made under s 67.
15 Companies Act 2006 s 67(2). The text refers to the power conferred by s 67 (see the text and notes 1–6): see s 67(2). At the date at which this volume states the law, no such regulations had been made.
16 Companies Act 2006 s 67(3)(a).
17 Companies Act 2006 s 67(3)(b).
18 Companies Act 2006 s 67(3).
19 Companies Act 2006 s 67(4)(a)(i). For these purposes, 'specified' means specified in the regulations: s 67(6).
20 Companies Act 2006 s 67(4)(a)(ii).
21 Companies Act 2006 s 67(4)(b).
22 As to the meaning of 'carry on business' generally see PARA 1 note 1.
23 *North Cheshire and Manchester Brewery Co v Manchester Brewery Co* [1899] AC 83, HL (injunction granted as businesses competing and appellant adopted name suggesting amalgamation); *Ewing v Buttercup Margarine Co Ltd* [1917] 2 Ch 1, CA (injunction granted as businesses competing and name adopted by defendants similar to that of Buttercup Dairy Co used by plaintiff); *Society of Motor Manufacturers and Traders Ltd v Motor Manufacturers' and Traders' Mutual Insurance Co Ltd* [1925] Ch 675, CA (injunction refused as businesses different and names consisted of words in ordinary use). See further TRADE MARKS AND TRADE NAMES vol 97A (2014) PARA 300 et seq.
24 See TRADE MARKS AND TRADE NAMES vol 97A (2014) PARA 419 et seq.
25 *Hendriks v Montagu* (1881) 17 ChD 638, CA; *Tussaud v Tussaud* (1890) 44 ChD 678.
26 As to the meaning of 'England' see PARA 1 note 5.
27 *Anciens Etablissements Panhard et Levassor SA v Panhard Levassor Motor Co Ltd* [1901] 2 Ch 513.

214. Direction to change company name due to irregularities. If it appears to the Secretary of State[1] that misleading information has been given for the purpose of a company's registration[2] with a particular name[3], or that an undertaking or assurance has been given for that purpose and has not been fulfilled[4], then he may direct the company to change its name[5].

Any such direction must be given within five years of the company's registration by the name in question[6], and must specify the period within which the company is to change its name[7], although the Secretary of State may by a further direction extend that period[8].

If a company fails to comply with such a direction, an offence is committed by the company and by every officer of the company who is in default[9].

1 As to the Secretary of State see PARA 6. See also PARA 195 note 4.
2 As to company registration under the Companies Act 2006 see PARA 104 et seq. As to companies registered but not formed under the Companies Act 2006, and as to overseas companies, see PARA 29. As to the meaning of 'company' under the Companies Acts see PARA 21; and as to the meaning of the 'Companies Acts' see PARA 13.
3 Companies Act 2006 s 75(1)(a). As to company names generally see PARAS 195 et seq, 215 et seq; and as to the registered name of an overseas company see PARA 2016.
4 Companies Act 2006 s 75(1)(b).
5 Companies Act 2006 s 75(1). A direction under s 75 must be in writing: s 75(4).
6 Companies Act 2006 s 75(2)(a).

7 Companies Act 2006 s 75(2)(b).
8 Companies Act 2006 s 75(3). Any such direction must be given before the end of the period for the time being specified: s 75(3).
9 Companies Act 2006 s 75(5). For these purposes, a shadow director is treated as an officer of the company: s 75(5). As to the meaning of 'shadow director' see PARA 513. As to the meaning of 'officer who is in default' see PARA 316. As to the meaning of 'officer' generally see PARA 679.
A person guilty of such an offence is liable on summary conviction to a fine not exceeding level 3 on the standard scale and for continued contravention to a daily default fine not exceeding one-tenth of level 3 on the standard scale: s 75(6). As to the standard scale and the powers of magistrates' courts to issue fines on summary conviction see SENTENCING vol 92 (2015) PARA 176; and as to the meaning of 'daily default fine' see PARA 1816.

215. Power to require company to abandon misleading name. If, in the opinion of the Secretary of State[1], the name by which a company is registered[2] gives so misleading an indication of the nature of its activities as to be likely to cause harm to the public[3], he may direct the company to change its name[4].

The direction must be complied with within a period of six weeks from the date of the direction or such longer period as the Secretary of State may think fit to allow[5]. However, this does not apply if, within the period of three weeks from the date of the direction, the company duly makes an application to the court[6] to set the direction aside[7].

The court may set the direction aside or confirm it[8]. If the direction is confirmed, the court must specify the period within which the direction is to be complied with[9].

If a company fails to comply with such a direction, an offence is committed by the company and by every officer of the company who is in default[10].

1 As to the Secretary of State see PARA 6. See also PARA 195 note 4.
2 As to company registration under the Companies Act 2006 see PARA 104 et seq. As to companies registered but not formed under the Companies Act 2006, and as to overseas companies, see PARA 29. As to the meaning of 'company' under the Companies Acts see PARA 21; and as to the meaning of the 'Companies Acts' see PARA 13. As to company names generally see PARAS 195 et seq, 216 et seq; and as to the registered name of an overseas company see PARA 2016.
3 It is not sufficient to show that the name is misleading; a likelihood of harm being caused to the public must also be shown: *Association of Certified Public Accountants of Britain v Secretary of State for Trade and Industry* [1998] 1 WLR 164, [1997] 2 BCLC 307.
4 Companies Act 2006 s 76(1). A direction under s 76 must be in writing: s 76(2). As to the procedure that must be followed on a change of company name, and the effect of such a change, see PARA 218. As to the methods generally by which a company name may be changed see PARA 216. Any notice of a change of the company's name is subject to the disclosure requirements in s 1078: see PARA 139.
5 Companies Act 2006 s 76(3).
6 As to the meaning of 'the court' see PARA 160 note 12.
7 Companies Act 2006 s 76(3), (4).
8 Companies Act 2006 s 76(5). The burden of proof is on the Secretary of State to show that the name is misleading at the time of the judgment of the court (and not at the date of the direction): *Association of Certified Public Accountants of Britain v Secretary of State for Trade and Industry* [1998] 1 WLR 164, [1997] 2 BCLC 307.
9 Companies Act 2006 s 76(5).
10 Companies Act 2006 s 76(6). For these purposes, a shadow director is treated as an officer of the company: s 76(6). As to the meaning of 'shadow director' see PARA 513. As to the meaning of 'officer who is in default' see PARA 316. As to the meaning of 'officer' generally see PARA 679.
A person guilty of such an offence is liable on summary conviction to a fine not exceeding level 3 on the standard scale and for continued contravention to a daily default fine not exceeding one-tenth of level 3 on the standard scale: Companies Act 2006 s 76(7). As to the standard scale and the powers of magistrates' courts to issue fines on summary conviction see SENTENCING vol 92 (2015) PARA 176; and as to the meaning of 'daily default fine' see PARA 1816.

(v) Changes of Company Name

216. Methods by which company name may be changed. A company[1] may change its name[2]:

(1) voluntarily by special resolution[3]; or

(2) by other means provided for by the company's articles[4].

However, the name of a company may also be changed:

(a) by resolution of the directors[5] in order to comply with a direction of Secretary of State[6];

(b) on the determination of a new name by a company names adjudicator[7] under his powers on upholding an objection to a company name[8];

(c) on the determination of a new name by the court[9] on appeal against a decision of a company names adjudicator[10];

(d) upon restoration to the register[11].

1 As to the meaning of 'company' under the Companies Acts see PARA 21; and as to the meaning of the 'Companies Acts' see PARA 13.

2 As to company names generally see PARAS 195 et seq, 217 et seq; and as to the registered name of an overseas company see PARA 2016. As to the procedure that must be followed on a change of company name, and the effect of such a change, see PARA 218.

As to transitional provisions that apply where, in the case of an existing or transitional company, the company's articles are deemed to contain a statement of its name by virtue of the Companies Act 2006 s 28 (provisions of memorandum treated as provisions of articles) (see PARA 227), and the company changes its name (by any means) on or after 1 October 2009, see the Companies Act 2006 (Consequential Amendments, Transitional Provisions and Savings) Order 2009, SI 2009/1941, art 5; and PARA 227.

3 Companies Act 2006 s 77(1)(a). Head (1) in the text refers to the special resolution that must be passed in accordance with s 283 (see PARA 686): see s 77(1)(a). As to the meaning of 'special resolution' see PARA 686.

4 Companies Act 2006 s 77(1)(b). As to the meaning of references to a company's 'articles' see PARA 227 note 2. As to a company's articles of association generally see PARA 227 et seq.

5 Ie acting under the Companies Act 2006 s 64 (see PARA 212): see s 77(2)(a). As to the meaning of 'director' see PARA 512. As to meetings of directors and the making of resolutions see PARA 568 et seq.

6 Companies Act 2006 s 77(2)(a). As to the Secretary of State see PARA 6. See also PARA 195 note 4.

7 Ie under the Companies Act 2006 s 73 (see PARA 210): see s 77(2)(b). As to company names adjudicators see PARA 205.

8 Companies Act 2006 s 77(2)(b). As to applications made objecting to a company's registered name see PARA 207 et seq.

9 Ie under the Companies Act 2006 s 74 (see PARA 211): see s 77(2)(c). As to the meaning of 'the court' see PARA 160 note 12.

10 Companies Act 2006 s 77(2)(c). As to decisions in hearings before a company names adjudicator see PARA 209.

11 Companies Act 2006 s 77(2)(d). Head (d) in the text refers to a change of name under s 1033 (see PARA 1723): see s 77(2)(d). As to the meaning of the 'register' see PARA 142. As to restoration to the register see PARA 1714 et seq.

217. Change of company name by the company by voluntary means. Where a change of name[1] has been agreed to by a company[2] by special resolution[3], the company must give notice to the registrar of companies[4]. Where a change of name by special resolution is conditional on the occurrence of an event, the notice given to the registrar of the change must specify that the change is conditional[5], and state whether the event has occurred[6]. If the notice states that the event has not occurred:

(1) the registrar is not required to enter the new name on the register[7] in place of the former name or to issue a certificate of incorporation[8] altered to meet the circumstances of the case[9] until further notice[10];

(2) when the event occurs, the company must give notice to the registrar stating that it has occurred[11]; and
(3) the registrar may rely on the statement as sufficient evidence of the matters stated in it[12].

Where a change of a company's name has been made by other means provided for by its articles[13], the company must give notice to the registrar[14], and the notice must be accompanied by a statement that the change of name has been made by means provided for by the company's articles[15]. The registrar may rely on the statement as sufficient evidence of the matters stated in it[16].

1 As to the methods by which a company name may be changed see PARA 216. As to company names generally see PARA 195 et seq. As to the procedure that must be followed on a change of company name, and the effect of such a change, see PARA 218.
2 As to the meaning of 'company' under the Companies Acts see PARA 21; and as to the meaning of the 'Companies Acts' see PARA 13.
3 As to the meaning of 'special resolution' see PARA 686. CPR 70.2A (replacing Sch 1 RSC Ord 45 r 8 (revoked)) (court's powers to order act to be done at expense of disobedient party: see CIVIL PROCEDURE vol 12A (2015) PARA 1298) does not empower the court to make an order to a third party or to the registrar to authorise a company name change without compliance with the Companies Act 2006 ss 78, 80 (replacing the Companies Act 1985 s 28 (repealed)): see *Halifax plc v Halifax Repossessions Ltd* [2004] EWCA Civ 331, [2004] FSR 903, [2004] 2 BCLC 455.
4 Companies Act 2006 s 78(1). This is in addition to the obligation to forward a copy of the resolution to the registrar (see PARA 688): s 78(1). As to the meaning of 'registrar of companies' see PARA 126 note 2. As to the delivery of documents to the registrar see PARA 136; and as to the requirements for the proper delivery of documents to the registrar see PARA 137. Any notice of a change of the company's name is subject to the disclosure requirements in s 1078: see PARA 139.
5 Companies Act 2006 s 78(2)(a).
6 Companies Act 2006 s 78(2)(b).
7 As to the meaning of the 'register' see PARA 142.
8 As to certificates issued by the registrar after a company's name has been altered see PARA 218.
9 Ie the registrar is not required to act under the Companies Act 2006 s 80 (see PARA 218): s 78(3)(a).
10 Companies Act 2006 s 78(3)(a).
11 Companies Act 2006 s 78(3)(b). Where a change of name is conditional on the occurrence of an event, the giving of notice of the event to the registrar under s 78(3)(b) is the required document for the registration of the change of name for the purposes of the Registrar of Companies (Fees) (Companies, Overseas Companies and Limited Liability Partnerships) Regulations 2012, SI 2012/1907, reg 3, Sch 1 (see PARA 218): Sch 1 para 9(2).
12 Companies Act 2006 s 78(3)(c).
13 As to the meaning of references to a company's 'articles' see PARA 227 note 2. As to a company's articles of association generally see PARA 227 et seq.
14 Companies Act 2006 s 79(1)(a).
15 Companies Act 2006 s 79(1)(b).
16 Companies Act 2006 s 79(2).

218. Procedure on change of name and effect. Where the registrar of companies[1] receives notice of a change of a company's name[2], then if he is satisfied that the new name complies with the requirements of the Companies Act 2006[3] so far as it governs a company's name[4], and that the requirements of the Companies Acts, and any relevant requirements of the company's articles[5], with respect to a change of name are complied with[6], the registrar must enter the new name on the register[7] in place of the former name[8]. On the registration of the new name, the registrar must issue a certificate of incorporation altered to meet the circumstances of the case[9]. The change of name is not complete until it has been made upon the register and the new certificate has been issued; and, until the certificate is obtained, the company exists under its original name, although notice of a call stating the new name which is sent before the certificate is obtained is sufficient[10].

A change of a company's name has effect from the date on which the new certificate of incorporation is issued[11]. The effect of the issue of the certificate of incorporation on change of name is not to re-form or reincorporate the company as a new entity but to recognise the continued existence of the company under its new name[12]. The change does not affect any rights or obligations of the company or render defective any legal proceedings by or against it[13]; and any legal proceedings that might have been continued or commenced against it by its former name may be continued or commenced against it by its new name[14]. If, after the issue of the certificate, it is found that the special resolution was not duly passed, application may be made to the registrar to vacate the registration[15].

1 As to the meaning of 'registrar of companies' see PARA 126 note 2.
2 Companies Act 2006 s 80(1). As to the meaning of 'company' under the Companies Acts see PARA 21; and as to the meaning of the 'Companies Acts' see PARA 13. As to the methods by which a company name may be changed see PARA 216. As to company names generally see PARA 195 et seq. As to the delivery of documents to the registrar see PARA 136; and as to the requirements for the proper delivery of documents to the registrar see PARA 137.
3 Ie the requirements of the Companies Act 2006 Pt 5 (ss 53–85) (as to which see PARAS 195 et seq, 219 et seq): see s 80(2)(a). References in the company law provisions of the Companies Act 2006 to the requirements of that Act include the requirements of regulations and orders made under it: s 1172. As to the meaning of the 'company law provisions' of the Companies Act 2006 see PARA 13 note 6.
4 Companies Act 2006 s 80(2)(a).
5 As to the meaning of references to a company's 'articles' see PARA 227 note 2. As to a company's articles of association generally see PARA 227 et seq.
6 Companies Act 2006 s 80(2)(b). As to a company's articles which provide for a change of name see PARA 217.
7 As to the meaning of the 'register' see PARA 142.
8 Companies Act 2006 s 80(2). As to fees payable under s 80 (other than a change made in response to a direction of the Secretary of State under s 64 (see PARA 212) or s 67 (see PARA 213), a determination by a company names adjudicator or a court under s 73(5) (see PARA 210) or s 74(5) (see PARA 211), or on the restoration of the company to the register under s 1033(2) (see PARA 1723)), see the Registrar of Companies (Fees) (Companies, Overseas Companies and Limited Liability Partnerships) Regulations 2012, SI 2012/1907, reg 3, Sch 1 para 8(g). The fee specified in Sch 1 para 8(g) is not payable where the change of name relates solely to the indication of the particular type of company that the company whose name is changed becomes on its re-registration under the Companies Act 2006 Pt 7 (ss 89–111) (see PARA 167 et seq): Registrar of Companies (Fees) (Companies, Overseas Companies and Limited Liability Partnerships) Regulations 2012, SI 2012/1907, Sch 1 para 9(1).
9 Companies Act 2006 s 80(3).
10 *Shackleford, Ford & Co Ltd v Dangerfield, Shackleford, Ford & Co Ltd v Owen* (1868) LR 3 CP 407 at 411 per Bovill CJ.
11 Companies Act 2006 s 81(1).
12 *Oshkosh B'Gosh Inc v Dan Marbel Inc Ltd* [1989] 1 CMLR 94, [1989] BCLC 507, CA.
13 Companies Act 2006 s 81(2). As to the company's name in litigation see PARA 302.
14 Companies Act 2006 s 81(3).
15 See *Re Australasian Mining Co* [1893] WN 74 (where the court expressed the opinion that it had no jurisdiction to order the registrar to vacate the registration).

(vi) Trading Disclosures

219. Provision made as to trading disclosures. The Secretary of State[1] may by regulations[2] make provision requiring companies[3]:

(1) to display specified[4] information in specified locations[5];
(2) to state specified information in specified descriptions of document or communication[6]; and
(3) to provide specified information on request to those they deal with in the course of their business[7].

The regulations must in every case require disclosure of the name of the company[8], and may make provision as to the manner in which any specified information is to be displayed, stated or provided[9]. The regulations may provide that, for the purposes of any requirement to disclose a company's name, any variation between a word or words required to be part of the name and a permitted abbreviation of that word or those words, or vice versa is to be disregarded[10]. Such regulations also may provide that where a company fails, without reasonable excuse, to comply with any specified[11] requirement of the regulations an offence is committed by the company, and by every officer of the company who is in default[12]; and that a person guilty of such an offence is liable on summary conviction to a fine not exceeding level 3 on the standard scale[13] and, for continued contravention, a daily default fine[14] not exceeding one-tenth of level 3 on the standard scale[15].

1 As to the Secretary of State see PARA 6. See also PARA 195 note 4.

2 Regulations under the Companies Act 2006 s 82 are subject to affirmative resolution procedure (ie the regulations must not be made unless a draft of the statutory instrument containing them has been laid before Parliament and approved by a resolution of each House of Parliament): see ss 82(5), 1290. As to the making of regulations under the Companies Act 2006 generally see ss 1288–1292. Partly in exercise of the powers so conferred by s 82, the Secretary of State has made the Company, Limited Liability Partnership and Business (Names and Trading Disclosures) Regulations 2015, SI 2015/17. See further PARA 220.

The provisions of the Companies Act 2006 ss 82, 84, 85 apply to unregistered companies by virtue of the Unregistered Companies Regulations 2009, SI 2009/2436, reg 3, Sch 1 para 4, but as modified thereby: see PARA 1857. As to the meaning of 'unregistered company' see PARA 1856.

3 Companies Act 2006 s 82(1). As to the meaning of 'company' under the Companies Acts see PARA 21; and as to the meaning of the 'Companies Acts' see PARA 13.

4 For these purposes, 'specified' means specified in the regulations: Companies Act 2006 s 82(4).

5 Companies Act 2006 s 82(1)(a).

6 Companies Act 2006 s 82(1)(b).

7 Companies Act 2006 s 82(1)(c).

8 Companies Act 2006 s 82(2)(a).

9 Companies Act 2006 s 82(2)(b).

10 Companies Act 2006 s 82(3). For the purposes of Pt 5 Ch 6 (ss 82–85) (see also PARA 221), in considering a company's name no account is to be taken of the following, provided there is no real likelihood of names differing only in those respects being taken to be different names (s 85(1)), ie:

(1) whether upper or lower case characters (or a combination of the two) are used;

(2) whether diacritical marks or punctuation are present or absent;

(3) whether the name is in the same format or style as is specified under s 57(1)(b) (see PARA 196) for the purposes of registration.

This provision does not affect the operation of regulations under s 57(1)(a) (see PARA 196) permitting only specified characters, diacritical marks or punctuation: s 85(2).

11 For these purposes, 'specified' means specified in the regulations: Companies Act 2006 s 84(3).

12 Companies Act 2006 s 84(1)(a). The regulations may provide that, for the purposes of any provision made under s 84(1), a shadow director of the company is to be treated as an officer of the company: s 84(2). Accordingly, see the Companies (Trading Disclosures) Regulations 2008, SI 2008/495, reg 28(3); and PARA 220. As to the meaning of 'shadow director' see PARA 513. As to the meaning of 'officer who is in default' see PARA 316. As to the meaning of 'officer' generally see PARA 679. As to provision made for civil consequences to flow from a failure to make required disclosures see PARA 221.

13 As to the standard scale and the powers of magistrates' courts to issue fines on summary conviction see SENTENCING vol 92 (2015) PARA 176.

14 As to the meaning of 'daily default fine' see PARA 1816.

15 Companies Act 2006 s 84(1)(b).

220. Requirements as to disclosure of company's name etc. A company[1] which has a common seal[2] must have its name[3] engraved in legible characters on its seal[4].

A company[5] must display[6] its registered name at its registered office[7], and at any inspection place[8]. A company also must display its registered name at any location, other than a company's registered office or any inspection place, at which it carries on business[9]. Where a company is required to display its registered name at any office, place or location:

(1) where that office, place or location is shared by no more than five companies, the registered name must be so positioned that it may be easily seen by any visitor to that office, place or location and must be displayed continuously[10];

(2) where any such office, place or location is shared by six or more companies, each such company must ensure that either its registered name is displayed for at least 15 continuous seconds at least once every three minutes or its registered name is available for inspection on a register by any visitor to that office, place or location[11].

A company also must disclose the address of its registered office, any inspection place, and the type of company records which are kept at that office or place, to any person it deals with in the course of business who makes a written request to the company for that information[12].

Every company must disclose its registered name on:

(a) its business letters, notices and other official publications[13];

(b) its bills of exchange, promissory notes, endorsements and order forms[14];

(c) cheques purporting to be signed by or on behalf of the company[15];

(d) orders for money, goods or services purporting to be signed by or on behalf of the company[16];

(e) its bills of parcels, invoices and other demands for payment, receipts and letters of credit[17];

(f) its applications for licences to carry on a trade or activity[18]; and

(g) all other forms of its business correspondence and documentation[19].

Every company also must disclose its registered name on its websites[20].

On its business letters, its order forms, and its websites, every company must disclose the following particulars[21]:

(i) the part of the United Kingdom[22] in which the company is registered[23];

(ii) the company's registered number[24];

(iii) the address of the company's registered office[25];

(iv) in the case of a limited company[26] that is exempt from the obligation to use the word 'limited' as part of its registered name[27], the fact that it is a limited company[28];

(v) in the case of a community interest company[29] that is not a public company[30], the fact that it is a limited company[31]; and

(vi) in the case of an investment company[32], the fact that it is such a company[33].

If, in the case of a company having a share capital[34], there is a disclosure as to the amount of share capital on its business letters, on its order forms, or on its websites, that disclosure must be as to paid up share capital[35].

Where a company's business letter includes the name of any director of that company[36], other than in the text or as a signatory, the letter must disclose the name of every director of that company[37].

Where a company fails, without reasonable excuse, to comply with any such requirement relating to trading disclosures[38], an offence is committed by the company, and by every officer of the company who is in default[39].

1 As to the meaning of 'company' under the Companies Acts see PARA 21; and as to the meaning of the 'Companies Acts' see PARA 13.

2 A company may have a common seal, but need not have one: see the Companies Act 2006 s 45; and PARA 282.

3 As to the company name generally see PARA 199 et seq. As to companies registered but not formed under the Companies Act 2006, and as to overseas companies, see PARA 29. As to the registered name of an overseas company see PARA 2016. As to permitted contractions in relation to the words 'limited', 'public limited company' and their Welsh equivalents, which may be included as part of the ordinary name of the company, see the Companies Act 2006 ss 58, 59; and PARA 199. It seems that 'Company' may be abbreviated for present purposes to 'Coy', 'limited' to 'ltd', and 'and' to '&': see *F Stacey & Co Ltd v Wallis* (1912) 106 LT 544; *Banque de l'Indochine et de Suez SA v Euroseas Group Finance Co Ltd* [1981] 3 All ER 198.

4 See the Companies Act 2006 s 45(2); and PARA 282. Where a bond had been entered into as a deed, but the company obtaining the bond had used a seal engraved with its trading name rather than its registered name, non-compliance with the statutory provisions did not in itself render the bond a nullity or unenforceable by a third party beneficiary against the surety which had validly sealed the bond: *OTV Birwelco Ltd v Technical and General Guarantee Co Ltd* [2002] EWHC 2240 (TCC), [2002] 4 All ER 668, [2002] 2 BCLC 723.

5 As to the meaning of 'company' generally see PARA 1. See also note 8.

6 Any display or disclosure of information required by the Company, Limited Liability Partnership and Business (Names and Trading Disclosures) Regulations 2015, SI 2015/17, Pt 6 (regs 20–29) must be in characters that can be read with the naked eye: reg 20. As to compliance with the requirement under previous legislation that the company's name must be 'mentioned' see *F Stacey & Co Ltd v Wallis* (1912) 106 LT 544.

7 As to a company's registered office see PARA 124. As to incorporation by registration under the Companies Act 2006 see PARA 104 et seq.

8 Company, Limited Liability Partnership and Business (Names and Trading Disclosures) Regulations 2015, SI 2015/17, reg 21(1). For these purposes, 'inspection place' means any location, other than a company's registered office, at which a company keeps available for inspection any company record which it is required under the Companies Acts to keep available for inspection: Company, Limited Liability Partnership and Business (Names and Trading Disclosures) Regulations 2015, SI 2015/17, reg 29(b). See further the Companies (Company Records) Regulations 2008, SI 2008/3006, reg 3, made under the Companies Act 2006 s 1136; and PARA 748. 'Company record' means any register, index, accounting records, agreement, memorandum, minutes or other document required by the Companies Acts to be kept by a company, and any register kept by a company of its debenture holders: Company, Limited Liability Partnership and Business (Names and Trading Disclosures) Regulations 2015, SI 2015/17, reg 29(a). A reference to any type of document is a reference to a document of that type in hard copy, electronic or any other form: reg 29(c). As to the meaning of the 'Companies Acts' see PARA 13. As to the keeping of company records (the 'register') by the registrar see PARA 142; as to the registers etc that must be kept at a company's registered office see PARA 125; and as to a company's register of debenture holders see PARA 1504.

Where the registrar changes the address of a company's registered office under the Companies Act 2006 s 1097A(7) or the Companies (Address of Registered Office) Regulations 2016, SI 2016/423 (see PARA 160), the company's duty to display its registered name at its registered office under the Company, Limited Liability Partnership and Business (Names and Trading Disclosures) Regulations 2015, SI 2015/17, reg 21(1)(a) is suspended for a period of 28 days beginning on the day the address was changed: see the Companies (Address of Registered Office) Regulations 2016, SI 2016/423, reg 11; and PARA 160.

The Company, Limited Liability Partnership and Business (Names and Trading Disclosures) Regulations 2015, SI 2015/17, reg 21(1) does not apply to any company which has at all times since its incorporation been dormant: reg 21(2). As to the meaning of a company that is 'dormant' see PARA 25. The provisions of reg 21(1) also do not apply to the registered office or an inspection place of a company where in respect of that company, a liquidator, administrator or administrative receiver has been appointed and the registered office or inspection place is also a place of business of that liquidator, administrator or administrative receiver: reg 21(3). As to administrators see COMPANY AND PARTNERSHIP INSOLVENCY vol 16 (2011) PARA 158 et seq; as to administrative receivers see COMPANY AND PARTNERSHIP INSOLVENCY vol 16 (2011) PARA 329 et seq; and as to the appointment of a liquidator see COMPANY AND PARTNERSHIP INSOLVENCY vol 17 (2011) PARA 909.

9 Company, Limited Liability Partnership and Business (Names and Trading Disclosures) Regulations 2015, SI 2015/17, reg 22(1), (2). As to the meaning of 'carry on business' generally see PARA 1 note 1.

The provisions mentioned in the text do not apply:

(1) to a location which is primarily used for living accommodation (reg 22(3)):

(2) to any location at which business is carried on by a company where: in respect of that company, a liquidator, administrator or administrative receiver has been appointed and the location is also a place of business of that liquidator, administrator or administrative receiver (reg 22(4));

(3) to any location at which business is carried on by a company of which every director who is an individual is a relevant director (reg 22(5)).

For these purposes, 'administrative receiver' has the meaning given by the Insolvency Act 1986 s 251 (see PARA 1518) and 'relevant director' means an individual in respect of whom the registrar of companies is required by regulations made pursuant to the Companies Act 2006 s 243(4) (see PARA 539) to refrain from disclosing protected information to a credit reference agency, where 'credit reference agency' has the meaning given in s 243(7) (see PARA 539) and 'protected information' has the meaning given in s 240 (see PARA 537): Company, Limited Liability Partnership and Business (Names and Trading Disclosures) Regulations 2015, SI 2015/17, reg 22(6). As to the registrar of companies see PARA 126 et seq.

10 Company, Limited Liability Partnership and Business (Names and Trading Disclosures) Regulations 2015, SI 2015/17, reg 23(1), (2).

11 Company, Limited Liability Partnership and Business (Names and Trading Disclosures) Regulations 2015, SI 2015/17, reg 23(1), (3).

12 Company, Limited Liability Partnership and Business (Names and Trading Disclosures) Regulations 2015, SI 2015/17, reg 27(1). The company must send a written response to that person within five working days of the receipt of that request: reg 27(2).

Where the registrar changes the address of a company's registered office under the Companies Act 2006 s 1097A(7) or the Companies (Address of Registered Office) Regulations 2016, SI 2016/423 (see PARA 160), the company's duty to provide information about its registered office under the Company, Limited Liability Partnership and Business (Names and Trading Disclosures) Regulations 2015, SI 2015/17, reg 27(1)(a) is suspended for a period of 28 days beginning on the day the address was changed: see the Companies (Address of Registered Office) Regulations 2016, SI 2016/423, reg 11; and PARA 160.

13 Company, Limited Liability Partnership and Business (Names and Trading Disclosures) Regulations 2015, SI 2015/17, reg 24(1)(a). As to whether an advertisement is included in 'other official publications' see *General Radio Co v General Radio Co (Westminster) Ltd* [1957] RPC 471 at 484–485 per Roxburgh J.

14 Company, Limited Liability Partnership and Business (Names and Trading Disclosures) Regulations 2015, SI 2015/17, reg 24(1)(b). As to a company's capacity to deal with bills and notes etc see PARA 291.

15 Company, Limited Liability Partnership and Business (Names and Trading Disclosures) Regulations 2015, SI 2015/17, reg 24(1)(c). See also PARA 221.

16 Company, Limited Liability Partnership and Business (Names and Trading Disclosures) Regulations 2015, SI 2015/17, reg 24(1)(d).

17 Company, Limited Liability Partnership and Business (Names and Trading Disclosures) Regulations 2015, SI 2015/17, reg 24(1)(e). As to bills and notes see further PARAS 291–294.

18 Company, Limited Liability Partnership and Business (Names and Trading Disclosures) Regulations 2015, SI 2015/17, reg 24(1)(f).

19 Company, Limited Liability Partnership and Business (Names and Trading Disclosures) Regulations 2015, SI 2015/17, reg 24(1)(g).

20 Company, Limited Liability Partnership and Business (Names and Trading Disclosures) Regulations 2015, SI 2015/17, reg 24(2). In relation to a company, a reference to 'its websites' includes a reference to any part of a website relating to that company which that company has caused or authorised to appear: reg 29(d).

21 Company, Limited Liability Partnership and Business (Names and Trading Disclosures) Regulations 2015, SI 2015/17, reg 25(1). Where the registrar changes the address of a company's registered office under the Companies Act 2006 s 1097A(7) or the Companies (Address of Registered Office) Regulations 2016, SI 2016/423 (see PARA 160), the company's duty to state information about the company's registered office under the Company, Limited Liability Partnership and Business (Names and Trading Disclosures) Regulations 2015, SI 2015/17, reg 25(1) is suspended for a period of 28 days beginning on the day the address was changed: see the Companies (Address of Registered Office) Regulations 2016, SI 2016/423, reg 11; and PARA 160.

22 As to the meaning of 'United Kingdom' see PARA 1 note 5.

23 Company, Limited Liability Partnership and Business (Names and Trading Disclosures) Regulations 2015, SI 2015/17, reg 25(2)(a).

24 Company, Limited Liability Partnership and Business (Names and Trading Disclosures) Regulations 2015, SI 2015/17, reg 25(2)(b). As to a company's registered number see PARAS 134–135.

25 Company, Limited Liability Partnership and Business (Names and Trading Disclosures) Regulations 2015, SI 2015/17, reg 25(2)(c).
26 As to the meaning of 'limited company' under the Companies Act 2006 see PARA 95.
27 Ie exempt under the Companies Act 2006 s 60 (see PARA 200).
28 Company, Limited Liability Partnership and Business (Names and Trading Disclosures) Regulations 2015, SI 2015/17, reg 25(2)(d).
29 As to community interest companies see PARA 75.
30 As to the meaning of 'public company' under the Companies Act 2006 see PARA 95.
31 Company, Limited Liability Partnership and Business (Names and Trading Disclosures) Regulations 2015, SI 2015/17, reg 25(2)(e).
32 Ie within the meaning of the Companies Act 2006 s 833 (see PARA 1567.
33 Company, Limited Liability Partnership and Business (Names and Trading Disclosures) Regulations 2015, SI 2015/17, reg 25(2)(f).
34 As to the meanings of 'share capital' and 'company having a share capital' under the Companies Act 2006 see PARA 1231.
35 Company, Limited Liability Partnership and Business (Names and Trading Disclosures) Regulations 2015, SI 2015/17, reg 25(3). As to paid up and unpaid shares see PARA 1231 et seq.
36 As to a company's directors see PARA 512 et seq.
37 Company, Limited Liability Partnership and Business (Names and Trading Disclosures) Regulations 2015, SI 2015/17, reg 26(1). For these purposes, in the case of a director who is an individual, 'name' has the meaning given in the Companies Act 2006 s 163(2) (see PARA 535) and, in the case of a director who is a body corporate or a firm that is a legal person under the law by which it is governed, 'name' means corporate name or firm name: Company, Limited Liability Partnership and Business (Names and Trading Disclosures) Regulations 2015, SI 2015/17, reg 26(2). As to companies, corporations and partnerships etc see PARAS 2–4.
38 Ie fails, without reasonable excuse, to comply with any requirement in the Company, Limited Liability Partnership and Business (Names and Trading Disclosures) Regulations 2015, SI 2015/17, regs 20–27 (see the text and notes 5–37): see reg 28(1). A breach of these provisions will not deprive the company of the right to protect a trade name used separately from its corporate name: *Pearks Gunston and Tee Ltd v Thompson Talmey & Co* (1901) 18 RPC 185, CA; *HE Randall Ltd v British and American Shoe Co* [1902] 2 Ch 354 (approved in *Employers' Liability Assurance Corpn v Sedgwick, Collins & Co* [1927] AC 95 at 120, HL, per Lord Blanesburgh). As to provision made for civil consequences to flow from a failure to make required disclosures see PARA 221.
39 Company, Limited Liability Partnership and Business (Names and Trading Disclosures) Regulations 2015, SI 2015/17, reg 28(1). For these purposes, a shadow director of the company is to be treated as an officer of the company: reg 28(3). As to the meaning of 'shadow director' under the Companies Act 2006 see PARA 513. As to the meaning of 'officer who is in default' under the Companies Act 2006 see PARA 316. As to the meaning of 'officer' generally under the Companies Act 2006 see PARA 679.

A person guilty of such an offence is liable on summary conviction to a fine not exceeding level 3 on the standard scale and for continued contravention to a daily default fine not exceeding one-tenth of level 3 on the standard scale: Company, Limited Liability Partnership and Business (Names and Trading Disclosures) Regulations 2015, SI 2015/17, reg 28(2). As to the standard scale and the powers of magistrates' courts to issue fines on summary conviction see SENTENCING vol 92 (2015) PARA 176; and as to the meaning of 'daily default fine' see PARA 1816.

221. Civil remedies for breach of trading disclosure provisions. In relation to any legal proceedings brought by a company[1] which is subject to the trading disclosures provisions[2] to enforce a right arising out of a contract made in the course of a business in respect of which the company was, at the time the contract was made, in breach of regulations made under those provisions[3], the proceedings must be dismissed if the defendant to the proceedings shows[4]:

(1) that he has a claim against the claimant arising out of the contract that he has been unable to pursue by reason of the latter's breach of the regulations[5]; or

(2) that he has suffered some financial loss in connection with the contract by reason of the claimant's breach of the regulations[6],

unless the court before which the proceedings are brought is satisfied that it is just and equitable to permit the proceedings to continue[7].

This provision does not affect the right of any person to enforce such rights as he may have against another person in any proceedings brought by that person[8].

1 As to the meaning of 'company' under the Companies Acts see PARA 21; and as to the meaning of the 'Companies Acts' see PARA 13.

2 Ie a company to which the Companies Act 2006 s 82 applies (as to which see PARA 219): see s 83(1).

3 Companies Act 2006 s 83(1). The text refers to a company that was, at the time the contract was made, in breach of regulations made under s 82 (as to which see PARA 219): see s 83(1). The provisions of s 83 apply to unregistered companies by virtue of the Unregistered Companies Regulations 2009, SI 2009/2436, reg 3, Sch 1 para 4, but as modified thereby: see PARA 1857. As to the meaning of 'unregistered company' see PARA 1856.

Under the Companies Act 1985 s 349(4) (repealed) (see now the Companies Act 2006 s 83), a director who signed a company cheque, bill of exchange etc which did not contain the name of the company was personally liable to the holder of the bill, etc, unless the amount was duly paid by the company: see *Scottish and Newcastle Breweries Ltd v Blair* 1967 SLT 72; *Fiorentino Comm Giuseppe Srl v Farnesi* [2005] EWHC 160 (Ch), [2005] 2 All ER 737, [2005] 1 WLR 3718. See also *Durham Fancy Goods Ltd v Michael Jackson (Fancy Goods) Ltd* [1968] 2 QB 839, [1968] 2 All ER 987 (holders estopped from enforcing personal liability as they had initiated the misdescription of the company); *Hendon v Adelman* (1973) 117 Sol Jo 631 (cheque printed by bank for 'L & R Agencies Ltd' gave as the company's name 'L R Agencies Ltd'; signatories to cheque personally liable); *British Airways Board v Parish* [1979] 2 Lloyd's Rep 361, CA ('limited' omitted). The director who signed is liable not as surety but for breach of statutory duty: *Maxform SpA v B Mariani and Goodville Ltd* [1981] 2 Lloyd's Rep 54, CA (signature in trading name not sufficient to avoid personal liability); *Banque de l'Indochine et de Suez SA v Euroseas Group Finance Co Ltd* [1981] 3 All ER 198 (abbreviation of 'Company' to 'Co' no breach); *John Wilkes (Footwear) Ltd v Lee International (Footwear) Ltd* [1985] BCLC 444, CA (officer of the company authorised the placing of an order for goods on the company's behalf by a company servant in a written form omitting the company's name); *Lindholst & Co A/S v Fowler* [1988] BCLC 166, CA ('Ltd' omitted); *Blum v OCP Repartition SA* [1988] BCLC 170, CA ('Ltd' omitted); *Rafsanjan Pistachio Producers Co-operative v Reiss* [1990] BCLC 352. Cf *Jenice Ltd v Dan* [1993] BCLC 1349 (company's name on cheques was misspelt in circumstances which did not lead to any of the vices against which the statutory provisions were directed and, accordingly, the defendant was not personally liable). Although documents omitting the company's name could not have been relied on as against the company, moneys paid under them to persons known to represent the company were not on that account payable over again: *Mahony v East Holyford Mining Co* (1875) LR 7 HL 869 at 893 per Lord Chelmsford; *Beer v London and Paris Hotel Co* (1875) LR 20 Eq 412; *OTV Birwelco Ltd v Technical and General Guarantee Co Ltd* [2002] EWHC 2240 (TCC), [2002] 4 All ER 668, [2002] 2 All ER (Comm) 1116, [2002] 2 BCLC 723. As to the liability of directors generally see PARA 599 et seq.

4 Companies Act 2006 s 83(2).

5 Companies Act 2006 s 83(2)(a).

6 Companies Act 2006 s 83(2)(b).

7 Companies Act 2006 s 83(2).

8 Companies Act 2006 s 83(3).

(vii) Business Names

222. Persons subject to the business names provisions of the Companies Act 2006. The business names provisions of the Companies Act 2006[1] apply to any person carrying on business in the United Kingdom[2]. However, those provisions do not prevent:

(1) an individual carrying on business under a name consisting of his surname without any addition other than a permitted addition[3]; or

(2) individuals carrying on business in partnership[4] under a name consisting of the surnames of all the partners without any addition other than a permitted addition[5].

The 'permitted additions' for these purposes are:

(a) in the case of an individual, his forename or initial[6];

(b) in the case of a partnership, the forenames of individual partners or the initials of those forenames[7] or, where two or more individual partners have the same surname, the addition of 's' at the end of that surname[8]; and

(c) in either case, an addition merely indicating that the business is carried on in succession to a former owner of the business[9].

1 Ie the Companies Act 2006 Pt 41 Ch 1 (ss 1192–1199) (see also PARA 223 et seq): see s 1192(1). As to Pt 41 Ch 2 (ss 1200–1206), which relates to trading disclosures required of individuals and partnerships, see PARTNERSHIP vol 79 (2014) PARA 8. (The equivalent provisions to Pt 41 Ch 2 that apply to companies are set out in ss 82–84: see PARAS 219, 221).

2 Companies Act 2006 s 1192(1). For these purposes, 'business' includes a profession: see s 1208. As to the meaning of 'carry on business' generally see PARA 1 note 1. As to the meaning of 'United Kingdom' see PARA 1 note 5.

However, s 1192 does not apply to the carrying on of a business by a person who:

(1) carried on the business immediately before 1 October 2009 (ie the date on which Pt 41 Ch 1 came into force: see the Companies Act 2006 (Commencement No 8, Transitional Provisions and Savings) Order 2008, SI 2008/2860, art 3(x)) (Companies Act 2006 s 1199(1), (2)(a)); and

(2) continues to carry it on under the name that immediately before that date was its lawful business name (s 1199(1), (2)(b)).

Where a business is transferred to a person on or after 1 October 2009, and that person carries on the business under the name that was its lawful business name immediately before the transfer, s 1192 does not apply in relation to the carrying on of the business under that name during the period of 12 months beginning with the date of the transfer: s 1199(3). For these purposes, 'lawful business name', in relation to a business, means a name under which the business was carried on without contravening the Business Names Act 1985 s 2(1) (repealed) (see now the Companies Act 2006 ss 1193–1196; and PARA 223) or, after 1 October 2009, the provisions of Pt 41 Ch 1: s 1199(4). The Business Names Act 1985 (repealed) (see now the Companies Act 2006 Pt 41 Ch 1) was capable of applying to educational establishments as it was intended to deal with situations where a contracting party fails to disclose its true identity in documents which could be evidence of a contract: *London College of Science and Technology Ltd v Islington London Borough Council* [1997] ELR 162, 140 Sol Jo LB 166.

3 Companies Act 2006 s 1192(2)(a). For these purposes, 'surname', in relation to a peer or person usually known by a British title different from his surname, means the title by which he is known: see s 1208.

4 For these purposes, 'partnership' means a partnership within the Partnership Act 1890 (see PARTNERSHIP vol 79 (2014) PARA 1 et seq), or a limited partnership registered under the Limited Partnerships Act 1907 (see PARTNERSHIP vol 79 (2014) PARA 217 et seq), or a firm or entity of a similar character formed under the law of a country or territory outside the United Kingdom: see the Companies Act 2006 s 1208. As to the meaning of 'firm' see PARA 105 note 15. As to the meanings of 'firm' and 'partnership' generally see PARTNERSHIP vol 79 (2014) PARA 1; and as to the legal personality of a partnership or firm generally see PARTNERSHIP vol 79 (2014) PARA 2.

5 Companies Act 2006 s 1192(2)(b).

6 Companies Act 2006 s 1192(3)(a). For these purposes, 'initial' includes any recognised abbreviation of a name: see s 1208.

7 Companies Act 2006 s 1192(3)(b)(i).

8 Companies Act 2006 s 1192(3)(b)(ii).

9 Companies Act 2006 s 1192(3)(c).

223. Business names requiring Secretary of State's approval. A person[1] must not, without the approval of the Secretary of State[2], carry on business in the United Kingdom[3] under a name that:

(1) would be likely to give the impression that the business is connected with Her Majesty's government or the Welsh Assembly Government[4], or with any local authority[5], or with any public authority[6] that is specified for these purposes[7] by regulations made by the Secretary of State[8]; or

(2) includes a word or expression for the time being specified in regulations made by the Secretary of State for these purposes[9].

A person who contravenes the prohibition under head (1) or head (2) above commits an offence[10]; and where such an offence is committed by a body corporate[11], an offence is also committed by every officer of the body who is in default[12]. Any person guilty of either such offence is liable on summary conviction to a fine not exceeding level 3 on the standard scale[13] and for continued contravention to a daily default fine[14] not exceeding one-tenth of level 3 on the standard scale[15].

The Secretary of State may by regulations made under head (1) or head (2) above require that, in connection with an application for the approval of the Secretary of State[16], the applicant must seek the view of a specified[17] government department or other body[18]. Where such a requirement applies, the applicant must request the specified department or other body, in writing, to indicate whether, and if so why, it has any objections to the proposed name[19]. He must submit to the Secretary of State a statement that such a request has been made and a copy of any response received from the specified body[20]. If these requirements are not complied with, the Secretary of State may refuse to consider the application for approval[21].

Where approval has been given for the purposes of head (1) or head (2) above, and it appears to the Secretary of State that there are overriding considerations of public policy that require such approval to be withdrawn, the approval may be withdrawn by notice in writing given to the person concerned[22]. The notice must state the date as from which approval is withdrawn[23].

1 As to the persons to whom the Companies Act 2006 Pt 41 Ch 1 (ss 1192–1199) (see also PARAS 222, 224 et seq) (business names) applies see PARA 222. However, ss 1193–1196 do not apply to the carrying on of a business by a person who:
   (1) carried on the business immediately before 1 October 2009 (ie the date on which Pt 41 Ch 1 came into force: see the Companies Act 2006 (Commencement No 8, Transitional Provisions and Savings) Order 2008, SI 2008/2860, art 3(x)) (Companies Act 2006 s 1199(1), (2)(a)); and
   (2) continues to carry it on under the name that immediately before that date was its lawful business name (s 1199(1), (2)(b)).

   Where a business is transferred to a person on or after 1 October 2009, and that person carries on the business under the name that was its lawful business name immediately before the transfer, ss 1193–1196 do not apply in relation to the carrying on of the business under that name during the period of 12 months beginning with the date of the transfer: s 1199(3). As to the meanings of 'business' and 'lawful business name' for these purposes see PARA 222 note 2. As to the meaning of 'carry on business' generally see PARA 1 note 1.

2 As to the Secretary of State see PARA 6. It is the duty of the Secretary of State to secure that the expression 'chamber of commerce' and its Welsh equivalent ('siambr fasnach') is specified in regulations under s 1194 (business names requiring approval of Secretary of State) (see head (2) in the text), as an expression for the registration of which as or as part of a company's name the approval of the Secretary of State is required: Company and Business Names (Chamber of Commerce, etc) Act 1999 s 1 (amended by SI 2009/1941). Before determining under the Companies Act 2006 s 1194 whether to approve the carrying on of a business under a name which includes the expression 'chamber of commerce' or 'siambr fasnach', or any other expression for the time being specified in regulations under s 1194 which begins with the words 'chamber of' or 'chambers of' (or the Welsh equivalents), the Secretary of State must consult at least one relevant representative body: Company and Business Names (Chamber of Commerce, etc) Act 1999 s 3(1) (amended by SI 2009/1941). The Secretary of State may publish guidance with respect to factors which may be taken into account in determining whether to approve the use of a business name to which the Company and Business Names (Chamber of Commerce, etc) Act 1999 s 3 applies: s 3(2). The relevant representative bodies for these purposes are the British Chambers of Commerce and the body known as the Scottish Chambers of Commerce (see s 4(1)); but the Secretary of State may by order made by statutory instrument amend s 4(1) by adding or deleting from it the name of any body (whether corporate or unincorporated) (see s 4(2), (3)). At the date at which this volume states the law, no such order had been made.

   The functions conferred on the Secretary of State by the Companies Act 2006 s 1193 (see head (1) in the text) or s 1194 (see head (2) in the text) (together formerly the Business Names Act 1985 s 2(1) (repealed)) may be exercised by, or by employees of, such person (if any) as may be authorised in that behalf by the Secretary of State: see the Contracting Out (Functions in relation to the Registration of Companies) Order 1995, SI 1995/1013, Sch 3 para 2 the Interpretation Act 1978 s 17(2)(b); and PARA 8.

All the regulatory functions of the Secretary of State under the Companies Act 2006 Pt 41 (ss 1192–1208) are functions to which the Legislative and Regulatory Reform Act 2006 ss 21, 22 apply: Legislative and Regulatory Reform (Regulatory Functions) Order 2007, SI 2007/3544, art 2, Schedule Pt 2 (amended by SI 2009/2981). This is subject to arts 3, 4, which exclude any regulatory function exercisable by Order in Council, order, rules, regulations, scheme, warrant, byelaw or other subordinate instrument under a public general Act or local Act (art 3), any function, so far as exercisable in Northern Ireland, if or to the extent that the function relates to matters which are transferred matters (art 4(b)) or any function exercisable only in or as regards Wales (art 4(c)). As to the Legislative and Regulatory Reform Act 2006 ss 21, 22 see PARA 126 note 2.

3 As to the meaning of 'United Kingdom' see PARA 1 note 5.

4 Companies Act 2006 s 1193(1)(a) (amended by SI 2009/2958). This provision also applies to a name that would be likely to give the impression that the business is connected with any part of the Scottish administration or Her Majesty's Government in Northern Ireland: see the Companies Act 2006 s 1193(1)(a) (as so amended).

5 Companies Act 2006 s 1193(1)(b). For these purposes, 'local authority' means a local authority within the meaning of the Local Government Act 1972 (see LOCAL GOVERNMENT vol 69 (2009) PARA 23) (or a council constituted under the Local Government etc (Scotland) Act 1994 s 2 or a district council in Northern Ireland), the Common Council of the City of London or the Council of the Isles of Scilly: Companies Act 2006 s 1193(2). As to the Common Council of the City of London see LONDON GOVERNMENT vol 71 (2013) PARA 34 et seq. As to the Council of the Isles of Scilly see LOCAL GOVERNMENT vol 69 (2009) PARA 36.

6 For these purposes, 'public authority' includes any person or body having functions of a public nature: Companies Act 2006 s 1193(2). As to public bodies and public authorities generally see CONSTITUTIONAL AND ADMINISTRATIVE LAW vol 20 (2014) PARAS 93 et seq (parliament), 126 et seq (the judiciary), 148 et seq (the executive) and 311 et seq (other public bodies).

7 Ie for the purposes of the Companies Act 2006 s 1193: see s 1193(1)(c).

8 Companies Act 2006 s 1193(1)(c). Regulations made under s 1193 are subject to affirmative resolution procedure (ie the regulations must not be made unless a draft of the statutory instrument containing them has been laid before Parliament and approved by a resolution of each House of Parliament): see ss 1193(3), 1290. As to the making of regulations under the Companies Act 2006 generally see ss 1288–1292. Partly in the exercise of the power under s 1193 the Secretary of State has made the Company, Limited Liability Partnership and Business (Names and Trading Disclosures) Regulations 2015, SI 2015/17. See reg 18, Sch 4. There is no requirement for the purposes of head (1) in the text for the court to have before it evidence that confusion had in fact been caused as a result of the use of a business name said to have given the impression that the business was connected to the government: *Department of Trade and Industry v Cedenio* [2001] All ER (D) 323 (Feb) (considering the Business Names Act 1985 s 2(1) (repealed)).

9 Companies Act 2006 s 1194(1). Head (2) in the text refers to regulations made by the Secretary of State under s 1194: see s 1194(1). Regulations made under s 1194 are subject to approval after being made: s 1194(2). As to the meaning of 'approval after being made' see s 1291; and PARA 195 note 13. Partly in exercise of the power under s 1194, the Secretary of State has made the Company, Limited Liability Partnership and Business Names (Sensitive Words and Expressions) Regulations 2014, SI 2014/3140. See reg 3, Sch 1 Pt 1.

10 Companies Act 2006 ss 1193(4), 1194(3). Because the statute carries criminal sanctions, it should not be given a purposive construction: *Department of Trade and Industry v Cedenio* [2001] All ER (D) 323 (Feb). The provisions of the Companies Act 2006 ss 1121–1123 (liability of officer in default) (see PARA 316) and 1125–1131 (general provisions about offences) (see PARA 1816 et seq) apply in relation to offences under Pt 41 (ss 1192–1208) (see also PARAS 222, 224–225; and TRADE MARKS AND TRADE NAMES vol 97A (2014) PARA 476) as in relation to offences under the Companies Acts: Companies Act 2006 s 1207. As to the meaning of the 'Companies Acts' see PARA 13.

11 As to the meaning of 'body corporate' for the purposes of the Companies Acts see PARA 1 note 5.

12 Companies Act 2006 ss 1193(5), 1194(4). As to the meaning of 'officer who is in default' see PARA 316. As to the meaning of 'officer' generally see PARA 679.

13 As to the standard scale and the powers of magistrates' courts to issue fines on summary conviction see SENTENCING vol 92 (2015) PARA 176.

14 As to the meaning of 'daily default fine' see PARA 1816.

15 Companies Act 2006 ss 1193(6), 1194(5).

16 Ie under the Companies Act 2006 s 1193 (see head (1) in the text) or under s 1194 (see head (2) in the text), as the case may be: see s 1195(1).

17 For these purposes, 'specified' means specified in the regulations: Companies Act 2006 s 1195(5). Accordingly, in connection with applications for the Secretary of State's approval where the situation of the registered office or principal place of business is irrelevant see the Company, Limited Liability Partnership and Business Names (Sensitive Words and Expressions) Regulations 2014, SI 2014/3140, reg 5, Sch 2 Pt 1; and as to applications where the situation of the registered office or principal place of business is relevant see reg 6, Sch 2 Pt 2.
18 Companies Act 2006 s 1195(1).
19 Companies Act 2006 s 1195(2).
20 Companies Act 2006 s 1195(3).
21 Companies Act 2006 s 1195(4).
22 Companies Act 2006 s 1196(1), (2).
23 Companies Act 2006 s 1196(1), (3).

224. Business name containing inappropriate indication of company type or legal form. The Secretary of State[1] may make provision by regulations[2] prohibiting a person[3] from carrying on business in the United Kingdom[4] under a name consisting of or containing specified[5] words, expressions or other indications[6]:

(1) that are associated with a particular type of company or form of organisation[7]; or
(2) that are similar to words, expressions or other indications associated with a particular type of company or form of organisation[8].

The regulations may prohibit the use of words, expressions or other indications either in a specified part, or otherwise than in a specified part, of a name[9], or in conjunction with, or otherwise than in conjunction with, such other words, expressions or indications as may be specified[10].

A person who uses a name in contravention of such regulations commits an offence[11]; and where such an offence is committed by a body corporate[12], an offence is also committed by every officer of the body who is in default[13].

1 As to the Secretary of State see PARA 6. See also PARA 223 note 2.
2 As to the making of regulations under the Companies Act 2006 generally see ss 1288–1292. Regulations under s 1197 are subject to negative resolution procedure (ie the statutory instrument containing the regulations is subject to annulment in pursuance of a resolution of either House of Parliament): see ss 1197(4), 1289. Partly in exercise of the power under s 1197, the Secretary of State has made the Company, Limited Liability Partnership and Business (Names and Trading Disclosures) Regulations 2015, SI 2015/17. See note 10.
3 As to the persons to whom the Companies Act 2006 Pt 41 Ch 1 (ss 1192–1199) (see also PARAS 222 et seq, 225) (business names) applies see PARA 222. However, s 1197 does not apply to the carrying on of a business by a person who:
   (1) carried on the business immediately before 1 October 2009 (ie the date on which Pt 41 Ch 1 came into force: see the Companies Act 2006 (Commencement No 8, Transitional Provisions and Savings) Order 2008, SI 2008/2860, art 3(x)) (Companies Act 2006 s 1199(1), (2)(a)); and
   (2) continues to carry it on under the name that immediately before that date was its lawful business name (s 1199(1), (2)(b)).

   Where a business is transferred to a person on or after 1 October 2009, and that person carries on the business under the name that was its lawful business name immediately before the transfer, s 1197 does not apply in relation to the carrying on of the business under that name during the period of 12 months beginning with the date of the transfer: s 1199(3). As to the meanings of 'business' and 'lawful business name' for these purposes see PARA 222 note 2. As to the meaning of 'carry on business' generally see PARA 1 note 1.
4 As to the meaning of 'United Kingdom' see PARA 1 note 5.
5 For these purposes, 'specified' means specified in the regulations: Companies Act 2006 s 1197(3).
6 Companies Act 2006 s 1197(1).
7 Companies Act 2006 s 1197(1)(a).
8 Companies Act 2006 s 1197(1)(b).
9 Companies Act 2006 s 1197(2)(a).
10 Companies Act 2006 s 1197(2)(b).

   Accordingly, no person may carry on business in the United Kingdom under a name that concludes with any word or abbreviation set out in inverted commas in the Company, Limited

Liability Partnership and Business (Names and Trading Disclosures) Regulations 2015, SI 2015/17, Sch 2 para 1(a), (b) unless that person is:

(1) a company or an overseas company registered in the United Kingdom by that name (reg 16(1)(a));

(2) an overseas company incorporated with that name (reg 16(1)(b));

(3) a society registered under the Co-operative and Community Benefit Societies Act 2014 or the Industrial and Provident Societies Act (Northern Ireland) 1969 by that name (Company, Limited Liability Partnership and Business (Names and Trading Disclosures) Regulations 2015, SI 2015/17, reg 16(1)(c));

(4) an incorporated friendly society (as defined in the Friendly Societies Act 1992 s 116: see FINANCIAL INSTITUTIONS vol 48 (2015) PARAS 556–557) which has that name (Company, Limited Liability Partnership and Business (Names and Trading Disclosures) Regulations 2015, SI 2015/17, reg 16(1)(d)); or

(5) a company to which the Companies Act 2006 s 1040 (companies authorised to register under the Companies Act 2006) (see PARA 30) applies which has that name (Company, Limited Liability Partnership and Business (Names and Trading Disclosures) Regulations 2015, SI 2015/17, reg 16(1)(e)).

Nor may any person carry on business in the United Kingdom under a name that concludes with any word or abbreviation specified as similar to any word or abbreviation set out in inverted commas in Sch 2 para 1(a), (b): reg 16(2). For these purposes, the words or abbreviations specified as similar to the words and abbreviations set out in inverted commas in Sch 2 para 1(a), (b) are any in which one or more permitted characters has been omitted, one or more permitted characters has been added, or each of one or more permitted characters has been substituted by one or more other permitted characters, in such a way as to be likely to mislead the public as to the legal form of a company if included in the registered name of the company or in a business name: reg 1(2), Sch 2 para 2. As to the meaning of 'overseas company' see PARA 2013. As to company registration under the Companies Act 2006 see PARA 104 et seq. As to companies registered but not formed under the Companies Act 2006, and as to overseas companies, see PARA 29. As to societies registered under the Co-operative and Community Benefit Societies Act 2014 see FINANCIAL INSTITUTIONS vol 48 (2015) PARA 898 et seq.

A person must not carry on business in the United Kingdom under a name that includes any expression or abbreviation set out in inverted commas in the Company, Limited Liability Partnership and Business (Names and Trading Disclosures) Regulations 2015, SI 2015/17, Sch 2 para 3 unless that person is such a company, partnership grouping or organisation as is indicated in that expression or abbreviation: reg 17(1). Nor may any person carry on business in the United Kingdom under a name that includes any expression or abbreviation specified as similar to any expression or abbreviation set out in inverted commas in Sch 2 para 3: reg 17(2). As to transitional provisions see reg 19. The expressions and abbreviations specified as similar to the expressions and abbreviations set out in inverted commas in Sch 2 para 3 are any in which one or more permitted characters has been omitted, one or more permitted characters has been added, or each of one or more permitted characters has been substituted by one or more other permitted characters, in such a way as to be likely to mislead the public as to the legal form of a company or business if included in the registered name of the company or in a business name: reg 1(2), Sch 2 para 4.

11 Companies Act 2006 s 1197(5). The provisions of ss 1121–1123 (liability of officer in default) (see PARA 316) and 1125–1131 (general provisions about offences) (see PARA 1816 et seq) apply in relation to offences under Pt 41 (ss 1192–1208) (see also PARAS 222 et seq, 225; and TRADE MARKS AND TRADE NAMES vol 97A (2014) PARA 476) as in relation to offences under the Companies Acts: Companies Act 2006 s 1207. As to the meaning of the 'Companies Acts' see PARA 13.

12 As to the meaning of 'body corporate' for the purposes of the Companies Acts see PARA 1 note 5.

13 Companies Act 2006 s 1197(6). As to the meaning of 'officer who is in default' see PARA 316. As to the meaning of 'officer' generally see PARA 679.

Any person guilty of such an offence is liable on summary conviction to a fine not exceeding level 3 on the standard scale and for continued contravention to a daily default fine not exceeding one-tenth of level 3 on the standard scale: Companies Act 2006 s 1197(7). As to the standard scale and the powers of magistrates' courts to issue fines on summary conviction see SENTENCING vol 92 (2015) PARA 176; and as to the meaning of 'daily default fine' see PARA 1816.

225. Offence of trading under misleading business name. A person[1] must not carry on business[2] in the United Kingdom[3] under a name that gives so misleading an indication of the nature of the activities of the business as to be likely to cause harm to the public[4].

A person who uses a name in contravention of this prohibition commits an offence[5]; and where such an offence is committed by a body corporate[6], an offence is also committed by every officer of the body who is in default[7].

1 As to the persons to whom the Companies Act 2006 Pt 41 Ch 1 (ss 1192–1199) (see also PARA 222 et seq) (business names) applies see PARA 222.
2 As to the meaning of 'business' for these purposes see PARA 222 note 2. As to the meaning of 'carry on business' generally see PARA 1 note 1.
3 As to the meaning of 'United Kingdom' see PARA 1 note 5.
4 Companies Act 2006 s 1198(1). See also PARA 215 note 3.
5 Companies Act 2006 s 1198(2). The provisions of ss 1121–1123 (liability of officer in default) (see PARA 316) and 1125–1131 (general provisions about offences) (see PARA 1816 et seq; and) apply in relation to offences under Pt 41 (ss 1192–1208) (see also PARA 222 et seq; and TRADE MARKS AND TRADE NAMES vol 97A (2014) PARA 476) as in relation to offences under the Companies Acts: Companies Act 2006 s 1207. As to the meaning of the 'Companies Acts' see PARA 13.
6 As to the meaning of 'body corporate' for the purposes of the Companies Acts see PARA 1 note 5.
7 Companies Act 2006 s 1198(3). As to the meaning of 'officer who is in default' see PARA 316. As to the meaning of 'officer' generally see PARA 679.
Any person guilty of such an offence is liable on summary conviction to a fine not exceeding level 3 on the standard scale and for continued contravention to a daily default fine not exceeding one-tenth of level 3 on the standard scale: s 1198(4). As to the standard scale and the powers of magistrates' courts to issue fines on summary conviction see SENTENCING vol 92 (2015) PARA 176; and as to the meaning of 'daily default fine' see PARA 1816.

(7) THE COMPANY CONSTITUTION

(i) Meaning of 'Constitution' of a Company

226. Meaning of references to a company's constitution. Unless the context otherwise requires, references in the Companies Acts[1] to the constitution of a company[2] (a 'company's constitution') include[3]:

(1) the company's articles of association[4]; and
(2) any of the following resolutions and agreements[5]:
   (a) any special resolution[6];
   (b) any resolution or agreement agreed to by all the members[7] of a company that, if not so agreed to, would not have been effective for its purpose unless passed as a special resolution[8];
   (c) any resolution or agreement agreed to by all the members of a class of shareholders[9] that, if not so agreed to, would not have been effective for its purpose unless passed by some particular majority or otherwise in some particular manner[10];
   (d) any resolution or agreement that effectively binds all members of a class of shareholders though not agreed to by all those members[11];
   (e) any other resolution or agreement which affects a company's constitution[12] by virtue of any enactment[13].

References to a company's constitution in the provisions of the Companies Act 2006 that (amongst other things) impose duties and limitations upon a company's directors[14] include, in addition to the matters mentioned in heads (1) and (2) above[15]:

(i) any resolution or other decision come to in accordance with the constitution[16]; and

(ii) any decision by the members of the company, or a class of members, that is treated by virtue of any enactment or rule of law as equivalent to a decision by the company[17].

1 As to the meaning of the 'Companies Acts' for these purposes see PARA 13.
2 As to the meaning of 'company' under the Companies Acts see PARA 21. As to the effect of a company's constitution see PARA 242 et seq.
3 Companies Act 2006 s 17. The use of the word 'include' indicates that the list given in heads (1)–(2) in the text is not exhaustive, eg a company's certificate of incorporation has constitutional relevance serving as it does to define a company and therefore to indicate its general nature, powers and limitations: see PARA 114.

In the case of an unregistered company (see PARA 1856 et seq), any reference to the company's constitution must be read as referring to any instrument constituting or regulating the company: see the Unregistered Companies Regulations 2009, SI 2009/2436, reg 5(1)(c); and PARA 1857. As to the meaning of 'unregistered company' see PARA 1856.
4 Companies Act 2006 s 17(a). As to the meaning of references to a company's 'articles' see PARA 227 note 2. As to articles of association generally see PARA 227 et seq.
5 Companies Act 2006 s 17(b). Head (2) in the text refers to any resolutions and agreements to which Pt 3 Ch 3 (ss 29–30) (resolutions and agreements affecting a company's constitution) applies (see s 29; heads (2)(a)–(2)(e) in the text; and PARA 230): see s 17(b). As to resolutions and decisions of the company generally see PARA 684 et seq.
6 See the Companies Act 2006 s 29(1)(a); and PARA 230. As to the meaning of 'special resolution' see PARA 686.
7 References in the Companies Act 2006 s 29(1) to a member of a company do not include the company itself where it is such a member by virtue only of its holding shares as treasury shares: see s 29(2); and PARA 230. As to the meaning of 'member' see PARA 323; and as to the meaning of 'shares' see PARA 1231. As to treasury shares see PARA 1437.
8 See the Companies Act 2006 s 29(1)(b); and PARA 230. The redenomination of shares does not affect any rights or obligations of members under the company's constitution, or any restrictions affecting members under the company's constitution: see s 624(1); and PARA 1355.
9 References in the Companies Act 2006 s 29(1) to a class of members of a company do not include the company itself where it is such a member by virtue only of its holding shares as treasury shares: see s 29(2); and PARA 230. As to classes of shares generally see PARA 1246 et seq.
10 See the Companies Act 2006 s 29(1)(c); and PARA 230.
11 See the Companies Act 2006 s 29(1)(d); and PARA 230.
12 Ie any other resolution or agreement to which the Companies Act 2006 Pt 3 Ch 3 applies (see note 5): see s 29(1)(e); and PARA 230.
13 See the Companies Act 2006 s 29(1)(e); and PARA 230. As to the meaning of 'enactment' see PARA 13 note 16.
14 Ie references to a company's constitution in the Companies Act 2006 Pt 10 (ss 154–259) (see PARA 512 et seq): see s 257(1); and PARA 580. A director of a company has a duty to act in accordance with the company's constitution: see s 171; and PARA 580. As to the meaning of 'director' see PARA 512.
15 Ie in addition to the matters mentioned in the Companies Act 2006 s 17: see s 257(2); and PARA 580.
16 See the Companies Act 2006 s 257(1)(a); and PARA 580.
17 See the Companies Act 2006 s 257(1)(b); and PARA 580.

(ii) Articles of Association

227. Power to prescribe model articles and their application. A company[1] must have articles of association[2] prescribing regulations for the company[3].

Unless it is a company to which model articles apply[4], it must register articles of association[5]; and articles of association registered by a company must[6] be contained in a single document[7] and be divided into paragraphs numbered consecutively[8].

The Secretary of State[9] may by regulations prescribe[10] model articles of association for companies[11]; and different model articles may be prescribed for different descriptions of company[12]. A company may adopt all or any of the provisions of model articles[13].

On the formation of a limited company[14]:

(1) if articles are not registered[15]; or

(2) if articles are registered, in so far as they do not exclude or modify the relevant model articles[16],

the relevant model articles, so far as applicable, form part of the company's articles in the same manner and to the same extent as if articles in the form of those articles had been duly registered[17].

According to the jurisprudence of the Court of Justice of the European Union, it may be that the articles should, in a case where the number of directors is only one, explicitly state, for the purpose of registration, that such one director may alone represent the company, even though this is in any event the position under the general law[18].

1 As to the meaning of 'company' under the Companies Acts see PARA 21; and as to the meaning of the 'Companies Acts' see PARA 13.

2 References in the Companies Acts to a company's 'articles' are to its articles of association (Companies Act 2006 s 18(4)); and, unless the context otherwise requires, references in the Companies Acts to a company's constitution include the company's articles (see s 17; and PARA 226). As to the articles of association of a community interest company see PARA 98.

In the case of an unregistered company (see PARA 1856 et seq), any reference to the company's articles of association must be read as referring to any instrument constituting or regulating the company: see the Unregistered Companies Regulations 2009, SI 2009/2436, reg 5(1)(c); and PARA 1857. As to the meaning of 'unregistered company' see PARA 1856.

3 Companies Act 2006 s 18(1). Any such article, at any rate when read with other articles, may be directory only: *Re Hansard Publishing Union Ltd* (1892) 8 TLR 280, CA; *Landowners West of England and South Wales Land Drainage and Inclosure Co v Ashford* (1880) 16 ChD 411.

Provisions that immediately before 1 October 2009 were contained in a company's memorandum but are not provisions of the kind mentioned in the Companies Act 2006 s 8 (which substantially altered the purpose of the memorandum of association) (see PARA 97) are to be treated after that date as provisions of the company's articles: s 28(1). This applies not only to substantive provisions but also to provision for entrenchment, as defined in s 22 (see PARA 232): s 28(2). The provisions of Pt 3 (ss 17–38) (a company's constitution) about provision for entrenchment apply to such provision as they apply to provision made on the company's formation, except that the company's duty under s 23(1)(a) (see PARA 232) to give notice to the registrar of any provision for entrenchment contained in the articles does not apply: s 28(3). Nothing in s 18(3) (see the text and notes 6–8) is to be read as affecting the operation of s 28: see the Companies Act 2006 (Commencement No 8, Transitional Provisions and Savings) Order 2008, SI 2008/2860, art 5, Sch 2 para 3(2). Nor is anything in the Companies Act 2006 as a whole to be read as enabling a company to amend or omit provisions of its articles that were formerly in its memorandum so as to change its status as a limited or unlimited company otherwise than in accordance with the relevant provisions of Pt 7 (ss 89–111) (re-registration as a means of changing company's status) (see PARA 167 et seq): see the Companies Act 2006 (Commencement No 8, Transitional Provisions and Savings) Order 2008, SI 2008/2860, Sch 2 para 10. The date of 1 October 2009 is the date by which all the provisions of the Companies Act 2006 Pt 3 had been commenced: see the Companies Act 2006 (Commencement No 8, Transitional Provisions and Savings) Order 2008, SI 2008/2860, art 3. Where, in the case of an existing or transitional company, the company's articles are deemed to contain a statement of its name by virtue of the Companies Act 2006 s 28, and the company changes its name (by any means) on or after 1 October 2009, the company is not required to amend its articles in order to effect the change of name (see the Companies Act 2006 (Consequential Amendments, Transitional Provisions and Savings) Order 2009, SI 2009/1941, art 5(1), (2)); and the company is not required to send a copy of its articles to the registrar in accordance with the Companies Act 2006 s 26 (see PARA 235) (see the Companies Act 2006 (Consequential Amendments, Transitional Provisions and Savings) Order 2009, SI 2009/1941, art 5(4)). The deemed statement in the company's articles ceases to have effect when the change of name takes effect: art 5(3). As to the meaning of 'existing company' for these purposes see PARA 14 note 2; and as to the meaning of 'transitional company' for these purposes see PARA 13 note 18 (definitions applied by art 5(6)).

Prior to the Companies Act 2006, the articles of association were considered subordinate to the memorandum of association; and any clause in them, if and so far as it was at variance with the memorandum, was to that extent overruled by it and inoperative: see *Guinness v Land Corpn of Ireland Ltd* (1882) 22 ChD 349 at 376 per Cotton LJ; *Angostura Bitters (Dr JGB Siegert & Sons) Ltd v Kerr* [1933] AC 550 at 554, PC; *Re Duncan Gilmour & Co Ltd, Duncan Gilmour & Co Ltd v Inman* [1952] 2 All ER 871 at 874 per Wynn-Parry J. The memorandum was regarded as the charter of the company, defining its powers, while the articles of association (in their subsidiary role) defined the duties, rights and powers of the governing body as between themselves and the company at large, and the mode and form in which the business of the company was to be carried on and in which changes in its internal regulations may from time to time be made: see *Ashbury v Watson* (1885) 30 ChD 376, CA. However, in certain circumstances, the memorandum and articles were read together, at all events so far as was necessary to explain any ambiguity appearing in the terms of one document or to supplement it upon any matter as to which it is silent: see *Angostura Bitters (Dr JGB Siegert & Sons) Ltd v Kerr* at 554; *Re Duncan Gilmour & Co Ltd, Duncan Gilmour & Co Ltd v Inman*. See also *Harrison v Mexican Rly Co* (1875) LR 19 Eq 358; *Re Wedgewood Coal and Iron Co, Anderson's Case* (1877) 7 ChD 75 at 99, CA, per Jessel MR; *London Financial Association v Kelk* (1884) 26 ChD 107 at 135 per Bacon V-C; *Ashbury v Watson* (explained in *Re Marshall, Fleming & Co* 1938 SC 873 at 877–878, Ct of Sess per Lord Keith); *Re South Durham Brewery Co* (1885) 31 ChD 261, CA; *Andrews v Gas Meter Co* [1897] 1 Ch 361 at 369, CA, per Lindley LJ; *Re Southern Brazilian Rio Grande do Sul Rly Co Ltd* [1905] 2 Ch 78.

Questions as to the true meaning of the memorandum or articles of a company may be decided by the court in the course of proceedings: see PARA 306.

4 Ie by virtue of the Companies Act 2006 s 20 (default application of model articles in case of limited company) (see the text and notes 14–17): see the Companies Act 2006 s 18(2).

5 Companies Act 2006 s 18(2). As to registration requirements see PARA 104 et seq. Articles duly registered and acted on for many years may be held binding: *Ho Tung v Man On Insurance Co* [1902] AC 232, PC.

6 Companies Act 2006 s 18(3). See also note 3.

7 Companies Act 2006 s 18(3)(a). See also note 3.

8 Companies Act 2006 s 18(3)(b). See also note 3.

9 As to the Secretary of State see PARA 6.

10 In the Companies Acts, 'prescribed' means prescribed (by order or by regulations) by the Secretary of State: Companies Act 2006 s 1167. As to the making of regulations under the Companies Act 2006 generally see ss 1288–1292. Regulations under s 19 are subject to negative resolution procedure (ie the statutory instrument containing the regulations is subject to annulment in pursuance of a resolution of either House of Parliament): ss 19(5), 1289. In exercise of the powers conferred by s 19, the Secretary of State has made the Companies (Model Articles) Regulations 2008, SI 2008/3229: see PARA 228. Any amendment of model articles by regulations under the Companies Act 2006 s 19 does not affect a company registered before the amendment takes effect; and, for these purposes, 'amendment' here includes addition, alteration or repeal: s 19(4).

11 Companies Act 2006 s 19(1). See also note 10. The default articles prescribed for the purposes of the Companies Act 1985 ('legacy articles'), ie the Companies (Tables A to F) Regulations 1985, SI 1985/805, have not been revoked and may, in their amended form, continue to be used by companies after the commencement of the Companies Act 2006: see PARA 229; and see note 16.

12 Companies Act 2006 s 19(2). See the Companies (Model Articles) Regulations 2008, SI 2008/3229, regs 2–4, Sch 1 (private companies limited by shares), Sch 2 (private companies limited by guarantee), Sch 3 (public companies); and PARA 228. No such model articles have been prescribed for unlimited companies.

13 Companies Act 2006 s 19(3). See also *Gaiman v National Association for Mental Health* [1971] Ch 317, [1970] 2 All ER 362 (provided that he follows the general form of the model articles, the draftsman is free to add, subtract or vary the articles as circumstances require). As to provision made for the alteration of articles see PARA 231 et seq.

14 Companies Act 2006 s 20(1). As to the meaning of 'limited company' see PARA 95.

15 Companies Act 2006 s 20(1)(a). As to the registration of articles see PARA 104 et seq.

16 Companies Act 2006 s 20(1)(b). For these purposes, the 'relevant model articles' means the model articles prescribed for a company of that description as in force at the date on which the company is registered (see notes 10–11): s 20(2). As to the importance of using words clearly excluding prescribed model articles see *Fisher v Black and White Publishing Co* [1901] 1 Ch 174, CA; *R Paterson & Sons Ltd v Paterson Publishing Co* [1916] WN 352, HL.

17 Companies Act 2006 s 20(1).

18 See Case 32/74 *Friedrich Haaga GmbH* ECLI:EU:C:1974:116, [1974] ECR 1201, [1975] 1 CMLR 32, ECJ. A private company need have only one director: see the Companies Act 2006 s 154(1); and PARA 517.

228. Model articles prescribed for the purposes of the Companies Act 2006. The Secretary of State[1] has by regulations prescribed[2] different versions of model articles[3] for the following different descriptions of company[4]:

(1) private companies limited by shares[5];

(2) private companies limited by guarantee[6]; and
(3) public companies[7].

The default articles prescribed for the purposes of the Companies Act 1985[8] have not been revoked and may, in their amended form[9], continue to be used by companies after the commencement of the Companies Act 2006[10].

1 As to the Secretary of State see PARA 6.
2 Ie by regulations made under the Companies Act 2006 s 19: see PARA 227. In the Companies Acts, 'prescribed' means prescribed (by order or by regulations) by the Secretary of State: Companies Act 2006 s 1167. In exercise of the powers conferred by s 19, the Secretary of State has made the Companies (Model Articles) Regulations 2008, SI 2008/3229: see heads (1)–(3) in the text.
3 As to the meaning of references to 'articles' see PARA 227 note 2. As to articles of association generally see PARAS 227, 229 et seq.
4 See the Companies Act 2006 s 19; and PARA 227. As to the meaning of 'company' under the Companies Acts see PARA 21; and as to the meaning of the 'Companies Acts' see PARA 13.
5 See the Companies (Model Articles) Regulations 2008, SI 2008/3229, reg 2, Sch 1 (amended by the Mental Health (Discrimination) Act 2013 s 3(1)(a)). As to the meanings of 'private company' and 'company limited by shares' see PARA 95.
6 See the Companies (Model Articles) Regulations 2008, SI 2008/3229, reg 3, Sch 2 (amended by the Mental Health (Discrimination) Act 2013 s 3(1)(b)). As to the meaning of 'company limited by guarantee' see PARA 95.
7 See the Companies (Model Articles) Regulations 2008, SI 2008/3229, reg 4, Sch 3 (amended by the Mental Health (Discrimination) Act 2013 s 3(1)(c)). As to the meaning of 'public company' see PARA 95.
8 Ie the Companies (Tables A to F) Regulations 1985, SI 1985/805: see PARA 229.
9 See PARA 229.
10 See PARA 229. As to the statutory authority of Table A etc see PARA 229 note 4.

229. Legacy articles and the Companies Act 2006. The Companies Act 2006 does not vary the rule that the version of the default articles[1] that applies to any given company is the version in force at the date that the company was registered[2].

Prior to 1 October 2009[3], a company would have adopted default articles (known as 'Table A') that were issued under the Companies Act 1985[4].

Where companies relied on the default articles prescribed for the purposes of the Companies Act 1985 ('Table A')[5], or indeed any preceding version (such as the Companies Act 1948 'Table A'[6]), those articles continue to regulate the company after the Companies Act 2006 came fully into force, unless action has been taken to replace them[7].

1 Ie the articles of association that govern a company's activities if it fails to register its own bespoke articles. As to the meaning of references to 'articles' see PARA 227 note 2. As to articles of association generally see PARAS 227–228, 230 et seq. As to the meaning of 'company' under the Companies Acts see PARA 21; and as to the meaning of the 'Companies Acts' see PARA 13. A limited company need not register its articles: see PARA 227. As to the meaning of 'limited company' see PARA 95.
2 See the Companies Act 2006 s 19; and PARA 227. As to articles applicable to companies incorporated under the Companies Act 2006 see PARA 227. As to incorporation and registration under the Companies Act 2006 see PARA 104 et seq; and as to the re-registration of a private company as a public company under the Companies Act 2006 see PARAS 168–172.
3 Ie the date by which all the provisions of the Companies Act 2006 that affect the law in England and Wales had come into force: see PARA 13 note 15. Companies formed and registered between 1 October 2007 and 30 September 2009, which elected to adopt Table A articles, would have adopted such articles that had been specifically amended in order to make the articles compatible with the requirements of the Companies Act 2006 ('compatible articles'): see the Companies (Tables A to F) Regulations 1985, SI 1985/805 (amended by SI 1985/1052; SI 2000/3373; SI 2007/2541; SI 2007/2826; SI 2008/739); and see the Companies (Tables A to F) (Amendment) Regulations 2007, SI 2007/2541 (applicable to a company registered on or after 1 October 2007 and before 1 October 2009 which adopted Table A or Table C as its articles of association); the Companies (Tables A to F) (Amendment) (No 2) Regulations 2007, SI 2007/2826 (applicable to a company registered on or after 1 October 2007 and before 1 October 2009 which adopted Table A as its articles of association); and the Companies (Tables A to F) (Amendment) Regulations 2008, SI 2008/739 (applicable to a company registered on or after 6 April 2008 and before 1 October 2009 which adopted Table C or Table E as its articles of association). The

requirement for compatibility also led, in some instances, to articles which had appeared in the Companies (Tables A to F) Regulations 1985, SI 1985/805, being revoked.

4 See the Companies (Tables A to F) Regulations 1985, SI 1985/805; and PARA 14. The expressions 'Table A', 'Table B' etc were not formally defined in statute, although they were referred to in statute, eg in the Companies Act 1985 s 8 (repealed).

The regulations in the Companies (Tables A to F) Regulations 1985, SI 1985/805, reg 2, Schedule Table A and the forms in Schedule Tables B, C, D, E and F were the regulations and forms of memorandum and articles of association prescribed for the purposes of the Companies Act 1985 ss 3, 8 (repealed): see the Companies (Tables A to F) Regulations 1985, SI 1985/805, reg 2. The Companies (Tables A to F) Regulations 1985, SI 1985/805, Schedule Table A contains a model set of regulations for the management of a company limited by shares; Table B sets out the model memorandum of association for a private company limited by shares; and Table F sets out the model memorandum of association for a public company limited by shares. The Companies (Tables A to F) Regulations 1985, SI 1985/805, Schedule, Table C sets out the model memorandum of association for a company limited by guarantee and not having a share capital and applies modified Table A as articles of association; Table D Pts I–III sets out the model memorandum of association for a public or private company limited by guarantee and having a share capital and applies unmodified Table A as articles of association; and Table E sets out the model memorandum of association for an unlimited company having a share capital and applies modified Table A as articles of association. As to the meanings of 'company limited by guarantee', 'company limited by shares', 'private company', 'public company' and 'unlimited company' see PARA 95. As to the meanings of 'company having a share capital' and 'share capital' see PARA 1231.

As to the statutory authority of Table A see *Re Barned's Banking Co, ex p Contract Corpn* (1867) 3 Ch App 105 at 113–114 per Lord Cairns LJ; *Re Pyle Works* (1890) 44 ChD 534 at 571, CA; *Lock v Queensland Investment and Land Mortgage Co* [1896] AC 461, HL; *New Balkis Eersteling Ltd v Randt Gold Mining Co* [1904] AC 165 at 167, HL, per Lord Davey; *Trevor v Whitworth* (1887) 12 App Cas 409, HL. Case law that was applicable to Table A can be assumed generally to apply to model articles prescribed under the Companies Act 2006: see eg the cases cited in PARA 227 notes 5, 13, 16.

5 See note 4.

6 See PARA 14 note 4.

7 Nothing in the Companies Act 2006 affects the application in relation to an existing company of Table B in the Joint Stock Companies Act 1856 or Table A in the former Companies Acts or the Companies (Tables A to F) Regulations 1985, SI 1985/805: see the Companies Act 2006 (Commencement No 8, Transitional Provisions and Savings) Order 2008, SI 2008/2860, art 5, Sch 2 para 1; and PARA 14. As to the general savings made for existing companies under the Companies Act 2006 see PARA 14. As to the general provision made for continuity in company law see PARA 13. As to the formal adoption of amended articles see PARA 231 et seq. There is, of course, nothing to prevent a company from replacing its existing articles (whether they are based on default articles of previous vintage or not) with the model articles prescribed for the purposes of the Companies Act 2006, so long as the articles are altered in accordance with s 21: see PARA 231 et seq.

(iii) Resolutions and Agreements relating to Company's Constitution

230. Resolutions and agreements affecting a company's constitution. A copy of every resolution or agreement[1] which falls under any of heads (1) to (5) below[2], namely:

(1) any special resolution[3];

(2) any resolution or agreement agreed to by all the members of a company[4] that, if not so agreed to, would not have been effective for its purpose unless passed as a special resolution[5];

(3) any resolution or agreement agreed to by all the members of a class of shareholders[6] that, if not so agreed to, would not have been effective for its purpose unless passed by some particular majority or otherwise in some particular manner[7];

(4) any resolution or agreement that effectively binds all members of a class of shareholders though not agreed to by all those members[8];

(5) any other resolution or agreement which affects a company's constitution[9] by virtue of any enactment[10],

or, in the case of a resolution or agreement that is not in writing, a written memorandum setting out its terms, must be forwarded to the registrar of companies[11] within 15 days after it is passed or made[12].

If a company fails to comply with this requirement[13], an offence is committed by the company, and by every officer of the company who is in default[14].

1 As to company resolutions and decisions generally see PARA 684 et seq.

2 Heads (1)–(5) in the text specify the resolutions and agreements to which the Companies Act 2006 Pt 3 Ch 3 (ss 29–30) (resolutions and agreements affecting a company's constitution) applies: see s 29(1).

3 Companies Act 2006 s 29(1)(a). As to the meaning of 'special resolution' see PARA 686.

4 References in the Companies Act 2006 s 29(1) to a member of a company do not include the company itself where it is such a member by virtue only of its holding shares as treasury shares: see s 29(2). As to the meaning of 'member' see PARA 323; and as to the meaning of 'shares' see PARA 1231. As to the meaning of 'company' under the Companies Acts see PARA 21; and as to the meaning of the 'Companies Acts' for these purposes see PARA 13. As to treasury shares see PARA 1437.

5 Companies Act 2006 s 29(1)(b). The redenomination of shares does not affect any rights or obligations of members under the company's constitution, or any restrictions affecting members under the company's constitution: see s 624(1); and PARA 1355.

6 References in the Companies Act 2006 s 29(1) to a class of members of a company do not include the company itself where it is such a member by virtue only of its holding shares as treasury shares: see s 29(2). As to classes of shares generally see PARA 1246 et seq.

7 Companies Act 2006 s 29(1)(c).

8 Companies Act 2006 s 29(1)(d).

9 Ie any other resolution or agreement to which the Companies Act 2006 Pt 3 Ch 3 applies (see note 2): see s 29(1)(e). As to the meaning of references in the Companies Acts to a company's constitution see PARA 226. As to the effect of a company's constitution see PARA 242 et seq.

10 Companies Act 2006 s 29(1)(e). As to the meaning of 'enactment' see PARA 13 note 16.

11 As to the meaning of 'registrar of companies' see PARA 126 note 2. As to the delivery of documents to the registrar see PARA 136; and as to the requirements generally for the proper delivery of documents to the registrar see PARA 137. Any amendment of the company's articles (including every resolution or agreement required to be embodied in or annexed to copies of the company's articles issued by the company) is subject to the disclosure requirements in the Companies Act 2006 s 1078: see PARA 139. As to the meaning of references to a company's 'articles' see PARA 227 note 2. As to a company's articles of association generally see PARA 227 et seq.

12 Companies Act 2006 s 30(1). Agreements which are required to be forwarded to the registrar under Pt 3 Ch 3 may be drawn up and delivered to the registrar in a language other than English, but when delivered to the registrar they must be accompanied by a certified translation into English: see s 1105; and PARA 164. A company must, on request by any member, send to him a copy of any resolution or agreement to which Pt 3 Ch 3 applies: see s 32(1)(b); and PARA 241.

13 Ie fails to comply with the Companies Act 2006 s 30: see s 30(2).

14 Companies Act 2006 s 30(2). For these purposes, a liquidator of the company is treated as an officer of it: s 30(4). As to the meaning of 'officer' generally see PARA 679; and as to the meaning of 'officer in default' see PARA 316. As to the appointment of liquidators see COMPANY AND PARTNERSHIP INSOLVENCY vol 17 (2011) PARA 909 et seq.

Any person guilty of such an offence is liable on summary conviction to a fine not exceeding level 3 on the standard scale and for continued contravention to a daily default fine not exceeding one-tenth of level 3 on the standard scale: Companies Act 2006 s 30(3). As to the standard scale and the powers of magistrates' courts to issue fines on summary conviction see SENTENCING vol 92 (2015) PARA 176; and as to the meaning of 'daily default fine' see PARA 1816.

(iv) Alterations to Company's Constitution

A. ALTERATION OF ARTICLES BY MEMBERS' RESOLUTION

231. How amendment of articles is effected. A company[1] may amend its articles of association[2] by special resolution[3]. A special resolution is not, however, required if immediately before 26 May 2015[4] the company's articles contain provision authorising the company to issue share warrants ('the offending provision')[5]. In such a case the company may alter its articles for the purpose of removing the offending provision without passing a special resolution as otherwise required[6] and without complying with any provision for entrenchment[7] which is relevant to the offending provision[8].

A member[9] of a company is not bound by any alteration to its articles after the date on which he became a member[10], if and so far as the alteration either requires him to take or subscribe for more shares[11] than the number held by him at the date on which the alteration is made, or in any way increases his liability as at that date to contribute to the company's share capital[12] or otherwise to pay money to the company, subject to agreement[13].

The power of alteration, which is statutory, cannot be modified by the articles[14]. Nor can a company contract itself out of the power to alter its articles[15], even by the express terms of the articles[16]. The conferring of special voting rights on a particular class of shares, which would in effect make it impossible to alter the articles without the consent of a particular person, would not, however, be a provision depriving the company of the power to alter the articles; it is otherwise if the provisions were merely that no alteration should be made without the consent of a particular person[17].

Directors cannot by resolution alter the articles[18]; but the words 'articles of association' as used in a contract may refer to provisions put forward by the company as its articles even if they have not been validly adopted[19].

1 As to the meaning of 'company' under the Companies Acts see PARA 21; and as to the meaning of the 'Companies Acts' see PARA 13.

2 As to the meaning of references to a company's 'articles' see PARA 227 note 2. As to a company's articles of association generally see PARA 227 et seq. As to the amendment of 'entrenched provisions': see PARA 232. As to alterations to a company's articles that are required to be made when the company alters it status by means of re-registration see PARA 167 et seq.

3 Companies Act 2006 s 21(1). As to the meaning of 'special resolution' see PARA 686. The registrar of companies must be sent a copy of the amended articles (see PARA 235); and he has power to issue a notice to comply where a company has failed to observe the procedural requirements with respect to amended articles (see PARA 236). See also PARA 140. See also the Companies Act 2006 (Consequential Amendments, Transitional Provisions and Savings) Order 2009, SI 2009/1941, art 5; and PARA 235.

If the company which is proposing to alter its articles is a charity, the Companies Act 2006 s 21(1) is subject, in England and Wales, to the procedure that must be observed in such cases (ie it is subject to the Charities the Charities Act 2011 ss 197, 198: see CHARITIES vol 8 (2015) PARA 242): see the Companies Act 2006 s 21(2) (amended by the Charities Act 2011 Sch 7 Pt 2 para 113). As to the meanings of 'England' and 'Wales' see PARA 1 note 5. As to the statement of a company's objects see PARA 239.

4 Ie the date when the Small Business, Enterprise and Employment Act 2015 s 84 came into force: see s 164(3)(g)(ii).

5 See the Small Business, Enterprise and Employment Act 2015 s 85(1), (2). The Companies Act 2006 s 26 (see PARA 235) sets out the duty of a company to send the registrar a copy of its articles where they have been amended: Small Business, Enterprise and Employment Act 2015 s 85(3).

6 Ie as required by the Companies Act 2006 s 21: see the text and notes 1–3.

7 See the Companies Act 2006 s 22; and PARA 232.

8 See note 5.

9 As to the meaning of 'member' see PARA 323.

10 Ie except where the member agrees in writing, either before or after the alteration is made, to be bound by the alteration: see the Companies Act 2006 s 25(2); and PARA 377.
11 As to the meaning of 'share' see PARA 1231.
12 As to the meanings of 'company having a share capital' and 'share capital' see PARA 1231.
13 See the Companies Act 2006 s 25(1), (2); and PARA 377. See also *Morshead Mansions Ltd v Di Marco* [2008] EWCA Civ 1371, [2008] All ER (D) 113 (Dec) (interaction between the Landlord and Tenant Act 1985 ss 18–30 (limits on the amount of service charges payable to a landlord of residential premises) (see LANDLORD AND TENANT vol 62 (2012) PARA 468 et seq) and the claimant's articles of association).
14 *Ayre v Skelsey's Adamant Cement Co Ltd* (1904) 20 TLR 587; affd (1905) 21 TLR 464, CA.
15 *Malleson v National Insurance and Guarantee Corpn* [1894] 1 Ch 200; *Andrews v Gas Meter Co* [1897] 1 Ch 361, CA. See also PARA 234.
16 *Walker v London Tramways Co* (1879) 12 ChD 705.
17 *Bushell v Faith* [1970] AC 1099, [1970] 1 All ER 53, HL. As to classes of shares and the rights attached to classes of shares generally see PARA 1246 et seq.
18 *Re British Provident Life and Guarantee Association, De Ruvigne's Case* (1877) 5 ChD 306, CA.
19 *Muirhead v Forth and North Sea Steamboat Mutual Insurance Association* [1894] AC 72, HL. Cf *Re Miller's Dale and Ashwood Dale Lime Co* (1885) 31 ChD 211, CA. Articles irregularly adopted may be treated as adopted by the company, if acted upon, amended and added to by the shareholders for many years without objection: *Ho Tung v Man On Insurance Co Ltd* [1902] AC 232, PC.

232. Entrenched provisions of the articles. The articles[1] of a company[2] may contain provision ('provision for entrenchment') to the effect that specified provisions of the articles may be amended or repealed[3] only if conditions are met, or procedures are complied with, that are more restrictive than those applicable in the case of a special resolution[4]. As from a day to be appointed[5], provision for entrenchment may only be made in this way either in the company's articles on formation, or by an amendment of the company's articles agreed to by all the members of the company[6]. Provision for entrenchment does not prevent amendment of the company's articles by agreement of all the members of the company[7], or by order of a court or other authority having power to alter the company's articles[8].

Where a company's articles:

(1) on formation contain provision for entrenchment[9];
(2) are amended so as to include such provision[10]; or
(3) are altered by order of a court or other authority so as to restrict or exclude the power of the company to amend its articles[11],

the company must give notice of that fact to the registrar of companies[12]. Similarly, where a company's articles:

(a) are amended so as to remove provision for entrenchment[13]; or
(b) are altered by order of a court or other authority so as to remove such provision[14], or so as to remove any other restriction on, or any exclusion of, the power of the company to amend its articles[15],

the company must give notice of that fact to the registrar[16].

Where a company's articles are subject either to provision for entrenchment[17], or to an order of a court or other authority restricting or excluding the company's power to amend the articles[18], if the company amends its articles[19], and is required to send to the registrar a document making or evidencing the amendment[20], then the company must deliver with that document a statement of compliance[21]. The statement of compliance required is a statement certifying that the amendment has been made in accordance with the company's articles and, where relevant, any applicable order of a court or other authority[22]. The registrar may rely on the statement of compliance as sufficient evidence of the matters stated in it[23].

1 As to the meaning of references to a company's 'articles' see PARA 227 note 2. As to a company's articles of association generally see PARA 227 et seq.
2 As to the meaning of 'company' under the Companies Acts see PARA 21; and as to the meaning of the 'Companies Acts' see PARA 13.
3 As to the amendment of a company's articles generally see PARA 231. As to alterations to a company's articles that are required to be made when the company alters it status by means of re-registration see PARA 167 et seq.
4 Companies Act 2006 s 22(1). However, nothing in s 22 affects any power of a court or other authority to alter a company's articles: s 22(4). As to the meaning of 'special resolution' see PARA 686.
5 The Companies Act 2006 s 22(2) comes into force on a day to be appointed under s 1300(2). However, at the date at which this volume states the law, no such day had been appointed. As to the commencement of s 22(1), (3), (4) see the Companies Act 2006 (Commencement No 8, Transitional Provisions and Savings) Order 2008, SI 2008/2860, art 3(c) (amended by SI 2009/2476).
6 Companies Act 2006 s 22(2) (not yet in force: see note 5). As to the meaning of 'member' see PARA 323. As to company formation and registration under the Companies Act 2006 see PARA 95 et seq.
7 Companies Act 2006 s 22(3)(a). See also note 4.
8 Companies Act 2006 s 22(3)(b). See also note 4.
9 Companies Act 2006 s 23(1)(a).
10 Companies Act 2006 s 23(1)(b).
11 Companies Act 2006 s 23(1)(c).
12 Companies Act 2006 s 23(1). As to the meaning of 'registrar of companies' see PARA 126 note 2. As to the delivery of documents to the registrar see PARA 136; and as to the requirements generally for the proper delivery of documents to the registrar see PARA 137. As to the meaning of 'document' for these purposes see PARA 136 note 2. Any amendment of the company's articles (including every resolution or agreement required to be embodied in or annexed to copies of the company's articles issued by the company) and, after any amendment of the company's articles, the text of the articles as amended are subject to the disclosure requirements in s 1078: see PARA 139.
13 Companies Act 2006 s 23(2)(a).
14 Companies Act 2006 s 23(2)(b)(i).
15 Companies Act 2006 s 23(2)(b)(ii).
16 Companies Act 2006 s 23(2). The registrar of companies must be sent a copy of any amended articles (see PARA 235); and he has power to issue a notice to comply where a company has failed to observe the disclosure requirements with respect to amended articles (see PARA 236). See also PARA 140.
17 Companies Act 2006 s 24(1)(a).
18 Companies Act 2006 s 24(1)(b).
19 Companies Act 2006 s 24(2)(a).
20 Companies Act 2006 s 24(2)(b).
21 Companies Act 2006 s 24(2).
22 Companies Act 2006 s 24(3).
23 Companies Act 2006 s 24(4).

233. Rectification of mistake in company's articles of association. A mistake in a company's articles of association[1] may be rectified only by altering the articles by special resolution[2] pursuant to the Companies Act 2006[3]; the court will not rectify the mistake in the course of proceedings[4]. A special resolution altering the articles may be followed immediately at the same meeting by a resolution operating under the articles as so altered[5]. Where the Companies Act 2006 requires the articles to give the necessary power, as in cases of a public company issuing redeemable shares[6], the resolution purporting to exercise the power is of no avail unless the power is already in the articles or has been added by special resolution[7].

1 As to the meaning of references to a company's 'articles' see PARA 227 note 2. As to the meaning of 'company' under the Companies Acts see PARA 21; and as to the meaning of the 'Companies Acts' see PARA 13. As to a company's articles of association generally see PARA 227 et seq.
2 As to the meaning of 'special resolution' see PARA 686.
3 As to the amendment of a company's articles under the Companies Act 2006 see PARAS 231–232.
4 *Evans v Chapman* (1902) 86 LT 381; *Scott v Frank F Scott (London) Ltd* [1940] Ch 794, [1940] 3 All ER 508, CA. The articles should, however, be regarded as a business document and should be construed so as to give them reasonable business efficacy: see PARA 242.
5 Cf *Re Imperial Hydropathic Hotel Co, Blackpool v Hampson* (1882) 23 ChD 1, CA (decided on its own special facts); *Re Patent Invert Sugar Co* (1885) 31 ChD 166, CA (decided at a time when it was necessary that a special resolution should be passed and confirmed, and it was held that, until a special resolution altering the articles to empower the company to reduce its capital had been passed and confirmed, a special resolution for its reduction could not be proposed; but a special resolution need not now be confirmed).
6 See the Companies Act 2006 s 684(3); and PARA 1416.
7 *James v Buena Ventura Nitrate Grounds Syndicate Ltd* [1896] 1 Ch 456 at 463, CA, per Lord Herschell; *Harben v Phillips* (1883) 23 ChD 14, CA; *Boschoek Pty Co Ltd v Fuke* [1906] 1 Ch 148 at 163 per Swinfen Eady J. This is not the case if the passing of the special resolution completes the transaction as far as is necessary for the company to act, the directors being able to do the rest under their general powers, as, for example, prior to the Companies Act 1929, to issue new capital (*Campbell's Case* (1873) 9 Ch App 1 at 7, 22 per Lord Selborne LC; followed in *Taylor v Pilsen Joel and General Electric Light Co* (1884) 27 ChD 268), or if sanction is given to what the company already has power to do (*Re Bank of Hindustan, China and Japan, Campbell's Case* (1873) 9 Ch App 1 at 22–23 per Lord Selborne LC; *James v Buena Ventura Nitrate Grounds Syndicate Ltd* [1896] 1 Ch 456, CA). Cf *Re Metropolitan Cemetery Co* 1934 SC 65, Ct of Sess. See also PARAS 1348, 1374.

234. How far company's articles of association may be altered. Any alterations to a company's articles[1] must be made in good faith for the benefit of the company as a whole[2], that is of the corporators as a general body[3]. Subject to this, articles may be freely altered. It is for the shareholders and not the court to determine whether or not the alteration is for the benefit of the company; and the court will not readily interfere with an alteration made in good faith unless it is of such a character that no reasonable person could have regarded it as made for the benefit of the company[4]. The alteration may affect the rights of a member as between himself and the company by retrospective operation, since the shares are held subject to the statutory power of altering the articles[5].

If a contract, whether with a member or an outsider, is so drawn as by its terms or implication to prohibit the company from altering its articles to the prejudice of the other contracting party, then, although the company cannot be precluded from altering its articles, thereby giving itself power to act upon the provisions of the altered articles, so to act may nevertheless be a breach of the contract[6].

The articles cannot be so altered as to increase the liability of a member to contribute to share capital or otherwise to pay money to the company without his consent[7]; and a special resolution altering articles of association may be impeached if its effect is to discriminate between the majority of shareholders and the minority shareholders so as to give the former an advantage of which the latter are deprived[8]. In a case where an order by the court by way of protection of a member of the company against unfair prejudice[9] requires the company not to make any, or any specified, alteration in its articles, the company has no power without leave of the court to make any such alteration[10].

1 As to the meaning of references to a company's 'articles' see PARA 227 note 2. As to the meaning of 'company' under the Companies Acts see PARA 21; and as to the meaning of the 'Companies Acts' see PARA 13. As to a company's articles of association generally see PARA 227 et seq; and as to the amendment of a company's articles under the Companies Act 2006 see PARAS 231, 232.

2 *Allen v Gold Reefs of West Africa Ltd* [1900] 1 Ch 656 at 671, CA, per Lindley MR (as explained in *Sidebottom v Kershaw, Leese & Co* [1920] 1 Ch 154, CA, and in *Shuttleworth v Cox Bros & Co (Maidenhead) Ltd* [1927] 2 KB 9, CA); *Greenhalgh v Arderne Cinemas Ltd* [1951] Ch 286 at 291, [1950] 2 All ER 1120 at 1126, CA, per Evershed MR. Cf *Brown v British Abrasive Wheel Co* [1919] 1 Ch 290; *Dafen Tinplate Co v Llanelly Steel Co (1907) Ltd* [1920] 2 Ch 124. The court will not allow the majority of the shareholders to benefit (as shareholders) at the expense of a minority: see PARA 654. It is for the benefit of a company to alter articles for the purpose of clarifying the rights of the various classes of shareholders: *Caledonian Insurance Co v Scottish-American Investment Co Ltd* 1951 SLT 23, Ct of Sess; *Edinburgh Railway Access and Property Co v Scottish Metropolitan Assurance Co* 1932 SC 2 at 9, Ct of Sess. As to whether it is permissible to alter the articles so as to introduce a compulsory transfer provision see *Constable v Executive Connections Ltd* [2005] EWHC 3 (Ch), [2005] 2 BCLC 638, applying *Allen v Gold Reefs of West Africa Ltd* [1900] 1 Ch 656, CA.

3 *Greenhalgh v Arderne Cinemas Ltd* [1951] Ch 286 at 291, [1950] 2 All ER 1120 at 1126, CA, per Evershed MR.

4 *Shuttleworth v Cox Bros & Co (Maidenhead) Ltd* [1927] 2 KB 9, CA; disapproving dicta in *Dafen Tinplate Co v Llanelly Steel Co (1907) Ltd* [1920] 2 Ch 124. See also *Citco Banking NV v Pusser's Ltd* [2007] UKPC 13, [2007] 2 BCLC 483, [2007] 4 LRC 626 (it was not necessary for the chairman and the company to prove to the judge that the arguments, as to whether the amendment was for the benefit of the company, were justified by the facts).

5 *Allen v Gold Reefs of West Africa Ltd* [1900] 1 Ch 656, CA (where the fully paid shares affected by the extension to them of the company's lien in respect of an existing debt were vendor's shares known by the company to be held by the shareholder as nominee for the vendor, and the alteration was intended to affect only this individual shareholder). See also *Last v Buller & Co Ltd* (1919) 36 TLR 35. The articles may be altered so as to allow for the issue of preference shares: *Andrews v Gas Meter Co* [1897] 1 Ch 361, CA. Cf *Pepe v City and Suburban Permanent Building Society* [1893] 2 Ch 311; *Botten v City and Suburban Permanent Building Society* [1895] 2 Ch 441; *James v Buena Ventura Nitrate Grounds Syndicate Ltd* [1896] 1 Ch 456, CA; *Swabey v Port Darwin Gold Mining Co* (1889) 1 Meg 385, CA. In *W and A M'Arthur Ltd (Liquidator) v Gulf Line Ltd* 1909 SC 732, Ct of Sess, it was held that the rights of a transferee could not be prejudiced by an alteration in the articles made after the lodgment of the transfer, following the ratio decidendi in *Re Cawley & Co* (1889) 42 ChD 209 at 227, CA, per Lord Esher MR. As to preference shares see PARA 1880.

6 See *Southern Foundries (1926) Ltd v Shirlaw* [1940] AC 701 at 740, [1940] 2 All ER 445 at 469, HL, per Lord Porter; *Re TN Farrer Ltd* [1937] Ch 352 at 356 per Simonds J; *Allen v Gold Reefs of West Africa Ltd* [1900] 1 Ch 656 at 673, CA, per Lindley MR, and at 676 per Vaughan Williams LJ; *Griffith v Paget* (1877) 5 ChD 894 (where the company had paid for property by preference shares and attempted to issue pre-preference shares). In *British Murac Syndicate Ltd v Alperton Rubber Co Ltd* [1915] 2 Ch 186, an injunction was granted to restrain an alteration of articles which would have involved a breach of contract; this was directly opposed to the decision in *Punt v Symons & Co Ltd* [1903] 2 Ch 506 (which was treated as being overruled by *Baily v British Equitable Assurance Co* [1904] 1 Ch 374, CA; revsd on other grounds sub nom *British Equitable Assurance Co Ltd v Baily* [1906] AC 35, HL), where it was held that a company could not contract itself out of its statutory powers of altering its articles as against an outside contractor (see *Re Barrow Haematite Steel Co* (1888) 39 ChD 582). However, the judgment of the Court of Appeal in *Baily v British Equitable Assurance Co* 1904] 1 Ch 374, CA did not cite *Punt v Symons & Co Ltd* [1903] 2 Ch 506, and seems only to restate the position that a company cannot justify a breach of contract by such alteration. It is implicit in both the majority and minority opinions in *Southern Foundries (1926) Ltd v Shirlaw* [1940] AC 701, [1940] 2 All ER 445, HL that *Punt v Symons & Co Ltd* [1903] 2 Ch 506 was correct (see *Southern Foundries (1926) Ltd v Shirlaw* [1940] AC 701 at 713, 717, [1940] 2 All ER 445 at 452, 454, HL, per Viscount Maugham, at 722 and 458 per Lord Wright, at 731 and 464 per Lord Romer, and at 739–740 and 468–469 per Lord Porter), and that *British Murac Syndicate Ltd v Alperton Rubber Co Ltd* [1915] 2 Ch 186 was wrongly decided (see *Southern Foundries (1926) Ltd v Shirlaw* [1940] AC 70 at 740, [1940] 2 All ER 445 at 469, HL, per Lord Porter). Cf *Shuttleworth v Cox Bros & Co (Maidenhead) Ltd* [1927] 2 KB 9, CA.

7 See the Companies Act 2006 s 25(1); and PARA 377.

8 *Greenhalgh v Arderne Cinemas Ltd* [1951] Ch 286 at 291, [1950] 2 All ER 1120 at 1126, CA, per Evershed MR. As to the meaning of 'special resolution' see PARA 686.

9 See PARA 657 et seq.

10 See the Companies Act 2006 s 996(2)(d); and PARA 666.

235. Registrar of companies to be sent copy of amended articles. Where a company[1] amends its articles of association[2] it must send to the registrar of companies[3] a copy of the articles as amended[4] not later than 15 days after the amendment takes effect[5]. If a company fails to comply with this requirement[6], an offence is committed by the company, and by every officer of the company who is in default[7].

1 As to the meaning of 'company' under the Companies Acts see PARA 21; and as to the meaning of the 'Companies Acts' see PARA 13.

2 As to the meaning of references to a company's 'articles' see PARA 227 note 2. As to a company's articles of association generally see PARA 227 et seq. As to the amendment of a company's articles generally see PARA 231. As to alterations to a company's articles that are required to be made when the company alters it status by means of re-registration see PARA 167 et seq.

3 As to the meaning of 'registrar of companies' see PARA 126 note 2. As to the delivery of documents to the registrar see PARA 136; and as to the requirements generally for the proper delivery of documents to the registrar see PARA 137.

4 The provisions of the Companies Act 2006 s 26 do not require a company to set out in its articles any provisions of model articles that either are applied by the articles, or apply by virtue of s 20 (default application of model articles) (see PARA 227): s 26(2). The provisions of s 26 apply to unregistered companies by virtue of the Unregistered Companies Regulations 2009, SI 2009/2436, reg 3, Sch 1 para 1, but as modified thereby: see PARA 1857. As to the meaning of 'unregistered company' see PARA 1856.

Nothing in the Companies Act 2006 s 28 (see PARA 227) requires a company to give notice to the registrar of an alteration of its articles: see the Companies Act 2006 (Commencement No 8, Transitional Provisions and Savings) Order 2008, SI 2008/2860, art 5, Sch 2 para 8. A company whose articles are deemed by virtue of the Companies Act 2006 s 28 to contain provisions formerly in its memorandum may comply with any obligation to send a person a copy of its articles either:

(1) by appending to a copy of the other provisions of the articles a copy of the provisions of its old-style memorandum that are deemed to be provisions of the articles (Companies Act 2006 (Commencement No 8, Transitional Provisions and Savings) Order 2008, SI 2008/2860, Sch 2 para 9(1)(a)); or

(2) by sending together with a copy of the other provisions of the articles a copy of its old-style memorandum indicating the provisions that are deemed to be provisions of the articles (Sch 2 para 9(1)(b)).

For these purposes, references to a company's 'old-style memorandum' are (in the case of an existing company) to its memorandum of association as it stood immediately before 1 October 2009, and (in the case of a transitional company) to its memorandum of association as it stood on its registration or re-registration (as the case may be) apart from the operation of the Companies Act 2006 s 28: see the Companies Act 2006 (Commencement No 8, Transitional Provisions and Savings) Order 2008, SI 2008/2860, Sch 2 para 9(2). As to the meaning of 'existing company' for these purposes see PARA 14 note 2; and as to the meaning of 'transitional company' for these purposes see PARA 13 note 18.

Where, in the case of an existing or transitional company, the company's articles are deemed to contain a statement of its name by virtue of the Companies Act 2006 s 28, and the company changes its name (by any means) on or after 1 October 2009, the company is not required to send a copy of its articles to the registrar in accordance with s 26: see the Companies Act 2006 (Consequential Amendments, Transitional Provisions and Savings) Order 2009, SI 2009/1941, art 5(1), (4). Where the company, in complying with any obligation to send a person a copy of its articles, relies on the Companies Act 2006 (Commencement No 8, Transitional Provisions and Savings) Order 2008, SI 2008/2860, Sch 2 para 9(1)(a) (see head (1) above) or Sch 2 para 9(1)(b) (see head (2) above), it must (if it relies on Sch 2 para 9(1)(a)) omit the provision stating the company's former name or (if it relies on Sch 2 para 9(1)(b)) indicate that the provision stating the company's former name is no longer effective: see the Companies Act 2006 (Consequential Amendments, Transitional Provisions and Savings) Order 2009, SI 2009/1941, art 5(5). As to the meaning of 'existing company' for these purposes see PARA 14 note 2; and as to the meaning of 'transitional company' for these purposes see PARA 13 note 18 (definitions applied by art 5(6)).

5 Companies Act 2006 s 26(1). Any amendment of the company's articles (including every resolution or agreement required to be embodied in or annexed to copies of the company's articles issued by the company) and, after any amendment of the company's articles, the text of the articles as amended are subject to the disclosure requirements in s 1078: see PARA 139.

6 Ie fails to comply with the Companies Act 2006 s 26: see s 26(3).

7 Companies Act 2006 s 26(3). As to the meaning of 'officer' see PARA 679; and as to the meaning of 'officer in default' see PARA 316.

Any person guilty of such an offence is liable on summary conviction to a fine not exceeding level 3 on the standard scale and for continued contravention to a daily default fine not exceeding one-tenth of level 3 on the standard scale: Companies Act 2006 s 26(4). As to the standard scale and the powers of magistrates' courts to issue fines on summary conviction see SENTENCING vol 92 (2015) PARA 176; and as to the meaning of 'daily default fine' see PARA 1816.

236. Registrar's notice to comply in case of failure with respect to amended articles. If it appears to the registrar of companies[1] that a company has failed to comply with any enactment[2] requiring it either to send to the registrar a document[3] making or evidencing an alteration in the company's articles[4], or to send to the registrar a copy of the company's articles as amended[5], the registrar may give notice to the company requiring it to comply[6]. The notice must state the date on which it is issued[7], and require the company to comply within 28 days from that date[8].

If the company complies with the notice within the specified time, no criminal proceedings may be brought in respect of the failure to comply with the relevant enactment[9].

However, if the company does not comply with the notice within the specified time, it is liable to a civil penalty of £200[10]; and this is in addition to any liability to criminal proceedings in respect of the failure[11] to comply with the relevant enactment[12]. The penalty may be recovered by the registrar and is to be paid into the Consolidated Fund[13].

1 As to the meaning of 'registrar of companies' see PARA 126 note 2. As to the meaning of 'company' under the Companies Acts see PARA 21; and as to the meaning of the 'Companies Acts' see PARA 13.
2 As to the meaning of 'enactment' see PARA 13 note 16.
3 As to the meaning of 'document' for these purposes see PARA 136 note 2. As to the delivery of documents to the registrar see PARA 136; and as to the requirements generally for the proper delivery of documents to the registrar see PARA 137.
4 Companies Act 2006 s 27(1)(a). As to the meaning of references to a company's 'articles' see PARA 227 note 2. As to a company's articles of association generally see PARA 227 et seq. As to the amendment of a company's articles generally see PARA 231. The provisions of s 27 apply to unregistered companies by virtue of the Unregistered Companies Regulations 2009, SI 2009/2436, reg 3, Sch 1 para 1, but as modified thereby: see PARA 1857. As to the meaning of 'unregistered company' see PARA 1856.
5 Companies Act 2006 s 27(1)(b).
6 Companies Act 2006 s 27(1).
7 Companies Act 2006 s 27(2)(a).
8 Companies Act 2006 s 27(2)(b).
9 Companies Act 2006 s 27(3). The text refers to the relevant enactment mentioned in s 27(1) (see the text and notes 1–6): see s 27(3).
10 Companies Act 2006 s 27(4).
11 Ie the failure mentioned in the Companies Act 2006 s 27(1) (see the text and notes 1–6): see s 27(4).
12 Companies Act 2006 s 27(4).
13 Companies Act 2006 s 27(5). Nothing in the Companies Acts or any other enactment as to the payment of receipts into the Consolidated Fund is to be read as affecting the operation in relation to the registrar of the Government Trading Funds Act 1973 s 3(1) (see CONSTITUTIONAL AND ADMINISTRATIVE LAW vol 20 (2014) PARA 521): see the Companies Act 2006 s 1118; and PARA 130. As to the Consolidated Fund see CONSTITUTIONAL AND ADMINISTRATIVE LAW vol 20 (2014) PARA 480 et seq; PARLIAMENT vol 78 (2010) PARAS 1028–1031.

B. ALTERATION OF COMPANY'S CONSTITUTION BY ENACTMENT OR ORDER

237. Notice to registrar required where company's constitution altered by enactment. Where a company's constitution[1] is altered by an enactment[2], other than an enactment amending the general law, the company must give notice of the alteration to the registrar of companies[3], specifying the enactment, not later than

15 days after the enactment comes into force[4]. In the case of a special enactment[5], the notice must be accompanied by a copy of the enactment[6].

If the enactment amends either the company's articles[7], or a resolution or agreement which affects the company's constitution[8], the notice must be accompanied by a copy of the company's articles, or the resolution or agreement in question, as amended[9].

If a company fails to comply with this requirement[10], an offence is committed by the company, and by every officer of the company who is in default[11].

1 As to the meaning of references to a company's constitution see PARA 226. As to the meaning of 'company' under the Companies Acts see PARA 21; and as to the meaning of the 'Companies Acts' see PARA 13.

2 As to the meaning of 'enactment' see PARA 13 note 16.

3 As to the meaning of 'registrar of companies' see PARA 126 note 2. As to the delivery of documents to the registrar see PARA 136; and as to the requirements generally for the proper delivery of documents to the registrar see PARA 137.

4 Companies Act 2006 s 34(1), (2). A company must, on request by any member, send to him a copy of any document required to be sent to the registrar of companies under s 34(2): see s 32(1)(c); and PARA 241. As to the meaning of 'member' see PARA 323. The provisions of s 34 apply to unregistered companies by virtue of the Unregistered Companies Regulations 2009, SI 2009/2436, reg 3, Sch 1 para 2, but as modified thereby: see PARA 1857. As to the meaning of 'unregistered company' see PARA 1856.

5 For these purposes, a 'special enactment' means an enactment that is not a public general enactment, and includes an Act for confirming a provisional order, any provision of a public general Act in relation to the passing of which any of the standing orders of the House of Lords or the House of Commons relating to Private Business applied, or any enactment to the extent that it is incorporated in or applied for the purposes of a special enactment: Companies Act 2006 s 34(4). As to the nature and classification of enactments see STATUTES AND LEGISLATIVE PROCESS vol 96 (2012) PARA 609 et seq.

6 Companies Act 2006 s 34(2).

7 Companies Act 2006 s 34(3)(a). As to the meaning of references to a company's 'articles' see PARA 227 note 2. As to a company's articles of association generally see PARA 227 et seq. As to the amendment of a company's articles by members' resolution see PARA 231.

8 Companies Act 2006 s 34(3)(b). The text refers to any resolution or agreement to which Pt 3 Ch 3 (ss 29–30) applies (see PARA 230): see s 34(3)(b).

9 Companies Act 2006 s 34(3).

A company whose articles are deemed by virtue of the Companies Act 2006 s 28 (see PARA 227) to contain provisions formerly in its memorandum may comply with any obligation to send a person a copy of its articles either by appending to a copy of the other provisions of the articles a copy of the provisions of its old-style memorandum that are deemed to be provisions of the articles, or by sending together with a copy of the other provisions of the articles a copy of its old-style memorandum indicating the provisions that are deemed to be provisions of the articles: see the Companies Act 2006 (Commencement No 8, Transitional Provisions and Savings) Order 2008, SI 2008/2860, Sch 2 para 9(1). As to the meaning of references to a company's 'old-style memorandum' for these purposes see PARA 235 note 4.

10 Ie fails to comply with the Companies Act 2006 s 34: see s 34(5).

11 Companies Act 2006 s 34(5). As to the meaning of 'officer' see PARA 679; and as to the meaning of 'officer in default' see PARA 316.

Any person guilty of such an offence is liable on summary conviction to a fine not exceeding level 3 on the standard scale and for continued contravention to a daily default fine not exceeding one-tenth of level 3 on the standard scale: Companies Act 2006 s 34(6). As to the standard scale and the powers of magistrates' courts to issue fines on summary conviction see SENTENCING vol 92 (2015) PARA 176; and as to the meaning of 'daily default fine' see PARA 1816.

238. Notice to registrar required where company's constitution altered by order. Where a company's constitution[1] is altered by an order of a court or other authority, the company must give notice to the registrar of companies[2] of the alteration not later than 15 days after the alteration takes effect[3].

The notice must be accompanied by a copy of the order[4] and, if the order amends either the company's articles[5], or a resolution or agreement which affects a company's constitution[6], the notice must be accompanied by a copy of the company's articles, or the resolution or agreement in question, as amended[7].

If a company fails to comply with this requirement[8], an offence is committed by the company, and by every officer of the company who is in default[9].

1 As to the meaning of references to a company's constitution see PARA 226. As to the meaning of 'company' under the Companies Acts see PARA 21; and as to the meaning of the 'Companies Acts' see PARA 13.

2 As to the meaning of 'registrar of companies' see PARA 126 note 2. As to the delivery of documents to the registrar see PARA 136; and as to the requirements generally for the proper delivery of documents to the registrar see PARA 137.

3 Companies Act 2006 s 35(1). However, s 35 does not apply where provision is made by another enactment for the delivery to the registrar of a copy of the order in question: s 35(5). As to the meaning of 'enactment' see PARA 13 note 16. The provisions of s 35 apply to unregistered companies by virtue of the Unregistered Companies Regulations 2009, SI 2009/2436, reg 3, Sch 1 para 2, but as modified thereby: see PARA 1857. As to the meaning of 'unregistered company' see PARA 1856.

4 Companies Act 2006 s 35(2)(a). A company must, on request by any member, send to him a copy of any document required to be sent to the registrar of companies under s 35(2)(a): see s 32(1)(c); and PARA 241. As to the meaning of 'member' see PARA 323.

5 Companies Act 2006 s 35(2)(b)(i). As to the meaning of references to a company's 'articles' see PARA 227 note 2. As to a company's articles of association generally see PARA 227 et seq. As to the amendment of a company's articles by members' resolution see PARA 231.

6 Companies Act 2006 s 35(2)(b)(ii). The text refers to any resolution or agreement to which Pt 3 Ch 3 (ss 29–30) applies (see PARA 230): see s 35(2)(b)(ii).

7 Companies Act 2006 s 35(2)(b).

A company whose articles are deemed by virtue of the Companies Act 2006 s 28 (see PARA 227) to contain provisions formerly in its memorandum may comply with any obligation to send a person a copy of its articles either by appending to a copy of the other provisions of the articles a copy of the provisions of its old-style memorandum that are deemed to be provisions of the articles, or by sending together with a copy of the other provisions of the articles a copy of its old-style memorandum indicating the provisions that are deemed to be provisions of the articles: see the Companies Act 2006 (Commencement No 8, Transitional Provisions and Savings) Order 2008, SI 2008/2860, Sch 2 para 9(1). As to the meaning of references to a company's 'old-style memorandum' for these purposes see PARA 235 note 4.

8 Ie fails to comply with the Companies Act 2006 s 35: see s 35(3).

9 Companies Act 2006 s 35(3). As to the meaning of 'officer' see PARA 679; and as to the meaning of 'officer in default' see PARA 316.

Any person guilty of such an offence is liable on summary conviction to a fine not exceeding level 3 on the standard scale and for continued contravention to a daily default fine not exceeding one-tenth of level 3 on the standard scale: s 35(4). As to the standard scale and the powers of magistrates' courts to issue fines on summary conviction see SENTENCING vol 92 (2015) PARA 176; and as to the meaning of 'daily default fine' see PARA 1816.

(v) Stating a Company's Objects

239. Statement of company's objects. Unless the articles of association[1] of a company[2] specifically restrict the objects of the company, its objects are unrestricted[3].

Where a company amends its articles[4] so as to add, remove or alter a statement of the company's objects[5]:

(1) it must give notice to the registrar of companies[6];
(2) on receipt of the notice, the registrar must register it[7]; and
(3) the amendment is not effective until entry of that notice on the register[8].

Any such amendment does not affect any rights or obligations of the company or render defective any legal proceedings by or against it[9].

1 As to the meaning of references to 'articles' see PARA 227 note 2. As to articles of association generally see PARA 227 et seq.

2 As to the meaning of 'company' under the Companies Acts see PARA 21; and as to the meaning of the 'Companies Acts' see PARA 13.

3 Companies Act 2006 s 31(1). This is a change from the situation that pertained under the Companies Act 1985 and earlier legislation where a company was obliged to state its objects in the memorandum of association. The role of the memorandum of association has been altered fundamentally under the Companies Act 2006, and provisions that immediately before 1 October 2009 were contained in a company's memorandum but are not provisions of the kind mentioned in the Companies Act 2006 s 8 are to be treated after that date as provisions of the company's articles: see s 28(1); and PARA 227. 1 October 2009 is the date by which s 8 had come fully into force: see the Companies Act 2006 (Commencement No 8, Transitional Provisions and Savings) Order 2008, SI 2008/2860, art 3(b). Where a company's objects are unrestricted, so is its capacity: see PARA 251. As to the consequences that may arise, in terms of a company's capacity to act, from stating a company's objects (or, in the case of companies formed before the Companies Act 2006 came into effect, from continuing to operate under existing objects) see the cases cited in PARAS 256–257.

4 As to provision made for the alteration of articles see PARA 231 et seq.

5 Companies Act 2006 s 31(2). The need to add, remove or alter a statement of the company's objects will be most applicable to existing companies which, because of s 28 (see PARA 227), will have objects in their articles.

In the case of a company that is a charity, the provisions of s 31 have effect subject, in England and Wales, to the Charities Act 2011 ss 197, 198 (see CHARITIES vol 8 (2015) PARA 242): see the Companies Act 2006 s 31(4) (amended by the Charities Act 2011 Sch 7 para 114). As to the meanings of 'England' and 'Wales' see PARA 1 note 5.

6 Companies Act 2006 s 31(2)(a). As to the meaning of 'registrar of companies' see PARA 126 note 2. As to the delivery of documents to the registrar see PARA 136; and as to the requirements generally for the proper delivery of documents to the registrar see PARA 137. Any amendment of the company's articles (including every resolution or agreement required to be embodied in or annexed to copies of the company's articles issued by the company) is subject to the disclosure requirements in the Companies Act 2006 s 1078: see PARA 139.

7 Companies Act 2006 s 31(2)(b).

8 Companies Act 2006 s 31(2)(c). As to the register see PARA 142.

9 Companies Act 2006 s 31(3).

(vi) Constitutional Documents issued or provided by the Company

240. Documents to be incorporated in or accompany copies of articles issued by company. Every copy of a company's articles[1] issued by the company must be accompanied by[2]:

(1) a copy of any resolution or agreement[3] relating to the company which affects its constitution[4];

(2) where the company has been required to give notice to the registrar of companies[5] under the provisions that apply where a company's constitution is altered by an enactment, other than an enactment amending the general law[6], a statement that the enactment in question alters the effect of the company's constitution[7];

(3) where the company's constitution is altered by a special enactment[8], a copy of the enactment[9]; and

(4) a copy of any order required to be sent to the registrar[10] under the provisions that apply where a company's constitution is altered by an order of a court or other authority[11].

This provision does not require the articles to be accompanied by a copy of a document or by a statement if the effect of the resolution, agreement, enactment or order, as the case may be, on the company's constitution has been incorporated into the articles by amendment[12], or if the resolution, agreement, enactment or order, as the case may be, is not for the time being in force[13].

If a company fails to comply with this requirement[14], an offence is committed by every officer of the company who is in default[15].

1 As to the meaning of references to 'articles' see PARA 227 note 2; as to the meaning of 'company' under the Companies Acts see PARA 21; and as to the meaning of the 'Companies Acts' see PARA 13. As to articles of association generally see PARA 227 et seq.

2 Companies Act 2006 s 36(1).

A company whose articles are deemed by virtue of the Companies Act 2006 s 28 (see PARA 227) to contain provisions formerly in its memorandum may comply with any obligation to send a person a copy of its articles either by appending to a copy of the other provisions of the articles a copy of the provisions of its old-style memorandum that are deemed to be provisions of the articles, or by sending together with a copy of the other provisions of the articles a copy of its old-style memorandum indicating the provisions that are deemed to be provisions of the articles: see the Companies Act 2006 (Commencement No 8, Transitional Provisions and Savings) Order 2008, SI 2008/2860, Sch 2 para 9(1). As to the meaning of references to a company's 'old-style memorandum' for these purposes see PARA 235 note 4.

3 As to resolutions and decisions of the company generally see PARA 684 et seq.

4 Companies Act 2006 s 36(1)(a). Head (1) in the text refers to any resolution or agreement to which Pt 3 Ch 3 (ss 29–30) (resolutions and agreements affecting a company's constitution) applies (see PARA 230): see s 36(1)(a). As to the meaning of references to a company's constitution see PARA 226.

5 As to the meaning of 'registrar of companies' see PARA 126 note 2. As to the meaning of references to delivering a document, and as to the meaning of 'document' for these purposes, see PARA 136 note 2. As to the delivery of documents to the registrar see PARA 136; and as to the requirements generally for the proper delivery of documents to the registrar see PARA 137.

6 Ie under the Companies Act 2006 s 34(2) (see PARA 237): see s 36(1)(b). As to the meaning of 'enactment' see PARA 13 note 16.

7 Companies Act 2006 s 36(1)(b).

8 Ie as mentioned in the Companies Act 2006 s 34(4) (see PARA 237): see s 36(1)(c). As to the meaning of 'special enactment' see PARA 237 note 5.

9 Companies Act 2006 s 36(1)(c).

10 Ie under the Companies Act 2006 s 35(2)(a) (see PARA 238): see s 36(1)(d).

11 Companies Act 2006 s 36(1)(d).

12 Companies Act 2006 s 36(2)(a). As to provision made for the alteration of articles see PARA 231 et seq.

13 Companies Act 2006 s 36(2)(b).

14 Ie fails to comply with the Companies Act 2006 s 36: see s 36(3).

15 Companies Act 2006 s 36(3). For these purposes, a liquidator of the company is treated as an officer of it: s 36(5). As to the meaning of 'officer' generally see PARA 679; and as to the meaning of 'officer in default' see PARA 316. As to the appointment of liquidators see COMPANY AND PARTNERSHIP INSOLVENCY vol 17 (2011) PARA 909 et seq.

Any person guilty of such an offence is liable on summary conviction to a fine not exceeding level 3 on the standard scale for each occasion on which copies are issued, or, as the case may be, requested: s 36(4). As to the standard scale and the powers of magistrates' courts to issue fines on summary conviction see SENTENCING vol 92 (2015) PARA 176.

241. Copies of constitutional documents to be provided to members. A company[1] must, on request by any member[2], send to him the following documents[3]:

(1) an up-to-date copy of the company's articles of association[4];

(2) a copy of any resolution or agreement[5] relating to the company which affects its constitution[6] and that is for the time being in force[7];

(3) a copy of any document required to be sent to the registrar of companies[8] under the provisions that apply where a company's constitution is altered either by an enactment, other than an enactment amending the general law[9], or by an order of a court or other authority[10];

(4) a copy of any court order which either sanctions a compromise or arrangement[11] or facilitates a reconstruction or amalgamation[12];

(5) a copy of any court order, made under the court's powers to protect members against unfair prejudice[13], that alters the company's constitution[14];
(6) a copy of the company's current certificate of incorporation[15], and of any past certificates of incorporation[16];
(7) in the case of a company with a share capital[17], a current statement of capital[18];
(8) in the case of a company limited by guarantee[19], a copy of the statement of guarantee[20].

If a company makes default in complying with these requirements[21], an offence is committed by every officer of the company who is in default[22].

1 As to the meaning of 'company' under the Companies Acts see PARA 21; and as to the meaning of the 'Companies Acts' see PARA 13.
2 As to the meaning of 'member' see PARA 323.
3 Companies Act 2006 s 32(1). As to the provision made for the sending or supplying of documents or information to or from a company (the 'company communications provisions') see PARA 750 et seq.
4 Companies Act 2006 s 32(1)(a). As to the meaning of references to a company's 'articles' see PARA 227 note 2. As to a company's articles of association generally see PARA 227 et seq. A limited company need not register its articles: see PARA 227.
A company whose articles are deemed by virtue of the Companies Act 2006 s 28 (see PARA 227) to contain provisions formerly in its memorandum may comply with any obligation to send a person a copy of its articles either by appending to a copy of the other provisions of the articles a copy of the provisions of its old-style memorandum that are deemed to be provisions of the articles, or by sending together with a copy of the other provisions of the articles a copy of its old-style memorandum indicating the provisions that are deemed to be provisions of the articles: see the Companies Act 2006 (Commencement No 8, Transitional Provisions and Savings) Order 2008, SI 2008/2860, Sch 2 para 9(1). As to the meaning of references to a company's 'old-style memorandum' for these purposes see PARA 235 note 4.
5 As to resolutions and decisions of the company generally see PARA 684 et seq.
6 Ie any resolution or agreement to which the Companies Act 2006 Pt 3 Ch 3 (ss 29–30) (resolutions and agreements affecting a company's constitution) applies (see PARA 230): see s 32(1)(b). As to the meaning of references to a company's constitution see PARA 226.
7 Companies Act 2006 s 32(1)(b).
8 As to the meaning of 'registrar of companies' see PARA 126 note 2. As to the meaning of references to delivering a document, and as to the meaning of 'document' for these purposes, see PARA 136 note 2. As to the delivery of documents to the registrar see PARA 136; and as to the requirements generally for the proper delivery of documents to the registrar see PARA 137.
9 Ie under the Companies Act 2006 s 34(2) (see PARA 237): see s 32(1)(c). As to the meaning of 'enactment' see PARA 13 note 16.
10 Companies Act 2006 s 32(1)(c). The text refers to the notice required to be sent to the registrar of companies under s 35(2)(a) (ie where an order of a court or other authority alters a company's constitution) (see PARA 238): see s 32(1)(c).
11 Ie under the Companies Act 2006 s 899 (see PARA 1611): see s 32(1)(d).
12 Companies Act 2006 s 32(1)(d). The text refers to any court order required to be sent to the registrar of companies under s 900 (ie where a court order facilitates a reconstruction or amalgamation) (see PARA 1614): see s 32(1)(d).
13 Ie under the Companies Act 2006 s 996 (see PARA 666): see s 32(1)(e).
14 Companies Act 2006 s 32(1)(e).
15 As to the issue of a company's certificate of incorporation upon successful completion of registration see PARA 114; and as to certificates issued by the registrar after a company's status has been altered following re-registration see PARA 167 et seq.
16 Companies Act 2006 s 32(1)(f).
17 As to the meanings of 'company having a share capital', 'share' and 'share capital' see PARA 1231.
18 Companies Act 2006 s 32(1)(g). The statement of capital required by s 32(1)(g) is a statement of:
(1) the total number of shares of the company (s 32(2)(a));
(2) the aggregate nominal value of those shares (s 32(2)(b));
(3) for each class of shares:
(a) prescribed particulars of the rights attached to the shares (s 32(2)(c)(i));
(b) the total number of shares of that class (s 32(2)(c)(ii)); and
(c) the aggregate nominal value of shares of that class (s 32(2)(c)(iii)); and

(4) either
(a) until 30 June 2016, the amount paid up and the amount, if any, unpaid on each share (whether on account of the nominal value of the share or by way of premium) (s 32(2)(d) (repealed by the Small Business, Enterprise and Employment Act 2015 Sch 6 paras 1, 3(b); and see the Small Business, Enterprise and Employment Act 2015 (Commencement No 4, Transitional and Savings Provisions) Regulations 2016, SI 2016/321, reg 6(e))); or
(b) as from that date, the aggregate amount if any unpaid on the shares described in heads (1)–(2) above, whether on account of their nominal value or by way of premium (Companies Act 2006 s 32(2)(ba) (added by the Small Business, Enterprise and Employment Act 2015 Sch 6 paras 1, 3(a)); and see head (a) above).

As to classes of shares generally see PARA 1246 et seq. As to the nominal value of shares, and as to paid up and unpaid shares, see PARA 1231 et seq. As to rights attached to classes of shares generally see PARA 1246 et seq. In the Companies Acts, 'prescribed' (see head (3)(a) above) means prescribed (by order or by regulations) by the Secretary of State: Companies Act 2006 s 1167. As to the making of orders and regulations under the Companies Act 2006 generally see ss 1288–1292. As to the Secretary of State see PARA 6. Partly in exercise of the powers conferred by s 32(2)(c)(i), the Secretary of State has made the Companies (Shares and Share Capital) Order 2009, SI 2009/388. Accordingly, the following particulars of the rights attached to shares are prescribed for the purposes of the Companies Act 2006 s 32(2)(c)(i) (see the Companies (Shares and Share Capital) Order 2009, SI 2009/388, art 2(1), (2)(a)):
(i) particulars of any voting rights attached to the shares, including rights that arise only in certain circumstances (art 2(3)(a));
(ii) particulars of any rights attached to the shares, as respects dividends, to participate in a distribution (art 2(3)(b));
(iii) particulars of any rights attached to the shares, as respects capital, to participate in a distribution (including on winding up) (art 2(3)(c)); and
(iv) whether the shares are to be redeemed or are liable to be redeemed at the option of the company or the shareholder (art 2(3)(d)).

As to redeemable shares see PARAS 1241, 1416 et seq; and as to distributions see PARA 1562 et seq. As to winding up in general see COMPANY AND PARTNERSHIP INSOLVENCY vol 16 (2011) PARA 380 et seq. As to the initial statement of capital and initial shareholdings required in the case of a company limited by shares see PARA 107. As to the meaning of 'company limited by shares' see PARA 95.

19 As to the meaning of 'company limited by guarantee' see PARA 95.
20 Companies Act 2006 s 32(1)(h). As to the statement of guarantee see PARA 109.
21 Ie in complying with the Companies Act 2006 s 32: see s 32(3).
22 Companies Act 2006 s 32(3). As to the meaning of 'officer' see PARA 679; and as to the meaning of 'officer in default' see PARA 316. Any person guilty of such an offence is liable on summary conviction to a fine not exceeding level 3 on the standard scale: s 32(4). As to the standard scale and the powers of magistrates' courts to issue fines on summary conviction see SENTENCING vol 92 (2015) PARA 176.

(vii) Effect of Company's Constitution

242. Provisions of company's constitution binding as if by covenant. The provisions of a company's constitution[1] bind the company and its members[2] to the same extent as if there were covenants on the part of the company and of each member to observe those provisions[3]. By virtue of this, the constitution becomes a contract between the company and its members; it is a 'statutory contract' of a special nature with its own distinctive features[4].

Once a company's articles are registered[5], the court has no power to rectify them even if they do not accord with what is proved to be the concurrent intention of the members[6]. The articles should, however, be regarded as a business document and should be construed so as to give them reasonable business efficacy[7], where a construction tending to that result is admissible on the language of the articles, in preference to a result which would or might prove unworkable[8]. A purely constructional implication is not precluded but the court will not imply a term from extrinsic circumstances[9].

Money payable by a member to the company under its constitution is a debt due from him to the company[10]; and it is[11] of the nature of an ordinary contract debt[12].

1 As to the meaning of 'company' under the Companies Acts see PARA 21; and as to the meaning of the 'Companies Acts' see PARA 13. As to the meaning of references to a company's constitution see PARA 226.

2 As to the meaning of 'member' see PARA 323.

3 Companies Act 2006 s 33(1). This provision gives effect to *Hickman v Kent or Romney Marsh Sheep Breeders' Association* [1915] 1 Ch 881 (see PARA 243).

The provision made by the Companies Act 2006 s 33(1) is subject to any overriding provisions of the Companies Act 2006 and may be modified by separate shareholder agreements and by amendment under s 21(1) (see PARA 231). As to shareholders' agreements see also PARA 250. In the case of any contract binding on a company and its members under s 33, the Contracts (Rights of Third Parties) Act 1999 s 1 (see CONTRACT vol 22 (2012) PARA 343) confers no rights on a third party: s 6(2) (amended by SI 2009/1941).

4 *Scott v Frank F Scott (London) Ltd* [1940] Ch 794, [1940] 3 All ER 508, CA; *Bratton Seymour Service Co Ltd v Oxborough* [1992] BCLC 693 at 698, CA, per Steyn LJ. A company may amend its articles of association (and, therefore, the statutory 'contract') by special resolution: see the Companies Act 2006 s 21(1); and PARA 231. As to contracts which are enforceable between a member and the company and between members *inter se* see PARA 243 et seq. As to outsider rights see PARA 246.

5 As to the meaning of references to a company's 'articles' see PARA 227 note 2. As to the registration of articles of association, and as to the articles generally, see PARA 227 et seq.

6 *Scott v Frank F Scott (London) Ltd* [1940] Ch 794, [1940] 3 All ER 508, CA.

7 The 'business efficacy' test is merely one way of stating the proposition that the implication of a term is an exercise in the construction of the instrument as a whole: *A-G of Belize v Belize Telecom Ltd* [2009] UKPC 10 at [19], [2009] 2 All ER 1127, [2009] 1 WLR 1988 (construction of the articles of association of Belize Telecom Ltd). It follows that in every case in which it is said that some provision ought to be implied in an instrument, the question for the court is whether such a provision would spell out in express words what the instrument, read against the relevant background, would reasonably be understood to mean; there is only one question: is that what the instrument, read as a whole against the relevant background, would reasonably be understood to mean?: see *A-G of Belize v Belize Telecom Ltd* [2009] UKPC 10 at [21], [2009] 2 All ER 1127, [2009] 1 WLR 1988. The fact that any proposed implied term would be inequitable or unreasonable, or contradict what the parties have expressly said, or is incapable of clear expression, are all good reasons for saying that a reasonable man would not have understood that to be what the instrument meant: see *A-G of Belize v Belize Telecom Ltd* [2009] UKPC 10 at [23], [27], [2009] 2 All ER 1127, [2009] 1 WLR 1988. The approach to the question when to imply a term into a contract or other instrument which is set out in that casehas been indorsed in eg *Mediterranean Salvage and Towage Ltd v Seamar Trading and Commerce Inc, The Reborn* [2009] EWCA Civ 531 at [8]–[18], [2009] All ER (D) 83 (Jun) per Lord Clarke of Stone-cum-Ebony MR (considering terms of a charterparty), *Stack v Ajar-Tec Ltd* [2015] EWCA Civ 46, [2015] IRLR 474, [2015] All ER (D) 63 (Feb) (terms of a contract of service) and *Rathbone Bros Plc v Novae Corporate Underwriting* [2014] EWCA Civ 1464, [2015] Lloyd's Rep IR 95, [2015] WTLR 301 (terms of a contract of insurance).

8 *Holmes v Lord Keyes* [1959] Ch 199 at 215, [1958] 2 All ER 129 at 318, CA, per Jenkins LJ; *Robert Batcheller & Sons Ltd v Batcheller* [1945] Ch 169 at 177, [1945] 1 All ER 522 at 531 per Romer J (disapproved in *Grundt v Great Boulder Pty Gold Mines Ltd* [1948] Ch 145, [1948] 1 All ER 21, CA, where the court refused to find any absurdity). See also *Folkes Group plc v Alexander* [2002] EWHC 51 (Ch), [2002] 2 BCLC 254 (court used additional words to construe an amended article whose natural and ordinary meaning gave a result so absurd that something had to have gone seriously wrong with its drafting); *BWE International Ltd v Jones* [2003] EWCA Civ 298, [2004] 1 BCLC 406; *Davenport v Cream Holdings Ltd* [2008] EWCA Civ 1363, [2008] All ER (D) 89 (Dec) (construction of articles proposed by defendant produced consequences so surprising that it was doubtful that they could have been within the contemplation of the parties).

9 *Bratton Seymour Service Co Ltd v Oxborough* [1992] BCLC 693, CA.

10 Companies Act 2006 s 33(2).

11 Ie in England and Wales and Northern Ireland: see the Companies Act 2006 s 33(2). As to the meanings of 'England' and 'Wales' see PARA 1 note 5.

12 Companies Act 2006 s 33(2). Such a debt will become time-barred after six years: see the Limitation Act 1980 s 5; and LIMITATION PERIODS vol 68 (2008) PARA 956. See also *St*

Johnstone Football Club Ltd v Scottish Football Association Ltd 1965 SLT 171, Ct of Sess (fines imposed pursuant to powers in articles). The debt referred to in the text was previously a specialty debt, ie under the Companies Act 1985 s 14(2) (repealed).

243. How far company's articles constitute a contract. The question of how far a company's articles[1] constitute a binding contract (on the one hand, between a company and its members[2] and, on the other hand, between its members among themselves) is one of great difficulty and the principles are not altogether clear[3]. It has, however, been held that the contractual force given to the articles of association is limited to those provisions which apply to the relationship of members in their capacity as members and does not extend to those provisions which govern the relationship of a company and its directors[4] as such[5].

1 As to the meaning of 'company' under the Companies Acts see PARA 21; and as to the meaning of the 'Companies Acts' see PARA 13. As to a company's articles of association generally see PARA 227 et seq. As to the relative force of the memorandum and articles see PARA 227.
2 As to membership of a company see PARA 323 et seq.
3 As to a general discussion of this question see *Hickman v Kent or Romney Marsh Sheep Breeders' Association* [1915] 1 Ch 881.
4 As to a company's directors see PARA 512 et seq.
5 *Beattie v E & F Beattie Ltd* [1938] Ch 708 at 721, [1938] 3 All ER 214 at 218, following *Hickman v Kent or Romney Marsh Sheep Breeders' Association* [1915] 1 Ch 881.

244. Articles as contract between company and member. A company's articles of association[1] constitute a contract between the company and a member[2] in respect of his rights[3] and liabilities as a shareholder[4]; and a company may sue a member and a member may sue a company to enforce and restrain breaches of the regulations contained in the articles dealing with such matters[5]. The purpose of the articles is to define the position of the shareholder as a shareholder, not to bind him in his capacity as an individual[6]. The articles do not constitute a contract between the company and a member in respect of rights and liabilities which he has in a capacity other than that of member, whether he becomes a member originally or subsequently[7]; and, where such rights and liabilities are the subject of a written agreement, the articles will not be imported unless they are referred to[8].

Where the articles provide that the company on incorporation is to enter into an agreement for the purchase of property and for the appointment of the vendor as a director[9], the vendor who becomes a shareholder cannot sue nor can any person claiming through the vendor sue or rely on the articles as constituting a contract[10]; and, where the articles provide that a solicitor who subsequently becomes a shareholder is to be the solicitor of the company, he cannot sue the company on the articles[11]. Similarly, where the articles provide that a director is to hold a certain number of shares[12], the provision does not constitute an agreement on his part to take the shares, even though he is already a member of the company[13].

The articles may be evidence of the terms upon which services are rendered to the company[14]; thus an agreement on the part of a director to act on the terms as to qualification contained in the articles[15], or on the part of the company to remunerate its directors on the terms of the articles[16], may be inferred from the subsequent action of the parties.

Any contract, so far as it relates to the constitution of the company, or the rights or obligations of its corporators or members, is exempt from the prohibitions on exclusion of liability imposed by the Unfair Contract Terms Act 1977[17].

1 As to a company's articles of association generally see PARA 227 et seq. As to the relative force of the memorandum and articles see PARA 227.
2 As to membership of a company see PARA 323 et seq.

3 A member may have legitimate expectations and interests not set out in the articles which the courts will be prepared to recognise in some circumstances: *Ebrahimi v Westbourne Galleries Ltd* [1973] AC 360, [1972] 2 All ER 492, HL. This is of particular importance in the context of petitions by members under the Companies Act 2006 s 994, alleging that the company's affairs are being or have been conducted in a manner which is unfairly prejudicial to their interests: see PARA 657.

4 As to shareholders generally see PARA 323 et seq.

5 *Johnson v Lyttle's Iron Agency* (1877) 5 ChD 687, CA; *Pender v Lushington* (1877) 6 ChD 70; *Re Imperial Hydropathic Hotel Co, Blackpool v Hampson* (1882) 23 ChD 1, CA; *Bradford Banking Co Ltd v Briggs, Son & Co Ltd* (1886) 12 App Cas 29 at 33, HL, per Lord Blackburn; *Wood v Odessa Waterworks Co* (1889) 42 ChD 636; *Welton v Saffery* [1897] AC 299 at 315, HL, per Lord Herschell; *Hickman v Kent or Romney Marsh Sheep Breeders' Association* [1915] 1 Ch 881; *Re Greene, Greene v Greene* [1949] Ch 333 at 340, [1949] 1 All ER 167 at 170 per Harman J (no contract where article invalid) (see contra *Re Tavarone Mining Co, Pritchard's Case* (1873) 8 Ch App 956 at 960 per Mellish LJ); *Eley v Positive Government Security Life Assurance Co Ltd* (1875) 1 ExD 20 at 26 per Amphlett B (on appeal (1876) 1 ExD 88 at 89, CA, per Lord Cairns LC); *Baring-Gould v Sharpington Combined Pick and Shovel Syndicate* [1899] 2 Ch 80 at 89, CA, per Lindley MR. See also *Quin & Axtens Ltd v Salmon* [1909] AC 442 at 443, HL, per Lord Loreburn LC. As to actions by a shareholder against the company see PARA 646 et seq.

6 *Bisgood v Henderson's Transvaal Estates Ltd* [1908] 1 Ch 743 at 759, CA, per Buckley LJ.

7 *Re Tavarone Mining Co, Pritchard's Case* (1873) 8 Ch App 956; *Eley v Positive Government Security Life Assurance Co* (1876) 1 ExD 88, CA; *Browne v La Trinidad* (1887) 37 ChD 1, CA; *Re Dale and Plant Ltd* (1889) 61 LT 206; *Re Famatina Development Corpn* [1914] 2 Ch 271 at 279 per Sargant J; *Hickman v Kent or Romney Marsh Sheep Breeders' Association* [1915] 1 Ch 881; *McEllistrim v Ballymacelligott Co-operative Agricultural and Dairy Society* [1919] AC 548 at 575, HL, per Lord Atkinson; *Beattie v E & F Beattie Ltd* [1938] Ch 708, [1938] 3 All ER 214.

8 *Re Alexander's Timber Co* (1901) 70 LJ Ch 767; *Boston Deep Sea Fishing and Ice Co v Ansell* (1888) 39 ChD 339, CA; *Re City Equitable Fire Insurance Co Ltd* [1925] Ch 407 at 521, CA, per Warrington LJ.

9 As to a company's directors see PARA 512 et seq.

10 *Re Tavarone Mining Co, Pritchard's Case* (1873) 8 Ch App 956; *Browne v La Trinidad* (1887) 37 ChD 1, CA.

11 *Eley v Positive Government Security Life Assurance Co* (1876) 1 ExD 88, CA.

12 As to shares and a company's share capital see PARA 1231 et seq.

13 *Re Wheal Buller Consols* (1888) 38 ChD 42, CA; *Re Printing Telegraph and Construction Co of the Agence Havas, ex p Cammell* [1894] 2 Ch 392, CA; *Re R Bolton & Co, Salisbury-Jones and Dale's Case* [1894] 3 Ch 356, CA.

14 See *Re City Equitable Fire Insurance Co Ltd* [1925] Ch 407 at 520–521, CA, per Warrington LJ; and the cases cited in notes 15, 16.

15 *Re Anglo-Austrian Printing and Publishing Union, Isaacs' Case* [1892] 2 Ch 158, CA; *Re Hercynia Copper Co* [1894] 2 Ch 403, CA; *Salton v New Beeston Cycle Co* [1899] 1 Ch 775; *Molineaux v London, Birmingham and Manchester Insurance Co Ltd* [1902] 2 KB 589, CA. Cf *Re International Cable Co Ltd, ex p Official Liquidator* (1892) 66 LT 253.

16 *Salton v New Beeston Cycle Co* [1899] 1 Ch 775; *Swabey v Port Darwin Gold Mining Co* (1889) 1 Meg 385, CA; *Re London and Scottish Bank, ex p Logan* (1870) LR 9 Eq 149; *Boston Deep Sea Fishing and Ice Co v Ansell* (1888) 39 ChD 339 at 366, CA, per Bowen LJ; *Re New British Iron Co, ex p Beckwith* [1898] 1 Ch 324. Cf *Re TN Farrer Ltd* [1937] Ch 352, [1937] 2 All ER 505.

17 Unfair Contract Terms Act 1977 s 1(2), Sch 1 para 1(d) (amended by the Consumer Rights Act 2015 Sch 4 paras 2, 3, 26(1), (3)). As to the exemptions from liability arising in contract referred to in the text generally see CONTRACT vol 22 (2012) PARA 416.

245. Whether articles are contract between members of company among themselves. While a company's articles of association[1] regulate the rights of the members[2] among themselves, the older authorities support the view that they do not constitute a contract between the members among themselves, but only a contract between the company and its members[3]. Therefore, the rights and liabilities of members as members under the articles may be enforced by or against the members only through the company[4]. However, more recent authorities support the direct enforcement by members of rights as members conferred by the articles[5].

1 As to a company's articles of association generally see PARA 227 et seq. As to the relative force of the memorandum and articles see PARA 227.
2 As to membership of a company see PARA 323 et seq.
3 *Welton v Saffery* [1897] AC 299 at 315, HL, per Lord Herschell; *Re Greene, Greene v Greene* [1949] Ch 333 at 340, [1949] 1 All ER 167 at 170 per Harman J; contra *Re Tavarone Mining Co, Pritchard's Case* (1873) 8 Ch App 956; *Eley v Positive Government Security Life Assurance Co Ltd* (1876) 1 ExD 88 at 89, CA, per Lord Cairns LC; *Browne v La Trinidad* (1887) 37 ChD 1, CA; *Borland's Trustee v Steel Bros & Co Ltd* [1901] 1 Ch 279 at 288 per Farwell J; *Re Famatina Development Corpn Ltd* [1914] 2 Ch 271 at 279 per Sargant J; and see *Salmon v Quin & Axtens Ltd* [1909] 1 Ch 311 at 318, CA, per Farwell LJ (affd sub nom *Quin & Axtens Ltd v Salmon* [1909] AC 442, HL), qualifying dicta of Stirling J in *Wood v Odessa Waterworks Co* (1889) 42 ChD 636 at 642; *Rayfield v Hands* [1960] Ch 1, [1958] 2 All ER 194 (directors, as members of the company, bound by provision in the articles that they would take at a fair value shares offered to them by the members).
4 See cases cited in PARA 244 note 5; and *MacDougall v Gardiner* (1875) 1 ChD 13, CA.
5 *Rayfield v Hands* [1960] Ch 1, [1958] 2 All ER 194 (where it was held to be unnecessary to join the company in the action); *Hurst v Crampton Bros (Coopers) Ltd* [2002] EWHC 1375 (Ch), [2003] 1 BCLC 304 (transfer of shares by member in breach of pre-emption requirements in articles defeasible at the suit of another member). As to the exercise of members' rights generally see PARA 378 et seq.

246. Articles not a contract between company and outsider. As between the company and a person who is not a member[1], the articles of association[2] do not in any circumstances constitute a contract of which that person may take advantage[3], as, for example, where they provide that the preliminary expenses of forming the company are to be paid out of the assets of the company[4] or that a solicitor is to be the solicitor of the company[5].

1 As to membership of a company see PARA 323 et seq.
2 As to a company's articles of association generally see PARA 227 et seq. As to the relative force of the memorandum and articles see PARA 227.
3 See *Hickman v Kent or Romney Marsh Sheep Breeders' Association* [1915] 1 Ch 881 at 897, 900 per Astbury J; *Beattie v E & F Beattie Ltd* [1938] Ch 708 at 721, [1938] 3 All ER 214 at 218 per Greene MR. See also PARA 242.
4 *Melhado v Porto Alegre Rly Co* (1874) LR 9 CP 503; *Re Rotherham Alum and Chemical Co* (1883) 25 ChD 103 at 110, CA, per Lindley LJ; and see PARA 57.
5 *Re Rhodesian Properties Ltd* (1901) 45 Sol Jo 580.

247. Notice of company's constitution. Members of a company[1] are deemed to be aware of the contents of the company's constitution[2], and to understand its meaning[3]. Notice is not, however, to be imputed to persons who have been induced by fraudulent misrepresentations to take shares[4], since they are entitled to repudiate the contract of membership[5].

In favour of a person dealing with a company[6] in good faith, the power of the directors[7] to bind the company, or authorise others to do so, is deemed to be free of any limitation under the company's constitution[8]; and such a person dealing with a company is not bound to inquire as to any limitation on the powers of the directors to bind the company or authorise others to do so, he is presumed to have acted in good faith unless the contrary is proved, and he is not to be regarded as acting in bad faith by reason only of his knowing that an act is beyond the powers of the directors under the company's constitution[9].

1 As to membership of a company see PARA 323 et seq. As to the meaning of 'company' under the Companies Acts see PARA 21; and as to the meaning of the 'Companies Acts' see PARA 13.
2 *Re Barned's Banking Co, Peel's Case* (1867) 2 Ch App 674 at 684 per Lord Cairns LJ; *Re New Zealand Banking Corpn, Sewell's Case* (1868) 3 Ch App 131 at 140 per Lord Cairns LJ; *Griffith*

v Paget (1877) 6 ChD 511 at 517 per Jessel MR. As to the meaning of references to a company's constitution under the Companies Act 2006 see PARA 226.

3 *Oakbank Oil Co v Crum* (1882) 8 App Cas 65 at 71, HL, per Lord Selborne LC.

4 As to shares and a company's share capital see PARA 1231 et seq.

5 *Central Rly Co of Venezuela (Directors etc) v Kisch* (1867) LR 2 HL 99 at 123 per Lord Cranworth, as explained in *Oakes v Turquand and Harding* (1867) LR 2 HL 325 at 345, 346 per Lord Chelmsford. Cf *Downes v Ship* (1868) LR 3 HL 343.

6 For these purposes, a person 'deals with' a company if he is a party to any transaction or other act to which the company is a party: see the Companies Act 2006 s 40(2); and PARA 262.

7 As to a company's directors see PARA 512 et seq.

8 See the Companies Act 2006 s 40(1); and PARA 262.

9 See the Companies Act 2006 s 40(2); and PARA 262.

248. Company's articles at variance with statutory provision. Any provision in a company's articles[1] which is at variance with the provisions of the Companies Act 2006 is void, as, for example, an article purporting to authorise a company to forfeit, instead of selling, shares for debts due from a member otherwise than as a contributory[2]; to pay dividends out of capital or allot shares at a discount[3]; to limit the right of a member to present a winding-up petition[4]; to shut dissentient shareholders[5] out of their statutory rights on a reconstruction of the company[6]; to fetter the power of the company to alter its articles[7], or to increase its share capital[8], or to register a transferee of shares without a proper instrument of transfer having been delivered[9].

A provision in any article which is in accordance with the model articles[10] is valid, subject to any subsequent legislation, as the model articles have statutory authority[11].

1 As to a company's articles of association generally see PARA 227 et seq.

2 *Hopkinson v Mortimer, Harley & Co Ltd* [1917] 1 Ch 646. As to shares and a company's share capital see PARA 1231 et seq; and as to membership of a company see PARA 323 et seq. As to the meaning of 'contributory' see COMPANY AND PARTNERSHIP INSOLVENCY vol 17 (2011) PARA 661. As to the meaning of 'contributory' under the Companies Acts see PARA 109 note 10.

3 *Welton v Saffery* [1897] AC 299, HL. As to the allotment of shares at a discount and the consequences of so allotting shares in contravention of the statutory prohibition see PARA 1300.

4 *Re Peveril Gold Mines Ltd* [1898] 1 Ch 122, CA. As to winding up in general see COMPANY AND PARTNERSHIP INSOLVENCY vol 16 (2011) PARA 380 et seq.

5 As to shareholders generally see PARA 323 et seq.

6 *Baring-Gould v Sharpington Combined Pick and Shovel Syndicate* [1899] 2 Ch 80, CA. As to reconstruction of a company see PARA 1605 et seq.

7 *Malleson v National Insurance and Guarantee Corpn* [1894] 1 Ch 200; *Russell v Northern Bank Development Corpn Ltd* [1992] 3 All ER 161, [1992] 1 WLR 588, HL. As to provision made for the alteration of articles see PARA 231 et seq. An agreement outside the articles between shareholders as to how they would exercise their voting rights on a resolution to alter the articles would, however, not necessarily be invalid: see PARA 250.

8 *Russell v Northern Bank Development Corpn Ltd* [1992] 3 All ER 161, [1992] 1 WLR 588, HL. See also note 10.

9 *Re Greene, Greene v Greene* [1949] Ch 333, [1949] 1 All ER 167.

10 Ie as they are in existence from time to time: see PARAS 227–229.

11 See *Lock v Queensland Investment and Land Mortgage Co* [1896] AC 461, HL; and PARA 229. See also *Movitex Ltd v Bulfield* [1988] BCLC 104.

249. Restrictions on articles of association under the Companies Act 2006. In certain cases, the Companies Act 2006 provides that certain provisions contained in the articles of association[1] are to be void or subject to restriction. Thus the production to a company of any document which is by law sufficient evidence of probate of the will, or letters of administration of the estate, or confirmation as executor of a deceased person, must be accepted by the company as sufficient evidence of the grant, notwithstanding anything in its articles[2]; and any provision of the company's articles is void in so far as it would have the effect of inhibiting or denying certain members' rights that are guaranteed under the Companies Act

2006[3]. A shareholder's right to petition the court on the grounds of unfair prejudice[4] is not, however, subject to such express guarantee and it seems that a provision in the articles obliging him instead to submit to arbitration would be valid[5].

1 As to a company's articles of association generally see PARA 227 et seq.
2 See the Companies Act 2006 s 774; and PARA 445.
3 See eg the Companies Act 2006 s 321 (cited in PARA 727), s 327 (cited in PARA 736).
4 See the Companies Act 2006 s 994; and PARA 657.
5 See *Fulham Football Club (1987) Ltd v Richards* [2011] EWCA Civ 855, [2012] Ch 333, [2012] 1 All ER 414.

250. Shareholders' agreements. Individual shareholders[1] may deal with their own interests by contract in such way as they may think fit; but such contracts, whether made by all or some only of the shareholders, create personal obligations, or a personal exception against themselves only, and do not become a regulation of the company or binding on the transferees of the parties to it or upon new or non-assenting shareholders[2].

Thus although a provision in a company's articles of association[3] which restricts the company's statutory power to alter the articles[4] or a formal undertaking by the company to that effect, would be invalid[5], an agreement outside the articles between shareholders as to how they are to exercise their voting rights on a resolution to alter the articles would not necessarily be so[6].

1 As to shareholders and the membership of companies generally see PARA 323 et seq.
2 *Welton v Saffery* [1897] AC 299 at 331, HL, per Lord Davey; applied in *Russell v Northern Bank Development Corpn Ltd* [1992] 3 All ER 161, [1992] 1 WLR 588, HL.
3 As to a company's articles of association generally see PARA 227 et seq.
4 Amendment might be subject to certain conditions being met if the articles in question are 'entrenched provisions': see PARA 232. As to provision made for the alteration of articles generally see PARA 231 et seq.
5 See PARA 248.
6 *Russell v Northern Bank Development Corpn Ltd* [1992] 3 All ER 161, [1992] 1 WLR 588, HL. See also *Greenwell v Porter* [1902] 1 Ch 530; *Puddephatt v Leith* [1916] 1 Ch 200; *Bushell v Faith* [1969] 2 Ch 438, [1969] 1 All ER 1002, CA (affd [1970] AC 1099, [1970] 1 All ER 53, HL).

(8) CAPACITY OF COMPANY

(i) Capacity of Company: in general

251. Capacity, and limits on capacity, deriving from corporate status. Under the Companies Act 2006, a company[1] may be incorporated[2] for carrying out any lawful purpose[3].

Moreover, a company is subject to the common law and to statutory provisions which affect the conduct of its affairs or business[4], like any other person[5], and may come within the scope of special statutory restrictions as, for example, those enabling restriction or winding-up orders to be made if the business is carried on by or on behalf of enemies or enemy subjects[6] or those restricting the transfer of businesses abroad[7], or those restricting insolvency proceedings or other legal processes while the company is in administration[8].

Unless it is a private company[9], a company registered under the Companies Act 2006 does not acquire the right to exercise all its powers immediately on incorporation, for it must comply with certain statutory requirements before it may either properly commence business or exercise its borrowing powers or enter into binding contracts[10].

1 As to the meaning of 'company' under the Companies Acts see PARA 21; and as to the meaning of the 'Companies Acts' see PARA 13.
2 As to incorporation upon registration under the Companies Act 2006 see PARA 114 et seq.
3 See the Companies Act 2006 s 7(2); and PARA 95. As to companies which are formed for an illegal purpose see PARA 99 et seq. The objects of a company are unrestricted unless its articles of association specifically restrict them: see s 31; and PARA 239. This is a change from the situation that pertained under the Companies Act 1985 where a company was obliged to state its objects in the memorandum of association (the role of which has been altered fundamentally under the Companies Act 2006). The case law that is cited in PARA 256 et seq derives from the time when the statement of a company's objects was a requirement.
4 See PARAS 253–255.
5 A limited company may be a 'respectable and responsible person' within the meaning of a proviso against assigning a lease without the landlord's consent: *Willmott v London Road Car Co Ltd* [1910] 2 Ch 525, CA; *Re Greater London Properties Ltd's Lease, Taylor Bros (Grocers) Ltd v Covent Garden Properties Co Ltd* [1959] 1 All ER 728, [1959] 1 WLR 503.
6 See the Trading with the Enemy Act 1939 s 3A; and ARMED CONFLICT AND EMERGENCY vol 3 (2011) PARA 203.
7 See PARA 118.
8 As to applications for administration orders see COMPANY AND PARTNERSHIP INSOLVENCY vol 16 (2011) PARA 158 et seq.
9 As to the meaning of 'private company' see PARA 95.
10 See PARA 67.

252. Company exceeding statutory powers. A company[1], even if apparently authorised to do so by its constitution[2], cannot lawfully do anything beyond the powers given by the Companies Acts[3]. Thus it cannot, for example[4]:

(1) purchase its own shares[5] save in compliance with the statutory requirements[6]; or
(2) in the case of a public company, give financial assistance for the purchase of its shares[7]; or
(3) reduce or repay capital without complying with the statutory requirements[8]; or
(4) distribute bonus shares gratuitously[9]; or
(5) allot shares at a discount[10]; or
(6) pay dividends on shares out of capital[11]; or
(7) make presents to directors out of capital[12]; or
(8) make payments for the benefit of a section only of the shareholders[13], such as paying the costs of a prosecution for libel[14] or the costs of pursuing proceedings not instituted by itself, even though it is for the company's benefit[15].

1 As to the meaning of 'company' under the Companies Acts see PARA 21; and as to the meaning of the 'Companies Acts' see PARA 13. As to the meaning of 'company' more generally see PARA 1.
2 *Trevor v Whitworth* (1887) 12 App Cas 409 at 430, HL, per Lord Watson; *Re Castle Crag Steamship Co, Raine's Case* (1888) 4 TLR 302; *Re Mersina and Adana Construction Co* (1889) 5 TLR 680; *General Property Investment Co v Matheson's Trustees* (1888) 16 R 282. As to the meaning of references to a company's constitution see PARA 226.
3 This position is not affected by the Companies Act 2006 ss 39–42 (as to which see PARAS 262–264).
4 This list is not exhaustive.
5 *Trevor v Whitworth* (1887) 12 App Cas 409, HL (overruling *Re Dronfield Silkstone Coal Co* (1880) 17 ChD 76); *Re Balgooley Distillery Co* (1886) 17 LR Ir 239, CA; *Taylor v Pilsen, Joel and General Electric Light Co* (1884) 27 ChD 268; *Phosphate of Lime Co Ltd v Green* (1871) LR 7 CP 43; *Cree v Somervail* (1879) 4 App Cas 648, HL. As to shares and a company's share capital see PARA 1231.
6 As to which see PARAS 1421, 1431.
7 See PARA 1409 et seq.

8 As to which see PARA 1360 et seq.
9 *Re Eddystone Marine Insurance Co* [1893] 3 Ch 9, CA; *Welton v Saffery* [1897] AC 299, HL.
10 As to the allotment of shares at a discount and the consequences of so allotting shares in contravention of the statutory prohibition see PARA 1300. As to the meaning of 'allotted' see PARA 1280.
11 See PARA 1563 et seq. As to the declaration and payment of dividends especially see PARA 1581 et seq.
12 *Re George Newman & Co* [1895] 1 Ch 674, CA. See also PARA 1409. As to a company's directors see PARA 512 et seq.
13 As to shareholders and membership of companies generally see PARAS 323 et seq, 1889 et seq.
14 *Pickering v Stephenson* (1872) LR 14 Eq 322 at 340 per Wickens V-C; *Studdert v Grosvenor* (1886) 33 ChD 528. These two decisions were adversely commented on in *Cullerne v London and Suburban General Permanent Building Society* (1890) 25 QBD 485 at 490, CA, per Lindley LJ, on the question of the directors' liability to repay funds improperly paid ultra vires the company.
15 *Kernaghan v Williams* (1868) LR 6 Eq 228; *Re Liverpool Household Stores Association* (1890) 59 LJ Ch 616.

253. Statutory powers exercisable subject to authorisation by, or restriction or prohibition in, articles. Many powers are conferred on a company[1] by the Companies Act 2006 unless they are restricted or excluded by the company's articles of association[2]; a small number of other powers are subject to authorisation.

For example, the following powers are conferred unless they are excluded or restricted, namely the power[3]:

(1) to increase its share capital[4] by sub-dividing its shares, or any of them, into shares of a smaller nominal amount[5] than its existing shares, or by consolidating and dividing all or any of its share capital into shares of a larger nominal amount than its existing shares[6], or to redenominate its share capital, or any class of its share capital, by converting shares from having a fixed nominal value in one currency to having a fixed nominal value in another currency[7];
(2) to reduce its share capital[8];
(3) to issue redeemable shares, if a private company[9];
(4) to purchase its own shares[10].

The following powers are subject to authorisation, namely the power[11]:

(a) to pay commission to a person in consideration of his subscribing or agreeing to subscribe, whether absolutely or conditionally, for shares in the company, or procuring or agreeing to procure subscriptions, whether absolute or conditional, for shares in the company[12];
(b) to make provision for different amounts to be paid on its shares, with proportionate dividends[13];
(c) to issue redeemable shares, if a public company[14];
(d) to provide, by a resolution of its directors[15], for employees on cessation or transfer of the business of the company or any of its subsidiaries[16].

1 As to the meaning of 'company' under the Companies Acts see PARA 21; and as to the meaning of the 'Companies Acts' see PARA 13.
2 As to the meaning of references to a company's 'articles' see PARA 227 note 2. As to a company's articles of association generally see PARA 227 et seq.
3 This list is not exhaustive.
4 As to the meanings of 'share capital' and 'company having a share capital' see PARA 1231. As to the meaning of 'share' see PARA 1231.
5 As to the nominal value of shares see PARA 1233.
6 See the Companies Act 2006 s 618; and PARA 1349 et seq.
7 See the Companies Act 2006 s 622; and PARA 1354.
8 See the Companies Act 2006 Pt 17 Ch 10 (ss 641–653); and PARA 1360 et seq.

9 See the Companies Act 2006 s 684; and PARA 1416. As to the meaning of 'private company' see PARA 95. As to rights attached to classes of shares generally see PARA 1246 et seq; as to redeemable shares see PARAS 1241, 1416 et seq.
10 See the Companies Act 2006 s 690; and PARA 1421.
11 This list is not exhaustive.
12 See the Companies Act 2006 s 553(1), (2); and PARA 1340.
13 See the Companies Act 2006 s 581; and PARAS 1301, 1583. As to the declaration and payment of dividends see PARA 1581 et seq.
14 See note 9. As to the meaning of 'public company' see PARA 95.
15 As to a company's directors generally see PARA 512 et seq. As to meetings of directors, and the taking of resolutions, see PARA 568 et seq.
16 See the Companies Act 2006 s 247; and PARA 586. As to the meaning of 'subsidiary' see PARA 22.

254. Powers exercisable under the Companies Act 2006 only by special resolution. A special resolution[1] is required by the Companies Act 2006 for the exercise of certain powers. These include[2] the power:

(1) to change the company's name[3];
(2) subject to one exception[4], to alter its articles of association[5];
(3) to redenominate some or all of the company's shares in order to reduce its share capital[6];
(4) to reduce its share capital, either supported by a solvency statement or subject to confirmation by the court[7];
(5) to make a payment out of capital (if a private company[8]) for the redemption or purchase of its own shares[9];
(6) to disapply pre-emption rights[10];
(7) to alter the company's status by re-registration[11];
(8) to opt in to, or out of, the takeover provisions[12];
(9) as a rule, to wind up voluntarily[13];
(10) to require the register[14] to be amended so that it states that the company's registered office[15] is to be situated in Wales[16] (rather than England[17] and Wales)[18].

1 As to special resolutions see PARA 686.
2 This list is not exhaustive.
3 See the Companies Act 2006 ss 77, 78; and PARAS 216–217. Head (1) in the text is not prescriptive; a company may change its name voluntarily by other means provided for by the company's articles: see s 77(1)(b); and PARA 216. As to the meaning of 'company' under the Companies Acts see PARA 21; and as to the meaning of the 'Companies Acts' see PARA 13.
4 A special resolution is not required to remove provision in the company's articles authorising the company to issue share warrants: see the Small Business, Enterprise and Employment Act 2015 s 85(1), (2); and PARA 231 text and notes 4–5.
5 See the Companies Act 2006 s 21; and PARA 231. As to a company's articles of association generally see PARA 227 et seq; and as to the amendment of a company's articles under the Companies Act 2006 see PARAS 231, 232.
6 See the Companies Act 2006 s 626; and PARA 1354 et seq. As to the meanings of 'share capital' and 'company having a share capital' see PARA 1231.
7 See the Companies Act 2006 Pt 17 Ch 10 (ss 641–653); and PARA 1360 et seq.
8 As to the meaning of 'private company' see PARA 95.
9 See the Companies Act 2006 Pt 18 Ch 5 (ss 709–723); and PARA 1431 et seq.
10 See the Companies Act 2006 ss 569–573; and PARA 1291 et seq.
11 See the Companies Act 2006 Pt 7 (ss 89–111); and PARA 167 et seq.
12 See the Companies Act 2006 Pt 28 Ch 2 (ss 966–973); and PARA 1689 et seq.
13 See the Insolvency Act 1986 s 84(1)(b); and COMPANY AND PARTNERSHIP INSOLVENCY vol 17 (2011) PARA 898. The company may also, by special resolution, resolve that it be wound up by the court: see s 122(1)(a); and COMPANY AND PARTNERSHIP INSOLVENCY vol 16 (2011) PARA 392 et seq.
14 As to the register see PARA 142.
15 As to a company's registered office see PARA 124.
16 As to the meaning of 'Wales' see PARA 1 note 5.

17 As to the meaning of 'England' see PARA 1 note 5.
18 See the Companies Act 2006 s 88; and PARA 124.

(ii) Company's Powers

A. COMPANY'S POWERS: IN GENERAL

255. Objects and capacity of company. Previously, the capacity of a company was determined by the breadth of the company's objects as expressed in the company's memorandum of association[1], and acts beyond those objects were ultra vires and void[2].

The Companies Act 2006 provides that, unless a company's articles[3] specifically restrict the objects of the company[4], its objects are unrestricted[5]. A company with unrestricted objects has an unrestricted capacity other than restrictions imposed by the requirements of the Companies Act 2006 and the general law[6]. However, it remains the duty of the directors to observe any limitation on their powers, whether flowing from the company's constitution or otherwise[7].

1 See PARA 239 note 3.
2 As to the authorities on ultra vires generally see PARA 258 et seq.
3 As to a company's articles of association generally see PARA 227 et seq.
4 As to restricting a company's objects see PARA 256.
5 See the Companies Act 2006 s 31(1); and PARA 239.
6 See PARAS 251–254.
7 See PARA 264 et seq.

B. STATEMENT OF COMPANY'S OBJECTS

256. Restricting a company's objects. For companies formed under the Companies Act 2006[1], the company's objects are unrestricted[2], unless the company's articles[3] specifically restrict them[4].

Existing companies[5] were required to have an objects clause in the memorandum of association and those clauses now are treated as forming part of the company's articles[6]. Those clauses, if retained[7], would be regarded, it seems, as restricting the company's objects, although the original drafting of such clauses was intended to expand and not to restrict a company's capacity[8].

Whether the company is a company formed under the Companies Act 2006 which chooses to restrict its objects, or is a company formed under the Companies Act 1985 or earlier enactments which retains its objects clause, the objects clause operates only to limit the powers of the directors[9], for the validity of an act done by the company cannot be called into question on the ground of a lack of capacity by reason of anything in the company's constitution[10]. No issue of ultra vires may be raised[11], but it remains the duty of the directors of a company (now a statutory duty) to act in accordance with the constitution and to exercise powers only for the purposes for which they are conferred[12]. The authorities on ultra vires[13], though obsolete on that issue, may remain of some value in determining whether the directors have complied with that duty.

Persons dealing with the company in good faith are afforded a considerable measure of statutory protection against limitations on the directors' powers to bind the company[14].

1 As to company formation under the Companies Act 2006 see PARA 104 et seq.
2 See PARA 239.
3 As to a company's articles of association generally see PARA 227 et seq.

4 See the Companies Act 2006 s 31(1); and PARA 239. See also *Cotman v Brougham* [1918] AC 514 at 522, 523, HL, per Lord Wrenbury (where the practice of inserting powers in the objects clause is criticised). The requirement to 'specifically restrict' suggests that the articles must delimit and identify the objects in such a manner that the reader may identify the field of industry within which the company's activities are to be confined: see *Cotman v Brougham* [1918] AC 514, HL

5 Ie those formed under the Companies Act 1985 and earlier enactments: see PARA 14.

6 See the Companies Act 2006 s 28(1); and PARA 227.

7 Ie because companies may remove objects clauses by amending their articles, subject to the need to give notice to the registrar, and subject to any such amendment not being effective until notice is entered on the register: see the Companies Act 2006 s 31(2); and PARA 239.

8 See *Cotman v Brougham* [1918] AC 514, HL; *Bell Houses Ltd v City Wall Properties Ltd* [1966] 2 QB 656, [1966] 2 All ER 674, CA.

9 As to a company's directors see PARA 512 et seq.

10 See the Companies Act 2006 s 39; and PARA 264. As to the meaning of references to a company's constitution see PARA 226.

11 See generally PARA 258 et seq.

12 See the Companies Act 2006 s 171; and PARA 580.

13 These are discussed below: see PARA 258 et seq.

14 See the Companies Act 2006 s 40; and PARA 262.

257. Construction of objects adopted by company. The ordinary rules applicable to construing documents apply to the construction of the objects adopted by a company[1]. The first question is: what is the fair construction of the company's constitution[2] as a whole? General words following a particular specification may be construed ejusdem generis, but there is no special rule of interpretation by reference to what are supposed to be the main or principal objects of a company where the question is whether something done or proposed to be done by the directors is ultra vires[3]. However, this consideration may be of importance where the question is whether the company ought to be wound up on the ground that its substratum is gone[4]. Although the subjective intent with which a transaction is carried out by the directors may result in a charge of misfeasance against them, and, if participated in by the other contracting party, may entitle the company to rescind the contract, such intent is irrelevant to the question whether the transaction is within the company's capacity[5].

It is possible to provide that the objects set out in the articles are to be construed as separate objects and are not limited by reference to any other clause or the name of the company[6], but such a provision does not operate to turn what is properly a power into an object in itself[7].

1 Under the Companies Act 2006, the objects of a company are unrestricted unless its articles of association specifically restrict them: see s 31; and PARA 239. This is a change from the situation that pertained under the Companies Act 1985 where a company was obliged to state its objects in the memorandum of association (the role of which has been altered fundamentally under the Companies Act 2006). The case law that is cited below and in PARA 256 derives from the time when the statement of a company's objects was a requirement. As to the meaning of 'company' under the Companies Acts see PARA 21; and as to the meaning of the 'Companies Acts' see PARA 13. As to the meaning of 'company' more generally see PARA 1. As to the meaning of references to 'articles' see PARA 227 note 2. As to articles of association generally see PARA 227 et seq.

2 As to the meaning of references to a company's constitution see PARA 226.

3 *Cotman v Brougham* [1918] AC 514, HL; *Pedlar v Road Block Gold Mines of India Ltd* [1905] 2 Ch 427. Cf *Stephens v Mysore Reefs (Kangundy) Mining Co Ltd* [1902] 1 Ch 745; *Re German Date Coffee Co* (1882) 20 ChD 169 at 188, CA, per Lindley LJ; *Re New Finance and Mortgage Co Ltd* [1975] Ch 420, [1975] 1 All ER 684 ('and merchants generally' covers all purely commercial occupations). The name of the company may be important in construing wide objects: see *Re Crown Bank* (1890) 44 ChD 634; *Re Coolgardie Consolidated Gold Mines Ltd* (1897) 76 LT 269, CA. See also *Re London and Edinburgh Shipping Co Ltd* 1909 SC 1, Ct of Sess; *Butler v Northern Territories Mines of Australia Ltd* (1906) 96 LT 41.

For some purposes, it is necessary to discover what is the main object of a company. This inquiry involves not merely the construction of the constitutional documents but also evidence on the further question of which activities have in fact been so far the main objects: *North of England Zoological Society v Chester RDC* [1959] 3 All ER 116, [1959] 1 WLR 773, CA.

4 See COMPANY AND PARTNERSHIP INSOLVENCY vol 16 (2011) PARA 398.

5 *Rolled Steel Products (Holdings) Ltd v British Steel Corpn* [1986] Ch 246, [1985] 3 All ER 52, CA; *Charterbridge Corpn Ltd v Lloyds Bank Ltd* [1970] Ch 62, [1969] 2 All ER 1185.

6 *Cotman v Brougham* [1918] AC 514, HL; *Anglo-Overseas Agencies Ltd v Green* [1961] 1 QB 1, [1960] 3 All ER 244.

7 *Re Introductions Ltd, Introductions Ltd v National Provincial Bank Ltd* [1970] Ch 199, [1969] 1 All ER 887, CA (where a clause conferring a power to borrow was held incapable of being a wholly independent object). Cf *Re Horsley & Weight Ltd* [1982] Ch 442, [1982] 3 All ER 1045, CA (where a provision of the memorandum relating to the granting of pensions was construed as an independent object of the company).

In the light of the statutory modifications of the ultra vires doctrine (see PARAS 239, 251–255, 258 et seq), the distinction between an object and a power, in that context, is irrelevant but it remains of importance to questions of directors exceeding their authority (see *Rolled Steel Products (Holdings) Ltd v British Steel Corpn* [1986] Ch 246, [1985] 3 All ER 52, CA), and to the statutory duty imposed on a director to act in the way he considers, in good faith, would be most likely to promote the success of the company for the benefit of its members as a whole (see the Companies Act 2006 s 172; and PARA 584).

258. Meaning of 'ultra vires'. The term 'ultra vires' in its proper sense denotes some act or transaction on the part of a corporation[1] which, although not unlawful or contrary to public policy if done by an individual, is yet beyond the corporation's legitimate powers as defined by the statute under which it is formed[2], or the statutes which are applicable to it, or by its constitution[3], although the scope of the ultra vires doctrine as it applies to companies and corporations is now restricted by statute[4]. The term is not appropriate in relation to any act or transaction which is beyond the lawful powers of any person. Thus the term is used in two senses:

(1) beyond the powers of the company; and
(2) beyond the powers of the directors[5] under the authority conferred on them by the company or its constitution[6].

Acts of directors which should not be undertaken by them without the sanction of the members[7] of the company are often described as acts ultra vires the directors[8]; and exercises by the directors of powers for purposes other than the promotion of the objects[9] of the company are also often denominated as being ultra vires[10].

1 As to companies and corporations see PARA 2.

2 As to the creation of corporations generally see CORPORATIONS vol 24 (2010) PARA 329 et seq.

3 As to the meaning of references to a company's constitution see PARA 226.

4 See PARAS 255, 263–264. Further, under the Companies Act 2006, the objects of a company are unrestricted unless its articles of association specifically restrict them: see s 31; and PARA 239.

5 As to a company's directors see PARA 512 et seq.

6 The term was also used in two different ways in relation exclusively to the powers of a company in *Rolled Steel Products (Holdings) Ltd v British Steel Corpn* [1982] Ch 478, [1982] 3 All ER 1057 per Vinelott J. On appeal, however, the Court of Appeal considered that such use of the term could lead to confusion and that the term should be confined rigidly to 'describing acts which are beyond the corporate capacity of a company': see *Rolled Steel Products (Holdings) Ltd v British Steel Corpn* [1986] Ch 246 at 297, [1985] 3 All ER 52 at 87, CA, per Slade LJ, and at 303 and 91 per Browne-Wilkinson LJ.

7 As to who qualifies as a member of a company see PARA 323.

8 As to a director's liability to the company for causing it to commit ultra vires acts see PARA 630. As to the personal liability of a director for any breach of duty in tort see PARA 633.

9 Under the Companies Act 2006, the objects of a company are unrestricted unless its articles of association specifically restrict them: see s 31; and PARA 239. As to the meaning of references to 'articles' see PARA 227 note 2. As to articles of association generally see PARA 227 et seq.

10 Directors are under a statutory duty to act in accordance with the company's constitution, and to only exercise powers for the purposes for which they are conferred: see the Companies Act 2006 s 171; and PARA 580.

259. Examples of ultra vires acts. Formerly, when the capacity of a company[1] was limited by the objects clause in the memorandum[2], and in the absence of a special power in the company's constitution[3], it was, for example, ultra vires[4]:

(1) for any company to take shares[5] in another carrying on a different class of business[6];

(2) for one company to amalgamate with another company[7];

(3) for a company which has power to invest on second mortgages, and which is a second mortgagee, to guarantee payment of the prior mortgage debt for good consideration[8];

(4) for a company with power to lend to guarantee the debts of a company promoted by it[9];

(5) unless first sanctioned[10], for a company to treat its former employees not merely generously but beyond all entitlement[11];

(6) for a company authorised by its constitution to make and deal in railway carriages to purchase a concession for a foreign railway[12];

(7) for a bill-broking company to take shares in a banking company for the purpose of increasing its own business[13]; and

(8) for a body dedicated to preventing cruelty to animals to pay money over to a political party whose aims include such an aim, but with no obligation to expend the money in any particular manner[14].

1 As to the meaning of 'company' under the Companies Acts see PARA 21; and as to the meaning of the 'Companies Acts' see PARA 13. As to the meaning of 'company' more generally see PARA 1.

2 As to a company's objects see PARA 239. Provisions that immediately before 1 October 2009 were contained in a company's memorandum but are not provisions of the kind mentioned in the Companies Act 2006 s 8 (see PARA 97) are to be treated after that date as provisions of the company's articles: see s 28(1); and PARA 227. See also PARA 256 et seq.

3 As to the meaning of references to a company's constitution see PARA 226.

4 This list is not exhaustive. As to the meaning of 'ultra vires' see PARA 258.

5 As to shares and a company's share capital see PARA 1231.

6 *Re Lands Allotment Co* [1894] 1 Ch 616, CA. As to the meaning of 'business' generally see PARA 1 note 1. Cf *Re Barned's Banking Co, ex p Contract Corpn* (1867) 3 Ch App 105 (where there was power in the company's memorandum). In the case of a banking company, no express power is required, as it is an inherent part of its business that it should advance money on securities such as shares: see *Re Asiatic Banking Corpn, Royal Bank of India's Case* (1869) 4 Ch App 252; *Re Financial Corpn, Goodson's Claim* (1880) 28 WR 760. In *Re William Thomas & Co* [1915] 1 Ch 325, a company with a power of amalgamating was held to have a power to sell part of its undertaking for shares, although apart from the power of amalgamating there was no other authority for it to hold shares in another company. As to accepting shares by way of compromise and not for investment see *Re Lands Allotment Co* [1894] 1 Ch 616, CA.

7 *Re European Society Arbitration Acts, ex p British Nation Life Assurance Association (Liquidators)* (1878) 8 ChD 679, CA. A power to amalgamate does not include a power to force partly paid shares on a member: *Re European Society Arbitration Acts, ex p British Nation Life Assurance Association (Liquidators)*. As to amalgamation generally see PARA 1614 et seq.

8 *Small v Smith* (1884) 10 App Cas 119, HL.

9 *Re Queen Anne and Garden Mansions Co* (1894) 1 Mans 460. As to the promotion of companies generally see PARA 42 et seq.

10 See PARA 1611.

11 *Parke v Daily News Ltd* [1962] Ch 927, [1962] 2 All ER 929. See, however, PARA 546.

12 *British and Foreign Railway Plant Co Ltd v Ashbury Carriage and Iron Co Ltd, Smith v Ashbury etc Co* (1869) 20 LT 360; *Ashbury Railway Carriage and Iron Co v Riche* (1875) LR 7 HL 653. See also *Guinness v Land Corpn of Ireland Ltd* (1882) 22 ChD 349, CA.

13 *Joint Stock Discount Co v Brown* (1866) LR 3 Eq 139 (subsequent proceedings (1869) LR 8 Eq 381). Cf *Re West of England Bank, ex p Booker* (1880) 14 ChD 317.

14 *Simmonds v Heffer* [1983] BCLC 298.

260. Examples of acts not ultra vires. Formerly, when the capacity of a company[1] was limited by the objects clause in the memorandum[2], it was not ultra vires[3] for a trading company[4], without any special powers to do so, to pay a pension to the family of a deceased officer[5]; or to give gratuities to its employees[6];

or to pay a loss not within the terms of a policy[7]; or to pay a reasonable brokerage for placing its shares[8]; or to let off a large part of a hotel for government offices[9]; or to take a larger house than necessary and underlet a portion[10]. A company established to buy a special brewery, but with general powers, may buy a different one, even though it will not have enough money left to buy the first[11]. A trading company may borrow, with or without security[12]; or accept bills of exchange[13]; or deposit its title deeds to secure an overdraft[14]; or issue debenture stock[15] as collateral security[16].

A company formed to work a patent may purchase it[17]. A company whose powers include that of promoting may promote another company, subscribe shares, and pay the expenses of the promotion[18]. A chemical company may distribute money to scientific institutions in the United Kingdom for the furtherance of scientific education and research[19]. A company formed for the development of salt concessions and the manufacture of salt may export salt[20].

In these and similar cases, it is a question dependent on the true construction of the company's constitution and all the circumstances of the case whether the proceeding in question will facilitate or is otherwise incidental to the business which the company was formed to carry on[21].

1 As to the meaning of 'company' under the Companies Acts see PARA 21; and as to the meaning of the 'Companies Acts' see PARA 13. As to the meaning of 'company' more generally see PARA 1.

2 As to a company's objects see PARA 239. Provisions that immediately before 1 October 2009 were contained in a company's memorandum but are not provisions of the kind mentioned in the Companies Act 2006 s 8 (see PARA 97) are to be treated after that date as provisions of the company's articles: see s 28(1); and PARA 227. See also PARA 256 et seq.

3 As to the meaning of 'ultra vires' see PARA 258.

4 Where a company is registered without the word 'limited' or words 'plc' but with limited liability, the power to give pensions depends on its constitution: *Cyclists' Touring Club v Hopkinson* [1910] 1 Ch 179. As to the meaning of references to a company's constitution see PARA 226.

5 *Henderson v Bank of Australasia* (1888) 40 ChD 170. Cf *Re Lee, Behrens & Co Ltd* [1932] 2 Ch 46, applied in *Re W & M Roith Ltd* [1967] 1 All ER 427, [1967] 1 WLR 432, but criticised in *Charterbridge Corpn Ltd v Lloyds Bank Ltd* [1970] Ch 62, [1969] 2 All ER 1185, and purportedly overruled in *Rolled Steel Products (Holdings) Ltd v British Steel Corpn* [1986] Ch 246, [1985] 3 All ER 52, CA.

6 *Hampson v Price's Patent Candle Co* (1876) 45 LJ Ch 437. Cf *Warren v Lambeth Waterworks* (1905) 21 TLR 685. See also *Re Birkbeck Permanent Benefit Building Society* [1913] 1 Ch 400.

7 *Taunton v Royal Insurance Co* (1864) 2 Hem & M 135. See also PARA 655.

8 *Metropolitan Coal Consumers' Association v Scrimgeour* [1895] 2 QB 604, CA. As to brokerage see PARA 1346. As to shares and a company's share capital see PARA 1231.

9 *Simpson v Westminster Palace Hotel Co* (1860) 8 HL Cas 712.

10 *Re London and Colonial Co, Horsey's Claim* (1868) LR 5 Eq 561.

11 *Syers v Brighton Brewery Co Ltd, Wright v Brighton Brewery Co Ltd* (1864) 11 LT 560. Cf *Re Langham Skating Rink Co* (1877) 5 ChD 669 at 685, CA, per Jessel MR.

12 As to a company's capacity to borrow see PARA 1442.

13 *Peruvian Rlys Co v Thames and Mersey Marine Insurance Co, Re Peruvian Rlys Co* (1867) 2 Ch App 617, distinguishing *Bateman v Mid-Wales Rly Co* (1866) LR 1 CP 499.

14 *Re Patent File Co, ex p Birmingham Banking Co* (1870) 6 Ch App 83.

15 As to the meaning of 'debenture' see PARA 1482; and as to the meaning of 'stock' see PARA 1351.

16 *Whitehaven Joint Stock Banking Co v Reed* (1886) 54 LT 360, CA.

17 *Re British and Foreign Cork Co, Leifchild's Case* (1865) LR 1 Eq 231.

18 *Butler v Northern Territories Mines of Australia Ltd* (1906) 96 LT 41; *Re Financial Corpn, Goodson's Claim* (1880) 28 WR 760. As to the promotion of companies generally see PARA 42 et seq.

19 *Evans v Brunner, Mond & Co Ltd* [1921] 1 Ch 359.

20 *Egyptian Salt and Soda Co Ltd v Port Said Association Ltd* [1931] AC 677, PC.

21 As to the meanings of 'carry on' and 'business' generally see PARA 1 note 1. A company may purchase land on a joint account (*London Financial Association v Kelk* (1884) 26 ChD 107); an insurance company may compromise claims (*Re Norwich Provident Insurance Society, Bath's Case* (1878) 8 ChD 334, CA); a banking company may be empowered to guarantee payment of interest on debentures in another company (*Re West of England Bank, ex p Booker*

(1880) 14 ChD 317); a company may be empowered to guarantee the debenture stock of another company (*Re Friary Holyroyd and Healy's Breweries Ltd* (1922) 67 Sol Jo 97, 126); a newspaper company may pay the cost of defending the editor in libel proceedings (*Breay v Royal British Nurses' Association* [1897] 2 Ch 272, CA); and a colliery company may purchase a colliery (*Re Baglan Hall Colliery Co* (1870) 5 Ch App 346; *Johns v Balfour* (1889) 5 TLR 389), or sell land to a builder for the erection of cottages (*Re Kingsbury Collieries Ltd and Moore's Contract* [1907] 2 Ch 259).

261. Failure to act in accordance with restricted objects. Any shareholder of a company[1] may bring proceedings to restrain the doing of an act that is beyond either the company's constitution[2] or the directors' powers[3].

If the directors act in breach of the constitution, the act may not be called into question on the grounds of a lack of capacity[4]. The breach of the constitution is a breach of the directors' duties[5] which may be ratified by an ordinary resolution of the members[6], although to authorise such acts in the future, an alteration to the articles by special resolution[7] is required[8]. The possibility of ratification is subject, in the case of ratification to relieve a director of the consequences of his action (rather than to affirm the transaction), to the statutory requirements as to voting on that ratification[9] and subject generally to the common law limits on ratification[10]. Even in the absence of ratification, the position of a person dealing with the company in good faith is protected by statute[11].

A corporation, in a matter within its powers, cannot be heard to deny a transaction to which all the shareholders have given their assent, even when such assent has been given in an informal manner, or by conduct, as distinct from a formal resolution at a duly convened meeting[12]. If shareholders require directors to make certain decisions, or approve the decisions which the directors have already taken, then such decisions become the acts of the company, and binding on it, so that thereafter it cannot sue its directors in negligence[13]. However, it is otherwise if the shareholders or directors are acting fraudulently[14].

1 As to shareholders and membership of companies generally see PARAS 323 et seq, 1889 et seq.

2 As to the meaning of references to a company's constitution under the Companies Act 2006 see PARA 226.

3 See the Companies Act 2006 s 40(4); and PARA 262. See also *Simpson v Westminster Palace Hotel Co* (1860) 8 HL Cas 712 at 717 per Lord Campbell LC. See also *Mosely v Koffyfontein Mines Ltd* [1911] 1 Ch 73, CA (affd sub nom *Koffyfontein Mines Ltd v Mosely* [1911] AC 409, HL). As to a company's directors see PARA 512 et seq.

4 This is the effect of the Companies Act 2006 s 39: see PARA 264.

5 See the Companies Act 2006 s 171; and PARA 580.

6 As to ordinary resolutions see PARA 685.

7 As to alterations in a company's articles of association by special resolution see PARA 231 et seq. As to special resolutions see PARA 686.

8 *Grant v United Kingdom Switchback Rlys Co* (1888) 40 ChD 135, CA. See also *Hogg v Cramphorn* [1967] Ch 254, [1966] 3 All ER 420; *Bamford v Bamford* [1970] Ch 212, [1968] 2 All ER 655; and PARA 277.

9 As to the ratification by a company of conduct by a director amounting to negligence, default, breach of duty or breach of trust in relation to the company, see the Companies Act 2006 s 239; and PARA 638. See also PARA 277.

10 Ie which have been retained by the Companies Act 2006 s 239(7) (see PARA 638). See also PARAS 654–655.

11 See the Companies Act 2006 s 40; and PARA 262.

12 *Walton v Bank of Nova Scotia* (1965) 52 DLR (2d) 506; *CPHC Holding Co Ltd v Western Pacific Trust Co* (1973) 36 DLR (3d) 431, BC SC; *Re Horsley & Weight Ltd* [1982] Ch 442, [1982] 3 All ER 1045, CA; *Multinational Gas and Petrochemical Co v Multinational Gas and Petrochemical Services Ltd* [1983] Ch 258, [1983] 2 All ER 563, CA.

13 *A-G for Canada v Standard Trust Co of New York* [1911] AC 498, PC; *Re Express Engineering Works Ltd* [1920] 1 Ch 466, CA; *Re Horsley & Weight Ltd* [1982] Ch 442, [1982] 3 All ER 1045, CA (where Cumming-Bruce LJ (at 455 and 1055) and Templeman LJ (at 456 and 1056) reserved their views on the situation where what had been done by the directors amounted to misfeasance).

14 *A-G's Reference (No 2 of 1982)* [1984] QB 624, [1984] 2 All ER 216, CA; applied in *Bilta (UK) Ltd (in liquidation) v Nazir* [2013] EWCA Civ 968, [2014] Ch 52, [2014] 1 All ER 168.

C. BINDING THE COMPANY

262. Powers of directors to bind the company. In favour of a person dealing with a company[1] in good faith, the power of the directors[2] to bind the company, or to authorise others to do so, is deemed to be free of any limitation under the company's constitution[3].

For these purposes:

(1) a person 'deals with' a company if he is a party to any transaction or other act to which the company is a party[4]; and

(2) a person dealing with a company:

(a) is not bound to inquire as to any limitation on the powers of the directors to bind the company or authorise others to do so[5];

(b) is presumed to have acted in good faith unless the contrary is proved[6]; and

(c) is not regarded as acting in bad faith by reason only of his knowing that an act is beyond the powers of the directors under the company's constitution[7].

These protections do not affect any right of a member of the company to bring proceedings to restrain the doing of an action that is beyond the powers of the directors[8]; but no such proceedings lie in respect of an act to be done in fulfilment of a legal obligation arising from a previous act of the company[9]. Nor do the statutory protections affect any liability incurred by the directors, or any other person, by reason of the directors' exceeding their powers[10].

1 As to the meaning of 'company' under the Companies Acts see PARA 21; and as to the meaning of the 'Companies Acts' see PARA 13.

2 As to the meaning of 'director' see PARA 512.

3 Companies Act 2006 s 40(1). The Companies Act 2006 s 40 has effect subject to s 41 (transactions with directors or their associates) (see PARA 263) and s 42 (charities) (see PARA 264): s 40(6). As to the meaning of references to a company's constitution see PARA 226. For these purposes, the references to limitations on the directors' powers under the company's constitution include limitations deriving:

(1) from a resolution of the company or of any class of shareholders (s 40(3)(a)); or

(2) from any agreement between the members of the company or of any class of shareholders (s 40(3)(b)).

As to resolutions of the company generally see PARA 684 et seq. As to shareholders and membership of companies generally see PARAS 323 et seq, 1889 et seq. As to classes of shares and the rights attached to classes of shares generally see PARA 1246 et seq. See also *Smith v Henniker-Major& Co (a firm)* [2002] EWCA Civ 762, [2003] Ch 182, [2002] 2 BCLC 655 (whether act of an inquorate board attracts the protection of the Companies Act 1985 s 35A (see now the Companies Act 2006 s 40)); *Ford v Polymer Vision Ltd* [2009] EWHC 945 (Ch), [2009] 2 BCLC 160 (on the difficulties of establishing bad faith where a meeting of directors which was quorate but not validly convened constituted a constitutional limitation under the Companies Act 2006 s 40).

Persons dealing with the company may also rely on the rule in *Royal British Bank v Turquand* (1856) 6 E & B 327, which provides that such persons are not obliged to inquire into the internal proceedings of a company but can assume that all acts of internal management had been properly carried out, save where an outsider knows or ought to know of a failure to adhere to procedures: see PARA 265.

The provisions of the Companies Act 2006 s 40 apply to unregistered companies by virtue of the Unregistered Companies Regulations 2009, SI 2009/2436, reg 3, Sch 1 para 3(a): see PARA 1857. As to the meaning of 'unregistered company' see PARA 1856.

4 Companies Act 2006 s 40(2)(a). See also note 3. As to a director as a 'person dealing with a company' see *Smith v Henniker-Major& Co (a firm)* [2002] EWCA Civ 762, [2003] Ch 182, [2002] 2 BCLC 655. However, the Companies Act 2006 s 40 is now qualified in s 40(6) (see note 3) so directors are governed by s 41 (transactions with directors or their associates) (see PARA 263) and not by s 40).A shareholder receiving bonus shares is not 'a person dealing with a

company' for these purposes: see *EIC Services Ltd v Phipps* [2004] EWCA Civ 1069, [2005] 1 All ER 338, [2005] 1 WLR 1377, [2004] 2 BCLC 589 (the Companies Act 1985 s 35A(1) (repealed; see now the Companies Act 2006 s 40(1)) contemplated a bilateral transaction between the company and the person dealing with the company or an act to which both were parties, such as would bind the company other than in good faith; such would not be the case where a bonus issue was made by a single resolution applicable to all shareholders) (reversing on this point *EIC Services Ltd v Phipps* [2003] EWHC 1507 (Ch), [2003] 3 All ER 804, [2003] 1 WLR 2360, [2004] 2 BCLC 589). See also *Cottrell v King* [2004] EWHC 397 (Ch), [2004] 2 BCLC 413 (it was not clear that the operation of a share transfer provision in the articles could amount to 'dealing' with the company for these purposes).

5 Companies Act 2006 s 40(2)(b)(i). See also notes 3, 7.

6 Companies Act 2006 s 40(2)(b)(ii). See also notes 3, 7. See *TCB Ltd v Gray* [1986] Ch 621, [1986] 1 All ER 587 (manner in which the company's seal is to be affixed; lack of good faith could not be presumed merely from failure to inquire); *Thompson v J Barke & Co (Caterers) Ltd* 1975 SLT 67, Ct of Sess (cheque drawn on company account by director for the purpose of paying off his private account; regularity of transaction suspect; other party put on inquiry); *Ford v Polymer Vision Ltd* [2009] EWHC 945 (Ch), [2009] 2 BCLC 160 (power in question has to be exercised for the purpose for which it was conferred; arguable that contract to dispose of company's assets to meet liabilities and indebtedness to claimant was proper exercise).

7 Companies Act 2006 s 40(2)(b)(iii). See also note 3.

In *Wrexham Association Football Club Ltd v Crucialmove Ltd* [2006] EWCA Civ 237, [2008] 1 BCLC 508, the dictum of Slade LJ in *Rolled Steel Products (Holdings) Ltd v British Steel Corpn* [1986] Ch 246 at 284, [1984] BCLC 466 at 498, CA, was applied to the Companies Act 1985 ss 35A, 35B (repealed; see now the Companies Act 2006 s 40) in holding that the statutory protections thereby afforded did not absolve a person dealing with a company from any duty to inquire whether the persons acting for the company were authorised by the board to enter into the transaction when the circumstances were such as to put that person on inquiry.

8 Companies Act 2006 s 40(4). See also note 3.

9 Companies Act 2006 s 40(4) proviso. See also note 3.

10 Companies Act 2006 s 40(5). See also note 3. As to directors' liabilities generally see para 599. Directors are under a statutory duty to act in accordance with the company's constitution, and to only exercise powers for the purposes for which they are conferred (see s 171; and para 580).

263. Transactions involving director or person connected with director. If, or to the extent that, the validity of a transaction[1] depends on the statutory protection[2] afforded a person dealing with the company[3] in good faith[4], then where:

(1) a company enters into such a transaction[5]; and

(2) the parties to the transaction include:

 (a) a director of the company[6] or of its holding company[7]; or

 (b) a person connected with any such director[8],

the transaction is voidable at the instance of the company[9].

Whether or not it is avoided, any such party to the transaction as is mentioned in head (2)(a) or head (2)(b) above, and any director of the company who authorised the transaction, is liable[10] to account to the company for any gain he has made directly or indirectly by the transaction[11], and to indemnify the company for any loss or damage resulting from the transaction[12].

The transaction ceases to be voidable if:

(i) restitution of any money or other asset which was the subject matter of the transaction is no longer possible[13]; or

(ii) the company is indemnified for any loss or damage resulting from the transaction[14]; or

(iii) rights acquired bona fide for value and without actual notice of the directors' exceeding their powers by a person who is not party to the transaction would be affected by the avoidance[15]; or

(iv) the transaction is affirmed by the company[16].

Nothing in these provisions[17] affects the rights of any party to the transaction not mentioned in head (2)(a) or head (2)(b) above[18]. The court may, however, on the application of the company or any such party, make an order affirming, severing or setting aside the transaction on such terms as appear to the court to be just[19].

1 For these purposes, 'transaction' includes any act: Companies Act 2006 s 41(7)(a).
2 Ie depends on the Companies Act 2006 s 40 (see PARA 262): see s 41(1).
3 As to the meaning of 'company' under the Companies Acts see PARA 21; and as to the meaning of the 'Companies Acts' see PARA 13.
4 See the Companies Act 2006 s 41(1). The provisions of s 41 apply to a transaction if or to the extent that its validity depends on s 40 (see PARA 262): see s 41(1). However, nothing in s 41 is to be read as excluding the operation of any other enactment or rule of law by virtue of which the transaction may be called in question or any liability of the company may arise: see s 41(1). As to the meaning of 'enactment' see PARA 13 note 16. See also *Smith v Henniker-Major & Co (a firm)* [2002] EWCA Civ 762 at [51], [2003] Ch 182, [2002] 2 BCLC 655 per Robert Walker LJ, at [109] per Carnwath LJ, and at [128] per Schiemann LJ.
The provisions of the Companies Act 2006 s 41 apply to unregistered companies by virtue of the Unregistered Companies Regulations 2009, SI 2009/2436, reg 3, Sch 1 para 3(b): see PARA 1857. As to the meaning of 'unregistered company' see PARA 1856.
5 Companies Act 2006 s 41(2)(a). See also note 4.
6 As to the meaning of 'director' see PARA 512.
7 Companies Act 2006 s 41(2)(b)(i). See also note 4. As to the meaning of 'holding company' see PARA 22.
8 Companies Act 2006 s 41(2)(b)(ii). For these purposes, the reference to a person connected with a director has the same meaning as in Pt 10 (ss 154–259) (see PARA 515): s 41(7)(b). See also note 4.
9 Companies Act 2006 s 41(2). See also note 4.
10 Companies Act 2006 s 41(3). A person other than a director of the company is not liable under s 41(3) if he shows that at the time the transaction was entered into he did not know that the directors were exceeding their powers: s 41(5). See also note 4.
11 Companies Act 2006 s 41(3)(a). See also note 4.
12 Companies Act 2006 s 41(3)(b). See also note 4.
13 Companies Act 2006 s 41(4)(a). See also note 4.
14 Companies Act 2006 s 41(4)(b). See also note 4.
15 Companies Act 2006 s 41(4)(c). See also note 4.
16 Companies Act 2006 s 41(4)(d). See also note 4.
17 Ie nothing in the Companies Act 2006 s 41(1)–(5) (see the text and notes 1–16): see s 41(6).
18 Companies Act 2006 s 41(6). See also note 4.
19 See the Companies Act 2006 s 41(6) proviso. See also note 4. In applying this power, it seems that the court is allowed a very wide and unfettered discretion: see *Re Torvale Group Ltd* [1999] 2 BCLC 605 (decided under the Companies Act 1985 s 322A(7) (repealed: see now the Companies Act 2006 s 41(6))).

264. Company's capacity not limited generally by its constitution; position with regard to charities. The validity of an act done by a company[1] may not be called into question on the ground of lack of capacity by reason of anything in the company's constitution[2].

However, this statutory protection applies to the acts of a company that is a charity only in favour of a person who:

(1) does not know at the time the act is done that the company is a charity[3]; or
(2) gives full consideration in money or money's worth in relation to the act in question and does not know, as the case may be, either that the act is not permitted by the company's constitution, or that the act is beyond the powers of the directors[4].

Where a company that is a charity purports to transfer or grant an interest in property, the fact that, as the case may be, either the act was not permitted by the company's constitution[5], or the directors in connection with the act exceeded any limitation on their powers under the company's constitution[6], does not affect the title of a person who subsequently acquires the property or any interest in it for full consideration without actual notice of any such circumstances affecting the validity of the company's act[7]. In any proceedings so arising[8], the burden of proving that a person knew that the company was a charity[9], or that a person knew that an act was not permitted by the company's constitution or was beyond the powers of the directors[10], lies on the person asserting that fact[11]. In the case of a company that is a charity, the affirmation of a transaction whose validity depends upon the power of the directors to bind the company, or to authorise others to do so, free of any limitation under the company's constitution[12] is ineffective without, in England and Wales[13], the prior written consent of the Charity Commission[14].

1 As to the meaning of 'company' under the Companies Acts see PARA 21; and as to the meaning of the 'Companies Acts' see PARA 13.

2 Companies Act 2006 s 39(1). As to the meaning of references to a company's constitution see PARA 226. The Companies Act 2006 s 39 has effect subject to s 42 (see the text and notes 3–14): s 39(2).

The provisions of the Companies Act 2006 ss 39, 42 apply to unregistered companies by virtue of the Unregistered Companies Regulations 2009, SI 2009/2436, reg 3, Sch 1 para 3(a), (c): see PARA 1857. As to the meaning of 'unregistered company' see PARA 1856.

3 Companies Act 2006 s 42(1)(a).

4 Companies Act 2006 s 42(1)(b). As to the meaning of 'director' see PARA 512. As to the powers of directors generally to bind the company see PARAS 262–263.

5 Companies Act 2006 s 42(2)(a).

6 Companies Act 2006 s 42(2)(b).

7 Companies Act 2006 s 42(2).

8 Ie in any proceedings arising out of the Companies Act 2006 s 42(1) (see the text and notes 3–4) or s 42(2) (see the text and notes 5–7): see s 42(3).

9 Companies Act 2006 s 42(3)(a).

10 Companies Act 2006 s 42(3)(b).

11 Companies Act 2006 s 42(3).

12 Ie a transaction to which the Companies Act 2006 s 41 (see PARA 263) applies: see s 42(4).

13 As to the meanings of 'England' and 'Wales' see PARA 1 note 5.

14 Companies Act 2006 s 42(4). As to the Charity Commission see CHARITIES vol 8 (2015) PARA 543 et seq.

265. Notice of company's constitution assumed. The doctrine of constructive notice means that persons contracting with a company, whether or not they are shareholders, are bound to know, or are precluded from denying that they know, the constitution of the company and its powers as given by statute and the constitution[1].

This doctrine of constructive notice of a company's registered documents is a purely negative one which does not operate against a company, but only in its favour[2]. Its effect, however, is now much modified by statute which provides that a person dealing in good faith with a company is not bound to inquire as to whether it is permitted by the company's constitution or as to any limitation on the powers of the directors to bind the company or authorise others to do so[3].

1 See *Re Barned's Banking Co, Peel's Case* (1867) 2 Ch App 674; *Re New Zealand Banking Corpn, Sewell's Case* (1868) 3 Ch App 131 at 140 per Lord Cairns LJ; *Re Bank of Hindustan, China and Japan, Campbell's Case* (1873) 9 Ch App 1; *Griffith v Paget* (1877) 6 ChD 511 at 517 per Jessel MR; *Oakbank Oil Co v Crum* (1882) 8 App Cas 65 at 70, HL, per Lord Selborne LC (as to shareholders). See *Ernest v Nicholls* (1857) 6 HL Cas 401 at 419 per Lord Wensleydale; *Mahony v East Holyford Mining Co* (1875) LR 7 HL 869 at 893 per Lord Chelmsford (as to outsiders). As to constructive notice in relation to companies generally see PARA 121. See also PARA 247. As to the meaning of references in the Companies Acts to a company's constitution see PARA 226.

2 *Houghton & Co v Nothard, Lowe and Wills Ltd* [1927] 1 KB 246, CA (affd [1928] AC 1, HL); *Rama Corpn Ltd v Proved Tin and General Investments Ltd* [1952] 2 QB 147, [1952] 1 All ER 554. As to the required registration of constitutional documents see PARA 104.

3 See the Companies Act 2006 s 40; and PARA 262.

266. Presumption as to matters of internal company management. Persons contracting with a company and dealing in good faith have always been entitled to assume that acts within its constitution and powers have been properly and duly performed[1], and were never bound to inquire whether acts of internal management have been regular[2]. This rule does not, however, apply to a director, or de facto director, who contracts with the company, as he should know the true position[3]. In any case, persons contracting with the company must take the articles of association in force to be those registered, and they are not entitled to assume that a special resolution has been passed pursuant to the articles, for that would have to be registered[4], and where the act is within the company's power only on the fulfilment of a statutory condition, persons dealing with the company are bound to ascertain whether the condition has been fulfilled[5]. An irregularity may be cured by a special article validating certain acts of the officers notwithstanding any irregularity[6]; but the particular act to be protected must on the face of it comply with the articles[7].

1 Cf *Rolled Steel Products (Holdings) Ltd v British Steel Corpn* [1986] Ch 246, [1985] 3 All ER 52, CA (where the dealing was not in good faith).

2 *Royal British Bank v Turquand* (1856) 6 E & B 327 (where a power to borrow could only be exercised with the sanction of a general meeting which had not been held). This statement in the text of the so-called 'rule in *Turquand's Case*' was cited with approval by Lord Simonds in *Morris v Kanssen* [1946] AC 459 at 474, [1946] 1 All ER 586 at 592, HL. See now the Companies Act 2006 ss 39–42; and PARAS 262–264. As to the interaction between the protection afforded by the Companies Act 2006 s 40 and the 'rule in *Turquand's Case*' see *Wrexham Association Football Club Ltd v Crucialmove Ltd* [2006] EWCA Civ 237, [2008] 1 BCLC 508.

See also *Landowners West of England and South Wales Land Drainage and Inclosure Co v Ashford* (1880) 16 ChD 411 (where the order of a statutory meeting was held to be directory only); *Heiton v Waverley Hydropathic Co* (1877) 4 R 830 (where the meeting had been irregularly summoned); *Agar v Athenaeum Life Assurance Society Official Manager* (1858) 3 CBNS 725; *Re Athenaeum Life Assurance Society, ex p Eagle Insurance Co* (1858) 4 K & J 549 (issue of debentures not duly authorised); *Prince of Wales Assurance Co v Harding* (1858) EB & E 183 (policies); *Re British Provident Life and Fire Assurance Society, Grady's Case* (1863) 1 De GJ & Sm 488 (no consent by a general meeting); *Reuter v Electric Telegraph Co* (1856) 6 E & B 341 (where an oral contract was upheld, the constitution requiring special formalities); *Bargate v Shortridge* (1855) 5 HL Cas 297 (irregular registration of transfer by directors); *GloucesterCounty Bank v Rudry Merthyr Steam and House Coal Colliery Co* [1895] 1 Ch 629, CA (mortgage executed at a board meeting of less than a quorum); *Cox v Dublin City Distillery (No 2)* [1915] 1 IR 345, CA; *Re Fireproof Doors Ltd, Umney v Fireproof Doors Ltd* [1916] 2 Ch 142 (debentures issued at a board meeting where there was an insufficient quorum); *Mahony v East Holyford Mining Co* (1875) LR 7 HL 869 at 893 per Lord Chelmsford (bankers honouring cheques signed by a self-appointed board); *Re County Life Assurance Co* (1870) 5 Ch App 288 at 293 per Giffard LJ (policy issued by de facto directors); *Montreal and St Lawrence Light and Power Co v Robert* [1906] AC 196, PC (contract made on a resolution of directors less than a quorum); *Re Bank of Syria, Owen and Ashworth's Claim, Whitworth's Claim* [1901] 1 Ch 115, CA (security given for debts in similar circumstances, following *Re Scottish Petroleum Co* (1883) 23 ChD 413, CA (allotment of shares)); *Duck v Tower Galvanizing Co* [1901] 2 KB 314 (debenture issued, although no directors had been appointed and no resolution of the company had been passed); *Gillies v Craigton Garage Co* 1935 SC 423, Ct of Sess (borrowing without sanction of a general meeting); *Freeman and Lockyer (a firm) v Buckhurst Park Properties (Mangal) Ltd* [1964] 2 QB 480, [1964] 1 All ER 630, CA (company bound by acts of person held out as managing director); *Hely-Hutchinson v Brayhead Ltd* [1968] 1 QB 549 at 584–585, [1967] 3 All ER 98 at 102–103 per Lord Denning MR (similar point); *Albert Gardens (Manly) Pty Ltd v Mercantile Credits Ltd* (1973) 9 ALR 653, Aust HC (security given by invalidly appointed directors); *IRC v Ufitec Group Ltd* [1977] 3 All ER 924 (company permitting chairman to continue negotiations estopped from denying his authority to contract). See also *Re David Payne & Co Ltd, Young v David Payne & Co Ltd* [1904] 2 Ch 608, CA; *Re Marseilles Extension Rly Co, ex p Crédit Foncier and Mobilier of England* (1871) 7 Ch App 161; *Totterdell v Fareham Blue Brick and Tile Co Ltd* (1866) LR 1 CP 674. As to bills of exchange see PARAS 291–294.

3 *Morris v Kanssen* [1946] AC 459, [1946] 1 All ER 586, HL (invalid allotment of shares to a de facto director). Cf *Hely-Hutchinson v Brayhead Ltd* [1968] 1 QB 549, [1967] 3 All ER 98, CA (director entitled to rely on managing director's ostensible authority). As to directors and de facto directors see PARA 512 et seq.

4 *Irvine v Union Bank of Australia* (1877) 2 App Cas 366, PC. As to articles of association generally see PARA 227 et seq. As to resolutions and decisions of the company generally see PARA 684 et seq.

5 *Pacific Coast Coal Mines Ltd v Arbuthnot* [1917] AC 607, PC.

6 As to the effect of defects in the appointment of directors or managers see PARA 520. As to an article validating acts notwithstanding such irregularity see PARA 520 note 6.

7 *Davies v R Bolton & Co* [1894] 3 Ch 678 at 688 per Vaughan Williams J.

267. Notice of irregularity of internal company management. Actual or constructive notice of an irregularity prevents a person contracting with the company obtaining the protection of the rule that the regularity of internal management may be relied on[1], except where he is claiming for value through another who had no notice[2]. A person does not obtain the protection of the rule where he was put on inquiry by the circumstances out of which the transaction with the company arose[3].

Further, the rule does not operate to protect a person who has accepted a document which is a forgery[4].

1 *Irvine v Union Bank of Australia* (1877) 2 App Cas 366, PC; *Wandsworth and Putney Gas-Light and Coke Co v Wright* (1870) 22 LT 404. Circumstances in which there is actual or constructive notice arise where a director is himself claiming (*Howard v Patent Ivory Manufacturing Co* (1888) 38 ChD 156 at 170 per Kay J; *Re Greymouth-Point Elizabeth Railway and Coal Co Ltd, Yuill v Greymouth-Point Elizabeth Railway and Coal Co Ltd* [1904] 1 Ch 32), although he is only a de facto director (*Morris v Kanssen* [1946] AC 459, [1946] 1 All ER 586, HL); where a copy of the articles was supplied to the creditor (*Davies v R Bolton & Co* [1894] 3 Ch 678); or where the company's solicitor was claiming (*Re General Provident Assurance Co Ltd* (1869) 38 LJ Ch 320). Cf *Hely-Hutchinson v Brayhead Ltd* [1968] 1 QB 549, [1967] 3 All ER 98, CA (director acting as an individual not in his capacity as a director; no notice). The employment by a woman of her husband as agent to apply for debentures has been held not to affect the woman with all the husband knew as a director: *Re Fireproof Doors Ltd, Umney v Fireproof Doors Ltd* [1916] 2 Ch 142. As to directors and de facto directors see PARA 512 et seq. As to the meaning of references to a company's 'articles' under the Companies Act 2006 see PARA 227 note 2. As to articles of association generally see PARA 227 et seq.

As to whether the fact that a person has actual notice of an internal irregularity may prevent him from taking advantage of the protection afforded persons dealing with the company in good faith under the Companies Act 2006 ss 39–42, modifying the common law 'ultra vires' rule (see PARAS 262–264), where the irregularity is not a limitation under the company's constitution for those purposes see *Smith v Henniker-Major& Co (a firm)* [2002] EWCA Civ 762, [2003] Ch 182, [2002] 2 BCLC 655; and PARA 262 note 3.

2 *Re Bank of Syria, Owen and Ashworth's Claim, Whitworth's Claim* [1901] 1 Ch 115, CA.

3 *AL Underwood Ltd v Bank of Liverpool and Martins* [1924] 1 KB 775; *Houghton & Co v Nothard, Lowe and Wills Ltd* [1927] 1 KB 246, CA (affd [1928] AC 1, HL, this point not being discussed); *B Liggett (Liverpool) Ltd v Barclays Bank Ltd* [1928] 1 KB 48.

4 *Kreditbank Cassel GmbH v Schenkers Ltd* [1927] 1 KB 826, CA (applying *Ruben v Great Fingall Consolidated* [1906] AC 439, HL); *South London Greyhound Racecourses Ltd v Wake* [1931] 1 Ch 496 (fact that board had not authorised affixing of the seal rendered certificate a forgery and a nullity). See further *Lovett v Carson Country Homes Ltd* [2009] EWHC 1143 (Ch), [2009] 2 BCLC 196 (company bound by debenture on which director's signature had been forged); but see also PARA 398.

(iii) Company Acting through Agents

268. How a company may act. A company[1], not being a physical person, may only act either by the resolution of its members[2], or by its agents[3]. It is not the agent of its members[4], and a member as such is not the agent of the company[5], the company being a separate entity or legal person apart from its members, who are not, even collectively, the company[6]. The legal position of a company, as so stated, must be regarded in relation to its contracts[7], to torts committed by it[8], and to such liabilities as regards acts which might bring it within the criminal law[9].

A company exists because there is a rule, usually in a statute, which says that an artificial person('persona ficta')is deemed to exist and to have certain powers, rights and duties of a natural person; and the company exercises these through natural persons as its agents, those acts being attributable to the company[10]. It also makes itself subject to the general rules by which liability for the acts of others can be attributed to natural persons, such as ostensible authority in contract and vicarious liability in tort[11].

1 As to the meaning of 'company' generally see PARA 1. As to the meaning of 'company' under the Companies Acts see PARA 21; and as to the meaning of the 'Companies Acts' see PARA 13.
2 As to resolutions of the company generally see PARA 684 et seq.
3 *Ferguson v Wilson* (1866) 2 Ch App 77 at 89 per Cairns LJ. As to a consideration of the position of a company's directors as agents of the company see PARA 270.
4 *Ferguson v Wilson* (1866) 2 Ch App 77 at 89 per Cairns LJ; *Salomon v A Salomon & Co Ltd* [1897] AC 22 at 31, HL, per Lord Halsbury LC, at 51 per Lord Macnaghten, and at 57 per Lord Davey.
5 *Oakes v Turquand and Harding* (1867) LR 2 HL 325 at 358 per Lord Cranworth.
6 *Re Exchange Banking Co, Flitcroft's Case* (1882) 21 ChD 519 at 536, CA, per Cotton LJ; *John Foster & Sons v IRC* [1894] 1 QB 516 at 528, CA, per Lindley LJ; *Society of Practical Knowledge v Abbott* (1840) 2 Beav 559 at 567 per Lord Langdale MR; *Re Sheffield and South Yorkshire Permanent Building Society* (1889) 22 QBD 470 at 476 per Cave J; *Farrar v Farrars Ltd* (1888) 40 ChD 395 at 410, CA, per Lindley LJ. See also PARA 115 text and note 16.
7 See PARAS 278–294.
8 See PARAS 298–301.
9 See PARA 313 et seq.
10 *Meridian Global Funds Management Asia Ltd v Securities Commission* [1995] 2 AC 500 at 506, [1995] 3 All ER 918 at 922–923, PC. See also *Odyssey Re (London) Ltd (formerly Sphere Drake Insurance plc) v OIC Run-Off Ltd (formerly Orion Insurance Co plc)* [2001] Lloyd's Rep IR 1, CA (fraudulent evidence given on behalf of company by natural person treated as evidence of company).
11 See note 10. As to an employer's vicarious liability in tort for the actions of an employee see TORT vol 97 (2015) PARA 767 et seq.

269. Appointment of agents by a company. The appointment of an agent by a company[1] need not be made under its corporate seal[2]; and it may employ an agent or employee to do ordinary services without a deed[3].

1 As to the meaning of 'company' generally see PARA 1. As to the meaning of 'company' under the Companies Acts see PARA 21; and as to the meaning of the 'Companies Acts' see PARA 13.
2 As to a company's seal see PARA 282.
3 See AGENCY vol 1 (2008) PARA 21; CORPORATIONS vol 24 (2010) PARA 323. As to the form of a company's contracts generally see PARA 281 et seq.

270. Directors' position as company's agents. A company's directors[1] are agents of the company[2]. Wherever an agent is liable, they are liable; and, where the liability would attach to the principal, and the principal only, the liability is the company's liability[3]. It does not follow that they are the only agents of the company; and they, or the company in general meeting where its powers in this respect are not exclusively vested in the directors, may appoint other agents of the company, by whose acts it will be bound[4]. For example, the secretary is able to bind the company in all administrative matters[5], and clerks in a company's registered office[6], in the absence of evidence to the contrary, are deemed to have authority during business hours in the absence of the secretary to receive notices on the company's behalf[7].

In practice, it is clear that in many companies most of the transactions are carried out by employees of the company, not by the directors; such employees will in most cases have actual authority to bind the company in the matters with which their employment is concerned. All agents are limited at all times by a requirement to act for the benefit of the principal[8].

1 As to a company's directors see PARA 512 et seq.
2 See PARA 584.
3 *Ferguson v Wilson* (1866) 2 Ch App 77 at 89–90 per Cairns LJ.
4 *Smith v Hull Glass Co* (1852) 11 CB 897. As to the authority of a secretary see PARA 672.
5 See PARA 672.
6 As to a company's registered office see PARA 124.
7 *Re Brewery Assets Corpn, Truman's Case* [1894] 3 Ch 272. See further PARA 127.
8 See eg *Criterion Properties v Stratford UK Properties* [2004] UKHL 28, [2004] 1 WLR 1846, [2006] 1 BCLC 729 (the test for determining whether the agreement was a valid and binding agreement, and therefore enforceable, turned solely on whether, applying the ordinary principles of agency, the directors who signed the agreement did so within the actual or apparent scope of their authority).

271. Exercise of powers delegated by company. Where there is a power of delegation to a committee of directors or a managing director, a person contracting with the company may assume that that power has been duly exercised[1]. Where there is a power of delegation to agents, a person is entitled to assume only that such powers as are within the ostensible authority of such an agent have been so delegated[2]; but where an agreement entered into by a director is unusual, a person contracting with the company through that director is put upon inquiry as to whether the necessary power has been delegated to that director[3]. A person who has only ostensible authority to do an act or make a representation cannot make a representation which may be relied upon as giving a further agent an ostensible authority which he would not otherwise have had[4].

Where a power of delegation has been exercised, the subsequent act of the agent within the scope of his authority is binding on the company as against the person with whom the company is contracting; but, if the power of delegation has not been exercised, a person is not entitled to rely on the supposed exercise of the power unless he actually knew of its existence, because there is no estoppel in such circumstances[5].

A company which has appointed a manager of its business is bound by contracts made by him in the usual course of the business, even though sufficient powers have not in fact been delegated to him; and, where goods are supplied to the order of unauthorised persons, the company is liable if the goods are received and used for the purposes of its trade[6].

1 *Biggerstaff v Rowatt's Wharf Ltd* [1896] 2 Ch 93, CA; *Re Fireproof Doors Ltd, Umney v Fireproof Doors Ltd* [1916] 2 Ch 142; *Clay Hill Brick and Tile Co Ltd v Rawlings* [1938] 4 All ER 100 (payment by valid cheque to managing director equivalent to payment in cash to company); *Hely-Hutchinson v Brayhead Ltd* [1968] 1 QB 549, [1967] 3 All ER 98, CA (act within managing director's ostensible authority). As to the importance, when entering into a contract on behalf of a company, of so stating in unmistakable terms, see *The Swan* [1968] 1 Lloyd's Rep 5; and AGENCY vol 1 (2008) PARA 156 et seq. As to delegation see generally AGENCY vol 1 (2008) PARA 48 et seq. As to statutory protections afforded a person dealing with the company in good faith see PARAS 255, 262 et seq. As to liability for contracts on the part of an agent see PARA 276.
2 *Kreditbank Cassel GmbH v Schenkers Ltd* [1927] 1 KB 826, CA; *British Thomson-Houston Co Ltd v Federated European Bank Ltd* [1932] 2 KB 176, CA; *Freeman and Lockyer (a firm) v Buckhurst Park Properties (Mangal) Ltd* [1964] 2 QB 480, [1964] 1 All ER 630, CA; *Hely-Hutchinson v Brayhead Ltd* [1968] 1 QB 549, [1967] 3 All ER 98, CA; *Armagas Ltd v Mundogas SA, The Ocean Forest* [1986] AC 717, [1986] 2 All ER 385, HL (no ostensible authority to make contract; no actual or ostensible authority to inform other party of alleged approval by board of company); *Hopkins v TL Dallas Group Ltd* [2004] EWHC 1379 (Ch), [2005] 1 BCLC 543 (agent acting fraudulently or in furtherance of his own interests nullifies actual authority, but not apparent authority). The grant of actual authority should be implied as

being subject to a condition that it is to be exercised honestly and on behalf of the principal: *Lysaght Bros & Co Ltd v Falk* (1905) 2 CLR 421; *Hopkins v TL Dallas Group Ltd*.

3 *Houghton & Co v Nothard, Lowe and Wills Ltd* [1927] 1 KB 246, CA (affd [1928] AC 1, HL, this point not being discussed); *Kreditbank Cassel GmbH v Schenkers Ltd* [1927] 1 KB 826, CA. See also *Rama Corpn Ltd v Proved Tin and General Investments Ltd* [1952] 2 QB 147, [1952] 1 All ER 554, which was a correct decision on its facts, but the suggestion of Slade J at 161 and 563 that the earlier cases were conflicting is not justified (see *Freeman and Lockyer (a firm) v Buckhurst Park Properties (Mangal) Ltd* [1964] 2 QB 480, [1964] 1 All ER 630, CA, at 493–494 and 638 per Willmer LJ, and at 508–509 and 647 per Diplock LJ).

4 *Crabtree-Vickers Pty Ltd v Australian Direct Mail Advertising and Addressing Co Pty Ltd* (1975) 7 ALR 527, Aust HC; *British Bank of the Middle East v Sun Life Assurance Co of Canada (UK) Ltd* [1983] 2 Lloyd's Rep 9, HL.

5 *Kreditbank Cassel GmbH v Schenkers Ltd* [1927] 1 KB 826, CA; *Houghton & Co v Nothard, Lowe and Wills Ltd* [1927] 1 KB 246 at 266, CA, per Sargant LJ. For reservations see *Houghton & Co v Nothard, Lowe and Wills Ltd* at 266 per Sargant LJ; *Rama Corpn Ltd v Proved Tin and General Investments Ltd* [1952] 2 QB 147, [1952] 1 All ER 554.

6 *Smith v Hull Glass Co* (1852) 11 CB 897. As to the meanings of 'trade' and 'business' generally see PARA 1 note 1.

272. Agent's liability for torts. An agent who commits a tort in the course of his employment is himself liable in damages to the full amount[1], and, if more than one agent, each agent is so liable[2]. This applies to a company's agent in the same way as to any person's agent; but one of two or more agents is not liable for the acts of the other or others unless he has expressly or impliedly authorised such acts[3].

Directors are not responsible to third persons for torts committed by sub-agents of the company properly appointed, unless they themselves committed or knowingly procured the commission of the tortious acts[4].

1 As to the liability of an agent for torts see AGENCY vol 1 (2008) PARA 164.

2 An officer of the company may be a joint tortfeasor with the company itself: *The Radiant* [1958] 2 Lloyd's Rep 596 (managing director aware of defects in equipment which contributed to accident); *C Evans & Sons Ltd v Spritebrand Ltd* [1985] 2 All ER 415, [1985] 1 WLR 317, CA. As to proceedings against and contributions between joint and several tortfeasors see the Civil Liability (Contribution) Act 1978; and TORT vol 97 (2015) PARA 450 et seq.

3 *Cargill v Bower* (1878) 10 ChD 502. See also AGENCY vol 1 (2008) PARA 28.

4 *Weir v Bell* (1878) 3 ExD 238, CA; *Betts v De Vitre* (1868) 3 Ch App 429 at 441, CA, per Lord Chelmsford LC; *Cargill v Bower* (1878) 10 ChD 502; *The Radiant* [1958] 2 Lloyd's Rep 596. See further AGENCY vol 1 (2008) PARAS 57–59, 150 et seq. As to directors' personal liability for breach of a duty in tort see PARA 633. As to the liability of directors for the torts of a company see PARA 630.

273. Position of company's agents. The agent of a company cannot normally obtain an injunction to prevent his discharge, since the court will not usually specifically enforce a contract of personal service; but he will be left to his claim for damages[1]. Agents of a company are in the position of agents of an individual, except that their principal is a corporate body and must act in accordance with its constitution[2]. An agent of a company has a right to be repaid the expenses incurred by him in the performance of his agency[3].

1 *Mair v Himalaya Tea Co* (1865) LR 1 Eq 411; *Johnson v Shrewsbury and Birmingham Rly Co* (1853) 3 De GM & G 914. See, however, *Hill v CA Parsons & Co Ltd* [1972] Ch 305, [1971] 3 All ER 1345, CA; and *CH Giles & Co Ltd v Morris* [1972] 1 All ER 960, [1972] 1 WLR 307 (specific performance of execution of service agreement). As to the discharge of directors, and a director's right to protest, see PARA 557.

2 *Imperial Hydropathic Hotel Co, Blackpool v Hampson* (1882) 23 ChD 1 at 13, CA, per Bowen LJ. As to the meaning of references to a company's constitution see PARA 226.

3 *Re Famatina Development Corpn Ltd* [1914] 2 Ch 271, CA. As to the expenses of defending criminal proceedings see *Tomlinson v Scottish Amalgamated Silks Ltd (Liquidators)* 1935 SC (HL) 1; and see AGENCY vol 1 (2008) PARA 111 et seq.

274. Admissions by agents of company. In cases of express authorisation, an admission by an agent of the company is an admission by the company itself, where the statement or act is made or done in the ordinary course of employment[1]. A statement made by a director to the shareholders at a general meeting is not an admission which may be used by a shareholder against the company, being a statement by the agent of the company and of the shareholders to his joint principals[2].

1 See AGENCY vol 1 (2008) PARA 136. See also *Lampson & Co v London and India Dock Joint Co* (1901) 17 TLR 663; *Simmons v London Joint Stock Bank* (1890) 62 LT 427; *Re Royal Bank of Australia, Meux's Executors' Case* (1852) 2 De GM & G 522 at 533 per Lord St Leonards LC; *Bruff v Great Northern Rly Co* (1858) 1 F & F 344. As to representations by agents generally see PARA 276.

2 *Re Devala Provident Gold Mining Co* (1883) 22 ChD 593; and see AGENCY vol 1 (2008) PARA 136.

275. Presumption that acts are properly performed. It is presumed in favour of third persons or members of the company that acts which are proved to have been performed have been properly performed, so that the burden of proving the contrary is thrown upon the company[1].

1 *Re North Hallenbeagle Mining Co, Knight's Case* (1867) 2 Ch App 321 (forfeiture of shares held to be valid although there was no proof of a directors' resolution to that effect); *Clarke v Imperial Gas Light and Coke Co* (1832) 4 B & Ad 315. See also *Re Fireproof Doors Ltd, Umney v Fireproof Doors Ltd* [1916] 2 Ch 142.

276. Respective liability for contracts on part of company and agent. A company is liable in respect of contracts made by its agents when acting within the scope of their authority, provided that the contract is within the company's powers[1], but not for acts or representations without that scope[2]. The question whether the act or representation was committed or made by the agent for his own benefit or for the benefit of the company is irrelevant[3]. Similarly, the company may be bound by the knowledge of, or notice given to, a subordinate official[4].

An agent may become liable on a contract made by him on behalf of a company if it is made in his own name and it does not appear from the document that he did not intend to contract as principal; and, where there is an ambiguity in this respect on the face of the document, parol evidence is admissible to explain it[5]. When an agent expressly contracts on behalf of his company or makes a contract in its name, he is not personally liable to the other contracting party in the absence of fraud or misrepresentation[6] unless he expressly or impliedly warrants an authority which he does not have or a state of facts which does not exist[7], in which case the contracting party has a remedy against him[8]. Thus borrowing by the directors is a warranty that they as directors, or the company, as the case may be, have or has power to borrow[9]. A director or other agent may, however, act in such a way as to expose himself to liability for breach of trust[10].

1 See AGENCY vol 1 (2008) PARA 121 et seq; CORPORATIONS vol 24 (2010) PARA 475. As to the limitations on a principal's liability in respect of contracts made by an agent see *Re International Contract Co, Pickering's Claim* (1871) 6 Ch App 525; and AGENCY vol 1 (2008) PARA 127 et seq. As to an analysis of this subject see *Meridian Global Funds Management Asia Ltd v Securities Commission* [1995] 2 AC 500 at 506, [1995] 3 All ER 918 at 922–923, PC.

2 *Kleinwort, Sons & Co v Associated Automatic Machine Corpn Ltd* (1934) 151 LT 1, HL; *George Whitechurch Ltd v Cavanagh* [1902] AC 117, HL (secretary falsely certifying transfers of shares); *Ruben v Great Fingall Consolidated* [1906] AC 439, HL (secretary issuing fraudulent certificates); *Shaw v Port Philip Colonial Gold Mining Co Ltd* (1884) 13 QBD 103. The effect of the first two cases in so far as they relate to certification of transfers was negatived by the Companies Act 1948 s 79 (repealed): see now the Companies Act 2006 s 775; and PARAS 416, 428. As to the exercise of delegated powers in making company contracts see PARA 271.

It is not within the scope of a manager's duties to make an unusual contract (*Re Cunningham & Co Ltd, Simpson's Claim* (1887) 36 ChD 532; *Houghton & Co v Nothard, Lowe and Wills Ltd*

[1927] 1 KB 246, CA (affd on other grounds [1928] AC 1, HL); cf *Re County Palatine Loan and Discount Co, Cartmell's Case* (1874) 9 Ch App 691); nor is it within the ostensible authority of a provincial manager of a bank to draw or indorse cheques (*Kreditbank Cassel GmbH v Schenkers Ltd* [1927] 1 KB 826, CA); nor is the resident agent of a mining company authorised to borrow money to pay wages, although warrants of distress have been issued (*Hawtayne v Bourne* (1841) 7 M & W 595); nor may a local agent grant a policy (*Linford v Provincial Horse and Cattle Insurance Co* (1864) 34 Beav 291); nor is it within the scope of a secretary's duties to make representations as to the financial arrangements of a company with its contractors (*Barnett v South London Tramways Co* (1887) 18 QBD 815, CA) or to make false statements to induce an investor to take shares (*Newlands v National Employers' Accident Association Ltd* (1885) 54 LJQB 428, CA). See further AGENCY vol 1 (2008) PARA 124.

3 *Lloyd v Grace, Smith & Co* [1912] AC 716, HL, which overruled many dicta to the effect that the act or representation had to be committed for the benefit of the principal (see also PARA 297 note 4).

4 *Evans v Employers' Mutual Insurance Association Ltd* [1936] 1 KB 505. As to notice of assignments see CHOSES IN ACTION vol 13 (2009) PARA 72.

5 *McCollin v Gilpin* (1881) 6 QBD 516, CA; *Re International Contract Co, Pickering's Claim* (1871) 6 Ch App 525. See also AGENCY vol 1 (2008) PARA 156 et seq.

6 *Godwin v Francis* (1870) LR 5 CP 295 (misrepresentation of authority); *Chapman v Smethurst* [1909] 1 KB 927, CA (promissory note); *Premier Industrial Bank Ltd v Carlton Manufacturing Co Ltd and Crabtree Ltd* [1909] 1 KB 106; *Landes v Marcus and Davids* (1909) 25 TLR 478; *HB Etlin & Co v Asselstyne* (1962) 34 DLR (2d) 191, Ont CA; *Elkington & Co v Hürter* [1892] 2 Ch 452; *Ferguson v Wilson* (1866) 2 Ch App 77; *Gadd v Houghton* (1876) 1 ExD 357, CA; *Bondina Ltd v Rollaway Shower Blinds Ltd* [1986] 1 All ER 564, [1986] 1 WLR 517, CA. See also AGENCY vol 1 (2008) PARA 142.

7 *Collen v Wright* (1857) 8 E & B 647, Ex Ch. See also AGENCY vol 1 (2008) PARA 160. Directors are liable on bills accepted by them for the company without authority: *West London Commercial Bank Ltd v Kitson* (1884) 13 QBD 360, CA; and see PARA 294. See also *ING Re (UK) Ltd v R&V Versicherung AG*, sub nom *ING Re (UK) Ltd v R* [2006] EWHC 1544 (Comm), [2006] 2 All ER (Comm) 870, [2007] 1 BCLC 108 (claimant had entered into contract in mistaken belief that defendant had assigned authority to act on its behalf).

8 See note 7.

9 *Chapleo v Brunswick Permanent Building Society* (1881) 6 QBD 696, CA; *Richardson v Williamson and Lawson* (1871) LR 6 QB 276; *Looker v Wrigley* (1882) 9 QBD 397; *Whitehaven Joint Stock Banking Co v Reed* (1886) 54 LT 360, CA. See also *Contex Drouzhba Ltd v Wiseman* [2007] EWCA Civ 1201, [2008] 1 BCLC 631 (affg [2006] EWHC 2708 (QB), [2007] 1 BCLC 758) (not every contact signed by a director would contain implied representations by the director but a director signing for a company might be making an implied representation about the ability of the company to pay since by promising terms of payment there was, by implication, a representation that the company had the capacity to meet the payment terms; if that was so, there might be situations in which, by the signing of contracts by directors, where those directors were guilty of fraudulent trading, the creditors might have a direct remedy against the director in deceit).

10 *Wilson v Lord Bury* (1880) 5 QBD 518, CA.

277. Ratification of agents' acts. A company cannot confirm or ratify anything which is beyond the powers conferred by statute[1]. At common law, it was not possible for a company to ratify an ultra vires transaction, in the sense of an act beyond the capacity of the company as expressed or implied in the company's constitution[2]. It is possible for a company to ratify conduct by a director[3] amounting to negligence, default, breach of duty or breach of trust in relation to the company if the decision to ratify such conduct is duly made by resolution of the members of the company[4].

A transaction by the directors which is beyond their own powers but within the company's powers may be ratified by a resolution of the company or even by acquiescence, provided the shareholders have knowledge of the facts relating to the transaction to be ratified or the means of knowledge are available to them[5].

By resolution at a subsequent meeting, a company may ratify any business which it has purported to transact at a meeting informally called[6]. Such a ratification will not be implied merely from the fact that the shareholders have seen and passed without comment the balance sheet or formal documents[7], but it may be implied from acquiescence[8]. A contract entered into by directors at a meeting irregularly constituted may be ratified at a subsequent duly constituted meeting, and is sufficiently ratified by proceedings being brought by the company to enforce it[9]. A company may ratify the institution and conduct of litigation commenced in its name without proper authority, but, until ratified, the proceedings may be stayed[10].

1 See PARA 251 et seq.

2 *Oakbank Oil Co v Crum* (1882) 8 App Cas 65 at 71, HL, per Lord Selborne LC; *Ashbury Railway Carriage and Iron Co v Riche* (1875) LR 7 HL 653 at 668 per Lord Cairns LC; *Preston v Liverpool, Manchester and Newcastle-upon-Tyne Junction Rly Co (Proprietors)* (1856) 5 HL Cas 605; *Athy Guardians v Murphy* [1896] 1 IR 65; *James v Eve* (1873) LR 6 HL 335; *Re Empress Engineering Co* (1880) 16 ChD 125, CA; *Re Exchange Banking Co, Flitcroft's Case* (1882) 21 ChD 519, CA; *Re Dale and Plant Ltd* (1889) 43 ChD 255; *Mann and Beattie v Edinburgh Northern Tramways Co* [1893] AC 69, HL. As to the meaning of 'ultra vires' see PARA 258. As to the meaning of references to a company's constitution see PARA 226.

3 As to a company's directors see PARA 512 et seq.

4 See the Companies Act 2006 s 239; and PARA 638. As to company resolutions and decisions generally see PARA 684 et seq. As to membership of a company see PARA 323 et seq. A director is under a statutory duty not only to act in accordance with the company's constitution and to only exercise powers for the purposes for which they are conferred (see s 171; and PARA 580 et seq) but also to exercise reasonable care, skill and diligence (see s 174; and PARA 588).

5 *Grant v United Kingdom Switchback Rlys Co* (1888) 40 ChD 135, CA; *Irvine v Union Bank of Australia* (1877) 2 App Cas 366, PC. See also *Srimati Premila Devi v Peoples Bank of Northern India Ltd* [1938] 4 All ER 337, PC; *Bamford v Bamford* [1970] Ch 212, [1969] 1 All ER 969, CA (issue of shares voidable on assumption of improper motives in directors ratified by company in general meeting after full and frank disclosure); *Baillie v Oriental Telephone and Electric Co Ltd* [1915] 1 Ch 503, CA (insufficient notice of effect of resolution to ratify irregular payment of remuneration); *Re Bank of Hindustan, China and Japan, Campbell's Case* (1873) 9 Ch App 1 (irregular amalgamation); *Sewell's Case* (1868) 3 Ch App 131; *Re London and New York Investment Corpn* [1895] 2 Ch 860 (increase of capital, made without the previous sanction of a resolution required by the articles, validated by a subsequent resolution); *Phosphate of Lime Co v Green* (1871) LR 7 CP 43 (what is a sufficient intimation to shareholders); *Spackman v Evans* (1868) LR 3 HL 171; *Houldsworth v Evans* (1868) LR 3 HL 263; *Re Republic of Bolivia Exploration Syndicate Ltd* [1914] 1 Ch 139 at 176 per Astbury J (approving of balance sheet). Cf *Re Railway and General Light Improvement Co, Marzetti's Case* (1880) 42 LT 206, CA. See also *Imperial Mercantile Credit Association (Liquidators) v Coleman* (1873) LR 6 HL 189; *London Financial Association v Kelk* (1884) 26 ChD 107 at 152 per Bacon V-C; and PARA 575. As to ratification after repudiation by the other party see AGENCY vol 1 (2008) PARA 66. A contract entered into by an agent in his own name and without authority cannot be ratified: *Keighley, Maxsted & Co v Durant* [1901] AC 240, HL. As to ratification generally see AGENCY vol 1 (2008) PARA 57 et seq.

6 *Briton Medical, General and Life Association v Jones (No 2)* (1889) 61 LT 384. It is possible that ratification may be effected by the individual consents of all the shareholders without a meeting: see PARA 738.

7 *Blackburn and District Benefit Building Society v Cunliffe, Brooks & Co* (1885) 29 ChD 902, CA.

8 *London Financial Association v Kelk* (1884) 26 ChD 107; *Evans v Smallcombe* (1868) LR 3 HL 249. See also *Maclae v Sutherland* (1854) 3 E & B 1; *Re Magdalena Steam Navigation Co* (1860) John 690; *Phosphate of Lime Co v Green* (1871) LR 7 CP 43; *Reuter v Electric Telegraph Co* (1856) 6 E & B 341.

9 *Re Portuguese Consolidated Copper Mines Ltd, ex p Badman, ex p Bosanquet* (1890) 45 ChD 16 at 26–27, CA, per Cotton LJ. See also *Re Land Credit Co of Ireland, ex p Overend, Gurney & Co* (1869) 4 Ch App 460 at 473 per Giffard LJ (not necessary for the directors to pass any resolution in order to make the acceptance of bills binding on the company); *Re State of Wyoming Syndicate* [1901] 2 Ch 431.

10 *Danish Mercantile Co Ltd v Beaumont* [1951] Ch 680, [1951] 1 All ER 925, CA (proceedings a nullity until ratified), approved in *Alexander Ward & Co Ltd v Samyang Navigation Co Ltd* [1975] 2 All ER 424, [1975] 1 WLR 673, HL (company without directors; two individuals brought proceedings on company's behalf to recover debt without authority; acts of individuals

subsequently ratified by liquidator). See also *Airways Ltd v Bowen* [1985] BCLC 355, CA. As to a solicitor's liability for costs where he institutes proceedings without authority see LEGAL PROFESSIONS vol 66 (2015) PARA 660.

(iv) Company Contracts

A. CONTRACTS BEFORE INCORPORATION OR COMMENCEMENT OF BUSINESS

278. Pre-incorporation contracts. A company is not bound by contracts purporting to be entered into on its behalf by its promoters or other persons before its incorporation[1]. After incorporation, it cannot ratify or adopt any such contract because in such cases there is no agency and the contract is that of the parties making it[2]. The adoption and confirmation by a directors' resolution of a contract made before the incorporation of the company by persons purporting to act on its behalf does not create any contractual relation between it and the other party to the contract, or impose any obligation on it towards him[3].

The principle that there is no agency before the company is incorporated does not apply where a company, awaiting a certificate of incorporation on change of name[4], purports to contract in the new name; in such a case no personal liability attaches to a director for contracts authorised by him or made by him on behalf of the company in the new name[5].

1 See PARA 56; *FJ Neale (Glasgow) Ltd v Vickery* 1973 SLT (Sh Ct) 88 (new company formed with same name as old company and taking over assets and goodwill not liable on old company's contracts). The person purporting to enter into such a contract is personally liable upon it: *Kelner v Baxter* (1866) LR 2 CP 174; *Wilson & Co v Baker, Lees & Co* (1901) 17 TLR 473. A contract which purports to be made by or on behalf of a company at a time when the company has not been formed has effect, subject to any agreement to the contrary, as one made with the person purporting to act for the company or as agent for it; and he is personally liable on the contract accordingly: see the Companies Act 2006 s 51 (cited in PARA 59); and the Overseas Companies (Execution of Documents and Registration of Charges) Regulations 2009, SI 2009/1917, reg 6. See also *Phonogram Ltd v Lane* [1982] QB 938, [1981] 3 All ER 182, CA. A contract cannot purport to be made on behalf of a company not yet formed if no one had thought of the new company at the time of contracting: *Cotronic (UK) Ltd v Dezonie* [1991] BCLC 721, CA (parties contracted with first company which in fact had been struck off the register and dissolved and, when this was discovered years later, a second company was incorporated; it was impossible to say that the contract purported to be made by or on behalf of the second company). The person actually issuing an invoice showing chargeable VAT is liable for that amount if he issues such invoices in the name of a company before its incorporation: *Customs and Excise Comrs v Wells* [1982] 1 All ER 920. A solicitor who prepares a company's constitutional documents cannot recover his costs for doing so from the company when it is incorporated (*Re English and Colonial Produce Co Ltd* [1906] 2 Ch 435, CA); or even the fees required to be paid on the registration of the company (*Re National Motor Mail-Coach Co Ltd, Clinton's Claim* [1908] 2 Ch 515, CA, overruling the decision of Buckley J in *Re English and Colonial Produce Co Ltd* [1906] 2 Ch 435 at 439, which was not appealed against on this point). See also *Smith v Brown* [1896] AC 614, PC.

2 *Kelner v Baxter* (1866) LR 2 CP 174; *Scott v Lord Ebury* (1867) LR 2 CP 255; *Re Northumberland Avenue Hotel Co* (1886) 33 ChD 16, CA; *Re Dale and Plant Ltd* (1889) 61 LT 206; *Falcke v Scottish Imperial Insurance Co* (1886) 34 ChD 234 at 249, CA, per Bowen LJ; *Natal Land and Colonization Co v Pauline Colliery and Development Syndicate* [1904] AC 120, PC; *Bagot Pneumatic Tyre Co v Clipper Pneumatic Tyre Co* [1901] 1 Ch 196 (affd [1902] 1 Ch 146, CA); *North Sydney Investment and Tramway Co v Higgins* [1899] AC 263 at 721, PC; *Bridgetown Co-operative Society v Whelan* [1917] 2 IR 39. See also AGENCY vol 1 (2008) PARA 61.

3 *North Sydney Investment and Tramway Co v Higgins* [1899] AC 263, PC; *Re Johannesburg Hotel Co, ex p Zoutpansberg Prospecting Co* [1891] 1 Ch 119 at 128, CA, per Lord Halsbury LC.

4 As to change of a company's name generally see PARAS 216–218.

5 *Oshkosh B'Gosh Inc v Dan Marbel Inc Ltd* [1989] 1 CMLR 94, [1989] BCLC 507, CA.

279. Adoption of pre-incorporation contracts. In order that the company may be bound by agreements entered into before its incorporation, there must be a new contract to the effect of the previous agreement[1]; although this new contract may be inferred from the company's acts when incorporated[2], except where such acts are done in the mistaken belief that the agreement is binding[3].

If the company has notice of a contract made before its incorporation between the persons under whom it claims property of which it takes possession and a former owner of the property, whereby a charge or incumbrance was imposed on the property, the company takes subject to the charge or incumbrance, although it is not liable to be sued for breach of the contract[4].

It is the duty of directors of a company which is formed to adopt and enter into a contract to make careful and full inquiries before finally committing the company to it and to act as prudent men of affairs would in their own business[5].

1 *Melhado v Porto Alegre Rly Co* (1874) LR 9 CP 503; *Re Hereford and South Wales Waggon and Engineering Co* (1876) 2 ChD 621, CA; *Re Empress Engineering Co* (1880) 16 ChD 125 at 128, CA, per Jessel MR (and see at 130 per James LJ, criticising *Spiller v Paris Skating Rink Co* (1878) 7 ChD 368); *Re Rotherham Alum and Chemical Co* (1883) 25 ChD 103, CA; *Tinnevelly Sugar Refining Co Ltd v Mirrlees, Watson and Varyan Co Ltd* (1894) 31 SLR 823. Cf *Hutchison v Surrey Consumers Gaslight and Coke Association* (1851) 11 CB 689; *Payne v New South Wales Coal and Intercolonial Steam Navigation Co* (1854) 10 Exch 283; *Kelner v Baxter* (1866) LR 2 CP 174; *Natal Land and Colonization Co v Pauline Colliery and Development Syndicate* [1904] AC 120, PC.

2 *Re Empress Engineering Co* (1880) 16 ChD 125 at 128, CA, per Jessel MR; *Re Rotherham Alum and Chemical Co* (1883) 25 ChD 103, CA; *Howard v Patent Ivory Manufacturing Co, Re Patent Ivory Manufacturing Co* (1888) 38 ChD 156. See also *Browning v Great Central Mining Co* (1860) 5 H & N 856; *Touche v Metropolitan Railway Warehousing Co* (1871) 6 Ch App 671 (and as to this case see *Gandy v Gandy* (1885) 30 ChD 57 at 67, CA, per Cotton LJ).

3 *Re Northumberland Avenue Hotel Co* (1886) 33 ChD 16, CA; *Bagot Pneumatic Tyre Co v Clipper Pneumatic Tyre Co* [1901] 1 Ch 196 at 203 per Kekewich J (affd [1902] 1 Ch 146, CA).

4 *Werderman v Société Générale d'Electricité* (1881) 19 ChD 246, CA, as explained in *Bagot Pneumatic Tyre Co v Clipper Pneumatic Tyre Co* [1902] 1 Ch 146 at 157, CA, per Vaughan Williams LJ. It may be, however, that the original assignor might succeed by suing in the name of the intermediate assignee: *Werderman v Société Générale d'Electricité* (1881) 19 ChD 246, CA, as explained in *Bagot Pneumatic Tyre Co v Clipper Pneumatic Tyre Co* [1902] 1 Ch 146 at 161–162, CA, per Romer LJ. As to lien see *Gifford v Mashonaland Development Co (Willoughby's) Ltd* (1902) 18 TLR 274, HL; and see generally LIEN.

5 See *Overend, Gurney & Co v Gibb and Gibb* (1872) LR 5 HL 480; *Twycross v Grant* (1877) 2 CPD 469 at 494, CA, per Bramwell LJ. As to the disclosures to be made to the company as regards profit and other matters see PARA 53. A director is under a statutory duty (amongst others) to exercise reasonable care, skill and diligence in relation to the company's affairs: see the Companies Act 2006 s 174; and PARA 588.

280. Contracts made before company entitled to commence business. A company[1] that is a public company[2] must not do business[3] or exercise any borrowing powers[4] unless the registrar of companies[5] has issued it with a certificate (a 'trading certificate') entitling it to do so[6].

Any contract made by a company before the issue of the registrar's certificate is, nevertheless, not invalid on that account[7]. If, however, the company fails to comply with its obligations under any such contract within 21 days from being called upon to do so, the directors[8] of the company are jointly and severally liable to indemnify any other party to the transaction in respect of any loss or damage suffered by him by reason of the company's failure to comply with its obligations[9].

1 As to the meaning of 'company' under the Companies Acts see PARA 21; and as to the meaning of the 'Companies Acts' see PARA 13.

2 Ie a company that is registered as a public company on its original incorporation rather than by virtue of its re-registration as a public company: see the Companies Act 2006 s 761(1); and PARA 67. As to incorporation by registration under the Companies Act 2006 see PARA 104 et seq; and as to the re-registration of a private company as a public company under the Companies Act 2006 see PARAS 168–172. As to the meanings of 'private company' and 'public company' see PARA 95. See also PARAS 65–66.

3 As to the meaning of 'business' generally see PARA 1 note 1.

4 As to a company's borrowing powers see PARA 1442 et seq.
5 As to the meaning of 'registrar of companies' see PARA 126 note 2.
6 See the Companies Act 2006 s 761(2); and PARA 67. As to the meaning of 'trading certificate' see PARA 67.
7 See the Companies Act 2006 s 767(3); and PARAS 69, 635. However, if a company does business or exercises borrowing powers in contravention of s 761 (see PARA 67), an offence is committed by the company, and by any officer of it who is in default: see s 767(1), (2); and PARA 67. As to the meaning of 'officer' see PARA 679; and as to the meaning of 'officer in default' see PARA 316.
8 As to a company's directors see PARA 512 et seq.
9 See the Companies Act 2006 s 767(3); and PARAS 69, 635. The directors who are so liable are those who were directors at the time the company entered into the transaction: see s 767(4); and PARAS 69, 1449.

B. FORM OF COMPANY CONTRACT; AUTHENTICATION OF DOCUMENTS

281. Form of company contracts. Under the law of England and Wales[1] a contract may be made[2]:

(1) by a company[3], by writing under its common seal[4]; or
(2) on behalf of a company, by any person acting under its authority, express or implied[5];

and any formalities required by law in the case of a contract made by an individual also apply, unless a contrary intention appears, to a contract made by or on behalf of a company[6].

Contracts may be validly made between companies on a Sunday[7].

1 As to the meanings of 'England' and 'Wales' see PARA 1 note 5.
2 Companies Act 2006 s 43(1).
The Secretary of State has made provision by regulations (see the Companies Act 2006 s 1045; and PARA 2014) applying s 43 to overseas companies, but with modifications: see the Overseas Companies (Execution of Documents and Registration of Charges) Regulations 2009, SI 2009/1917, reg 4. As to the meaning of 'overseas company' see PARA 2013. The provisions of the Companies Act 2006 s 43 apply also to unregistered companies by virtue of the Unregistered Companies Regulations 2009, SI 2009/2436, Sch 1 para 3(d): see PARA 1857. As to the meaning of 'unregistered company' see PARA 1856.
3 As to the meaning of 'company' under the Companies Acts see PARA 21; and as to the meaning of the 'Companies Acts' see PARA 13.
4 Companies Act 2006 s 43(1)(a). See also note 2. A company may have a common seal, but need not have one: see s 45; and PARA 282. As to contracts under seal see further PARA 286; and DEEDS AND OTHER INSTRUMENTS vol 32 (2012) PARA 210 et seq; and as to written contracts see PARA 283.
5 Companies Act 2006 s 43(1)(b). See also note 2.
6 Companies Act 2006 s 43(2). See also note 2. See also PARA 59 note 2. As to the name of the company being engraved on its seal see PARA 220. As to appointing an attorney to execute deeds see PARA 288. As to the company's power to have an official seal for use abroad see PARA 289. As to execution of deeds by corporations generally see CORPORATIONS vol 24 (2010) PARA 463 et seq. See also DEEDS AND OTHER INSTRUMENTS vol 32 (2012) PARA 240 et seq.
7 *Rolloswin Investments Ltd v Chromolit Portugal Cutelarias e Produtos Metálicos SARL* [1970] 2 All ER 673, [1970] 1 WLR 912. See also TIME vol 97 (2015) PARA 324 et seq.

282. Company seal. A company[1] may have a common seal[2], but need not have one[3].

A company which has a common seal must have its name[4] engraved in legible characters on the seal[5]. If a company fails to comply with this requirement[6], an offence is committed by the company, and by every officer of the company who is in default[7]. An officer of a company, or a person acting on behalf of a company, also commits an offence if he uses, or authorises the use of, a seal purporting to be a seal of the company on which its name is not engraved as so required[8]. A person guilty of either such offence[9] is liable on summary conviction to a fine not exceeding level 3 on the standard scale[10].

Under the model articles of association[11], any common seal may only be used by the authority of the directors[12], who may decide by what means and in what form any common seal is to be used[13]. Unless otherwise decided by the directors, if the company has a common seal and it is affixed to a document, the document must also be signed by at least one authorised person[14] in the presence of a witness who attests the signature[15].

Where the company is a public company, the directors also may decide under the model articles by what means and in what form any securities seal is to be used[16]; and if the company has a securities seal, it may only be affixed to securities by the company secretary or a person authorised to apply it to securities by the company secretary[17]. If a public company has an official seal for use abroad, it may only be affixed to a document if its use on that document, or documents of a class to which it belongs, has been authorised by a decision of the directors[18].

1 As to the meaning of 'company' under the Companies Acts see PARA 21; and as to the meaning of the 'Companies Acts' see PARA 13.

2 As to the use of the company's seal for making company contracts see PARA 281; for use in the execution of documents see PARA 287; for use outside the United Kingdom see PARA 289; and for use for sealing securities issued by the company, or for sealing documents creating or evidencing securities so issued, see PARA 290. As to the appointment of an attorney to execute deeds see PARA 288. See also PARAS 269, 286.

3 Companies Act 2006 s 45(1).

The Secretary of State may make provision by regulations applying the Companies Act 2006 ss 43–52 (see PARAS 281, 283 et seq) to overseas companies, subject to such exceptions, adaptations or modifications as may be specified in the regulations: see s 1045; and PARA 2014. However, at the date at which this volume states the law, no such provision had been made in relation to s 45.

The provisions of the Companies Act 2006 s 45(1) apply to unregistered companies by virtue of the Unregistered Companies Regulations 2009, SI 2009/2436, Sch 1 para 3(d): see PARA 1857. As to the meaning of 'unregistered company' see PARA 1856. In the case of an unregistered company, any reference to the common seal of the company must be read as referring to the common or other authorised seal of the company: see reg 5(1)(d); and PARA 1857.

4 As to the requirements for, and limitations on, the name of a company registered under the Companies Acts see PARA 199 et seq.

5 Companies Act 2006 s 45(2). As to the name of the company being engraved on its common seal see further PARA 220. Where a bond had been entered into as a deed, but the company obtaining the bond had used a seal engraved with its trading name rather than its registered name, non-compliance with the Companies Act 1985 s 350 (see now the Companies Act 2006 s 45) did not in itself render the bond a nullity or unenforceable by a third party beneficiary against the surety which had validly sealed the bond: *OTV Birwelco Ltd v Technical and General Guarantee Co Ltd* [2002] EWHC 2240 (TCC), [2002] 4 All ER 668, [2002] 2 BCLC 723.

6 Ie fails to comply with the Companies Act 2006 s 45(2) (see the text and notes 4–5): see s 45(3).

7 Companies Act 2006 s 45(3). As to the meaning of 'officer' see PARA 679; and as to the meaning of 'officer in default' see PARA 316.

8 Companies Act 2006 s 45(4). The text refers to a seal of the company on which its name is not engraved as required by s 45(2) (see the text and notes 4–5): see s 45(4).

9 Ie guilty of an offence under the Companies Act 2006 s 45: see s 45(5).

10 Companies Act 2006 s 45(5). As to the standard scale and the powers of magistrates' courts to issue fines on summary conviction see SENTENCING vol 92 (2015) PARA 176.

11 As to model articles of association prescribed for the purposes of the Companies Act 2006, and their application generally, see PARA 227 et seq. Different versions of model articles have been so prescribed for use by private companies limited by shares (see the Companies (Model Articles) Regulations 2008, SI 2008/3229, reg 2, Sch 1), private companies limited by guarantee (see reg 3, Sch 2), and public companies (see reg 4, Sch 3). As to the meanings of 'company limited by guarantee', 'company limited by shares', 'private company' and 'public company' see PARA 95. The default articles prescribed for the purposes of the Companies Act 1985 ('legacy articles'), ie the Companies (Tables A to F) Regulations 1985, SI 1985/805, have not been revoked and may, in their amended form, continue to be used by companies after the commencement of the Companies Act 2006: see PARA 229.

12 Companies (Model Articles) Regulations 2008, SI 2008/3229, Sch 1 art 49(1), Sch 2 art 35(1), Sch 3 art 81(1). Under the Companies (Tables A to F) Regulations 1985, SI 1985/805, the seal

may only be used by the authority of the directors or of a committee of directors authorised by the directors: see reg 2, Schedule Table A art 101. As to a company's directors see PARA 512 et seq.

13 Companies (Model Articles) Regulations 2008, SI 2008/3229, Sch 1 art 49(2), Sch 2 art 35(2), Sch 3 art 81(2). This wording is not used in the Companies (Tables A to F) Regulations 1985, SI 1985/805.

14 For these purposes, an authorised person is any director of the company, the company secretary (if any), or any person authorised by the directors for the purpose of signing documents to which the common seal is applied: Companies (Model Articles) Regulations 2008, SI 2008/3229, Sch 1 art 49(4), Sch 2 art 35(4), Sch 3 art 81(4). This wording is not used in the Companies (Tables A to F) Regulations 1985, SI 1985/805. As to the company secretary and other officers see PARA 671. Private companies are not required to have a secretary: see PARA 669.

15 Companies (Model Articles) Regulations 2008, SI 2008/3229, Sch 1 art 49(3), Sch 2 art 35(3), Sch 3 art 81(3). The wording used for the purposes of the Companies (Tables A to F) Regulations 1985, SI 1985/805, allows the directors to determine who is to sign any instrument to which the seal is affixed and, unless otherwise so determined, it must be signed by a director and by the secretary or by a second director: see Schedule Table A art 101.

16 Companies (Model Articles) Regulations 2008, SI 2008/3229, Sch 3 art 81(2).

17 Companies (Model Articles) Regulations 2008, SI 2008/3229, Sch 3 art 81(6). For these purposes, references to the securities seal being affixed to any document include the reproduction of the image of that seal on or in a document by any mechanical or electronic means which has been approved by the directors in relation to that document or documents of a class to which it belongs: Sch 3 art 81(7). As to documents or information sent or supplied by electronic means see PARA 751.

18 Companies (Model Articles) Regulations 2008, SI 2008/3229, Sch 3 art 81(5).

283. Written contracts made by, or on behalf of, a company. A contract which, if made between private persons, would be required under law to be in writing, signed by the parties to be charged therewith, may be made on behalf of the company in writing signed[1] by any person acting under its authority, express or implied[2]. A contract so made is effectual in law and binds the company and its successors and all other parties to it; it may be varied or discharged in the same manner in which it is authorised so to be made.

It is not essential to the validity of a contract made on behalf of a company that the company should be described with precision, since the normal rule can be applied that a contract was to be construed by reference to the surrounding circumstances or in the light of the known facts[3].

Many contracts when made by individuals are required by statute to be in writing and duly signed[4]; and such a contract, if made by a company, must comply with the like formalities[5]. A director's signature to a resolution referring to a draft agreement may be sufficient for this purpose[6].

1 The signature may consist of the company's stamp: *McDonald v John Twiname Ltd* [1953] 2 QB 304, [1953] 2 All ER 589, CA (apprenticeship agreement). An instrument which fails as a deed because of lack of delivery may yet take effect as an instrument in writing: *Windsor Refrigerator Co Ltd v Branch Nominees Ltd* [1961] Ch 375, [1961] 1 All ER 277, CA.

2 See the Companies Act 2006 s 43(1); and PARA 281. See also *Beer v London and Paris Hotel Co* (1875) LR 20 Eq 412. As to bills and notes see PARAS 291–294. The Corporate Bodies' Contracts Act 1960 (see CORPORATIONS vol 24 (2010) PARA 474 et seq) does not apply to a company registered under the Companies Act 2006, to a company incorporated outside the United Kingdom, or to a limited liability partnership: Corporate Bodies' Contracts Act 1960 s 2 (substituted by SI 2009/1941). As to the meaning of 'United Kingdom' see PARA 1 note 5. As to formation and registration under the Companies Act 2006 see PARA 95 et seq. As to companies incorporated outside the United Kingdom ('overseas companies') see PARA 2013 et seq. As to limited liability partnerships incorporated in the United Kingdom see PARTNERSHIP vol 79 (2014) PARA 233 et seq.

3 *F Goldsmith (Sicklesmere) Ltd v Baxter* [1970] Ch 85, [1969] 3 All ER 733 (company named as 'Goldsmith Coaches (Sicklesmere) Ltd').

4 See CONTRACT vol 22 (2012) PARA 222 et seq; DEEDS AND OTHER INSTRUMENTS vol 32 (2012) PARA 208.

5 See the Companies Act 2006 s 43(2); and PARA 281.

6 *Jones v Victoria Graving Dock Co* (1877) 2 QBD 314, CA; *Howard v Patent Ivory Manufacturing Co, Re Patent Ivory Manufacturing Co* (1888) 38 ChD 156; *Wilson v West Hartlepool Rly Co* (1865) 2 De GJ & Sm 475.

284. Parol contracts made on behalf of company. A contract which, if made between private persons, would under law be valid, although made by parol only, and not reduced into writing, may be made by parol on behalf of the company by any person acting under its authority, express or implied[1]. A contract so made is effectual in law and binds the company and its successors; it may be varied or discharged in the same manner in which it is authorised so to be made[2].

A company is liable, equally with an individual, to be estopped by the acts of its agents, for example by a parol consent to an act, even though no resolution on the subject has been passed[3].

1 See the Companies Act 2006 s 43(1); and PARA 281.
2 This proposition contains the provisions of the Companies Act 1985 s 36(2) (as originally enacted). Those provisions are not re-enacted word by word in the Companies Act 2006 s 43 (see PARA 281) but as the Explanatory Notes to the Companies Act 2006 para 133 states, the Companies Act 2006 s 43 restates the provisions of the Companies Act 1985 s 36 which means that the proposition nevertheless remains correct.
3 See *Bourke v Alexandra Hotel Co Ltd* (1877) 25 WR 393 (on appeal 25 WR 782, CA).

285. Assignment of contracts by or to company. The question how far the benefit of a commercial contract is assignable by or to a company is decided on the same principles as in the case of an individual, and depends on the circumstances of each case[1].

1 *Tolhurst v Associated Portland Cement Manufacturers (1900) Ltd* [1903] AC 414, HL; *Kemp v Baerselman* [1906] 2 KB 604, CA. See also CONTRACT vol 22 (2012) PARA 497.

C. EXECUTION OF DOCUMENTS BY COMPANY

286. Execution of documents under seal. A document is executed by a company by the affixing of its common seal[1]; but while a company may have a common seal, there is no requirement to have one[2]. If the company does have a common seal, and if it has adopted prescribed articles of association[3], its articles will almost invariably contain provisions as to its affixation[4]. If these provisions are apparently complied with, the company will be bound as against a person dealing with it in good faith[5]. If no particular formalities are prescribed, whoever, as a matter of practice, manages the affairs of a company may use the seal for those acts which he is authorised to perform[6].

A document that is a forgery does not ordinarily bind the company[7].

1 As to use of a company's common seal in the execution of documents see PARA 287; as to a company's common seal generally see PARA 282. As to the use of the company's seal for making company contracts see PARA 281; for use outside the United Kingdom see PARA 289; and for use for sealing securities issued by the company, or for sealing documents creating or evidencing securities so issued, see PARA 290. As to the appointment of an attorney to execute deeds abroad see PARA 288. See also PARA 269.
2 See the Companies Act 2006 s 45; and PARA 282.
3 As to articles of association generally see PARA 227 et seq.
4 See eg the Companies (Tables A to F) Regulations 1985, SI 1985/805, reg 2, Schedule Table A art 101; the Companies (Model Articles) Regulations 2008, SI 2008/3229, Sch 1 art 49, Sch 2 art 35, Sch 3 art 81; and PARA 282.
5 *Re County Life Assurance Co* (1870) 5 Ch App 288 at 293 per Giffard LJ. See also *Re Athenaeum Life Assurance Society, ex p Eagle Insurance Co* (1858) 4 K & J 549; *Re Barned's Banking Co, ex p Contract Corpn* (1867) 3 Ch App 105; *Gloucester County Bank v Rudry Merthyr Steam and House Coal Colliery Co* [1895] 1 Ch 629, CA; *Ruben v Great Fingall Consolidated* [1906] AC 439, HL; *Re Fireproof Doors Ltd, Umney v Fireproof Doors Ltd* [1916] 2 Ch 142. Cf *Mayor Constables and Co of Merchants of the Staple of England v Governors and Co of the Bank of England* (1887) 21 QBD 160, CA; *Davies v R Bolton & Co* [1894] 3 Ch 678. Directors who

subscribe a deed in accordance with articles of association are not signing as witnesses attesting its execution: see *Shears v Jacob* (1866) LR 1 CP 513; *Deffell v White* (1866) LR 2 CP 144 (bills of sale).

Under the Companies Act 2006, in favour of a purchaser, a document is deemed to have been duly executed by a company if it purports to be signed on behalf of the company either by two authorised signatories, or by a director of the company in the presence of a witness who attests the signature: see s 44(5); and PARA 287.

6 *Re Barned's Banking Co, ex p Contract Corpn* (1867) 3 Ch App 105 at 116 per Lord Cairns LJ.

7 *Ruben v Great Fingall Consolidated* [1906] AC 439, HL. However, there may be circumstances in which a company is estopped from denying the validity of a document (see DEEDS AND OTHER INSTRUMENTS vol 32 (2012) PARA 272) and the company may be bound where the person executing the document has ostensible authority to warrant that all formalities relating to execution have been complied with (see *Lovett v Carson Country Homes Ltd* [2009] EWHC 1143 (Ch), [2009] 2 BCLC 196, [2009] All ER (D) 95 (Jun) (distinguishing *Ruben v Great Fingall Consolidated* [1906] AC 439, HL; and see PARA 398). The court in *Lovett v Carson Country Homes Ltd* [2009] EWHC 1143 (Ch), [2009] 2 BCLC 196, [2009] All ER (D) 95 (Jun) also doubted (obiter) whether the Companies Act 2006 s 44(5) (see also note 5) should be subject to an implied proviso that it operates subject to *Ruben v Great Fingall Consolidated* [1906] AC 439, HL: see *Lovett v Carson Country Homes Ltd* [2009] EWHC 1143 (Ch) at [99], [2009] 2 BCLC 196, [2009] All ER (D) 95 (Jun).

287. Execution of documents by signature. Under the law of England and Wales[1], a document is executed by a company[2] either:

(1) by the affixing of its common seal[3]; or

(2) by signature[4].

If head (2) above applies, a document is validly executed by a company only if it is signed on behalf of the company either by two authorised signatories[5], or by a director of the company in the presence of a witness who attests the signature[6]. A document signed in this way[7] and expressed, in whatever words, to be executed by the company has the same effect as if executed under the common seal of the company[8].

Where a document is to be signed by a person on behalf of more than one company, it is not duly signed by that person for these purposes[9] unless he signs it separately in each capacity[10].

In favour of a purchaser[11], a document is deemed to have been duly executed by a company if it purports to be signed on behalf of the company either by two authorised signatories, or by a director of the company in the presence of a witness who attests the signature[12].

A document is validly executed by a company as a deed[13] if, and only if it is duly executed by the company[14], and it is delivered as a deed[15].

1 As to the meanings of 'England' and 'Wales' see PARA 1 note 5.

2 The Companies Act 2006 s 44 applies to a document that is (or purports to be) executed by a company in the name of or on behalf of another person whether or not that person is also a company: s 44(8). As to the meaning of 'company' under the Companies Acts see PARA 21; and as to the meaning of the 'Companies Acts' see PARA 13. As to the execution of deeds or other documents by an attorney appointed by a company for the purpose see PARA 288. A document that is a forgery does not ordinarily bind the company: see PARA 286.

The Secretary of State has made provision by regulations (see the Companies Act 2006 s 1045; and PARA 2014) applying ss 44, 46 to overseas companies, but with modifications: see the Overseas Companies (Execution of Documents and Registration of Charges) Regulations 2009, SI 2009/1917, reg 4. As to the meaning of 'overseas company' see PARA 2013. The provisions of the Companies Act 2006 ss 44, 46 apply also to unregistered companies by virtue of the Unregistered Companies Regulations 2009, SI 2009/2436, Sch 1 para 3(d): see PARA 1857. As to the meaning of 'unregistered company' see PARA 1856.

3 Companies Act 2006 s 44(1)(a). See also note 2. A company may have a common seal, but need not have one: see s 45; and PARA 282.

4 Companies Act 2006 s 44(1)(b). Where head (2) in the text applies, the procedure for execution must be in accordance with s 44(2)–(8) (see the text and notes 2, 5–12): see s 44(1)(b). See also note 2.

5 Companies Act 2006 s 44(2)(a). For these purposes, the following are 'authorised signatories':

(1) every director of the company (s 44(3)(a)); and
(2) in the case of a private company with a secretary or a public company, the secretary (or any joint secretary) of the company (s 44(3)(b)).

References in s 44 to a document being (or purporting to be) signed by a director or secretary are to be read, in a case where that office is held by a firm, as references to its being (or purporting to be) signed by an individual authorised by the firm to sign on its behalf: s 44(7). See also note 2. As to the meaning of 'director' see PARA 512; and as to the meaning of 'firm' see PARA 105 note 15. As to the meanings of 'private company' and 'public company' see PARA 95. As to the company secretary and other officers see PARA 671. Private companies are not required to have a secretary: see PARA 669.

See *Re Armstrong Brands Ltd (in administration)* [2015] EWHC 3303 (Ch), [2015] All ER (D) 172 (Nov) (document signed by two authorised signatories validly executed although not dated until four months after signature).

6 Companies Act 2006 s 44(2)(b). See also note 2.

7 Ie in accordance with the Companies Act 2006 s 44(2) (see the text and notes 5–6): see s 44(4).

8 Companies Act 2006 s 44(4). See also note 2. See *OTV Birwelco Ltd v Technical and General Guarantee Co Ltd* [2002] EWHC 2240 (TCC), [2002] 4 All ER 668, [2002] 2 All ER (Comm) 1116, [2002] 2 BCLC 723 (there is nothing in the Companies Act 1985 s 36A (repealed; see now the Companies Act 2006 s 44) which requires a company to use its registered name rather than its trading name in the body of a deed or bond, as such a requirement would abrogate the common law rule that extraneous evidence was admissible to identify a contracting party when its identity was not clear from the face of the deed). A valid execution of a document does not require the express words 'by or on behalf of the company': *Williams v Redcard Ltd* [2011] EWCA Civ 466, [2011] 4 All ER 444, [2011] Bus LR 1479.

9 Ie for the purposes of the Companies Act 2006 s 44: see s 44(6).

10 Companies Act 2006 s 44(6). See also note 2.

11 For these purposes, 'purchaser' means a purchaser in good faith for valuable consideration and includes a lessee, mortgagee or other person who for valuable consideration acquires an interest in property: Companies Act 2006 s 44(5). See also note 2. See *Lovett v Carson Country Homes Ltd* [2009] EWHC 1143 (Ch), [2009] 2 BCLC 196, [2009] All ER (D) 95 (Jun) (forbearance may be valuable consideration for these purposes).

12 Companies Act 2006 s 44(5). The text refers to a document that purports to be signed in accordance with s 44(2) (see the text and notes 5–6): see s 44(5). See also notes 2, 5. See *Lovett v Carson Country Homes Ltd* [2009] EWHC 1143 (Ch), [2009] 2 BCLC 196, [2009] All ER (D) 95 (Jun) (company bound by debenture on which director's signature had been forged; bank had been a 'purchaser' for the purpose of the Companies Act 2006 s 44(5), and the debenture 'purported' (ie that was the impression conveyed by the document) to have been signed on behalf of the company by two authorised signatories).

In relation to the execution of a document by a company where the Companies Act 2006 s 44(2) applies by virtue of the Land Registration Act 2002 s 91(4) (electronic dispositions), the effect of s 91(4) is modified in relation to the Companies Act 2006 s 44(2) and the other provisions of s 44 apply accordingly: see the Land Registration Act 2002 s 91(9) (substituted by SI 2008/948); and REAL PROPERTY AND REGISTRATION vol 87 (2012) PARA 540.

13 Ie for the purposes of the Law of Property (Miscellaneous Provisions) Act 1989 s 1(2)(b) (see DEEDS AND OTHER INSTRUMENTS vol 32 (2012) PARA 208): see the Companies Act 2006 s 46(1).

14 Companies Act 2006 s 46(1)(a).

15 Companies Act 2006 s 46(1)(b). For the purposes of s 46(1)(b), a document is presumed to be delivered upon its being executed, unless a contrary intention is proved: s 46(2).

288. Appointment of attorney to execute deeds. Under the law of England and Wales[1], a company[2] may, by instrument executed as a deed, empower any person, either generally or in respect of specified matters, as its attorney to execute deeds or other documents on its behalf[3]. A deed or other document so executed, whether in the United Kingdom[4] or elsewhere, has effect as if executed by the company[5].

1 As to the meanings of 'England' and 'Wales' see PARA 1 note 5.

2 As to the meaning of 'company' under the Companies Acts see PARA 21; and as to the meaning of the 'Companies Acts' see PARA 13.

3 Companies Act 2006 s 47(1).

The Secretary of State may make provision by regulations applying the Companies Act 2006 ss 43–52 (see PARAS 281 et seq, 289 et seq) to overseas companies, subject to such exceptions, adaptations or modifications as may be specified in the regulations: see s 1045; and PARA 2014. As to the meaning of 'overseas company' see PARA 2013.

4 As to the meaning of 'United Kingdom' see PARA 1 note 5.

5 Companies Act 2006 s 47(2).

289. Company's official seal for use outside the United Kingdom. A company[1] that has a common seal[2] may have for use outside the United Kingdom[3] an official seal[4], which must be a facsimile of the company's common seal, with the addition on its face of the place or places where it is to be used[5].

A company having an official seal for use outside the United Kingdom may, by writing under its common seal, authorise any person appointed for the purpose to affix the official seal to any deed or other document to which the company is party[6].

As between the company and a person dealing with such an agent, the agent's authority continues, during the period mentioned in the instrument conferring the authority[7], or, if no period is mentioned, then until notice of the revocation or determination of the agent's authority has been given to the person dealing with him[8].

The person affixing the official seal must certify in writing on the deed or other document to which the seal is affixed the date on which, and the place at which, it is affixed[9].

When duly affixed to a document, the official seal has the same effect as the company's common seal[10].

1 As to the meaning of 'company' under the Companies Acts see PARA 21; and as to the meaning of the 'Companies Acts' see PARA 13.

2 A company may have a common seal, but need not have one: see the Companies Act 2006 s 45; and PARA 282.

3 As to the meaning of 'United Kingdom' see PARA 1 note 5.

4 Companies Act 2006 s 49(1).

The Secretary of State may make provision by regulations applying the Companies Act 2006 ss 43–52 (see PARAS 281 et seq, 290 et seq) to overseas companies, subject to such exceptions, adaptations or modifications as may be specified in the regulations: see s 1045; and PARA 2014. However, at the date at which this volume states the law, no such provision has been made in relation to s 49. As to the meaning of 'overseas company' see PARA 2013.

5 Companies Act 2006 s 49(2).

6 Companies Act 2006 s 49(4).

7 Companies Act 2006 s 49(5)(a).

8 Companies Act 2006 s 49(5)(b).

9 Companies Act 2006 s 49(6).

10 Companies Act 2006 s 49(3).

290. Company's official seal for share certificates etc. A company[1] that has a common seal[2] may have, for use for sealing securities issued by the company[3], or for sealing documents creating or evidencing securities so issued[4], an official seal[5], which must be a facsimile of the company's common seal, with the addition on its face of the word 'Securities'[6]. When duly affixed to a document, the official seal has the same effect as the company's common seal[7].

1 As to the meaning of 'company' under the Companies Acts see PARA 21; and as to the meaning of the 'Companies Acts' see PARA 13.

2 A company may have a common seal, but need not have one: see the Companies Act 2006 s 45; and PARA 282.

3 Companies Act 2006 s 50(1)(a).

The provisions of the Companies Act 2006 s 50 apply to unregistered companies by virtue of the Unregistered Companies Regulations 2009, SI 2009/2436, reg 3, Sch 1 para 3(f): see PARA 1857. As to the meaning of 'unregistered company' see PARA 1856. The Secretary of State also may make provision by regulations applying the Companies Act 2006 ss 43–52 (see

PARAS 281 et seq, 292) to overseas companies, subject to such exceptions, adaptations or modifications as may be specified in the regulations: see s 1045; and PARA 2014. As to the meaning of 'overseas company' see PARA 2013.

4 Companies Act 2006 s 50(1)(b).

5 Companies Act 2006 s 50(1).

6 Companies Act 2006 s 50(2)(a). A share certificate evidenced in this way imputes a prima facie entitlement to the shares: see PARA 391.

7 Companies Act 2006 s 50(2)(b).

D. BILLS AND NOTES

291. Company's power to deal with bills and notes. A company incorporated under the Companies Act 2006 with unrestricted objects[1] has power to deal with bills of exchange or promissory notes. This power is limited only by the statutory duty imposed on a director to act in the way he considers, in good faith, would be most likely to promote the success of the company for the benefit of its members as a whole[2]. A company which restricts its objects, or a company incorporated under earlier legislation which retains its statement of objects, does not have as an incident of its incorporation[3] the power of accepting bills or issuing negotiable instruments[4]; such power is to be determined on the construction of the company's constitution[5]. If the constitutional documents are silent on the subject, the power may be inferred where the nature of the company's business involves such a power[6]. Thus a non-trading company has no general power to incur liability on bills of exchange or promissory notes[7] and, although it may transfer the property in a bill or note, it cannot incur liability on it unless its instrument of incorporation expressly or by clear implication confers the power[8].

A proviso in a bill of exchange by an unlimited company professing to limit the liability under the bill is void[9].

1 See the Companies Act 2006 s 31; and PARA 239.

2 See the Companies Act 2006 s 172; and PARA 584.

3 As to incorporation by registration under the Companies Act 2006, and its effects, see PARA 104 et seq.

4 As to provision made in the Companies Act 2006 in relation to the making, acceptance or indorsement of bills of exchange or promissory notes on behalf of a company see PARA 292.

5 *Peruvian Rlys Co v Thames and Mersey Marine Insurance Co, Re Peruvian Rlys Co* (1867) 2 Ch App 617. As to the meaning of references in the Companies Acts to a company's constitution see PARA 226.

6 *Re General Estates Co, ex p City Bank* (1868) 3 Ch App 758 (where a land and building company was held to have the power). See also *East London Waterworks Co v Bailey* (1827) 4 Bing 283 at 288; *Slark v Highgate Archway Co* (1814) 5 Taunt 792; *Murray v East India Co* (1821) 5 B & Ald 204; *Dickinson v Valpy* (1829) 10 B & C 128; *Steele v Harmer* (1845) 14 M & W 831. As to the power of a liquidator see COMPANY AND PARTNERSHIP INSOLVENCY vol 16 (2011) PARA 527 et seq.

7 As to liability of the parties on bills of exchange or promissory notes generally see FINANCIAL INSTRUMENTS AND TRANSACTIONS vol 49 (2015) PARA 358 et seq. As to the personal liability of a company's officers see PARA 294.

8 *Peruvian Rlys Co v Thames and Mersey Marine Insurance Co, Re Peruvian Rlys Co* (1867) 2 Ch App 617 at 623 per Lord Cairns LJ. As to inferring the power from the course of dealing see *Bramah v Roberts* (1837) 5 Scott 172. The following companies have been held not to be trading companies which have as such the implied power: a waterworks company (*Broughton v Manchester and Salford Waterworks Co* (1819) 3 B & Ald 1); a cemetery company (*Steele v Harmer* (1845) 14 M & W 831); a gas company (*Bramah v Roberts* (1837) 5 Scott 172); a salt company (*Bult v Morrell* (1840) 12 Ad & El 745); a salvage company (*Thompson v Universal Salvage Co* (1848) 1 Exch 694); a mining company (*Hawtayne v Bourne* (1841) 7 M & W 595; *Dickinson v Valpy* (1829) 10 B & C 128 at 137); a railway company incorporated by statute (*Bateman v Mid-Wales Rly Co* (1866) LR 1 CP 499). 'Trade' probably has a more restricted significance than 'business': see PARA 1 note 1.

9 *Re State Fire Insurance Co, ex p Meredith's and Conver's Claim* (1863) 1 New Rep 510. As to the meaning of 'unlimited company' see PARA 95.

292. Signature on bill or note. Where, in the case of an individual, a bill of exchange or promissory note is required to be signed[1], it is sufficient, in the case of a company, if it is signed on behalf of the company by any person acting on its authority or if it is sealed with the corporate seal[2]. However, a company's bill or note is not required to be under seal[3].

A bill of exchange or promissory note is deemed to have been made, accepted or indorsed on behalf of a company[4] if made, accepted or indorsed in the name of, or by or on behalf or on account of, the company by a person acting under its authority[5]. It is not necessary that a formal resolution of the directors should be passed that bills should be accepted[6]; and, where a director without authority accepts bills on behalf of a company whose articles give power to delegate the duty of accepting bills to one director, the company is liable to a holder in due course, even though the delegation has not in fact taken place[7].

1 Ie under the Bills of Exchange Act 1882: see s 91; and FINANCIAL INSTRUMENTS AND TRANSACTIONS vol 49 (2015) PARAS 249–250.

2 See the Bills of Exchange Act 1882 s 91; and FINANCIAL INSTRUMENTS AND TRANSACTIONS vol 49 (2015) PARAS 249–250. See also *Re General Estates Co, ex p City Bank* (1868) 3 Ch App 758 at 762 per Page Wood LJ, and at 763 per Selwyn LJ; and PARA 283. A company may have a common seal, but need not have one: see the Companies Act 2006 s 45; and PARA 282. As to the use of a company's common seal in the execution of documents generally see PARA 287.

3 See the Bills of Exchange Act 1882 s 91; and FINANCIAL INSTRUMENTS AND TRANSACTIONS vol 49 (2015) PARAS 249–250.

4 As to the meaning of 'company' under the Companies Acts see PARA 21; and as to the meaning of the 'Companies Acts' see PARA 13.

5 Companies Act 2006 s 52. See also *Re Barber & Co, ex p Agra Bank* (1870) LR 9 Eq 725. Cf *Herald v Connah* (1876) 34 LT 885.

The Secretary of State may make provision by regulations applying the Companies Act 2006 ss 43–52 (see PARA 281 et seq) to overseas companies, subject to such exceptions, adaptations or modifications as may be specified in the regulations: see s 1045; and PARA 2014. As to the meaning of 'overseas company' see PARA 2013.

6 *Re Land Credit Co of Ireland, ex p Overend, Gurney & Co* (1869) 4 Ch App 460 at 473 per Giffard LJ.

7 *Dey v Pullinger Engineering Co* [1921] 1 KB 77 (dissenting from *Premier Industrial Bank Ltd v Carlton Manufacturing Co Ltd and Crabtree Ltd* [1909] 1 KB 106). Cf *Kreditbank Cassel GmbH v Schenkers Ltd* [1927] 1 KB 826, CA (branch manager of bank); *AL Underwood Ltd v Bank of Liverpool and Martins* [1924] 1 KB 775, CA; *B Liggett (Liverpool) Ltd v Barclays Bank Ltd* [1928] 1 KB 48 (as to being put on inquiry). See also PARA 267. A signature 'for and on behalf of a company, X, director' is not a signature by procuration within the Bills of Exchange Act 1882 s 25 (as to which seeFINANCIAL INSTRUMENTS AND TRANSACTIONS vol 49 (2015) PARA 258), and does not put the person taking the bill on inquiry as to the actual authority of the director to sign: *Alexander Stewart & Son of Dundee Ltd v Westminster Bank Ltd* [1926] WN 126; revsd on other grounds [1926] WN 271, CA.

293. Duties of holder of bill of exchange to inquire as to agent's authority. A holder in due course[1] is not concerned to see that the agent's authority has been strictly followed[2]. Where no express authority has been given to the agent, the company is not liable if the bill is given to meet an unusual occurrence or emergency not in the ordinary course of business[3]. Where a holder has notice that the agent had only a limited authority, he is in the same position as if he had inquired into the extent of that authority[4].

1 As to the meaning of 'holder in due course' see FINANCIAL INSTRUMENTS AND TRANSACTIONS vol 49 (2015) PARA 191.

2 *Re Land Credit Co of Ireland, ex p Overend, Gurney & Co* (1869) 4 Ch App 460 (where bills were authorised on condition that security was deposited); *Hambro v Burnard* [1904] 2 KB 10, CA (where the agent acted for his own purposes); *Thompson v Wesleyan Newspaper Association* (1849) 8 CB 849 (where the authorised amount was exceeded); *Re State Fire Insurance Co, ex p Meredith's and Conver's Claim* (1863) 1 New Rep 510.

3 *Re Cunningham & Co Ltd, Simpson's Claim* (1887) 36 ChD 532; *Hawtayne v Bourne* (1841) 7 M & W 595; *Re Moseley Green Coal and Coke Co, ex p Official Liquidator* (1864) 10 LT 819.
4 *Reckitt v Barnett, Pembroke and Slater Ltd* [1929] AC 176, HL: *John v Dodwell & Co* [1918] AC 563, PC; *Bryant, Powis and Bryant v La Banque du Peuple* [1893] AC 170, PC; *Gompertz v Cook* (1903) 20 TLR 106; *Reid v Rigby & Co* [1894] 2 QB 40; *Stagg v Elliott* (1862) 12 CBNS 373; *National Bank of Scotland Ltd v Dewhurst, The Gonchar and The Izgar* (1896) 1 Com Cas 318; *Jacobs v Morris* [1902] 1 Ch 816, CA. See further AGENCY vol 1 (2008) PARA 123.

294. Liability of company's officers on bill of exchange. If the company is liable on a bill of exchange[1], its authorised agents are not personally liable, even though they used words apparently sufficient to render them so liable, such as 'I promise' or 'We promise'[2], provided the signatures are expressed to be on behalf of the company as principal or in a representative capacity[3]. Thus if a bill is directed to a company and accepted by its directors describing themselves as directors of the (named) company, the company alone is liable[4]; but words describing them as being officers of the company may not of themselves exempt them[5].

Where a company has no power to accept, an acceptance by directors and secretary 'for and on behalf of the company' makes them personally liable on a warranty of authority[6], but there is no implied warranty that the company has funds at its bank to meet a cheque or acceptance[7]. If a loan is made to a director who has become liable on a bill accepted for the company's purposes, it is a question of evidence whether the loan is made to him personally or to the company[8].

The company's name is not properly mentioned on a bill of exchange or similar document if the word 'limited' or words 'public limited company' (or their Welsh equivalents) is or are omitted from the name on the document[9], or if additions are made to it[10]; but if the company's name appears on the face of the bill, it is a sufficient mention and the name need not appear again in the acceptance[11].

1 As to a company's power to deal with bills and notes see PARA 291. As to liability of the parties on bills of exchange or promissory notes generally see FINANCIAL INSTRUMENTS AND TRANSACTIONS vol 49 (2015) PARA 358 et seq.
2 *Chapman v Smethurst* [1909] 1 KB 927, CA; *HB Etlin Co Ltd v Asselstyne* (1962) 34 DLR (2d) 191, Ont CA; *Bondina Ltd v Rollaway Shower Blinds Ltd* [1986] 1 All ER 564, [1986] 1 WLR 517, CA; *Lindus v Melrose* (1858) 3 H & N 177, Ex Ch; *Halford v Cameron's Coalbrook Steam Coal and Swansea and Loughor Rly Co* (1851) 16 QB 442; *Forbes v Marshall* (1855) 11 Exch 166; *Aggs v Nicholson* (1856) 1 H & N 165.
3 *Alexander v Sizer* (1869) LR 4 Exch 102; *Dutton v Marsh* (1871) LR 6 QB 361 at 364 per Cockburn CJ; *Landes v Marcus and Davids* (1909) 25 TLR 478; *Leadbitter v Farrow* (1816) 5 M & S 345; *Mare v Charles* (1856) 5 E & B 978; *Liverpool Borough Bank v Walker* (1859) 4 De G & J 24; *W and T Avery Ltd v Charlesworth* (1914) 31 TLR 52, CA. Even so, evidence is admissible to show the defendant signed in his personal capacity: *Rolfe Lubell & Co v Keith* [1979] 1 All ER 860.

Alternatively, the form of the document may indicate that the signatories are intended to be liable jointly with the company: *Glatt v Ritt* (1973) 34 DLR (3d) 295, Ont HC. See further AGENCY vol 1 (2008) PARA 159.
4 *Okell v Charles* (1876) 34 LT 822, CA. As to a company's directors see PARA 512 et seq.
5 *Courtauld v Saunders (or Sanders)* (1867) 16 LT 562; *Dutton v Marsh* (1871) LR 6 QB 361 (notwithstanding that the company's seal was also affixed to the note); *Penkivil v Connell* (1850) 5 Exch 381; *Jones v Jackson* (1870) 22 LT 828; *Kettle v Dunster and Wakefield* (1927) 138 LT 158 (signed by the receiver of a company); *F Stacey & Co Ltd v Wallis* (1912) 106 LT 544; *Brebner v Henderson* 1925 SC 643, Ct of Sess. See also *Elliott v Bax-Ironside* [1925] 2 KB 301, CA (where bills were accepted by two directors on behalf of a company and indorsed by the company and the two directors, and it was held that the signatures were intended to create a personal liability on the directors), explained in *Britannia Electric Lamp Works Ltd v Mandler & Co Ltd and Mandler* [1939] 2 KB 129 at 135, [1939] 2 All ER 469 at 472 per Branson J. See also AGENCY vol 1 (2008) PARA 159; FINANCIAL INSTRUMENTS AND TRANSACTIONS vol 49 (2008) PARAS 259–260, 279.

6 *West London Commercial Bank v Kitson* (1884) 13 QBD 360, CA. Cf *Liverpool Borough Bank v Walker* (1859) 4 De G & J 24. As to the company secretary and other officers see PARA 671.
7 *Beattie v Lord Ebury* (1874) LR 7 HL 102.
8 *Colley v Smith* (1838) 2 Mood & R 96. Cf *McCollin v Gilpin* (1881) 6 QBD 516, CA.
9 *Penrose v Martyr* (1858) EB & E 499; *Atkins (or Atkin) & Co v Wardle* (1889) 58 LJQB 377. The abbreviation 'Ltd' has always been sufficient for this purpose: *F Stacey & Co Ltd v Wallis* (1912) 106 LT 544. It seems that 'company' may be abbreviated for present purposes to 'Coy', and 'and' to '&': see *F Stacey & Co Ltd v Wallis*; *Banque de l'Indochine et de Suez SA v Euroseas Group Finance Co Ltd* [1981] 3 All ER 198. See also *Scottish and Newcastle Breweries Ltd v Blair* 1967 SLT 72. Cf *Durham Fancy Goods Ltd v Michael Jackson (Fancy Goods) Ltd* [1968] 2 QB 839, [1968] 2 All ER 987 (holders estopped from enforcing personal liability as they had initiated the misdescription of the company). A trading name is not sufficient: *Maxform SpA v B Mariani and Goodville Ltd* [1981] 2 Lloyd's Rep 54, CA. As to permitted wordings which may be included as part of the ordinary name of the company see PARA 196. As to the obligation to put the company's name on business correspondence etc and the penalty for non-compliance see PARA 219.
10 *Nassau Steam Press v Tyler* (1894) 70 LT 376.
11 *F Stacey & Co Ltd v Wallis* (1912) 106 LT 544; *Dermatine Co Ltd v Ashworth* (1905) 21 TLR 510 (where the word 'limited' was omitted by accident, the words of acceptance being on a rubber stamp which overlapped the edge of the bill).

E. BUSINESS PAYMENT PRACTICES AND TRANSPARENCY IN SUPPLY CHAINS

295. Duty of certain companies to publish report on payment practices and performance. The Secretary of State[1] may by regulations[2] impose a requirement, on such descriptions of companies[3] as may be prescribed[4], to publish, at such intervals and in such manner as may be prescribed, prescribed information about:

(1) the company's payment practices and policies[5] relating to relevant contracts[6] of a prescribed description; and
(2) the company's performance by reference to those practices and policies[7].

The regulations may not impose a requirement on a company in relation to any time during which:

(a) it qualifies[8] as a micro-entity[9];
(b) the small companies regime[10] applies to it[11];
(c) it qualifies[12] as medium-sized[13].

The regulations may:

(i) require that information published in accordance with the regulations must be approved or signed by such description of person as may be prescribed[14];
(ii) require such of the information required to be published as may be prescribed to be given, in such form as may be prescribed, to prescribed persons[15];
(iii) make provision for a prescribed breach by a prescribed description of person of a requirement imposed by the regulations to be an offence punishable on summary conviction by a fine[16].

At the date at which this volume states the law, no such regulations had been made.

1 As to the Secretary of State see PARA 6.
2 Before making such regulations, the Secretary of State must consult such persons as he considers appropriate: Small Business, Enterprise and Employment Act 2015 s 3(8). Regulations under s 3 are subject to affirmative resolution procedure (ie the regulations may not be made unless a draft of the statutory instrument containing them has been laid before Parliament and approved by a resolution of each House of Parliament: s 161(4)): s 3(9). As to the making of regulations generally see s 161(1)–(3), (5)–(6).
3 For these purposes, 'company' has the meaning given by the Companies Act 2006 s 1(1) (see PARA 21) (but see the Small Business, Enterprise and Employment Act 2015 s 3(3); and heads (a)–(c) in the text): s 3(2).

4 'Prescribed' means prescribed by the regulations: Small Business, Enterprise and Employment Act 2015 s 3(2).
5 'The company's payment practices and policies' has such meaning as may be prescribed and the information which may be prescribed may, in particular, include the following information (Small Business, Enterprise and Employment Act 2015 s 3(4)), ie information:
   (1) about the standard payment terms of the company and whether these are part of any code of conduct or code of ethics of the company;
   (2) about payment terms of the company which are not standard;
   (3) about the processing and payment of invoices;
   (4) by reference to such codes of conduct or standards as may be prescribed and as are applicable to companies generally or to companies of a prescribed description;
   (5) about disputes relating to the payment of invoices, including any dispute resolution mechanism that the company uses;
   (6) about payments owed or paid by the company due to late payment of invoices, whether in respect of interest or otherwise.
6 For these purposes, a contract is a 'relevant contract' if it is a contract for goods, services or intangible assets (including intellectual property), and the parties to the contract have entered into it in connection with the carrying on of a business: Small Business, Enterprise and Employment Act 2015 s 3(2).
7 Small Business, Enterprise and Employment Act 2015 s 3(1).
8 Ie for the purposes of the Companies Act 2006 s 384A: see PARA 767.
9 Small Business, Enterprise and Employment Act 2015 s 3(3)(a).
10 As to the small companies regime see the Companies Act 2006 s 381; and PARA 766.
11 Small Business, Enterprise and Employment Act 2015 s 3(3)(b).
12 Ie for the purposes of the Companies Act 2006 s 465 or s 466: see PARA 768.
13 Small Business, Enterprise and Employment Act 2015 s 3(3)(c).
14 Small Business, Enterprise and Employment Act 2015 s 3(5).
15 Small Business, Enterprise and Employment Act 2015 s 3(6).
16 Small Business, Enterprise and Employment Act 2015 s 3(7).

296. Duty of certain companies to prepare slavery and human trafficking statement for each financial year. As from 29 October 2015[1], the following provisions have effect.

A commercial organisation[2] which supplies goods or services, and has a total turnover[3] of not less than an amount prescribed by regulations made by the Secretary of State[4], must prepare a slavery and human trafficking[5] statement for each financial year of the organisation[6]. A slavery and human trafficking statement for a financial year is:

(1) a statement of the steps the organisation has taken during the financial year to ensure that slavery and human trafficking is not taking place in any of its supply chains, and in any part of its own business[7]; or
(2) a statement that the organisation has taken no such steps[8].

An organisation's slavery and human trafficking statement may include information about:

(a) the organisation's structure, its business and its supply chains[9];
(b) its policies in relation to slavery and human trafficking[10];
(c) its due diligence processes in relation to slavery and human trafficking in its business and supply chains[11];
(d) the parts of its business and supply chains where there is a risk of slavery and human trafficking taking place, and the steps it has taken to assess and manage that risk[12];
(e) its effectiveness in ensuring that slavery and human trafficking is not taking place in its business or supply chains, measured against such performance indicators as it considers appropriate[13];
(f) the training about slavery and human trafficking available to its staff[14].

If the organisation is a body corporate other than a limited liability partnership, a slavery and human trafficking statement must be approved by the board of directors[15] or equivalent management body and signed by a director or equivalent[16].

If the organisation has a website, it must publish the slavery and human trafficking statement on that website, and include a link to the slavery and human trafficking statement in a prominent place on that website's homepage[17]. If the organisation does not have a website, it must provide a copy of the slavery and human trafficking statement to anyone who makes a written request for one, and must do so before the end of the period of 30 days beginning with the day on which the request is received[18].

The Secretary of State may issue guidance about the duties so imposed on commercial organisations[19] and must publish any such guidance in a way he considers appropriate[20]. The guidance may in particular include further provision about the kind of information which may be included in a slavery and human trafficking statement[21].

The duties imposed on commercial organisations by the above provisions are enforceable by the Secretary of State bringing civil proceedings in the High Court for an injunction[22].

1 See the Modern Slavery Act 2015 (Commencement No 3 and Transitional Provision) Regulations 2015, SI 2015/1816, reg 2. The provisions set out in the text and notes 2–22 do not have effect in respect of a financial year ending before 31 March 2016: see reg 3.

2 For these purposes, 'commercial organisation' means a body corporate (wherever incorporated) which carries on a business, or part of a business, in any part of the United Kingdom, or a partnership (wherever formed) which carries on a business, or part of a business, in any part of the United Kingdom; and 'business' includes a trade or profession: Modern Slavery Act 2015 s 54(12). 'Partnership' means a partnership within the Partnership Act 1890 (see PARTNERSHIP vol 79 (2014) PARA 1 et seq), a limited partnership registered under the Limited Partnerships Act 1907 (see PARTNERSHIP vol 79 (2014) PARA 217 et seq), or a firm, or an entity of a similar character, formed under the law of a country outside the United Kingdom: Modern Slavery Act 2015 s 54(12).

3 For these purposes, an organisation's total turnover is to be determined in accordance with regulations made by the Secretary of State: Modern Slavery Act 2015 s 54(3). As to the Secretary of State see PARA 6.

4 See the Modern Slavery Act 2015 s 54(1), (2). The total amount of turnover prescribed for these purposes is £36m (Modern Slavery Act 2015 (Transparency in Supply Chains) Regulations 2015, SI 2015/1833, reg 2); and the total turnover of a commercial organisation is the turnover of that organisation and the turnover of any of its subsidiary undertakings (reg 3(1)). For the purposes of reg 3(1), 'turnover' means the amount derived from the provision of goods and services falling within the ordinary activities of the commercial organisation or subsidiary undertaking, after deduction of trade discounts, value added tax and any other taxes based on the amounts so derived: reg 3(2).

The Secretary of State must from time to time carry out a review of the 2015 Regulations, set out the conclusions of the review in a report and publish the report: reg 4(1). The report must in particular set out the objectives intended to be achieved by those Regulations, assess the extent to which those objectives are achieved and assess whether those objectives remain appropriate and, if so, the extent to which they could be achieved with a system that imposes less regulation: reg 4(2). The first such report must be published before the end of the period of five years beginning with 29 October 2015 (ie the day on which the 2015 Regulations came into force): regs 1(1), 4(3). Reports under reg 4 are afterwards to be published at intervals not exceeding five years: reg 4(4).

5 For these purposes, 'slavery and human trafficking' means the following (see the Modern Slavery Act 2015 s 54(12)), ie:

(1) conduct which constitutes an offence under any of the following: the Modern Slavery Act 2015 s 1, s 2 or s 4 or the equivalent Northern Ireland provisions; the Criminal Justice (Scotland) Act 2003 s 22 (traffic in prostitution etc); the Asylum and Immigration (Treatment of Claimants, etc) Act 2004 s 4 (trafficking for exploitation); the Criminal Justice and Licensing (Scotland) Act 2010 s 47 (slavery, servitude and forced or compulsory labour); or

(2) conduct which would constitute an offence in a part of the United Kingdom under any of those provisions if the conduct took place in that part of the United Kingdom.

6 Modern Slavery Act 2015 s 54(1).
7 Modern Slavery Act 2015 s 54(4)(a).
8 Modern Slavery Act 2015 s 54(4)(b).
9 Modern Slavery Act 2015 s 54(5)(a).
10 Modern Slavery Act 2015 s 54(5)(b).
11 Modern Slavery Act 2015 s 54(5)(c).
12 Modern Slavery Act 2015 s 54(5)(d).
13 Modern Slavery Act 2015 s 54(5)(e).
14 Modern Slavery Act 2015 s 54(5)(f).
15 As to the directors of a company see PARA 512 et seq.
16 Modern Slavery Act 2015 s 54(6)(a).
17 Modern Slavery Act 2015 s 54(7).
18 Modern Slavery Act 2015 s 54(8).
19 Modern Slavery Act 2015 s 54(9)(a).
20 Modern Slavery Act 2015 s 54(9)(b).
21 Modern Slavery Act 2015 s 54(10).
22 Modern Slavery Act 2015 s 54(11).

(v) Torts involving a Company

297. Company's liability in tort for agent's acts. Although every tort is ultra vires[1], on the basis that no corporation is formed for the purpose of committing wrongs[2], a company is not thereby exempted from tortious liability[3].

A company is liable for torts committed by its agents in the course of their employment, and proceedings may be brought if an individual would be liable for the tort that has been committed, if the agent is acting in the course of his employment (or within the actual or ostensible scope of his authority), and if the act complained of is one which the company might possibly be authorised by its constitution to commit[4]. No express command or privity of the company need be proved[5] but, in general, the claim arises whenever the relevant person or body, not necessarily the directors, made the relevant decision[6].

A company may also be liable for the torts and contracts of its agents under the doctrine of estoppel[7], when they are either acting within their apparent authority[8] or apparently acting within their actual authority[9].

Proceedings based on fraudulent misrepresentation as to the credit, trade or dealings of third persons made for the purpose of such persons obtaining credit, money or goods cannot be maintained unless the misrepresentation is in writing signed by the party to be charged[10]. For these purposes, a representation signed on behalf of a limited company by a duly authorised agent acting within the scope of his authority, or by an officer or employee of the company acting in the course of his duties in the business of the company, constitutes a representation made by the company and signed by it[11], but it may also constitute the personal signature of the agent signing so as to make him personally liable in deceit too[12].

1 As to the meaning of 'ultra vires' see PARA 258.
2 As to the legal effect of companies formed for an illegal purpose see PARA 99.
3 See *Yarborough v Bank of England* (1812) 16 East 6; and CORPORATIONS vol 24 (2010) PARA 477 et seq. See also note 7.
4 See AGENCY vol 1 (2008) PARA 150 et seq; CORPORATIONS vol 24 (2010) PARA 477. As to the meaning of references to a company's constitution see PARA 226. See also *New Brunswick and Canada Rly and Land Co v Conybeare* (1862) 9 HL Cas 711 at 738 per Lord Cranworth (shares taken on directors' fraudulent representations); *Ranger v Great Western Rly Co* (1854) 5 HL Cas 72; *Western Bank of Scotland v Addie* (1867) LR 1 Sc & Div 145, HL (managers); *Houldsworth v City of Glasgow Bank* (1880) 5 App Cas 317, HL; *Refuge Assurance Co Ltd v Kettlewell* [1909] AC 243, HL; *Barwick v English Joint Stock Bank* (1867) LR 2 Exch 259 (fraud of agents); *Re United Service Co, Johnston's Claim* (1870) 6 Ch App 212; *Mackay v Commercial Bank of*

New Brunswick (1874) LR 5 PC 394; *Swire v Francis* (1877) 3 App Cas 106, PC (deceit); *Mersey Docks and Harbour Board Trustees v Gibbs* (1866) LR 1 HL 93 (negligence); *Edwards v Midland Rly Co* (1880) 6 QBD 287; *Kemp v Courage & Co* (1890) 7 TLR 50 (malicious prosecution; trover); *Goff v Great Northern Rly Co* (1861) 3 E & E 672; *Cornford v Carlton Bank* [1899] 1 QB 392 (malicious prosecution) (cf *Bank of New South Wales v Owston* (1879) 4 App Cas 270, PC; *Bank of New South Wales v Piper* [1897] AC 383, PC); *Lambert v Great Eastern Rly Co* [1909] 2 KB 776, CA (false imprisonment); *Yarborough v Bank of England* (1812) 16 East 6; *Butler v Manchester, Sheffield and Lincolnshire Rly Co* (1888) 21 QBD 207, CA (assault); *Pratt v British Medical Association* [1919] 1 KB 244 (boycotting medical practitioner); *Nevill v Fine Arts and General Insurance Co* [1897] AC 68, HL (libel); *Citizens' Life Assurance Co v Brown* [1904] AC 423, PC (malicious libel); *Whitfield v South Eastern Rly Co* (1858) EB & E 115; *E Hulton & Co v Jones* [1910] AC 20, HL (libel); *Finburgh v Moss Empires Ltd* 1908 SC 928, Ct of Sess (slander); *M'Adam v City and Suburban Dairies Ltd* 1911 SC 430, Ct of Sess (slander); *Aiken v Caledonian Rly Co* 1913 SC 66 (slander); *Mandelston v North British Rly Co* 1917 SC 442, Ct of Sess (slander); *Maund v Monmouthshire Canal Co* (1842) 4 Man & G 452; *Eastern Counties Rly Co v Broom* (1851) 6 Exch 314, Ex Ch (trespass); *Green v London General Omnibus Co* (1859) 7 CBNS 290 (obstruction in business); *United Telephone Co v London and Globe Telephone and Maintenance Co* (1884) 26 ChD 766 (infringement of patent).

As to fraudulent misrepresentation see *Lloyd v Grace, Smith & Co* [1912] AC 716, HL, overruling a dictum in *Barwick v English Joint Stock Bank* (1867) LR 2 Exch 259 at 266 per Willes J, which had been approved in subsequent cases. See also *London County Freehold and Leasehold Properties Ltd v Berkeley Property and Investment Co Ltd* [1936] 2 All ER 1039, CA. Cf *Briess v Woolley* [1954] AC 333, [1954] 1 All ER 909, HL (where the negotiations for the sale of shares by the managing director in which the false representations were made were held to have been authorised by the shareholders and the shareholders were in consequence liable). As to the rescission of contracts to take shares on the ground of misrepresentation see MISREPRESENTATION vol 76 (2013) PARA 780 et seq. Liability for fraud will not be established against a company in the absence of specific allegations against officials: see *Smith and Houston Ltd v Metal Industries (Salvage) Ltd* (1953) 103 L Jo 734, Ct of Sess.

5 It is possible that a company may sometimes be liable for the tortious acts of its liquidator: see *Metropolitan Bank Ltd v Pooley* (1885) 10 App Cas 210 at 218, HL, per Lord Selborne LC.

6 *Multinational Gas and Petrochemical Co v Multinational Gas and Petrochemical Services Ltd* [1983] Ch 258, [1983] 2 All ER 563, CA; *Meridian Global Funds Management Asia Ltd v Securities Commission* [1995] 2 AC 500, [1995] 3 All ER 918, PC. As to the personal liability of directors for any breach of duty in tort see PARA 633.

7 *Smith v Hull Glass Co* (1852) 11 CB 897 at 928; *Re Henry Bentley & Co and Yorkshire Breweries, ex p Harrison* (1893) 69 LT 204, CA. Thus, as a principal is estopped from denying the full authority of his agent where the limitation of it is not disclosed, an application for shares which is conditional in the hands of the applicant's agent may be absolute in the hands of the company: *Re Henry Bentley & Co and Yorkshire Breweries, ex p Harrison*; and see AGENCY vol 1 (2008) PARA 25. A concealed limitation of the directors' powers does not bind third persons without notice: *Commercial Mutual Marine Insurance Co v Union Mutual Insurance Co* (1856) 19 Howard 318. See also the Companies Act 2006 ss 39–42; and PARAS 262–264.

8 *Sutton v Tatham* (1839) 10 Ad & El 27 at 30 per Litterdale J; *Trott v National Discount Co* (1900) 17 TLR 37.

9 *Bryant, Powis and Bryant v La Banque du Peuple* [1893] AC 170, PC; *Hambro v Burnand* [1904] 2 KB 10, CA; *Cuthbert v Robarts, Lubbock & Co* [1909] 2 Ch 226 at 235, CA, per Buckley LJ; *Re Land Credit Co of Ireland, ex p Overend, Gurney & Co* (1869) 4 Ch App 460 (distinguished in *Premier Industrial Bank Ltd v Carlton Manufacturing Co Ltd and Crabtree Ltd* [1909] 1 KB 106). The last-named case was expressly dissented from in *Dey v Pullinger Engineering Co* [1921] 1 KB 77, where the principle laid down in *Royal British Bank v Turquand* (1856) 6 E & B 327 (see PARA 265) was applied (see also PARA 262 note 3). As to agency by estoppel see AGENCY vol 1 (2008) PARA 25.

10 See the Statute of Frauds Amendment Act 1828 s 6; and MISREPRESENTATION vol 76 (2013) PARA 803.

11 *UBAF Ltd v European American Banking Corpn, The Pacific Colcotronis* [1984] QB 713, [1984] 2 All ER 226, CA. On proper examination, *Swift v Jewsbury and Goddard* (1874) LR 9 QB 301, Ex Ch and *Hirst v West Riding Union Banking Co Ltd* [1901] 2 KB 560, CA, which had been presumed to support the contrary, do not preclude such a finding.

12 *Contex Drouzhba Ltd v Wiseman* [2007] EWCA Civ 1201, [2008] 1 BCLC 631 (affg [2006] EWHC 2708 (QB), [2007] 1 BCLC 758) (director liable).

298. Company's liability for misrepresentation. Persons who have been induced to enter into transactions with a company for the purchase of chattels or goods by misrepresentation may, instead of claiming rescission with a return of money paid, elect to retain the goods or chattels and recover any damages which have been sustained[1].

The statutory liability[2] as to misstatements in listing particulars[3] or a prospectus[4] does not affect any liability which any person may incur under the general law apart from that liability[5]. In respect of the liability so incurred, the remedies for misrepresentation open to an allottee of shares, but not necessarily to a transferee of his shares[6], or to a person in whose favour an allotment of shares is renounced[7], are:

(1) rectification of the register of members by the court and consequent relief[8];
(2) rescission of the contract[9];
(3) damages in a claim of deceit[10] or negligent misrepresentation[11] or negligent misstatement[12];
(4) compensation or damages under the relevant provision of the Financial Services and Markets Act 2000[13]; and
(5) criminal proceedings[14].

Issuers of securities are liable to pay compensation to persons who have suffered loss as a result of a misleading statement or dishonest omission in certain published information relating to the securities, or a dishonest delay in publishing such information[15].

1 See the Misrepresentation Act 1967 s 2(2); and MISREPRESENTATION vol 76 (2013) PARA 832. Section 2 does not entitle a person to be paid damages in respect of a misrepresentation if the person has a right to redress under the Consumer Protection from Unfair Trading Regulations 2008, SI 2008/1277, Pt 4A (regs 27A–27L) (consumers' rights to redress: see CONSUMER PROTECTION vol 21 (2011) PARAS 509A–509F) in respect of the conduct constituting the misrepresentation: Misrepresentation Act 1967 s 2(4) (added by SI 2014/870).
2 Ie under the Financial Services and Markets Act 2000 s 90 (see FINANCIAL SERVICES REGULATION vol 50A (2016) PARAS 641–642). See also PARA 1259.
3 As to listing particulars see the Financial Services and Markets Act 2000 s 79; and FINANCIAL SERVICES REGULATION vol 50A (2016) PARA 597 et seq. See also PARA 1259.
4 As to prospectuses see FINANCIAL SERVICES REGULATION vol 50A (2016) PARA 601 et seq. See also PARA 1259.
5 See the Financial Services and Markets Act 2000 s 90(6) (see FINANCIAL SERVICES REGULATION vol 50A (2016) PARA 641). See also PARA 1259. As to the exemptions from liability for non-compliance (in relation to listed securities) see FINANCIAL SERVICES REGULATION vol 50A (2016) PARA 642.
6 *Hyslop v Morel* (1891) 7 TLR 263; *Andrews v Mockford* [1896] 1 QB 372, CA. As to sub-underwriters see PARA 1345.
7 *Collins v Associated Greyhound Racecourses Ltd* [1930] 1 Ch 1.
8 See PARA 352. As to the register of members see PARA 336 et seq.
9 See PARA 1260.
10 See PARA 1270 et seq.
11 See the Misrepresentation Act 1967 s 2; and MISREPRESENTATION vol 76 (2013) PARA 797. See also PARA 1276.
12 See NEGLIGENCE vol 78 (2010) PARA 14. See also PARA 1276.
13 See note 2.
14 Eg, in circumstances where criminal liability for fraud may be proved (as to which see CRIMINAL LAW vol 25 (2016) PARA 346 et seq).
15 See the Financial Services and Markets Act 2000 s 90A, Sch 10A; and FINANCIAL SERVICES REGULATION vol 50A (2016) PARA 641. See also PARA 1259.

299. Defamation at company meetings etc. At common law, a claim cannot be brought for slanders uttered at a meeting of a company, provided the allegations are germane to its affairs and there is no malice, for to that extent the occasion is privileged; complaints made to the directors or managers touching the conduct of its affairs are similarly privileged[1]. Even away from meetings of the company, a shareholder has a qualified privilege in making communications to another shareholder as such[2].

Neither a company nor its directors are liable in proceedings for libel if, without malice, they circulate among the shareholders an auditor's report reflecting on one of the agents[3].

1 *Harris v Thompson* (1853) 13 CB 333. As to company meetings generally see PARA 701 et seq. As to the defence of privilege in the law of defamation see DEFAMATION vol 32 (2012) PARA 594 et seq.

2 *Quartz Hill Consolidated Gold Mining Co v Beall* (1882) 20 ChD 501, CA.

3 *Lawless v Anglo-Egyptian Cotton and Oil Co* (1869) LR 4 QB 262. Cf *Nevill v Fine Arts and General Insurance Co* [1897] AC 68, HL; *Philadelphia, Wilmington and Baltimore Railroad Co v Quigley* 62 US (21 How) 202 (1858). As to statements in official reports in a winding up by official receivers and other officials see COMPANY AND PARTNERSHIP INSOLVENCY vol 16 (2011) PARA 477 et seq.

300. Defamation in published reports of proceedings or in published documents. For the purposes of defamation proceedings[1], the publication[2] of any of the following reports or statements[3] is subject to a statutory defence of qualified privilege[4] unless the publication is shown to be made with malice[5]:

(1) a fair and accurate report of proceedings at a general meeting of a listed company[6];

(2) a fair and accurate copy of, extract from or summary of any document circulated to members of a listed company[7]:

(a) by or with the authority of the board of directors of the company[8];

(b) by the auditors of the company[9]; or

(c) by any member of the company in pursuance of a right conferred by any statutory provision[10];

(3) a fair and accurate copy of, extract from or summary of any document circulated to members of a listed company which relates to the appointment, resignation, retirement or dismissal of directors of the company or its auditors[11].

However, in defamation proceedings in respect of the publication of such a report or statement, the statutory defence of qualified privilege is not available if the claimant shows that the defendant[12]:

(i) was requested by him to publish in a suitable manner[13] a reasonable letter or statement by way of explanation or contradiction[14]; and

(ii) refused or neglected to do so[15].

Nor is the statutory defence available to protect the publication of matter the publication of which is prohibited by law[17].

1 As to defamation proceedings generally see DEFAMATION.

2 For these purposes, 'publication' and 'publish', in relation to a statement, have the meaning they have for the purposes of the law of defamation generally (see DEFAMATION vol 32 (2012) PARA 560 et seq): Defamation Act 1996 s 17(1). The provisions of s 15 (see DEFAMATION vol 32 (2012) PARAS 633–634) do not apply to the publication to the public, or a section of the public, of matter which is not of public interest and the publication of which is not for the public benefit: s 15(3) (amended by the Defamation Act 2013 s 7(2)). Publication of a report of charges against a company's officers is not for the public benefit: *Ponsford v Financial Times Ltd and Hart* (1900) 16 TLR 248 (a meeting of company shareholders is a public meeting).

3 A statement may be in the form of words or pictures or visual images or gestures or any other method of signifying meaning: see Defamation Act 1996 s 17(1); and DEFAMATION vol 32 (2012) PARA 510 et seq.

4 Ie under the Defamation Act 1996 s 15 (see DEFAMATION vol 32 (2012) PARAS 633–634). As to the defence of qualified privilege generally see DEFAMATION vol 32 (2012) PARA 609 et seq.

5 Defamation Act 1996 s 15(1). As to malice sufficient to defeat a defence raised in defamation proceedings see DEFAMATION vol 32 (2012) PARA 651 et seq.
6 Defamation Act 1996 Sch 1 para 13(1) (amended by the Defamation Act 2013 s 7(3), (7)(a)). For the purposes of heads (1)–(3) in the text, 'listed company' has the same meaning as in the Corporation Tax Act 2009 Pt 12 (ss 1001–1038B) (see s 1005): Defamation Act 1996 Sch 1 para 13(4) (Sch 1 para 13(2)–(4) substituted by the Defamation Act 2013 s 7(3), (7)(b)). The Corporation Tax Act 2009 s 1005 defines a 'listed company' as a company whose shares are listed on a recognised stock exchange, and which is neither a close company nor a company that would be a close company if it were UK resident.
7 Defamation Act 1996 Sch 1 para 13(2) (as substituted: see note 6).
8 Defamation Act 1996 Sch 1 para 13(2)(a) (as substituted: see note 6). As to a company's directors see PARA 512 et seq.
9 Defamation Act 1996 Sch 1 para 13(2)(b) (as substituted: see note 6). As to company auditors see PARA 983 et seq.
10 Defamation Act 1996 Sch 1 para 13(2)(c) (as substituted: see note 6).
11 Defamation Act 1996 Sch 1 para 13(3) (as substituted: see note 6).
12 Defamation Act 1996 s 15(2).
13 For this purpose, 'in a suitable manner' means in the same manner as the publication complained of or in a manner that is adequate and reasonable in the circumstances: Defamation Act 1996 s 15(2). The terms of the letter or statement which the claimant requires must be sent by him to the defendant as part of the request: see *Khan v Ahmed* [1957] 2 QB 149, [1957] 2 All ER 385 (a decision on an earlier similar provision under the Defamation Act 1952).
14 Defamation Act 1996 s 15(2)(a).
15 Defamation Act 1996 s 15(2)(b).
17 Defamation Act 1996 s 15(4)(a). Nothing in these provisions is to be construed as limiting or abridging any privilege subsisting otherwise: s 15(4)(b).

301. Torts committed against companies. A company may claim for any damage done to it in its corporate capacity by a tort not of a purely personal nature, such as a libel affecting its property, or a libel reflecting on the management of its trade or business[1], or attacking its financial position[2]. It is not necessary to prove special damage[3].

A claim is available to a trading company in respect of the malicious and unreasonable presentation of a winding-up petition against it[4].

Where the company is a victim of a conspiracy to which its directors acting on its behalf are parties, the company will not be considered a co-conspirator, and may recover damages from the directors if it suffers loss as a result of the conspiracy[5].

A company is not a 'person' for the purpose of seeking injunctive relief[6] against harassment[7].

1 As to the meanings of 'trade' and 'business' generally see PARA 1 note 1.
2 *Metropolitan Saloon Omnibus Co v Hawkins* (1859) 4 H & N 87; *Thorley's Cattle Food Co v Massam* (1880) 14 ChD 763, CA; *Slazengers Ltd v C Gibbs & Co* (1916) 33 TLR 35. See also *Rubber Improvement Ltd v Daily Telegraph Ltd* [1964] AC 234, sub nom *Lewis v Daily Telegraph Ltd* [1963] 2 All ER 151, HL (subsequent proceedings sub nom *Lewis v Daily Telegraph Ltd (No 2)* [1964] 2 QB 601, [1964] 1 All ER 705, CA); and CORPORATIONS vol 24 (2010) PARA 481.
3 *South Hetton Coal Co v North-Eastern News Association* [1894] 1 QB 133, CA; *Linotype Co Ltd v British Empire Type-setting Machine Co Ltd* (1899) 81 LT 331, HL.
4 *Quartz Hill Consolidated Gold Mining Co v Eyre* (1883) 11 QBD 674, CA. See also COMPANY AND PARTNERSHIP INSOLVENCY vol 16 (2011) PARA 399. As to winding up in general see COMPANY AND PARTNERSHIP INSOLVENCY vol 16 (2011) PARA 380 et seq.
5 *Belmont Finance Corpn Ltd v Williams Furniture Ltd* [1979] Ch 250, [1979] 1 All ER 118, CA (conspiracy to cause company to breach the Companies Act 1948 s 54 (see now the Companies Act 2006 ss 678, 679; and see PARAS 1411–1412)).
6 Ie under the Protection from Harassment Act 1997 s 3: see TORT vol 97 (2015) PARA 558.
7 *Daiichi UK Ltd v Stop Huntingdon Animal Cruelty* [2003] EWHC 2337 (QB), [2004] 1 WLR 1503, [2005] 1 BCLC 27.

(vi) Civil Proceedings involving a Company

302. Company's name in litigation. As from the date of a company's incorporation[1], the subscribers of the memorandum of association[2], together with such other persons as may from time to time become members of the company[3], are a body corporate[4] by the name stated in the certificate of incorporation[5]. As such, the company may only proceed or be proceeded against in its corporate name[6].

A change of a company's name has effect from the date on which the new certificate of incorporation is issued[7]; and the effect of the issue of the certificate of incorporation on change of name is not to re-form or reincorporate the company as a new entity but to recognise the continued existence of the company under its new name[8]. The change does not affect any rights or obligations of the company or render defective any legal proceedings by or against it[9]; and any legal proceedings that might have been continued or commenced against it by its former name may be continued or commenced against it by its new name[10].

If the name of the company has been wrongly used as claimant, it will be struck out as claimant[11], but may be added as defendant[12]. The solicitor[13] or the person who instructed him and who was also claimant[14] may be ordered to pay the costs of a company improperly made claimant and of the defendant[15]. However, where, in bringing the proceedings in the company's name, the claimants substantially represent the wishes of the majority of the shareholders, the claimants' costs may be directed to be paid by the company[16]. Where proceedings are properly brought in the company's name, the solicitors for those who unsuccessfully apply in its name for a stay may be ordered to pay the costs personally[17].

A company which purports to have been incorporated in a foreign country may be recognised as a corporation in England and, as such, English law will allow it to sue and be sued in England in its corporate capacity[18].

1 Ie the date mentioned in the certificate of incorporation, following the registration of a company: see PARA 114 note 7. As to the meaning of 'company' under the Companies Acts see PARA 21; and as to the meaning of the 'Companies Acts' see PARA 13. As to a company's incorporation by registration under the Companies Act 2006 see PARA 104 et seq. As to companies registered but not formed under the Companies Act 2006, and as to overseas companies, see PARA 29.

2 As to the memorandum of association, and subscribers of the memorandum, see PARA 97.

3 As to membership of a company see PARA 323 et seq.

4 As to the meaning of 'body corporate' see PARA 1 note 5.

5 See the Companies Act 2006 s 16; and PARA 115. As to the company's name see PARA 199 et seq.

6 *Re Hodges* (1873) 8 Ch App 204; *Pilbrow v Pilbrow's Atmospheric Rly Co* (1846) 3 CB 730. In *Springate v Questier* [1952] 2 All ER 21, notice of an intended prosecution for a road traffic offence was held to have been validly served on a limited company, though the word 'limited' was omitted. See generally CORPORATIONS vol 24 (2010) PARA 493. As to the amendment of misnomers for the purpose of proceedings see *Etablissement Baudelot v RS Graham & Co Ltd* [1953] 2 QB 271, [1953] 1 All ER 149, CA (French trading firm wrongly described as incorporated company). As to the rules that apply to proceedings under companies legislation generally see PARA 306.

7 See the Companies Act 2006 s 81(1); and PARA 218.

8 *Oshkosh B'Gosh Inc v Dan Marbel Inc Ltd* [1989] 1 CMLR 94, [1989] BCLC 507, CA.

9 See the Companies Act 2006 s 81(2); and PARA 218.

10 See the Companies Act 2006 s 81(3); and PARA 218. Where a company changes its name in the course of proceedings, the title of any claim form, application, affidavit, witness statement, notice or other document in such proceedings must be altered by substituting the new name for the old, and by inserting the old name in brackets at the end of the title: see CPR PD 49A—*Applications under the Companies Acts and Related Legislation* para 4(2).

11 *Atwool v Merryweather* (1867) LR 5 Eq 464n at 468n per Page Wood V-C; *Pender v Lushington* (1877) 6 ChD 70; *Oystermouth Rly or Tramroad Co v Morris* [1876] WN 129 (on appeal [1876] WN 192 (dismissed with costs)); *West End Hotels Syndicate Ltd v Bayer* (1912) 29 TLR 92.

12 *Silber Light Co v Silber* (1879) 12 ChD 717.

13 *Newbiggin-by-the-Sea Gas Co v Armstrong* (1879) 13 ChD 310, CA; *John Morley Building Co v Barras* [1891] 2 Ch 386; *Gold Reefs of Western Australia Ltd v Dawson* [1897] 1 Ch 115; *West End Hotels Syndicate Ltd v Bayer* (1912) 29 TLR 92.

14 *Compagnie de Mayville v Whitley* [1896] 1 Ch 788 at 810, CA, per Smith LJ. See also *Wandsworth and Putney Gas-Light and Coke Co v Wright* (1870) 22 LT 404.

15 See *Silber Light Co v Silber* (1879) 12 ChD 717. Where a solicitor had originally authority to defend an action for a company which was afterwards dissolved, he was ordered to pay the costs of the plaintiff as from the date on which he might with due diligence have known of the dissolution: *Salton v New Beeston Cycle Co* [1900] 1 Ch 43. The proper order would now date from the dissolution itself: see *Yonge v Toynbee* [1910] 1 KB 215, CA. As to the effect of solicitors acting without authority see LEGAL PROFESSIONS vol 66 (2015) PARA 660.

16 *Re Imperial Hydropathic Hotel Co, Blackpool v Hampson* (1882) 23 ChD 1, CA.

17 *Marshall's Valve Gear Co Ltd v Manning, Wardle & Co Ltd* [1909] 1 Ch 267 at 275 per Neville J.

18 *Henriques v General Privileged Dutch Co Trading to West Indies* (1728) 2 Ld Raym 1532; *Newby v von Oppen and Colt's Patent Firearms Manufacturing Co* (1872) LR 7 QB 293; *Lazard Bros & Co v Midland Bank Ltd* [1933] AC 289 at 297, HL. As to the principles on which recognition is accorded or withheld see CONFLICT OF LAWS vol 19 (2011) PARA 763 et seq. The universal succession of one foreign corporate body to another will also be recognised: *National Bank of Greece and Athens SA v Metliss* [1958] AC 509, [1957] 3 All ER 608, HL (creditor's action against successor to foreign guarantor company).

303. Control of company's litigation. As regards litigation by an incorporated company[1], where management powers are vested generally in the board of directors[2], it is the directors who have authority to act for the company[3]. In the absence of any provision to the contrary in the articles of association, the majority of the members of a company[4] are not entitled to decide whether an action in the company's name should be begun or allowed to proceed[5]. The secretary[6] of a company cannot institute proceedings in its name in the absence of express authority to do so[7]; but proceedings begun without proper authority may subsequently be ratified[8].

Any objection that proceedings in the name of the company are not properly authorised should be raised at the outset by an application to have the name of the company struck out; if not so raised, it may be raised when it comes to the attention of the court or the defendant that this is the case[9]. Where appropriate, the proceedings may be adjourned so that the issue as to the initial authorisation, or subsequent ratification, of the proceedings may be tried[10].

1 As to incorporated companies generally see PARA 2.

2 Ie in the manner provided for by the company's articles of association: see PARA 581. As to a company's articles of association generally see PARA 227 et seq. As to a company's directors see PARA 512 et seq.

3 See PARA 584; *Harben v Phillips* (1883) 23 ChD 14 at 29 per Chitty J. See also *Mitchell & Hobbs (UK) Ltd v Mill* [1996] 2 BCLC 102 (managing director does not have power to bring proceedings in the name of the company without reference to the other directors unless that power has been specifically delegated to him). As to delegation see also PARA 577.

4 As to membership of a company see PARA 323 et seq.

5 *Automatic Self-Cleansing Filter Syndicate Co Ltd v Cuninghame* [1906] 2 Ch 34, CA; *Gramophone and Typewriter Ltd v Stanley* [1908] 2 KB 89 at 98, CA, per Fletcher Moulton LJ, and at 105 per Buckley LJ; *Quin & Axtens Ltd v Salmon* [1909] AC 442, HL; *Breckland Group Holdings Ltd v London & Suffolk Properties Ltd* [1989] BCLC 100. Cf *Marshall's Valve Gear Co Ltd v Manning, Wardle & Co Ltd* [1909] 1 Ch 267 at 272 per Neville J; *Pender v Lushington* (1877) 6 ChD 70; *Duckett v Gover* (1877) 6 ChD 82; *Harben v Phillips* (1883) 23 ChD 14, CA. See also PARA 646.

6 As to the company secretary see PARA 669 et seq.

7 *Daimler Co Ltd v Continental Tyre and Rubber Co (Great Britain) Ltd* [1916] 2 AC 307, HL. As to the court procedure where there is want of authority to sue see *Russian Commercial and Industrial Bank v Comptoir d'Escompte de Mulhouse* [1925] AC 112, HL; *John Shaw & Sons (Salford) Ltd v Shaw* [1935] 2 KB 113, CA; and CIVIL PROCEDURE vol 11 (2015) PARA 470.

8 *Danish Mercantile Co Ltd v Beaumont* [1951] Ch 680, [1951] 1 All ER 925, CA; approved in *Alexander Ward & Co Ltd v Samyang Navigation Co Ltd* [1975] 2 All ER 424, [1975] 1 WLR

673, HL (company without directors; two individuals brought proceedings on company's behalf to recover debt without authority; acts of individuals subsequently ratified by liquidator).

9 *Airways Ltd v Bowen* [1985] BCLC 355, CA.

10 *Airways Ltd v Bowen* [1985] BCLC 355, CA.

304. Representative parties. Where more than one person has the same interest in a claim[1], as where a member of a company seeks to enforce or protect the rights of members generally, the claim may be begun, or the court may order that the claim be continued, by or against one or more of the persons who have the same interest, as representatives of any other persons who have that interest[2]. Unless the court otherwise directs, any judgment or order given in a claim in which a party is acting as a representative under the rules governing representative parties is binding on all persons represented in the claim, but may only be enforced by or against a person who is not a party to the claim with the permission of the court[3].

No consent is required from those on whose behalf the claimant purports to sue[4]. A claimant suing on behalf of a class must specify the class as accurately as possible[5]; but the fact that the interest of some members of the class is different from that of the claimant does not make the proceedings defective[6]. The fact that the claimant is suing on behalf of himself and others should be stated in the title of the pleading, and not merely in the statement of claim[7].

Whatever is a defence against the party making a claim in a representative capacity is a defence to the proceedings, even though other persons on whose behalf he is making a claim might maintain the proceedings[8]. If anyone objects to the claimant suing on his behalf, he should apply to have himself added as a defendant[9]; but the application must be made promptly[10].

The court will not allow a person to represent himself and others as defendants unless it is satisfied that he is authorised to represent the others[11].

If the claimant is suing as a creditor and a trustee is appointed in his bankruptcy whilst the proceedings are pending, the right of action vests in his trustee, and, unless the trustee intervenes, the proceedings will be dismissed[12].

1 Ie other than proceedings under CPR 19.7 (representation of interested persons who cannot be ascertained): see CIVIL PROCEDURE vol 11 (2015) PARA 492.

2 See CPR 19.6(1); and CIVIL PROCEDURE vol 11 (2015) PARA 491.

3 See CPR 19.6(4); and CIVIL PROCEDURE vol 11 (2015) PARA 491. See also *City of London Sewers Comrs v Gellatly* (1876) 3 ChD 610 at 615 per Jessel MR; *Friends Provident and Century Life Office v Investment Trust Corpn Ltd* [1951] 2 All ER 632 at 634, HL, per Lord Simonds. As to a judgment against trustees for debenture holders binding the debenture holders see *Cox v Dublin City Distillery Co Ltd (No 3)* [1917] 1 IR 203, CA.

4 *White v Carmarthen etc Rly Co* (1863) 1 Hem & M 786; *Bloxam v Metropolitan Rly Co* (1868) 3 Ch App 337. As to the claimant's right to discontinue proceedings see *Handford v Storie* (1825) 2 Sim & St 196; *Re Alpha Co Ltd, Ward v Alpha Co* [1903] 1 Ch 203.

5 *Marshall v South Staffordshire Tramways Co* [1895] 2 Ch 36, CA.

6 *Hallows v Fernie* (1868) 3 Ch App 467; *Watson v Cave* (1881) 17 ChD 19, CA.

7 *Re Tottenham, Tottenham v Tottenham* [1896] 1 Ch 628 (explaining *Eyre v Cox* (1876) 24 WR 317); *Worraker v Pryer* (1876) 2 ChD 109; *Dover Picture Palace Ltd and Pessers v Dover Corpn and Crundall, Wraith, Gurr and Knight* (1913) 11 LGR 971, CA.

8 *Burt v British Nation Life Assurance Association* (1859) 4 De G & J 158; *Scarth v Chadwick* (1850) 14 Jur 300.

9 *Wilson v Church* (1878) 9 ChD 552; *Watson v Cave* (1881) 17 ChD 19, CA; *Fraser v Cooper, Hall & Co* (1882) 21 ChD 718; *May v Newton* (1887) 34 ChD 347.

10 *Conybeare v Lewis* (1883) 48 LT 527.

11 *Morgan's Brewery Co v Crosskill* [1902] 1 Ch 898. As to appointing parties to represent absent persons see CPR 19.7; and CIVIL PROCEDURE vol 11 (2015) PARA 492.

12 *Wolff v Van Boolen* (1906) 94 LT 502. As to trustees in bankruptcy see BANKRUPTCY AND INDIVIDUAL INSOLVENCY vol 5 (2013) PARA 314 et seq.

305. When representative claim may be brought. A representative claim is properly brought[1] by a shareholder to prevent the improper declaration or payment of dividends[2], or the misapplication of the company's funds[3], or purchase by the company of its own shares[4], or an improper reduction of capital[5], or improper forfeiture of shares[6], or to stop directors from making calls unfairly[7], or to prevent loans to them[8], or to impeach the validity of resolutions as to the issue of shares or otherwise[9].

Proceedings may be brought by an applicant for shares on behalf of himself and other depositors when the company is abortive and no shares have been issued[10].

Where another class of shareholders has a conflicting interest, they should be made defendants[11].

In proceedings against directors for misrepresentation, several persons may join as claimants[12].

1 As to representative claims by debenture holders see COMPANY AND PARTNERSHIP INSOLVENCY.

2 *Hoole v Great Western Rly Co* (1867) 3 Ch App 262; *Bloxam v Metropolitan Rly Co* (1868) 3 Ch App 337; *Wood v Odessa Waterworks Co* (1889) 42 ChD 636. Cf *Carlisle v South Eastern Rly Co* (1850) 1 Mac & G 689 (payment of dividends actually declared; not restrained); *Salisbury v Metropolitan Rly Co* (1870) 18 WR 484 at 486 per James V-C; *Will v United Lankat Plantations Co Ltd* [1912] 2 Ch 571, CA (affd [1914] AC 11, HL). Cf *Fawcett v Laurie* (1860) 1 Drew & Sm 192 at 202–203 per Kindersley V-C. As to proceedings by creditors or debenture holders to restrain the payment of improper dividends see PARA 1580.

3 *Guinness v Land Corpn of Ireland Ltd* (1882) 22 ChD 349, CA; *Smith v Duke of Manchester* (1883) 24 ChD 611 (costs of dismissed winding-up petition by directors); *Studdert v Grosvenor* (1886) 33 ChD 528 (as to the points decided in this case see *Peel v London and North Western Rly Co* [1907] 1 Ch 5, CA); *Tomkinson v South-Eastern Rly Co* (1887) 35 ChD 675; *Lyde v Eastern Bengal Rly Co* (1866) 36 Beav 10; *Vance v East Lancashire Rly Co* (1856) 3 K & J 50 (application to Parliament); *Warburton v Huddersfield Industrial Society* [1892] 1 QB 817, CA; *Evans v Brunner, Mond & Co Ltd* [1921] 1 Ch 359.

4 *Hope v International Financial Society* (1876) 4 ChD 327, CA; *Rowell v John Rowell & Sons Ltd* [1912] 2 Ch 609. A company may obtain authorisation to purchase its own shares: see PARA 1416 et seq.

5 *Bannatyne v Direct Spanish Telegraph Co* (1886) 34 ChD 287, CA.

6 *Sweny v Smith* (1869) LR 7 Eq 324.

7 *Alexander v Automatic Telephone Co* [1900] 2 Ch 56, CA.

8 *Bluck v Mallalue* (1859) 27 Beav 398.

9 *Andrews v Gas Meter Co* [1897] 1 Ch 361, CA; *Preston v Grand Collier Dock Co* (1840) 11 Sim 327; *McEllistrim v Ballymacelligott Co-operative Agricultural and Dairy Society Ltd* [1919] AC 548, HL.

10 *Moseley v Cressey's Co* (1865) LR 1 Eq 405.

11 *Hoole v Great Western Rly Co* (1867) 3 Ch App 262 at 277–278 per Rolt LJ.

12 *Drincqbier v Wood* [1899] 1 Ch 393.

306. Procedure for making claims and applications to court under companies legislation. The legislation relating to companies provides for many applications to be made to the court with reference to the companies which are subject to its provisions[1].

The Civil Procedure Rules[2] apply to proceedings under the Companies Act 1985[3], the Companies Act 2006[4] and other legislation relating to companies and limited liability partnerships[5], subject to the provision of the relevant practice direction which applies to those proceedings[6]. The claim form will be issued (where issued in the High Court) out of the Companies Court or a Chancery district registry or (where issued out of a County Court hearing centre), out of a County Court office[7]. Where, in a claim under the Companies Act 2006, the company concerned is not the claimant, the company is to be made a defendant to the claim unless any other enactment, the Civil Procedure Rules or a relevant practice direction[8] makes a different provision or unless the court orders otherwise[9]; and where an application is made in the course of proceedings to which the company is or is required to be a defendant, the company must be made a respondent to the application unless any other enactment, the Civil Procedure Rules or a relevant practice direction[10] makes a different provision or unless the court orders otherwise[11].

Provisions in the Companies Act 2006[12], supplemented by Civil Procedure Rules[13], introduce a two-stage procedure for permission to continue a derivative claim:

(1) the applicant is required to make a prima facie case for permission to continue a derivative claim and the court is required to consider the issue on the basis of the evidence filed by the applicant only, without requiring evidence from the defendant[14];

(2) before the substantive action begins, the court may require evidence to be provided by the company, and the matters which the court must take into account in considering whether to give permission and the circumstances in which the court is bound to refuse permission are set out[15].

Questions as to the true meaning of a company's constitution[16] may be decided by the court in the course of proceedings. The court may decide the question as between the company and the shareholder who is the other party to the claim[17], but will not usually appoint a defendant shareholder to represent a class, or decide the question so as to bind the class unless a meeting of the members of the class is first called and nominates a person to represent the class[18].

1 As to the procedure that applies generally to such applications see the text and notes 2–7. See also the Insolvency Rules 1986, SI 1986/1925; and COMPANY AND PARTNERSHIP INSOLVENCY vol 17 (2011) PARA 1002 et seq. The mode in which applications are to be made is dealt with in this title where the provisions under which the applications may be made are dealt with.

2 As to the Civil Procedure Rules generally see CIVIL PROCEDURE vol 11 (2016) PARA 6 et seq.

3 CPR 49(a). As to proceedings under the Companies Act 1985 see PARA 1725 et seq.

4 CPR 49(b).

5 CPR 49(c).

6 CPR 49. CPR PD 49A—*Applications under the Companies Acts and Related Legislation* applies to proceedings under the Companies Act 1985 (as to which see PARA 1725 et seq), under the Companies Act 2006 (except proceedings under Pt 11 Ch 1 (ss 260–264) (derivative claims in England and Wales or Northern Ireland) (see PARA 646 et seq) or under Pt 30 (ss 994–999) (protection of members against unfair prejudice) (see PARA 657 et seq)), under Council Regulation (EC) 2157/2001 (OJ L294, 10.11.2001, p 1) arts 22, 25 and 26 (see PARA 1835), under the Financial Services and Markets Act 2000 Pt VII (ss 103A–117) (control of business transfers) (see FINANCIAL SERVICES REGULATION vol 50A (2016) PARA 826 et seq) and under the Companies (Cross-Border Mergers) Regulations 2007, SI 2007/2974 (see PARA 1631): see CPR PD 49A—*Applications under the Companies Acts and Related Legislation* para 2. CPR Pt 19 and CPR PD 19C—*Derivative Claims* contain provisions about proceedings under the Companies Act 2006 Pt 11 Ch 1: see CPR PD 49A—*Applications under the Companies Acts and Related Legislation* para 2; and see PARA 646 et seq.

7 SeeCPR PD 49A—*Applications under the Companies Acts and Related Legislation* para 5(2). Proceedings to which CPR PD 49A—*Applications under the Companies Acts and Related Legislation* applies must be started by a Part 8 claim form (as to which see CIVIL PROCEDURE vol 11 (2015) PARAS 139, 150 et seq) unless a provision of that practice direction or another practice direction provides otherwise, but subject to any modification of that procedure by that or any other practice direction: CPR PD 49A—*Applications under the Companies Acts and Related Legislation* para 5(1). Where CPR PD 49A—*Applications under the Companies Acts and Related Legislation* requires a party to proceedings to notify another person of an application, such notification must, unless the court orders otherwise, be given by sending to that other person a copy of the claim form as soon as reasonably practicable after the claim form has been issued: see para 5(3).

The claim form in proceedings under the Companies Act 1985 (as to which see PARA 1725 et seq), under the Companies Act 2006, under the Financial Services and Markets Act 2000 Pt VII (control of business transfers) (see FINANCIAL SERVICES REGULATION vol 50A (2016) PARA 826 et seq), under Council Regulation (EC) 2157/2001 (OJ L294, 10.11.2001, p 1) (see PARA 1835) or under the Companies (Cross-Border Mergers) Regulations 2007, SI 2007/2974 (see PARA 1631), and any application, affidavit, witness statement, notice or other document in such proceedings, must be entitled 'In the matter of [*the name of the company in question*] and in the matter of [*the relevant law*]', where the 'relevant law' means the 'Companies Act 1985', the 'Companies Act 2006', 'Part VII of the Financial Services and Markets Act 2000', 'Council Regulation (EC) No 2157/2001 of 8 October 2001 on the Statute for a European Company (SE)' or the 'Companies (Cross-Border Merger) Regulations 2007', as the case may be: see CPR PD 49A—*Applications under the Companies Acts and Related Legislation* para 4(1). A statement of claim against a company, if it states the corporate title, need not allege that the company is a corporation or state how it was incorporated: *Woolf v City Steam Boat Co* (1849) 7 CB 103.

8 Ie CPR PD 49A—*Applications under the Companies Acts and Related Legislation* or another practice direction.

9 CPR PD 49A—*Applications under the Companies Acts and Related Legislation* para 7(1).

10 See note 8.

11 CPR PD 49A—*Applications under the Companies Acts and Related Legislation* para 7(2).

12 Ie the Companies Act 2006 Pt 11 Ch 1 (derivative claims in England and Wales or Northern Ireland): see PARA 646 et seq.

13 Ie CPR 19.9–19.9F: see PARA 647 et seq.

14 See PARA 648 et seq.

15 See PARA 650 et seq.

16 As to the meaning of references to a company's constitution see PARA 226.

17 *Mason v Schuppisser* (1899) 81 LT 147; *Re William Thomas & Co Ltd* [1915] 1 Ch 325.

18 *Morgan's Brewery Co v Crosskill* [1902] 1 Ch 898.

307. Practice relating to claims and applications to court under companies legislation. A company may be represented, with the permission of the court, by a duly-authorised employee[1]. In relation to the small-claims track, a corporate party may be represented by any of its officers or employees[2].

Where a transaction by a company is within its powers but is about to be carried out without the necessary sanction of the shareholders, an injunction may be granted until the meeting has been held to sanction the transaction[3].

1 See CPR 39.6; and CIVIL PROCEDURE vol 12 (2015) PARA 1066.

2 See CPR PD 27—*Small Claims Track* para 3.2(4); and CIVIL PROCEDURE vol 11 (2015) PARA 219.

3 *Kaye v Croydon Tramways Co* [1898] 1 Ch 358, CA; *Towers v African Tug Co* [1904] 1 Ch 558, CA; *Lawson v Financial News Ltd* (1917) 34 TLR 52, CA.

308. Disclosure of documents to or by company. An officer of a company[1] need not be made a party to proceedings in order to obtain disclosure of documents[2].

If a company is a party to proceedings, the opposite party may apply to the court for an order asking the company to clarify any matter which is in dispute in the proceedings or to give additional information in relation to any such matter, whether or not the matter is contained, or referred to, in a statement of case[3].

A response to such a request must be in writing, dated and signed by the party from whom the information is sought or his legal representative[4], and must be verified by a statement of truth[5]. A responsible or proper officer or member[6] of the company, normally the company secretary[7], should make the statement of truth, but the order may name any officer or member who has personal knowledge as to the information in the company's possession[8].

1 As to officers of the company see PARA 679.

2 *Cooke v Oceanic Steam Co* [1875] WN 220; *Dyke v Stephens* (1885) 30 ChD 189 at 191 per Pearson J. Cf *Wilson v Church* (1878) 9 ChD 552 (interrogatories).

3 See CPR 18.1(1); and CIVIL PROCEDURE vol 11 (2015) PARA 361. However, before applying for such an order, the party seeking clarification or information should first serve on the party from whom it is sought a written request for that clarification or information stating a date by which the response to the request should be served; the date must allow the second party a reasonable time to respond: see CPR PD 18—*Further Information* para 1.1; and CIVIL PROCEDURE vol 11 (2015) PARA 361. The request should be concise and strictly confined to matters which are reasonably necessary and proportionate in order to enable the requesting party to prepare his case or to understand the case he has to meet: see para 1.2; and CIVIL PROCEDURE vol 11 (2015) PARA 361.

4 See CPR PD 18—*Further Information* para 2.1; and CIVIL PROCEDURE vol 11 (2015) PARA 361.

5 See CPR PD 18—*Further Information* para 3; and CIVIL PROCEDURE vol 11 (2015) PARA 361. See also CPR Pt 22; and CIVIL PROCEDURE vol 11 (2015) PARA 363.
6 As to who qualifies as a member of a company see PARA 323.
7 As to the company secretary see PARA 669 et seq.
8 See *A-G v North Metropolitan Tramways Co* [1892] 3 Ch 70 at 74 per North J.

309. Security for costs in company claims. A defendant to any claim may apply[1] for security for his costs of the proceedings[2].

In exercising its discretion, the court will have regard to all the circumstances of the case, and must balance the injustice to the claimant (if he should be prevented from pursuing a proper claim by an order for security) against the injustice to the defendant (if no security is ordered and at the trial the claim fails and the defendant finds himself unable to recover from the claimant the costs which have been incurred by him in his defence of the claim)[3]. In considering all the circumstances, the court will have regard to the claimant company's prospects of success but without going into the merits in detail unless it can clearly be demonstrated that there is a high degree of probability of success or failure[4]. The court will not refuse to order security on the ground that it would unfairly stifle a valid claim unless it is satisfied that in all the circumstances, including whether the company can fund the litigation from outside sources, it is probable that the claim would be stifled[5].

Pre-action costs could be the subject of an application for security but the court should be slow to exercise its discretion in favour of an applicant in such circumstances because of the risk that, if the pre-action period were lengthy, the costs might be extensive and any subsequent attempt to obtain security in respect of such costs might become penal in nature[6].

The requirement for security does not enable security to be ordered to be given by the liquidator of a company taking proceedings in his own name, even where he has no means, either when he is conducting proceedings for misfeasance or is coming to the court in exercise of any other statutory duty[7].

The fact of a company being in liquidation is prima facie evidence that it will, if unsuccessful, be unable to pay the defendant's costs, even if the liquidation occurs while proceedings are pending[8]. The mere fact that a company has issued a debenture charging all its assets to secure the repayment of money then or at any time owing to a particular person is not itself a sufficient reason for ordering security[9]. A defendant company is not obliged to give security[10]; nor need it do so if it is claimant in proceedings against a person who is suing it in other proceedings in regard to the same subject matter[11].

If, however, there is a counterclaim or separate proceedings to impeach the transaction in respect of which the original proceedings are brought, security may be ordered[12], but the amount of the security should be determined by the claim alone, and not by the cross claim[13]. In interpleader proceedings, if both parties are in substance claimants, and are in a similar financial position, an order for security may only be made by one upon giving the like security as the other is ordered to give[14].

Where the court makes an order for security for costs, it will determine the amount of security[15] and direct the manner in which[16] and the time within which the security must be given[17].

1 Ie under CPR Pt 25 Section II (CPR 25.12–CPR 25.15): see CPR 25.12(1); and CIVIL PROCEDURE vol 12 (2015) PARA 617.
2 See CPR 25.12; and CIVIL PROCEDURE vol 12 (2015) PARA 617. Security for costs is dealt with among the interim remedies ordered under CPR Pt 25: see CIVIL PROCEDURE vol 12 (2015) PARA 617 et seq. As to the court's power to order indemnity against liability for costs in favour

of the claimant in derivative claims see PARA 652. The court will only have jurisdiction to award security if it appears by credible testimony that there is reason to believe that the company will, and not merely may, be unable to pay the defendant's costs if successful in its defence: *Europa Holdings Ltd v Circle Industries (UK) plc* [1993] BCLC 320, CA. There is a critical difference between a conclusion that there is 'reason to believe' that a company will be unable to pay costs and a conclusion that this has been proved to be the case: *Jirehouse Capital v Beller* [2008] EWCA Civ 908, [2009] 1 WLR 751, [2008] BPIR 1498.

The Companies Act 1985 provided that where a limited company was a claimant in any legal proceeding, the court having jurisdiction in the matter had power, if it appeared by credible testimony that there was reason to believe that the company would have been unable to pay the costs of the defendant if successful in his defence, to require sufficient security to be given for those costs, and to stay all proceedings until the security was given: see s 726 (repealed). This provision, which covered proceedings commenced by petition (*Re Unisoft Group Ltd* [1993] BCLC 528) and patent proceedings before the Comptroller-General of Patents, Designs and Trade Marks (*Abdulhayoglu's Application* [2000] RPC 18) has not been re-enacted in the Companies Act 2006. However, the cases cited in the text remain relevant to applications for security for costs under CPR 25.12, which used to interact with the Companies Act 1985 s 726 (repealed). As to the interaction between CPR Pt 25 and the Companies Act 1985 s 726 (repealed) see *Classic Catering Ltd v Donnington Park Leisure Ltd* [2001] 1 BCLC 537; *Anglo Petroleum Ltd v Hocking* [2002] EWHC 2375 (Ch), [2002] All ER (D) 444 (Oct) (application made by receivers for security for costs under CPR 25.13 and the Companies Act 1985 s 726 (repealed) allowed as it was clear that, if a costs order were to be made in favour of the receivers following the trial of the claim, the company would be unable to pay it). As to the Comptroller-General of Patents, Designs and Trade Marks see PATENTS AND REGISTERED DESIGNS vol 79 (2014) PARA 575.

Remission of the case to a county court (now the County Court) did not deprive the county court judge of his power under the Companies Act 1985 s 726 (repealed) to order security: *Plasycoed Collieries Co Ltd v Partridge, Jones & Co Ltd* (1911) 104 LT 807, DC. Security may be ordered up to a certain stage of the proceedings, with liberty to apply: *Western of Canada Oil, Lands and Works Co v Walker* (1875) 10 Ch App 628. The fact that there was another claimant, whose claim only slightly overlapped the claimant company's claim, was held not to be a ground for excusing the company from giving security in *John Bishop (Caterers) Ltd v National Union Bank Ltd* [1973] 1 All ER 707. In *Bilcon Ltd v Fegmay Investments Ltd* [1966] 2 QB 221, [1966] 2 All ER 513, security was ordered in a reference to arbitration. See also *Pearson v Naydler* [1977] 3 All ER 531, [1977] 1 WLR 899 (security ordered where there was a natural person as co-plaintiff with the company).A successful claimant will not be entitled to have the security paid out to him where the defendant has lodged an appeal and the interests of justice require that the payment stays with the court: *Stabilad Ltd v Stephens & Carter Ltd* [1998] 4 All ER 129, [1999] 1 WLR 1201, CA.

3 *Sir Lindsay Parkinson & Co Ltd v Triplan Ltd* [1973] QB 609, [1973] 2 All ER 273, CA (discretion exercisable according to all the circumstances of the particular case); *Porzelack KG v Porzelack (UK) Ltd* [1987] 1 All ER 1074, [1987] 1 WLR 420; *Keary Developments Ltd v Tarmac Construction Ltd* [1995] 3 All ER 534, [1995] 2 BCLC 395, CA.

4 *Trident International Freight Services Ltd v Manchester Ship Canal Co* [1990] BCLC 263, CA; *Keary Developments Ltd v Tarmac Construction Ltd* [1995] 3 All ER 534, [1995] 2 BCLC 395, CA. Account should also be taken of the conduct of the litigation, including any open offer or payment into court, any changes of stance by the parties and the lateness of the application, if appropriate: *Keary Developments Ltd v Tarmac Construction Ltd* [1995] 3 All ER 534, [1995] 2 BCLC 395, CA.

5 *Trident International Freight Services Ltd v Manchester Ship Canal Co* [1990] BCLC 263, CA; *Keary Developments Ltd v Tarmac Construction Ltd* [1995] 3 All ER 534, [1995] 2 BCLC 395, CA. In this regard, it is for the claimant company to satisfy the court that it would be prevented by an order for security from continuing the litigation (*Keary Developments Ltd v Tarmac Construction Ltd* [1995] 3 All ER 534, [1995] 2 BCLC 395, CA); but it is not necessary for the company, in order to have the application dismissed, to adduce evidence that it will or may be unable to pursue the proceedings if the order is granted (*Trident International Freight Services Ltd v Manchester Ship Canal Co* [1990] BCLC 263, CA).

6 *Lobster Group Ltd v Heidelberg Graphic Equipment Ltd* [2008] EWHC 413 (TCC), [2008] 2 All ER 1173, [2008] 1 BCLC 722. Moreover, the greater the distance in time between the incurring of the costs and the commencement of the proceedings, the greater would be the likelihood that the losing party would have good grounds to dispute its liability to reimburse such costs in any event and/or would have a stronger argument to the effect that the court should not

exercise its discretion under CPR Pt 25 and order security in respect of such historic costs: *Lobster Group Ltd v Heidelberg Graphic Equipment Ltd* [2008] EWHC 413 (TCC), [2008] 2 All ER 1173, [2008] 1 BCLC 722.

7 *Re Strand Wood Co Ltd* [1904] 2 Ch 1, CA. In such a case, the liquidator may be ordered to pay the costs personally: see COMPANY AND PARTNERSHIP INSOLVENCY vol 16 (2011) PARA 546. As to security for costs by a foreign company as petitioning creditor see COMPANY AND PARTNERSHIP INSOLVENCY vol 16 (2011) PARA 424.

8 *Northampton Coal, Iron and Waggon Co v Midland Waggon Co* (1878) 7 ChD 500, CA; *Pure Spirit Co v Fowler* (1890) 25 QBD 235; *Re Diamond Fuel Co* (1879) 13 ChD 400, CA; *Re Photographic Artists' Co-operative Supply Association* (1883) 23 ChD 370, CA; *Lydney and Wigpool Iron Ore Co v Bird* (1883) 23 ChD 358 at 359; *City of Moscow Gas Co v International Financial Society Ltd* (1872) 7 Ch App 225 at 229.

9 *Universal Aircraft Ltd v Hickey* (4 May 1943, unreported); *Tudor Furnishers Ltd v Montague & Co and Finer Production Co Ltd* [1950] Ch 113 at 115, [1950] 1 All ER 65 at 66 per Wynn-Parry J.

10 *Accidental and Marine Insurance Co v Mercati* (1866) LR 3 Eq 200; *Maatshappij Voor Fondsenbezit v Shell Transport and Trading Co* [1923] 2 KB 166, CA; *Naamlooze Vennootschap Beleggings Compagnie 'Uranus' v Bank of England* [1948] 1 All ER 465, CA; *CT Bowring & Co (Insurance) Ltd v Corsi & Partners Ltd* [1994] 2 Lloyd's Rep 567, [1995] 1 BCLC 148, CA.

11 *Accidental and Marine Insurance Co v Mercati* (1866) LR 3 Eq 200.

12 *Strong v Carlyle Press (No 2)* (1893) 37 Sol Jo 357; *City of Moscow Gas Co v International Financial Society* (1872) 7 Ch App 225; *Washoe Mining Co v Ferguson* (1866) LR 2 Eq 371. See also *Sinclair v Glasgow and London Contract Corpn* (1904) 6 F 818; *Freehold Land and Brickmaking Co v Spargo* [1868] WN 94; *Hutchison Telephone (UK) Ltd v Ultimate Response Ltd* [1993] BCLC 307, CA; *Thistle Hotels Ltd v Orb Estates plc* [2004] All ER (D) 326 (Feb). In *Hart Investments Ltd v Larchpark Ltd* [2007] EWHC 291 (TCC), [2008] 1 BCLC 589, the claimant's claim and the defendant's counterclaim both had a reasonable prospect of success, but security was ordered on the grounds that it had not been shown that the grant of security would stifle the claim or that the claimant was responsible for the defendant's financial difficulties or that the application for security was made at a late stage of the proceedings, and because the defendant had refused to comply with previous costs orders made against it.

13 *T Sloyan & Sons (Builders) Ltd v Brothers of Christian Instruction* [1974] 3 All ER 715 (arbitration).

14 *Tudor Furnishers Ltd v Montague & Co and Finer Production Co Ltd* [1950] Ch 113, [1950] 1 All ER 65.

15 See CPR 25.12(3)(a); and CIVIL PROCEDURE vol 12 (2015) PARA 617. See also *Imperial Bank of China, India, and Japan v Bank of Hindustan, China and Japan* (1866) 1 Ch App 437; *Dominion Brewery Ltd v Foster* (1897) 77 LT 507, CA. In considering the amount of security that might be ordered, the court will have regard to the fact that it is not required to order the full amount claimed by way of security and it is not even bound to make an order of a substantial amount: *Keary Developments Ltd v Tarmac Construction Ltd* [1995] 3 All ER 534, [1995] 2 BCLC 395, CA.

16 The manner in which security is ordered to be given is usually that the amount of security is to be paid into court. As to the payment of money into court see CPR Pt 37; and CIVIL PROCEDURE vol 11 (2015) PARA 72 et seq.

17 See CPR 25.12(3)(b); and CIVIL PROCEDURE vol 12 (2015) PARA 617.

310. Non-party costs orders against directors. Generally, where the court is considering whether to exercise its power[1] to make a costs order in favour of or against a person who is not a party to proceedings, that person must be added as a party to the proceedings for the purposes of costs only[2].

Although the circumstances in which it is appropriate to make an order for costs against a person who was not a party to the litigation always have to be exceptional[3], liability for costs has been ordered in this way where a non-party director has been described as the 'real party', seeking his own benefit, in controlling or funding a company's litigation[4], even where he has acted in good faith or without any impropriety[5].

However, the mere fact that an action brought by a company has been held to be an abuse of process does not necessarily mean that the company's managing director should be personally liable to pay the costs owed by the company[6].

1 Ie under the Senior Courts Act 1981 s 51 (costs are in the discretion of the court): see CIVIL PROCEDURE vol 12A (2015) PARA 1707.

2 See CPR 46.2(1); and CIVIL PROCEDURE vol 11 (2015) PARA 486.

3 See *Metalloy Supplies Ltd (in liquidation) v MA (UK) Ltd* [1997] 1 All ER 418 at 424–425, [1997] 1 WLR 1613 at 1620, CA, per Millett LJ. See also note 6.

4 *Goodwood Recoveries Ltd v Breen* [2005] EWCA Civ 414, [2006] 2 All ER 533, [2006] 1 WLR 2723. See also *Dymocks Franchise Systems (NSW) Pty Ltd v Todd* [2004] UKPC 39, [2005] 4 All ER 195, [2004] 1 WLR 2807 (non-party who promoted and funded proceedings by an insolvent company solely or substantially for his own financial benefit was liable for costs as the appeals would not have been made without this assistance; applied in *Re Gatnom Capital and Finance Ltd, Macaria Investments Ltd v Saunders* [2011] EWHC 3716 (Ch), [2012] BPIR 299, [2011] All ER (D) 218 (Nov)); *Halton International Inc (Holdings) SARL v Guernroy Ltd* [2005] EWHC 1968 (Ch), [2006] 1 BCLC 78 (where the claimant company had been used by its sole director and shareholder as an investment vehicle, and had no other assets of its own, there was a strong inference that the shareholder had funded the proceedings on behalf of the company for his own personal benefit); *BE Studios Ltd v Smith & Williamson Ltd* [2005] EWHC 2730 (Ch), [2006] 2 All ER 811 (company could not realistically be regarded as the real party interested in the result of speculative litigation which could have resulted in the repayment of certain loan creditors of the company, of whom the non-party director was by far the largest); *CIBC Mellon Trust Co v Stolzenberg* [2005] EWCA Civ 628, [2005] 2 BCLC 618 (order for costs against shareholder who had funded and controlled litigation by the company); *Equitas Ltd v Horace Holman & Co Ltd* [2008] EWHC 2287 (Comm), [2009] 1 BCLC 662 (no justification for piercing the corporate veil where company funding litigation was controlled and indirectly owned by another company if any benefit accruing to first company from the litigation could not be treated as tantamount to a financial benefit accruing to latter company); and see *Petromec Inc v Petroleo Brasileiro SA Petrobras* [2006] EWCA Civ 1038 at [10]–[16], 150 Sol Jo LB 984, [2006] All ER (D) 260 per Longmore LJ (jurisdiction not limited to directors; costs can be ordered against a corporate controller); and *Alan Phillips Associates Ltd v Dowling (t/a The Joseph Dowling Partnership)* [2007] EWCA Civ 64 at [20]–[22], [2007] BLR 151, [2007] All ER (D) 37 (Jan) per Chadwick LJ (there was so close an identity between director and substantial shareholder of the company and the company itself, and so close an identity between his interests and the interests of the company, that it was just to make a third party costs order against him personally).

5 *Goodwood Recoveries Ltd v Breen* [2005] EWCA Civ 414, [2006] 2 All ER 533, [2006] 1 WLR 2723; *BE Studios Ltd v Smith & Williamson Ltd* [2005] EWHC 2730 (Ch), [2006] 2 All ER 811.

6 *Landare Investments Ltd v Welsh Development Agency* [2004] EWHC 946 (QB), [2006] 1 BCLC 451 (where an action brought by a company had been dismissed, with indemnity costs, as constituting an abuse of process, the defendants' application for an order for costs against the managing director was refused, on the grounds that he could not be blamed for the company's failure to prove its loss, since he had received professional advice at all stages, had acted bona fide throughout and had not acted improperly at any stage, and that making an order for costs against him would amount to an erosion of the principle of limited liability).

See also *Taylor v Pace Developments Ltd* [1991] BCC 406, CA (where the court refused to order the sole director and shareholder personally liable for costs where an insolvent company had unsuccessfully defended court proceedings; although it may be possible so to order in certain cases, as eg where the company's defence was not bona fide); *Metalloy Supplies Ltd (in liquidation) v MA (UK) Ltd* [1997] 1 All ER 418 at 424–425, [1997] 1 WLR 1613 at 1620, CA, per Millett LJ; *Floods of Queensferry Ltd v Shand Construction Ltd* [2002] EWCA Civ 918, [2003] Lloyd's Rep IR 181.

311. Enforcement of judgments and orders against company. Judgment against a company may be enforced by writ or warrant[1], as in the case of a natural person[2]. Any judgment or order against the company requiring it to do an act within a specified time or requiring it to abstain from doing an act may, with the permission of the court, be enforced by sequestration against its property or the property of any director or other officer of the company[3], or by a committal order against any director or other officer of the company[4]. For this purpose, an undertaking given to the court and embodied in a court order has the same effect as a judgment or order[5]. A company cannot be attached for contempt of court[6], but the court may inflict an appropriate fine[7]; and sequestration will be ordered if the company contumaciously refuses to obey, though not in the case of casual or accidental and unintentional disobedience[8].

1 As to the forms of writ or warrant see CIVIL PROCEDURE vol 12A (2015) PARA 1379 et seq.
2 *Worral Waterworks Co v Lloyd* (1866) LR 1 CP 719; *Spokes v Banbury Board of Health* (1865) LR 1 Eq 42. See also CIVIL PROCEDURE vol 12A (2015) PARA 1309.
3 See CPR 81.20(1), (3); and CIVIL PROCEDURE vol 12A (2015) PARA 1298. As to writs of sequestration see CIVIL PROCEDURE vol 12A (2015) PARA 1380.
4 See CPR 81.4(1), (3); and CONTEMPT OF COURT vol 22 (2012) PARA 94 et seq. As to orders of committal see CIVIL PROCEDURE vol 12A (2015) PARA 1502 et seq. The remedies against the company, and against its directors for committal, are alternative: *Iberian Trust Ltd v Founders Trust and Investment Co Ltd* [1932] 2 KB 87. See also *Benabo v William Jay & Partners Ltd* [1941] Ch 52, [1940] 4 All ER 196. It was formerly not necessary that the judgment or order which had been disobeyed should have been served personally on the company, as service on the company's solicitors was sufficient (*Aberdonia Cars Ltd v Brown, Hughes and Strachan Ltd* (1915) 59 Sol Jo 598 (sequestration)), at all events where the order was merely prohibitive (see *Ronson Products Ltd v Ronson Furniture Ltd* [1966] Ch 603, [1966] 2 All ER 381). Personal service on the director affected is now essential: see CPR 81.5(2), 81.21(2); and CIVIL PROCEDURE vol 12A (2015) PARA 1298. Execution may be issued against shareholders or public officers of joint stock companies which were registered under 7 & 8 Vict c 110 (Joint Stock Companies) (1844), or the Country Bankers Act 1826, and have not been re-registered under the Joint Stock Companies Acts (see PARA 21 note 5); but such a proceeding is now so rare as to be practically obsolete. Cf PARA 1903. As to the power of a court to punish by committal or sequestration see CONTEMPT OF COURT vol 22 (2012) PARA 72.
5 *Biba Ltd v Stratford Investments Ltd* [1973] Ch 281, [1972] 3 All ER 1041.
6 *R v Windham* (1776) 1 Cowp 377; *Re Hooley, ex p Hooley* (1899) 79 LT 706.
7 *R v JG Hammond & Co Ltd* [1914] 2 KB 866; *R v Hutchison, ex p McMahon* [1936] 2 All ER 1514.
8 *Fairclough & Sons v Manchester Ship Canal Co (No 2)* [1897] WN 7, CA. It has been held under the previous rules (CPR Sch 1 RSC Ord 45 r 5 (revoked)) that where a director or other officer of a company may be committed or have his property sequestrated if the company disobeys an injunction, such a person is not rendered liable in contempt merely by virtue of his office and his knowledge that the order sought to be enforced was made, but will be liable only if he can otherwise be shown to be in contempt under the general law of contempt; in the absence of mens rea or an actus reus, such a director or other officer of a company will not be liable in contempt: *Director General of Fair Trading v Buckland* [1990] 1 All ER 545, [1990] 1 WLR 920. Where, however, a company is ordered by the court not to do certain acts or to give an undertaking to the like effect and a director of the company is aware of that order or undertaking, the director is under a duty to take reasonable steps to ensure that the order or undertaking is obeyed; and if he wilfully fails to take those steps and the order or undertaking is breached, he may be punished for contempt unless he reasonably believes that some other director or officer of the company is taking them: *A–G for Tuvalu v Philatelic Distribution Corpn Ltd* [1990] 2 All ER 216, [1990] 1 WLR 926, CA.

(vii) Company's Liability for Criminal Acts etc

312. Potential criminal liability of a company. The activities of a registered company[1] are subject to the criminal law in the same way as those of a natural person[2]; and a company may be convicted of offences both at common law[3] and under statute[4], including those offences which require mens rea[5]. Where an offence requires mens rea, a company may be convicted if the offence is committed in the course of business by a person in control of its affairs to such a degree that the company may fairly be said to think and act through him so that his actions and intent are the actions and intent of the company[6]; in such a case, those who 'constitute the directing mind and will of the company' are the company for this purpose[7]. Although the 'directing mind' may delegate its functions, it is not enough, for criminal liability to attach, that the person whose conduct it is sought to impute to the company is a manager or responsible agent or high executive[8]; whether persons are the 'directing mind and will' of a company, so that their conduct in its affairs becomes the conduct of the company, must depend on all the circumstances[9].

A company cannot be guilty of any criminal offences which, by their very nature, may be committed only by natural persons[10]. Nor can a company be indicted for a crime where the only punishment is imprisonment[11].

1 As to the meaning of 'company' generally see PARA 1. As to the meaning of 'company' under the Companies Acts see PARA 21; and as to the meaning of the 'Companies Acts' see PARA 13.

2 Ie subject to the proviso that there are certain offences that can be committed only by natural persons or for which only natural persons may be convicted: see the text and notes 10–11. In any Act, unless the contrary intention appears, 'person' includes a body of persons corporate or unincorporate: see the Interpretation Act 1978 ss 5, 22(1), Sch 1; and STATUTES AND LEGISLATIVE PROCESS vol 96 (2012) PARA 1214. This definition of 'person', so far as it includes bodies corporate, applies to any provision of an Act whenever passed relating to an offence punishable on indictment or on summary conviction: see s 22(1), Sch 2 para 4(5). As to corporate liability for criminal acts generally see CORPORATIONS vol 24 (2010) PARA 482; CRIMINAL LAW vol 25 (2016) PARA 40 et seq. As to corporate personality generally see PARA 2; and CORPORATIONS vol 24 (2010) PARAS 426–427. As to the effect of a petition for administration, an administration order or a winding-up order on the initiation or pursuit of proceedings against a company see PARA 41; COMPANY AND PARTNERSHIP INSOLVENCY vol 16 (2011) PARAS 158, 159, 395; COMPANY AND PARTNERSHIP INSOLVENCY vol 17 (2011) PARAS 845, 851. As to the criminal liability of partnerships as distinct from the liability of individual partners see *R v W Stevenson & Sons (a partnership)* [2008] EWCA Crim 273, [2008] Bus LR 1200, [2008] All ER (D) 351 (Feb); and PARTNERSHIP vol 79 (2014) PARA 2.

3 See eg *R v Great North of England Rly Co* (1846) 2 Cox CC 70 (public nuisance); *R v JG Hammond & Co Ltd* [1914] 2 KB 866 (contempt of court); *R v ICR Haulage Ltd* [1944] KB 551, [1944] 1 All ER 691, CCA (conspiracy to defraud); *Triplex Safety Glass Co Ltd v Lancegaye Safety Glass* (1939) Ltd [1939] 2 KB 395, [1939] 2 All ER 613, CA (criminal libel).

4 See eg *R v Birmingham and Gloucester Rly Co* (1842) 3 QB 223 (non-repair of highway); *A-G v London and North Western Rly Co* [1900] 1 QB 78, CA (excessive speed of trains); *Pearks, Gunston and Tee Ltd v Ward* [1902] 2 KB 1, DC; *R v Ascanio Puck & Co and Paice* (1912) 76 JP 487 (sale of food); *Provincial Motor Cab Co Ltd v Dunning* [1909] 2 KB 599 (breach of road traffic regulations); *R v Gainsford Justices* (1913) 29 TLR 359 (breach of Factory and Workshop Acts); *Evans & Co Ltd v LCC* [1914] 3 KB 315 (breach of the Shops Act 1912 s 4 (repealed)); *Mousell Bros Ltd v London and North Western Rly Co* [1917] 2 KB 836 (giving false account of goods to toll collector); *Brentnall and Cleland Ltd v LCC* [1945] 1 KB 115, [1944] 2 All ER 552, DC (offence against the Weights and Measures Act 1889 s 29 (repealed)); *Orpen v Haymarket Capitol Ltd* (1931) 145 LT 614; *Houghton-Le Touzel v Mecca Ltd* [1950] 2 KB 612, [1950] 1 All ER 638 (offence against the Sunday Observance Act 1780 (repealed)); *Worthy v Gordon Plant (Services) Ltd* [1989] RTR 7n, DC (breach of road traffic legislation concerning drivers' hours); *R v Associated Octel Co Ltd* [1996] 4 All ER 846, [1996] 1 WLR 1543, HL (breach of Health and Safety at Work etc Act 1974 s 3(1)); *R v Gateway Foodmarkets Ltd* [1997] 3 All ER 78, [1997] 2 Cr App Rep 40, CA (breach of Health and Safety at Work etc Act 1974 s 2(1)). As to the liability of officers of the company for failing to comply with requirements imposed by the Companies Acts see PARAS 315–316; and see eg *R v Tyler and International Commercial Co* [1891] 2 QB 588 at 592–594, CA (default in complying with the Companies Act 1862 s 26 (now repealed) (forwarding annual list of members to registrar)).

5 *DPP v Kent and Sussex Contractors Ltd* [1944] KB 146, [1944] 1 All ER 119, DC; *R v ICR Haulage Ltd* [1944] KB 551, [1944] 1 All ER 691, CCA (doubting *R v Cory Bros & Co* [1927] 1 KB 810).

6 One source of difficulty in attaching criminal liability to a company lies in the principle of separate corporate personality: see PARA 115 note 16. Since a company is an artificial person, the knowledge of those who manage and control it must be treated as the knowledge of the company: see *Houghton & Co v Nothard, Lowe and WillsLtd* [1928] AC 1, [1927] All ER Rep 97.

Historically, cases of 'corporate manslaughter' have tested this principle: see *R v P & O European Ferries (Dover) Ltd (1991)* 93 Cr App Rep 72; *R v HM Coroner for East Kent, ex p Spooner* (1987) 88 Cr App Rep 10, 3 BCC 636, DC. In *A-G's Reference (No 2 of 1999)* [2000] QB 796, [2000] 3 All ER 182, CA, which was made partly on the question of whether a non-human defendant can be convicted of the criminal offence of manslaughter by gross negligence in the absence of evidence establishing the guilt of an identified human individual for the same crime, the court held that a corporation's liability for manslaughter was based solely on the principle of 'identification', which was just as relevant to actus reus as to mens rea, and that unless an identified individual's conduct, characterisable as gross criminal negligence, could be attributed to the corporation, the corporation was not, at common law, liable for manslaughter; the court on that reference also held that civil negligence rules were not apt to confer criminal liability on a corporation: see *A-G's Reference (No 2 of 1999)* at 815–816, 191–192. This position, as it relates to the common law offence of manslaughter by gross negligence in its application to corporations, has been modified by statute: see the Corporate Manslaughter and Corporate Homicide Act 2007; and PARA 314.

A corporation may be vicariously liable for a crime committed by its servant or agent in the course of his employment or agency in the same circumstances as an employer or principal who is a natural person: see CRIMINAL LAW vol 25 (2016) PARA 61 et seq.

7 *Tesco Supermarkets Ltd v Nattrass* [1972] AC 153, [1971] 2 All ER 127, HL. See also *DPP v Kent and Sussex Contractors Ltd* [1944] KB 146, [1944] 1 All ER 119, DC; *R v ICR Haulage Ltd* [1944] KB 551, [1944] 1 All ER 691, CCA; *Moore v I Bressler Ltd* [1944] 2 All ER 515, DC; *Magna Plant Ltd v Mitchell* (1966) 110 Sol Jo 349, DC; *John Henshall (Quarries) Ltd v Harvey* [1965] 2 QB 233, [1965] 1 All ER 725, DC; *HL Bolton (Engineering) Co Ltd v TJ Graham & Sons Ltd* [1957] 1 QB 159, [1956] 3 All ER 624, CA. It is not possible to aggregate the acts and states of mind of two or more controlling officers (none of whom could be criminally liable) so as to render the corporation liable: *R v HM Coroner for East Kent, ex p Spooner* (1987) 88 Cr App Rep 10, 3 BCC 636, DC; *R v P & O European Ferries (Dover) Ltd* (1990) 93 Cr App Rep 72; *A-G's Reference (No 2 of 1999)* [2000] QB 796, [2000] 3 All ER 182, CA. As to the 'identification principle', which attributes the directing mind and will of the company, see PARA 313.

The principle of non-attribution, by which knowledge of a fraud would not be attributed to a company when the fraud was practised on the company itself, could apply where the fraud or dishonesty of the company's directing mind and will was targeted against the company itself, depending on whether the company was to be regarded as the villain or victim of the fraud: see *Stone & Rolls Ltd (in liquidation) v Moore Stephens (a firm)* [2008] EWCA Civ 644, [2008] 3 WLR 1146, [2008] 2 BCLC 461 (where a company's sole directing mind and will procured the company to enter into fraudulent transactions with the bank, and it was the company that dealt with the bank, his dishonesty was to be imputed to the company; the company was therefore itself liable for the frauds and, being the fraudster rather than the target of the fraud, the adverse consequences which it suffered from the fraud did not make it a victim; where the fraudulent conduct of the directing mind and will of the company was to be treated as the conduct of the company, ex turpi causa would defeat a claim by the company against its auditors for failure to detect the fraud); affd [2009] UKHL 39, [2009] 3 WLR 455.

Where a company is the victim of fraud or wrongdoing by its directors or of which its directors have notice, the wrongdoing or knowledge of the directors cannot be attributed to the company as a defence to a claim brought against the directors by the company's liquidator in the name of the company and/or on behalf of its creditors for the loss suffered by the company as a result of the wrongdoing, even where the directors are the only directors and shareholders of the company and even though the wrongdoing or knowledge of the directors may be attributed to the company in other types of proceedings: *Bilta (UK) Ltd (in liquidation) v Nazir* [2015] UKSC 23, [2015] 2 All ER 1083, [2015] 2 All ER (Comm) 281. See also *Top Brands Ltd v Sharma* [2015] EWCA Civ 1140, [2015] All ER (D) 77 (Nov).

8 *HL Bolton (Engineering) Co Ltd v TJ Graham & Sons Ltd* [1957] 1 QB 159, [1956] 3 All ER 624, CA; *R v Andrews Weatherfoil Ltd* [1972] 1 All ER 65, [1972] 1 WLR 118, CA. It would bring the law into disrepute if every act and state of mind of an individual employee was attributed to a company which was entirely blameless: see *Tesco Supermarkets Ltd v Nattrass* [1972] AC 153 at 169, [1971] 2 All ER 127 at 131, HL, per Lord Reid; and see *Canadian Dredge & Dock Co Ltd v R* (1985) 19 DLR (4th) 314, 19 CCC (3d) 1, Can SC.

9 An important circumstance is the constitution of the corporation and the extent to which it identifies the natural persons who, by the constitution or as a result of action taken by the directors or by the corporation in general meeting pursuant to the articles, are entrusted with the exercise of the powers of the corporation: see *Tesco Supermarkets Ltd v Nattrass* [1972] AC 153 at 199–200, [1971] 2 All ER 127 at 155, HL, per Lord Diplock. As to the meaning of references to a company's constitution see PARA 226.

10 See *DPP v Kent and Sussex Contractors Ltd* [1944] KB 146, [1944] 1 All ER 119, DC, where earlier cases are also discussed. There appears to be a conflict in the case law as to whether a corporation can commit perjury: cf *R v ICR Haulage Ltd* [1944] KB 551 at 554, [1944] 1 All ER 691 at 693, CCA ('[there] are the cases in which, from its very nature, the offence cannot be committed by a corporation, as, for example, perjury, an offence which cannot be vicariously committed, or bigamy, an offence which a limited company, not being a natural person, cannot commit vicariously or otherwise'); *Wych v Meal* (1734) 3 P Wms 310 (corporation cannot commit perjury); *Odyssey Re (London) Ltd (formerly Sphere Drake Insurance plc) v OIC Run-Off Ltd*

(formerly Orion Insurance Co plc) [2001] Lloyd's Rep IR 1, CA (where a party is a corporation, it is possible for evidence perjured by a natural person to be treated as that of the company, the test to be adopted being whether the natural person in question has the status and authority which in law make his acts in the matter under consideration the acts of the company, so that he is to be treated as the company itself). A corporation cannot be convicted of conspiracy where the only other party to it is the sole director of the corporation: *R v McDonnell* [1966] 1 QB 233, 50 Cr App Rep 5. As to manslaughter see note 6.

A corporation cannot be guilty as a principal of dangerous driving or of driving without due care and attention. In *R v Robert Millar (Contractors) Ltd, R v Millar* [1970] 2 QB 54, 54 Cr App Rep 158, CA, the corporation was convicted as a secondary party to the offence of causing death through dangerous driving (contrary to what is now the Road Traffic Act 1988 s 1: see ROAD TRAFFIC vol 90 (2011) PARA 720).

11 *R v ICR Haulage Ltd* [1944] KB 551 at 554, 557, [1944] 1 All ER 691 at 693, 694, CCA, per Stable J. See also *Pharmaceutical Society v London and Provincial Supply Association* (1880) 5 App Cas 857 at 869, HL, per Lord Blackburn; *R v Cory Bros & Co Ltd* [1927] 1 KB 810; *Law Society v United Service Bureau Ltd* [1934] 1 KB 343 at 350, DC, per Avory J. However, the Companies Act 2006 provides copiously for individual 'officers in default' to become liable to terms of imprisonment for contravention of its provisions: see PARA 316.

313. Directing mind of company. Since a company cannot act of itself, but only through an individual, and even then not necessarily through one and the same individual, the question arises whether, on the one hand, a person so acting is acting as a living embodiment of the company, or whether, on the other hand, he is merely acting as the company's employee or agent[1].

For most civil purposes, it is not necessary to decide the matter, since usually as a result of the doctrine of ostensible authority the company will be bound by the acts of the person acting on its behalf[2]. The question is, however, often a live one so far as the criminal law is concerned, since for the acts of a person who may properly be classified as the 'directing mind of the company'[3] the company will undoubtedly be liable criminally[4] if those acts are in breach of any of the provisions of the criminal law[5]; but if the person who has acted is merely an employee or agent, the company may well be able to refute any charge or take advantage of any exempting provision based on actual fault in the actor[6].

The directors may delegate part of their functions of management in such a way as to make their delegate an embodiment of the company within the sphere of the delegation; but they do not do this merely because, of necessity, ministerial functions have to be delegated[7]. Once the facts relating to the precise position of the person alleged to form the directing mind of the company have been ascertained, it is a question of law whether that person, in doing a particular act, is or is not to be regarded as the company[8]. The main considerations are the relative position in the company which he holds and the extent to which, as a matter of fact, he is in actual control of its operations or a section of them without effective superior control[9].

1 See *Tesco Supermarkets Ltd v Nattrass* [1972] AC 153 at 170, [1971] 2 All ER 127 at 131–132, HL, per Lord Reid. Where a company's rights and obligations cannot be determined either by the primary rules of attribution, expressed in its constitution or implied by law, for determining what acts are to be attributed to the company, or by the application of the general principles of agency or vicarious liability, the question of attribution for a particular substantive rule is a matter of interpretation or construction of that rule. If the court decides that the substantive rule is intended to apply to a company, it then has to decide how the rule is intended to apply and whose act or knowledge or state of mind is for that purpose intended to count as the act, knowledge or state of mind of the company. Although in some cases that can be determined by applying the test of whose was the 'directing mind and will' of the company so that his fault or knowledge becomes the company's fault or knowledge, that test is not appropriate in all cases: *Meridian Global Funds Management Asia Ltd v Securities Commission* [1995] 2 AC 500, [1995] 3 All ER 918, PC, applying *Tesco Supermarkets Ltd v Nattrass* [1972] AC 153, [1971] 2 All ER 127, HL. See also

KR v Royal & Sun Alliance plc [2006] EWCA Civ 1454, [2007] 1 All ER (Comm) 161, [2007] Lloyd's Rep IR 368 (acts of managing director and majority shareholder attributed to company).

2 See PARA 265 et seq. As to cases under the Landlord and Tenant Act 1954 s 30(1)(f), involving a consideration of the landlord's intention, see LANDLORD AND TENANT vol 63 (2012) PARA 858 et seq.

3 The line of authority for attributing the 'directing mind of the company' ('identification') is usually traced back to *Lennard's Carrying Co Ltd v Asiatic Petroleum Co Ltd* [1915] AC 705 at 713, HL, per Viscount Haldane LC ('a corporation is an abstraction. It has no mind of its own any more than it has a body of its own; its active and directing will must consequently be sought in the person of somebody who for some purposes may be called an agent, but who is really the directing mind and will of the corporation, the very ego and centre of the personality of the corporation'). See also *HL Bolton (Engineering) Co Ltd v TJ Graham & Sons Ltd* [1957] 1 QB 159 at 172, [1956] 3 All ER 624 at 630, CA, per Denning LJ; and *Tesco Supermarkets Ltd v Nattrass* [1972] AC 153 at 170, [1971] 2 All ER 127 at 131–132, HL, per Lord Reid. If there is just one person classified as the 'directing mind of the company', he cannot conspire with the company, since conspiracy requires two minds: *R v McDonnell* [1966] 1 QB 233, [1966] 1 All ER 193.

4 This doctrine, sometimes known as the 'alter ego' doctrine, has been developed in both civil and criminal jurisdictions with no divergence of approach, the authorities in each being cited indifferently in the other. A company having no mind or will of its own, the need for it arises because the criminal law often requires mens rea as a constituent of the crime and the civil law often requires intention or knowledge as an ingredient of the cause of action or defence: *El Ajou v Dollar Land Holdings plc* [1994] 2 All ER 685 at 472–473, CA, per Nourse LJ.

5 This will not be so, however, where the directors or other directing minds are acting for their own benefit at the expense of the company, or in order to deprive the company of part of its assets: see eg *Belmont Finance Corpn Ltd v Williams Furniture Ltd* [1979] Ch 250, [1979] 1 All ER 118, CA.

6 *Tesco Supermarkets Ltd v Nattrass* [1972] AC 153, [1971] 2 All ER 127, HL; *Dumfries and Maxwelltown Co-operative Society v Williamson* 1950 JC 76; *John Henshall (Quarries) Ltd v Harvey* [1965] 2 QB 233, [1965] 1 All ER 725, DC (lorry of excessive weight allowed on road); *Magna Plant Ltd v Mitchell* (1966) 110 Sol Jo 349, DC (unmaintained vehicle allowed on road).

7 *Tesco Supermarkets Ltd v Nattrass* [1972] AC 153, [1971] 2 All ER 127, HL (delegation to branch managers).

8 *Tesco Supermarkets Ltd v Nattrass* [1972] AC 153 at 170, 173, [1971] 2 All ER 127 at 131, 134, HL, per Lord Reid; *Essendon Engineering Co Ltd v Maile* [1982] RTR 260, DC (no evidence as to responsibilities of guilty employee, so company not liable). See also *El Ajou v Dollar Land Holdings plc* [1994] 2 All ER 685, CA; *Morris v Bank of India* [2005] EWCA Civ 693, [2005] 2 BCLC 328 (it would in practice defeat the effectiveness of the Insolvency Act 1986 s 213 (as to which see COMPANY AND PARTNERSHIP INSOLVENCY vol 17 (2011) PARA 869) if liability were limited to those cases in which the board of directors was actually a direct privy to the fraud of the company with whom the transactions were entered into; the scheme of delegation of authority might provide only an incomplete picture of what was done and might not be sufficient for the purposes of determining whether the company should be treated as possessing the requisite knowledge); *Stone & Rolls Ltd (in liquidation) v Moore Stephens (a firm)* [2008] EWCA Civ 644, [2008] 3 WLR 1146, [2008] 2 BCLC 461 (the essence of the case was that it was one in which the sole directing mind and will of the company procured it to enter into fraudulent transactions with banks).

9 *DPP v Kent and Sussex Contractors Ltd* [1944] KB 146, [1944] 1 All ER 119, DC; *R v ICR Haulage Ltd* [1944] KB 551, [1944] 1 All ER 691, CCA. Cf *R v Andrews Weatherfoil Ltd* [1972] 1 All ER 65, [1972] 1 WLR 118, CA (not every 'high executive' binds the company). See also *Odyssey Re (London) Ltd (formerly Sphere Drake Insurance plc) v OIC Run-Off Ltd (formerly Orion Insurance Co plc)* [2001] Lloyd's Rep IR 1, CA (where a party is a corporation, it is possible for evidence perjured by a natural person to be treated as that of the company, the test to be adopted being whether the natural person in question has the status and authority which in law make his acts in the matter under consideration the acts of the company, so that he is to be treated as the company itself).

314. Liability for corporate manslaughter. The common law offence of manslaughter by gross negligence[1] is abolished in its application to corporations[2], and in any application it has to other organisations to which the Corporate Manslaughter and Corporate Homicide Act 2007[3] applies[4].

Under the 2007 Act, a corporation or other such organisation[5] is guilty of the offence of corporate manslaughter if the way in which its activities are managed or organised causes a person's death, amounting to a gross breach of a relevant duty of care owed by the organisation to the deceased, but only if the way in which its activities are managed or organised by its senior management is a substantial element in that breach[6]. For these purposes, the term 'relevant duty of care', in relation to an organisation, is defined by reference to specified duties owed under the law of negligence[7]. In assessing whether an organisation's breach of a relevant duty of care was 'gross', the jury is required to consider whether the organisation failed to comply with relevant health and safety legislation, the seriousness of such a failure, how much of a risk of death it posed, and the wider context of the failure[8].

An organisation that is guilty of corporate manslaughter is liable on conviction on indictment to a fine[9].

1 As to manslaughter by gross negligence generally see CRIMINAL LAW vol 25 (2016) PARA 112.

2 For these purposes, 'corporation' does not include a corporation sole but includes any body corporate wherever incorporated: see the Corporate Manslaughter and Corporate Homicide Act 2007 s 25; and CRIMINAL LAW vol 25 (2016) PARA 115. As to corporations sole see CORPORATIONS vol 24 (2010) PARAS 314–315. As to the criminal liability of companies generally see PARAS 312–313.

3 Ie by virtue of the Corporate Manslaughter and Corporate Homicide Act 2007 s 1 (as to which see note 4): see s 20; and CRIMINAL LAW vol 25 (2016) PARA 115.

4 See the Corporate Manslaughter and Corporate Homicide Act 2007 s 20; and CRIMINAL LAW vol 25 (2016) PARA 112.

5 Ie any organisation to which the Corporate Manslaughter and Corporate Homicide Act 2007 s 1 applies: see s 1; and CRIMINAL LAW vol 25 (2016) PARA 115.

6 See the Corporate Manslaughter and Corporate Homicide Act 2007 s 1; and CRIMINAL LAW vol 25 (2016) PARA 115. For these purposes, a breach of a duty of care by an organisation is a 'gross' breach if the conduct alleged to amount to a breach of that duty falls far below what can reasonably be expected of the organisation in the circumstances (see also the text and note 8); and 'senior management', in relation to an organisation, means the persons who play significant roles in the making of decisions about how the whole or a substantial part of its activities are to be managed or organised, or in the actual managing or organising of the whole or a substantial part of those activities: see s 1(4); and CRIMINAL LAW vol 25 (2016) PARA 115.

An individual cannot be guilty of aiding, abetting, counselling or procuring the commission of an offence of corporate manslaughter: see s 18(1); and CRIMINAL LAW vol 25 (2016) PARA 115.

7 See the Corporate Manslaughter and Corporate Homicide Act 2007 s 2, which is subject to the modifications and exceptions contained in ss 3–7; and CRIMINAL LAW vol 25 (2016) PARA 116.

8 See the Corporate Manslaughter and Corporate Homicide Act 2007 s 8; and CRIMINAL LAW vol 25 (2016) PARA 117. See also note 6.

9 See the Corporate Manslaughter and Corporate Homicide Act 2007 s 1(6); and CRIMINAL LAW vol 25 (2016) PARA 115. A court before which an organisation is convicted of corporate manslaughter may make an order (a 'remedial order') requiring the organisation to take specified steps to remedy the relevant breach, and any matter that appears to the court to have resulted from the relevant breach and to have been a cause of the death, and any deficiency, as regards health and safety matters, in the organisation's policies, systems or practices of which the relevant breach appears to the court to be an indication: see s 9; and CRIMINAL LAW vol 25 (2016) PARA 118. A court before which an organisation is convicted of corporate manslaughter also may make an order (a 'publicity order') requiring the organisation to publicise in a specified manner the fact that it has been convicted of the offence, specified particulars of the offence, the amount of any fine imposed and the terms of any remedial order made: see s 10; and CRIMINAL LAW vol 25 (2016) PARA 119. The fact that an organisation is charged with, or has been convicted of, corporate manslaughter does not preclude a further charge of a health and safety offence which arises out of the same set of circumstances: see s 19; and CRIMINAL LAW vol 25 (2016) PARA 115.

315. Criminal liability attaching to officers of a company. Where a company is criminally liable for an offence, a natural person involved may also be convicted of it, as a joint principal or as an accomplice[1]. In addition, many statutes now provide for the guilt of controlling officers of the company who would not be criminally liable under ordinary principles, or whose guilt it would otherwise be hard to prove[2].

Directors, officers and members may be liable for the general offences of theft in relation to the company's property (if any such person dishonestly appropriates property belonging to the company with the intention of permanently depriving the company of it)[3] or for false accounting[4]. Where an offence of false accounting is committed by a body corporate and the offence is proved to have been committed with the consent or connivance of any director, manager, secretary or other similar officer[5] of the body corporate, he, as well as the body corporate, is guilty of the offence, and is liable to be proceeded against and punished accordingly[6]. A person, on the basis that to do otherwise would incriminate either himself or his spouse or civil partner, cannot refuse to give evidence in civil proceedings, or to comply with any order made in any such proceedings; but no statement or admission made by him in answering a question put or in complying with such an order will be admissible in evidence against that person in proceedings for any offence under the Theft Act 1968[7].

Where an officer of a body corporate or unincorporated association, or person purporting to act as such, with intent to deceive members or creditors of the body corporate or association about its affairs, publishes or concurs in publishing a written statement or account which to his knowledge is or may be misleading, false or deceptive in a material particular, he is liable on conviction on indictment to imprisonment for a term not exceeding seven years[8].

Any person may become liable under the general offence of fraud, which may be committed by false representation, by failing to disclose information, or by abuse of position[9]. In all cases of fraud where two or more persons such as directors co-operate, an indictment for conspiracy will normally lie[10]; but, where only one person is the directing mind of the company[11], a charge of conspiracy with the company will not lie, as there are not the necessary two minds concerned[12]. Where the conspiracy is to commit a fraud on the company or to deprive it of part of its assets, the natural persons to the conspiracy being the company's directors, a charge of conspiracy will not lie against the company, even though the company, through the agency of the conspiring directors, carries out part of the conspired acts[13].

The Companies Act 2006, the Insolvency Act 1986 and the Company Directors Disqualification Act 1986 include many provisions rendering directors and others liable to imprisonment[14]. Many of the offences punishable are those committed in connection with a company which is being wound up[15].

Provision is made under the Companies Acts in relation to the criminal liability of an officer in default[16].

1 See PARAS 312, 313.
2 The most pertinent example is the Corporate Manslaughter and Corporate Homicide Act 2007: see PARA 314. However, more commonly, statutes provide that, where an offence created by the particular statute which has been committed by a body corporate is proved to have been committed with the consent or connivance of, or to be attributable to any neglect on the part of, a director, manager, secretary or other similar officer of the body corporate, or any person who was purporting to act in any such capacity, he, as well as the body corporate, is guilty of that offence: see eg the Trade Descriptions Act 1968 s 20(1) (see CONSUMER PROTECTION vol 21 (2011) PARA 518); the Insolvency Act 1986 s 432(2) (see COMPANY AND PARTNERSHIP INSOLVENCY vol 17 (2011) PARA 886); the Consumer Protection Act 1987 s 40(2) (see CONSUMER PROTECTION vol 21 (2011) PARA 678); the Food Safety Act 1990 s 36 (see FOOD AND DRINK vol 51 (2013) PARA 827); the Clean Air Act 1993 s 52 (see ENVIRONMENTAL QUALITY AND PUBLIC HEALTH vol 45 (2010) PARA 247); and the Railways Act 1993 s 147 (see RAILWAYS AND TRAMWAYS vol 86 (2013) PARA 432). See further CRIMINAL LAW vol 25 (2016) PARA 40. See also the text and note 16; and the Fraud Act 2006 s 12 (cited in PARA 317).
3 See the Theft Act 1968 s 1; and CRIMINAL LAW vol 25 (2016) PARA 315. See also *R (on the application of A) v Crown Court at Snaresbrook* (2001) Times, 12 July, [2001] All ER (D) 123 (Jun) (director could be found guilty of theft where appropriation was dishonest).
4 See the Theft Act 1968 s 17; and CRIMINAL LAW vol 25 (2016) PARA 353.
5 This extends also to a person purporting to act as such: see the Theft Act 1968 s 18(1).

6 Theft Act 1968 s 18(1) (amended by the Fraud Act 2006 Sch 1 para 4, Sch 3). Where the affairs of a company are managed by its members, the Theft Act 1968 s 18 applies in relation to the member's acts and defaults in connection with his management functions as if he were a director: s 18(2).

7 Theft Act 1968 s 31(1) (amended by the Civil Partnership Act 2004 Sch 27 para 28). When an act done by a person is first disclosed by him without making any objection during cross-examination in civil proceedings, it is not disclosed by him 'in consequence of any compulsory process of any court of law' (the phrase used in the Larceny Act 1861 s 85 (repealed), which is now replaced by the Theft Act 1968 s 31(1)): *R v Noel* [1914] 3 KB 848, CCA. See also *R v Gunnell* (1886) 55 LT 786, CCR; *R v Strahan, Paul and Bates* (1855) 7 Cox CC 85; *R v Oliver* (1909) 3 Cr App Rep 246, CCA; and CRIMINAL PROCEDURE vol 28 (2015) PARA 466.

8 Theft Act 1968 s 19(1). For these purposes, a person who has entered into a security for the benefit of a body corporate or association is to be treated as a creditor of it: s 19(2). Where the affairs of a body corporate or association are managed by its members, s 19 applies to any statement which a member publishes or concurs in publishing in connection with his functions of management as if he were an officer of the body corporate or association: s 19(3). An offence under s 19 is triable either way; the penalty on summary conviction is imprisonment for a term not exceeding six months or a fine, or both: see the Magistrates' Courts Act 1980 ss 17, 32(1), Sch 1 para 28. In the case of liability on summary conviction the fine is one not exceeding the prescribed sum. By virtue of the Legal Aid, Sentencing and Punishment of Offenders Act 2012 s 85, however, where the offence is committed on or after 12 March 2015, it is punishable by a fine of an unlimited amount. As to the standard scale, the statutory maximum, the prescribed sum, and magistrates' powers to levy unlimited fines see SENTENCING vol 92 (2015) PARA 176. As from a day to be appointed, the maximum term of imprisonment on summary conviction under these provisions is increased to 12 months: see s 32(1) (prospectively amended by the Criminal Justice Act 2003 s 282). At the date at which this volume states the law, no such day had been appointed.

9 See the Fraud Act 2006 ss 1–5; and CRIMINAL LAW vol 25 (2016) PARA 346. The general offence of fraud mentioned in the text replaces various deception offences contained in the Theft Act 1968 s 15 (repealed) and s 16 (repealed).

10 *Twycross v Grant* (1877) 2 CPD 469 at 493, CA, per Bramwell LJ (directors receiving presents etc from promoters); *Re Gold Co* (1879) 11 ChD 701 at 723, CA, per Bramwell LJ (directors may have deluded the public by allotting gratuitous shares to existing shareholders, thereby diluting the capital); *Burnes v Pennell* (1849) 2 HL Cas 497 at 524 per Lord Campbell (publishing false statements); *R v De Berenger* (1814) 3 M & S 67 (inducing purchase of shares); *Scott v Brown, Doering, McNab & Co* [1892] 2 QB 724 at 730, CA, per Lopes LJ; *R v Aspinall* (1876) 2 QBD 48, CA (inducing the Committee of the Stock Exchange to grant a quotation of shares); *R v Barber* (1887) 3 TLR 491 (paying a concealed profit to a broker). An agreement between two or more persons to purchase shares in a company in order to induce persons thereafter purchasing shares in it to believe, contrary to the fact, that there is a bona fide market in the shares, and that there is a real premium, being an offence indictable as a conspiracy, no claim may be maintained in respect of such an agreement or purchase of shares: *Scott v Brown, Doering, McNab & Co*. See also *Taylor v Chester* (1869) LR 4 QB 309; *Begbie v Phosphate Sewage Co* (1876) 1 QBD 679.

11 See PARA 313.

12 *R v McDonnell* [1966] 1 QB 233, [1966] 1 All ER 193.

13 *Belmont Finance Corpn Ltd v Williams Furniture Ltd* [1979] Ch 250, [1979] 1 All ER 118, CA.

14 See eg the Companies Act 2006 s 119 (offences in connection with request for or disclosure of information from register of members) (see PARA 350); s 350 (offences relating to failure to provide information to independent assessor) (see PARA 731); s 387 (officer of company failing to keep accounting records) (see PARA 782); s 389 (where and for how long records to be kept) (see PARA 783); s 418 (contents of directors' report: statement as to disclosure to auditors) (see PARA 897); s 501 (auditor's rights to information) (see PARA 1030); s 572 (authorising the inclusion of misleading, false or deceptive matter in a statement setting out the reasons for a resolution disapplying pre-emption rights) (see PARA 1292); s 643(4), (5) (directors making a solvency statement without having reasonable grounds for the opinions expressed in it) (see PARA 1365); s 658 (company acquiring its own shares otherwise than in accordance with statutory provisions) (see PARA 1384); s 680 (company giving financial assistance towards acquisition of own shares) (see PARA 1413); s 715 (making statutory declaration relating to a payment out of capital for redemption or purchase of own shares) (see PARA 1433); s 993 (being a party to carrying on company's business with intent to defraud creditors, or for any fraudulent purpose) (see PARA 317); s 1153 (making misleading, false or deceptive statement to valuer of non-cash asset) (see PARA 1311); the Insolvency Act 1986 s 89 (making statutory declaration of company's solvency without reasonable grounds for opinion) (see COMPANY AND PARTNERSHIP INSOLVENCY vol 17 (2011) PARA 900); s 206 (fraud in anticipation of winding

up) (see COMPANY AND PARTNERSHIP INSOLVENCY vol 17 (2011) PARA 863); s 207 (entering into transactions in fraud of company's creditors) (see COMPANY AND PARTNERSHIP INSOLVENCY vol 17 (2011) PARA 866); s 208 (misconduct in course of winding up) (see COMPANY AND PARTNERSHIP INSOLVENCY vol 17 (2011) PARA 864); s 209 (destroying, falsifying etc the company's books) (see COMPANY AND PARTNERSHIP INSOLVENCY vol 17 (2011) PARA 865); s 210 (making material omission from statement relating to company's affairs) (see COMPANY AND PARTNERSHIP INSOLVENCY vol 17 (2011) PARA 867); s 211 (making false representation or fraud for purpose of obtaining creditors' consent to an agreement in connection with winding up) (see COMPANY AND PARTNERSHIP INSOLVENCY vol 17 (2011) PARA 869); and the Company Directors Disqualification Act 1986 s 13 (undischarged bankrupt acting as director or director acting in contravention of a disqualification order or undertaking) (see PARAS 1780, 1806). This list is not exhaustive.

15 See COMPANY AND PARTNERSHIP INSOLVENCY vol 17 (2011) PARA 863 et seq.

16 See PARA 316.

316. Criminal liability of officer in default under the Companies Acts. Certain provisions of the Companies Acts[1] are worded to the effect that, in the event of contravention of an enactment[2] in relation to a company[3], an offence is committed by every officer of the company who is in default[4]. For these purposes, 'officer' includes any director[5], manager or secretary[6], and any person who is to be treated as an officer of the company for the purposes of the provision in question[7]; and an officer is 'in default' for the purposes of the provision if he authorises or permits, participates in, or fails to take all reasonable steps to prevent, the contravention[8].

Where a company is an officer[9] of another company, it does not commit an offence as an officer in default[10] unless one of its officers is in default[11]. Where any such offence is committed by a company the officer in question also commits the offence and is liable to be proceeded against and punished accordingly[12].

1 As to the meaning of the 'Companies Acts' see PARA 13.

2 As to the meaning of 'enactment' see PARA 13 note 16.

3 As to the meaning of 'company' under the Companies Acts see PARA 21. The provisions of the Companies Act 2006 s 1121 apply to a body other than a company as they apply to a company: s 1123(1). See further notes 5–6.

4 Companies Act 2006 s 1121(1). See eg s 32(3) (constitutional documents to be provided to members) (see PARA 241); and s 36(3) (documents to be incorporated in or accompany copies of articles issued by company) (see PARA 240).

In most cases under the Companies Act 2006, however, liability falls upon both the company and the 'officer in default': see eg s 26(3) (registrar to be sent copy of amended articles) (see PARA 235); s 30(2) (copies of resolutions or agreements to be forwarded to registrar) (see PARA 230); s 34(5) (notice to registrar where company's constitution altered by enactment) (see PARA 237).

5 As to the meaning of 'director' see PARA 512. As the Companies Act 2006 s 1121 applies in relation to a body corporate other than a company (see note 3), the reference to a director of the company must be read as referring, where the body's affairs are managed by its members, to a member of the body and, in any other case, to any corresponding officer of the body: s 1123(2)(a). As s 1121 applies in relation to a partnership, the reference to a director of the company must be read as referring to a member of the partnership (s 1123(3)(a)); and, as it applies in relation to an unincorporated body other than a partnership, the reference to a director of the company must be read as referring, where the body's affairs are managed by its members, to a member of the body and, in any other case, to a member of the governing body (s 1123(4)(a)). As to the meaning of 'body corporate' for the purposes of the Companies Acts see PARA 1 note 5. As to the meaning of 'member' see PARA 323; and as to the meaning of 'officer' generally see PARA 679. As to companies, corporations and partnerships etc see PARAS 2–4.

6 Companies Act 2006 s 1121(2)(a). As to the company secretary and other officers see PARA 669. As s 1121 applies in relation to a body corporate other than a company, the reference to a manager or secretary of the company must be read as referring to any manager, secretary or similar officer of the body: s 1123(2)(b). As it applies in relation to a partnership, the reference to a manager or secretary of the company must be read as referring to any manager, secretary or similar officer of the partnership (s 1123(3)(b)); and, as it applies in relation to an unincorporated body other than a partnership, the reference to a manager or secretary of the company must be read as referring to any manager, secretary or similar officer of the body (s 1123(4)(b)).

7 Companies Act 2006 s 1121(2)(b).

8 Companies Act 2006 s 1121(3).

9 For these purposes, 'officer' has the meaning given by the Companies Act 2006 s 1121 (see the text and notes 5–7): s 1122(3).
10 For these purposes, 'in default' has the meaning given by the Companies Act 2006 s 1121 (see the text and note 8): s 1122(3).
11 Companies Act 2006 s 1122(1).
12 Companies Act 2006 s 1122(2).

317. Punishment for fraudulent trading. If any business of a company[1] is carried on[2] with intent to defraud[3] creditors of the company or creditors of any other person, or for any fraudulent purpose[4], every person who is knowingly a party to the carrying on[5] of the business in that manner commits an offence[6]. The allegation of intent to defraud contains an ingredient of dishonesty without which finding no jury would be entitled to convict[7]. It must be dishonesty on the part of those who are carrying on the business of the company[8]. Where a person carries on the business of two companies with the fraudulent intent of defrauding the companies' customers, he commits the offence of fraudulent trading[9].

Where a business is carried on by a person who is outside the reach of this offence of fraudulent trading[10], and with intent to defraud creditors of any person or for any other fraudulent purpose[11], and if he is knowingly a party to the carrying on of such a business, that person is guilty of an offence[12]. If such an offence[13] is committed by a body corporate[14], and if the offence is proved to have been committed with the consent or connivance of a director, manager, secretary or other similar officer of the body corporate, or a person who was purporting to act in any such capacity, he, as well as the body corporate, is guilty of the offence and liable to be proceeded against and punished accordingly[15].

1 As to the meaning of 'company' under the Companies Acts see PARA 21; and as to the meaning of the 'Companies Acts' see PARA 13.
2 'Carrying on of the business' is not necessarily synonymous with actively carrying on trade: *Re Sarflax Ltd* [1979] Ch 592, [1979] 1 All ER 529. It is necessary to show an act which could be described as carrying on the business of the company: *Re Augustus Barnett & Son Ltd* [1986] BCLC 170 (letters of comfort provided by parent did not themselves constitute the carrying on of the subsidiary's business). One transaction may be sufficient: *Re Gerald Cooper Chemicals Ltd* [1978] Ch 262, [1978] 2 All ER 49. However, it does not follow that whenever a fraud on a creditor is perpetrated in the course of carrying on business that the business is being carried on with intent to defraud creditors: *Morphitis v Bernasconi* [2003] EWCA Civ 289, [2003] Ch 552, [2003] 2 WLR 1521. Where the only allegation is the bare fact of preferring one creditor over another, such preference will not per se be sufficient to constitute fraud: *Re Sarflax Ltd* [1979] Ch 592, [1979] 1 All ER 529. As to the meanings of 'business', 'carry on business' and 'trade' generally see PARA 1 note 1.
3 The persons who actually carry on the business must be guilty of fraud, and a holding company cannot be liable otherwise than as a knowing party to such conduct: *Re Augustus Barnett & Son Ltd* [1986] BCLC 170. See also note 11. As to the general offence of fraud see CRIMINAL LAW vol 25 (2016) PARA 346 et seq.
4 'Defraud' and 'fraudulent purpose' connote actual dishonesty: *Re Patrick & Lyon Ltd* [1933] Ch 786. 'Intent to defraud creditors' may in general be properly inferred if the company continues to carry on business and incurs debts when to the knowledge of the persons liable there is no reasonable prospect of those debts being paid: *Re William C Leitch Bros Ltd* [1932] 2 Ch 71. One transaction may constitute fraudulent trading: *Re Gerald Cooper Chemicals Ltd* [1978] Ch 262, [1978] 2 All ER 49. Where the only allegation is the bare fact of preferring one creditor to another, such preference per se cannot constitute fraud within the meaning of the Insolvency Act 1986 s 213 (as to which see COMPANY AND PARTNERSHIP INSOLVENCY vol 17 (2011) PARA 869): *Re Sarflax Ltd* [1979] Ch 592, [1979] 1 All ER 529. It is not necessary to prove knowledge that there was no reasonable prospect of the debts ever being paid; proof of knowledge that there was no reason for thinking that funds would become available to pay the debt when it became due or shortly thereafter may be sufficient: *R v Grantham* [1984] QB 675, [1984] 3 All ER 166, CA. See also *R v Cox, R v Hodges* [1983] BCLC 169, CA; *R v Lockwood* [1986] Crim LR 244, CA. An intent to defraud customers as potential creditors is sufficient even where those customers, through want of assets, have not obtained judgment or pursued other civil remedies against the company: *R v Kemp* [1988] QB 645, [1988] 2 WLR 975, CA. The word 'creditor' in its ordinary meaning denotes one to whom money is owed; and whether that debt can presently

be sued for is immaterial: *R v Smith* [1996] 2 BCLC 109, CA. In order to fall within the Insolvency Act 1986 s 213 the behaviour of the respondent must be deserving of real moral blame: *Re L Todd (Swanscombe) Ltd* [1990] BCLC 454, [1990] BCC 125. A receiver carrying on the business of a company is exposed to a claim for fraudulent trading if he allows debts or liabilities to be incurred by a company under continuing contracts during the receivership for which he has no personal liability and in respect of which he knows that there is no good reason for thinking that they can or will be paid: *Powdrill v Watson, Re Leyland DAF Ltd, Re Ferranti International plc* [1995] 2 AC 394, [1995] 2 All ER 65, HL (receivers not liable where, in pursuance of their duties to the debenture holder, they postponed the sale of properties on which unoccupied business rates continued to accrue); cf *Brown v City of London Corpn* [1996] 1 WLR 1070, sub nom *Re Sobam BV (in receivership)* [1996] 1 BCLC 446.

5 A person who, although not a director, manages the business in consultation with a director is within this description: *Re Peake and Hall* [1985] PCC 87, Isle of Man HC. A creditor who knowingly receives money procured by carrying on a business with intent to defraud may be liable (see *Re Gerald Cooper Chemicals Ltd* [1978] Ch 262, [1978] 2 All ER 49); but not a secretary who merely performs the duties appropriate to that office (*Re Maidstone Buildings Provisions Ltd* [1971] 3 All ER 363, [1971] 1 WLR 1085). Similarly, a financial adviser who fails to give advice is not liable by reason of that fact alone (*Re Maidstone Buildings Provisions Ltd* [1971] 3 All ER 363, [1971] 1 WLR 1085); nor is a director who did not concern himself with the company's financial affairs (*Re Peake and Hall* [1985] PCC 87, Isle of Man HC). A company which was involved in and assisted and benefited from an offending business or a business carried on in an offending way and did so knowingly and therefore dishonestly may fall within this provision: *Re Bank of Credit and Commerce International SA (No 2), Banque Arabe et Internationale D'Investissement SA v Morris* [2001] 1 BCLC 263. Where there is an issue as to whether the accused falls within what is now the Companies Act 2006 s 993, that issue must be put to the jury with clear guidance as to the meaning of 'a party to the carrying on of the business of the company': *R v Miles* [1992] Crim LR 657, CA.

6 Companies Act 2006 s 993(1). The provisions of s 993 apply whether or not the company has been, or is in the course of being, wound up: s 993(2). As to the possible unlimited liability of persons in a winding up see further COMPANY AND PARTNERSHIP INSOLVENCY vol 17 (2011) PARA 869.

A person guilty of such an offence is liable on conviction on indictment to imprisonment for a term not exceeding ten years or a fine, or to both, or on summary conviction to imprisonment for a term not exceeding 12 months or a fine, or to both: see s 993(3). In the case of liability on summary conviction the fine is one not exceeding the statutory maximum: see s 993(b). By virtue of the Legal Aid, Sentencing and Punishment of Offenders Act 2012 s 85, however, where the offence is committed on or after 12 March 2015, it is punishable by a fine of an unlimited amount. As to the statutory maximum and the powers of magistrates' courts to issue fines on summary conviction see SENTENCING vol 92 (2015) PARA 176. In relation to an offence committed before the coming into force of the Criminal Justice Act 2003 s 154(1) (not yet in force), the maximum term of imprisonment on summary conviction is six months: see the Companies Act 2006 s 1131; and PARA 1818.

The provisions of the Companies Act 2006 s 993 apply to unregistered companies by virtue of the Unregistered Companies Regulations 2009, SI 2009/2436, Sch 1 para 15: see PARA 1857. As to the meaning of 'unregistered company' see PARA 1856.

A deferred prosecution agreement (as to which see CRIMINAL PROCEDURE vol 27 (2015) PARA 58 et seq) may be entered into in relation to an offence under the Companies Act 2006 s 993 committed by an organisation: see the Crime and Courts Act 2013 Sch 17 paras 4(1), 24(c).

As to any civil liability that might arise see the Insolvency Act 1986 s 213; and COMPANY AND PARTNERSHIP INSOLVENCY vol 17 (2011) PARA 869.

7 See *RePatrick and Lyon Ltd* [1933] Ch 786; *DPP v Schildkamp* [1971] AC 1, [1969] 3 All ER 1640, HL; *R v Rollafson* [1969] 2 All ER 833, [1969] 1 WLR 815, CA. To establish an intent to defraud it is not necessary to prove knowledge that there was no reasonable prospect of the debts ever being paid; proof of knowledge that there was no reason for thinking that funds would become available to pay the debt when it became due or shortly thereafter may be sufficient: *R v Grantham* [1984] QB 675, [1984] 3 All ER 166, CA.

8 *Re Augustus Barnett & Son Ltd* [1986] BCLC 170.

9 *R v Kemp* [1988] QB 645, [1988] 2 WLR 975, CA. See also *R v Seillon* [1982] Crim LR 676, CA.

10 Ie outside the reach of the Companies Act 2006 s 993 (see the text and notes 1–6): see the Fraud Act 2006 s 9(2) (s 9(2), (3) amended by SI 2007/2194). The following are within the reach of the Companies Act 2006 s 993 (Fraud Act 2006 s 9(3) (as so amended)):

(1) a company, as defined in the Companies Act 2006 s 1(1) (see PARA 21) (Fraud Act 2006 s 9(3)(a) (amended by SI 2009/1941));

(2) a person to whom the Companies Act 2006 s 993 applies (with or without adaptations or modifications) as if the person were a company (Fraud Act 2006 s 9(3)(b));
(3) a person exempted from the application of the Companies Act 2006 s 993 (Fraud Act 2006 s 9(3)(c)).

11 Fraud Act 2006 s 9(2) (as amended: see note 11). For these purposes, 'fraudulent purpose' has the same meaning as in the Companies Act 2006 s 993 (which depends upon common law for that meaning: see note 4): Fraud Act 2006 s 9(5) (amended by SI 2007/2194).

12 Fraud Act 2006 s 9(1). See also note 5. A person guilty of such an offence is liable on summary conviction to imprisonment for a term not exceeding 12 months or to a fine, or to both, or on conviction on indictment to imprisonment for a term not exceeding ten years or to a fine, or to both: see s 9(6). In the case of liability on summary conviction the fine is one not exceeding the statutory maximum: see s 9(6)(a). By virtue of the Legal Aid, Sentencing and Punishment of Offenders Act 2012 s 85, however, where the offence is committed on or after 12 March 2015, it is punishable by a fine of an unlimited amount. As to the statutory maximum and the powers of magistrates' courts to issue fines on summary conviction see SENTENCING vol 92 (2015) PARA 176.

13 Ie any offence under the Fraud Act 2006: see s 12(1).

14 Fraud Act 2006 s 12(1).

15 Fraud Act 2006 s 12(2). If the affairs of a body corporate are managed by its members, s 12(2) applies in relation to the acts and defaults of a member in connection with his functions of management as if he were a director of the body corporate: s 12(3).

318. Liability for bribery or for failure to prevent bribery. If an offence under the Bribery Act 2010 of bribing another person[1], being bribed[2], or bribing a foreign public official[3] is committed by a body corporate or a Scottish partnership[4], then if the offence is proved to have been committed with the consent or connivance of a senior officer[5] of the body corporate or Scottish partnership, or a person purporting to act in such a capacity, the senior officer or person, as well as the body corporate or partnership, is guilty of the offence and liable to be proceeded against and punished accordingly[6].

A relevant commercial organisation[7] ('C') is guilty of an offence if a person ('A') associated with C[8] bribes another person[9] intending to obtain or retain business for C, or to obtain or retain an advantage in the conduct of business for C[10]. It is, however, a defence for C to prove that C had in place adequate procedures designed to prevent persons associated with C from undertaking such conduct[11]. A person guilty of such an offence is liable on conviction on indictment to a fine[12].

1 Ie an offence under the Bribery Act 2010 s 1: see CRIMINAL LAW vol 26 (2016) PARA 369.

2 Ie an offence under the Bribery Act 2010 s 2: see CRIMINAL LAW vol 26 (2016) PARA 369.

3 Ie an offence under the Bribery Act 2010 s 6: see CRIMINAL LAW vol 26 (2016) PARA 370.

4 Bribery Act 2010 s 14(1).

5 For these purposes, 'senior officer' means, in relation to a body corporate, a director, manager, secretary or other similar officer of the body corporate, and in relation to a Scottish partnership, a partner in the partnership; and 'director', in relation to a body corporate whose affairs are managed by its members, means a member of the body corporate: Bribery Act 2010 s 14(4).

6 Bribery Act 2010 s 14(2). This does not, however, apply, in the case of an offence which is committed under s 1, 2 or 6 by virtue of section 12(2)–(4) (territorial application: see CRIMINAL LAW vol 26 (2016) PARA 369), to a senior officer or person purporting to act in such a capacity unless the senior officer or person has a close connection with the United Kingdom (within the meaning given by s 12(4)): s 14(3). As to penalties and consents to prosecutions see ss 10, 11; and CRIMINAL LAW vol 26 (2016) PARA 369. For a statutory defence for certain bribery offences see s 13; and CRIMINAL LAW vol 26 (2016) PARA 372.

7 'Relevant commercial organisation' means the following (Bribery Act 2010 s 7(5)), ie;
(1) a body which is incorporated under the law of any part of the United Kingdom and which carries on a business, whether there or elsewhere;
(2) any other body corporate, wherever incorporated, which carries on a business, or part of a business, in any part of the United Kingdom;
(3) a partnership which is formed under the law of any part of the United Kingdom and which carries on a business, whether there or elsewhere; or
(4) any other partnership, wherever formed, which carries on a business, or part of a business, in any part of the United Kingdom.

For these purposes, a trade or profession is a business: s 7(5). 'Partnership' means a partnership within the Partnership Act 1890 (see PARTNERSHIP vol 79 (2014) PARA 1 et seq), or a limited partnership registered under the Limited Partnerships Act 1907 (see PARTNERSHIP vol 79 (2014) PARA 217 et seq), or a firm or entity of a similar character formed under the law of a country or territory outside the United Kingdom: Bribery Act 2010 s 7(5). As to the meanings of 'firm' and 'partnership' generally see PARTNERSHIP vol 79 (2014) PARA 1; and as to the legal personality of a partnership or firm generally see PARTNERSHIP vol 79 (2014) PARA 2.

8 As to the meaning of 'a person associated with C' see the Bribery Act 2010 s 8; and CRIMINAL LAW vol 26 (2016) PARA 371.

9 For these purposes, A bribes another person if, and only if, A either is, or would be, guilty of an offence under the Bribery Act 2010 s 1 (bribing another person: see CRIMINAL LAW vol 26 (2016) PARA 369) or s 6 (bribing a foreign public official: see CRIMINAL LAW vol 26 (2016) PARA 370), whether or not A has been prosecuted for such an offence, or would be guilty of such an offence if s 12(2)(c), (4) (territorial application: see CRIMINAL LAW vol 26 (2016) PARA 369) were omitted: s 7(3).

10 Bribery Act 2010 s 7(1).

11 Bribery Act 2010 s 7(2).

12 Bribery Act 2010 s 11(3).

(viii) Ownership and Disposition of Property by Company

319. Company's power to hold land. Any company incorporated under the Companies Act 2006[1] or the former Companies Acts[2], or registered, though not formed, under that Act or the former Companies Acts[3], has always had power to hold land in the United Kingdom[4].

The fact that a company holds land does not make its shares an interest in land within the Law of Property (Miscellaneous Provisions) Act 1989[5], or, where it is established for charitable purposes, render it necessary to obtain any consent of the Charity Commission[6] to the sale of its land which would not be required if it was not incorporated[7].

The power of holding land imposes no restriction on the mode in which the company may acquire land, which may therefore be taken on lease[8]. The company may let the land acquired unless the company's objects expressly or impliedly restrict the letting of its property[9].

1 As to incorporation under the Companies Act 2006 see PARA 95 et seq. As to the meaning of 'company' under the Companies Acts see PARA 21; and as to the meaning of the 'Companies Acts' see PARA 13.

2 As to the meaning of the 'former Companies Acts' see PARA 14 note 1.

3 As to predecessor legislation to the Companies Act 2006 and the continuity maintained in the law see PARA 13 et seq.

4 As to the power to hold personal property see PARA 320. As to the meaning of 'United Kingdom' see PARA 1 note 5. Formerly, a company formed for the purpose of promoting art, science, religion, charity or any other like object, not involving the acquisition of gain by the company or by its individual members, could not without the licence of the Board of Trade hold more than two acres of land, although the Board might license any such company to hold land in such quantity and subject to such conditions as the Board thought fit: see the Companies Act 1948 s 14(1) proviso (repealed).

5 Ie within the Law of Property (Miscellaneous Provisions) Act 1989 s 2 (see CONVEYANCING vol 23 (2013) PARA 151). See also the Companies Act 2006 ss 541, 544, under which the shares or other interest of any company member are personal property, transferable as provided by the articles, and are not of the nature of real estate (see PARA 1244); and *Bligh v Brent* (1837) 2 Y & C Ex 268; *Humble v Mitchell* (1839) 11 Ad & El 205.

6 As to the Charity Commission see CHARITIES vol 8 (2015) PARA 543 et seq.

7 *Re Church Army* (1906) 75 LJ Ch 467, CA. See also *Re Society for Training Teachers of the Deaf and Whittle's Contract* [1907] 2 Ch 486. As to restrictions on the disposition of charity land see and CHARITIES vol 8 (2015) PARA 401.

8 If the company takes premises which are the best for its purposes, it is no objection to the validity of the lease that the premises are too large and that part will have to be sublet: *Re London and Colonial Co, Horsey's Claim* (1868) LR 5 Eq 561 (judgment of Wood V-C cited at 562n(1)). Directors entering into an agreement for a lease in their own names are personally liable: *Kay v*

Johnson (1864) 2 Hem & M 118. As to the effect of the dissolution of the company on leases see COMPANY AND PARTNERSHIP INSOLVENCY vol 17 (2011) PARAS 892–894.

9 A lease of the company's undertaking may be sanctioned as a term in a scheme of arrangement under the Companies Act 2006 s 899 (see PARA 1611): see *Re Dynevor, Dyffryn and Neath Abbey Collieries Co* (1879) 11 ChD 605, CA. As to schemes of arrangement see PARA 1605 et seq. As to a company's objects (which are no longer a required part of a company's constitution) see PARA 239.

320. Company's power to hold personalty. An incorporated company[1] may hold personal property to any extent without licence from any government department[2]. Its powers in this respect may, however, be limited by its constitution[3].

Regardless of whether such limitations exist or not, a company cannot, save in the manner provided by the Companies Act 2006[4], purchase its own shares[5], although it may buy up its debentures[6] for the purpose of redeeming or reissuing them[7], or redeem redeemable shares[8].

Where a person transfers property to a company for the purpose of defeating his creditors, its title to the property may in certain cases be displaced in favour of his trustee in bankruptcy[9].

A bill of sale to a company must state its address and description[10].

1 As to incorporated companies see PARA 2.
2 As to corporations' ownership of property generally see CORPORATIONS vol 24 (2010) PARA 447 et seq.
3 As to the meaning of references to a company's constitution see PARA 226.
4 See PARA 1416 et seq.
5 *Trevor v Whitworth* (1887) 12 App Cas 409, HL.
6 As to the meaning of 'debenture' see PARA 1482.
7 See the Companies Act 2006 s 752; and PARA 1501.
8 See PARA 1416 et seq.
9 As to the vesting of property in a trustee in bankruptcy and the property available for creditors see BANKRUPTCY AND INDIVIDUAL INSOLVENCY vol 5 (2013) PARA 397 et seq.
10 *Altree v Altree* [1898] 2 QB 267. See also FINANCIAL INSTRUMENTS AND TRANSACTIONS vol 49 (2015) PARA 498 et seq.

321. Joint ownership by company. Being a body corporate[1], a company[2] is capable of acquiring and holding any real or personal property in joint tenancy[3] in the same manner as if it were an individual[4]. Where it and an individual, or two or more bodies corporate, become entitled to any such property under circumstances or by virtue of any instrument which would, if the company had been an individual, have created a joint tenancy, they are entitled to the property as joint tenants[5]. Such acquisition and holding of property in joint tenancy are, however, subject to the like conditions and restrictions which attach to the acquisition and holding of property by a body corporate in severalty[6].

1 As to companies and corporations generally see PARA 2.
2 As to the general meaning of 'company' see PARA 1.
3 See generally REAL PROPERTY AND REGISTRATION vol 87 (2012) PARA 198 et seq. See also PERSONAL PROPERTY vol 80 (2013) PARA 829.
4 Bodies Corporate (Joint Tenancy) Act 1899 s 1(1). As to corporations as joint tenants see also REAL PROPERTY AND REGISTRATION vol 87 (2012) PARA 200.
5 Bodies Corporate (Joint Tenancy) Act 1899 s 1(1). On the dissolution of a body corporate which is a joint tenant the property devolves on the other joint tenant: s 1(2).
6 Bodies Corporate (Joint Tenancy) Act 1899 s 1(1) proviso.

322. Company's power to sell property. Unless specifically restricted to do so by its constitution[1], a company may have, for example, extensive powers to sell its personal property[2], or to sell its business for shares in another company[3].

Even if its constitution purports to give it power to do so, a company which is proposed to be wound up cannot sell all its assets and undertaking and provide for the distribution of the proceeds in the winding up otherwise than in accordance with the statutory provisions[4].

An agreement for sale is not necessarily bad on the ground that one of its terms is the payment of a bonus to the directors of the selling company, unless the bonus is in fact a bribe to them[5]; but it is not lawful to make any such payment to a director unless a memorandum setting out particulars of the proposed payment, including its amount, is made available to the members of the company, whose approval is sought, and a resolution approving the payment has been duly passed[6].

1 See PARA 239. As to the meaning of references to a company's constitution see PARA 226.
2 *Wilson v Miers* (1861) 10 CBNS 348 at 366.
3 *Re European Society Arbitration Acts, ex p British Nation Life Assurance Association (Liquidators)* (1878) 8 ChD 679, CA (power had to be implied at time when company's objects had to be specified in the memorandum of association). See also *Re Barned's Banking Co* (1867) 3 Ch App 105; *Grant v United Kingdom Switchback Rly Co* (1888) 40 ChD 135, CA; *Wall v London and Northern Assets Corpn* [1898] 2 Ch 469, CA; *Re HH Vivian & Co Ltd, Metropolitan Bank of England and Wales Ltd v HH Vivian & Co Ltd* [1900] 2 Ch 654; *Re Borax Co, Foster v Borax Co* [1901] 1 Ch 326, CA (disapproving *Re Borax Co, Foster v Borax Co* [1899] 2 Ch 130); *Loeffler v Donna Thereza Christina Rly Co Ltd* (1901) 18 TLR 149; *Booth v New Afrikander Gold Mining Co Ltd* [1903] 1 Ch 295 at 313, CA, per Vaughan Williams LJ; *Mason v Motor Traction Co Ltd* [1905] 1 Ch 419; *Bisgood v Henderson's Transvaal Estates Ltd* [1908] 1 Ch 743, CA; *Re William Thomas & Co Ltd* [1915] 1 Ch 325.
4 *Bisgood v Henderson's Transvaal Estates Ltd* [1908] 1 Ch 743, CA; and see *MacPherson v European Strategic Bureau Ltd* [2000] 2 BCLC 683. As to the statutory provisions referred to in the text regarding distributions in a winding up see COMPANY AND PARTNERSHIP INSOLVENCY vol 17 (2011) PARA 770 et seq. As to reconstructions and amalgamations see PARA 1614.
5 *Southall v British Mutual Life Assurance Society* (1871) 6 Ch App 614.
6 See the Companies Act 2006 s 218; and PARA 622.

(9) COMPANY MEMBERSHIP

(i) Membership of a Company: in general

323. Who are members of a company. The subscribers of a company's memorandum of association[1] are deemed to have agreed to become members of the company and, on its registration[2], become members and must be entered as such in its register of members[3]. However, neither this entry in the register nor any allotment[4] of shares[5] is a condition precedent to their becoming members[6]. Furthermore, as from 30 June 2016[7], where an election to keep membership information on the central register[8] is in force in relation to a company, the above requirement to enter particulars of members in the company's register of members does not apply[9].

Every other person who agrees to become a member of a company[10], and whose name is entered in its register of members[11], is a 'member of the company'[12].

As from the date of incorporation[13], the subscribers of the memorandum of association, together with such other persons as may from time to time become members of the company, are a body corporate[14] by the name stated in the certificate of incorporation[15]. Accordingly, the members of a company are those persons (including corporations[16], if any), who collectively constitute the company, or, in other words, are its corporators. A member is not necessarily a shareholder[17], because an unlimited company[18] or a company limited by guarantee may exist without a share capital[19]. However, where a company has a capital limited by shares, the shareholders are the only members[20].

The bearer of a share warrant[21] may, if the articles of the company so provide, be deemed a member of the company within the meaning of the Companies Act 2006, either to the full extent or for any purposes defined in the articles[22]. No share warrant may, however, be issued by a company on or after 26 May 2015[23].

1 As to the meaning of 'memorandum of association' see PARA 97. As to subscribers of the memorandum see PARA 97. As to the meaning of 'company' under the Companies Acts see PARA 21; and as to the meaning of the 'Companies Acts' see PARA 13.

2 As to company registration under the Companies Act 2006 see PARA 104 et seq. As to companies registered but not formed under the Companies Act 2006, and as to overseas companies, see PARA 29.

3 Companies Act 2006 s 112(1). As to the register of members see PARA 336 et seq. As to subscribers' liability see PARA 324.

4 As to the meaning of 'allotted' see PARA 1280.

5 As to shares generally see PARA 1231 et seq.

6 *Re Florence Land and Public Works Co,Nicol's Case, Tufnell and Ponsonby's Case* (1885) 29 ChD 421 at 445, CA, per Fry LJ; *Evans's Case* (1867) 2 Ch App 427; *Hall's Case* (1870) 5 Ch App 707; *Sidney's Case* (1871) LR 13 Eq 228; *Re London and Provincial Consolidated Coal Co* (1877) 5 ChD 525; *Re Argyle Coal and Cannell Co Ltd, ex p Watson* (1885) 54 LT 233.

7 See the Small Business, Enterprise and Employment Act 2015 (Commencement No 4, Transitional and Savings Provisions) Regulations 2016, SI 2016/321, reg 6(c).

8 Ie an election under the Companies Act 2006 s 128B: see PARA 364.

9 Companies Act 2006 s 112(3)(a) (s 112(3) added by the Small Business, Enterprise and Employment Act 2015 Sch 5 Pt 2 paras 11, 13).

10 See PARA 327.

11 As from 30 June 2016 (see note 7), if an election under the Companies Act 2006 s 128B (see PARA 364) is in force in relation to a company, s 112(2) has effect as if the reference to a person whose name is entered in the company's register of members were a reference to a person with respect to whom the following steps have been taken (s 112(3)(b) (as added: see note 9)), ie:

(1) the person's name has been delivered to the registrar under s 128E (see PARA 366); and

(2) the document containing that information has been registered by the registrar.

12 Companies Act 2006 s 112(2).

Under the Companies (Tables A to F) Regulations 1985, SI 1985/805, reg 2, Schedule Table C (which applies modified Table A articles of association to companies limited by guarantee and not having a share capital), it is specified that the subscribers to the memorandum of association of the company and such other persons as are admitted to membership in accordance with the articles are members of the company: see Schedule Table C art 3. However, no person may be admitted a member of the company unless he is approved by the directors; and every person who wishes to become a member must deliver to the company an application for membership in such form as the directors require executed by him: Schedule Table C art 3. Such a member may at any time withdraw from the company by giving at least seven clear days' notice to the company but membership is not transferable and it ceases on death: Schedule Table C art 4. As to the meaning of 'company limited by guarantee' see PARA 95. As to the meanings of 'company having a share capital' and 'share capital' see PARA 1231. As to the meanings of 'Table A' and 'Table C', and as to the treatment of legacy articles under the Companies Act 2006, see PARA 229. As to a company's directors see PARA 512 et seq. As to the meaning of references to a company's 'articles' see PARA 227 note 2. As to a company's articles of association generally see PARA 227 et seq. Similar provision is made by the model articles which have been made for the purposes of the Companies Act 2006 and intended for adoption by private companies limited by guarantee (see the Companies (Model Articles) Regulations 2008, SI 2008/3229, reg 3, Sch 2; and PARA 227 et seq). Under those model articles, no person may become a member of the company unless that person has completed an application for membership in a form approved by the directors, and the directors have approved the application: see Sch 2 art 21. A member may withdraw from membership of the company by giving seven days' notice to the company in writing: Sch 2 art 22(1). However, membership is not transferable (Sch 2 art 22(2)); and a person's membership terminates when that person dies or ceases to exist (Sch 2 art 22(3)). As to the meaning of 'private company' see PARA 95.

13 Ie the date stated in the certificate of incorporation, following the registration of a company: see PARA 114 note 7.

14 As to the meaning of 'body corporate' see PARA 1 note 5.

15 See the Companies Act 2006 s 16; and PARA 115. As to the company's name see PARA 199 et seq.
16 See the Companies Act 2006 s 16; and PARA 115. As to the company's name see PARA 199 et seq.
17 *Re Barned's Banking Co, ex p Contract Corpn* (1867) 3 Ch App 105 at 113 per Lord Cairns LC. As to membership of a corporation generally see CORPORATIONS vol 24 (2010) PARA 347 et seq. As to companies and corporations generally see PARA 2. As to shareholders and membership of companies generally see PARAS 323 et seq, 1889 et seq.
18 As to the meaning of 'unlimited company' see PARA 95.
19 *Re South London Fish Market Co* (1888) 39 ChD 324, CA. As to share capital and companies limited by guarantee see PARA 72. As to share capital and unlimited companies see PARA 74.
20 As to the meaning of 'company limited by shares' see PARA 95.
21 As to the meaning of 'share warrant' see PARA 392.
22 See the Companies Act 2006 s 122(3); and PARA 338.
23 See the Companies Act 2006 s 779(4); and PARA 392.

324. Subscribers' liability for shares. By subscribing, each subscriber at once irrevocably agrees to take from the company the subscribed number of shares[1], being at least one share each, unless all its share capital has been duly allotted to other persons[2]. The fact that no shares are allotted to him and that he has ceased to be treated as a member for a considerable time does not relieve him from liability[3], though a valid surrender will do so[4]. A subscriber who is a director is bound to see that the allotment is made[5].

The subscriber's obligation to take shares is not satisfied by a transfer to him, or by an allotment to him of shares, credited as fully paid up, to which a third person is entitled[6]. The obligation of a person who subscribes in his own name, but in fact as an agent, is satisfied by his principal taking the number of shares subscribed for[7].

Shares taken by a subscriber of the memorandum of association[8] of a public company[9] in pursuance of an undertaking of his in the memorandum, and any premium on the shares, must be paid up in cash[10]; and if the company contravenes this provision, it, and any officer of it, who is in default[11] is liable on conviction on indictment or on summary conviction to a fine[12]. Otherwise, the shares so subscribed for may be paid for either in cash or in money's worth[13]. The shares paid for in money's worth must, however, be identified with the shares subscribed for[14].

A subscriber for preference shares[15] may take the like amount of ordinary shares instead[16]. If a person subscribes for shares, some of which are to be allotted as fully paid up, he is liable only as contributory in respect of the others; but, if he subscribes for fully paid up shares only, he is liable for them as unpaid[17], except in so far as he has actually paid for them.

1 *Alexander v Automatic Telephone Co* [1900] 2 Ch 56, CA. Unless otherwise agreed, by the articles or otherwise, the subscriber is bound to pay only when calls are made: *Alexander v Automatic Telephone Co*. As to a company's articles of association generally see PARA 227 et seq. As to a shareholder's liability for calls or capital not paid up generally see PARA 1895 et seq. See also *Re Freen & Co Ltd* (1866) 15 LT 406; *Gilman's Case* (1886) 31 ChD 420; *Re China Steamship and Labuan Coal Co Ltd, Drummond's Case* (1869) 4 Ch App 772; *Dunster's Case* [1894] 3 Ch 473, CA.

Prior to the commencement of the Companies Act 2006, the number of shares agreed to be taken by a subscriber on formation was placed opposite the subscriber's signature on the memorandum of association (the role of which has been altered fundamentally under the Companies Act 2006): see PARA 97. This information is not amongst the information that is required to be included in the form of memorandum prescribed by regulations made under the Companies Act 2006 (see the Companies (Registration) Regulations 2008, SI 2008/3014, reg 2(a), Sch 1 (memorandum of association of a company having a share capital)), but this information does have to be included in the statement of capital and initial shareholdings that is required to be delivered in the case of a company limited by shares: see the Companies Act 2006 s 10(4), (5); and PARA 107. As to shares, share capital and allotments generally see PARA 1231 et seq.

2 *Mackley's Case* (1875) 1 ChD 247. See also *Evans's Case* (1867) 2 Ch App 427; *Re China Steamship and Labuan Coal Co Ltd, Drummond's Case* (1869) 4 Ch App 772 at 780 per Giffard LJ.
3 *Re Imperial Land Co of Marseilles Ltd, Levick's Case* (1870) 40 LJ Ch 180; *Ex p London and Colonial Co Ltd, Tooth's Case* (1868) 19 LT 599; *Sidney's Case* (1871) LR 13 Eq 228.
4 *Re Freen & Co Ltd* (1866) 15 LT 406; *Snell's Case* (1869) 5 Ch App 22; *Hall's Case* (1870) 5 Ch App 707; *Re London and Provincial Consolidated Coal Co* (1877) 5 ChD 525.
5 *Evans's Case* (1867) 2 Ch App 427; *Re United Service Co, Hall's Case* (1870) 5 Ch App 707 at 711 per James LJ. As to a company's directors see PARA 512 et seq.
6 *Migotti's Case* (1867) LR 4 Eq 238; *Forbes and Judd's Case* (1870) 5 Ch App 270; *Dent's Case, Forbes' Case* (1873) 8 Ch App 768. Cf *Re Pen'Allt Silver Lead Mining Co Ltd, Fraser's Case* (1873) 42 LJ Ch 358. As to paid up and unpaid shares see PARA 1231 et seq.
7 *Dunster's Case* [1894] 3 Ch 473, CA.
8 As to the meaning of 'memorandum of association' see PARA 97.
9 As to the meaning of 'public company' see PARA 95.
10 See the Companies Act 2006 s 584; and PARA 1303. As to the meaning of 'cash' for these purposes see PARA 1280 note 10. As to the meaning of 'premium' see PARA 1335.
11 As to the meaning of 'officer who is in default' see PARA 316.
12 See the Companies Act 2006 s 590; and PARA 1303. In the case of liability on summary conviction the fine is one not exceeding the statutory maximum. By virtue of the Legal Aid, Sentencing and Punishment of Offenders Act 2012 s 85, however, where the offence is committed on or after 12 March 2015, it is punishable by a fine of an unlimited amount. As to the statutory maximum and the powers of magistrates' courts to issue fines on summary conviction see SENTENCING vol 92 (2015) PARA 176.
13 *Re China Steamship and Labuan Coal Ltd, Drummond's Case* (1869) 4 Ch App 772; *Pell's Case* (1869) 5 Ch App 11; *Re Baglan Hall Colliery Co* (1870) 5 Ch App 346; *Jones' Case* (1870) 6 Ch App 48; *Maynard's Case* (1873) 9 Ch App 60. As to payments in cash see also PARA 1298. Directors cannot pay for the shares out of fees paid to themselves ultra vires: *Re Great Northern and Midland Coal Co Ltd, Currie's Case* (1863) 3 De GJ & Sm 367 at 371. Nor can they pay for the shares out of money of the company paid to other persons ultra vires: *Hay's Case* (1875) 10 Ch App 593. Cf *Re Canadian Oil Works Corpn, Eastwick's Case* (1876) 45 LJ Ch 225, CA.
14 *Fothergill's Case* (1873) 8 Ch App 270.
15 As to preference shares see PARA 1880.
16 *Duke's Case* (1876) 1 ChD 620.
17 *Baron De Beville's Case* (1868) LR 7 Eq 11.

325. Shareholders not debarred from damages. Formerly a shareholder could not both retain his shares[1] and bring proceedings against a company for deceit inducing him to buy from the company its shares or, by analogy, to take up shares of the company[2]. A person is, however, no longer debarred from obtaining damages or other compensation from a company[3] by reason only of his holding or having held shares in the company or any right to apply or subscribe for shares or to be included in the company's register of members[4] or, as from 30 June 2016[5], to have his name and other particulars delivered to the registrar of companies[6] and registered by the registrar in respect of shares[7].

1 As to the meaning of 'share' see PARA 1231. As to shareholders and membership of companies generally see PARAS 323–324, 326 et seq, 1889 et seq.
2 *Houldsworth v City of Glasgow Bank* (1880) 5 App Cas 317, HL; *Re Addlestone Linoleum Co* (1887) 37 ChD 191, CA. In principle, it was thought that such a claim was inconsistent with the contract into which the claimant had entered and the claimant had, therefore, to have severed his connection with the company by agreement or judgment for rescission before he could sue the company for misrepresentation: see *Houldsworth v City of Glasgow Bank* (1880) 5 App Cas 317 at 324–325, HL, per Lord Cairns LC. This principle did not prevent proceedings being maintained for rescission in a proper case: see *Western Bank of Scotland v Addie* (1867) LR 1 Sc & Div 145 at 163–164, HL, per Lord Chelmsford. As to the grounds for claims of deceit see PARA 1270 et seq.
3 As to the meaning of 'company' under the Companies Acts see PARA 21; and as to the meaning of the 'Companies Acts' see PARA 13.
4 As to the register of members see PARA 336 et seq.
5 See the Small Business, Enterprise and Employment Act 2015 (Commencement No 4, Transitional and Savings Provisions) Regulations 2016, SI 2016/321, reg 6(c).

6 Ie under the Companies Act 2006 Pt 8 Ch 2A (ss 128A–128K): see PARA 363 et seq. As to the meaning of 'registrar of companies' see PARA 126 note 2; as to the meaning of 'company' under the Companies Acts see PARA 21; and as to the meaning of the 'Companies Acts' see PARA 13.
7 Companies Act 2006 s 655 (amended by the Small Business, Enterprise and Employment Act 2015 Sch 5 Pt 2 paras 11, 24).

326. Service of notice on members of company. Provisions in a company's articles of association[1] as to service of notices on members[2] generally apply only to notices relating to the ordinary business of the company, and service in the manner set out by them is not in itself sufficient to fix a shareholder with knowledge of the falsity of a misrepresentation which would entitle him to repudiate his shares[3]. Similarly, such a provision that service of a notice at the registered address was to be good did not necessarily apply to give validity to substituted service of a debtor's summons at the address on the company register[4].

When a member has died[5], a notice addressed to him at his registered address is good, if the company has no notice of his death[6]; but not if the directors[7] are aware of the death[8], in which case, unless the articles themselves otherwise provide[9], a notice required by the articles to be served on members need not be sent at all, even to the personal representatives, unless they have been registered as members[10].

A notice sent to all the members on the register at the date of sending out is good, even though the register is subsequently rectified with effect retrospective to a day prior to that date[11].

1 As to articles of association generally see PARA 227 et seq.
2 The default articles prescribed for the purposes of the Companies Act 1985 ('legacy articles'), ie the Companies (Tables A to F) Regulations 1985, SI 1985/805, have not been revoked and may, in their amended form, continue to be used by companies after the commencement of the Companies Act 2006: see PARA 229. They make extensive provision as to the service of notices on members: see the Companies (Tables A to F) Regulations 1985, SI 1985/805, reg 2, Schedule Table A arts 111–116 (art 111 substituted by, arts 112, 115 amended by, SI 2000/3373). The Companies (Tables A to F) Regulations 1985, SI 1985/805, Schedule Table A arts 112, 113 are modified by Schedule, Table C arts 12, 13, and Schedule Table A arts 114, 116 are disapplied by Schedule, Table C art 1, in relation to companies limited by guarantee and not having a share capital). Table A arts 112 and 115 do not require that service of a notice on a member by the company by post had to be to his registered address; rather, a notice was 'properly addressed' if it was accurately addressed: *Hunter v Senate Support Services Ltd* [2004] EWHC 1085 (Ch), [2005] 1 BCLC 175, applying *Rayfield v Hands* [1958] 2 All ER 194 at 196 per Vaisey J. See also *Bradman v Trinity Estates plc* [1989] BCLC 757 (notices not timeously served because of postal strike; injunction granted restraining the holding of the meeting until a later date). As to the meaning of 'company having a share capital' see PARA 1231. As to the meaning of 'company limited by guarantee' see PARA 95. As to notices which must be served on members to convene a meeting of the company see PARA 706 et seq.

Model articles have been prescribed under the Companies Act 2006 for use by public companies (see the Companies (Model Articles) Regulations 2008, SI 2008/3229, reg 4, Sch 3) and these make general provision as to notice. Accordingly, if the company sends two consecutive documents to a member over a period of at least 12 months, and if each of those documents is returned undelivered, or the company receives notification that it has not been delivered, that member ceases to be entitled to receive notices from the company: Sch 3 art 80(1). A member who has ceased to be entitled to receive notices from the company becomes entitled to receive such notices again by sending the company either a new address to be recorded in the register of members or (if the member has agreed that the company should use a means of communication other than sending things to such an address) the information that the company needs to use that means of communication effectively: Sch 3 art 80(2). As to the meaning of 'public company' see PARA 95.
3 *Re London and Staffordshire Fire Insurance Co* (1883) 24 ChD 149. See also *Peek v Gurney* (1873) LR 6 HL 377.
4 *Re Studer, ex p Chatteris* (1875) 10 Ch App 227.
5 See the Companies (Tables A to F) Regulations 1985, SI 1985/805, Schedule Table A art 116; andnote 2.

6 *New Zealand Gold Extraction Co (Newbery-Vautin Process) v Peacock* [1894] 1 QB 622, CA (notice of a call).
7 As to directors of a company see PARA 512 et seq.
8 *James v Buena Ventura Nitrate Grounds Syndicate Ltd* [1896] 1 Ch 456 at 465, CA, per Lord Herschell (offer of new shares), followed in *Ward v Dublin North City Milling Co Ltd* [1919] 1 IR 5 (forfeiture of unclaimed dividends).
9 See the Companies (Tables A to F) Regulations 1985, SI 1985/805, Schedule Table A art 116; andnote 2.
10 *Allen v Gold Reefs of West Africa Ltd* [1900] 1 Ch 656, CA (meeting to alter articles to prejudice of deceased).
11 *Re Sussex Brick Co* [1904] 1 Ch 598, CA.

(ii) Agreement to become a Member

327. Requirement for an agreement to become a member of a company. Except in the case of the subscribers to a company's memorandum of association[1], the Companies Act 2006 requires an agreement to become a member[2] and entry in the register of members[3] or, as from a day to be appointed[4], delivery of a person's name to the registrar of companies[5] and registration of the document containing that information by the registrar in order to constitute membership[6]. No particular form of agreement is required[7] and it may be express or implied, written or oral[8].

By agreement it is meant that a person assents to become a member and it does not require that there should be a binding contract between the person and the company[9]. Accordingly, where the name of a person is entered on the register of members with his consent, he is a member of the company, subject to the power vested in the court to rectify the register in cases of error[10].

1 Ie whose membership of a company may be deemed: see PARA 323. As to the meaning of 'memorandum of association' see PARA 97. As to subscribers of the memorandum see PARA 97. As to the meaning of 'company' under the Companies Acts see PARA 21; and as to the meaning of the 'Companies Acts' see PARA 13.
2 As to who qualifies as a member of a company see PARA 323. Any contract, so far as it relates to the constitution of a company or the rights or obligations of its corporators or members, is exempt from the prohibitions on exclusion of liability imposed by the Unfair Contract Terms Act 1977: see s 1(2), Sch 1para1(d); and PARA 244. As to the exemptions from liability referred to see CONTRACT vol 22 (2012) PARA 416.

For cases where it was held that there was no agreement to become a member of a company limited by guarantee see *Re Premier Underwriting Association Ltd (No 2), Cory's Case* [1913] 2 Ch 81; *WR Corfield & Co v Buchanan* (1913) 29 TLR 258, HL. As to the meaning of 'company limited by guarantee' see PARA 95.
3 As to the register of members see PARA 336 et seq. References in any enactment or instrument to a company's register of members, unless the context otherwise requires, is to be construed in relation to a company which is a participating issuer as referring to the company's issuer register of members and operator register of members: see the Uncertificated Securities Regulations 2001, SI 2001/3755, reg 20(4); and PARA 341. As to the meaning of 'participating issuer' see PARA 432 note 9. As to the meaning of 'issuer register of members' and 'operator register of members' see PARA 341.
4 See the Small Business, Enterprise and Employment Act 2015 (Commencement No 4, Transitional and Savings Provisions) Regulations 2016, SI 2016/321, reg 6(c).
5 Ie under the Companies Act 2006 s 128E: see PARA 366. As to the meaning of 'registrar of companies' see PARA 126 note 2; and as to the meaning of 'company' under the Companies Acts see PARA 21.
6 See the Companies Act 2006 s 112; and PARA 323 et seq. As to share warrant bearers being deemed members by provisions in the articles sees 122(3); and PARA 338; but note that no share warrant may be issued by a company on or after 26 May 2015 (see PARA 392).The entry of a person's name and address in a company's issuer register of members must not be treated as showing that person to be a member of the company unless certain conditions are met: see the Uncertificated Securities Regulations 2001, SI 2001/3755, reg 24(3); and PARA 347.
7 *Ritso's Case* (1877) 4 ChD 774, CA.

See, however, the Companies (Tables A to F) Regulations 1985, SI 1985/805, reg 2, Schedule Table C (which applies modified Table A articles of association to companies limited by guarantee and not having a share capital) and the Companies (Model Articles) Regulations 2008, SI 2008/3229, reg 3, Sch 2 (the model articles which have been made for the purposes of the Companies Act 2006 and intended for adoption by private companies limited by guarantee) making membership conditional on the submission of a formal application to the directors who must approve: see PARA 323 note 12. As to the meanings of 'company limited by guarantee' and 'private company' see PARA 95. As to the meanings of 'company having a share capital' and 'share capital' see PARA 1231. As to the meanings of 'Table A' and 'Table C', and as to the treatment of legacy articles under the Companies Act 2006, see PARA 229. As to a company's directors see PARA 512 et seq. As to the meaning of references to a company's 'articles' see PARA 227 note 2. As to a company's articles of association generally see PARA 227 et seq.

8 *Re New Theatre Co Ltd, Bloxam's Case* (1864) 33 LJ Ch 574, which shows that contracts to take shares were not within the Statute of Frauds (1677) s 17 (repealed). As to express contracts see PARA 328; and as to implied contracts see PARA 329.

9 *Re Nuneaton Borough Association Football Club Ltd* [1989] BCLC 454 at 456, 459, CA. See also *Re Railway Time Tables Publishing Co, ex p Sandys* (1889) 42 ChD 98, CA.

10 See the cases cited in note 9. As to the power to rectify the register in cases of error see PARA 357 et seq. See *POW Services Ltd v Clare* [1995] 2 BCLC 435 (entry of individuals with their consent on register of company limited by guarantee did not confer membership when this was in breach of an express provision on membership in the articles).

328. Express contract to take shares. While there is no requirement that there should be a binding contract between a person and the company in order for a person to agree to become a member[1], in most instances there will be a contractual relationship[2] governed by the ordinary law of contract.

To constitute an express agreement to take shares, there must be an absolute and unqualified acceptance of a proposal to take or allot them and a communication of the acceptance to the proposer; but, in the case of a qualified acceptance, there is a contract if the qualification is agreed to, or if the applicant pays for the shares within the specified time[3]. Where an application for shares is subject to a condition precedent, the condition must be performed to create a liability to take them[4]. Where, however, the application is subject to a condition subsequent, the liability arises although the condition is never complied with[5]. An application for shares, being a mere offer, may be withdrawn before it is accepted[6].

1 See PARA 327.

2 It may be a contract between the shareholder and the company or one between the shareholder and the transferor of shares to him. In *Re Nuneaton Borough Association Football Club Ltd* [1989] BCLC 454, CA (cited in PARA 327 note 7), there would have been a contract had there been a properly constituted board of directors of the company.

3 *Re Adelphi Hotel Co Ltd, Best's Case* (1865) 2 De GJ & Sm 650; *Addinell's Case* (1865) LR 1 Eq 225; *Jackson v Turquand* (1869) LR 4 HL 305; *Oriental Steam Navigation Co, ex p Briggs* (1861) 4 De GF & J 191; *Pentelow's Case* (1869) 4 Ch App 178; *Ex p Capper* (1850) 1 Sim NS 178; *Gustard's Case* (1869) LR 8 Eq 438; *Beck's Case* (1874) 9 Ch App 392; *Re Leeds Banking Co, ex p Barrett* (1865) 2 Drew & Sm 415. As to shares, allotments of shares, and payments for shares generally see PARA 1231 et seq.

4 *Roger's Case, Harrison's Case* (1868) 3 Ch App 633. Cf *Wood's Case* (1873) LR 15 Eq 236. See also *Re London and Provincial Provident Association Ltd, Re Mogridge* (1888) 57 LJ Ch 932; *Simpson's Case* (1869) 4 Ch App 184; *Gorrissen's Case* (1873) 8 Ch App 507; *Humphrey and Denman Ltd v Kavanagh* (1925) 41 TLR 378, CA.

5 *Elkington's Case* (1867) 2 Ch App 511; *Re Matlock Old Bath Hydropathic Co Ltd, Wheatcroft's Case* (1873) 42 LJ Ch 853; *Bridger's Case* (1870) 5 Ch App 305; *Black & Co's Case* (1872) 8 Ch App 254; *Gore and Durant's Case* (1866) LR 2 Eq 349; *Re Alexandra Park Co, Sharon's Claim* (1866) 12 Jur NS 482; *Re Life Association of England, Thomson's Case* (1865) 4 De GJ & Sm 749; *Re Southport and West Lancashire Banking Co, Fisher's Case, Sherrington's Case* (1885) 31 ChD 120, CA; *Mare, Holmwood & Co v Anglo-Indian Steamship Co Ltd* (1886) 3 TLR 142, CA.

6 *Ramsgate Victoria Co v Montefiore, Ramsgate Victoria Hotel Co v Goldsmid* (1866) LR 1 Exch 109; *Re Bowron, Baily & Co, ex p Baily* (1868) 3 Ch App 592. As to offer and acceptance in relation to contracts generally see CONTRACT vol 22 (2012) PARA 233 et seq. As to acceptance by allotment see PARA 1277.

329. Implied contract to take shares. An agreement to take shares may be implied from conduct[1]. Although a person's name is entered in the register as the holder of shares allotted to him, no agreement will be implied, by reason only of his receiving notice of the allotment, if he forthwith repudiates them[2], or if he has not acted as the holder of the shares or otherwise accepted them[3]. In such a case, even when a winding up has supervened, he may have his name removed from the register in respect of the shares[4].

Where a company's articles of association[5] require a director to have a share qualification[6], the fact of a person becoming a director does not in itself constitute an agreement to take the required qualification shares from the company[7]. The company's constitution[8] may, however, constitute a contract to take shares, as where they require every original holder of a founders' share to apply for and take a specified number of ordinary shares[9]. A statement in a prospectus that the directors will take all the ordinary shares not taken by the vendors does not constitute a contract which can be enforced against them to take such shares[10].

A person may be estopped by his conduct from denying that he agreed to accept shares, as, for example, where, being the registered holder of shares forming part of an irregular or invalid issue of capital, he deals with them as his own, by paying calls or receiving dividends, or by attempting to transfer them[11], or where he has held himself out as having in fact subscribed[12].

1 See PARA 1277 et seq. As to shares, allotments of shares, and payments for shares generally see PARA 1231 et seq.
2 *Austin's Case* (1866) LR 2 Eq 435; *Re Imperial Land Credit Corpn Ltd, ex p Eve* (1868) 37 LJ Ch 844. As to the necessity of assent on the part of the member see *Re Nuneaton Borough Association Football Club Ltd* [1989] BCLC 454 at 456, CA, per Fox LJ, and at 459 per Nicholls LJ; and see PARA 327.
3 *Re Imperial Mercantile Credit Association, Chapman and Barker's Case* (1867) LR 3 Eq 361 at 365 per Page Wood V-C; *Oakes v Turquand and Harding* (1867) LR 2 HL 325 at 350–351 per Lord Chelmsford LC; *Re Empire Assurance Corpn, Challis's Case, Somerville's Case* (1871) 6 Ch App 266; *Wynne's Case* (1873) 8 Ch App 1002; *Baillie's Case* [1898] 1 Ch 110.
4 *Arnot's Case* (1887) 36 ChD 702, CA.
5 As to a company's articles of association generally see PARA 227 et seq.
6 See PARA 531.
7 *Brown's Case* (1873) 9 Ch App 102. See also PARA 532.
8 As to the meaning of references to a company's constitution see PARA 226.
9 *General Phosphate Corpn v Horrocks* (1892) 8 TLR 350.
10 *Re Moore Bros & Co Ltd* [1899] 1 Ch 627, CA; *Todd v Millen* 1910 SC 868, Ct of Sess. As to potential liability with respect to misstatements in offer documents see PARA 298.
11 *Re Bank of Hindustan, China and Japan, Campbell's Case, Hippisley's Case* (1873) 9 Ch App 1 at 15 per Lord Selborne LC.
12 *New Brunswick and Canada Railway and Land Co Ltd v Boore* (1858) 3 H & N 249; *Re Oola Lead and Copper Mining Co, Palmer's Case* (1868) 2 IR Eq 573. See also *Re Llanharry Hematite Iron Ore Co Ltd, Roney's Case* (1864) 33 LJ Ch 731; *Tothill's Case* (1865) 1 Ch App 85; *Re Patent File Co Ltd, ex p White* (1867) 16 LT 276.

330. Agent's contract to take shares. A person who agrees, on behalf of another, to take shares, without disclosing the agency, is personally liable to take them[1]. Where he purports to agree to take shares on behalf of another, but is without authority[2], he is liable, unless the other person ratifies the act[3], to pay damages for breach of warranty of authority, the measure of damages being the amount which the company has lost by losing the contract to take shares[4].

A person purporting to contract to take shares on behalf of a fictitious or non-existent person is himself bound to take them[5].

If an application is made for shares on behalf of a person who is ignorant of the matter, and he is registered as the holder, and the directors know that the person applying does not intend to take the shares himself, neither the person registered nor the applicant is liable as a shareholder; but the applicant is liable to those who are deceived for breach of an implied warranty of authority[6].

1 *Re Southampton, Isle of Wight and Portsmouth Improved Steam Boat Co Ltd, Bird's Case* (1864) 4 De GJ & Sm 200.
2 A person applying for shares in the name of a minor is himself liable: *Richardson's Case* (1875) LR 19 Eq 588; *Re North of England Joint Stock Banking Co, ex p Reavely* (1849) 1 H & Tw 118; *Re Electric Telegraph Co of Ireland, Maxwell's Case* (1857) 24 Beav 321.
3 *Levita's Case* (1870) 5 Ch App 489.
4 *Re National Coffee Palace Co, ex p Panmure* (1883) 24 ChD 367, CA (where, the alleged applicant being solvent, and the shares having become unsaleable, the loss was equivalent to the nominal value of the shares). As to the liabilities of agents on breach of warranty of authority see generally AGENCY vol 1 (2008) PARA 160.
5 *Re Wheal Emily Mining Co, Cox's Case* (1863) 4 De GJ & Sm 53; *Pugh and Sharman's Case* (1872) LR 13 Eq 566; *Savigny's Case* (1898) 5 Mans 336.
6 *Re Britannia Fire Association, Coventry's Case* [1891] 1 Ch 202 at 210, CA, per Lindley LJ, and at 211 per Bowen LJ; *Collen v Wright* (1857) 8 E & B 647. Cf *Re London, Bombay, and Mediterranean Bank* (1881) 18 ChD 581.

331. Contract by company to take shares. A contract by a company to take shares in another company is binding[1] even if the former company lacks the capacity to purchase such shares[2].

1 Ie provided that it is not a subsidiary of the latter, unless one of the statutory exceptions applies: see the Companies Act 2006 s 136; and PARA 335. As to the meaning of 'subsidiary' see PARA 22.
2 This is the effect of the Companies Act 2006 s 39: see PARA 264. As to a company's capacity and the effect of s 39 generally see PARA 264 et seq.

332. Effect of minor's agreement to take or transfer shares. A minor[1] may repudiate his membership and his holding in the company, either during his minority or upon attaining full age, because his agreement to take shares is voidable[2]; but he cannot recover money paid by him for shares unless there has been a total failure of consideration[3]. If, however, he does not repudiate[4] within a reasonable time after attaining full age, he will thenceforth be subject to all the liabilities of membership[5].

Where shares are transferred into the name of a minor, the transferor remains liable for calls in respect of the shares[6], whether at the time of the transfer he was aware that the transferee was a minor or not[7]; but, if he was ignorant of that fact, he may claim to have his liability transferred to the person who effected the transaction[8]. If, however, a company or the liquidator of a company, knowing the transferee to be a minor, is guilty of laches in making a claim against the transferor, the transferor is relieved from his liability[9]. He is also relieved by a subsequent transfer by the minor to an adult[10].

1 As to the attainment of majority at the age of 18 see the Family Law Reform Act 1969 s 1; and CHILDREN AND YOUNG PERSONS vol 9 (2012) PARA 1.
2 *Newry and Enniskillen Rly Co v Coombe* (1849) 3 Exch 565; *North Western Rly Co v M'Michael, Birkenhead, Lancashire and Cheshire Junction Rly Co v Pilcher* (1850) 5 Exch 114; *Re Alexandra Park Co, Hart's Case* (1868) LR 6 Eq 512; *Re Financial Corpn, Sassoon's Case* (1869) 20 LT 161 (affd 20 LT 424); *Hamilton v Vaughan-Sherrin Electrical Engineering Co* [1894] 3 Ch 589. See also the Minors' Contracts Act 1987 s 1 (with regard to contracts made by a minor after 9 June 1987); and CHILDREN AND YOUNG PERSONS vol 9 (2012) PARA 14; CONTRACT vol 22 (2012) PARA 613. As to subscription of the memorandum of association by a minor see PARA 96.

3 *Steinberg v Scala (Leeds) Ltd* [1923] 2 Ch 452, CA. If and in so far as *Hamilton v Vaughan-Sherrin Electrical Engineering Co* [1894] 3 Ch 589 decides the contrary, it must be treated as having been overruled: *Steinberg v Scala (Leeds) Ltd* [1923] 2 Ch 452 at 457, 461, CA, per Lord Sterndale MR, at 462 per Warrington LJ, and at 465 per Younger LJ.

4 As to confirmation see *Baker's Case* (1871) 7 Ch App 115; *Wilson's Case* (1869) LR 8 Eq 240; *Castello's Case* (1869) LR 8 Eq 504; *Mitchell's Case* (1870) LR 9 Eq 363; *Symons' Case* (1870) 5 Ch App 298; *Re Ottoman Financial Association, Cheetham's Case* [1869] WN 201. See also the Minors' Contracts Act 1987; and CHILDREN AND YOUNG PERSONS vol 9 (2012) PARA 14.

5 *Cork and Bandon Rly Co v Cazenove* (1847) 10 QB 935; *Leeds and Thirsk Rly Co v Fearnley* (1849) 4 Exch 26; *North Western Rly Co v M'Michael, Birkenhead, Lancashire and Cheshire Junction Rly Co v Pilcher* (1850) 5 Exch 114; *Dublin and Wicklow Rly Co v Black* (1852) 8 Exch 181; *Lumsden's Case* (1868) 4 Ch App 31; *Mitchell's Case* (1870) LR 9 Eq 363; *Ebbetts' Case* (1870) 5 Ch App 302; *Re Yeoland Consols Ltd (No 2)* (1888) 58 LT 922. A director knowingly allotting shares to a minor is liable to the company for any loss thereby occasioned: *Re Crenver and Wheal Abraham United Mining Co, ex p Wilson* (1872) 8 Ch App 45.

6 *Re St George's Steam Packet Co, Litchfield's Case* (1850) 3 De G & Sm 141; *Re Electric Telegraph Co of Ireland, Reid's Case* (1857) 24 Beav 318; *Curtis's Case* (1868) LR 6 Eq 455; *Castello's Case* (1869) LR 8 Eq 504; *Re Imperial Mercantile Credit Association, Edwards' Case* [1869] WN 211; *Weston's Case* (1870) 5 Ch App 614; *Re Crenver and Wheal Abraham United Mining Co, ex p Wilson* (1872) 8 Ch App 45. As to transfer of shares by a minor see PARA 409. As to a shareholder's liability for calls or capital not paid up generally see PARA 1895 et seq.

7 *Re Joint Stock Discount Co, Mann's Case* (1867) 3 Ch App 459n; *Capper's Case* (1868) 3 Ch App 458.

8 *Nickalls v Furneaux* [1869] WN 118; *Re National Provincial Marine Insurance Co, Maitland's Case* (1869) 38 LJ Ch 554; *Brown v Black* (1873) 8 Ch App 939; *Richardson's Case* (1875) LR 19 Eq 588; *Watson v Miller* [1876] WN 18.

9 *Capper's Case* (1868) 3 Ch App 458 at 461 per Page Wood LJ; *Parson's Case* (1869) LR 8 Eq 656; *Re National Bank of Wales Ltd, Massey and Giffin's Case* [1907] 1 Ch 582.

10 *Gooch's Case* (1872) 8 Ch App 266.

333. Enforcement of contract for shares. Specific performance of an agreement to take and pay for shares[1] or to allot shares[2] may be obtained[3].

In addition to obtaining a decree for the specific performance of a contract to allot shares, the disappointed allottee may obtain damages equal to the dividends at the rates declared by the company between the date when the shares should have been allotted and the date of actual allotment, together with interest on the dividends until payment[4].

When a contract to take shares is disclaimed by a trustee in bankruptcy, the contract is at an end and the company's remedy is a claim for damages against the bankrupt's estate[5].

An agreement with a company to take shares proposed to be issued at a discount cannot be enforced and an allottee of shares pursuant to such an agreement may have the register rectified in order to remove his name. He may, however, lose his remedy if he has assented to the registration or has not sought the remedy promptly[6].

1 *Odessa Tramways Co v Mendel* (1878) 8 ChD 235, CA. See also *New Brunswick and Canada Rly and Land Co v Muggeridge* (1859) 4 Drew 686; *Oriental Inland Steam Co v Briggs* (1861) 2 John & H 625 (on appeal sub nom *Oriental Steam Navigation Co, ex p Briggs* (1861) 4 De GF & J 191); and SPECIFIC PERFORMANCE vol 95 (2013) PARA 325 et seq. As to shares, allotments of shares, and payments for shares generally see PARA 1231 et seq.

2 *Sri Lanka Omnibus Co Ltd v Perera* [1952] AC 76, PC.

3 A distinction must, however, be drawn between cases where shares are readily available in the market (*Re Schwabacher* (1907) 98 LT 127) and where they are not (*Jobson v Johnson* [1989] 1 All ER 621, [1989] 1 WLR 1026, CA; *Harvela Investments Ltd v Royal Trust Co of Canada (CI) Ltd* [1986] AC 207, [1985] 2 All ER 966, HL). See also SPECIFIC PERFORMANCE vol 95 (2013) PARA 325 et seq.

4 *Sri Lanka Omnibus Co Ltd v Perera* [1952] AC 76, PC.

5 *Re Hooley, ex p United Ordnance and Engineering Co Ltd* [1899] 2 QB 579. See also BANKRUPTCY AND INDIVIDUAL INSOLVENCY vol 5 (2013) PARA 534.

6 See *Re Railway Time Tables Publishing Co, ex p Sandys* (1889) 42 ChD 98, CA; *Re Nuneaton Borough Association Football Club Ltd* [1989] BCLC 454, CA.

(iii) Prohibition on Subsidiary being Member of its Holding Company

334. General rule against company acquiring own shares. The general rule is that a limited company[1] must not acquire its own shares[2], whether by purchase, subscription, or otherwise[3]. If a company purports to act in contravention of this prohibition, an offence is committed by the company, and by every officer of the company who is in default[4]; and a person guilty of such an offence is liable on conviction on indictment to imprisonment for a term not exceeding two years or a fine, or to both[5] and on summary conviction to imprisonment for a term not exceeding 12 months[6] or a fine[7], or to both[8]. Also in the event of such a contravention, the purported acquisition is void[9].

The general prohibition on a limited company acquiring its own shares[10] does not prohibit[11]:

(1) acquisition in accordance with the statutory scheme[12] for the purchase by a company of its own shares[13];
(2) the acquisition of shares in a reduction of share capital duly made[14];
(3) the purchase of shares in pursuance of an order of the court[15] under the powers conferred in relation to:
    (a) proceedings objecting to a resolution proposing that the company be re-registered as a private company[16];
    (b) an objection to the redemption or purchase of shares out of capital[17];
    (c) a breach of the prohibition on public offers being made by a private company[18]; or
    (d) the protection of company members against unfair prejudice[19]; or
(4) the forfeiture of shares, or the acceptance of shares surrendered in lieu, in pursuance of the company's articles[20], for failure to pay any sum payable in respect of the shares[21].

As a general rule, shares so acquired are cancelled, save with respect to treasury shares, which may be held by a company[22]; and, where shares are held by the company in this way, the company must be entered in its register of members or, as from 30 June 2016[23] and where an election to keep membership information on the central register is in force in relation to the company, the company's name must be delivered to the registrar of companies[24] as the member holding the shares[25].

A limited company may acquire any of its own fully paid[26] shares otherwise than for valuable consideration[27].

1 As to the meaning of 'limited company' see PARA 95. As to the meaning of 'company' under the Companies Acts see PARA 21; and as to the meaning of the 'Companies Acts' see PARA 13.

2 Ie except in accordance with the Companies Act 2006 Pt 18 (ss 658–737) (see PARA 1384 et seq): see s 658(1); and PARA 1384. As to the meaning of 'share' see PARA 1231.

3 See the Companies Act 2006 s 658(1); and PARA 1384. This gives statutory force to *Trevor v Whitworth* (1887) 12 App Cas 409, HL; *Kirby v Wilkins* [1929] 2 Ch 444; *Vision Express (UK) Ltd v Wilson* [1995] 2 BCLC 419. This does not prohibit a company from acquiring the shares of another company (the 'acquired company') in circumstances where the sole asset of the acquired company is shares in the acquiring company: *Acatos & Hutcheson plc v Watson* [1995] 1 BCLC 218 (in view of the potential for abuse, the court will, however, look carefully at the transaction to ensure that the directors have fulfilled their fiduciary duties to safeguard the interests of shareholders and creditors alike). See also *British and Commonwealth Holdings plc v Barclays Bank plc* [1996] 1 All ER 381, [1996] 1 WLR 1, CA.

As to the prohibition on a body corporate being a member of a company which is its holding company see PARA 335.

4 See the Companies Act 2006 s 658(2)(a); and PARA 1384. As to the meaning of 'officer who is in default' see PARA 316. As to the meaning of 'officer' generally see PARA 679.

5 See the Companies Act 2006 s 658(3)(a); and PARA 1384.

6 In relation to an offence committed after the commencement of the Companies Act 2006 s 1131 (summary proceedings) (see PARA 1818), but before a day is appointed in relation to the commencement of the Criminal Justice Act 2003 s 154(1) (general limit on magistrates' courts' power to impose imprisonment), the reference in the Companies Act 2006 s 658(3)(b) to '12 months' must be read as a reference to 'six months': see ss 658(3)(b), 1131, 1133; and see PARA 1818.

7 In the case of liability on summary conviction the fine is one not exceeding the statutory maximum. By virtue of the Legal Aid, Sentencing and Punishment of Offenders Act 2012 s 85, however, where the offence is committed on or after 12 March 2015, it is punishable by a fine of an unlimited amount. As to the statutory maximum and the powers of magistrates' courts to issue fines on summary conviction see SENTENCING vol 92 (2015) PARA 176.

8 See the Companies Act 2006 s 658(3)(b); and PARA 1384.

9 See the Companies Act 2006 s 658(2)(b); and PARA 1384.

10 Ie the Companies Act 2006 s 658 (see PARA 1384): see s 659(2); and PARA 1385.

11 See the Companies Act 2006 ss 658(1), 659(2); and PARAS 1384, 1385.

12 Ie in accordance with the Companies Act 2006 Pt 18 (see PARA 1384 et seq): see s 658(1); and PARA 1384.

13 See the Companies Act 2006 s 658(1); and PARA 1384.

14 See the Companies Act 2006 s 659(2)(a); and PARA 1385. As to the meaning of 'share capital' see PARA 1231. As to a reduction of capital see PARA 1360 et seq.

15 As to the meaning of 'the court' see PARA 160 note 12.

16 See the Companies Act 2006 s 659(2)(b)(i); and PARA 1385. Head (3)(a) in the text refers to an order of the court under s 98 (see PARA 174): see s 659(2)(b)(i). As to the meaning of 'private company' see PARA 95.

17 See the Companies Act 2006 s 659(2)(b)(ii); and PARA 1385. Head (3)(b) in the text refers to an order of the court under s 721(6) (see PARA 1436): see s 659(2)(b)(ii).

18 See the Companies Act 2006 s 659(2)(b)(iii); and PARA 1385. Head (3)(c) in the text refers to an order of the court under s 759 (see PARA 1255): see s 659(2)(b)(iii).

19 See the Companies Act 2006 s 659(2)(b)(iv); and PARA 1385. Head (3)(d) in the text refers to an order of the court under Pt 30 (ss 994–999) (see PARA 657 et seq): see s 659(2)(b)(iv).

20 As to the meaning of references to a company's 'articles' see PARA 227 note 2. As to a company's articles of association generally see PARA 227 et seq. As to the power given by articles in relation to the forfeiture and surrender of shares see PARA 1400.

21 See the Companies Act 2006 s 659(2)(c); and PARA 1385. As to payment for shares comprised in a company's share capital see PARA 1302 et seq.

22 See the Companies Act 2006 s 724(5); and PARA 1437.

23 See the Small Business, Enterprise and Employment Act 2015 (Commencement No 4, Transitional and Savings Provisions) Regulations 2016, SI 2016/321, reg 6(c).

24 Ie under the Companies Act 2006 Pt 8 Ch 2A (ss 128A–128K): see PARA 363 et seq. As to the meaning of 'registrar of companies' see PARA 126 note 2; and as to the meaning of 'company' under the Companies Acts see PARA 21.

25 See the Companies Act 2006 s 724(4); and PARA 1437.

26 As to the meaning of 'fully paid' see PARA 1237.

27 See the Companies Act 2006 s 659(1); and PARA 1385. See eg *Re Castiglione's Will Trusts, Hunter v Mackenzie* [1958] Ch 549, [1958] 1 All ER 480.

335. Membership of holding company. A body corporate[1] cannot, except as provided by statute[2], be a member of a company[3] that is its holding company[4]; and any allotment[5] or transfer of shares[6] in a company to its subsidiary is[7] void[8]. The prohibition does not, however, apply:

(1) where the subsidiary is concerned only as personal representative[9] or as trustee unless, in the latter case, the holding company or a subsidiary of it is beneficially interested under the trust[10];

(2) where the shares in the holding company are held by the subsidiary in the ordinary course of its business as an intermediary[11].

Where a body corporate became a holder of shares in a company before 1 July 1948[12] or on or after that date and before 1 October 2009[13] in circumstances in which the prohibition on membership as it then had effect[14] did not apply, or at any time on or after 1 October 2009[15] in circumstances in which the prohibition on membership did not apply, it may continue to be a member of that company[16]. So long as a body corporate is permitted in this way[17] to continue as a member of a company, an allotment to it of fully paid[18] shares in the company may be validly made by way of capitalisation of reserves of the company[19]; but, for so long as the prohibition on membership would otherwise apply[20], it has no right to vote in respect of any shares so allotted[21], or in respect of any shares it acquired before the prohibition came to apply[22], either on a written resolution[23] or at meetings of the company[24] or of any class of its members[25].

1 As to the meaning of 'body corporate' see PARA 1 note 5.

2 Ie except as provided by the Companies Act 2006 Pt 8 Ch 4 (ss 136–144): see s 136(1). The exceptions are provided for in s 138 (subsidiary acting as personal representative or trustee) (see head (1) in the text), and in s 141 (subsidiary acting as authorised dealer in securities) (see head (2) in the text): s 136(2). The provisions of Pt 8 Ch 4 apply to a nominee acting on behalf of a subsidiary as to the subsidiary itself: s 144. As to the meaning of 'subsidiary' see PARA 22. As to shares held by a company's nominee generally see PARA 1386.

3 As to the meaning of 'member of a company' see PARA 323. As to the meaning of 'company' under the Companies Acts see PARA 21; and as to the meaning of the 'Companies Acts' see PARA 13.

4 Companies Act 2006 s 136(1)(a). As to the meaning of 'holding company' see PARA 22. See also note 10.

5 As to the meaning of 'allotted' see PARA 1280.

6 For these purposes, in relation to a company other than a company limited by shares, the references to shares in the Companies Act 2006 Pt 8 Ch 4 are to be read as references to the interest of its members as such, whatever the form of that interest: s 143. As to the meaning of 'company limited by shares' see PARA 95. As to the meaning of 'share' see PARA 1231.

7 See note 2.

8 Companies Act 2006 s 136(1)(b).

9 As to the meaning of 'personal representative' see WILLS AND INTESTACY vol 103 (2010) PARA 608.

10 Companies Act 2006 s 138(1). For the purpose of ascertaining whether the holding company or a subsidiary is so interested, the following must be disregarded:

(1) any interest held only by way of security for the purposes of a transaction entered into by the holding company or subsidiary in the ordinary course of a business that includes the lending of money (s 138(2)(a));

(2) any interest within s 139 (residual interest under pension scheme or employees' share scheme to be disregarded), or within s 140 (employer's rights of recovery under pension scheme or employees' share scheme to be disregarded) (s 138(2)(b));

(3) any rights that the company or subsidiary has in its capacity as trustee, including in particular, any right to recover its expenses or be remunerated out of the trust property, and any right to be indemnified out of the trust property for any liability incurred by reason of any act or omission in the performance of its duties as trustee (s 138(2)(c)).

Further to head (2) above, where shares in a company are held on trust for the purposes of a pension scheme or employees' share scheme, there must be disregarded for the purposes of s 138 any residual interest that has not vested in possession: s 139(1). For these purposes, a 'residual interest' means a right of the company or subsidiary (the 'residual beneficiary') to receive any of the trust property in the event of:

(a) all the liabilities arising under the scheme having been satisfied or provided for (s 139(2)(a)); or

(b) the residual beneficiary ceasing to participate in the scheme (s 139(2)(b)); or

(c) the trust property at any time exceeding what is necessary for satisfying the liabilities arising or expected to arise under the scheme (s 139(2)(c)).

For the purposes of s 139(2), the reference to a right includes a right dependent on the exercise of a discretion vested by the scheme in the trustee or another person, and the reference to liabilities arising under a scheme includes liabilities that have resulted, or may result, from the exercise of any such discretion: s 139(3). A residual interest vests in possession, in a case within head (a) above, on the occurrence of the event mentioned there (whether or not the amount of the property receivable pursuant to the right is ascertained) or, in a case within head (b) or head (c) above, when the residual beneficiary becomes entitled to require the trustee to transfer to him any of the property receivable pursuant to the right: s 139(4). 'Pension scheme' means a scheme for the provision of benefits consisting of or including relevant benefits for or in respect of employees or former employees (s 139(5)), where 'relevant benefits' means any pension, lump sum, gratuity or other like benefit given or to be given on retirement or on death or in anticipation of retirement or, in connection with past service, after retirement or death, and 'employee' must be read as if a director of a company were employed by it (s 139(6)). Where shares in a company are held on trust for the purposes of a pension scheme or employees' share scheme, there must be disregarded for the purposes of s 138 any charge or lien on, or set-off against, any benefit or other right or interest under the scheme for the purpose of enabling the employer or former employer of a member of the scheme to obtain the discharge of a monetary obligation due to him from the member: s 140(1). Until 6 April 2016, in the case of a trust for the purposes of a pension scheme, there was also to be disregarded any right to receive from the trustee of the scheme, or as trustee of the scheme to retain, an amount that could be recovered or retained, under the Pension Schemes Act 1993 s 61 (repealed as from that date) (deduction of contributions equivalent premium from refund of scheme contributions) (see PERSONAL AND OCCUPATIONAL PENSIONS vol 80 (2013) PARA 434) or otherwise, as reimbursement or partial reimbursement for any contributions equivalent premium paid in connection with the scheme under Pt 3 (ss 7–68) (see PERSONAL AND OCCUPATIONAL PENSIONS vol 80 (2013) PARA 393 et seq): Companies Act 2006 s 140(2) (amended as from that date, so as to remove the reference to the Pension Schemes Act 1993 s 61 and leave only a reference to corresponding Northern Ireland legislation, by the Pensions Act 2014 Sch 13 Pt 2 paras 74, 75). For these purposes, 'pension scheme' means a scheme for the provision of benefits consisting of or including relevant benefits for or in respect of employees or former employees, where 'relevant benefits' means any pension, lump sum, gratuity or other like benefit given or to be given on retirement or on death or in anticipation of retirement or, in connection with past service, after retirement or death (Companies Act 2006 s 140(3)); and 'employer' and 'employee' must be read as if a director of a company were employed by it (s 140(4)). As to the meaning of 'director' see PARA 512. As to the meaning of 'employees' share scheme' see PARA 169 note 20.

11 Companies Act 2006 s 141(1). For this purpose, a person is an intermediary if he:

(1) carries on a bona fide business of dealing in securities (s 141(2)(a));
(2) is a member of or has access to a regulated market (s 141(2)(b)); and
(3) does not carry on an excluded business (s 141(2)(c)).

For these purposes, 'securities' includes options, futures and contracts for differences; and rights or interests in those investments: s 141(4)(d). As to the meanings of 'business' and 'carry on business' generally see PARA 1 note 1. In the Companies Acts, 'regulated market' means a multilateral system operated and/or managed by a market operator, which brings together or facilitates the bringing together of multiple third-party buying and selling interests in financial instruments, in the system and in accordance with its non-discretionary rules, in a way that results in a contract, in respect of the financial instruments admitted to trading under its rules and/or systems, and which is authorised and functions regularly and in accordance with the provisions of European Parliament and Council Directive (EC) 2004/39 (OJ L145, 30.4.2004, p 1) Title III (arts 36–47) (see further FINANCIAL SERVICES REGULATION vol 50 (2016) PARA 113 et seq): art 4.1(14) (definition applied by the Companies Act 2006 s 1173(1)). Further to head (3) above, the excluded businesses are:

(a) any business that consists wholly or mainly in the making or managing of investments (s 141(3)(a));
(b) any business that consists wholly or mainly in, or is carried on wholly or mainly for the purpose of, providing services to persons who are connected with the person carrying on the business (s 141(3)(b));
(c) any business that consists in insurance business (s 141(3)(c));
(d) a business that consists in managing or acting as trustee in relation to a pension scheme or which is carried on by the manager or trustee of such a scheme in connection with or for the purposes of the scheme (s 141(3)(d));
(e) a business that consists in operating or acting as trustee in relation to a collective investment scheme or is carried on by the operator or trustee of such a scheme in connection with or for the purposes of the scheme (s 141(3)(e)).

For these purposes, the question whether a person is connected with another is to be determined in accordance with the Corporation Tax Act 2010 s 1122 (see INCOME TAXATION vol 59 (2014) PARA 1825): Companies Act 2006 s 141(4)(a) (amended by the Corporation Tax Act 2010 Sch 1 Pt 2 paras 487, 488). 'Collective investment scheme' has the meaning given in the Financial Services and Markets Act 2000 s 236 (ie an open-ended investment company) (see FINANCIAL SERVICES REGULATION vol 50A (2016) PARA 841): Companies Act 2006 s 141(4)(b). 'Insurance business' means business which consists of the effecting or carrying out of contracts of insurance: s 141(4)(c). 'Trustee' and 'operator', in relation to a collective investment scheme, must be construed in accordance with the Financial Services and Markets Act 2000 s 237(2) (see FINANCIAL SERVICES REGULATION vol 50A (2016) PARA 844): Companies Act 2006 s 141(4)(e). Expressions used in s 141 that are also used in the provisions regulating activities under the Financial Services and Markets Act 2000 have the same meaning here as they do in those provisions (see s 22, orders made under s 22, Sch 2; and FINANCIAL SERVICES REGULATION vol 50 (2016) PARA 101 et seq): Companies Act 2006 s 141(5). Where:

(i) a subsidiary that is a dealer in securities has purportedly acquired shares in its holding company in contravention of the prohibition in s 136 (see the text and notes 1–8) (s 142(1)(a)); and

(ii) a person acting in good faith has agreed, for value and without notice of that contravention, to acquire shares in the holding company, either from the subsidiary or from someone who has purportedly acquired the shares after their disposal by the subsidiary (s 142(1)(b)),

any transfer to that person of the shares mentioned in head (i) above has the same effect as it would have had if their original acquisition by the subsidiary had not been in contravention of the prohibition (s 142(2)).

12 Ie the date on which the Companies Act 1948 (repealed) came into force. As to the Companies Act 1948 generally see PARA 10.

13 Ie before the commencement of the Companies Act 2006 Pt 8 Ch 4 (see the Companies Act 2006 (Commencement No 8, Transitional Provisions and Savings) Order 2008, SI 2008/2860, art 3(h)): see the Companies Act 2006 s 137(1).

14 Ie the prohibition in the Companies Act 1985 s 23(1) (repealed) (or any corresponding earlier enactment): see the Companies Act 2006 s 137(1). As to the meaning of 'enactment' see PARA 13 note 16. As to predecessor legislation from which the Companies Act 2006 is derived see PARA 10 et seq.

15 Ie on or after the commencement of the Companies Act 2006 Pt 8 Ch 4 (see the Companies Act 2006 (Commencement No 8, Transitional Provisions and Savings) Order 2008, SI 2008/2860, art 3(h)): see the Companies Act 2006 s 137(1).

16 Companies Act 2006 s 137(1), (2).

17 Ie by virtue of the Companies Act 2006 s 137 (see the text and notes 12–16): see s 137(3).

18 As to the meaning of 'fully paid' see PARA 1237.

19 Companies Act 2006 s 137(3).

20 Ie so long as the prohibition in the Companies Act 2006 s 136 (see the text and notes 1–8) would, apart from s 137, apply: see s 137(4).

21 Ie it has no right to vote in respect of any shares allotted as mentioned in the Companies Act 2006 s 137(3) (see the text and notes 17–19): see s 137(4).

22 Ie it has no right to vote in respect of the shares mentioned in the Companies Act 2006 s 137(1) (see the text and notes 12–16): see s 137(4).

23 As to the meaning of 'written resolution' see PARA 695.

24 As to resolutions and meetings of members see PARA 684 et seq. As to voting at meetings see PARA 725 et seq.

25 Companies Act 2006 s 137(4). As to classes of shares and class rights see PARA 1246 et seq.

(iv) Register of Members

A. CONTENTS OF REGISTER OF MEMBERS

336. Requirement for register of members. Every company[1] must keep a register of its members[2]; and there must be entered in the register the following particulars[3]:

(1) the names and addresses of members[4];

(2) the date on which each person was registered as a member[5]; and

(3) the date at which any person ceased to be a member[6].

In the case of a company having a share capital[7]:

(a) there must be entered in the register, with the names and addresses of the members, a statement of the shares held by each member, distinguishing each share by its number (so long as the share has a number)[8], and, where the company has more than one class of issued shares[9], by its class[10], and a statement of the amount paid or agreed to be considered as paid on the shares of each member[11];

(b) where the company has converted any of its shares into stock[12] and given notice of the conversion to the registrar of companies[13], the register must show the amount and class of stock held by each member, instead of the amount of shares and the particulars relating to shares specified in head (a) above[14].

The subscribers of the company's memorandum of association[15], as well as other persons agreeing to become members[16], must be entered in the register[17].

In the case of a company which does not have a share capital, but has more than one class of members, there must be entered in the register, with the names and addresses of the members, a statement of the class to which each member belongs[18].

If a company makes default in complying with these requirements[19], an offence is committed by the company, and by every officer of the company who is in default[20]; and a person guilty of such an offence is liable on summary conviction to a fine not exceeding level 3 on the standard scale[21] and for continued contravention to a daily default fine[22] not exceeding one-tenth of level 3 on the standard scale[23].

An entry relating to a former member of the company may be removed from the register after the expiration of ten years from the date on which he ceased to be a member[24].

Liability incurred by a company from the making or deletion of an entry in its register of members[25], or from a failure to make or delete any such entry[26], is not enforceable more than ten years after the date on which the entry was made or deleted or, as the case may be, the failure first occurred[27].

The company must not enter in the register a statement that it has a lien on the shares of a member[28], and cannot insist on putting on the register anything except what is required by statute to be inserted in it[29].

Where the name of a firm is entered in the register as the holder of shares, the members of the firm are jointly liable for the shares[30]. A firm which has no separate legal persona is not entitled to be registered in the name of the firm, but only in the names of its partners[31].

1 As to the meaning of 'company' under the Companies Acts see PARA 21; and as to the meaning of the 'Companies Acts' see PARA 13.

2 Companies Act 2006 s 113(1). As to the option for a private company to keep membership information on the central register see PARA 363 et seq. As to the meaning of 'member' see PARA 323. An overseas branch register is regarded as part of the company's register of members: see s 131; and PARA 360. As to the meaning of 'overseas company' see PARA 2013. The register of members falls within the definition of 'company records' that is used for the purposes of the Companies Act 2006: see PARA 746. As to the form of company records, their inspection and the duty to take precautions against their falsification see PARAS 746–748. Prior to the Companies Act 1948, it had been held that rough memoranda on sheets of paper intended as materials from which a register might be prepared are not a register (*Re Printing, Telegraph and Construction Co of Agence Havas, ex p Cammell* [1894] 2 Ch 392, CA), and this is presumably still good law in spite of the relaxations as to the form of company records now provided for under the Companies Act 2006.

References in any enactment or instrument to a company's register of members, unless the context otherwise requires, are to be construed in relation to a company which is a participating issuer as referring to the company's issuer register of members and operator register of members: see the Uncertificated Securities Regulations 2001, SI 2001/3755, reg 20(4); and PARA 341. As to the meaning of 'participating issuer' see PARA 432 note 9. As to the meanings of 'issuer register of members' and 'operator register of members' see PARA 341; and as to the meaning of 'operator' see PARA 432 note 1. As to the entries to be made generally in registers regarding uncertificated securities see PARA 341.

3 Companies Act 2006 s 113(2). As to the entries to be made in the registers regarding uncertificated securities see PARA 341; as to the entries and amendments to be made where there are share warrants see PARA 338; as to the statements required to be made in the register where a private

company has only one member see PARA 337; and as to the registration requirements where a company holds its own shares as treasury shares see PARA 339.

4 Companies Act 2006 s 113(2)(a). Any obligation under the Companies Acts to give a person's address is, unless otherwise expressly provided, to give a service address for that person: Companies Act 2006 s 1142. As to service of documents on a company generally see PARA 743.

In the case of joint holders of shares or stock in a company, the company's register of members must state the names of each joint holder: s 113(5). Where two or more persons hold a share or shares jointly, they may insist on having their names registered in such order as they choose, or to have their holding split into several joint holdings with their names in different orders: *Re TH Saunders & Co Ltd* [1908] 1 Ch 415; *Burns v Siemens Bros Dynamo Works Ltd* [1919] 1 Ch 225. In other respects, joint holders are regarded for the purposes of the Companies Act 2006 Pt 8 Ch 2 (ss 113–128) (see also PARA 337 et seq) as a single member (so that the register must show a single address): s 113(5). As to the meaning of 'share' see PARA 1231. As to the meaning of 'stock' see PARA 1351.

5 Companies Act 2006 s 113(2)(b).

6 Companies Act 2006 s 113(2)(c). As to cessation of company membership see PARAS 389, 390.

7 Companies Act 2006 s 113(3). As to the meanings of 'share capital' and 'company having a share capital' see PARA 1231.

8 Companies Act 2006 s 113(3)(a)(i). As to the numbering of shares see PARA 1239.

9 As to classes of shares generally see PARA 1246 et seq; and as to the meaning of 'issued shares' see PARA 1234.

10 Companies Act 2006 s 113(3)(a)(ii).

11 Companies Act 2006 s 113(3)(b). As to payments for shares and paid up shares see PARA 1231 et seq.

12 As to the conversion of shares into stock see PARA 1351 et seq. A company's shares may no longer be converted into stock: see the Companies Act 2006 s 540(2); and PARA 1231.

13 As to the meaning of 'registrar of companies' see PARA 126 note 2. As to the notice required to be given to the registrar of the reconversion of stock into shares see PARA 1353.

14 Companies Act 2006 s 113(4).

15 As to the meaning of 'memorandum of association' see PARA 97. As to subscribers of the memorandum see PARA 97.

16 As to the requirement for persons other than subscribers of the memorandum to agree to become members before their membership is duly constituted see PARA 327.

17 Seethe Companies Act 2006 s 112; and PARA 323 et seq.

18 Companies Act 2006 s 113(6). This nullifies the decision in *Re Performing Right Society Ltd, Lyttleton v Performing Right Society Ltd* [1978] 3 All ER 972, [1978] 1 WLR 1197, CA.

19 Ie in complying with the Companies Act 2006 s 113: see s 113(7). See note 23.

20 Companies Act 2006 s 113(7). As to the meaning of 'officer who is in default' see PARA 316. As to the meaning of 'officer' generally see PARA 679.

21 As to the standard scale and the powers of magistrates' courts to issue fines on summary conviction see SENTENCING vol 92 (2015) PARA 176.

22 As to the meaning of 'daily default fine' see PARA 1816.

23 Companies Act 2006 s 113(8). Although s 113 does not apply to a company which is a participating issuer (other than as respects any overseas branch register) (Uncertificated Securities Regulations 2001, SI 2001/3755, reg 23(4), Sch 4 para 2(4) (amended by SI 2009/1889)), the Companies Act 2006 s 113(7), (8) applies to a participating issuer which is a company which makes default in complying with the Uncertificated Securities Regulations 2001, SI 2001/3755, Sch 4 para 2 (see PARA 341) and every officer of it who is in default as if such a default were a default in complying with the Companies Act 2006 s 113 (Uncertificated Securities Regulations 2001, SI 2001/3755, Sch 4 para 2(5) (amended by SI 2009/1889)). An officer of a participating issuer is in default in complying with, or in contravention of the Uncertificated Securities Regulations 2001, SI 2001/3755, Sch 4 para 2, if, and only if, he knowingly and wilfully authorised or permitted the default or contravention: Sch 4 para 20. Notwithstanding any other enactment, a participating issuer may not close a register of securities relating to a participating security without the consent of the operator: reg 26 (amended by SI 2009/1889). As to the meaning of 'officer' (in relation to an operator or a participating issuer) see PARA 432 note 4; and as to the meaning of 'operator register of securities' see PARA 432 note 3. As to the overseas branch register of members see PARA 359.

24 Companies Act 2006 s 121. The power conferred by s 121 is exercisable on and after 6 April 2018, whenever the period of ten years referred to in that provision expired: see the Companies Act 2006 (Commencement No 5, Transitional Provisions and Savings) Order 2007, SI 2007/3495, art 9, Sch 4 para 2(1) (amended by SI 2008/674). A copy of any details that were included in the register immediately before that date and that are removed from the register under that power

must be retained by the company until 6 April 2008 or, if earlier, 20 years after the member concerned ceased to be a member: see the Companies Act 2006 (Commencement No 5, Transitional Provisions and Savings) Order 2007, SI 2007/3495, Sch 4 para 2(2).

25 Companies Act 2006 s 128(1)(a).

26 Companies Act 2006 s 128(1)(b).

27 Companies Act 2006 s 128(1). This is without prejudice to any lesser period of limitation: s 128(2). The provisions of s 128 apply to causes of action arising on or after 6 April 2008: see the Companies Act 2006 (Commencement No 5, Transitional Provisions and Savings) Order 2007, SI 2007/3495, Sch 4 para 3(1). The time limit for causes of action arising before that date is ten years from 6 April 2008, or 20 years (as provided by the Companies Act 1985 s 352(7) (repealed)) from when the cause of action arose, whichever expires first: see the Companies Act 2006 (Commencement No 5, Transitional Provisions and Savings) Order 2007, SI 2007/3495, Sch 4 para 3(2). This is without prejudice to any lesser period of limitation: see Sch 4 para 3(3).

28 *Re W Key & Son Ltd* [1902] 1 Ch 467. As to a company's lien on shares for moneys owing see PARAS 1393–1398.

29 *Re TH Saunders & Co Ltd* [1908] 1 Ch 415.

30 *Weikersheim's Case* (1873) 8 Ch App 831. See also *Dunster's Case* [1894] 3 Ch 473, CA.

31 *Re Vagliano Anthracite Collieries Ltd* (1910) 79 LJ Ch 769.

337. Statement in register that private company has only one member. If a limited company[1] is formed under the Companies Act 2006[2] with only one member[3] there must be entered in the company's register of members[4], with the name and address of the sole member, a statement that the company has only one member[5].

If the number of members of a limited company falls to one, or if an unlimited company[6] with only one member becomes a limited company on re-registration[7], there must, upon the occurrence of that event, be entered in the company's register of members, with the name and address of the sole member[8]:

(1) a statement that the company has only one member[9]; and

(2) the date on which the company became a company having only one member[10].

If the membership of a limited company increases from one to two or more members, there must, upon the occurrence of that event, be entered in the company's register of members, with the name and address of the person who was formerly the sole member, a statement that the company has ceased to have only one member[11] together with the date on which that event occurred[12].

If a company makes default in complying with these requirements[13], an offence is committed by the company, and by every officer of the company who is in default[14].

1 As to the meaning of 'limited company' see PARA 95. As to the meaning of 'company' under the Companies Acts see PARA 21; and as to the meaning of the 'Companies Acts' see PARA 13.

2 As to company formation and registration under the Companies Act 2006, and the different forms that such a company may take, see PARA 65 et seq.

3 As to the meaning of 'member of a company' see PARA 323. By virtue of the Companies Act 2006 s 7(1), (2), a company is duly formed under the Act by one or more persons: see PARA 95.

4 As to the register of members see PARA 336 et seq. As to the option for a private company to keep membership information on the central register see PARA 363 et seq.

5 Companies Act 2006 s 123(1). An unlimited company is not required to make such a statement whether it is formed with, or becomes, a company with one member. See also the text and notes 6–9.

6 As to the meaning of 'unlimited company' see PARA 95.

7 As to the re-registration of an unlimited company as a private limited company see PARA 178 et seq.

8 Companies Act 2006 s 123(2).

9 Companies Act 2006 s 123(2)(a).

10 Companies Act 2006 s 123(2)(b).

11 Companies Act 2006 s 123(3)(a).

12 Companies Act 2006 s 123(3)(b).

13 Ie in complying with the Companies Act 2006 s 123: see s 123(4).

14 Companies Act 2006 s 123(4). As to the meaning of 'officer who is in default' see PARA 316. As to the meaning of 'officer' generally see PARA 679.

A person guilty of such an offence is liable on summary conviction to a fine not exceeding level 3 on the standard scale and for continued contravention to a daily default fine not exceeding one-tenth of level 3 on the standard scale: s 123(5). As to the standard scale and the powers of magistrates' courts to issue fines on summary conviction see SENTENCING vol 92 (2015) PARA 176; and as to the meaning of 'daily default fine' see PARA 1816.

338. Entries and amendments to be made where there are share warrants. Until a share warrant issued by a company[1] is surrendered the following are deemed to be the particulars required to be entered in the register of members[2] in respect of the warrant:

(1) the fact of the issue of the warrant;

(2) a statement of the shares[3] included in the warrant, distinguishing each share by its number so long as the share has a number[4]; and

(3) the date of the issue of the warrant[5].

The bearer of a share warrant may, if the company's articles[6] so provide, be deemed a member of the company within the meaning of the Companies Act 2006, either to the full extent or for any purposes defined in the articles[7]. The company is responsible for any loss incurred by any person by reason of the company entering in the register the name of a bearer of a share warrant in respect of the shares specified in it without the warrant being surrendered and cancelled[8]. On the surrender of a share warrant, the date of the surrender must be entered in the register[9].

1 No share warrant may be issued by a company on or after 26 May 2015: see the Companies Act 2006 s 779(4); and PARA 392. As to the meaning of 'company' under the Companies Acts see PARA 21; and as to the meaning of the 'Companies Acts' see PARA 13.

2 As to the meaning of 'member' see PARA 323. As to the register of members see PARA 336 et seq. The Companies Act 2006 s 122 applies to a company which is a participating issuer as if references to the company's register of members were references instead to its issuer register of members: Uncertificated Securities Regulations 2001, SI 2001/3755, reg 23(4), Sch 4 para 8 (amended by SI 2009/1889). As to the meaning of 'participating issuer' see PARA 432 note 9. As to the meaning of 'issuer register of members' see PARA 341.

3 As to the meaning of 'share' see PARA 1231.

4 As to the numbering of shares see PARA 1239.

5 Companies Act 2006 s 122(1) (substituted by the Small Business, Enterprise and Employment Act 2015 Sch 4 Pt 2 paras 22, 23(a)).

6 As to the meaning of references to a company's 'articles' see PARA 227 note 2. As to a company's articles of association generally see PARA 227 et seq.

7 Companies Act 2006 s 122(3). As to articles providing that share warrant bearers be deemed members see PARA 323.

8 Companies Act 2006 s 122(5).

9 Companies Act 2006 s 122(6).

339. Registration requirements where company holds own shares as treasury shares. Where a company[1] purchases its own shares[2] in circumstances where it is deemed to be holding them as treasury shares[3]:

(1) the requirements to make entries in the register of members[4] need not be complied with if the company cancels all of the shares forthwith after the purchase[5]; and

(2) if the company does not cancel all of the shares forthwith after the purchase, any share that is so cancelled must be disregarded for the purposes of that requirement[6].

Subject to these provisions[7], where a company holds shares as treasury shares the company must be entered in the register as the member holding those shares[8].

1 As to the meaning of 'company' under the Companies Acts see PARA 21; and as to the meaning of the 'Companies Acts' see PARA 13.

2 Ie in accordance with the Companies Act 2006 Pt 18 Ch 4 (ss 690–708): see PARA 1421 et seq. As to the meaning of 'share' see PARA 1231.
3 Ie in circumstances in which the Companies Act 2006 s 724 (treasury shares) applies (see PARA 1437): see s 124(1). As to treasury shares see PARA 1437.
4 Ie the requirements of the Companies Act 2006 s 113 (see PARA 336): see s 124(1)(a). As to the register of members see PARA 336 et seq. As to the meaning of 'member' see PARA 323. As to the option for a private company to keep membership information on the central register see PARA 363 et seq.
5 Companies Act 2006 s 124(1)(a).
6 Companies Act 2006 s 124(1)(b). Head (2) in the text refers to the purposes of s 113 (see PARA 336): see s 124(1)(b).
7 Ie subject to the Companies Act 2006 s 124(1) (see the text and notes 1–6): see s 124(2).
8 Companies Act 2006 s 124(2).

340. Index of names of members. Every company[1] having more than 50 members[2] must keep an index of the names of the members of the company, unless the register of members[3] is in such a form as to constitute in itself an index[4]. The company must, within 14 days after the date on which any alteration is made in the register of members, make any necessary alteration in the index[5]. The index must contain, in respect of each member, a sufficient indication to enable the account of that member in the register to be readily found[6]; and the index must be at all times kept available for inspection at the same place as the register of members[7].

If default is made in complying with these requirements[8], an offence is committed by the company, and by every officer of the company who is in default[9].

1 As to the meaning of 'company' under the Companies Acts see PARA 21; and as to the meaning of the 'Companies Acts' see PARA 13.
2 As to the meaning of 'member' see PARA 323.
3 As to the register of members see PARA 336 et seq. As to the option for a private company to keep membership information on the central register see PARA 363 et seq.
4 Companies Act 2006 s 115(1). The index of members' names falls within the definition of 'company records' that is used for the purposes of the Companies Act 2006: see PARA 746. As to the form of company records, their inspection and the duty to take precautions against their falsification see PARAS 746–748. As to the index of names of members to be kept regarding uncertificated securities see PARA 342.
5 Companies Act 2006 s 115(2).
6 Companies Act 2006 s 115(3).
7 Companies Act 2006 s 115(4). As to the custody and inspection of the register and index see PARA 348 et seq.
8 Ie in complying with the Companies Act 2006 s 115: see s 115(5).
9 Companies Act 2006 s 115(5). As to the meaning of 'officer who is in default' see PARA 316. As to the meaning of 'officer' generally see PARA 679.

A person guilty of such an offence is liable on summary conviction to a fine not exceeding level 3 on the standard scale and for continued contravention to a daily default fine not exceeding one-tenth of level 3 on the standard scale: s 115(6). As to the standard scale and the powers of magistrates' courts to issue fines on summary conviction see SENTENCING vol 92 (2015) PARA 176; and as to the meaning of 'daily default fine' see PARA 1816.

Although s 115 does not apply to a company which is a participating issuer (Uncertificated Securities Regulations 2001, SI 2001/3755, reg 23(4), Sch 4 para 7(4) (amended by SI 2009/1889)), the Companies Act 2006 s 115(5), (6) applies to a participating issuer which is a company which makes default in complying with the Uncertificated Securities Regulations 2001, SI 2001/3755, Sch 4 para 7 (see PARA 342) and every officer of it who is in default as if such a default were a default in complying with the Companies Act 2006 s 115 (Uncertificated Securities Regulations 2001, SI 2001/3755, Sch 4 para 7(5) (amended by SI 2009/1889)). An officer of a participating issuer is in default in complying with, or in contravention of the Uncertificated Securities Regulations 2001, SI 2001/3755, Sch 4 para 7, if, and only if, he knowingly and wilfully authorised or permitted the default or contravention: Sch 4 para 20. As to the meaning of 'participating issuer' see PARA 432 note 9. As to the meaning of 'officer' (in relation to an operator or a participating issuer) see PARA 432 note 4.

341. Entries to be made in registers regarding uncertificated securities. In respect of every company[1] which is a participating issuer[2], there must be a register maintained by the participating issuer (an 'issuer register of members')[3]; and a register maintained by the operator[4] (an 'operator register of members')[5]. References in any enactment or instrument to a company's register of members, unless the context otherwise requires, is to be construed in relation to a company which is a participating issuer as referring to the company's issuer register of members and operator register of members[6].

Every participating issuer[7] which is a company must enter in its issuer register of members[8]:

(1) the names and addresses of the members[9];
(2) the date on which each person was registered as a member[10]; and
(3) the date at which any person ceased to be a member[11].

With the names and addresses of the members there must be entered a statement of the certificated shares[12] held by each member[13], distinguishing each share by its number (so long as the share has a number) and, where the company has more than one class of issued shares, by its class[14], and a statement of the amount paid or agreed to be considered as paid on the certificated shares of each member[15]. Where the company has converted any of its shares into stock[16] and given notice of the conversion to the registrar of companies[17], the issuer register of members must show the amount and class of the certificated stock[18] held by each member, instead of the amount of shares and the particulars relating to shares so specified[19]. Provision is made in respect of persons who make default in complying with these requirements[20].

An entry relating to a former member of the company may be removed from the issuer register of members after the expiration of ten years beginning with the day on which he ceased to be a member[21].

In relation to every participating issuer which is a company, an operator of a relevant system must, in respect of any class of shares which is a participating security for the purposes of that system, enter on an operator register of members[22]:

(a) the names and addresses of the members who hold uncertificated shares in the company[23];
(b) with those names and addresses, a statement of the uncertificated shares held by each member, distinguishing, where the company has more than one class of issued uncertificated shares, each share by its class[24]; and
(c) where the company has converted any of its shares into stock and given notice of the conversion to the registrar of companies, the operator register of members must show the amount and class of uncertificated stock held by each member, instead of the amount of shares and the particulars relating to shares specified in head (b) above[25].

An entry relating to a member of a company who has ceased to hold any uncertificated shares in the company may be removed from the operator register of members after the expiration of ten years beginning with the day on which he ceased to hold any such shares[26]. Members of a company who hold shares in uncertificated form may not be entered as holders of those shares on an overseas branch register[27].

The obligations of an operator to maintain and to keep and enter up any register of securities, imposed by the Uncertificated Securities Regulations 2001[28]:

(i) does not give rise to any form of duty or liability on the operator, except such as is expressly provided for in the Regulations or as arises from fraud or other wilful default, or negligence, on the part of the operator[29];

(ii) does not give rise to any form of duty or liability on a participating issuer, other than where the operator acts on the instructions of that participating issuer, in the absence of fraud or other wilful default, or negligence, on the part of that participating issuer[30]; and

(iii) does not give rise to any form of duty or liability enforceable by civil proceedings for breach of statutory duty[31].

Without prejudice to the above, or to any lesser period of limitation or to any rule as to the prescription of rights, any liability incurred by a participating issuer or by an operator arising either from the making or deletion of an entry in a register of securities or record of securities pursuant to the Uncertificated Securities Regulations 2001[32], or from a failure to make or delete any such entry, is not enforceable more than ten years after the date on which the entry was made or deleted or, in the case of a failure, the failure first occurred[33].

A participating issuer which is a company must maintain a record[34] of the entries made in its operator register of members (a 'record of uncertificated[35] shares')[36]. Every participating issuer which is a company must enter in its record of uncertificated shares[37]:

(A) the same particulars, so far as practicable, as are required[38] to be entered in the operator register of members[39]; and

(B) a statement of the amount paid or agreed to be considered as paid on the uncertificated shares of each member[40].

Such a company must, unless it is impracticable to do so by virtue of circumstances beyond its control, ensure that the record of uncertificated shares is regularly reconciled with the operator register of members[41]. Provided that it has so complied, a company is not liable in respect of any act or thing done or omitted to be done by or on behalf of the company in reliance upon the assumption that the particulars entered in any record of uncertificated shares which the company is required to keep by the Uncertificated Securities Regulations 2001 accord with the particulars entered in its operator register of members[42].

Such sanctions as apply to a company and its officers in the event of a default in complying with keeping a register of members under the Companies Act 2006[43] apply to a company which is a participating issuer and its officers[44], or an operator and his officers[45], as the case may be[46].

1 For these purposes, 'company' means a company within the meaning of the Companies Act 2006 s 1(1): Uncertificated Securities Regulations 2001, SI 2001/3755, reg 3(1) (definition amended by SI 2009/1889). As to the meaning of 'company' under the Companies Acts see PARA 21; and as to the meaning of the 'Companies Acts' see PARA 13.

2 As to the meaning of 'participating issuer' see PARA 432 note 9.

3 Uncertificated Securities Regulations 2001, SI 2001/3755, reg 20(1)(a). A participating issuer which is a company must keep and enter up the issuer register of members in accordance with reg 23(4), Sch 4 para 2 (see the text and notes 7–21): reg 20(2).

4 As to the meaning of 'operator' see PARA 432 note 1.

5 Uncertificated Securities Regulations 2001, SI 2001/3755, reg 20(1)(b). In respect of every company which is a participating issuer, the operator must keep and enter up the operator register of members in accordance with Sch 4 para 4 (see the text and notes 22–27): reg 20(3). Every register which an operator is required to maintain by virtue of the Uncertificated Securities Regulations 2001, SI 2001/3755 (other than an operator register of eligible debt securities) which relates to securities issued by a company is deemed to be kept (in the case of a company registered in England and Wales), in England and Wales, or (in the case of a company registered in Scotland), in Scotland: Sch 4 para 16(2) (amended by SI 2009/1889; SI 2003/1633). For these purposes, 'register of members' means either or both of an issuer register of members and an operator

register of members: Uncertificated Securities Regulations 2001, SI 2001/3755, reg 3(1). As to the meanings of 'England' and 'Wales' see PARA 1 note 5. As to the operator register of eligible debt securities see PARA 436.

6 Uncertificated Securities Regulations 2001, SI 2001/3755, reg 20(4). This provision does not apply in relation to a company's issuer register of members to the extent that any of the particulars entered in that register in accordance with Sch 4 para2(1) (see the text and notes 7–11) are inconsistent with the company's operator register of members: reg 20(5).

7 The Companies Act 2006 s 123 (see PARA 337) applies to a participating issuer which is a private company limited by shares as if references therein to the company's register of members were references to its issuer register of members: Uncertificated Securities Regulations 2001, SI 2001/3755, Sch 4 para 3 (amended by SI 2009/1889). As to the meanings of 'company limited by shares' and 'private company' see PARA 95.

8 Uncertificated Securities Regulations 2001, SI 2001/3755, Sch 4 para 2(1). For these purposes, references to an issuer register of members must not be taken to include an overseas branch register: Sch 4 para 2(7). As to the overseas branch register of members see PARA 359.

9 Uncertificated Securities Regulations 2001, SI 2001/3755, Sch 4 para 2(1)(a).

10 Uncertificated Securities Regulations 2001, SI 2001/3755, Sch 4 para 2(1)(b).

11 Uncertificated Securities Regulations 2001, SI 2001/3755, Sch 4 para 2(1)(c). As to cessation of company membership see PARAS 389–390.

12 For this purpose, 'certificated shares' means shares which are not uncertificated shares; and 'uncertificated shares' means shares title to which may be transferred by means of a relevant system: Uncertificated Securities Regulations 2001, SI 2001/3755, Sch 4 para 1. As to the meaning of 'share' for these purposes see PARA 432 note 2. Nothing in the Uncertificated Securities Regulations 2001, SI 2001/3755, requires a participating issuer or its officers to maintain a register which records how many units of a wholly dematerialised security are held in certificated form: reg 45(a). As to the meaning of 'wholly dematerialised security' see PARA 432 note 8. As to the meaning of 'officer' (in relation to an operator or a participating issuer) see PARA 432 note 4; and as to the meaning of 'relevant system' see PARA 432 note 1.

13 As to who qualifies as a member of a company see PARA 323.

14 Uncertificated Securities Regulations 2001, SI 2001/3755, Sch 4 para 2(2)(a). As to the numbering of shares see PARA 1239; and as to classes of shares see PARA 1246 et seq.

15 Uncertificated Securities Regulations 2001, SI 2001/3755, Sch 4 para 2(2)(b).

16 As to the meaning of 'stock' see PARA 1351.

17 As to the meaning of 'registrar of companies' see PARA 126 note 2. As to the notice required to be given to the registrar of the reconversion of stock into shares see PARA 1353.

18 For these purposes, 'certificated stock' means stock which is not uncertificated stock; and 'uncertificated stock' means stock title to which may be transferred by means of a relevant system: Uncertificated Securities Regulations 2001, SI 2001/3755, Sch 4 para 1.

19 Uncertificated Securities Regulations 2001, SI 2001/3755, Sch 4 para 2(3).

20 See PARA 336.

21 Uncertificated Securities Regulations 2001, SI 2001/3755, Sch 4 para 2(6) (amended by SI 2009/1889). See also note 5.

22 Uncertificated Securities Regulations 2001, SI 2001/3755, Sch 4 para 4(1). For these purposes, references to an operator register of members must not be taken to include an overseas branch register: Sch 4 para4(3).

23 Uncertificated Securities Regulations 2001, SI 2001/3755, Sch 4 para 4(1)(a).

24 Uncertificated Securities Regulations 2001, SI 2001/3755, Sch 4 para 4(1)(b).

25 Uncertificated Securities Regulations 2001, SI 2001/3755, Sch 4 para 4(1)(c).

26 Uncertificated Securities Regulations 2001, SI 2001/3755, Sch 4 para 4(2) (amended by SI 2009/1889).

27 Uncertificated Securities Regulations 2001, SI 2001/3755, Sch 4 para 4(4).

28 Ie imposed by the Uncertificated Securities Regulations 2001, SI 2001/3755: see reg 23(1).

29 Uncertificated Securities Regulations 2001, SI 2001/3755, reg 23(1)(a).

30 Uncertificated Securities Regulations 2001, SI 2001/3755, reg 23(1)(b).

31 Uncertificated Securities Regulations 2001, SI 2001/3755, reg 23(1)(c).

32 Ie pursuant to the Uncertificated Securities Regulations 2001, SI 2001/3755: see reg 23(2). An entry in a register of securities or in a record of securities (see the text and notes 34–42) relating to a person who no longer holds the securities which are the subject of the entry may be removed from the register or the record (as the case may be) after the expiration of 20 years beginning with the day on which the person ceased to hold any of those securities: Sch 4 para 17(1). It is submitted that the reference to 20 years in Sch 4 para 17(1) should be a reference to ten years. This does not apply in respect of an entry in a register of members: Sch 4 para 17(2).

33 Uncertificated Securities Regulations 2001, SI 2001/3755, reg 23(2) (amended by SI 2009/1889). In relation to the keeping of registers and records of participating securities, the Uncertificated Securities Regulations 2001, SI 2001/3755, Sch 4, which also excludes, or applies with appropriate modifications, certain provisions of the Companies Act 2006, has effect (see the text and notes 6–27, 32, 37–46): Uncertificated Securities Regulations 2001, SI 2001/3755, reg 23(4) (amended by SI 2009/1889). As to entries relating to trusts and equitable interests see PARA 344.
34 The record must be kept and entered up in accordance with the Uncertificated Securities Regulations 2001, SI 2001/3755, Sch 4 para 5 (see the text and notes 37–42): reg 20(6)(b).
35 As to the meaning of 'uncertificated' see PARA 432 note 3.
36 Uncertificated Securities Regulations 2001, SI 2001/3755, reg 20(6)(a). See also note 33.
37 Uncertificated Securities Regulations 2001, SI 2001/3755, Sch 4 para 5(1).
38 Ie required by the Uncertificated Securities Regulations 2001, SI 2001/3755, Sch 4 para 4(1) (see heads (a)–(c) in the text): see Sch 4 para 5(1)(a).
39 Uncertificated Securities Regulations 2001, SI 2001/3755, Sch 4 para 5(1)(a).
40 Uncertificated Securities Regulations 2001, SI 2001/3755, Sch 4 para 5(1)(b).
41 Uncertificated Securities Regulations 2001, SI 2001/3755, Sch 4 para 5(2).
42 Uncertificated Securities Regulations 2001, SI 2001/3755, Sch 4 para 5(3).
43 Ie the Companies Act 2006 s 113(7), (8) (see PARA 336): see the Uncertificated Securities Regulations 2001, SI 2001/3755, reg 20(7), Sch 4 para 5(4) (amended by SI 2009/1889).
44 Ie in the event of a default in complying with the Uncertificated Securities Regulations 2001, SI 2001/3755, reg 20(1)(a) (see the text and notes 1–3) or reg 20(6)(a) (see the text and notes 35–36): see reg 20(7), Sch 4 para 5(4) (as amended: see note 43).
45 Ie in the event of a default in complying with the Uncertificated Securities Regulations 2001, SI 2001/3755, reg 20(1)(b) (see the text and notes 4–5): see reg 20(7), Sch 4 para 5(4) (as amended: see note 43). Such sanctions as apply to a company and its officers in the event of a default in complying with the Companies Act 2006 s 113 (see PARA 336) apply also to an operator and his officers in the event of a default in complying with the Uncertificated Securities Regulations 2001, SI 2001/3755, Sch 4 para 4 (see the text and notes 22–27): Sch 4 para 19(1) (amended by SI 2009/1889). An officer of an operator is in default in complying with, or in contravention of, the provisions of the Uncertificated Securities Regulations 2001, SI 2001/3755, Sch 4 para 4, if, and only if, he knowingly and wilfully authorised or permitted the default or contravention: see Sch 4 para 21 (amended by SI 2009/1889).
46 Uncertificated Securities Regulations 2001, SI 2001/3755, reg 20(7), Sch 4 para 5(4) (as amended: see note 43). For the purposes of the Uncertificated Securities Regulations 2001, SI 2001/3755, reg 20(7), an officer of a participating issuer, or an officer of an operator, is in default in complying with, or in contravention of, the provision mentioned in that regulation if, and only if, he knowingly and wilfully authorised or permitted the default or contravention: reg 47(1), (2). An officer of a participating issuer is in default in complying with, or in contravention of, Sch 4 para 5, if, and only if, he knowingly and wilfully authorised or permitted the default or contravention: Sch 4 para 20.

342. Index of names of members regarding uncertificated securities. Every participating issuer[1] which is a company[2] having more than 50 members[3] must (unless the particulars required[4] to be entered in the issuer register of members[5] are kept in such a form as to constitute in themselves an index) keep an index of the names of the members of the company and must, within 14 days after the date on which any alteration is made in the issuer register of members or the operator register of members[6], make any necessary alteration in the index[7]. The index must in respect of each member contain a sufficient indication to enable the account of that member in the issuer register of members (and, in the case of a member who holds uncertificated shares[8] in the company, in the record of uncertificated shares) to be readily found[9]. The index must be at all times kept available for inspection at the same place as the issuer register of members and the record of uncertificated shares[10].

1 As to the meaning of 'participating issuer' see PARA 432 note 9.
2 As to the meaning of 'company' for these purposes see PARA 341 note 1.
3 As to who qualifies as a member of a company see PARA 323.
4 Ie required by the Uncertificated Securities Regulations 2001, SI 2001/3755, reg 23(4), Sch 4 para 2(1) (see PARA 341): see Sch 4 para 7(1).
5 As to the meaning of 'issuer register of members' see PARA 341.
6 As to the meaning of 'operator register of members' see PARA 341.

7 Uncertificated Securities Regulations 2001, SI 2001/3755, Sch 4 para 7(1).
8 As to the meaning of 'uncertificated shares' see PARA 341 note 12.
9 Uncertificated Securities Regulations 2001, SI 2001/3755, Sch 4 para 7(2).
10 Uncertificated Securities Regulations 2001, SI 2001/3755, Sch 4 para 7(3) (amended by SI 2009/1889). As to the meaning of 'record of uncertificated shares' see PARA 341. As to the location of the register see PARA 349. Where, under the Uncertificated Securities Regulations 2001, SI 2001/3755, Sch 4 para 6(1) (see PARA 349), a company's issuer register of members and record of uncertificated shares is kept available for inspection at the office of some person other than the company, and by reason of any default of his the company fails to comply with Sch 4para 6(2) (record of uncertificated shares to be kept available for inspection with issuer register of members) (see PARA 349), Sch 4 para 6(3) (notice to registrar) (see PARA 349), Sch 4 para 7(3) or the Companies Act 2006 s 116 (rights to inspect and require copies) (see PARA 350), or with any requirement of the 2006 Act as to the production of the register of members or any part thereof, that other person is liable to the same penalties as if he were an officer of the company who was in default, and the power of the court under s 118(3) extends to the making of orders against that other and his officers and servants: Uncertificated Securities Regulations 2001, SI 2001/3755, Sch 4 para 10 (amended by SI 2009/1889). An officer of a participating issuer is in default in complying with, or in contravention of the Uncertificated Securities Regulations 2001, SI 2001/3755, Sch 4 paras 6, 7, if, and only if, he knowingly and wilfully authorised or permitted the default or contravention: Sch 4 para 20. As to the meaning of 'participating issuer' see PARA 432 note 9; and as to the meaning of 'officer' (in relation to an operator or a participating issuer) see PARA 432 note 4.

343. How far entry on register necessary for membership. In order to constitute membership of a company[1], entry on the register is necessary[2], except in the case of signatories or persons deemed to be signatories to the memorandum of association[3].

1 As to membership of a company see PARA 323 et seq.
2 *Nicol's Case, Tufnell and Ponsonby's Case* (1885) 29 ChD 421, CA; *Re Macdonald, Sons & Co* [1894] 1 Ch 89, CA. As to the register of members see PARA 336 et seq. As to the option for a private company to keep membership information on the central register see PARA 363 et seq.
3 See PARA 323. As to the meaning of 'memorandum of association' see PARA 97. As to subscribers of the memorandum see PARA 97.

344. Trusts and equitable interests not to be entered on register of members. No notice of any trust, expressed, implied or constructive[1], is to be entered on the register of members[2] of a company[3] registered in England and Wales[4], or to be receivable by the registrar of companies[5].

The entry of the Public Trustee by that name in the books of a company does not constitute notice of a trust, and a company is not entitled to object to enter the name of the Public Trustee on its books by reason only that the Public Trustee is a corporation, and in dealings with property the fact that the person or one of the persons dealt with is the Public Trustee does not of itself constitute notice of a trust[6].

Although a member, to the knowledge of the company, is merely a trustee or legal mortgagee[7] of shares registered in his name, he is liable to the company for calls and other obligations of membership[8], and this liability is not limited to the amount of the trust estate[9]. He is, however, entitled to be indemnified against all such liabilities by the beneficiary[10]; but he cannot maintain a claim to enforce this right, unless the liability has been or is about to be enforced against him[11]. The right of indemnity may be assigned to the liquidator of the company, and enforced by him[12].

Where a company's articles of association[13] supplement the statutory provision by expressly providing that the company is entitled to treat a shareholder as the absolute owner of his registered shares, and is not to be bound to recognise any equitable interest in shares[14], the company is not bound to accept or preserve notices of equitable interests, and such notices do not affect the company or its officers or agents with any trust[15]; but, where the company in which the shares are held claims to have a lien or charge on the shares for its own benefit, the company is liable to be affected with notice of the interests of third parties, and the provisions of the articles will not protect the company if, in the face of notice that the shareholder is not the beneficial owner of the shares, it makes advances or gives credit to the shareholder[16].

Notice to the company does not give any priority as between two persons claiming title to shares registered in the name of a third[17].

No notice of any trust, expressed, implied or constructive, may be entered on an operator register of securities[18], or a part of such a register, or be receivable by an operator[19]. Unless expressly prohibited from transferring units of a security[20] by means of any computer-based system[21], a trustee or personal representative is not chargeable with a breach of trust or, as the case may be, with default in administering the estate by reason only of the fact that[22]:

(1) for the purpose of acquiring units of a security which he has the power to acquire in connection with the trust or estate, he has paid for the units under arrangements which provide for them to be transferred to him from a system-member but not to be so transferred until after the payment of the price[23];

(2) for the purpose of disposing of units of a security which he has power to dispose of in connection with the trust or estate, he has transferred the units to a system-member under arrangements which provide that the price is not to be paid to him until after the transfer is made[24]; or

(3) for the purpose of holding units of a security belonging to the trust or estate in uncertificated form and for transferring title to them by means of a relevant system[25], he has become a system-member[26].

1 As to express, implied or constructive trusts etc see TRUSTS AND POWERS vol 98 (2013) PARA 24 et seq.

2 As to the register of members see PARA 336 et seq. As to the meaning of 'member' see PARA 323.

3 As to the meaning of 'company' under the Companies Acts see PARA 21; and as to the meaning of the 'Companies Acts' see PARA 13.

4 As to the meanings of 'England' and 'Wales' see PARA 1 note 5. As to company formation and registration in England and Wales under the Companies Act 2006 see PARA 95 et seq. As to companies registered, but not formed, under the Companies Act 2006, and as to overseas companies, see PARA 29. As to the position in Scotland see *Muir v City of Glasgow Bank* (1879) 4 App Cas 337 at 360, HL, per Earl Cairns LC.

5 Companies Act 2006 s 126. As to the meaning of 'registrar of companies' see PARA 126 note 2. As to the delivery of documents to the registrar see PARA 136; and as to the requirements generally for the proper delivery of documents to the registrar see PARA 137.

Without prejudice to the Companies Act 2006 s 126 or to the Uncertificated Securities Regulations 2001, SI 2001/3755, reg 23(3) (see the text and notes 18–19), the operator is not bound by or compelled to recognise any express, implied or constructive trust or other interest in respect of uncertificated units of a security, even if he has actual or constructive notice of the said trust or interest: reg 40(3) (amended by SI 2009/1889). This provision does not prevent, however, in the case of a participating issuer constituted under the law of Scotland, an operator giving notice of a trust to the participating issuer on behalf of a system-member: Uncertificated Securities Regulations 2001, SI 2001/3755, reg 40(4). As to the meaning of 'operator' see PARA 432 note 1; as to the meaning of 'participating issuer' see PARA 432 note 9; as to the meaning of 'system-member' see PARA 433 note 9; and as to the meaning of 'uncertificated' see PARA 432 note 3. See further the text and notes 18–26.

6 See the Public Trustee Act 1906 s 11(5); and TRUSTS AND POWERS vol 98 (2013) PARA 226. Note that the offices of the Public Trustee and the Official Solicitor have been reorganised, and functions relating to trusts have been transferred from the Public Trustee to the Official Solicitor: see TRUSTS AND POWERS vol 98 (2013) PARA 206.

7 *Royal Bank of India's Case* (1869) 4 Ch App 252; *Weikersheim's Case* (1873) 8 Ch App 831.

8 *Chapman and Barker's Case* (1867) LR 3 Eq 361; *Muir v City of Glasgow Bank* (1879) 4 App Cas 337, HL. Cf *Re Moseley Green Coal and Coke Co Ltd, Barrett's Case* (1864) 4 De GJ & Sm 416; *Re Phoenix Life Assurance Co, Hoare's Case* (1862) 2 John & H 229; *Gray's Case* (1876)

1 ChD 664; *Re Electric Telegraph Co of Ireland, Bunn's Case* (1860) 2 De GF & J 275; *Re East of England Banking Co, ex p Bugg* (1865) 2 Drew & Sm 452. As to trust shares being sufficient to qualify a director see PARA 533; and as to lien on trust shares see PARA 1394.

9 *Re British and Foreign Cork Co, Leifchild's Case* (1865) LR 1 Eq 231 at 235–236 per Kindersley V-C; *Muir v City of Glasgow Bank* (1879) 4 App Cas 337, HL.

10 *Hardoon v Belilios* [1901] AC 118, PC; *Hemming v Maddick* (1872) 7 Ch App 395; *Hughes-Hallett v Indian Mammoth Gold Mines Co* (1882) 22 ChD 561; *Butler v Cumpston* (1868) LR 7 Eq 16; *James v May* (1873) LR 6 HL 328; *Cruse v Paine* (1869) 4 Ch App 441; *Chapman and Barker's Case* (1867) LR 3 Eq 361 (trusts for the company). See also *Re European Society Arbitration Acts, ex p Liquidators of the British Nation Life Assurance Association* (1878) 8 ChD 679 at 708, CA, per James LJ (enforcement against the beneficiary through and in name of trustee). As to a trustee's right of indemnity under the Trustee Act 2000 in respect of expenses and liabilities generally see TRUSTS AND POWERS vol 98 (2013) PARA 342 et seq.

A person holding shares as a trustee is accountable to the beneficiary: *Rooney v Stanton* (1900) 17 TLR 28, CA. See also *Merlo v Duffy* [2009] EWHC 296 (Ch), [2009] All ER (D) 91 (Feb) (claimant did not have to prove that he was entitled to half of company's share capital which had been held by a legal owner as a nominee on a trust established by agreement, the beneficiaries of which were the claimant and defendant; although the legal ownership of the shares had changed several times, the claimant had not disposed of his beneficial interest to the defendant at any point).

11 *Hughes-Hallett v Indian Mammoth Gold Mines Co* (1882) 22 ChD 561; *Hobbs v Wayet* (1887) 36 ChD 256. See also *Re National Financial Co, ex p Oriental Commercial Bank* (1868) 3 Ch App 791.

12 *Hemming v Maddick* (1872) 7 Ch App 395; *Massey v Allen* (1878) 9 ChD 164; *Heritage v Paine* (1876) 2 ChD 594.

13 As to the meaning of references to a company's 'articles' see PARA 227 note 2. As to a company's articles of association generally see PARA 227 et seq.

14 Provision is made by the model articles which have been made for the purposes of the Companies Act 2006 and intended for adoption by private companies limited by shares (see the Companies (Model Articles) Regulations 2008, SI 2008/3229, reg 2, Sch 1; and PARA 227 et seq) and by public companies (see reg 4, Sch 3; and PARA 227 et seq). As to the meanings of 'company limited by shares', 'private company' and 'public company' see PARA 95. Accordingly, where those articles are adopted, it is provided that, except as required by law, no person is to be recognised by the company as holding any share upon any trust, and except as otherwise required by law or the articles, the company is not in any way to be bound by or recognise any interest in a share other than the holder's absolute ownership of it and all the rights attaching to it: Sch 1 art 23, Sch 3 art 45. Very similar provision is made in the regulations for management of a company limited by shares contained in the Companies (Tables A to F) Regulations 1985, SI 1985/805, reg 2, Schedule Table A: see art 5 (which is disapplied by reg 2, Schedule Table C art 1, in relation to companies limited by guarantee and not having a share capital). As to the meaning of 'company limited by guarantee' see PARA 95. As to the meanings of 'company having a share capital' and 'share capital' see PARA 1231. As to 'Table A' and 'Table C', and as to the treatment of legacy articles under the Companies Act 2006, see PARA 229.

15 *Société Générale de Paris v Walker* (1885) 11 App Cas 20 at 30, HL, per Earl of Selborne; *Simpson v Molson's Bank* [1895] AC 270, PC. Probably, even where the articles contain no such provision, the company is not bound to accept notices of equitable interests, but may treat a registered shareholder as the absolute owner of shares registered in his name. Such provisions do not operate to prevent an equitable owner of shares obtaining a court order to protect his equitable interests: *McGrattan v McGrattan* [1985] NI 28, CA.

16 *Rearden v Provincial Bank of Ireland* [1896] 1 IR 532; *Mackereth v Wigan Coal and Iron Co Ltd* [1916] 2 Ch 293; *Bradford Banking Co v Briggs, Son & Co Ltd* (1886) 12 App Cas 29, HL (applying the principle of *Hopkinson v Rolt* (1861) 9 HL Cas 514). See also *Bank of Africa v Salisbury Gold Mining Co* [1892] AC 281, PC. As to the equitable claims where shares have been transferred by an assignment for the benefit of creditors see *Peat v Clayton* [1906] 1 Ch 659.

17 *Roots v Williamson* (1888) 38 ChD 485; *Moore v North Western Bank* [1891] 2 Ch 599. The principle of *Dearle v Hall* (1828) 3 Russ 1 (see CHOSES IN ACTION vol 13 (2009) PARA 41) does not apply: *Société Générale de Paris v Walker* (1885) 11 App Cas 20 at 30, HL, per Earl of Selborne.

18 As to the meaning of 'operator register of securities' see PARA 432 note 3; and as to the meaning of 'operator' see PARA 432 note 1. As to the entries to be made generally in registers regarding uncertificated securities see PARA 341.

19 Uncertificated Securities Regulations 2001, SI 2001/3755, reg 23(3). See also note 5.

20 As to the meaning of 'securities' see PARA 431 note 2; and as to the meaning of 'unit' (of a security) see PARA 431 note 38.

21 As to the transfer of uncertificated securities by means of a computer-based system see PARA 431.

22 Uncertificated Securities Regulations 2001, SI 2001/3755, reg 40(1).
23 Uncertificated Securities Regulations 2001, SI 2001/3755, reg 40(1)(a).
24 Uncertificated Securities Regulations 2001, SI 2001/3755, reg 40(1)(b).
25 As to the meaning of 'relevant system' see PARA 432 note 1.
26 Uncertificated Securities Regulations 2001, SI 2001/3755, reg 40(1)(c).

345. Stop notice and charging order. A person who has an equitable claim to shares may prevent his claim from being prejudiced by the registered holder dealing with them, by serving upon the company a stop notice[1], after which the company cannot permit the shares claimed to be dealt with by the registered holder, except after proper notice to the claimant[2].

A charging order[3] cannot be made on shares for a debt due from the registered shareholder, if he is a trustee of the shares; for they are not stock (including shares, debentures and debenture stock) in which the judgment debtor has a beneficial interest[4].

A charging order may, however, be made in respect of a judgment debt due from a debtor who holds any beneficial interest in any shares, debentures or securities of any company incorporated in England and Wales[5], or incorporated outside England and Wales, or of any state or territory outside the United Kingdom[6] if registered in a register kept at any place within England and Wales in relation to that interest[7].

1 As to stop notices see CIVIL PROCEDURE vol 12A (2015) PARA 1487 et seq.
2 *Société Générale de Paris v Tramways Union Co* (1884) 14 QBD 424 at 453, CA, per Lindley LJ; affd sub nom *Société Générale de Paris v Walker* (1885) 11 App Cas 20, HL. Any person claiming to be beneficially entitled to an interest in the securities may apply to the High Court for a stop order which may prohibit (amongst other things) the registration of any transfer of the securities or the making of any payment by way of dividend, interest or otherwise in respect of the securities: see CPR 73.14(1); and CIVIL PROCEDURE vol 12A (2015) PARA 1483 et seq.
3 As to charging orders see CIVIL PROCEDURE vol 12A (2015) PARA 1467 et seq.
4 The charge affects the beneficial interest: *Cragg v Taylor* (1867) LR 2 Exch 131; *South Western Loan and Discount Co v Robertson* (1881) 8 QBD 17; *Dixon v Wrench* (1869) LR 4 Exch 154; *Bolland v Young* [1904] 2 KB 824, CA; *Ideal Bedding Co Ltd v Holland* [1907] 2 Ch 157; *Hawks v McArthur* [1951] 1 All ER 22. As to charging orders on stocks and shares generally see CIVIL PROCEDURE vol 12A (2015) PARA 1462 et seq.
5 As to the meanings of 'England' and 'Wales' see PARA 1 note 5.
6 As to the meaning of 'United Kingdom' see PARA 1 note 5.
7 See CIVIL PROCEDURE vol 12A (2015) PARA 1462 et seq.

346. Register of members as evidence. The register of members[1] is prima facie evidence of any matters which are by the Companies Act 2006 directed or authorised to be inserted in it, except, as from 30 June 2016[2], for any matters of which the central register is[3] prima facie evidence[4]. Where a company is being wound up[5], it is, as between the contributories of the company[6], prima facie evidence of the truth of all matters purporting to be recorded in it (along with all books and papers of the company and of the liquidators)[7]. However, the register is not conclusive evidence, although the courts endeavour to make it as conclusive as they can consistently with the statutory provisions[8].

Inaccuracies or omissions do not necessarily prevent the register from being evidence[9]. As, however, it is only prima facie evidence, a person whose name is registered, or omitted from the register, may adduce evidence to show that he ought not or ought to have been registered[10].

A book or document, intended to be a register of members[11], may be admitted in evidence as such, although the statutory requirements as to how it should be kept have not been regularly complied with[12].

1 As to the register of members see PARA 336 et seq. As to the option for a private company to keep membership information on the central register see PARA 363 et seq.

2 See the Small Business, Enterprise and Employment Act 2015 (Commencement No 4, Transitional and Savings Provisions) Regulations 2016, SI 2016/321, reg 6(c).

3 Ie by virtue of the Companies Act 2006 s 128H: see PARA 369.

4 Companies Act 2006 s 127 (amended by the Small Business, Enterprise and Employment Act 2015 Sch 5 Pt 2 paras 11, 14). The provisions of the Companies Act 2006 s 127 do not apply with respect to a company which is a participating issuer: Uncertificated Securities Regulations 2001, SI 2001/3755, reg 24(4) (amended by SI 2009/1889). As to the meaning of 'participating issuer' see PARA 432 note 9. As to the effect of entries on registers relating to uncertificated securities see PARA 347.

5 As to winding up in general see COMPANY AND PARTNERSHIP INSOLVENCY vol 16 (2011) PARA 380 et seq.

6 As to the meaning of 'contributory' see COMPANY AND PARTNERSHIP INSOLVENCY vol 17 (2011) PARA 661. As to the meaning of 'contributory' under the Companies Acts see PARA 109 note 10.

7 See the Insolvency Act 1986 s 191; and COMPANY AND PARTNERSHIP INSOLVENCY vol 17 (2011) PARA 1029.

8 See *Reese River Silver Mining Co v Smith* (1869) LR 4 HL 64 at 80 per Lord Cairns; *Re Briton Medical and General Life Association* (1888) 39 ChD 61 at 71 per Stirling J.

9 *Wills v Murray* (1850) 4 Exch 843; *Bain v Whitehaven and Furness Junction Rly Co* (1850) 3 HL Cas 1; *Southampton Dock Co v Richards* (1840) 1 Man & G 448; *London and Brighton Rly Co v Fairclough* (1841) 2 Man & G 674.

10 *Carmarthen Rly Co v Wright* (1858) 1 F & F 282; *Portal v Emmens* (1876) 1 CPD 201 at 212 per Lindley J (affd (1876) 1 CPD 664, CA); *Hallmark's Case* (1878) 9 ChD 329, CA. As to rectification of the register see PARA 357 et seq.

11 See the cases cited in note 10.

12 *Re Printing, Telegraph and Construction Co of the Agence Havas, ex p Cammell* [1894] 2 Ch 392, CA.

347. Effect of entries on registers relating to uncertificated securities. Any purported registration of a transfer of title to an uncertificated[1] unit of a security[2] other than in accordance with the due provisions[3] is of no effect[4]. Subject to this restriction, a register of members[5] is prima facie evidence of any matters which are by the Uncertificated Securities Regulations 2001[6] directed or authorised to be inserted in it[7].

The entry of a person's name and address in a company's issuer register of members must not be treated as showing that person to be a member of the company unless[8]:

(1) the issuer register of members also shows him as holding shares[9] in the company in certificated form[10];

(2) the operator register of members shows him as holding shares in the company in uncertificated form[11]; or

(3) he is deemed to be a member of the company[12].

1 As to the meaning of 'uncertificated' see PARA 432 note 3.

2 As to the meaning of 'securities' see PARA 431 note 2. As to the transfer of uncertificated shares see PARA 431.

3 Ie other than in accordance with the Uncertificated Securities Regulations 2001, SI 2001/3755, reg 27 (see PARA 437) or reg 28 (see PARA 438): see reg 29.

4 Uncertificated Securities Regulations 2001, SI 2001/3755, reg 29.

5 As to the meaning of 'register of members' where the company is a participating issuer see PARA 341 note 5.

6 Ie the Uncertificated Securities Regulations 2001, SI 2001/3755: see reg 24(1).

7 Uncertificated Securities Regulations 2001, SI 2001/3755, reg 24(1). This provision does not apply to a company's issuer register of members to the extent that any of the particulars entered in that register in accordance with reg 23(4), Sch 4 para 2(1) (see PARA 341) are inconsistent with the company's operator register of members: reg 24(2). Reg 24(1) is also subject to reg 24(3): see text and notes 8–12. As to the meaning of 'issuer register of members' see PARA 341. As to the meaning of 'operator register of members' see PARA 341.

8 Uncertificated Securities Regulations 2001, SI 2001/3755, reg 24(3).

9 As to the meaning of 'share' for these purposes see PARA 432 note 2.

10 Uncertificated Securities Regulations 2001, SI 2001/3755, reg 24(3)(a). As to the meaning of 'certificated' see PARA 432 note 3.
11 Uncertificated Securities Regulations 2001, SI 2001/3755, reg 24(3)(b).
12 Uncertificated Securities Regulations 2001, SI 2001/3755, reg 24(3)(c). Head (3) in the text refers to a person who is deemed to be a member of the company by reg 32(6)(b) (see PARA 433): see reg 24(3)(c).

B. CUSTODY AND INSPECTION OF REGISTER OF MEMBERS

348. Custody of register and index. A company's register of members[1] must be kept available for inspection[2] either at its registered office[3] or at a place specified in regulations[4] made for the purposes of specifying where certain company records are to so kept[5].

A company must give notice to the registrar of companies[6] of the place where its register of members is kept available for inspection, and of any change in that place[7]. If a company makes default for 14 days in complying with the requirement to give such notice[8], an offence is committed by the company, and by every officer of the company who is in default[9]; and a person guilty of such an offence is liable on summary conviction to a fine not exceeding level 3 on the standard scale[10] and for continued contravention to a daily default fine[11] not exceeding one-tenth of level 3 on the standard scale[12]. However, no such notice is required if the register has, at all times since it came into existence (or, in the case of a register in existence on 1 July 1948[13], at all times since then) been kept available for inspection at the company's registered office[14].

The index of the names of members[15] must at all times be kept at the same place as the register of members[16].

Neither the register nor the index may be dealt with by way of charge or otherwise in such a way as to interfere with the purposes for which they must be kept[17].

1 As to the register of members see PARA 336 et seq. As to the meaning of 'member' see PARA 323. As to the meaning of 'company' under the Companies Acts see PARA 21; and as to the meaning of the 'Companies Acts' see PARA 13. As to the option for a private company to keep membership information on the central register see PARA 363 et seq.
2 Companies Act 2006 s 114(1). Where the registrar changes the address of a company's registered office under the Companies Act 2006 s 1097A(7) or the Companies (Address of Registered Office) Regulations 2016, SI 2016/423 (see PARA 160), the company's duties under the Companies Act 2006 s 114 are suspended for a period of 28 days beginning on the day the address was changed: see the Companies (Address of Registered Office) Regulations 2016, SI 2016/423, reg 11; and PARA 160.

Shares in a company are choses in action which are situated at the place where the existence of the choses in action is recorded. The situs of shares in a company is, therefore, at the registered office, or some other specified place at which the register of members should be kept, which place must be within England and Wales or Scotland, as the case may be: *International Credit and Investment Co (Overseas) Ltd v Adham* [1994] 1 BCLC 66 at 72 per Harman J. See also PARA 117 text and notes 13–14; and CONFLICT OF LAWS vol 19 (2011) PARAS 684–685. As to the meanings of 'England' and 'Wales' see PARA 1 note 5. As to a company's registered office see PARA 124. As to the form of company records, their inspection and the duty to take precautions against their falsification see PARAS 746–748. As to the location of the issuer register of members and records of uncertificated shares see PARA 349.
3 Companies Act 2006 s 114(1)(a).
4 Ie regulations made under the Companies Act 2006 s 1136 (see PARA 748): see s 114(1)(b). See the Companies (Company Records) Regulations 2008, SI 2008/3006; and PARA 748.
5 Companies Act 2006 s 114(1)(b).
6 As to the meaning of 'registrar of companies' see PARA 126 note 2. As to the delivery of documents to the registrar see PARA 136; and as to the requirements generally for the proper delivery of documents to the registrar see PARA 137.
7 Companies Act 2006 s 114(2).
8 Ie in complying with the Companies Act 2006 s 114(2) (see the text and notes 6–7): see s 114(5).

9 Companies Act 2006 s 114(5). As to the meaning of 'officer who is in default' see PARA 316. As to the meaning of 'officer' generally see PARA 679.
10 As to the standard scale and the powers of magistrates' courts to issue fines on summary conviction see SENTENCING vol 92 (2015) PARA 176.
11 As to the meaning of 'daily default fine' see PARA 1816.
12 Companies Act 2006 s 114(6). Although s 114 does not apply to a company which is a participating issuer (Uncertificated Securities Regulations 2001, SI 2001/3755, reg 23(4), Sch 4 para 6(5) (amended by SI 2009/1889)), the Companies Act 2006 s 114(6) applies to a participating issuer which is a company which makes default in complying with the Uncertificated Securities Regulations 2001, SI 2001/3755, Sch 4 para 6(2) (see PARA 349) and every officer of it who is in default as if such a default were a default in complying with the Companies Act 2006 s 114(2) (Uncertificated Securities Regulations 2001, SI 2001/3755, Sch 4 para 6(6) (amended by SI 2009/1889)). An officer of a participating issuer is in default in complying with, or in contravention of the Uncertificated Securities Regulations 2001, SI 2001/3755, Sch 4 para 6, if, and only if, he knowingly and wilfully authorised or permitted the default or contravention: Sch 4 para 20. As to the meaning of 'participating issuer' see PARA 432 note 9; and as to the meaning of 'officer' (in relation to an operator or a participating issuer) see PARA 432 note 4.
13 Ie the day on which the Companies Act 1948 (now repealed) came into force. As to the Companies Act 1948 see PARA 10.
14 Companies Act 2006 s 114(3), (4).
15 As to the index of members see PARA 340.
16 See the Companies Act 2006 s 115(4); and PARA 340.
17 *Re Capital Fire Insurance Association* (1883) 24 ChD 408 at 418, CA, per Cotton LJ (where it was held that a solicitor had not acquired a lien as against the liquidator).

349. Location of issuer register of members and records of uncertificated shares. A company's issuer register of members[1] and its record of uncertificated shares[2] must be kept available for inspection at its registered office[3], or at a place specified in regulations[4]. However, the issuer register of members must not be kept available for inspection, in the case of a company registered in England and Wales[5], at any place elsewhere than in England and Wales or, in the case of a company registered in Scotland, at any place elsewhere than in Scotland[6]. A company's issuer register of members and its record of uncertificated shares must at all times be kept available for inspection at the same place[7].

Every participating issuer[8] which is a company must send notice to the registrar of companies[9] of the place where its issuer register of members and its record of uncertificated shares are kept available for inspection, and of any change in that place, provided that any notice sent by such a company[10], and which has effect on the coming into force of the Uncertificated Securities Regulations 2001[11], is treated as being a notice sent in compliance with this provision[12]. However, the notice need not be sent if the issuer register of members and the record of uncertificated shares have at all times since they came into existence been kept available for inspection at the company's registered office[13].

1 As to the meaning of 'issuer register of members' see PARA 341. As to the meaning of 'company' for these purposes see PARA 341 note 1.
2 As to the meaning of 'record of uncertificated shares' see PARA 341. As to the meaning of 'share' for these purposes see PARA 432 note 2; and as to the meaning of 'uncertificated' see PARA 432 note 3.
3 As to a company's registered office see PARA 124. As to the custody of a company's register and index of members that are required to be kept under the Companies Act 2006 see PARA 348.
4 Uncertificated Securities Regulations 2001, SI 2001/3755, reg 23(4), Sch 4 para 6(1) (amended by SI 2009/1889). The text refers to regulations made under the Companies Act 2006 s 1136 (see PARA 748): see the Uncertificated Securities Regulations 2001, SI 2001/3755, Sch 4 para 6(1) (as so amended). Where, under Sch 4 para 6(1), a company's issuer register of members and record of uncertificated shares is kept available for inspection at the office of some person other than the company, and by reason of any default of his the company fails to comply with Sch 4 para 6(2) (record of uncertificated shares to be kept available for inspection with issuer register of members) (see the text and note 7), Sch 4 para 6(3) (notice to registrar) (see the text and notes 8–12), Sch 4 para 7(3) (see PARA 342) or the Companies Act 2006 s 116 (rights to inspect and require copies) (see PARA 350), or with any requirement of the 2006 Act as to the production of the register of

members or any part thereof, that other person is liable to the same penalties as if he were an officer of the company who was in default, and the power of the court under s 118(3) (see PARAS 350–351) extends to the making of orders against that other and his officers and servants: Uncertificated Securities Regulations 2001, SI 2001/3755, Sch 4 para 10 (amended by SI 2009/1889). An officer of a participating issuer is in default in complying with, or in contravention of the Uncertificated Securities Regulations 2001, SI 2001/3755, Sch 4 paras 6, 7, if, and only if, he knowingly and wilfully authorised or permitted the default or contravention: Sch 4 para 20. As to the meaning of 'participating issuer' see PARA 432 note 9; and as to the meaning of 'officer' (in relation to an operator or a participating issuer) see PARA 432 note 4.

5 As to company registration under the Companies Act 2006 see PARA 104 et seq. As to the meanings of 'England' and 'Wales' see PARA 1 note 5.

6 Uncertificated Securities Regulations 2001, SI 2001/3755, Sch 4 para 6(1) (as amended: see note 4).

7 Uncertificated Securities Regulations 2001, SI 2001/3755, Sch 4 para 6(2) (amended by SI 2009/1889). See also notes 4, 8.

8 The Companies Act 2006 s 114 (see PARA 348) does not apply to a company which is a participating issuer: Uncertificated Securities Regulations 2001, SI 2001/3755, Sch 4 para 6(5) (amended by SI 2009/1889). However, the Companies Act 2006 s 114(6) applies to a participating issuer which is a company which makes default in complying with the Uncertificated Securities Regulations 2001, SI 2001/3755, Sch 4 para 6(2) (see the text and note 7) or makes default for 14 days in complying with Sch 4 para 6(3) (see the text and notes 9–12), and every officer of it who is in default, as if such a default were a default in complying with the Companies Act 2006 s 114(2): Uncertificated Securities Regulations 2001, SI 2001/3755, Sch 4 para 6(6) (amended by SI 2009/1889). An officer of a participating issuer is in default in complying with, or in contravention of the Uncertificated Securities Regulations 2001, SI 2001/3755, Sch 4 para 6, if, and only if, he knowingly and wilfully authorised or permitted the default or contravention: Sch 4 para 20.

9 As to the meaning of 'registrar of companies' see PARA 126 note 2. As to the delivery of documents to the registrar see PARA 136; and as to the requirements for the proper delivery of documents to the registrar see PARA 137.

10 Ie in accordance with the Companies Act 2006 s 114(2) (see PARA 348): see the Uncertificated Securities Regulations 2001, SI 2001/3755, Sch 4 para 6(3) (amended by SI 2009/1889).

11 Ie 26 November 2001 (see the Uncertificated Securities Regulations 2001, SI 2001/3755, reg 1): see Sch 4 para 6(3).

12 Uncertificated Securities Regulations 2001, SI 2001/3755, Sch 4 para 6(3) (as amended: see note 10). See also notes 4, 8.

13 Uncertificated Securities Regulations 2001, SI 2001/3755, Sch 4 para 6(4) (amended by SI 2009/1889).

350. Inspection of register of members and index. The company's register of members[1] and the index of members' names[2] must be open to the inspection[3]:

(1) of any member of the company without charge[4]; and
(2) of any other person on payment of such fee as may be prescribed[5].

A person seeking to exercise the right of inspection so conferred must make a request to the company to that effect[6]; and such a request must contain the following information[7]:

(a) in the case of an individual, his name and address[8];
(b) in the case of an organisation, the name and address of an individual responsible for making the request on behalf of the organisation[9];
(c) the purpose for which the information is to be used[10]; and
(d) whether the information will be disclosed to any other person[11], and if so:
    (i) where that person is an individual, his name and address[12];
    (ii) where that person is an organisation, the name and address of an individual responsible for receiving the information on its behalf[13]; and
    (iii) the purpose for which the information is to be used by that person[14].

Where a company receives such a request, it must within five working days either comply with the request[15], or apply to the court[16]. If the company applies to the court, it must notify the person making the request[17]. If, on such an application, the court is satisfied that the inspection is not sought for a proper purpose[18]:

(A) it must direct the company not to comply with the request[19]; and

(B) it may further order that the company's costs on the application be paid in whole or in part by the person who made the request, even if he is not a party to the application[20].

If the court makes such a direction and it appears to the court that the company is or may be subject to other requests made for a similar purpose (whether made by the same person or different persons), it may direct that the company is not to comply with any such request[21]. The order must contain such provision as appears to the court appropriate to identify the requests to which it applies[22]. If, on such an application[23], the court does not direct the company not to comply with the request, the company must comply with the request immediately upon the court giving its decision or, as the case may be, the proceedings being discontinued[24].

If an inspection required under the right to inspect the register and index[25] is refused, otherwise than in accordance with an order of the court, an offence is committed by the company, and by every officer of the company who is in default[26]; and a person guilty of such an offence is liable on summary conviction to a fine not exceeding level 3 on the standard scale[27] and for continued contravention to a daily default fine[28] not exceeding one-tenth of level 3 on the standard scale[29]. In the case of any such refusal, the court may by order compel an immediate inspection[30].

The right of inspection ceases when the company is being wound up[31]. The inspection may be made, under proper restrictions, by an agent of the member desiring inspection[32].

It is an offence for a person knowingly or recklessly to make, in a request to inspect the register and/or index[33], a statement that is misleading, false or deceptive in a material particular[34]; and it is an offence for a person in possession of information obtained by exercise of the right of inspection[35] to do anything that results in the information being disclosed to another person[36], or to fail to do anything with the result that the information is disclosed to another person[37], knowing, or having reason to suspect, that person may use the information for a purpose that is not a proper purpose[38]. A person guilty of such an offence is liable on conviction on indictment to imprisonment for a term not exceeding two years or a fine, or to both[39]; and on summary conviction to imprisonment for a term not exceeding 12 months[40] or a fine, or to both[41].

When a person inspects the register, the company must inform him of the most recent date, if any, on which alterations were made to the register and whether there are further alterations to be made[42]; and when a person inspects the index of members' names, the company must inform him whether there is any alteration to the register that is not reflected in the index[43]. If a company fails to provide the information so required[44], an offence is committed by the company, and by every officer of the company who is in default[45]; and a person guilty of such an offence is liable on summary conviction to a fine not exceeding level 3 on the standard scale[46].

1 As to the register of members see PARA 336 et seq. As to the meaning of 'member' see PARA 323. As to the meaning of 'company' under the Companies Acts see PARA 21; and as to the meaning of the 'Companies Acts' see PARA 13. As to the option for a private company to keep membership information on the central register see PARA 363 et seq.

2 As to the index of members see PARA 340.

The Companies Act 2006 s 116 applies to a company which is a participating issuer as if references to the company's register of members were references to its issuer register of members and its record of uncertificated shares; and as if references in s 116 to the company's index of members' names were references to the index required to be kept by the Uncertificated Securities Regulations 2001, SI 2001/3755, reg 23(4), Sch 4 para 7 (see PARA 342): Sch 4 para 9 (amended by SI 2009/1889). References to the Companies Act 2006 in the Companies (Fees for Inspection and Copying of Company Records) Regulations 2007, SI 2007/2612, and in the Companies (Fees for Inspection of Company Records) Regulations 2008, SI 2008/3007, are to be construed accordingly: Uncertificated Securities Regulations 2001, SI 2001/3755, Sch 4 para 9 (as so amended). As to the meaning of 'issuer register of members' see PARA 341. As to the meaning of 'record of uncertificated shares' see PARA 341.

3 Companies Act 2006 s 116(1). As to the inspection of company records generally see PARA 748. As to the right conferred on any person to require a copy of the register see PARA 351.

4 Companies Act 2006 s 116(1)(a).

5 Companies Act 2006 s 116(1)(b). In the Companies Acts, 'prescribed' means prescribed (by order or by regulations) by the Secretary of State: Companies Act 2006 s 1167. As to the Secretary of State see PARA 6. As to the making of orders and regulations under the Companies Act 2006 generally see ss 1288–1292. Partly in exercise of the powers conferred by s 116(1)(b), the Secretary of State has made the Companies (Fees for Inspection and Copying of Company Records) Regulations 2007, SI 2007/2612. As to the fee prescribed for the purpose of the Companies Act 2006 s 116(1)(b) see the Companies (Fees for Inspection and Copying of Company Records) Regulations 2007, SI 2007/2612, reg 2.

The object of giving non-members a right of inspection is to enable them to ascertain what assets they may rely on: *Oakes v Turquand and Harding, Peek v Turquand and Harding, Re Overend, Gurney & Co* (1867) LR 2 HL 325 at 366 per Lord Cranworth. Cf the provision under the Companies Clauses Consolidation Act 1845 (see PARA 1892).

6 Companies Act 2006 s 116(3).

7 Companies Act 2006 s 116(4).

8 Companies Act 2006 s 116(4)(a). Any obligation under the Companies Acts to give a person's address is, unless otherwise expressly provided, to give a service address for that person: Companies Act 2006 s 1142. As to service of documents on a company generally see PARA 743.

9 Companies Act 2006 s 116(4)(b).

10 Companies Act 2006 s 116(4)(c).

11 Companies Act 2006 s 116(4)(d).

12 Companies Act 2006 s 116(4)(d)(i).

13 Companies Act 2006 s 116(4)(d)(ii).

14 Companies Act 2006 s 116(4)(d)(iii).

15 Companies Act 2006 s 117(1)(a). As to the meaning of 'working day' see PARA 140 note 16.

16 Companies Act 2006 s 117(1)(b). As to the meaning of 'the court' see PARA 160 note 12. As to the procedure that applies to proceedings under companies legislation generally see PARA 306.

17 Companies Act 2006 s 117(2).

18 Companies Act 2006 s 117(3). See *Burry & Knight Ltd v Knight* [2014] EWCA Civ 604, [2015] 1 All ER 37, [2014] 1 WLR 4046 (purpose in circulating shareholders with details of past irregularities not a proper one); applied in *Burberry Group plc v Fox-Davies* [2015] EWHC 222 (Ch), [2015] 2 BCLC 66, [2015] All ER (D) 185 (Feb).

19 Companies Act 2006 s 117(3)(a).

20 Companies Act 2006 s 117(3)(b).

21 Companies Act 2006 s 117(4).

22 See note 21.

23 Ie an application under the Companies Act 2006 s 117 (see the text and notes 15–22): see s 117(5).

24 Companies Act 2006 s 117(5).

25 Ie an inspection required under the Companies Act 2006 s 116 (see the text and notes 1–14): see s 118(1).

26 Companies Act 2006 s 118(1). As to the meaning of 'officer who is in default' see PARA 316. As to the meaning of 'officer' generally see PARA 679.

27 As to the standard scale and the powers of magistrates' courts to issue fines on summary conviction see SENTENCING vol 92 (2015) PARA 176.

28 As to the meaning of 'daily default fine' see PARA 1816.

29 Companies Act 2006 s 118(2).

30 Companies Act 2006 s 118(3). The court has discretion to refuse an application for an order requiring a company to disclose its register of members: *Pelling v Families Need Fathers Ltd* [2001] EWCA Civ 1280, [2002] 2 All ER 440, [2002] 1 BCLC 645. As to the extension of the

power of the court under the Companies Act 2006 s 118(3) where a company's issuer register of members and record of uncertificated shares is kept at the office of some person other than the company see PARAS 342 note 10, 349 note 4.

31 *Re Kent Coalfields Syndicate* [1898] 1 QB 754, CA; *Re Yorkshire Fibre Co* (1870) LR 9 Eq 650. As to winding up in general see COMPANY AND PARTNERSHIP INSOLVENCY vol 16 (2011) PARA 380 et seq.

32 *Re Joint-Stock Discount Co, Buchanan's Case* (1866) 15 LT 261; *Bevan v Webb* [1901] 2 Ch 59, CA; *Norey v Keep* [1909] 1 Ch 561.

33 Ie in a request under the Companies Act 2006 s 116 (see the text and notes 1–14): see s 119(1).

34 Companies Act 2006 s 119(1).

35 Ie the right conferred by the Companies Act 2006 s 116 (see the text and notes 1–14): see s 119(2).

36 Companies Act 2006 s 119(2)(a).

37 Companies Act 2006 s 119(2)(b).

38 Companies Act 2006 s 119(2).

39 Companies Act 2006 s 119(3)(a).

40 In relation to an offence committed after the commencement of the Companies Act 2006 s 1131 (summary proceedings) (see PARA 1818), but before a day is appointed in relation to the commencement of the Criminal Justice Act 2003 s 154(1) (general limit on magistrates' courts' power to impose imprisonment), the reference in the Companies Act 2006 s 119(3)(b) to '12 months' must be read as a reference to 'six months': see ss 119(3)(b), 1131, 1133; and see PARA 1818.

41 Companies Act 2006 s 119(3)(b). In the case of liability on summary conviction the fine is one not exceeding the statutory maximum: see s 119(30(b). By virtue of the Legal Aid, Sentencing and Punishment of Offenders Act 2012 s 85, however, where the offence is committed on or after 12 March 2015, it is punishable by a fine of an unlimited amount. As to the statutory maximum and the powers of magistrates' courts to issue fines on summary conviction see SENTENCING vol 92 (2015) PARA 176.

42 Companies Act 2006 s 120(1) (amended by the Small Business, Enterprise and Employment Act 2015 Sch 3 Pt 2 paras 3, 6). Note that this amendment operates from 6 April 2016: see the Small Business, Enterprise and Employment Act 2015 (Commencement No 3) Regulations 2015, SI 2015/2029, reg 4(a). The provisions of the Companies Act 2006 s 120 do not apply with respect to a company which is a participating issuer: Uncertificated Securities Regulations 2001, SI 2001/3755, reg 23(5) (added by SI 2009/1889). As to the meaning of 'participating issuer' see PARA 432 note 9.

43 Companies Act 2006 s 120(2). See also note 42.

44 Ie under either the Companies Act 2006 s 120(1) (see the text and note 42) or under s 120(2) (see the text and note 43): see s 120(3).

45 Companies Act 2006 s 120(3). See also note 42.

46 Companies Act 2006 s 120(4). See also note 42.

351. Copies of register of members. Any person may require a copy of a company's register of members[1], or of any part of it, on payment of such fee as may be prescribed[2]. A person seeking to exercise the right that is so conferred[3] to require a copy must make a request to the company to that effect[4]. The information that must be contained in such a request, and the action to be taken by the company on receiving it, are the same as those applicable to a request to inspect the register[5]. Failure to provide a copy of the register on such a request, otherwise than in accordance with an order of the court, is an offence[6]. The company, and every officer of the company who is in default[7], is liable if guilty of such an offence to the like penalties as for failure to permit inspection of the register[8]. In the case of any such default, the court may by order direct that the copy required be sent to the person requesting it[9].

It is an offence for a person knowingly or recklessly to make, in a request that requires a company to provide a copy of its register or any part of it[10], a statement that is misleading, false or deceptive in a material particular[11]; and it is an offence for a person in possession of information obtained by exercise of the right to require a copy of the register or any part of it to be provided[12] to do anything that results in the information being disclosed to another person[13], or to fail to do anything with the result that the information is disclosed to another person[14], knowing, or having reason to suspect, that person may use the information for a purpose that is not a proper purpose[15]. A person guilty of such an offence is liable on conviction on indictment to imprisonment for a term not exceeding two years or a fine, or to both[16]; and on summary conviction to imprisonment for a term not exceeding 12 months[17] or a fine, or to both[18].

When the company provides a person with a copy of the register, or any part of it, the company must inform him of the most recent date, if any, on which alterations were made to the register and whether there are further alterations to be made[19]. If a company fails to provide the information so required[20], an offence is committed by the company, and by every officer of the company who is in default[21]; and a person guilty of such an offence is liable on summary conviction to a fine not exceeding level 3 on the standard scale[22].

1 As to the register of members see PARA 336 et seq. As to the meaning of 'member' see PARA 323. As to the meaning of 'company' under the Companies Acts see PARA 21; and as to the meaning of the 'Companies Acts' see PARA 13. As to the option for a private company to keep membership information on the central register see PARA 363 et seq.

2 Companies Act 2006 s 116(2). As to the provision of copies of company records generally see PARA 748. As to the right conferred on members and others to inspect the register and index see PARA 350. In the Companies Acts, 'prescribed' means prescribed (by order or by regulations) by the Secretary of State: Companies Act 2006 s 1167. As to the making of orders and regulations under the Companies Act 2006 generally see ss 1288–1292. As to the Secretary of State see PARA 6. Partly in exercise of the powers conferred by s 116(2), the Secretary of State has made the Companies (Fees for Inspection and Copying of Company Records) Regulations 2007, SI 2007/2612. As to the fee prescribed for the purpose of the Companies Act 2006 s 116(2) see the Companies (Fees for Inspection and Copying of Company Records) Regulations 2007, SI 2007/2612, reg 3.

As to the application of the Companies Act 2006 ss 116–118 to a company which is a participating issuer see PARA 350 note 2.

3 Ie conferred by the Companies Act 2006 s 116 (see the text and notes 1–2): see s 116(3).

4 Companies Act 2006 s 116(3).

5 See the Companies Act 2006 ss 116(4), 117; and PARA 350.

6 See the Companies Act 2006 s 118(1).

7 As to the meaning of 'officer who is in default' see PARA 316. As to the meaning of 'officer' generally see PARA 679.

8 As to the penalties referred to in the text see the Companies Act 2006 s 118(2), (3); and PARA 350.

9 Companies Act 2006 s 118(3). The court has discretion to refuse an application for an order requiring a company to disclose its register of members: *Pelling v Families Need Fathers Ltd* [2001] EWCA Civ 1280, [2002] 2 All ER 440. As a general rule, the court will make a mandatory order to give effect to the legal right to be supplied with a copy of the register upon request, the importance of the right and the obligation of the company to give effect to it being underscored by the penalties to which the company would otherwise be exposed; but it is not a matter of unqualified right. As to mandatory orders see JUDICIAL REVIEW vol 61 (2010) PARA 703 et seq. As to the extension of the power of the court under the Companies Act 2006 s 118(3) where a company's issuer register of members and record of uncertificated shares is kept at the office of some person other than the company see PARAS 342 note 10, 349 note 4.

10 Ie in a request under the Companies Act 2006 s 116.

11 Companies Act 2006 s 119(1).

12 Ie the right conferred by the Companies Act 2006 s 116 (see the text and notes 1–2): see s 119(2).

13 Companies Act 2006 s 119(2)(a).

14 Companies Act 2006 s 119(2)(b).

15 Companies Act 2006 s 119(2).

16 Companies Act 2006 s 119(3)(a).

17 In relation to an offence committed after the commencement of the Companies Act 2006 s 1131 (summary proceedings) (see PARA 1818), but before a day is appointed in relation to the commencement of the Criminal Justice Act 2003 s 154(1) (general limit on magistrates' courts' power to impose imprisonment), the reference in the Companies Act 2006 s 119(3)(b) to '12 months' must be read as a reference to 'six months': see ss 119(3)(b), 1131, 1133; and see PARA 1818.

18 Companies Act 2006 s 119(3)(b). In the case of liability on summary conviction the fine is one not exceeding the statutory maximum: see s 119(3)(b). By virtue of the Legal Aid, Sentencing and Punishment of Offenders Act 2012 s 85, however, where the offence is committed on or after

12 March 2015, it is punishable by a fine of an unlimited amount. As to the statutory maximum and the powers of magistrates' courts to issue fines on summary conviction see SENTENCING vol 92 (2015) PARA 176.

19 Companies Act 2006 s 120(1) (amended by the Small Business, Enterprise and Employment Act 2015 Sch 3 Pt 2 paras 3, 6). See further PARA 350 note 42.

20 Ie required under the Companies Act 2006 s 120(1) (see the text and note 19): see s 120(3).

21 Companies Act 2006 s 120(3).

22 Companies Act 2006 s 120(4).

C. RECTIFICATION OF REGISTER OF MEMBERS

352. Application to court for rectification of company's register. A person aggrieved, or any member of the company[1], or the company itself, may apply to the court[2] for rectification of the register of members[3], if[4]:

(1) the name of any person is, without sufficient cause, entered in or omitted from the register[5]; or

(2) default is made, or unnecessary delay takes place, in entering on the register the fact of any person having ceased to be a member[6].

On such an application, the court may decide any question relating to the title of any person who is a party to the application to have his name entered in or omitted from the register, whether the question arises between members or alleged members, or between members or alleged members on the one hand and the company on the other hand; and generally the court may decide any question necessary or expedient to be decided for rectification of the register[7]. The court may either refuse the application, or may order rectification of the register and payment by the company of any damages sustained by any party aggrieved[8]. However, the company may be ordered to pay damages only when the register is ordered to be rectified[9]. If money has been paid on the shares, the amount will be ordered to be returned with interest at an appropriate rate[10], and the amount with costs is provable in a winding up[11].

1 As to the meaning of 'member of a company' see PARA 323. As to the meaning of 'company' under the Companies Acts see PARA 21; and as to the meaning of the 'Companies Acts' see PARA 13.

2 As to the meaning of 'the court' see PARA 160 note 12. For an example of an unmeritorious application by a member who was not affected see *Re Piccadilly Radio plc* [1989] BCLC 683 (cited in PARA 353 note 5).

3 As to the register of members see PARA 336 et seq. Rectification of the share register is a matter for the court of the country of incorporation of the company: *International Credit and Investment Co (Overseas) Ltd v Adham* [1994] 1 BCLC 66 at 78 per Harman J. See also *Re Fagin's Bookshop plc* [1992] BCLC 118. As to custody of the register see PARA 348. For instances of applications by the company itself see *Re Indo-China Steam Navigation Co* [1917] 2 Ch 100; *Re London Electrobus Co Ltd* (1906) 22 TLR 677; *Re Cleveland Trust plc* [1991] BCLC 424, [1991] BCC 33.

4 Companies Act 2006 s 125(1).

5 Companies Act 2006 s 125(1)(a). The jurisdiction of the court under this provision is not limited to cases where a name has been entered improperly but extends to cases where a name stands on the register without sufficient cause: *Re Imperial Chemical Industries Ltd* [1936] 2 All ER 463. See *Re New Cedos Engineering Co Ltd* (1975) [1994] 1 BCLC 797; *Re Transatlantic Life Assurance Co Ltd* [1979] 3 All ER 352, [1980] 1 WLR 79. There is no necessity to show any wrongdoing by the company and any question of omission by error or entry by error can be raised. The phrase 'without sufficient cause' is a requirement that the court must be shown at the hearing that there is no sufficient cause for the omission or entry, as the case may be: *Re Diamond Rock Boring Co Ltd, ex p Shaw* (1877) 2 QBD 463 at 482, CA, per Brett LJ; *Re Fagin's Bookshop plc* [1992] BCLC 118 at 123 per Harman J. There is, however, no jurisdiction to rectify on the grounds of omission if there never was an entitlement to entry in the register in the first place: *Re BTR plc* (1988) 4 BCC 45; *Re Welsh Highland Railway Light Railway Co* [1993] BCLC 338. For a case where the register had been lost, and rectification of an entirely blank new register was ordered, see *Re Data Express Ltd* (1987) Times, 27 April.

6 Companies Act 2006 s 125(1)(b). As to the power of the court to rectify the register when a company is being wound up see PARA 355; and COMPANY AND PARTNERSHIP INSOLVENCY vol 17 (2011) PARA 684 et seq. As to winding up in general see COMPANY AND PARTNERSHIP INSOLVENCY vol 16 (2011) PARA 380 et seq.

7 Companies Act 2006 s 125(3). For an example where a court granted the relief sought in respect of the rectification of the register see *Domoney v Godinho* [2004] EWHC 328 (Ch), [2004] 2 BCLC 15. It was held in *Re Hoicrest,Keene v Martin* [2000] 1 WLR 414, [2000] 1 BCLC 194, CA that the court's general discretionary power under the Companies Act 2006 s 125(3) is not limited by the scope of its jurisdiction to rectify the register of members under s 125(1) (see the text and notes 1–6); but this decision was doubted and not followed in *Nilon Ltd v Royal Westminster Investments SA* [2015] UKPC 2, [2015] 3 All ER 372, [2015] 2 BCLC 1. See also PARA 353. *Nilon Ltd v Royal Westminster Investments SA* [2015] UKPC 2, [2015] 3 All ER 372, [2015] 2 BCLC 1 does not, however, lay down a rule that a signed transfer is always essential before a register of members may be rectified; rather, it establishes that a dispute between shareholders as to the ownership of shares in equity, namely a pure contractual dispute, is not properly the subject to an application to rectify a company's share register: see *Intellimedia Technologies Ltd v Richards, Intellimedia Systems Ltd v Doyle* [2015] EWHC 1200 (Ch) at [58], [2015] All ER (D) 58 (Jun).

8 Companies Act 2006 s 125(2). Where, under s 125, the court orders rectification of the register of members of a company which is a participating issuer, it must not order the payment of any damages under s 125(2) to the extent that such rectification relates to the company's operator register of members and does not arise from an act or omission of the operator on the instructions of that company or from fraud or other wilful default, or negligence, on the part of that company: Uncertificated Securities Regulations 2001, SI 2001/3755, Sch 4 para 11 (amended by SI 2009/1889). As to the meaning of 'register of members' for these purposes see PARA 341 note 5; as to the meaning of 'participating issuer' see PARA 432 note 9; and as to the meaning of 'operator register of members' see PARA 341.

9 *Re Ottos Kopje Diamond Mines Ltd* [1893] 1 Ch 618, CA. As to the measure of damages see *Re Ottos Kopje Diamond Mines Ltd*; *Skinner v City of London Marine Insurance Corpn* (1885) 14 QBD 882, CA.

10 *Karberg's Case* [1892] 3 Ch 1, CA; *Re Metropolitan Coal Consumers' Association, Wainwright's Case* (1889) 62 LT 30 (affd (1890) 63 LT 429, CA) (no fixed rate applicable). See also *Re Railway Time Tables Publishing Co, ex p Sandys* (1889) 42 ChD 98 at 108 per Stirling J.

11 *Re British Gold Fields of West Africa* [1899] 2 Ch 7, CA.

353. General jurisdiction to rectify company's register of members. The jurisdiction to rectify a company's register of members is discretionary[1]; and it is not limited by the provisions of the Companies Act 2006[2]. Thus the court will rectify the register, apart from that Act, to enable the members of a company to have a fair and reasonable exercise of their rights[3].

When the court entertains the application, it is bound to go into all the circumstances of the case, and to consider what equity the applicant has to call for its interposition[4] and the purpose for which relief is sought[5].

The power to rectify has been exercised where there has been misrepresentation in the prospectus[6]; where it is expedient to have an order which will bind all the shareholders and effectually bar any subsequent application for restoration of a name struck out by the directors[7]; where shares have been illegally allotted at a discount[8]; where the application for shares has been made in the name of a person, as, for example, an underwriter, without his authority[9]; where there is no valid allotment of shares[10]; or the allotment is not made within a reasonable time[11], or is irregular[12]; where a transfer of shares has been improperly registered or registration has been refused[13]; where there are joint holders of shares who wish to divide the shares so held into two parts with their names entered in the register in respect of each part in a different order[14]; where the company puts on its register matters which are not required by the statute[15]; in order to set right allotments of shares which have been issued as fully paid without a proper contract being filed[16]; and where an overseas company was entered in the register without the permission of the Treasury, which was at the time required[17].

1 *Re Diamond Rock Boring Co Ltd, ex p Shaw* (1877) 2 QBD 463, CA; *Re Kimberley North Block Diamond Co, ex p Wernher* (1888) 59 LT 579, CA. Cf *Ward and Henry's Case* (1867) 2 Ch App 431 at 441 per Lord Cairns LJ; *Re Tahiti Cotton Co, ex p Sargent* (1874) LR 17 Eq 273 at 276 per Jessel MR; *Re Piccadilly Radio plc* [1989] BCLC 683 at 697 per Millett J. As to the register of members see PARA 336 et seq. As to membership of a company see PARA 323 et seq.
2 As to the provisions of the Companies Act 2006 which allow for rectification of the register see s 125; and PARA 352.
3 *Burns v Siemens Bros Dynamo Works Ltd* [1919] 1 Ch 225. Cf *Re Welsh Highland Railway Light Railway Co* [1993] BCLC 338 at 351 per Vinelott J.
4 *Trevor v Whitworth* (1887) 12 App Cas 409 at 440, HL, per Lord Macnaghten; *Re Joint Stock Discount Co, Sichell's Case* (1867) 3 Ch App 119; *Bellerby v Rowland and Marwood's Steamship Co Ltd* [1902] 2 Ch 14, CA; *Re Onward Building Society* [1891] 2 QB 463, CA; *Re Hannan's King (Browning) Gold Mining Co Ltd* (1898) 14 TLR 314, CA. By virtue of the corresponding provision in the Companies Act 1862 s 35 (repealed), the court might have made an order for rectification 'if satisfied of the justice of the case'. The words last quoted have been omitted from the later Companies Acts, but, it seems, without affecting the law. See also PARA 1268.
5 *Re Piccadilly Radio plc* [1989] BCLC 683 (shares in a radio company were transferred without obtaining the consent of the broadcasting authority as required by the articles of association; rectification was refused; the applicants had no interest in the shares and were not seeking to have their own names restored to the register but were searching for a means to disenfranchise opposition to proposals to be put to the general meeting; the broadcasting authority had not complained; the transferor did not seek rectification and the company itself did not support the application). Cf *Dempsey v Celtic Football and Athletic Co Ltd* [1993] BCC 514, Ct of Sess.
6 See PARA 1268.
7 *Re Bank of Hindustan, China and Japan, ex p Martin* (1865) 2 Hem & M 669; *Re Bank of Hindustan, China and Japan, Higgs's Case* (1865) 2 Hem & M 657; *Re Bank of Hindustan, China and Japan, ex p Los* (1865) 6 New Rep 327.
8 See PARA 1300.
9 *Re Consort Deep Level Gold Mines Ltd, ex p Stark* [1897] 1 Ch 575, CA. Cf *Re Henry Bentley & Co Ltd and Yorkshire Breweries, ex p Harrison* (1893) 69 LT 204, CA; *Hindley's Case* [1896] 2 Ch 121, CA; *Re Hannan's Empress Gold Mining and Development Co, Carmichael's Case* [1896] 2 Ch 643, CA.
10 *Re Consolidated Gold Mines, ex p Smith* (1888) 39 ChD 546 at 551 per North J; *Re Portuguese Consolidated Copper Mines Ltd* (1889) 42 ChD 160, CA. This arises eg where a director has, without his authority, been placed on the register in respect of qualification shares (*Re Printing, Telegraph and Construction Co of the Agence Havas, ex p Cammell* [1894] 2 Ch 392, CA) or where the allotment was made at an improperly constituted meeting of directors (*Re Sly, Spink & Co* [1911] 2 Ch 430).
11 *Re Bowron, Baily & Co, ex p Baily* (1868) 3 Ch App 592.
12 *Re Homer District Consolidated Gold Mines, ex p Smith* (1888) 39 ChD 546; *Re Cleveland Trust plc* [1991] BCLC 424, [1991] BCC 33 (register rectified by deletion of bonus shares after bonus issue mistakenly made); *Re Thundercrest Ltd* [1995] 1 BCLC 117 (register rectified by cancellation of allotment to two members who were also directors when the third member of the company, to their knowledge, had not received a provisional letter of allotment of those shares to him, a letter which was in any event defective as it allowed insufficient time for acceptance).
13 *Pulbrook v Richmond Consolidated Mining Co* (1878) 9 ChD 610 at 615 per Jessel MR; *Re Bahia and San Francisco Rly Co* (1868) LR 3 QB 584 (forged transfer); *Re Stranton Iron and Steel Co* (1873) LR 16 Eq 559 (transfer to increase voting power); *Re Manchester and Oldham Bank* (1885) 54 LJ Ch 926. See also *Re Tahiti Cotton Co, ex p Sargent* (1874) LR 17 Eq 273 (dispute between transferor and transferee); *Re Diamond Rock Boring Co Ltd, ex p Shaw* (1877) 2 QBD 463, CA (dispute between transferor and transferee); *Re Stockton Malleable Iron Co* (1875) 2 ChD 101 (lien); *Re Ystalyfera Gas Co* (1887) 3 TLR 321; *Re Violet Consolidated Gold Mining Co* (1899) 68 LJ Ch 535; *Re Copal Varnish Co Ltd* [1917] 2 Ch 349; *Re Imperial Chemical Industries Ltd* [1936] 2 All ER 463 (entry of name proper, but name standing on register without good cause); *Welch v Bank of England* [1955] Ch 508, [1955] 1 All ER 811 (restoration of status quo after forged transfers); *International Credit and Investment Co (Overseas) Ltd v Adham* [1994] 1 BCLC 66 (restoration of status quo; no proper share transfers were executed, merely entries made in the share register purporting to deprive the true owner of entire holding); *Re New Cedos Engineering Co Ltd* (1975) [1994] 1 BCLC 797 (on their true construction right to be

registered existed under the articles); *Stothers v William Steward (Holdings) Ltd* [1994] 2 BCLC 266, CA (directors purported to exercise their discretion to refuse registration, which power on the true construction of the articles they did not possess); *Re Claygreen Ltd, Romer-Ormiston v Claygreen Ltd* [2005] EWHC 2032 (Ch), [2006] 1 BCLC 715 (transfer provisions not triggered so claimant entitled to have register rectified and name re-entered on register). See also PARA 404.

14 *Burns v Siemens Bros Dynamo Works Ltd* [1919] 1 Ch 225. See also PARA 336 note 4.

15 *Re W Key & Son Ltd* [1902] 1 Ch 467; *Re TH Saunders & Co Ltd* [1908] 1 Ch 415.

16 *Re New Zealand Kapanga Gold Mining Co, ex p Thomas* (1873) LR 18 Eq 17n; *Re Denton Colliery Co, ex p Shaw* (1874) LR 18 Eq 16; *Re Broad Street Station Dwellings Co* [1887] WN 149; *Re Nottingham Brewery Ltd and Reduced* (1888) 4 TLR 429; *Re Maynards Ltd* [1898] 1 Ch 515; *Re Henry Lovibond & Sons (1900) Ltd* (1901) 17 TLR 315; *Re Darlington Forge Co* (1887) 34 ChD 522 (where the contract was oral).

17 *Re Transatlantic Life Assurance Co Ltd* [1979] 3 All ER 352, [1980] 1 WLR 79. As to overseas companies see PARA 2013 et seq. As to the Treasury see CONSTITUTIONAL AND ADMINISTRATIVE LAW vol 20 (2014) PARA 262 et seq.

354. Procedure on application to court for rectification of register of members. The application to the court[1] for rectification of a company's register of members[2] may be made by the person aggrieved, by any member of the company, or by the company[3]. Such an application must be made by the issue of a claim form[4]. The jurisdiction of the court is summary in nature with affidavit evidence and ought not to be invoked where there is a substantial dispute as to fact[5].

A claim may be instituted for rectification of the register[6] without any direction by the court, a course which should be followed where there is much complexity, or where other relief is required. The court will not give substantive relief by way of rectification of the register on an interim application in a claim[7], nor will it rectify the register in the absence of third parties whose rights will be affected by the rectification[8]. The application to rectify must be made promptly[9].

The proper respondents to an application to rectify the register are the company and the registered holder or holders of the shares whose registration is in question, if not the applicant[10]. It is not necessary to join other shareholders who are registered in respect of shares other than those in respect of which rectification is sought[11]. Nor is it necessary to join the directors of the company where rectification is sought unless an order for costs is sought against them[12].

The right to challenge the court's exercise of discretion to make an order for rectification must depend upon the applicant having a sufficient interest in the rectification of the share register to give it a right to do so[13].

1 As to the meaning of 'the court' see PARA 160 note 12.

2 As to the register of members see PARA 336 et seq. As to the meaning of 'member of a company' see PARA 323. As to the meaning of 'company' under the Companies Acts see PARA 21; and as to the meaning of the 'Companies Acts' see PARA 13.

3 See the Companies Act 2006 s 125(1); and PARA 352. For instances of applications by the company see *Re Indo-China Steam Navigation Co* [1917] 2 Ch 100; *Re London Electrobus Co Ltd* (1906) 22 TLR 677; *Re Cleveland Trust plc* [1991] BCLC 424, [1991] BCC 33.

4 As to the procedure that applies to proceedings under companies legislation generally see PARA 306.

5 *Nilon Ltd v Royal Westminster Investments SA* [2015] UKPC 2, [2015] 3 All ER 372, [2015] 2 BCLC 1. See also *Re National and Provincial Marine Insurance Co, ex p Parker* (1867) 2 Ch App 685; *Simpson's Case* (1869) LR 9 Eq 91; *Stewart's Case* (1866) 1 Ch App 574 at 585; *Re Gresham Life Assurance Society, ex p Penney* (1872) 8 Ch App 446 at 448; *Askew's Case* (1874) 9 Ch App 664; *Re Bagnall & Co, ex p Dick* (1875) 32 LT 536; *Re Greater Britain Insurance Corpn Ltd, ex p Brockdorff* (1920) 124 LT 194, CA; *Re Greater Britain Products Development Corpn Ltd* (1924) 40 TLR 488. in such a case, the court will look to actively manage the dispute by making appropriate directions rather than simply striking out the application for rectification: *Re Hoicrest,Keene v Martin* [2000] 1 WLR 414, [2000] 1 BCLC 194, CA (doubted on other grounds in *Nilon Ltd v Royal Westminster Investments SA* [2015] UKPC 2, [2015] 3 All ER 372, [2015] 2 BCLC 1).

6 *Bloxam v Metropolitan Cab and Carriage Co* (1864) 4 New Rep 51; *Roots v Williamson* (1888) 38 ChD 485; *Moore v North Western Bank* [1891] 2 Ch 599; *Lynde v Anglo-Italian Hemp Spinning Co* [1896] 1 Ch 178; *McKeown v Boudard-Peveril Gear Co* (1896) 65 LJ Ch 735, CA.

7 *Siemens Bros & Co Ltd v Burns* [1918] 2 Ch 324 at 338 per Swinfen Eady MR.

8 *Re Greater Britain Insurance Corpn Ltd, ex p Brockdorff* (1920) 124 LT 194, CA.

9 *Sewells's Case* (1868) 3 Ch App 131 at 138 per Lord Cairns LJ; *Re Isis Factors plc, Dulai v Isis Factors plc* [2003] EWHC 1653 (Ch), [2003] 2 BCLC 411 (application refused because applicant had failed to act for seven years and third party had purchased what it believed to be the company's entire share capital in ignorance of the applicant's claim to a large number of shares).

10 *Morgan v Morgan Insurance Brokers Ltd* [1993] BCLC 676 at 678 per Millett J.

11 See *Morgan v Morgan Insurance Brokers Ltd* [1993] BCLC 676.

12 In *Morgan v Morgan Insurance Brokers Ltd* [1993] BCLC 676, it was held to be unjust to order the company to pay costs where rectification was sought by a shareholder owning three-quarters of the shares following a bona fide but improper refusal by the directors to register a transfer; but an order for costs was made against the directors personally. Cf *Re Keith Prowse & Co Ltd* [1918] 1 Ch 487; *Re Copal Varnish Co Ltd* [1917] 2 Ch 349 at 355 per Eve J. See also *Re Fisher* [1894] 1 Ch 450, CA; the Senior Courts Act 1981 s 51(1); and CIVIL PROCEDURE vol 12A (2015) PARA 1707.

13 *Re New Millennium Experience Co Ltd, Greenwich Millennium Exhibition Ltd v New Millennium Experience Co Ltd* [2003] EWHC 1823 (Ch), [2004] 1 All ER 687, [2004] 1 BCLC 19 (there was a distinction between a person who might be affected by something and in a loose sense, 'interested', and a person with a legitimate interest in a matter, such as to require that person to be given notice and be heard); *Re Joint Stock Discount Co, Sichell's Case* (1867) 3 Ch App 119.

355. Rectification of register of members after winding up. Notwithstanding that the winding up of a company has commenced[1], the court has power to rectify the register of members[2] under the statutory power[3]. However, a strong case must be made out[4]. When giving directions as to the distribution of surplus assets in a winding up, the court may treat as members those who would be entitled to have their names placed on the register without insisting on the formality of an application to rectify the register[5].

1 As to winding up in general see COMPANY AND PARTNERSHIP INSOLVENCY vol 16 (2011) PARA 380 et seq.

2 As to the register of members see PARA 336 et seq.

3 Ie under the Companies Act 2006 s 125(1) (as to which see PARA 352), as applied in winding up by the Insolvency Act 1986 s 148(1) (as to which see COMPANY AND PARTNERSHIP INSOLVENCY vol 17 (2011) PARA 678): see *Re Joint Stock Discount Co, Sichell's Case* (1867) 3 Ch App 119 at 122 per Lord Cairns LJ; *Re Sussex Brick Co* [1904] 1 Ch 598, CA; *Re New Millennium Experience Co Ltd, Greenwich Millennium Exhibition Ltd v New Millennium Experience Co Ltd* [2003] EWHC 1823 (Ch), [2004] 1 All ER 687, [2004] 1 BCLC 19; and COMPANY AND PARTNERSHIP INSOLVENCY vol 17 (2011) PARA 684.

4 *Re Onward Building Society* [1891] 2 QB 463, CA. See further COMPANY AND PARTNERSHIP INSOLVENCY vol 17 (2011) PARA 684 et seq.

5 See *Re Baku Consolidated Oilfields Ltd* [1994] 1 BCLC 173 (liquidator sought directions under the Insolvency Act 1986 s 112 as to the distribution of funds to the members of a company, the assets of which had been seized by the Soviet government in 1920 and in respect of which compensation was paid by the Soviet authorities in 1990; the share register was necessarily incomplete, not having been maintained since 1920).

356. Order for rectification of register of members. In the case of a company[1] required by the Companies Act 2006[2] to send a list of its members[3] to the registrar of companies[4], the court[5], when making an order for rectification of the register of members[6], must by its order direct notice of the rectification to be given to the registrar[7].

Where the court orders the register to be rectified by removing a name from it, the name should not be erased, but a line should be drawn through it, and an abstract of the order signed by the secretary of the company should be added[8].

Where a company does not rectify the register pursuant to an order of the court, the court may direct that the person by whom the order was obtained or some other person appointed by the court may do so[9]. In ordering rectification, the court has power to fix a particular date at which the registration will become operative, even to the extent of making it retrospective; but subject, if necessary, to conditions protecting the rights of third persons[10].

1 As to the meaning of 'company' under the Companies Acts see PARA 21; and as to the meaning of the 'Companies Acts' see PARA 13.
2 As to such a requirement see eg the Companies Act 2006 s 856A (repealed subject to transitional provisions); and PARA 1596.
3 As to the meaning of 'member of a company' see PARA 323.
4 As to the meaning of 'registrar of companies' see PARA 126 note 2. As to the delivery of documents to the registrar see PARA 136; and as to the requirements generally for the proper delivery of documents to the registrar see PARA 137.
5 As to the meaning of 'the court' see PARA 160 note 12.
6 Ie under the Companies Act 2006 s 125(2): see PARA 352. As to the register of members see PARA 336 et seq.
7 Companies Act 2006 s 125(4).
8 *Re Iron Ship Building Co* (1865) 34 Beav 597.
9 See CPR 70.2A(2); and CIVIL PROCEDURE vol 12A (2015) PARA 1298. As to the position where the company by reason of resignations had no directors or secretary to carry out the original order of the court see *Re LL Syndicate Ltd* (1901) 17 TLR 711; *Re Manihot Rubber Plantations Ltd* (1919) 63 Sol Jo 827.
10 *Re Sussex Brick Co* [1904] 1 Ch 598, CA; *Re New Millennium Experience Co Ltd, Greenwich Millennium Exhibition Ltd v New Millennium Experience Co Ltd* [2003] EWHC 1823 (Ch), [2004] 1 All ER 687, [2004] 1 BCLC 19.

357. Rectification of register of members by directors. The directors of a company[1] may rectify the register of members[2] without any application to the court[3], if there is no dispute, and the circumstances are such that the court would order rectification[4]; but ordinarily the protection of the court's order is essential to any rectification by the removal of the name of a registered holder of shares[5].

1 As to a company's directors see PARA 512 et seq.
2 As to the register of members see PARA 336 et seq. As to membership of a company see PARA 323 et seq.
3 As to rectification by the court see PARA 352.
4 *Re London and Mediterranean Bank, Wright's Case* (1871) 7 Ch App 55; *Reese River Silver Mining Co v Smith* (1869) LR 4 HL 64 at 74 per Lord Hatherley LC; *Hartley's Case* (1875) 10 Ch App 157; *Smith v Brown* [1896] AC 614 at 622, PC; *First National Reinsurance Co Ltd v Greenfield* [1921] 2 KB 260 at 279 per McCardie J.
5 *Re Derham and Allen Ltd* [1946] Ch 31 at 36 per Cohen J.

358. Rectification of issuer and operator register of securities. A participating issuer[1] must not rectify an issuer register of securities[2] if such rectification would also require the rectification of an operator register of securities[3] unless the rectification of an issuer register of securities is effected either with the consent of the operator or by order of a court in the United Kingdom[4]. A participating issuer who rectifies an issuer register of securities in order to give effect to an order of a court in the United Kingdom must immediately give the operator written notification of the change to the entry, if any rectification of the operator register of securities may also be required, unless the change to the issuer register is made in response to an operator-instruction[5].

An operator who rectifies an operator register of securities must immediately generate an operator-instruction to inform the relevant participating issuer of the change to the entry, unless the change is made in response to an issuer-instruction[6], and must generate an operator-instruction to inform the system-members[7] concerned of the change to the entry[8].

1 As to the meaning of 'participating issuer' see PARA 432 note 9.
2 As to the meaning of 'issuer register of securities' see PARA 433 note 20.

3 Uncertificated Securities Regulations 2001, SI 2001/3755, reg 25(1). As to the meaning of 'operator register of securities' see PARA 432 note 3; and as to the meaning of 'operator' see PARA 432 note 1. A default in complying with, or a contravention of, reg 25(1) is actionable at the suit of a person who suffers loss as a result of the default or contravention, or who is otherwise adversely affected by it, subject to the defences and other incidents applying to claims for breach of statutory duty: reg 46(1). However, this does not affect the liability which any person may incur, nor affect any right which any person may have, apart from reg 46(1): reg 46(2).
4 Uncertificated Securities Regulations 2001, SI 2001/3755, reg 25(2). As to the meaning of 'United Kingdom' see PARA 1 note 5.
5 Uncertificated Securities Regulations 2001, SI 2001/3755, reg 25(3). As to the meaning of 'operator-instruction' see PARA 432 note 1.
6 Uncertificated Securities Regulations 2001, SI 2001/3755, reg 25(4)(a). As to the meaning of 'issuer-instruction' see PARA 434 note 6.
7 As to the meaning of 'system-member' see PARA 433 note 9.
8 Uncertificated Securities Regulations 2001, SI 2001/3755, reg 25(4)(b).

D. OVERSEAS BRANCH REGISTER AND REGISTERS IN FOREIGN COUNTRIES

359. Overseas branch register of members. A company[1] having a share capital[2] may, if it transacts business in any part of Her Majesty's dominions[3] outside the United Kingdom[4], the Channel Islands, the Isle of Man, or certain other overseas countries and territories[5], cause to be kept there a branch register of members[6] resident in that country or territory (an 'overseas branch register')[7]. As from 30 June 2016[8], however, this right to keep an overseas branch register does not apply during or with respect to any period when an election to keep membership information on the central register[9] is in force in respect of the company[10].

The Secretary of State[11] may make provision by regulations[12] as to the circumstances in which a company is to be regarded as keeping a register in a particular country or territory[13].

A company that begins to keep an overseas branch register must give notice to the registrar of companies[14] within 14 days of doing so, stating the country or territory in which the register is kept[15]. If default is made in complying with this requirement to give notice, an offence is committed by the company and by every officer of the company who is in default[16]; and any person guilty of such an offence is liable on summary conviction to a fine not exceeding level 3 on the standard scale[17] and for continued contravention to a daily default fine[18] not exceeding one-tenth of level 3 on the standard scale[19].

An overseas branch register is regarded as part of the company's register of members (the 'main register')[20].

1 As to the meaning of 'company' under the Companies Acts see PARA 21; and as to the meaning of the 'Companies Acts' see PARA 13.
2 As to the meanings of 'share capital' and 'company having a share capital' see PARA 1231.
3 As to the meaning of 'Her Majesty's dominions' see COMMONWEALTH vol 13 (2009) PARA 707.
4 As to the meaning of 'United Kingdom' see PARA 1 note 5.
5 The Companies Act 2006 Pt 8 Ch 3 (ss 129–135) (see also PARA 360 et seq) applies to a company which transacts business not only in any part of Her Majesty's dominions outside the United Kingdom, the Channel Islands and the Isle of Man, but also in the following countries or territories: Bangladesh, Cyprus, Dominica, the Gambia, Ghana, Guyana, The Hong Kong Special Administrative Region of the People's Republic of China, India, Ireland, Kenya, Kiribati, Lesotho, Malawi, Malaysia, Malta, Nigeria, Pakistan, Seychelles, Sierra Leone, Singapore, South Africa, Sri Lanka, Swaziland, Trinidad and Tobago, Uganda and Zimbabwe: see s 129(1), (2).
6 As to the general duty under the Companies Act 2006 to keep a register of company members see PARA 336 et seq. As to membership of a company see PARA 323 et seq.
7 Companies Act 2006 s 129(1), (2). As to the keeping of the overseas branch register see PARA 360. Under the Companies (Consolidation) Act 1908 s 34(1) (repealed), the corresponding provision in that Act, the register was called the colonial register. References to a colonial register occurring in articles registered before 1 November 1929 (ie the date on which the consolidating act, the Companies Act 1929 (repealed), came into force) are to be read, unless the context otherwise requires, as a reference to an overseas branch register kept under the Companies Act 2006 s 129

(s 129(5)(b)). Under the Companies Act 1948 s 119 (repealed) such a register was called a dominion register. Accordingly, references in any Act or instrument (including, in particular, a company's articles) to a company's dominion register is to be read, unless the context otherwise requires, as a reference to an overseas branch register kept under the Companies Act 2006 s 129 (s 129(5)(a)). As to the meaning of references to a company's 'articles' see PARA 227 note 2. As to a company's articles of association generally see PARA 227 et seq. As to predecessor legislation from which the Companies Act 2006 is derived see PARA 10 et seq. As to the form of company records, their inspection and the duty to take precautions against their falsification see PARAS 746–748.

8 See the Small Business, Enterprise and Employment Act 2015 (Commencement No 4, Transitional and Savings Provisions) Regulations 2016, SI 2016/321, reg 6(c).

9 Ie an election under the Companies Act 2006 s 128B: see PARA 364.

10 Companies Act 2006 s 129(6) (added by the Small Business, Enterprise and Employment Act 2015 Sch 5 Pt 1 paras 1, 4).

11 As to the Secretary of State see PARA 6 et seq.

12 As to the making of regulations under the Companies Act 2006 generally see ss 1288–1292. Regulations under s 129 are subject to negative resolution procedure (ie the statutory instrument containing the regulations is subject to annulment in pursuance of a resolution of either House of Parliament): see ss 129(4), 1289. At the date at which this volume states the law, no such regulations had been made.

13 Companies Act 2006 s 129(3). See also note 12.

14 As to the meaning of 'registrar of companies' see PARA 126 note 2. As to the delivery of documents to the registrar see PARA 136; and as to the requirements for the proper delivery of documents to the registrar see PARA 137.

15 Companies Act 2006 s 130(1).

16 Companies Act 2006 s 130(2). As to the meaning of 'officer who is in default' see PARA 316. As to the meaning of 'officer' generally see PARA 679.

17 As to the standard scale and the powers of magistrates' courts to issue fines on summary conviction see SENTENCING vol 92 (2015) PARA 176.

18 As to the meaning of 'daily default fine' see PARA 1816.

19 Companies Act 2006 s 130(3).

20 Companies Act 2006 s 131(1).

360. How the overseas branch register is kept. The Secretary of State[1] may make provision by regulations[2] modifying any provision of the Companies Act 2006, so far as it relates to the main register of members[3], as it applies in relation to an overseas branch register[4]. Subject to the provisions of the Companies Act 2006, a company[5] may by its articles[6] make such provision as it thinks fit as to the keeping of overseas branch registers[7]. A competent court in a country or territory where an overseas branch register is kept may exercise the same jurisdiction as is exercisable by a court[8] in the United Kingdom[9] either:

(1) to rectify a register of members[10]; or
(2) in relation to a request for inspection of, or a copy of, the register[11];

and the offences of:

(a) refusing inspection of, or failing to provide a copy of, the register[12]; and
(b) making a false, misleading or deceptive statement in a request for inspection or a copy[13],

may be prosecuted summarily before any tribunal having summary criminal jurisdiction in the country or territory where the register is kept[14].

A company that keeps an overseas branch register must keep available for inspection either the register[15], or a duplicate of the register duly entered up from time to time[16], at the place in the United Kingdom where the company's main register is kept available for inspection[17]. If default is made in complying with this requirement to keep the overseas branch register (or a duplicate) available for inspection in the United Kingdom, an offence is committed by the company and by every officer of the company who is in default[18]; and any person guilty of such an offence is liable on summary conviction to a fine not exceeding level 3 on the standard scale[19] and for continued contravention to a daily default fine[20] not exceeding one-tenth of level 3 on the standard scale[21].

Shares[22] registered in an overseas branch register must be distinguished from the shares registered in the main register[23]; and no transaction with respect to any shares registered in an overseas branch register may be registered in any other register[24].

1 As to the Secretary of State see PARA 6 et seq.
2 As to the making of regulations under the Companies Act 2006 generally see ss 1288–1292. Regulations under s 131 are subject to negative resolution procedure (ie the statutory instrument containing the regulations is subject to annulment in pursuance of a resolution of either House of Parliament): see ss 131(3), 1289. At the date at which this volume states the law, no such regulations had been made.
3 Ie modifying any provision of the Companies Act 2006 Pt 8 Ch 2 (ss 113–128) (see PARA 336 et seq): s 131(2). As to the meaning of the 'main register' see PARA 359. As to the general duty under the Companies Act 2006 to keep a register of company members see PARA 336 et seq; and as to the option to keep membership information on the central register instead see PARA 363 et seq. As to membership of a company see PARA 323 et seq.
4 Companies Act 2006 s 131(2). See also note 2. As to the meaning of 'overseas branch register' see PARA 359.
5 As to the meaning of 'company' under the Companies Acts see PARA 21; and as to the meaning of the 'Companies Acts' see PARA 13.
6 As to the meaning of references to a company's 'articles' see PARA 227 note 2. As to a company's articles of association generally see PARA 227 et seq.
7 Companies Act 2006 s 131(4).
8 As to the meaning of 'the court' see PARA 160 note 12.
9 Companies Act 2006 s 134(1). As to the meaning of 'United Kingdom' see PARA 1 note 5. As to how far Acts of Parliament of the United Kingdom extend to dominions as part of their law otherwise than by consent see COMMONWEALTH vol 13 (2009) PARA 867 et seq. As to the application of the provisions which govern overseas branch registers to other countries see PARA 359 text and notes 1–7. The Companies Act 2006 s 134 extends only to those countries and territories to which the Companies Act 1985 s 362(1), Sch 14 Pt II para 3 (repealed), which made similar provision, extended immediately before 1 October 2009 (ie immediately before the coming into force of the Companies Act 2006 Pt 8 Ch 3 (ss 129–135) (see also PARAS 359, 361–161): see the Companies Act 2006 (Commencement No 8, Transitional Provisions and Savings) Order 2008, SI 2008/2860, art 3(h)): Companies Act 2006 s 134(3). The Companies Act 1985 Sch 14 Pt II para 3 (repealed) provided for the extension of jurisdiction to apply only to those countries and territories where, immediately before 1 July 1985 (ie the date of the coming into force of the Companies Act 1985), provision to the same effect made under the corresponding provision of the Companies Act 1948 s 120(2) (repealed), had effect as part of the local law: see the Companies Act 1985 Sch 14 Pt II para 3(2) (repealed). The Companies Act 1948 ss 119–121 (repealed) applied in relation to the Republic of South Africa (see the South Africa Act 1962 s 2(1), Sch 2para4(1) (Sch 2 para 4 now substituted by SI 1986/1035)) and the whole of Malaysia (see the Companies Registers (Malaysia) Order 1964, SI 1964/911, made under the Federation of Malaya Independence Act 1957 s 2(3); and the Malaysia Act 1963 s 4(1)) as if they were parts of Her Majesty's dominions and to Pakistan as if it had not withdrawn from the Commonwealth and as if the Pakistan (Consequential Provisions) Act 1956 had not been repealed (see the Pakistan Act 1973 s 4(1), Sch 3 para 3(1) (repealed)). Such a register was under the Companies Act 1948 known as a dominion register: see s 119(1) (repealed); and PARA 359 note 7.

These statutory provisions might also apply to Kenya, Malawi, Swaziland, Zanzibar and Tanzania (formerly Tanganyika). The first four named countries were the subject matter of an Order in Council dated 26 October 1931, SR & O 1931/931, which applied the Companies Act 1929 ss 103–105 (repealed) and, if it was in force on 1 July 1948, was continued in force as if made under the Companies Act 1948: see s 459(2) (repealed). The provisions were applied to Tanganyika by the Tanganyika (Companies Dominion Register) Order in Council 1951, SI 1951/752. Both these orders were made under, or under provisions corresponding to, the Companies Act 1948 s 122 (repealed) (see PARA 10) and under the Foreign Jurisdiction Act 1890. The countries concerned all became part of the Commonwealth, and, when this happened, they were no longer such countries as are referred to in the Companies Act 1948 s 122 (repealed), more especially as they then became part of Her Majesty's dominions to which ss 119–121 (repealed) applied automatically. These orders would then presumably have lapsed, and would not automatically revive when these countries ceased to be part of Her Majesty's dominions and became independent under the Kenya Independence Act 1963, the Malawi Republic Act 1966, the Swaziland Independence Act 1968, the Zanzibar Act 1963 and the Tanganyika Independence Act 1961 respectively.

A further order made under provisions corresponding to the Companies Act 1948 s 122 (repealed), the Aden Protectorate (Application of Acts) Order 1938, SR & O 1938/1603, applied these provisions in relation to the Aden Protectorate. This order was not revoked, but is considered spent, having been overtaken by events.

The Companies Act 1948 s 122 (repealed) was applied to Pakistan: see the Pakistan Act 1973 s 4(1), Sch 3 para 3(1) (repealed).

Where a register of members of a company is kept in Bangladesh, it is not to be treated as improperly kept by reason only that, at any time after 3 February 1972 and before 1 September 1974, it included members resident in Pakistan: see the Bangladesh Act 1973 Schedule para 10(1).

10 Companies Act 2006 s 134(1)(a). Head (1) in the text refers to rectification of the register by the court under s 125 (see PARA 352 et seq): see s 134(1)(a). See also note 9.

11 Companies Act 2006 s 134(1)(b). Head (2) in the text refers to requests for inspection of, or a copy of, the registers under s 117 (see PARAS 350–351): see s 134(1)(b). See also note 9.

12 Companies Act 2006 s 134(2)(a). Head (a) in the text refers to the offence of refusing inspection of, or failing to provide a copy of, the register under s 118 (see PARA 350): see s 134(2)(a). See also note 9.

13 Companies Act 2006 s 134(2)(b). Head (b) in the text refers to the offence of making a false, misleading or deceptive statement in a request for inspection or a copy under s 119 (see PARA 350): see s 134(2)(b). See also note 9.

14 Companies Act 2006 s 134(2). See also note 9.

15 Companies Act 2006 s 132(1)(a).

16 Companies Act 2006 s 132(1)(b). Any such duplicate is treated for all purposes of the Companies Act 2006 as part of the main register: s 132(2).

17 Companies Act 2006 s 132(1). As to the custody and inspection of the main register and index see PARA 348 et seq.

18 Companies Act 2006 s 132(3). As to the meaning of 'officer who is in default' see PARA 316. As to the meaning of 'officer' generally see PARA 679.

19 As to the powers of magistrates' courts to issue fines on summary conviction see SENTENCING vol 92 (2015) PARA 176.

20 As to the meaning of 'daily default fine' see PARA 1816.

21 Companies Act 2006 s 132(4).

22 As to the meaning of 'share' see PARA 1231.

23 Companies Act 2006 s 133(1).

24 Companies Act 2006 s 133(2). As to transfers of shares see PARA 361.

361. Transfers of shares registered in overseas branch register. An instrument of transfer of a share[1] registered in an overseas branch register[2] is regarded as a transfer of property situated outside the United Kingdom[3] and is, unless executed in a part of the United Kingdom, exempt from stamp duty[4].

1 As to the meaning of 'share' see PARA 1231.

2 As to the meaning of 'overseas branch register' see PARA 359.

3 Companies Act 2006 s 133(3)(a). As to the meaning of 'United Kingdom' see PARA 1 note 5.

4 Companies Act 2006 s 133(3)(b).

362. Ceasing to keep overseas branch register. A company[1] may discontinue an overseas branch register[2]. If it does so, all the entries in that register must be transferred either to some other overseas branch register kept in the same country or territory[3], or to the main register[4].

The company must give notice to the registrar of companies[5] within 14 days of the discontinuance[6]. If default is made in complying with this requirement to give notice, an offence is committed by the company and by every officer of the company who is in default[7].

1 As to the meaning of 'company' under the Companies Acts see PARA 21; and as to the meaning of the 'Companies Acts' see PARA 13.

2 Companies Act 2006 s 135(1). As to the meaning of 'overseas branch register' see PARA 359.

3 Companies Act 2006 s 135(2)(a). As to the countries or territories to which Pt 8 Ch 3 (ss 129–135) (see also PARA 359 et seq) applies see PARA 359 note 5.

4 Companies Act 2006 s 135(2)(b). As to the meaning of the 'main register' see PARA 359. As to the option to keep membership information on the central register instead of the main membership register see PARA 363 et seq.

5 As to the meaning of 'registrar of companies' see PARA 126 note 2. As to the delivery of documents to the registrar see PARA 136; and as to the requirements for the proper delivery of documents to the registrar see PARA 137.

6 Companies Act 2006 s 135(3). A company that begins to keep an overseas branch register must give notice to the registrar of companies stating the country or territory in which the register is kept: see s 130(1); and PARA 359. As to the application of this provision to other countries see PARA 359 text and notes 1–7.

7 Companies Act 2006 s 135(4). As to the meaning of 'officer who is in default' see PARA 316. As to the meaning of 'officer' generally see PARA 679.

Any person guilty of such an offence is liable on summary conviction to a fine not exceeding level 3 on the standard scale and for continued contravention to a daily default fine not exceeding one-tenth of level 3 on the standard scale: s 135(5). As to the standard scale and the powers of magistrates' courts to issue fines on summary conviction see SENTENCING vol 92 (2015) PARA 176; and as to the meaning of 'daily default fine' see PARA 1816.

E. OPTION TO KEEP MEMBERS' INFORMATION ON CENTRAL REGISTER

363. Option for private companies to keep members' information on central register and power to extend option to public companies. As from 30 June 2016[1], the relevant provisions of the Companies Act 2006[2] have effect to set out rules allowing private companies[3] to keep information on the register kept by the registrar of companies[4] ('the central register') instead of entering it in their register of members[5]. The Secretary of State[6] may by regulations[7] amend the Companies Act 2006 to extend those rules[8], with or without modification, to public companies[9] or public companies of a class specified in the regulations, and to make such other amendments as he thinks fit in consequence of that extension[10].

1 See the Small Business, Enterprise and Employment Act 2015 (Commencement No 4, Transitional and Savings Provisions) Regulations 2016, SI 2016/321, reg 6(c).

2 Ie the Companies Act 2006 Pt 8 Ch 2A (ss 128A–128K): see the text and notes 3–10; and PARA 364 et seq.

3 As to the meaning of 'private company' see PARA 95.

4 As to the meaning of 'registrar of companies' see PARA 126 note 2. As to the meaning of 'company' under the Companies Acts see PARA 21. As to the central register see PARA 142 et seq.

5 Companies Act 2006 s 128A(1), (2) (ss 128A, 128K added by the Small Business, Enterprise and Employment Act 2015 Sch 5 Pt 1 paras 1, 3).

6 As to the Secretary of State see PARA 6.

7 Regulations so made are subject to affirmative resolution procedure (ie the regulations must not be made unless a draft of the statutory instrument containing them has been laid before Parliament and approved by a resolution of each House of Parliament): see the Companies Act 2006 s 128K(2) (as added: see note 5), s 1290. As to the making of regulations under the Companies Act 2006 generally see ss 1288–1292.

8 Ie to extend the Companies Act 2006 Pt 8 Ch 2A (ss 128A–128J).

9 As to the meaning of 'public company' see PARA 95.

10 Companies Act 2006 s 128K(2) (as added: see note 5).

364. Right to make an election that members' information be kept on central register. As from 30 June 2016[1], the following provisions have effect.

An election may be made[2] by giving notice of it to the registrar of companies[3] under these provisions[4]:

(1) by the subscribers wishing to form a private company[5] under the Companies Act 2006[6]; or

(2) by the private company itself once it is formed and registered[7].

In the latter case, the election is of no effect unless, before it is made:

(a) all the members of the company have assented to the making of the election[8]; and

(b) any overseas branch registers that the company was keeping[9] have been discontinued and all the entries in those registers transferred[10] to the company's register of members[11].

If the notice is given by subscribers wishing to form a private company:

(i) it must be given when the registration documents required to be delivered[12] are delivered to the registrar[13]; and

(ii) it must be accompanied by a statement containing all the information that would be required, in the absence of the notice, to be entered in the company's register of members on incorporation of the company, and is not otherwise included in the documents delivered as described in head (a) above[14].

If the notice is given by the company, it must be accompanied by:

(A) a statement by the company:

 (I) that all the members of the company have assented to the making of the election[15]; and

 (II) if the company was keeping any overseas branch registers, that all such registers have been discontinued and all the entries in them transferred[16] to the company's register of members[17];

(B) a statement containing all the information that is required to be contained in the company's register of members as at the date of the notice in respect of matters that are current[18] as at that date[19].

The company must where necessary update the statement sent under head (B) above to ensure that the final version delivered to the registrar contains all the information that is required to be contained in the company's register of members as at the time immediately before the election takes effect[20] in respect of matters that are current as at that time[21]. This obligation to update the statement includes an obligation to rectify it, where necessary, in consequence of the company's register of members being rectified, whether before or after the election takes effect[22]. If default is made in complying with the obligation to update the statement sent under head (B) above, an offence is committed by the company, and by every officer of the company[23] who is in default[24].

Once notice of such an election is registered by the registrar[25], the election remains in force until either the company ceases to be a private company[26], or a notice of withdrawal sent by the company[27] is registered by the registrar, whichever occurs first[28].

1 See the Small Business, Enterprise and Employment Act 2015 (Commencement No 4, Transitional and Savings Provisions) Regulations 2016, SI 2016/321, reg 6(c).
2 Ie under the Companies Act 2006 s 126B: see the text and notes 3–27.
3 As to the meaning of 'registrar of companies' see PARA 126 note 2. As to the meaning of 'company' under the Companies Acts see PARA 21.
4 See the Companies Act 2006 s 128B(3) (ss 128B, 128C added by the Small Business, Enterprise and Employment Act 2015 Sch 5 Pt 1 paras 1, 3).
5 As to the meaning of 'private company' see PARA 95. As to the Secretary of State's power to extend the right to make such an election to public companies see PARA 363.
6 Companies Act 2006 s 128B(1)(a) (as added: see note 4). As to the formation of a company under the Companies Act 2006 see PARA 95 et seq.
7 Companies Act 2006 s 128B(1)(b) (as added: see note 4).
8 Companies Act 2006 s 128B(2)(a) (as added: see note 4). As to the members of a company see PARA 323 et seq.
9 Ie under the Companies Act 2006 Pt 8 Ch 3 (ss 129–135): see PARA 359 et seq.
10 Ie in accordance with the Companies Act 2006 s 135: see PARA 362.
11 Companies Act 2006 s 128B(2)(b) (as added: see note 4).
12 Ie the documents required to be delivered under the Companies Act 2006 s 9: see PARA 104.
13 Companies Act 2006 s 128B(4)(a) (as added: see note 4).

14 Companies Act 2006 s 128B(4)(b) (as added: see note 4).
15 Companies Act 2006 s 128B(5)(a)(i) (as added: see note 4).
16 See note 10.
17 Companies Act 2006 s 128B(5)(a)(ii) (as added: see note 4).
18 For these purposes, a reference to matters that are current as at a given date or time is a reference to persons who are members of the company as at that date or time, and to any other matters that are current as at that date or time: Companies Act 2006 s 128B(10) (as added: see note 4).
19 Companies Act 2006 s 128B(5)(b) (as added: see note 4). The Companies Act 2006 s 128H(1) (central register as evidence: see PARA 369) does not apply to information to be included in a statement under s 128B(5)(b): see PARA 369 note 2.
20 An election made under the Companies Act 2006 s 128B takes effect when the notice of election is registered by the registrar: s 128C(1) (as added: see note 4).
21 Companies Act 2006 s 128B(6) (as added: see note 4). The Companies Act 2006 s 128H(1) (central register as evidence: see PARA 369) does not apply to information to be included in any updated statement under s 128B(6): see PARA 369 note 2.
22 Companies Act 2006 s 128B(7) (as added: see note 4).
23 For this purpose a shadow director is treated as an officer of the company: Companies Act 2006 s 128B(8) (as added: see note 4). As to the meaning of 'shadow director' see PARA 513. As to the meaning of 'officer' generally under the Companies Act 2006 see PARA 679; and as to the meaning of 'officer in default' see PARA 316.
24 Companies Act 2006 s 128B(8) (as added: see note 4). A person guilty of such an offence is liable on summary conviction to a fine not exceeding level 3 on the standard scale and, for continued contravention, to a daily default fine not exceeding one-tenth of level 3 on the standard scale: s 128B(9) (as so added). As to the standard scale and the powers of magistrates' courts to issue fines on summary conviction see SENTENCING vol 92 (2015) PARA 176; and as to the meaning of 'daily default fine' see PARA 1816.
25 See the Companies Act 2006 s 128C(1), cited in note 20.
26 See, however, note 5.
27 Ie under the Companies Act 2006 s 128J: see PARA 371.
28 Companies Act 2006 s 128C(2) (as added: see note 4).

365. Effect of election that members' information be kept on central register on obligations with regard to register of members. As from 30 June 2016[1], the following provisions have effect. The effect of an election that members' information be kept on the central register[2] on a company's obligations with regard to a register of members[3] is as follows[4].

The company's obligation to maintain a register of members does not apply with respect to the period when the election is in force[5]. This means that, during that period:

(1) the company must continue to keep a register of members[6] (a 'historic' register) containing all the information that was required to be stated in that register as at the time immediately before the election took effect[7]; but
(2) the company does not have to update that register to reflect any changes that occur after that time[8];

and this applies to the index of members[9], if the company is obliged to keep an index of members, as it applies to the register of members[10].

The provisions of the Companies Act 2006 with regard to the register of members[11], including the rights to inspect or require copies of the register and to inspect the index, continue to apply to the historic register and, if applicable, the historic index during the period when the election is in force[12]. The company must place a note in its historic register:

(a) stating that an election is in force[13];
(b) recording when that election took effect[14]; and
(c) indicating that up-to-date information about its members is available for public inspection on the central register[15].

If a company makes default in complying with these requirements[16], an offence is committed by the company, and by every officer of the company who is in default[17].

The above obligations with respect to a historic register and historic index do not apply in a case where the election was made by subscribers wishing to form a private company[18].

1 See the Small Business, Enterprise and Employment Act 2015 (Commencement No 4, Transitional and Savings Provisions) Regulations 2016, SI 2016/321, reg 6(c).
2 Ie an election under the Companies Act 2006 s 128B: see PARA 364.
3 Ie its obligations under the Companies Act 2006 Pt 8 Sch 2 (ss 113–128): see PARA 336 et seq.
4 Companies Act 2006 s 128D(1) (s 128D (ss 126B, 126C added by the Small Business, Enterprise and Employment Act 2015 Sch 5 Pt 1 paras 1, 3).
5 Companies Act 2006 s 128D(2) (as added: see note 4). As to when an election is in force see PARA 364 text and notes 20, 28–31.
6 Ie in accordance with the Companies Act 2006 Pt 8 Sch 2.
7 Companies Act 2006 s 128D(3)(a) (as added: see note 4). As to when the election took effect see PARA 364 note 20.
8 Companies Act 2006 s 128D(3)(b) (as added: see note 4).
9 As to the index of members see PARA 340.
10 Companies Act 2006 s 128D(4) (as added: see note 4).
11 Ie the Companies Act 2006 Pt 8 Sch 2.
12 Companies Act 2006 s 128D(5) (as added: see note 4). See also note 5.
13 Ie an election under the Companies Act 2006 s 128B (see PARA 364): see s 128D(6)(a) (as added: see note 4).
14 Companies Act 2006 s 128D(6)(b) (as added: see note 4).
15 Companies Act 2006 s 128D(6)(c) (as added: see note 4). As to the meaning of 'the central register' see PARA 363; and as to that register see PARA 142 et seq.
16 Ie in complying with the Companies Act 2006 s 128D(6): see the text and notes 13–15.
17 Companies Act 2006 s 113(7) (s 113(7), (8) applied for these purposes by s 128D(7) (as added: see note 4)). As to the meaning of 'officer who is in default' see PARA 316. As to the meaning of 'officer' generally see PARA 679.

A person guilty of such an offence is liable on summary conviction to a fine not exceeding level 3 on the standard scale and for continued contravention to a daily default fine not exceeding one-tenth of level 3 on the standard scale: s 113(8) (as so applied). As to the standard scale and the powers of magistrates' courts to issue fines on summary conviction see SENTENCING vol 92 (2015) PARA 176; and as to the meaning of 'daily default fine' see PARA 1816.
18 Companies Act 2006 s 128D(8) (as added: see note 4).

366. Duty to notify registrar of companies of changes to membership information. As from 30 June 2016[1], the following provisions have effect.

During the period when an election that members' information be kept on the central register[2] is in force[3], the company[4] must deliver to the registrar of companies[5] any relevant information[6] that the company would during that period have been obliged[7] to enter in its register of members[8], had the election not been in force[9]. The relevant information must be delivered as soon as reasonably practicable after the company becomes aware of it and, in any event, no later than the time by which the company would have been required to enter the information in its register of members[10].

If default is made in complying with these provisions, an offence is committed by the company, and by every officer of the company[11] who is in default[12].

1 See the Small Business, Enterprise and Employment Act 2015 (Commencement No 4, Transitional and Savings Provisions) Regulations 2016, SI 2016/321, reg 6(c).
2 Ie an election under the Companies Act 2006 s 128B: see PARA 364. As to the meaning of 'the central register' see PARA 363; and as to that register see PARA 142 et seq.
3 As to when an election is in force see PARA 364 text and notes 20, 28–31.
4 As to the meaning of 'company' under the Companies Acts see PARA 21.
5 As to the meaning of 'registrar of companies' see PARA 126 note 2.

6 For these purposes, 'relevant information' means information other than the following (Companies Act 2006 s 128E(3) (s 128E added by the Small Business, Enterprise and Employment Act 2015 Sch 5 Pt 1 paras 1, 3)), ie:
(1) the date mentioned in the Companies Act 2006 113(2)(b) (date when person registered as member: see PARA 336);
(2) the date mentioned in s 123(3)(b) (date when membership of limited company increases from one to two or more members: see PARA 337); and
(3) the dates mentioned in the following provisions, but only in cases where the date to be recorded in the central register is to be the date on which the document containing information of the relevant change is registered by the registrar:
(a) s 113(2)(c) (date when person ceases to be member: see PARA 336);
(b) s 123(2)(b) (date when company becomes single member company: see PARA 337).

In a case of the kind described in head (3) above, the company must, when it delivers information under s 128E(2) of the relevant change, indicate to the registrar that, in accordance with s 1081(1A) (see PARA 143), the date to be recorded in the central register is to be the date on which the document containing that information is registered by the registrar: s 128E(5) (as so added).

7 Ie under the Companies Act 2006.
8 As to the register of members see PARA 336 et seq.
9 Companies Act 2006 s 128E(1), (2) (as added: see note 6).
10 Companies Act 2006 s 128E(4) (as added: see note 6).
11 For this purpose a shadow director is treated as an officer of the company: Companies Act 2006 s 128E(6) (as added: see note 6). As to the meaning of 'officer' generally see PARA 679.
12 Companies Act 2006 s 128E(6) (as added: see note 6). As to the meaning of 'officer who is in default' see PARA 316. See also note 11.

A person guilty of such an offence is liable on summary conviction to a fine not exceeding level 3 on the standard scale and for continued contravention to a daily default fine not exceeding one-tenth of level 3 on the standard scale: s 128E(7) (as so added). As to the standard scale and the powers of magistrates' courts to issue fines on summary conviction see SENTENCING vol 92 (2015) PARA 176; and as to the meaning of 'daily default fine' see PARA 1816.

367. Court's power to order company to remedy default or delay with regard to membership information. As from 30 June 2016[1], the following provisions apply if:

(1) the name of a person is without sufficient cause included in, or omitted from, information that a company delivers to the registrar of companies[2] concerning its members[3]; or
(2) default is made or unnecessary delay takes place in informing the registrar[4] of:
(a) the name of a person who is to be a member of the company[5]; or
(b) the fact that a person has ceased or is to cease to be a member of the company[6].

The person aggrieved, or any member of the company, or the company, may apply to the court[7] for an order:

(i) requiring the company to deliver to the registrar the information, or statements, necessary to rectify the position[8]; and
(ii) where applicable, requiring the registrar to record[9] the date determined by the court[10].

The court may either refuse the application or may make the order and order the company to pay any damages sustained by any party aggrieved[11]. On such an application the court may decide:

(A) any question relating to the title of a person who is a party to the application to have the person's name included in or omitted from information delivered to the registrar[12] about the company's members, whether the question arises between members or alleged members, or between members or alleged members on the one hand and the company on the other hand[13]; and

(B) any question necessary or expedient to be decided for rectifying the position[14].

Nothing in these provisions, however, affects a person's rights under the provisions of the Companies Act 2006 regarding rectification of the register on application to the registrar[15] or under a court order[16].

1 See the Small Business, Enterprise and Employment Act 2015 (Commencement No 4, Transitional and Savings Provisions) Regulations 2016, SI 2016/321, reg 6(c).
2 Ie under the Companies Act 2006 Pt 8 Ch 2A (ss 128A–128K): see PARAS 363 et seq, 368 et seq. As to the meaning of 'registrar of companies' see PARA 126 note 2. As to the meaning of 'company' under the Companies Acts see PARA 21.
3 Companies Act 2006 s 128G(1)(a) (s 128G added by the Small Business, Enterprise and Employment Act 2015 Sch 5 Pt 1 paras 1, 3).
4 See note 2.
5 Companies Act 2006 s 128G(1)(b)(i) (as added: see note 3). As to who is a member of a company see PARA 323 et seq.
6 Companies Act 2006 s 128G(1)(b)(ii) (as added: see note 3).
7 As to the meaning of 'the court' see PARA 160 note 12.
8 Companies Act 2006 s 128G(2)(a) (as added: see note 3).
9 Ie under the Companies Act 2006 s 1081(1A): see PARA 143.
10 Companies Act 2006 s 128G(2)(b) (as added: see note 3).
11 Companies Act 2006 s 128G(3) (as added: see note 3).
12 See note 2.
13 Companies Act 2006 s 128G(4)(a) (as added: see note 3).
14 Companies Act 2006 s 128G(4)(b) (as added: see note 3).
15 Ie under the Companies Act 2006 s 1095: see PARA 158.
16 Companies Act 2006 s 128G(5) (as added: see note 3). The reference in the text is to rectification under a court order under s 1096 (see PARA 161): see s 128G(5) (as so added).

368. Time limits for claims arising from delivery to registrar of company of membership information. As from 30 June 2016[1], the following provisions have effect.

Liability incurred by a company[2] from the delivery to the registrar of companies[3] of membership information[4] or from a failure to deliver any such information is not enforceable more than ten years after the date on which the information was delivered or, as the case may be, the failure first occurred[5]. This is without prejudice to any lesser period of limitation[6].

1 See the Small Business, Enterprise and Employment Act 2015 (Commencement No 4, Transitional and Savings Provisions) Regulations 2016, SI 2016/321, reg 6(c).
2 As to the meaning of 'company' under the Companies Acts see PARA 21.
3 As to the meaning of 'registrar of companies' see PARA 126 note 2.
4 Ie information under the Companies Act 2006 Pt 8 Ch 2A (ss 128A–128K): see PARAS 363 et seq, 369 et seq.
5 See the Companies Act 2006 s 128I(1) (s 128I added by the Small Business, Enterprise and Employment Act 2015 Sch 5 Pt 1 paras 1, 3).
6 Companies Act 2006 s 128I(2) (as added: see note 5). As to limitation periods generally see LIMITATION PERIODS vol 68 (2008) PARA 901 et seq.

369. Central register to be evidence of certain matters concerning membership. As from 30 June 2016[1], the following provisions have effect.

Subject to certain exceptions[2], the central register[3] is prima facie evidence of any matters about which a company[4] is required to deliver information to the registrar of companies[5] under the provisions of the Companies Act 2006[6] setting out rules allowing private companies[7] to keep information on that register instead of entering it in their register of members[8].

1 See the Small Business, Enterprise and Employment Act 2015 (Commencement No 4, Transitional and Savings Provisions) Regulations 2016, SI 2016/321, reg 6(c).

2 The Companies Act 2006 s 128H(1) (see the text and notes 3–8) does not apply to information to be included in a statement under s 128B(5)(b) (see PARA 364) or in any updated statement under s 128B(6) (see PARA 364): s 128H(2) (s 128H added by the Small Business, Enterprise and Employment Act 2015 Sch 5 Pt 1 paras 1, 3).
3 As to the meaning of 'the central register' see PARA 363; and as to that register see PARA 142 et seq.
4 As to the meaning of 'company' under the Companies Acts see PARA 21.
5 As to the meaning of 'registrar of companies' see PARA 126 note 2.
6 Ie under the Companies Act 2006 Pt 8 Ch 2A (ss 128A–128K): see PARAS 363 et seq, 370–371.
7 As to the meaning of 'private company' see PARA 95. As to the Secretary of State's power to extend the right to make an election under the Companies Act 2006 Pt 8 Ch 2A to public companies see PARA 363.
8 Companies Act 2006 s 128H(1) (as added: see note 2).

370. Information as to state of central register. As from 30 June 2016[1], the following provisions have effect.

When a person inspects or requests a copy of material on the central register[2] relating to a company[3] in respect of which an election to keep membership information on that register[4] is in force, the person may ask the company to confirm that all information that the company is required to deliver to the registrar of companies[5] under the relevant statutory provisions[6] has been delivered[7]. If a company fails to respond to such a request, an offence is committed by the company, and by every officer of the company who is in default[8].

1 See the Small Business, Enterprise and Employment Act 2015 (Commencement No 4, Transitional and Savings Provisions) Regulations 2016, SI 2016/321, reg 6(c).
2 As to the meaning of 'the central register' see PARA 363; and as to that register see PARA 142 et seq.
3 As to the meaning of 'company' under the Companies Acts see PARA 21.
4 Ie an election under the Companies Act 2006 s 128B: see PARA 364.
5 As to the meaning of 'registrar of companies' see PARA 126 note 2.
6 Ie under the Companies Act 2006 Pt 8 Ch 2A (ss 128A–128K): see PARAS 363 et seq, 371.
7 See the Companies Act 2006 s 128F(1) (s 128F added by the Small Business, Enterprise and Employment Act 2015 Sch 5 Pt 1 paras 1, 3).
8 Companies Act 2006 s 128F(2) (as added: see note 7). As to the meaning of 'officer who is in default' see PARA 316. As to the meaning of 'officer' generally see PARA 679.
A person guilty of such an offence is liable on summary conviction to a fine not exceeding level 3 on the standard scale: s 128F(3) (as so added). As to the standard scale and the powers of magistrates' courts to issue fines on summary conviction see SENTENCING vol 92 (2015) PARA 176.

371. Withdrawing the election to keep membership information on central register. As from 30 June 2016[1], the following provisions have effect.

A company[2] may withdraw an election to keep membership information on the central register made[3] by or in respect of it[4].

Withdrawal is achieved by giving notice of withdrawal to the registrar of companies[5] and the withdrawal takes effect when the notice is registered by the registrar[6].

The effect of withdrawal is that the company's obligation[7] to maintain a register of members applies from then on with respect to the period going forward[8]. This means that, when the withdrawal takes effect:

(1) the company must enter in its register of members all the information that is required to be contained in that register in respect of matters that are current[9] as at that time[10];
(2) the company must also retain in its register all the information that it was required[11] to keep in a historic register while the election was in force[12]; but

(3) the company is not required to enter in its register information relating to the period when the election was in force that is no longer current[13].

The company must place a note in its register of members:

(a) stating that the election[14] has been withdrawn[15];

(b) recording when that withdrawal took effect[16]; and

(c) indicating that information about its members relating to the period when the election was in force that is no longer current is available for public inspection on the central register[17].

If a company makes default in complying with these requirements[18], an offence is committed by the company, and by every officer of the company who is in default[19].

1 See the Small Business, Enterprise and Employment Act 2015 (Commencement No 4, Transitional and Savings Provisions) Regulations 2016, SI 2016/321, reg 6(c).

2 As to the meaning of 'company' under the Companies Acts see PARA 21.

3 Ie an election made under the Companies Act 2006 s 128B: see PARA 364.

4 Companies Act 2006 s 128J(1) (s 128J added by the Small Business, Enterprise and Employment Act 2015 Sch 5 Pt 1 paras 1, 3).

5 Companies Act 2006 s 128J(2) (as added: see note 4).

6 Companies Act 2006 s 128J(3) (as added: see note 4).

7 Ie under the Companies Act 2006 Pt 8 Ch 2 (ss 113–128): see PARA 336 et seq.

8 Companies Act 2006 s 128J(4) (as added: see note 4).

9 As to the meaning of 'matters that are current' see PARA 364 note 18.

10 Companies Act 2006 s 128J(5)(a) (as added: see note 4).

11 Ie under the Companies Act 2006 s 128D(3)(a): see PARA 365.

12 Companies Act 2006 s 128J(5)(b) (as added: see note 4).

13 Companies Act 2006 s 128J(5)(c) (as added: see note 4).

14 Ie the election under the Companies Act 2006 s 128B: see PARA 364.

15 Companies Act 2006 s 128J(6)(a) (as added: see note 4).

16 Companies Act 2006 s 128J(6)(b) (as added: see note 4).

17 Companies Act 2006 s 128J(6)(c) (as added: see note 4).

18 Ie in complying with the Companies Act 2006 s 128J(6): see s 128J(7) (as added: see note 4).

19 Companies Act 2006 s 113(7) (s 113(7), (8) applied for these purposes by s 128J(7) (as added: see note 4). As to the meaning of 'officer who is in default' see PARA 316. As to the meaning of 'officer' generally see PARA 679.

A person guilty of such an offence is liable on summary conviction to a fine not exceeding level 3 on the standard scale and for continued contravention to a daily default fine not exceeding one-tenth of level 3 on the standard scale: s 113(8) (as so applied). As to the standard scale and the powers of magistrates' courts to issue fines on summary conviction see SENTENCING vol 92 (2015) PARA 176; and as to the meaning of 'daily default fine' see PARA 1816.

(v) Liability of Members of Company

372. Liability of members of company: in general. Merely as such, members of a company[1] are not liable to anyone except on a winding up to the extent and manner provided by the Insolvency Act 1986[2].

A past member is not liable to contribute (that is, he is not liable as a 'contributory'[3]) if he has ceased to be a member for one year or more before the commencement of the winding up[4]; nor is he liable to contribute in respect of any debt or liability of the company contracted after he ceased to be a member[5]; nor unless it appears to the court that the existing members are unable to satisfy their required contributions[6]. In the case of a company limited by shares[7], no contribution is required from any member exceeding the amount, if any, unpaid on the shares in respect of which he is liable as a present or past member[8].

1 As to who qualifies as a member of a company see PARA 323.

2 See COMPANY AND PARTNERSHIP INSOLVENCY vol 17 (2011) PARAS 661–701. As to winding up in general see COMPANY AND PARTNERSHIP INSOLVENCY vol 16 (2011) PARA 380 et seq.

3 As to the meaning of 'contributory' see COMPANY AND PARTNERSHIP INSOLVENCY vol 17 (2011) PARA 661. As to the meaning of 'contributory' under the Companies Acts see PARA 109 note 10.
4 See the Insolvency Act 1986 s 74(2)(a); and COMPANY AND PARTNERSHIP INSOLVENCY vol 17 (2011) PARA 663.
5 See the Insolvency Act 1986 s 74(2)(b); and COMPANY AND PARTNERSHIP INSOLVENCY vol 17 (2011) PARA 663.
6 See the Insolvency Act 1986 s 74(2)(c); and COMPANY AND PARTNERSHIP INSOLVENCY vol 17 (2011) PARA 663. As to possible liability to contribute if the member has had shares which have been purchased or redeemed by the company see PARA 376.
7 As to companies limited by shares generally see PARA 71.
8 See the Insolvency Act 1986 s 74(2)(d); and COMPANY AND PARTNERSHIP INSOLVENCY vol 17 (2011) PARA 663.

373. Liability of members of unlimited company. Where a company which is being wound up[1] is registered[2] as unlimited[3], the liability of each past and present member[4] extends to the whole amount of the company's debts and liabilities, and the expenses of its winding up[5], subject to a right of contribution from the other solvent members ('contributories')[6]. With regard to any policy of insurance or other contract, the liability of individual members may, however, by the terms of the policy or contract be restricted, or the funds of the company alone made liable[7]. If an unlimited company has a share capital[8], the liability on the shares may be defined by its articles of association[9]. The liability on the shares[10], if any, is the only liability which may be enforced by the company whilst it is carrying on business[11], although there is then an unlimited liability to creditors[12].

1 As to winding up in general see COMPANY AND PARTNERSHIP INSOLVENCY vol 16 (2011) PARA 380 et seq.
2 As to company registration under the Companies Act 2006 generally see PARA 104 et seq.
3 As to unlimited companies generally see PARA 74.
4 As to who qualifies as a member of a company generally see PARA 323.
5 See the Insolvency Act 1986 s 74(1); and COMPANY AND PARTNERSHIP INSOLVENCY vol 17 (2011) PARA 662. See also *Re Mayfair Property Co, Bartlett v Mayfair Property Co* [1898] 2 Ch 28 at 36, CA, per Lindley MR. This is a liability which neither the company nor its directors may dispose of to the prejudice of the creditors: *Re Mayfair Property Co* 1898] 2 Ch 28, CA.
6 See the Insolvency Act 1986 s 74(1); and COMPANY AND PARTNERSHIP INSOLVENCY vol 17 (2011) PARA 662. As to the meaning of 'contributory' see COMPANY AND PARTNERSHIP INSOLVENCY vol 17 (2011) PARA 661. The right of contribution arises under the ordinary law of partnership, except so far as controlled by the company's constitution: *Robinson's Executor's Case* (1856) 6 De GM & G 572 at 588, CA, per Lord Cranworth LC. As to the meaning of references to a company's constitution under the Companies Act 2006 see PARA 226.
7 See the Insolvency Act 1986 s 74(2)(e); and COMPANY AND PARTNERSHIP INSOLVENCY vol 17 (2011) PARA 663.
8 As to a company's share capital see PARA 1231.
9 As to a company's articles of association generally see PARA 227 et seq.
10 As to the nature of shares see PARA 1244.
11 As to the meaning of 'carry on business' generally see PARA 1 note 1.
12 *Re Mayfair Property Co, Bartlett v Mayfair Property Co* [1898] 2 Ch 28, CA.

374. Liability of members where company is limited by guarantee. In the case of a company limited by guarantee[1] being wound up[2], if the company is without a share capital[3], no contribution is required from any member[4] exceeding the amount undertaken to be contributed by him to the company's assets in the event of its being wound up[5]. The statement of guarantee required to be delivered in the case of a company that is to be limited by guarantee[6] must state that each member undertakes that, if the company is wound up while he is a member, or within one year after he ceases to be a member, he will contribute to the assets of the company such amount as may be required for:

(1) payment of the debts and liabilities of the company contracted before he ceases to be a member[7];
(2) payment of the costs, charges and expenses of winding up[8]; and
(3) adjustment of the rights of the contributories among themselves[9],

not exceeding a specified amount[10]. If the company has a share capital[11], every member of it is liable (in addition to the amount so undertaken to be contributed to the assets), to contribute to the extent of any sums unpaid on any shares[12] held by him[13]; and he may further under the articles of association[14], as regards his fellow members, incur an additional liability, which in the event of winding up must be enforced by bringing proceedings[15].

A past member is not liable to contribute if he has ceased to be a member for one year or more before the commencement of the winding up[16]; nor is he liable to contribute in respect of any debt or liability of the company contracted after he ceased to be a member[17]; nor unless it appears to the court that the existing members are unable to satisfy their required contributions[18].

1 As to companies limited by guarantee generally see PARAS 72–73.
2 As to winding up in general see COMPANY AND PARTNERSHIP INSOLVENCY vol 16 (2011) PARA 380 et seq.
3 As to a company's share capital see PARA 1231.
4 As to who qualifies as a member of a company generally see PARA 323.
5 See the Insolvency Act 1986 s 74(3); and COMPANY AND PARTNERSHIP INSOLVENCY vol 17 (2011) PARA 673.
6 See the Companies Act 2006 s 11(1); and PARA 109. As to the meaning of 'company' under the Companies Acts see PARA 21; and as to the meaning of the 'Companies Acts' see PARA 13.
7 See the Companies Act 2006 s 11(3)(a); and PARA 109.
8 See the Companies Act 2006 s 11(3)(b); and PARA 109.
9 See the Companies Act 2006 s 11(3)(c); and PARA 109. As to the meaning of 'contributory' under the Companies Acts see PARA 109 note 10.
10 See the Companies Act 2006 s 11(3); and PARA 109.
11 With effect from 22 December 1980 (ie the date on which the corresponding provisions of the Companies Act 1980 (now repealed) came into force) a company cannot be formed as, or become, a company limited by guarantee with a share capital: see the Companies Act 2006 s 5(1), (2)(a); and PARA 72. As to the Companies Act 1980 generally see PARA 10.
12 As to the nature of shares see PARA 1244.
13 See the Insolvency Act 1986 s 74(3); and COMPANY AND PARTNERSHIP INSOLVENCY vol 17 (2011) PARA 673.
14 As to a company's articles of association generally see PARA 227 et seq. Provision similar to that made by heads (1)–(3) in the text is made by the model articles which have been made for the purposes of the Companies Act 2006 and intended for adoption by private companies limited by guarantee (see the Companies (Model Articles) Regulations 2008, SI 2008/3229, reg 3, Sch 2; and PARA 227 et seq). Under those model articles, the liability of each member is limited to £1, being the amount that each member undertakes to contribute to the assets of the company in the event of its being wound up while he is a member or within one year after he ceases to be a member, for payment of the company's debts and liabilities contracted before he ceases to be a member, payment of the costs, charges and expenses of winding up, and adjustment of the rights of the contributories among themselves: see Sch 2 art 2.
15 See COMPANY AND PARTNERSHIP INSOLVENCY vol 17 (2011) PARA 673.
16 See the Insolvency Act 1986 s 74(2)(a); and COMPANY AND PARTNERSHIP INSOLVENCY vol 17 (2011) PARA 663.
17 See the Insolvency Act 1986 s 74(2)(b); and COMPANY AND PARTNERSHIP INSOLVENCY vol 17 (2011) PARA 663.
18 See the Insolvency Act 1986 s 74(2)(c); and COMPANY AND PARTNERSHIP INSOLVENCY vol 17 (2011) PARA 663. As to possible liability to contribute if the member has had shares which have been purchased or redeemed by the company see PARA 376.

375. Liability of members where company is limited by shares. Save that a past member[1] of a company being wound up, which was at some former time registered as unlimited[2] but which has re-registered as a limited company[3], who was a member of the company at the time of re-registration, is liable to contribute to the assets of the company in respect of its debts and liabilities contracted before that time if a winding up commences within three years of such re-registration[4], the liability of a past or present member of a company limited by shares[5] is limited to the amount, if any, unpaid on the shares in respect of which he is liable as a present or past member[6]. A company's articles of association[7] may, however, impose a further liability on him in relation to other members[8]. Except where the articles otherwise provide, or by the terms of some special contract, there is no liability to pay for shares even in the case of signatories to the memorandum of association[9], except in pursuance of calls duly made in accordance with the articles[10], while the company is a going concern[11], or of calls duly made in the winding up of the company[12].

The liability of a past member can arise only if a winding up supervenes within 12 months of his ceasing to be a member[13], and he is not liable to contribute in respect of any debt or liability of the company contracted after he ceased to be a member[14]. Nor is he liable to contribute unless it appears to the court that the existing members are unable to satisfy the required contributions[15].

A person cannot become a member of a company in a representative capacity so as to be free from personal liability in respect of his shares[16]; but a trustee shareholder is entitled to be indemnified out of the trust estate if the shares are an investment authorised by the trust instrument or by statute[17], and he is entitled to be indemnified by a beneficial owner who is sui juris, whether such owner created the trust or accepted a transfer of the beneficial ownership[18].

1 As to who qualifies as a member of a company generally see PARA 323.

2 As to unlimited companies see PARA 74.

3 As to applications to re-register an unlimited company as a private limited company see PARA 178 et seq. As to private companies and limited companies generally see PARA 65 et seq.

4 See the Insolvency Act 1986 s 77(2); and COMPANY AND PARTNERSHIP INSOLVENCY vol 17 (2011) PARA 664.

5 As to companies limited by shares generally see PARA 71.

6 See the Insolvency Act 1986 s 74(2)(d); and COMPANY AND PARTNERSHIP INSOLVENCY vol 17 (2011) PARA 663. Thus a shareholder in an English company carrying on business in a country where shareholders are liable for all the debts of the company cannot be made liable beyond the amount remaining payable on his shares unless he had assented to being made so liable: *Risdon Iron and Locomotive Works v Furness* [1906] 1 KB 49, CA. As to shares generally see PARA 1231 et seq.

7 As to a company's articles of association generally see PARA 227 et seq.

8 See COMPANY AND PARTNERSHIP INSOLVENCY vol 17 (2011) PARA 673. Provision similar to that made in the text and notes 5–6, ie that the liability of the members is limited to the amount, if any, unpaid on the shares held by them, is made by the model articles which have been made for the purposes of the Companies Act 2006 and intended for adoption by private companies limited by shares (see the Companies (Model Articles) Regulations 2008, SI 2008/3229, Sch 1 art 2 (private company limited by shares), Sch 3 art 2 (public company). As to the model articles generally see PARA 227 et seq. As to public companies generally see PARA 66 et seq.

9 As to a company's memorandum of association generally see PARA 97 et seq.

10 *Alexander v Automatic Telephone Co* [1900] 2 Ch 56, CA; *Nicol's Case, Tufnell and Ponsonby's Case* (1885) 29 ChD 421, CA.

11 See PARA 1301 et seq.

12 See COMPANY AND PARTNERSHIP INSOLVENCY vol 17 (2011) PARA 691 et seq.

13 See the Insolvency Act 1986 s 74(2)(a); and COMPANY AND PARTNERSHIP INSOLVENCY vol 17 (2011) PARA 663. See also *Re Premier Underwriting Association Ltd* [1913] 2 Ch 29.

14 See the Insolvency Act 1986 s 74(2)(b); and COMPANY AND PARTNERSHIP INSOLVENCY vol 17 (2011) PARA 663.

15 See the Insolvency Act 1986 s 74(2)(c); and COMPANY AND PARTNERSHIP INSOLVENCY vol 17 (2011) PARA 663. As to possible liability to contribute if the member has had shares which have been purchased or redeemed by the company see PARA 376.

16 *Re Leeds Banking Co, Fearnside and Dean's Case, Dobson's Case* (1866) 1 Ch App 231. See *Buchan's Case* (1879) 4 App Cas 549, HL (where the liability was unlimited); and PARA 445.

17 As to authorised investments and a trustee's implied indemnity see TRUSTS AND POWERS vol 98 (2013) PARA 446 et seq.

18 *Hardoon v Belilios* [1901] AC 118, PC. See the cases cited in PARA 344 note 10. The liability to indemnify the trustee will not be limited by the fact that the trustee is incapable of meeting the liability on the shares: *Liverpool Mortgage Insurance Co's Case* [1914] 2 Ch 617, CA; *British Union and National Insurance Co v Rawson* [1916] 2 Ch 476, CA.

376. Liability of persons whose shares have been redeemed or purchased by company. Where a company is being wound up[1] and it has made a payment out of capital in respect of the redemption or purchase of any of its own shares[2] (the 'relevant payment')[3] and the aggregate amount of the company's assets and the amounts paid by way of contribution to its assets, apart from these provisions, are not sufficient for payment of its debts and liabilities, and the expenses of the winding up[4], and if the winding up commenced[5] within one year of the date on which the relevant payment was made, then[6]:

(1) the person from whom the shares were redeemed or purchased[7]; and
(2) the directors[8] who signed the statement that is required[9] for the purposes of the redemption or purchase, except a director who shows that he had reasonable grounds for forming the opinion set out in the statement[10],

are, so as to enable that insufficiency to be met, liable to contribute to the company's assets[11]. A person from whom any of the shares were so redeemed or purchased is liable to contribute an amount not exceeding so much of the relevant payment as was made by the company in respect of his shares; and the directors are jointly and severally liable with that person to contribute that amount[12]. A person who has contributed any amount to the assets in pursuance of these provisions may apply to the court for an order directing any other person jointly and severally liable in respect of that amount to pay him such amount as the court thinks just and equitable[13].

1 As to winding up in general see COMPANY AND PARTNERSHIP INSOLVENCY vol 17 (2011) PARA 380 et seq.

2 Ie under the Companies Act 2006 Pt 18 Ch 5 (ss 709–723) (acquisition by limited company of its own shares; redemption or purchase by private company out of capital) (see PARA 1431 et seq): see the Insolvency Act 1986 s 76(1)(a); and COMPANY AND PARTNERSHIP INSOLVENCY vol 17 (2011) PARA 671.

3 See the Insolvency Act 1986 s 76(1)(a); and COMPANY AND PARTNERSHIP INSOLVENCY vol 17 (2011) PARA 671.

4 See the Insolvency Act 1986 s 76(1)(b); and COMPANY AND PARTNERSHIP INSOLVENCY vol 17 (2011) PARA 671.

5 As to the commencement of the winding up see COMPANY AND PARTNERSHIP INSOLVENCY vol 16 (2011) PARA 439.

6 See the Insolvency Act 1986 s 76(2); and COMPANY AND PARTNERSHIP INSOLVENCY vol 17 (2011) PARA 671.

7 See the Insolvency Act 1986 s 76(2)(a); and COMPANY AND PARTNERSHIP INSOLVENCY vol 17 (2011) PARA 671.

8 As to a company's directors see PARA 512 et seq.

9 Ie under the Companies Act 2006 s 714(1) (see PARA 1433): see the Insolvency Act 1986 s 76(2)(b); and COMPANY AND PARTNERSHIP INSOLVENCY vol 17 (2011) PARA 671.

10 See the Insolvency Act 1986 s 76(2)(b); and COMPANY AND PARTNERSHIP INSOLVENCY vol 17 (2011) PARA 671.

11 See the Insolvency Act 1986 s 76(2); and COMPANY AND PARTNERSHIP INSOLVENCY vol 17 (2011) PARA 671.

12 See the Insolvency Act 1986 s 76(3); and COMPANY AND PARTNERSHIP INSOLVENCY vol 17 (2011) PARA 671.

13 See the Insolvency Act 1986 s 76(4); and COMPANY AND PARTNERSHIP INSOLVENCY vol 17 (2011) PARA 671. Section 74 (see COMPANY AND PARTNERSHIP INSOLVENCY vol 17 (2011) PARA 662 et seq) and s 75 (see COMPANY AND PARTNERSHIP INSOLVENCY vol 17 (2011) PARA 675) do not apply in relation to liability accruing by virtue of s 76: see s 76(5); and COMPANY AND PARTNERSHIP INSOLVENCY vol 17 (2011) PARA 671.

377. Effect of alterations of articles as to members' liability. A company[1] may amend its articles of association[2] by special resolution[3].

However, a member of a company[4] is not bound by any such alteration to its articles after the date on which he became a member[5], if and so far as the alteration either:

(1) requires him to take or subscribe for more shares[6] than the number held by him at the date on which the alteration is made[7]; or

(2) in any way increases his liability as at that date to contribute to the company's share capital[8] or otherwise to pay money to the company[9].

1 As to the meaning of 'company' under the Companies Acts see PARA 21; and as to the meaning of the 'Companies Acts' see PARA 13.

2 As to the meaning of references to a company's 'articles' see PARA 227 note 2. As to a company's articles of association generally see PARA 227 et seq. Amendment might be subject to certain conditions being met if the articles in question are 'entrenched provisions': see PARA 232. As to alterations to a company's articles that are required to be made when the company alters it status by means of re-registration see PARA 167 et seq.

3 See the Companies Act 2006 s 21(1); and PARA 231. As to the meaning of 'special resolution' see PARA 686. A special resolution is not required where the sole purpose of the amendment is to remove provision authorising the company to issue share warrants: see the Small Business, Enterprise and Employment Act 2015 s 85; and PARA 231. The registrar of companies must be sent a copy of the amended articles (see PARA 235); and he has power to issue a notice to comply where a company has failed to observe the procedural requirements with respect to amended articles (see PARA 236). See also PARA 140.

4 As to the meaning of 'member of a company' see PARA 323.

5 Ie except where the member agrees in writing, either before or after the alteration is made, to be bound by the alteration: see the Companies Act 2006 s 25(2).

6 As to the meaning of 'share' see PARA 1231.

7 Companies Act 2006 s 25(1)(a).

8 As to the meanings of 'company having a share capital' and 'share capital' see PARA 1231.

9 Companies Act 2006 s 25(1)(b).

(vi) Exercise of Members' Rights

A. MEMBERS' RIGHTS: IN GENERAL

378. Rights of members of company generally. The rights of a member of a 'company'[1], as that word is defined for the purposes of the Companies Acts[2], are:

(1) statutory;

(2) given by the company's constitution[3];

(3) given by the general law, more particularly such rules as relate to contracts[4] and members of corporations[5].

A shareholder[6] seeking to enforce an individual right against the company is not entitled to an advance order for an indemnity as to costs[7].

1 As to who qualifies as a member of a company see PARA 323.

2 As to the meaning of 'company' under the Companies Acts see PARA 21; and as to the meaning of the 'Companies Acts' see PARA 13.

3 As to the meaning of references to a company's constitution for the purposes of the Companies Act 2006 see PARA 226.

4 See generally CONTRACT vol 22 (2012) PARA 201 et seq.

5 See generally CORPORATIONS vol 24 (2012) PARA 301 et seq.

6 As to shareholders and membership of companies generally see PARAS 323 et seq, 1889 et seq.

7 *Re a Company (No 005136 of 1986)* [1987] BCLC 82. The principle of *Wallersteiner v Moir (No 2)* [1975] QB 373, [1975] 1 All ER 849, CA, is confined to derivative claims: see PARA 646 et seq.

379. Statutory rights of individual members of company. The statutory rights of an individual company member[1] include:

(1) his right to have his name properly inserted in the company's register of members, where the company maintains such a register[2], to make an inspection (unless the court rules otherwise) and to have copies of the register, and to have the register rectified when defective[3];
(2) unless excluded or disapplied[4], rights of pre-emption on the issue of further shares[5];
(3) to inspect copies of instruments creating and amending charges[6];
(4) to obtain upon request copies of the company's constitutional documents[7];
(5) to recover compensation for misrepresentation, although not fraudulent, by directors or promoters[8];
(6) to obtain repayment from the company of money paid in respect of shares which cannot legally be allotted[9];
(7) to petition for a winding-up order[10];
(8) to petition for relief when the affairs of the company are being conducted in a manner which is unfairly prejudicial to his interests[11];
(9) to take proceedings for misfeasance against directors[12] and officers[13] of the company in a winding up[14];
(10) to make application to the court in a voluntary winding up[15];
(11) to require his interest to be purchased on a reconstruction of the company[16];
(12) to be sent a copy of the company's annual accounts, together with a copy of the directors' report and of the auditors' report on those accounts[17]; and
(13) to require the company to hold an annual general meeting in a year when it has elected not to do so[18], except in the case of a company without a share capital[19], in any case where he has a right to attend and vote at a meeting of the company, and the right to appoint a proxy[20] and demand or join in demanding a poll[21].

1 As to who qualifies as a member of a company see PARA 323. As to the meaning of 'company' under the Companies Acts see PARA 21; and as to the meaning of the 'Companies Acts' see PARA 13.
2 As to the register of members see PARA 336 et seq. As to the option to keep membership information on the central register see PARA 363 et seq.
3 See PARA 352.
4 See PARAS 1289, 1292.
5 See PARA 1287 et seq.
6 See PARA 1472.
7 See PARA 241.
8 See PARAS 51, 1276.
9 See PARA 1286.
10 See COMPANY AND PARTNERSHIP INSOLVENCY vol 16 (2011) PARAS 399, 403.
11 See PARA 657.
12 As to a company's directors see PARA 512 et seq.
13 As to officers of the company see PARA 679.
14 See COMPANY AND PARTNERSHIP INSOLVENCY vol 17 (2011) PARA 646 et seq.
15 See COMPANY AND PARTNERSHIP INSOLVENCY vol 17 (2011) PARA 972.
16 See PARA 1618.
17 See PARA 935.
18 See PARA 702.
19 As to a company's share capital see PARA 1231 et seq.
20 See PARA 734.
21 See PARA 727.

380. Statutory rights of members collectively. The members of a company[1] collectively have statutory rights, some of which are exercisable by a bare majority[2], others by a particular majority[3].

Statutory rights cannot be taken away or modified by any provisions of the company's constitution[4].

1 As to who qualifies as a member of a company see PARA 323. As to the meaning of 'company' under the Companies Acts see PARA 21; and as to the meaning of the 'Companies Acts' see PARA 13.

2 Eg by ordinary resolution under the Companies Act 2006 s 168 (removal of director from office; director's right to protest): see PARA 557. As to ordinary resolutions see PARA 685.

3 Eg:

(1) shareholders holding an aggregate of 5% or more of the total voting rights can object to the resolution proposing re-registration as a private limited company (see the Companies Act 2006 s 98; and PARA 174); can circulate a written resolution in the case of a private company (see s 292; and PARA 697), or a resolution in the case of a general meeting of a public company (see s 338; and PARA 715); can require directors to call a general meeting (see s 303; and PARA 713); can circulate a statement to a general meeting (see s 314; and PARA 714); can demand an independent report on a poll (see s 342; and PARA 729); can prevent the deemed re-appointment of an auditor (see s 488; and PARA 998); and can publish audit concerns on a website (see s 527; and PARA 1050);

(2) shareholders holding an aggregate of 10% or more of the total voting rights can demand a poll (see s 321(1); and PARA 727); can require an audit of accounts to be made where the company would otherwise be entitled to exemption (see s 476; and PARA 984); and can require a company to exercise its powers to give notice requiring information about interests in its shares (see s 803; and PARA 461);

(3) where the rights attached to any class of shares in a company having a share capital are varied, the holders of not less in the aggregate than 15% of the issued shares of the class in question can object to a variation of class rights (see s 633; and PARA 1250);

(4) a 'special resolution' of the members (or of a class of members) of a company, being a resolution passed by a majority of not less than 75% (see PARA 686), must be passed eg to amend a company's articles, unless the amendment is solely to remove provision authorising the company to issue share warrants (see s 21; the Small Business, Enterprise and Employment Act 2015 s 85; and PARA 231).

4 See PARAS 248–249. As to the meaning of references to a company's constitution for the purposes of the Companies Act 2006 see PARA 226. A shareholders' agreement as to how to vote on a particular matter may effectively block the exercise of statutory rights: see PARAS 248, 250, 382.

381. Members' rights under company's constitution. Rights may be expressly conferred on the members of a company[1] by its constitution[2].

Some statutory rights of members may be exercised only if expressly authorised by the company's articles of association[3] or may require confirmation in any case by the court[4].

The rights usually conferred on members by the express terms of the articles include those with regard to dividends, the transfer and transmission of shares, attending and voting at meetings of the company, and appointment of directors[5].

1 As to who qualifies as a member of a company see PARA 323. As to the meaning of 'company' under the Companies Acts see PARA 21; and as to the meaning of the 'Companies Acts' see PARA 13.

2 Whether they are enforceable or not is another matter: see PARA 244. As to the meaning of references to a company's constitution for the purposes of the Companies Act 2006 see PARA 226. As to the necessity of registration of particulars of newly created class rights see PARA 1254.

3 See PARA 244. As to a company's articles of association generally see PARA 227 et seq.

4 Eg in the case of a reduction of capital which must be confirmed by the court: see the Companies Act 2006 s 641(1)(b); and PARA 1360.

5 As to model articles of association prescribed for the purposes of the Companies Act 2006, and their application generally, see PARA 227 et seq. Different versions of model articles have been so prescribed for use by private companies limited by shares (see the Companies (Model Articles) Regulations 2008, SI 2008/3229, reg 2, Sch 1), private companies limited by guarantee (see reg 3, Sch 2), and public companies (see reg 4, Sch 3). As to the meanings of 'company limited by

guarantee', 'company limited by shares', 'private company' and 'public company' see PARA 95. The default articles prescribed for the purposes of the Companies Act 1985 ('legacy articles'), ie the Companies (Tables A to F) Regulations 1985, SI 1985/805, have not been revoked and may, in their amended form, continue to be used by companies after the commencement of the Companies Act 2006: see PARA 229.

382. Members' rights under the general law. The rights of a company member[1] under the general law include the right, where he has been induced to take shares[2] by misrepresentation, to recover damages for misrepresentation if fraudulent or negligent[3], or to obtain a rescission of his contract to take shares, and rectification of the share register, together with a return of the money paid by him on the shares[4]; and the right to restrain directors[5] from acting ultra vires the company or in excess of their own powers or acting unfairly to the members[6].

To supplement their rights under the company's constitution[7] some or all of the shareholders[8] may decide to enter into a shareholders' agreement, that is to say a separate contract apart from the articles; and shareholders who are parties to such an agreement can enforce that agreement among themselves in the same manner as any other contract[9].

1 As to who qualifies as a member of a company see PARA 323. As to the meaning of 'company' under the Companies Acts see PARA 21; and as to the meaning of the 'Companies Acts' see PARA 13.
2 As to shares generally see PARA 1231 et seq.
3 See PARA 1276.
4 See PARA 298.
5 As to a company's directors see PARA 512 et seq.
6 See PARAS 261, 646 et seq.
7 See PARA 381. As to the meaning of references to a company's constitution for the purposes of the Companies Act 2006 see PARA 226.
8 As to shareholders and membership of companies generally see PARAS 323 et seq, 1889 et seq.
9 See PARAS 248, 250.

383. Member cannot recover reflective loss. Proceedings may be maintained by a member of a company when the matter is one which affects his individual rights[1]; and in a proper case he may obtain an injunction against the company in aid of his right[2]. Where a company suffers loss caused by a breach of duty owed to it, only the company may undertake proceedings in respect of that loss[3]; and no action lies in favour of a shareholder suing in that capacity, and no other, to make good a diminution in the value of the shareholder's shareholding by taking action against the responsible party where that merely reflects the loss suffered by the company (the principle of 'no reflective loss')[4].

However, a personal claim may be brought by a shareholder where he can show a breach of duty owed personally to the shareholder and a personal loss separate and distinct from any loss suffered by the company[5]. A shareholder's claim may survive also in circumstances where a defendant's wrong has disabled the company from pursuing its own claim against him[6].

1 *Pender v Lushington* (1877) 6 ChD 70 at 80; *Edwards v Halliwell* [1950] 2 All ER 1064, CA. See also PARA 244.
2 See *Pulbrook v Richmond Consolidated Mining Co* (1878) 9 ChD 610; *Munster v Cammell Co* (1882) 21 ChD 183; *Kyshe v Alturas Gold Co* (1888) 36 WR 496; *Turnbull v West Riding Athletic Club Leeds Ltd* (1894) 70 LT 92; *Catesby v Burnett* [1916] 2 Ch 325 (where an injunction was granted restraining two former directors from continuing to act, and restraining the company from refusing to allow two duly elected directors to act as such); *Norman v Mitchell* (1854) 5 De GM & G 648; *Johnson v Lyttle's Iron Agency* (1877) 5 ChD 687, CA; *Goulton v London Architectural Brick and Tile Co* [1877] WN 141 (where an injunction was granted to restrain an illegal forfeiture of shares); *Jones v Pacaya Rubber and Produce Co Ltd* [1911] 1 KB 455, CA (forfeiture restrained pending trial of action for rescission of contract to take shares); *Lawson v Financial News Ltd* (1917) 34 TLR 52, CA (issue of debenture stock to directors and

employees restrained); *Nelson v Anglo-American Land Mortgage Agency Co* [1897] 1 Ch 130 (where an injunction was granted to restrain interference by a company with shareholders and debenture holders, in the exercise of their statutory rights to inspect, at all reasonable times, the register of mortgages of the company); *Cory v Reindeer Steamship Ltd* (1915) 31 TLR 530 (where an interlocutory injunction was granted to restrain the company from acting upon resolutions which had been passed against the wishes of the majority of the shareholders); *Last v Buller & Co Ltd* (1919) 36 TLR 35; *Tatham v Palace Restaurants Ltd* (1909) 53 Sol Jo 743; *Hayes v Bristol Plant Hire Ltd* [1957] 1 All ER 685, [1957] 1 WLR 499 (action for wrongful exclusion of a director from the boardroom).

A shareholder seeking to enforce an individual right against the company is not entitled to an advance order for an indemnity as to costs: *Re a Company (No 005136 of 1986)* [1987] BCLC 82. The principle in *Wallersteiner v Moir (No 2)* [1975] QB 373, [1975] 1 All ER 849, CA, is confined to derivative claims: see PARA 646 et seq. See also *Royal Westminster Investments SA v Varma* [2012] EWHC 3439 (Ch), [2012] All ER (D) 370 (Nov) (shareholder suing exclusively on his own behalf lacked standing to bring claim for interim relief to prevent director from causing company to incur expenditure).

3 See *Foss v Harbottle* (1843) 2 Hare 461; and PARA 653 note 4.

4 *Johnson v Gore Wood & Co* [2002] 2 AC 1 at 35, [2001] 1 All ER 481 at 503, HL, per Lord Bingham; *Prudential Assurance Co Ltd v Newman Industries Ltd (No 2)* [1982] Ch 204 at 222–223, [1982] 1 All ER 354 at 366–367, CA.See also *Stein v Blake* [1998] 1 All ER 724, [1998] 1 BCLC 573, CA (loss sustained by a member by a diminution in the value of his shares, by reason of the misappropriation of the company's assets, is recoverable by the company only, as the member has not suffered a distinct loss); *Ellis v Property Leeds (UK) Ltd* [2002] EWCA Civ 32, [2002] 2 BCLC 175 (director of company precluded from suing in personal capacity as his loss reflected the company's loss). The principle in *Prudential Assurance Co Ltd v Newman Industries Ltd (No 2)* [1982] Ch 204, [1982] 1 All ER 354 is not precluded from applying simply because the defendant also owes fiduciary duties to the claimant, unless the defendants could show that the whole of the claimed profit reflected what the company had lost and which it had a cause of action to recover: *Shaker v Al-Bedrawi* [2002] EWCA Civ 1452, [2003] Ch 350, [2002] 4 All ER 835 (proceedings brought by a claimant not as a shareholder but as a beneficiary under a trust, against his trustee for a profit). See also *Gardner v Parker* [2004] EWCA Civ 781, [2004] 2 BCLC 554. The rule against reflective loss is not concerned with barring causes of action but with barring recovery of certain types of loss and therefore whether the cause of action lay in common law or equity and whether the remedy lay in damages or restitution makes no difference as to its applicability: *Shaker v Al-Bedrawi*; *Gardner v Parker* [2002] EWCA Civ 1452, [2003] Ch 350, [2002] 4 All ER 835. See also *Royal Westminster Investments SA v Varma* [2012] EWHC 3439 (Ch), [2012] All ER (D) 370 (Nov) (shareholder suing exclusively on his own behalf lacked standing to bring claim for interim relief to prevent director from causing company to incur expenditure).

5 *Johnson v Gore Wood & Co* [2002] 2 AC 1, [2001] 1 All ER 481, HL.

Where there is a risk of double recovery created by a wrong done both to the company and to the shareholder, the shareholder's claim must give way: *Johnson v Gore Wood & Co* [2002] 2 AC 1, [2001] 1 All ER 481, HL; *Day v Cook* [2001] EWCA Civ 592, [2002] 1 BCLC 1 (where the company's cause of action was in fact statute-barred). See also *Gardner v Parker* [2004] EWCA Civ 781, [2004] 2 BCLC 554 (since the foundation of the rule against reflective loss was the need to avoid double recovery, there was a powerful case for saying that it should be applied in a case where, in its absence, both the beneficiary and the company would be able to recover effectively the same damages from a defaulting trustee-director, even where the cause of action that may be asserted by the shareholder is different from the one that may be asserted by the company). Cf *Barings plc (in administration) v Coopers & Lybrand* [1997] 1 BCLC 427, CA. See also *Pearce v European Reinsurance* [2005] EWHC 1493 (Ch), [2005] 2 BCLC 366 (reflective loss principle did not prevent a member from bringing a claim against auditors simply because his claim involved allegations that the auditors' valuation of shares had failed to take into account in their valuation claims which the company had against a director).

6 *Giles v Rhind* [2002] EWCA Civ 1428, [2003] Ch 618, [2002] 4 All ER 977; *Perry v Day* [2004] EWHC 3372 (Ch), [2005] 2 BCLC 405. In *Gardner v Parker* [2004] EWCA Civ 781, [2004] 2 BCLC 554, where the claim was judged on the facts to have failed to fall within this exception, it was held that the mere fact that the company chose not to claim against the defendant, or settled with him on comparatively generous terms, would not, without more, justify disapplying the principle in *Prudential Assurance Co Ltd v Newman Industries Ltd (No 2)* [1982] Ch 204, [1982] 1 All ER 354, CA. Since this principle is an exclusionary rule, denying a claimant

what otherwise would be his right to take action, the onus is on the defendants to establish its applicability: *Shaker v Al-Bedrawi* [2002] EWCA Civ 1452 at [83], [2003] Ch 350 at [83], [2002] 4 All ER 835 at [83] per Peter Gibson LJ.

As the law stands, the principles in *Johnson v Gore Wood & Co* [2002] 2 AC 1, [2001] 1 All ER 481, HL (see the text and notes 4–5) as qualified by the Court of Appeal in *Giles v Rhind* [2002] EWCA Civ 1428, [2003] Ch 618, [2002] 4 All ER 977 are binding: *Webster v Sanderson* [2009] EWCA Civ 830 at [36], [2009] All ER (D) 352 (Jul) per Lord Clarke of Stone-cum-Ebony MR (refusing to follow *Waddington Ltd v Chan Chun Hoo Thomas* [2008] HKCU 1381 at [85]–[87], [2009] 2 BCLC 82 per Lord Millett, where doubt had been expressed as to whether it was right that *Giles v Rhind* [2002] EWCA Civ 1428, [2003] Ch 618, [2002] 4 All ER 977 should allow the shareholder to bring an action for his own benefit, as this would entail recovery by the wrong party to the prejudice of the company and its creditors and would produce the result which was identified as unacceptable in *Johnson v Gore Wood & Co* [2002] 2 AC 1, [2001] 1 All ER 481, HL). See also *International Leisure Ltd v First National Trustee Co UK Ltd* [2012] EWHC 1971 (Ch), [2013] Ch 346, [2014] 1 BCLC 128 (claims by debenture holders for loss resulting from breach of duty by administrative receivers did not offend reflective loss rule).

B. EXERCISE OF MEMBERS' RIGHTS BY NOMINEE

384. Provisions of articles as to enjoyment and exercise of members' rights by nominated person. Where provision is made by a company's articles[1] enabling a member[2] to nominate another person or persons as entitled to enjoy or exercise all or any specified rights of the member in relation to the company[3], then, so far as is necessary to give effect to that provision, anything required or authorised by any provision of the Companies Acts to be done by or in relation to the member must instead be done (or, as the case may be, may instead be done) by or in relation to the nominated person or each of them as if he were a member of the company[4]. This applies, in particular, to the rights conferred in relation to the following:

(1) the right[5] to be sent a resolution that is proposed to be moved as a written resolution[6];
(2) the right[7] to require circulation of a resolution that is proposed to be moved as a written resolution[8];
(3) the right[9] to require directors[10] to call a general meeting[11];
(4) the right[12] to receive notice of general meetings[13];
(5) the right[14] to require circulation of a statement[15];
(6) the right[16] to ask questions at a meeting of a traded company[17];
(7) the right[18] to appoint a proxy to act at a meeting[19];
(8) the right[20] to require circulation of a resolution for a general meeting of a public company[21];
(9) the right[22] to request a traded company to include in the business to be dealt with at an annual general meeting any matter (other than a proposed resolution) which may properly be included in the business[23]; and
(10) the right[24] to be sent a copy of annual accounts and reports[25].

However, these provisions[26] do not confer rights enforceable against the company by anyone other than the member[27]; nor do they affect the requirements for an effective transfer or other disposition of the whole or part of a member's interest in the company[28].

As regards the rights conferred by such a nomination[29]:

(a) enjoyment by the nominated person of the rights conferred by the nomination is enforceable against the company by the member as if they were rights conferred by the company's articles[30]; and

(b) any enactment[31], and any provision of the company's articles, having effect in relation to communications with members has a corresponding effect (subject to any necessary adaptations) in relation to communications with the nominated person[32].

The rights conferred by the nomination are in addition to the rights of the member himself[33], and they do not affect any rights exercisable by virtue of any provisions of company's articles as to the enjoyment or exercise of members' rights[34].

A failure to give effect to the rights conferred by the nomination does not affect the validity of anything done by or on behalf of the company[35].

The Secretary of State[36] may by regulations[37] amend the provisions relating to information rights[38] so as to extend or restrict the classes of companies to which the nomination of a person to enjoy information rights applies[39], so as to make other provision as to the circumstances in which such a nomination may be made, or so as to extend or restrict the rights conferred by such a nomination[40].

1 As to the meaning of references to a company's 'articles' see PARA 227 note 2. As to a company's articles of association generally see PARA 227 et seq. As to the meaning of 'company' under the Companies Acts see PARA 21; and as to the meaning of the 'Companies Acts' see PARA 13.
2 As to the meaning of 'member of a company' see PARA 323.
3 Companies Act 2006 s 145(1).
4 Companies Act 2006 s 145(2).
5 Ie the rights conferred by the Companies Act 2006 s 291 (see PARA 696) or s 293 (see PARA 697): see s 145(3)(a).
6 Companies Act 2006 s 145(3)(a). As to the meaning of 'written resolution' see PARA 695. As to resolutions and meetings of the company generally see PARA 684 et seq.
7 Ie the right conferred by the Companies Act 2006 s 292 (see PARA 697): see s 145(3)(b).
8 Companies Act 2006 s 145(3)(b).
9 Ie the right conferred by the Companies Act 2006 s 303 (see PARA 713): see s 145(3)(c).
10 As to the meaning of 'director' see PARA 512.
11 Companies Act 2006 s 145(3)(c).
12 Ie the right conferred by the Companies Act 2006 s 310 (see PARA 707): see s 145(3)(d).
13 Companies Act 2006 s 145(3)(d).
14 Ie the right conferred by the Companies Act 2006 s 314 (see PARA 714): see s 145(3)(e).
15 Companies Act 2006 s 145(3)(e).
16 Ie the right conferred by the Companies Act 2006 s 319A (see PARA 723): see s 145(3)(ea) (added by SI 2009/1632).
17 Companies Act 2006 s 145(3)(ea) (as added: see note 16). As to the meaning of 'traded company' for these purposes see PARA 702 note 6. As to the modified application of the Companies Act 2006 s 145(3), so as to omit s 145(3)(ea), see the Bank Recovery and Resolution (No 2) Order 2014, SI 2014/3348, art 220(4), Sch 4 Pt 1 para 2.
18 Ie the right conferred by the Companies Act 2006 s 324 (see PARA 734): see s 145(3)(f).
19 Companies Act 2006 s 145(3)(f).
20 Ie the right conferred by the Companies Act 2006 s 338 (see PARA 715): see s 145(3)(g).
21 Companies Act 2006 s 145(3)(g).
22 Ie the right conferred by the Companies Act 2006 s 338A (see PARA 716): see s 145(3)(ga) (added by SI 2009/1632).
23 Companies Act 2006 s 145(3)(ga) (as added: see note 22). As to the modified application of the Companies Act 2006 s 145(3), so as to omit s 145(3)(ga), see the Bank Recovery and Resolution (No 2) Order 2014, SI 2014/3348, art 220(4), Sch 4 Pt 1 para 2.
24 Ie the right conferred by the Companies Act 2006 s 423 (see PARA 935): see s 145(3)(h).
25 Companies Act 2006 s 145(3)(h).
26 Ie the Companies Act 2006 s 145 and any such provision as is mentioned in s 145(1) (see the text and notes 1–3): see s 145(4).
27 Companies Act 2006 s 145(4)(a). Thus they do not confer rights on indirect investors: see *Re DNick Holding plc, Eckerle v Wickeder Westfalenstahl GmbH* [2013] EWHC 68 (Ch), [2014] Ch 196, [2013] NLJR 107.
28 Companies Act 2006 s 145(4)(b).

29 Companies Act 2006 s 150(1). References in s 150 to the rights conferred by the nomination are to the rights referred to in s 146(3) (information rights) (see PARA 385) and, where applicable, the rights conferred by s 147(3) (right to hard copy communications) (see PARA 385) and s 149 (information as to possible voting rights) (see PARA 385): s 150(7). As to the meaning of 'information rights' see PARA 385 note 4.
30 Companies Act 2006 s 150(2).
31 As to the meaning of 'enactment' see PARA 13 note 16.
32 Companies Act 2006 s 150(3). In particular, where under any enactment, or any provision of the company's articles, the members of a company entitled to receive a document or information are determined as at a date or time before it is sent or supplied, the company need not send or supply it to a nominated person whose nomination was received by the company after that date or time, or if that date or time falls in a period of suspension of his nomination (s 150(4)(a)); and where under any enactment, or any provision of the company's articles, the right of a member to receive a document or information depends on the company having a current address for him, the same applies to any person nominated by him (s 150(4)(b)). Any obligation under the Companies Acts to give a person's address is, unless otherwise expressly provided, to give a service address for that person: Companies Act 2006 s 1142. As to the service of documents on a company generally see PARA 743 et seq; and as to the provision made for the sending or supplying of documents or information to or from a company (the 'company communications provisions') see PARA 750 et seq. As to the termination or suspension of a nomination to enjoy information rights see PARA 386.
33 Companies Act 2006 s 150(5)(a).
34 Companies Act 2006 s 150(5)(b). The text refers to the rights exercisable by virtue of any such provision as is mentioned in s 145 (see the text and notes 1–25): see s 150(5)(b).
35 Companies Act 2006 s 150(6).
36 As to the Secretary of State see PARA 6 et seq.
37 As to the making of regulations under the Companies Act 2006 generally see ss 1288–1292. Regulations under s 151 are subject to affirmative resolution procedure (ie the regulations must not be made unless a draft of the statutory instrument containing them has been laid before Parliament and approved by a resolution of each House of Parliament): see ss 151(3), 1290. The regulations may make such consequential modifications of any other provisions of Pt 9 (ss 145–153), or of any other enactment, as appear to the Secretary of State to be necessary: s 151(2). At the date at which this volume states the law, no such regulations had been made.
38 Ie amend the Companies Act 2006 s 150 (see the text and notes 29–35) (as well as ss 146–149: see PARAS 385–386): see s 151(1).
39 Ie extend or restrict the classes of companies to which the Companies Act 2006 s 146 (see PARA 385) applies: see s 151(1).
40 Companies Act 2006 s 151(1).

385. Information rights enjoyed by person nominated by member of traded company. A member of a company[1], whose shares[2] are admitted to trading on a regulated market[3], who holds shares on behalf of another person may nominate that person to enjoy information rights[4]. However, a company need not act on a nomination purporting to relate to certain information rights only[5].

If the person to be nominated wishes to receive hard copy communications[6], he must request the person making the nomination to notify the company of that fact[7], and provide an address to which such copies may be sent[8]; and this must be done before the nomination is made[9]. If, having received such a request, the person making the nomination notifies the company that the nominated person wishes to receive hard copy communications[10], and provides the company with that address[11], the right of the nominated person is to receive hard copy communications accordingly[12]. If no such notification is given, or no address is provided, the nominated person is taken to have agreed that documents or information may be sent or supplied to him by the company by means of a website[13]. However, that agreement may be revoked by the nominated person[14], and it does not affect his right[15] to require a hard copy version of a document or information provided in any other form[16].

Where a company sends a copy of a notice of a meeting to a person nominated to enjoy a member's information rights[17], the copy of the notice must be accompanied by a statement that:

(1) he may have a right under an agreement between him and the member by whom he was nominated to be appointed, or to have someone else appointed, as a proxy for the meeting[18]; and

(2) if he has no such right or does not wish to exercise it, he may have a right under such an agreement to give instructions to the member as to the exercise of voting rights[19].

1 As to the meaning of 'member of a company' see PARA 323. As to the meaning of 'company' under the Companies Acts see PARA 21; and as to the meaning of the 'Companies Acts' see PARA 13.

2 As to the meaning of 'share' see PARA 1231.

3 As to the meaning of 'regulated market' see PARA 335 note 11.

4 Companies Act 2006 s 146(1), (2). For these purposes, 'information rights' means the following (s 146(3)), ie:

(1) the right to receive a copy of all communications that the company sends to its members generally or to any class of its members that includes the person making the nomination; and

(2) the rights conferred by s 431 or s 432 (right to require copies of accounts and reports) (see PARA 941), and s 1145 (right to require hard copy version of document or information provided in another form) (see PARA 753).

The reference in head (1) above to communications that a company sends to its members generally includes the company's annual accounts and reports; and as to the application of s 426 (option to provide strategic report with supplementary material) (see PARA 938) in relation to a person nominated to enjoy information rights see s 426(5): s 146(4) (amended by SI 2013/1970). As to the Secretary of State's power to amend the Companies Act 2006 s 146 see s 151; and PARA 384. As to classes of shares and class rights see PARA 1246 et seq. As to the termination or suspension of a nomination to enjoy information rights see PARA 386.

5 Companies Act 2006 s 146(5).

6 The Companies Act 2006 s 147 applies as regards the form in which copies are to be provided to a person nominated under s 146 (see the text and notes 1–5): s 147(1). However, this is subject to the provisions of s 1144(2), Sch 5 Pt 3 (paras 5–7) (communications in electronic form) (see PARA 754) and Sch 5 Pt 4 (paras 8–13) (communications by means of a website) (see PARA 755) under which the company may take steps to enable it to communicate in electronic form or by means of a website: s 147(4). As to the Secretary of State's power to amend s 147 see s 151; and PARA 384. As to documents or information in electronic form see PARA 751.

7 Companies Act 2006 s 147(2)(a). See also note 6. As to the service of documents on a company generally see PARA 743 et seq; and as to the provision made for the sending or supplying of documents or information to or from a company (the 'company communications provisions') see PARA 750 et seq.

8 Companies Act 2006 s 147(2)(b). See also note 6. Any obligation under the Companies Acts to give a person's address is, unless otherwise expressly provided, to give a service address for that person: Companies Act 2006 s 1142. A company must at all times have a registered office to which all communications and notices may be addressed: see s 86; and PARA 124.

9 Companies Act 2006 s 147(2). See also note 6.

10 Companies Act 2006 s 147(3)(a). See also note 6.

11 Companies Act 2006 s 147(3)(b). See also note 6.

12 Companies Act 2006 s 147(3). See also note 6.

13 Companies Act 2006 s 147(5). See also note 6.

14 Companies Act 2006 s 147(6)(a). See also note 6.

15 Ie under the Companies Act 2006 s 1145 (see PARA 753): see s 147(6)(b). See also note 6.

16 Companies Act 2006 s 147(6)(b). See also note 6.

17 Companies Act 2006 s 149(1). The text refers to a person nominated under s 146 (see the text and notes 1–5): see s 149(1). As to the Secretary of State's power to amend s 149 see s 151; and PARA 384.

18 Companies Act 2006 s 149(2)(a). The requirements of s 325 (notice of meeting to contain statement of member's rights in relation to appointment of proxy) (see PARA 734) do not apply

to the copy, and the company must either omit the notice required by s 325, or include it but state that it does not apply to the nominated person: s 149(3). See also note 17. As to voting by proxy at meetings see PARA 734 et seq.

19 Companies Act 2006 s 149(2)(b). See also notes 17–18.

386. Termination or suspension of nomination to enjoy information rights. The nomination of a person to enjoy a member's information rights[1] may be terminated at the request either of the member or of the nominated person[2].

In any case, such a nomination ceases to have effect on the occurrence, in relation either to the member or to the nominated person, of:

(1) in the case of an individual, death or bankruptcy[3]; or

(2) in the case of a body corporate[4], dissolution or the making of an order for the winding up of the body otherwise than for the purposes of reconstruction[5].

The effect of any nominations made by a member is suspended at any time when there are more nominated persons than the member has shares in the company[6]; and where the member holds different classes of shares[7] with different information rights[8], and where there are more nominated persons than he has shares conferring a particular right[9], the effect of any nominations made by him is suspended to the extent that they confer that right[10].

Where the company inquires of a nominated person whether he wishes to retain information rights[11], and where the company does not receive a response within the period of 28 days beginning with the date on which the company's inquiry was sent[12], the nomination ceases to have effect at the end of that period[13].

The termination or suspension of a nomination means that the company is not required to act on it[14]; but it does not prevent the company from continuing to do so, to such extent or for such period as it thinks fit[15].

1 The Companies Act 2006 s 148 has effect in relation to a nomination under s 146 (see PARA 385): s 148(1). As to the Secretary of State's power to amend s 148 see s 151; and PARA 384. As to the meaning of 'information rights' see PARA 385 note 4. As to the meaning of 'member' see PARA 323.

2 Companies Act 2006 s 148(2). See also note 1.

3 Companies Act 2006 s 148(3)(a). For these purposes, the reference to bankruptcy includes the sequestration of a person's estate: s 148(4)(a). See also note 1.

4 As to the meaning of 'body corporate' see PARA 1 note 5.

5 Companies Act 2006 s 148(3)(b). For these purposes, the reference to the making of an order for winding up is to the making of such an order under the Insolvency Act 1986 or any corresponding proceeding under the law of a country or territory outside the United Kingdom: s 148(4)(b). See also note 1. As to the meaning of 'United Kingdom' see PARA 1 note 5. As to orders for winding up made under the Insolvency Act 1986 see COMPANY AND PARTNERSHIP INSOLVENCY vol 16 (2011) PARA 438 et seq; and as to the dissolution of a company in respect of which a winding-up order has been made see COMPANY AND PARTNERSHIP INSOLVENCY vol 17 (2011) PARA 888 et seq. As to the making of orders to facilitate reconstruction see PARA 1616.

6 Companies Act 2006 s 148(5). See also note 1. As to the meaning of 'company' under the Companies Acts see PARA 21; and as to the meaning of the 'Companies Acts' see PARA 13. As to the meaning of 'share' see PARA 1231.

7 As to classes of shares generally see PARA 1246 et seq.

8 Companies Act 2006 s 148(6)(a). See also note 1.

9 Companies Act 2006 s 148(6)(b). See also note 1.

10 Companies Act 2006 s 148(6). See also note 1.

11 Companies Act 2006 s 148(7)(a). Such an inquiry is not to be made of a person more than once in any 12 month period: s 148(7). See also note 1.

12 Companies Act 2006 s 148(7)(b). See also note 1.

13 Companies Act 2006 s 148(7). See also note 1.

14 Companies Act 2006 s 148(8). See also note 1.

15 Companies Act 2006 s 148(8) proviso. See also note 1.

387. Exercise of members' rights where shares held on behalf of others. Where a member[1] holds shares[2] in a company[3] on behalf of more than one person, then rights attached to the shares[4], and rights under any enactment[5] exercisable by virtue of holding the shares[6], need not all be exercised (and, if exercised, need not all be exercised in the same way)[7]. A member who exercises such rights, but does not exercise all his rights, must inform the company to what extent he is exercising the rights[8]; and a member who exercises such rights in different ways must inform the company of the ways in which he is exercising them and to what extent they are exercised in each way[9]. If a member exercises such rights without informing the company either that he is not exercising all his rights[10], or that he is exercising his rights in different ways[11], the company is entitled to assume that he is exercising all his rights and is exercising them in the same way[12].

A company is required to act under any of the following provisions[13]:

(1) the members' power[14] to require circulation of a statement[15];

(2) the members' power[16] to require circulation of a resolution for a general meeting of a public company[17];

(3) the members' power[18] to request a traded company[19] to include in the business to be dealt with at an annual general meeting any matter (other than a proposed resolution) which may properly be included in the business[20];

(4) the members' power[21] to require an independent report on a poll taken at a meeting[22]; and

(5) the members' power[23] to require website publication of audit concerns[24],

if it receives a request in relation to which the following conditions are met[25]:

(a) it is made by at least 100 persons[26];

(b) it is authenticated by all the persons making it[27];

(c) in the case of any of those persons who is not a member of the company, it is accompanied by a statement[28]:

  (i) of the full name and address[29] of a person (the 'member') who is a member of the company and holds shares on behalf of that person[30];

  (ii) that the member is holding those shares on behalf of that person in the course of a business[31];

  (iii) of the number of shares in the company that the member holds on behalf of that person[32];

  (iv) of the total amount paid up on those shares[33];

  (v) that those shares are not held on behalf of anyone else or, if they are, that the other person or persons are not among the other persons making the request[34];

  (vi) that some or all of those shares confer voting rights that are relevant for the purposes of making a request under the provision in heads (1) to (5) above which is in question[35]; and

  (vii) that the person has the right to instruct the member how to exercise those rights[36];

(d) in the case of any of those persons who is a member of the company, it is accompanied by a statement[37]:

  (i) that he holds shares otherwise than on behalf of another person[38]; or

(ii) that he holds shares on behalf of one or more other persons but those persons are not among the other persons making the request[39];

(e) it is accompanied by such evidence as the company may reasonably require of the matters mentioned in heads (c) and (d) above[40];

(f) the total amount of the sums paid up on[41] shares held as mentioned in head (c) above[42] and shares held as mentioned in head (d) above[43], divided by the number of persons making the request, is not less than £100[44];

(g) the request complies with any other requirements of the provision in heads (1) to (5) above which is in question as to contents, timing and otherwise[45].

1 As to the meaning of 'member' see PARA 323.
2 As to the meaning of 'share' see PARA 1231.
3 As to the meaning of 'company' under the Companies Acts see PARA 21; and as to the meaning of the 'Companies Acts' see PARA 13.
4 Companies Act 2006 s 152(1)(a). As to classes of shares and class rights see PARA 1246 et seq.
5 As to the meaning of 'enactment' see PARA 13 note 16.
6 Companies Act 2006 s 152(1)(b).
7 Companies Act 2006 s 152(1).
8 Companies Act 2006 s 152(2). A company must at all times have a registered office to which all communications and notices may be addressed: see s 86; and PARA 124. As to the service of documents on a company generally see PARA 743 et seq; and as to the provision made for the sending or supplying of documents or information to or from a company (the 'company communications provisions') see PARA 750 et seq.
9 Companies Act 2006 s 152(3).
10 Companies Act 2006 s 152(4)(a).
11 Companies Act 2006 s 152(4)(b).
12 Companies Act 2006 s 152(4).
13 Companies Act 2006 s 153(2).
14 Ie the power contained in the Companies Act 2006 s 314 (see PARA 714): see s 153(1)(a).
15 Companies Act 2006 s 153(1)(a).
16 Ie the power contained in the Companies Act 2006 s 338 (see PARA 715): see s 153(1)(b).
17 Companies Act 2006 s 153(1)(b).
18 Ie the power contained in the Companies Act 2006 s 338A (see PARA 716): see s 153(1)(ba) (added by SI 2009/1632).
19 As to the meaning of 'traded company' for these purposes see PARA 702 note 6.
20 Companies Act 2006 s 153(1)(ba) (as added: see note 18). As to the modified application of the Companies Act 2006 s 1153(1), so as to omit s 153(1)(ba), see the Bank Recovery and Resolution (No 2) Order 2014, SI 2014/3348, art 220(4), Sch 4 Pt 1 para 3.
21 Ie the power contained in the Companies Act 2006 s 342 (see PARA 729): see s 153(1)(c).
22 Companies Act 2006 s 153(1)(c).
23 Ie the power contained in the Companies Act 2006 s 527 (see PARA 1050): see s 153(1)(d).
24 Companies Act 2006 s 153(1)(d).
25 Companies Act 2006 s 153(2).
26 Companies Act 2006 s 153(2)(a).
27 Companies Act 2006 s 153(2)(b). In relation to the authentication of a document under the Companies Act 2006 see s 1146; and PARA 750 et seq.
28 Companies Act 2006 s 153(2)(c).
29 Any obligation under the Companies Acts to give a person's address is, unless otherwise expressly provided, to give a service address for that person: Companies Act 2006 s 1142.
30 Companies Act 2006 s 153(2)(c)(i).
31 Companies Act 2006 s 153(2)(c)(ii).
32 Companies Act 2006 s 153(2)(c)(iii).
33 Companies Act 2006 s 153(2)(c)(iv).
34 Companies Act 2006 s 153(2)(c)(v).
35 See the Companies Act 2006 s 153(2)(c)(vi).
36 Companies Act 2006 s 153(2)(c)(vii).
37 Companies Act 2006 s 153(2)(d).
38 Companies Act 2006 s 153(2)(d)(i).

39 Companies Act 2006 s 153(2)(d)(ii).
40 Companies Act 2006 s 153(2)(e).
41 Companies Act 2006 s 153(2)(f).
42 Companies Act 2006 s 153(2)(f)(i). As to payments for shares and paid up shares see PARA 1231 et seq.
43 Companies Act 2006 s 153(2)(f)(ii).
44 Companies Act 2006 s 153(2)(f).
45 See the Companies Act 2006 s 153(2)(g).

388. Information as to exercise of voting rights by institutional investors. The Treasury[1] or the Secretary of State[2] may make provision by regulations[3] requiring the institutions listed in heads (1) to (5) below to provide information about the exercise of voting rights attached to the shares[4] listed in heads (a) and (b) below[5].

The institutions to which this provision[6] applies are[7]:

(1) unit trust schemes[8] in respect of which an order declaring them to be authorised unit trust schemes[9] is in force[10];
(2) open-ended investment companies[11] incorporated by virtue of regulations under the Financial Services and Markets Act 2000[12];
(3) companies[13] approved as investment trusts[14] as respects any accounting period[15];
(4) pension schemes as defined in the Pension Schemes Act 1993[16];
(5) undertakings authorised under the Financial Services and Markets Act 2000 to carry on long-term insurance business[17].

The shares to which this provision[18] applies are[19]:

(a) shares of a description traded on a specified market[20]; and
(b) shares in which the institution has, or is taken to have, an interest[21].

Regulations so made[22] may require the provision of specified information about[23]:

(i) the exercise or non-exercise of voting rights by the institution or any person acting on its behalf[24];
(ii) any instructions[25] given by the institution or any person acting on its behalf as to the exercise or non-exercise of voting rights[26]; and
(iii) any delegation by the institution or any person acting on its behalf of any functions in relation to the exercise or non-exercise of voting rights or the giving of such instructions[27].

Where instructions are given to act on the recommendations or advice of another person, the regulations may require the provision of information about what recommendations or advice were given[28].

The regulations may provide that an institution may discharge its obligations under the regulations by referring to information disclosed by a person acting on its behalf[29], and that, in such a case, it is sufficient, where that other person acts on behalf of more than one institution, that the reference is to information given in aggregated form[30], that is:

(A) relating to the exercise or non-exercise by that person of voting rights on behalf of more than one institution[31]; or
(B) relating to the instructions given by that person in respect of the exercise or non-exercise of voting rights on behalf of more than one institution[32]; or

(C) relating to the delegation by that person of functions in relation to the exercise or non-exercise of voting rights, or the giving of instructions in respect of the exercise or non-exercise of voting rights, on behalf of more than one institution[33].

1 As to the Treasury see CONSTITUTIONAL AND ADMINISTRATIVE LAW vol 20 (2014) PARA 262 et seq.

2 As to the Secretary of State see PARA 6 et seq.

3 As to the making of regulations under the Companies Act 2006 generally see ss 1288–1292. Regulations under s 1277 are subject to affirmative resolution procedure (ie the regulations must not be made unless a draft of the statutory instrument containing them has been laid before Parliament and approved by a resolution of each House of Parliament): see ss 1277(6), 1290. Regulations under s 1277 may make different provision for different descriptions of institution, different descriptions of shares and for other different circumstances: s 1277(5). At the date at which this volume states the law, no such regulations had been made.

4 As to the meaning of 'share' see PARA 1231. As to classes of shares and class rights see PARA 1246 et seq.

5 Companies Act 2006 s 1277(1). This power is exercisable in accordance with s 1278 (see the text and notes 6–17), s 1279 (see the text and notes 18–21) and s 1280 (see the text and notes 23–33): s 1277(2). The obligation imposed by regulations under s 1277 is enforceable by civil proceedings brought either by any person to whom the information should have been provided, or by a specified regulatory authority: s 1277(4). For the purposes of ss 1277–1280, 'specified' means specified in the regulations: s 1277(3)(b).

6 Ie the Companies Act 2006 s 1277 (see the text and notes 1–5): see s 1278(1).

7 Companies Act 2006 s 1278(1). Regulations under s 1277 (see the text and notes 1–5) may provide that s 1277 applies to other descriptions of institution, or provide that s 1277 does not apply to a specified description of institution: s 1278(2). As to the meaning of 'specified' see note 5. The regulations must specify by whom, in the case of any description of institution, the duty imposed by the regulations is to be fulfilled: s 1278(3).

8 Ie within the meaning of the Financial Services and Markets Act 2000 (see FINANCIAL SERVICES REGULATION vol 50A (2016) PARA 841): see the Companies Act 2006 s 1278(1)(a).

9 Ie an order under the Financial Services and Markets Act 2000 s 243 (see FINANCIAL SERVICES REGULATION vol 50A (2016) PARA 847): see the Companies Act 2006 s 1278(1)(a).

10 Companies Act 2006 s 1278(1)(a).

11 As to open-ended investment companies authorised in the United Kingdom see FINANCIAL SERVICES REGULATION vol 50A (2016) PARA 873 et seq.

12 Companies Act 2006 s 1278(1)(b). Head (2) in the text refers to open-ended investment companies incorporated by virtue of regulations under the Financial Services and Markets Act 2000 s 262 (see FINANCIAL SERVICES REGULATION vol 50A (2016) PARA 873): see the Companies Act 2006 s 1278(1)(b).

13 As to the meaning of 'company' under the Companies Acts see PARA 21; and as to the meaning of the 'Companies Acts' see PARA 13.

14 Ie approved for the purposes of the Corporation Tax Act 2010 Pt 24 Ch 4 (ss 1158–1159) (see INCOME TAXATION vol 59 (2014) PARA 1951): see the Companies Act 2006 s 1278(1)(c) (amended by the Corporation Tax Act 2010 Sch 1 Pt 2 paras 487, 490).

15 Companies Act 2006 s 1278(1)(c) (as amended: see note 14).

16 Companies Act 2006 s 1278(1)(d). Head (4) in the text refers to pension schemes as defined in the Pension Schemes Act 1993 s 1(5): see the Companies Act 2006 s 1278(1)(d). In the Pension Schemes Act 1993 s 1(1), 'pension scheme' (except in the phrases 'occupational pension scheme', 'personal pension scheme' and 'public service pension scheme') means a scheme or other arrangements, comprised in one or more instruments or agreements, having or capable of having effect so as to provide benefits to or in respect of people on retirement, on having reached a particular age, or on termination of service in an employment: see s 1(5); and PERSONAL AND OCCUPATIONAL PENSIONS vol 80 (2013) PARA 208.

17 Companies Act 2006 s 1278(1)(e). Head (5) in the text refers to the activity of effecting or carrying out contracts of long-term insurance within the meaning of the Financial Services and Markets (Regulated Activities) Order 2001, SI 2001/544 (see INSURANCE vol 60 (2011) PARA 20): see the Companies Act 2006 s 1278(1)(e).

18 Ie the Companies Act 2006 s 1277 (see the text and notes 1–5): see s 1279(1).

19 Companies Act 2006 s 1279(1). Regulations under s 1277 (see the text and notes 1–5) may provide that s 1277 does not apply to shares of a specified description: s 1279(1). As to the meaning of 'specified' see note 5.

20 Companies Act 2006 s 1279(1)(a).
21 Companies Act 2006 s 1279(1)(b). For this purpose, an institution has an interest in shares if the shares, or a depositary certificate in respect of them, are held by it, or on its behalf: s 1279(2). A 'depositary certificate' means an instrument conferring rights (other than options) in respect of shares held by another person, and the transfer of which may be effected without the consent of that person: s 1279(2). Where an institution has an interest in a specified description of collective investment scheme, within the meaning of the Financial Services and Markets Act 2000 (ie an open-ended investment company) (see FINANCIAL SERVICES REGULATION vol 50A (2016) PARA 841), or in any other specified description of scheme or collective investment vehicle, it is taken to have an interest in any shares in which that scheme or vehicle has or is taken to have an interest: Companies Act 2006 s 1279(3). For this purpose, a scheme or vehicle is taken to have an interest in shares if it would be regarded as having such an interest in accordance with s 1279(2) if it was an institution to which s 1277 applied: s 1279(4).
22 Ie made under the Companies Act 2006 s 1277 (see the text and notes 1–5): see s 1280(1).
23 Companies Act 2006 s 1280(1). The regulations may require information to be provided in respect of specified occasions or specified periods (s 1280(2)) and in such manner as may be specified, and to such persons as may be specified, or to the public (or both) (s 1280(4)).
24 Companies Act 2006 s 1280(1)(a). For these purposes, references to a person acting on behalf of an institution include any person to whom authority has been delegated by the institution to take decisions as to any matter relevant to the subject matter of the regulations, and such other persons as may be specified: s 1277(3)(a).
25 References in the Companies Act 2006 s 1280 to instructions are to instructions of any description, whether general or specific, whether binding or not and whether or not acted upon: s 1280(6).
26 Companies Act 2006 s 1280(1)(b).
27 Companies Act 2006 s 1280(1)(c).
28 Companies Act 2006 s 1280(3).
29 Companies Act 2006 s 1280(5)(a).
30 Companies Act 2006 s 1280(5)(b).
31 Companies Act 2006 s 1280(5)(b)(i).
32 Companies Act 2006 s 1280(5)(b)(ii).
33 Companies Act 2006 s 1280(5)(b)(iii).

(vii) Cessation of Company Membership

389. Cessation of membership of a company. Membership of a company[1] ceases:

(1) on death[2];
(2) on the registration of a transfer of all the shares held by a member[3];
(3) by a valid surrender or forfeiture of his shares[4];
(4) on the registration as a member of a purchaser of shares under a sale to satisfy a lien[5]; or
(5) on the dissolution of the company[6].

Provision may be made in a company's articles of association[7] for cessation of membership in accordance with these principles[8].

1 As to who qualifies as a member of a company see PARA 323.
2 See PARA 409. A company's articles may make provision for the transmission of shares by operation of law, including devolution by death or bankruptcy: see PARA 445.
3 See PARA 419. As to the transfer of shares see PARA 400 et seq. As to a member's liability as a past member where the company is being wound up see COMPANY AND PARTNERSHIP INSOLVENCY vol 17 (2011) PARA 663. See also PARA 372 et seq.
4 See PARA 1400 et seq.
5 See PARA 1393.
6 See COMPANY AND PARTNERSHIP INSOLVENCY vol 17 (2011) PARA 891. As to orders for winding up made under the Insolvency Act 1986 see COMPANY AND PARTNERSHIP INSOLVENCY vol 16 (2011) PARA 438 et seq; and as to the dissolution of a company in respect of which a winding-up order has been made see COMPANY AND PARTNERSHIP INSOLVENCY vol 17 (2011) 888 et seq.
7 As to a company's articles of association see PARA 227 et seq.

8 Under the Companies (Tables A to F) Regulations 1985, SI 1985/805, reg 2, Schedule Table C (which applies modified Table A articles of association to companies limited by guarantee and not having a share capital), it is specified that a member of the company may at any time withdraw from the company by giving at least seven clear days' notice to the company but membership is not transferable and it ceases on death: Schedule Table C art 4. As to the meaning of 'company limited by guarantee' see PARA 95. As to the meanings of 'company having a share capital' and 'share capital' see PARA 1231. As to 'Table A' and 'Table C', and as to the treatment of legacy articles under the Companies Act 2006, see PARA 229. Similar provision is made by the model articles which have been made for the purposes of the Companies Act 2006 and intended for adoption by private companies limited by guarantee (see the Companies (Model Articles) Regulations 2008, SI 2008/3229, reg 3, Sch 2; and PARA 227 et seq). Under those model articles, a member may withdraw from membership of the company by giving seven days' notice to the company in writing: Sch 2 art 22(1). However, membership is not transferable (Sch 2 art 22(2)); and a person's membership terminates when that person dies or ceases to exist (Sch 2 art 22(3)). As to the meaning of 'private company' see PARA 95.

390. Bankruptcy or insolvency of company member. A company member[1] who becomes bankrupt ceases to be a member when the trustee is registered as a member in his place, as he may be, if the company's articles of association permit it[2], or when the trustee disclaims the share and the name of the bankrupt is removed from the register[3], or when the trustee's transferee is registered[4]. Where a company is a member, its membership ceases when the transferee of the liquidator is registered or when the liquidator disclaims the shares[5].

1 As to who qualifies as a member of a company see PARA 323.

2 *Re Bentham Mills Spinning Co* (1879) 11 ChD 900, CA; *Morgan v Gray* [1953] Ch 83 at 87, [1953] 1 All ER 213 at 217 per Danckwerts J. As to a company's articles of association generally see PARA 227 et seq; and as to such articles that make provision specifically as indicated in the text see PARAS 407, 445, 1589.

3 *Wise v Lansdell* [1921] 1 Ch 420.

4 As to a shareholder's bankruptcy generally see BANKRUPTCY AND INDIVIDUAL INSOLVENCY vol 5 (2013) PARA 435.

5 This occurs under the Insolvency Act 1986 s 178: see COMPANY AND PARTNERSHIP INSOLVENCY vol 17 (2011) PARA 824 et seq.

(10) CERTIFICATION AND TRANSFER OF SECURITIES

(i) Certification and Transfer of Shares

A. SHARE CERTIFICATES AND WARRANTS: IN GENERAL

391. Share certificates as evidence of title. In the case of a company[1] registered in England and Wales[2] or Northern Ireland, a certificate under the common seal[3] of the company specifying any shares[4] held by a member[5] is prima facie evidence of his title to the shares[6]. This provision does not, however, apply to any document issued with respect to uncertificated shares; and a document issued by or on behalf of a participating issuer purportedly evidencing title to an uncertificated unit of a participating security is not evidence of title to the unit of the security[7].

A company has power[8] to issue a certificate certifying that the shareholder named in the certificate is the registered holder of the shares specified in it, the object being to give shareholders the opportunity of more easily dealing with their shares in the market and at once showing a marketable title[9]. The certificate is the only documentary evidence of title in the possession of a shareholder[10]. It is not a negotiable instrument or a warranty of title by the company issuing it[11]. It declares to all the world that the person who is named in it is the registered holder of certain shares in the company[12], and that the shares are paid up to the extent mentioned in it[13]; and it is given with the intention that it shall be used as such a declaration[14].

1 As to the meaning of 'company' see PARA 21.
2 As to the registration of companies see PARA 104. As to the meanings of 'England' and 'Wales' see PARA 1 note 5.
3 A company may have a common seal, but need not have one: see Companies Act 2006 s 45; and PARA 282. A company that has a common seal may have an official seal for use for sealing securities issued by the company, or for sealing documents creating or evidencing securities so issued: see s 50; and PARA 290. A share certificate is not a deed within the meaning of the word as used in the Law of Property Act 1925 s 74 relating to the execution of deeds by or on behalf of corporations (see DEEDS AND OTHER INSTRUMENTS vol 32 (2012) PARAS 240–242): *South London Greyhound Racecourses Ltd v Wake* [1931] 1 Ch 496 at 503 per Clauson J. See also *R v Morton* (1873) LR 2 CCR 22.
4 As to the meaning of 'share' see PARA 1231.
5 As to the meaning of 'member of a company' see PARA 323.
6 Companies Act 2006 s 768(1). As to the equivalent provision in relation to Scotland see s 768(2). The provisions of s 768 apply to unregistered companies by virtue of the Unregistered Companies Regulations 2009, SI 2009/2436, Sch 1 para 12(1)(a): see PARA 1857. As to the meaning of 'unregistered company' see PARA 1856.

While membership of a company requires entry on the register of members (unless the company has made an election under the Companies Act 2006 s 128B to keep membership information on the central register (see PARA 364)), a liquidator may distribute surplus assets in a winding up to the possessors of share certificates without requiring them to perfect their title by registration where the liquidator is satisfied that they are beneficially entitled to the shares to which the certificate relates; but, where certificates have been purchased by collectors for their ornamental value, the holders of those certificates are not beneficially entitled to the shares to which the certificate relates: *Re Baku Consolidated Oilfields Ltd* [1994] 1 BCLC 173.
7 See the Uncertificated Securities Regulations 2001, SI 2001/3755, reg 38(3); and PARA 432. As to uncertificated shares generally see PARA 431 et seq.
8 A person cannot insist on having a certificate of his title as a shareholder until he has done everything required to make him a shareholder: *Wilkinson v Anglo-Californian Gold Mining Co* (1852) 18 QB 728.
9 *Re Bahia and San Francisco Rly Co* (1868) LR 3 QB 584 at 595 per Cockburn CJ.
10 *Société Générale de Paris v Walker* (1885) 11 App Cas 20 at 29, HL, per Earl of Selborne. It applies only to the legal and not to the equitable title to the shares: *Shropshire Union Railways and Canal Co v R* (1875) LR 7 HL 496 at 509 per Lord Cairns LC.
11 *Longman v Bath Electric Tramways Ltd* [1905] 1 Ch 646, CA. See also *Royal Bank of Scotland plc v Sandstone Properties Ltd* [1998] 2 BCLC 429 at 431, 432 per Tuckey J.
12 *Re Bahia and San Francisco Rly Co* (1868) LR 3 QB 584; *Shropshire Union Railways and Canal Co v R* (1875) LR 7 HL 496.
13 *Bloomenthal v Ford* [1897] AC 156, HL; *Burkinshaw v Nicolls* (1878) 3 App Cas 1004, HL; *Barrow's Case* (1880) 14 ChD 432, CA; *Waterhouse v Jamieson* (1870) LR 2 Sc & Div 29 at 33, HL, per Lord Hatherley LC. Cf *Re AW Hall & Co* (1887) 37 ChD 712.
14 *Re Bahia and San Francisco Rly Co* (1868) LR 3 QB 584; *Webb v Bay Comrs* (1870) LR 5 QB 642; *Balkis Consolidated Co v Tomkinson* [1893] AC 396, HL; *Dixon v Kennaway & Co* [1900] 1 Ch 833. A company is estopped from disputing the truth of any statement in a share certificate: see PARA 398.

392. Prohibition on issue of new share warrants; effect of existing share warrants. No share warrant may be issued by a company[1], irrespective of whether its articles[2] purport to authorise it to do so, on or after 26 May 2015[3]. Prior to that date, a company limited by shares[4] might, if so authorised by its articles[5], issue with respect to any fully paid shares[6] a warrant (a 'share warrant') stating that the bearer of the warrant was entitled to the shares specified in it[7]. A share warrant issued under the company's common seal[8] entitles the bearer to the shares specified in it and the shares may be transferred by delivery of the warrant[9]. A share warrant is a negotiable instrument[10].

A company that has issued a share warrant may, if so authorised by its articles, provide, by coupons or otherwise, for the payment of the future dividends on the shares included in the warrant[11].

An application for voluntary striking off[12] on behalf of a company must not be made at a time when there is a share warrant issued by the company[13]. It is an offence for a person to make an application in contravention of this provision[14]. In proceedings for such an offence it is, however, a defence for the accused to prove that the accused did not know, and could not reasonably have known, of the existence of the share warrant[15].

1 As to the meaning of 'company' see PARA 21..
2 As to the meaning of references to a company's 'articles' see PARA 227 note 2.
3 See the Companies Act 2006 s 779(4) (added by the Small Business, Enterprise and Employment Act 2015 s 84(1)). The date referred to in the text is the date on which s 84 came into force: see s 164(3)(g)(ii).

The Secretary of State must, as soon as reasonably practicable after the end of the period of five years beginning with the day on which s 84 came into force, carry out a review of section 84, and prepare and publish a report setting out the conclusions of the review: s 86(1). The report must, in particular, set out the objectives intended to be achieved by s 84, and assess the extent to which those objectives have been achieved: s 86(2). The Secretary of State must lay the report before Parliament: s 86(3). As to the Secretary of State see PARA 6.
4 As to the meaning of 'limited by shares' see PARA 95. As to the meaning of 'share' see PARA 1231
5 As to the provision made for share warrants in the model articles see the Companies (Model Articles) Regulations 2008, SI 2008/3229, Sch 3 art 51 (public company). As to the model articles see PARA 227. Such a provision in the articles may be removed without the necessity for a special resolution: see PARA 231.

In *Pilkington v United Railways of the Havana and Regla Warehouses Ltd* [1930] 2 Ch 108, it was unsuccessfully contended that the corresponding provision of the Companies Act 1929 had altered the law so as to preclude the issue of warrants in respect of stock.
6 The fact that in the Companies Act 1867 s 31 (repealed); see now the Companies Act 2006 s 122; and PARA 338) each share must, so long as the share has a number, be distinguished by that number in the statement to be inserted in the register of members on the issue of a warrant is not sufficient indication of an intention that the provisions of the Act relating to share warrants do not apply to stock: see *Pilkington v United Railways of the Havana and Regla Warehouses Ltd* [1930] 2 Ch 108.
7 See the Companies Act 2006 s 779(1). Such unregistered shares were known as 'bearer shares'.
8 A company may have a common seal, but need not have one: see the Companies Act 2006 s 45; and PARA 282. A company that has a common seal may have an official seal for use for sealing securities issued by the company, or for sealing documents creating or evidencing securities so issued: see s 50; and PARA 290.
9 Companies Act 2006 s 779(2). This will not apply, however, after the end of the surrender period: see PARA 393.
10 *Webb, Hale & Co v Alexandria Water Co* (1905) 93 LT 339. Cf *Stern v R* [1896] 1 QB 211. This will not apply, however, after the end of the surrender period: see PARA 393. See also FINANCIAL INSTRUMENTS AND TRANSACTIONS vol 49 (2015) PARA 401.
11 Companies Act 2006 s 779(3). This will not apply, however, after the end of the surrender period: see PARA 393.
12 Ie under the Companies Act 2006 s 1003: see PARAS 1707, 1712.
13 Small Business, Enterprise and Employment Act 2015 Sch 4 para 13(1).
14 Small Business, Enterprise and Employment Act 2015 Sch 4 para 13(2). A person guilty of such an offence is liable on conviction on indictment, or on summary conviction, to a fine: Sch 4 para 18(2).
15 Small Business, Enterprise and Employment Act 2015 Sch 4 para 13(3).

393. Arrangements for conversion and cancellation of existing share warrants. In relation to a company[1] which has issued a share warrant[2] which has not been surrendered for cancellation before 26 May 2015[3] (the 'commencement date')[4], during the period of nine months beginning with the commencement date (the 'surrender period') the bearer of the share warrant has a right of surrender in relation to the warrant[5]. If the bearer of a share warrant has a right of surrender in relation to the warrant, the bearer is entitled on surrendering the warrant for cancellation:

(1) to have the bearer's name entered as a member in the register of members[6] of the company concerned; or

(2) where an election[7] is in force in respect of the company to keep membership information on the central register[8], to have the bearer's name and other particulars delivered to the registrar of companies[9], and the document containing that information registered by the registrar and the date recorded, as if the information were information required[10] to be delivered[11].

A company must, as soon as reasonably practicable and in any event before the end of the period of two months beginning with the day on which a share warrant is surrendered for cancellation pursuant to a right of surrender, complete and have ready for delivery the certificates of the shares specified in the warrant[12]. If a company fails to comply with this requirement, an offence is committed by every officer of the company[13] who is in default[14].

A company must, as soon as reasonably practicable and in any event before the end of the period of one month beginning with the commencement date, give notice[15] to the bearer of a share warrant issued by the company of:

(a) the bearer's right of surrender;

(b) the consequences of not exercising that right before the end of the period of seven months beginning with the commencement date[16];

(c) the fact that the right will cease to be exercisable at the end of the surrender period; and

(d) the consequences of not exercising the right before the end of that period[17].

If a company fails to comply with this requirement an offence is committed by every officer of the company who is in default[18].

In relation to a share warrant of a company which has not been surrendered by the bearer for cancellation before the end of the period of seven months beginning with the commencement date, any transfer of, or agreement to transfer, the share warrant made after the end of that period is void[19]. With effect from the end of that period, all rights which are attached to the shares specified in the warrant are suspended, including any voting rights and any right to receive a dividend or other distribution[20]. The company must pay into a separate bank account that complies with the statutory conditions[21] any dividend or other distribution which the bearer of the share warrant would, but for the suspension, have been entitled to receive[22]. If the share warrant is subsequently surrendered[23], the suspension ceases to have effect on surrender, and the suspension period amount[24] must be paid to the bearer by the company[25].

A company must, before the end of the period of eight months beginning with the commencement date, give further notice to the bearer of a share warrant of the company of:

(i) the bearer's right of surrender;

(ii) the consequences of not having exercised the right of surrender before the end of the period of seven months beginning with the commencement date[26]; and

(iii) the matters referred to in heads (c) and (d) above[27].

If a company fails to comply with this requirement an offence is committed by every officer of the company who is in default[28].

In relation to a company which has issued a share warrant which has not been surrendered for cancellation before the end of the surrender period, the company must, as soon as reasonably practicable and in any event before the end of the period of three months beginning with the day after the end of the surrender period, apply to the court[29] for an order (a 'cancellation order') cancelling with effect from the date of the order both the share warrant and the shares specified in it[30]. The company must give notice to the bearer of the share warrant of the fact that an application has been so made before the end of the period of 14 days beginning with the day on which it is made; and the notice must include a copy of the application[31]. If a company fails to comply with these requirements an offence is committed by every officer of the company who is in default[32]. A company must, on making an application for a cancellation order, immediately give notice to the registrar[33]. If a company fails to comply with this requirement an offence is committed by the company, and by every officer of the company who is in default[34].

The court must make a cancellation order in respect of a share warrant if, on an application duly made[35], it is satisfied either that the company has given notice to the bearer of the share warrant as required[36], or that the bearer had actual notice by other means of the matters mentioned in heads (a) to (d) above[37]. If, on such an application, the court is not so satisfied, it must instead make a suspended cancellation order[38] in respect of the share warrant[39]. Where a share warrant is cancelled by an order under this provision, the company concerned must, as soon as reasonably practicable:

(A) enter the cancellation date[40] in its register of members; or

(B) where an election[41] to keep membership information on the central register[42] is in force in respect of the company, deliver that information to the registrar as if it were information required[43] to be delivered[44].

In relation to a company, if a share warrant of the company and the shares specified in it are cancelled by a cancellation order or a suspended cancellation order, the company must, before the end of the period of 15 days beginning with the cancellation date, deliver to the registrar:

(I) a copy of the order;

(II) in the case of a suspended cancellation order, a statement confirming that the share warrant and the shares specified in it have been cancelled by the order with effect from the cancellation date; and

(III) a statement of capital[45].

If the company fails to comply with this requirement an offence is committed by the company, and by every officer of the company who is in default[46]. In the case of a public company[47], a statement of capital so delivered is to be treated as a document subject to the Directive disclosure requirements[48] for the purposes of the Companies Act 2006[49].

Where the court makes a cancellation order or a suspended cancellation order in relation to a public company and either, in the case of a cancellation order, the order has the effect of bringing the nominal value of its allotted share capital below the authorised minimum[50], or, in the case of a suspended cancellation order, the order may have that effect from the end of the grace period[51], the registrar must not register the cancellation order or, as the case may be, the suspended cancellation order if it has that effect from the end of the grace period unless either the court so directs in the order concerned, or the company is first re-registered as a private company[52].

Where a share warrant is cancelled by a cancellation order or suspended cancellation order, the company concerned must, before the end of the period of 14 days beginning with the cancellation date, make a payment into court of an amount equal to the aggregate nominal value of the shares specified in the warrant and the whole of any premium paid on them[53], plus the suspension period amount[54]. If a company fails to comply with this requirement an offence is committed by every officer of the company who is in default[55]. A person who, at the end of the period of seven months beginning with the commencement date, was the bearer of a share warrant which has been cancelled by a cancellation order or a suspended cancellation order may apply to the court for the sum so paid into court in respect of the shares specified in the warrant to be paid to that person[56]. Such an application may only be made during the period beginning with the day which is six months after the cancellation date, and ending with the day which is three years after the cancellation date[57]. The court may grant such an application only if it is satisfied that there are exceptional circumstances justifying the failure of the bearer of the share warrant to exercise the right of surrender either, in the case of a warrant cancelled by a cancellation order, before the end of the surrender period, or, in the case of a warrant cancelled by a suspended cancellation order, before the end of the grace period[58].

In relation to a company in respect of which a cancellation order or suspended cancellation order has been made, if any of the following is appointed in relation to the company after the cancellation date, namely an administrator, an administrative receiver or a liquidator (the 'office-holder'[59]), the office-holder may apply to the court for the sum paid into court which is equal to the aggregate nominal value of the shares specified in the warrant and the whole of any premium paid on them[60] to be paid to the office-holder by way of a contribution to the company's assets[61]. Such an application may only be made during the period beginning with the cancellation date, and ending with the day which is three years after that date[62]. Anything left of a sum paid into court[63] immediately after the end of that period must be paid into the Consolidated Fund[64].

1 As to the meaning of 'company' under the Companies Acts see PARA 21 (definition applied for these purposes by the Small Business, Enterprise and Employment Act 2015 Sch 4 para 20(2)).
2 As to share warrants see PARA 392.
3 Ie date on which the Small Business, Enterprise and Employment Act 2015 s 84 (see PARA 392) came into force: see s 164(3)(g)(ii).
4 Small Business, Enterprise and Employment Act 2015 Sch 4 para 1(1).
5 Small Business, Enterprise and Employment Act 2015 Sch 4 para 1(2).
6 As to the register of members see PARA 336 et seq; and as to the option to keep membership information on the central register see PARA 363 et seq.
7 Ie an election under the Companies Act 2006 s 128B: see PARA 364.
8 As to the central register see PARA 142.
9 As to the meaning of 'registrar of companies' see PARA 126 note 2 (definition as applied: see note 1).
10 Ie under the Companies Act 2006 s 128E: see PARA 366.
11 Small Business, Enterprise and Employment Act 2015 Sch 4 para 1(3).

The Companies Act 2006 ss 1103, 1104, 1107 (language requirements: see PARAS 164–165) apply to all documents required to be delivered to the registrar under the Small Business, Enterprise and Employment Act 2015 Sch 4 Pt 1 (paras 1–21): Sch 4 para 15.
12 Small Business, Enterprise and Employment Act 2015 Sch 4 para 1(4).
13 For the purposes of any offence under the Small Business, Enterprise and Employment Act 2015 Sch 4 Pt 1, a shadow director is treated as an officer of the company: Sch 4 para 17. As to the meaning of 'officer who is in default' see PARA 316; as to the meaning of 'officer' generally see PARA 679; and as to shadow directors see PARA 513 (definitions as applied: see note 1). The Companies Act 2006 ss 1121, 1122 (liability of officer in default: see PARA 316) apply for the purposes of the Small Business, Enterprise and Employment Act 2015 Sch 4 Pt 1 as they apply for the purposes of the Companies Acts: Small Business, Enterprise and Employment Act 2015 Sch 4 para 19(a). As to the meaning of the 'Companies Acts' see PARA 13 (definition applied by the Small Business, Enterprise and Employment Act 2015 Sch 4 para 20(1)).
14 Small Business, Enterprise and Employment Act 2015 Sch 4 para 1(5). A person guilty of such an offence is liable on summary conviction to a fine not exceeding level 3 on the standard scale and, for continued contravention, to a daily default fine not exceeding one-tenth of level 3 on the standard scale: Sch 4 para 18(1). As to the meaning of 'daily default fine' see the Companies Act 2006 s 1125; and PARA 1816 (applied for these purposes by the Small Business, Enterprise and

Employment Act 2015 Sch 4 para 19(b)). As to the standard scale and the powers of magistrates' courts to issue fines on summary conviction see SENTENCING vol 92 (2015) PARA 176.

The Companies Act 2006 ss 1127, 1128 (general provision about summary proceedings: see PARA 1818), s 1129 (legal professional privilege: see PARA 1821) and s 1132 (production and inspection of documents: see PARA 1820) apply for the purposes of the Small Business, Enterprise and Employment Act 2015 Sch 4 Pt 1 as they apply for the purposes of the Companies Acts: Small Business, Enterprise and Employment Act 2015 Sch 4 para 19(c)–(e).

15 A notice required by virtue of any provision of the Small Business, Enterprise and Employment Act 2015 to be given to the bearer of a share warrant must be:
(1) published in the Gazette (Sch 4 para 14(1)(a));
(2) communicated to that person in the same way, if any, as the company concerned normally communicates with that person for other purposes relating to the shares specified in the warrant (Sch 4 para 14(1)(b)); and
(3) made available in a prominent position on the company's website, if it has one, during the period mentioned in Sch 4 para 14(2) (see heads (a)–(d) below; and see Sch 4 para 14(3)) (Sch 4 para 14(1)(c)).

That period is the period beginning with the day on which the notice is published in the Gazette and ending with:
(a) in the case of a notice required by Sch 4 para 2, the day on which a notice required by Sch 4 para 4 is made available on the company's website (Sch 4 para 14(2)(a));
(b) in the case of a notice required by Sch 4 para 4, the day on which a notice required by Sch 4 para 5(3) is made available on the company's website (Sch 4 para 14(2)(b));
(c) in the case of a notice required by Sch 4 para 5(3), the day on which the court makes a cancellation order or (as the case may be) suspended cancellation order in respect of the share warrant (Sch 4 para 14(2)(c));
(d) in the case of a notice required by virtue of Sch 4 para 6(3)(a), the end of the grace period (Sch 4 para 14(2)(d)).

'Grace period' has the meaning given by Sch 4 para 6(3)(b) (see note 38 head (2)): Sch 4 para 20(1). Nothing in Sch 4 para 14 requires a notice to be made available on the company's website after the day on which the last of the share warrants issued by the company to be surrendered is surrendered: Sch 4 para 14(3). The Companies Act 2006 ss 1143–1148 (company communications provisions: see PARA 749 et seq) apply for the purposes of the Small Business, Enterprise and Employment Act 2015 Sch 4 Pt 1 as they apply for the purposes of the Companies Acts: Small Business, Enterprise and Employment Act 2015 Sch 4 para 14(4).

16 See the Small Business, Enterprise and Employment Act 2015 Sch 4 para 14(3); and note 15.

17 Small Business, Enterprise and Employment Act 2015 Sch 4 para 2(1).

18 Small Business, Enterprise and Employment Act 2015 Sch 4 para 2(2). A person guilty of an offence under any provision Sch 4 except Sch 4 para 1(5) (see note 14) is liable on conviction on indictment, or on summary conviction in England and Wales, to a fine: Sch 4 para 18(2). See also note 13.

The Companies Act 2006 s 1112 (general false statement offence: see PARA 132) and s 1113 (enforcement of company's filing obligations: see PARA 166) apply for the purposes of the Small Business, Enterprise and Employment Act 2015 Sch 4 Pt 1 as they apply for the purposes of the Companies Acts: Small Business, Enterprise and Employment Act 2015 Sch 4 para 16.

19 Small Business, Enterprise and Employment Act 2015 Sch 4 para 3(1), (2).

20 Small Business, Enterprise and Employment Act 2015 Sch 4 para 3(3).

21 Ie the conditions in the Small Business, Enterprise and Employment Act 2015 Sch 4 para 3(5). A bank account complies with this provision if the balance of the account bears interest at an appropriate rate, and can be withdrawn by such notice (if any) as is appropriate: Sch 4 para 3(5).

22 Small Business, Enterprise and Employment Act 2015 Sch 4 para 3(4).

23 Ie in accordance with the Small Business, Enterprise and Employment Act 2015 Sch 4.

24 The 'suspension period amount', in relation to a share warrant, is the aggregate amount of any dividends or other distributions which the bearer of the warrant would, but for the suspension, have been entitled to receive, plus any interest accrued on that amount: Small Business, Enterprise and Employment Act 2015 Sch 4 para 3(7).

25 Small Business, Enterprise and Employment Act 2015 Sch 4 para 3(6).

26 See the Small Business, Enterprise and Employment Act 2015 Sch 4 para 3; and the text and notes 19–25.

27 Small Business, Enterprise and Employment Act 2015 Sch 4 para 4(1).

28 Small Business, Enterprise and Employment Act 2015 Sch 4 para 4(2). See further notes 13–14, 18.

29 As to the meaning of 'the court' see PARA 160 note 12 (definition as applied: see note 1).

30 Small Business, Enterprise and Employment Act 2015 Sch 4 para 5(1), (2).

31 Small Business, Enterprise and Employment Act 2015 Sch 4 para 5(3).
32 Small Business, Enterprise and Employment Act 2015 Sch 4 para 5(4). See further notes 13–14, 18.
33 Small Business, Enterprise and Employment Act 2015 Sch 4 para 5(5).
34 Small Business, Enterprise and Employment Act 2015 Sch 4 para 5(6). See further notes 13–14, 18.
35 Ie an application under the Small Business, Enterprise and Employment Act 2015 Sch 4 para 5: see the text and notes 29–34.
36 Ie as required by the Small Business, Enterprise and Employment Act 2015 Sch 4 para 2 or Sch 4 para 4: see the text and notes 16–18, 27–28.
37 Small Business, Enterprise and Employment Act 2015 Sch 4 para 6(1).
38 A 'suspended cancellation order' is an order:
(1) requiring the company to give notice to the bearer of the share warrant containing the information set out in the Small Business, Enterprise and Employment Act 2015 Sch 4 para 6(4) before the end of the period of five working days beginning with the day the order is made (Sch 4 para 6(3)(a));
(2) providing that the bearer of the share warrant has a right of surrender during the period of two months beginning with the day the order is made ('the grace period') (Sch 4 para 6(3)(b)); and
(3) if the share warrant is not so surrendered, cancelling it and the shares specified in it with effect from the end of the grace period Sch 4 para 6(3)(c)).

A notice required to be given by a suspended cancellation order must:
(a) inform the bearer of the share warrant of the fact that the bearer has a right of surrender during the grace period (Sch 4 para 6(4)(a));
(b) inform the bearer of the consequences of not having exercised that right before the end of the period of seven months beginning with the commencement date (see Sch 4 para 3) (Sch 4 para 6(4)(b)); and
(c) explain that the share warrant will be cancelled with effect from the end of the grace period if it is not surrendered before then ((Sch 4 para 6(4)(c)).

39 Small Business, Enterprise and Employment Act 2015 Sch 4 para 6(2).
40 For these purposes, 'the cancellation date', in relation to a share warrant, means the day its cancellation by a cancellation order or suspended cancellation order takes effect: Small Business, Enterprise and Employment Act 2015 Sch 4 para 6(6).
41 See note 7.
42 See note 8.
43 See note 10.
44 Small Business, Enterprise and Employment Act 2015 Sch 4 para 6(5).
45 Small Business, Enterprise and Employment Act 2015 Sch 4 para 7(1), (2). The statement of capital must state with respect to the company's share capital as reduced by the cancellation of the share warrant and the shares specified in it the following matters (Sch 4 para 7(3)), ie:
(1) the total number of shares of the company;
(2) the aggregate nominal value of those shares;
(3) the aggregate amount, if any, unpaid on those shares, whether on account of their nominal value or by way of premium; and
(4) for each class of shares:
  (a) such particulars of the rights attached to the shares as are prescribed by the Secretary of State under the Companies Act 2006 s 644(2)(c)(i) (see PARA 1366);
  (b) the total number of shares of that class; and
  (c) the aggregate nominal value of shares of that class.

46 Small Business, Enterprise and Employment Act 2015 Sch 4 para 7(4). See further notes 13–14, 18.
47 As to the meaning of 'public company' see PARA 95 (definition as applied: see note 1).
48 As to the Directive disclosure requirements see the Companies Act 2006 s 1078; and PARA 139.
49 Small Business, Enterprise and Employment Act 2015 Sch 4 para 7(5).
50 Small Business, Enterprise and Employment Act 2015 Sch 4 para 8(1)(a).
51 Small Business, Enterprise and Employment Act 2015 Sch 4 para 8(1)(b).
52 Small Business, Enterprise and Employment Act 2015 Sch 4 para 8(2). As to the meaning of 'private company' see PARA 95 (definition as applied: see note 1). The expedited procedure for re-registration provided by the Companies Act 2006 s 651 (see PARA 1381) applies for these purposes as it applies for the purposes of s 650: Small Business, Enterprise and Employment Act 2015 Sch 4 para 8(3). Where the court makes an order under the Companies Act 2006 s 651 of that Act in connection with a suspended cancellation order, the order under s 651 must be

conditional on the suspended cancellation order having the effect mentioned in the Small Business, Enterprise and Employment Act 2015 Sch 4 para 8(1)(b) (see the text and note 51) from the end of the grace period: Sch 4 para 8(4).
53 Small Business, Enterprise and Employment Act 2015 Sch 4 para 9(1)(a).
54 Small Business, Enterprise and Employment Act 2015 Sch 4 para 9(1)(b).
55 Small Business, Enterprise and Employment Act 2015 Sch 4 para 9(2). See further notes 13–14, 18.
56 Small Business, Enterprise and Employment Act 2015 Sch 4 para 10(1).
57 Small Business, Enterprise and Employment Act 2015 Sch 4 para 10(2).
58 Small Business, Enterprise and Employment Act 2015 Sch 4 para 10(3).
59 Small Business, Enterprise and Employment Act 2015 Sch 4 para 11(1).
60 Ie the sum paid into court under the Small Business, Enterprise and Employment Act 2015 Sch 4 para 9(1)(a): see the text and note 53.
61 Small Business, Enterprise and Employment Act 2015 Sch 4 para 11(2).
62 Small Business, Enterprise and Employment Act 2015 Sch 4 para 11(3).
63 Ie under the Small Business, Enterprise and Employment Act 2015 Sch 4 para 9(1): see the text and notes 53–54.
64 Small Business, Enterprise and Employment Act 2015 Sch 4 para 12(1). This does not, however, apply to any amount in respect of which an application under Sch 4 para 10(1) or Sch 4 para 11(2) has been made but not yet determined before the end of that period unless and until the application is dismissed and either the period for bringing an appeal against the dismissal has expired, or, in a case where an appeal is brought before the end of that period, the appeal is dismissed, abandoned or otherwise ceases to have effect: Sch 4 para 12(2). As to the Consolidated Fund see CONSTITUTIONAL AND ADMINISTRATIVE LAW vol 20 (2014) PARA 480 et seq; PARLIAMENT vol 78 (2010) PARAS 1028–1031.

B. ISSUE OF CERTIFICATES ON ALLOTMENT OF SHARES

394. Issue of certificates on the allotment of shares. A company[1] must, within two months[2] after the allotment of any of its shares[3], complete and have ready for delivery, the certificates of the shares allotted[4]. This requirement does, however, not apply:

(1) if the conditions of issue of the shares provide otherwise[5];
(2) in the case of allotment to a financial institution[6]; or
(3) in the case of an allotment of shares if, following the allotment, the company has issued a share warrant[7] in respect of the shares[8]; but no new share warrant may be issued on or after 26 May 2015[9].

If default is made in complying with the requirement to complete and have ready for delivery the certificates of the shares allotted, an offence is committed by every officer of the company who is in default[10].

1 As to the meaning of 'company' under the Companies Acts see PARA 21; and as to the meaning of the 'Companies Acts' see PARA 13.
2 As to the meaning of 'month' see PARA 1818 note 10. As to enforcement of the duty see PARA 395.
3 As to the meaning of 'share' see PARA 1231. As to when shares are allotted see the Companies Act 2006 s 558; and PARA 1280. As to the issue of certificates on the allotment of debentures and debenture stock see PARA 421.
4 Companies Act 2006 s 769(1)(a). As to share certificates see PARA 391. As to the provision made in the model articles for the issue of share certificates see the Companies (Model Articles) Regulations 2008, SI 2008/3229, Sch 1 arts 24, 25 (private company limited by shares), Sch 3 arts 46–49 (public company). As to the model articles see PARA 227.
5 Companies Act 2006 s 769(2)(a).
6 Companies Act 2006 s 769(2)(b). A company of which shares are allotted to a financial institution (see s 778(1)(a)), or with which a transfer for transferring shares to a financial institution is lodged (see s 778(1)(c)), is not required in consequence of that allotment or transfer to comply with s 769(1): s 778(1). For these purposes, a 'financial institution' means:
(1) a recognised clearing house acting in relation to a recognised investment exchange (s 778(2)(a)); or
(2) a nominee of a recognised clearing house acting in that way (s 778(2)(b)(i)), or a recognised investment exchange (s 778(2)(b)(ii)), designated for these purposes in the rules of the recognised investment exchange in question (s 778(2)(b)).

Expressions used in s 778(2) have the same meaning as in the Financial Services and Markets Act 2000 Pt XVIII (ss 285–313): Companies Act 2006 s 778(3). Accordingly, 'recognised clearing house' means either a central counterparty in relation to which a recognition order is in force (a 'recognised central counterparty'), or a clearing house which provides clearing services in the United Kingdom without doing so as a central counterparty, and in relation to which a recognition order is in force: see the Financial Services and Markets Act 2000 ss 285(1)(b), 417(1) (s 285(1)(b) substituted by SI 2013/504); and FINANCIAL SERVICES REGULATION vol 50A (2016) PARA 939.

The provisions of the Companies Act 2006 s 778 apply to unregistered companies by virtue of the Unregistered Companies Regulations 2009, SI 2009/2436, Sch 1 para 12(1)(b), (2), but as modified thereby: see PARA 1857. As to the meaning of 'unregistered company' see PARA 1856.

7 Ie under the Companies Act 2006 s 779: see PARA 392.
8 Companies Act 2006 s 769(2)(c).
9 See the Companies Act 2006 s 779(4); and PARA 392.
10 Companies Act 2006 s 769(3). As to the meaning of 'officer' see PARA 679; and as to the meaning of 'officer in default' see PARA 316.

A person guilty of such an offence is liable on summary conviction to a fine not exceeding level 3 on the standard scale and for continued contravention to a daily default fine not exceeding one-tenth of level 3 on the standard scale: . s 769(4). As to the standard scale and the powers of magistrates' courts to issue fines on summary conviction see SENTENCING vol 92 (2015) PARA 176; and as to the meaning of 'daily default fine' see PARA 1816.

395. Enforcement of issue of certificate of shares allotted. If a company[1] on which a notice has been served[2] requiring it to make good any default in complying with the duty[3] of the company to complete and have ready for delivery the certificates of shares allotted[4] fails to make good the default within ten days after service of the notice, the person[5] entitled to have the certificates delivered to him may apply to the court[6]. The court may on such an application make an order directing the company and any officer[7] of it to make good the default within such time as may be specified in the order[8]; and the order may provide that all costs of and incidental to the application are to be borne by the company or by an officer of it responsible for the default[9].

1 As to the meaning of 'company' under the Companies Acts see PARA 21; and as to the meaning of the 'Companies Acts' see PARA 13.
2 As to the service of documents on a company see PARA 743 et seq.
3 Ie the duty under the Companies Act 2006 s 769(1) (see PARA 394): see s 782(1)(a).
4 See the Companies Act 2006 s 782(1)(a). As to the meaning of 'share' see PARA 1231.
5 As to the meaning of 'person' see PARA 312 note 2.
6 Companies Act 2006 s 782(1). As to the meaning of 'the court' see PARA 160 note 12. As to the procedure that applies on application to the court under companies legislation generally see PARA 306.
7 As to the meaning of 'officer' see PARA 679.
8 Companies Act 2006 s 782(2).
9 Companies Act 2006 s 782(3).

396. Split certificates in respect of shareholding. Whether a shareholder[1] has the right to divide his shareholding and accordingly force the company to give him two or more certificates[2] in respect of it depends entirely on the construction of the articles of the company[3].

1 As to shareholders and membership of companies generally see PARAS 323 et seq, 1889 et seq.
2 As to share certificates see PARA 391.
3 *Sharpe v Tophams Ltd* [1939] Ch 373, [1939] 1 All ER 123, CA. As to the provision made in the model articles see the Companies (Model Articles) Regulations 2008, SI 2008/3229, Sch 1 art 24 (private company limited by shares), Sch 3 arts 46–48 (public company). Similar provision is made in the Companies (Tables A to F) Regulations 1985, SI 1985/805: see Schedule Table A art 6 (disapplied by Table C art 1 in relation to companies limited by guarantee and not having a share capital). As to the model articles see PARA 227. As to the continuing application of the Companies (Tables A to F) Regulations 1985, SI 1985/805, see PARA 229.

397. 'Clean' share certificates. A member[1] is entitled to a 'clean' certificate[2], that is one which does not contain on it any statement derogatory to his title[3].

1 As to who qualifies as a member of a company see PARA 323.
2 As to share certificates see PARA 391.
3 *Re W Key & Son Ltd* [1902] 1 Ch 467. As to the order in which the names of joint holders appear in the register see PARA 336 note 4.

398. Estoppel in relation to share certificates. A company is estopped[1] from disputing the truth of any statement in a share certificate[2] as against any person not knowing that the statement is untrue, who has acted or refrained from acting on the faith of it, and has thereby altered his position to his detriment[3].

Where a person, who lends money to a company on the terms of having as security fully paid shares, receives certificates of the shares as fully paid, and the shares are allotted, and he is registered accordingly[4], the company is estopped from asserting against him any liability in respect of them[5]. The company is also estopped where an allottee accepts a certificate for fully paid shares in such circumstances that he may have reason to believe, when he accepts it, that the balance of the money due on the shares had been paid by another person[6].

The test is whether the shares were taken honestly on the faith of the certificate, and, if so, whether the holder afterwards honestly acted on the certificate or relied on it to his detriment[7]. If a person did not take the shares on the faith of the certificate, or ought to have known that the statements in it were untrue, there is no estoppel as against the company[8]. A company may be estopped although the certificate was signed by a director in favour of a firm of which he is the partner, provided that the director can prove that he did not at the time of signing know the true facts[9]. The company is, however, estopped or liable in respect of its share certificate only where it is issued by those who have authority or apparent authority to issue it; where the certificate is a forgery, as where the secretary forges the signatures of directors, the company is not estopped[10]. Payment of dividends on shares does not estop the company from denying the title of the payee to the shares[11].

If the company is estopped from denying that a share is fully paid as against a holder without notice, such a holder can give a good title to the share as fully paid even to a transferee who has notice that the shares are not fully paid[12].

A person who by reason of the issue of a certificate is entitled to shares by estoppel, and who acts on the certificate to his detriment, may recover from the company as damages the value of the shares at the time of the refusal of the company to recognise him as a shareholder, together with interest from that date[13]. Similarly, a person who as a consequence of relying on a certificate loses his power to get redress against a third party may recover damages from the company[14]. If, however, he has not altered his position on the faith of the certificate, he cannot recover damages[15].

1 As to the meaning of estoppel see ESTOPPEL vol 47 (2014) PARA 301.
2 As to share certificates see PARA 391.
3 *Balkis Consolidated Co v Tomkinson* [1893] AC 396, HL; *Bloomenthal v Ford* [1897] AC 156, HL; *Dixon v Kennaway & Co* [1900] 1 Ch 833; *Parbury's Case* [1896] 1 Ch 100; *Barrow's Case* (1880) 14 ChD 432, CA; *Burkinshaw v Nicolls* (1878) 3 App Cas 1004, HL; *Re Ottos Kopje Diamond Mines Ltd* [1893] 1 Ch 618, CA; *Shaw v Port Philip Colonial Gold Mining Co* (1884) 13 QBD 103; *Monarch Motor Car Co v Pease* (1903) 19 TLR 148. Cf *Simm v Anglo-American Telegraph Co, Anglo-American Telegraph Co v Spurling* (1879) 5 QBD 188, CA; *Re Railway Time Tables Publishing Co, ex p Sandys* (1889) 42 ChD 98, CA; *Re London Celluloid Co* (1888) 39 ChD 190, CA; *Markham and Darter's Case* [1899] 1 Ch 414; *Re Newport and South Wales Shipowners' Co, Rowland's Case* (1880) 42 LT 785, CA; *Penang Foundry Co Ltd v Gardiner* 1913 SC 1203, Ct of Sess.

The three essential elements of an estoppel by representation are: the representation that the person named in the certificate was the holder of the shares; reliance upon that representation; and detriment suffered by way of reliance: *Cadbury Schweppes Ltd v Halifax Share Dealing Ltd* [2006] EWHC 1184 (Ch) at [31], [2007] 1 BCLC 497 at [31] per Lindsay J. See also note 7.

4 As to the register of shareholders see PARA 1891.

5 *Bloomenthal v Ford* [1897] AC 156, HL. This case, together with *Christchurch Gas Co v Kelly* (1887) 3 TLR 634, *Parbury's Case* [1896] 1 Ch 100, and *Penang Foundry Co Ltd v Gardiner* 1913 SC 1203, Ct of Sess, extend the doctrine of *Burkinshaw v Nicolls* (1878) 3 App Cas 1004, HL (a case of a transferee) to the case of an original allottee.

6 *Penang Foundry Co Ltd v Gardiner* 1913 SC 1203, Ct of Sess.

7 *Hart v Frontino and Bolivia South American Gold Mining Co Ltd* (1870) LR 5 Exch 111; *Dixon v Kennaway & Co* [1900] 1 Ch 833. A detriment suffered by reliance on a share certificate arises where an innocent party puts forward a share transfer (together with the certificate) for registration to the company so becoming obliged to indemnify the company for any liability arising as a consequence of the company acting on the request for registration (as to which see *Sheffield Corpn v Barclay* [1905] AC 392, HL; and PARA 442): see *Cadbury Schweppes Ltd v Halifax Share Dealing Ltd* [2006] EWHC 1184 (Ch) at [30], [2007] 1 BCLC 497, [2006] BCC 707 per Lindsay J. The estoppel defeats the company's claim to the indemnity in a situation where there is nothing unconscionable in raising the estoppel: *Cadbury Schweppes Ltd v Halifax Share Dealing Ltd* [2006] EWHC 1184 (Ch), [2007] 1 BCLC 497, [2006] BCC 707.

8 *Blyth's Case* (1876) 4 ChD 140, CA; *Simm v Anglo-American Telegraph Co, Anglo-American Telegraph Co v Spurling* (1879) 5 QBD 188, CA; *Re Vulcan Ironworks Co* [1885] WN 120.

9 *Re Coasters Ltd* [1911] 1 Ch 86.

10 *Ruben v Great Fingall Consolidated* [1906] AC 439, HL; *Dixon v Kennaway & Co* [1900] 1 Ch 833; *South London Greyhound Racecourses Ltd v Wake* [1931] 1 Ch 496. Cf *Shaw v Port Philip Colonial Gold Mining Co* (1884) 13 QBD 103. See also *Lovett v Carson Country Homes Ltd* [2009] EWHC 1143 (Ch), [2011] BCC 789, [2009] All ER (D) 95 (Jun), where the court sought to distinguish *Ruben v Great Fingall Consolidated* [1906] AC 439, HL and was highly critical of *South London Greyhound Racecourses Ltd v Wake* [1931] 1 Ch 496 and held that, while those authorities treat a forged share certificate as a nullity not binding on the company and not giving rise to an estoppel, the company may still be bound by a forged document if the person executing the document can be found to have ostensible authority to warrant that the formalities of execution have been properly complied with.

11 *Foster v Tyne Pontoon and Dry Docks Co and Renwick* (1893) 63 LJQB 50.

12 *Barrow's Case* (1880) 14 ChD 432, CA. Cf *Re London Celluloid Co* (1888) 39 ChD 190, CA.

13 *Re Bahia and San Francisco Rly Co* (1868) LR 3 QB 584; *Hart v Frontino and Bolivia South American Gold Mining Co Ltd* (1870) LR 5 Exch 111; *Re Ottos Kopje Diamond Mines Ltd* [1893] 1 Ch 618, CA; *Balkis Consolidated Co v Tomkinson* [1893] AC 396, HL.

14 *Dixon v Kennaway & Co* [1900] 1 Ch 833.

15 *Simm v Anglo-American Telegraph Co, Anglo-American Telegraph Co v Spurling* (1879) 5 QBD 188, CA (where the person claiming under estoppel had acted upon a forged transfer); *Platt v Rowe (t/a Chapman & Rowe) and CM Mitchell & Co* (1909) 26 TLR 49 (a transferee who paid for shares comprised in a transfer to him which were not registered in the name of the vendor recovered the purchase price as on a total failure of consideration even though the company had sent him a certificate).

399. Note on share certificate. The usual note on a share certificate, that without its production no transfer will be registered, is a mere warning to take care of it, and not a representation to or a contract with the holder of the certificate that a transfer will not be registered without its production[1].

1 *Rainford v James Keith and Blackman Co Ltd* [1905] 1 Ch 296 per Farwell J (revsd on another ground [1905] 2 Ch 147, CA); *Guy v Waterlow Bros and Layton Ltd* (1909) 25 TLR 515. Cf *Société Générale de Paris v Walker* (1885) 11 App Cas 20, HL. As to the company's duties with regard to certificates deposited with it for the purpose of certification of transfers see PARA 416.

C. TRANSFER OF CERTIFICATED SHARES

(A) Contract for Sale of Shares

400. Contract to sell shares. A contract for the sale of shares[1] may be made orally[2]. Specific performance may be ordered of a contract to sell shares[3], even though the company, pending the litigation, has gone into liquidation[4], and also of a contract to take a transfer of shares on which nothing has been paid[5].

1 See further PARAS 401–402.
2 *Humble v Mitchell* (1839) 11 Ad & El 205; *Watson v Spratley* (1854) 10 Exch 222; *Bowlby v Bell* (1846) 3 CB 284; *Bradley v Holdsworth* (1838) 3 M & W 422.
3 *Duncuft v Albrecht* (1841) 12 Sim 189; *Poole v Middleton* (1861) 4 LT 631; *Llewellin v Grossman* (1950) 83 Ll L Rep 462. See CPR PD 24—*The Summary Disposal of Claims* para 7; SPECIFIC PERFORMANCE vol 95 (2013) PARA 326 et seq; and *Woodlands v Hind* [1955] 2 All ER 604, [1955] 1 WLR 688. See also *Langen and Wind Ltd v Bell* [1972] Ch 685, [1972] 1 All ER 296 (specific performance not granted where vendor's equitable lien for unpaid purchase money would not be safeguarded); *Grant v Cigman* [1996] 2 BCLC 24 (on the question of specific performance of an agreement to sell shares, there was an arguable case that time was of the essence given that, due to the nature of the shares to be sold, their value was volatile). As to damages for breach of contract see DAMAGES vol 29 (2014) PARA 499 et seq.
4 *Paine v Hutchinson* (1868) 3 Ch App 388.
5 *Cheale v Kenward* (1858) 3 De G & J 27.

401. Vendor's obligation under a contract for the sale of shares. Under an ordinary contract for sale of shares[1], made subject to the rules of the Stock Exchange, the vendor's only duty is to execute a valid transfer, hand it and the certificate to the purchaser, and do all that is necessary on his part to enable the purchaser to be registered, it being the purchaser's duty to obtain registration of the transfer[2]. Unless registration is refused because the transferor has no right to execute the transfer, the transferee must pay the consideration for the transfer, although registration is refused[3] in which case the transferor, so long as his name remains on the register, holds the shares in trust for the transferee[4] unless the transferor annuls the bargain[5]. Unless the transferor takes this course, the transferee becomes in equity the owner of the shares[6] and the transferor is bound not to prevent or delay the registration of the transferee as owner[7]. A vendor who contracts to sell registered shares is not entitled to complete the transaction by delivery of share warrants[8].

For breach of the vendor's obligations, a claim for damages will lie at the suit of the purchaser[9]. Alternatively, unless the shares are freely available in the market, a claim for specific performance will lie[10].

1 A sale may be subject to a special term eg 'with registration guaranteed': see *Cruse v Paine* (1869) 4 Ch App 441. As to contracts for the sale of shares see PARA 400. As to stocks see PARA 392 note 6.
2 *Neilson v James* (1882) 9 QBD 546, CA. As to the register of shareholders see PARA 1891. See also *RGI International Ltd v Synergy Classic Ltd* [2011] EWHC 3417 (Comm), [2012] 03 LS Gaz R 18, [2011] All ER (D) 172 (Dec) (meaning of term 'investor' in contract for sale of shares).
3 *Stray v Russell* (1859) 1 E & E 888 (affd (1860) 1 E & E 916, Ex Ch); *Skinner v City of London Marine Insurance Corpn* (1885) 14 QBD 882, CA; *London Founders' Association v Clarke* (1888) 20 QBD 576, CA; *Re London, Hamburg and Continental Exchange Bank, Ward and Henry's Case* (1867) 2 Ch App 431 at 438 per Lord Cairns LJ. See also *East Wheal Martha Mining Co* (1863) 33 Beav 119 at 121. For the vendor's obligation where he is not the transferor see *Hichens, Harrison, Woolston & Co v Jackson & Sons* [1943] AC 266, [1943] 1 All ER 128, HL.
4 *Stevenson v Wilson* 1907 SC 445, Ct of Sess. A registered shareholder who is the vendor under an uncompleted but specifically enforceable contract for the sale of his shares is a fiduciary but not a nominee: *Michaels v Harley House (Marylebone) Ltd* [2000] Ch 104, [1999] 1 All ER 356, CA.
5 *Lyle and Scott Ltd v Scott's Trustees* [1959] AC 763, [1959] 2 All ER 661, HL.
6 *Re London, Hamburg and Continental Exchange Bank, Ward and Henry's Case* (1867) 2 Ch App 431 at 438 per Lord Cairns LJ; *Hawks v McArthur* [1951] 1 All ER 22.
7 *Hooper v Herts* [1906] 1 Ch 549, CA.
8 *Iredell v General Securities Corpn Ltd* (1916) 33 TLR 67, CA (where the contract provided that registration of transfers was to be carried out by the vendors free of charge; the company went into liquidation and the liquidator declined to register the transfer).

9 The measure of damages will be the market price at the contractual date for delivery less the contract price: *Shaw v Holland* (1846) 15 M & W 136; *Powell v Jessopp* (1856) 18 CB 336.
10 See SPECIFIC PERFORMANCE vol 95 (2013) PARAS 314, 326–327.

402. Purchaser's obligation under a contract for the sale of shares. On a sale of shares[1] the purchaser is liable on an implied promise to indemnify the vendor, so long as he remains registered, against calls, whether made while the purchaser was beneficially entitled or after the purchaser sold them to a sub-purchaser[2].

For breach of the purchaser's obligations in all cases a claim for damages will lie at the suit of the vendor[3]. Alternatively, unless the shares are freely disposable in the market, a claim for specific performance will lie[4].

1 As to contracts for the sale of shares see PARA 400. As to the vendor's obligations on such a contract see PARA 401.
2 *Walker v Bartlett* (1856) 18 CB 845; *Kellock v Enthoven* (1874) LR 9 QB 241; *Spencer v Ashworth, Partington & Co* [1925] 1 KB 589, CA.
3 The measure of damages will be the contract price less the market price at the contractual date for completion: *AKAS Jamal v Moolla Dawood, Sons & Co* [1916] 1 AC 175, PC.
4 See SPECIFIC PERFORMANCE vol 95 (2013) PARAS 314, 326–327.

(B) Transfer of Shares: in general

403. Restrictions on transfer of shares. The shares[1] or other interest of any member[2] in a company[3] are transferable in accordance with the company's articles[4]. The articles of many companies contain restrictions on the right of transfer of shares[5].

A restriction on the right to transfer shares is not repugnant to the absolute ownership of the shares, but is one of the original incidents of the shares attached to them by the contract contained in the articles[6]. Any condition precedent to transfer, such as obtaining the consent of the directors, must be observed[7], although the consent may be inferred from entries in the company's books[8], or from a constant disregard of the prescribed mode[9]. The rule against perpetuities has no application in such cases[10].

Restrictive provisions are strictly construed[11] because shares, being personal property, are prima facie transferable[12]. Nevertheless if the intent and existence of the restrictions are sufficiently certain, they will not be rejected as being unworkable if a term can be implied which will give them business efficacy[13]. Articles restricting the transfer of a share are construed as restricting only a transfer of the legal title, and not as preventing the transfer of a beneficial interest therein[14]. Accordingly, a transfer for full consideration made in defiance of binding restrictive provisions will suffice to pass the equitable as distinct from the legal interest in the shares[15], although the transferor is entitled to annul the transaction if registration cannot be effected within a reasonable time[16]. Depending on the context[17], a restriction on transfer may include parting with the shares by way of gift[18].

Where the scheme and intent of the restrictions are to accord rights of pre-emption[19] to the other members of the company, if there is no substantial compliance with the procedure laid down, the shareholder denied such rights is entitled to an appropriate injunction to protect his position[20].

Where shares have been issued to an officer of a company, and a provision, which prohibits the transfer of the shares for a period of years, has been inserted in the articles for the protection of the company, a valid transfer may be effected in spite of the prohibition, prior to the expiration of the period, if the consent of the company is obtained[21].

1 As to the meaning of 'share' see PARA 1231.

2 As to the meaning of 'member of a company' see PARA 323.

3 As to the meaning of 'company' see PARA 21.

4 See the Companies Act 2006 s 544(1); and PARA 1244. This provision is subject to certain requirements: see s 544(2); and PARA 1244. As to the meaning of references to a company's 'articles' see PARA 227 note 2.

5 As to model articles of association prescribed for the purposes of the Companies Act 2006, and their application generally, see PARA 227 et seq. Different versions of model articles have been so prescribed for use by private companies limited by shares (see the Companies (Model Articles) Regulations 2008, SI 2008/3229, reg 2, Sch 1), private companies limited by guarantee (see reg 3, Sch 2), and public companies (see reg 4, Sch 3). As to the meanings of 'company limited by guarantee', 'company limited by shares', 'limited company', 'private company' and 'public company' see PARA 95. The default articles prescribed for the purposes of the Companies Act 1985 ('legacy articles'), ie the Companies (Tables A to F) Regulations 1985, SI 1985/805, have not been revoked and may, in their amended form, continue to be used by companies after the commencement of the Companies Act 2006: see PARA 229.

The Companies (Model Articles) Regulations 2008, SI 2008/3229, Sch 1 provides that directors of a private company limited by shares may refuse to register the transfer of a share, and if they do so, the instrument of transfer must be returned to the transferee with the notice of refusal unless they suspect that the proposed transfer may be fraudulent: see Sch 1 art 26(5).

Similarly, the directors of a public company may refuse to register the transfer of a certificated share if:

(1) the share is not fully paid (Sch 3 art 63(5)(a));
(2) the transfer is not lodged at the company's registered office or such other place as the directors have appointed (art 63(5)(b));
(3) the transfer is not accompanied by the certificate for the shares to which it relates, or such other evidence as the directors may reasonably require to show the transferor's right to make the transfer, or evidence of the right of someone other than the transferor to make the transfer on the transferor's behalf (art 63(5)(c));
(4) the transfer is in respect of more than one class of share (art 63(5)(d)); or
(5) the transfer is in favour of more than four transferees (art 63(5)(e)).

If the directors refuse to register the transfer of a share, the instrument of transfer must be returned to the transferee with the notice of refusal unless they suspect that the proposed transfer may be fraudulent: art 63(6). As to a company's registered office see PARA 124. As to classes of shares generally see PARA 1246 et seq.

For companies still using the 'legacy articles' (ie the Companies (Tables A to F) Regulations 1985, SI 1985/805) provision is made for the directors to refuse to register the transfer of a share which is not fully paid to a person of whom they do not approve and they may refuse to register the transfer of a share on which the company has a lien: Schedule Table A art 24. They may also refuse to register a transfer unless:

(a) it is lodged at the office or at such other place as the directors may appoint and is accompanied by the certificate for the shares to which it relates and such other evidence as the directors may reasonably require to show the right of the transferor to make the transfer (Table A art 24(a));
(b) it is in respect of only one class of shares (Table A art 24(b)); and
(c) it is in favour of not more than four transferees (Table A art 24(c)).

If the directors refuse to register a transfer of a share, they must within two months after the date on which the transfer was lodged with the company send to the transferee notice of the refusal: Table A art 25. The registration of transfers of shares or of transfers of any class of shares may be suspended at such times and for such periods (not exceeding 30 days in any year) as the directors may determine: Table A art 26. The Companies (Tables A to F) Regulations 1985, SI 1985/805, Schedule Table A provides regulations for the management of a company limited by shares but arts 24–26 are applied by Table D Pt III (regulations for the management of a company limited by guarantee and having a share capital), and Table E (an unlimited company having a share capital) but are disapplied by Table C art 1 (regulations for the management of a company limited by guarantee and not having a share capital). As to the meaning of 'unlimited company' see PARA 95. As to the meanings of 'company having a share capital' and 'share capital' see PARA 1231. As to the exercise by the directors of the power to refuse registration see PARA 404.

The discretion to refuse transfers of shares refers only to transfers and does not apply to a renunciation of a rights issue (*Re Pool Shipping Co* [1920] 1 Ch 251) or to an allotment of shares or a renunciation of an allotment (*System Control plc v Munro Corporate plc* [1990] BCLC 659 at 662–663 per Hoffmann J) or to a transmission of shares (*Re Bentham Mills Spinning Co* (1879) 11 ChD 900, CA; *Moodie v W and J Shepherd (Bookbinders) Ltd* [1949] 2 All ER 1044, HL). In some cases articles provide that no transfer shall be made without the consent of the directors; to comply with such an article it is not necessary to obtain their consent before executing the transfer; consent to the registration of the transfer is sufficient: *Re Copal Varnish Co Ltd* [1917] 2 Ch 349.

6 *Borland's Trustee v Steel Bros & Co Ltd* [1901] 1 Ch 279 at 289 per Farwell J.

7 *Re Royal British Bank, Nicol's Case* (1859) 3 De G & J 387; *Roots v Williamson* (1888) 38 ChD 485; *Re Dublin North City Milling Co* [1909] 1 IR 179; *Hunter v Hunter* [1936] AC 222, HL; *Lyle and Scott Ltd v Scott's Trustees* [1959] AC 763, [1959] 2 All ER 661, HL ('desire to sell' covered situation where registration of transfer was to be delayed). The secretary has no authority to pass transfers: *Chida Mines Ltd v Anderson* (1905) 22 TLR 27. Consent of directors in an article means consent to the registration of a transfer not consent to the execution of the transfer: see note 5.

8 *Re Royal British Bank, ex p Walton, ex p Hue* (1857) 26 LJ Ch 545; *Re Branksea Island Co, ex p Bentinck (No 2)* (1888) 1 Meg 23, CA.

9 *Re Vale of Neath and South Wales Brewery Co, Walter's Case* (1850) 3 De G & Sm 149; affd 19 LJ Ch 501.

10 *Witham v Vane* (1883) Challis' Real Property (3rd Edn) App V, 440, HL; *Walsh v Secretary of State for India* (1863) 10 HL Cas 367; *Borland's Trustee v Steel Bros & Co Ltd* [1901] 1 Ch 279; *A-G for Ireland v Jameson* [1905] 2 IR 218, CA. As to the rule against perpetuities see PERPETUITIES AND ACCUMULATIONS vol 80 (2013) PARA 9.

11 See *Re Bentham Mills Spinning Co* (1879) 11 ChD 900, CA (cited in PARA 407 note 5); *Delavenne v Broadhurst* [1931] 1 Ch 234; *Greenhalgh v Mallard* [1943] 2 All ER 234, CA (where the court refused to imply a prohibition on transfers to existing members of the company which was not expressed in terms). Cf *Re Cannock and Rugeley Colliery Co, ex p Harrison* (1885) 28 ChD 363, CA. See also *Chappell's Case* (1871) 6 Ch App 902; *Re Hobson, Houghton & Co Ltd* [1929] 1 Ch 300. As to the effect of informality on transfer see *Smellie's Trustees v Smellie* (1952) 103 LJo 139.

12 *Greenhalgh v Mallard* [1943] 2 All ER 234 at 237, CA, per Lord Greene MR; *Re Smith and Fawcett Ltd* [1942] Ch 304 at 306, [1942] 1 All ER 542 at 543, CA, per Lord Greene MR; *BWE International Ltd v Jones* [2003] EWCA Civ 298, [2004] 1 BCLC 406. The importance of the principle of protecting a shareholders' property rights is underscored by the European Convention on Human Rights First Protocol art 1 (protection of property) (as incorporated into English law by the Human Rights Act 1998 s 1(3), Sch I Pt II art 1: see RIGHTS AND FREEDOMS vol 88A (2013) PARA 14): *Martyn Rose Ltd v AKG Group Ltd* [2003] EWCA Civ 375 at [44]–[45], [2003] 2 BCLC 102, [2003] All ER (D) 104 (Mar) per Arden LJ. In the absence of special circumstances, a member of a company cannot be said to have been deprived of his property other than 'subject to the conditions provided for by law' or 'by the general principles of international law' (ie other than in accordance with the European Convention on Human Rights First Protocol art 1) if the manner and circumstances in which he is so deprived are pursuant to the very agreement under which he acquired the property, provided that those provisions are enforceable according to the domestic law in the country concerned: *Money Markets International Stockbrokers Ltd (in liquidation) v London Stock Exchange Ltd* [2001] 2 All ER (Comm) 344 at [142], [2001] 4 All ER 223, [2002] 1 WLR 1151 per Neuberger J.

13 *Tett v Phoenix Property and Investment Co Ltd* [1986] BCLC 149, CA (provision as to giving reasonable notice to persons entitled to take the benefit of the restrictive provisions implied; notice to be given to non-members, so entitled, being family of members, sufficiently satisfied if notice given to member himself).

14 See *Safeguard Industrial Investments Ltd v National Westminster Bank Ltd* [1982] 1 All ER 449, [1982] 1 WLR 589, CA; *Theakston v London Trust plc* [1984] BCLC 390; *Re Sedgefield Steeplechase Co (1927) Ltd, Scotto v Petch* [2001] BCC 889, (2001) Times, 8 February, CA. A member's dealings go beyond dealings with the beneficial interest when nothing except registration remains to be done: *Hurst v Crampton Bros (Coopers) Ltd* [2002] EWHC 1375 (Ch) at [31], [2003] 1 BCLC 304 per Jacob J; *Re Macro (Ipswich) Ltd, Re Earliba Finance Co Ltd* [1994] 2 BCLC 354 at 402 per Arden J.

15 *Hawks v McArthur* [1951] 1 All ER 22, distinguishing *Hunter v Hunter* [1936] AC 222, HL (mortgagee not authorised to sell beneficial apart from legal interest). See also *Re Hafner, Olhausen v Powderley* [1943] IR 264.

16 *Lyle and Scott Ltd v Scott's Trustees* [1959] AC 763, [1959] 2 All ER 661, HL.

17 *Lyle and Scott Ltd v Scott's Trustees* [1959] AC 763 at 778, [1959] 2 All ER 661 at 670, HL, per Lord Reid.

18 *Hurst v Crampton Bros (Coopers) Ltd* [2002] EWHC 1375 (Ch), [2003] 1 BCLC 304.

19 As to rights of pre-emption see PARA 1287 et seq.

20 *Curtis v JJ Curtis & Co Ltd* [1986] BCLC 86, [1984] 2 NZLR 267, NZ CA. See also *Hurst v Crampton Bros (Coopers) Ltd* [2002] EWHC 1375 (Ch), [2003] 1 BCLC 304 (transfer of shares

by member in breach of pre-emption requirements in articles defeasible at the suit of another member).

21 *London and Westminster Supply Association Ltd v Griffiths* (1883) Cab & El 15.

404. Exercise of power to refuse registration of transfer of shares. The power of refusal to register a transfer of shares[1] may be conferred on the directors of a company[2], and in such a case must be exercised by a decision of the board of directors[3]. This power must be exercised within two months of the transfer being lodged with the company[4]. Thereafter the directors will no longer be able to exercise their discretion[5] and an application can be made to have the register rectified by the inclusion of the name of the transferee[6]. If a company[7] refuses to register a transfer of shares[8], it must provide the transferee with such further information about the reasons for the refusal as the transferee may reasonably request[9]. If a company fails to comply with this provision[10], an offence is committed by the company, and by every officer of the company who is in default[11]. A person guilty of such an offence is liable on summary conviction to a fine not exceeding level 3 on the standard scale[12] and for continued contravention to a daily default fine[13] not exceeding one-tenth of level 3 on the standard scale[14].

The power to refuse to register a transfer is a discretionary power and must be exercised reasonably and in good faith for the company's benefit, and not arbitrarily[15], although, in the absence of evidence to the contrary, the power will be presumed to have been properly exercised[16]. Where there are several grounds on which the power may be exercised, the directors are bound to state on which ground they act[17]. They need not in any case give the reasons which influenced them in exercising their discretion on that ground[18], whether they do so under an absolute power[19] or under a power to refuse in specified circumstances[20]. Where shares may be freely transferred to other members of the company, registration of a transfer to another member may not be refused because that member has entered into equitable obligations with a non-member affecting such shares[21].

Where the directors' consent is required to a transfer, they must exercise their powers as trustees for the company and a consent given corruptly for their own benefit may be treated as a nullity[22]. Where their consent is necessary, they may refuse to consent to a transfer where the price payable is merely nominal, and the company is insolvent[23], but they may approve of an out-and-out transfer for a nominal consideration to the transferor's clerk if the transferor agrees to guarantee the payment of a call about to be made[24]. It is their duty to refuse to register a transfer giving a misleadingly false description of the transferee and falsely stating the consideration[25].

Having given their reasons, the court will examine them, but it will not overrule the decision of the directors because it disagrees with the conclusion they reached as to the advisability of refusing the transfer[26]. It will, however, do so if the directors have acted on a wrong principle[27].

As a general rule, a director is just as free to deal with his shares as any other person, although he may, by parting with his qualification shares, cease to hold office as a director[28]. The mere fact that a transfer of shares is made in order to increase the voting power of the transferor, or in his interest, is no ground of objection to the transfer[29], nor is the fact that the transfer is made to avoid a prospective call[30]. If a transfer is real, in the sense that it was intended to effect an out-and-out assignment, and there is no covert agreement or understanding to the contrary, it is immaterial that the transferee is insolvent and unable to pay any future calls[31], but a colourable transfer, as to a clerk or other nominee of the transferor, will not discharge the transferor from liability[32], nor will a transfer in a case where some benefit is reserved to the transferor[33]. A purported transfer by a member in breach of the articles of the company[34] is defeasible at the suit of a member[35] and no transfer of shares so made may be registered and the board of directors is bound to refuse registration accordingly[36].

1 As to the power to refuse to register a transfer of shares see PARA 403.

2 As to such provision made in the model articles of association see PARA 403 note 5.

3 *Re Hackney Pavilion Ltd* [1924] 1 Ch 276. See also *Moodie v W and J Shepherd (Bookbinders) Ltd* [1949] 2 All ER 1044, 1950 SC (HL) 60, HL (right of refusal not exercised by failure to pass resolution approving transfer). See *Re Swaledale Cleaners Ltd* [1968] 3 All ER 619, [1968] 1 WLR 1710, CA (power lost by delay); *Re New Cedos Engineering Co Ltd* (1976) [1994] 1 BCLC 797 (no properly appointed directors; power not exercisable). As to meetings and decisions of a company's directors see PARA 568 et seq.

4 This period is dictated by the Companies Act 2006 s 771(1) (notice of refusal to register transfer) (see the text and notes 7–14). See also *Re Swaledale Cleaners Ltd* [1968] 3 All ER 619, [1968] 1 WLR 1710, CA; *Re Zinotty Properties Ltd* [1984] 3 All ER 754, [1984] 1 WLR 1249.

5 Provision to this effect is not made in the Companies Act 2006 s 771, which imposes a fine for default: see s 771(3), (4) (cited in notes 10–14); and PARA 425. However, it was accepted under the previous law, which made similar provision, that this can be the only consequence of requiring the power to be exercised within two months of the transfer being lodged with the company: see *Re Swaledale Cleaners Ltd* [1968] 3 All ER 619, [1968] 1 WLR 1710, CA. See also *Re Inverdeck Ltd* [1998] 2 BCLC 242 (directors' right to refuse to register a transfer lost after failure in their duty to register the transfer within two months or give notice of refusal to do so). Where the directors' decision is taken within the two month period, a failure to inform the transferee of the exercise of their discretion does not render the directors' decision ineffective: *Popely v Planarrive Ltd* [1997] 1 BCLC 8. Quaere whether in some circumstances the company might be estopped from relying on the directors' decision: *Popely v Planarrive Ltd* [1997] 1 BCLC 8 at 15 per Laddie J.

6 Ie under the Companies Act 2006 s 125: see PARA 352.

7 As to the meaning of 'company' under the Companies Acts see PARA 21; and as to the meaning of the 'Companies Acts' see PARA 13.

8 If an election is in force under the Companies Act 2006 Pt 8 Ch 2A (ss 128A–128K) (see PARA 363 et seq) in respect of the company, references in s 771 to registering the transfer are to be read as references to delivering particulars of the transfer to the registrar of companies in accordance with Pt 8 Ch 2A: s 771(2A) (added by the Small Business, Enterprise and Employment Act 2015 Sch 5 Pt 2 paras 11, 27).

The Companies Act 2006 s 771 does not apply in relation to a transfer of shares if the company has issued a share warrant in respect of the shares (see s 779; and PARA 392; but note that no new share warrants may be issued: see PARA 392), or in relation to the transmission of shares by operation of law: see s 771(5). As to registration of share transfers see PARA 410. As to the meaning of 'share' see PARA 1231. The Companies Act 2006 s 771 applies also to a transfer of debentures of a company: see PARA 425.

9 See the Companies Act 2006 s 771(2). However, this does not include copies of minutes of meetings of directors: see s 771(2). As to the meaning of 'director' see PARA 512.

10 Ie fails to comply with the Companies Act 2006 s 771: see s 771(3).

11 Companies Act 2006 s 771(3). As to the meaning of 'officer who is in default' see PARA 316. As to the meaning of 'officer' generally see PARA 679.

12 As to the standard scale and the powers of magistrates' courts to issue fines on summary conviction see SENTENCING vol 92 (2015) PARA 176.

13 As to the meaning of 'daily default fine' see PARA 1816.

14 Companies Act 2006 s 771(4).

15 *Re Smith and Fawcett Ltd* [1942] Ch 304, [1942] 1 All ER 542, CA; *Heron International Ltd v Grade* [1983] BCLC 244, CA; *Popely v Planarrive Ltd* [1997] 1 BCLC 8. See also *Re Coalport China Co* [1895] 2 Ch 404, CA. See also *Poole v Middleton* (1861) 29 Beav 646 at 651; *Slee v International Bank* (1868) 17 LT 425; *Shepherd's Case* (1866) 2 Ch App 16; *Re Yuruari Co Ltd* (1889) 6 TLR 119, CA; *Re South Yorkshire Wine, Spirit and Mineral Water Co* (1892) 8 TLR 413; *Re Hannan's King (Browning) Gold Mining Co Ltd* (1898) 14 TLR 314, CA; *Re Faure Electric Accumulator Co* (1888) 40 ChD 141; *Re Gresham Life Assurance Society, ex p Penney* (1872) 8 Ch App 446; *Re Bede Steam Shipping Co Ltd* [1917] 1 Ch 123, CA; *Kennedy v North British Wireless Schools Ltd* (1916) 53 SLR 543; *Mactra Properties Ltd v Morshead Mansions Ltd* [2008] EWHC 2843 (Ch), [2009] 1 BCLC 179, [2008] All ER (D) 49 (Nov).

16 *Berry v Tottenham Hotspur Football and Athletic Co Ltd* [1936] 3 All ER 554 (where evidence as to systematic rejections of transfers of shares was held to be inadmissible); *Re Smith and Fawcett Ltd* [1942] Ch 304, [1942] 1 All ER 542, CA. It is axiomatic that the onus of proof is

on those challenging the exercise of the power: see also *Popely v Planarrive Ltd* [1997] 1 BCLC 8; *Village Cay Marine Ltd v Acland* [1998] 2 BCLC 327, PC. See, however, *Re Hafner, Olhausen v Powderley* [1943] IR 264 (evidence of improper motive in refusal; court entitled to draw an inference from the omission to state grounds of refusal, and to hold, in the absence of an explanation, that the refusal was not the result of a bona fide exercise of discretion); *Charles Forte Investments Ltd v Amanda* [1964] Ch 240, [1963] 2 All ER 940, CA (refusal to register does not normally give rise to a right to present a winding-up petition; other remedies are available if refusal wrongful). See also *Morgan v Morgan Insurance Brokers Ltd* [1993] BCLC 676 (where exceptionally directors were personally liable for the costs of an application to have the register of members rectified; rectification was sought by a shareholder owning three-quarters of the shares following a bona fide but improper refusal by the directors to register a transfer).

The Companies Act 2006 s 994 (petition by company member: see PARA 657) may provide an alternative remedy where this power has been exercised improperly.

17 *Berry and Stewart v Tottenham Hotspur Football and Athletic Co Ltd* [1935] Ch 718.

18 *Duke of Sutherland v British Dominions Land Settlement Corpn* [1926] Ch 746; *Berry v Tottenham Hotspur Football and Athletic Co Ltd* [1936] 3 All ER 554.

19 *Re Gresham Life Assurance Society, ex p Penney* (1872) 8 Ch App 446.

20 *Re Coalport China Co* [1895] 2 Ch 404, CA.

21 *Theakston v London Trust plc* [1984] BCLC 390.

22 *Bennett's Case* (1854) 5 De GM & G 284; *Re Mitre Assurance Co, Eyre's Case* (1862) 31 Beav 177.

23 *Taft v Harrison* (1853) 10 Hare 489.

24 *Re Bank of Hindustan, China and Japan,Harrison's Case* (1871) 6 Ch App 286 at 292 per James LJ. A transfer is not invalidated by the fact that the directors would have refused to register it if they had known all the facts, unless they have been deliberately misled by the transferor: *Re Discoverers Finance Corpn Ltd* [1910] 1 Ch 312, CA.

25 *Payne's Case* (1869) LR 9 Eq 223; *William's Case* (1869) 9 LR Eq 225n. As to false description see further *Masters' Case* (1872) 7 Ch App 292; *Re Financial Insurance Co, Bishop's Case* (1869) 7 Ch App 296n; *Re Smith, Knight & Co, Battie's Case* (1870) 39 LJ Ch 391. See also the Companies Act 2006 s 113(2) (no provision made for entry of occupation of the members of the company on the register); and PARA 336. As to approving the transfer of a director's shares see *Re Agriculturist Cattle Insurance Co, Bush's Case* (1870) 6 Ch App 246 (affd sub nom *Murray v Bush* (1873) LR 6 HL 37); *Re London and County Assurance Co, Jessopp's Case* (1858) 2 De G & J 638; *Re Kilbricken Mines Co, Libri's Case* (1857) 30 LTOS 185; *Re Cawley & Co* (1889) 42 ChD 209, CA; *Re South London Fish Market Co* (1888) 39 ChD 324, CA.

26 *Re Bell Bros Ltd, ex p Hodgson* (1891) 65 LT 245; *Re Bede Steam Shipping Co Ltd* [1917] 1 Ch 123, CA.

27 *Re Bede Steam Shipping Co Ltd* [1917] 1 Ch 123, CA; *Robinson v Chartered Bank of India* (1865) LR 1 Eq 32 (explained in *Re Gresham Life Assurance Society, ex p Penney* (1872) 8 Ch App 446); *Moffatt v Farquhar* (1878) 7 ChD 591; *Re Stranton Iron and Steel Co* (1873) LR 16 Eq 559; *Tett v Phoenix Property and Investment Co Ltd* [1984] BCLC 599 (revsd on appeal [1986] BCLC 149, CA).

28 *Re National Provincial Marine Insurance Co,Gilbert's Case* (1870) 5 Ch App 559; *Re Cawley & Co* (1889) 42 ChD 209, CA. Cf *Re South London Fish Market Co* (1888) 39 ChD 324, CA.

29 *Re Stranton Iron and Steel Co* (1873) LR 16 Eq 559; *Cannon v Trask* (1875) LR 20 Eq 669; *Pender v Lushington* (1877) 6 ChD 70; *Moffatt v Farquhar* (1878) 7 ChD 591.

30 *Re Cawley & Co* (1889) 42 ChD 209, CA; *Re Hafod Lead Mining Co, Slater's Case* (1866) 35 Beav 391. If the making of the call has been postponed on the faith of a representation that no transfer will be made, registration of the transfer may be refused: *Re National and Provincial Marine Insurance Co, ex p Parker* (1867) 2 Ch App 685. See also *Re National Provincial Marine Insurance Co,Gilbert's Case* (1870) 5 Ch App 559.

31 *R v Lambourn Valley Rly Co* (1888) 22 QBD 463 at 465 per Pollock B; *Re Hafod Lead Mining Co, Slater's Case* (1866) 35 Beav 391; *Masters' Case* (1872) 7 Ch App 292; *Re Mexican and South American Co, De Pass Case* (1859) 4 De G & J 544; *M'Lintock v Campbell* 1916 SC 966, Ct of Sess.

32 *Re Mexican and South American Co, Hyam's Case* (1859) 1 De GF & J 75; *Re Mexican and South American Co, Costello's Case* (1860) 2 De GF & J 302. Cf *Re National and Provincial Marine Insurance Co, ex p Parker* (1867) 2 Ch App 685; *Re Bank of Hindustan, China and Japan, ex p Kintrea* (1869) 5 Ch App 95; *Re Imperial Mercantile Credit Association, Wilkinson's Case* [1869] WN 211.

33 *Re Athenaeum Life Assurance Society, Chinnocks's Case* (1860) John 714. Cf *Re Esgair Mwyn Mining Co, Alexander's Case* (1861) 3 LT 883.

34 As to a company's articles of association see PARA 227 et seq. As to model articles of association prescribed for the purposes of the Companies Act 2006, and their application generally, see PARA 227 et seq. Different versions of model articles have been so prescribed for use by private companies limited by shares (see the Companies (Model Articles) Regulations 2008, SI 2008/3229, reg 2, Sch 1), private companies limited by guarantee (see reg 3, Sch 2), and public companies (see reg 4, Sch 3). As to the meanings of 'company limited by guarantee', 'company limited by shares', 'limited company', 'private company' and 'public company' see PARA 95. The default articles prescribed for the purposes of the Companies Act 1985 ('legacy articles'), ie the Companies (Tables A to F) Regulations 1985, SI 1985/805, have not been revoked and may, in their amended form, continue to be used by companies after the commencement of the Companies Act 2006: see PARA 229.

35 *Hurst v Crampton Bros (Coopers) Ltd* [2002] EWHC 1375 (Ch), [2003] 1 BCLC 304.

36 *Tett v Phoenix Property and Investment Co Ltd* [1986] BCLC 149, CA.

405. Provisions for compulsory transfer of shares. Provisions made in good faith for the compulsory sale and transfer of shares at a fixed price, on the happening of a certain event, such as bankruptcy, are valid[1]. It is common for the articles of a company to grant pre-emption rights to existing members so that a member wishing to transfer may find himself obliged to offer his shares first to the existing members, and at a price to be fixed by the company's auditors, although in appropriate circumstances a member may be able to prevent the company from exercising such powers by relying on statutory provisions protecting shareholders against inequitable or unfairly prejudicial conduct[2].

The articles of a company often provide that such a pre-emption provision is triggered by a member 'wishing' or 'desiring' or 'intending' to transfer his shares and much will depend on whether, on a proper construction of the articles, and in the light of the conduct of the member, such an intention has been evidenced[3]. A shareholder who has made a contract to sell his shares and has been paid the purchase price and is ready but not asked to execute an instrument of transfer, cannot say that he does not propose to, or is not desirous of, or does not wish to, sell his shares[4]. The mere fact that a shareholder is under a duty to transfer or sell when called upon to do so does not, however, mean that he desires or proposes to transfer[5]. A conditional agreement to sell shares subject to several events occurring (which were not within the control of either party to the agreement) did not constitute a present and unequivocal desire to transfer or dispose of the shares[6]. A gift of shares will trigger a pre-emption provision arising on the 'transfer' of a share where, in the articles, the term 'transfer' has a business meaning and, properly construed, means to 'part with' or to 'hand over'[7]. Share transfers may also be subject to pre-emption rights conferred not in the articles but, for example, in an agreement evidenced by letters between certain of the company's shareholders[8].

When the company has power to fix the purchase price not below a minimum stated in the articles, if it fixes the price at the minimum, which is in fact far less than the actual value of the shares, its action is not of itself fraudulent or oppressive[9]. When the value of the shares is to be ascertained by reference to the proportion of the value of the assets appearing in the books of the company to which the holders of the shares would be entitled in a winding up, deduction for depreciation of the assets is allowed[10].

Where the value of the shares[11] is to be certified by the auditors or other independent valuer[12], and their opinion is expressed to be final and binding for all purposes, a valuation can be questioned only where the valuer departs from his instructions in a material respect[13], though an action will lie against the auditors for making their valuation negligently[14].

Such provisions may constitute a contract of which the transferring shareholder is entitled to the benefit, so as to force the directors to purchase his shares where the articles designate the directors as the purchasers of shares of which the holder wishes to dispose[15].

1 *Borland's Trustee v Steel Bros & Co Ltd* [1901] 1 Ch 279; but see *Money Markets International Stockbrokers Ltd (in liquidation) v London Stock Exchange Ltd* [2001] 4 All ER 223, [2002] 1 WLR 1151; and see *Constable v Executive Connections Ltd* [2005] EWHC 3 (Ch), [2005] 2 BCLC 638 (regarding precisely where the line is to be drawn between those cases where the introduction of a compulsory transfer provision will be upheld and those where it will not). As to the alteration of articles by including provisions for the compulsory sale and transfer of shares see *Brown v British Abrasive Wheel Co* [1919] 1 Ch 290; *Sidebottom v Kershaw, Leese & Co Ltd* [1920] 1 Ch 154, CA; *Dafen Tinplate Co v Llanelly Steel Co (1907) Ltd* [1920] 2 Ch 124. See also *Greenhalgh v Arderne Cinemas Ltd* [1951] Ch 286, [1950] 2 All ER 1120, CA. As to the meaning of references to a company's 'articles' see PARA 227 note 2. As to the alteration of articles see PARA 231 et seq.

2 See *Re Abbey Leisure Ltd, Virdi v Abbey Leisure Ltd* [1990] BCLC 342, CA (member entitled to seek winding up on the just and equitable ground under the Insolvency Act 1986 s 122(1)(g) (see COMPANY AND PARTNERSHIP INSOLVENCY vol 16 (2011) PARA 392) rather than submit to transfer and valuation procedures under the articles); *Re a company (No 00330 of 1991), ex p Holden* [1991] BCLC 597 (member entitled to relief under the Companies Act 1985 s 459 (repealed: see now the Companies Act 2006 s 994; and PARA 657) rather than submit to transfer and valuation procedures under the articles); *Re Coroin Ltd, McKillen v Misland (Cyprus) Investments Ltd* [2012] EWCA Civ 179, [2012] 2 BCLC 611, [2012] BCC 575 (sale of parent company not subject to pre-emption provisions).

3 On a pre-emption provision being triggered, a member is commonly required to serve a transfer notice on the existing members indicating the number of shares that he is 'wishing' or 'desiring' or 'intending' to sell. A requirement in the articles to 'specify' a price in the transfer notice and to 'state' that price in the offer notice, properly construed, is a requirement that the price must be stated in detail, wholly and completely, and the use of a formula to determine the price renders the notice invalid: *BWE International Ltd v Jones* [2003] EWCA Civ 298, [2004] 1 BCLC 406. See also *Martyn Rose Ltd v AKG Group Ltd* [2003] EWCA Civ 375, [2003] 2 BCLC 102 (an article requiring notice to indicate the price to be paid for shares, properly construed, did not allow for some or all of the price to be paid subsequent to completion and a notice to that effect was held to be invalid).

4 *Theakston v London Trust plc* [1984] BCLC 390 at 401 per Harman J; *Lyle and Scott Ltd v Scott's Trustees* [1959] AC 763, [1959] 2 All ER 661, HL. See also *Re Macro (Ipswich) Ltd, Re Earliba Finance Co Ltd, Macro v Thompson (No 2)* [1994] 2 BCLC 354 at 401–402 per Arden J.

5 *Safeguard Industrial Investments Ltd v National Westminster Bank Ltd* [1982] 1 All ER 449, [1982] 1 WLR 589; *Theakston v London Trust plc* [1984] BCLC 390.

6 *Re a company (No 005685 of 1988), ex p Schwarcz (No 2)* [1989] BCLC 427.

7 *Hurst v Crampton Bros (Coopers) Ltd* [2002] EWHC 1375 (Ch), [2003] 1 BCLC 304. See also *Lyle and Scott Ltd v Scott's Trustees* [1959] AC 763 at 778, [1959] 2 All ER 661 at 668, HL, per Lord Reid.

8 See *Dixon v Blindley Heath Investments Ltd* [2015] EWCA Civ 1023, [2015] All ER (D) 80 (Oct) (where, however, the parties concerned were later estopped by convention from relying on and enforcing the pre-emption rights). As to estoppel by convention see ESTOPPEL vol 47 (2014) PARA 368.

9 *Phillips v Manufacturers' Securities Ltd* (1917) 86 LJ Ch 305 (reported on interlocutory application (1915) 31 TLR 451). This is now subject to the text to note 2.

10 *Jacobsen v Jamaica Times Ltd* (1921) 90 LJPC 100. Where shares are required by the articles to be first offered for sale to the other shareholders, the offer must be accepted or rejected as a whole: *Ocean Coal Co Ltd v Powell Duffryn Steam Coal Co Ltd* [1932] 1 Ch 654.

11 As to valuation see *Re Howie and Crawford's arbitration* [1990] BCLC 686, [1990] BCC 330 (where an asset was a holding of shares in a private company, the market price of that asset would normally depend on the proportion of the shares of the company comprised in the holding and on any special rights or restrictions contained in the articles of association of the company as well as on the value of the net assets of the company and its profit and dividend record). The addition of the word 'fair' (as in 'fair market value') adds nothing except to remind the valuer that the market price is to be ascertained on the assumption that no one is excluded from the bidding and to exclude the exceptional or freak price which might otherwise have to be taken into account if an agreement as to valuation refers to the 'open market price': *Re Howie and Crawford's arbitration*[1990] BCLC 686, [1990] BCC 330.

12 The appointment by directors of auditors as valuers who are not 'independent' and who have compromised their ability to be an independent valuer as required by the articles may warrant a petition under the Companies Act 1985 s 459 (repealed) (unfair prejudice) (see now the Companies Act 2006 s 994; and PARA 657): *Re Benfield Greig Group, Nugent v Benfield Group plc* [2001] EWCA Civ 397, [2002] 1 BCLC 65. See also *Davenport v Cream Holdings Ltd* [2008] EWCA Civ 1363, [2009] BCC 183, [2008] All ER (D) 89 (Dec) (shareholder not bound by accountants' valuation where he had not agreed to their appointment and the articles required his agreement). Agreed formal requirements are aimed at eliminating, or at least reducing, the risk of avoidable, time wasting and cost consuming disputes about whether or not a person has been appointed to a position and on what terms. There is, in general, more to the appointment of a person to perform any duties than simply selecting a name to fill the position. Appointment is a process which should be formal and precise: *Davenport v Cream Holdings Ltd* [2008] EWCA Civ 1363 at [32], [2009] BCC 183, [2008] All ER (D) 89 (Dec) per Mummery LJ. See further *Cream Holdings Ltd v Davenport* [2010] All ER (D) 100 (Nov).

13 *Arenson v Arenson* [1973] Ch 346 at 363–364, [1973] 2 All ER 235 at 241–242, CA, per Lord Denning MR (dissenting), applied in *Campbell v Edwards* [1976] 1 All ER 785, [1976] 1 WLR 403, CA; *Baber v Kenwood Manufacturing Co Ltd* [1978] 1 Lloyd's Rep 175, CA; *Re Belfield Furnishings Ltd, Isaacs v Belfield Furnishings Ltd* [2006] EWHC 183 (Ch), [2006] 2 BCLC 705, [2006] All ER (D) 216 (Jan) (where the auditor's valuation of the petitioners' shares was alleged to be tainted).

Having agreed that the expert's opinion will be conclusive and binding for all purposes, it is not sufficient to allege that the expert's opinion is mistaken; it must be shown that the expert departed from his instructions in a material respect, eg if he valued the wrong number of shares, or valued shares in the wrong company, or the wrong person had acted as valuer: *Jones v Sherwood Computer Services plc* [1992] 2 All ER 170 at 179, [1992] 1 WLR 277 at 287, CA, per Dillon LJ. In assessing the validity of a valuation there was a distinction between the identity of the object (eg shares) being valued and the attributes of that object, since only a mistake as to the object's identity could found an attack on a valuation certificate: *Doughty Hanson & Co Ltd v Roe* [2007] EWHC 2212 (Ch), [2008] 1 BCLC 404, [2009] BCC 126 (even if it could be shown that the valuation of the defendant's shares had been made on the basis of a hypothesis that would not be adopted by other valuers, all that would show is that, in applying a particular valuation technique, the valuers had valued the right thing but on an erroneous hypothesis, which was a mistake that an expert was permitted to make without invalidating the certificate). See also *Macro v Thompson (No 2)* [1997] 1 BCLC 626, CA (valuation open to challenge by the court when expert required to value shares in a company using the value of its assets used those of another company); *Baber v Kenwood Manufacturing Co Ltd* [1978] 1 Lloyd's Rep 175 at 179, CA, per Megaw LJ. In *Veba Oil Supply & Trading GmbH v Petrotrade Inc* [2001] EWCA Civ 1832 at [26], [2002] 1 All ER 703, [2002] 1 Lloyd's Rep 295, Simon Brown LJ noted that it was time that *Dean v Prince* [1954] Ch 409, [1954] 1 All ER 749, CA (a previously significant authority on these issues) received its quietus. To the same effect see also *Jones v Sherwood Computer Services plc* [1992] 2 All ER 170 at 179, [1992] 1 WLR 277 at 287, CA, per Dillon LJ.

14 *Killick v PriceWaterhouseCoopers (a firm)* [2001] 1 BCLC 65; *Arenson v Casson Beckman, Rutley & Co* [1977] AC 405, [1975] 3 All ER 901, HL.

15 *Rayfield v Hands* [1960] Ch 1, [1958] 2 All ER 194.

406. Transfer of shares where individual shareholding limited. Where a limited number of shares only may be held by a shareholder[1], a transfer to a person already holding the prescribed number by a transferor with notice of the fact is invalid. If the transferor is a director, he is deemed to have notice, and will remain a contributory[2].

1 As to shareholders and membership of companies generally see PARAS 323 et seq, 1889 et seq.

2 *Re Newcastle-upon-Tyne Marine Insurance Co, ex p Brown* (1854) 19 Beav 97. As to the meaning of 'contributory' under the Companies Acts see PARA 109 note 10.

407. Transfer of shares by a member indebted to the company. In the absence of express power to do so[1], directors cannot decline to register transfers of shares[2] because calls on them are in arrear; but, if empowered to decline to register a transfer by a member[3] who is indebted to the company, they may refuse to register a transfer made by a shareholder who is indebted to the company on any account whatever[4], and whether solely or jointly with others[5]. If directors with such a power register transfers, the transfers are valid, although the directors may be liable to make good any loss thereby caused to the company[6]. The power to decline to register for indebtedness is exercisable although the company holds unmatured bills of the shareholder in respect of the debt[7]. If a company delays registration of a transfer because of indebtedness where there is no indebtedness, nominal damages are recoverable by the transferor[8].

Where articles give a discretion to refuse registration of a transfer by a shareholder who is indebted to the company, the time for ascertaining whether he is so indebted is when the transfer is sent to the proper officer for registration, and not when it afterwards comes before a board meeting for registration[9].

1 As to the restrictions on the transfer of shares contained in the model articles and the Companies (Tables A to F) Regulations 1985, SI 1985/805, see PARA 403. As to the model articles see PARA 227. As to the continuing application of the Companies (Tables A to F) Regulations 1985, SI 1985/805, see PARA 229.
2 As to registration of share transfers see PARA 410.
3 As to who is a member of a company see PARA 323.
4 *Ex p Stringer* (1882) 9 QBD 436.
5 *Re Bentham Mills Spinning Co* (1879) 11 ChD 900, CA. In *Re Stockton Malleable Iron Co* (1875) 2 ChD 101 the term 'indebted' as used in the articles of a company was held to mean owing a debt due and payable. Where an article provided that the company might refuse to register a transfer by a member who was indebted, and another article provided for the registration of persons becoming entitled to a share in consequence of bankruptcy, it was held that the company was not justified in refusing to register a member's trustee in bankruptcy: see *Re Bentham Mills Spinning Co* (1879) 11 ChD 900, CA; *Re W Key & Son Ltd* [1902] 1 Ch 467 (trustee in bankruptcy entitled to a 'clean' registration). Cf *Re Cannock and Rugeley Colliery Co, ex p Harrison* (1885) 28 ChD 363, CA (trustee in bankruptcy not 'entitled' to the share by reason of a prior charge). As to the transmission of shares see PARA 445.
6 *Re Hoylake Rly Co, ex p Littledale* (1874) 9 Ch App 257. Cf *Anderson's Case* (1869) LR 8 Eq 509 (where the registration of transfers, registered in ignorance that calls were in arrear, was cancelled).
7 *Re London, Birmingham and South Staffordshire Banking Co Ltd* (1865) 34 Beav 332; *Bank of Africa v Salisbury Gold Mining Co* [1892] AC 281, PC. Cf *Holden's Case* (1869) LR 8 Eq 444.
8 *Skinner v City of London Marine Insurance Corpn* (1885) 14 QBD 882, CA.
9 *Re Cawley & Co* (1889) 42 ChD 209, CA; *R v Inns of Court Hotel Co, ex p Rudolf* (1863) 11 WR 806.

408. Transfer of shares when company becomes insolvent. Where the company has stopped payment or ceased to be a going concern, although no winding up has commenced, the directors may refuse registration of transfers of shares[1] executed for the purpose of avoiding liability[2]. The mere fact that the company is in difficulties is not, however, a ground for refusing registration[3].

1 As to registration of share transfers see PARA 410.
2 *Mitchell v City of Glasgow Bank* (1879) 4 App Cas 624, HL: *Mitchell's Case* (1879) 4 App Cas 547, 567, HL. Cf *Chappell's Case* (1871) 6 Ch App 902; *Lankester's Case* (1870) 6 Ch App 905n; *Allin's Case* (1873) LR 16 Eq 449; *Dodds v Cosmopolitan Insurance Corpn Ltd* 1915 SC 992, Ct of Sess. As to transfers made after, or not registered before, a winding up see COMPANY AND PARTNERSHIP INSOLVENCY vol 17 (2011) PARA 659. See also *Mills v Sportsdirect.com Retail Ltd* [2010] EWHC 1072 (Ch), [2010] 2 P & CR D45, [2010] 2 BCLC 143 (contract for sale of shares made on same day as company became insolvent).
3 *Re Mexican and South American Co, De Pass's Case* (1859) 4 De G & J 544; *Re Smith, Knight & Co, Battie's Case* (1870) 39 LJ Ch 391; *Nation's Case* (1866) LR 3 Eq 77; *Re Taurine Co* (1883) 25 ChD 118, CA. Cf *Re Mexican and South American Co, Hyam's Case* (1859) 1 De GF & J 75.

409. Persons who may transfer shares. The proper person to transfer shares is the registered holder[1] or his attorney[2], or such other person as is by the articles[3] or by statute empowered to transfer.

An instrument of transfer of the share[4] or other interest of a deceased member of a company[5] may be made by his personal representative[6] although the personal representative is not himself a member of the company[7], and is as effective as if the personal representative had been such a member at the time of the execution of the instrument[8].

Shares or stock registered in the name of a person who, by reason of mental disorder, is incapable of managing his affairs may only be transferred under the authority of the person having jurisdiction in relation to his affairs under the Mental Capacity Act 2005[9]. Where he is a trustee, a vesting order of shares may be made by the court[10].

A transfer of shares by or to a minor is voidable during his minority or within a reasonable time after his attaining full age[11]. Shares held by a married person or civil partner as registered holder, or one of several registered joint holders, may be transferred without the concurrence of his or her spouse or civil partner[12].

Any shares or stock belonging to a bankrupt will vest automatically in his trustee in bankruptcy and may be transferred by him accordingly[13].

1 As to the registered holder of shares see PARA 323 et seq.
2 See *Chatenay v Brazilian Submarine Telegraph Co* (1890) 6 TLR 408; affd [1891] 1 QB 79, CA. A vesting declaration does not extend to shares or stock only transferable in the books of a company: see the Trustee Act 1925 s 40(4)(c); and TRUSTS AND POWERS vol 98 (2013) PARA 307. As to powers of attorney see AGENCY vol 1 (2008) PARA 16.
3 As to the meaning of references to a company's 'articles' see PARA 227 note 2.
4 As to the meaning of 'share' see PARA 1231.
5 As to the meaning of 'member of a company' see PARA 323.
6 As to personal representatives see WILLS AND INTESTACY vol 103 (2010) PARA 605 et seq.
7 Companies Act 2006 s 773(a).
8 Companies Act 2006 s 773(b). See also *Simpson v Molson's Bank* [1895] AC 270 at 279, PC. As to the transmission of shares on death see PARA 445.
9 See MENTAL HEALTH AND CAPACITY vol 75 (2013) PARA 597 et seq.
10 See the Trustee Act 1925 s 51; and TRUSTS AND POWERS vol 98 (2013) PARA 324 et seq. As to jurisdiction in regard to mental patients see s 54; and TRUSTS AND POWERS vol 98 (2013) PARA 291; MENTAL HEALTH AND CAPACITY vol 75 (2013) PARA 730.
11 See PARA 332. As to the attainment of majority at the age of 18 see the Family Law Reform Act 1969 s 1; and CHILDREN AND YOUNG PERSONS vol 9 (2012) PARA 1.
12 See the Law Reform (Married Women and Tortfeasors) Act 1935 s 1(a); *Re London, Bombay and Mediterranean Bank* (1881) 18 ChD 581; and MATRIMONIAL AND CIVIL PARTNERSHIP LAW vol 72 (2015) PARA 252.
13 See the Insolvency Act 1986 ss 306(1), 311(3); and BANKRUPTCY AND INDIVIDUAL INSOLVENCY vol 5 (2013) PARAS 398, 409, 435.

(C) Formalities required by Transfer of Shares

410. Necessity for proper instrument of transfer of shares. A company[1] may not register a transfer of shares[2] in the company unless:

(1) a proper instrument of transfer has been delivered to it[3]; or
(2) the transfer is an exempt transfer[4] or is in accordance with regulations[5] relating to the evidencing and transfer of title to securities without written instrument[6].

This does not, however, affect any power of the company to register as shareholder a person[7] to whom the right to any shares in the company has been transmitted by operation of law[8]. When a transfer of shares in a company has been lodged with the company[9], the company must, as soon as practicable and in any event within two months[10] after the date on which the transfer is lodged with it[11], either register the transfer[12], or give the transferee notice of refusal to register the transfer, together with its reasons for the refusal[13]. If a company fails to comply with these requirements, an offence[14] is committed by the company[15] and every officer[16] of the company who is in default[17].

Articles of association usually require that shares to be transferred in any usual form or any other form approved by the directors[18]. Registration of a transfer cannot be refused because it omits particulars which would be found in the form but are in the circumstances immaterial[19]; and irregularities in the form of transfer have been often condoned on such grounds as the usage of the company, lapse of time, and the acceptance of the transfer as valid[20].

In order to ascertain whether a transfer is valid, and whether the transferee ought to be registered, the directors must have a reasonable time to consider the matter[21]; but this is subject to the obligation to notify the transferee within two months of the transfer being lodged[22]. Usually the directors notify the registered holder that a transfer has been lodged for registration[23]. If the registered holder does not reply to such a notification and a forged transfer is registered, he is not estopped from having the register rectified by substituting his name for that of the transferee[24].

On the application of the transferor of any share or interest in a company, the company must enter in its register of members the name of the transferee or, as the case may be[25], deliver the name of the transferee to the registrar[26], in the same manner and subject to the same conditions as if the application for the entry or delivery were made by the transferee[27]. However, this does not affect the transferee's duty[28] to obtain registration[29]. The transferor may enforce the registration by obtaining an order for rectification of the register[30].

The secretary has no implied authority from the directors or the company to register transfers[31].

1 As to the meaning of 'company' under the Companies Acts see PARA 21; and as to the meaning of the 'Companies Acts' see PARA 13.

2 If an election under the Companies Act 2006 Pt 8 Ch 2A (ss 128A–128K) (see PARA 363 et seq) is in force in respect of the company, references in s 770 to registering a transfer or a person are to be read as references to delivering particulars of that transfer or person to the registrar of companies under Pt 8 Ch 2A: s 770(3) (added by the Small Business, Enterprise and Employment Act 2015 Sch 5 Pt 2 paras 11, 26). As to the meaning of 'registrar of companies' see PARA 126 note 2. As to the meaning of 'share' see PARA 1231. As to the nature, transferability and numbering of shares see PARAS 1239, 1244 et seq. As to transfers of shares see PARA 400 et seq. As to the register of shares see PARA 1891. For restrictions on the transfer of securities by or on behalf of enemies, or to enemy subjects, see the Trading with the Enemy Act 1939 s 5; and ARMED CONFLICT AND EMERGENCY vol 3 (2011) PARA 205. The Companies Act 2006 ss 770, 771 apply also to a transfer of company debentures: see PARA 425.

3 Companies Act 2006 s 770(1)(a). See *Re Greene, Greene v Greene* [1949] Ch 333, [1949] 1 All ER 167 (articles providing for automatic transfer on death invalid); and PARA 244. As to the provision made for the sending or supplying of documents or information to or from a company (the 'company communications provisions') see PARA 750 et seq. For the purposes of an equitable assignment of shares by way of gift, delivery of the share transfer form, though required, may be dispensed with in some circumstances, as where it would have been unconscionable for the donor to have recalled the gift: *Pennington v Waine* [2002] EWCA Civ 227, [2002] 4 All ER 215, [2002] 1 WLR 2075 (donor had intended to make an immediate gift, and gift had been perfected, but the share transfer form, though signed by the donor, had not been delivered either to the donee or to the company).

4 Companies Act 2006 s 770(1)(b)(i). An exempt transfer is one within the Stock Transfer Act 1982 (see PARA 441): see s 770(1)(b)(i).

5 Ie regulations under the Companies Act 2006 Pt 21 Ch 2 (ss 783–790) (see PARA 431 et seq): see s 770(1)(b)(ii).

6 See the Companies Act 2006 s 770(1)(b)(ii).

7 As to the meaning of 'person' see PARA 312 note 2.

8 Companies Act 2006 s 770(2). As to transmission by operation of law see PARA 445. See also note 18.

9 The Companies Act 2006 s 771 does not apply in relation to a transfer of shares if the company has issued a share warrant in respect of the shares (see s 779; and PARA 392); but note that no new share warrants may be issued (see PARA 392), or in relation to the transmission of shares by operation of law: see s 771(5).

10 As to the meaning of 'month' see PARA 1818 note 10.
11 Companies Act 2006 s 771(1).
12 Companies Act 2006 s 771(1)(a). If an election under the Companies Act 2006 Pt 8 Ch 2A (see PARA 363 et seq) is in force in respect of the company, references in s 771 to registering the transfer are to be read as references to delivering particulars of the transfer to the registrar in accordance with Pt 8 Ch 2A: s 771(2A) (added by the Small Business, Enterprise and Employment Act 2015 Sch 5 Pt 2 paras 11, 27).
13 Companies Act 2006 s 771(1)(b). As to notice of refusal to register a transfer of debentures see PARA 426. As to the provision made for the sending or supplying of documents or information to or from a company (the 'company communications provisions') see PARA 750 et seq.
14 A person guilty of such an offence is liable on summary conviction to a fine not exceeding level 3 on the standard scale and, for continued contravention, a daily default fine not exceeding one-tenth of level 3 on the standard scale: Companies Act 2006 s 771(4). As to the standard scale and the powers of magistrates' courts to issue fines on summary conviction see SENTENCING vol 92 (2015) PARA 176. As to the meaning of 'daily default fine' see PARA 1816. As to offences generally see PARA 1816 et seq.
15 See the Companies Act 2006 s 771(3)(a).
16 As to the meaning of 'officer' generally see PARA 679.
17 See the Companies Act 2006 s 771(3)(b). As to the meaning of 'officer who is in default' see PARA 316.
18 As to a company's articles of association see PARA 227 et seq. As to model articles of association prescribed for the purposes of the Companies Act 2006, and their application generally, see PARA 227 et seq. Different versions of model articles have been so prescribed for use by private companies limited by shares (see the Companies (Model Articles) Regulations 2008, SI 2008/3229, reg 2, Sch 1), private companies limited by guarantee (see reg 3, Sch 2), and public companies (see reg 4, Sch 3). As to the meanings of 'company limited by guarantee', 'company limited by shares', 'limited company', 'private company' and 'public company' see PARA 95. The default articles prescribed for the purposes of the Companies Act 1985 ('legacy articles'), ie the Companies (Tables A to F) Regulations 1985, SI 1985/805, have not been revoked and may, in their amended form, continue to be used by companies after the commencement of the Companies Act 2006: see PARA 229.

The Companies (Model Articles) Regulations 2008, SI 2008/3229, Sch 1 provides that shares may be transferred by means of an instrument of transfer in any usual form or any other form approved by the directors, which is executed by or on behalf of the transferor: Sch 1 art 26(1). No fee may be charged for registering any instrument of transfer or other document relating to or affecting the title to any share: art 26(2). The company may retain any instrument of transfer which is registered (art 26(3)); and the transferor remains the holder of a share until the transferee's name is entered in the register of members as holder of it (art 26(4)). If title to a share passes to a transmittee, the company may only recognise the transmittee as having any title to that share: art 27(1). As to the register of members see PARA 336 et seq.

The Companies (Model Articles) Regulations 2008, SI 2008/3229, Sch 3 provides that certificated shares may be transferred by means of an instrument of transfer in any usual form or any other form approved by the directors, which is executed by or on behalf of the transferor, and (if any of the shares is partly paid) the transferee: Sch 3 art 63(1). No fee may be charged for registering any instrument of transfer or other document relating to or affecting the title to any share: art 63(2). The company may retain any instrument of transfer which is registered (art 63(3)); and the transferor remains the holder of a certificated share until the transferee's name is entered in the register of members as holder of it (art 63(4)).

For companies still using the 'legacy articles' (ie the Companies (Tables A to F) Regulations 1985, SI 1985/805), it is provided that the instrument of transfer of a share may be in any usual form or in any other form which the directors may approve and must be executed by or on behalf of the transferor and, unless the share is fully paid, by or on behalf of the transferee: Schedule Table A art 23. No fee is to be charged for the registration of any instrument of transfer or other document relating to or affecting the title to any share: Table A art 27. The company is entitled to retain any instrument of transfer which is registered, but any instrument of transfer which the directors refuse to register must be returned to the person lodging it when notice of the refusal is given: Table A art 28. The Companies (Tables A to F) Regulations 1985, SI 1985/805, Schedule Table A provides regulations for the management of a company limited by shares but arts 23–28 are applied by Table D Pt III (regulations for the management of a company limited by guarantee and having a share capital), and Table E (an unlimited company having a share capital) but are disapplied by Table C art 1 (regulations for the management of a company limited by guarantee and not having a share capital). As to the meaning of 'unlimited company' see PARA 95. As to the meanings of 'company having a share capital' and 'share capital' see PARA 1231.

As to the power to refuse to register a transfer see PARA 403.

19 *Re Letheby and Christopher Ltd* [1904] 1 Ch 815 (where the transferor's address and the denoting number of the share were omitted).
20 *Bargate v Shortridge* (1855) 5 HL Cas 297; *Straffon's Executors' Case* (1852) 1 De GM & G 576; *Burnes v Pennell* (1849) 2 HL Cas 497; *Barrow Mutual Ship Insurance Co v Ashburner* (1885) 54 LJQB 377, CA; *Ind's Case* (1872) 7 Ch App 485 (wrong denoting number); *Feiling's and Rimington's Case* (1867) 2 Ch App 714; *Murray v Bush* (1873) LR 6 HL 37; *Re General Floating Dock Co Ltd* (1867) 15 LT 526; *Re Taurine Co* (1883) 25 ChD 118, CA; *Smellie's Trustees v Smellie* (1952) 103 LJo 139. See also *Nisbet v Shepherd* [1994] 1 BCLC 300, CA (transfer relied on for more than seven years). Errors in the dates of transfers as entered on the register were held to be immaterial in *Weikersheim's Case* (1873) 8 Ch App 831.
21 *Société Générale de Paris v Walker* (1885) 11 App Cas 20, HL; *Re Ottos Kopje Diamond Mines Ltd* [1893] 1 Ch 618, CA; *Ireland v Hart* [1902] 1 Ch 522. The directors are not entitled to refuse to register a transfer on the assumption that the transfer is a breach of trust, but should give notice to any person objecting thereto that they will register the transfer unless proceedings to restrain its registration are taken within a reasonable time: see *Grundy v Briggs* [1910] 1 Ch 444.
22 See PARA 404.
23 See *Tayler v Great Indian Peninsula Rly Co* (1859) 28 LJ Ch 285 at 288 per Wood V-C (affd 28 LJ Ch 709); *Re North British Australasian Co Ltd, ex p Swan* (1860) 7 CBNS 400 at 438–439; *Swan v North British Australasian Co* (1862) 7 H & N 603 at 631 per Wilde B (affd (1863) 2 H & C 175, Ex Ch); *Johnston v Renton* (1870) LR 9 Eq 181.
24 *Barton v London and North Western Rly Co* (1889) 24 QBD 77, CA. As to forged transfers see PARAS 442–444. As to the meaning of estoppel see ESTOPPEL vol 47 (2014) PARA 301.
25 Ie if an election is in force as described in notes 2, 12.
26 Ie under the Companies Act 2006 Pt 8 Ch 2A (ss 128A–128K) (see PARA 363 et seq).
27 See the Companies Act 2006 s 772 (amended by the Small Business, Enterprise and Employment Act 2015 Sch 5 Pt 2 paras 11, 28). This provision does not apply in relation to the transfer of uncertificated units of a security by means of a relevant system: Uncertificated Securities Regulations 2001, SI 2001/3755, reg 38(7) (amended by SI 2009/1889). As to the meaning of 'relevant system' see PARA 432 note 1. As to the execution of a share transfer by a personal representative see the Companies Act 2006 s 773; and PARA 409.
28 See PARA 402.
29 *Skinner v City of London Marine Insurance Corpn* (1885) 14 QBD 882, CA.
30 *Re Stranton Iron and Steel Co* (1873) LR 16 Eq 559. See also PARA 352.
31 See *Chida Mines v Anderson* (1905) 22 TLR 27; *Re Matlock Old Bath Hydropathic Co, Wheatcroft's Case* (1873) 42 LJ Ch 853.

411. Simplified form of transfer of securities. Certain registered securities[1] may be transferred by means of an instrument under hand in the statutory form[2] known as a 'stock transfer'[3]. The transfer is executed by the transferor only, but specifies the full name and address of the transferee[4]. Particulars of the consideration, of the description and number or amount of the securities, and of the person by whom the transfer is made are also to be specified[5].

In the case of a transfer to a stock exchange nominee[6] neither particulars of the consideration nor the address of the transferee need be inserted[7]. A form used to transfer securities from a stock exchange nominee which is a body corporate need not be executed under hand but will be sufficiently executed if it bears a facsimile of the corporate seal of the transferor authenticated by the signature, whether actual or facsimile of a director or the secretary of the transferor[8].

The execution of a stock transfer need not be attested[9]. Where a stock transfer has been executed for the purpose of a stock exchange transaction[10], the particulars of the consideration and of the transferee may either be inserted in that transfer or, as the case may require, supplied by means of separate instruments in the statutory form[11] known as 'brokers' transfers'[12]. A brokers' transfer must identify the stock transfer and specify the securities to which each instrument relates and the consideration paid for the securities[13].

The provisions described above[14] have effect in relation to a transfer of specified securities notwithstanding anything to the contrary in any enactment or instrument relating to the transfer of those securities[15]. However, any right to refuse to register a person as the holder of any securities on any ground other than the form in which the securities purport to be transferred to him is unaffected[16]. Also unaffected is any enactment or rule of law regulating the execution of documents by companies or other bodies corporate, or any articles of association or other instrument regulating the execution of documents by any particular company or body corporate[17].

1 The securities which may be so transferred are fully paid-up registered securities of any description, as follows (Stock Transfer Act 1963 s 1(4) (amended by the Finance Act 1964 ss 24, 26(7), Sch 8 para 10, Sch 9; the Post Office Act 1969 s 108(1)(f); the Companies Consolidation (Consequential Provisions) Act 1985 s 30, Sch 2; the Building Societies Act 1986 s 120(1), Sch 18 Pt I para 5; the Financial Services Act 1986 s 212(2), Sch 16 para 4(a); the Co-operative and Community Benefit Societies Act 2014 Sch 4 Pt 2 para 21; and by SI 2001/1228; SI 2001/3649; SI 2009/1941; SI 2013/1388), ie:

(1) securities issued by any company as defined in the Companies Act 2006 s 1(1) (see PARA 21) except a company limited by guarantee or an unlimited company;

(2) securities issued by any body (other than a company as so defined) incorporated in Great Britain by or under any enactment or by royal charter except a building society within the meaning of the Building Societies Act 1986 (see FINANCIAL INSTITUTIONS vol 48 (2015) PARA 330) or a registered society within the meaning of the Co-operative and Community Benefit Societies Act 2014 (see FINANCIAL INSTITUTIONS vol 48 (2015) PARA 880);

(3) securities issued by the government of the United Kingdom, except stock or bonds in the National Savings Stock Register, and except national savings certificates (see FINANCIAL INSTRUMENTS AND TRANSACTIONS vol 49 (2015) PARA 122 et seq);

(4) securities issued by any local authority;

(5) units of an authorised unit trust scheme, an authorised contractual scheme or a recognised scheme within the meaning of the Financial Services and Markets Act 2000 Pt XVII (ss 235–284) (see FINANCIAL SERVICES REGULATION vol 50A (2016) PARA 841);

(6) shares issued by an open-ended investment company within the meaning of the Open-Ended Investment Companies Regulations 2001, SI 2001/1228 (see FINANCIAL SERVICES REGULATION vol 50A (2016) PARA 875).

For these purposes, 'securities' means shares, stock, debentures, debenture stock, loan stock, bonds, units of a collective investment scheme within the meaning of the Financial Services and Markets Act 2000 (see FINANCIAL SERVICES REGULATION vol 50A (2016) PARA 841), and other securities of any description: Stock Transfer Act 1963 s 4(1) (definition amended by the Financial Services Act 1986 Sch 16 para 4(b); and by SI 2001/3649). 'Registered securities' means transferable securities the holders of which are entered in a register (whether maintained in Great Britain or not): Stock Transfer Act 1963 s 4(1). As to the meaning of 'company limited by guarantee' see PARA 95. As to the meaning of 'unlimited company' see PARA 95. As to the meaning of 'company' see PARA 21. As to the meanings of 'Great Britain' and 'United Kingdom' see PARA 1 note 5. As to incorporated bodies in Great Britain generally (other than a company within the meaning of the Companies Act 2006) see PARAS 1–2. For these purposes, 'local authority' means the following (Stock Transfer Act 1963 s 4(1) (definition amended by the Local Government Finance Act 1992 s 117(1), Sch 13 para 12; the Police and Magistrates' Courts Act 1994 s 93, Sch 9 Pt I; SI 1990/776; the Fire and Rescue Services Act 2004 s 53(1), Sch 1 para 18), ie:

(a) a billing authority or a precepting authority as defined in the Local Government Finance Act 1992 s 69;

(b) a fire and rescue authority in Wales constituted by a scheme under the Fire and Rescue Services Act 2004 s 2 or a scheme to which s 4 of that Act applies;

(c) a levying body within the meaning of the Local Government Finance Act 1988 s 74; or

(d) a body as regards which the Local Government Finance Act 1988 s 75 applies.

As to the meaning of 'Wales' see PARA 1 note 5.

2 References in the Stock Transfer Act 1963 to the forms set out in Schs 1, 2 (see below; and note 11) include references to forms substantially corresponding to those forms respectively: s 3(1). For the prescribed form of stock transfer and the prescribed forms for use as alternatives where the transfer is to a stock exchange nominee or from a stock exchange nominee see Sch 1 (amended by SI 1974/1214; SI 1990/18; SI 1996/1571). 'Stock exchange' means the London Stock Exchange, and any other stock exchange (whether in Great Britain or not) which is declared by order of the Treasury to be a recognised stock exchange for the purposes of the Stock Transfer Act 1963: s 4(1). Any such order must be made by statutory instrument, and may be varied or revoked by a subsequent order: s 4(2). As to an order so made see the Stock Transfer (Recognised Stock

Exchanges) Order 1973, SI 1973/536, which specifies the Stock Exchange as being a recognised stock exchange for the purposes of the Stock Transfer Act 1963. As to the London Stock Exchange see FINANCIAL SERVICES REGULATION vol 50 (2016) PARA 96. The Treasury may by order amend the forms either by altering them as they are set out in Sch 1 or by substituting different forms for those forms or by the addition of forms for use as alternatives to those forms; and references to the forms set out in the Stock Transfer Act 1963 Sch 1 (including references in s 3) must be construed accordingly: s 3(2). Any such order must be made by statutory instrument, and may be varied or revoked by a subsequent order; and any statutory instrument so made is subject to annulment in pursuance of a resolution of either House of Parliament: s 3(4). As to the provision which may be made by any order made under s 3 see s 3(3), (5) (s 3(5) added by the Stock Exchange (Completion of Bargains) Act 1976 s 6). As to the orders made see the Stock Transfer (Amendment of Forms) Order 1974, SI 1974/1214; the Stock Transfer (Addition of Forms) Order 1979, SI 1979/277; the Stock Transfer (Substitution of Forms) Order 1990, SI 1990/18; the Stock Transfer (Addition and Substitution of Forms) Order 1996, SI 1996/1571. As to the Treasury see CONSTITUTIONAL AND ADMINISTRATIVE LAW vol 20 (2014) PARA 262 et seq.

3 See the Stock Transfer Act 1963 s 1(1). Nothing in s 1 is to be construed as affecting the validity of any instrument which would otherwise be effective to transfer securities: s 1(3). Any instrument purporting to be made in any form for which the form set out in the Stock Transfer (Substitution of Forms) Order 1990, SI 1990/18, Schedule, is substituted, or in any other form otherwise authorised or required for that purpose, is sufficient, whether or not it is completed in accordance with the form, if it complies with the requirements as to execution and contents which apply to a stock transfer: Stock Transfer Act 1963 s 1(3) (amended by SI 1990/18). In relation to the transfer of securities by means of a stock transfer and a brokers' transfer:

(1) any reference in any enactment or instrument (including in particular the Companies Act 2006 s 770(1)(a): see PARA 410) to the delivery or lodging of an instrument, or proper instrument, of transfer, is to be construed as a reference to the delivery or lodging of the stock transfer and the brokers' transfer (Stock Transfer Act 1963 s 2(3)(a) (amended by the Finance Act 1999 s 139, Sch 20 Pt V(5); and by SI 2008/948)); and

(2) any such reference to the date on which an instrument of transfer is delivered or lodged is to be construed as a reference to the date by which the later of those transfers to be delivered or lodged has been delivered or lodged (Stock Transfer Act 1963 s 2(3)(b)).

Subject to this, the brokers' transfer (and not the stock transfer) is deemed to be the conveyance or transfer for stamp duty purposes: s 2(3)(c). Section 2(3)(c) is repealed, as from a day to be appointed, by the Finance Act 1990 s 132, Sch 19 Pt VI. However, at the date at which this volume states the law, no such day had been appointed.

4 See the Stock Transfer Act 1963 s 1(1). Where the transfer is executed for the purpose of a stock exchange transaction (see note 10) by the donee of a power of attorney, it is conclusively to be presumed in favour of the transferee that the power had not been revoked at the date of the instrument if a statutory declaration to that effect is made by the donee of the power on or within three months after that date: Powers of Attorney Act 1971 s 6. As to statutory declarations see the Statutory Declarations Act 1835; and CIVIL PROCEDURE vol 12 (2015) PARA 827. As to the meaning of 'month' see PARA 1818 note 10. As to the position where the terms of an offer for all or any uncertificated units of a participating security provide that a person accepting the offer creates an irrevocable power of attorney in favour of the offeror, or a person nominated by the offeror, in the terms set out in the offer see the Uncertificated Securities Regulations 2001, SI 2001/3755, reg 43. As to the meaning of 'participating securities' see PARA 432. As to the transfer of uncertificated securities see PARA 431. As to uncertificated securities generally see PARA 432.

5 See the Stock Transfer Act 1963 s 1(1). Section 1 has effect:

(1) subject to the amendment that a sold transfer form, and a stock transfer form used to transfer securities to a stock exchange nominee, need not specify particulars of the consideration or the address of the transferee (Stock Transfer (Addition of Forms) Order 1979, SI 1979/277, art 3(1)); and

(2) in relation to the form set out in the Stock Transfer (Substitution of Forms) Order 1990, SI 1990/18, Schedule, subject to the amendment that that form need not specify particulars of the consideration or the address of the transferee (art 4).

6 As to the meaning of 'stock exchange nominee' see the Stock Transfer (Addition of Forms) Order 1979, SI 1979/277, art 4. As to the meaning of 'person' see PARA 312 note 2. As to the Secretary of State see PARA 6.

7 See the Stock Transfer (Addition of Forms) Order 1979, SI 1979/277, art 3(1); and note 5 head (1).

8 Stock Transfer (Addition of Forms) Order 1979, SI 1979/277, art 3(2).

9 See the Stock Transfer Act 1963 s 1(2).

10 'Stock exchange transaction' means a sale and purchase of securities in which each of the parties is a member of a stock exchange acting in the ordinary course of his business as such or is acting through the agency of such a member: Stock Transfer Act 1963 s 4(1).
11 For the prescribed form of brokers' transfer see the Stock Transfer Act 1963 Sch 2 (amended by SI 1974/1214). A form substantially corresponding to the prescribed form is permissible: see Stock Transfer Act 1963 s 3(1); and note 2.
12 See the Stock Transfer Act 1963 s 1(2). As to the prohibition of circulation of blank transfers see PARA 412.
13 See the Stock Transfer Act 1963 s 1(2).
14 Ie the Stock Transfer Act 1963 s 1: see the text and notes 1–13.
15 Stock Transfer Act 1963 s 2(1).
16 Stock Transfer Act 1963 s 2(1)(a).
17 Stock Transfer Act 1963 s 2(1)(b). Any enactment or instrument relating to the transfer of securities specified for the purposes of s 1 applies with any necessary modifications to a transfer authorised by s 1: see s 2(2) (amended by SI 2008/948).

412. Transfer of securities in blank. Where shares are transferable only by deed, a blank transfer, although executed by the shareholder, gives no security to an equitable mortgagee, because the filling in of the transferee's name would be a material alteration in the deed rendering the instrument void unless made under an authority conferred by a deed[1]. The same principle is applied where blank spaces are left in the deed for the purchaser's name[2], the consideration and name of the transferee[3], and the names of the transferees and attesting witnesses[4]. Where, as is the usual position, transfers are not required to be made by deed, an equitable mortgagee has an implied authority to complete the blank transfer for the purpose of protecting his security, and to procure it to be registered[5], although he cannot delegate such authority to another person to be used for a different purpose[6]. If the company refuses to register a transfer so completed, the court may direct an account of what is due, and, if the borrower declines to have the account taken within the time limited, may rectify[7] the register by substituting the name of the transferee[8]. The delivery by executors to a broker of a blank transfer signed by them with the certificates, so that the shares may be registered in their own names, does not estop them from setting up their title against persons who advance money to the broker on a deposit of the certificates, although in good faith and without notice of any fraud[9].

Where a transfer in blank relating to registered stock of any description has been delivered, pursuant to a sale or gift to or to the order of the purchaser or any person acting on his behalf, or to the donee, any person who in Great Britain parts with possession of that transfer, or who removes it or causes or permits it to be removed from Great Britain before it has been duly completed is liable to a penalty[10].

1 *Société Générale de Paris v Walker* (1885) 11 App Cas 20, HL; *France v Clark* (1884) 26 ChD 257, CA; *Powell v London and Provincial Bank* [1893] 2 Ch 555, CA. Registration does not validate the transfer: *Hare v London and North Western Rly Co* (1860) John 722. Cf *Tayler v Great Indian Peninsula Rly Co* (1859) 4 De G & J 559. As to equitable mortgages see MORTGAGE vol 77 (2016) PARA 105. There is no requirement for share transfers to be by deed: see DEEDS AND OTHER INSTRUMENTS vol 32 (2012) PARA 222. See also the Stock Transfer Act 1963 s 1; and PARA 411.
2 *Hibblewhite v M'Morine* (1840) 6 M & W 200.
3 *Tayler v Great Indian Peninsular Rly Co* (1859) 4 De G & J 559; *Société Générale de Paris v Walker* (1885) 11 App Cas 20, HL; *France v Clark* (1884) 26 ChD 257, CA; *Powell v London and Provincial Bank* [1893] 2 Ch 555, CA.
4 *Swan v North British Australasian Co* (1863) 2 H & C 175, Ex Ch. As to the signature of documents in blank see generally *Lloyds Bank Ltd v Cooke* [1907] 1 KB 794, CA; *Smith v Prosser* [1907] 2 KB 735, CA; and DEEDS AND OTHER INSTRUMENTS vol 32 (2012) PARA 228.
5 *Re Tahiti Cotton Co, ex p Sargent* (1874) LR 17 Eq 273; *Re Tees Bottle Co, Davies' Case* (1876) 33 LT 834. As to filling in description and number of shares after execution see *Re*

Barned's Banking Co, ex p Contract Corpn (1867) 3 Ch App 105; *Re Financial Insurance Co, Bishop's Case* (1869) 7 Ch App 296n; *Re Blakely Ordnance Co, Bailey's Case* [1869] WN 196. As to gaining priority over earlier equitable interests, of which a creditor had no notice when he advanced his money, by perfecting his security by registration even after he had notice of such prior interest see *Dodds v Hills* (1865) 2 Hem & M 424; *Macmillan Inc v Bishopsgate Investment Trust plc (No 3)* [1995] 3 All ER 747, [1995] 1 WLR 978 (affd on other grounds [1996] 1 All ER 585, [1996] 1 WLR 387, CA).

6 Ie such as to secure a sub-mortgage: *France v Clark* (1884) 26 ChD 257, CA. Cf *Fox v Martin* (1895) 64 LJ Ch 473; *Fry v Smellie* [1912] 3 KB 282, CA; *Fuller v Glyn, Mills, Currie & Co* [1914] 2 KB 168.

7 Ie under the Companies Act 2006 s 125: see PARA 352.

8 *Re Tees Bottle Co, Davies' Case* (1876) 33 LT 834.

9 *Colonial Bank v Cady and Williams* (1890) 15 App Cas 267, HL; *Colonial Bank v Hepworth* (1887) 36 ChD 36; *Fox v Martin* (1895) 64 LJ Ch 473; *Fry v Smellie* [1912] 3 KB 282, CA; *Fuller v Glyn, Mills, Currie & Co* [1914] 2 KB 168; *Hutchinson v Colorado United Mining Co and Hamill* (1886) 3 TLR 265, CA.

10 See the Finance Act 1963 s 67; and STAMP TAXES vol 96 (2012) PARA 388. The Finance Act 1963 s 67 is repealed, as from a day to be appointed, by the Finance Act 1990 ss 109(3), 132, Sch 19 Pt VI. Such repeal will apply where the sale is made on or after the abolition day, being such day as may be appointed by the Treasury by order made by statutory instrument: see ss 109(3), 111(1). However, at the date at which this volume states the law, no such day had been appointed.

413. Non-execution by transferee. When a company's articles of association[1] provide that the instrument of transfer must be executed or signed both by the transferor and transferee[2], non-execution by the transferee only makes the transfer irregular and not a nullity; and, if it has been acted on for a long period, it cannot be impeached[3]. In the absence of such a provision, a transfer executed by the transferor only passes the property in the shares, subject to the transferee's right, on discovering any defect, to repudiate the shares[4]. If it is the practice of the company, the directors may decline to register a transfer where it has not been executed by the transferee[5], and it is their duty not to permit registration of a transfer of shares on which there is any liability except when satisfied that the consent of the transferee has been given. They may refuse to register a bona fide transfer to a minor because he is unable to accept it[6], but not a bona fide transfer to a person who is destitute[7].

1 As to a company's articles of association generally see PARA 227 et seq.

2 See the Companies (Model Articles) Regulations 2008, SI 2008/3229, Sch 3 art 63(1) which provides, in the case of a public company, that an instrument of transfer be executed by or on behalf of the transferor and, if any of the shares is partly paid, the transferee. Similar provision is made in the Companies (Tables A to F) Regulations 1985, SI 1985/805, Schedule Table A art 23. In the case of a private company the model articles provide for execution by or on behalf of the transferor only: see the Companies (Model Articles) Regulations 2008, SI 2008/3229, Sch 1 art 26(1). As to the provisions for simplified transfer by a stock transfer: see PARA 411. As to the model articles see PARA 227. As to the continuing application of the Companies (Tables A to F) Regulations 1985, SI 1985/805, see PARA 227.

3 *Re Taurine Co* (1883) 25 ChD 118, CA. Cf *Royal Bank of India's Case* (1869) 4 Ch App 252; *Cuninghame v City of Glasgow Bank* (1879) 4 App Cas 607, HL. See also *Re Paradise Motor Co Ltd* [1968] 2 All ER 625, [1968] 1 WLR 1125, CA (transfer not signed by transferee); *Dempsey v Celtic Football and Athletic Co Ltd* [1993] BCC 514, Ct of Sess.

4 *Heritage's Case* (1869) LR 9 Eq 5; *Fitch Lovell Ltd v IRC* [1962] 3 All ER 685 at 694, [1962] 1 WLR 1325 at 1338–1339 per Wilberforce J. Cf *Standing v Bowring* (1885) 31 ChD 282, CA.

5 *Marino's Case* (1867) 2 Ch App 596. Cf the provisions for simplified transfer by a stock transfer: see PARA 411.

6 *R v Midland Counties and Shannon Junction Rly Co* (1862) 15 ICLR 514. Cf *Lumsden's Case* (1868) 4 Ch App 31. See also PARA 332. As to the attainment of majority at the age of 18 see the Family Law Reform Act 1969 s 1; and CHILDREN AND YOUNG PERSONS vol 9 (2012) PARA 1.

7 *R v Midland Counties and Shannon Junction Rly Co* (1862) 15 ICLR 514; *Re Discoverers' Finance Corpn Ltd, Lindlar's Case* [1910] 1 Ch 312, CA.

414. Position before registration of transfer of shares. Until the instrument of transfer is registered[1], the transfer of shares is not complete[2]; the transferor is the legal owner of the shares, and, if they are not fully paid, he is liable to pay all the calls made on them while his name remains on the register of members[3]. A transferee who has accepted the transfer, although he has not executed it, is, however, liable to indemnify the transferor as from its date[4].

1 As to the registration of shares see PARA 410.
2 See *Re Fry, Chase National Executors and Trustees Corpn v Fry* [1946] Ch 312, [1946] 2 All ER 106. Cf *Re Rose, Rose v IRC* [1952] Ch 499, [1952] 1 All ER 1217, CA (gift complete even though delay in registration); *Pennington v Waine* [2002] EWCA Civ 227, [2002] 4 All ER 215, [2002] 1 WLR 2075 (for the purposes of an equitable assignment of shares by way of gift, delivery of the share transfer form, though required, could be dispensed with in some circumstances.). An attempted transfer will not, prima facie, be validated as a declaration of trust (see TRUSTS AND POWERS vol 98 (2013) PARA 77), but an assignment of a chose or thing in action will be enforced, although voluntary, if everything required to be done by the donor has been done by him (see CHOSES IN ACTION).
3 *Sayles v Blane* (1849) 14 QB 205. Cf *Symons' Case* (1870) 5 Ch App 298 at 300 per Giffard LJ. Even after the transfer is registered, it seems that he is liable for calls already made: *Taylor, Phillips and Rickards' Cases* [1897] 1 Ch 298 at 306, CA, per Lindley LJ; *Re Hoylake Rly Co, ex p Littledale* (1874) 9 Ch App 257 at 262 per Mellish LJ. Cf *Watson v Eales* (1857) 23 Beav 294. As to the effect of delay on the part of the company in registering see COMPANY AND PARTNERSHIP INSOLVENCY vol 17 (2011) PARA 688. He is also liable as a contributory in a winding up: see COMPANY AND PARTNERSHIP INSOLVENCY vol 17 (2011) PARA 661 et seq. As to the effect of an uncompleted contract for sale on voting rights see PARA 725.
4 *Loring v Davis* (1886) 32 ChD 625; *Levi v Ayers* (1878) 3 App Cas 842, PC. Cf *Hardoon v Belilios* [1901] AC 118, PC. The transferor must hold as a trustee all the dividends declared on the shares from that date: *Stevenson v Wilson* 1907 SC 445, Ct of Sess.

415. Production of share certificate. A company's articles of association[1] generally require a transfer of shares lodged for registration[2] to be accompanied by the certificate of such shares[3]. The articles generally also provide for the granting of a new certificate on proof of the loss or destruction of the old certificate, or upon a satisfactory indemnity being given[4]. Where the articles provide that transfers must be registered on presentation of the transfer accompanied by such evidence as the company may require of the transferor's title, the directors may refuse to register if the certificate is not so produced[5].

1 As to a company's articles of association see PARA 227.
2 As to the registration of shares see PARA 410.
3 See the Companies (Model Articles) Regulations 2008, SI 2008/3229, Sch 3 art 63(5)(c) (public company); the Companies (Tables A to F) Regulations 1985, SI 1985/805, Schedule Table A art 24(a). The model articles provide that no fee may be charged for registering any instrument of transfer or other document relating to or affecting the title to any share, and that the company may retain any instrument of transfer which is registered: see the Companies (Model Articles) Regulations 2008, SI 2008/3229, Sch 1 art 26(2), (3) (private company), Sch 3 art 63(2), (3) (public company). Similar provision is made in the Companies (Tables A to F) Regulations 1985, SI 1985/805: see Schedule Table A arts 27, 28. As to the model articles see PARA 227. As to the continuing application of the Companies (Tables A to F) Regulations 1985, SI 1985/805, see PARA 229. As to share certificates see PARA 391.
4 See the Companies (Model Articles) Regulations 2008, SI 2008/3229, Sch 1 art 25 (private company), Sch 3 art 49 (public company); the Companies (Tables A to F) Regulations 1985, SI 1985/805, Schedule Table A art 7. As to the splitting of certificates see PARA 396.
5 *Re East Wheal Martha Mining Co* (1863) 33 Beav 119.

416. Certification of transfers of shares. Where a shareholder[1] sells some only of the shares comprised in one certificate[2], or sells some to one person and the rest to another, on the deposit of the transfer and certificate with the company[3], the secretary[4] generally indorses a note on the transfer or transfers that the certificate has been lodged. This practice, called 'certification of transfers', arose from the difficulty felt by members of the Stock Exchange[5] in settling their accounts as buyers and sellers of shares where the seller's certificate does not accompany his transfer.

The certification by a company[6] of an instrument of transfer of any shares[7] in the company is to be taken as a representation by the company to any person acting on the faith of the certification that there have been produced to the company such documents as on their face show a prima facie title to the shares in the transferor named in the instrument[8]. The certification is not to be taken as a representation that the transferor has any title to the shares[9]. Where a person acts on the faith of a false certification by a company made negligently, the company is under the same liability to him as if the certification had been made fraudulently[10].

These provisions impose very serious liabilities upon a company, which, however, is not bound to certify transfers at all.

If the company by mistake returns the share certificate to the transferor, and the transferor is thereby enabled to obtain money on another transfer of the shares, the company is not liable to the second transferee, as it has no duty to the public with regard to the custody of the certificate[11].

1 As to shareholders and membership of companies generally see PARAS 323 et seq, 1889 et seq.
2 As to share certificates see PARA 391.
3 As to the production of share certificates see PARA 415.
4 As to the company secretary see PARA 669 et seq.
5 As to the London Stock Exchange see FINANCIAL SERVICES REGULATION vol 50 (2016) PARA 96.
6 For these purposes:
   (1) an instrument of transfer is certificated if it bears the words 'certificate lodged' (or words to the like effect) (Companies Act 2006 s 775(4)(a));
   (2) the certification of an instrument of transfer is made by a company if the person issuing the instrument is a person authorised to issue certificated instruments of transfer on the company's behalf (s 775(4)(b)(i)), and if the certification is signed by a person authorised to certificate transfers on the company's behalf or by an officer or employee either of the company or of a body corporate so authorised (s 775(4)(b)(ii));
   (3) a certification is treated as signed by a person if it purports to be authenticated by his signature or initials (whether handwritten or not) (s 775(4)(c)(i)), and if it is not shown that the signature or initials was or were placed there neither by himself nor by a person authorised to use the signature or initials for the purpose of certificating transfers on the company's behalf (s 775(4)(c)(ii)).

   As to the meaning of 'company' see PARA 21; as to the meaning of 'person' see PARA 312 note 2; as to the meaning of 'officer' see PARA 679; and as to the meaning of 'body corporate' see PARA 1 note 5.
7 As to the meaning of 'share' see PARA 1231. As to the transfer of shares see PARA 400 et seq. As to the transfer of debentures see PARA 423 et seq.
8 Companies Act 2006 s 775(1). See *Bishop v Balkis Consolidated Co Ltd* (1890) 25 QBD 512 at 519–520, CA.
9 Companies Act 2006 s 775(2).
10 Companies Act 2006 s 775(3). This, together with s 775(4) (see note 6) negatives the effect of *George Whitechurch Ltd v Cavanagh* [1902] AC 117, HL, and *Kleinwort, Sons & Co v Associated Automatic Machine Corpn Ltd* (1934) 151 LT 1, HL, in so far as they relate to fraudulent certifications made by an agent of the company but not for the company's benefit. Cf *McKay's Case* [1896] 2 Ch 757.
11 *Longman v Bath Electric Tramways Ltd* [1905] 1 Ch 646, CA.

417. Issue of certificates on transfer of shares. A company[1] must, within two months[2] after the date on which a transfer[3] of any of its shares[4] is lodged with the company, complete and have ready for delivery the certificates of the shares transferred[5]. However, this duty does not apply:

(1) if the conditions of issue of the shares provide otherwise[6];
(2) in the case of a transfer to a financial institution[7];

(3) in the case of a transfer of shares if, following the transfer, the company has issued a share warrant[8] in respect of the shares[9]; or

(4) in the case of a transfer to a person[10] where he is not entitled[11] to a certificate or other document of or evidencing title in respect of the securities transferred[12].

If default is made in complying with this duty[13] an offence is committed by every officer[14] of the company who is in default[15].

1 As to the meaning of 'company' see PARA 21.
2 As to the meaning of 'month' see PARA 1818 note 10.
3 For these purposes a 'transfer' means a transfer duly stamped and otherwise valid (Companies Act 2006 s 776(2)(a)) or an exempt transfer within the Stock Transfer Act 1982 (see PARA 441) (s 776(2)(b)), but does not include a transfer that the company is for any reason entitled to refuse to register and does not register (s 776(2)). As to powers to refuse to register transfers of shares see PARA 404. As to the registration of shares see PARA 410. As to the transfer of debentures see PARA 423 et seq.
4 As to the meaning of 'share' see PARA 1231.
5 Companies Act 2006 s 776(1)(a). As to share certificates see PARA 391. As to the enforcement of this duty see PARA 418.
6 Companies Act 2006 s 776(3)(a).
7 Companies Act 2006 s 776(3)(b). A company of which shares are allotted to a financial institution (see s 778(1)(a)), or with which a transfer for transferring shares to a financial institution is lodged (see s 778(1)(c)), is not required in consequence of that allotment or transfer to comply with s 776(1) (see s 778(1)). As to the meaning of 'financial institution' see PARA 394 note 6.
8 See the Companies Act 2006 s 779; and PARA 392.
9 Companies Act 2006 s 776(3)(c).
10 As to the meaning of 'person' see PARA 312 note 2.
11 Ie by virtue of regulations under the Stock Transfer Act 1982 s 3: see PARA 441.
12 See the Companies Act 2006 ss 776(4), 777(1). If in such a case the transferee subsequently becomes entitled to such a certificate or other document by virtue of any provision of those regulations (s 777(2)(a)), and gives notice in writing of that fact to the company (s 777(2)(b)), s 776 has effect as if the reference in s 776(1) (see the text and notes 1–5) to the date of the lodging of the transfer were a reference to the date of the notice (s 777(2)). As to the provision made for the sending or supplying of documents or information to or from a company (the 'company communications provisions') see PARA 750 et seq.
13 Ie with the Companies Act 2006 s 776(1): see the text and notes 1–5.
14 As to the meaning of 'officer' see PARA 679.
15 Companies Act 2006 s 776(5). A person guilty of such an offence is liable on summary conviction to a fine not exceeding level 3 on the standard scale and, for continued contravention, a daily default fine not exceeding one-tenth of level 3 on the standard scale: s 776(6). As to the standard scale and the powers of magistrates' courts to issue fines on summary conviction see SENTENCING vol 92 (2015) PARA 176. As to the meaning of 'daily default fine' see PARA 1816. As to offences generally see PARA 1816 et seq.

418. Enforcement of issue of certificate on transfer. If a company[1] on which a notice has been served[2] requiring it to make good any default in complying with the duty[3] as to the issue of certificates on the transfer of any of its shares[4], fails to make good the default within ten days after service of the notice, the person[5] entitled to have the certificates delivered to him may apply to the court[6]. The court may on such an application make an order directing the company and any officer[7] of it to make good the default within such time as may be specified in the order[8]. The order may provide that all costs of and incidental to the application are to be borne by the company or by an officer of it responsible for the default[9].

1 As to the meaning of 'company' see PARA 21.
2 As to the service of documents on a company see PARA 743.
3 Ie the duty under the Companies Act 2006 s 776(1) (see PARA 417): see s 782(1)(b).
4 See the Companies Act 2006 s 782(1)(b).
5 As to the meaning of 'person' see PARA 312 note 2.

6 Companies Act 2006 s 782(1). As to the meaning of 'the court' see PARA 160 note 12. As to the procedure that applies on application to the court under companies legislation generally see PARA 306. Failure to comply with the duty under s 776(1) is also a criminal offence: see PARA 417.
7 As to the meaning of 'officer' see PARA 679.
8 Companies Act 2006 s 782(2).
9 Companies Act 2006 s 782(3).

419. Transferor's liability after registration of transfer of shares. When a transfer of shares has been duly registered[1], the transferor ceases to be a member of the company[2] in respect of the shares transferred. Thereupon he becomes a 'past member' of the company, and in case of a winding up is liable to contribute towards the payment of its debts and liabilities and the expenses of the winding up and for the adjustment of the rights of contributors among themselves[3], to the extent of the amount remaining unpaid on the shares, where it appears to the court that the existing members are unable to satisfy the contributions required to be made by them under the Insolvency Act 1986[4], unless the debt or liability was contracted after he has ceased to be a member[5], or unless he has ceased to be a member for a year or upwards before the commencement of the winding up[6].

Where a limited company is re-registered as unlimited[7], a person[8] who, at the time when the application for it to be re-registered was lodged, was a past member of the company, and did not thereafter again become a member, does not have his liability increased[9].

Where an unlimited company is re-registered as limited[10], a past member of the company who was a member of it at the time of re-registration is, if the winding up commences within a period of three years from re-registration, liable to contribute to the assets of the company without limit in respect of debts and liabilities contracted before such re-registration[11]. Where no persons who were members of the company at that time are existing members of the company, a person who at such time was a present or past member of the company will (unless he has ceased to be a member for one year or upwards), if the winding up takes place within a period of three years from re-registration, be liable to contribute without limit notwithstanding that the existing members have satisfied the contributions required to be made by them under the Insolvency Act 1986[12].

1 As to the registration of shares see PARA 410.
2 As to who qualifies as a member of a company see PARA 323.
3 As to the liability of past and present members see the Insolvency Act 1986 s 74(1); and COMPANY AND PARTNERSHIP INSOLVENCY vol 17 (2011) PARA 662. As to liability for calls already made see PARA 414. As to contributories generally see COMPANY AND PARTNERSHIP INSOLVENCY vol 17 (2011) PARA 661 et seq.
4 See the Insolvency Act 1986 s 74(2)(c); and COMPANY AND PARTNERSHIP INSOLVENCY vol 17 (2011) PARA 663.
5 See the Insolvency Act 1986 s 74(2)(b); and COMPANY AND PARTNERSHIP INSOLVENCY vol 17 (2011) PARA 663.
6 See the Insolvency Act 1986 s 74(2)(a); and COMPANY AND PARTNERSHIP INSOLVENCY vol 17 (2011) PARA 663.
7 See the Insolvency Act 1986 s 78(1); and COMPANY AND PARTNERSHIP INSOLVENCY vol 17 (2011) PARA 664. As to re-registration as an unlimited company see PARAS 176–177. As to the meanings of 'limited company' and 'unlimited company' see PARA 95.
8 As to the meaning of 'person' see PARA 312 note 2.
9 See the Insolvency Act 1986 s 78(2); and COMPANY AND PARTNERSHIP INSOLVENCY vol 17 (2011) PARA 664.
10 See the Insolvency Act 1986 s 77(1); and COMPANY AND PARTNERSHIP INSOLVENCY vol 17 (2011) PARA 664. As to re-registration as a limited company see PARA 178.
11 See the Insolvency Act 1986 s 77(2), (4); and COMPANY AND PARTNERSHIP INSOLVENCY vol 17 (2011) PARA 664.

12 See the Insolvency Act 1986 ss 74(2)(a), 77(3); and COMPANY AND PARTNERSHIP INSOLVENCY vol 17 (2011) PARAS 663–664.

420. Stamp duty reserve tax in respect of agreements to transfer securities. Until a day to be appointed the following provisions have effect[1].

Stamp duty reserve tax is charged in respect of agreements to transfer certain securities for money or money's worth and in respect of arrangements involving depositary receipts and clearance services[2]. The principal charge in respect of agreements is deferred and will not arise if certain conditions are satisfied[3]; but there is also an immediate and unconditional charge in respect of agreements to transfer chargeable securities which are constituted by or transferable by means of certain renounceable instruments as soon as they are made, without regard to whether or not the agreement is implemented by an instrument of transfer[4]. In each case, tax is imposed at the rate of 50 pence for every £100 or part of £100 of the amount or value of the consideration[5]. A higher rate charge of £1.50 per £100 or part of £100 of the amount or value of the consideration is imposed in respect of certain transactions involving depositary receipts or clearance services which do not give rise to a transfer chargeable with ad valorem stamp duty in the same amount as the tax[6].

1 The Finance Act 1986 Pt IV (ss 86–99A) is repealed by the Finance Act 1990 s 132, Sch 19 Pt VII as from a day to be appointed in accordance with s 110: see Sch 19 Pt VII; and STAMP TAXES vol 96 (2012) PARA 393. At the date at which this volume states the law no such day had been appointed.

2 Stamp duty reserve tax was introduced by the Finance Act 1986 Pt IV (ss 86–99): see s 86(1). As to stamp duty reserve tax generally see STAMP TAXES vol 96 (2012) PARA 392 et seq. As to exceptions and exemptions see STAMP TAXES vol 96 (2012) PARA 355 et seq.

3 As to agreements to transfer chargeable securities see STAMP TAXES vol 96 (2012) PARA 394 et seq.

4 As to stamp duties generally see STAMP TAXES.

5 As to the principal charge see STAMP TAXES vol 96 (2012) PARA 394.

6 As to the higher rate charge in respect of depositary receipts and clearance services see STAMP TAXES vol 96 (2012) PARAS 397–398.

(ii) Certification and Transfer of Debentures

A. ISSUE OF CERTIFICATES ON ALLOTMENT OF DEBENTURES ETC

421. Issue of certificates etc on allotment of debentures. A company[1] must, within two months after the allotment of any of its debentures[2] or debenture stock[3], complete and have ready for delivery the debentures allotted[4], or the certificates of the debenture stock allotted[5]. This requirement does, however, not apply:

(1) if the conditions of issue of the debentures or debenture stock provide otherwise[6]; or

(2) in the case of allotment to a financial institution[7].

If default is made in complying with the requirement to complete and have ready for delivery the debentures allotted, or the certificates of the debenture stock allotted, an offence is committed by every officer of the company who is in default[8]. A person guilty of such an offence is liable on summary conviction to a fine not exceeding level 3 on the standard scale[9] and for continued contravention to a daily default fine[10] not exceeding one-tenth of level 3 on the standard scale[11].

1 As to the meaning of 'company' under the Companies Acts see PARA 21; and as to the meaning of the 'Companies Acts' see PARA 13.

2 As to the meaning of 'debenture' see PARA 1482. As to the issue of certificates on the allotment of shares see PARA 394.

3 As to debenture stock see PARA 1492. As to the meaning of 'stock' generally see PARA 1351.
4 Companies Act 2006 s 769(1)(b). As to enforcement see PARA 422.
5 Companies Act 2006 s 769(1)(c).
6 Companies Act 2006 s 769(2)(a).
7 Companies Act 2006 s 769(2)(b). A company of which debentures are (or of which debenture stock is) allotted to a financial institution (s 778(1)(a), (b)), or with which a transfer for transferring debentures or debenture stock to a financial institution is lodged (s 778(1)(c)), is not required in consequence of that allotment or transfer to comply with s 769(1) (s 778(1)). As to the meaning of 'financial institution' for these purposes see PARA 394 note 6.
8 Companies Act 2006 s 769(3). As to the meaning of 'officer' see PARA 679; and as to the meaning of 'officer in default' see PARA 316.
9 As to the standard scale and the powers of magistrates' courts to issue fines on summary conviction see SENTENCING vol 92 (2015) PARA 176.
10 As to the meaning of 'daily default fine' see PARA 1816.
11 Companies Act 2006 s 769(4).

422. Enforcement of issue of certificate. If a company[1] on which a notice has been served[2] requiring it to make good any default in complying with the duty[3] of that company to complete and have ready for delivery the debentures[4] allotted, or the certificates of the debenture stock[5] allotted[6], fails to make good the default within ten days after service of the notice, the person entitled to have the certificates or the debentures delivered to him may apply to the court[7]. The court may on such an application make an order directing the company and any officer[8] of it to make good the default within such time as may be specified in the order[9]; and the order may provide that all costs of and incidental to the application are to be borne by the company or by an officer of it responsible for the default[10].

1 As to the meaning of 'company' under the Companies Acts see PARA 21; and as to the meaning of the 'Companies Acts' see PARA 13.
2 As to the service of documents on a company see PARA 743.
3 Ie the duty under the Companies Act 2006 s 769(1) (see PARA 421); see s 782(1)(a).
4 As to the meaning of 'debenture' see PARA 1482. As to the issue of certificates on the allotment of debentures see PARA 421.
5 As to debenture stock see PARA 1492. As to the meaning of 'stock' generally see PARA 1351.
6 See the Companies Act 2006 s 782(1)(a).
7 Companies Act 2006 s 782(1). As to the meaning of 'the court' see PARA 160 note 12. As to the procedure that applies on application to the court under companies legislation generally see PARA 306.
8 As to the meaning of 'officer' see PARA 679.
9 Companies Act 2006 s 782(2).
10 Companies Act 2006 s 782(3).

B. TRANSFER OF DEBENTURES

(A) Transfer of Debentures: in general

423. Transfer of debentures by delivery. Being a negotiable instrument[1], a bearer debenture[2] is transferable by delivery so as to pass the property in it to a holder for value in good faith, and entitle him, upon delivery of it to the company, to obtain payment of the principal secured when due, and to sue in his own name upon the debenture[3].

1 *Bechuanaland Exploration Co v London Trading Bank* [1898] 2 QB 658; *Edelstein v Schuler & Co* [1902] 2 KB 144. Cf *Goodwin v Robarts* (1876) 1 App Cas 476, HL, apparently overruling *Crouch v Crédit Foncier of England* (1873) LR 8 QB 374 (where it was held that the company might lawfully refuse to pay the bona fide transferee for value of a stolen debenture payable to bearer, even though he had no notice of the theft). As to negotiable instruments generally see FINANCIAL INSTRUMENTS AND TRANSACTIONS vol 49 (2015) PARA 184 et seq.
2 As to debentures payable to bearer see PARA 1487. As to the meaning of 'debenture' see PARA 1482.
3 In certain cases decided before the negotiability of bearer debentures had been fully established (see note 1), the holder for value in good faith of a bearer debenture was held entitled to prove on

the debentures without being subject to equities between the company and the persons to whom the debentures were originally issued: see *Re Blakely Ordnance Co, ex p New Zealand Corpn* (1867) 3 Ch App 154; *Re General Estates Co, ex p City Bank* (1868) 3 Ch App 758 (where the question arose whether the instrument was not in fact a promissory note); *Re Imperial Land Co of Marseilles, ex p Colborne and Strawbridge* (1870) LR 11 Eq 478 at 490–491, 494 per Malins V-C (question whether the instrument was a promissory note). Contrast *Re Natal Investment Co, Financial Corpn Claim* (1868) 3 Ch App 355; but see comments on this case in *Re General Estates Co, ex p City Bank* at 762 per Page Wood LJ; *Re Imperial Land Co of Marseilles, ex p Colborne and Strawbridge* at 493 per Malins V-C; *Higgs v Assam Tea Co* (1869) LR 4 Exch 387 at 395 per Bramwell B; *Crouch v Crédit Foncier of England* (1873) LR 8 QB 374 at 385 per Blackburn J; *Re Romford Canal Co, Pocock's Claim, Trickett's Claim, Carew's Claim* (1883) 24 ChD 85 at 91–92 per Kay J.

424. Transfer of debentures by instrument. According to the ordinary form, a registered debenture[1] is legally transferable only by an instrument of transfer duly executed or signed and by registration in the company's books. The conditions of registered debentures usually provide that the company must keep a register of the debentures at its registered office, containing the names, addresses and descriptions of the registered holders and particulars of the debentures held by them respectively; that every transfer must be in writing under the hand of the registered holder or his legal personal representatives; that, upon delivery of the transfer at the registered office with the prescribed fee and such evidence of identity or title as the company may reasonably require, the transfer is to be registered, and a note of the registration is to be indorsed on the debenture; and that the company will be entitled to retain the transfer[2]. The simplified form of transfer introduced by the Stock Transfer Act 1963 applies to debentures[3].

When the principal and interest secured by the debenture are to be paid to the registered holder for the time being without regard to any equities subsisting between the company and the original or any intermediate holder, and the conditions as to transfer are similar to those mentioned above, a liquidator is bound to register the transfer, even if made after the liquidation commenced, and after judgment in a claim by debenture holders, but before any notice of a claim by the company against the transferor[4].

1 As to which see PARA 1474 et seq. As to the meaning of 'debenture' see PARA 1482.
2 Under such provisions, a person entitled by transmission is not bound to produce a transfer before registration: *Edwards v Ransomes and Rapier Ltd* (1930) 143 LT 594.
3 See the Stock Transfer Act 1963 ss 1, 4(1); and PARA 411.
4 *Re Goy & Co Ltd, Farmer v Goy & Co Ltd* [1900] 2 Ch 149. Cf *Re Palmer's Decoration and Furnishing Co* [1904] 2 Ch 743; *Re Brown and Gregory Ltd, Shepheard v Brown and Gregory Ltd, Andrews v Brown and Gregory Ltd* [1904] 1 Ch 627; *Re Richard Smith & Co* [1901] 1 IR 73; *Re Rhodesia Goldfields Ltd* [1910] 1 Ch 239.

(B) Formalities required by Transfer of Debentures

425. Necessity for proper instrument of transfer of debentures. A company[1] may not register a transfer of debentures[2] of the company unless:

(1) a proper instrument of transfer has been delivered to it[3]; or
(2) the transfer is an exempt transfer[4] or is in accordance with regulations[5] relating to the evidencing and transfer of title to securities without written instrument[6].

This requirement[7] does not, however, affect any power of the company to register as debenture holder a person to whom the right to any debentures of the company has been transmitted by operation of law[8].

1 As to the meaning of 'company' under the Companies Acts see PARA 21; and as to the meaning of the 'Companies Acts' see PARA 13.

2 As to the meaning of 'debenture' see PARA 1482. As to transfers of debentures see PARAS 423, 424. The Companies Act 2006 ss 770, 771 apply also to a transfer of shares in a company: see PARA 410. Accordingly, see also the cases cited in PARA 410.
3 Companies Act 2006 s 770(1)(a). As to the provision made for the sending of documents or information from a company (the 'company communications provisions') see PARA 750 et seq.
4 Companies Act 2006 s 770(1)(b)(i). For these purposes, an exempt transfer is one within the Stock Transfer Act 1982: see s 770(1)(b)(i). As to exempt transfers within the Stock Transfer Act 1982, which in its relation to companies affects only debentures issued by the Agricultural Mortgage Corpn plc, the Commonwealth Development Finance Co Ltd, Finance for Industry plc and the Scottish Agricultural Securities Corpn Ltd, see s 2, Sch 1para6(1); and PARA 441. See also *Re Greene, Greene v Greene* [1949] Ch 333, [1949] 1 All ER 167.
5 Ie under the Companies Act 2006 Pt 21 Ch 2 (ss 783–790) (see PARA 431 et seq): see s 770(1)(b)(ii).
6 See the Companies Act 2006 s 770(1)(b)(ii). As to the transfer and registration of uncertificated securities other than shares see PARA 436.
7 Ie the Companies Act 2006 s 770(1) (see the text and notes 1–6): see s 770(2).
8 Companies Act 2006 s 770(2). As to transmission by operation of law see PARA 445.

426. Procedure on transfer of debentures being lodged. When a transfer of debentures[1] of a company[2] has been lodged with the company[3], the company must, as soon as practicable and in any event within two months after the date on which the transfer is lodged with it[4], either register the transfer[5], or give the transferee notice of refusal to register the transfer, together with its reasons for the refusal[6]. If a company fails to comply with these requirements[7], an offence is committed by the company and by every officer of the company who is in default[8]. A person guilty of such an offence is liable on summary conviction to a fine not exceeding level 3 on the standard scale[9] and for continued contravention to a daily default fine[10] not exceeding one-tenth of level 3 on the standard scale[11].

If the company refuses to register a transfer of debentures, it must provide the transferee with such further information about the reasons for the refusal as the transferee may reasonably request[12]. If a company fails to comply with these requirements[13], an offence is committed by the company and by every officer of the company who is in default[14]. A person guilty of such an offence is liable on summary conviction to a fine not exceeding level 3 on the standard scale and for continued contravention to a daily default fine not exceeding one-tenth of level 3 on the standard scale[15].

A company's articles of association[16] usually require that securities are to be transferred in any usual form or any other form approved by the directors[17].

1 As to the meaning of 'debenture' see PARA 1482. As to transfers of debentures see PARAS 423–424.
2 As to the meaning of 'company' under the Companies Acts see PARA 21; and as to the meaning of the 'Companies Acts' see PARA 13.
3 The Companies Act 2006 s 771 does not apply in relation to the transmission of debentures by operation of law: see s 771(5)(b). As to the application of s 771 to a transfer of shares see PARA 410.
4 See the Companies Act 2006 s 771(1).
5 Companies Act 2006 s 771(1)(a).
6 Companies Act 2006 s 771(1)(b).
7 Ie fails to comply with the Companies Act 2006 s 771(1) (see the text and notes 1–6): see s 771(3).
8 Companies Act 2006 s 771(3). As to the meaning of 'officer who is in default' see PARA 316. As to the meaning of 'officer' generally see PARA 679.
9 As to the standard scale and the powers of magistrates' courts to issue fines on summary conviction see SENTENCING vol 92 (2015) PARA 176.
10 As to the meaning of 'daily default fine' see PARA 1816.
11 Companies Act 2006 s 771(4).
12 Companies Act 2006 s 771(2). This does not, however, include copies of minutes of meetings of directors: s 771(2). As to the meaning of 'director' under the Companies Acts see PARA 512. As to meetings of directors see PARA 567 et seq.
13 Ie fails to comply with the Companies Act 2006 s 771(2) (see the text and note 12): see s 771(3).

14 Companies Act 2006 s 771(3).
15 Companies Act 2006 s 771(4).
16 As to a company's articles of association see PARA 227 et seq.
17 Neither the model articles of association that have been prescribed under the Companies Act 2006 (see PARA 227 et seq) nor the model articles that were prescribed under the Companies Act 1985 (the 'legacy articles', which have not been revoked: see PARA 229) make provision explicitly in relation to the transfer and registration of debentures, although such provision is made in relation to shares: see PARAS 403, 410.

427. Transfer of debenture by way of mortgage. The principles applicable to mortgages of shares apply to mortgages of debentures which are transferable by registration of an instrument of transfer in the company's books[1].

1 See PARA 1399.

428. Certification of instrument of transfer of debentures. The certification by a company[1] of an instrument of transfer of any debentures[2] of the company is to be taken as a representation by the company to any person acting on the faith of the certification that there have been produced to the company such documents as on their face show a prima facie title to the debentures in the transferor named in the instrument[3]. The certification is not to be taken as a representation that the transferor has any title to the debentures[4]. Where a person acts on the faith of a false certification by a company made negligently, the company is under the same liability to him as if the certification had been made fraudulently[5].

These provisions impose very serious liabilities upon a company, which, however, is not bound to certify transfers at all.

If the company by mistake returns the debenture to the transferor, and the transferor is thereby enabled to obtain money on another transfer, the company is not liable to the second transferee, as it has no duty to the public with regard to the custody of the debenture[6].

1 As to the meaning of 'company' under the Companies Acts see PARA 21; and as to the meaning of the 'Companies Acts' see PARA 13.
2 As to the meaning of 'debenture' see PARA 1482. As to transfers of debentures see PARAS 423–427. For these purposes:
   (1) an instrument of transfer is certificated if it bears the words 'certificate lodged' (or words to the like effect) (Companies Act 2006 s 775(4)(a));
   (2) the certification of an instrument of transfer is made by a company if the person issuing the instrument is a person authorised to issue certificated instruments of transfer on the company's behalf (s 775(4)(b)(i)), and if the certification is signed by a person authorised to certificate transfers on the company's behalf or by an officer or employee either of the company or of a body corporate so authorised (s 775(4)(b)(ii));
   (3) a certification is treated as signed by a person if it purports to be authenticated by his signature or initials (whether handwritten or not) (s 775(4)(c)(i)), and if it is not shown that the signature or initials was or were placed there neither by himself nor by a person authorised to use the signature or initials for the purpose of certificating transfers on the company's behalf (s 775(4)(c)(ii)).

   As to the meaning of 'officer' see PARA 679. As to the meaning of 'body corporate' see PARA 1 note 5.
3 Companies Act 2006 s 775(1). See *Bishop v Balkis Consolidated Co Ltd* (1890) 25 QBD 512 at 519–520, CA.
4 Companies Act 2006 s 775(2).
5 Companies Act 2006 s 775(3). This, together with s 755(4) (see note 2) negatives the effect of *George Whitechurch Ltd v Cavanagh* [1902] AC 117, HL, and *Kleinwort, Sons & Co v Associated Automatic Machine Corpn Ltd* (1934) 151 LT 1, HL, in so far as they relate to fraudulent certifications made by an agent of the company but not for the company's benefit. Cf *McKay's Case* [1896] 2 Ch 757.
6 *Longman v Bath Electric Tramways Ltd* [1905] 1 Ch 646, CA.

429. Issue of certificates etc on transfer of debentures. A company[1] must, within two months after the date on which a transfer[2] of any of its debentures[3] or debenture stock[4] is lodged with the company, complete and have ready for delivery, the debentures transferred[5], or the certificates of the debenture stock transferred[6].

However, this duty does not apply:

(1) if the conditions of issue of the debentures or debenture stock provide otherwise[7];
(2) in the case of a transfer to a financial institution[8];
(3) in the case of a transfer to a person where he is not entitled[9] to a certificate or other document of or evidencing title in respect of the securities transferred[10].

If default is made in complying with this duty[11] to complete and have ready for delivery, the debentures transferred, or the certificates of the debenture stock transferred, an offence is committed by every officer of the company who is in default[12]. A person guilty of such an offence is liable on summary conviction to a fine not exceeding level 3 on the standard scale[13] and for continued contravention a daily default fine[14] not exceeding one-tenth of level 3 on the standard scale[15].

1 As to the meaning of 'company' under the Companies Acts see PARA 21; and as to the meaning of the 'Companies Acts' see PARA 13.
2 For these purposes, a 'transfer' means a transfer duly stamped and otherwise valid (Companies Act 2006 s 776(2)(a)), or an exempt transfer within the Stock Transfer Act 1982 (s 776(2)(b)); but does not include a transfer that the company is for any reason entitled to refuse to register and does not register (s 776(2)). As to exempt transfers within the Stock Transfer Act 1982, which in its relation to companies affects only debentures issued by the Agricultural Mortgage Corpn plc, the Commonwealth Development Finance Co Ltd, Finance for Industry plc and the Scottish Agricultural Securities Corpn Ltd, see s 2, Sch 1para6(1); and PARA 441. As to powers to refuse to register transfers of debentures see PARA 426.
3 As to the meaning of 'debenture' see PARA 1482.
4 As to debenture stock see PARA 1492. As to the meaning of 'stock' generally see PARA 1351.
5 Companies Act 2006 s 776(1)(b). As to the enforcement of this duty see PARA 430.
6 Companies Act 2006 s 776(1)(c).
7 Companies Act 2006 s 776(3)(a).
8 Companies Act 2006 s 776(3)(b). A company of which debentures are (or of which debenture stock is) allotted to a financial institution (see s 778(1)(a), (b)), or with which a transfer for transferring debentures or debenture stock to a financial institution is lodged (see s 778(1)(c)), is not required in consequence of that allotment or transfer to comply with s 776(1) (see s 778(1)). As to the meaning of 'financial institution' for these purposes see PARA 394 note 6.
9 Ie by virtue of regulations under the Stock Transfer Act 1982 s 3 (see PARA 441): see the Companies Act 2006 ss 776(4), 777(1). The provisions of s 776(1) (see the text and notes 1–6) are subject to s 777: s 776(4).
10 See the Companies Act 2006 ss 776(4), 777(1). If in such a case the transferee subsequently becomes entitled to such a certificate or other document by virtue of any provision of those regulations (s 777(2)(a)), and gives notice in writing of that fact to the company (s 777(2)(b)), s 776 has effect as if the reference in s 776(1) (see the text and notes 1–6) to the date of the lodging of the transfer were a reference to the date of the notice (s 777(2)). As to the provision made for the sending or supplying of documents or information to or from a company (the 'company communications provisions') see PARA 750 et seq.
11 Ie in complying with the Companies Act 2006 s 776(1) (see the text and notes 1–6): see s 776(5).
12 Companies Act 2006 s 776(5). As to the meaning of 'officer who is in default' see PARA 316. As to the meaning of 'officer' generally see PARA 679.
13 As to the standard scale and the powers of magistrates' courts to issue fines on summary conviction see SENTENCING vol 92 (2015) PARA 176.
14 As to the meaning of 'daily default fine' see PARA 1816.
15 Companies Act 2006 s 776(6).

430. Enforcement of issue of certificate on transfer of debentures. If a company[1] on which a notice has been served[2] requiring it to make good any default in complying with the duty[3] to complete and have ready for delivery, debentures[4] transferred, or certificates of the debenture stock[5] transferred[6], fails to make good the default within ten days after service of the notice, the person entitled to have the certificates delivered to him may apply to the court[7]. The court may on such an application make an order directing the company and any officer[8] of it to make good the default within such time as may be specified in the order[9]. The order may provide that all costs of and incidental to the application are to be borne by the company or by an officer of it responsible for the default[10].

1 As to the meaning of 'company' under the Companies Acts see PARA 21; and as to the meaning of the 'Companies Acts' see PARA 13.
2 As to the provision made for the sending or supplying of documents or information to or from a company (the 'company communications provisions') see PARA 750 et seq.
3 Ie the duty under the Companies Act 2006 s 776(1) (see PARA 417): see s 782(1)(b).
4 As to the meaning of 'debenture' see PARA 1482.
5 As to debenture stock see PARA 1492. As to the meaning of 'stock' generally see PARA 1351.
6 See the Companies Act 2006 s 782(1)(b).
7 Companies Act 2006 s 782(1). As to the meaning of 'the court' see PARA 160 note 12. As to the procedure that applies on application to the court under companies legislation generally see PARA 306. Failure to comply with the duty under s 776(1) is also a criminal offence: see PARA 429.
8 As to the meaning of 'officer' see PARA 679.
9 Companies Act 2006 s 782(2).
10 Companies Act 2006 s 782(3).

(iii) Uncertificated Securities

431. Provision to allow securities to be evidenced without certificate and transferred without written instrument. Provision may be made by regulations[1] for enabling title to securities to be evidenced and transferred without a written instrument[2]. The regulations must contain such safeguards as appear to the authority making the regulations appropriate for the protection of investors and for ensuring that competition is not restricted, distorted or prevented[3]. The regulations may:

(1) make provision for procedures for recording and transferring title to securities[4], and for the regulation of those procedures and the persons[5] responsible for or involved in their operation[6];
(2) for the purpose of enabling or facilitating the operation of the procedures provided for by the regulations, make provision with respect to the rights and obligations of persons in relation to securities dealt with under the procedures[7];
(3) include provision for the purpose of giving effect to:
 (a) the transmission of title to securities by operation of law[8];
 (b) any restriction on the transfer of title to securities arising by virtue of the provisions of any enactment[9] or instrument, court order or agreement[10];
 (c) any power conferred by any such provision on a person to deal with securities on behalf of the person entitled[11];
(4) make provision with respect to the persons responsible for the operation of the procedures provided for by the regulations as to the consequences of their insolvency or incapacity[12], or as to the transfer from them to other persons of their functions in relation to those procedures[13];
(5) confer functions on any person, including:
 (a) the function of giving guidance or issuing a code of practice in relation to any provision made by the regulations[14]; and
 (b) the function of making rules for the purposes of any provision made by the regulations[15];

(6) in prescribed cases[16], confer immunity from liability in damages[17].

Regulations[18] may also make provision:

(i) enabling the members of a company[19] or of any designated class of companies[20] to adopt, by ordinary resolution[21], arrangements under which title to securities is required to be evidenced or transferred, or both, without a written instrument[22]; or

(ii) requiring companies, or any designated class of companies, to adopt such arrangements[23].

Such regulations may make such provision in respect of all securities issued by a company[24], or in respect of all securities of a specified description[25]. The regulations may prohibit the issue of any certificate by the company in respect of the issue or transfer of securities[26], require the provision by the company to holders of securities of statements, at specified intervals or on specified occasions, of the securities held in their name[27], and make provision as to the matters of which any such certificate or statement is, or is not, evidence[28].

Regulations under these provisions[29] may:

(A) modify or exclude any provision of any enactment or instrument, or any rule of law[30];

(B) apply, with such modifications as may be appropriate, the provisions of any enactment or instrument (including provisions creating criminal offences)[31];

(C) require the payment of fees, or enable persons to require the payment of fees, of such amounts as may be specified in the regulations or determined in accordance with them[32];

(D) empower the authority making the regulations to delegate to any person willing and able to discharge them any functions of the authority under the regulations[33].

Before making regulations under these provisions[34], or any order[35] enabling or requiring arrangements to be adopted, the authority having power to make regulations must carry out such consultation as appears to it to be appropriate[36].

The Uncertificated Securities Regulations 2001[37] enable title to units of a security[38] to be evidenced otherwise than by a certificate[39] and transferred otherwise than by a written instrument by means of a relevant system[40], and make provision for certain supplementary and incidental matters[41]. Where a title to a unit of a security is evidenced otherwise than by a certificate by virtue of those regulations, the transfer of title to such a unit of a security is subject to the regulations[42].

1 The power to make regulations under the Companies Act 2006 Pt 21 Ch 2 (ss 783–790) is exercisable by the Treasury and the Secretary of State, either jointly or concurrently (s 784(1)); and references to the authority having power to make regulations must accordingly be read as references to both or either of them, as the case may require (s 784(2)). Any such regulations are subject to affirmative resolution procedure (ie the order must not be made unless a draft of the statutory instrument containing it has been laid before Parliament and approved by a resolution of each House of Parliament) (ss 784(3), 1290); and, before making such regulations, the authority having power to make such regulations must carry out such consultation as appears to it to be appropriate(s 789). See the Uncertificated Securities Regulations 2001, SI 2001/3755, made under the Companies Act 1989 s 207 (now repealed and replaced by provisions of the Companies Act 2006 Pt 21 Ch 2); and the statutory instruments amending those regulations. As to the making of regulations under the Companies Act 2006 generally see ss 1288–1292. As to the Treasury see CONSTITUTIONAL AND ADMINISTRATIVE LAW vol 20 (2014) PARA 262 et seq. As to the Secretary of State see PARA 6.

2 Companies Act 2006 s 785(1). In Pt 21 Ch 2:

(1) 'securities' means shares, debentures, debenture stock, loan stock, bonds, units of a collective investment scheme within the meaning of the Financial Services and Markets

Act 2000 (see FINANCIAL SERVICES REGULATION vol 50A (2008) PARA 841) and other securities of any description (s 783(a));

(2) references to title to securities include any legal or equitable interest in securities (s 783(b));

(3) references to a transfer of title include a transfer by way of security (s 783(c));

(4) references to transfer without a written instrument include, in relation to bearer securities, transfer without delivery (s 783(d)).

As to the meaning of 'share' see PARA 1231. As to the meaning of 'debenture' see PARA 1482. As to bearer securities see PARA 1487.

3 Companies Act 2006 s 785(3).

4 Companies Act 2006 s 785(2)(a).

5 As to the meaning of 'person' see PARA 312 note 2.

6 Companies Act 2006 s 785(2)(b).

7 Companies Act 2006 s 785(4).

8 Companies Act 2006 s 785(5)(a).

9 As to the meaning of 'enactment' see PARA 13 note 16.

10 Companies Act 2006 s 785(5)(b).

11 Companies Act 2006 s 785(5)(c).

12 Companies Act 2006 s 785(6)(a).

13 Companies Act 2006 s 785(6)(b).

14 Companies Act 2006 s 785(7)(a) (s 785(7), (8) added by the Financial Services Act 2012 s 112).

15 Companies Act 2006 s 785(7)(b) (as added: see note 14).

16 In the Companies Acts, 'prescribed' means prescribed (by order or by regulations) by the Secretary of State: Companies Act 2006 s 1167. As to the meaning of the 'Companies Acts' see PARA 13.

17 Companies Act 2006 s 785(8) (as added: see note 14).

18 Ie under the Companies Act 2006 Pt 21 Ch 2.

19 As to the meaning of 'member of a company' see PARA 323. As to the meaning of 'company' see PARA 21.

20 In the Companies Act 2006 s 786, references to a designated class of companies are to a class designated in the regulations or by order under s 787 (s 786(5)(a)); and 'specified' means specified in the regulations (s 786(5)(b)). The authority having power to make regulations may by order:

(1) designate classes of companies for the purposes of s 786 (s 787(1)(a));

(2) provide that, in relation to securities of a specified description in a designated class of companies (s 787(1)(b)(i)), or in a specified company or class of companies (s 787(1)(b)(ii)), specified provisions of regulations made by virtue of s 786 either do not apply or apply subject to specified modifications (s 787(1)(b)).

In this context, 'specified' means specified in the order: s 787(2). Such an order is subject to negative resolution procedure (ie the statutory instrument containing the order being subject to annulment in pursuance of a resolution of either House of Parliament) (ss 787(3), 1289); and, before making any order under s 787, the authority having power to make regulations under Pt 21 Ch 2 must carry out such consultation as appears to it to be appropriate (s 789). At the date at which this volume states the law, no such order had been made. As to the making of orders under the Companies Act 2006 generally see ss 1288–1292.

21 As to the meaning of 'ordinary resolution' see PARA 685. The Companies Act 2006 Pt 3 Ch 3 (ss 29–30) (see PARA 230) applies to a resolution passed by virtue of regulations under Pt 21 Ch 2 (ss 783–790): see s 790.

22 Companies Act 2006 s 786(1)(a). The arrangements provided for by the regulations making such provision as is mentioned in s 786(1):

(1) must not be such that a person who but for the arrangements would be entitled to have his name entered in the company's register of members or, as the case may be, delivered to the registrar of companies under Pt 8 Ch 2A (ss 128A–128K) (see PARA 363 et seq), ceases to be so entitled (s 786(3)(a) (amended by the Small Business, Enterprise and Employment Act 2015 Sch 5 Pt 2 paras 11, 29));

(2) must be such that a person who but for the arrangements would be entitled to exercise any rights in respect of the securities continues to be able effectively to control the exercise of those rights (Companies Act 2006 s 786(3)(b)).

As to the register of members see PARA 336 et seq; as to the option to keep membership information on the central register see PARA 363 et seq; and as to the meaning of 'registrar of companies' see PARA 126 note 2.

23 Companies Act 2006 s 786(1)(b). See also note 22.

24 Companies Act 2006 s 786(2)(a).

25 Companies Act 2006 s 786(2)(b).

26 Companies Act 2006 s 786(4)(a).

27 Companies Act 2006 s 786(4)(b).

28 Companies Act 2006 s 786(4)(c).
29 Ie regulations under the Companies Act 2006 Pt 21 Ch 2 (ss 783–790).
30 Companies Act 2006 s 788(a).
31 Companies Act 2006 s 788(b).
32 Companies Act 2006 s 788(c).
33 Companies Act 2006 s 788(d).
34 See note 29.
35 Ie under the Companies Act 2006 s 787: see note 20.
36 Companies Act 2006 s 789. As to the exercise of the duty to consult see JUDICIAL REVIEW vol 61 (2010) PARA 627.
37 Ie the Uncertificated Securities Regulations 2001, SI 2001/3755, which were made under the Companies Act 1989 s 207 (repealed) and which now have effect as if made under the Companies Act 2006 ss 784, 785, 788 (see the text and notes 1–36) by virtue of s 1297 (see PARAS 13–14).
38 'Unit', in relation to a security, means the smallest possible transferable unit of the security (for example a single share): Uncertificated Securities Regulations 2001, SI 2001/3755, reg 3(1).
39 'Certificate' means any certificate, instrument or other document of, or evidencing, title to units of a security: Uncertificated Securities Regulations 2001, SI 2001/3755, reg 3(1). As to share certificates see PARA 391.
40 As to the meaning of 'relevant system' see PARA 432 note 1.
41 See the Uncertificated Securities Regulations 2001, SI 2001/3755, reg 2(1).
42 Uncertificated Securities Regulations 2001, SI 2001/3755, reg 2(2).

432. Uncertificated shares. Where an operator[1] permits title to shares[2] of the appropriate class[3], or in relation to which a directors' resolution duly passed[4] is effective, to be transferred by means of a relevant system[5], and the company in question permits the holding of shares of that class in uncertificated form and the transfer of title to any such shares by means of a relevant system[6], then title to shares of that class which are recorded on an operator register of members may be transferred by means of that relevant system[7]. Such securities are known as 'participating securities'[8]; and the issuer of such a security is known as a 'participating issuer'[9].

Any requirements in an enactment or rule of law which apply in respect of the transfer of securities otherwise than by means of a relevant system do not prevent an operator from registering a transfer of title to uncertificated units of a security[10] upon settlement of a transfer of such units in accordance with his rules[11], or an operator-instruction from requiring a participating issuer to register a transfer of title to uncertificated units of a security[12]. Notwithstanding any enactment, instrument or rule of law, a participating issuer must not issue a certificate in relation to any uncertificated units of a participating security[13]; and a document issued by or on behalf of a participating issuer purportedly evidencing title to an uncertificated unit of a participating security is not evidence of title to the unit of the security[14]. Any requirement in or under any enactment to indorse any statement or information on a certificate evidencing title to a unit of a security does not prohibit the conversion into, or issue of, units of the security in uncertificated form[15]; and, in relation to uncertificated units of the security, must be taken to be a requirement for the relevant participating issuer to provide the holder of the units with the statement or information on request by him[16].

1 'Operator' means a person approved by the Bank of England under the Uncertificated Securities Regulations 2001, SI 2001/3755, as operator of a relevant system: reg 3(1) (definition amended by SI 2013/632). As to the continuing effect of the Uncertificated Securities Regulations 2001, SI 2001/3755, see PARA 431 note 37. As to the meaning of 'person' see PARA 312 note 2. 'Relevant system' means a computer-based system, and procedures, which enable title to units of a security to be evidenced and transferred without a written instrument, and which facilitate supplementary and incidental matters: see reg 2(1). 'Relevant system' includes an 'operator-system', that is to say those facilities and procedures which are part of the relevant system, which are maintained and operated by or for an operator, by which he generates operator-instructions and receives dematerialised instructions from system-participants and by which persons change the form in

which units of a participating security are held (see PARAS 433–434): reg 3(1). As to the meaning of 'securities', and of references to title to securities, to a transfer of title, and to transfer without a written instrument see PARA 431 note 2. As to the meaning of As to the meaning of 'unit' see PARA 431 note 38. 'Operator-instruction' means a properly authenticated dematerialised instruction attributable to an operator; and 'dematerialised instruction' means an instruction sent or received by means of a relevant system: reg 3(1). 'Instruction' includes any instruction, election, acceptance or any other message of any kind: reg 3(1). For this purpose, a dematerialised instruction is properly authenticated if it complies with the specifications referred to in reg 5(1), Sch 1 para 5(3) (reg 3(2)(a)); and a dematerialised instruction is attributable to a person if it is expressed to have been sent by that person, or if it is expressed to have been sent on behalf of that person, in accordance with the rules and specifications referred to in Sch 1 para 5(4) (reg 3(2)(b)). A dematerialised instruction may be attributable to more than one person: reg 3(2)(b). As to properly authenticated dematerialised instructions see also reg 35. As to liability for forged dematerialised instructions and induced operator-instructions see reg 36. 'System-participant', in relation to a relevant system, means a person who is permitted by an operator to send and receive properly authenticated dematerialised instructions: reg 3(1). 'Generate', in relation to an operator-instruction, means to initiate the procedures by which the operator-instruction comes to be sent: reg 3(1). The settlement service for the London Stock Exchange is provided by CRESTCo: see FINANCIAL SERVICES REGULATION vol 50 (2015) PARAS 96–97. Nothing in the Uncertificated Securities Regulations 2001, SI 2001/3755, prevents an operator from charging a fee for carrying out any function under Pt 3 (regs 14–34) (reg 39(1)), except that an operator may not charge a fee to a participating issuer (see note 9) for maintaining or keeping and entering up an operator register of securities (see note 3) (reg 39(2)).

2 'Share' means share (or stock) in the share capital of a company: Uncertificated Securities Regulations 2001, SI 2001/3755, reg 3(1). As to the meaning of 'share' generally see PARA 1231. As to the meaning of 'share capital' see PARA 1231. As to the meaning of 'company' see PARA 21.

3 Ie in relation to which the Uncertificated Securities Regulations 2001, SI 2001/3755, reg 15 applies. Regulation 15 applies to a class of shares if the company's articles of association are in all respects consistent with the following (reg 15):

(1) the holding of shares of that class in uncertificated form;
(2) the transfer of title to shares of that class by means of a relevant system; and
(3) the Uncertificated Securities Regulations 2001, SI 2001/3755.

As to a company's articles of association see PARA 227 et seq. As to companies whose articles of association in any respect are inconsistent with these requirements see note 4. As to the provision made in the model articles as to uncertificated shares see the Companies (Model Articles) Regulations 2008, SI 2008/3229, Sch 3 arts 50, 64. As to the model articles see PARA 227. 'Uncertificated', in relation to a unit of a security, means (subject to the Uncertificated Securities Regulations 2001, SI 2001/3755, reg 42(11)(a): see PARA 1698) that title to the unit is recorded on the relevant operator register of securities, and may, by virtue of the Uncertificated Securities Regulations 2001, SI 2001/3755, be transferred by means of a relevant system; and 'certificated', in relation to a unit of a security, means that the unit is not an uncertificated unit: reg 3(1). 'Operator register of securities', in relation to shares, means an operator register of members: reg 3(1). As to the meaning of 'operator register of members' see PARA 341. As to liability for induced amendments to operator registers of securities see reg 36. For the purposes of regs 15, 16 (see note 4) and reg 17, any shares with respect to which share warrants to bearer were issued under the Companies Act 2006 s 779 (see PARA 392) are regarded as forming a separate class of shares: see the Uncertificated Securities Regulations 2001, SI 2001/3755, reg 18 (amended by SI 2009/1889). No share warrant may be issued by a company on or after 26 May 2015: see the Companies Act 2006 s 779(4); and PARA 392.

A class of shares in relation to which, immediately before 26 November 2001 (ie the date on which the Uncertificated Securities Regulations 2001, SI 2001/3755, came into force: see reg 1), the Uncertificated Securities Regulations 1995, SI 1995/3272, reg 15 (now revoked) applied is taken to be a class of shares in relation to which the Uncertificated Securities Regulations 2001, SI 2001/3755, reg 15 applies: reg 17(1)(a). As from 26 November 2001, a company's articles of association in relation to any such class of shares, and the terms of issue of any such class of shares, cease to apply to the extent that they are inconsistent with any provision of the Uncertificated Securities Regulations 2001, SI 2001/3755: reg 17(2).

4 Ie in accordance with the Uncertificated Securities Regulations 2001, SI 2001/3755, reg 16. Regulation 16 applies to a class of shares if a company's articles of association in any respect are inconsistent with the following (reg 16(1)):

(1) the holding of shares of that class in uncertificated form;
(2) the transfer of title to shares of that class by means of a relevant system; or
(3) any provision of the Uncertificated Securities Regulations 2001, SI 2001/3755.

As to what constitutes a class of shares see also reg 18; and note 3. A company may resolve by resolution of its directors (a 'director's resolution') that title to shares of a class issued or to be issued by it may be transferred by means of a relevant system: reg 16(2). As to the meaning of 'director' see PARA 512. Upon a directors' resolution becoming effective in accordance with its terms, and for as long as it is in force, the articles of association in relation to the class of shares which were the subject of the directors' resolution do not apply to any uncertificated shares of that class to the extent that they are inconsistent with heads (1)–(3) above: reg 16(3). Unless a company has given notice to every member of the company in accordance with its articles of association of its intention to pass a directors' resolution before the passing of such a resolution, it must give such notice within 60 days of the passing of the resolution: reg 16(4). As to who qualifies as a member of a company see PARA 323. In the event of default in complying with reg 16(4), an offence is committed by every officer of the issuer who is in default: reg 16(7) (reg 16(7) substituted, (7A) added by SI 2007/2194). A person guilty of such an offence is liable, on conviction on indictment, to a fine, or on summary conviction to a fine: Uncertificated Securities Regulations 2001, SI 2001/3755, reg 16(7A) (as so added). In the case of liability on summary conviction the fine is one not exceeding the statutory maximum: see reg 16(7A) (as so added). By virtue of the Legal Aid, Sentencing and Punishment of Offenders Act 2012 s 85, however, where the offence is committed on or after 12 March 2015, it is punishable by a fine of an unlimited amount. As to the statutory maximum and the powers of magistrates' courts to issue fines on summary conviction see SENTENCING vol 92 (2015) PARA 176.

An officer of a participating issuer is in default in complying with, or in contravention of, the Uncertificated Securities Regulations 2001, SI 2001/3755, reg 16(4) if, and only if, he knowingly and wilfully authorised or permitted the default: see reg 47(1). 'Officer', in relation to an operator or a participating issuer, includes the following (reg 3(1) (definition amended by SI 2009/1889)):

(a) where the operator or the participating issuer is a company, such persons as are mentioned in the Companies Act 2006 s 1173(1) (see PARA 679);
(b) where the operator or the participating issuer is a partnership, a partner or, in the event that no partner is situated in the United Kingdom, a person in the United Kingdom who is acting on behalf of a partner; and
(c) where the operator or the participating issuer is neither a company nor a partnership, any member of its governing body or, in the event that no member of its governing body is situated in the United Kingdom, a person in the United Kingdom who is acting on behalf of any member of its governing body.

As to companies and partnerships etc see PARAS 1–4. As to the meaning of 'United Kingdom' see PARA 1 note 5. Notice given by the company before 26 November 2001 (ie the date on which the Uncertificated Securities Regulations 2001, SI 2001/3755, came into force: see reg 1), of its intention to pass a directors' resolution which, if it had been given after the coming into force of the regulations would have satisfied the requirements of reg 16(4), is taken to satisfy those requirements: reg 16(5). In respect of a class of shares, the members of a company may by ordinary resolution:

(i) if a directors' resolution has not been passed, resolve that the directors of the company may not pass a directors' resolution;
(ii) if a directors' resolution has been passed but not yet come into effect in accordance with its terms, resolve that it may not come into effect;
(iii) if a directors' resolution has been passed and is effective in accordance with its terms but the class of shares has not yet been permitted by the operator to be a participating security, resolve that the directors' resolution ceases to have effect; or
(iv) if a directors' resolution has been passed and is effective in accordance with its terms and the class of shares has been permitted by the operator to be a participating security, resolve that the directors must take the necessary steps to ensure that title to shares of the class that was the subject of the directors' resolution cease to be transferable by means of a relevant system and that the directors' resolution ceases to have effect,

and the directors are bound by the terms of any such ordinary resolution: reg 16(6). The Companies Act 2006 Pt 3 Ch 3 (ss 29–30) (resolutions affecting a company's constitution: see PARA 230) applies to a directors' resolution passed by virtue of the Uncertificated Securities Regulations 2001, SI 2001/3755, reg 16(2), or a resolution of a company passed by virtue of reg 16(6) preventing or reversing such a resolution: reg 16(8A) (added by SI 2007/2194; amended by SI 2009/1889). As to the meaning of 'ordinary resolution' see PARA 685. A company may not permit the holding of shares in such a class as is referred to in the Uncertificated Securities Regulations 2001, SI 2001/3755, reg 16(1) in uncertificated form, or the transfer of title to shares in such a class by means of a relevant system, unless in relation to that class of shares a directors' resolution is effective: reg 16(8). A default in complying with, or a contravention of, reg 16(8) is actionable at the suit of a person who suffers loss as a result of the default or contravention, or who is otherwise adversely affected by it, subject to the defences and other incidents applying to claims for breach of statutory duty: reg 46(1). However, this does not affect the liability which any person may incur, nor affect any right which any person may have, apart from reg 46(1): reg 46(2). As to breach of statutory duty see TORT vol 97 (2015) PARA 500 et seq. The Uncertificated Securities Regulations 2001, SI 2001/3755, reg 16 must not be taken to exclude the right of the members of a company to amend the articles of association of the company, in accordance with the articles, to allow the holding of any class of its shares in uncertificated form and the transfer of title to shares in such a class by means of a relevant system: reg 16(9). A class of shares in relation to which, immediately before 26 November 2001, the Uncertificated Securities Regulations 1995, SI 1995/3272, reg 16 (revoked) applied is taken to be a class of shares in relation to which a directors' resolution passed in accordance with the Uncertificated Securities Regulations 2001, SI 2001/3755, reg 16 is effective: reg 17(1)(b).

5 Uncertificated Securities Regulations 2001, SI 2001/3755, reg 14(a).

6 Uncertificated Securities Regulations 2001, SI 2001/3755, reg 14(b).

7 Uncertificated Securities Regulations 2001, SI 2001/3755, reg 14. References in any enactment or rule of law to a proper instrument of transfer or to a transfer with respect to securities, or any expression having like meaning, is taken to include a reference to an operator-instruction to a participating issuer to register a transfer of title on the relevant issuer register of securities in accordance with the operator-instruction: reg 37. As to the meaning of 'issuer register of securities' see PARA 433 note 20. As to the transfer and registration of uncertificated securities other than shares see PARA 436.

8 'Participating security' means a security title to units of which is permitted by an operator to be transferred by means of a relevant system: Uncertificated Securities Regulations 2001, SI 2001/3755, reg 3(1). Where the terms of issue of a participating security which is a share, or the articles of association of the company in question, provide that its units may only be held in uncertificated form, and title to them may only be transferred by means of a relevant system, that security is known as a 'wholly dematerialised security': see reg 3(1). As to the conversion of securities into certificated form, by means of a rematerialisation notice, see PARA 433. As to the conversion of securities into uncertificated form see PARA 434.

9 'Participating issuer' means, subject to certain provisions relating to general public sector securities (ie the Uncertificated Securities Regulations 2001, SI 2001/3755, reg 3(3)), a person who has issued a security which is a participating security: reg 3(1).

10 As to the transfer of uncertificated shares see PARA 431.

11 'Settlement', in relation to a transfer of uncertificated units of a security between two system-members by means of a relevant system, means the delivery of those units to the transferee and, where appropriate, the creation of any associated obligation to make payments, in accordance with the rules and practices of the operator; and 'settle' is to be construed accordingly: Uncertificated Securities Regulations 2001, SI 2001/3755, reg 3(1). 'Rules', in relation to an operator, means rules made or conditions imposed by him with respect to the provision of the relevant system: reg 3(1). As to the meaning of 'system-member' see PARA 433 note 9.

12 Uncertificated Securities Regulations 2001, SI 2001/3755, reg 38(1).

13 Uncertificated Securities Regulations 2001, SI 2001/3755, reg 38(2). This provision is expressed to be subject to reg 32(7): see PARA 433 note 21.

14 See the Uncertificated Securities Regulations 2001, SI 2001/3755, reg 38(3). In particular, the Companies Act 2006 s 768 (see PARA 391) does not apply to any document issued with respect to uncertificated shares: Uncertificated Securities Regulations 2001, SI 2001/3755, reg 38(3)(a) (amended by SI 2009/1889). Nor do the provisions of the Law of Property Act 1925 s 53(1)(c) (see DEEDS AND OTHER INSTRUMENTS vol 32 (2012) PARA 224) or s 136 (see CHOSES IN ACTION vol 13 (2009) PARA 72 et seq) (which impose requirements for certain dispositions and assignments to be in writing) apply, if they would otherwise do so, to any transfer of title to uncertificated units of a security by means of a relevant system; and any disposition or assignment of an interest in uncertificated units of a security title to which is held by a relevant nominee: Uncertificated Securities Regulations 2001, SI 2001/3755, reg 38(5). For this purpose, 'relevant nominee' means a subsidiary undertaking of an operator designated by him as a relevant nominee in accordance with his rules and practices: reg 38(6). As to the requirements to be met by an operator's rules and practices see Sch 1 paras 25–27 (amended by SI 2003/1633).

15 Uncertificated Securities Regulations 2001, SI 2001/3755, reg 38(4)(a).

16 Uncertificated Securities Regulations 2001, SI 2001/3755, reg 38(4)(b).

433. Conversion of uncertificated securities into certificated form. Except as provided for by the Uncertificated Securities Regulations 2001[1], a unit of a participating security[2] must not be converted from uncertificated[3] form into certificated[4] form unless an operator[5] generates an operator-instruction[6] (known as a 'rematerialisation notice') to notify the relevant participating issuer[7] that a conversion event has occurred[8]. A conversion event occurs:

(1) where such a conversion is permitted by the operator's conversion rules[9]; or

(2) following receipt by an operator of a system-member instruction[10] requiring the conversion into certificated form of uncertificated units of a participating security registered in the name of the system-member[11]; or

(3) following receipt by an operator of written notification from a participating issuer which is a company[12] requiring the conversion into certificated form of uncertificated units of a participating security, issued by that participating issuer and registered in the name of a system-member, and containing a statement that the conversion is required to enable the participating issuer to deal with the units in question in accordance with provisions in that participating issuer's memorandum or articles[13] or in the terms of issue of the units in question[14].

An operator may generate a rematerialisation notice following a conversion event occurring in the circumstances specified in head (1) above[15]; he must generate such a notice following a conversion event occurring in the circumstances specified in head (2) above unless the participation in the relevant system, by the system-member in whose name the uncertificated units in question are registered, has been suspended pursuant to the operator's rules[16]; and he must also generate such a notice following a conversion event occurring in the circumstances specified in head (3) above[17].

On the generation of a rematerialisation notice, the operator must delete any entry in an operator register of securities[18] which shows the relevant system-member as the holder of the unit or units specified in the rematerialisation notice[19].

On receipt of a rematerialisation notice, the participating issuer to whom the rematerialisation notice is addressed must, where relevant, enter the name of the system-member on an issuer register of securities[20] as the holder of the unit or units specified in the rematerialisation notice[21]. Such sanctions as apply to a company and its officers in the event of a default in complying with the provisions of the Companies Act 2006 if a company refuses to register a transfer of shares or debentures[22] apply to an operator and his officers in the event of a default in complying with the above requirement[23] to delete entries in an operator register of securities[24], and apply to a participating issuer and his officers in the event of a default in complying with the above requirement[25] to enter the name of the system-member on an issuer register of securities[26].

During any period between the required deletion of any entry in an operator register of securities and the required making of the entry in an issuer register of securities, the relevant system-member retains title to the units of the security specified in the rematerialisation notice notwithstanding the deletion of any entry in the operator register of securities[27]; and, where those units are shares, the relevant system-member is deemed to continue to be a member of the company[28].

1 Ie by the Uncertificated Securities Regulations 2001, SI 2001/3755, reg 42: see PARA 1698. As to the continuing effect of the Uncertificated Securities Regulations 2001, SI 2001/3755, see PARA 431 note 37.

2 As to the meaning of 'participating security' see PARA 432 note 8; as to the meaning of 'unit' see PARA 431 note 38; and as to the meaning of 'securities' see PARA 431 note 2.

3 As to the meaning of 'uncertificated' see PARA 432 note 3.

4 As to the meaning of 'certificated' see PARA 432 note 3.

5 As to the meaning of 'operator' see PARA 432 note 1.

6 As to the meaning of 'operator-instruction' see PARA 432 note 1.

7 As to the meaning of 'participating issuer' see PARA 432 note 9.

8 See the Uncertificated Securities Regulations 2001, SI 2001/3755, reg 32(1). Nothing in the Uncertificated Securities Regulations 2001, SI 2001/3755, requires an operator or participating issuer, or their officers, to take any action to change a unit of a wholly dematerialised security from uncertificated form to certificated form or vice versa: reg 45(b). As to the meaning of 'officer' (in relation to an operator or a participating issuer) see PARA 432 note 4. As to the meaning of 'wholly dematerialised security' see PARA 432 note 8.

9 Uncertificated Securities Regulations 2001, SI 2001/3755, reg 32(2)(a). 'Operator's conversion rules' means the rules made and practices instituted by the operator in order to comply with Sch 1 para 18: reg 3(1). As to the meaning of 'rules' (in relation to an operator) see PARA 432 note 11. A relevant system must enable system-members to change the form in which they hold units of a participating security and, where appropriate, to require participating issuers to issue certificates relating to units of a participating security held or to be held by them: Sch 1 para 18. As to the meaning of 'relevant system' see PARA 432 note 1. 'System-member', in relation to a relevant system, means a person who is permitted by an operator to transfer by means of that system title to uncertificated units of a security held by him, and includes, where relevant, two or more persons who are jointly so permitted: reg 3(1). As to the meaning of 'certificate' see PARA 431 note 39; as to the meaning of 'person' see PARA 312 note 2; and as to the meaning of references to title to securities, and to a transfer of title, see PARA 431 note 2.

10 'System-member instruction' means a properly authenticated dematerialised instruction attributable to a system-member: Uncertificated Securities Regulations 2001, SI 2001/3755, reg 3(1). As to the meaning of 'dematerialised instruction' see PARA 432 note 1.

11 Uncertificated Securities Regulations 2001, SI 2001/3755, reg 32(2)(b).

12 As to the meaning of 'company' see PARA 21.

13 As to the meaning of references to a company's 'articles' see PARA 227 note 2. As to the meaning of 'memorandum of association' see PARA 97.

14 Uncertificated Securities Regulations 2001, SI 2001/3755, reg 32(2)(c).

15 Uncertificated Securities Regulations 2001, SI 2001/3755, reg 32(3)(a).

16 Uncertificated Securities Regulations 2001, SI 2001/3755, reg 32(3)(b).

17 Uncertificated Securities Regulations 2001, SI 2001/3755, reg 32(3)(c).

18 As to the meaning of 'operator register of securities' see PARA 432 note 3.

19 Uncertificated Securities Regulations 2001, SI 2001/3755, reg 32(4).

20 'Issuer register of securities', in relation to shares, means an issuer register of members: Uncertificated Securities Regulations 2001, SI 2001/3755, reg 3(1). As to the meaning of 'issuer register of members' see PARA 341.

21 Uncertificated Securities Regulations 2001, SI 2001/3755, reg 32(5). A default in complying with, or a contravention of, reg 32(5) is actionable at the suit of a person who suffers loss as a result of the default or contravention, or who is otherwise adversely affected by it, subject to the defences and other incidents applying to claims for breach of statutory duty: see reg 46(1). However, this does not affect the liability which any person may incur, nor affect any right which any person may have, apart from reg 46(1): reg 46(2). As to breach of statutory duty see TORT vol 97 (2015) PARA 500 et seq. Following the making of an entry in an issuer register of securities in accordance with reg 32(5) or registration of a transfer of title to units of a security in accordance with reg 28 (see PARA 438), the relevant participating issuer must, where the terms of issue of the security in question provide for a certificate to be issued, issue a certificate in respect of the units of the security to the relevant person: reg 32(7). The Companies Act 2006 s 776(1) (duty of company as to issue of certificates: see PARA 417) applies in relation to the issue of a certificate by a participating issuer pursuant to the Uncertificated Securities Regulations 2001, SI 2001/3755, reg 32(7) as it applies in relation to the completion and having ready for delivery by a company of share certificates, debentures or certificates of debenture stock: reg 32(8) (amended by SI 2009/1889). The reference in the Companies Act 2006 s 776(1)(b) (as it so applies) to the date on which a transfer is lodged with the company is a reference to the date on which the participating issuer receives the relevant rematerialisation notice in accordance with the Uncertificated Securities Regulations 2001, SI 2001/3755, reg 32, or the relevant operator-instruction in accordance with reg 27(7) (see PARA 437): reg 32(8) (as so amended). Such sanctions as apply to a company and its officers in the event of a default in complying with the Companies Act 2006 s 776(1) (see PARA 417) apply to a participating issuer and his officers in the event of a default in complying with the Uncertificated Securities Regulations 2001, SI 2001/3755, reg 32(7) in accordance with the requirements laid down in reg 32(8): reg 32(10) (amended by SI 2009/1889). For the purposes of the Uncertificated Securities Regulations 2001, SI 2001/3755, reg 32(10), an officer of a participating issuer is in default in complying with the Companies Act 2006 s 776(1) if, and only if, he knowingly and wilfully authorised or permitted the default or contravention: see the Uncertificated Securities Regulations 2001, SI 2001/3755, reg 47(1). However, reg 32(9), (10) does not apply to any of the following or its officers (reg 48 (amended by SI 2004/1662)):

(1) the Crown;

(2) any person acting on behalf of the Crown;

(3) the Bank of England;
(4) the Registrar of Government Stock;
(5) any previous Registrar of Government Stock; or
(6) in respect of a security which immediately before it became a participating security was transferable by exempt transfer within the meaning of the Stock Transfer Act 1982 (see PARA 441), a participating issuer.

As to the Bank of England see FINANCIAL INSTITUTIONS vol 48 (2015) PARA 97 et seq; and as to the Registrar of Government Stock see FINANCIAL INSTRUMENTS AND TRANSACTIONS vol 49 (2015) PARA 123.

22 Ie the Companies Act 2006 s 771(1), (2) (see PARA 426): see the Uncertificated Securities Regulations 2001, SI 2001/3755, reg 32(9) (amended by SI 2009/1889).
23 Ie the requirement contained in the Uncertificated Securities Regulations 2001, SI 2001/3755, reg 32(4): see the text and notes 18–19.
24 Uncertificated Securities Regulations 2001, SI 2001/3755, reg 32(9)(a). For these purposes, an officer of an operator is in default in complying with the provision mentioned in that regulation if, and only if, he knowingly and wilfully authorised or permitted the default or contravention: see reg 47(2). See also reg 48; and note 21.
25 Ie the requirement contained in the Uncertificated Securities Regulations 2001, SI 2001/3755, reg 32(5): see the text and notes 20–21.
26 Uncertificated Securities Regulations 2001, SI 2001/3755, reg 32(9)(b). For these purposes, an officer of a participating issuer is in default if, and only if, he knowingly and wilfully authorised or permitted the default or contravention: see the Uncertificated Securities Regulations 2001, SI 2001/3755, reg 47(1). See also reg 48; and note 21.
27 Uncertificated Securities Regulations 2001, SI 2001/3755, reg 32(6)(a).
28 Uncertificated Securities Regulations 2001, SI 2001/3755, reg 32(6)(b). As to the meaning of 'member of a company' see PARA 323.

434. Conversion of certificated securities into uncertificated form. A unit of a participating security[1] must not be converted from certificated[2] form into uncertificated[3] form unless the participating issuer[4] notifies the operator[5] by means of an issuer-instruction[6] (referred to as a 'dematerialisation notice') that any of the following circumstances have arisen[7], namely that:

(1) where the unit of the participating security is held by a system-member[8], the participating issuer:
 (a) has received a request in writing from the system-member in the form required by the operator's conversion rules[9] that the unit be converted from certificated form to uncertificated form[10]; and
 (b) has received the certificate[11] relating to that unit[12]; or
(2) where the unit of the participating security is to be registered on an operator register of securities[13] in the name of a system-member following a transfer of the unit to him, the participating issuer:
 (a) has received (by means of the operator-system[14] unless the operator's conversion rules permit otherwise) a proper instrument of transfer in favour of the system-member relating to the unit to be transferred[15];
 (b) has received (by means of the operator-system unless the operator's conversion rules permit otherwise) the certificate relating to that unit[16]; and
 (c) may accept by virtue of the operator's conversion rules that the system-member to whom the unit is to be transferred wishes to hold it in uncertificated form[17].

Upon giving a dematerialisation notice, a participating issuer must delete any entry in any issuer register of securities[18] which evidences title to the unit or units of the participating security in question[19]; and following receipt of a dematerialisation notice, an operator must enter the name of the relevant system-member on an operator register of securities as the holder of the relevant unit or units of the participating security in question[20].

When a dematerialisation notice is given, the relevant system-member, or the transferor of the unit or units of the security in question, as the case may be, retains (without prejudice to any equitable interest which the transferee may have acquired in the unit or units in question) title[21] to the units of the security specified in the dematerialisation notice notwithstanding the deletion of any entry in any issuer register of securities that is required[22] to be made[23] and, where those units are shares[24], is deemed to continue to be a member of the company[25]. Where a dematerialisation notice is given in the circumstances specified in head (2) above, such title is retained, and, where appropriate, such membership is deemed to continue, until the time at which the operator enters[26] the name of the relevant system-member on an operator register of securities[27].

Within two months[28] of receiving a dematerialisation notice, an operator must generate an operator-instruction[29] informing the participating issuer whether an entry has been made in an operator register of securities in response to the dematerialisation notice[30].

Such sanctions as apply to a company and its officers in the event of a default in complying with the provisions of the Companies Act 2006 if a company refuses to register a transfer of shares or debentures[31] apply, in the event of a default, to a participating issuer and his officers[32] or to an operator and his officers[33], as the case may be[34].

1 As to the meaning of 'participating security' see PARA 432 note 8. As to the meaning of 'unit' see PARA 431 note 38.
2 As to the meaning of 'certificated' see PARA 432 note 3.
3 As to the meaning of 'uncertificated' see PARA 432 note 3.
4 As to the meaning of 'participating issuer' see PARA 432 note 9.
5 As to the meaning of 'operator' see PARA 432 note 1.
6 'Issuer-instruction' means a properly authenticated dematerialised instruction attributable to a participating issuer: Uncertificated Securities Regulations 2001, SI 2001/3755, reg 3(1). As to the meaning of 'dematerialised instruction' see PARA 432 note 1. As to the continuing effect of the Uncertificated Securities Regulations 2001, SI 2001/3755, see PARA 431 note 37.
7 Uncertificated Securities Regulations 2001, SI 2001/3755, reg 33(1). Subject to reg 33(3) (see note 15) and reg 33(4) (see note 12), a participating issuer must not give a dematerialisation notice except in the circumstances specified in reg 33(2) (see the text and notes 8–17): reg 33(5). A default in complying with, or a contravention of, reg 33(5) is actionable at the suit of a person who suffers loss as a result of the default or contravention, or who is otherwise adversely affected by it, subject to the defences and other incidents applying to claims for breach of statutory duty: see reg 46(1). However, this does not affect the liability which any person may incur, nor affect any right which any person may have, apart from reg 46(1): reg 46(2). As to breach of statutory duty see TORT vol 97 (2015) PARA 500 et seq. Nothing in the Uncertificated Securities Regulations 2001, SI 2001/3755, requires an operator or participating issuer, or their officers, to take any action to change a unit of a wholly dematerialised security from uncertificated form to certificated form or vice versa: reg 45(b). As to the meaning of 'officer' (in relation to an operator or a participating issuer) see PARA 432 note 4. As to the meaning of 'wholly dematerialised security' see PARA 432 note 8.
8 As to the meaning of 'system-member' see PARA 433 note 9.
9 As to the meaning of 'operator's conversion rules' see PARA 433 note 9.
10 Uncertificated Securities Regulations 2001, SI 2001/3755, reg 33(2)(a)(i).
11 As to the meaning of 'certificate' see PARA 431 note 39.
12 Uncertificated Securities Regulations 2001, SI 2001/3755, reg 33(2)(a)(ii). The requirements in reg 33(2)(a)(ii) and reg 33(2)(b)(ii) (see head (2)(b) in the text) that the participating issuer must have received a certificate relating to the unit of the participating security does not apply in a case where the system-member or transferor, as the case may be, does not have a certificate in respect of the unit to be converted into uncertificated form because no certificate has yet been issued to him or is due to be issued to him in accordance with the terms of issue of the relevant participating security: reg 33(4).
13 As to the meaning of 'operator register of securities' see PARA 432 note 3.
14 As to the meaning of 'operator-system' see PARA 432 note 1.

15 Uncertificated Securities Regulations 2001, SI 2001/3755, reg 33(2)(b)(i). The requirement in reg 33(2)(b)(i) that the participating issuer must have received an instrument of transfer relating to the unit of the participating security does not apply in a case where for a transfer of a unit of that security no instrument of transfer is required: reg 33(3).
16 Uncertificated Securities Regulations 2001, SI 2001/3755, reg 33(2)(b)(ii). See also note 12.
17 Uncertificated Securities Regulations 2001, SI 2001/3755, reg 33(2)(b)(iii).
18 As to the meaning of 'issuer register of securities' see PARA 433 note 20.
19 Uncertificated Securities Regulations 2001, SI 2001/3755, reg 33(6).
20 Uncertificated Securities Regulations 2001, SI 2001/3755, reg 33(7). This obligation is subject to reg 27 (see PARA 437) if the notice was given in the circumstances specified in reg 33(2)(b) (see heads (2)(a)–(c) in the text): see reg 33(7).
21 As to the meaning of references to title to securities see PARA 431 note 2.
22 Ie required to be made by the Uncertificated Securities Regulations 2001, SI 2001/3755, reg 33(6): see the text and notes 18–19.
23 Uncertificated Securities Regulations 2001, SI 2001/3755, reg 33(8)(a).
24 As to the meaning of 'share' see PARA 432 note 2.
25 Uncertificated Securities Regulations 2001, SI 2001/3755, reg 33(8)(b). As to the meaning of 'member of a company' see PARA 323.
26 Ie in accordance with the Uncertificated Securities Regulations 2001, SI 2001/3755, reg 33(7): see the text and note 20.
27 Uncertificated Securities Regulations 2001, SI 2001/3755, reg 33(9).
28 As to the meaning of 'month' see PARA 1818 note 10.
29 As to the meaning of 'operator-instruction' see PARA 432 note 1.
30 Uncertificated Securities Regulations 2001, SI 2001/3755, reg 33(10).
31 Ie the Companies Act 2006 s 771(1), (2) (see PARA 426): see the Uncertificated Securities Regulations 2001, SI 2001/3755, reg 33(11) (amended by SI 2009/1889).
32 Ie in the event of a default in complying with the Uncertificated Securities Regulations 2001, SI 2001/3755, reg 33(6) (see the text and notes 18–19): see the Uncertificated Securities Regulations 2001, SI 2001/3755, reg 33(11)(a).
33 Ie in the event of a default in complying with the Uncertificated Securities Regulations 2001, SI 2001/3755, reg 33(7) (see the text and note 20) or reg 33(10) (see the text and notes 28–30): see the Uncertificated Securities Regulations 2001, SI 2001/3755, reg 33(11)(b).
34 See the Uncertificated Securities Regulations 2001, SI 2001/3755, reg 33(11) (as amended: see note 31). For the purposes of reg 33(11), an officer of a participating issuer, or an officer of an operator, is in default if, and only if, he knowingly and wilfully authorised or permitted the default or contravention: see reg 47(1), (2). However, reg 33(11) does not apply to any of the following or its officers (reg 48 (amended by SI 2004/1662)):
(1) the Crown;
(2) any person acting on behalf of the Crown;
(3) the Bank of England;
(4) the Registrar of Government Stock;
(5) any previous Registrar of Government Stock; or
(6) in respect of a security which immediately before it became a participating security was transferable by exempt transfer within the meaning of the Stock Transfer Act 1982 (see PARA 441), a participating issuer.

As to the Bank of England see FINANCIAL INSTITUTIONS vol 48 (2015) PARA 97 et seq; and as to the Registrar of Government Stock see FINANCIAL INSTRUMENTS AND TRANSACTIONS vol 49 (2015) PARA 123.

435. New issues in uncertificated form. For the purposes of an issue of units of a participating security[1], a participating issuer[2] may require the operator[3] to enter the name of a person in an operator register of securities[4] as the holder of new units of that security in uncertificated[5] form if, and only if, that person is a system-member[6]; and compliance with any such requirement is subject to the rules of the operator[7]. Such a requirement made by a participating issuer may be made by means of an issuer-instruction[8] and must specify the names of the persons to be entered in the operator register of securities as the holders of new uncertificated units of the security, and the number of such units to be issued to each of those persons[9].

An operator who receives such a requirement made by a participating issuer must notify the participating issuer, by operator-instruction[10] or in writing, if he has not entered the name of any one or more of the persons in question in the operator register of securities as the holder of new units of the security[11].

1 As to the meaning of 'participating security' see PARA 432 note 8. As to the meaning of 'unit' see PARA 431 note 38. 'Issue', in relation to a new unit of a security, means to confer title to a new unit on a person: Uncertificated Securities Regulations 2001, SI 2001/3755, reg 3(1). As to the meaning of references to title to securities see PARA 431 note 2. As to the meaning of 'person' see PARA 312 note 2. As to the continuing effect of the Uncertificated Securities Regulations 2001, SI 2001/3755, see PARA 431 note 37.
2 As to the meaning of 'participating issuer' see PARA 432 note 9.
3 As to the meaning of 'operator' see PARA 432 note 1.
4 As to the meaning of 'operator register of securities' see PARA 432 note 3.
5 As to the meaning of 'uncertificated' see PARA 432 note 3.
6 Uncertificated Securities Regulations 2001, SI 2001/3755, reg 34(1). As to the meaning of 'system-member' see PARA 433 note 9. For the purposes of calculating the number of new units to which a system-member is entitled, a participating issuer may treat a system-member's holdings of certificated and uncertificated units of a security as if they were separate holdings: reg 34(2). As to the meaning of 'certificated' see PARA 432 note 3.
7 Uncertificated Securities Regulations 2001, SI 2001/3755, reg 34(1). As to the meaning of 'rules' see PARA 432 note 11.
8 As to the meaning of 'issuer-instruction' see PARA 434 note 6.
9 Uncertificated Securities Regulations 2001, SI 2001/3755, reg 34(3).
10 As to the meaning of 'operator-instruction' see PARA 432 note 1.
11 Uncertificated Securities Regulations 2001, SI 2001/3755, reg 34(4).

436. Transfer and registration of uncertificated securities. Where an operator[1] permits title to a security[2] other than a share[3] to be transferred by means of a relevant system[4], and the issuer permits the holding of units[5] of that security in uncertificated[6] form and the transfer of title to units of that security by means of a relevant system[7], title to units of that security which are recorded on an operator register of securities[8] may be transferred by means of that relevant system[9]. However, in relation to any security other than a share, if the law under which it is constituted is not the law of England and Wales[10], Northern Ireland or Scotland, or if the current terms of its issue[11] are in any respect inconsistent with:

(1) the holding of title to units of that security in uncertificated form[12];
(2) the transfer of title to units of that security by means of a relevant system[13]; or
(3) the Uncertificated Securities Regulations 2001[14],

an issuer of that security must not permit the holding of units of that security in uncertificated form, or the transfer of title to units of that security by means of a relevant system[15].

Where a participating issuer[16] is required by or under an enactment[17] or instrument to maintain in the United Kingdom[18] a register of persons[19] holding securities (other than shares, general public sector securities[20] or eligible debt securities[21]) issued by him[22], then in so far as the register in question relates to any class of security which is a participating security[23]:

(a) the operator must maintain a register (an 'operator register of corporate securities'[24]); and
(b) the participating issuer must not maintain the register to the extent that it relates to securities held in uncertificated form[25], but must maintain a record of the entries made in any operator register of corporate securities (a 'record of uncertificated corporate securities')[26].

Where an operator of a relevant system is required to maintain an operator register of corporate securities, that register must comprise, and the operator must enter on it, the names and addresses of the persons holding units of the relevant participating security in uncertificated form and how many units of that security each such person holds in that form[27]. The same particulars must be entered in a record of uncertificated corporate securities by a participating issuer, so far as practicable[28], and he must, unless it is impracticable to do so by virtue of circumstances beyond his control, ensure that the record of uncertificated corporate securities is regularly reconciled with the operator register of corporate securities[29].

Where a participating issuer is not required by or under an enactment or instrument to maintain in the United Kingdom in respect of a participating security, other than an eligible debt security, issued by him a register of persons holding units of that participating security, the operator must maintain a register in respect of that participating security and record in that register the names and addresses of the persons holding units of that security in uncertificated form, and how many units of that security each such person holds in that form[30].

In respect of every participating security which is an eligible debt security, the operator must maintain a register (an 'operator register of eligible debt securities') and record in that register the names and addresses of the persons holding units of that security and how many units of that security each such person holds[31].

1 As to the meaning of 'operator' see PARA 432 note 1.
2 As to the meanings of 'securities' and references to title to securities and to a transfer of title see PARA 431 note 2.
3 As to the meaning of 'share' see PARA 432 note 2. As to the transfer of uncertificated shares see PARA 431. As to entries to be made in registers regarding uncertificated shares see PARA 341. As to the power to make regulations relating to the evidencing and transfer of title to securities without a written instrument see the Companies Act 2006 Pt 21 Ch 2 (ss 783–790); and PARA 431.
4 Uncertificated Securities Regulations 2001, SI 2001/3755, reg 19(1)(a). As to the meaning of 'relevant system' see PARA 432 note 1. As to the continuing effect of the Uncertificated Securities Regulations 2001, SI 2001/3755, see PARA 431 note 37.
5 As to the meaning of 'unit' see PARA 431 note 38.
6 As to the meaning of 'uncertificated' see PARA 432 note 3.
7 Uncertificated Securities Regulations 2001, SI 2001/3755, reg 19(1)(b).
8 As to the meaning of 'operator register of securities' see PARA 432 note 3.
9 Uncertificated Securities Regulations 2001, SI 2001/3755, reg 19(1).
10 As to the meanings of 'England' and 'Wales' see PARA 1 note 5.
11 On 26 November 2001 (ie the coming into force of the Uncertificated Securities Regulations 2001, SI 2001/3755: see reg 1), the current terms of issue of a relevant participating security ceased to apply to the extent that they were inconsistent with any provision of the regulations: see reg 19(3). For these purposes, a relevant participating security is a participating security (other than a share) the terms of issue of which, immediately before 26 November 2001 (ie the coming into force of the regulations), were in all respects consistent with the Uncertificated Securities Regulations 1995, SI 1995/3272 (revoked); and the terms of issue of a security is taken to include the terms prescribed by the issuer on which units of the security are held and title to them is transferred: Uncertificated Securities Regulations 2001, SI 2001/3755, reg 19(4). As to the meaning of 'participating security' see PARA 432 note 8.
12 Uncertificated Securities Regulations 2001, SI 2001/3755, reg 19(2)(a).
13 Uncertificated Securities Regulations 2001, SI 2001/3755, reg 19(2)(b).
14 Ie the Uncertificated Securities Regulations 2001, SI 2001/3755: see reg 19(2)(c).
15 Uncertificated Securities Regulations 2001, SI 2001/3755, reg 19(2) (amended by SI 2003/1633).
16 As to the meaning of 'participating issuer' see PARA 432 note 9.
17 As to the meaning of 'enactment' see PARA 13 note 16.
18 As to the meaning of 'United Kingdom' see PARA 1 note 5.
19 As to the meaning of 'person' see PARA 312 note 2.
20 'General public sector security' means a public sector security that is not an eligible debt security (see note 21): Uncertificated Securities Regulations 2001, SI 2001/3755, reg 3(1) (definition added by SI 2003/1633). 'Public sector securities' means UK Government securities and local authority securities; and 'UK Government security' means a security issued by Her Majesty's Government in the United Kingdom or by a Northern Ireland department: Uncertificated Securities Regulations 2001, SI 2001/3755, reg 3(1). 'Local authority security' means a security which is either of the following (Uncertificated Securities Regulations 2001, SI 2001/3755, reg 3(1) (definition substituted by SI 2003/1633; amended by SI 2004/2044)), ie:

(1) a security other than an eligible debt security which, when held in certificated form is transferable in accordance with the Local Authority (Stocks and Bonds) Regulations 1974, SI 1974/519, reg 7(1) and title to which must be registered in accordance with reg 5 of those Regulations; or

(2) an eligible debt security issued by a local authority.

As to the meaning of 'certificated' see PARA 432 note 3. 'Local authority', in relation to a security referred to in head (1) of the definition of 'local authority security', has the same meaning as in the Local Authority (Stocks and Bonds) Regulations 1974, SI 1974/519; and in relation to a security referred to in head (2) of that definition has the same meaning as in the Local Government Act 2003 s 23 (see LOCAL GOVERNMENT vol 69 (2009) PARA 23): Uncertificated Securities Regulations 2001, SI 2001/3755, reg 3(1) (definition added by SI 2003/1633; amended by SI 2004/2044). As to the registration of general public sector securities see the Uncertificated Securities Regulations 2001, SI 2001/3755, reg 21 (amended by SI 2003/1633; SI 2004/1662; SI 2004/2044; SI 2009/1889). Notwithstanding the repeal of the enabling authority, ie the Local Government Act 1972 Sch 13 para 4(1), by the Local Government and Housing Act 1989 s 194(2), Sch 12 Pt I, the Local Authority (Stocks and Bonds) Regulations 1974, SI 1974/519, continue in force in relation to stock issued before 1 April 1990, by virtue of the Local Government and Housing Act 1989 (Commencement No 5 and Transitional Provisions) Order 1990, SI 1990/431, art 4, Sch 1 para 3 (amended by SI 1990/762).

21 'Eligible debt security' means the following (Uncertificated Securities Regulations 2001, SI 2001/3755, reg 3(1) (definition added by SI 2003/1633)), ie:

(1) a security that is constituted by an order, promise, engagement or acknowledgement to pay on demand, or at a determinable future time, a sum in money to, or to the order of, the holder of one or more units of the security and the current terms of issue of the security provide that its units may only be held in uncertificated form and title to them may only be transferred by means of a relevant system;

(2) an eligible Northern Ireland Treasury Bill; or

(3) an eligible Treasury Bill.

'Eligible Northern Ireland Treasury Bill' means a security constituted by a Northern Ireland Treasury Bill issued in accordance with the Exchequer and Financial Provisions Act (Northern Ireland) 1950 (as modified by the Uncertificated Securities (Amendment) (Eligible Debt Securities) Regulations 2003, SI 2003/1633, Sch 1 Pt 2) and whose current terms of issue provide that its units may only be held in uncertificated form and title to them may only be transferred by means of a relevant system: Uncertificated Securities Regulations 2001, SI 2001/3755, reg 3(1) (definition added by SI 2003/1633). 'Eligible Treasury Bill' means a security constituted by a Treasury Bill issued in accordance with the Treasury Bills Act 1877 and the Treasury Bills Regulations 1968, SI 1968/414 (as modified by SI 2003/1633, Sch 1 Pt 1) and whose current terms of issue provide that its units may only be held in uncertificated form and title to them may only be transferred by means of a relevant system: Uncertificated Securities Regulations 2001, SI 2001/3755, reg 3(1) (definition added by SI 2003/1633). As to Treasury Bills see CONSTITUTIONAL AND ADMINISTRATIVE LAW vol 20 (2014) PARA 504.

22 Uncertificated Securities Regulations 2001, SI 2001/3755, reg 22(1) (amended by SI 2003/1633).

23 Uncertificated Securities Regulations 2001, SI 2001/3755, reg 22(2).

24 Uncertificated Securities Regulations 2001, SI 2001/3755, reg 22(2)(a)(i). The operator register of corporate securities must be kept and entered up in accordance with Sch 4 para 14 (see the text and note 27): reg 22(2)(a)(ii). Such sanctions as apply to a company and its officers in the event of a default in complying with the Companies Act 2006 s 113 (see PARA 336) apply to an operator and his officers in the event of a default in complying with the Uncertificated Securities Regulations 2001, SI 2001/3755, reg 22(2)(a)(i): reg 22(4) (amended by SI 2003/1633; SI 2009/1889). As to the meaning of 'officer' for these purposes see PARA 432 note 4.

25 Uncertificated Securities Regulations 2001, SI 2001/3755, reg 22(2)(b)(i).

26 Uncertificated Securities Regulations 2001, SI 2001/3755, reg 22(2)(b)(ii). The record of uncertificated corporate securities must be kept and entered up in accordance with Sch 4 para 15: reg 22(2)(b)(iii). In the case of a participating issuer which is a company, the record of uncertificated corporate securities must be kept at the same place as the part of any register of debenture holders maintained by the company would be required to be kept: Sch 4 para 15(4). As to the meaning of 'company' see PARA 21. As to the keeping of the register of debenture holders see PARA 1504. The Companies Act 2006 ss 744(1)–(4), 746 (see PARA 1505) apply in relation to a record of uncertificated corporate securities maintained by a participating issuer which is a company, so far as that record relates to debentures, as they apply or would apply to any register of debenture holders maintained by the company; and references to the Companies Act 2006 in the Companies (Fees for Inspection and Copying of Company Records) Regulations 2007, SI 2007/2612, and in the Companies (Fees for Inspection of Company Records) Regulations 2008, SI 2008/3007 must be construed accordingly: Uncertificated Securities Regulations 2001, SI 2001/3755, Sch 4 para 15(5) (amended by SI 2009/1889). Any provision of an enactment or

instrument which requires a register of persons holding securities (other than shares or public sector securities) to be open to inspection also applies to the record of uncertificated corporate securities relating to any units of those securities which are participating securities: Uncertificated Securities Regulations 2001, SI 2001/3755, Sch 4 para 15(6). Such sanctions as apply in the event of a default in complying with the requirement to maintain a register imposed by the relevant enactment or instrument referred to in reg 22(1) (see the text and notes 16–22) apply to a participating issuer and his officers in the event of a default in complying with reg 22(2)(b)(ii): reg 22(5). For the purposes of reg 22(5), an officer of a participating issuer is in default in complying with, or in contravention of, the provision mentioned therein if, and only if, he knowingly and wilfully authorised or permitted the default or contravention: reg 47(1). Such sanctions as apply in the event of a default in complying with the requirement to maintain a register imposed by the relevant enactment or instrument referred to in reg 22(1) apply to:

(1) a participating issuer other than a company;
(2) a participating issuer which is a company, in relation to so much of the record of uncertificated corporate securities as does not relate to debentures,

and to his officers in the event of a default in complying with Sch 4 para 15: Sch 4 para 19(3). However, this provision does not apply to any of the following or its officers (Sch 4 para 19(4) (amended by SI 2004/1662)), ie:

(a) the Crown;
(b) any person acting on behalf of the Crown;
(c) the Bank of England;
(d) the Registrar of Government Stock;
(e) any previous Registrar of Government Stock; or
(f) in respect of a security which immediately before it became a participating security was transferable by exempt transfer within the meaning of the Stock Transfer Act 1982 (see PARA 441), a participating issuer.

As to the Bank of England see FINANCIAL INSTITUTIONS vol 48 (2015) PARA 97 et seq; and as to the Registrar of Government Stock see FINANCIAL INSTRUMENTS AND TRANSACTIONS vol 49 (2015) PARA 123. An officer of a participating issuer is in default in complying with, or in contravention of Sch 4 para 15 if, and only if, he knowingly and wilfully authorised or permitted the default or contravention: Sch 4 para 20.

27 Uncertificated Securities Regulations 2001, SI 2001/3755, Sch 4 para 14(1). The Companies Act 2006 ss 743–748 (see PARAS 1504–1506) do not apply to any part of an operator register of corporate securities: Uncertificated Securities Regulations 2001, SI 2001/3755, Sch 4 para 14(2) (amended by SI 2009/1889). An entry on a register of corporate securities which records a person as holding units of a security in uncertificated form is evidence of such title to the units as would be evidenced if the entry on that register were an entry on the part maintained by the participating issuer of such register as is mentioned in the Uncertificated Securities Regulations 2001, SI 2001/3755, reg 22(1) (see the text and notes 16–22), and, where appropriate, related to units of that security held in certificated form: reg 24(6). This is subject to the proviso that any purported registration of a transfer of title to an uncertificated unit of a security other than in accordance with regs 27, 28 (see PARAS 437–438) is of no effect: regs 24(6), 29. Such sanctions as apply to a company and its officers in the event of a default in complying with the Companies Act 2006 s 113 (see PARA 336) apply also to an operator and his officers in the event of a default in complying with the Uncertificated Securities Regulations 2001, SI 2001/3755, Sch 4 para 14: Sch 4 para 19(1) (amended by SI 2009/1889). An officer of an operator is in default in complying with, or in contravention of, the provisions referred to in the Uncertificated Securities Regulations 2001, SI 2001/3755, Sch 4 para 19(1) if, and only if, he knowingly and wilfully authorised or permitted the default or contravention: Sch 4 para 21.

28 Uncertificated Securities Regulations 2001, SI 2001/3755, Sch 4 para 15(1).

29 Uncertificated Securities Regulations 2001, SI 2001/3755, Sch 4 para 15(2). Provided that it has complied with Sch 4 para 15(2), a participating issuer is not liable in respect of any act or thing done or omitted to be done by it or on its behalf in reliance upon the assumption that the particulars entered in any record of uncertificated corporate securities which the participating issuer is required to keep by the Uncertificated Securities Regulations 2001, SI 2001/3755, accord with particulars entered in any operator register of corporate securities relating to it: Sch 4 para 15(3).

30 Uncertificated Securities Regulations 2001, SI 2001/3755, reg 22(3) (amended by SI 2003/1633). Subject to the Uncertificated Securities Regulations 2001, SI 2001/3755, reg 29 (see note 27), an entry on a register maintained by virtue of reg 22(3) is (where the units are capable of being held in certificated form) prima facie evidence, and in Scotland sufficient evidence unless the contrary is shown, that the person to whom the entry relates has such title to the units of the security which he is recorded as holding in uncertificated form as he would have if he held the units in certificated form: reg 24(7). Such sanctions as apply to a company and its officers in the event of a default in complying with the Companies Act 2006 s 113 (see PARA 336) apply to an operator and his officers in the event of a default in complying with the Uncertificated Securities Regulations 2001,

SI 2001/3755, reg 22(3): reg 22(4) (amended by SI 2003/1633; SI 2009/1889). For the purposes of the Uncertificated Securities Regulations 2001, SI 2001/3755, reg 22(4), an officer of an operator is in default in complying with, or in contravention of, the provision mentioned in that regulation if, and only if, he knowingly and wilfully authorised or permitted the default or contravention: reg 47(2).

31 Uncertificated Securities Regulations 2001, SI 2001/3755, reg 22(3A) (added by SI 2003/1633). Subject to the Uncertificated Securities Regulations 2001, SI 2001/3755, reg 29 (see note 27), an entry on an operator register of eligible debt securities is prima facie evidence, and in Scotland sufficient evidence unless the contrary is shown, of any matters which are by those regulations directed or authorised to be inserted in it: reg 24(8) (added by SI 2003/1633). Such sanctions as apply to a company and its officers in the event of a default in complying with the Companies Act 2006 s 113 (see PARA 336) apply to an operator and his officers in the event of a default in complying with the Uncertificated Securities Regulations 2001, SI 2001/3755, reg 22(3A): reg 22(4) (amended by SI 2003/1633; SI 2009/1889).

437. Registration by an operator of transfers of uncertificated securities. Except where relevant units of a security[1] are transferred by means of a relevant system[2] to a person[3] who is to hold them thereafter in certificated form[4], and subject to the provisions relating to refusal of registration[5], an operator[6] must register on the relevant operator register of securities[7] the transfer of title[8] to those units of that security[9]:

(1) upon settlement of a transfer of uncertificated units of a security in accordance with his rules[10];

(2) following receipt of an issuer-instruction[11] notifying him that the circumstances allowing conversion of securities into uncertificated form[12] have arisen in respect of a transfer of units of a participating security[13]; or

(3) following receipt of an issuer-instruction informing him of the name of the transferee[14].

An operator must refuse to register a transfer of title to units of a participating security in accordance with a system-member instruction[15] or an issuer-instruction, as the case may be, if he has actual notice that the transfer is[16]:

(a) prohibited by order of a court in the United Kingdom[17];

(b) prohibited or avoided by or under an enactment[18];

(c) a transfer to a deceased person[19]; or

(d) where the participating issuer[20] is constituted under the law of Scotland, prohibited by or under an arrestment[21].

Notwithstanding that an operator has received such notice in respect of a transfer of title to units of a participating security, the operator may register that transfer of title on the relevant operator register of securities if at the time that he received the actual notice it was not practicable for him to halt the process of registration[22].

Without prejudice to his rules, an operator may refuse to register a transfer of title to units of a participating security in accordance with a system-member instruction or an issuer-instruction, as the case may be, if the instruction requires a transfer of units:

(i) to an entity which is not a natural or legal person[23];

(ii) to a minor (which, in relation to a participating issuer constituted under the law of Scotland, means a person under 16 years of age)[24];

(iii) to be held jointly in the names of more persons than is permitted under the terms of the issue of the security[25]; or

(iv) where, in relation to the system-member instruction or the issuer-instruction, as the case may be, the operator has actual notice of any specified[26] matters[27].

An operator must not register a transfer of title to uncertificated units of a security on an operator register of securities otherwise than in accordance with the provisions described above[28] unless he is required to do so by order of a court in the United Kingdom or by or under an enactment[29]; however, this must not be taken to prevent an operator from entering on an operator register of securities a person who is a system-member to whom title to uncertificated units of a security has been transmitted by operation of law[30].

Immediately upon:

(A) the registration by an operator of the transfer of title to units of a participating security in accordance with the above provisions[31], or an order of a court in the United Kingdom[32], or a requirement arising by or under an enactment[33]; or

(B) the making or deletion by an operator of an entry on an operator register of securities following the transmission of title to uncertificated units of a security by operation of law[34], or upon the transfer of uncertificated units of a security to a person who is to hold them thereafter in certificated form[35],

the operator must generate an operator-instruction[36] to inform the relevant participating issuer of the registration, or of the making or deletion of the entry, as the case may be; and where appropriate the participating issuer must register[37] the transfer or transmission of title to those units on an issuer register of securities[38].

If an operator refuses to register a transfer of securities in any of the circumstances specified above[39], the operator must, within two months of the date on which the relevant system-member instruction or issuer-instruction, as the case may be, was received by the operator, send an operator-instruction, or written notification, informing the relevant system-member or participating issuer, as the case may be, of the refusal[40].

1 As to the meaning of 'securities' see PARA 431 note 2. As to the meaning of 'unit' see PARA 431 note 38.
2 As to the meaning of 'relevant system' see PARA 432 note 1.
3 As to the meaning of 'person' see PARA 312 note 2.
4 As to the meaning of 'certificated' see PARA 432 note 3. As to the registration of the transfer of uncertificated securities to certificated form see PARA 438.
5 Ie subject to the Uncertificated Securities Regulations 2001, SI 2001/3755, reg 27(2)–(4): see the text and notes 15–27.
6 As to the meaning of 'operator' see PARA 432 note 1.
7 As to the meaning of 'operator register of securities' see PARA 432 note 3.
8 As to the meaning of references to title to securities, and to a transfer of title, see PARA 431 note 2.
9 Uncertificated Securities Regulations 2001, SI 2001/3755, reg 27(1). Any purported registration of a transfer of title to an uncertificated unit of a security other than in accordance with reg 27 or reg 28 (see PARA 438) is of no effect: reg 29. See also PARA 347. As to the meaning of 'uncertificated' see PARA 432 note 3. As to the transfer of uncertificated securities see PARA 431. As to the continuing effect of the Uncertificated Securities Regulations 2001, SI 2001/3755, see PARA 431 note 37.
10 Uncertificated Securities Regulations 2001, SI 2001/3755, reg 27(1)(a). As to the meaning of 'rules' see PARA 432 note 11. As to the requirements to be met by an operator's rules and practices see reg 5(1), Sch 1 paras 25–27 (Sch 1 para 25 amended by SI 2003/1633). The operator must make transparent and non-discriminatory rules, based on objective criteria, governing access to his settlement facilities: see the Uncertificated Securities Regulations 2001, SI 2001/3755, Sch 1 para 28(1) (added by SI 2007/124).
11 As to the meaning of 'issuer-instruction' see PARA 434 note 6.
12 Ie the circumstances specified in the Uncertificated Securities Regulations 2001, SI 2001/3755, reg 33(2)(b): see PARA 434.
13 Uncertificated Securities Regulations 2001, SI 2001/3755, reg 27(1)(b). As to the meaning of 'participating security' see PARA 432 note 8.
14 Uncertificated Securities Regulations 2001, SI 2001/3755, reg 27(1)(c). The issuer-instruction referred to in the text is one given under reg 42(8)(b) (see PARA 1698).

15 As to the meaning of 'system-member instruction' see PARA 433 note 10.

16 Uncertificated Securities Regulations 2001, SI 2001/3755, reg 27(2). For the purpose of determining under these regulations whether a person has actual notice of a fact, matter or thing, that person must not under any circumstances be taken to be concerned to establish whether or not it exists or has occurred: reg 44.

17 Uncertificated Securities Regulations 2001, SI 2001/3755, reg 27(2)(a). As to the meaning of 'United Kingdom' see PARA 1 note 5.

18 Uncertificated Securities Regulations 2001, SI 2001/3755, reg 27(2)(b). As to the meaning of 'enactment' see PARA 13 note 16.

19 Uncertificated Securities Regulations 2001, SI 2001/3755, reg 27(2)(c).

20 As to the meaning of 'participating issuer' see PARA 432 note 9.

21 Uncertificated Securities Regulations 2001, SI 2001/3755, reg 27(2)(d).

22 Uncertificated Securities Regulations 2001, SI 2001/3755, reg 27(3).

23 Uncertificated Securities Regulations 2001, SI 2001/3755, reg 27(4)(a).

24 Uncertificated Securities Regulations 2001, SI 2001/3755, reg 27(4)(b). As to the meaning of 'minor' see the Family Law Reform Act 1969 s 1; and CHILDREN AND YOUNG PERSONS vol 9 (2012) PARA 1.

25 Uncertificated Securities Regulations 2001, SI 2001/3755, reg 27(4)(c).

26 Ie the matters specified in the Uncertificated Securities Regulations 2001, SI 2001/3755, reg 35(5)(a)(i)–(iii), namely that he was a person other than a participating issuer or a sponsoring system-participant receiving properly authenticated dematerialised instructions on behalf of a participating issuer, and he had actual notice:

(1) that any information contained in it was incorrect (reg 35(5)(a)(i));

(2) that the system-participant or the operator, as the case may be, expressed to have sent the instruction did not send the instruction (reg 35(5)(a)(ii)); or

(3) where relevant, that the person on whose behalf it was expressed to have been sent had not given to the operator or the sponsoring system-participant (as the case may be), identified in the properly authenticated dematerialised instruction as having sent it, his authority to send the properly authenticated dematerialised instruction on his behalf (reg 35(5)(a)(iii)).

'Sponsoring system-participant' means a system-participant who is permitted by an operator to send properly authenticated dematerialised instructions attributable to another person and to receive properly authenticated dematerialised instructions on another person's behalf: reg 3(1). As to the meanings of 'dematerialised instruction' and 'system-participant' see PARA 432 note 1.

27 Uncertificated Securities Regulations 2001, SI 2001/3755, reg 27(4)(d).

28 Ie in accordance with the Uncertificated Securities Regulations 2001, SI 2001/3755, reg 27(1): see the text and notes 1–14.

29 Uncertificated Securities Regulations 2001, SI 2001/3755, reg 27(5).

30 Uncertificated Securities Regulations 2001, SI 2001/3755, reg 27(6).

31 Uncertificated Securities Regulations 2001, SI 2001/3755, reg 27(7)(a)(i). The provisions referred to in the text are those of reg 27(1): see the text and notes 1–14.

32 Uncertificated Securities Regulations 2001, SI 2001/3755, reg 27(7)(a)(ii).

33 Uncertificated Securities Regulations 2001, SI 2001/3755, reg 27(7)(a)(iii).

34 Uncertificated Securities Regulations 2001, SI 2001/3755, reg 27(7)(b)(i).

35 Uncertificated Securities Regulations 2001, SI 2001/3755, reg 27(7)(b)(ii).

36 As to the meaning of 'operator-instruction' see PARA 432 note 1.

37 Ie in accordance with the Uncertificated Securities Regulations 2001, SI 2001/3755, reg 28: see PARA 438.

38 Uncertificated Securities Regulations 2001, SI 2001/3755, reg 27(7) (amended by SI 2003/1633). This provision does not apply in relation to units of an eligible debt security: Uncertificated Securities Regulations 2001, SI 2001/3755, reg 27(7A) (added by SI 2003/1633). As to the meaning of 'issuer register of securities' see PARA 433 note 20. As to the meaning of 'eligible debt security' see PARA 436 note 21.

39 Ie any of the circumstances specified in the Uncertificated Securities Regulations 2001, SI 2001/3755, reg 27(2) (see the text and notes 15–21) and reg 27(4) (see the text and notes 23–27): see reg 27(8) (substituted by SI 2009/1889).

40 Uncertificated Securities Regulations 2001, SI 2001/3755, reg 27(8) (as substituted: see note 39). Such sanctions as apply to a company and its officers in the event of a default in complying with the Companies Act 2006 s 771(1), (2) (see PARA 426) apply to an operator and his officers in the event of a default in complying with that provision as applied by the Uncertificated Securities Regulations 2001, SI 2001/3755, reg 27(8): reg 27(9) (amended by SI 2009/1889). For the purposes of the Uncertificated Securities Regulations 2001, SI 2001/3755, reg 27(9), an officer of an operator is in default if, and only if, he knowingly and wilfully authorised or permitted the

default or contravention: Uncertificated Securities Regulations 2001, SI 2001/3755, reg 47(2). As to the meaning of 'officer' (in relation to an operator or a participating issuer) see PARA 432 note 4.

438. Registration of transfers of uncertificated securities to be held in certificated form. Where uncertificated units of a security[1] are transferred by means of a relevant system[2] to a person[3] who is to hold them thereafter in certificated form[4], a participating issuer[5] must, where appropriate, register a transfer of title[6] to uncertificated units of a security on an issuer register of securities[7] in accordance with an operator-instruction[8] unless he has actual notice[9] that the transfer is:

(1) prohibited by order of a court in the United Kingdom[10];
(2) prohibited or avoided by or under an enactment[11];
(3) a transfer to a deceased person[12]; or
(4) where the participating issuer is constituted under the law of Scotland, prohibited by or under an arrestment[13].

A participating issuer may refuse to register a transfer of title to uncertificated units of a security in accordance with an operator-instruction if the instruction requires a transfer of units:

(a) to an entity which is not a natural or legal person[14];
(b) to a minor (which in relation to a participating issuer constituted under the law of Scotland means a person under 16 years of age)[15];
(c) to be held jointly in the names of more persons than is permitted under the terms of the issue of the security[16]; or
(d) where, in relation to the operator-instruction, the participating issuer has actual notice from the operator of any of the specified[17] matters[18].

A participating issuer must notify the operator by issuer-instruction[19] whether he has registered a transfer in response to an operator-instruction to do so[20]. A participating issuer must not register a transfer of title to uncertificated units of a security on an issuer register of securities unless he is required to do so by an operator-instruction[21], an order of a court in the United Kingdom[22], or by or under an enactment[23].

1 Ie units of a security that, immediately before the transfer in question, were held by the transferor in uncertificated form: see the Uncertificated Securities Regulations 2001, SI 2001/3755, reg 28(7). As to the meaning of 'securities' see PARA 431 note 2. As to the meaning of 'unit' see PARA 431 note 38. As to the meaning of 'uncertificated' see PARA 432 note 3. As to the continuing effect of the Uncertificated Securities Regulations 2001, SI 2001/3755, see PARA 431 note 37.
2 As to the meaning of 'relevant system' see PARA 432 note 1.
3 As to the meaning of 'person' see PARA 312 note 2.
4 Uncertificated Securities Regulations 2001, SI 2001/3755, reg 28(1). As to the meaning of 'certificated' see PARA 432 note 3.
5 As to the meaning of 'participating issuer' see PARA 432 note 9.
6 As to the meaning of references to title to securities, and to a transfer of title, see PARA 431 note 2.
7 As to the meaning of 'issuer register of securities' see PARA 433 note 20.
8 Uncertificated Securities Regulations 2001, SI 2001/3755, reg 28(2). Any purported registration of a transfer of title to an uncertificated unit of a security other than in accordance with reg 27 (see PARA 437) or reg 28 is of no effect: reg 29. See also PARA 347. As to the meanings of 'operator-instruction' and 'operator' see PARA 432 note 1. If a participating issuer refuses to register under reg 28(2) a transfer of securities in any of the circumstances specified in reg 28(3) and reg 28(4), the participating issuer must, within two months of the date on which the operator-instruction was received by the participating issuer, send to the transferee notice of the refusal: reg 28(8) (substituted by SI 2009/1889). Such sanctions as apply to a company and its officers in the event of a default in complying with the Companies Act 2006 s 771(1), (2) (see PARA 426) apply to a participating issuer and his officers in the event of default in complying with that provision as applied by the Uncertificated Securities Regulations 2001, SI 2001/3755, reg 28(8): reg 28(9) (amended by SI 2009/1889). For the purposes of the Uncertificated Securities Regulations 2001, SI 2001/3755, reg 28(9), an officer of a participating issuer is in default if, and

only if, he knowingly and wilfully authorised or permitted the default or contravention: Uncertificated Securities Regulations 2001, SI 2001/3755, reg 47(1). However, reg 28(9) does not apply to any of the following or its officers (Uncertificated Securities Regulations 2001, SI 2001/3755, reg 48 (amended by SI 2004/1662)):

(1) the Crown;
(2) any person acting on behalf of the Crown;
(3) the Bank of England;
(4) the Registrar of Government Stock;
(5) any previous Registrar of Government Stock; or
(6) in respect of a security which immediately before it became a participating security was transferable by exempt transfer within the meaning of the Stock Transfer Act 1982 (see PARA 441), a participating issuer.

As to the meaning of 'share' see PARA 432 note 2. As to the meaning of 'officer' (in relation to an operator or a participating issuer) see PARA 432 note 4. As to the Bank of England see FINANCIAL INSTITUTIONS vol 48 (2015) PARA 97 et seq; and as to the Registrar of Government Stock see FINANCIAL INSTRUMENTS AND TRANSACTIONS vol 49 (2015) PARA 123.

9 As to actual notice see PARA 437 note 16.
10 Uncertificated Securities Regulations 2001, SI 2001/3755, reg 28(3)(a). As to the meaning of 'United Kingdom' see PARA 1 note 5.
11 Uncertificated Securities Regulations 2001, SI 2001/3755, reg 28(3)(b). As to the meaning of 'enactment' see PARA 13 note 16.
12 Uncertificated Securities Regulations 2001, SI 2001/3755, reg 28(3)(c).
13 Uncertificated Securities Regulations 2001, SI 2001/3755, reg 28(3)(d).
14 Uncertificated Securities Regulations 2001, SI 2001/3755, reg 28(4)(a).
15 Uncertificated Securities Regulations 2001, SI 2001/3755, reg 28(4)(b). As to the meaning of 'minor' see the Family Law Reform Act 1969 s 1; and CHILDREN AND YOUNG PERSONS vol 9 (2012) PARA 1.
16 Uncertificated Securities Regulations 2001, SI 2001/3755, reg 28(4)(c).
17 Ie the matters specified in the Uncertificated Securities Regulations 2001, SI 2001/3755, reg 35(5)(a)(i)–(iii): see PARA 437 note 26.
18 Uncertificated Securities Regulations 2001, SI 2001/3755, reg 28(4)(d).
19 As to the meaning of 'issuer-instruction' see PARA 434 note 6.
20 Uncertificated Securities Regulations 2001, SI 2001/3755, reg 28(5). A default in complying with, or a contravention of, reg 28(5) or reg 28(6) (see the text and notes 21–23) is actionable at the suit of a person who suffers loss as a result of the default or contravention, or who is otherwise adversely affected by it, subject to the defences and other incidents applying to claims for breach of statutory duty: reg 46(1). However, this does not affect the liability which any person may incur, nor affect any right which any person may have, apart from reg 46(1): reg 46(2). As to breach of statutory duty see TORT vol 97 (2015) PARA 500 et seq.
21 Uncertificated Securities Regulations 2001, SI 2001/3755, reg 28(6)(a). See also note 20.
22 Uncertificated Securities Regulations 2001, SI 2001/3755, reg 28(6)(b). See also note 20.
23 Uncertificated Securities Regulations 2001, SI 2001/3755, reg 28(6)(c). See also note 20.

439. Registration of linked transfers of uncertificated securities. Where an operator[1] receives two or more system-member instructions[2] requesting him to register two or more transfers of title[3] to uncertificated[4] units of a security[5], and it appears to the operator[6]:

(1) either that there are fewer units of the security registered on an operator register of securities[7] in the name of a person[8] identified in any of the system-member instructions as a transferor than the number of units to be transferred from him under those system-member instructions[9], or that it has not been established[10], in relation to any of the transfers taken without regard to the other transfers, that a settlement bank has agreed to make a payment[11]; and
(2) that registration of all of the transfers would result in each of the persons identified in the system-member instructions as a transferor having title to a number of uncertificated units of a security equal to or greater than nil[12]; and
(3) that the combined effect of all the transfers taken together would result in the necessary condition[13] being satisfied[14],

the operator may either register the combined effect of all the transfers taken together[15], or register all the transfers simultaneously[16], unless:

(a) one or more of those transfers may not be registered by virtue of the fact that the operator has actual notice[17] of any of the circumstances specified[18]; or

(b) one or more of those transfers is to be[19] refused registration[20].

Notwithstanding that an operator has received such actual notice, in respect of two or more such system-member instructions as are referred to in head (1), head (2) or head (3) above, the operator may register all the transfers in question or their combined effect if at the time that he received the actual notice it was not practicable for him to halt the process of registration[21].

1 As to the meaning of 'operator' see PARA 432 note 1.
2 As to the meaning of 'system-member instruction' see PARA 433 note 10.
3 As to the meaning of references to title to securities, and to a transfer of title, see PARA 431 note 2. As to the transfer of uncertificated securities see PARA 431.
4 As to the meaning of 'uncertificated' see PARA 432 note 3.
5 As to such requests for registration see PARAS 437–438. As to the meaning of 'securities' see PARA 431 note 2. As to the meaning of 'unit' see PARA 431 note 38.
6 Uncertificated Securities Regulations 2001, SI 2001/3755, reg 30(1). As to the continuing effect of the Uncertificated Securities Regulations 2001, SI 2001/3755, see PARA 431 note 37.
7 As to the meaning of 'operator register of securities' see PARA 432 note 3.
8 As to the meaning of 'person' see PARA 312 note 2.
9 Uncertificated Securities Regulations 2001, SI 2001/3755, reg 30(1)(a)(i).
10 Ie in accordance with the Uncertificated Securities Regulations 2001, SI 2001/3755, Sch 1 para 21(1)(c). A relevant system must comprise procedures which provide that an operator only registers a transfer of title to uncertificated units of a security or generates an operator-instruction requiring a participating issuer to register such a transfer, and only generates an operator-instruction informing a settlement bank of its payment obligations in respect of such a transfer, if (in the case of a transfer to a system-member for value) it has established that a settlement bank has agreed to make payment in respect of the transfer, whether alone or taken together with another transfer for value: see Sch 1 para 21(1)(c). As to the meanings of 'relevant system' and 'operator-instruction' see PARA 432 note 1; and as to the meaning of 'participating issuer' see PARA 432 note 9. 'Settlement bank', in relation to a relevant system, means a person who has contracted to make payments in connection with transfers of title to uncertificated units of a security by means of that system: reg 3(1). As to the meaning of 'system-member' see PARA 433 note 9.
11 Uncertificated Securities Regulations 2001, SI 2001/3755, reg 30(1)(a)(ii).
12 Uncertificated Securities Regulations 2001, SI 2001/3755, reg 30(1)(b).
13 Ie the Uncertificated Securities Regulations 2001, SI 2001/3755, Sch 1 para 21(1)(c): see note 10.
14 Uncertificated Securities Regulations 2001, SI 2001/3755, reg 30(1)(c).
15 Uncertificated Securities Regulations 2001, SI 2001/3755, reg 30(2)(a).
16 Uncertificated Securities Regulations 2001, SI 2001/3755, reg 30(2)(b).
17 As to actual notice see PARA 437 note 16.
18 Ie specified in the Uncertificated Securities Regulations 2001, SI 2001/3755, reg 27(2): see PARA 437.
19 Ie by virtue of the Uncertificated Securities Regulations 2001, SI 2001/3755, reg 27(4): see PARA 437.
20 Uncertificated Securities Regulations 2001, SI 2001/3755, reg 30(2).
21 Uncertificated Securities Regulations 2001, SI 2001/3755, reg 30(3).

440. Transferor retains title until transferee entered as holder on issuer register of securities. When an operator[1] deletes an entry on an operator register of securities[2] in consequence of which:

(1) the operator must generate[3] an operator-instruction[4]; and

(2) by virtue of that instruction a participating issuer[5] must register, on an issuer register of securities[6], a transfer of title to units of a participating security[7] constituted under the law of England and Wales[8] or Northern Ireland[9],

then, subject to any enactment[10] or rule of law, the transferor[11], notwithstanding the deletion of the entry in the operator register of securities, retains title to the requisite number of units of the relevant participating security until the transferee[12] is entered on the relevant issuer register of securities as the holder thereof[13], and the transferee acquires an equitable interest in the requisite number of units of that security[14].

When an operator deletes an entry on an operator register of securities in consequence of which:

(a) the operator must generate[15] an operator-instruction[16]; and
(b) by virtue of that instruction a participating issuer must register, on an issuer register of securities, a transfer of title to units of a participating security constituted under the law of Scotland[17],

then, subject to any enactment or rule of law, the transferor, notwithstanding the deletion of the entry in the operator register of securities, retains title to the requisite number of units of the relevant participating security until the transferee is entered on the relevant issuer register of securities as the holder thereof[18], and the transferor holds the requisite number[19] of units of that security on trust for the benefit of the transferee[20].

These provisions have effect notwithstanding that the units to which the deletion of the entry in the operator register of securities relates, or in which an interest arises by virtue of these provisions[21], or any of them, may be unascertained[22]. Subject thereto, these provisions must not be construed as conferring a proprietary interest[23] in units of a security if the conferring of such an interest at the time specified[24] would otherwise be void by or under any enactment or rule of law[25].

1 As to the meaning of 'operator' see PARA 432 note 1.
2 As to the meaning of 'operator register of securities' see PARA 432 note 3.
3 Ie in accordance with the Uncertificated Securities Regulations 2001, SI 2001/3755, reg 27(7): see PARA 437.
4 Uncertificated Securities Regulations 2001, SI 2001/3755, reg 31(1)(a). As to the meaning of 'operator-instruction' see PARA 432 note 1. As to the continuing effect of the Uncertificated Securities Regulations 2001, SI 2001/3755, see PARA 431 note 37.
5 As to the meaning of 'participating issuer' see PARA 432 note 9.
6 As to the meaning of 'issuer register of securities' see PARA 433 note 20.
7 As to the meaning of 'participating security' see PARA 432 note 8; as to the meaning of 'unit' see PARA 431 note 38; and as to the meaning of references to title to securities, and to a transfer of title, see PARA 431 note 2.
8 As to the meanings of 'England' and 'Wales' see PARA 1 note 5.
9 Uncertificated Securities Regulations 2001, SI 2001/3755, reg 31(1)(b).
10 As to the meaning of 'enactment' see PARA 13 note 16.
11 'Transferor' means the person to be identified in the operator-instruction as the transferor: Uncertificated Securities Regulations 2001, SI 2001/3755, reg 31(9)(b). As to the meaning of 'person' see PARA 312 note 2.
12 'Transferee' means the person to be identified in the operator-instruction as the transferee: Uncertificated Securities Regulations 2001, SI 2001/3755, reg 31(9)(a).
13 Uncertificated Securities Regulations 2001, SI 2001/3755, reg 31(2)(a).
14 Uncertificated Securities Regulations 2001, SI 2001/3755, reg 31(2)(b). As to equitable interests in personal property see REAL PROPERTY AND REGISTRATION vol 87 (2012) PARA 191.
15 Ie in accordance with the Uncertificated Securities Regulations 2001, SI 2001/3755, reg 27(7): see PARA 437.
16 Uncertificated Securities Regulations 2001, SI 2001/3755, reg 31(3)(a).
17 Uncertificated Securities Regulations 2001, SI 2001/3755, reg 31(3)(b).
18 Uncertificated Securities Regulations 2001, SI 2001/3755, reg 31(4)(a).
19 For these purposes, the requisite number is the number of units which are to be specified in the operator-instruction which the operator must generate in accordance with the Uncertificated Securities Regulations 2001, SI 2001/3755, reg 27(7) (see PARA 437): reg 31(5).
20 Uncertificated Securities Regulations 2001, SI 2001/3755, reg 31(4)(b).

21 Ie by virtue of the Uncertificated Securities Regulations 2001, SI 2001/3755, reg 31(2)(b) (see the text and note 14) or reg 31(4)(b) (see the text and notes 19–20).
22 Uncertificated Securities Regulations 2001, SI 2001/3755, reg 31(6). As to the position in Scotland see reg 31(7).
23 Ie whether of the kind referred to in the Uncertificated Securities Regulations 2001, SI 2001/3755, reg 31(2)(b) (see the text and note 14) or reg 31(4)(b) (see the text and notes 19–20), or of any other kind.
24 Ie in the Uncertificated Securities Regulations 2001, SI 2001/3755.
25 Uncertificated Securities Regulations 2001, SI 2001/3755, reg 31(8).

(iv) Special Provisions relating to Certain Transfers of Securities

441. Computerised transfer of certain government and public authority securities. In the exercise of the appropriate power[1], provision may be made permitting a transfer in certain cases of specified securities[2] to which the power extends through the medium of a computer-based system to be established by the Bank of England and the London Stock Exchange[3]. Such a transfer effected in this way is referred to as an 'exempt transfer'[4]. However, no provision may be made, in the exercise of the appropriate power, for the application of the procedure of an exempt transfer to any securities or securities of any class except with the agreement of the person issuing the securities or, as the case may be, securities of that class or, if the liability for those securities or securities of that class has vested in another person, of that other person[5].

The Treasury may by regulations made by statutory instrument make provision in connection with the operation of such a system[6]. Such regulations may provide[7]:

(1) that, for the purposes of any provision made by or under any enactment or contained in any prospectus or other document and requiring or relating to the lodging or deposit of any instrument of transfer, notification of an exempt transfer in the manner required by the regulations is to be regarded as lodging or depositing an instrument of the transfer concerned[8]; and
(2) that, in such circumstances as may be specified in the regulations, certificates or other documents of or evidencing title to specified securities are or are not to be issued to persons who (by virtue of their participation in the system) are or have been able to transfer such securities by exempt transfers[9].

The Secretary of State[10] may by order made by statutory instrument repeal or amend any provision of any local Act, including an Act confirming a provisional order, or any order or other instrument made under a local Act, if it appears to him that the provision has become unnecessary or requires alteration in consequence of any of the provisions described above[11].

1 'Appropriate power' means the power to make regulations or orders under:

(1) the Finance Act 1942 s 47 (government stock: see FINANCIAL INSTRUMENTS AND TRANSACTIONS vol 49 (2015) PARA 122) or the Exchequer and Financial Provisions Act (Northern Ireland) 1950 s 11(1)(c) (Northern Ireland Exchequer stock) (Stock Transfer Act 1982 s 1(3)(a)); or
(2) the Local Government (Scotland) Act 1975 Sch 3 para 5 or the Local Government Act (Northern Ireland) 1972 s 70 (local authority stocks) (Stock Transfer Act 1982 s 1(3)(b) (amended by the Local Government Act 2003 s 127(1), (2), Sch 7 para 6, Sch 8 Pt 1)); or
(3) the Stock Transfer Act 1982 s 1(4) (s 1(3)(e)).

With respect to any specified securities to which none of the provisions referred to in heads (1)–(2) above apply, the Treasury may make the provision referred to in the Stock Transfer Act 1982 s 1(1) (see the text and note 3) by regulations made by statutory instrument subject to annulment in pursuance of a resolution of either House of Parliament: s 1(4). In exercise of this power, the Treasury has made the Stock Transfer (Gilt-edged Securities) (Exempt Transfer) Regulations 1985, SI 1985/1145; the Stock Transfer (Gilt-edged Securities) (Exempt Transfer) Regulations 1987, SI 1987/1294; the Stock Transfer (Gilt-edged Securities) (Exempt Transfer) Regulations 1988, SI 1988/232; the Stock Transfer (Gilt-edged Securities) (Exempt Transfer) Regulations 1989, SI 1989/880; the Stock Transfer (Gilt-edged Securities) (Exempt Transfer) (Amendment) Regulations 1990, SI 1990/1027; the Stock Transfer (Gilt-edged Securities) (Exempt Transfer) Regulations 1990, SI 1990/1211; the Stock Transfer (Gilt-edged Securities) (Exempt Transfer) (No 2) Regulations 1990, SI 1990/2547; the Stock Transfer (Gilt-edged Securities) (Exempt Transfer) Regulations 1991, SI 1991/1145; and the Stock Transfer (Gilt-edged Securities) (Exempt Transfer) (Amendment) Regulations 1999, SI 1999/1210. As to the Treasury see CONSTITUTIONAL AND ADMINISTRATIVE LAW vol 20 (2014) PARA 262 et seq.

2 For these purposes, 'specified securities' means:

(1) securities issued by Her Majesty's government in the United Kingdom or the government of Northern Ireland, not being excluded securities (ie securities in respect of which a stock certificate issued under the National Debt Act 1870 Pt V (ss 26–42) (repealed) (see FINANCIAL INSTRUMENTS AND TRANSACTIONS vol 49 (2015) PARA 125)) is for the time being outstanding; or any other bearer securities; or any securities for the time being registered on the National Savings Stock Register (see FINANCIAL INSTRUMENTS AND TRANSACTIONS vol 49 (2015) PARA 134) (Stock Transfer Act 1982 s 2(1), Sch 1 para 1);

(2) securities the payment of interest on which is guaranteed by Her Majesty's government in the United Kingdom or the government of Northern Ireland (Sch 1 para 2);

(3) securities issued in the United Kingdom by any public authority or nationalised industry or undertaking in the United Kingdom (Sch 1 para 3);

(4) securities issued in the United Kingdom by the government of any overseas territory, being securities registered in the United Kingdom, where 'overseas territory' means any territory or country outside the United Kingdom and where the reference to the government of any overseas territory includes a reference to a government constituted for two or more overseas territories, and to any authority established for the purpose of providing or administering services which are common to, or relate to matters of common interest to, two or more such territories (Sch 1 para 4 (amended by the International Development Act 2002 Sch 3 para 8));

(5) securities issued in the United Kingdom by the International Bank for Reconstruction and Development, the Inter-American Development Bank, the European Investment Bank or the European Coal and Steel Community, being, in each case, securities registered in the United Kingdom (Stock Transfer Act 1982 Sch 1 para 5);

(6) debentures (including debenture stock and bonds, whether constituting a charge on assets or not, and loan stock or notes) issued by the Agricultural Mortgage Corpn plc, the Commonwealth Development Finance Co Ltd, Finance for Industry plc or the Scottish Agricultural Securities Corpn Ltd (Sch 1 para 6);

(7) securities issued by any local authority in the United Kingdom, any authority all or the majority of the members of which are appointed or elected by one or more local authorities in the United Kingdom, or any police and crime commissioner (Stock Transfer Act 1982 Sch 1 para 7(1) (amended by the Police and Magistrates' Courts Act 1994 s 43, Sch 4 Pt II para 56; the Police Act 1996 s 103, Sch 7 para 1(2)(t); the Greater London Authority Act 1999 ss 392(1), (2), 423, Sch 34 Pt I; the Serious Organised Crime and Police Act 2005 Sch 4 para 41, Sch 17, Pt 2; the Police Reform and Social Responsibility Act 2011 Sch 16 Pt 3 para 158));

(8) securities issued in the United Kingdom by the African Development Bank, the Asian Development Bank, Caisse Centrale de Coopération Economique, Crédit Foncier de France, Electricité de France (EDF), Service National or Hydro-Québec, being, in each case, securities registered in the United Kingdom (Stock Transfer Act 1982 Sch 1 para 8 (added by SI 1988/231));

(9) securities issued in the United Kingdom by the European Bank for Reconstruction and Development, being securities registered in the United Kingdom (Stock Transfer Act 1982 Sch 1 para 9 (added by SI 1991/340)).

Notwithstanding that a security may at any time be so specified, it is not at that time a specified security for the purposes of the Stock Transfer Act 1982 if, on a transfer of it at that time effected by a written instrument, that instrument would be liable to stamp duty: s 2(2). The Treasury may from time to time, after consultation with the Bank of England, by order either add a security or class of securities to those listed above or remove a security or class of securities from that list (whether the security or class of securities was included in the list as originally enacted or was so added): s 2(3). The power to make such an order is exercisable by statutory instrument which must be laid before Parliament after being made: s 2(4). As to the orders made see the Stock Transfer (Specified Securities) Order 1988, SI 1988/231; Stock Transfer (Specified Securities) Order 1991, SI 1991/340. As to the meaning of 'United Kingdom' see PARA 1 note 5. As to the Bank of England see FINANCIAL INSTITUTIONS vol 48 (2015) PARA 97 et seq; as to the International Bank for

Reconstruction and Development see FINANCIAL INSTRUMENTS AND TRANSACTIONS vol 49 (2015) PARA 174; and as to the former Agricultural Mortgage Corporation see AGRICULTURAL LAND vol 1 (2008) PARA 618. For the purposes of head (7) above, 'local authority' means:

(a) the Greater London Authority, a county council, a district council, a London borough council, the Common Council of the City of London, a functional body within the meaning of the Greater London Authority Act 1999 (see LONDON GOVERNMENT vol 71 (2013) PARA 148 et seq), a joint authority established by the Local Government Act 1985 Pt IV (ss 23–42), an economic prosperity board established under the Local Democracy, Economic Development and Construction Act 2009 s 88, a combined authority established under s 103 or the Council of the Isles of Scilly;

(b) any council constituted under the Local Government etc (Scotland) Act 1994 s 2; or

(c) a council within the meaning of the Local Government Act (Northern Ireland) 1972,

and any reference to a security issued by a local authority includes a reference to a security the liability for which is for the time being vested in a local authority (being a security issued by an authority which has ceased to exist): Stock Transfer Act 1982 Sch 1 para 7(2) (amended by the Local Government Act 1985 ss 84, 102, Sch 14 para 62, Sch 17; the Education Reform Act 1988 s 237, Sch 13 Pt I; the Local Government etc (Scotland) Act 1994 s 180(1), Sch 13 para 127; the Greater London Authority Act 1999 s 392(1), (3)(a), (b); the Local Government and Public Involvement in Health Act 2007 s 209(2), Sch 13 Pt 2, para 39; the Local Democracy, Economic Development and Construction Act 2009 s 119 Sch 6 para 57; the Deregulation Act 2015 Sch 13 Pt 3 para 6(1), (17)). As to the meaning of 'England' see PARA 1 note 5. As to local authorities in England and Wales see LOCAL GOVERNMENT vol 69 (2009) PARA 22 et seq. As to administrative areas and authorities in London see LONDON GOVERNMENT vol 71 (2013) PARA 14 et seq. As to joint authorities see LOCAL GOVERNMENT vol 69 (2009) PARA 47 et seq.

3 Stock Transfer Act 1982 s 1(1). The responsibility for operating the CGO Service (ie the computer-based system established to facilitate the transfer of gilt-edged securities) was transferred from the Bank of England to CRESTCo Ltd on 24 May 1999: see the Stock Transfer (Gilt-edged Securities) (CGO Service) (Amendment) Regulations 1999, SI 1999/1208. As to the functions and duties of the London Stock Exchange and recognised clearing houses such as CRESTCo see FINANCIAL SERVICES REGULATION vol 50 (2016) PARAS 96–97.

4 Stock Transfer Act 1982 s 1(2). Notwithstanding anything in any enactment or in any prospectus or other document relating to the terms of issue, holding or transfer of specified securities, an exempt transfer is effective without the need for an instrument in writing: s 1(2).

5 Stock Transfer Act 1982 s 1(5). As to the meaning of 'person' see PARA 312 note 2.

6 Stock Transfer Act 1982 s 3(1). A statutory instrument made in the exercise of the power conferred by s 3(1) is subject to annulment in pursuance of a resolution of either House of Parliament: s 3(5). In exercise of the power conferred under s 3(1), (2), (the Treasury has made the Stock Transfer (Gilt-edged Securities) (CGO Service) Regulations 1985, SI 1985/1144; the Stock Transfer (Gilt-edged Securities) (CGO Service) (Amendment) Regulations 1987, SI 1987/1293; the Stock Transfer (Gilt-Edged Securities) (CGO Service) (Amendment) Regulations 1997, SI 1997/1329; the Stock Transfer (Gilt-edged Securities) (CGO Service) (Amendment) Regulations 1999, SI 1999/1208.

7 Stock Transfer Act 1982 s 3(2). Such regulations are without prejudice to the generality of s 3(1) (see the text and note 6), but are subject to any express provision made by or by virtue of any amendment contained in s 3(3), Sch 2 (which amends the Forged Transfers Act 1891 s 1, the Finance Act 1942 s 47 and the Colonial Stock Act 1948 s 1): Stock Transfer Act 1982 s 3(2).

8 Stock Transfer Act 1982 s 3(2)(a).

9 Stock Transfer Act 1982 s 3(2)(b).

10 As to the Secretary of State see PARA 6.

11 Stock Transfer Act 1982 s 3(4). A statutory instrument made in exercise of the power conferred by s 3(4) is subject to annulment in pursuance of a resolution of either House of Parliament: s 3(5). At the date at which this volume states the law, no order had been made under s 3(4).

(v) Forged Transfers of Securities

442. Forged transfers of shares. The company owes a duty to each of its shareholders not to take his shares out of his name unless he has executed a valid transfer of them, and this duty involves the corresponding obligation not to give effect to a forged transfer[1]. If, however, the forged transfer is registered, the true owner of the shares may sue the company jointly with the transferee for rectification of the register of shareholders by striking out the name of the transferee and restoring his own[2]. Where this remedy is no longer possible (as in the case of the intervention of third party rights) he may sue the company alone for an order that the company purchase and register in his name the necessary shares[3]. The period of limitation[4] does not begin to run against him in favour of the company until the company resists his claim, as his cause of action is not the invalid transfer of his shares but the company's refusal, when the forgery is made known, to treat him as the shareholder[5]. Negligence on the part of the shareholder does not create an estoppel disentitling him to succeed, unless it is the proximate cause of what the company has done[6].

The mere registration of the transferee does not entitle him to compel the company to recognise him as the holder of the shares[7], since registration only gives effect to a prior valid transfer[8]. Nor is the company necessarily estopped from disputing, as against the transferee, the validity of the transfer[9]. The only duty which the company owes to the transferee is to consult the register[10]; but, even where such reference would have shown that the alleged transferor was not on the register, the company is not ipso facto liable by estoppel to the transferee[11]. However, the issue of a certificate for the shares in favour of the transferee can undoubtedly create an estoppel in favour of the transferee himself, or any third party, if he acts to his detriment on the faith of it[12].

A person who, innocently, and even without negligence, brings about the transfer is bound to indemnify the company against any liability to the owner of the shares who has been displaced by a forged transfer[13].

The provisions of the Forged Transfers Acts 1891 and 1892 apply to shares[14].

1 *Simm v Anglo-American Telegraph Co* (1879) 5 QBD 188 at 214, CA, per Cotton LJ.
2 *Re Bahia and San Francisco Rly Co* (1868) LR 3 QB 584; *Barton v London North Western Rly Co* (1889) 24 QBD 77, CA. Cf *Midland Rly Co v Taylor* (1862) 8 HL Cas 751 at 756 per Lord Westbury LC.
3 *Barton v London and North Western Rly Co* (1888) 38 ChD 144 at 149, CA, per Cotton LJ, and at 152 per Lindley LJ; *Johnston v Renton* (1870) LR 9 Eq 181 at 188 per James V-C; *Welch v Bank of England* [1955] Ch 508, [1955] 1 All ER 811.
4 Ie under the Limitation Act 1980 s 2: see LIMITATION PERIODS vol 68 (2008) PARA 979.
5 *Barton v North Staffordshire Rly Co* (1888) 38 ChD 458 at 463 per Kay J; *Welch v Bank of England* [1955] Ch 508, [1955] 1 All ER 811.
6 *Mayor, Constables & Co of Merchants of the Staple of England v Governor & Co of Bank of England* (1887) 21 QBD 160 at 173, CA, per Lord Esher MR, and at 174 per Bowen LJ. Cf *Swan v North British Australasian Co* (1863) 2 H & C 175, Ex Ch. Failure to reply to an intimation by the company that the transfer is about to be made unless objected to is not negligence on the part of the shareholder: *Barton v London and North Western Rly Co* (1889) 24 QBD 77, CA; *Welch v Bank of England* [1955] Ch 508, [1955] 1 All ER 811.
7 *Simm v Anglo-American Telegraph Co* (1879) 5 QBD 188, CA.
8 *France v Clark* (1884) 26 ChD 257, CA; *Barton v London and North Western Rly Co* (1888) 38 ChD 144 at 149, CA, per Cotton LJ.
9 *Waterhouse v London and South Western Rly Co* (1879) 41 LT 553. Cf *Simm v Anglo-American Telegraph Co* (1879) 5 QBD 188, CA. As to estoppel see further PARA 398.
10 *Balkis Consolidated Co v Tomkinson* [1893] AC 396 at 412–413, HL, per Lord Field; *Dixon v Kennaway & Co* [1900] 1 Ch 833.
11 *Balkis Consolidated Co v Tomkinson* [1893] AC 396, HL; *Dixon v Kennaway & Co* [1900] 1 Ch 833 (following *Knights v Wiffen* (1870) LR 5 QB 660); *Platt v Rowe (t/a Chapman & Rowe) and CM Mitchell & Co* (1909) 26 TLR 49. Cf *Foster v Tyne Pontoon and Dry Docks Co and Renwick* (1893) 63 LJQB 50 at 55 per Collins J (where it was held that the fact that the fraudulent person had been insolvent from the first precluded the plaintiff from getting damages from the company).
12 See PARA 398.
13 *Sheffield Corpn v Barclay* [1905] AC 392, HL. See also *Yeung Kai Yung v Hong Kong and Shanghai Banking Corpn* [1981] AC 787, [1980] 2 All ER 599, PC. As to the liability of a stockbroker who, without fraud on his part, by acting on a forged transfer or by identification of a forger brings about a transfer, see *Starkey v Bank of England* [1903] AC 114, HL; *Bank of England v Cutler* [1908] 2 KB 208, CA. A stockbroker is liable to indemnify a company or its

registrar against the expense of restoring the true owner of shares to his previous position not only where the stockbroker requests the company or registrar to register a false transfer of shares but also where the broker makes the request for transfer after the company or registrar had issued a duplicate share certificate which a fraudster used to sell the shares through the broker: *Royal Bank of Scotland plc v Sandstone Properties Ltd* [1998] 2 BCLC 429 (the indemnity is sought against the consequence of complying with the request contained in the transfer form and/or for breach of a warranty that the form was genuine, without relying on anything which happened before that to establish the claim). *Royal Bank of Scotland plc v Sandstone Properties Ltd* was distinguished in *Cadbury Schweppes Ltd v Halifax Share Dealing Ltd* [2006] EWHC 1184 (Ch), [2007] 1 BCLC 497, on the basis that the company's claim for an indemnity in the latter case was defeated by the estoppel arising from the issue of the certificates (see also PARA 398).

As to costs of third parties see *Welch v Bank of England* [1955] Ch 508 at 548, [1955] 1 All ER 811 at 830 per Harman J.

14 See PARA 444.

443. Forged transfers of debentures. If the company registers a forged transfer of debentures, the true owner may obtain a cancellation of the registration and the delivery of the debentures[1]; and if the debentures are redeemed by the company and the sums secured are paid to the transferee under a forged transfer, the company is primarily liable to the true owner for the sums so paid, without prejudice to any rights it may have against the transferee[2].

The provisions of the Forged Transfers Acts 1891 and 1892 apply to the debentures and debenture stock of a company, as well as to shares[3].

1 *Cottam v Eastern Counties Rly Co* (1860) 1 John & H 243 (where one of three trustees forged the signatures of his co-trustees).

2 See the cases relating to transfers of shares and stock cited in PARA 442.

3 See PARA 444.

444. Compensation for loss under forged transfers of shares etc. A company may impose such reasonable restrictions on the transfer of its shares, stock or securities, or with respect to powers of attorney for the transfer of such, as it may consider requisite for guarding against losses arising from forgery[1]. Out of its funds it may grant compensation for losses caused by forged instruments[2] or transfers under forged powers of attorney[3]; and it also may borrow on the security of its property to meet claims for such compensation[4]. Compensation may be paid whether the person receiving compensation or any person through whom he claims has or has not paid any fee or otherwise contributed to any fund out of which compensation is paid[5]. Where the company pays compensation, it is subrogated to the rights of the person compensated against the person liable for the loss[6].

1 Forged Transfers Act 1891 s 1(4). As to forgery generally see CRIMINAL LAW vol 25 (2016) PARA 404 et seq. The manner in which shares may be transferred is governed by the articles of the company and the general law: see PARA 410. As to restrictions in the articles of a company on the transfer of shares see PARA 403. As to forged transfers see PARAS 442–443.

2 As to the meaning of 'instrument' for these purposes see the Forgery and Counterfeiting Act 1981 s 8; and CRIMINAL LAW vol 25 (2016) PARA 404 (definition applied by the Forged Transfers Act 1891 s 1(1A) (added by the Stock Transfer Act 1982 s 3, Sch 2)).

3 See the Forged Transfers Act 1891 s 1(1) (amended by the Stock Transfer Act 1982 Sch 2). The company may, if it thinks fit, charge a fee at a rate not exceeding five pence on every £100 transferred, with a minimum charge equal to that for £25, to provide for such compensation: see the Forged Transfers Act 1891 s 1(2) (amended by the Forged Transfers Act 1892 ss 2, 3; and the Decimal Currency Act 1969 s 11(1)). This provision is obsolete in practice.

4 See the Forged Transfers Act 1891 s 1(3) (amended by SI 1990/1285).

5 See the Forged Transfers Act 1891 s 1(1) (amended by the Forged Transfers Act 1892 ss 2, 3; the Stock Transfer Act 1982 Sch 2; the Statute Law (Repeals) Act 2004).

6 See the Forged Transfers Act 1891 s 1(5). These provisions apply to all companies incorporated by or in pursuance of any Act of Parliament or by royal charter or amalgamated with such a company: s 2; Forged Transfers Act 1892 s 4.

(vi) Transmission of Securities

445. Transmission of securities on death etc. In the model articles[1], and in articles of association generally[2], the word 'transmission' is used in relation to shares in contradistinction to the word 'transfer'; the former means transmission by operation of law, including devolution by death or bankruptcy[3], and the latter a transfer by the act of a member[4]. Unless the articles otherwise provide, the survivors or survivor of registered joint holders of shares[5] are alone entitled to and liable upon such shares[6], even where one of the joint holders is a corporation[7].

Upon the death of the sole holder of shares, the title to his shares devolves upon his personal representatives[8], who, subject to any provisions in the articles of association, may transfer his shares without being registered as shareholders[9], or, in the absence of any right of veto conferred on the company by its articles, may have their names entered on the register[10]. The production to a company[11] of any document that is by law sufficient evidence of the grant of probate of the will of a deceased person[12], letters of administration of the estate of a deceased person[13], or confirmation as executor of a deceased person[14], must be accepted by the company as sufficient evidence of the grant[15]. The personal representatives are liable for calls only in their representative capacity until they are registered as members with their consent; but after registration they become personally liable[16]. It is the duty of the representatives to give notice of the member's death as soon as possible[17]. Where executors are entitled to be registered as members, they are entitled to have their names inserted in such order as they please and the company cannot state on the register that they are executors[18]. On the death of a shareholder domiciled abroad the company may act only upon a grant of probate or administration in this country[19]. If, therefore, the company registers the name of or a transfer by any person who has not obtained such a grant or pays dividends to any such person, it becomes an executor without authority, and is liable to penalties and to pay such duties as would have been payable on a grant of probate[20].

When new shares are offered to the members in proportion to their holdings while the name of a deceased member is on the register, the executors may claim their testator's proportion[21]. They must, however, be registered themselves as members in respect of the new shares, and become liable to the company as individuals[22], though as between them and the beneficiaries they hold the shares as part of the estate and have a right of indemnity against the estate[23].

On a registered member having a person appointed as trustee of his estate in bankruptcy, the right to transfer his shares will vest in the trustee in bankruptcy[24].

1 As to the model articles see PARA 227.

2 As to a company's articles of association generally see PARA 227 et seq.

3 *Barton v London and North Western Rly Co* (1889) 24 QBD 77 at 88, CA, per Lindley LJ. As to the provision made in respect of the transmission of shares in the model articles see the Companies (Model Articles) Regulations 2008, SI 2008/3229, Sch 1 arts 27–29 (private company), Sch 3 arts 65–68 (public company). Similar provision is made in the Companies (Tables A to F) Regulations 1985, SI 1985/805: see Schedule Table A arts 29–31. As to the continuing application of the Companies (Tables A to F) Regulations 1985, SI 1985/805, see PARA 229.

4 *Re Bentham Mills Spinning Co* (1879) 11 ChD 900 at 904, CA, per Jessel MR; *Moodie v W and J Shepherd (Bookbinders) Ltd* [1949] 2 All ER 1044 at 1054, HL, per Lord Reid; *Stothers v William Steward (Holdings) Ltd* [1994] 2 BCLC 266 at 273, CA, per Peter Gibson LJ. The distinction between transfer and transmission is also recognised by the Companies Act 2006 s 770(2), which permits a company to register as shareholder or debenture holder a person to whom the right to any shares in or debentures of the company has been transmitted by operation of law: see PARA 410. As to the transfer of shares generally see PARA 400 et seq.

5 As to shareholders and membership of companies generally see PARAS 323 et seq, 1889 et seq.
6 *Re Maria Anna and Steinbank Coal and Coke Co, Maxwell's Case, Hill's Case* (1875) LR 20 Eq 585. It is usually so provided in the articles: see the Companies (Model Articles) Regulations 2008, SI 2008/3229, Sch 1 art 27 (private company), Sch 3 art 65 (public company), the latter of which also provides that nothing in the articles releases the estate of a deceased member from any liability in respect of a share solely or jointly held by that member. The Companies (Tables A to F) Regulations 1985, SI 1985/805, makes similar provision: see Schedule Table A art 29.
7 See the Bodies Corporate (Joint Tenancy) Act 1899 s 1 (passed in consequence of *Law Guarantee and Trust Society Ltd and Hunter v Governor & Co of Bank of England* (1890) 24 QBD 406); and *Re Thompson's Settlement Trusts, Thompson v Alexander* [1905] 1 Ch 229. As to companies and corporations generally see PARA 2. As to corporations as joint tenants under the Bodies Corporate (Joint Tenancy) Act 1899 see REAL PROPERTY AND REGISTRATION vol 87 (2012) PARA 200.
8 See *Re Greene, Greene v Greene* [1949] Ch 333, [1949] 1 All ER 167. As to the meaning of 'personal representative' see WILLS AND INTESTACY vol 103 (2010) PARA 608.
9 See the Companies Act 2006 s 773; Companies (Model Articles) Regulations 2008, SI 2008/3229, Sch 1 art 27 (private company), Sch 3 art 66 (public company); the Companies (Tables A to F) Regulations 1985, SI 1985/805, Schedule Table A arts 29–31; and PARA 409. See also *Stothers v William Steward (Holdings) Ltd* [1994] 2 BCLC 266, CA (articles properly construed permitted transfers by personal representatives to the same extent as transfers to privileged relations were permitted by members while alive; hence the personal representatives were able to transfer the shares of the deceased member to his widow (a privileged relation) without obtaining the consent of the directors to the transfer). As to voting by a person entitled by transmission see PARA 725.
10 *Scott v Frank F Scott (London) Ltd* [1940] Ch 794, [1940] 3 All ER 508, CA. As to the register of members see PARA 336 et seq.
11 As to the meaning of 'company' see PARA 21.
12 Companies Act 2006 s 774(a). As to the grant of probate see WILLS AND INTESTACY vol 103 (2010) PARA 707 et seq.
13 Companies Act 2006 s 774(b). As to letters of administration see WILLS AND INTESTACY vol 103 (2010) PARA 754 et seq.
14 Companies Act 2006 s 774(c). As to appointment as executor see WILLS AND INTESTACY vol 103 (2010) PARA 610 et seq.
15 Companies Act 2006 s 774.
16 *Duff's Executors' Case* (1886) 32 ChD 301, CA; *Buchan's Case* (1879) 4 App Cas 549, 583, HL. As to the personal representatives being put on the list of contributories see COMPANY AND PARTNERSHIP INSOLVENCY vol 17 (2011) PARA 669.
17 *New Zealand Gold Extraction Co (Newberg-Vautin Process) v Peacock* [1894] 1 QB 622 at 632–633, CA, per Davey LJ.
18 *Re TH Saunders & Co Ltd* [1908] 1 Ch 415; *Edwards v Ransomes and Rapier Ltd* (1930) 143 LT 594. As to the exclusion of trusts from the register see the Companies Act 2006 s 126; and PARA 344.
19 See *Commercial Bank Corpn of India and the East, Fernandes' Executors' Case* (1870) 5 Ch App 314. As to the resealing of dominion and colonial grants see WILLS AND INTESTACY vol 103 (2010) PARA 835 et seq. As to foreign domicile grants see WILLS AND INTESTACY vol 103 (2010) PARA 844 et seq.
20 *New York Breweries Co v A-G* [1899] AC 62, HL. See also *Re Baku Consolidated Oilfields Ltd* [1994] 1 BCLC 173 at 176 per Chadwick J (liquidator not bound to insist on an English grant being obtained if satisfied that the personal representatives would be so entitled and can distribute a deceased member's share of surplus assets without the formality of an English grant; he may seek a suitable indemnity to protect himself against liability as an executor de son tort). As to an executor without authority (formerly an 'executor de son tort') see WILLS AND INTESTACY vol 103 (2010) PARA 1263 et seq.
21 *James v Buena Ventura Nitrate Grounds Syndicate Ltd* [1896] 1 Ch 456, CA.
22 *Re Leeds Banking Co, Fearnside and Dean's Case, Dobson's Case* (1866) 1 Ch App 231; *Duff's Executors' Case* (1886) 32 ChD 301, CA.
23 *Duff's Executors' Case* (1886) 32 ChD 301 at 309, CA, per Cotton LJ, and at 310 per Fry LJ.
24 See the Insolvency Act 1986 ss 306, 311(3); and BANKRUPTCY AND INDIVIDUAL INSOLVENCY vol 5 (2013) PARAS 398, 409, 435.

(11) DISCLOSURE OF INTERESTS IN SHARES OF PUBLIC COMPANIES

(i) Disclosure of Interests: in general

446. Interaction between the Companies Act 2006 and rules made under the Financial Services and Markets Act 2000. Although the Companies Act 2006 makes provision in relation to the disclosure of information about interests in public company shares[1], the rules that have been made under the Financial Services and Markets Act 2000 for the purposes of the Transparency Obligations Directive[2] also have effect[3]. Of particular relevance in this context are the provisions contained in those chapters of the Disclosure Rules and Transparency Rules which set out:

(1) the notification obligations of issuers, persons discharging managerial responsibilities and their connected persons in respect of transactions conducted on their own account in shares of the issuer, or derivatives or any other financial instrument relating to those shares[4]; and

(2) the notification obligations that a person must make to an issuer of the percentage of its voting rights he holds as shareholder or holds or is deemed to hold through his direct or indirect holding of financial instruments, if, subject to certain exemptions, the percentage of those voting rights reaches, exceeds or falls below certain thresholds as a result of an acquisition or disposal of shares or certain financial instruments, or reaches, exceeds or falls below an applicable threshold as a result of events changing the breakdown of voting rights and on the basis of information disclosed by the issuer[5].

1 See the Companies Act 2006 Pt 22 (ss 791–828); and PARA 448 et seq.

2 Ie European Parliament and Council Directive (EC) 2004/109 (OJ L390, 31.12.2004, p 38) relating to the harmonisation of transparency requirements in relation to information about issuers whose securities are admitted to trading on a regulated market: see FINANCIAL SERVICES REGULATION vol 50A (2016) PARA 623 et seq.

3 See the Financial Services and Markets Act 2000 s 89A; and FINANCIAL SERVICES REGULATION vol 50A (2016) PARA 623. Rules under the Financial Services and Markets Act 2000 s 89A are referred to as 'transparency rules': see s 89A(5), s 103(1); and FINANCIAL SERVICES REGULATION vol 50A (2016) PARA 623.The rules so made, which are not statutory instruments, are set out in the FCA Handbook, are referred to as 'Disclosure Rules and Transparency Rules' ('DTR') and are accessible, at the date at which this volume states the law, on the Financial Conduct Authority's website. As to the rules made by the Financial Conduct Authority generally see FINANCIAL SERVICES REGULATION vol 50A (2016) PARA 584.

4 See DTR 3.1.

5 See DTR 5.1, especially DTR 5.1.2.

(ii) Interests in Public Company Shares

447. Information about interests in public company shares. The Companies Act 2006 makes specific provision[1] in relation to the disclosure of information about interests in public company shares[2]. References in those provisions to a company's shares are to the company's issued shares of a class carrying rights to vote in all circumstances at general meetings of the company[3], including any shares held as treasury shares[4]. The temporary suspension of voting rights in respect of any shares does not affect the application of the statutory provisions in relation to interests in those or any other shares[5].

1 See the Companies Act 2006 Pt 22 (ss 791–828); and PARA 448 et seq).

2 See the Companies Act 2006 s 791. As to the meaning of 'public company' see PARA 95. The repeal of the Companies Act 1985 ss 198–210, 220 does not affect any obligation to which a person became subject under s 198 before 20 January 2007: see the Companies Act 2006 (Commencement No 1, Transitional Provisions and Savings) Order 2006, SI 2006/3428, art 8(1), Sch 5 para 2(1).
3 As to meetings of members see PARA 701 et seq. As to voting at meetings see PARA 725 et seq.
4 Companies Act 2006 s 792(1). As to treasury shares see PARA 1437. As to the power of the Secretary of State to amend the definition of shares see PARA 448.
5 Companies Act 2006 s 792(2).

448. Secretary of State's power to make further provision about disclosure of interests. The Secretary of State[1] may by regulations[2] amend:

(1) the definition of shares[3] to which the statutory provisions relating to interests in a public company's shares[4] apply[5];
(2) the provisions as to notice by a company requiring information about interests in its shares[6]; and
(3) the provisions as to what is taken to be an interest in shares[7].

The regulations may amend, repeal or replace those provisions and make such other consequential amendments or repeals of provisions as appear to the Secretary of State to be appropriate[8].

1 As to the Secretary of State see PARA 6.
2 Regulations under the Companies Act 2006 s 828 are subject to affirmative resolution procedure (ie the regulations must not be made unless a draft of the statutory instrument containing them has been laid before Parliament and approved by a resolution of each House of Parliament): see the Companies Act 2006 ss 828(3), 1290. At the date at which this volume states the law, no such regulations had been made.
3 Ie the definition set out in the Companies Act 2006 s 792 (see PARA 447).
4 Ie the Companies Act 2006 Pt 22 (ss 791–828). As to the meaning of 'public company' see PARA 95.
5 Companies Act 2006 s 828(1)(a).
6 Companies Act 2006 s 828(1)(b). The provisions as to notice are set out in s 793 (see PARA 453).
7 Companies Act 2006 s 828(1)(c). The provisions as to what is taken to be an interest in shares are set out in ss 820, 821 (see PARA 449).
8 Companies Act 2006 s 828(2).

449. Determining whether a person has a disclosable interest. The following provisions apply to determine[1] whether a person has an interest in public company shares[2]. For this purpose[3], a reference to an interest in shares includes an interest of any kind whatsoever in the shares, and any restraints or restrictions to which the exercise of any right attached to the interest is or may be subject are to be disregarded[4].

Where an interest in shares is comprised in property held on trust, every beneficiary of the trust is treated as having an interest in the shares[5].

A person is treated as having an interest in shares if:

(1) he enters into a contract to acquire them; or
(2) not being the registered holder, he is entitled to exercise any right conferred by the holding of the shares, or to control the exercise of any such right[6].

A person is treated as having an interest in shares if:

(a) he has a right to call for delivery of the shares to himself or to his order; or
(b) he has a right to acquire an interest in shares or is under an obligation to take an interest in shares[7].

This applies whether the right or obligation is conditional or absolute[8].

Persons having a joint interest are treated as each having that interest[9].

It is immaterial that shares in which a person has an interest are unidentifiable[10].

1 Ie for the purposes of the Companies Act 2006 Pt 22 (ss 791–828).
2 Companies Act 2006 s 820(1). See s 791; and PARA 447. As to the meaning of 'public company' see PARA 95. The repeal of the Companies Act 1985 ss 212–220 (power of public company to require disclosure of interests in shares) does not affect the operation of those provisions in relation to a notice issued by a company under s 212 before 20 January 2007: see the Companies Act 2006 (Commencement No 1, Transitional Provisions and Savings) Order 2006, SI 2006/3428, art 8(1), Sch 5 para 2(2).
3 Ie for the purposes of the Companies Act 2006 Pt 22.
4 Companies Act 2006 s 820(2). The provisions of s 793 (notice by company requiring information about interests in its shares) (see PARA 453) apply in relation to a person who has, or previously had, or is or was entitled to acquire, a right to subscribe for shares in the company as it applies in relation to a person who is or was interested in shares in that company; and references in s 793 to an interest in shares are to be read accordingly: s 821(1), (2).
5 Companies Act 2006 s 820(3).
6 Companies Act 2006 s 820(4). A person is entitled to exercise or control the exercise of a right conferred by the holding of shares if he either has a right, whether subject to conditions or not, the exercise of which would make him so entitled or is under an obligation, whether subject to conditions or not, the fulfilment of which would make him so entitled: s 820(5).
7 Companies Act 2006 s 820(6)(a), (b).
8 Companies Act 2006 s 820(6).
9 Companies Act 2006 s 820(7).
10 Companies Act 2006 s 820(8).

450. Family and corporate interests in public company shares. A person is taken[1] to be interested in public company shares[2] in which his spouse or civil partner, or any infant child or step-child of his, is interested[3].

A person is taken[4] to be interested in public company shares[5] if a body corporate[6] is interested in them and:

(1) the body or its directors are accustomed to act in accordance with his directions or instructions; or
(2) he is entitled to exercise or control the exercise of one-third or more of the voting power at general meetings of the body[7].

1 Ie for the purposes of the Companies Act 2006 Pt 22 (ss 791–828).
2 See PARA 447. As to the meaning of 'public company' see PARA 95.
3 Companies Act 2006 s 822(1).
4 Ie for the purposes of the Companies Act 2006 Pt 22.
5 See PARA 447.
6 As to the meaning of 'body corporate' see PARA 1 note 5.
7 Companies Act 2006 s 823(1). As to meetings of members see PARA 701 et seq. As to voting at meetings see PARA 725 et seq. For the purposes of s 823, a person is treated as entitled to exercise or control the exercise of voting power if another body corporate is entitled to exercise or control the exercise of that voting power and he is entitled to exercise or control the exercise of one-third or more of the voting power at general meetings of that body corporate: s 823(2). A person is also treated as entitled to exercise or control the exercise of voting power if either he has a right (whether or not subject to conditions) the exercise of which would make him so entitled, or he is under an obligation (whether or not subject to conditions) the fulfilment of which would make him so entitled: s 823(3).

451. Agreement to acquire interests in a particular public company. An interest in public company shares[1] may arise[2] from an agreement[3] between two or more persons that includes provision for the acquisition by any one or more of them of interests in shares of a particular public company (the 'target company' for that agreement)[4].

An interest arises in relation to such an agreement if:

(1) the agreement includes provision imposing obligations or restrictions on any one or more of the parties to it with respect to their use[5], retention or disposal of their interests in the shares of the target company acquired

in pursuance of the agreement (whether or not together with any other interests of theirs in the company's shares to which the agreement relates)[6]; and

(2) an interest in the target company's shares is in fact acquired by any of the parties in pursuance of the agreement[7].

Once an interest in shares in the target company has been acquired in pursuance of the agreement, then the interest continues so long as the agreement continues to include provisions of any description mentioned in heads (1) and (2) above[8]. This applies irrespective of:

(a) whether or not any further acquisitions of interests in the company's shares take place in pursuance of the agreement;

(b) any change in the persons who are for the time being parties to it;

(c) any variation of the agreement[9].

An interest does not arise in relation to an agreement that is not legally binding unless it involves mutuality in the undertakings, expectations or understandings of the parties to it[10]. Nor does it arise in relation to an agreement to underwrite or sub-underwrite an offer of shares in a company, provided the agreement is confined to that purpose and any matters incidental to it[11].

1 See PARA 447. As to the meaning of 'public company' see PARA 95.
2 Ie for the purposes of the Companies Act 2006 Pt 22 (ss 791–828).
3 'Agreement' includes any agreement or arrangement: Companies Act 2006 s 824(5)(a). References to provisions of an agreement include: (1) undertakings, expectations or understandings operative under an arrangement; and (2) any provision whether express or implied and whether absolute or not: s 824(5)(b). References elsewhere in Pt 22 to an agreement to which s 824 applies have a corresponding meaning: s 824(5).
4 Companies Act 2006 s 824(1). See also the relevant rules on 'concert parties' in the *City Code on Takeovers and Mergers* (11th Edn, 20 May 2013) (as amended from time to time) Section E. As to that code see PARA 1662.
5 The reference in head (1) in the text to the use of interests in shares in the target company is to the exercise of any rights or of any control or influence arising from those interests (including the right to enter into an agreement for the exercise, or for control of the exercise, of any of those rights by another person): Companies Act 2006 s 824(3).
6 Companies Act 2006 s 824(2)(a).
7 Companies Act 2006 s 824(2)(b).
8 Companies Act 2006 s 824(4). References in s 824(4) to the agreement include any agreement having effect (whether directly or indirectly) in substitution for the original agreement: s 824(4).
9 Companies Act 2006 s 824(4).
10 Companies Act 2006 s 824(6)(a).
11 Companies Act 2006 s 824(6)(b). As to underwriting see PARA 1339 et seq.

452. Extent of obligation in case of share acquisition agreement. Each party to a share acquisition agreement[1] is treated[2] for the purposes of disclosure[3] as interested in all shares in the target company[4] in which any other party to the agreement is interested apart from the agreement[5] (whether or not the interest of the other party was acquired, or includes any interest that was acquired, in pursuance of the agreement)[6]. Accordingly, any such interest of the person, apart from the agreement, includes for those purposes any family or corporate interest treated as his[7] in relation to any other agreement with respect to shares in the target company to which he is a party[8].

A notification with respect to his interest in shares in the target company made to the company[9] by a person who is for the time being a party to a share acquisition agreement must[10]:

(1) state that the person making the notification is a party to such an agreement[11];

(2) include the names and, so far as known to him, the addresses of the other parties to the agreement, identifying them as such[12]; and
(3) state whether or not any of the shares to which the notification relates are shares in which he is interested[13] and, if so, the number of those shares[14].

1 Ie an agreement to which the Companies Act 2006 s 824 applies (see PARA 451).
2 Ie for the purposes of the Companies Act 2006 Pt 22 (ss 791–828).
3 See PARA 453.
4 See PARA 451.
5 For these purposes, an interest of a party to such an agreement in shares in the target company is an interest apart from the agreement if he is interested in those shares otherwise than by virtue of the application of the Companies Act 2006 s 824 (see PARA 451) and s 825 in relation to the agreement: s 825(2).
6 Companies Act 2006 s 825(1).
7 Ie under the Companies Act 2006 s 822 or s 823 (see PARA 450) or by the application of s 824 (see PARA 451) and s 825.
8 Companies Act 2006 s 825(3).
9 Ie under the Companies Act 2006 Pt 22.
10 Companies Act 2006 s 825(4).
11 Companies Act 2006 s 825(4)(a).
12 Companies Act 2006 s 825(4)(b).
13 Ie by virtue of the Companies Act 2006 s 824 (see PARA 451) and s 825.
14 Companies Act 2006 s 825(4)(c).

(iii) Company Notice requiring Information about Interests in Shares

453. Notice by company requiring information about interests. A public company[1] may give notice[2] to any person whom the company knows or has reasonable cause to believe:

(1) to be interested in the company's shares[3]; or
(2) to have been so interested at any time during the three years immediately preceding the date on which the notice is issued[4].

The notice may require the person:

(a) to confirm that fact or, as the case may be, to state whether or not it is the case; and
(b) if he holds, or has during that time held, any such interest, to give such further information as may be required by the notice[5].

The notice may require the person to whom it is addressed:

(i) to give particulars[6] of his own present or past interest in the company's shares, held by him at any time during the three years immediately preceding the date on which the notice is issued[7];
(ii) where his interest is a present interest and another interest in the shares subsists, or another interest in the shares subsisted during that three year period at a time when his interest subsisted, to give, so far as lies within his knowledge, such particulars with respect to that other interest as may be required by the notice[8];
(iii) where his interest is a past interest, to give, so far as lies within his knowledge, particulars of the identity of the person who held that interest immediately upon his ceasing to hold it[9].

The information required by the notice must be given within such reasonable time as may be specified in the notice[10].

1 As to the meaning of 'public company' see PARA 95.
2 Ie under the Companies Act 2006 s 793: see the text and notes 3–10.
3 The provisions of the Companies Act 2006 s 793 (notice by company requiring information about interests in its shares) apply in relation to a person who has, or previously had, or is or was entitled

to acquire, a right to subscribe for shares in the company as they apply in relation to a person who is or was interested in shares in that company; and references in s 793 to an interest in shares are to be read accordingly: s 821(1), (2).

4 Companies Act 2006 s 793(1). Under the Financial Conduct Authority's Disclosure Rules and Transparency Rules ('DTR'), an issuer must notify a Regulatory Information Service ('RIS') of any information notified to it in accordance with the Companies Act 2006 s 793 to the extent that it relates to the interests of a director or, as far as the issuer is aware, any connected person: see DTR 3.1.4(c). As to the meaning of 'Regulatory Information Service' under the Listing Rules see PARA 517 note 7. See further the rules governing obligations of notification and disclosure regarding interests in voting rights under the DTR, especially DTR 5; and see PARA 446. As to the rules made by the Financial Conduct Authority generally see FINANCIAL SERVICES REGULATION vol 50A (2016) PARA 584.

5 Companies Act 2006 s 793(2).

6 The particulars referred to in heads (i)–(ii) in the text include the following (Companies Act 2006 s 793(5)), ie
- (1) the identity of persons interested in the shares in question; and
- (2) whether persons interested in the same shares are or were parties to
  - (a) an agreement to which s 824 applies (certain share acquisition agreements) (see PARA 451); or
  - (b) an agreement or arrangement relating to the exercise of any rights conferred by the holding of the shares.

7 Companies Act 2006 s 793(3). See also note 6.

8 Companies Act 2006 s 793(4). See also note 6.

9 Companies Act 2006 s 793(6).

10 Companies Act 2006 s 793(7).

454. Persons exempted from obligation to comply with notice by company. A person is not obliged to comply with a notice requiring information about interests in public company shares[1] if he is for the time being exempted[2] by the Secretary of State[3]. The Secretary of State must not grant any such exemption unless he:
- (1) has consulted the Governor of the Bank of England[4]; and
- (2) is satisfied that, having regard to any undertaking given by the person in question with respect to any interest held or to be held by him in any shares, there are special reasons why that person should not be subject to the obligation to comply with the notice[5].

1 Ie a notice under the Companies Act 2006 s 793 (see PARA 453). As to the meaning of 'public company' see PARA 95.

2 Ie exempted from the operation of the Companies Act 2006 s 793 (see PARA 453).

3 Companies Act 2006 s 796(1). As to the Secretary of State see PARA 6.

4 As to the Governor of the Bank of England see FINANCIAL INSTITUTIONS vol 48 (2015) PARA 97.

5 Companies Act 2006 s 796(2).

455. Failure to comply with notice requiring information about interests: offences. An offence is committed by a person who:
- (1) fails to comply with a notice requiring information about interests in public company shares[1]; or
- (2) in purported compliance with such a notice makes a statement that he knows to be false in a material particular, or recklessly makes a statement that is false in a material particular[2].

A person does not, however, commit an offence under head (1) above if he proves that the requirement to give information was frivolous or vexatious[3].

1 Ie a notice under the Companies Act 2006 s 793 (see PARA 453). As to the meaning of 'public company' see PARA 95.

2 Companies Act 2006 s 795(1). A person guilty of an offence under s 795 is liable on conviction on indictment, to imprisonment for a term not exceeding two years or a fine, or to both or on summary conviction, to imprisonment for a term not exceeding 12 months or to a fine, or to both: s 795(3). In the case of liability on summary conviction the fine is one not exceeding the statutory

maximum. By virtue of the Legal Aid, Sentencing and Punishment of Offenders Act 2012 s 85, however, where the offence is committed on or after 12 March 2015, it is punishable by a fine of an unlimited amount. As to the statutory maximum and the powers of magistrates' courts to issue fines on summary conviction see SENTENCING vol 92 (2015) PARA 176. In relation to an offence committed before the coming into force of the Criminal Justice Act 2003 s 154(1) (not yet in force), the maximum term of imprisonment on summary conviction is six months: see the Companies Act 2006 s 1131; and PARA 1818.

3 Companies Act 2006 s 795(2).

456. Failure to comply with notice requiring information about interests: imposing restrictions on shares. Where a notice requiring information about interests in a public company's shares[1] is served by a company on a person who is or was interested in shares in the company, and that person fails to give the company the information required by the notice within the time specified in it, the company may apply to the court for an order directing that the shares in question be subject to restrictions[2].

If the court is satisfied that such an order may unfairly affect the rights of third parties in respect of the shares, the court may, for the purpose of protecting those rights and subject to such terms as it thinks fit, direct that such acts by such persons or descriptions of persons and for such purposes as may be set out in the order are not to constitute a breach of the restrictions[3].

On an application, the court may make an interim order[4]. Any such order may be made unconditionally or on such terms as the court thinks fit[5].

Where a company's articles[6] empower the directors, without applying to the court, to impose restrictions on the exercise of rights attaching to shares if those interested in them fail to comply with a disclosure notice, the proper purpose rule[7] applies to the imposition of such restrictions[8].

1 Ie a notice under the Companies Act 2006 s 793 (see PARA 453). As to the meaning of 'public company' see PARA 95.

2 Companies Act 2006 s 794(1). For the effect of such an order see s 797; and PARA 457. As to the meaning of 'the court' see PARA 160 note 12.

The Secretary of State may by regulations made by statutory instrument make such amendments of the provisions of s 794 relating to orders imposing restrictions on shares as appear to him necessary or expedient, for enabling orders to be made in a form protecting the rights of third parties, or with respect to the circumstances in which restrictions may be relaxed or removed, or with respect to the making of interim orders by a court: Companies Act 1989 s 135(1), (2) (amended by SI 2008/948; the Companies Act 1989 s 135 prospectively repealed by the Companies Act 2006 s 1295, Sch 16, as from a day to be appointed under s 1300(2); at the date at which this volume states the law, no such day had been appointed). The regulations may make different provision for different cases and may contain such transitional and other supplementary and incidental provisions as appear to the Secretary of State to be appropriate (Companies Act 1989 s 135(3) (prospectively repealed)); but such regulations are not to be made unless a draft of the regulations has been laid before Parliament and approved by resolution of each House of Parliament (s 135(4) (prospectively repealed)). As to the Secretary of State see PARA 6. At the date at which this volume states the law, no such regulations had been made.

3 Companies Act 2006 s 794(2).

4 Companies Act 2006 s 794(3). Further provision about orders under s 794 is made in ss 798–802 (see PARAS 458–460): s 794(4).

5 Companies Act 2006 s 794(3).

6 As to the meaning of references to a company's 'articles' see PARA 227 note 2. As to a company's articles of association generally see PARA 227 et seq.

7 Ie the Companies Act 2006 s 171(b): see PARA 580.

8 *See Eclairs Group Ltd v JKX Oil & Gas plc, Glengary Overseas Ltd v JKX Oil & Gas plc* [2015] UKSC 71, [2016] 1 BCLC 1, [2015] All ER (D) 20 (Dec).

457. Effect of court order imposing restrictions on shares. The effect of an order[1] that public company shares are subject to restrictions is as follows[2]:

(1) any transfer of the shares, or agreement to transfer the shares, is void[3];

(2) no voting rights are exercisable in respect of the shares[4];

(3) no further shares may be issued in right of the shares or in pursuance of an offer made to their holder[5];

(4) except in a liquidation, no payment may be made of sums due from the company on the shares, whether in respect of capital or otherwise[6].

Where shares are subject to the restriction in head (3) or head (4) above, an agreement to transfer any right to be issued with other shares in right of those shares, or to receive any payment on them, otherwise than in a liquidation, is void[7].

The provisions set out above are subject to any directions for the protection of third parties[8], and to the terms of any interim order[9].

1 Ie an order under the Companies Act 2006 s 794 (see PARA 456).
2 Companies Act 2006 s 797(1). As to the meaning of 'public company' see PARA 95.
3 Companies Act 2006 s 797(1)(a), (2). As to the transfer of shares see PARA 400 et seq. Head (1) in the text does not apply to an agreement to transfer the shares on the making of an order under s 800 made by virtue of s 800(3)(b) (removal of restrictions in case of court-approved transfer) (see PARA 459): s 797(2).
4 Companies Act 2006 s 797(1)(b). As to voting rights see PARA 725 et seq.
5 Companies Act 2006 s 797(1)(c). As to the issue of shares see PARAS 1234, 1281.
6 Companies Act 2006 s 797(1)(d). As to the appointment of a liquidator where a company goes into voluntary liquidation see COMPANY AND PARTNERSHIP INSOLVENCY vol 17 (2011) PARA 909.
7 Companies Act 2006 s 797(3). This does not apply to an agreement to transfer any such right on the making of an order under s 800 made by virtue of s 800(3)(b) (removal of restrictions in case of court-approved transfer) (see PARA 459): s 797(3).
8 Ie any directions under the Companies Act 2006 s 794(2) (see PARA 456) or s 799(3) (see PARA 459).
9 Companies Act 2006 s 797(4). An interim order is made under s 794(3) (see PARA 456).

458. Penalty for attempted evasion of restrictions on shares imposed by court order. Where public company shares are subject to restrictions by virtue of an order[1], a person commits an offence if he[2]:

(1) exercises or purports to exercise any right to dispose of shares that to his knowledge are for the time being subject to restrictions, or to dispose of any right to be issued with any such shares[3];

(2) votes in respect of any such shares, whether as holder or proxy, or appoints a proxy to vote in respect of them[4]; or

(3) being the holder of any such shares, fails to notify of their being subject to those restrictions a person whom he does not know to be aware of that fact but does know to be entitled, apart from the restrictions, to vote in respect of those shares whether as holder or as proxy[5]; or

(4) being the holder of any such shares, or being entitled to a right to be issued with other shares in right of them, or to receive any payment on them, otherwise than in a liquidation, enters into an agreement which is void[6].

If shares in a company are issued in contravention of the restrictions, an offence is committed by the company and by every officer of the company who is in default[7].

The provisions set out above are subject to directions for the protection of third parties[8], or any directions as to the relaxation or removal of restrictions[9], and, in the case of an interim order[10], to the terms of the order[11].

1 Ie an order under the Companies Act 2006 s 794 (see PARA 456). As to the meaning of 'public company' see PARA 95.
2 Companies Act 2006 s 798(1), (2).
3 Companies Act 2006 s 798(2)(a).
4 Companies Act 2006 s 798(2)(b).
5 Companies Act 2006 s 798(2)(c).

6 Companies Act 2006 s 798(2)(d). An agreement is void under s 797(2) or (3) (see PARA 457).
7 Companies Act 2006 s 798(3). A person guilty of such an offence is liable on conviction on indictment to a fine, and, on summary conviction, to a fine: s 798(4). In the case of liability on summary conviction the fine is one not exceeding the statutory maximum: see s 798(4). By virtue of the Legal Aid, Sentencing and Punishment of Offenders Act 2012 s 85, however, where the offence is committed on or after 12 March 2015, it is punishable by a fine of an unlimited amount. As to the statutory maximum and the powers of magistrates' courts to issue fines on summary conviction see SENTENCING vol 92 (2015) PARA 176.
8 Ie any directions under the Companies Act 2006 s 794(2) (see PARA 456).
9 Ie any directions under the Companies Act 2006 s 799 (see PARA 459) or s 800 (see PARA 459).
10 Ie an interim order under the Companies Act 2006 s 794(3) (see PARA 456).
11 Companies Act 2006 s 798(5).

459. Relaxation and removal of restrictions on shares imposed by court order. An application may be made to the court on the ground that an order directing that public company shares are to be subject to restrictions unfairly affects the rights of third parties in respect of the shares[1]. An application may be made by the company or by any person aggrieved[2]. If the court is satisfied that the application is well founded, it may, for the purpose of protecting the rights of third parties in respect of the shares, and subject to such terms as it thinks fit, direct that such acts by such persons or descriptions of persons and for such purposes as may be set out in the order do not constitute a breach of the restrictions[3].

An application may also be made to the court for an order directing that the shares cease to be subject to restrictions[4]. An application may be made by the company or by any person aggrieved[5]. The court must not make such an order unless:

(1) it is satisfied that the relevant facts about the shares have been disclosed to the company and no unfair advantage has accrued to any person as a result of the earlier failure to make that disclosure[6]; or
(2) the shares are to be transferred for valuable consideration and the court approves the transfer[7].

1 Companies Act 2006 s 799(1). As to the meaning of 'public company' see PARA 95; and As to the meaning of 'the court' see PARA 160 note 12. Such an application must be made by the issue of a CPR Pt 8 claim form (as to which see CIVIL PROCEDURE vol 11 (2015) PARAS 139, 150 et seq): see CPR PD 49A—*Applications under the Companies Acts and Related Legislation* para 5. For cases illustrating the adverse effect restrictions can have on third parties see *Re Geers Gross plc* [1988] 1 All ER 224, [1987] 1 WLR 1649, CA; *Re Lonrho plc (No 3)* [1989] BCLC 480; *Re Lonrho plc (no 2)* [1990] Ch 695, sub nom *Re Lonrho plc (No 4)* [1990] BCLC 151.

Where a genuine dispute arises as to the validity or regularity of steps taken under the Companies Act 2006 Pt 22 (ss 791–828), the law ought to afford the widest scope for persons economically affected by the taking of those steps to challenge them in court: *Eclairs Group Ltd v JKX Oil & Gas plc* [2014] EWCA Civ 640 at [37], [2014] 4 All ER 463, [2014] 2 All ER (Comm) 1018 (revsd without affecting this point sub nom *Eclairs Group Ltd v JKX Oil & Gas plc, Glengary Overseas Ltd v JKX Oil & Gas plc* [2015] UKSC 71, [2016] 1 BCLC 1, [2015] All ER (D) 20 (Dec).
2 Companies Act 2006 s 799(2).
3 Companies Act 2006 s 799(3).
4 Companies Act 2006 s 800(1).
5 Companies Act 2006 s 800(2).
6 Companies Act 2006 s 800(3)(a). Once the information to which the company is entitled is supplied, the order imposing the restrictions should be discharged; a desire to produce evidence of new failures is no ground for adjournment of the hearing or continuation of the restrictions: *Re Ricardo Group plc* [1989] BCLC 566. Cf *Re Lonrho plc* [1988] BCLC 53 (the provision empowers the court to free shares subject to a restriction but does not require the court to do so, particularly where it appears that the applicant to have the restriction lifted has not disclosed information reasonably required in relation to other shares of the company). See also *Re Ricardo Group plc (No 3)* [1989] BCLC 771 (restrictions released without disclosure of information where their continuation would prevent a take-over bid from going ahead to the prejudice of those shareholders who wanted to accept the bid).

7 Companies Act 2006 s 800(3)(b). An order made by virtue of s 800(3)(b) may continue, in whole or in part, the restrictions on issue of further shares or making of payments mentioned in s 797(1)(c), (d) (see PARA 457 heads (3)–(4)) so far as they relate to a right acquired or offer made before the transfer: s 800(4). Where any restrictions continue in force under s 800(4), an application may be made under s 800 for an order directing that the shares are to cease to be subject to those restrictions, and s 800(3) does not apply in relation to the making of such an order: s 800(5).

As to the type of circumstances requiring the maintenance of any restrictions see *Re TR Technology Investment Trust plc* [1988] BCLC 256. See also *Eclairs Group Ltd v JKX Oil & Gas plc, Glengary Overseas Ltd v JKX Oil & Gas plc* [2015] UKSC 71, [2016] 1 BCLC 1, [2015] All ER (D) 20 (Dec). In exercising its discretion whether to approve a sale, the court is entitled to take into account the refusal to disclose relevant facts: *Re Geers Gross plc* [1988] 1 All ER 224, [1987] 1 WLR 1649, CA.

460. Order for sale of shares subject to restrictions. The court may order that the public company shares subject to restrictions be sold, subject to the court's approval as to the sale[1]. An application for such an order may only be made by the company[2]. Where the court has made an order, it may make such further order relating to the sale or transfer of the shares as it thinks fit[3]. An application for a further order may be made by the company, by the person appointed by or in pursuance of the order to effect the sale, or by any person interested in the shares[4]. On making an order or a further order, the court may order that the applicant's costs be paid out of the proceeds of sale[5].

Where shares are sold in pursuance of an order of the court[6], the proceeds of the sale, less the costs of the sale, must be paid into court for the benefit of the persons who are beneficially interested in the shares[7]. A person who is beneficially interested in the shares may apply to the court for the whole or part of those proceeds to be paid to him[8]. On such an application the court must order the payment to the applicant of the whole of the proceeds of sale together with any interest on them[9], unless another person had a beneficial interest in the shares at the time of their sale, in which case the court must order the payment of such proportion of the proceeds and interest as the value of the applicant's interest in the shares bears to the total value of the shares[10]. If, however, the court has ordered[11] that the costs of an applicant are to be paid out of the proceeds of sale, the applicant is entitled to payment of his costs out of those proceeds before any person interested in the shares receives any part of those proceeds[12].

1 Companies Act 2006 s 801(1). As to the meaning of 'public company' see PARA 95. As to the meaning of 'the court' see PARA 160 note 12.
2 Companies Act 2006 s 801(2). Such an application must be made by the issue of a CPR Pt 8 claim form (as to which see CIVIL PROCEDURE vol 11 (2015) PARAS 1397, 150 et seq): CPR PD 49A—*Applications under the Companies Acts and Related Legislation* para 5.
3 Companies Act 2006 s 801(3).
4 Companies Act 2006 s 801(4).
5 Companies Act 2006 s 801(5).
6 Ie under the Companies Act 2006 s 801 (see the text and notes 1–5).
7 Companies Act 2006 s 802(1).
8 Companies Act 2006 s 802(2).
9 Companies Act 2006 s 802(3)(a).
10 See the Companies Act 2006 s 802(3)(b).
11 Ie under the Companies Act 2006 s 801(5) (see the text and note 5).
12 Companies Act 2006 s 802(4).

(iv) Requisition by Members with regard to Interests in Shares

461. Power of members to require company to act by giving notice requiring information about interests. The members of a public company[1] may require it to exercise its powers[2] to give notice requiring information about interests in shares[3].

A company is required to do so once it has received requests, to the same effect, from members of the company holding at least 10 per cent of such of the paid-up capital[4] of the company as carries a right to vote at general meetings of the company[5] (excluding any voting rights attached to any shares in the company held as treasury shares)[6].

A request may be in hard copy form or in electronic form[7]. It must:

(1) state that the company is requested to exercise its powers to give notice requiring information about interests in shares[8];
(2) specify the manner in which the company is requested to act; and
(3) give reasonable grounds for requiring the company to exercise those powers in the manner specified[9].

The request must be authenticated by the person or persons making it[10].

A company that is required[11] to exercise its powers to give notice requiring information about interests in shares must exercise those powers in the manner specified in the requests[12]. If default is made in complying with this requirement, an offence is committed by every officer of the company who is in default[13].

1 As to the meaning of 'public company' see PARA 95. As to who qualifies as a member of a company see PARA 323.
2 Ie under the Companies Act 2006 s 793 (see PARA 453).
3 Companies Act 2006 s 803(1).
4 As to the meaning of 'paid up capital' see PARA 1237.
5 As to meetings of members see PARA 701 et seq. As to voting at meetings see PARA 725 et seq.
6 Companies Act 2006 s 803(2). As to treasury shares see PARA 1437.
7 Companies Act 2006 s 803(3)(a). As to documents or information sent or supplied in hard copy form see PARA 750; and as to documents or information sent or supplied in electronic form (or by electronic means) see PARA 751.
8 See note 2.
9 Companies Act 2006 s 803(3)(b).
10 Companies Act 2006 s 803(3)(c).
11 Ie under the Companies Act 2006 s 803 (see the text and notes 1–10).
12 Companies Act 2006 s 804(1).
13 Companies Act 2006 s 804(2). As to the meaning of 'officer who is in default' see PARA 316. As to the meaning of 'officer' generally see PARA 679. A person guilty of such an offence is liable on conviction on indictment to a fine, and on summary conviction to a fine: s 804(3). In the case of liability on summary conviction the fine is one not exceeding the statutory maximum: see s 804(3). By virtue of the Legal Aid, Sentencing and Punishment of Offenders Act 2012 s 85, however, where the offence is committed on or after 12 March 2015, it is punishable by a fine of an unlimited amount. As to the statutory maximum and the powers of magistrates' courts to issue fines on summary conviction see SENTENCING vol 92 (2015) PARA 176.

462. Report by company to members on outcome of investigation. On the conclusion of an investigation carried out by a public company[1] in pursuance of a requirement of the members[2] the company must cause a report of the information received in pursuance of the investigation to be prepared[3]. The report must be made available for inspection within a reasonable period, of not more than 15 days[4], after the conclusion of the investigation[5].

Where a company undertakes an investigation and the investigation is not concluded within three months after the date on which the company became subject to the requirement, the company must cause to be prepared in respect of that period, and in respect of each succeeding period of three months ending before the conclusion of the investigation, an interim report of the information received during that period in pursuance of the investigation[6]. Each such report must be made available for inspection within a reasonable period, of not more than 15 days, after the end of the period to which it relates[7].

The reports must be retained by the company for at least six years from the date on which they are first made available for inspection and must be kept available for inspection during that time at the company's registered office[8], or at the company's alternative inspection location[9]. The company must give notice to the registrar of companies[10] of the place at which the reports are kept available for inspection and of any change in that place, unless they have at all times been kept at the company's registered office[11]. The company must within three days of making any report prepared available for inspection, notify the members who made the requests[12] where the report is so available[13].

If default is made in complying with the above provisions[14], an offence is committed by every officer of the company who is in default[15].

Any report prepared[16] must be open to inspection by any person without charge[17]. Any person is entitled, on request and on payment of such fee as may be prescribed[18], to be provided with a copy of any such report or any part of it[19]. The copy must be provided within ten days after the request is received by the company[20].

In the case of any refusal of an inspection or default in providing a copy of a report, the court may by order compel an immediate inspection or, as the case may be, direct that the copy required be sent to the person requiring it[21].

1 As to the meaning of 'public company' see PARA 95.

2 Ie under the Companies Act 2006 s 803 (see PARA 461). As to who qualifies as a member of a company see PARA 323.

3 Companies Act 2006 s 805(1). Information in respect of which a company is for the time being entitled to any exemption conferred by regulations under s 409(3) (information about related undertakings to be given in notes to accounts: exemption where disclosure harmful to company's business) (see PARA 834) must not be included in a report under s 805: s 826(1)(a). Where any such information is omitted from a report under s 805, that fact must be stated in the report: s 826(2).

Where the registrar changes the address of a company's registered office under the Companies Act 2006 s 1097A(7) or the Companies (Address of Registered Office) Regulations 2016, SI 2016/423 (see PARA 160), the company's duties under the Companies Act 2006 s 805 are suspended for a period of 28 days beginning on the day the address was changed: see the Companies (Address of Registered Office) Regulations 2016, SI 2016/423, reg 11; and PARA 160.

4 Where the period allowed by any provision of the Companies Act 2006 Pt 22 (ss 791–828) for fulfilling an obligation is expressed as a number of days, any day that is not a working day is to be disregarded in reckoning that period: s 827. As to the meaning of 'working day' see PARA 140 note 16.

5 Companies Act 2006 s 805(1). For the purposes of s 805, an investigation carried out by a company in pursuance of a requirement under s 803 (see PARA 461) is concluded when the company has made all such inquiries as are necessary or expedient for the purposes of the requirement and in the case of each such inquiry either a response has been received by the company, or the time allowed for a response has elapsed: s 805(7).

6 Companies Act 2006 s 805(2).

7 Companies Act 2006 s 805(3).

8 As to a company's registered office see PARA 124.

9 Companies Act 2006 ss 805(4), 1136(2); Companies (Company Records) Regulations 2008, SI 2008/3006, reg 3. As to inspection of company records see PARA 748.

10 As to the registrar of companies see PARA 126 et seq.

11 Companies Act 2006 s 805(5). If default is made for 14 days in complying with s 805(5) (notice to registrar of place at which reports made available for inspection) an offence is committed by the company, and by every officer of the company who is in default: s 806(1). A person guilty of such an offence is liable on summary conviction to a fine not exceeding level 3 on the standard scale and, for continued contravention, a daily default fine not exceeding one-tenth of level 3 on the standard scale: s 806(2). As to the meaning of 'officer who is in default' see PARA 316. As to the meaning of 'officer' generally see PARA 679; As to the standard scale and the powers of magistrates' courts to issue fines on summary conviction see SENTENCING vol 92 (2015) PARA 176; and as to the meaning of 'daily default fine' see PARA 1816.

12 Ie under the Companies Act 2006 s 803 (see PARA 461).

13 Companies Act 2006 s 805(6).

14 Ie any provision of the Companies Act 2006 s 805 apart from s 805(5) (see note 11).

15 Companies Act 2006 s 806(3). A person guilty of an offence under s 806(3) is liable on conviction on indictment, to a fine, and on summary conviction, to a fine: s 806(4). In the case of liability on summary conviction the fine is one not exceeding the statutory maximum: see s 806(4). By virtue of the Legal Aid, Sentencing and Punishment of Offenders Act 2012 s 85, however, where the offence is committed on or after 12 March 2015, it is punishable by a fine of an unlimited amount. As to the statutory maximum and the powers of magistrates' courts to issue fines on summary conviction see SENTENCING vol 92 (2015) PARA 176.

16 Ie under the Companies Act 2006 s 805 (see the text and notes 1–13).

17 Companies Act 2006 s 807(1). If an inspection required under s 807(1) is refused, or default is made in complying with s 807(2) (see the text and notes 18–20), an offence is committed by the company, and every officer of the company who is in default: s 807(3). A person guilty of an offence under s 807 is liable on summary conviction to a fine not exceeding level 3 on the standard scale and, for continued contravention, a daily default fine not exceeding one-tenth of level 3 on the standard scale: s 807(4).

18 As to the prescribed fee see the Companies (Fees for Inspection and Copying of Company Records) Regulations 2007, SI 2007/2612, reg 4.

19 Companies Act 2006 s 807(2). See also notes 17–18.

20 Companies Act 2006 s 807(2). See also note 17.

21 Companies Act 2006 s 807(5). As to the meaning of 'the court' see PARA 160 note 12.

(v) Register of Interests Disclosed

463. Register of interests disclosed following notice requiring information. A public company[1] must keep a register of information received by it in pursuance of a notice requiring information about interests in company's shares[2]. A company which receives any such information must, within three days[3] of the receipt, enter in the register:

(1) the fact that the requirement was imposed and the date on which it was imposed; and

(2) the information received in pursuance of the requirement[4].

The information must be entered against the name of the present holder of the shares in question or, if there is no present holder or the present holder is not known, against the name of the person holding the interest[5]. The register must be made up so that the entries against the names entered in it appear in chronological order[6]. If default is made in complying with these requirements, an offence is committed by the company, and by every officer[7] of the company who is in default[8].

The company is not by virtue of anything done for the purposes of the provisions set out above affected with notice of, or put upon inquiry as to, the rights of any person in relation to any shares[9].

Unless the register[10] is kept in such a form as itself to constitute an index, the company must keep an index of the names entered in it[11]. The company must make any necessary entry or alteration in the index within ten days after the date on which any entry or alteration is made in the register[12]. The index must contain, in respect of each name, a sufficient indication to enable the information entered against it to be readily found[13]. The index must be at all times kept available for inspection at the same place as the register[14]. If default is made in complying with these requirements, an offence is committed by the company, and by every officer of the company who is in default[15].

If a company ceases to be a public company, it must continue to keep any register and any associated index, until the end of the period of six years after it ceased to be such a company[16]. If default is made in complying with this requirement, an offence is committed by the company, and by every officer of the company who is in default[17].

1 As to the meaning of 'public company' see PARA 95.
2 Companies Act 2006 s 808(1). Information is received in pursuance of a requirement imposed under s 793 (see PARA 453).
3 Where the period allowed by any provision of the Companies Act 2006 Pt 22 (ss 791–828) for fulfilling an obligation is expressed as a number of days, any day that is not a working day is to be disregarded in reckoning that period: s 827. As to the meaning of 'working day' see PARA 140 note 16.
4 Companies Act 2006 s 808(2).
5 Companies Act 2006 s 808(3).
6 Companies Act 2006 s 808(4).
7 As to the meaning of 'officer' see PARA 679.
8 Companies Act 2006 s 808(5). A person guilty of an offence under s 808 is liable on summary conviction to a fine not exceeding level 3 on the standard scale and, for continued contravention, a daily default fine not exceeding one-tenth of level 3 on the standard scale: s 808(6). As to the meaning of 'officer who is in default' see PARA 316. As to the meaning of 'officer' generally see PARA 679. As to the meaning of 'daily default fine' see PARA 1816. As to the standard scale and the powers of magistrates' courts to issue fines on summary conviction see SENTENCING vol 92 (2015) PARA 176.
9 Companies Act 2006 s 808(7).
10 Ie the register kept under the Companies Act 2006 s 808 (see the text and notes 1–9).
11 Companies Act 2006 s 810(1).
12 Companies Act 2006 s 810(2).
13 Companies Act 2006 s 810(3).
14 Companies Act 2006 s 810(4).
15 Companies Act 2006 s 810(5). A person guilty of an offence under s 810 is liable on summary conviction to a fine not exceeding level 3 on the standard scale and, for continued contravention, a daily default fine not exceeding one-tenth of level 3 on the standard scale: s 810(6).
16 Companies Act 2006 s 819(1).
17 Companies Act 2006 s 819(2). A person guilty of an offence under s 819 is liable on summary conviction to a fine not exceeding level 3 on the standard scale and, for continued contravention, a daily default fine not exceeding one-tenth of level 3 on the standard scale: s 819(3).

464. Rights to inspect and require copy of entries. The register of interests disclosed[1] must be kept available for inspection at the company's registered office[2], or at the company's alternative inspection location[3]. A public company[4] must give notice to the registrar of companies[5] of the place where the register is kept available for inspection and of any change in that place[6]. No such notice is required if the register has at all times been kept available for inspection at the company's registered office[7]. If default is made in complying with the requirement to keep the register available for inspection, or a company makes default for 14 days[8] in giving notice to the registrar, an offence is committed by the company, and by every officer[9] of the company who is in default[10].

The register of interests disclosed, and any associated index, must be open to inspection by any person without charge[11]. Any person is entitled, on request and on payment of such fee as may be prescribed[12], to be provided with a copy of any entry in the register[13]. A person seeking to exercise either of these rights must make a request to the company to that effect[14], containing the following information:

(1) in the case of an individual, his name and address;
(2) in the case of an organisation, the name and address of an individual responsible for making the request on behalf of the organisation;
(3) the purpose for which the information is to be used; and
(4) whether the information will be disclosed to any other person, and if so
 (a) where that person is an individual, his name and address;

(b) where that person is an organisation, the name and address of an individual responsible for receiving the information on its behalf; and

(c) the purpose for which the information is to be used by that person[15].

Where a company receives a request[16] to inspect or require a copy of the register, it must comply with the request if it is satisfied that it is made for a proper purpose, or refuse the request if it is not so satisfied[17]. If the company refuses the request, it must inform the person making the request, stating the reason why it is not satisfied[18]. A person whose request is refused may apply to the court[19]. If an application is made to the court, the person who made the request must notify the company, and the company must use its best endeavours to notify any persons whose details would be disclosed if the company were required to comply with the request[20]. If the court is not satisfied that the inspection or copy is sought for a proper purpose, it must direct the company not to comply with the request[21]. If the court makes such a direction and it appears to the court that the company is or may be subject to other requests made for a similar purpose, whether made by the same person or different persons, it may direct that the company is not to comply with any such request[22]. If the court does not direct the company not to comply with the request, the company must comply with the request immediately upon the court giving its decision or, as the case may be, the proceedings being discontinued[23].

If an inspection of the register is refused or default is made in providing a copy required, otherwise than in accordance with the above provisions[24], an offence is committed by the company, and by every officer of the company who is in default[25]. In the case of any such refusal or default the court may by order compel an immediate inspection or, as the case may be, direct that the copy required be sent to the person requesting it[26].

It is an offence for a person knowingly or recklessly to make, in a request to inspect or require a copy of the register of interests, a statement that is misleading, false or deceptive in a material particular[27]. It is also an offence for a person in possession of information obtained by exercise of the right to inspect or require a copy of the register to do anything that results in the information being disclosed to another person, or to fail to do anything with the result that the information is disclosed to another person, knowing, or having reason to suspect, that person may use the information for a purpose that is not a proper purpose[28].

1 Ie the register kept under the Companies Act 2006 s 808 (see PARA 463).
2 As to a company's registered office see PARA 124.
3 Companies Act 2006 ss 809(1), 1136(2); Companies (Company Records) Regulations 2008, SI 2008/3006, reg 3. As to inspection of company records see PARA 748.

Where the registrar changes the address of a company's registered office under the Companies Act 2006 s 1097A(7) or the Companies (Address of Registered Office) Regulations 2016, SI 2016/423 (see PARA 160), the company's duties under the Companies Act 2006 s 809 are suspended for a period of 28 days beginning on the day the address was changed: see the Companies (Address of Registered Office) Regulations 2016, SI 2016/423, reg 11; and PARA 160.
4 As to the meaning of 'public company' see PARA 95.
5 As to the registrar see PARA 126 et seq.
6 Companies Act 2006 s 809(2).
7 Companies Act 2006 s 809(3).
8 Where the period allowed by any provision of the Companies Act 2006 Pt 22 (ss 791–828) for fulfilling an obligation is expressed as a number of days, any day that is not a working day is to be disregarded in reckoning that period: s 827. As to the meaning of 'working day' see PARA 140 note 16.

9 As to the meaning of 'officer' see PARA 679.
10 Companies Act 2006 s 809(4). A person guilty of an offence under s 809 is liable on summary conviction to a fine not exceeding level 3 on the standard scale and, for continued contravention, a daily default fine not exceeding one-tenth of level 3 on the standard scale: s 809(5). As to the meaning of 'officer who is in default' see PARA 316. As to the meaning of 'officer' generally see PARA 679. As to the standard scale and the powers of magistrates' courts to issue fines on summary conviction see SENTENCING vol 92 (2015) PARA 176; and as to the meaning of 'daily default fine' see PARA 1816.
11 Companies Act 2006 s 811(1). Information in respect of which a company is for the time being entitled to any exemption conferred by regulations under s 409(3) (information about related undertakings to be given in notes to accounts: exemption where disclosure harmful to company's business) (see PARA 834) must not be made available under s 811: s 826(1)(b).
12 As to the prescribed fee see the Companies (Fees for Inspection and Copying of Company Records) Regulations 2007, SI 2007/2612, reg 3.
13 Companies Act 2006 s 811(2).
14 Companies Act 2006 s 811(3).
15 Companies Act 2006 s 811(4).
16 Ie a request under the Companies Act 2006 s 811 (see the text and notes 11–15).
17 Companies Act 2006 s 812(1). Compare the situation under s 117, by virtue of which, where a company receives a request to inspect the company's register of members and/or the index of members' names, a company must within five working days either comply with the request, or apply to the court: see PARA 350.
18 Companies Act 2006 s 812(2).
19 Companies Act 2006 s 812(3). As to the meaning of 'the court' see PARA 160 note 12.
20 Companies Act 2006 s 812(4).
21 Companies Act 2006 s 812(5).
22 Companies Act 2006 s 812(6). The order must contain such provision as appears to the court appropriate to identify the requests to which it applies: s 812(6).
23 Companies Act 2006 s 812(7).
24 Ie otherwise than in accordance with the Companies Act 2006 s 812: see the text and notes 16–23.
25 Companies Act 2006 s 813(1) (amended by the Small Business, Enterprise and Employment Act 2015 s 83). A person guilty of an offence under the Companies Act 2006 s 813 is liable on summary conviction to a fine not exceeding level 3 on the standard scale and, for continued contravention, a daily default fine not exceeding one-tenth of level 3 on the standard scale: s 813(2).
26 Companies Act 2006 s 813(3).
27 Companies Act 2006 s 814(1). A person guilty of an offence under s 814 is liable on conviction on indictment, to imprisonment for a term not exceeding two years or a fine, or to both, or on summary conviction, to imprisonment for a term not exceeding 12 months or to a fine, or to both: s 814(3). In the case of liability on summary conviction the fine is one not exceeding the statutory maximum: see s 814(3). By virtue of the Legal Aid, Sentencing and Punishment of Offenders Act 2012 s 85, however, where the offence is committed on or after 12 March 2015, it is punishable by a fine of an unlimited amount. As to the statutory maximum and the powers of magistrates' courts to issue fines on summary conviction see SENTENCING vol 92 (2015) PARA 176. In relation to an offence committed before the coming into force of the Criminal Justice Act 2003 s 154(1) (not yet in force), the maximum term of imprisonment on summary conviction is six months: see the Companies Act 2006 s 1131; and PARA 1818.
28 Companies Act 2006 s 814(2). As to the penalty see note 27.

465. Entries not to be removed from the register of interests disclosed or adjusted except in accordance with statute. Entries in the register of interests disclosed[1] must not be deleted[2] unless:

(1) more than six years have elapsed since the entry was made[3]; or
(2) there is an incorrect entry relating to a third party[4].

If an entry is wrongly deleted, the company must restore it as soon as reasonably practicable[5]. If default is made in complying with these requirements, an offence is committed by the company, and by every officer[6] of the company who is in default[7].

If a person who is identified in the register of interests disclosed as being a party to a share acquisition agreement[8] ceases to be a party to the agreement, he may apply to the company for the inclusion of that information in the register[9]. If the company is satisfied that he has ceased to be a party to the agreement, it must record that information, if not already recorded, in every place where his name appears in the register as a party to the agreement[10]. If an application is refused, otherwise than on the ground that the information has already been recorded, the applicant may apply to the court for an order directing the company to include the information in question in the register, and the court may make such an order if it thinks fit[11].

1 Ie the register kept under the Companies Act 2006 s 808 (see PARA 463).
2 Companies Act 2006 s 815(1).
3 Companies Act 2006 s 816.
4 Where, in pursuance of an obligation imposed by a notice under the Companies Act 2006 s 793 (notice requiring information about interests in company's shares) (see PARA 453), a person gives to a company the name and address of another person as being interested in shares in the company, that other person may apply to the company for the removal of the entry from the register: s 817(1), (2). If the company is satisfied that the information in pursuance of which the entry was made is incorrect, it must remove the entry: s 817(3). If an application is refused, the applicant may apply to the court for an order directing the company to remove the entry in question from the register; and the court may make such an order if it thinks fit: s 817(4). As to the meaning of 'the court' see PARA 160 note 12.
5 Companies Act 2006 s 815(2).
6 As to the meaning of 'officer' see PARA 679.
7 Companies Act 2006 s 815(3). As to the meaning of 'officer who is in default' see PARA 316. A person guilty of an offence under s 815 is liable on summary conviction to a fine not exceeding level 3 on the standard scale and, for continued contravention of the duty to restore a entry wrongly deleted, a daily default fine not exceeding one-tenth of level 3 on the standard scale: s 815(4). As to the standard scale and the powers of magistrates' courts to issue fines on summary conviction see SENTENCING vol 92 (2015) PARA 176; and as to the meaning of 'daily default fine' see PARA 1816
8 Ie an agreement to which the Companies Act 2006 s 824 applies (see PARA 451).
9 Companies Act 2006 s 818(1).
10 Companies Act 2006 s 818(2).
11 Companies Act 2006 s 818(3).

(12) INFORMATION ABOUT PEOPLE WITH SIGNIFICANT CONTROL OVER COMPANY

(i) Companies to which Part 21A of the Companies Act 2006 applies

466. Outline of the provisions concerning people with significant control over certain companies. As from 6 April 2016 for most purposes[1], Part 21A of the Companies Act 2006[2]:

(1) requires certain companies[3] to keep a register, referred to as a register of people with significant control over the company, and to make the register available to the public[4];
(2) imposes duties on companies to gather information, and on others to supply information, to enable companies to keep the required register[5];
(3) makes provision for excluding certain material from the information available to the public[6];
(4) gives private companies[7] the option of using an alternative method of record-keeping[8]; and
(5) explains some key terms, including what it means to have 'significant control' over a company[9].

1 6 April 2016 was the day appointed for the coming into force of the Small Business, Enterprise and Employment Act 2015 s 81, Sch 3 (which add the Companies Act 2006 Pt 21A (ss 790A–790ZG)) except to the extent that they had already been commenced, and subject to the Small Business,

Enterprise and Employment Act 2015 (Commencement No 3) Regulations 2015, SI 2015/2029, reg 5: see reg 4. The Companies Act 2006 s 790M(9)(c) (see PARA 480) and ss 790W–790ZE (see PARA 484 et seq) (which are set out in the Small Business, Enterprise and Employment Act 2015 Sch 3 Pt 1) came into force on 30 June 2016, as did the Small Business, Enterprise and Employment Act 2015 Sch 3 Pt 2 paras 4, 5, 7: Small Business, Enterprise and Employment Act 2015 (Commencement No 3) Regulations 2015, SI 2015/2029, reg 4. 26 May 2015 was the day appointed for the coming into force of the Small Business, Enterprise and Employment Act 2015 s 81, Sch 3 for the purposes of enabling the exercise of any power to make provision by regulations, rules or order made by statutory instrument or to prepare and issue guidance: see the Small Business, Enterprise and Employment Act 2015 (Commencement No 1) Regulations 2015, SI 2015/1329, reg 3(a).

2 Ie the Companies Act 2006 Pt 21A (ss 790A–790ZG) (added by the Small Business, Enterprise and Employment Act 2015 Sch 3 Pt 1 para 1): see the text and notes 3–8; and PARA 467 et seq.

3 The Companies Act 2006 Pt 21A applies to companies other than the following (s 790B(1) (as added: see note 2)), ie:

(1) DTR5 issuers; and

(2) companies of any description specified by the Secretary of State by regulations.

A 'DTR5 issuer' is an issuer to which Chapter 5 of the Disclosure Rules and Transparency Rules sourcebook made by the Financial Conduct Authority (as amended or replaced from time to time) applies: Companies Act 2006 s 790B(3) (as so added). As to the Disclosure Rules and Transparency Rules see PARA 446; and as to the rules made by the Financial Conduct Authority generally see FINANCIAL SERVICES REGULATION vol 50A (2016) PARA 584. As to the meaning of 'company' under the Companies Acts see PARA 21.

In deciding whether to specify a description of company, the Secretary of State is to have regard to the extent to which companies of that description are bound by disclosure and transparency rules, in the United Kingdom or elsewhere, broadly similar to the ones applying to DTR5 issuers: Companies Act 2006 s 790B(2) (as so added). Regulations under s 790B are subject to affirmative resolution procedure (affirmative resolution procedure (ie the regulations must not be made unless a draft of the statutory instrument containing them has been laid before Parliament and approved by a resolution of each House of Parliament): see ss 790B(4), 1290 (s 790B(4) as so added). As to the Secretary of State see PARA 6; and as to the meaning of 'United Kingdom' see PARA 1 note 5.

A company is specified for the purpose of 790B(1)(b) (see head (2) above) if it has voting shares admitted to trading on a regulated market in an EEA state other than the United Kingdom, or on a market listed in the Register of People with Significant Control Regulations 2016, SI 2016/339, Sch 1: reg 3. For these purposes, 'voting shares' means shares carrying voting rights; and 'voting rights' means rights to vote at general meetings of the company or legal entity in question, including rights that arise only in certain circumstances, and in relation to a legal entity that does not have general meetings at which matters are decided by the exercise of voting rights, a reference to voting rights is to be read as a reference to rights in relation to the entity that are equivalent to those of a person entitled to exercise voting rights in a company: reg 2. As to the meaning of 'regulated market' see para 335 note 11; and as to the meaning of 'EEA state' see PARA 26 note 5.

4 See the Companies Act 2006 ss 790A(c), 790M–790V (as added; see note 2); and PARA 480 et seq.

5 See the Companies Act 2006 ss 790A(b), 790D–790L (as added: see note 2); and PARA 468 et seq.

6 See the Companies Act 2006 ss 790A(e), 790ZF–790ZG (as added: see note 2); and PARAS 491–492.

7 As to the meaning of 'private company' see PARA 95.

8 See the Companies Act 2006 ss 790A(d), 790W–790ZE (added: see note 2); and PARA 484 et seq. As to the power to extend this option to public companies see PARA 484. As to the meaning of 'public company' see PARA 95.

9 See the Companies Act 2006 ss 790A(a), 790B–790C (as added: see note 2); note 3; and PARA 467.

467. Persons with, or having, 'significant control' over a company; registrable and non-registrable persons and legal entities. As from 6 April 2016[1], the following provisions have effect.

References[2] to a person with, or having, 'significant control' over a company are to an individual[3] who meets one or more of the specified conditions[4] in relation to the company[5]. The conditions at least one of which must be met by an individual ('X') in relation to a company ('company Y') in order for the individual to be a person with 'significant control' over the company are as follows[6]:

(1) that X holds, directly or indirectly, more than 25 per cent of the shares in company Y[7];
(2) that X holds, directly or indirectly, more than 25 per cent of the voting rights in company Y[8];
(3) that X holds the right, directly or indirectly, to appoint or remove a majority of the board of directors of company Y[9];
(4) that X has the right to exercise, or actually exercises, significant influence or control over company Y[10]; and
(5) that:
   (a) the trustees of a trust or the members of a firm that, under the law by which it is governed, is not a legal person meet any of the other specified conditions, in their capacity as such, in relation to company Y, or would do so if they were individuals; and
   (b) X has the right to exercise, or actually exercises, significant influence or control over the activities of that trust or firm[11].

For these purposes[12]:
(i) if two or more persons each hold a share or right jointly, each of them is treated as holding that share or right[13];
(ii) if shares or rights held by a person and shares or rights held by another person are the subject of a joint arrangement[14] between those persons, each of them is treated as holding the combined shares or rights of both of them[15].

Individuals with significant control over a company are either 'registrable' or 'non-registrable' in relation to the company[16]. They are 'non-registrable' if they do not hold any interest in the company[17] except through one or more other legal entities[18] over each of which they have significant control and which are, or at least one of which is, a 'relevant legal entity'[19] in relation to the company as respects certain shares or rights in the company which they hold indirectly[20]. Otherwise, they are 'registrable'[21]. References to a 'registrable person' in relation to a company are to an individual with significant control over the company who is registrable in relation to that company[22].

A relevant legal entity is either 'registrable' or 'non-registrable' in relation to a company[23]. It is 'non-registrable' if it does not hold any interest in the company except through one or more other legal entities over each of which it has significant control and which are, or at least one of which is, also a relevant legal entity in relation to the company as respects certain shares or rights in the company which it holds indirectly[24]. Otherwise, it is 'registrable'[25]. References to a 'registrable relevant legal entity' in relation to a company are to a relevant legal entity which is registrable in relation to that company[26].

1 See PARA 466 note 1.

2 Ie references in the Companies Act 2006 Pt 21A (ss 790A–790ZG) (added by the Small Business, Enterprise and Employment Act 2015 Sch 3 Pt 1 para 1): see the text and notes 3–26; and PARAS 466, 468 et seq.

3 Subject to express provision in the Companies Act 2006 Pt 21A and to any modification prescribed by regulations under s 790C(12), Pt 21A is to be read and have effect as if each of the following were an individual, even if they are legal persons under the laws by which they are governed (s 790C(12) (as added: see note 2)):
   (1) a corporation sole;
   (2) a government or government department of a country or territory or a part of a country or territory;
   (3) an international organisation whose members include two or more countries or territories (or their governments);
   (4) a local authority or local government body in the United Kingdom or elsewhere.

The following modification is prescribed for the purpose of section 790C(12): Register of People with Significant Control Regulations 2016, SI 2016/339, reg 5(1). The Companies Act 2006 s 790M(2)–(6), (10) (see PARA 480) are not to be read and do not have effect as if a person within s 790C(12) were an individual: Register of People with Significant Control Regulations 2016, SI 2016/339, reg 5(2).

Subject to the Companies Act 2006 s 790C(13) (see note 19), regulations under s 790C are subject to negative resolution procedure (ie the statutory instrument containing the regulations is subject to annulment in pursuance of a resolution of either House of Parliament): ss 790C(14), 1289 (s 790C(14) as so added). As to the making of regulations under the Companies Act 2006 generally see ss 1288–1292.

4 The 'specified conditions' are those specified in the Companies Act 2006 Sch 1A Pt 1 (paras 1–6) (see the text and notes 6–11): s 790C(3) (as added: see note 2).

An individual does not meet the specified condition in the Companies Act 2006 Sch 1A para 2, para 3 or para 4 (see heads (1)–(3) in the text) in relation to a company by virtue only of being a limited partner, or by virtue only of, directly or indirectly, holding shares, or holding a right, in or in relation to a limited partner which (in its capacity as such) would meet the condition if it were an individual: Sch 1A para 25(1), (2) (as added: see note 6). This does not, however, apply for the purposes of determining whether the requirement set out in paragraph (a) of the specified condition in Sch 1A para 6 (see head (5)(a) in the text) is met: Sch 1A para 25(3) (as so added). For these purposes, 'limited partner' means a limited partner in a limited partnership registered under the Limited Partnerships Act 1907 (other than one who takes part in the management of the partnership business), or a foreign limited partner; and 'foreign limited partner' means an individual who participates in arrangements established under the law of a country or territory outside the United Kingdom, and has the characteristics prescribed by regulations made by the Secretary of State: Sch 1A para 25(4), (5) (as so added). Such regulations may, in particular, prescribe characteristics by reference to the nature of arrangements and the nature of an individual's participation in the arrangements: Sch 1A para 25(7) (as so added). Such regulations are subject to affirmative resolution procedure (ie the regulations must not be made unless a draft of the statutory instrument containing them has been laid before Parliament and approved by a resolution of each House of Parliament: see s 1290): Sch 1A para 25(8) (as so added). The characteristics prescribed for the purposes of Sch 1A para 25(5)(b) are that the individual either participates in a foreign limited partnership as a limited liability participant or, directly or indirectly, holds shares or a right in or in relation to a legal entity which participates in a foreign limited partnership as a limited liability participant: Register of People with Significant Control Regulations 2016, SI 2016/339, reg 8(1). For these purposes, a 'foreign limited partnership' is an arrangement which is established under the law of a country or territory outside the United Kingdom, consists of at least one person who has unlimited liability for the debts and obligations of the arrangement and consists of at least one person who has no, or limited, liability for the debts and obligations of the arrangement for so long as that person does not take part in the management of the arrangement's business (reg 8(2)(a)); and a 'limited liability participant' is a person who has no, or limited, liability for the debts and obligations of the foreign limited partnership for so long as that person does not take part in the management of the foreign limited partnership's business, and does not take part in the management of the foreign limited partnership's business (reg 8(2)(b)).

The Secretary of State may by regulations amend Sch 1A for a permitted purpose: Sch 1A para 26(1) (as so added). The permitted purposes are as follows (Sch 1A para 26(2) (as so added)):

(1) to replace any or all references in Sch 1A to a percentage figure with references to some other (larger or smaller) percentage figure;

(2) to change or supplement the specified conditions in Sch 1A Pt 1 so as to include circumstances (for example, circumstances involving more complex structures) that give individuals a level of control over company Y broadly similar to the level of control given by the other specified conditions;

(3) in consequence of any provision made by virtue of head (2) above, to change or supplement Sch 1A Pt 2 (paras 7–9) so that circumstances specified therein in which a person is to be regarded as holding an interest in a company correspond to any of the specified conditions, or would do so but for the extent of the interest.

Regulations under Sch 1A para 26 are subject to affirmative resolution procedure: Sch 1A para 26(3) (as so added).

5 Companies Act 2006 s 790C(1), (2) (as added: see note 2). As to the meaning of 'company' under the Companies Acts see PARA 21. As to the companies to which these provisions apply see PARA 466.

6 Companies Act 2006 Sch 1A para 1 (Sch 1A added by the Small Business, Enterprise and Employment Act 2015 Sch 3 Pt 1 para 2). See also note 4.

7 Companies Act 2006 Sch 1A para 2 (as added: see note 6). See also note 4. In relation to a legal entity that has a share capital, a reference to holding 'more than 25% of the shares' in that entity is to holding shares comprised in the issued share capital of that entity of a nominal value exceeding (in aggregate) 25% of that share capital: Sch 1A para 13(1) (as added: see note 6). In relation to a legal entity that does not have a share capital, a reference to holding shares in that entity is to holding a right to share in the capital or, as the case may be, profits of that entity; and a reference to holding 'more than 25% of the shares' in that entity is to holding a right or rights to share in more than 25% of the capital or, as the case may be, profits of that entity: Sch 1A para 13(2) (as so added). As to the meaning of 'legal entity' see note 18.

A person holds a share 'indirectly' if the person has a majority stake in a legal entity and that entity either holds the share in question, or is part of a chain of legal entities each of which (other than the last) has a majority stake in the entity immediately below it in the chain, and the last of which holds the share: Sch 1A para 18(1) (as so added). For these purposes, A has a 'majority stake' in B if:

(1) A holds a majority of the voting rights in B (Sch 1A para 18(3)(a) (as so added));
(2) A is a member of B and has the right to appoint or remove a majority of the board of directors of B (Sch 1A para 18(3)(b) (as so added));
(3) A is a member of B and controls alone, pursuant to an agreement with other shareholders or members, a majority of the voting rights in B (Sch 1A para 18(3)(c) (as so added)); or
(4) A has the right to exercise, or actually exercises, dominant influence or control over B (Sch 1A para 18(3)(d) (as so added)).

A share held by a person as nominee for another is to be treated for the purposes of Sch 1A as held by the other (and not by the nominee): Sch 1A para 19 (as so added).

8 Companies Act 2006 Sch 1A para 3 (as added: see note 6). See also note 4. A reference to the voting rights in a legal entity is to the rights conferred on shareholders in respect of their shares (or, in the case of an entity not having a share capital, on members) to vote at general meetings of the entity on all or substantially all matters: Sch 1A para 14(1) (as so added). In relation to a legal entity that does not have general meetings at which matters are decided by the exercise of voting rights, a reference to exercising voting rights in the entity is to be read as a reference to exercising rights in relation to the entity that are equivalent to those of a person entitled to exercise voting rights in a company; and a reference to exercising more than 25% of the voting rights in the entity is to be read as a reference to exercising the right under the constitution of the entity to block changes to the overall policy of the entity or to the terms of its constitution: Sch 1A para 14(2) (as so added). In applying Sch 1A, the voting rights in a legal entity are to be reduced by any rights held by the entity itself: Sch 1A para 15 (as so added).

A person holds a right 'indirectly' if the person has a majority stake in a legal entity and that entity either holds that right, or is part of a chain of legal entities each of which (other than the last) has a majority stake in the entity immediately below it in the chain, and the last of which holds that right: Sch 1A para 18(2) (as so added). As to holding a majority stake see note 7.

Where a person controls a right, the right is to be treated for the purposes of Sch 1A as held by that person (and not by the person who in fact holds the right, unless that person also controls it): Sch 1A para 20(1) (as so added). A person 'controls' a right if, by virtue of any arrangement between that person and others, the right is exercisable only by that person, in accordance with that person's directions or instructions, or with that person's consent or concurrence: Sch 1A para 20(2) (as so added). As to the meaning of 'arrangement' see note 14.

Rights that are exercisable only in certain circumstances are to be taken into account only when the circumstances have arisen, and for so long as they continue to obtain, or when the circumstances are within the control of the person having the rights: Sch 1A para 22(1) (as so added). But rights that are exercisable by an administrator or by creditors while a legal entity is in relevant insolvency proceedings are not to be taken into account even while the entity is in those proceedings: Sch 1A para 22(2) (as so added). 'Relevant insolvency proceedings' means administration within the meaning of the Insolvency Act 1986, administration within the meaning of the Insolvency (Northern Ireland) Order 1989, SI 1989/2405 (NI 19), or proceedings under the insolvency law of another country or territory during which an entity's assets and affairs are subject to the control or supervision of a third party or creditor: Companies Act 2006 Sch 1A para 22(3) (as so added). Rights that are normally exercisable but are temporarily incapable of exercise are to continue to be taken into account: Sch 1A para 22(4) (as so added).

Rights attached to shares held by way of security provided by a person are to be treated for the purposes of Sch 1A as held by that person where apart from the right to exercise them for the purpose of preserving the value of the security, or of realising it, the rights are exercisable only in accordance with that person's instructions, and where the shares are held in connection with the granting of loans as part of normal business activities and apart from the right to exercise them for the purpose of preserving the value of the security, or of realising it, the rights are exercisable only in that person's interests: Sch 1A para 23 (as so added).

9 Companies Act 2006 Sch 1A para 4 (as added: see note 6). See also note 4. A reference to the right to appoint or remove a majority of the board of directors of a legal entity is to the right to appoint or remove directors holding a majority of the voting rights at meetings of the board on all or substantially all matters: Sch 1A para 16 (as so added). References to a board of directors, in the case of an entity that does not have such a board, are to be read as references to the equivalent management body of that entity: Sch 1A para 17 (as so added).

In the application of Sch 1A para 18 (see notes 7–8) to the right to appoint or remove a majority of the board of directors, a legal entity is to be treated as having the right to appoint a director if a person's appointment as director follows necessarily from that person's appointment as director of the legal entity, or the directorship is held by the legal entity itself: Sch 1A para 18(4) (as so added). As to the exercise of rights see also note 9.

10 Companies Act 2006 Sch 1A para 5 (as added: see note 6). See also note 4. The Secretary of State must issue guidance about the meaning of 'significant influence or control' for these purposes: Sch 1A para 24(1) (as so added). Regard must be had to that guidance in interpreting references in Sch 1A to 'significant influence or control': Sch 1A para 24(2) (as so added). Before issuing such guidance the Secretary of State must lay a draft of it before Parliament: Sch 1A para 24(3) (as so added). If, within the 40-day period, either House of Parliament resolves not to approve the draft guidance, the Secretary of State must take no further steps in relation to it; but this does not prevent a new draft of proposed guidance from being laid before Parliament: Sch 1A para 24(4), (6) (as so added). If no such resolution is made within that period, the Secretary of State must issue and publish the guidance in the form of the draft: Sch 1A para 24(5) (as so added). For this purpose, 'the 40-day period', in relation to draft guidance, means the period of 40 days beginning with the day on which the draft is laid before Parliament (or, if it is not laid before each House on the same day, the later of the days on which it is laid): Sch 1A para 24(7) (as so added). In calculating the 40-day period, no account is to be taken of any period during which Parliament is dissolved or prorogued, or both Houses are adjourned for more than four days: Sch 1A para 24(8) (as so added). The Secretary of State may revise guidance so issued, and a reference Sch 1A para 24 to guidance includes a reference to revised guidance: Sch 1A para 24(9) (as so added). See *Statutory Guidance on the meaning of 'significant influence or control' over companies in the context of the Register of People with Significant Control* (Department for Business Innovation and Skills, April 2016).

11 Companies Act 2006 Sch 1A para 6 (as added: see note 6). See also note 4.

12 Ie for the purposes of the Companies Act 2006 Sch 1A.

13 Companies Act 2006 Sch 1A paras 10, 11 (as added: see note 6).

14 A 'joint arrangement' is an arrangement between the holders of shares (or rights) that they will exercise all or substantially all the rights conferred by their respective shares (or rights) jointly in a way that is predetermined by the arrangement: Companies Act 2006 Sch 1A para 12(2) (as added: see note 6). 'Arrangement' includes any scheme, agreement or understanding, whether or not it is legally enforceable, and any convention, custom or practice of any kind; but something does not count as an arrangement unless there is at least some degree of stability about it (whether by its nature or terms, the time it has been in existence or otherwise): Sch 1A paras 12(3), 21(1), (2) (as so added).

15 Companies Act 2006 Sch 1A para 12(1) (as added: see note 6).

16 Companies Act 2006 s 790C(4) (as added: see note 2).

17 For the purposes of s 790C(4) (see the text and note 16) and s 790C(8) (see the text and notes 23–26), whether someone holds an interest in a company, or holds that interest through another legal entity, is to be determined in accordance with Sch 1A Pt 2 (paras 7–9) (see below); and whether someone has significant control over that other legal entity is to be determined in accordance with s 790C(2), (3) and Sch 1A Pt 1 (see the text and notes 1–11), reading references in those provisions to the company as references to that other entity: s 790C(9) (as added: see note 2). Schedule 1A Pt 2 (paras 7–9) specifies the circumstances in which, for the purposes of s 790C(4) or (8), a person ('V') is to be regarded as holding an interest in a company ('company W') and an interest held by V in company W is to be regarded as held through a legal entity: Sch 1A para 7 (as added: see note 6).

V holds an interest in company W if:

(1) V holds shares in company W, directly or indirectly (Sch 1A para 8(1)(a) (as so added)):

(2) V holds, directly or indirectly, voting rights in company W (Sch 1A para 8(1)(b) (as so added));

(3) V holds, directly or indirectly, the right to appoint or remove any member of the board of directors of company W (Sch 1A para 8(1)(c) (as so added));

(4) V has the right to exercise, or actually exercises, significant influence or control over company W (Sch 1A para 8(1)(d) (as so added)); or
(5) Sch 1A para 8(2) is satisfied (Sch 1A para 8(1)(e) (as so added)).

Schedule 1A para 8(2) is satisfied where the trustees of a trust or the members of a firm that, under the law by which it is governed, is not a legal person hold an interest in company W in a way mentioned in heads (1)–(4) above, and V has the right to exercise, or actually exercises, significant influence or control over the activities of that trust or firm: Sch 1A para 8(2) (as so added).

Where:
(a) V holds an interest in company W by virtue of indirectly holding shares or a right; and
(b) does so by virtue of having a majority stake (see note 7) in
  (i) a legal entity ('L') which holds the shares or right directly; or
  (ii) a legal entity that is part of a chain of legal entities such as is described in Sch 1A para 18(1)(b) or (2)(b) (see notes 7–8) that includes L,

then V holds the interest in company W through L, and through each other legal entity in the above-mentioned chain: see Sch 1A para 9 (as so added).

As to the Secretary of State's power to amend Sch 1A Pt 2 see note 4.

18 A 'legal entity' is a body corporate or a firm that is a legal person under the law by which it is governed: Companies Act 2006 s 790C(5) (as added: see note 2.

19 In relation to a company, a legal entity is a 'relevant legal entity' if
(1) it would have come within the definition of a person with significant control over the company if it had been an individual (Companies Act 2006 s 790C(6)(a)(as added: see note 2); and
(2) it is subject to its own disclosure requirements (Companies Act 2006 s 790C(6)(b) (as so added).

A legal entity is 'subject to its own disclosure requirements' if:
(a) Pt 21A applies to it (whether by virtue of s 790B (see PARA 466) or another enactment that extends the application of Pt 21A (s 790C(7)(a) (as so added));
(b) it is a DTR5 issuer (s 790C(7)(b) (as so added));
(c) it is of a description specified in regulations under s 790B (or s 790B as extended) (s 790C(7)(c) (as so added); or
(d) it is of a description specified by the Secretary of State by regulations made under s 790C(7) (s 790C(7)(d) (as so added).

As to the meaning of 'DTR5 issuer' see PARA 466 note 3. In deciding whether to specify a description of legal entity under s 790C(7)(d) (see head (d) above), the Secretary of State is to have regard to the extent to which entities of that description are bound by disclosure and transparency rules (in the United Kingdom or elsewhere) broadly similar to the ones applying to an entity falling within any of s 790C(7)(a)–(c) (see heads (a)–(c) above): see s 790C(11) (as so added). Regulations under s 790C(7)(d) are subject to affirmative resolution procedure (ie the regulations must not be made unless a draft of the statutory instrument containing them has been laid before Parliament and approved by a resolution of each House of Parliament): see ss 790C(13), 1290 (s 790C(13) as so added). As to the Secretary of State see PARA 6; and as to the meaning of 'United Kingdom' see PARA 1 note 5.

A legal entity, other than one to which s 790C(7)(c) (see head (c) above) applies, is specified for the purpose of s 790C(7)(d) (see head (d) above) if it has voting shares admitted to trading on a regulated market in an EEA state other than the United Kingdom, or on a market listed in the Register of People with Significant Control Regulations 2016, SI 2016/339, Sch 1: reg 4. As to the meaning of 'voting shares' see PARA 466 note 3; as to the meaning of 'regulated market' see PARA 335 note 11; and as to the meaning of 'EEA state' see PARA 26 note 5.

20 See the Companies Act 2006 s 790C(4)(a) (as added (see note 2); substituted by SI 2016/136). As respects:
(1) any shares or right in the company which they hold indirectly as described in the Companies Act 2006 Sch 1A para 9(1)(b)(i) (see note 17 head (b)(i)), the legal entity through which the shares or right are held must be a relevant legal entity in relation to the company (see s 790C(4)(a)(i) (as so added and substituted)); and
(2) any shares or right in the company which they hold indirectly as described in Sch 1A para 9(1)(b)(ii) (see note 17 head (b)(ii)), at least one of the legal entities in the chain must be a relevant legal entity in relation to the company (see s 790C(4)(a)(ii) (as so added and substituted)).

21 Companies Act 2006 s 790C(4)(b) (as added: see note 2).

22 Companies Act 2006 s 790C(4) (as added: see note 2).

23 Companies Act 2006 s 790C(8) (as added: see note 2).

24 See the Companies Act 2006 s 790C(8)(a) (as added (see note 2); substituted by SI 2016/136). As respects:

(1) any shares or right in the company which it holds indirectly as described in the Companies Act 2006 Sch 1A para 9(1)(b)(i) (see note 17 head (b)(i)), the legal entity through which the shares or right are held must also be a relevant legal entity in relation to the company (see sO790C(8)(a)(i) (as so added and substituted)); and

(2) any shares or right in the company which it holds indirectly as described in Sch 1A para 9(1)(b)(ii) (see note 17 head (b)(ii)), at least one of the legal entities in the chain must also be a relevant legal entity in relation to the company (see s 790C(8)(a)(ii) (as so added and substituted)).

25 Companies Act 2006 s 790C(8)(b) (as added: see note 2).

26 Companies Act 2006 s 790C(8) (as added: see note 2).

(ii) Gathering Information about People with Significant Control

A. COMPANY'S DUTY TO OBTAIN PSC INFORMATION

468. Company's duty to investigate and obtain information about people with significant control. As from 6 April 2016[1], the following provisions have effect.

A company to which Part 21A of the Companies Act 2006[2] applies[3] must take reasonable steps:

(1) to find out if there is anyone who is a registrable person[4] or a registrable relevant legal entity[5] in relation to the company; and

(2) if so, to identify them[6].

Without limiting heads (1) and (2) above, such a company must give notice to anyone whom it knows or has reasonable cause to believe to be a registrable person or a registrable relevant legal entity in relation to it[7]. The notice:

(a) if addressed to an individual[8], must require the addressee to state whether or not he is a registrable person in relation to the company[9], and, if so, to confirm or correct any particulars[10] of his that are included in the notice, and supply any that are missing[11];

(b) if addressed to a legal entity[12], must require the addressee to state whether or not it is a registrable relevant legal entity in relation to the company[13], and, if so, to confirm or correct any of its particulars that are included in the notice, and supply any that are missing[14].

A company to which Part 21A of the Companies Act 2006 applies may also give notice to a person under these provisions if it knows or has reasonable cause to believe that the person knows the identity[15] of someone who falls within heads (i) to (iii) below, or knows the identity of someone likely to have that knowledge[16]. The persons whose identity is sought are:

(i) any registrable person in relation to the company;

(ii) any relevant legal entity in relation to the company;

(iii) any entity which would be a relevant legal entity[17] in relation to the company but for the fact that it is not subject[18] to its own disclosure requirements[19].

Such a notice[20] may require the addressee to state whether or not the addressee knows the identity of any person who falls within heads (i) to (iii) above, or any person likely to have that knowledge, and, if so, to supply any particulars of theirs that are within the addressee's knowledge, and state whether or not the particulars are being supplied with the knowledge of each of the persons concerned[21]. A person to whom a notice is so given is not, however, required by that notice to disclose any information in respect of which a claim to legal professional privilege could be maintained in legal proceedings[22].

A notice under the above provisions[23] must state that the addressee is to comply with the notice by no later than the end of the period of one month beginning with the date of the notice[24]. The Secretary of State may by regulations make further provision about the giving of such notices, including the form and content of any such notices and the manner in which they must be given[25].

A company is not, however, required to take steps or give notice under these provisions with respect to a registrable person or registrable relevant legal entity if the company has already been informed of the person's status as a registrable person or registrable relevant legal entity in relation to it, and been supplied with all the particulars, and, in the case of a registrable person, the information and particulars were provided either by the person concerned or with his knowledge[26].

If a company fails to comply with a duty under the above provisions to take steps or give notice, an offence is committed by the company, and by every officer of the company[27] who is in default[28].

A person to whom a notice under the above provisions is addressed commits an offence if the person:

(A) fails to comply with the notice; or
(B) in purported compliance with the notice, makes a statement that the person knows to be false in a material particular, or recklessly makes a statement that is false in a material particular[29];

and where the person is a legal entity, an offence is also committed by every officer of the entity who is in default[30]. A person or an officer of a legal entity does not, however, commit an offence under head (A) above if the person proves that the requirement to give information was frivolous or vexatious[31].

The Secretary of State has power to make exemptions from the requirements of the above provisions[32].

1 See PARA 466 note 1.
2 Ie the Companies Act 2006 Pt 21A (ss 790A–790ZG) (added by the Small Business, Enterprise and Employment Act 2015 Sch 3 Pt 1 para 1): see PARAS 466–467; the text and notes 3–28; and PARA 469 et seq.
3 As to the companies to which the Companies Act 2006 Pt 21A applies see PARA 466. As to the meaning of 'company' under the Companies Acts see PARA 21. As to the companies to which these provisions apply see PARA 466.
4 As to the meaning of 'registrable person' see PARA 467 text and note 22.
5 As to the meaning of 'registrable relevant legal entity' see PARA 467 text and note 26.
6 Companies Act 2006 s 790D(1) (as added: see note 2).
7 Companies Act 2006 s 790D(2) (as added: see note 2).
8 As to the meaning of 'individual' for these purposes see PARA 467 note 3.
9 Ie within the meaning of the Companies Act 2006 Pt 21A: see note 4.
10 For these purposes, 'particulars' means, in the case of a registrable person or a registrable relevant legal entity, the required particulars (see the Companies Act 2006 s 790K; and PARA 469), and in any other case, any particulars that will allow the person to be contacted by the company: Companies Act 2006 s 790D(13)(b) (as added: see note 2).
11 Companies Act 2006 s 790D(3) (as added: see note 2).
12 As to the meaning of 'legal entity' for these purposes see PARA 467 note 18.
13 Ie within the meaning of the Companies Act 2006 Pt 21A: see note 5.
14 Companies Act 2006 s 790D(4) (as added: see note 2).
15 For these purposes, a reference to knowing the identity of a person includes knowing information from which that person can be identified: Companies Act 2006 s 790D(13)(a) (as added: see note 2).
16 Companies Act 2006 s 790D(5) (as added: see note 2).
17 As to the meaning of 'relevant legal entity' for these purposes see PARA 467 note 19.
18 Ie but for the fact that the Companies Act 2006 s 790C(6)(b) (see PARA 467 note 19 head (2)) does not apply in respect of it.
19 Companies Act 2006 s 790D(6) (as added: see note 2).
20 Ie a notice under the Companies Act 2006 s 790D(5): see the text and notes 15–16.
21 Companies Act 2006 s 790D(7) (as added: see note 2).

22 Companies Act 2006 s 790D(12) (as added: see note 2). As to legal professional privilege see LEGAL PROFESSIONS vol 65 (2015) PARAS 351, 538; LEGAL PROFESSIONS vol 66 (2015) PARA 877.
23 Ie under the Companies Act 2006 s 790D: see the text and notes 1–22.
24 Companies Act 2006 s 790D(8) (as added: see note 2).
25 Companies Act 2006 s 790D(9) (as added: see note 2). Regulations under s 790D(9) are subject to negative resolution procedure (ie the statutory instrument containing the regulations is subject to annulment in pursuance of a resolution of either House of Parliament): ss 790D(10), 1289 (s 790D(10) as added: see note 2). As to the making of regulations under the Companies Act 2006 generally see ss 1288–1292. As to the Secretary of State see PARA 6.
26 Companies Act 2006 s 790D(11) (as added: see note 2).
27 As to the meaning of 'officer who is in default' see PARA 316. As to the meaning of 'officer' generally see PARA 679.
28 Companies Act 2006 s 790F(1) (as added: see note 2). A person guilty of such an offence is liable on conviction on indictment, to imprisonment for a term not exceeding two years or a fine, or to both, or on summary conviction to imprisonment for a term not exceeding 12 months or a fine, or to both: see s 790F(2)(a), (b)(i) (as so added). In the case of liability on summary conviction the fine is one not exceeding the statutory maximum: see s 790F(2)(b)(i) (as so added). By virtue of the Legal Aid, Sentencing and Punishment of Offenders Act 2012 s 85, however, where the offence is committed on or after 12 March 2015, it is punishable by a fine of an unlimited amount. As to the statutory maximum and the powers of magistrates' courts to issue fines on summary conviction see SENTENCING vol 92 (2015) PARA 176.In relation to an offence committed before the coming into force of the Criminal Justice Act 2003 s 154(1) (not yet in force), the maximum term of imprisonment on summary conviction is six months: see the Companies Act 2006 s 1131; and PARA 1818.
29 Companies Act 2006 Sch 1B para 13(1) (Sch 1B added by the Small Business, Enterprise and Employment Act 2015 Sch 3 Pt 1 para 2). A person guilty of such an offence is liable on conviction on indictment, to imprisonment for a term not exceeding two years or a fine, or to both, or on summary conviction to imprisonment for a term not exceeding 12 months or to a fine, or to both: Sch 1B para 13(4)(a), (b)(i) (as so added). In relation to an offence committed before the coming into force of the Criminal Justice Act 2003 s 154(1) (not yet in force), the maximum term of imprisonment on summary conviction is six months: see the Companies Act 2006 s 1131; and PARA 1818.

As to enforcement by means of a restrictions notice see PARA 474 et seq.
30 Companies Act 2006 Sch 1B para 13(2) (as added: see note 29). As to the penalty for such an offence see note 29.
31 See the Companies Act 2006 Sch 1B para 13(3) (as added: see note 29).
32 See PARA 479.

469. Required particulars of registrable person and registrable relevant legal entity. As from 6 April 2016[1], the following provisions have effect.

The 'required particulars' of an individual[2] who is a registrable person[3] are:

(1) name;
(2) a service address;
(3) the country or state, or part of the United Kingdom[4], in which the individual is usually resident;
(4) nationality;
(5) date of birth;
(6) usual residential address;
(7) the date on which the individual became a registrable person in relation to the company in question[5];
(8) the nature of his control over that company[6]; and
(9) if, in relation to that company, restrictions on using or disclosing any of the individual's PSC particulars[7] are in force under regulations[8], that fact[9].

In the case of a person in relation to which Part 21A of the Companies Act 2006[10] has effect as if the person were an individual[11], the 'required particulars' are:

(a) name;

(b) principal office;
(c) the legal form of the person and the law by which it is governed;
(d) the date on which it became a registrable person in relation to the company in question; and
(e) the nature of its control[12] over the company[13].

The 'required particulars' of a registrable relevant legal entity[14] are:
(i) corporate or firm name;
(ii) registered or principal office;
(iii) the legal form of the entity and the law by which it is governed;
(iv) if applicable, the register of companies in which it is entered, including details of the state, and its registration number in that register;
(v) the date on which it became a registrable relevant legal entity in relation to the company in question; and
(vi) the nature of its control[15] over that company[16].

The Secretary of State may by regulations make further provision about the particulars required by heads (8), (e) and (vi) above[17]. The regulations made in the exercise of this power[18] provide that the particulars required by those heads are:
(A) where the person meets the first specified condition[19], the prescribed statement[20] which is applicable to that person[21];
(B) where the person meets the second specified condition[22], the prescribed statement[23] which is applicable to that person[24];
(C) where the person meets the third specified condition[25], the prescribed statement[26];
(D) where the person meets the fourth specified condition[27] and does not meet the first, second or third specified condition, the prescribed statement[28];
(E) where the person meets the fifth specified condition[29] in connection with a trust, every prescribed statement[30] which is applicable to that person[31];
(F) where the person meets the fifth specified condition in connection with a firm[32], every prescribed statement[33] which is applicable to that person[34].

The Secretary of State may also by regulations amend the provisions of the Companies Act 2006 set out above[35] so as to add to or remove from any of the lists of required particulars[36].

1 See PARA 466 note 1.
2 The Companies Act 2006 s 163(2) (particulars of directors to be registered: individuals) (see PARA 535) applies for the purposes of s 790K(1) (see heads (1)–(8) in the text): s 790K(4) (ss 790K, 790L, 790ZG added by the Small Business, Enterprise and Employment Act 2015 Sch 3 Pt 1 para 1).
3 As to the meaning of 'registrable person' see PARA 467 text and note 22.
4 As to the meaning of 'United Kingdom' see PARA 1 note 5.
5 Where an individual or a relevant legal entity was registrable in relation to a company on 6 April 2016, the date on which the individual or entity became a registrable person or a registrable relevant legal entity, as the case may be, in relation to the company in question is deemed to be 6 April 2016 for the purposes of s 790K(1)(g) (see head (7) in the text), s 790K(2)(d) (see head (d) in the text) and s 790K(3)(e) (see head (v) in the text): Register of People with Significant Control Regulations 2016, SI 2016/339, reg 47.
6 As to control over a company see the Companies Act 2006 Sch 1A; and PARA 467. As to the meaning of 'company' under the Companies Acts see PARA 21. As to the companies to which these provisions apply see PARA 466.
7 'PSC particulars' are particulars of a person with significant control over the company, including a person who used to be such a person, but excluding any person in relation to which the Companies Act 2006 Pt 21A has effect by virtue of s 790C(12) (see PARA 467 note 3) as if the person were an individual: s 790ZG(2) (as added: see note 2). As to persons with significant control over a company see PARA 467.

8 Ie regulations under the Companies Act 2006 s 790ZG: see PARA 492.
9 Companies Act 2006 s 790K(1) (as added: see note 2).
10 Ie the Companies Act 2006 Pt 21A (ss 790A–790ZG): see PARAS 466–468; the text and notes 1–9, 11–18; and PARA 470 et seq.
11 Ie by virtue of the Companies Act 2006 s 790C(12): see PARA 467 note 3.
12 See note 6.
13 Companies Act 2006 s 790K(2) (as added: see note 2). See also note 5.
14 As to the meaning of 'registrable relevant legal entity' see PARA 467 text and note 26.
15 See note 5.
16 Companies Act 2006 s 790K(3) (as added: see note 2). See also note 5.
17 Companies Act 2006 s 790K(5) (as added: see note 2). Such regulations are subject to negative resolution procedure (ie the statutory instrument containing the regulations is subject to annulment in pursuance of a resolution of either House of Parliament): ss 790K(6), 1289 (s 790K(6) (as so added). As to the making of regulations under the Companies Act 2006 generally see ss 1288–1292; and as to the Secretary of State see PARA 6.
18 Ie the Register of People with Significant Control Regulations 2016, SI 2016/339, reg 7; see heads (I)–(VI) in the text.
19 As to the meaning of 'specified conditions' see the Companies Act 2006 s 790C(3); and PARA 467 note 4; and as to the first such condition see PARA 467 head (1).
20 Ie the statement listed in the Register of People with Significant Control Regulations 2016, SI 2016/339, Sch 2 Pt 1. The statements so listed are as follows (Sch 2 Pt 1 (paras 1–3)):
    (1) a statement that the person holds, directly or indirectly, more than 25% but not more than 50% of the shares in the company;
    (2) a statement that the person holds, directly or indirectly, more than 50% but less than 75% of the shares in the company;
    (3) a statement that the person holds, directly or indirectly, 75% or more of the shares in the company.

    For the purposes of Sch 2, in relation to a company that does not have a share capital, a reference to holding a particular percentage of shares in a company is to holding a right or rights to share in that percentage of capital or, as the case may be, profits of that company: Sch 2 para 25.
21 Register of People with Significant Control Regulations 2016, SI 2016/339, reg 7(a).
22 As to the second specified condition see PARA 467 head (2).
23 Ie the statement listed in the Register of People with Significant Control Regulations 2016, SI 2016/339, Sch 2 Pt 2. The statements so listed are as follows (Sch 2 Pt 2 (paras 4–6)):
    (1) a statement that the person holds, directly or indirectly, more than 25% but not more than 50% of the voting rights in the company;
    (2) a statement that the person holds, directly or indirectly, more than 50% but less than 75% of the voting rights in the company;
    (3) a statement that the person holds, directly or indirectly, 75% or more of the voting rights in the company.

    As to the meaning of 'voting rights' see PARA 466 note 3.
24 Register of People with Significant Control Regulations 2016, SI 2016/339, reg 7(b).
25 As to the third specified condition see PARA 467 head (3).
26 Register of People with Significant Control Regulations 2016, SI 2016/339, reg 7(c). The statement referred to in head (iii) in the text is the statement listed in Sch 2 Pt 3. That statement is a statement that the person holds the right, directly or indirectly, to appoint or remove a majority of the board of directors of the company: Sch 2 Pt 3 (para 7).
27 As to the fourth specified condition see PARA 467 head (4).
28 Register of People with Significant Control Regulations 2016, SI 2016/339, reg 7(d). The statement referred to in head (iv) in the text is the statement listed in Sch 2 Pt 4. That statement is a statement that the person has the right to exercise, or actually exercises, significant influence or control over the company: Sch 2 Pt 4 (para 8).
29 As to the fifth specified condition see PARA 467 head (5).
30 Ie every statement listed in the Register of People with Significant Control Regulations 2016, SI 2016/339, Sch 2 Pt 5. The statements so listed are as follows (Sch 2 Pt 5 (paras 9–16)):
    (1) a statement that:
        (a) the person has the right to exercise, or actually exercises, significant influence or control over the activities of a trust; and
        (b) the trustees of that trust, in their capacity as such, hold, directly or indirectly, more than 25% but not more than 50% of the shares in the company;
    (2) a statement that:
        (a) the person has the right to exercise, or actually exercises, significant influence or control over the activities of a trust; and

(b) the trustees of that trust, in their capacity as such, hold, directly or indirectly, more than 50% but less than 75% of the shares in the company;
(3) a statement that:
(a) the person has the right to exercise, or actually exercises, significant influence or control over the activities of a trust; and
(b) the trustees of that trust, in their capacity as such, hold, directly or indirectly, 75% or more of the shares in the company;
(4) a statement that:
(a) the person has the right to exercise, or actually exercises, significant influence or control over the activities of a trust; and
(b) the trustees of that trust, in their capacity as such, hold, directly or indirectly, more than 25% but not more than 50% of the voting rights in the company;
(5) a statement that:
(a) the person has the right to exercise, or actually exercises, significant influence or control over the activities of a trust; and
(b) the trustees of that trust, in their capacity as such, hold, directly or indirectly, more than 50% but less than 75% of the voting rights in the company;
(6) a statement that:
(a) the person has the right to exercise, or actually exercises, significant influence or control over the activities of a trust; and
(b) the trustees of that trust, in their capacity as such, hold, directly or indirectly, 75% or more of the voting rights in the company;
(7) a statement that:
(a) the person has the right to exercise, or actually exercises, significant influence or control over the activities of a trust; and
(b) the trustees of that trust, in their capacity as such, hold the right, directly or indirectly, to appoint or remove a majority of the board of directors of the company;
(8) a statement that:
(a) the person has the right to exercise, or actually exercises, significant influence or control over the activities of a trust; and
(b) the trustees of that trust, in their capacity as such, have the right to exercise, or actually exercise, significant influence or control over the company.

31 Register of People with Significant Control Regulations 2016, SI 2016/339, reg 7(e).

32 As to the meaning of 'firm' for the purposes of the Companies Acts see PARA 105 note 15.

33 Ie every statement listed in the Register of People with Significant Control Regulations 2016, SI 2016/339, Sch 2 Pt 6. The statements so listed are as follows (Sch 2 Pt 6 (paras 17–24)):
(1) a statement that:
(a) the person has the right to exercise, or actually exercises, significant influence or control over the activities of a firm that, under the law by which it is governed, is not a legal person; and
(b) the members of that firm, in their capacity as such, hold, directly or indirectly, more than 25% but not more than 50% of the shares in the company;
(2) a statement that:
(a) the person has the right to exercise, or actually exercises, significant influence or control over the activities of a firm that, under the law by which it is governed, is not a legal person; and
(b) the members of that firm, in their capacity as such, hold, directly or indirectly, more than 50% but less than 75% of the shares in the company;
(3) a statement that:
(a) the person has the right to exercise, or actually exercises, significant influence or control over the activities of a firm that, under the law by which it is governed, is not a legal person; and
(b) the members of that firm, in their capacity as such, hold, directly or indirectly, 75% or more of the shares in the company;
(4) a statement that:
(a) the person has the right to exercise, or actually exercises, significant influence or control over the activities of a firm that, under the law by which it is governed, is not a legal person; and
(b) the members of that firm, in their capacity as such, hold, directly or indirectly, more than 25% but not more than 50% of the voting rights in the company;
(5) a statement that:

(a) the person has the right to exercise, or actually exercises, significant influence or control over the activities of a firm that, under the law by which it is governed, is not a legal person; and

(b) the members of that firm, in their capacity as such, hold, directly or indirectly, more than 50% but less than 75% of the voting rights in the company;

(6) a statement that:

(a) the person has the right to exercise, or actually exercises, significant influence or control over the activities of a firm that, under the law by which it is governed, is not a legal person; and

(b) the members of that firm, in their capacity as such, hold, directly or indirectly, 75% or more of the voting rights in the company;

(7) a statement that:

(a) the person has the right to exercise, or actually exercises, significant influence or control over the activities of a firm that, under the law by which it is governed, is not a legal person; and

(b) the members of that firm, in their capacity as such, hold the right, directly or indirectly, to appoint or remove a majority of the board of directors of the company;

(8) a statement that:

(a) the person has the right to exercise, or actually exercises, significant influence or control over the activities of a firm that, under the law by which it is governed, is not a legal person; and

(b) the members of that firm, in their capacity as such, have the right to exercise, or actually exercise, significant influence or control over the company.

34 Register of People with Significant Control Regulations 2016, SI 2016/339, reg 7(f).

35 Ie the Companies Act 2006 s 790K: see the text and notes 1–17.

36 Companies Act 2006 s 790L(1) (as added: see note 2). Such regulations are subject to affirmative resolution procedure (ie the regulations must not be made unless a draft of the statutory instrument containing them has been laid before Parliament and approved by a resolution of each House of Parliament): see ss 790L(2), 1290 (s 790L(2) as added: see note 2).

470. Company's duty to keep PSC information up to date. As from 6 April 2016[1], the following provisions have effect.

If particulars[2] of a registrable person[3] or registrable relevant legal entity[4] are stated in a company's PSC register[5], the company must give notice to the person or entity if the company knows or has reasonable cause to believe that a relevant change has occurred[6]. In the case of a registrable person, a 'relevant change' occurs if:

(1) the person ceases to be a registrable person in relation to the company; or

(2) any other change occurs as a result of which the particulars stated for the person in the PSC register are incorrect or incomplete[7].

In the case of a registrable relevant legal entity, a 'relevant change' occurs if:

(a) the entity ceases to be a registrable relevant legal entity in relation to the company; or

(b) any other change occurs as a result of which the particulars stated for the entity in the PSC register are incorrect or incomplete[8].

The company must give the notice as soon as reasonably practicable after it learns of the change or first has reasonable cause to believe that the change has occurred[9]. The notice must require the addressee to confirm whether or not the change has occurred, and, if so, to state the date of the change, and to confirm or correct the particulars included in the notice, and supply any that are missing from the notice[10].

A notice under the above provisions must state that the addressee is to comply with the notice by no later than the end of the period of one month beginning with the date of the notice[11]. The Secretary of State may by regulations make further provision about the giving of such notices, including the form and content of any such notices and the manner in which they must be given[12].

A company is not, however, required to give notice under these provisions if the company has already been informed of the relevant change, and, in the case of a registrable person, that information was provided either by the person concerned or with his or her knowledge[13].

If a company fails to comply with a duty under the above provisions to give notice, an offence is committed by the company, and by every officer of the company[14] who is in default[15].

A person to whom a notice under the above provisions is addressed commits an offence if the person:

(i) fails to comply with the notice; or
(ii) in purported compliance with the notice, makes a statement that the person knows to be false in a material particular, or recklessly makes a statement that is false in a material particular[16];

and where the person is a legal entity, an offence is also committed by every officer of the entity who is in default[17]. A person or an officer of a legal entity does not, however, commit an offence under head (i) above if the person proves that the requirement to give information was frivolous or vexatious[18].

The Secretary of State has power to make exemptions from the requirements of the above provisions[19].

1 See PARA 466 note 1. Note, however, that the Companies Act 2006 s 790W(5), cited in note 5, was not brought into force until 30 June 2016: see PARA 466 note 1.
2 As to the meaning of 'particulars' see PARA 468 note 10; and as to the required particulars see PARA 469.
3 As to the meaning of 'registrable person' see PARA 467 text and note 22.
4 As to the meaning of 'registrable relevant legal entity' see PARA 467 text and note 26.
5 The register that a company is required to keep under the Companies Act 2006 s 790M (register of people with significant control over a company: see PARA 480) is referred to as the company's 'PSC register': s 790C(10) (ss 790C–790F, 790W added by the Small Business, Enterprise and Employment Act 2015 Sch 3 Pt 1 para 1). Where an election under the Companies Act 2006 s 790X is in force in respect of a company (see PARA 485), references in Pt 21A Ch 2 (ss 790D–790L) to the company's PSC register are to be read as references to the central register: s 790W(5) (as so added). As to the central register see PARA 142 et seq.
As to the meaning of 'company' under the Companies Acts see PARA 21. As to the companies to which these provisions apply see PARA 466.
6 Companies Act 2006 s 790E(1), (2) (as added: see note 5).
7 Companies Act 2006 s 790E(3) (as added: see note 5).
8 Companies Act 2006 s 790E(4) (as added: see note 5).
9 Companies Act 2006 s 790E(5) (as added: see note 5).
10 Companies Act 2006 s 790E(6) (as added: see note 5).
11 Companies Act 2006 s 790D(8) (as added: see note 5); applied for these purposes by s 790E(7) (as so added).
12 Companies Act 2006 s 790D(9) (as added (see note 5); applied for these purposes (see note 11)). Regulations under s 790D(9) are subject to negative resolution procedure (ie the statutory instrument containing the regulations is subject to annulment in pursuance of a resolution of either House of Parliament): ss 790D(10), 1289 (s 790D(10) as so added; applied for these purposes (see note 11)). As to the making of regulations under the Companies Act 2006 generally see ss 1288–1292. As to the Secretary of State see PARA 6.
13 Companies Act 2006 s 790E(8) (as added: see note 5).
14 As to the meaning of 'officer who is in default' see PARA 316. As to the meaning of 'officer' generally see PARA 679.
15 Companies Act 2006 s 790F(1) (as added: see note 5). A person guilty of such an offence is liable on conviction on indictment, to imprisonment for a term not exceeding two years or a fine, or to both, or on summary conviction to imprisonment for a term not exceeding 12 months or a fine, or to both: see s 790F(2)(a), (b)(i) (as so added). In the case of liability on summary conviction the fine is one not exceeding the statutory maximum: see s 790F(2)(b)(i) (as so added) By virtue of the Legal Aid, Sentencing and Punishment of Offenders Act 2012 s 85, however, where the offence is

committed on or after 12 March 2015, it is punishable by a fine of an unlimited amount. As to the statutory maximum and the powers of magistrates' courts to issue fines on summary conviction see SENTENCING vol 92 (2015) PARA 176. In relation to an offence committed before the coming into force of the Criminal Justice Act 2003 s 154(1) (not yet in force), the maximum term of imprisonment on summary conviction is six months: see the Companies Act 2006 s 1131; and PARA 1818.

16 Companies Act 2006 Sch 1B para 13(1) (Sch 1B as added, as from a day to be appointed (see note 1), by the Small Business, Enterprise and Employment Act 2015 Sch 3 Pt 1 para 2). A person guilty of such an offence is liable on conviction on indictment, to imprisonment for a term not exceeding two years or a fine, or to both, or on summary conviction to imprisonment for a term not exceeding 12 months or to a fine, or to both: Sch 1B para 13(4)(a), (b)(i) (as so added). In relation to an offence committed before the coming into force of the Criminal Justice Act 2003 s 154(1) (not yet in force), the maximum term of imprisonment on summary conviction is six months: see the Companies Act 2006 s 1131; and PARA 1818.

As to enforcement by means of a restrictions notice see PARA 474 et seq.

17 Companies Act 2006 Sch 1B para 13(2) (as added: see note 16). As to the penalty for such an offence see note 16.

18 See the Companies Act 2006 Sch 1B para 13(3) (as added: see note 16).

19 See PARA 479.

B. OTHERS' DUTY TO SUPPLY AND UPDATE PSC INFORMATION

471. Duty on others to supply and update information about people with significant control. As from 6 April 2016[1], the following provisions have effect.

The duty set out in heads (a) to (c) below applies to a person if:

(1) the person is a registrable person[2] or a registrable relevant legal entity[3] in relation to a company;
(2) the person knows that to be the case or ought reasonably to do so;
(3) the required particulars[4] of the person are not stated in the company's PSC register[5];
(4) the person has not received notice from the company requiring information about that person's status and particulars[6]; and
(5) the circumstances described in heads (1) to (4) above have continued for a period of at least one month[7].

The person must:

(a) notify the company of the person's status, as a registrable person or registrable relevant legal entity, in relation to the company;
(b) state the date, to the best of the person's knowledge, on which the person acquired that status; and
(c) give the company the required particulars[8];

and that duty must be complied with by the end of the period of one month beginning with the day on which all the conditions in heads (1) to (5) above were first met with respect to the person[9].

The duty under heads (A) to (C) below applies to a person if:

(i) the required particulars of the person, whether a registrable person or a registrable relevant legal entity, are stated in a company's PSC register;
(ii) a relevant change[10] occurs;
(iii) the person knows of the change or ought reasonably to do so;
(iv) the company's PSC register has not been altered to reflect the change; and
(v) the person has not received notice from the company requiring that person to give information concerning such a change[11] by the end of the period of one month beginning with the day on which the change occurred[12].

The person must:

(A) notify the company of the change;

(B) state the date on which it occurred; and

(C) give the company any information needed to update the PSC register[13],

and that duty must be complied with by the later of:

(I) the end of the period of 2 months beginning with the day on which the change occurred; and

(II) the end of the period of one month beginning with the day on which the person discovered the change[14].

A person commits an offence if the person fails to comply with a duty under the above provisions[15], or, in purported compliance with such a duty, either makes a statement that the person knows to be false in a material particular, or recklessly makes a statement that is false in a material particular[16]. Where the person is a legal entity[17], an offence is also committed by every officer[18] of the entity who is in default[19].

The Secretary of State has power to make exemptions from the requirements of the above provisions[20].

1 See PARA 466 note 1. Note, however, that the Companies Act 2006 s 790W(5), cited in note 5, was not brought into force until 30 June 2016: see PARA 466 note 1.
2 As to the meaning of 'registrable person' see PARA 467 text and note 22.
3 As to the meaning of 'registrable relevant legal entity' see PARA 467 text and note 26.
4 As to the meaning of 'particulars' see PARA 468 note 10; and as to the required particulars see PARA 469.
5 As to the meaning of 'company's PSC register' see PARA 470 note 5; and as to that register see PARA 480. As to the meaning of 'company' under the Companies Acts see PARA 21. As to the companies to which these provisions apply see PARA 466. Where an election under the Companies Act 2006 s 790X is in force in respect of a company (see PARA 485), references in Pt 21A Ch 2 (ss 790D–790L) to the company's PSC register are to be read as references to the central register: s 790W(5) (as added: see note 7). As to the central register see PARA 142 et seq.
6 Ie notice under the Companies Act 2006 s 790D(2): see PARA 468.
7 Companies Act 2006 s 790G(1) (ss 790G–790H, 790W added by the Small Business, Enterprise and Employment Act 2015 Sch 3 Pt 1 para 1).
8 Companies Act 2006 s 790G(2) (as added: see note 7).
9 Companies Act 2006 s 790G(3) (as added: see note 7).
10 For these purposes, 'relevant change' has the same meaning as in the Companies Act 2006 s 790E (see PARA 470 heads (1)–(2), (a)–(b)): s 790H(4) (as added: see note 7).
11 Ie notice under the Companies Act 2006 s 790E (see PARA 470.
12 Companies Act 2006 s 790H(1) (as added: see note 7).
13 Companies Act 2006 s 790H(2) (as added: see note 7).
14 Companies Act 2006 s 790H(3) (as added: see note 7).
15 Ie a duty under the Companies Act 2006 s 790G or s 790H: see the text and notes 2–15.
16 Companies Act 2006 Sch 1B para 14(1) (Sch 1B added by the Small Business, Enterprise and Employment Act 2015 Sch 3 Pt 1 para 2). A person guilty of such an offence is liable on conviction on indictment, to imprisonment for a term not exceeding two years or a fine, or to both, or on summary conviction to imprisonment for a term not exceeding 12 months or to a fine, or to both: Sch 1B para 14(3)(a), (b)(i) (as so added). In relation to an offence committed before the coming into force of the Criminal Justice Act 2003 s 154(1) (not yet in force), the maximum term of imprisonment on summary conviction is six months: see the Companies Act 2006 s 1131.

As to enforcement by means of a restrictions notice see PARA 474 et seq.
17 As to the meaning of 'legal entity' for these purposes see PARA 467 note 18.
18 As to the meaning of 'officer who is in default' see PARA 316. As to the meaning of 'officer' generally see PARA 679.
19 Companies Act 2006 Sch 1B para 14(2) (as added: see note 16). As to the penalty for such an offence see note 16.
20 See PARA 479.

C. ENFORCEMENT OF PSC DISCLOSURE REQUIREMENTS

472. Enforcement of disclosure requirements regarding people with significant control: in general. As from 6 April 2016[1], provisions of the Companies Act 2006[2] have effect with regard to when a person, whether an individual[3] or a legal entity[4], fails to comply with a notice from a company requiring information as to that person's status[5] or a relevant change to that status[6] or with a duty to supply[7] or update[8] information as to people with significant control[9].

1 See PARA 466 note 1.
2 Ie the Companies Act 2006 Sch 1B (paras 1–14): see PARAS 468, 470–471, 473 et seq.
3 As to the meaning of 'individual' for these purposes see PARA 467 note 3.
4 As to the meaning of 'legal entity' for these purposes see PARA 467 note 18.
5 Ie a notice under the Companies Act 2006 s 790D: see PARA 468.
6 Ie a notice under the Companies Act 2006 s 790E: see PARA 470.
7 Ie a duty under the Companies Act 2006 s 790G: see PARA 471.
8 Ie a duty under the Companies Act 2006 s 790H: see PARA 471.
9 See the Companies Act 2006 s 790I (added by the Small Business, Enterprise and Employment Act 2015 Sch 3 Pt 1 para 1).

473. Power to serve restrictions notice. As from 6 April 2016[1], the following provisions have effect.

If a notice requiring information as to a person's status[2] or a relevant change to that status[3] is served by a company on a person who has a relevant interest[4] in the company, and the person fails to comply with that notice within the time specified in it, the company may give the person a notice (a 'warning notice') informing the person that it is proposing to issue the person with a notice (a 'restrictions notice') with respect to the relevant interest[5]. The company may issue the restrictions notice[6] if, by the end of the period of one month beginning with the date on which the warning notice was given, the person has not complied with the notice served as mentioned above[7], and the company has not been provided with a valid reason sufficient to justify the person's failure to comply with the notice so served[8]. In deciding whether to issue a restrictions notice, the company must have regard to the effect of the notice on the rights of third parties in respect of the relevant interest[9].

The effect of a restrictions notice with regard to a relevant interest is as follows[10]:

(1) any transfer of the interest is void;
(2) no rights are exercisable in respect of the interest;
(3) no shares may be issued in right of the interest or in pursuance of an offer made to the interest-holder;
(4) except in a liquidation, no payment may be made of sums due from the company in respect of the interest, whether in respect of capital or otherwise[11].

An agreement to transfer an interest that is subject to the restriction in head (1) above is void[12]; but this does not apply to an agreement to transfer the interest on the making of an order[13] for the removal of restrictions in the case of a court-approved transfer[14]. An agreement to transfer any associated right[15], otherwise than in a liquidation, is also void[16]; but this does not apply to an agreement to transfer any such right on the making of an order[17] for the removal of restrictions in the case of a court-approved transfer[18].

These provisions are subject to any directions given[19] by the court for the protection of third party rights[20].

1 See PARA 466 note 1.
2 Ie a notice under the Companies Act 2006 s 790D: see PARA 468.
3 Ie a notice under the Companies Act 2006 s 790E: see PARA 470.
4 For these purposes, a person has a relevant interest in a company if the person holds any shares in the company, holds any voting rights in the company, or holds the right to appoint or remove any member of the board of directors of the company; and references to 'the relevant interest' are to the shares or right in question: Companies Act 2006 Sch 1B para 2(1), (2) (Sch 1B added by

the Small Business, Enterprise and Employment Act 2015 Sch 3 Pt 1 para 2). The Companies Act 2006 Sch 1A Pt 3 (paras 10–26) (see PARA 467) applies for the interpretation of Sch 1B para 2(1) save that, where the relevant interest is, by virtue of Sch 1A para 19 (see PARA 467 note 7) or Sch 1A para 20 (see PARA 467 note 8), treated for the purposes of Sch 1A as held by a person other than the person who in fact holds the interest, both the holder and the other person are to be regarded for these purposes as having the relevant interest: Sch 1B para 2(3) (as so added). As to the meaning of 'company' under the Companies Acts see PARA 21. As to the companies to which these provisions apply see PARA 466.

5 See the Companies Act 2006 Sch 1B para 1(1), (2) (as added: see note 4). A warning notice so given must:
   (1) specify the date on which the warning notice is given (Register of People with Significant Control Regulations 2016, SI 2016/339, reg 18(a));
   (2) be accompanied by a copy of the notice given under the Companies Act 2006 s 790D or s 790E to which the warning notice relates (Register of People with Significant Control Regulations 2016, SI 2016/339, reg 18(b));
   (3) identify the addressee's relevant interest in the company by reference to the shares or right in question (reg 18(c));
   (4) state that the company will consider reasons provided to it as to why the addressee failed to comply with the notice given under the Companies Act 2006 s 790D or s 790E (Register of People with Significant Control Regulations 2016, SI 2016/339, reg 18(d));
   (5) explain the effect of a restrictions notice (reg 18(e)); and
   (6) state that, by virtue of a restrictions notice, certain acts or failures to act may constitute an offence (reg 18(f)).

6 A restrictions notice is issued on a person by sending the notice to the person: Companies Act 2006 Sch 1B para 1(4) (as added: see note 4). The Secretary of State may by regulations make provision about the procedure to be followed by companies in issuing and withdrawing restrictions notices: Sch 1B para 12(1) (as so added). The regulations may in particular make provision about the following matters (Sch 1B para 12(2) (as so added)) ie:
   (1) the form and content of warning notices and restrictions notices, and the manner in which they must be given;
   (2) the factors to be taken into account in deciding what counts as a 'valid reason' sufficient to justify a person's failure to comply with a notice under s 790D or s 790E; and
   (3) the effect of withdrawing a restrictions notice on matters that are pending with respect to the relevant interest when the notice is withdrawn.

Such regulations are subject to negative resolution procedure (ie the statutory instrument containing the regulations is subject to annulment in pursuance of a resolution of either House of Parliament): s 1289, Sch 1B para 12(3) (Sch 1B para 12(3) (as so added). As to the making of regulations under the Companies Act 2006 generally see ss 1288–1292; and as to the Secretary of State see PARA 6. As to the withdrawal of a restrictions notice see PARA 478. As to the contents of a warning notice see note 5.

A restrictions notice issued under Sch 1B para 1 must:
   (a) specify the date on which the restrictions notice is issued (Register of People with Significant Control Regulations 2016, SI 2016/339, reg 19(a));
   (b) be accompanied by a copy of the warning notice which preceded the restrictions notice (reg 19(b));
   (c) identify the addressee's relevant interest in the company by reference to the shares or right in question (reg 19(c));
   (d) explain the effect of the restrictions notice (reg 19(d));
   (e) state that, by virtue of the restrictions notice, certain acts or failures to act may constitute an offence (reg 19(e)); and
   (f) state that an aggrieved person may apply to the court for an order directing that the relevant interest cease to be subject to restrictions (reg 19(f)).

7 Ie the notice served under the Companies Act 2006 s 790D (see PARA 468) or s 790E (see PARA 470).

8 Companies Act 2006 Sch 1B para 1(3) (as added: see note 4). A company must take into account any incapacity of the addressee of a notice given under s 790D or s 790E in deciding what counts as a 'valid reason' sufficient to justify the addressee's failure to comply with the notice: Register of People with Significant Control Regulations 2016, SI 2016/339, reg 20.

9 Companies Act 2006 Sch 1B para 1(6) (as added: see note 4).

10 Companies Act 2006 Sch 1B paras 1(5), 3(1) (as added: see note 4).

11 Companies Act 2006 Sch 1B para 3(1)(a)–(d) (as added: see note 4).

12 Companies Act 2006 Sch 1B para 3(2) (as added: see note 4).

13 Ie an order under the Companies Act 2006 Sch 1B para 8 (see PARA 476) made by virtue of Sch 1B para 8(3)(b) (removal of restrictions in case of court-approved transfer).
14 See the Companies Act 2006 Sch 1B para 3(3) (as added: see note 4).
15 An 'associated right', in relation to a relevant interest, is a right to be issued with any shares issued in right of the relevant interest, or a right to receive payment of any sums due from the company in respect of the relevant interest: Companies Act 2006 Sch 1B para 3(6) (as added: see note 4).
16 Companies Act 2006 Sch 1B para 3(4) (as added: see note 4).
17 See note 13.
18 Companies Act 2006 Sch 1B para 3(5) (as added: see note 4).
19 Ie under the Companies Act 2006 Sch 1B para 4 (see PARA 474).
20 Companies Act 2006 Sch 1B para 3(7) (as added: see note 4).

474. Protection of third party rights after issue of restrictions notice. As from 6 April 2016[1], the following provisions have effect.

The court[2] may give a direction under these provisions if, on application by any person aggrieved, the court is satisfied that a restrictions notice[3] issued by the company[4] unfairly affects the rights of third parties in respect of the relevant interest[5]. The direction is given for the purpose of protecting those third party rights[6] and is a direction that certain acts will not constitute a breach of the restrictions placed on the relevant interest by the restrictions notice[7].

An order containing such a direction must specify the acts that will not constitute a breach of the restrictions, and may confine the direction to cases where those acts are done by persons, or for purposes, described in the order[8].

The direction may be given subject to such terms as the court thinks fit[9].

1 See PARA 466 note 1.
2 As to the meaning of 'the court' see PARA 160 note 12.
3 As to the meaning of 'restrictions notice' see PARA 473.
4 Ie issued under the Companies Act 2006 Sch 1B para 1: see PARA 473. As to the meaning of 'company' under the Companies Acts see PARA 21. As to the companies to which these provisions apply see PARA 466.
5 Companies Act 2006 Sch 1B para 4(1) (Sch 1B added, partly as from a day to be appointed (see note 1), by the Small Business, Enterprise and Employment Act 2015 Sch 3 Pt 1 para 2). As to the meaning of 'relevant interest' for these purposes see para 473 note 4.
6 Companies Act 2006 Sch 1B para 4(2) (as added: see note 5).
7 Companies Act 2006 Sch 1B para 4(3) (as added: see note 5). As to breach of the restrictions placed on the relevant interest by a restrictions notice see PARA 475.
8 Companies Act 2006 Sch 1B para 4(4) (as added: see note 5).
9 Companies Act 2006 Sch 1B para 4(5) (as added: see note 5).

475. Breach of restrictions in restrictions notice. As from 6 April 2016[1], the following provisions have effect, subject to any direction given[2] by the court[3].

A person commits an offence if the person does anything listed in heads (1) to (3) below knowing that the interest is subject to restrictions[4]. Those things are:

(1) exercising or purporting to exercise any right to dispose of a relevant interest[5];
(2) exercising or purporting to exercise any right to dispose of any right to be issued with a relevant interest[6]; or
(3) voting in respect of a relevant interest, whether as holder of the interest or as proxy, or appointing a proxy to vote in respect of a relevant interest[7].

A person who has a relevant interest that the person knows to be subject to restrictions commits an offence if the person:

(a) knows a person to be entitled, apart from the restrictions, to vote in respect of the interest, whether as holder or as proxy;
(b) does not know the person to be aware of the fact that the interest is subject to restrictions; and
(c) fails to notify the person of that fact[8].

A person commits an offence if the person:

(i) either has a relevant interest that the person knows to be subject to restrictions or is entitled to an associated right[9]; and

(ii) enters in that capacity into an agreement that is void[10] by virtue of the effect of a restrictions notice[11].

If shares in a company are issued in contravention of a restriction imposed by virtue of a restrictions notice[12], an offence is committed by the company, and by every officer of the company who is in default[13].

A person guilty of an offence under the above provisions[14] is liable, on conviction on indictment or on summary conviction, to a fine[15].

1 See PARA 466 note 1.

2 Ie any direction given under the Companies Act 2006 Sch 1B para 4 (see PARA 474) or Sch 1B para 8 (see PARA 476).

3 See the Companies Act 2006 Sch 1B para 7(2) (Sch 1B paras 5–7 added by the Small Business, Enterprise and Employment Act 2015 Sch 3 Pt 1 para 2).

4 Companies Act 2006 Sch 1B para 5(1) (as added: see note 3). References in Sch 1B to an interest being 'subject to restrictions' are to an interest being subject to restrictions by virtue of a restrictions notice under Sch 1B para 1 (see PARA 473): Sch 1B para 5(5) (as so added). Proceedings for an offence under Sch 1B para 5 or Sch 1B para 6 require the consent of the Secretary of State: see PARA 1817.

5 Companies Act 2006 Sch 1B para 5(2)(a) (as added: see note 3). As to the meaning of 'relevant interest' for these purposes see PARA 473 note 4.

6 Companies Act 2006 Sch 1B para 5(2)(b) (as added: see note 3).

7 Companies Act 2006 Sch 1B para 5(2)(c) (as added: see note 3).

8 Companies Act 2006 Sch 1B para 5(3) (as added: see note 3). See also note 4.

9 Companies Act 2006 Sch 1B para 5(4)(a) (as added: see note 3). As to the meaning of 'associated right' see PARA 473 note 15.

10 Ie void by virtue of the Companies Act 2006 Sch 1B para 3(2) or (4): see PARA 473.

11 See the Companies Act 2006 Sch 1B para 5(4)(b) (as added: see note 3). See also note 4.

12 Ie a restrictions notice under the Companies Act 2006 Sch 1B para 1: see PARA 473. As to the meaning of 'company' under the Companies Acts see PARA 21. As to the companies to which these provisions apply see PARA 466.

13 Companies Act 2006 Sch 1B para 6 (as added: see note 3). As to the meaning of 'officer who is in default' see PARA 316. As to the meaning of 'officer' generally see PARA 679. See also note 4.

14 Ie an offence under the Companies Act 2006 Sch 1B para 5 or Sch 1B para 6: see the text and notes 2–13.

15 See the Companies Act 2006 Sch 1B para 7(1)(a), (b)(i) (as added: see note 3). As to the powers of magistrates' courts to issue fines on summary conviction see SENTENCING vol 92 (2015) PARA 176.

476. Relaxation of restrictions in restrictions notice. As from 6 April 2016[1], the following provisions have effect.

An application may be made to the court[2] by the company in question or by any person aggrieved[3] for an order directing that the relevant interest[4] cease to be subject to restrictions[5]. The court must not make an order under these provisions unless:

(1) it is satisfied that the information required by the notice requiring information as to a person's status[6] or the notice requiring information as to a relevant change to that status[7] has been disclosed to the company and no unfair advantage has accrued to any person as a result of the earlier failure to make that disclosure[8]; or

(2) the relevant interest is to be transferred for valuable consideration and the court approves the transfer[9].

An order under these provisions made by virtue of head (2) above may continue, in whole or in part, the restrictions on issuing shares in right of the interest or in pursuance of an offer made to the interest-holder[10] and the restrictions, except in a liquidation, on payment of sums due from the company in respect of the interest, whether in respect of capital or otherwise[11], so far as they relate to a right acquired or offer made before the transfer[12]. Where any restrictions so continue in force, an application may be made under these provisions for an order directing that the relevant interest cease to be subject to those restrictions, and heads (1) and (2) above do not apply in relation to the making of such an order[13].

1 See PARA 466 note 1.
2 As to the meaning of 'the court' see PARA 160 note 12.
3 Companies Act 2006 Sch 1B para 8(2) (Sch 1B para 8 added by the Small Business, Enterprise and Employment Act 2015 Sch 3 Pt 1 para 2). As to the meaning of 'company' under the Companies Acts see PARA 21. As to the companies to which these provisions apply see PARA 466.
4 As to the meaning of 'relevant interest' for these purposes see para 473 note 4.
5 Companies Act 2006 Sch 1B para 8(1) (as added: see note 3). As to the meaning of references to an interest being 'subject to restrictions' see PARA 475 note 4.
6 Ie the notice served under the Companies Act 2006 s 790D: see PARA 468.
7 Ie the notice served under the Companies Act 2006 s 790E: see PARA 470.
8 See the Companies Act 2006 Sch 1B para 8(3)(a) (as added: see note 3).
9 Companies Act 2006 Sch 1B para 8(3)(b) (as added: see note 3).
10 Ie the restrictions mentioned in the Companies Act 2006 Sch 1B para 3(1)(c): see PARA 473 head (3).
11 Ie the restrictions mentioned in the Companies Act 2006 Sch 1B para 3(1)(d): see PARA 473 head (4).
12 See the Companies Act 2006 Sch 1B para 8(4) (as added: see note 3).
13 Companies Act 2006 Sch 1B para 8(5) (as added: see note 3).

477. Orders for sale of relevant interest subject to restrictions. As from 6 April 2016[1], the following provisions have effect.

The court[2] may order that the relevant interest subject to restrictions[3] be sold subject to the court's approval as to the sale[4]. An application for such an order may only be made by the company in question[5].

If the court makes such an order, it may make such further order relating to the sale or transfer of the interest as it thinks fit[6]. An application for a further order may be made by the company in question, by the person appointed by or in pursuance of the order to effect the sale, or by any person with an interest in the relevant interest[7].

On making an order for sale[8] or a further order[9], the court may order that the applicant's costs be paid out of the proceeds of sale[10].

If a relevant interest is sold in pursuance of an order under the above provisions, the proceeds of the sale, less the costs of the sale, must be paid into court for the benefit of those who are beneficially interested in the relevant interest[11]. A person who is beneficially interested in the relevant interest may apply to the court for the whole or part of those proceeds to be paid to that person[12]. On such an application, the court must order the payment to the applicant of:

(1) the whole of the proceeds of sale together with any interest on the proceeds; or
(2) if another person was also beneficially interested in the relevant interest at the time of the sale, such proportion of the proceeds, and any interest, as the value of the applicant's interest bears to the total value of the relevant interest[13].

If the court has ordered[14] that the costs of an applicant[15] are to be paid out of the proceeds of sale, the applicant is entitled to payment of those costs out of the proceeds before any person receives[16] any part of the proceeds[17].

1 See PARA 466 note 1.
2 As to the meaning of 'the court' see PARA 160 note 12.

3 As to the meaning of 'relevant interest' for these purposes see para 473 note 4; and as to the meaning of references to an interest being 'subject to restrictions' see PARA 475 note 4.
4 Companies Act 2006 Sch 1B para 9(1) (Sch 1B paras 9, 10 added by the Small Business, Enterprise and Employment Act 2015 Sch 3 Pt 1 para 2).
5 Companies Act 2006 Sch 1B para 9(2) (as added: see note 4). As to the meaning of 'company' under the Companies Acts see PARA 21. As to the companies to which these provisions apply see PARA 466.
6 Companies Act 2006 Sch 1B para 9(3) (as added: see note 4).
7 Companies Act 2006 Sch 1B para 9(4) (as added: see note 4).
8 Ie an order under the Companies Act 2006 Sch 1B para 9(1): see the text and notes 2–4.
9 Ie an order under the Companies Act 2006 Sch 1B para 9(1): see the text and note 6.
10 Companies Act 2006 Sch 1B para 9(5) (as added: see note 4).
11 Companies Act 2006 Sch 1B para 10(1) (as added: see note 4).
12 Companies Act 2006 Sch 1B para 10(2) (as added: see note 4).
13 Companies Act 2006 Sch 1B para 10(3) (as added: see note 4).
14 Ie under the Companies Act 2006 Sch 1B para 9: see the text and notes 2–10.
15 Ie an applicant under the Companies Act 2006 Sch 1B para 9: see the text and notes 2–10.
16 Ie under the Companies Act 2006 Sch 1B para 10: see the text and notes 11–13.
17 Companies Act 2006 Sch 1B para 10(4) (as added: see note 4.

478. Withdrawal of restrictions notice. As from 6 April 2016[1], the following provisions have effect.

A company that issues a person with a restrictions notice[2] must by notice withdraw the restrictions notice if:

(1) it is satisfied that there is a valid reason sufficient to justify the person's failure to comply with the notice requiring information as to a person's status[3] or the notice requiring information as to a relevant change to that status[4];
(2) the notice mentioned under head (1) above is complied with; or
(3) it discovers that the rights of a third party in respect of the relevant interest[5] are being unfairly affected by the restrictions notice[6].

Where a company is so required to withdraw a restrictions notice (a 'withdrawal notice'), the withdrawal notice must:

(a) be given before the end of the period of 14 days beginning with the day on which the company became required to withdraw the restrictions notice;
(b) specify the date on which the withdrawal notice is given;
(c) identify the addressee's relevant interest in the company by reference to the shares or right in question; and
(d) state that the relevant interest is no longer subject to restrictions[7].

1 See PARA 466 note 1.
2 Ie under the Companies Act 2006 Sch 1B para 1: see PARA 473. As to the meaning of 'company' under the Companies Acts see PARA 21. As to the companies to which these provisions apply see PARA 466.
3 Ie the notice served under the Companies Act 2006 s 790D: see PARA 468.
4 Ie the notice served under the Companies Act 2006 s 790E: see PARA 470.
5 As to the meaning of 'relevant interest' for these purposes see para 473 note 4.
6 Companies Act 2006 Sch 1B para 11 (added by the Small Business, Enterprise and Employment Act 2015 Sch 3 Pt 1 para 2).
7 Register of People with Significant Control Regulations 2016, SI 2016/339, reg 21.

D. EXEMPTION FROM PSC INFORMATION AND REGISTRATION REQUIREMENTS

479. Exemption from information and registration requirements. As from 6 April 2016[1], the following provisions have effect.

The Secretary of State may exempt a person, whether an individual[2] or a legal entity[3], under these provisions[4]; and the effect of an exemption is:

(1) the person is not required to comply with any notice requiring information as to a person's status[5] or requiring information as to a relevant change to that status[6], but if a notice is received, the person must bring the existence of the exemption to the attention of the company that sent it;

(2) companies are not obliged to take steps or give notice with regard to information[7] to or with respect to that person;

(3) notices requiring information as to identity[8] do not require anyone else to give any information about that person;

(4) the duties imposed on others to supply and update information[9] do not apply to that person; and

(5) the person does not count[10] as a registrable person[11] or, as the case may be, a registrable relevant legal entity[12] in relation to any company[13].

The Secretary of State must not grant such an exemption unless he is satisfied that, having regard to any undertaking given by the person to be exempted, there are special reasons why that person should be exempted[14].

1 See PARA 466 note 1.
2 As to the meaning of 'individual' for these purposes see PARA 467 note 3.
3 As to the meaning of 'legal entity' for these purposes see PARA 467 note 18.
4 Companies Act 2006 s 790J(1) (s 790J added by the Small Business, Enterprise and Employment Act 2015 Sch 3 Pt 1 para 1). As to the Secretary of State see PARA 6.
5 Ie any notice under the Companies Act 2006 s 790D(2) (see PARA 468).
6 Ie any notice under the Companies Act 2006 s 790E (see PARA 470).
7 Ie under the Companies Act 2006 s 790D (see PARA 468) or s 790E (see PARA 470). As to the meaning of 'company' under the Companies Acts see PARA 21. As to the companies to which these provisions apply see PARA 466.
8 Ie notices under the Companies Act 2006 s 790D(5) (see PARA 468).
9 Ie the duties imposed by the Companies Act 2006 ss 790G, 790H (see PARA 471).
10 Ie for the purposes of the Companies Act 2006 s 790M (see PARA 480).
11 As to the meaning of 'registrable person' see PARA 467 text and note 22.
12 As to the meaning of 'registrable relevant legal entity' see PARA 467 text and note 26.
13 Companies Act 2006 s 790J(2) (as added: see note 4).
14 Companies Act 2006 s 790J(3) (as added: see note 4).

(iii) Register of People with Significant Control

480. Duties to keep PSC register and to keep it available for inspection. As from 6 April 2016 for most purposes[1], the following provisions have effect.

A company to which Part 21A of the Companies Act 2006[2] applies[3] must keep a register of people with significant control over the company[4] (a 'PSC register'[5]).

The required particulars[6] of any individual[7] with significant control over the company who is 'registrable'[8] in relation to the company must be entered in the register once all the required particulars of that individual have been confirmed[9]. The company must not enter any of the individual's particulars in the register until they have all been confirmed[10].

Particulars of any individual with significant control over the company who is 'non-registrable'[11] in relation to the company must not be entered in the register[12]; but the required particulars of any entity that is a registrable relevant legal entity[13] in relation to the company must be noted in the register once the company becomes aware of the entity's status as such[14].

If the company becomes aware of a relevant change[15] with respect to a registrable person[16] or registrable relevant legal entity whose particulars are stated in the register, details of the change and the date on which it occurred must be entered in the register, but, in the case of a registrable person, the details and date must not be entered there until they have all been confirmed[17].

The Secretary of State may by regulations require additional matters to be noted in a company's PSC register[18].

If a company makes default in complying with the above provisions, an offence is committed by the company, and by every officer of the company who is in default[19].

A company to which Part 21A of the Companies Act 2006 applies is not, by virtue of anything done for the purposes of the above provisions, affected with notice of, or put upon inquiry as to, the rights of any person in relation to any shares or rights in or with respect to the company[20].

A company's PSC register must be kept available for inspection at its registered office[21], or at a specified[22] place[23]. A company must give notice to the registrar of companies[24] of the place where its PSC register is kept available for inspection and of any change in that place[25]; but no such notice is required if the register has, at all times since it came into existence, been kept available for inspection at the company's registered office[26]. If a company makes default for 14 days in complying with the duty to give notice[27], an offence is committed by the company, and by every officer of the company who is in default[28].

The above provisions[29] must be read with the provisions setting out rules[30] for an alternative method of record keeping[31].

1 See PARA 466 note 1. Note, however, that the Companies Act 2006 s 790M(9)(c) (see note 9 head (3)) and s 790W(3) (cited in note 31) were not brought into force until 30 June 2016: see PARA 466 note 1.

2 Ie the Companies Act 2006 Pt 21A (ss 790A–790ZG) (added by the Small Business, Enterprise and Employment Act 2015 Sch 3 Pt 1 para 1): see PARA 466 et seq; the text and notes 3–21; and PARA 481 et seq.

3 As to companies to which the Companies Act 2006 Pt 21A applies see PARA 466. As to the meaning of 'company' under the Companies Acts see PARA 21.

4 Companies Act 2006 s 790M(1) (as added: see note 2). As to persons with significant control over the company see PARA 467.

5 See the Companies Act 2006 s 790C(10), cited in PARA 470 note 5.

6 As to the meaning of 'particulars' see PARA 468 note 10; and as to the required particulars see PARA 469.

7 As to the meaning of 'individual' for these purposes see PARA 467 note 3.

8 As to when an individual is 'registrable' see PARA 467 text and notes 21–22. The Secretary of State has power to make exemptions whereby an individual does not count as registrable for these purposes: see PARA 479. See also the Companies Act 2006 s 790M(11)(c) (as added: see note 2).

9 Companies Act 2006 s 790M(2) (as added: see note 2).

A person's required particulars, and the details and date of any relevant change with respect to a person, are considered for these purposes to have been 'confirmed' (Companies Act 2006 s 790M(9) (as so added), if:

(1) the person supplied or confirmed them to the company (whether voluntarily, pursuant to a duty imposed by Pt 21A or otherwise);

(2) another person did so but with that person's knowledge; or

(3) they were included in a statement of initial significant control delivered to the registrar of companies under s 9 (see PARA 104) by subscribers wishing to form the company.

Section 790M(9)(c) (see head (3) above) is modified in its application to SEs so that it reads as follows: 'they were included in a statement of initial significant control delivered to the registrar under the European Public Limited-Liability Company Regulations 2004, SI 2004/2326, regs 5–10 or reg 85': European Public Limited-Liability Company (Register of People with Significant Control) Regulations 2016, SI 2016/375, reg 5. As to the meaning of 'SE' for these purposes see PARA 106 note 3; and as to such companies see PARA 1825 et seq.

In the case of someone who was a registrable person or a registrable relevant legal entity in relation to the company on its incorporation, the date to be entered in the register as the date on which the individual became a registrable person, or the entity became a registrable relevant legal entity, is to be the date of incorporation, and, in the case of a registrable person, that particular is deemed to have been 'confirmed': Companies Act 2006 s 790M(10) (as so added). Section

790M(10) is modified in its application to SEs so that references to 'incorporation' are read as references to 'registration': European Public Limited-Liability Company (Register of People with Significant Control) Regulations 2016, SI 2016/375, reg 6.

For these purposes:

(a) if a person's usual residential address is the same as his service address, the entry for him in the register may state that fact instead of repeating the address; but this does not apply in a case where the service address is stated to be 'The company's registered office' (Companies Act 2006 s 790M(11)(a) (as so added));

(b) nothing in s 126 (trusts not to be entered on register: see PARA 344) affects what may be entered in a company's PSC register or is receivable by the registrar in relation to people with significant control over a company (even if they are members of the company) (s 790M(11)(b) (as so added)).

Information as to a person's usual residential address may be protected from disclosure: see s 790ZF; and PARA 491.

10 Companies Act 2006 s 790M(3) (as added: see note 2). As to confirmation see note 9.

11 As to when an individual is 'non-registrable' see PARA 467 text and notes 16–20.

12 Companies Act 2006 s 790M(4) (as added: see note 2).

13 As to the meaning of 'registrable relevant legal entity' see PARA 467 text and note 26. The Secretary of State has power to make exemptions whereby a legal entity does not count as registrable for these purposes: see PARA 479. See also the Companies Act 2006 s 790M(11)(c) (as added: see note 2).

14 Companies Act 2006 s 790M(5) (as added: see note 2).

15 Ie a relevant change within the meaning of the Companies Act 2006 s 790E (not yet in force): see PARA 470.

16 As to the meaning of 'registrable person' see PARA 467 text and note 22.

17 Companies Act 2006 s 790M(6) (as added: see note 2). As to confirmation see note 9.

18 Companies Act 2006 s 790M(7) (as added: see note 2). Such regulations are subject to affirmative resolution procedure (ie the regulations must not be made unless a draft of the statutory instrument containing them has been laid before Parliament and approved by a resolution of each House of Parliament): see ss 790M(8), 1290 (s 790M(8) as so added). As to the making of regulations under the Companies Act 2006 generally see ss 1288–1292; and as to the Secretary of State see PARA 6.

The additional matters required to be noted in a company's PSC register under s 790M(7) are the matters required to be noted by the Register of People with Significant Control Regulations 2016, SI 2016/339, regs 10–17 (see heads (1)–(10) below): reg 9(1). Where any additional matter noted in a company's PSC register in accordance with reg 10, reg 11, reg 12 or reg 13 (see heads (1)–(4) below) ceases to be true, the company must note in its PSC register that the additional matter has ceased to be true and the date on which the additional matter ceased to be true: reg 9(2).

Where:

(1) a company knows or has reasonable cause to believe that there is no registrable person or registrable relevant legal entity in relation to the company, the company must note in its PSC register that it knows or has reasonable cause to believe that there is no registrable person or registrable relevant legal entity in relation to the company (reg 10(1), (2));

(2) a company knows or has reasonable cause to believe that there is a registrable person in relation to the company, and has not been able to identify the registrable person, the company must note in its PSC register that it knows or has reasonable cause to believe that there is a registrable person in relation to the company but it has not identified the registrable person, and make a separate note in its PSC register in respect of each registrable person which the company has been unable to identify (reg 11(1), (2));

(3) a company has identified a registrable person in relation to the company, and all the required particulars of that person have not been confirmed for the purposes of the Companies Act 2006 s 790M, the company must note in its PSC register that it has identified a registrable person in relation to the company but all the required particulars of that person have not been confirmed, and make a separate note in its PSC register in respect of each such registrable person (see the Register of People with Significant Control Regulations 2016, SI 2016/339, reg 12(1), (2));

(4) a company is not required to place a note in its PSC register by reg 10, reg 11 or reg 12 (see heads (1)–(3) above), has not entered, and is not required to enter, the required particulars of any registrable person or registrable relevant legal entity in its PSC register, and has not yet completed taking reasonable steps to find out if there is anyone who is a registrable person or a registrable relevant legal entity in relation to the company under the Companies Act 2006 s 790D (see PARA 468), the company must

note in its PSC register that it has not yet completed taking reasonable steps to find out if there is anyone who is a registrable person or a registrable relevant legal entity in relation to the company (Register of People with Significant Control Regulations 2016, SI 2016/339, reg 13(1), (2));

(5) a company has given a notice under the Companies Act 2006 s 790D (see PARA 468) and the addressee of the notice has failed to comply with the notice within the time specified in it, the company must note in its PSC register that it has given a notice under s 790D which has not been complied with, and make a separate note in its PSC register in respect of each notice under s 790D which has not been complied with (Register of People with Significant Control Regulations 2016, SI 2016/339, reg 14(1), (2));

(6) a company has given a notice under the Companies Act 2006 s 790E (see PARA 470) and the addressee of the notice has failed to comply with the notice within the time specified in it, the company must note in the entry in its PSC register for the addressee that the addressee has failed to comply with a notice given by the company under s 790E (Register of People with Significant Control Regulations 2016, SI 2016/339, reg 15(1), (2));

(7) a note has been placed in a company's register under reg 14 or reg 15 (see heads (5)–(6) above) and the addressee of the notice to which the note relates has complied with the notice after the time specified in the notice, the company must note in its PSC register that the notice has been complied with after the time specified in the notice, and the date on which the notice was complied with (reg 16(1), (2));

(8) a company has issued a restrictions notice under the Companies Act 2006 Sch 1B para 1 (see PARA 473), the company must note in its PSC register that it has so issued a restrictions notice and make a separate note in its PSC register in respect of each registrable person which the company has been unable to identify (see the Register of People with Significant Control Regulations 2016, SI 2016/339, reg 17(1), (2));

(9) the company withdraws the restrictions notice under the Companies Act 2006 Sch 1B para 11 (see PARA 478), the company must note in its PSC register that it has withdrawn the restrictions notice by giving a withdrawal notice, and the date specified in the withdrawal notice as the date on which the withdrawal notice was given (Register of People with Significant Control Regulations 2016, SI 2016/339, reg 17(3));

(10) a court makes an order under the Companies Act 2006 Sch 1B para 8 (see PARA 476) directing that a relevant interest in the company cease to be subject to restrictions, the company must note in its PSC register that the court has made such an order and the date on which that order takes effect (see the Register of People with Significant Control Regulations 2016, SI 2016/339, reg 17(4)).

The statutory wording of reg 12(1), (2) (see head (3) above) requires the company to make a separate note in its PSC register in respect of each registrable person which the company has been unable to identify, but it is submitted that this is a drafting error and that reg 12 should read as set out in head (3) above.

19 Companies Act 2006 s 790M(12) (as added: see note 2). A person guilty of such an offence is liable on summary conviction to a fine not exceeding level 3 on the standard scale and, for continued contravention, a daily default fine not exceeding one-tenth of level 3 on the standard scale: s 790M(13) (as so added). As to the meaning of 'officer who is in default' see PARA 316. As to the meaning of 'officer' generally see PARA 679. As to the standard scale and the powers of magistrates' courts to issue fines on summary conviction see SENTENCING vol 92 (2015) PARA 176; and as to the meaning of 'daily default fine' see PARA 1816.

20 Companies Act 2006 s 790M(14) (as added: see note 2).

21 As to a company's registered office see PARA 124.

22 Ie a place specified in regulations made under the Companies Act 2006 s 1136 (see PARA 748).

23 Companies Act 2006 s 790N(1) (as added: see note 2). Section 790N is subject to s 790ZF (protection of information as to usual residential address: see PARA 491), and to any provision of regulations made under s 790ZG (protection of material: see PARA 492); but this is not to be taken to affect the generality of the power conferred by virtue of s 790ZG(3)(f): s 790T(1), (2) (as so added).

24 As to the meaning of 'registrar of companies' see PARA 126 note 2.

25 Companies Act 2006 s 790N(2) (as added: see note 2). See also note 23.

26 Companies Act 2006 s 790N(3) (as added: see note 2). See also note 23.

27 Ie the duty under the Companies Act 2006 s 790N(2): see the text and notes 24–25.

28 Companies Act 2006 s 790N(4) (as added: see note 2). A person guilty of such an offence is liable on summary conviction to a fine not exceeding level 3 on the standard scale and, for continued contravention, to a daily default fine not exceeding one-tenth of level 3 on the standard scale: s 790N(5) (as so added). See also note 23.

29 Ie the provisions set out in the text and notes 1–28.

30 Ie the Companies Act 2006 Pt 21A Ch 4 (ss 790W–790ZE): see PARA 484 et seq.

31 See the Companies Act 2006 s 790W(3) (as added: see note 2).

481. Rights to inspect and require copies of PSC register and company's response to request to exercise those rights. As from 6 April 2016 for most purposes[1], the following provisions have effect.

A company's PSC register[2] must be open to the inspection of any person without charge[3].

Any person may require a copy of a company's PSC register, or any part of it, on payment of such fee as may be prescribed[4].

A person seeking to exercise either of the rights conferred by these provisions must make a request to the company to that effect[5]. The request must contain the following information:

(1) in the case of an individual[6], his or her name and address;
(2) in the case of an organisation, the name and address of an individual responsible for making the request on behalf of the organisation; and
(3) the purpose for which the information is to be used[7].

Where a company receives such a request, it must within five working days[8] either comply with the request or apply to the court[9]. If it applies to the court, the company must notify the person making the request[10]. If on such an application the court is satisfied that the inspection or copy is not sought for a proper purpose:

(a) it must direct the company not to comply with the request; and
(b) it may further order that the company's costs on the application be paid in whole or in part by the person who made the request, even if that person is not a party to the application[11].

If the court makes such a direction and it appears to the court that the company is or may be subject to other requests made for a similar purpose, whether made by the same person or different persons, it may direct that the company is not to comply with any such request[12]. The order must contain such provision as appears to the court appropriate to identify the requests to which it applies[13]. If on such an application the court does not direct the company not to comply with the request, the company must comply with the request immediately upon the court giving its decision or, as the case may be, the proceedings being discontinued[14].

If a required inspection[15] is refused or default is made in providing a required copy[16], otherwise than in accordance with an order of the court, an offence is committed by the company and by every officer of the company[17] who is in default[18]. In the case of any such refusal or default the court may by order compel an immediate inspection or, as the case may be, direct that the copy required be sent to the person requesting it[19].

Where a person inspects the PSC register, or the company provides a person with a copy of the register or any part of it, the company must inform the person of the most recent date, if any, on which alterations were made to the register and whether there are further alterations to be made[20]. If a company fails to provide the information so required, an offence is committed by the company, and by every officer of the company who is in default[21].

It is an offence for a person in possession of information obtained by exercise of either the right of inspection or the right to require a copy of a company's PSC register or any part of it[22] to do anything that results in the information being disclosed to another person, or to fail to do anything with the result that the information is disclosed to another person, knowing, or having reason to suspect, that person may use the information for a purpose that is not a proper purpose[23].

The above provisions[24] must be read with the provisions setting out rules[25] for an alternative method of record keeping[26].

1 See PARA 466 note 1. Note, however, that the Companies Act 2006 s 790W(3) (cited in note 26) was not brought into force until 30 June 2016: see PARA 466 note 1.
2 As to the meaning of 'company's PSC register' see PARA 470 note 5; and as to that register see PARA 480. As to the meaning of 'company' under the Companies Acts see PARA 21. As to the companies to which these provisions apply see PARA 466.
3 Companies Act 2006 s 790O(1) (ss790O–790T, 790W added by the Small Business, Enterprise and Employment Act 2015 Sch 3 Pt 1 para 1). Section 790O(1), (2) is subject to s 790ZF (protection of information as to usual residential address: see PARA 491), and to any provision of regulations made under s 790ZG (protection of material: see PARA 492); but this is not to be taken to affect the generality of the power conferred by virtue of s 790ZG(3)(f): s 790T(1), (2) (as so added).
4 Companies Act 2006 s 790O(2) (as added: see note 3). The fee prescribed for the purpose of s 790O(2) is £12: Register of People with Significant Control Regulations 2016, SI 2016/339, reg 6(1). That fee applies to any single request for a copy of a company's PSC register, or any part of it, regardless of how many parts are required to be copied: reg 6(2).

In the Companies Acts, 'prescribed' means prescribed (by order or by regulations) by the Secretary of State: Companies Act 2006 s 1167. As to the meaning of the 'Companies Acts' see PARA 13. As to the making of orders and regulations under the Companies Act 2006 generally see ss 1288–1292.
5 Companies Act 2006 s 790O(3) (as added: see note 3). It is an offence for a person knowingly or recklessly to make in such a request a statement that is misleading, false or deceptive in a material particular: s 790R(1) (as so added). A person guilty of an offence under s 790R is liable on conviction on indictment, to imprisonment for a term not exceeding two years or a fine, or to both, or on summary conviction in England and Wales, to imprisonment for a term not exceeding 12 months or to a fine, or to both: see s 790R(3)(a), (b)(i) (as so added). In relation to an offence committed before the coming into force of the Criminal Justice Act 2003 s 154(1) (not yet in force), the maximum term of imprisonment on summary conviction is six months: see the Companies Act 2006 s 1131.
6 As to the meaning of 'individual' for these purposes see PARA 467 note 3.
7 Companies Act 2006 s 790O(4) (as added: see note 3).
8 As to the meaning of 'working day' see PARA 140 note 16.
9 Companies Act 2006 s 790P(1) (as added: see note 3). As to the meaning of 'the court' see PARA 160 note 12.
10 Companies Act 2006 s 790P(2) (as added: see note 3).
11 Companies Act 2006 s 790P(3) (as added: see note 3).
12 Companies Act 2006 s 790P(4) (as added: see note 3).
13 See note 12.
14 Companies Act 2006 s 790P(5) (as added: see note 3).
15 Ie an inspection required under the Companies Act 2006 s 790O: see the text and notes 1–7.
16 Ie a copy required under the Companies Act 2006 s 790O: see the text and notes 1–7.
17 As to the meaning of 'officer who is in default' see PARA 316. As to the meaning of 'officer' generally see PARA 679.
18 Companies Act 2006 s 790Q(1) (as added: see note 3). A person guilty of such an offence is liable on summary conviction to a fine not exceeding level 3 on the standard scale and, for continued contravention, to a daily default fine not exceeding one-tenth of level 3 on the standard scale: s 790Q(2) (as so added). as to the meaning of 'daily default fine' see PARA 1816; and As to the standard scale and the powers of magistrates' courts to issue fines on summary conviction see SENTENCING vol 92 (2015) PARA 176.
19 Companies Act 2006 s 790Q(3) (as added: see note 3).
20 Companies Act 2006 s 790S(1) (as added: see note 3).
21 Companies Act 2006 s 790S(2) (as added: see note 3). A person guilty of such an offence is liable on summary conviction to a fine not exceeding level 3 on the standard scale: s 790S(3) (as so added).
22 Ie by exercise of either of the rights conferred by the Companies Act 2006 s 790O: see the text and notes 1–7.
23 Companies Act 2006 s 790R(2) (as added: see note 3). As to the penalty for such an offence see note 5.
24 Ie the provisions set out in the text and notes 1–23.
25 Ie the Companies Act 2006 Pt 21A Ch 4 (ss 790W–790ZE): see PARA 484 et seq.
26 See the Companies Act 2006 s 790W(3) (as added: see note 3).

482. Removal of entries from the PSC register. As from 6 April 2016 for most purposes[1], the following provisions have effect.

An entry relating to an individual[2] who used to be a registrable person[3] may be removed from the company's PSC register[4] after the expiration of ten years from the date on which the individual ceased to be a registrable person in relation to the company[5].

An entry relating to an entity that used to be a registrable relevant legal entity[6] may be removed from the company's PSC register after the expiration of ten years from the date on which the entity ceased to be a registrable relevant legal entity in relation to the company[7].

The above provisions[8] must be read with the provisions setting out rules[9] for an alternative method of record keeping[10].

1 See PARA 466 note 1. Note, however, that the Companies Act 2006 s 790W(3) (cited in note 10) was not brought into force until 30 June 2016: see PARA 466 note 1.
2 As to the meaning of 'individual' for these purposes see PARA 467 note 3.
3 As to the meaning of 'registrable person' see PARA 467 text and note 22.
4 As to the meaning of 'company's PSC register' see PARA 470 note 5; and as to that register see PARA 480. As to the meaning of 'company' under the Companies Acts see PARA 21. As to the companies to which these provisions apply see PARA 466.
5 Companies Act 2006 s 790U(1) (ss 790U, 790W added by the Small Business, Enterprise and Employment Act 2015 Sch 3 Pt 1 para 1).
6 As to the meaning of 'registrable relevant legal entity' see PARA 467 text and note 26.
7 Companies Act 2006 s 790U(2) (as added: see note 5).
8 Ie the provisions set out in the text and notes 1–7.
9 Ie the Companies Act 2006 Pt 21A Ch 4 (ss 790W–790ZE): see PARA 484 et seq.
10 See the Companies Act 2006 s 790W(3) (as added: see note 5).

483. Power of court to rectify company's PSC register. As from 6 April 2016 for most purposes[1], the following provisions have effect. If:

(1) the name of any person is, without sufficient cause, entered in or omitted from a company's PSC register[2] as a registrable person[3] or registrable relevant legal entity[4]; or
(2) default is made or unnecessary delay takes place in entering on the PSC register the fact that a person has ceased to be a registrable person or registrable relevant legal entity,

the person aggrieved or any other interested party[5] may apply to the court[6] for rectification of the register[7]. The court may either refuse the application or may order rectification of the register and payment by the company of any damages sustained by any party aggrieved[8].

On such an application, the court may:

(a) decide any question as to whether the name of any person who is a party to the application should or should not be entered in or omitted from the register; and
(b) more generally, decide any question necessary or expedient to be decided for rectification of the register[9].

In the case of a company required by the Companies Act 2006 to send information stated in its PSC register to the registrar of companies[10], the court, when making an order for rectification of the register, must by its order direct notice of the rectification to be given to the registrar[11].

The above provisions[12] must be read with the provisions setting out rules[13] for an alternative method of record keeping[14].

1 See PARA 466 note 1. Note, however, that the Companies Act 2006 s 790W(3) (cited in note 14) was not brought into force until 30 June 2016: see PARA 466 note 1.

2 As to the meaning of 'company's PSC register' see PARA 470 note 5; and as to that register see PARA 480. As to the meaning of 'company' under the Companies Acts see PARA 21. As to the companies to which these provisions apply see PARA 466.
3 As to the meaning of 'registrable person' see PARA 467 text and note 22.
4 As to the meaning of 'registrable relevant legal entity' see PARA 467 text and note 26.
5 The reference in the text to 'any other interested party' is to any member of the company, and any other person who is a registrable person or a registrable relevant legal entity in relation to the company: Companies Act 2006 s 790V(5) (ss 790V, 790W added by the Small Business, Enterprise and Employment Act 2015 Sch 3 Pt 1 para 1).
6 As to the meaning of 'the court' see PARA 160 note 12.
7 Companies Act 2006 s 790V(1) (as added: see note 5).
8 Companies Act 2006 s 790V(2) (as added: see note 5).
9 Companies Act 2006 s 790V(3) (as added: see note 5).
10 As to the meaning of 'registrar of companies' see PARA 126 note 2.
11 Companies Act 2006 s 790V(4) (as added: see note 5).
12 Ie the provisions set out in the text and notes 1–11.
13 Ie the Companies Act 2006 Pt 21A Ch 4 (ss 790W–790ZE): see PARA 484 et seq.
14 See the Companies Act 2006 s 790W(3) (as added: see note 5).

(iv) Alternative Method of Record Keeping with regard to Persons with Significant Control

484. Rules allowing companies to keep information about persons with significant control on the central register: in general. As from 30 June 2016[1], the following provisions have effect.

Rules are set out in the Companies Act 2006[2] allowing private companies[3] to keep information on the register kept by the registrar of companies[4] ('the central register')[5] instead of entering it in their PSC register[6]. Nothing in the provisions setting out those rules[7], however, affects the information-gathering duties imposed[8] on a company[9].

The Secretary of State may by regulations amend the Companies Act 2006 to extend the provisions setting out those rules[10], with or without modification, to public companies[11] or public companies of a class specified in the regulations, and to make such other amendments as he thinks fit in consequence of that extension[12].

1 See PARA 466 note 1.
2 Ie in the Companies Act 2006 Pt 21A Ch 4 (ss 790W–790ZE) (added by the Small Business, Enterprise and Employment Act 2015 Sch 3 Pt 1 para 1): see the text and notes 3–12; and PARA 485 et seq.
3 As to the meaning of 'private company' see PARA 95.
4 As to the meaning of 'registrar of companies' see PARA 126 note 2.
5 As to the central register see PARA 142 et seq.
6 See the Companies Act 2006 s 790W(1), (2) (as added: see note 2). As to the meaning of 'company's PSC register' see PARA 470 note 5; and as to that register see PARA 480. As to the meaning of 'company' under the Companies Acts see PARA 21. As to the companies to which the Companies Act 2006 Pt 21A applies see PARA 466.
7 Ie nothing in the Companies Act 2006 Pt 21A Ch 4 (ss 790W–790ZE).
8 Ie the duties imposed by the Companies Act 2006 Pt 21A Ch 2 (ss 790D–790L): see PARA 468 et seq.
9 Companies Act 2006 s 790W(4) (as added: see note 2).
10 Ie to extend the Companies Act 2006 Pt 21A Ch 4 (ss 790W–790ZE).
11 As to the meaning of 'public company' see PARA 95.
12 Companies Act 2006 s 790ZE(1) (as added: see note 2). Such regulations are subject to affirmative resolution procedure (ie the regulations must not be made unless a draft of the statutory instrument containing them has been laid before Parliament and approved by a resolution of each House of Parliament): see ss 790ZE(2), 1290 (s 790ZE(2) as so added). As to the making of regulations under the Companies Act 2006 generally see ss 1288–1292; and as to the Secretary of State see PARA 6.

485. Right to make an election to keep information about persons with significant control on the central register. As from 30 June 2016[1], the following provisions have effect.

An election to keep information about persons with significant control on the central register may be made[2] by the subscribers wishing to form a private company[3] under the Companies Act 2006, or by the private company itself once it is formed and registered[4]. Such an election is made by giving notice of election to the registrar of companies[5]. If the notice is given by subscribers wishing to form a private company:

(1) it must be given when the documents required to be delivered for registration[6] are delivered to the registrar; and
(2) it must be accompanied by a statement confirming that no objection was received as mentioned in head (ii) below[7].

If the notice is given by the company, it must be accompanied by:

(a) a statement confirming that no objection was received as mentioned in head (ii) below; and
(b) a statement containing all the information that is required to be contained in the company's PSC register[8] as at the date of the notice in respect of matters that are current[9] as at that date[10];

and the company must where necessary update the statement sent under head (b) above to ensure that the final version delivered to the registrar contains all the information that is required to be contained in the company's PSC register as at the time immediately before the election takes effect[11] in respect of matters that are current as at that time[12]. This obligation to update the statement includes an obligation to rectify it, where necessary, in consequence of the company's PSC register being rectified[13], whether before or after the election takes effect[14]. If default is made in complying with the obligation to update the statement, an offence is committed by the company, and by every officer of the company[15] who is in default[16].

The election is of no effect unless:

(i) notice of the intention to make the election was given to each eligible person[17] at least 14 days before the day on which the election was made; and
(ii) no objection was received by the subscribers or, as the case may be, the company from any eligible person within that notice period[18].

1 See PARA 466 note 1.
2 Ie under the Companies Act 2006 s 790X: see the text and notes 3–18. As to persons with significant control over a company see PARA 467. As to the central register see PARA 142 et seq.
3 As to the meaning of 'private company' see PARA 95. As to the power to extend this option to public companies see PARA 484. As to the meaning of 'company' under the Companies Acts see PARA 21. As to the companies to which these provisions apply see PARA 466.
4 See the Companies Act 2006 s 790X(1) (s 790X added by the Small Business, Enterprise and Employment Act 2015 Sch 3 Pt 1 para 1). As to the formation and registration of companies see PARA 65 et seq.
5 Companies Act 2006 s 790X(4) (as added: see note 4). As to the meaning of 'registrar of companies' see PARA 126 note 2.
6 Ie the documents required to be delivered under the Companies Act 2006 s 9: see PARA 104.
7 Companies Act 2006 s 790X(5) (as added: see note 4).
8 As to the meaning of 'company's PSC register' see PARA 470 note 5; and as to that register see PARA 480.
9 A reference in the Companies Act 2006 Pt 21A Ch 4 (ss 790W–790ZE) (see PARA 484; the text and notes 1–8, 10–18; and PARA 486 et seq) to matters that are current as at a given date or time is a reference to persons who are a registrable person or registrable relevant legal entity in relation to the company as at that date or time and whose particulars are required to be contained in the company's PSC register as at that date or time, and to any other matters that are current as at that

date or time: s 790X(11) (as added: see note 4). As to the meaning of 'registrable person' see PARA 467 text and note 22; and as to the meaning of 'relevant legal entity' for these purposes see PARA 467 note 19.

10 Companies Act 2006 s 790X(6) (as added: see note 4).

11 As to when the election takes effect see PARA 486.

12 Companies Act 2006 s 790X(7) (as added: see note 4).

13 As to rectification of the company's PSC register see PARA 483; and as to removal of entries from the register see PARA 482.

14 Companies Act 2006 s 790X(8) (as added: see note 4).

15 For this purpose a shadow director is treated as an officer of the company: Companies Act 2006 s 790X(9) (as added: see note 4). As to shadow directors see PARA 513. As to the meaning of 'officer who is in default' see PARA 316; and as to the meaning of 'officer' generally see PARA 679.

16 Companies Act 2006 s 790X(9) (as added: see note 4). A person guilty of such an offence is liable on summary conviction to a fine not exceeding level 3 on the standard scale, and for continued contravention to a daily default fine not exceeding one-tenth of level 3 on the standard scale: s 790X(10) (as so added). As to the standard scale and the powers of magistrates' courts to issue fines on summary conviction see SENTENCING vol 92 (2015) PARA 176; and as to the meaning of 'daily default fine' see PARA 1816.

17 For these purposes, a person is an 'eligible person' if:

(1) in a case of an election by the subscribers wishing to form a private company, the person's particulars would, but for the election, be required to be entered in the company's PSC register on its incorporation (Companies Act 2006 s 790X(3)(a) (as added (see note 4)); and

(2) in the case of an election by the company itself, the person is a registrable person or a registrable relevant legal entity in relation to the company, and the person's particulars are stated in the company's PSC register (s 790X(3)(b) (as so added)).

As to the meaning of 'particulars' see PARA 468 note 10.

18 Companies Act 2006 s 790X(2) (as added: see note 4).

486. Date and effect of election to keep information about persons with significant control on the central register. As from 30 June 2016[1], the following provisions have effect.

An election to keep information about persons with significant control on the central register[2] takes effect when the notice of election[3] is registered by the registrar of companies[4]. The election remains in force until either the company ceases to be a private company[5], or a notice of withdrawal sent by the company[6] is registered by the registrar, whichever occurs first[7].

The effect of such an election on a company's obligations regarding a PSC register[8] is as follows[9]. The company's obligation to maintain a PSC register does not apply with respect to the period when the election is in force[10]. This means that, during that period:

(1) the company must continue to keep a PSC register in accordance with the relevant statutory provisions[11] (a 'historic' register) containing all the information that was required to be stated in that register as at the time immediately before the election took effect; but

(2) the company does not have to update that register to reflect any changes that occur after that time[12].

The statutory provisions with regard to the PSC register[13], including the rights to inspect or require copies of the PSC register[14], continue to apply to the historic register during the period when the election is in force[15]. The company must place a note in its historic register:

(a) stating that an election to keep information about persons with significant control on the central register[16] is in force;

(b) recording when that election took effect; and

(c) indicating that up-to-date information about people with significant control over the company is available for public inspection on the central register[17].

If a company makes default in complying with heads (a) to (c) above, an offence is committed by the company, and by every officer of the company who is in default[18]. The obligations under these provisions with respect to a historic register do not, however, apply in a case where the election was made by subscribers wishing to form a private company[19].

1 See PARA 466 note 1.
2 Ie an election made under the Companies Act 2006 s 790X: see PARA 485. As to persons with significant control over a company see PARA 467. As to the central register see PARA 142 et seq.
3 As to the notice of election see PARA 485.
4 See the Companies Act 2006 s 790Y(1) (ss 790M, 790Y, 790Z added by the Small Business, Enterprise and Employment Act 2015 Sch 3 Pt 1 para 1).
5 As to the meaning of 'private company' see PARA 95. As to the power to extend this option to public companies see PARA 484. As to the meaning of 'company' under the Companies Acts see PARA 21. As to the companies to which these provisions apply see PARA 466.
6 Ie sent under the Companies Act 2006 s 790ZD): see PARA 490.
7 Companies Act 2006 s 790Y(2) (as added: see note 7).
8 Ie its obligations under the Companies Act 2006 Pt 21A Ch 3 (ss 790M–790V): see PARA 480 et seq. As to the meaning of 'company's PSC register' see PARA 470 note 5; and as to that register see PARA 480.
9 See the Companies Act 2006 s 790Z(1) (as added: see note 7).
10 Companies Act 2006 s 790Z(2) (as added: see note 7).
11 Ie in accordance with the Companies Act 2006 Pt 21A Ch 3: see PARA 480 et seq.
12 Companies Act 2006 s 790Z(3) (as added: see note 7).
13 Ie the Companies Act 2006 Pt 21A Ch 3: see PARA 480 et seq.
14 As to the rights to inspect or require copies of the PSC register see PARA 481.
15 Companies Act 2006 s 790Z(4) (as added: see note 7).
16 See note 2.
17 Companies Act 2006 s 790Z(5) (as added: see note 7).
18 Companies Act 2006 s 790M(12) (as added: see note 7); applied for these purposes by s 790Z(6) (as so added). A person guilty of such an offence is liable on summary conviction to a fine not exceeding level 3 on the standard scale and, for continued contravention, a daily default fine not exceeding one-tenth of level 3 on the standard scale: s 790M(13) (as so added and applied). As to the meaning of 'officer who is in default' see PARA 316. As to the meaning of 'officer' generally see PARA 679. As to the standard scale and the powers of magistrates' courts to issue fines on summary conviction see SENTENCING vol 92 (2015) PARA 176; and as to the meaning of 'daily default fine' see PARA 1816.
19 Companies Act 2006 s 790Z(7) (as added; see note 7).

487. Duty to notify registrar of changes to information about persons with significant control. As from 30 June 2016[1], the following provisions have effect.

During the period when an election to keep information about persons with significant control on the central register[2] is in force, the company must deliver to the registrar of companies[3] any information that the company would during that period have been obliged[4] to enter in its PSC register[5], had the election not been in force[6]. The information must be delivered as soon as reasonably practicable after the company becomes aware of it and, in any event, no later than the time by which the company would have been required to enter the information in its PSC register[7]. If default is made in complying with these provisions, an offence is committed by the company, and by every officer of the company[8] who is in default[9].

1 See PARA 466 note 1.
2 Ie an election made under the Companies Act 2006 s 790X: see PARA 485. As to persons with significant control over a company see PARA 467. As to the central register see PARA 142 et seq.
3 As to the meaning of 'registrar of companies' see PARA 126 note 2.
4 Ie obliged under the Companies Act 2006 Pt 21A Ch 3 (ss 790M–790V): see PARA 480 et seq.
5 As to the meaning of 'company's PSC register' see PARA 470 note 5; and as to that register see PARA 480. As to the meaning of 'company' under the Companies Acts see PARA 21. As to the companies to which these provisions apply see PARA 466.

6 See the Companies Act 2006 s 790ZA(1), (2) (s 790ZA added by the Small Business, Enterprise and Employment Act 2015 Sch 3 Pt 1 para 1).

7 Companies Act 2006 s 790ZA(3) (as added: see note 6).

8 For this purpose a shadow director is treated as an officer of the company: Companies Act 2006 s 790ZA(4) (as added: see note 6). As to shadow directors see PARA 513. As to the meaning of 'officer who is in default' see PARA 316; and as to the meaning of 'officer' generally see PARA 679.

9 Companies Act 2006 s 790ZA(4) (as added: see note 6). A person guilty of such an offence is liable on summary conviction to a fine not exceeding level 3 on the standard scale, and for continued contravention to a daily default fine not exceeding one-tenth of level 3 on the standard scale: s 790ZA(5) (as so added). As to the standard scale and the powers of magistrates' courts to issue fines on summary conviction see SENTENCING vol 92 (2015) PARA 176; and as to the meaning of 'daily default fine' see PARA 1816.

488. Information as to state of central register. As from 30 June 2016[1], the following provisions have effect.

When a person inspects or requests a copy of material on the central register[2] relating to a company in respect of which an election to keep information about persons with significant control on that register[3] is in force, the person may ask the company to confirm that all information that the company is required to deliver to the registrar of companies[4] under the relevant statutory provisions[5] has been delivered[6]. If a company fails to respond to such a request, an offence is committed by the company, and by every officer of the company[7] who is in default[8].

1 See PARA 466 note 1.

2 As to the central register see PARA 142 et seq.

3 Ie an election made under the Companies Act 2006 s 790X: see PARA 485. As to persons with significant control over a company see PARA 467. As to the meaning of 'company' under the Companies Acts see PARA 21; and as to the companies to which these provisions apply see PARA 466.

4 As to the meaning of 'registrar of companies' see PARA 126 note 2.

5 Ie under the Companies Act 2006 Pt 21A Ch 4 (ss 790W–790ZE) (see PARAS 484–487; the text and notes 1–4, 6–7; and PARAS 489–490).

6 Companies Act 2006 s 790ZB(1) (s 790ZB added by the Small Business, Enterprise and Employment Act 2015 Sch 3 Pt 1 para 1).

7 As to the meaning of 'officer who is in default' see PARA 316. As to the meaning of 'officer' generally see PARA 679.

8 Companies Act 2006 s 790ZB(2) (as added: see note 6). A person guilty of such an offence is liable on summary conviction to a fine not exceeding level 3 on the standard scale: s 790ZB(3) (as so added). As to the standard scale and the powers of magistrates' courts to issue fines on summary conviction see SENTENCING vol 92 (2015) PARA 176.

489. Court's power to order company to remedy default or delay relating to information on central register about persons with significant control. As from 30 June 2016[1], the following provisions have effect if:

(1) the name of a person is without sufficient cause included in, or omitted from, information that a company delivers to the registrar of companies[2] concerning persons who are a registrable person[3] or a registrable relevant legal entity[4] in relation to the company; or

(2) default is made or unnecessary delay takes place in informing the registrar[5] that a person has become a registrable person or a registrable relevant legal entity in relation to the company, or has ceased to be a registrable person or a registrable relevant legal entity in relation to it[6].

The person aggrieved, or any other interested party[7], may apply to the court[8] for an order requiring the company to deliver to the registrar the information, or statements, necessary to rectify the position[9]. The court may either refuse the application or may make the order and order the company to pay any damages sustained by any party aggrieved[10]. On such an application the court may decide:

(a) any question as to whether the name of any person who is a party to the application should or should not be included in or omitted from information delivered to the registrar[11] about persons who are a registrable person or a registrable relevant legal entity in relation to the company; and
(b) any question necessary or expedient to be decided for rectifying the position[12].

Nothing in the above provisions affects a person's rights under the statutory provisions[13] with regard to rectification of register on application to the registrar or under court order[14].

1 See PARA 466 note 1.
2 Ie under the Companies Act 2006 Pt 21A Ch 4 (ss 790W–790ZE) (see PARAS 484–488; the text and notes 3–14; and PARA 490). As to the meaning of 'registrar of companies' see PARA 126 note 2. As to the meaning of 'company' under the Companies Acts see PARA 21. As to the companies to which these provisions apply see PARA 466.
3 As to the meaning of 'registrable person' see PARA 467 text and note 22.
4 As to the meaning of 'registrable relevant legal entity' see PARA 467 text and note 26.
5 See note 2.
6 See the Companies Act 2006 s 790ZC(1) (s 790ZC added by the Small Business, Enterprise and Employment Act 2015 Sch 3 Pt 1 para 1).
7 The reference in the text to 'any other interested party' is to any member of the company, and any other person who is a registrable person or a registrable relevant legal entity in relation to the company: Companies Act 2006 s 790ZC(6) (as added: see note 6).
8 As to the meaning of 'the court' see PARA 160 note 12.
9 Companies Act 2006 s 790ZC(2) (as added: see note 6).
10 Companies Act 2006 s 790ZC(3) (as added: see note 6).
11 See note 2.
12 Companies Act 2006 s 790ZC(4) (as added: see note 6).
13 Ie under the Companies Act 2006 s 1095 (see PARA 1248) or s 1096 (see PARA 1250).
14 Companies Act 2006 s 790ZC(5) (as added: see note 6).

490. Withdrawing the election to keep information about persons with significant control on the central register. As from 30 June 2016[1], the following provisions have effect.

A company may withdraw an election to keep information about persons with significant control on the central register[2] made by or in respect of it[3]. Withdrawal is achieved by giving notice of withdrawal to the registrar of companies[4] and takes effect when the notice is registered by the registrar[5].

The effect of withdrawal is that the company's obligation[6] to maintain a PSC register[7] applies from then on with respect to the period going forward[8]. This means that, when the withdrawal takes effect:

(1) the company must enter in its PSC register all the information that is required to be contained in that register in respect of matters that are current[9] as at that time;
(2) the company must also retain in its register all the information that it was required[10] to keep in a historic register while the election was in force; but
(3) the company is not required to enter in its register information relating to the period when the election was in force that is no longer current[11].

The company must place a note in its PSC register:

(a) stating that the election[12] has been withdrawn;
(b) recording when that withdrawal took effect; and

(c) indicating that information about people with significant control over the company relating to the period when the election was in force that is no longer current is available for public inspection on the central register[13].

If a company makes default in complying with heads (a) to (c) above, an offence is committed by the company, and by every officer of the company who is in default[14].

1 See PARA 466 note 1.
2 Ie an election made under the Companies Act 2006 s 790X: see PARA 485. As to persons with significant control over a company see PARA 467. As to the meaning of 'company' under the Companies Acts see PARA 21. As to the companies to which these provisions apply see PARA 466.
3 Companies Act 2006 s 790ZD(1) (ss 790M, 790ZD added by the Small Business, Enterprise and Employment Act 2015 Sch 3 Pt 1 para 1).
4 Companies Act 2006 s 790ZD(2) (as added: see note 3). As to the meaning of 'registrar of companies' see PARA 126 note 2.
5 Companies Act 2006 s 790ZD(3) (as added: see note 3).
6 Ie under the Companies Act 2006 Pt 21A Ch 3 (ss 790M–790V): see PARA 480 et seq.
7 As to the meaning of 'company's PSC register' see PARA 470 note 5; and as to that register see PARA 480.
8 Companies Act 2006 s 790ZD(4) (as added: see note 3).
9 As to the meaning of 'matters that are current' see PARA 485 note 9.
10 Ie under the Companies Act 2006 s 790Z(3)(a) (not yet in force): see PARA 486.
11 Companies Act 2006 s 790ZD(5) (as added: see note 3).
12 Ie the election under the Companies Act 2006 s 790X: see PARA 485.
13 Companies Act 2006 s 790ZD(6) (as added: see note 3).
14 Companies Act 2006 s 790M(12) (as added (see note 3); applied for these purposes by s 790ZD(7) (as so added). A person guilty of such an offence is liable on summary conviction to a fine not exceeding level 3 on the standard scale and, for continued contravention, a daily default fine not exceeding one-tenth of level 3 on the standard scale: s 790M(13) (as so added and applied). As to the meaning of 'officer who is in default' see PARA 316. As to the meaning of 'officer' generally see PARA 679. As to the standard scale and the powers of magistrates' courts to issue fines on summary conviction see SENTENCING vol 92 (2015) PARA 176; and as to the meaning of 'daily default fine' see PARA 1816.

(v) Protection from Disclosure under Part 21A of the Companies Act 2006

A. PROTECTION OF CERTAIN INFORMATION AS TO PERSONS WITH SIGNIFICANT CONTROL: IN GENERAL

491. Protection of information as to usual residential address of person with significant control: in general. As from 6 April 2016[1], the following provisions have effect.

The provisions of the Companies Act 2006 protecting directors' residential addresses from disclosure[2] apply to:

(1) information as to the usual residential address of a person with significant control over a company[3]; and
(2) the information that such a person's service address[4] is his or her usual residential address,

as they apply to protected information within the meaning of those provisions[5].

This does not, however, apply to information relating to a person if an application under regulations protecting material[6] has been granted with respect to that information and has not been revoked[7].

1 See PARA 466 note 1.
2 Ie the Companies Act 2006 ss 240–244: see PARAS 537–539, 548.
3 As to persons with significant control over a company see PARA 467.
4 As to the meaning of 'service address' see PARA 745.

5 Companies Act 2006 s 790ZF(1), (2) (s 790ZF added by the Small Business, Enterprise and Employment Act 2015 Sch 3 Pt 1 para 1).
6 Ie regulations made under the Companies Act 2006 s 790ZG: see PARA 492 et seq.
7 Companies Act 2006 s 790ZF(3) (as added: see note 5).

492. Power to make regulations protecting PSC particulars. The Secretary of State may by regulations[1] make provision requiring the registrar of companies[2] and the company to refrain from using or disclosing PSC particulars[3] of a prescribed kind[4], or to refrain from doing so except in prescribed circumstances, where an application is made to the registrar requesting them to refrain from so doing[5]. Such regulations may make provision as to:

(1) who may make an application;
(2) the grounds on which an application may be made;
(3) the information to be included in and documents to accompany an application;
(4) how an application is to be determined;
(5) the duration of and procedures for revoking the restrictions on use and disclosure;
(6) the operation of the statutory provisions relating to inspection of the PSC register[6], offences in connection with a request for, or disclosure of, information on that register and information as to the state of that register[7] in cases where an application is made; and
(7) the charging of fees by the registrar for disclosing PSC particulars where the regulations permit disclosure, by way of exception, in prescribed circumstances[8].

Provision under heads (4) and (5) above may in particular:

(a) confer a discretion on the registrar;
(b) provide for a question to be referred to a person other than the registrar for the purposes of determining the application or revoking the restrictions[9].

Nothing in the above provisions or in regulations made under them affects the use or disclosure of particulars of a person in any other capacity, for example, the use or disclosure of particulars of a person in that person's capacity as a member[10] or director[11] of the company[12].

The Register of People with Significant Control Regulations 2016[13] are partly made in the exercise of these powers.

1 Regulations under the Companies Act 2006 s 790ZG (see the text and notes 2–12) are subject to affirmative resolution procedure (ie the regulations must not be made unless a draft of the statutory instrument containing them has been laid before Parliament and approved by a resolution of each House of Parliament): see ss790ZG(5), 1290 (s 790ZG added by the Small Business, Enterprise and Employment Act 2015 Sch 3 Pt 1 para 1). As to the Secretary of State see PARA 6; and as to the making of regulations under the Companies Act 2006 generally see ss 1288–1292. As to the date when s 790ZG came into force see PARA 466 note 1.
2 As to the meaning of 'registrar of companies' see PARA 126 note 2. As to the meaning of 'company' under the Companies Acts see PARA 21. As to the companies to which these provisions apply see PARA 466.
3 As to the meaning of 'PSC particulars' see PARA 469 note 6.
4 In the Companies Acts, 'prescribed' means prescribed (by order or by regulations) by the Secretary of State: Companies Act 2006 s 1167. As to the meaning of the 'Companies Acts' see PARA 13.
5 Companies Act 2006 s 790ZG(1) (as added: see note 1).
6 As to the meaning of 'company's PSC register' see PARA 470 note 5; and as to that register see PARA 480.
7 Ie the operation of the Companies Act 2006 ss 790N–790S (not yet fully in force): see PARAS 480–481.
8 Companies Act 2006 s 790ZG(3) (as added: see note 1).
9 Companies Act 2006 s 790ZG(4) (as added: see note 1).

10 As to the members of a company see PARA 323 et seq.
11 As to the meaning of 'director' see PARA 512.
12 Companies Act 2006 s 790ZG(6) (as added: see note 1).
13 Ie the Register of People with Significant Control Regulations 2016, SI 2016/339: see PARA 493 et seq.

B. PROTECTION OF USUAL RESIDENTIAL ADDRESS INFORMATION ABOUT PERSONS WITH SIGNIFICANT CONTROL

493. Permitted disclosure of usual residential address information by the registrar to specified public authorities. The registrar of companies[1] may disclose usual residential address information[2] to a public authority[3] specified for these purposes[4] by regulations made by the Secretary of State[5].

The conditions specified for the disclosure of information to such a public authority are as follows[6]:

(1) the specified public authority has delivered to the registrar a statement that it intends to use the information only for the purpose of facilitating the carrying out by that specified public authority of a public function[7] ('the permitted purpose')[8];

(2) except where the specified public authority is the National Crime Agency, Secret Intelligence Service, Security Service or Government Communications Headquarters[9], the specified public authority has delivered to the registrar a statement that, where it supplies a copy of the information to a processor[10] for the purpose of processing the information for use in respect of the permitted purpose, the specified public authority will:
   (a) ensure that the processor is one who carries on business in the European Economic Area;
   (b) require that the processor does not transmit the information outside the European Economic Area; and
   (c) require that the processor does not disclose the information except to that specified public authority or an employee of that specified public authority[11];

(3) the specified public authority has delivered any information or evidence required by the registrar for the purpose of enabling the registrar to determine[12] whether to disclose the information[13];

(4) the specified public authority has complied with any requirement by the registrar to confirm the accuracy of the statements, information or evidence delivered to the registrar pursuant to these provisions[14].

1 As to the meaning of 'registrar of companies' see PARA 126 note 2.
2 Ie information within the Companies Act 2006 s 790ZF(2): see PARA 491 heads (1)–(2).
3 For these purposes, 'public authority' includes any person or body having functions of a public nature: see the Companies Act 2006 s 243(7) (s 243 applied for these purposes by s 790ZF(1): see PARA 491).
4 Ie specified for the purposes of the Companies Act 2006 s 243 (see s 243(2)(a) as applied by s 790ZF(1)). The public authorities specified for the purposes of the Companies Act 2006 s 243 as applied by s 790ZF are listed in the Register of People with Significant Control Regulations 2016, SI 2016/339, Sch 3: reg 22(1).
5 Companies Act 2006 s 243(2)(a), as applied by s 790ZF(1). As to the Secretary of State see PARA 6. As to the making of regulations under the Companies Act 2006 generally see ss 1288–1292. The Register of People with Significant Control Regulations 2016, SI 2016/339, are partly made in the exercise of this power.

The Companies Act 2006 s 243 does not, however, apply to information relating to a person if an application under regulations made under s 790ZG (see PARA 492) has been granted with respect to that information and has not been revoked: see s 790ZF(3); and PARA 491.

6 Register of People with Significant Control Regulations 2016, SI 2016/339, reg 22(2). As to the fee payable for an application by a specified public authority under reg 22 see the Registrar of Companies (Fees) (Companies, Overseas Companies and Limited Liability Partnerships) Regulations 2012, SI 2012/1907, Sch 3 (substituted with efefct from 30 June by SI 2016/621).

7 For these purposes, 'public function' includes the following (Register of People with Significant Control Regulations 2016, SI 2016/339, Sch 4 para 13(b)), ie:

(1) any function conferred by or in accordance with any provision contained in any enactment;

(2) any function conferred by or in accordance with any provision contained in the EU Treaties or any EU instrument;

(3) any similar function conferred on persons by or under provisions having effect as part of the law of a country or territory outside the United Kingdom; and

(4) any function exercisable in relation to the investigation of any criminal offence or for the purpose of any criminal proceedings.

Any reference to the disclosure for the purpose of facilitating the carrying out of a public function includes disclosure in relation to, and for the purpose of, any proceedings whether civil, criminal or disciplinary in which the specified public authority engages while carrying out its public functions: Sch 4 para 13(d).

8 Register of People with Significant Control Regulations 2016, SI 2016/339, Sch 4 para 1.

9 See the Register of People with Significant Control Regulations 2016, SI 2016/339, Sch 4 para 3.

10 For these purposes, 'processor' means any person who provides a service which consists of putting information into data form or processing information in data form and any reference to a processor includes a reference to the processor's employees: Register of People with Significant Control Regulations 2016, SI 2016/339, Sch 4 para 13(a). Any reference to an employee of any person who has access to information within the Companies Act 2006 s 790ZF(2) includes any person working or providing services for the purposes of that person or employed by or on behalf of, or working for, any person who is so working or who is supplying such a service: Register of People with Significant Control Regulations 2016, SI 2016/339, Sch 4 para 13(c).

11 Register of People with Significant Control Regulations 2016, SI 2016/339, Sch 4 para 2.

12 Ie in accordance with the Register of People with Significant Control Regulations 2016, SI 2016/339.

13 Register of People with Significant Control Regulations 2016, SI 2016/339, Sch 4 para 4.

14 Register of People with Significant Control Regulations 2016, SI 2016/339, Sch 4 para 5.

494. Permitted disclosure of usual residential address information by the registrar to a credit reference agency. The registrar of companies[1] may disclose usual residential address information[2] to a credit reference agency[3]. The conditions specified for the disclosure of such information by the registrar to a credit reference agency in accordance with this provision are as follows[4]:

(1) the credit reference agency:

(a) is carrying on in the United Kingdom[5] or in another EEA state[6] a business comprising the furnishing of information relevant to the financial standing of individuals, being information collected by the agency for that purpose;

(b) maintains appropriate procedures to ensure that an independent person can investigate and audit the measures maintained by the agency for the purposes of ensuring the security of any usual residential address information disclosed to that agency and for the purposes of ensuring that it complies with its obligations under the Data Protection Act 1998, or, where the agency carries on business in an EEA state other than the United Kingdom, with its obligations under legislation implementing the Directive on the protection of individuals with regard to the processing of personal data and on the free movement of such data[7]; and

(c) has not been found guilty of a specified offence[8];

(2) the credit reference agency has delivered to the registrar a statement[9] that it meets the conditions in head (1) above[10];

(3) the credit reference agency has delivered to the registrar a statement that it intends to use the usual residential address information only for the purposes of:
   (a) providing an assessment of the financial standing of a person;
   (b) meeting any obligations contained in the specified legislation[11];
   (c) conducting conflict of interest checks required or made necessary by any enactment;
   (d) providing such information to a specified public authority[12] which has satisfied the specified conditions[13] or to a credit reference agency which has satisfied the specified requirements[14]; or
   (e) conducting checks for the prevention and detection of crime and fraud[15];

(4) the credit reference agency has delivered to the registrar a statement that it intends to take delivery of and to use the usual residential address information only in the United Kingdom or in another EEA state[16];

(5) the credit reference agency has delivered to the registrar a statement that it will, where it supplies a copy of the usual residential address information to a processor[17] for the purpose of processing the information for use in respect of the purposes referred to in head (3) above:
   (a) ensure that the processor is one who carries on business in the European Economic Area;
   (b) require that the processor does not transmit the information outside the European Economic Area; and
   (c) require that the processor does not disclose the information except to the credit reference agency or an employee of the credit reference agency[18];

(6) the credit reference agency has delivered any information or evidence required by the registrar for the purpose of enabling the registrar to determine[19] in whether to disclose the usual residential address information[20];

(7) the credit reference agency has complied with any requirement by the registrar to confirm the accuracy of the statements, information or evidence delivered to him pursuant to these provisions[21].

1 As to the meaning of 'registrar of companies' see PARA 126 note 2.
2 Ie information within the Companies Act 2006 s 790ZF(2): see PARA 491 heads (1)–(2).
3 Companies Act 2006 s 243(2)(b) (s 243 applied for these purposes by s 790ZF(1): see PARA 491). For these purposes, 'credit reference agency' means a person carrying on a business comprising the furnishing of information relevant to the financial standing of individuals, being information collected by the agency for that purpose: see s 243(7) (as so applied).
   Section 243 does not, however, apply to information relating to a person if an application under regulations made under s 790ZG (see PARA 492) has been granted with respect to that information and has not been revoked: see s 790ZF(3); and PARA 491. As to such applications see PARA 495 et seq.
4 See the Register of People with Significant Control Regulations 2016, SI 2016/339, reg 23(1). As to the fee payable for an application by a credit reference agency under reg 23 see the Registrar of Companies (Fees) (Companies, Overseas Companies and Limited Liability Partnerships) Regulations 2012, SI 2012/1907, Sch 3 (substituted with efefct from 30 June by SI 2016/621).
5 As to the meaning of 'United Kingdom' see PARA 1 note 5.
6 As to the meaning of 'EEA state' see PARA 26 note 5.
7 Ie European Parliament and Council Directive (EC) 95/46 (OJ L 281, 23.11.1995, p 31) (amended by European Parliament and Council Regulation (EC) 1882/2003 (OJ L284, 31.10.2003, p 1): see CONFIDENCE AND INFORMATIONAL PRIVACY vol 19 (2011) PARA 95.

8 See the Register of People with Significant Control Regulations 2016, SI 2016/339, Sch 4 para 6. The reference in head (1)(c) in the text to a specified offence is a reference to an offence under the following (Sch 4 para 6(c)), ie:
(1) the Companies Act 2006 s 1112 (general false statement offence: see PARA 132);
(2) the Fraud Act 2006 s 2 (fraud by false representation: see CRIMINAL LAW vol 25 (2016) PARA 346); or
(3) the Data Protection Act 1998 s 47 (failure to comply with enforcement notice: see CONFIDENCE AND INFORMATIONAL PRIVACY vol 19 (2011) PARA 166) in circumstances where it has used the information within the Companies Act 2006 s 790ZF(2) for purposes other than those described in the Register of People with Significant Control Regulations 2016, SI 2016/339, Sch 4 para 8(a)–(e) (see head (3)(a)–(e) in the text).

9 The registrar may rely on a statement delivered to him by a credit reference agency under the Register of People with Significant Control Regulations 2016, SI 2016/339, Sch 4 Pt 2 (paras 6–12) as sufficient evidence of the matters stated in it: reg 23(2).

10 Register of People with Significant Control Regulations 2016, SI 2016/339, Sch 4 para 7.

11 Ie any obligations contained in the following (Register of People with Significant Control Regulations 2016, SI 2016/339, Sch 4 para 8(b)):
(1) the Money Laundering Regulations 2007, SI 2007/2157 (see FINANCIAL SERVICES REGULATION vol 50A (2016) PARA 759 et seq);
(2) any rules made pursuant to the Financial Services and Markets Act 2000 s 137A (see FINANCIAL SERVICES REGULATION vol 50 (2016) PARA 59) which relate to the prevention and detection of money laundering in connection with the carrying on of regulated activities by authorised persons; or
(3) any legislation of another EEA state implementing European Parliament and Council Directive (EC) 2005/60 (OJ L309, 25.11.2005, p 15) (with subsequent amendments) on the prevention of the use of the financial system for the purpose of money laundering and terrorist financing.

12 As to the meaning of 'specified public authority' see PARA 493.

13 Ie the conditions of the Register of People with Significant Control Regulations 2016, SI 2016/339, Sch 4 paras 1–2: see PARA 493 heads (1)–(2).

14 Ie the requirements of the Register of People with Significant Control Regulations 2016, SI 2016/339, Sch 4 Pt 2: see heads (1)–(7) in the text.

15 Register of People with Significant Control Regulations 2016, SI 2016/339, Sch 4 para 8.

16 Register of People with Significant Control Regulations 2016, SI 2016/339, Sch 4 para 9.

17 As to the meaning of 'processor' see PARA 493 note 10.

18 Register of People with Significant Control Regulations 2016, SI 2016/339, Sch 4 para 10.

19 Ie in accordance with the Register of People with Significant Control Regulations 2016, SI 2016/339.

20 Register of People with Significant Control Regulations 2016, SI 2016/339, Sch 4 para 11.

21 Register of People with Significant Control Regulations 2016, SI 2016/339, Sch 4 para 12.

495. Circumstances where the registrar must refrain from disclosure of usual residential address information. The registrar of companies[1] must not disclose usual residential address information[2] to a credit reference agency[3] if in relation to that information an application has been made[4] by an individual[5], a company[6] or a subscriber to a memorandum of association[7] requiring him to refrain from such disclosure:

(1) which has not yet been determined by the registrar and has not been withdrawn[8];
(2) which has been determined by the registrar in favour of the applicant, except where the determination has ceased[9] to have effect[10];
(3) which was unsuccessful and the period for applying for permission to appeal[11] has not passed[12];
(4) which was unsuccessful and an appeal to the court[13] in respect of that application[14] has not been determined by the court[15]; or
(5) which was unsuccessful and the applicant has successfully appealed the determination[16].

1 As to the meaning of 'registrar of companies' see PARA 126 note 2.

2 Ie information within the Companies Act 2006 s 790ZF(2): see PARA 491 heads (1)–(2).

3 As to disclosure to a credit reference agency see PARA 494.
4 For these purposes, an application is made when it has been registered by the registrar: Register of People with Significant Control Regulations 2016, SI 2016/339, reg 24(3).
5 Ie under the Register of People with Significant Control Regulations 2016, SI 2016/339, reg 25: see PARA 496.
6 Ie under the Register of People with Significant Control Regulations 2016, SI 2016/339, reg 26: see PARA 497.
7 Ie under the Register of People with Significant Control Regulations 2016, SI 2016/339, reg 27: see PARA 498.
8 Register of People with Significant Control Regulations 2016, SI 2016/339, reg 24(1)(a). As to withdrawal of an application see reg 29; and PARAS 496–498.
9 Ie under the Register of People with Significant Control Regulations 2016, SI 2016/339, reg 31: see PARA 499.
10 Register of People with Significant Control Regulations 2016, SI 2016/339, reg 24(1)(b), (2).
11 Ie in the Register of People with Significant Control Regulations 2016, SI 2016/339, reg 30(3): see PARA 501.
12 Register of People with Significant Control Regulations 2016, SI 2016/339, reg 24(1)(c).
13 As to the meaning of 'the court' see PARA 160 note 12.
14 Ie under the Register of People with Significant Control Regulations 2016, SI 2016/339, reg 30: see PARA 501.
15 Register of People with Significant Control Regulations 2016, SI 2016/339, reg 24(1)(d).
16 Register of People with Significant Control Regulations 2016, SI 2016/339, reg 24(1)(e).

496. Application by an individual requiring the registrar to refrain from disclosing that individual's usual residential address information to a credit reference agency. An individual who is, or proposes to become, a registrable person[1] in relation to a company[2] may make an application to the registrar of companies[3] requiring him to refrain from disclosing to a credit reference agency[4] usual residential address information[5] relating to that individual[6]. The grounds on which an application may be made are that:

(1) the applicant reasonably believes that there is a serious risk that the applicant, or a person who lives with the applicant, will be subjected to violence or intimidation as a result of the activities of at least one of:
   (a) the companies in relation to which the applicant is, or proposes to become, a registrable person;
   (b) the companies in relation to which the applicant used to be a registrable person;
   (c) the limited liability partnerships[7] in relation to which the applicant is, or proposes to become, a registrable person under the relevant regulations[8];
   (d) the limited liability partnerships in relation to which the applicant used to be a registrable person under those regulations;
   (e) the limited liability partnerships in relation to which the applicant is or proposes to become a member;
   (f) the limited liability partnerships in relation to which the applicant used to be a member;
   (g) the companies in relation to which the applicant is, or proposes to become, a director[9];
   (h) the companies in relation to which the applicant used to be a director; or
   (i) the overseas companies[10] of which the applicant is or used to be a director, secretary or permanent representative[11]; or

(2) a section 243 decision[12] has been made in respect of the applicant which has not ceased[13] to have effect[14].

The application must contain:

(i) a statement of the grounds on which the application is made[15];

(ii) the name and any former name[16] of the applicant[17];
(iii) the date of birth of the applicant[18];
(iv) the usual residential address of the applicant[19];
(v) the e-mail address of the applicant, if any[20];
(vi) the name and registered number[21] of each company in relation to which the applicant is, or proposes to become, a registrable person[22];
(vii) where the grounds of the application are those described in heads (1)(b) to (1)(i) above, the names and registered numbers of the companies, limited liability partnerships and overseas companies whose activities are relevant to the application[23]; and
(viii) where the grounds of the application are those described in head (2) above, the name and registered number of the company in relation to which the section 243 decision was made, unless the section 243 decision relates to a proposed company which was never incorporated[24].

Where the grounds of the application are those described in head (1)(a) above, the application must be accompanied by evidence which supports the applicant's statement of the grounds on which the application is made[25].

For the purpose of determining an application the registrar may:

(A) direct that additional information or evidence should be delivered to him;
(B) refer any question relating to an assessment of the nature or extent of any risk of violence or intimidation to a relevant body[26] or to any other person the registrar considers may be able to assist in making the assessment; and
(C) accept any answer to a question referred under head (B) above as providing sufficient evidence of the nature or extent of any risk[27].

A person who makes an application must inform the registrar in writing without delay upon becoming aware of any change to any information or evidence provided to the registrar in connection with the application[28].

If a person in relation to whom an application has been made that has not yet been determined notifies the registrar in writing that the person no longer wishes the registrar to determine the application, the registrar is not required to determine it[29]. Otherwise, the registrar must determine the application and, within seven days beginning with the date that the determination is made, send to the applicant notice of the determination[30]. Where the application is unsuccessful, that notice must inform the applicant of his right to apply for permission to appeal against the determination within 28 days beginning with the date of the notice[31].

The registrar must not make available for public inspection any application, any documents provided in support of that application or any notice[32] of withdrawal of the application[33].

1 As to the meaning of 'registrable person' see PARA 467 text and note 22.
2 As to the meaning of 'company' under the Companies Acts see PARA 21; and as to the meaning of the 'Companies Acts' see PARA 13.
3 As to the meaning of 'registrar of companies' see PARA 126 note 2.
4 As to disclosure to a credit reference agency see PARA 494.
5 Ie information within the Companies Act 2006 s 790ZF(2): see PARA 491 heads (1)–(2).
6 Register of People with Significant Control Regulations 2016, SI 2016/339, reg 25(1).
7 For these purposes, 'limited liability partnership' means a limited liability partnership incorporated under the Limited Liability Partnerships Act 2000 (see PARTNERSHIP vol 79 (2014) PARA 233 et seq): Register of People with Significant Control Regulations 2016, SI 2016/339, reg 2.
8 Ie under the Limited Liability Partnerships (Register of People with Significant Control) Regulations 2016, SI 2016/340: see PARTNERSHIP.

9 As to the meaning of 'director' see PARA 512.
10 As to the meaning of 'overseas company' see PARA 2013.
11 Register of People with Significant Control Regulations 2016, SI 2016/339, reg 25(2)(a).
12 For these purposes, 'section 243 decision' means a determination under the Companies (Disclosure of Address) Regulations 2009, SI 2009/214, which is a section 243 decision within the meaning of those Regulations (see PARA 151 head (3)): Register of People with Significant Control Regulations 2016, SI 2016/339, reg 2.
13 Ie under the Companies (Disclosure of Address) Regulations 2009, SI 2009/214, reg 15: see PARA 545.
14 Register of People with Significant Control Regulations 2016, SI 2016/339, reg 25(2)(b).
15 Register of People with Significant Control Regulations 2016, SI 2016/339, reg 25(3)(a).
16 For these purposes, 'name' means a person's, except that in the case of a peer or an individual usually known by a title, the title may be stated instead of that person's forename and surname or in addition to either or both of them: Register of People with Significant Control Regulations 2016, SI 2016/339, reg 2. 'Former name' means a name by which an individual was formerly known for business purposes: reg 2.
17 Register of People with Significant Control Regulations 2016, SI 2016/339, reg 25(3)(b).
18 Register of People with Significant Control Regulations 2016, SI 2016/339, reg 25(3)(c).
19 Register of People with Significant Control Regulations 2016, SI 2016/339, reg 25(3)(d).
20 Register of People with Significant Control Regulations 2016, SI 2016/339, reg 25(3)(e).
21 As to a company's registered number see PARAS 134–135.
22 Register of People with Significant Control Regulations 2016, SI 2016/339, reg 25(3)(f).
23 Register of People with Significant Control Regulations 2016, SI 2016/339, reg 25(3)(g).
24 Register of People with Significant Control Regulations 2016, SI 2016/339, reg 25(3)(h).
25 Register of People with Significant Control Regulations 2016, SI 2016/339, reg 25(4).
26 For these purposes, 'relevant body' means a police force within the meaning of the Police Act 1996 s 101(1) (see POLICE AND INVESTIGATORY POWERS vol 84 (2013) PARA 2 note 11), the Police Service of Northern Ireland and the Police Service of Scotland: Register of People with Significant Control Regulations 2016, SI 2016/339, reg 2.
27 Register of People with Significant Control Regulations 2016, SI 2016/339, reg 28(1).
28 Register of People with Significant Control Regulations 2016, SI 2016/339, reg 28(3).
29 Register of People with Significant Control Regulations 2016, SI 2016/339, reg 29.
30 Register of People with Significant Control Regulations 2016, SI 2016/339, reg 25(5).
31 Register of People with Significant Control Regulations 2016, SI 2016/339, reg 25(6).
32 Ie any notice provided under the Register of People with Significant Control Regulations 2016, SI 2016/339, reg 29: see the text and note 29.
33 Register of People with Significant Control Regulations 2016, SI 2016/339, reg 28(2)(a)–(c).

497. Application by a company requiring the registrar to refrain from disclosing an individual's usual residential address information to a credit reference agency. A company[1] ('the applicant') may make an application to the registrar of companies[2] requiring the registrar to refrain from disclosing to a credit reference agency[3] usual residential address information[4] relating to an individual ('R') who is, or proposes to become, a registrable person[5] in relation to the company[6]. A company may only make such an application, however, where R has given consent for the company to make the application on his behalf[7].

The grounds on which such an application may be made are that:

(1) the applicant reasonably believes that there is a serious risk that R, or a person who lives with R, will be subjected to violence or intimidation as a result of the applicant's activities[8]; or
(2) a section 243 decision[9] has been made in respect of R which has not ceased[10] to have effect[11].

Where the grounds of the application are those described in head (2) above, the application must only relate to one individual who is, or proposes to become, a registrable person in relation to the company[12].

The application must contain:

(a) a statement of the grounds on which the application is made[13];
(b) confirmation that R consents to the making of the application[14];
(c) the name and registered number[15] of the applicant[16];

(d) the address of the registered office[17] of the applicant[18];
(e) the e-mail address of the applicant, if any[19];
(f) the name and any former name of R[20];
(g) the date of birth of R[21];
(h) the usual residential address of R[22];
(i) the e-mail address of R, if any[23];
(j) where R is a registrable person in relation to another company, the name and registered number of that company[24]; and
(k) where the grounds of the application are those described in head (2) above, the name and registered number of the company in relation to which the section 243 decision was made, unless the section 243 decision relates to a proposed company which was never incorporated[25].

Where the grounds of the application are those described in head (1) above, the application must be accompanied by evidence which supports the applicant's statement of the grounds on which the application is made[26].

For the purpose of determining an application the registrar may:
(i) direct that additional information or evidence should be delivered to him;
(ii) refer any question relating to an assessment of the nature or extent of any risk of violence or intimidation to a relevant body[27] or to any other person the registrar considers may be able to assist in making the assessment; and
(iii) accept any answer to a question referred under head (ii) above as providing sufficient evidence of the nature or extent of any risk[28].

A person who makes an application must inform the registrar in writing without delay upon becoming aware of any change to any information or evidence provided to the registrar in connection with the application[29].

If a person in relation to whom an application has been made that has not yet been determined notifies the registrar in writing that the person no longer wishes the registrar to determine the application, the registrar is not required to determine it[30]. Otherwise the registrar must determine the application and, within seven days beginning with the date that the determination is made, send to the applicant and to R notice of the determination[31]. Where the application is unsuccessful, that notice must inform the applicant of the applicant's right to apply for permission to appeal against the determination within 28 days beginning with the date of the notice[32].

The registrar must not make available for public inspection any application, any documents provided in support of that application or any notice[33] of withdrawal of the application[34].

1 As to the meaning of 'company' under the Companies Acts see PARA 21; and as to the meaning of the 'Companies Acts' see PARA 13.
2 As to the meaning of 'registrar of companies' see PARA 126 note 2.
3 As to disclosure to a credit reference agency see PARA 494.
4 Ie information within the Companies Act 2006 s 790ZF(2): see PARA 491 heads (1)–(2).
5 As to the meaning of 'registrable person' see PARA 467 text and note 22.
6 Register of People with Significant Control Regulations 2016, SI 2016/339, reg 26(1).
7 Register of People with Significant Control Regulations 2016, SI 2016/339, reg 26(2).
8 Register of People with Significant Control Regulations 2016, SI 2016/339, reg 26(3)(a).
9 As to the meaning of 'section 243 decision' for these purposes see PARA 496 note 12.
10 Ie under the Companies (Disclosure of Address) Regulations 2009, SI 2009/214, reg 15: see PARA 545.
11 Register of People with Significant Control Regulations 2016, SI 2016/339, reg 26(3)(b).
12 Register of People with Significant Control Regulations 2016, SI 2016/339, reg 26(4).
13 Register of People with Significant Control Regulations 2016, SI 2016/339, reg 26(5)(a).

14 Register of People with Significant Control Regulations 2016, SI 2016/339, reg 26(5)(b).
15 As to a company's registered number see PARAS 134–135.
16 Register of People with Significant Control Regulations 2016, SI 2016/339, reg 26(5)(c).
17 As to a company's registered office see PARA 124.
18 Register of People with Significant Control Regulations 2016, SI 2016/339, reg 26(5)(d).
19 Register of People with Significant Control Regulations 2016, SI 2016/339, reg 26(5)(e).
20 Register of People with Significant Control Regulations 2016, SI 2016/339, reg 26(5)(f). As to the meanings of 'name' and 'former name' see PARA 496 note 16.
21 Register of People with Significant Control Regulations 2016, SI 2016/339, reg 26(5)(g).
22 Register of People with Significant Control Regulations 2016, SI 2016/339, reg 26(5)(h).
23 Register of People with Significant Control Regulations 2016, SI 2016/339, reg 26(5)(i).
24 Register of People with Significant Control Regulations 2016, SI 2016/339, reg 26(5)(j).
25 Register of People with Significant Control Regulations 2016, SI 2016/339, reg 26(5)(k).
26 Register of People with Significant Control Regulations 2016, SI 2016/339, reg 26(6).
27 As to the meaning of 'relevant body' see PARA 496 note 26.
28 Register of People with Significant Control Regulations 2016, SI 2016/339, reg 28(1).
29 Register of People with Significant Control Regulations 2016, SI 2016/339, reg 28(3).
30 Register of People with Significant Control Regulations 2016, SI 2016/339, reg 29.
31 Register of People with Significant Control Regulations 2016, SI 2016/339, reg 26(7).
32 Register of People with Significant Control Regulations 2016, SI 2016/339, reg 26(8).
33 Ie any notice provided under the Register of People with Significant Control Regulations 2016, SI 2016/339, reg 29: see the text and note 30.
34 Register of People with Significant Control Regulations 2016, SI 2016/339, reg 28(2)(a)–(c).

498. Application by a subscriber to a memorandum of association requiring the registrar to refrain from disclosing an individual's usual residential address information to a credit reference agency. A subscriber to a memorandum of association[1] ('the applicant') may make an application to the registrar of companies[2] requiring him to refrain from disclosing to a credit reference agency[3] usual residential address information[4] relating to an individual ('R') who proposes to become, on or after the formation of the company to which the memorandum relates, a registrable person[5] in relation to the company[6]. A subscriber to a memorandum of association may only make such an application, however, where R has given consent for the subscriber to make the application on R's behalf[7].

The grounds on which an application may be made are that:

(1) the applicant reasonably believes that there is a serious risk that R, or a person who lives with R, will be subjected to violence or intimidation as a result of the proposed activities of the company to which the memorandum relates[8]; or
(2) a section 243 decision[9] has been made in respect of R which has not ceased[10] to have effect[11].

Where the grounds of the application are those described in head (2) above, the application must only relate to one individual who proposes to become a registrable person in relation to the proposed company[12].

The application must contain:

(a) a statement of the grounds on which the application is made[13];
(b) confirmation that R consents to the making of the application[14];
(c) the name and any former name of the applicant[15];
(d) the usual residential address of the applicant[16];
(e) the e-mail address of the applicant, if any[17];
(f) the name of the proposed company to which the memorandum relates[18];
(g) the name and any former name of R[19];
(h) the date of birth of R[20];
(i) the usual residential address of R[21];
(j) the e-mail address of R, if any[22];

(k) where R is a registrable person in relation to another company, the name and registered number[23] of that company[24]; and
(l) where the grounds of the application are those described in head (2) above, the name and registered number of the company in relation to which the section 243 decision was made, unless the section 243 decision relates to a proposed company which was never incorporated[25].

Where the grounds of the application are those described in head (1) above, the application must be accompanied by evidence which supports the applicant's statement of the grounds on which the application is made[26].

For the purpose of determining an application the registrar may:
(i) direct that additional information or evidence should be delivered to him;
(ii) refer any question relating to an assessment of the nature or extent of any risk of violence or intimidation to a relevant body[27] or to any other person the registrar considers may be able to assist in making the assessment; and
(iii) accept any answer to a question referred under head (ii) above as providing sufficient evidence of the nature or extent of any risk[28].

A person who makes an application must inform the registrar in writing without delay upon becoming aware of any change to any information or evidence provided to the registrar in connection with the application[29].

If a person in relation to whom an application has been made that has not yet been determined notifies the registrar in writing that the person no longer wishes the registrar to determine the application, the registrar is not required to determine it[30]. Otherwise the registrar must determine the application and, within seven days beginning with the date that the determination is made, send to the applicant and to R notice of the determination[31]. Where the application is unsuccessful, that notice must inform the applicant of the applicant's right to apply for permission to appeal against the determination within 28 days beginning with the date of the notice[32].

The registrar must not make available for public inspection any application, any documents provided in support of that application or any notice[33] of withdrawal of the application[34].

1 As to a company's memorandum of association and its subscribers see PARA 97 et seq.
2 As to the meaning of 'registrar of companies' see PARA 126 note 2.
3 As to disclosure to a credit reference agency see PARA 494.
4 Ie information within the Companies Act 2006 s 790ZF(2): see PARA 491 heads (1)–(2).
5 As to the meaning of 'registrable person' see PARA 467 text and note 22.
6 Register of People with Significant Control Regulations 2016, SI 2016/339, reg 27(1).
Regulation 27 is modified in relation to its application to SEs: see the European Public Limited-Liability Company (Register of People with Significant Control) Regulations 2016, SI 2016/375, reg 7. As to the meaning of 'SE' for these purposes see PARA 106 note 3; and as to such companies see PARA 1825 et seq.
7 Register of People with Significant Control Regulations 2016, SI 2016/339, reg 27(2).
8 Register of People with Significant Control Regulations 2016, SI 2016/339, reg 27(3)(a).
9 As to the meaning of 'section 243 decision' for these purposes see PARA 496 note 12.
10 Ie under the Companies (Disclosure of Address) Regulations 2009, SI 2009/214, reg 15: see PARA 545.
11 Register of People with Significant Control Regulations 2016, SI 2016/339, reg 27(3)(b).
12 Register of People with Significant Control Regulations 2016, SI 2016/339, reg 27(4).
13 Register of People with Significant Control Regulations 2016, SI 2016/339, reg 27(5)(a).
14 Register of People with Significant Control Regulations 2016, SI 2016/339, reg 27(5)(b).
15 Register of People with Significant Control Regulations 2016, SI 2016/339, reg 27(5)(c). As to the meanings of 'name' and 'former name' see PARA 496 note 16.
16 Register of People with Significant Control Regulations 2016, SI 2016/339, reg 27(5)(d).

17 Register of People with Significant Control Regulations 2016, SI 2016/339, reg 27(5)(e).
18 Register of People with Significant Control Regulations 2016, SI 2016/339, reg 27(5)(f).
19 Register of People with Significant Control Regulations 2016, SI 2016/339, reg 27(5)(g).
20 Register of People with Significant Control Regulations 2016, SI 2016/339, reg 27(5)(h).
21 Register of People with Significant Control Regulations 2016, SI 2016/339, reg 27(5)(i).
22 Register of People with Significant Control Regulations 2016, SI 2016/339, reg 27(5)(j).
23 As to a company's registered number see PARAS 134–135.
24 Register of People with Significant Control Regulations 2016, SI 2016/339, reg 27(5)(k).
25 Register of People with Significant Control Regulations 2016, SI 2016/339, reg 27(5)(h).
26 Register of People with Significant Control Regulations 2016, SI 2016/339, reg 27(6).
27 As to the meaning of 'relevant body' see PARA 496 note 26.
28 Register of People with Significant Control Regulations 2016, SI 2016/339, reg 28(1).
29 Register of People with Significant Control Regulations 2016, SI 2016/339, reg 28(3).
30 Register of People with Significant Control Regulations 2016, SI 2016/339, reg 29.
31 Register of People with Significant Control Regulations 2016, SI 2016/339, reg 27(7).
32 Register of People with Significant Control Regulations 2016, SI 2016/339, reg 27(8).
33 Ie any notice provided under the Register of People with Significant Control Regulations 2016, SI 2016/339, reg 29: see the text and note 30.
34 Register of People with Significant Control Regulations 2016, SI 2016/339, reg 28(2)(a)–(c).

499. Duration of a determination that an application to refrain from disclosure of usual residential address information to a credit reference agency is successful. A determination[1] that an application to refrain from disclosure of usual residential address information[2] to a credit reference agency[3] is successful continues to have effect until:

(1) either the person to whom the determination relates, or that person's personal representative[4], notifies the registrar of companies[5] in writing that he wishes the determination to cease to have effect[6]; or

(2) the registrar revokes[7] the determination[8].

The registrar must not make available for public inspection any notice provided under head (1) above[9].

1 Ie a determination made under the Register of People with Significant Control Regulations 2016, SI 2016/339, reg 25(5) (see PARA 496), reg 26(7) (see PARA 497) or reg 27(7) (see PARA 498).
2 Ie information within the Companies Act 2006 s 790ZF(2): see PARA 491 heads (1)–(2).
3 As to disclosure to a credit reference agency see PARA 494.
4 For these purposes, 'personal representative' means the executor or administrator for the time being of a deceased person: Register of People with Significant Control Regulations 2016, SI 2016/339, reg 2. See further WILLS AND INTESTACY vol 103 (2010) PARA 608.
5 As to the meaning of 'registrar of companies' see PARA 126 note 2.
6 See the Register of People with Significant Control Regulations 2016, SI 2016/339, reg 31(a).
7 Ie under the Register of People with Significant Control Regulations 2016, SI 2016/339, reg 32: see PARA 500.
8 Register of People with Significant Control Regulations 2016, SI 2016/339, reg 31(b).
9 See the Register of People with Significant Control Regulations 2016, SI 2016/339, reg 28(2)(e).

500. Revocation of a determination that an application to refrain from disclosure of usual residential address information to a credit reference agency is successful. The registrar of companies[1] may revoke a determination[2] that an application to refrain from disclosure of usual residential address information[3] to a credit reference agency[4] is successful if:

(1) the applicant in relation to the determination or, if different, any person to whom the application relates has been found guilty of a general false statement offence[5] in respect of purported compliance with any provision of the regulations[6] relating to the protection of usual residential address information[7];

(2) the registrar has sent a notice[8] to the applicant in relation to the determination and, if different, the person to whom the determination relates[9], which must inform the addressee:

(a) of the registrar's intention to revoke the determination;

(b) that the addressee may, within 28 days beginning with the date of the notice, deliver representations in writing to the registrar as to why the registrar should not revoke the determination; and

(c) that if the registrar receives such representations within that period, the registrar will have regard to the representations in deciding whether to revoke the determination[10]; and

(3) the period of 28 days beginning with the date of that notice has expired[11].

If within the period specified in head (2)(b) above the addressee of the notice delivers representations in writing to the registrar as to why he should not revoke the determination, the registrar must have regard to the representations in deciding whether to revoke the determination[12]. He must not make available for public inspection any representations so delivered[13].

The registrar must send notice of his decision as to whether to revoke a determination to the applicant in relation to the determination and, if different, the person to whom the determination relates within seven days beginning with the date of the decision[14].

1 As to the meaning of 'registrar of companies' see PARA 126 note 2.
2 Ie a determination made under the Register of People with Significant Control Regulations 2016, SI 2016/339, reg 25(5) (see PARA 496), reg 26(7) (see PARA 497) or reg 27(7) (see PARA 498).
3 Ie information within the Companies Act 2006 s 790ZF(2): see PARA 491 heads (1)–(2).
4 As to disclosure to a credit reference agency see PARA 494.
5 Ie an offence under the Companies Act 2006 s 1112: see PARA 132.
6 Ie any provision of the Register of People with Significant Control Regulations 2016, SI 2016/339, Pt 6 (regs 22–32): see PARA 493 et seq.
7 See the Register of People with Significant Control Regulations 2016, SI 2016/339, reg 32(1)(a).
8 Ie in accordance with the Register of People with Significant Control Regulations 2016, SI 2016/339, reg 32(2): see heads (a)–(c) in the text.
9 Register of People with Significant Control Regulations 2016, SI 2016/339, reg 32(1)(b).
10 Register of People with Significant Control Regulations 2016, SI 2016/339, reg 32(2).
11 Register of People with Significant Control Regulations 2016, SI 2016/339, reg 32(1)(c).
12 Register of People with Significant Control Regulations 2016, SI 2016/339, reg 32(3).
13 Register of People with Significant Control Regulations 2016, SI 2016/339, reg 28(2)(f).
14 Register of People with Significant Control Regulations 2016, SI 2016/339, reg 32(4).

501. Appealing against a determination that an application to refrain from disclosure of usual residential address information to a credit reference agency has been unsuccessful. Provided that the permission of the court[1] has been obtained[2], an applicant who has received notice[3] that his application to refrain from disclosure of usual residential address information[4] to a credit reference agency[5] has been unsuccessful may appeal to the High Court on the grounds that the determination is unlawful, is irrational or unreasonable, or has been made on the basis of a procedural impropriety or otherwise contravenes the rules of natural justice[6].

An applicant who seeks permission to appeal must serve written notice of the application on the registrar of companies[7] within seven days beginning with the date on which the application for permission was issued[8]. The registrar must not make available for public inspection any notice of an appeal so provided[9].

The court determining an appeal may either dismiss the appeal or quash the determination[10]. Where the court quashes a determination it may refer the matter to the registrar with a direction to reconsider it and make a determination in accordance with the findings of the court[11].

1 As to the meaning of 'the court' see PARA 160 note 12.

2 See the Register of People with Significant Control Regulations 2016, SI 2016/339, reg 30(2). No application for such permission may be made after 28 days beginning with the date of the notice under reg 25(5) (see PARA 496), reg 26(7) (see PARA 497) or reg 27(7) (see PARA 498), unless the court is satisfied that there was good reason for the failure of the applicant to seek permission before the end of that period: reg 30(3).
3 Ie under the Register of People with Significant Control Regulations 2016, SI 2016/339, reg 25(5) (see PARA 496), reg 26(7) (see PARA 497) or reg 27(7) (see PARA 498).
4 Ie information within the Companies Act 2006 s 790ZF(2): see PARA 491 heads (1)–(2).
5 As to disclosure to a credit reference agency see PARA 494.
6 Register of People with Significant Control Regulations 2016, SI 2016/339, reg 30(1). As to the rules of natural justice see JUDICIAL REVIEW vol 61 (2010) PARA 629 et seq; and see RIGHTS AND FREEDOMS vol 88A (2013) PARA 244.
7 As to the meaning of 'registrar of companies' see PARA 126 note 2.
8 Register of People with Significant Control Regulations 2016, SI 2016/339, reg 30(4).
9 Register of People with Significant Control Regulations 2016, SI 2016/339, reg 28(2)(d).
10 Register of People with Significant Control Regulations 2016, SI 2016/339, reg 30(5).
11 Register of People with Significant Control Regulations 2016, SI 2016/339, reg 30(6).

C. PROTECTION OF SECURED INFORMATION ABOUT PERSONS WITH SIGNIFICANT CONTROL

502. Circumstances where the registrar must omit secured information from material on the register available for public inspection. The registrar of companies[1] must omit secured information[2] from the material on the register that is available for public inspection if:

(1) in relation to that information an application has been made[3] by an individual[4], a company[5], or a subscriber to a memorandum of association[6] requiring him to refrain from using or disclosing it:
  (a) which has not yet been determined by the registrar and has not been withdrawn[7];
  (b) which has been determined by the registrar in favour of the applicant, except where the determination has ceased[8] to have effect[9];
  (c) which was unsuccessful and a period of 42 days beginning with the date of the notice of determination[10] has not passed[11];
  (d) which was unsuccessful and an appeal to the court in respect of that application[12] has not been determined by the court[13]; or
  (e) which was unsuccessful and the applicant has successfully appealed the determination[14]; and

(2) that information is contained in a document delivered to the registrar in which such information is required to be stated and, in the case of a document having more than one part, the information is contained in a part of the document in which such information is required to be stated[15].

The registrar is not obliged to check documents, other than those described in head (2) above, to ensure the absence of secured information in relation to which an application for its non-use and non-disclosure[16] has been made[17].

If the secured information in relation to which an application an application for its non-use and non-disclosure[18] is made is available for public inspection on the register at the time that the application is made, the registrar must comply with heads (1) and (2) above as soon as reasonably practicable[19].

1 As to the meaning of 'registrar of companies' see PARA 126 note 2.
2 'Secured information' means the required particulars (other than the particular required by the Companies Act 2006 s 790K(1)(i): see PARA 469 head (9)) of a registrable person in relation to a company: Register of People with Significant Control Regulations 2016, SI 2016/339, reg 2. As to the meaning of 'required particulars' see PARA 469; as to the meaning of 'registrable person'

see PARA 467 text and note 22; as to the meaning of 'company' under the Companies Acts see PARA 21; and as to the meaning of the 'Companies Acts' see PARA 13.

3 For these purposes, an application under the Register of People with Significant Control Regulations 2016, SI 2016/339, reg 36 (see PARA 504), reg 37 (see PARA 505) or reg 38 (see PARA 506) is made when it has been registered by the registrar: reg 33(5).

4 Ie under the Register of People with Significant Control Regulations 2016, SI 2016/339, reg 36 (see PARA 504).

5 Ie under the Register of People with Significant Control Regulations 2016, SI 2016/339, reg 37 (see PARA 505).

6 Ie under the Register of People with Significant Control Regulations 2016, SI 2016/339, reg 38 (see PARA 506). As to a company's memorandum of association and its subscribers see PARA 97 et seq.

7 Register of People with Significant Control Regulations 2016, SI 2016/339, reg 33(1)(a)(i). As to withdrawal of an application see reg 40; and PARAS 504–506.

8 Ie under the Register of People with Significant Control Regulations 2016, SI 2016/339, reg 43: see PARA 508.

9 Register of People with Significant Control Regulations 2016, SI 2016/339, reg 33(1)(a)(ii), (4).

10 Ie the notice sent under Register of People with Significant Control Regulations 2016, SI 2016/339, reg 36(5) (see PARA 504), reg 37(5) (see PARA 505) or reg 38(5) (see PARA 506).

11 Register of People with Significant Control Regulations 2016, SI 2016/339, reg 33(1)(a)(iii).

12 Ie an appeal under the Register of People with Significant Control Regulations 2016, SI 2016/339, reg 41: see PARA 510. As to the meaning of 'the court' see PARA 160 note 12.

13 Register of People with Significant Control Regulations 2016, SI 2016/339, reg 33(1)(a)(iv).

14 Register of People with Significant Control Regulations 2016, SI 2016/339, reg 33(1)(a)(v).

15 Register of People with Significant Control Regulations 2016, SI 2016/339, reg 33(1)(b).

16 Ie an application under the Register of People with Significant Control Regulations 2016, SI 2016/339, reg 36 (see PARA 504), reg 37 (see PARA 505) or reg 38 (see PARA 506).

17 Register of People with Significant Control Regulations 2016, SI 2016/339, reg 33(2).

18 See note 16.

19 Register of People with Significant Control Regulations 2016, SI 2016/339, reg 33(3).

503. Circumstances where the registrar must not use or disclose secured information. Subject to certain exceptions[1], the registrar of companies[2] must not use or disclose secured information[3] if in relation to that information an application has been made[4] by an individual[5], a company[6], or a subscriber to a memorandum of association[7] requiring him to refrain from using or disclosing it:

(1) which has not yet been determined by the registrar and has not been withdrawn[8];

(2) which has been determined by the registrar in favour of the applicant, except where the determination has ceased[9] to have effect[10];

(3) which was unsuccessful and a period of 42 days beginning with the date of the notice of determination[11] has not passed[12];

(4) which was unsuccessful and an appeal to the court in respect of that application[13] has not been determined by the court[14]; or

(5) which was unsuccessful and the applicant has successfully appealed the determination[15].

Where, however, the above prohibition applies in relation to secured information, the registrar may:

(a) use or disclose that secured information for communicating with the person to whom the application for its non-use and non-disclosure[16] relates and, if different, the applicant[17]; and

(b) disclose the secured information to a specified public authority[18] where the specified conditions[19] are satisfied[20].

On the disclosure of secured information under head (b) above the specified public authority to which the information is disclosed must pay a fee to the registrar for the disclosure of that information[21].

1 Ie subject to the Register of People with Significant Control Regulations 2016, SI 2016/339, reg 34(3): see heads (a)–(b) in the text.
2 As to the meaning of 'registrar of companies' see PARA 126 note 2.
3 As to the meaning of 'secured information' see PARA 502 note 2.
4 For these purposes, an application under the Register of People with Significant Control Regulations 2016, SI 2016/339, reg 36 (see PARA 504), reg 37 (see PARA 505) or reg 38 (see PARA 506) is made when it has been registered by the registrar: reg 34(4).
5 Ie under the Register of People with Significant Control Regulations 2016, SI 2016/339, reg 36 (see PARA 504).
6 Ie under the Register of People with Significant Control Regulations 2016, SI 2016/339, reg 37 (see PARA 505). As to the meaning of 'company' under the Companies Acts see PARA 21; and as to the meaning of the 'Companies Acts' see PARA 13.
7 Ie under the Register of People with Significant Control Regulations 2016, SI 2016/339, reg 38 (see PARA 506). As to a company's memorandum of association and its subscribers see PARA 97 et seq.
8 Register of People with Significant Control Regulations 2016, SI 2016/339, reg 34(1)(a). As to withdrawal of an application see reg 40; and PARAS 504–505.
9 Ie under the Register of People with Significant Control Regulations 2016, SI 2016/339, reg 43: see PARA 508.
10 Register of People with Significant Control Regulations 2016, SI 2016/339, reg 34(1)(b), (2).
11 Ie the notice sent under Register of People with Significant Control Regulations 2016, SI 2016/339, reg 36(5) (see PARA 504), reg 37(5) (see PARA 505) or reg 38(5) (see PARA 506).
12 Register of People with Significant Control Regulations 2016, SI 2016/339, reg 34(1)(c).
13 Ie an appeal under the Register of People with Significant Control Regulations 2016, SI 2016/339, reg 41: see PARA 510. As to the meaning of 'the court' see PARA 160 note 12.
14 Register of People with Significant Control Regulations 2016, SI 2016/339, reg 34(1)(d).
15 Register of People with Significant Control Regulations 2016, SI 2016/339, reg 34(1)(e).
16 Ie the application under the Register of People with Significant Control Regulations 2016, SI 2016/339, reg 36 (see PARA 504), reg 37 (see PARA 505) or reg 38 (see PARA 506).
17 Register of People with Significant Control Regulations 2016, SI 2016/339, reg 34(3)(a).
18 As to the meaning of 'specified public authority' see the Register of People with Significant Control Regulations 2016, SI 2016/339, reg 22(1); and PARA 493.
19 Ie the conditions specified in the Register of People with Significant Control Regulations 2016, SI 2016/339, Sch 4 Pt 1 (paras 1–5): see PARA 493.
20 Register of People with Significant Control Regulations 2016, SI 2016/339, reg 34(3)(b).
21 Register of People with Significant Control Regulations 2016, SI 2016/339, reg 35(1). The fee so payable is, where the request for secured information by the specified public authority is made by reference to an individual, £5 per individual specified in the request, or where the request for secured information by the specified public authority is made by reference to a company, £5 per company specified in the request: reg 35(2).

504. Application by an individual requiring the registrar to refrain from using or disclosing that individual's secured information. An individual may make an application to the registrar of companies[1] requiring him to refrain from using or disclosing secured information[2] relating to that individual if that individual:

(1) is a registrable person[3] in relation to a company[4];
(2) proposes to become a registrable person in relation to a company[5]; or
(3) used to be a registrable person in relation to a company[6].

The grounds on which an application may be made are that the applicant reasonably believes that if that secured information is disclosed by the registrar the activities of that company, or one or more characteristics or personal attributes of the applicant when associated with that company, will put the applicant or a person living with the applicant at serious risk of being subjected to violence or intimidation[7].

The application must contain:

(a) a statement of the grounds on which the application is made[8];

(b) the name and any former name[9] of the applicant[10];
(c) the date of birth of the applicant[11];
(d) the usual residential address of the applicant[12];
(e) the e-mail address of the applicant, if any[13];
(f) the name and registered number[14] of the company in relation to which the applicant is, proposes to become, or used to be a registrable person[15]; and
(g) if relevant, a statement that in relation to the applicant an application has also been made[16] requiring the registrar to refrain from disclosing the applicant's usual residential address information to a credit reference agency or a determination has been made[17] in relation to such an application in favour of the applicant[18].

It must be accompanied by evidence which supports the applicant's statement of the grounds on which the application is made[19].

Where an individual who is or used to be a registrable person in relation to a company sends such an application to the registrar in relation to that company, that individual must inform that company of that fact as soon as reasonably practicable[20].

For the purpose of determining such an application the registrar may:
(i) direct that additional information or evidence should be delivered to him;
(ii) refer any question relating to an assessment of the nature or extent of any risk of violence or intimidation to a relevant body or to any other person the registrar considers may be able to assist in making that assessment; and
(iii) accept any answer to a question referred under head (ii) above as providing sufficient evidence of the nature or extent of any risk[21].

A person who makes an application must inform the registrar in writing without delay upon becoming aware of any change to any information or evidence provided to the registrar in connection with the application[22].

If a person in relation to whom an application has been made that has not yet been determined notifies the registrar in writing that the person no longer wishes the registrar to determine the application, the registrar is not required to determine the application[23]. Otherwise the registrar must determine the application and, within seven days beginning with the date that the determination is made, send to the applicant notice of the determination[24]. Where the application is unsuccessful, that notice must inform the applicant of the applicant's right to apply for permission to appeal against the determination within 28 days beginning with the date of the notice[25].

The registrar must not make available for public inspection any application, any documents provided in support of that application or any notice[26] of withdrawal of the application[27].

1 As to the meaning of 'registrar of companies' see PARA 126 note 2.
2 As to the meaning of 'secured information' see PARA 502 note 2.
3 As to the meaning of 'registrable person' see PARA 467 text and note 22.
4 Register of People with Significant Control Regulations 2016, SI 2016/339, reg 36(1)(a). As to the meaning of 'company' under the Companies Acts see PARA 21; and as to the meaning of the 'Companies Acts' see PARA 13.
5 Register of People with Significant Control Regulations 2016, SI 2016/339, reg 36(1)(b).
6 Register of People with Significant Control Regulations 2016, SI 2016/339, reg 36(1)(c).
7 Register of People with Significant Control Regulations 2016, SI 2016/339, reg 36(2).
8 Register of People with Significant Control Regulations 2016, SI 2016/339, reg 36(3)(a)(i).
9 As to the meanings of 'name' and 'former name' see PARA 496 note 16.

10 Register of People with Significant Control Regulations 2016, SI 2016/339, reg 36(3)(a)(ii).
11 Register of People with Significant Control Regulations 2016, SI 2016/339, reg 36(3)(a)(iii).
12 Register of People with Significant Control Regulations 2016, SI 2016/339, reg 36(3)(a)(iv).
13 Register of People with Significant Control Regulations 2016, SI 2016/339, reg 36(3)(a)(v).
14 As to a company's registered number see PARAS 134–135.
15 Register of People with Significant Control Regulations 2016, SI 2016/339, reg 36(3)(a)(vi).
16 Ie under the Register of People with Significant Control Regulations 2016, SI 2016/339, reg 25 (see PARA 496), reg 26 (see PARA 497) or reg 27 (see PARA 498).
17 Ie under the Register of People with Significant Control Regulations 2016, SI 2016/339, reg 25(5) (see PARA 496), reg 26(6) (see PARA 497) or reg 27(7) (see PARA 498).
18 See the Register of People with Significant Control Regulations 2016, SI 2016/339, reg 36(3)(a)(vii).
19 Register of People with Significant Control Regulations 2016, SI 2016/339, reg 36(3)(b).
20 Register of People with Significant Control Regulations 2016, SI 2016/339, reg 36(4).
21 Register of People with Significant Control Regulations 2016, SI 2016/339, reg 39(1).
22 Register of People with Significant Control Regulations 2016, SI 2016/339, reg 39(3). For these purposes, an application is made when it has been registered by the registrar: reg 39(4).
23 Register of People with Significant Control Regulations 2016, SI 2016/339, reg 40(1). For these purposes, an application is made when it has been registered by the registrar: reg 40(4). Where a person in relation to whom an application under reg 36 has been made sends a notice to the registrar under reg 40(1), that person must notify the company to which the application related of this fact as soon as reasonably practicable: reg 40(2).
24 Register of People with Significant Control Regulations 2016, SI 2016/339, reg 36(5).
25 Register of People with Significant Control Regulations 2016, SI 2016/339, reg 36(6).
26 Ie any notice provided under the Register of People with Significant Control Regulations 2016, SI 2016/339, reg 40: see the text and note 23.
27 Register of People with Significant Control Regulations 2016, SI 2016/339, reg 39(2)(a)–(c).

505. Application by a company requiring the registrar to refrain from using or disclosing an individual's secured information. A company[1] ('the applicant') may make an application to the registrar of companies[2] requiring him to refrain from using or disclosing secured information[3] relating to an individual ('S') who is a registrable person[4], proposes to become a registrable person, or used to be a registrable person, in relation to that company[5]. A company may only make such an application, however, where S has given consent for the company to make the application on S's behalf[6].

The grounds on which an application may be made are that the applicant reasonably believes that if the secured information is disclosed by the registrar the activities of the applicant, or one or more characteristics or personal attributes of S when associated with the applicant, will put S or a person living with S at serious risk of being subjected to violence or intimidation[7].

The application must contain:

(1) a statement of the grounds on which the application is made[8];
(2) confirmation that S consents to the making of the application[9];
(3) the name and registered number[10] of the applicant[11];
(4) the address of the registered office[12] of the applicant[13];
(5) the e-mail address of the applicant, if any[14];
(6) the name and any former name of S[15];
(7) the date of birth of S[16];
(8) the usual residential address of S[17]; and
(9) the e-mail address of S, if any[18].

It must be accompanied by evidence which supports the applicant's statement of the grounds on which the application is made[19].

For the purpose of determining such an application the registrar may:

(a) direct that additional information or evidence should be delivered to him;

(b) refer any question relating to an assessment of the nature or extent of any risk of violence or intimidation to a relevant body or to any other person the registrar considers may be able to assist in making that assessment; and

(c) accept any answer to a question referred under head (b) above as providing sufficient evidence of the nature or extent of any risk[20].

A person who makes an application must inform the registrar in writing without delay upon becoming aware of any change to any information or evidence provided to the registrar in connection with the application[21].

If a person in relation to whom an application has been made that has not yet been determined notifies the registrar in writing that the person no longer wishes the registrar to determine the application, the registrar is not required to determine the application[22]. Otherwise the registrar must determine the application and, within seven days beginning with the date that the determination is made, send to the applicant and to S notice of the determination[23]. Where the application is unsuccessful, that notice must inform the applicant of the applicant's right to apply for permission to appeal against the determination within 28 days beginning with the date of the notice[24].

The registrar must not make available for public inspection any application, any documents provided in support of that application or any notice[25] of withdrawal of the application[26].

1 As to the meaning of 'company' under the Companies Acts see PARA 21; and as to the meaning of the 'Companies Acts' see PARA 13.
2 As to the meaning of 'registrar of companies' see PARA 126 note 2.
3 As to the meaning of 'secured information' see PARA 502 note 2.
4 As to the meaning of 'registrable person' see PARA 467 text and note 22.
5 Register of People with Significant Control Regulations 2016, SI 2016/339, reg 37(1).
6 Register of People with Significant Control Regulations 2016, SI 2016/339, reg 37(2).
7 Register of People with Significant Control Regulations 2016, SI 2016/339, reg 37(3).
8 Register of People with Significant Control Regulations 2016, SI 2016/339, reg 37(4)(a)(i).
9 Register of People with Significant Control Regulations 2016, SI 2016/339, reg 37(4)(a)(ii).
10 As to a company's registered number see PARAS 134–135.
11 Register of People with Significant Control Regulations 2016, SI 2016/339, reg 37(4)(a)(iii).
12 As to a company's registered office see PARA 124.
13 Register of People with Significant Control Regulations 2016, SI 2016/339, reg 37(4)(a)(iv).
14 Register of People with Significant Control Regulations 2016, SI 2016/339, reg 37(4)(a)(v).
15 Register of People with Significant Control Regulations 2016, SI 2016/339, reg 37(4)(a)(vi). As to the meanings of 'name' and 'former name' see PARA 496 note 16.
16 Register of People with Significant Control Regulations 2016, SI 2016/339, reg 37(4)(a)(vii).
17 Register of People with Significant Control Regulations 2016, SI 2016/339, reg 37(4)(a)(viii).
18 Register of People with Significant Control Regulations 2016, SI 2016/339, reg 37(4)(a)(ix).
19 Register of People with Significant Control Regulations 2016, SI 2016/339, reg 37(4)(b).
20 Register of People with Significant Control Regulations 2016, SI 2016/339, reg 39(1).
21 Register of People with Significant Control Regulations 2016, SI 2016/339, reg 39(3). For these purposes, an application is made when it has been registered by the registrar: reg 39(4).
22 Register of People with Significant Control Regulations 2016, SI 2016/339, reg 40(1). For these purposes, an application is made when it has been registered by the registrar: reg 40(4). Where a person in relation to whom an application under reg 37 has been made sends a notice to the registrar under reg 40(1), that person must notify the company to which the application related of this fact as soon as reasonably practicable: reg 40(2).
23 Register of People with Significant Control Regulations 2016, SI 2016/339, reg 37(5).
24 Register of People with Significant Control Regulations 2016, SI 2016/339, reg 37(6).
25 Ie any notice provided under the Register of People with Significant Control Regulations 2016, SI 2016/339, reg 40: see the text and note 22.
26 Register of People with Significant Control Regulations 2016, SI 2016/339, reg 39(2)(a)–(c).

506. Application by a subscriber to a memorandum of association requiring the registrar to refrain from using or disclosing an individual's secured information. A subscriber to a memorandum of association[1] ('the applicant') may make an application to the registrar of companies[2] requiring him to refrain from using or disclosing secured information[3] relating to an individual ('S') who proposes to become, on or after the formation of the company to which the memorandum relates, a registrable person[4] in relation to the company[5]. A subscriber to a memorandum of association may, however, only make such an where S has given consent for the subscriber to make the application on S's behalf[6].

The grounds on which an application may be made are that the applicant reasonably believes that if the secured information is disclosed by the registrar the proposed activities of the company to which the memorandum relates, or one or more characteristics or personal attributes of S when associated with the company to which the memorandum relates, will put S or a person living with S at serious risk of being subjected to violence or intimidation[7].

The application must contain:

(1) a statement of the grounds on which the application is made[8];
(2) confirmation that S consents to the making of the application[9];
(3) the name and any former name of the applicant[10];
(4) the usual residential address of the applicant[11];
(5) the e-mail address of the applicant, if any[12];
(6) the name of the company to which the memorandum relates[13];
(7) the name and any former name of S[14];
(8) the date of birth of S[15];
(9) the usual residential address of S[16]; and
(10) the e-mail address of S, if any[17].

It must be accompanied by evidence which supports the applicant's statement of the grounds on which the application is made[18].

For the purpose of determining such an application the registrar may:

(a) direct that additional information or evidence should be delivered to him;
(b) refer any question relating to an assessment of the nature or extent of any risk of violence or intimidation to a relevant body or to any other person the registrar considers may be able to assist in making that assessment; and
(c) accept any answer to a question referred under head (b) above as providing sufficient evidence of the nature or extent of any risk[19].

A person who makes an application must inform the registrar in writing without delay upon becoming aware of any change to any information or evidence provided to the registrar in connection with the application[20].

If a person in relation to whom an application has been made that has not yet been determined notifies the registrar in writing that the person no longer wishes the registrar to determine the application, the registrar is not required to determine the application[21]. Otherwise, the registrar must determine the application and, within seven days beginning with the date that the determination is made, send to the applicant and to S notice of the determination[22]. Where the application is unsuccessful, that notice must inform the applicant of the applicant's right to apply for permission to appeal against the determination within 28 days beginning with the date of the notice[23].

The registrar must not make available for public inspection any application, any documents provided in support of that application or any notice[24] of withdrawal of the application[25].

1 As to a company's memorandum of association and its subscribers see PARA 97 et seq.

2 As to the meaning of 'registrar of companies' see PARA 126 note 2.
3 As to the meaning of 'secured information' see PARA 502 note 2.
4 As to the meaning of 'registrable person' see PARA 467 text and note 22.
5 Register of People with Significant Control Regulations 2016, SI 2016/339, reg 38(1). As to the meaning of 'company' under the Companies Acts see PARA 21; and as to the meaning of the 'Companies Acts' see PARA 13.

Regulation 38 is modified in relation to its application to SEs: see the European Public Limited-Liability Company (Register of People with Significant Control) Regulations 2016, SI 2016/375, reg 8. As to the meaning of 'SE' for these purposes see PARA 106 note 3; and as to such companies see PARA 1825 et seq.
6 Register of People with Significant Control Regulations 2016, SI 2016/339, reg 38(2).
7 Register of People with Significant Control Regulations 2016, SI 2016/339, reg 38(3).
8 Register of People with Significant Control Regulations 2016, SI 2016/339, reg 38(4)(a)(i).
9 Register of People with Significant Control Regulations 2016, SI 2016/339, reg 38(4)(a)(ii).
10 Register of People with Significant Control Regulations 2016, SI 2016/339, reg 38(4)(a)(iii). As to the meanings of 'name' and 'former name' see PARA 496 note 16.
11 Register of People with Significant Control Regulations 2016, SI 2016/339, reg 38(4)(a)(iv).
12 Register of People with Significant Control Regulations 2016, SI 2016/339, reg 38(4)(a)(v).
13 Register of People with Significant Control Regulations 2016, SI 2016/339, reg 38(4)(a)(vi).
14 Register of People with Significant Control Regulations 2016, SI 2016/339, reg 38(4)(a)(vii).
15 Register of People with Significant Control Regulations 2016, SI 2016/339, reg 38(4)(a)(viii).
16 Register of People with Significant Control Regulations 2016, SI 2016/339, reg 38(4)(a)(ix).
17 Register of People with Significant Control Regulations 2016, SI 2016/339, reg 38(4)(a)(x).
18 Register of People with Significant Control Regulations 2016, SI 2016/339, reg 38(4)(b).
19 Register of People with Significant Control Regulations 2016, SI 2016/339, reg 39(1).
20 Register of People with Significant Control Regulations 2016, SI 2016/339, reg 39(3). For these purposes, an application is made when it has been registered by the registrar: reg 39(4).
21 Register of People with Significant Control Regulations 2016, SI 2016/339, reg 40(1). For these purposes, an application is made when it has been registered by the registrar: reg 40(4). Where a person in relation to whom an application under reg 38 has been made sends a notice to the registrar under reg 40(1), that person must notify the subscriber to the memorandum of association who made the application and, if incorporated, the company to which the application related of this fact as soon as reasonably practicable: reg 40(3).
22 Register of People with Significant Control Regulations 2016, SI 2016/339, reg 38(5).
23 Register of People with Significant Control Regulations 2016, SI 2016/339, reg 38(6).
24 Ie any notice provided under the Register of People with Significant Control Regulations 2016, SI 2016/339, reg 40: see the text and note 22.
25 Register of People with Significant Control Regulations 2016, SI 2016/339, reg 39(2)(a)–(c).

507. Duration of successful determination not to use or disclose secured information. A determination[1] that an application for the non-use or non-disclosure of secured information[2] is successful continues to have effect until:

(1) either the person to whom the determination relates, or that person's personal representative[3], notifies the registrar in writing that he or she wishes the determination to cease to have effect[4]; or
(2) the registrar of companies[5] revokes[6] the determination[7].

Where a notice is given under head (1) above, the person giving the notice must also notify the company[8] to which the application that was determined relates of the notice given to the registrar[9].

The registrar must not make available for public inspection any notice provided under head (1) above[10].

1 Ie a determination under the Register of People with Significant Control Regulations 2016, SI 2016/339, reg 36(5) (see PARA 504), reg 37(5) (see PARA 505), or reg 38(5) (see PARA 506).
2 As to the meaning of 'secured information' see PARA 502 note 2.
3 As to the meaning of 'personal representative' see PARA 499 note 4.
4 See the Register of People with Significant Control Regulations 2016, SI 2016/339, reg 43(1)(a).
5 As to the meaning of 'registrar of companies' see PARA 126 note 2.
6 Ie under the Register of People with Significant Control Regulations 2016, SI 2016/339, reg 44: see PARA 508.
7 See the Register of People with Significant Control Regulations 2016, SI 2016/339, reg 43(1)(b).

8 As to the meaning of 'company' under the Companies Acts see PARA 21; and as to the meaning of the 'Companies Acts' see PARA 13.
9 Register of People with Significant Control Regulations 2016, SI 2016/339, reg 43(2).
10 Register of People with Significant Control Regulations 2016, SI 2016/339, reg 39(2)(e).

508. Revocation of determination not to use or disclose secured information. The registrar of companies[1] may revoke a determination[2] that an application for the non-use or non-disclosure of secured information[3] is successful if:

(1) the applicant in relation to the determination or, if different, any person to whom the application relates has been found guilty of a general false statement offence[4] in respect of purported compliance with any provision of the regulations[5] relating to the protection of secured information[6];

(2) the registrar has sent a notice[7] to the applicant in relation to the determination and, if different, to the person to whom the determination relates[8] which must inform the addressee:

(a) of the registrar's intention to revoke the determination;

(b) that the addressee may, within 28 days beginning with the date of the notice, deliver representations in writing to the registrar as to why the registrar should not revoke the determination; and

(c) that if the registrar receives such representations within that period, the registrar will have regard to the representations in deciding whether to revoke the determination[9]; and

(3) the period of 28 days beginning with the date of that notice has expired[10].

If within the period specified in head (2)(b) above an addressee of the notice delivers representations in writing to the registrar as to why he should not revoke the determination, the registrar must have regard to the representations in deciding whether to revoke the determination[11]. He must not make available for public inspection any representations so delivered[12].

The registrar must send notice of his decision as to whether to revoke a determination to the applicant in relation to the determination and, if different, to the person to whom the determination relates within seven days beginning with the date of the decision[13]. Where the registrar has made a decision to revoke a determination, he must make secured information on the register to which the determination relates available for public inspection as soon as reasonably practicable after sending that notice[14]. Where he makes secured information available for public inspection on the register under this provision, he must notify the person to whom the secured information relates and the company to which the application for its non-use or non-disclosure[15] related of that action as soon as reasonably practicable[16].

1 As to the meaning of 'registrar of companies' see PARA 126 note 2.
2 Ie a determination made under the Register of People with Significant Control Regulations 2016, SI 2016/339, reg 36(5) (see PARA 504), reg 37(5) (see PARA 505), or reg 38(5) (see PARA 506).
3 As to the meaning of 'secured information' see PARA 502 note 2.
4 Ie an offence under the Companies Act 2006 s 1112: see PARA 132.
5 Ie any provision of the Register of People with Significant Control Regulations 2016, SI 2016/339, Pt 7 (regs 33–45): see PARA 502 et seq.
6 See the Register of People with Significant Control Regulations 2016, SI 2016/339, reg 44(1)(a).
7 Ie in accordance with the Register of People with Significant Control Regulations 2016, SI 2016/339, reg 44(2): see heads (a)–(c) in the text.
8 Register of People with Significant Control Regulations 2016, SI 2016/339, reg 44(1)(b).
9 Register of People with Significant Control Regulations 2016, SI 2016/339, reg 44(2).
10 Register of People with Significant Control Regulations 2016, SI 2016/339, reg 44(1)(c).
11 Register of People with Significant Control Regulations 2016, SI 2016/339, reg 44(3).

12 Register of People with Significant Control Regulations 2016, SI 2016/339, reg 39(2)(f).
13 Register of People with Significant Control Regulations 2016, SI 2016/339, reg 44(4).
14 Register of People with Significant Control Regulations 2016, SI 2016/339, reg 44(5).
15 Ie the application under the Register of People with Significant Control Regulations 2016, SI 2016/339, reg 36 (see PARA 504), reg 37 (see PARA 505), or reg 38 (see PARA 506).
16 Register of People with Significant Control Regulations 2016, SI 2016/339, reg 44(6).

509. Action by the registrar after an unsuccessful determination of an application requiring him to refrain from using or disclosing an individual's secured information. Where the registrar of companies[1] has made a determination in respect of an application[2] for the non-use or non-disclosure of secured information[3] that is not in favour of the applicant, the registrar must make secured information on the register to which that application relates available for public inspection:

(1) where notice of an application for permission to appeal has not been served on the registrar[4], as soon as reasonably practicable after the end of the period of 42 days beginning with the date of the notice[5] of determination[6];
(2) where notice of an application for permission to appeal has been served on the registrar[7], as soon as reasonably practicable after:
  (a) the court[8] has dismissed the application for permission to appeal or the appeal and there is no further appeal pending; or
  (b) the registrar becomes aware that the application for permission to appeal or the appeal has been subsequently withdrawn or abandoned[9].

Where the registrar makes secured information available for public inspection on the register under these provisions, he must notify the person to whom the secured information relates and the company to which the application[10] related of that action as soon as reasonably practicable[11].

Transitional provision is made where an individual was a registrable person[12] on 6 April 2016 (a 'protectable person'), an application by an individual or a company[13] was made[14] in relation to the protectable person's secured information on or before 30 June 2016, and the registrar makes a determination that the application is unsuccessful[15]. Subject to an exception whereby the registrar may use or disclose the secured information for communicating with the protectable person and, where the application was made by a company[16], for communicating with the company which made the application[17]:

(i) for the protected period[18], the registrar must not use or disclose that secured information and must omit that secured information from the material on the register that is available for public inspection; and
(ii) where, before the expiry of the protected period, the protectable person ceases to be a registrable person in relation to the company to which the application relates and notifies the registrar in writing of that fact, after the expiry of the protected period the registrar must not use or disclose the secured information and must omit that secured information from the material on the register that is available for public inspection[19].

Where the registrar has not received a notice under head (ii) above before the expiry of the protected period, he must, as soon as reasonably practicable after the expiry of that period, make the secured information on the register available for public inspection and notify the protectable person and the company to which the application[20] related of that action[21].

1 As to the meaning of 'registrar of companies' see PARA 126 note 2.

2 Ie an application made under the Register of People with Significant Control Regulations 2016, SI 2016/339, reg 36 (see PARA 504), reg 37 (see PARA 505), or reg 38 (see PARA 506).
3 As to the meaning of 'secured information' see PARA 502 note 2.
4 Ie in accordance with the Register of People with Significant Control Regulations 2016, SI 2016/339, reg 41(4): see PARA 510.
5 Ie the notice given under the Register of People with Significant Control Regulations 2016, SI 2016/339, reg 36(5) (see PARA 504), reg 37(5) (see PARA 505), or reg 38(5) (see PARA 506).
6 See the Register of People with Significant Control Regulations 2016, SI 2016/339, reg 42(1), (2)(a).
7 See note 4.
8 As to the meaning of 'the court' see PARA 160 note 12.
9 See the Register of People with Significant Control Regulations 2016, SI 2016/339, reg 42(1), (2)(b).
10 Ie the application under the Register of People with Significant Control Regulations 2016, SI 2016/339, reg 36 (see PARA 504), reg 37 (see PARA 505), or reg 38 (see PARA 506).
11 Register of People with Significant Control Regulations 2016, SI 2016/339, reg 42(3).
12 As to the meaning of 'registrable person' see PARA 467 text and note 22.
13 Ie an application under the Register of People with Significant Control Regulations 2016, SI 2016/339, reg 36 (see PARA 504) or reg 37 (see PARA 505).
14 For these purposes, an application under the Register of People with Significant Control Regulations 2016, SI 2016/339, reg 36 or reg 37 is made when it is registered by the registrar: reg 46(6)(a).
15 See the Register of People with Significant Control Regulations 2016, SI 2016/339, reg 46(1).
16 Ie where the application was made under the Register of People with Significant Control Regulations 2016, SI 2016/339, reg 37.
17 See the Register of People with Significant Control Regulations 2016, SI 2016/339, reg 46(4).
18 For these purposes, 'protected period' means the following (Register of People with Significant Control Regulations 2016, SI 2016/339, reg 46(6)(b)), ie:
  (1) where an appeal under reg 41 (see PARA 510) has not been brought, 12 weeks beginning with the date of the notice sent under reg 36(5) or reg 37(5);
  (2) where an appeal under reg 41 has been brought and dismissed, 12 weeks beginning with the date the court dismissed the appeal in accordance with reg 41(5); or
  (3) where an appeal under reg 41 has been brought and subsequently withdrawn or abandoned, 12 weeks beginning with the date of the registrar becoming aware that such appeal has been withdrawn or abandoned.
19 Register of People with Significant Control Regulations 2016, SI 2016/339, reg 46(2). A protectable person who sends a notice to the registrar under reg 46(2)(b) (see head (ii) in the text) must include in the notice the date on which that protectable person ceased to be a registrable person in relation to the company, and must send a copy of the notice to the company: reg 46(3).
20 Ie the application under the Register of People with Significant Control Regulations 2016, SI 2016/339, reg 36 (see PARA 504) or reg 37 (see PARA 505).
21 Register of People with Significant Control Regulations 2016, SI 2016/339, reg 46(5).

510. Appealing against a determination that an application for the non-use or non-disclosure of secured information has been unsuccessful. Provided that the permission of the court[1] has been obtained[2], an applicant who has received notice[3] that his application for the non-use or non-disclosure of secured information[4] has been unsuccessful may appeal to the High Court on the grounds that the determination is unlawful, is irrational or unreasonable, or has been made on the basis of a procedural impropriety or otherwise contravenes the rules of natural justice[5].

An applicant who seeks permission to appeal must serve written notice of the application on the registrar of companies[6] within seven days beginning with the date on which the application for permission was issued[7]. The registrar must not make available for public inspection any notice of an appeal so provided[8].

The court determining an appeal may dismiss the appeal or quash the determination[9]. Where the court quashes a determination it may refer the matter to the registrar with a direction to reconsider it and make a determination in accordance with the findings of the court[10].

1 As to the meaning of 'the court' see PARA 160 note 12.

2 See the Register of People with Significant Control Regulations 2016, SI 2016/339, reg 41(2). No application for such permission may be made after 28 days beginning with the date of the notice under reg 36(5) (see PARA 504), reg 37(5) (see PARA 504), or reg 38(5) (see PARA 504), unless the court is satisfied that there was good reason for the failure of the applicant to seek permission before the end of that period: reg 41(3).
3 Ie under the Register of People with Significant Control Regulations 2016, SI 2016/339, reg 36(5) (see PARA 504), reg 37(5) (see PARA 504), or reg 38(5) (see PARA 504).
4 As to the meaning of 'secured information' see PARA 502 note 2.
5 Register of People with Significant Control Regulations 2016, SI 2016/339, reg 41(1). As to the rules of natural justice see JUDICIAL REVIEW vol 61 (2010) PARA 629 et seq; and see RIGHTS AND FREEDOMS vol 88A (2013) PARA 244.
6 As to the meaning of 'registrar of companies' see PARA 126 note 2.
7 Register of People with Significant Control Regulations 2016, SI 2016/339, reg 41(4).
8 Register of People with Significant Control Regulations 2016, SI 2016/339, reg 39(2)(d).
9 Register of People with Significant Control Regulations 2016, SI 2016/339, reg 41(5).
10 Register of People with Significant Control Regulations 2016, SI 2016/339, reg 41(6).

511. Protection by a company of secured information. Subject to certain exceptions[1], a company[2] must not use or disclose secured information[3] relating to a person ('S') if:

(1) in relation to that information an application has been made for its non-use or non-disclosure[4]; and
(2) the company has not received the specified notification which would allow its use or disclosure[5].

The company may, however, use or disclose secured information relating to S:

(a) for communicating with S;
(b) in order to comply with a requirement of the Companies Act 2006 as to particulars to be sent to the registrar; or
(c) where S has given consent for the company to use or disclose secured information relating to S[6].

Where a company is prohibited under heads (1) and (2) above from using or disclosing any secured information, the company's PSC register[7] is to be treated for certain statutory purposes[8] as not including that information[9].

1 Ie subject to the Register of People with Significant Control Regulations 2016, SI 2016/339, reg 45(2): see the text and note 6.
2 As to the meaning of 'company' under the Companies Acts see PARA 21; and as to the meaning of the 'Companies Acts' see PARA 13.
3 As to the meaning of 'secured information' see PARA 502 note 2.
4 Ie an application has been made under the Register of People with Significant Control Regulations 2016, SI 2016/339, reg 36 (see PARA 504), reg 37 (see PARA 504), or reg 38 (see PARA 504). For these purposes, an application has been made:
(1) under reg 36(1)(a) or (1)(c) when the applicant has informed the company under reg 36(4) that the applicant has made an application (reg 45(3)(a));
(2) under reg 36(1)(b) when the company has received the particular required by the Companies Act 2006 s 790K(1)(i) (see PARA 469 head (9)) in relation to that individual (Register of People with Significant Control Regulations 2016, SI 2016/339, reg 45(3)(b));
(3) under reg 37 when the company sends the application to the registrar (reg 45(3)(c)); or
(4) under reg 38 when the subscriber to the memorandum sends an application to the registrar (reg 45(3)(d)).

Regulation 45(3)(d) is modified in relation to its application to SEs: see the European Public Limited-Liability Company (Register of People with Significant Control) Regulations 2016, SI 2016/375, reg 9(1), (3). As to the meaning of 'SE' for these purposes see PARA 106 note 3; and as to such companies see PARA 1825 et seq.
5 See the Register of People with Significant Control Regulations 2016, SI 2016/339, reg 45(1). The notification referred to in the text is notification under reg 40(2), (3) (see PARAS 504–506), reg 42(3) (see PARA 509), reg 43(2) (see PARA 507), reg 44(6) (see PARA 508) or reg 46(5)(b) (see PARA 509).
6 Register of People with Significant Control Regulations 2016, SI 2016/339, reg 45(2).

Regulation 45(2)(b) (see head (b) in the text) is modified in relation to its application to SEs: see the European Public Limited-Liability Company (Register of People with Significant Control) Regulations 2016, SI 2016/375, reg 9(1), (2).

7 As to the meaning of 'company's PSC register' see PARA 470 note 5; and as to that register see PARA 480.

8 Ie for the purposes of the Companies Act 2006 s 790N(1) (see PARA 480) and s 790O(1), (2) (see PARA 481).

9 Register of People with Significant Control Regulations 2016, SI 2016/339, reg 45(4).

(13) COMPANY DIRECTORS

(i) Types of Director

512. Meaning of 'director' under the Companies Acts. In the Companies Acts[1], 'director' includes any person occupying the position of director, by whatever name called[2]. This term is defined in almost identical words for the purposes of the Company Directors Disqualification Act 1986[3] and for the purposes of the Insolvency Act 1986[4] and the case law that has built up in relation to the term is often 'read across' in the different statutory contexts[5]. Directors may be of three kinds[6]:

(1) de jure directors, that is to say, those who have been validly appointed to the office[7];

(2) de facto directors (or 'directors in fact'), that is to say, directors who assume to act as directors without having been appointed validly or at all[8]; and

(3) shadow directors, a term which is defined by statute for the purposes of both companies and insolvency legislation[9].

1 As to the meaning of the 'Companies Acts' see PARA 13.

2 Companies Act 2006 s 250. The meaning of 'director' may vary according to the context in which it is to be found: see *Re Lo-Line Electric Motors Ltd* [1988] Ch 477, [1988] 2 All ER 692; and see the text and notes 3–9.

3 See the Company Directors Disqualification Act 1986 s 22; and PARA 1759.

4 See the Insolvency Act 1986 s 251; and COMPANY AND PARTNERSHIP INSOLVENCY vol 16 (2011) PARA 6.

5 The law as to what constitutes a de facto director, for instance (see head (2) in the text) has developed largely in the context of decisions relating to applications under the Company Directors Disqualification Act 1986: see PARA 1761.

6 As to this formulation, and the categorisation given in heads (1)–(3) in the text, see *Re Hydrodam (Corby) Ltd* [1994] 2 BCLC 180 at 182, [1994] BCC 161 at 162 (decided under the Insolvency Act 1986 s 214 (declaration of liability for wrongful trading) (see COMPANY AND PARTNERSHIP INSOLVENCY vol 17 (2011) PARA 872) in reliance upon the definition of 'shadow director' given in s 251 (see COMPANY AND PARTNERSHIP INSOLVENCY vol 16 (2011) PARA 6) whose terms are identical to the definition of 'shadow director' given for the purposes of the Company Directors Disqualification Act 1986 s 22 (see PARA 1760) and that given for the purposes of the Companies Acts (see the Companies Act 2006 s 251; and PARA 513).

7 See *Re Hydrodam (Corby) Ltd* [1994] 2 BCLC 180 at 182, [1994] BCC 161 at 162. See also note 6. As to the appointment of directors see PARA 517 et seq. Persons properly and formally appointed as directors (de jure directors) owe fiduciary duties to the company: see PARA 584 et seq. The Companies Act 2006 contains for the first time a statutory statement of the general duties of directors (including the extent to which they apply to shadow directors: see s 170(5); and PARA 573): see Pt 10 Ch 2 (ss 170–181); and PARA 572 et seq.

8 See *Re Hydrodam (Corby) Ltd* [1994] 2 BCLC 180 at 182, [1994] BCC 161 at 162. See also note 6. It has been held for the purposes of the Companies Acts that, since the definition of 'director' is inclusive and not exhaustive, it is capable of including de facto directors but may not do so; the meaning of 'director' varies according to the context in which it is to be found: see *Re Lo-Line Electric Motors Ltd* [1988] Ch 477 at 489, [1988] 2 All ER 692 at 699 per Sir Nicolas Browne-Wilkinson V-C (decided under the Companies Act 1985 s 300 (repealed), which was a

predecessor of the Company Directors Disqualification Act 1986 but in more limited terms) (see PARA 1759)). Thus, in the Companies Acts, the word 'director' must be referring to de jure directors alone for the purposes of specifying eg a minimum number of directors (see PARA 517), or in relation to the register of directors (see PARA 535 et seq): see *Re Lo-Line Electric Motors Ltd* [1988] Ch 477, [1988] 2 All ER 692; *John Morley Building Co v Barras* [1891] 2 Ch 386. On the other hand, in some contexts, the word 'director' must include a person who is not a de jure director, eg where the acts of a person acting as a director are deemed to be valid notwithstanding that it is afterwards discovered that there was a defect in his appointment (see PARA 520): see *Re Lo-Line Electric Motors Ltd* [1988] Ch 477, [1988] 2 All ER 692. A de facto director owes the same fiduciary duties as a de jure director: *Re Canadian Land Reclaiming and Colonizing Co, Coventry and Dixon's Case* (1880) 14 ChD 660 at 670 (decided under the Companies Act 1862); *Ultraframe (UK) Ltd v Fielding, Northstar Systems Ltd v Fielding* [2005] EWHC 1638 (Ch) at [1257], [2005] All ER (D) 397 (Jul); *Primlake Ltd v Matthew Associates* [2006] EWHC 1227 (Ch) at [284], [2007] 1 BCLC 666. However, a person acting as director but not in fact duly appointed to that office is not liable under a penal enactment as a director of the company: *Dean v Hiesler* [1942] 2 All ER 340, DC. Consideration has to be given to what a person actually did to see whether he assumed a director's responsibilities in relation to the company. There is no single test in identifying what functions are, in essence, the sole responsibility of a de facto director, but the director has to be part of the corporate governance structure of the company: *Re Mumtaz Properties Ltd, Wetton (as liquidator of Mumtaz Properties Ltd) v Ahmed* [2011] EWCA Civ 610, [2012] 2 BCLC 109, [2011] NLJR 779. As to the relationship between de facto directors and 'shadow directors' as defined for the purposes of the Companies Acts see PARA 513. As to de facto directors under the Company Directors Disqualification Act 1986 see PARA 1761. As to the circumstances in which an individual director of a corporate director of a company in liquidation will be held to be a de facto director see *Revenue and Customs Comrs v Holland, Re Paycheck Services 3 Ltd* [2010] UKSC 51, [2011] 1 All ER 430, [2010] 1 WLR 2793 (so long as the relevant acts are done by the individual entirely within the ambit of the discharge of his duties and responsibilities as a director of the corporate director, it is to that capacity that his acts must be attributed). As to the prospective prohibition on the appointment of corporate directors see PARA 526.

9 See *Re Hydrodam (Corby) Ltd* [1994] 2 BCLC 180 at 182, [1994] BCC 161 at 162. See also note 6.

513. Meaning of 'shadow director' under the Companies Acts. In the Companies Acts[1], 'shadow director', in relation to a company[2], means a person in accordance with whose directions or instructions the directors[3] of the company are accustomed to act[4]. A person is not, however, to be regarded as a shadow director by reason only that the directors act:

(1) on advice given by that person in a professional capacity[5];

(2) in accordance with instructions, a direction, guidance or advice given by that person in the exercise of a function conferred by or under an enactment[6];

(3) in accordance with guidance or advice given by that person in that person's capacity as a Minister of the Crown[7].

The term is defined in almost identical words for the purposes of the Company Directors Disqualification Act 1986[8] and for the purposes of the Insolvency Act 1986[9] and the case law that has built up in relation to the term is often 'read across' in the different statutory contexts[10].

A body corporate[11] is not to be regarded as a shadow director of any of its subsidiary[12] companies for the purposes of those provisions of the Companies Act 2006 which govern:

(a) the general duties of directors[13];

(b) transactions requiring members' approval[14]; or

(c) contracts with a sole member who is also a director[15],

by reason only that the directors of the subsidiary are accustomed to act in accordance with its directions or instructions[16].

As from 26 May 2015[17], the general duties of a director set out in Part 10 of the Companies Act 2006[18] apply to a shadow director of a company where and to the extent that they are capable of so applying[19]. This is meant to clarify the uncertainty, whereby it was suggested that the mere fact that a person falls within the statutory definition of 'shadow director' may not be enough to impose upon him the same fiduciary duties to the relevant company as are owed by a de jure or de facto director[20]. A person is unlikely to be a de facto director and a shadow director simultaneously, although he may be both in succession[21].

1 As to the meaning of the 'Companies Acts' see PARA 13.
2 As to the meaning of 'company' under the Companies Acts see PARA 21.
3 As to the meaning of 'director' under the Companies Acts see PARA 512.
4 Companies Act 2006 s 251(1). For these purposes, the mere giving of instructions is not sufficient; the board must act upon those instructions for the person to be regarded as a shadow director: *Ultraframe (UK) Ltd v Fielding, Northstar Systems Ltd v Fielding* [2005] EWHC 1638 (Ch), [2005] All ER (D) 397 (Jul). In construing the phrase 'the directors of the company', the policy underlying the definition (ie that a person who effectively controlled the activities of a company is to be subject to the same statutory liabilities and disabilities as a person who is a de jure director) must be taken into account and, since a de jure director was subject to those liabilities and disabilities even if he was non-executive (or even inactive) it would undermine the policy of the definition if the fact that an inactive director did not act on the instructions of an alleged shadow director (because he did not act at all) could prevent that person from being a shadow director, even though in reality he controlled the activities of the company: see *Ultraframe (UK) Ltd v Fielding, Northstar Systems Ltd v Fielding* [2005] EWHC 1638 (Ch) at [1272], [2005] All ER (D) 397 (Jul) (a person at whose direction a governing majority of the board was accustomed to act was capable of being a shadow director). As to de jure directors see PARA 512.
The Companies Act 2006 contains for the first time a statutory statement of directors' duties (including the extent to which they apply to shadow directors: see s 170(5); the text and notes 17–19; and PARA 573): see Pt 10 Ch 2 (ss 170–181); and PARA 572 et seq.
5 Companies Act 2006 s 251(2)(a) (s 251(2)(a)–(c) substituted by the Small Business, Enterprise and Employment Act 2015 s 90(3)).
6 Companies Act 2006 s 251(2)(b) (as substituted: see note 5). As to the meaning of 'enactment' see PARA 13 note 16.
7 Companies Act 2006 s 251(2)(c) (as substituted: see note 5). The reference in the text to a Minister of the Crown is to such a minister within the meaning of the Ministers of the Crown Act 1975 (see s 8(1); and CONSTITUTIONAL AND ADMINISTRATIVE LAW vol 20 (2014) para 162 note 3): see the Companies Act 2006 s 251(2)(c) (as so substituted).
8 See the Company Directors Disqualification Act 1986 s 22(5) (amended by the Small Business, Enterprise and Employment Act 2015 s 90(2)); and PARA 1760.
9 See the Insolvency Act 1986 s 251 (definition amended by the Small Business, Enterprise and Employment Act 2015 s 90(1)); and COMPANY AND PARTNERSHIP INSOLVENCY vol 16 (2011) PARA 6.
10 The law as to what constitutes a de facto director, for instance (see the text and notes 17–18) has developed largely in the context of decisions relating to applications under the Company Directors Disqualification Act 1986: see PARA 1761.
11 As to the meaning of 'body corporate' for the purposes of the Companies Acts see PARA 1 note 5.
12 As to the meaning of 'subsidiary' see PARA 22.
13 Ie for the purposes of the Companies Act 2006 Pt 10 Ch 2 (see PARA 572 et seq): see s 251(3).
14 Ie for the purposes of the Companies Act 2006 Pt 10 Ch 4 (ss 188–225) (see PARA 601 et seq): see s 251(3).
15 Ie for the purposes of the Companies Act 2006 Pt 10 Ch 6 (s 231) (see PARA 629): see s 251(3).
16 Companies Act 2006 s 251(3).
17 See the Small Business, Enterprise and Employment Act 2015 s 164(3)(g)(iii).
18 Ie the general duties set out in the Companies Act 2006 Pt 10 Ch 2: see PARA 572 et seq.
19 Companies Act 2006 s 170(5) (substituted by the Small Business, Enterprise and Employment Act 2015 s 89(1)). As to the power to make provision about the application of the general duties of directors to shadow directors see PARA 573.
20 It was held in *Ultraframe (UK) Ltd v Fielding, Northstar Systems Ltd v Fielding* [2005] EWHC 1638 (Ch) at [1289], [2005] All ER (D) 397 (Jul) that the indirect influence exerted by a paradigm shadow director who did not directly deal with, or claim the right to deal directly with, the company's assets would not usually be sufficient to impose fiduciary duties upon him, although the case for this position was the stronger where the shadow director had been acting throughout in furtherance of his own, rather than the company's, interests. Cf, however, *Vivendi SA v Richards* [2013] EWHC 3006 (Ch) at [143], [2013] Bus LR D63, [2013] All ER (D) 112 (Oct), where it is suggested that *Ultraframe (UK) Ltd v Fielding, Northstar Systems Ltd v Fielding* [2005] EWHC 1638 (Ch), [2005] All ER (D) 397 (Jul) understates the extent to which shadow

directors owe fiduciary duties and that a shadow director will typically owe such duties in relation at least to the directions or instructions that he gives to the de jure directors. As to de facto directors, and the duties which they owe, see PARA 512 note 8.

21 *Ultraframe (UK) Ltd v Fielding, Northstar Systems Ltd v Fielding* [2005] EWHC 1638 (Ch), [2005] All ER (D) 397 (Jul) (a de facto director is held out to be a director but a shadow director will not be held out as having authority to act and directs activities only through the properly appointed board). As to the development of discussion on this point in relation to applications under the Company Directors Disqualification Act 1986 see PARA 1760 note 10.

514. Nominee directors. The position of a nominee director, that is, a director of a company who is nominated by a shareholder of that company to represent his interests[1], is not immediately clear, especially in relation to whom he owes his duties when the interests of all concerned in the arrangement are not in harmony[2]. The fact that a director of a company was nominated to that office by a shareholder does not, of itself, impose any duty on the director owed to his nominator[3]. The director might owe duties to his nominator if he were an employee or officer of the nominator, or by reason of a formal or informal agreement with his nominator[4], but such duties could not detract from his duty to the company of which he was a director when he was acting as such[5]. An appointed director, without being in breach of his duties to the company, could take the interests of his nominator into account, provided that his decisions as a director were in what he genuinely considered to be the best interests of the company; but that was a very different thing from his being under a duty to his nominator by reason of his appointment by it[6].

1 See *Boulting v Association of Cinematograph, Television and Allied Technicians* [1963] 2 QB 606 at 626, [1963] 1 All ER 716 at 723, CA, per Lord Denning MR.

2 The position of a nominee director has been summarised in *Re Southern Counties Fresh Foods Ltd* [2008] EWHC 2810 (Ch) at [67], [2008] All ER (D) 195 (Nov) per Warren J. It is clear that the nominee cannot do his duty to all parties when there is conflict within the nominee arrangement but if he agrees to subordinate the interests of the company to the interests of his patron, it is conduct oppressive to the other shareholders for which the patron can be made answerable: *Scottish Co-operative Wholesale Society Ltd v Meyer* [1959] AC 324, [1958] 3 All ER 66, HL. See also *Kuwait Asia Bank EC v National Mutual Life Nominees Ltd* [1991] 1 AC 187, [1990] 3 All ER 404, PC (in the performance of their duties as directors, the nominees were bound to ignore the interests and wishes of their employer). Cf *Re Broadcasting Station 2 GB Pty Ltd* [1964–5] NSWR 1648, NSW SC (it is consistent with a director's duty for the director to follow the wishes of a particular interest which has brought about his appointment, without the need for a close personal analysis of the issues, unless the director is of the view that in doing so he or she is not acting in the best interests of the company as a whole); *Re News Corpn Ltd* (1987) 70 ALR 419 at 437 per Bowen CJ (nominee directors will follow the interests of the company which appointed them subject to the qualification that they will not so act if of the view that their acts would not be in the interests of the company as a whole); *CanWest Global Communications Corp v Australian Broadcasting Authority* (1997) 24 ACSR 405, Aust FC (directors usually act in accordance with the wishes and interests of a party that has brought about their appointment and on whose goodwill their continuation in office depends unless that places them in breach of their duties).

3 *Hawkes v Cuddy, Re Neath Rugby Ltd* [2009] EWCA Civ 291 at [32], [2009] 2 BCLC 427, [2010] BCC 597 per Stanley Burnton LJ. See also *Re Neath Rugby Ltd, Hawkes v Cuddy* [2007] EWHC 2999 (Ch), [2008] BCC 390, [2008] All ER (D) 252 (Nov).

4 Ie which was the case on the facts of *Hawkes v Cuddy, Re Neath Rugby Ltd* [2009] EWCA Civ 291, [2009] 2 BCLC 427, [2010] BCC 597; *Re Neath Rugby Ltd, Hawkes v Cuddy* [2007] EWHC 2999 (Ch), [2008] BCC 390, [2008] All ER (D) 252 (Nov).

5 *Hawkes v Cuddy, Re Neath Rugby Ltd* [2009] EWCA Civ 291 at [32], [2009] 2 BCLC 427, [2010] BCC 597 per Stanley Burnton LJ. See also *Re Neath Rugby Ltd, Hawkes v Cuddy* [2007] EWHC 2999 (Ch), [2008] BCC 390, [2008] All ER (D) 252 (Nov).

6 *Hawkes v Cuddy, Re Neath Rugby Ltd* [2009] EWCA Civ 291 at [33], [2009] 2 BCLC 427, [2010] BCC 597 per Stanley Burnton LJ, citing with approval the Australian cases cited in note 2. See also *Re Neath Rugby Ltd, Hawkes v Cuddy* [2007] EWHC 2999 (Ch), [2008] BCC 390, [2008] All ER (D) 252 (Nov).

515. Meaning of references to persons 'connected' with director or director 'connected' with person. For the purposes of the Companies Act 2006 provisions[1] that govern the directors[2] of a company[3], the meaning of references to a person being 'connected' with a director of a company (or to a director being 'connected' with a person) has been defined[4].

Accordingly, the following persons (and only those persons) are 'connected' with a director of a company[5]:

(1) members of the director's family[6];

(2) a body corporate[7] with which the director is connected[8];

(3) a person acting in his capacity as trustee of a trust[9] the beneficiaries of which include the director or a person who by virtue of head (1) or head (2) above is connected with him[10], or the terms of which confer a power on the trustees that may be exercised for the benefit of the director or any such person[11], other than a trust for the purposes of an employees' share scheme[12] or a pension scheme[13];

(4) a person acting in his capacity as partner[14], either of the director[15], or of a person who, by virtue of head (1), head (2) or head (3) above, is connected with that director[16];

(5) a firm[17] that is a legal person under the law by which it is governed and in which[18]:

(a) the director is a partner[19];

(b) a partner is a person who, by virtue of head (1), head (2) or head (3) above, is connected with the director[20]; or

(c) a partner is a firm in which the director is a partner or in which there is a partner who, by virtue of head (1), head (2) or head (3) above, is connected with the director[21].

1 Ie the Companies Act 2006 Pt 10 (ss 154–259) (see PARAS 512 et seq, 516 et seq): see s 252(1).

2 As to the meaning of 'director' under the Companies Acts see PARA 512; and as to the meaning of the 'Companies Acts' see PARA 13.

3 As to the meaning of 'company' under the Companies Acts see PARA 21.

4 Companies Act 2006 s 252(1).

5 Companies Act 2006 s 252(2). References in Pt 10 to a person connected with a director of a company do not include a person who is himself a director of the company: s 252(3). The references in Pt 10 to a person connected with a director apply also for the purposes of s 41 (transactions involving director or person connected with director): see s 41(7)(b); and PARA 263. It is implicit in s 239(5) (ratification of acts giving rise to liability) (see PARA 638), which excludes s 252(3), that the definition given in the text applies also to define who is a member 'connected with' a director for the purposes of s 239: see PARA 638.

6 Companies Act 2006 s 252(2)(a). The meaning of references in Pt 10 to members of a director's family is defined by s 253: see ss 252(2)(a), 253(1). Accordingly, for the purposes of Pt 10, the members of a director's family are:

(1) the director's spouse or civil partner (s 253(2)(a));

(2) any other person (whether of a different sex or the same sex) with whom the director lives as partner in an enduring family relationship (s 253(2)(b));

(3) the director's children or step-children (s 253(2)(c));

(4) any children or step-children of a person within head (2) above (and who are not children or step-children of the director) who live with the director and have not attained the age of 18 (s 253(2)(d));

(5) the director's parents (s 253(2)(e)).

However, head (2) above does not apply if the other person is the director's grandparent or grandchild, sister, brother, aunt or uncle, or nephew or niece: s 253(3).

7 As to the meaning of 'body corporate' for the purposes of the Companies Acts see PARA 1 note 5.

8 Companies Act 2006 s 252(2)(b). The meaning of references in Pt 10 to a director being 'connected with' a body corporate is defined by s 254 (see PARA 516): see ss 252(2)(b), 254(1).

9 Companies Act 2006 s 252(2)(c).

10 Companies Act 2006 s 252(2)(c)(i).

11 Companies Act 2006 s 252(2)(c)(ii).
12 As to the meaning of 'employees' share scheme' see PARA 169 note 20.
13 Companies Act 2006 s 252(2)(c).
14 Companies Act 2006 s 252(2)(d).
15 Companies Act 2006 s 252(2)(d)(i).
16 Companies Act 2006 s 252(2)(d)(ii).
17 As to the meaning of 'firm' see PARA 105 note 15.
18 Companies Act 2006 s 252(2)(e).
19 Companies Act 2006 s 252(2)(e)(i).
20 Companies Act 2006 s 252(2)(e)(ii).
21 Companies Act 2006 s 252(2)(e)(iii).

516. Meaning of references to director 'connected' with or 'controlling' body corporate. A director[1] is 'connected with' a body corporate[2] if, but only if, he and the persons connected with him together either[3]:

(1) are interested in shares[4] comprised in the equity share capital[5] of that body corporate of a nominal value[6] equal to at least 20 per cent of that share capital[7]; or
(2) are entitled to exercise or control the exercise of more than 20 per cent of the voting power at any general meeting of that body[8].

A director of a company is taken to 'control' a body corporate[9] if, but only if:

(a) he or any person connected with him is interested in any part of the equity share capital of that body[10], or is entitled to exercise or control the exercise of any part of the voting power at any general meeting of that body[11]; and
(b) he, the persons connected with him, and the other directors of that company, together are interested in more than 50 per cent of that share capital[12], or together are entitled to exercise or control the exercise of more than 50 per cent of that voting power[13].

For these purposes, a reference to an interest in shares includes any interest of any kind whatsoever in shares[14]. Any restraints or restrictions to which the exercise of any right attached to the interest is or may be subject must be disregarded[15].

A person is taken to have an interest in shares if:

(i) he enters into a contract to acquire them[16]; or
(ii) he has a right to call for delivery of the shares to himself or to his order[17], or he has a right to acquire an interest in shares or is under an obligation to take an interest in shares[18], whether the right or obligation is conditional or absolute[19].

A person ceases[20] to have an interest in shares for these purposes:

(A) on the shares being delivered to another person at his order[21], either in fulfilment of a contract for their acquisition by him[22], or in satisfaction of a right of his to call for their delivery[23];
(B) on a failure to deliver the shares in accordance with the terms of such a contract or on which such a right falls to be satisfied[24];
(C) on the lapse of his right to call for the delivery of shares[25].

A person is taken to have an interest in shares if, not being the registered holder, he is entitled either to exercise any right conferred by the holding of the shares[26], or to control the exercise of any such right[27]. For this purpose, a person is taken to be entitled to exercise or control the exercise of a right conferred by the holding of shares if he has a right, whether subject to conditions or not, the exercise of which would make him so entitled[28], or if he is under an obligation, whether or not so subject, the fulfilment of which would make him so entitled[29]. A person is not[30] so taken to be interested in shares by reason only that he has been appointed a proxy to exercise any of the rights attached to the shares[31], or by reason only that he has been appointed by a body corporate to act as its representative at any meeting of a company or of any class of its members[32].

A person is taken to be interested in shares if a body corporate is interested in them[33], and if either the body corporate or its directors are accustomed to act in accordance with his directions or instructions[34], or he is entitled to exercise or control the exercise of more than one-half of the voting power at general meetings of the body corporate[35].

Where an interest in shares is comprised in property held on trust, every beneficiary of the trust is taken to have an interest in shares[36]. This is subject to the proviso that, so long as a person is entitled to receive, during the lifetime of himself or another, income from trust property comprising shares, an interest in the shares in reversion or remainder must be disregarded[37]. Further, a person is treated as not interested in shares if and so long as he holds them, under the law in force in any part of the United Kingdom[38], as a bare trustee or as a custodian trustee[39]. Any interest of a person subsisting by virtue of an authorised unit trust scheme[40], a local authority investment scheme[41], a common investment scheme or common deposit scheme[42], or the Church Funds Investment Scheme[43] is to be disregarded[44].

1 As to the meaning of 'director' under the Companies Acts see PARA 512; and as to the meaning of the 'Companies Acts' see PARA 13.

2 As to the meaning of 'body corporate' for the purposes of the Companies Acts see PARA 1 note 5. For the avoidance of circularity in the application of the Companies Act 2006 s 252 (meaning of 'connected person') (see PARA 515):
   (1) a body corporate with which a director is connected is not treated for the purposes of s 254 as connected with him unless it is also connected with him by virtue of s 252(2)(c) or s 252(2)(d) (connection as trustee or partner) (see PARA 515 heads (3)–(4)) (s 254(6)(a)); and
   (2) a trustee of a trust the beneficiaries of which include (or may include) a body corporate with which a director is connected is not treated for the purposes of s 254 as connected with a director by reason only of that fact (s 254(6)(b)).

3 Companies Act 2006 s 254(2).

4 The provisions of the Companies Act 2006 Sch 1 (see the text and notes 14–44) have effect for the interpretation of references in ss 254, 255 to an interest in shares or debentures: ss 254(3), 255(3), Sch 1 para 1(1). The provisions are expressed in relation to shares but apply to debentures as they apply to shares: Sch 1 para 1(2). However, shares in a company held as treasury shares, and any voting rights attached to such shares (see heads (2), (a)–(b) in the text), are disregarded for the purposes of ss 254, 255: ss 254(5), 255(5). As to the meaning of 'company' under the Companies Acts see PARA 21; and as to the meaning of the 'Companies Acts' see PARA 13. As to the meaning of 'share' see PARA 1231. As to the meaning of 'debenture' see PARA 1482. As to treasury shares see PARA 1437.

5 As to the meaning of 'equity share capital' see PARA 1236.

6 As to the meaning of 'nominal' see PARA 1231.

7 Companies Act 2006 s 254(2)(a).

8 Companies Act 2006 s 254(2)(b). References in s 254 to voting power the exercise of which is controlled by a director include voting power whose exercise is controlled by a body corporate controlled by him: s 254(4). As to company meetings see PARA 701 et seq.

9 The meaning of references in the Companies Act 2006 Pt 10 (ss 154–259) (see PARAS 512 et seq, 517 et seq) to a director 'controlling' a body corporate is defined by s 255: s 255(1). For the avoidance of circularity in the application of s 252 (meaning of 'connected person') (see PARA 515):
   (1) a body corporate with which a director is connected is not treated for the purposes of s 255 as connected with him unless it is also connected with him by virtue of s 252(2)(c) or s 252(2)(d) (connection as trustee or partner) (see PARA 515 heads (3)–(4)) (s 255(6)(a)); and
   (2) a trustee of a trust the beneficiaries of which include (or may include) a body corporate with which a director is connected is not treated for the purposes of s 255 as connected with a director by reason only of that fact (s 255(6)(b)).

10 Companies Act 2006 s 255(2)(a)(i). See also note 4.

11 Companies Act 2006 s 255(2)(a)(ii). References in s 255 to voting power the exercise of which is controlled by a director include voting power whose exercise is controlled by a body corporate controlled by him: s 255(4).
12 Companies Act 2006 s 255(2)(b)(i).
13 Companies Act 2006 s 255(2)(b)(ii).
14 Companies Act 2006 Sch 1 para 2(1). It is immaterial that the shares in which a person has an interest are not identifiable: Sch 1 para 2(3). Persons having a joint interest in shares are deemed each of them to have that interest: Sch 1 para 2(4).
15 Companies Act 2006 Sch 1 para 2(2).
16 Companies Act 2006 Sch 1 para 3(1).
17 Companies Act 2006 Sch 1 para 3(2)(a).
18 Companies Act 2006 Sch 1 para 3(2)(b).
19 Companies Act 2006 Sch 1 para 3(2). Rights or obligations to subscribe for shares are not to be taken for the purposes of Sch 1 para 3(2) to be rights to acquire or obligations to take an interest in shares: Sch 1 para 3(3).
20 Ie by virtue of the Companies Act 2006 Sch 1 para 3: see Sch 1 para 3(4).
21 Companies Act 2006 Sch 1 para 3(4)(a).
22 Companies Act 2006 Sch 1 para 3(4)(a)(i).
23 Companies Act 2006 Sch 1 para 3(4)(a)(ii).
24 Companies Act 2006 Sch 1 para 3(4)(b).
25 Companies Act 2006 Sch 1 para 3(4)(c).
26 Companies Act 2006 Sch 1 para 4(1)(a).
27 Companies Act 2006 Sch 1 para 4(1)(b).
28 Companies Act 2006 Sch 1 para 4(2)(a).
29 Companies Act 2006 Sch 1 para 4(2)(b).
30 Ie by virtue of the Companies Act 2006 Sch 1 para 4: see Sch 1 para 4(3).
31 Companies Act 2006 Sch 1 para 4(3)(a). As to class rights associated with certain shares see PARA 1246. As to voting by proxy see PARA 734 et seq.
32 Companies Act 2006 Sch 1 para 4(3)(b). As to who qualifies as a member of a company see PARA 323.
33 Companies Act 2006 Sch 1 para 5(1).
34 Companies Act 2006 Sch 1 para 5(1)(a). See also the case law cited in PARA 513 note 4, which relates to the equivalent wording in s 251(1).
35 Companies Act 2006 Sch 1 para 5(1)(b). For the purposes of Sch 1 para 5(1)(b), where a person is entitled to exercise or control the exercise of more than one-half of the voting power at general meetings of a body corporate and that body corporate is entitled to exercise or control the exercise of any of the voting power at general meetings of another body corporate, the latter voting power is taken to be exercisable by that person: Sch 1 para 5(2).
36 Companies Act 2006 Sch 1 para 6(1).
37 Companies Act 2006 Sch 1 para 6(2).
38 As to the meaning of 'United Kingdom' see PARA 1 note 5.
39 Companies Act 2006 Sch 1 para 6(3)(a). See also TRUSTS AND POWERS vol 98 (2013) PARAS 232–237.
40 Ie within the meaning of the Financial Services and Markets Act 2000 s 237: see FINANCIAL SERVICES REGULATION vol 50A (2016) PARA 841.
41 Ie a scheme made under the Trustee Investments Act 1961 s 11: see LOCAL GOVERNMENT FINANCE vol 70 (2012) PARA 2.
42 Ie a scheme made under the Charities Act 1960 s 22 (repealed), s 22A (repealed), the Charities Act 1993 s 24 (repealed) or s 25 (repealed), the Charities Act 2011 s 96 or s 100 (see CHARITIES vol 8 (2015) PARAS 426–427) or under the Administration of Justice Act 1982 s 42 (see CIVIL PROCEDURE vol 11 (2015) PARA 74).
43 Ie the scheme set out in the Church Funds Investment Measure 1958 Schedule: see ECCLESIASTICAL LAW vol 34 (2011) PARA 1009.
44 Companies Act 2006 Sch 1 para 6(4) (amended by the Charities Act 2011 Sch 7 Pt 2 para 116). Also to be disregarded is any interest of the Church of Scotland General Trustees or of the Church of Scotland Trust in shares or debentures held by them, or of any other person in shares or debentures held by those Trustees or that Trust otherwise than as simple trustees: see Sch 1 para 6(5). The 'Church of Scotland General Trustees' are the body incorporated by the order confirmed by the Church of Scotland (General Trustees) Order Confirmation Act 1921; and the 'Church of Scotland Trust' is the body incorporated by the order confirmed by the Church of Scotland Trust Order Confirmation Act 1932: see the Companies Act 2006 Sch 1 para 6(5).

(ii) Appointment and Removal of Directors

A. REQUIREMENT TO HAVE DIRECTORS

517. Requirement of directors. The affairs of a company[1] are conducted by directors[2], whether under that name or some other name such as 'trustees', 'members of the council', or 'governors'[3].

A private company[4] must have at least one director[5]. A public company[6] must have at least two directors[7].

If it appears to the Secretary of State[8] that a company is in breach of the requirements as to the minimum number of directors it must have[9], the Secretary of State may give the company a direction[10], which must specify:

(1) the statutory requirement the company appears to be in breach of[11];
(2) what the company must do in order to comply with the direction[12]; and
(3) the period within which it must do so[13].

The direction must also inform the company of the consequences of failing to comply[14].

Where the company is in breach of the requirements as to the minimum number of directors[15], it must comply with the direction by making the necessary appointment or appointments[16], and by giving notice of them[17], before the end of the period specified in the direction[18]. If the company has already made the necessary appointment or appointments, or so far as it has done so, it must comply with the direction by giving notice of them[19] before the end of the period specified in the direction[20].

If a company fails to comply with a direction so given[21], an offence is committed by the company, and by every officer of the company who is in default[22].

A provision requiring or authorising a thing to be done by or to a director and the secretary[23] is not satisfied by its being done by or to the same person acting both as director and as, or in place of, the secretary[24].

1 As to the meaning of 'company' under the Companies Acts see PARA 21; and as to the meaning of the 'Companies Acts' see PARA 13.
2 As to the meaning of 'director' under the Companies Acts see PARA 512.
3 As to the restrictions on classes of persons acting as directors see PARA 525 et seq.
4 As to the meaning of 'private company' see PARA 95.
5 Companies Act 2006 s 154(1). By virtue of s 155(1) (prospectively repealed), at least one director must be a natural person (and hence capable of being held accountable for company actions): see PARA 525. As from a day to be appointed, and subject to certain exceptions, each director must be a natural person: see PARA 526.
The model articles of association that have been prescribed under the Companies Act 2006 (as to which see PARA 227 et seq) make no provision for the number of directors. However, the default articles that were prescribed for the purposes of the Companies Act 1985, ie the Companies (Tables A to F) Regulations 1985, SI 1985/805 (which have not been revoked and may, in their amended form, continue to be used by companies after the commencement of the Companies Act 2006: see PARA 229) provide that the number of directors (other than alternate directors), unless otherwise determined by ordinary resolution, is not subject to any maximum but must be not less than two: see the Companies (Tables A to F) Regulations 1985, SI 1985/805, reg 2, Schedule Table A art 64. Table A provides regulations for the management of a company limited by shares but art 64 is applied by Table C (regulations for the management of a company limited by guarantee and not having a share capital), Table D Pt III (regulations for the management of a company limited by guarantee and having a share capital), and Table E (an unlimited company having a share capital). As to the meanings of 'company limited by shares', 'company limited by guarantee', 'limited company' and 'unlimited company' see PARA 95. As to the meanings of 'company having a share capital' and 'share capital' see PARA 1231. As to the meaning of 'ordinary resolution' see PARA 685. As to alternate directors see PARA 523.
6 As to the meaning of 'public company' see PARA 95.
7 Companies Act 2006 s 154(2). See also note 5.

A company which has obtained admission to the official list of the UK Listing Authority must notify a Regulatory Information Service ('RIS'), as soon as possible and in any event by the end of the business day following the decision or receipt of notice about the change by the company, of any change to the board including the following matters (see the Listing Rules r 9.6.11):

(1) the appointment of a new director (stating the appointee's name and whether the position is executive, non-executive or chairman and the nature of any specific function or responsibility of the position);
(2) the resignation, removal or retirement of a director (unless the director retires by rotation and is re-appointed at a general meeting of the listed company's shareholders);
(3) important changes to the role, functions or responsibilities of a director; and
(4) the effective date of the change if it is not with immediate effect.

A listed company also must notify a RIS of the following information in respect of any new director appointed to the board as soon as possible following the decision to appoint the director and in any event within five business days of the decision (see the Listing Rules r 9.6.13):

(a) details of all directorships held by the director in any other publicly quoted company at any time in the previous five years, indicating whether or not he is still a director;
(b) any unspent convictions in relation to indictable offences;
(c) details of any receiverships, compulsory liquidations, creditors voluntary liquidations, administrations, company voluntary arrangements or any composition or arrangement with its creditors generally or any class of its creditors of any company where the director was an executive director at the time of, or within the 12 months preceding, such events;
(d) details of any compulsory liquidations, administrations or partnership voluntary arrangements of any partnerships where the director was a partner at the time of, or within the 12 months preceding, such events;
(e) details of receiverships of any asset of such person or of a partnership of which the director was a partner at the time of, or within the 12 months preceding, such event; and
(f) details of any public criticisms of the director by statutory or regulatory authorities (including designated professional bodies) and whether the director has ever been disqualified by a court from acting as a director of a company or from acting in the management or conduct of the affairs of any company.

A listed company must, in respect of any current director, notify a RIS as soon as possible of any changes in the information set out in heads (b)–(f) above and any new directorships held by the director in any other publicly quoted company: see the Listing Rules r 9.6.14. A regulatory information service (or 'RIS') is a regulatory information service that is either a primary information provider or an incoming information society service that has its establishment in an EEA state other than the United Kingdom and that disseminates regulated information in accordance with the minimum standards set out in Commission Directive (EC) 2007/14 (OJ L69, 9.3.2007, p 27) ('the Transparency Directive implementing Directive') art 12. see the Listing Rules Appendix 1.1. As to the Listing Rules generally see FINANCIAL SERVICES REGULATION vol 50A (2016) PARA 584. As to the retirement and re-appointment of directors see PARA 555. As to directors and executive offices see PARA 578.

8 As to the Secretary of State see PARA 6.
9 Ie in breach of the Companies Act 2006 s 154 (see the text and notes 4–7): see s 156(1).
10 Companies Act 2006 s 156(1)(a). The direction referred to in the text is a direction under s 156: see s 156(1).
11 Companies Act 2006 s 156(2)(a).
12 Companies Act 2006 s 156(2)(b).
13 Companies Act 2006 s 156(2)(c). The period mentioned in the text must be not less than one month or more than three months after the date on which the direction is given: see s 156(2).
14 Companies Act 2006 s 156(3).
15 Ie in breach:

(1) at the date at which this volume states the law, of the Companies Act 2006 s 154 (see the text and notes 4–7) or s 155 (see PARA 525) (see s 156(4) (as originally enacted));
(2) as from a day to be appointed under the Small Business, Enterprise and Employment Act 2015 s 164(1), as mentioned in the Companies Act 2006 s 156(1) (see s 156(4) (prospectively amended by the Small Business, Enterprise and Employment Act 2015 s 87(1), (3)(b) (not yet in force)).

As to the Secretary of State's duty to keep the Small Business, Enterprise and Employment Act 2015 s 87 (see head (2) above) under review see PARA 526.

16 Companies Act 2006 s 156(4)(a).
17 Companies Act 2006 s 156(4)(b). The text refers to the giving of notice under s 167 (duty to notify registrar of changes) (see PARA 550): see s 156(4)(b).

18 Companies Act 2006 s 156(4).
19 Ie under the Companies Act 2006 s 167 (duty to notify registrar of changes) (see PARA 550): see s 156(5).
20 Companies Act 2006 s 156(5).
21 Ie a direction under the Companies Act 2006 s 156 (see the text and notes 8–20): see s 156(6).
22 Companies Act 2006 s 156(6). For these purposes, a shadow director is treated as an officer of the company: s 156(6). As to the meaning of 'shadow director' see PARA 512. As to the meaning of 'officer who is in default' see PARA 316; and as to the meaning of 'officer' generally see PARA 679.
A person guilty of such an offence is liable on summary conviction to a fine and for continued contravention to a daily default fine not exceeding one-tenth of the greater of £5,000 or level 4 on the standard scale: s 156(7) (amended by SI 2015/664). In the case of liability on summary conviction the fine is one not exceeding level 5 on the standard scale:see the Companies Act 2006 s 156(7) (as so amended). By virtue of the Legal Aid, Sentencing and Punishment of Offenders Act 2012 s 85, however, where the offence is committed on or after 12 March 2015, it is punishable by a fine of an unlimited amount. As to the standard scale and the powers of magistrates' courts to issue fines on summary conviction see SENTENCING vol 92 (2015) PARA 176. As to the meaning of 'daily default fine' see PARA 1816.
23 As to the company secretary and other officers see PARA 669 et seq.
24 See the Companies Act 2006 s 280; and PARA 669.

B. APPOINTMENT OF DIRECTORS

(A) Procedure for Appointment of Directors

518. Appointment of first directors. The person or persons named in the statement of proposed officers[1] as directors[2] of the company[3], is or are, as from the date of the company's incorporation[4], deemed to have been appointed to that office[5].

1 As to the statement of proposed officers see PARA 105. As to the meaning of 'officer' see PARA 679.
2 As to the meaning of 'director' under the Companies Acts see PARA 512; and as to the meaning of the 'Companies Acts' see PARA 13.
3 As to the meaning of 'company' under the Companies Acts see PARA 21.
4 Ie the date mentioned in the certificate of incorporation, following the registration of a company: see PARA 114 note 7. As to incorporation by registration under the Companies Act 2006 see PARA 104 et seq.
5 See the Companies Act 2006 s 16(1), (6); and PARA 115. See also *Re Great Northern Salt and Chemical Works, ex p Kennedy* (1890) 44 ChD 472 (as the subscribers to the memorandum of association had all concurred in appointing the first directors of the company, the fact that they had not met together for the purpose of coming to their determination did not invalidate their act).

519. Procedure for subsequent appointments of directors. Under the model articles of association[1], any person who is willing to act as a director[2], and is permitted by law to do so, may be appointed to be a director, either by ordinary resolution[3], or by a decision of the directors[4]. It is not competent for the directors to enter into contracts restricting the right of the company to appoint its own directors[5].

At a general meeting of a public company[6], a motion for the appointment of two or more persons as directors of the company by a single resolution must not be made unless a resolution that it should be so made has first been agreed to by the meeting without any vote being given against it[7]. A resolution moved in contravention of this restriction is void, whether or not its being so moved was objected to at the time[8]. Although the acts of any directors so appointed will be valid[9] in such circumstances, no provision for the automatic re-appointment of retiring directors in default of another appointment[10] will apply[11].

Sometimes provision is made for an outside body, for example debenture holders[12], to appoint a director; under such a provision, the court will not enforce the appointment of a person who is objectionable to the company[13].

The company is not entitled to rely against other persons on any change among the company's directors unless certain conditions are met[14].

1 As to model articles of association that have been prescribed for the purposes of the Companies Act 2006, and their application generally, see PARA 227 et seq. Different versions of model articles have been so prescribed for use by private companies limited by shares (see the Companies (Model Articles) Regulations 2008, SI 2008/3229, reg 2, Sch 1), private companies limited by guarantee (see reg 3, Sch 2), and public companies (see reg 4, Sch 3). As to the meanings of 'company limited by guarantee', 'company limited by shares', 'limited company', 'private company' and 'public company' see PARA 95. The default articles prescribed for the purposes of the Companies Act 1985 ('legacy articles'), ie the Companies (Tables A to F) Regulations 1985, SI 1985/805, have not been revoked and may, in their amended form, continue to be used by companies after the commencement of the Companies Act 2006: see PARA 229.

2 For these purposes, 'director' means a director of the company, and includes any person occupying the position of director, by whatever name called: see the Companies (Model Articles) Regulations 2008, SI 2008/3229, Sch 1 art 1, Sch 2 art 1, Sch 3 art 1. This wording is in almost identical terms to that used for the purposes of the Companies Acts: see PARA 512. As to the meaning of the 'Companies Acts' see PARA 13. As to the meaning of 'company' under the Companies Acts see PARA 21 (definition applied by the Companies (Model Articles) Regulations 2008, SI 2008/3229, Sch 1 art 1, Sch 2 art 1, Sch 3 art 1). As to the appointment of first directors see PARA 518; and as to casual vacancies see PARA 521.

3 As to the meaning of 'ordinary resolution' see PARA 685 (definition applied by the Companies (Model Articles) Regulations 2008, SI 2008/3229, Sch 1 art 1, Sch 2 art 1, Sch 3 art 1).

4 See the Companies (Model Articles) Regulations 2008, SI 2008/3229, Sch 1 art 17(1), Sch 2 art 17(1), Sch 3 art 20. No further provision in the model articles is made in relation to a public company but in relation to a private company it is provided that in any case where, as a result of death, the company has no members (or, in the case of a company limited by shares, no shareholders) and no directors, the personal representatives of the last member (or shareholder) to have died have the right, by notice in writing, to appoint a person to be a director: see Sch 1 art 17(2), Sch 2 art 17(2). For these purposes, where two or more members (or shareholders) die in circumstances rendering it uncertain who was the last to die, a younger member (or shareholder) is deemed to have survived an older member (or shareholder): see Sch 1 art 17(3), Sch 2 art 17(3). For companies that are still using legacy articles of association (ie the Companies (Tables A to F) Regulations 1985, SI 1985/805: see note 1), provision for the appointment of directors is made in Schedule Table A arts 78, 79, subject to Table A arts 73–77 (arts 73–75 revoked, arts 76–79 amended, in relation to a private company limited by shares, by SI 2007/2541). See further *Transport Ltd v Schonberg* (1905) 21 TLR 305; *Catesby v Burnett* [1916] 2 Ch 325. The Companies (Tables A to F) Regulations 1985, SI 1985/805, Schedule Table A provides regulations for the management of a company limited by shares but arts 73–79 are applied by Table C (regulations for the management of a company limited by guarantee and not having a share capital), Table D Pt III (regulations for the management of a company limited by guarantee and having a share capital), and Table E (an unlimited company having a share capital). As to the meaning of 'unlimited company' see PARA 95. As to the meanings of 'company having a share capital' and 'share capital' see PARA 1231.

5 *James v Eve* (1873) LR 6 HL 335. Cf *Stace and Worth's Case* (1869) 4 Ch App 682.

6 As to meetings of the company see PARA 701 et seq.

7 Companies Act 2006 s 160(1). For the purposes of s 160, a motion to approve a person's appointment, or to nominate a person for appointment, is to be treated as a motion for his appointment: s 160(3). Nothing in s 160 applies to a resolution amending the company's articles (as to which see PARA 227 et seq): s 160(4). The precise effect of this saving is obscure. As to the meaning of references in the Companies Acts to a company's 'articles' see PARA 227 note 2.

8 Companies Act 2006 s 160(2).

9 See the Companies Act 2006 s 161; and PARA 520.

10 Ie such as in accordance with the provision made under the Companies (Tables A to F) Regulations 1985, SI 1985/805, Schedule Table A art 80 (revoked in relation to a private company limited by shares by SI 2007/2541); and see PARA 555.

11 Companies Act 2006 s 160(2).

12 As to the meaning of 'debenture' see PARA 1482.

13 *British Murac Syndicate Ltd v Alperton Rubber Co Ltd* [1915] 2 Ch 186. Cf *Plantations Trust Ltd v Bila (Sumatra) Rubber Lands Ltd* (1916) 85 LJ Ch 801 (where the power was one of nomination and not appointment, and the court would not force the company to appoint the person nominated).

14 See the Companies Act 2006 s 1079(2)(b); and PARA 140.

520. Defect in appointment of person acting as director. If the company[1] has caused proper minutes of all proceedings at meetings of its directors[2] or of its general meetings[3] to be recorded[4] then, until the contrary is proved, all appointments made at such meetings are deemed to be valid[5]. The acts of a person acting as a director are valid[6] notwithstanding that it is afterwards discovered[7]:

(1) that there was a defect in his appointment[8];
(2) that he was disqualified from holding office[9];
(3) that he had ceased to hold office[10];
(4) that he was not entitled to vote on the matter in question[11].

This presumption as to validity applies only to cases where there has been an appointment, albeit an invalid one[12]; it has no application to cases where in fact there has never been any appointment or where there has been a fraudulent usurpation of authority[13].

This deemed validity operates not only as between the company and outsiders, but also as between the company and its members[14], as where, for example, de facto directors make a call[15], summon meetings of the company[16], elect other directors[17], or allot shares[18]. A de facto director may be ordered to furnish a statement of affairs in a winding up[19]. Directors cannot take advantage of any informality in company proceedings in which they have themselves participated; they are estopped as between themselves and the company[20]; they are also estopped from saying they have been improperly appointed, if they have acted after their appointment[21]. Persons dealing with them who know of the invalidity are likewise estopped[22].

1 As to the meaning of 'company' under the Companies Acts see PARA 21; and as to the meaning of the 'Companies Acts' see PARA 13.

2 As to the meaning of 'director' under the Companies Acts see PARA 512. As to meetings of directors generally see PARA 568 et seq.

3 As to meetings of the company see PARA 701 et seq.

4 Ie in accordance with the Companies Act 2006 s 248 (directors' meetings) (see PARA 570) or s 355 (general meetings) (see PARA 740), as the case may be.

5 See the Companies Act 2006 s 249 (directors' meetings) (see PARA 570) or s 356 (general meetings) (see PARA 740), as the case may be. However, a person having notice that there is an irregularity or invalidity cannot avail himself of this provision: *Re Staffordshire Gas and Coke Co, ex p Nicholson* (1892) 66 LT 413; *Re Bridport Old Brewery Co* (1867) 2 Ch App 191; *Woolf v East Nigel Gold Mining Co Ltd* (1905) 21 TLR 660. A subsequent meeting may effectually ratify and confirm the acts of an irregularly constituted meeting: *Re Portuguese Consolidated Copper Mines Ltd, ex p Badman, ex p Bosanquet* (1890) 45 ChD 16, CA. An injunction may be obtained to restrain improperly appointed directors from acting: *Cheshire v Gordon Hotels* (1953) Times, 13 February. A director need not be appointed at the company's office: *Smith v Paringa Mines Ltd* [1906] 2 Ch 193. Cf *Barron v Potter* [1914] 1 Ch 895. As to the company's registered office see PARA 124.

6 The liabilities incurred by persons acting as director are also as great as if they had been properly appointed: *Western Bank of Scotland v Bairds' Trustees* (1872) 11 M 96. As to directors' liabilities generally see PARA 599. See also *Briton Medical, General and Life Association v Jones (2)* (1889) 61 LT 384; *Coventry and Dixon's Case* (1880) 14 ChD 660, CA; *Re Western Counties Steam Bakeries and Milling Co* [1897] 1 Ch 617, CA.

For companies that are still using the default articles that were prescribed originally for the purposes of the Companies Act 1985 ('legacy articles') (ie the Companies (Tables A to F) Regulations 1985, SI 1985/805: see PARA 229), Schedule Table A art 92 provides that all acts done by any meeting of the directors or of a committee of directors, or by any person acting as a director, are, notwithstanding that it is afterwards discovered that there was a defect in the appointment of any such director, or that any of them were disqualified from holding office, or had vacated office, or were not entitled to vote, as valid as if every such person had been duly appointed and was qualified and had continued to be a director and had been entitled to vote. The reference to subsequent discovery of a defect means a discovery that there is a defect, not a discovery of the facts which cause the defect: *British Asbestos Co Ltd v Boyd* [1903] 2 Ch 439 at 444 per Farwell J; *Channel Collieries Trust Ltd v Dover, St Margaret's and Martin Mill Light Rly Co* [1914] 2 Ch 506, CA; *Albert Gardens (Manly) Pty Ltd v Mercantile Credits Ltd* (1973) 9 ALR 653, Aust HC. As to the limitations upon the effectiveness of this article see also *Morris v Kanssen* [1946] AC 459,

[1946] 1 All ER 586, HL. The Companies (Tables A to F) Regulations 1985, SI 1985/805, Schedule Table A provides regulations for the management of a company limited by shares but art 92 is applied by Table C (regulations for the management of a company limited by guarantee and not having a share capital), Table D Pt III (regulations for the management of a company limited by guarantee and having a share capital), and Table E (an unlimited company having a share capital). As to the meanings of 'company limited by guarantee', 'company limited by shares', 'limited company' and 'unlimited company' see PARA 95. As to the meanings of 'company having a share capital' and 'share capital' see PARA 1231. As to the extent to which directors may delegate powers, including to committees, see PARA 577.

7 Companies Act 2006 s 161(1). A defect that the person appointed had no share qualification was held to have been 'afterwards discovered' in *Albert Gardens (Manly) Pty Ltd v Mercantile Credits Ltd* (1973) 9 ALR 653, Aust HC. If the holding of a share qualification is required, this is not a condition of the power of appointment; if it is not complied with, there will still be an appointment, although it will be defective. As to qualification shares see PARA 531 et seq.

8 Companies Act 2006 s 161(1)(a). The provisions of s 161 apply even if the resolution to appoint is void under s 160 (as to which see PARA 519): s 161(2). A company which has put forward a resolution as being validly passed cannot, at any rate after lapse of considerable time, repudiate it as invalid: *Montreal and St Lawrence Light and Power Co v Robert* [1906] AC 196, PC.

9 Companies Act 2006 s 161(1)(b). As to company directors' disqualification generally see PARA 1759 et seq.

10 Companies Act 2006 s 161(1)(c). As to the retirement or removal of directors see PARA 555 et seq.

11 Companies Act 2006 s 161(1)(d). The provisions of s 161 are worded more broadly than their predecessor provisions, the Companies Act 1985 s 285 (repealed).

12 *Albert Gardens (Manly) Pty Ltd v Mercantile Credits Ltd* (1973) 9 ALR 653, Aust HC. See also notes 7–8.

13 *Morris v Kanssen* [1946] AC 459, [1946] 1 All ER 586, HL; *Re New Cedos Engineering Co Ltd* [1994] 1 BCLC 797 at 812–813 per Oliver J; *Tyne Mutual Steamship Insurance Association v Brown* (1896) 74 LT 283 at 285 per Lord Russell CJ.

14 *Dawson v African Consolidated Land and Trading Co* [1898] 1 Ch 6, CA, doubting *Howbeach Coal Co Ltd v Teague* (1860) 5 H & N 151. See also *Channel Collieries Trust Ltd v Dover, St Margaret's and Martin Mill Light Rly Co* [1914] 2 Ch 506, CA, following *Dawson v African Consolidated Land and Trading Co*. As to who qualifies as a member of a company see PARA 323.

15 *Dawson v African Consolidated Land and Trading Co* [1898] 1 Ch 6, CA; *Briton Medical, General, and Life Association v Jones (2)* (1889) 61 LT 384. As to calls see PARA 1321 et seq. As to de facto directors, and the duties which they owe, see PARA 512 note 8; and as to de facto directors under the Company Directors Disqualification Act 1986 see PARA 1761.

16 *Southern Counties Deposit Bank v Rider and Kirkwood* (1895) 73 LT 374, CA. As to the convening of meetings see PARA 704 et seq.

17 *British Asbestos Co Ltd v Boyd* [1903] 2 Ch 439. See also *Transport Ltd v Schonberg* (1905) 21 TLR 305.

18 *Channel Collieries Trust Ltd v Dover, St Margaret's and Martin Mill Light Rly Co* [1914] 2 Ch 506, CA; *Ellett v Sternberg* (1910) 27 TLR 127. As to allotment of shares see PARA 1277 et seq.

19 *Re New Par Consols* [1898] 1 QB 573.

20 *Faure Electric Accumulator Co v Phillipart* (1888) 58 LT 525; *Murray v Bush* (1873) LR 6 HL 37; *Bank of Hindustan, China and Japan Ltd v Alison* (1871) LR 6 CP 222. Cf *Re Miller's Dale and Ashwood Dale Lime Co* (1885) 31 ChD 211, CA; *Morris v Kanssen* [1946] AC 459, [1946] 1 All ER 586, HL; *Re New Cedos Engineering Co Ltd* [1994] 1 BCLC 797. Likewise, although the expression 'person dealing with the company' in the Companies Act 1985 s 35A(1) (repealed; see now the Companies Act 2006 s 40(1); and PARA 262) was wide enough to include a director of the company and, accordingly, might have allowed him to rely upon the protection so afforded, that provision did not apply to a director seeking to rely on his own mistake: *Smith v Henniker-Major & Co (a firm)* [2002] EWCA Civ 762, [2003] Ch 182, [2002] 2 BCLC 655.

21 *Tyne Mutual Steamship Insurance Association v Brown* (1896) 74 LT 283; *York Tramways Co v Willows* (1882) 8 QBD 685, CA (following *Harward's Case* (1871) LR 13 Eq 30 and *Fowler's Case* (1872) LR 14 Eq 316, and dissenting on this point from *Howbeach Coal Co Ltd v Teague* (1860) 5 H & N 151).

22 *Re New Cedos Engineering Co Ltd* [1994] 1 BCLC 797. It is not sufficient to establish that they knew of the facts giving rise to the defect; it is necessary in addition to prove that they were aware that these facts gave rise to an invalidity: *Channel Collieries Trust Ltd v Dover, St Margaret's and Martin Mill Light Rly Co* [1914] 2 Ch 506 at 512, CA, per Lord Cozens-Hardy MR; *AM Spicer & Son Pty Ltd* (1931) 47 CLR 151 at 176 per Starke J (with whom Evatt J concurred), Aust HC; *Albert Gardens (Manly) Pty Ltd v Mercantile Credits Ltd* (1973) 9 ALR 653 at 659, Aust HC, per Gibbs J. See further PARAS 265–267.

521. Casual vacancies for directors. A power to fill vacancies may be vested in the continuing directors[1]. If any such vacancy is not filled before a general meeting, it may be filled then, and if not, the power of filling the casual vacancy remains in the continuing directors[2]. If a qualified person must be appointed, he must hold the qualification shares at the time of appointment[3].

1 As to a company's directors see PARA 512 et seq. For companies that are still using model articles of association that were prescribed originally for the purposes of the Companies Act 1985 ('legacy articles') (ie the Companies (Tables A to F) Regulations 1985, SI 1985/805: see PARA 229), Schedule Table A art 79 (amended in relation to a private company limited by shares by SI 2007/2541) (cited in PARA 519 note 4) carries a proviso that the director so appointed is to hold office only during the natural term of office of the retiring director or until the next annual general meeting of the company and will not be taken into account in determining the directors who are to retire by rotation at the meeting. If not re-appointed at such an annual general meeting, he must vacate office at the conclusion of that meeting. See further *Eyre v Milton Pty Ltd* [1936] Ch 244, CA. As to the requirement to hold an annual general meeting see PARA 702. Where the articles provide that only qualified persons, ie persons with the requisite share qualification, may be appointed, a person is not qualified until he is registered as the holder of the necessary number of shares: *Channel Collieries Trust Ltd v Dover, St Margaret's and Martin Mill Light Rly Co* [1914] 2 Ch 506, CA; *Spencer v Kennedy* [1926] Ch 125; *Pollock v Garrett* 1957 SLT (Notes) 8. As to qualification shares see PARA 531. As to a company's articles of association generally see PARA 227 et seq.

2 *Munster v Cammell Co* (1882) 21 ChD 183 at 187 per Fry J (where casual vacancies are referred to as vacancies occurring otherwise than by retirement in rotation); *Bennett Bros (Birmingham) v Lewis* (1903) 20 TLR 1, CA.

If the number of directors is reduced below a quorum for a directors' meeting, a company's articles of association usually prescribe measures that must be taken to appoint the required number: see the Companies (Tables A to F) Regulations 1985, SI 1985/805, reg 2, Schedule Table A art 90; the Companies (Model Articles) Regulations 2008, SI 2008/3229, Sch 1 art 11(3), Sch 2 art 11(3), Sch 3 art 11; and PARA 569. The provisions of what is now the Companies Act 2006 s 161 (see PARA 520) would not seem to apply: see *Morris v Kanssen* [1946] AC 459, [1946] 1 All ER 586, HL. Appointments may be validly made without duly complying with the formalities required by the articles of association: *Smith v Paringa Mines Ltd* [1906] 2 Ch 193. Cf *Barron v Potter* [1914] 1 Ch 895. Whether a person was appointed to fill a casual vacancy or as an additional director may depend on the determination of the question whether or not a vacancy was treated by the company as still subsisting at the time when the appointment was made: see *Zimmers Ltd v Zimmer* (1951) 95 Sol Jo 803. As to the requirement of official notification see PARA 519. As to the quorum required for a meeting of directors see PARA 569.

3 See *Pollock v Garrett* 1957 SLT (Notes) 8.

522. Additional directors. The directors of a company[1] may be invested with the power of appointing additional directors[2]. In face of such a provision, a company cannot usurp the power entrusted to the directors[3], unless it is shown that the power could not be exercised by the directors owing to dissension or deadlock[4]. Where the appointment of an additional director is desired to resolve a company deadlocked both at general meeting level and at board level, the court[5] may make an order under its statutory powers[6] convening a meeting for the single act of enabling the appointment of a new director to be considered and voted on[7].

1 As to a company's directors see PARA 512 et seq.

2 For companies that are still using model articles of association that were prescribed originally for the purposes of the Companies Act 1985 ('legacy articles') (ie the Companies (Tables A to F) Regulations 1985, SI 1985/805: see PARA 229), Schedule Table A art 79 (amended in relation to a private company limited by shares by SI 2007/2541) (cited in PARA 519 note 4) provides (inter alia) that the directors may appoint any person who is willing to act to be a director as an additional director, provided that the appointment does not cause the number of directors to exceed any number fixed by or in accordance with the articles as the maximum number of directors. A director so appointed holds office only until the next following annual general meeting and, if not re-appointed at such a meeting, he must vacate his office. As to the requirement of official notification see PARA 519. As to a company's articles of association generally see PARA 227 et seq.

3 *Blair Open Hearth Furnace Co v Reigart* (1913) 29 TLR 449. There may be a concurrent power: see *Isaacs v Chapman* (1916) 32 TLR 237, CA; *Worcester Corsetry Ltd v Witting* [1936] Ch 640, CA (where similar provisions to those in note 2 were held not to exclude the inherent power of the company to appoint directors).

4 *Barron v Potter* [1914] 1 Ch 895. See also *Monnington v Easier plc* [2005] EWHC 2578 (Ch), [2006] 2 BCLC 283 (court had no jurisdiction to order an extraordinary general meeting of the company to be convened for the purpose of considering the replacement of board members where it had not become impracticable to call or to conduct such a meeting in the manner prescribed by the company's articles and by the Companies Acts).

5 As to the meaning of 'the court' see PARA 160 note 12; and see note 4.

6 Ie under what is now the Companies Act 2006 s 306 (see PARA 711).

7 *Union Music Ltd v Watson* [2003] EWCA Civ 180, [2003] 1 BCLC 453 (order made even though only one member would be present at the meeting so convened). However, the court will not exercise its powers where to do so would override class rights (*Harman v BML Group Ltd* [1994] 1 WLR 893, [1994] 2 BCLC 674, CA), or where the deadlock has arisen as a result of a division of power within the company which had been agreed to by the parties (*Ross v Telford* [1998] 1 BCLC 82, CA; *Alvona Developments Ltd v Manhattan Loft Corporation (AC) Ltd* [2005] EWHC 1567 (Ch), [2005] All ER (D) 252 (Jul), [2006] BCC 119). As to classes of shares and class rights see PARA 1246 et seq.

523. Alternate directors. A company's articles of association[1] may permit the appointment of alternate directors[2]. Such an alternate may be another director, or a third person, depending upon the provisions of the articles. Normally, such a person has the same rights and responsibilities, in relation to any directors' meeting or directors' written resolution, as the alternate's appointor[3]. His appointment cannot outlast the directorship of the person to whom he is an alternate, but may be made to continue notwithstanding such person's retirement by rotation and re-appointment[4]. Whilst the alternate is acting as a director, he stands in a fiduciary position in relation to the company, and accordingly owes the company all the same duties as are owed by a director[5].

1 As to a company's articles of association generally see PARA 227 et seq.

2 As to a company's directors generally see PARA 512 et seq. Under the model articles of association prescribed for the purposes of the Companies Act 2006 for use by public companies (see the Companies (Model Articles) Regulations 2008, SI 2008/3229, Sch 3), Sch 3 art 25(1) provides that any director (the 'appointor') may appoint as an alternate any other director, or any other person approved by resolution of the directors, to exercise that director's powers, and to carry out that director's responsibilities, in relation to the taking of decisions by the directors in the absence of the alternate's appointor. Any appointment or removal of an alternate must be effected by notice in writing to the company signed by the appointor, or in any other manner approved by the directors: Sch 3 art 25(2). The notice must identify the proposed alternate and, in the case of a notice of appointment, contain a statement signed by the proposed alternate that the proposed alternate is willing to act as the alternate of the director giving the notice: Sch 3 art 25(3). Other types of company apart from public companies may have alternates if they choose to make such provision in their articles. The default articles prescribed for the purposes of the Companies Act 1985 ('legacy articles'), ie the Companies (Tables A to F) Regulations 1985, SI 1985/805, have not been revoked and may, in their amended form, continue to be used by companies after the commencement of the Companies Act 2006: see PARA 229. Under those articles, Schedule Table A art 65 provides that any director (other than an alternate director) may appoint any other director, or any other person approved by resolution of the directors and willing to act, to be an alternate director and may remove from office an alternate director so appointed by him; and art 68 provides that any appointment or removal of an alternate director must be by notice to the company signed by the director making or revoking the appointment or in any other manner approved by the directors. The Companies (Tables A to F) Regulations 1985, SI 1985/805, Schedule Table A provides regulations for the management of a company limited by shares but arts 65–69 (see also notes 3–4) are applied by Table C (regulations for the management of a company limited by guarantee and not having a share capital), Table D Pt III (regulations for the management of a company limited by guarantee and having a share capital), and Table E (an unlimited company having a share capital). As to the meanings of 'company limited by guarantee', 'company limited by shares', 'limited company', 'public company' and 'unlimited company' see PARA 95. As to the meanings of 'company having a share capital' and 'share capital' see PARA 1231.

3 See the Companies (Model Articles) Regulations 2008, SI 2008/3229, Sch 3 art 26(1). Except as the articles specify otherwise, alternate directors are deemed for all purposes to be directors, are liable for their own acts and omissions, are subject to the same restrictions as their appointors, and

are not deemed to be agents of or for their appointors: Sch 3 art 26(2). A person who is an alternate director but not a director may be counted as participating for the purposes of determining whether a quorum is participating (but only if that person's appointor is not participating), and may sign a written resolution (but only if it is not signed or to be signed by that person's appointor): Sch 3 art 26(3). However, no alternate may be counted as more than one director for such purposes: see Sch 3 art 26(3). An alternate director is not entitled to receive any remuneration from the company for serving as an alternate director except such part of the alternate's appointor's remuneration as the appointor may direct by notice in writing made to the company: Sch 3 art 26(4). As to the quorum required for a meeting of directors see PARA 569. As to board meetings of directors generally see PARA 568. As to the extent to which directors may delegate powers, including to committees, see PARA 577.

Under the 'legacy articles' (ie the Companies (Tables A to F) Regulations 1985, SI 1985/805: see note 2), Schedule Table A art 66 provides that an alternate director is entitled to receive notice of all meetings of directors and of all meetings of committees of directors of which his appointor is a member, to attend and vote at any such meeting at which the director appointing him is not personally present and generally to perform all the functions of his appointor as a director in his absence but is not entitled to receive any remuneration from the company for his services as an alternate director. However, it is not necessary to give notice of a meeting to an alternate director who is absent from the United Kingdom: art 66. Save as otherwise provided in the articles, an alternate director is deemed for all purposes to be a director and is alone responsible for his own acts and defaults and must not be deemed to be the agent of the director appointing him: art 69. There are thus obvious advantages in appointing a person who is already a director as an alternate. A director who is also an alternate director is entitled in the absence of his appointor to a separate vote on behalf of his appointor in addition to his own vote: see art 88; and PARA 568.

4 Under the Companies (Model Articles) Regulations 2008, SI 2008/3229, Sch 3 art 27, an alternate director's appointment as an alternate terminates:
   (1) when the alternate's appointor revokes the appointment by notice to the company in writing specifying when it is to terminate (see Sch 3 art 27(a));
   (2) on the occurrence in relation to the alternate of any event which, if it occurred in relation to the alternate's appointor, would result in the termination of the appointor's appointment as a director (see Sch 3 art 27(b));
   (3) on the death of the alternate's appointor (see Sch 3 art 27(c)); or
   (4) when the alternate's appointor's appointment as a director terminates, except that an alternate's appointment as an alternate does not terminate when the appointor retires by rotation at a general meeting and is then re-appointed as a director at the same general meeting (see Sch 3 art 27(d)).

As to the rotation and re-appointment of directors see PARA 555.

Under the 'legacy articles' (ie the Companies (Tables A to F) Regulations 1985, SI 1985/805: see note 2), Schedule Table A art 67 provides that an alternate director must cease to be an alternate director if his appointor ceases to be a director; however, if a director retires by rotation or otherwise but is re-appointed or deemed to have been re-appointed at the meeting at which he retires, any appointment of an alternate director made by him which was in force immediately prior to his retirement continues after his re-appointment.

5 See PARA 512 et seq. As to the fiduciary duties owed by a director see PARA 587.

524. Continuing directors after expiry of term. When the first board of directors[1] or any subsequent board[2] continues to act after the period for which the directors were appointed has expired, or where the directors are due to retire and no valid appointment of new directors has been made[3], the acting directors (as de facto directors) can continue to act[4], and the validity of their acts cannot be challenged on the ground that they have ceased to hold office[5].

1 As to the appointment of first directors see PARA 518. As to the meaning of 'director' under the Companies Acts see PARA 512. As to board meetings of directors see PARA 568.

2 As to the procedure for appointment of directors other than first directors or directors to fill casual vacancies see PARA 519.

3 As to the retirement of directors see PARA 555.

4 *Muir v Forman's Trustee* (1903) 5 F 546, Ct of Sess. Cf *Tyne Mutual Steamship Insurance Association v Brown* (1896) 74 LT 283; *Garden Gully United Quartz Mining Co v McLister* (1875) 1 App Cas 39, PC. As to a company's articles of association generally see PARA 227 et seq.

5 See the Companies Act 2006 s 161; and PARA 520.

(B) Restrictions on Appointment of Directors

(a) Restrictions on Appointment of Directors who are not Natural Persons

525. Current requirement for at least one director to be a natural person. At the date at which this volume states the law, a company[1] must have at least one director[2] who is a natural person[3]. This requirement is met if the office of director is held by a natural person as a corporation sole[4] or otherwise by virtue of an office[5]; and, subject to this requirement, a limited company may be appointed to perform the duties and exercise the powers usually performed and exercised by individuals appointed as directors[6].

As from a day to be appointed[7], however, there will, subject to some limited exceptions, be a prohibition on appointing any directors who are not natural persons[8].

1 As to the meaning of 'company' under the Companies Acts see PARA 21; and as to the meaning of the 'Companies Acts' see PARA 13.

2 As to the meaning of 'director' under the Companies Acts see PARA 512.

3 Companies Act 2006 s 155(1) (s 155 prospectively repealed by the Small Business, Enterprise and Employment Act 2015 s 87(1), (2), as from a day to be appointed under s 164(1)). At the date at which this volume states the law, no such day had been appointed. This provision is intended to ensure that every company will have at least one individual who can, if necessary, be held to account for the company's actions; it is also consistent with the increased thrust being placed on the importance of directors understanding their statutory duties: see White Paper *Company Law Reform* (Cm 6456) (2005) para 3.3.

4 As to corporations sole see CORPORATIONS vol 24 (2010) PARAS 314–315.

5 Companies Act 2006 s 155(2) (prospectively repealed: see note 3).

6 *Re Bulawayo Market and Offices Co Ltd* [1907] 2 Ch 458. See also *Bank of Ireland v Cogry Flax Spinning Co* [1900] 1 IR 219. As to nominee directors see PARA 514.

7 See note 3.

8 See PARA 526.

526. Prospective requirement for each director to be a natural person. As from a day to be appointed[1], the following provisions have effect.

A person may not be appointed a director[2] of a company[3] unless the person is a natural person[4]. This does not, however, prohibit the holding of the office of director by a natural person as a corporation sole or otherwise by virtue of an office[5].

An appointment made in contravention of this prohibition is void[6]; but nothing in this prohibition affects any liability of a person under any provision of the Companies Acts or any other enactment[7] if the person purports to act as director, or acts as shadow director[8], although the person could not, by virtue of this prohibition, be validly appointed as a director[9].

If a purported appointment is made in contravention of this prohibition, an offence is committed by:

(1) the company purporting to make the appointment;

(2) where the purported appointment is of a body corporate[10] or a firm[11] that is a legal person under the law by which it is governed, that body corporate or firm; and

(3) every officer[12] of a person falling within head (1) or head (2) above who is in default[13].

The Secretary of State[14] may, however, make provision by regulations[15] for cases in which a person who is not a natural person may be appointed a director of a company[16]. The regulations must specify the circumstances in which, and any conditions subject to which, the appointment may be made[17]; and provision so made may in particular include provision that an appointment may be made only with the approval of a regulatory body specified in the regulations[18]. The regulations must include provision that a company must have at least one director who is a natural person; and for this purpose the requirement is met if the office of director is held by a natural person as a corporation sole or otherwise by virtue of an office[19]. Such regulations may require particulars relating to exceptions to be contained in a company's register of directors[20].

Where a person appointed a director of a company before the prohibition set out above comes into force[21] is not a natural person, and the case is not one excepted from that prohibition by regulations[22], that person ceases to be a director on the relevant day[23]. The company must:

(a) make the necessary consequential alteration in its register of directors[24]; and

(b) give notice[25] to the registrar of companies[26] of the change[27];

or, if an election to keep information about directors on the central register[28] is in force in respect of the company, the company must[29] deliver to the registrar[30] the information of which the company would otherwise have been obliged to give notice under head (b) above[31]. If it appears to the registrar that a notice should have, but has not, been given in accordance with head (b) above, or information should have, but has not, been delivered[32], he must place a note in the register recording the fact[33].

The Secretary of State must, before the end of each review period[34], carry out a review of the above provisions[35], and prepare and publish a report setting out the conclusions of the review[36]. The report must in particular:

(i) set out the objectives intended to be achieved by those provisions;

(ii) assess the extent to which those objectives have been achieved; and

(iii) assess whether those objectives remain appropriate and, if so, the extent to which they could be achieved in another way which imposed less regulation[37].

The Secretary of State must lay the report before Parliament[38].

1 Ie as from a day to be appointed under the Small Business, Enterprise and Employment Act 2015 s 164(1). At the date at which this volume states the law, no such day had been appointed.

2 As to the meaning of 'director' see PARA 512. As to the company secretary and other officers see PARA 671.

3 As to the meaning of 'company' under the Companies Acts see PARA 21; and as to the meaning of the 'Companies Acts' see PARA 13.

4 Companies Act 2006 s 156A(1) (ss 156A–156C prospectively added, as from a day to be appointed (see note 1), by the Small Business, Enterprise and Employment Act 2015 s 87(1), (4); not yet in force). As to the meaning of 'person' see PARA 312 note 2. The Companies Act 2006 s 156A has effect subject to s 156B (power to provide for exceptions from requirement that each director be a natural person: see the text and notes 14–19): s 156A(5) (prospectively added; not yet in force).

5 Companies Act 2006 s 156A(2) (prospectively added (see note 4); not yet in force). As to corporations sole see CORPORATIONS vol 24 (2010) PARAS 314–315.

6 Companies Act 2006 s 156A(3) (prospectively added (see note 4); not yet in force).

7 As to the meaning of 'enactment' see PARA 13 note 16.

8 As to shadow directors see PARA 513.

9 Companies Act 2006 s 156A(4) (prospectively added (see note 4); not yet in force).

10 As to the meaning of 'body corporate' for the purposes of the Companies Acts see PARA 1 note 5.

11 As to the meaning of 'firm' for the purposes of the Companies Acts see PARA 105 note 15.

12 For this purpose a shadow director is treated as an officer of a company: Companies Act 2006 s 156A(6) (prospectively added (see note 4); not yet in force). As to the meaning of 'officer' generally see PARA 679.

13 Companies Act 2006 s 156A(6) (prospectively added (see note 4); not yet in force). As to the meaning of 'officer who is in default' see PARA 316. A person guilty of such an offence is liable on summary conviction in England and Wales to a fine: s 156A(7)(a) (prospectively added; not yet in force).
14 As to the Secretary of State see PARA 6.
15 The regulations may make different provision for different parts of the United Kingdom: Companies Act 2006 s 156B(6) (prospectively added (see note 4); not yet in force). This is without prejudice to the general power to make different provision for different cases: s 156B(6) (prospectively added; not yet in force). As to the meaning of 'United Kingdom' see PARA 1 note 5. Regulations under s 156B are subject to affirmative resolution procedure (ie the regulations must not be made unless a draft of the statutory instrument containing them has been laid before Parliament and approved by a resolution of each House of Parliament): see ss 156B(7), 1290 (s 156B(7) (prospectively added; not yet in force). As to the making of regulations under the Companies Act 2006 generally see ss 1288–1292.
16 Companies Act 2006 s 156B(1) (prospectively added (see note 4); not yet in force).
17 Companies Act 2006 s 156B(2) (prospectively added (see note 4); not yet in force).
18 Companies Act 2006 s 156B(3) (prospectively added (see note 4); not yet in force).
19 Companies Act 2006 s 156B(4) (prospectively added (see note 4); not yet in force).
20 Ie the regulations may amend the Companies Act 2006 s 164 (see PARA 535) to that effect: see the Companies Act 2006 s 156B(5) (prospectively added (see note 4); not yet in force).
21 Ie before the Companies Act 2006 s 156A (see the text and notes 1–13) comes into force.
22 Ie regulations under the Companies Act 2006 s 156B (not yet in force): see the text and notes 14–19.
23 Companies Act 2006 s 156C(2) (prospectively added (see note 4); not yet in force). For these purposes, 'the relevant day' is the day after the end of the period of 12 months beginning with the day on which s 156A comes into force: s 156C(1) (prospectively added; not yet in force).
24 Companies Act 2006 s 156C(3)(a) (prospectively added (see note 4); not yet in force). As to the register of directors see PARA 535.
25 Ie in accordance with the Companies Act 2006 s 167: see PARA 550.
26 As to the meaning of 'registrar of companies' see PARA 126 note 2.
27 Companies Act 2006 s 156C(3)(b) (prospectively added (see note 4); not yet in force).
28 Ie an election under the Companies Act 2006 s 167A (not yet in force): see PARA 551.
29 Ie in place of doing the things required by the Companies Act 2006 s 156C(3): see the text and notes 24–27.
30 Ie in accordance with the Companies Act 2006 s 167D (not yet in force): see PARA 553.
31 Companies Act 2006 s 156C(4) (prospectively added (see note 4); not yet in force).
32 Ie in accordance with the Companies Act 2006 s 156C(4): see the text and notes 28–31.
33 Companies Act 2006 s 156C(5) (prospectively added (see note 4); not yet in force).
34 Each of the following is a review period for these purposes (Small Business, Enterprise and Employment Act 2015 s 88(4) (not yet in force)):
 (1) the period of five years beginning with the day on which s 87 (see note 4) comes into force (whether wholly or partly); and
 (2) each successive period of five years.
35 Ie a review of the Small Business, Enterprise and Employment Act 2015 s 87: see note 4.
36 Small Business, Enterprise and Employment Act 2015 s 88(1) (not yet in force).
37 Small Business, Enterprise and Employment Act 2015 s 88(2) (not yet in force).
38 Small Business, Enterprise and Employment Act 2015 s 88(3) (not yet in force).

527. Direction requiring company to appoint director who is a natural person. If it appears to the Secretary of State[1] that a company is in breach:

(1) of the current statutory requirement to have at least one director who is a natural person[2]; or
(2) as from a day to be appointed[3], of provision to that effect made by regulations[4],

he may give the company a direction[5], which must specify:

(a) the statutory requirement the company appears to be in breach of[6];
(b) what the company must do in order to comply with the direction[7]; and
(c) the period within which it must do so[8].

The direction must also inform the company of the consequences of failing to comply[9].

Where the company is in breach as mentioned above[10], it must comply with the direction by making the necessary appointment[11], and by giving the required notice[12], before the end of the period specified in the direction[13]. If the company has already made the necessary appointment, or so far as it has done so, it must comply with the direction by giving the required notice[14] before the end of the period specified in the direction[15].

If a company fails to comply with a direction so given[16], an offence is committed by the company, and by every officer of the company who is in default[17].

1 As to the Secretary of State see PARA 6.
2 Ie in breach of the Companies Act 2006 s 155 (prospectively repealed): see PARA 525. As to the meaning of 'director' see PARA 512.
3 Ie as from a day to be appointed under the Small Business, Enterprise and Employment Act 2015 s 164(1). At the date at which this volume states the law, no such day had been appointed.
4 Ie provision by virtue of the Companies Act 2006 s 156B(4) (not yet in force): see PARA 526.
5 Companies Act 2006 s 156(1)(b) (prospectively amended, as from a day to be appointed (see note 3), by the Small Business, Enterprise and Employment Act 2015 s 87(1), (3)(a)). As to the Secretary of State's duty to keep the Small Business, Enterprise and Employment Act 2015 s 87 under review see PARA 526.
6 Companies Act 2006 s 156(2)(a).
7 Companies Act 2006 s 156(2)(b).
8 Companies Act 2006 s 156(2)(c). The period mentioned in the text must be not less than one month or more than three months after the date on which the direction is given: see s 156(2).
9 Companies Act 2006 s 156(3).
10 Ie where, at the date at which this volume states the law, it is in breach of the Companies Act 2006 s 155 (prospectively repealed) or, as from a day to be appointed (see note 3), where it is in breach as mentioned in s 156(1) (see head (2) in the text): see s 156(4) (prospectively amended, as from a day to be appointed (see note 3), by the Small Business, Enterprise and Employment Act 2015 s 87(1), (3)(b)). See also note 5.
11 Companies Act 2006 s 156(4)(a). As to the appointment of directors see PARA 518 et seq.
12 Companies Act 2006 s 156(4)(b). The text refers to the giving of notice under s 167 (duty to notify registrar of changes) (see PARA 550): see s 156(4)(b).
13 Companies Act 2006 s 156(4).
14 Ie under the Companies Act 2006 s 167 (duty to notify registrar of changes) (see PARA 550): see s 156(5).
15 Companies Act 2006 s 156(5).
16 Ie a direction under the Companies Act 2006 s 156 (see the text and notes 1–15): see s 156(6).
17 Companies Act 2006 s 156(6). For these purposes, a shadow director is treated as an officer of the company: s 156(6). As to the meaning of 'shadow director' see PARA 513. As to the meaning of 'officer who is in default' see PARA 316. As to the meaning of 'officer' generally see PARA 679.
A person guilty of such an offence is liable on summary conviction to a fine and for continued contravention to a daily default fine not exceeding one-tenth of the greater of £5,000 or level 4 on the standard scale: Companies Act 2006 s 156(7) (amended by SI 2015/664). In the case of liability on summary conviction the fine is one not exceeding level 5 on the standard scale: see the Companies Act 2006 s 156(7) (as so amended). By virtue of the Legal Aid, Sentencing and Punishment of Offenders Act 2012 s 85, however, where the offence is committed on or after 12 March 2015, it is punishable by a fine of an unlimited amount. As to the standard scale and the powers of magistrates' courts to issue fines on summary conviction see SENTENCING vol 92 (2015) PARA 176. As to the meaning of 'daily default fine' see PARA 1816.

(b) Age Restrictions for Directors

528. Minimum age requirement for director. A person may not be appointed a director[1] of a company[2] unless he has attained the age of 16 years[3]. However, this does not affect the validity of an appointment that is not to take effect until the person appointed attains that age[4]. Where the office of director of a company is held by a corporation sole, or otherwise by virtue of another office, the appointment to that other office of a person who has not attained the age of 16 years is not effective also to make him a director of the company until he attains the age of 16 years[5]. Any appointment made in contravention of the minimum age requirement[6] is void[7] but any liability of a person under any provision of the Companies Acts is not affected[8] if he purports to act as director[9], or if he acts as a shadow director[10], although he could not, by virtue of the minimum age requirement[11], be validly appointed as a director[12].

The Secretary of State[13] may make provision by regulations[14] for cases in which a person who has not attained the age of 16 years may be appointed a director of a company[15]. The regulations must specify the circumstances in which, and any conditions subject to which, the appointment may be made[16]. If the specified circumstances cease to obtain, or any specified conditions cease to be met, a person who was appointed by virtue of the regulations and who has not since attained the age of 16 years ceases to hold office[17].

1 As to the meaning of 'director' under the Companies Acts see PARA 512; and as to the meaning of the 'Companies Acts' see PARA 13. As to the appointment of directors see PARA 518 et seq.
2 As to the meaning of 'company' under the Companies Acts see PARA 21.
3 Companies Act 2006 s 157(1). The provisions of s 157 have effect subject to s 158 (see the text and notes 13–17): s 157(6). Where a person appointed a director of a company before 1 October 2008 (ie before s 157 came into force: see the Companies Act 2006 (Commencement No 5, Transitional Provisions and Savings) Order 2007, SI 2007/3495, art 5(1)(c)) had not attained the age of 16 on that date or where the office of director of a company was held by a corporation sole, or otherwise by virtue of another office, and the person appointed to that other office had not attained the age of 16 years on that date, and the case was not one excepted from the Companies Act 2006 s 157 by regulations under s 158, that person ceased to be a director as from that date (ie 1 October 2008): see s 159(1), (2); and see also s 159(3), (4). As to corporations sole see CORPORATIONS vol 24 (2010) PARAS 314–315.
4 Companies Act 2006 s 157(2). See also note 3.
5 Companies Act 2006 s 157(3). See also note 3.
6 Ie in contravention of the Companies Act 2006 s 157: see s 157(1).
7 Companies Act 2006 s 157(4). See also note 3.
8 Ie by anything in the Companies Act 2006 s 157: see s 157(5).
9 Companies Act 2006 s 157(5)(a). See also note 3.
10 Companies Act 2006 s 157(5)(b). See also note 3. As to the meaning of 'shadow director' see PARA 513.
11 Ie by virtue of the Companies Act 2006 s 157: see s 157(5).
12 Companies Act 2006 s 157(5). See also note 3.
13 As to the Secretary of State see PARA 6 et seq.
14 As to the making of regulations under the Companies Act 2006 generally see ss 1288–1292. Regulations under s 158 are subject to negative resolution procedure (ie the statutory instrument containing the regulations is subject to annulment in pursuance of a resolution of either House of Parliament): see ss 158(5), 1289. Without prejudice to the general power to make different provision for different cases, the regulations may make different provision for different parts of the United Kingdom: see s 158(4). At the date at which this volume states the law, no such regulations had been made. As to the meaning of 'United Kingdom' see PARA 1 note 5.
15 Companies Act 2006 s 158(1).
16 Companies Act 2006 s 158(2).
17 Companies Act 2006 s 158(3).

(c) Restrictions on Undischarged Bankrupts etc or Disqualified Persons acting as Directors

529. Restriction on undischarged bankrupt etc acting as director. It is an offence for a person to act as director[1] of a company[2] or directly or indirectly to take part in or be concerned in the promotion, formation or management of a company, without the leave of the court[3], at a time when any of the following circumstances apply to him[4]:

(1) he is an undischarged bankrupt[5];

(2) a bankruptcy restrictions order or undertaking[6] is in force in respect of him;
(3) a debt relief restrictions order or undertaking[7] is in force in respect of him;
(4) a moratorium period under a debt relief order applies in relation to him[8].

The offence is one of strict liability[9].

A person who acts in contravention of these provisions is also personally responsible for all the relevant debts of the company incurred whilst he was involved in its management[10].

In England and Wales[11], the leave of the court may not be given unless notice of intention to apply for it has been served on the official receiver[12]; and it is the latter's duty, if he is of the opinion that it is contrary to the public interest that the application should be granted, to attend on the hearing of the application and oppose it[13].

1 As to the meaning of 'director' for the purposes of the Company Directors Disqualification Act 1986 see PARA 1759.
2 As to the meaning of 'company' for these purposes see PARA 1780 note 2.
3 As to the meaning of 'court' for these purposes see the Company Directors Disqualification Act 1986 s 11(2A); and PARA 1780 note 4.
4 See the Company Directors Disqualification Act 1986 s 11(1); and PARA 1780.
5 As to discharge from bankruptcy see BANKRUPTCY AND INDIVIDUAL INSOLVENCY vol 5 (2013) PARA 638 et seq.
6 A reference in an enactment to a person in respect of whom a bankruptcy restrictions order has effect (or who is 'the subject of' a bankruptcy restrictions order) includes a reference to a person in respect of whom a bankruptcy restrictions undertaking has effect: see the Insolvency Act 1986 Sch 4A para 8; and BANKRUPTCY AND INDIVIDUAL INSOLVENCY vol 5 (2013) PARA 657. As to bankruptcy orders see BANKRUPTCY AND INDIVIDUAL INSOLVENCY vol 5 (2013) PARA 198 et seq.
7 A reference in an enactment to a person in respect of whom a debt relief restrictions order has effect, or who is the subject of a debt relief restrictions order, includes a reference to a person in respect of whom a debt relief restrictions undertaking has effect: see the Insolvency Act 1986 Sch 4ZB para 8; and BANKRUPTCY AND INDIVIDUAL INSOLVENCY vol 5 (2013) PARA 127. As to debt relief restrictions orders see BANKRUPTCY AND INDIVIDUAL INSOLVENCY vol 5 (2013) PARA 125.
8 See the Company Directors Disqualification Act 1986 s 11(2); and PARA 1780. As to moratorium periods under debt relief orders see the Insolvency Act 1986 s 251H; and BANKRUPTCY AND INDIVIDUAL INSOLVENCY vol 5 (2013) PARA 109.
9 See *R v Brockley* [1994] 1 BCLC 606, CA.
10 See the Company Directors Disqualification Act 1986 s 15(1)(a); and PARA 1808.
11 As to the meanings of 'England' and 'Wales' see PARA 1 note 5.
12 As to the meaning of references in the Company Directors Disqualification Act 1986 to the official receiver, in relation to the winding up of a company or the bankruptcy of an individual, see PARA 1780 note 16.
13 See the Company Directors Disqualification Act 1986 s 11(3); and PARA 1780.

530. Restrictions on persons subject to disqualification orders: in general. In circumstances that are specified under statute[1], the court[2] may, and in some circumstances must, make a disqualification order[3] against a person, to the effect that for a period specified in the order:

(1) he must not be a director of a company[4]; or
(2) he must not act as receiver of a company's property[5]; or
(3) he must not in any way, whether directly or indirectly, be concerned or take part in the promotion, formation or management of a company[6],

unless, in each case, he has the leave of the court[7]; nor may he act as an insolvency practitioner[8].

1 Ie in the circumstances specified in the Company Directors Disqualification Act 1986: see PARA 1759 et seq.
2 As to the meaning of 'court' for these purposes see PARA 1762 note 1.
3 As to disqualification orders generally see PARA 1759 et seq.
4 See the Company Directors Disqualification Act 1986 s 1(1)(a); and PARA 1762. As to the meaning of 'director' for the purposes of the Company Directors Disqualification Act 1986 see PARA 1759; and as to the meaning of 'company' see PARA 1760 note 1.
5 See the Company Directors Disqualification Act 1986 s 1(1)(a); and PARA 1762. As to the construction of references to receivers for these purposes see PARA 1762 note 5. As to administrative receivers generally see COMPANY AND PARTNERSHIP INSOLVENCY vol 16 (2011) PARA 329 et seq.
6 See the Company Directors Disqualification Act 1986 s 1(1)(a); and PARA 1762. See also PARA 1762 notes 6–8.
7 See the Company Directors Disqualification Act 1986 s 1(1)(a); and PARA 1762.
8 See the Company Directors Disqualification Act 1986 s 1(1)(b); and PARA 1762. As to the meaning of references to acting as an insolvency practitioner for these purposes see PARA 1762 note 9.

C. DIRECTORS' QUALIFICATION SHARES

531. Whether a share qualification is required. Whether or not a company director[1] is required to possess any shareholding[2] at all in the company depends on the provisions of the company's articles of association[3]. Where such a qualification is so specified, the holding of shares as one of several joint holders constitutes good qualification[4].

The acts of a director or manager are valid if done before he is bound by law or by the articles to acquire his qualification[5], or notwithstanding that a defect may afterwards be discovered in his share qualification[6].

1 As to a company's directors see PARA 512 et seq.
2 As to share capital generally see PARA 1231 et seq.
3 *Re British Provident Life And Guarantee Association, De Ruvigne's Case* (1877) 5 ChD 306 at 321, CA, per James LJ, at 323 per Brett JA, and at 326 per Amphlett JA. As to a company's articles of association generally see PARA 227 et seq. No such qualification as is mentioned in the text is specified as being required either under the model articles of association which have been prescribed for the purposes of the Companies Act 2006 (see PARA 227 et seq) or under the default articles prescribed for the purposes of the Companies Act 1985 ('legacy articles') (ie the Companies (Tables A to F) Regulations 1985, SI 1985/805, which have not been revoked and may, in their amended form, continue to be used by companies after the commencement of the Companies Act 2006: see PARA 229). Where such a qualification is, however, specified, and a time limit on acquiring the qualification is also specified, as was the case under the Companies Act 1985 s 291 (repealed), time runs, when the election of directors is determined by a poll, only when the result of the poll is ascertained: *Holmes v Lord Keyes* [1959] Ch 199, [1958] 2 All ER 129, CA. Where the share qualification is increased, an existing director does not thereby cease to hold that larger qualification, but has a reasonable time in which to acquire it: *Molineaux v London, Birmingham and Manchester Insurance Co* [1902] 2 KB 589, CA. Under the Companies Act 1985 s 291 (repealed), criminal sanctions could be imposed on a person who acted as director without meeting the qualification requirement. See also *Re Barry and Staines Linoleum Ltd* [1934] Ch 227; *Re Gilt Edge Safety Glass Ltd* [1940] Ch 495, [1940] 2 All ER 237.
4 *Re Glory Paper Mills Co, Dunster's Case* [1894] 3 Ch 473 at 480, CA, per Lindley LJ; *Grundy v Briggs* [1910] 1 Ch 444.
5 *Re International Cable Co, ex p Official Liquidator* (1892) 66 LT 253.
6 See the Companies Act 2006 s 161; and PARA 520.

532. Liability for qualification shares. If a company director[1] resigns[2] before the time fixed as the date after which, unless already qualified, he is under the articles of association[3] to be deemed to have agreed to take his qualification shares from the company[4], he is not liable in respect of the shares to the company, although he acted as director without qualification[5]. If, however, he does not resign until after that date, he is liable, although he has never acted after accepting office[6].

A director who is bound by the articles to acquire a qualification, but who has not expressly agreed to take the shares from the company, is under no obligation to take the shares from the company[7], at any rate where it is possible for him to acquire his shares elsewhere[8].

Where a director applies for his qualification shares, but no allotment is made and the company does not undertake the business for which it was incorporated, or any other business, within the period during which he is to qualify or else be deemed bound, he cannot be put on the list of contributories[9]. Again, if his appointment as director is void, and the only agreement to take shares as qualification shares consists in his acting as director and the registration of shares in his name, the acting director is not liable on them[10].

If shares sufficient to qualify a director are registered in his name before his resignation, even without his knowledge, he will be liable to pay for them unless he has acquired other shares before the time when he was bound to qualify; for as director he must be taken to know the contents of the register and therefore that the shares have been registered in his name[11].

A transfer of qualification shares with a view to avoid liability may be void for fraud[12].

1 As to a company's directors see PARA 512 et seq.
2 As to resignation by a director see PARA 556.
3 As to a company's articles of association generally see PARA 227 et seq.
4 As to whether a director requires a share qualification see PARA 531. As to share capital generally see PARA 1231 et seq. A time limit on acquiring a share qualification was specified under the Companies Act 1985 s 291 (repealed): see PARA 531.
5 *Re Pandora Theatre Co* (1884) 28 Sol Jo 238; *Karuth's Case* (1875) LR 20 Eq 506; *Green's Case* (1874) LR 18 Eq 428; *Re Self-Acting Sewing Machine Co* (1886) 54 LT 676 (where the conduct of the director was held equivalent to refusal to act or to resignation); *Austin's Case* (1866) LR 2 Eq 435; *Re Imperial Land Credit Corpn Ltd, ex p Eve* (1868) 37 LJ Ch 844; *Salisbury-Jones and Dale's Case* [1894] 3 Ch 356, CA.
6 *Re Hercynia Copper Co* [1894] 2 Ch 403, CA; *Isaacs' Case* [1892] 2 Ch 158, CA.
7 *Re Printing, Telegraph and Construction Co of the Agence Havas, ex p Cammell* [1894] 2 Ch 392, CA (where shares were allotted to a director without his knowledge before his resignation, and registered afterwards); *Re Wheal Buller Consols* (1888) 38 ChD 42, CA; *Brown's Case* (1873) 9 Ch App 102 at 105 per Lord Selborne LC; *Green's Case* (1874) LR 18 Eq 428; *Austin's Case* (1866) LR 2 Eq 435; *Karuth's Case* (1875) LR 20 Eq 506 at 511; *Re Colombia Chemical Factory, Manure and Phosphate Works, Hewitt's Case, Brett's Case* (1883) 25 ChD 283, CA. See, however, *Harward's Case* (1871) LR 13 Eq 30; *Re Esparto Trading Co* (1879) 12 ChD 191. In *Re Bread Supply Association, Konrath's Case* (1893) 62 LJ Ch 376, Kekewich J held that the mere acting as director obliged him to qualify, and to do so by buying shares from the company, if he did not buy them elsewhere within a reasonable time, following, it was said, *Isaacs' Case* [1892] 2 Ch 158, CA, which case, however, is clearly distinguishable, as the clause ran 'he shall be deemed to have agreed to take his qualification shares from the company'. It seems that *Re Bread Supply Association, Konrath's Case* (1893) 62 LJ Ch 376is not consistent with *Re Medical Attendance Association, Onslow's Case* (1887) 57 LJ Ch 338n, CA, and *Re Wheal Buller Consols* (1888) 38 ChD 42, CA.
8 *Hamley's Case* (1877) 5 ChD 705. It may be different where he cannot obtain them elsewhere: see *Hamley's Case* 1877) 5 ChD 705 at 707 per Jessel MR.
9 *Re Youde's Billposting Ltd, Clayton's Case* (1902) 18 TLR 656, 731, CA. See also *General International Agency Co, Chapman's Case* (1866) LR 2 Eq 567 (where an allotment of a qualification was refused); *Tothill's Case* (1865) 1 Ch App 85 (where a smaller number was allotted); *Re Medical Attendance Association, Onslow's Case* (1887) 57 LJ Ch 338n, CA (where a smaller number of shares than the original qualification applied for was allotted, the company shortly afterwards reducing the required number to the same figure). As to the meaning of 'contributory' see COMPANY AND PARTNERSHIP INSOLVENCY vol 17 (2011) PARA 661.

10 *Stace and Worth's Case* (1869) 4 Ch App 682; *Re Wheal Buller Consols* (1888) 38 ChD 42, CA. See also *Hamley's Case* (1877) 5 ChD 705; and the other cases cited in PARA 534 note 3. Acting as a director without qualification is not a misfeasance under the Insolvency Act 1986 s 212: see COMPANY AND PARTNERSHIP INSOLVENCY vol 17 (2011) PARA 646 et seq. See also *Coventry and Dixon's Case* (1880) 14 ChD 660, CA.

11 *Re Portuguese Consolidated Copper Mines Ltd, ex p Lord Inchiquin* [1891] 3 Ch 28, CA; *Leeke's Case* (1871) 6 Ch App 469; *Molineaux v London, Birmingham and Manchester Insurance Co* [1902] 2 KB 589, CA. See also *Re Esparto Trading Co* (1879) 12 ChD 191 at 203 per Hall V-C (where the shares were not registered, but the calls were debited and the director was held to have assented to the entries); *Harward's Case* (1871) LR 13 Eq 30 (where the allotment committee was said to be the agent of the director to make an allotment to him); *Fowler's Case* (1872) LR 14 Eq 316 (where a director applied for further shares in ignorance that the qualifying number had been allotted to him). See also *Duke's Case* (1876) 1 ChD 620, doubting *Fowler's Case*.

12 *Gilbert's Case* (1870) 5 Ch App 559; *Re South London Fish Market Co* (1888) 39 ChD 324 at 331 per Kay J. See also PARA 410.

533. Qualification shares held as trustee etc. A company director[1] who is bound to hold his qualification shares[2] 'in his own right' is properly qualified if he holds in his name shares of which he is trustee[3]; and, if he is not bound to acquire his qualification shares from the company, is properly qualified if he holds shares which he receives as a present from the promoter by transfer or allotment[4]. In the latter case he may, however, be liable for misfeasance, and may be ordered to pay to the company the value of the shares[5].

Although a director fulfils the requirement of holding shares 'in his own right' if he holds shares as trustee, in spite of the beneficial interest being elsewhere, it is not sufficient if they are registered as held by the director in a representative capacity, as, for example, where he is registered as trustee in bankruptcy or as executor or as liquidator[6]; nor is it sufficient where he is bankrupt and his shares have, therefore, vested in his trustee, after which the company may no longer deal with the shares as the director's own[7]. No notice of any trust, expressed, implied or constructive may, however, be entered on the register[8] and the persons holding shares in a representative capacity are entitled to have a clean entry[9].

1 As to a company's directors see PARA 512 et seq.

2 As to whether a director requires a share qualification see PARA 531. As to share capital generally see PARA 1231 et seq. A time limit on acquiring a share qualification was specified under the Companies Act 1985 s 291 (repealed): see PARA 531.

3 *Pulbrook v Richmond Consolidated Mining Co* (1878) 9 ChD 610; *Cooper v Griffin* [1892] 1 QB 740, CA; *Howard v Sadler* [1893] 1 QB 1; *Bainbridge v Smith* (1889) 41 ChD 462 at 475, CA, per Lindley LJ; *Re Bainbridge, Reeves v Bainbridge* [1889] WN 228; *Sutton v English and Colonial Produce Co* [1902] 2 Ch 502.

4 *Brown's Case* (1873) 9 Ch App 102; *Carling, Hespeler and Walsh's Cases* (1875) 1 ChD 115, CA. See also *Miller's Case* (1877) 5 ChD 70, CA (where by the articles of association the qualification was to be provided by the company, and was forfeited on retirement, and the director was held not liable as shareholder). If shares are allotted and paid for out of money of the company fraudulently obtained by a promoter, they will be treated as unpaid although the director is innocent: *Leeke's Case* (1871) 6 Ch App 469; *Hay's Case* (1875) 10 Ch App 593. See also PARA 58.

5 *De Ruvigne's Case* (1877) 5 ChD 306, CA; *Pearson's Case* (1877) 5 ChD 336, CA; *Re Great Northern and Midland Coal Co, Currie's Case* (1863) 3 De GJ & Sm 367; *Re London and South Western Canal Ltd* [1911] 1 Ch 346. See PARA 47; and COMPANY AND PARTNERSHIP INSOLVENCY vol 17 (2011) PARA 646 et seq.

6 *Boschoek Pty Co Ltd v Fuke* [1906] 1 Ch 148 (in which instances the company could not deal with the shares as those of the registered holder). The articles of association may, however, contemplate that a person may be a director in a representative capacity: *Grundy v Briggs* [1910] 1 Ch 444 at 451 per Eve J.

7 *Sutton v English and Colonial Produce Co* [1902] 2 Ch 502 (where registration of subsequently acquired shares was enforced, the trustee not objecting). As to the restriction on undischarged bankrupts acting as directors see PARA 529.

8 See the Companies Act 2006 s 126; and PARA 344. As to the register of members see PARA 336 et seq. As to express, implied or constructive trusts etc see TRUSTS AND POWERS vol 98 (2013) PARA 24 et seq.
9 *Re TH Saunders & Co* [1908] 1 Ch 415. See also PARA 353.

534. Shares as condition precedent to holding office. If the holding of shares is a condition precedent to becoming a director of a company[1], the director must actually be registered as the holder of qualification shares before he is appointed[2], otherwise his election is void[3]; but, where it is not a condition precedent, he may be appointed and act before he qualifies[4].

1 As to a company's directors see PARA 512 et seq. As to whether a director requires a share qualification see PARA 531.
2 *Channel Collieries Trust Ltd v Dover, St Margaret's and Martin Mill Light Rly Co* [1914] 2 Ch 506, CA; *Spencer v Kennedy* [1926] Ch 125. A time limit on acquiring a shares qualification was specified under the Companies Act 1985 s 291 (repealed): see PARA 531.
3 *Hamley's Case* (1877) 5 ChD 705; *Re Elham Valley Rly Co, Biron's Case* (1878) 26 WR 606; *Barber's Case* (1877) 5 ChD 963, CA; *Jenner's Case* (1877) 7 ChD 132, CA; cf *Stace and Worth's Case* (1869) 4 Ch App 682.
4 *Re International Cable Co Ltd* (1892) 66 LT 253; *Re Portuguese Consolidated Copper Mines Ltd* (1889) 42 ChD 160, CA.

D. REGISTERS TO BE KEPT RELATING TO DIRECTORS

(A) Register of Directors

535. The register of directors. Every company[1] must keep a register of its directors[2].

The register must contain the required particulars[3] of each person who is a director of the company[4]. Accordingly, a company's register of directors must contain the following particulars in the case of an individual[5]:

(1) name[6] and any former name[7];
(2) a service address[8];
(3) the country or state (or part of the United Kingdom[9]) in which he is usually resident[10];
(4) nationality[11];
(5) business occupation (if any)[12];
(6) date of birth[13].

In the case of a body corporate[14], or a firm[15] that is a legal person under the law by which it is governed, a company's register of directors must contain the following particulars[16]:

(a) corporate or firm name[17];
(b) registered or principal office[18];
(c) in the case of an EEA company[19] to which the First Company Law Directive[20] (now repealed and replaced) applies, particulars of[21] the register in which the company file[22] is kept, including details of the relevant state[23] and the registration number in that register[24];
(d) in any other case, particulars of[25] the legal form of the company or firm and the law by which it is governed[26] and, if applicable, the register in which it is entered, including details of the state, and its registration number in that register[27].

The register must be kept available for inspection either at the company's registered office[28], or at a place specified in regulations[29]. The company must give notice to the registrar of companies[30] of the place at which the register is kept available for inspection[31], and of any change in that place[32], unless it has at all times been kept at the company's registered office[33]. The register must be open to the inspection of any member of the company[34] without charge[35], and to the inspection of any other person on payment of such fee as may be prescribed[36].

If default is made in complying with the requirements to keep a register[37], or to maintain the required particulars to be contained therein[38], or to keep the register available for inspection[39], or if default is made for 14 days in complying with the giving of notice to the registrar of the place where inspection may be made[40], or if an inspection[41] is refused, an offence is committed by the company, and by every officer of the company who is in default[42]. In the case of a refusal of inspection of the register, the court[43] may by order compel an immediate inspection of it[44].

The above provisions must be read with the provisions of the Companies Act 2006[45] which allow for an alternative method of record-keeping in the case of private companies[46].

1 As to the meaning of 'company' under the Companies Acts see PARA 21; and as to the meaning of the 'Companies Acts' see PARA 13.

2 Companies Act 2006 s 162(1). See, however, the text and notes 45–46. As to the meaning of 'director' under the Companies Acts see PARA 512. On and after 1 October 2009, the register of directors and secretaries kept by a company under the Companies Act 1985 s 288(1) (repealed) is to be treated as two separate registers, namely a register of directors kept under and for the purposes of the Companies Act 2006 s 162, and a register of secretaries kept under and for the purposes of s 275 (see PARA 673): see the Companies Act 2006 (Commencement No 8, Transitional Provisions and Savings) Order 2008, SI 2008/2860, Sch 2 para 25. As to the register of directors' residential addresses see PARA 536 et seq.

The provisions of the Companies Act 2006 ss 162–164, 166 apply to unregistered companies by virtue of the Unregistered Companies Regulations 2009, SI 2009/2436, reg 3, Sch 1 para 6(1), (2), but with the Companies Act 2006 s 162 as modified thereby: see PARA 1857. As to the meaning of 'unregistered company' see PARA 1856.

Where the registrar changes the address of a company's registered office under the Companies Act 2006 s 1097A(7) or the Companies (Address of Registered Office) Regulations 2016, SI 2016/423 (see PARA 160), the company's duties under the Companies Act 2006 s 162 are suspended for a period of 28 days beginning on the day the address was changed: see the Companies (Address of Registered Office) Regulations 2016, SI 2016/423, reg 11; and PARA 160.

3 Ie as specified in the Companies Act 2006 s 163 (particulars of directors to be registered: individuals) (see the text and notes 5–13), s 164 (particulars of directors to be registered: corporate directors and firms) (see the text and notes 14–27) and s 166 (particulars of directors to be registered: power to make regulations): see s 162(2). The Secretary of State may make provision by regulations amending s 163 or s 164, so as to add to or remove items from the particulars required to be contained in a company's register of directors: s 166(1). As to the Secretary of State see PARA 6. As to the making of regulations under the Companies Act 2006 generally see ss 1288–1292. Regulations under s 166 are subject to affirmative resolution procedure (ie the regulations must not be made unless a draft of the statutory instrument containing them has been laid before Parliament and approved by a resolution of each House of Parliament): see ss 166(2), 1290. At the date at which this volume states the law, no such regulations had been made.

The statement of proposed officers that is required to be delivered in accordance with the Companies Act 2006 s 9(1), (4) (see PARA 104) to the registrar of companies must contain the required particulars (ie the particulars that are, or, as from a day to be appointed (see note 48) would be, in the absence of an election under s 167A (see PARA 551), required to be stated in the company's register of directors and register of directors' residential addresses) of the person who is, or persons who are, to be the first director or directors of the company: see s 12; and PARA 105. As to the appointment of first directors see PARA 518.

4 Companies Act 2006 s 162(2).

5 Companies Act 2006 s 163(1). See also note 3.

6 For these purposes, 'name' means a person's Christian name (or other forename) and surname, except that in the case of a peer, or an individual usually known by a title, the title may be stated instead of his Christian name (or other forename) and surname or in addition to either or both of them: Companies Act 2006 s 163(2). See also note 3.

7 Companies Act 2006 s 163(1)(a). For these purposes, a 'former name' means a name by which the individual was formerly known for business purposes; and, where a person is or was formerly known by more than one such name, each of them must be stated: s 163(3). However, it is not necessary for the register to contain particulars of a former name in the following cases:

(1) in the case of a peer or an individual normally known by a British title, where the name is one by which the person was known previous to the adoption of or succession to the title (s 163(4)(a));

(2) in the case of any person, where the former name either was changed or disused before the person attained the age of 16 years, or has been changed or disused for 20 years or more (s 163(4)(b)).

See also note 3.

8 Companies Act 2006 s 163(1)(b). A person's service address may be stated to be 'The company's registered office': s 163(5). See also note 3. As to a company's registered office see PARA 124. As to requirements relating to service addresses generally see PARA 745.

In the case of an existing company, the relevant existing address of a director is deemed, on and after 1 October 2009, to be a service address, and any entry in the company's register of directors stating that address is treated, on and after that date, as complying with the obligation in the Companies Act 2006 s 163(1)(b) to state a service address: Companies Act 2006 (Commencement No 8, Transitional Provisions and Savings) Order 2008, SI 2008/2860, Sch 2 para 27(1). The relevant existing address is the address that immediately before 1 October 2009 appeared in the company's register of directors and secretaries as having been notified to the company under the Companies Act 1985 s 289(1A) (repealed) (service address notified by individual applying for confidentiality order in respect of usual residential address) or, if no such address appeared, the address that immediately before that date appeared in the company's register of directors and secretaries as the director's usual residential address: Companies Act 2006 (Commencement No 8, Transitional Provisions and Savings) Order 2008, SI 2008/2860, Sch 2 para 27(2). Any notification of a change of a relevant existing address occurring before 1 October 2009 that is received by the company on or after that date is treated as being or, as the case may be, including notification of a change of service address: Sch 2 para 27(3). However, the operation of Sch 2 para 27 does not give rise to any duty to notify the registrar under the Companies Act 2006 s 167 (duty to notify registrar of changes in particulars contained in register) (see PARA 550): Companies Act 2006 (Commencement No 8, Transitional Provisions and Savings) Order 2008, SI 2008/2860, Sch 2 para 27(4). As to the meaning of 'existing company' for these purposes see PARA 14 note 2. As to the company's register of directors and secretaries see note 2.

The registrar of companies may make such entries in the register of companies as appear to be appropriate having regard to Sch 2 para 27 and the information appearing on the register immediately before 1 October 2009 or notified to the registrar in accordance with Sch 2 para 31(2) (effect of repealed provisions): Sch 2 para 32(1). In particular, the registrar may record as a service address a relevant existing address (within the meaning of Sch 2 para 27) or, in the case of a company formed and registered on an application to which Sch 2 para 2(3) applies (see PARA 21 note 4), an address notified to the registrar in connection with that application as a director's usual residential address: Sch 2 para 32(2). Any notification of a change of a relevant existing address occurring before 1 October 2009 that is received by the registrar on or after that date is treated as being or, as the case may be, including notification of a change of service address: Sch 2 para 32(3). As to the registrar of companies see PARA 126 et seq. As to the register of companies see PARA 142 et seq.

9 As to the meaning of 'United Kingdom' see PARA 1 note 5.

10 Companies Act 2006 s 163(1)(c). See also note 3.

11 Companies Act 2006 s 163(1)(d). See also note 3.

12 Companies Act 2006 s 163(1)(e). See also note 3.

13 Companies Act 2006 s 163(1)(f). See also note 3.

14 As to the meaning of 'body corporate' see PARA 1 note 5.

15 As to the meaning of 'firm' see PARA 105 note 15.

16 Companies Act 2006 s 164. See also note 3. It seems that for these purposes 'director' does not include a de facto director: see *Re Lo-Line Electric Motors Ltd* [1988] Ch 477 at 489, [1988] 2 All ER 692 at 699, obiter per Sir Nicholas Browne-Wilkinson. As to de facto directors, and the duties which they owe, see PARA 512 note 8; and as to de facto directors under the Company Directors Disqualification Act 1986 see PARA 1761. As to the prospective prohibition on the appointment of corporate directors see PARA 526.

17 Companies Act 2006 s 164(a). See also note 3.

18 Companies Act 2006 s 164(b). See also note 3.

19 As to the meaning of 'EEA company' see PARA 26.

20 Ie Council Directive (EEC) 68/151 (OJ L65, 14.3.68, p 8), now repealed and replaced by European Parliament and Council Directive (EC) 2009/101 (OJ L258, 1.10.2009, p 11) (see PARA 20): see the Companies Act 2006 s 164(c). See also note 3.

21 Companies Act 2006 s 164(c). See also note 3.

22 Ie the company file mentioned in European Parliament and Council Directive (EC) 2009/101, (OJ L258, 1.10.2009, p 11) art 3 (which provides that, in each member state, a file must be opened in a central register, commercial register or companies register, for each of the companies registered therein: see art 3(1) (amended by European Parliament and Council Directive (EU) 2012/17 (OJ L156, 16.6.2012, p 1)); and see PARA 136 note 16): see the Companies Act 2006 s 164(c)(i). See also note 3.
23 Companies Act 2006 s 164(c)(i). See also note 3.
24 Companies Act 2006 s 164(c)(ii). See also note 3.
25 Companies Act 2006 s 164(d). See also note 3.
26 Companies Act 2006 s 164(d)(i). See also note 3.
27 Companies Act 2006 s 164(d)(ii). See also note 3. As to a company's registered number see ss 1066, 1067; and PARAS 134–135.
28 Companies Act 2006 s 162(3)(a).
29 Companies Act 2006 s 162(3)(b). The text refers to a place specified in regulations made under s 1136 (see PARA 748): see s 162(3)(b).
30 As to the meaning of 'registrar of companies' see PARA 126 note 2. As to the delivery of documents to the registrar see PARA 136; and as to the requirements for the proper delivery of documents to the registrar see PARA 137. As to a company's general duty to notify the registrar of changes relating to directors or their particulars see PARA 550.
31 Companies Act 2006 s 162(4)(a).
32 Companies Act 2006 s 162(4)(b).
33 Companies Act 2006 s 162(4).
34 As to the meaning of 'member of the company' see PARA 323.
35 Companies Act 2006 s 162(5)(a).
36 Companies Act 2006 s 162(5)(b). In the Companies Acts, 'prescribed' means prescribed (by order or by regulations) by the Secretary of State: s 1167. Partly in exercise of the powers conferred by s 162(5)(b), the Secretary of State has made the Companies (Fees for Inspection of Company Records) Regulations 2008, SI 2008/3007. As to the prescribed fee for these purposes see reg 2(a).
37 Ie in complying with the Companies Act 2006 s 162(1) (see the text and notes 1–2): see s 162(6).
38 Ie in complying with the Companies Act 2006 s 162(2) (see the text and notes 3–4): see s 162(6).
39 Ie in complying with the Companies Act 2006 s 162(3) (see the text and notes 28–29): see s 162(6).
40 Ie in complying with the Companies Act 2006 s 162(4) (see the text and notes 30–33): see s 162(6).
41 Ie an inspection required under the Companies Act 2006 s 162(5) (see the text and notes 34–36): see s 162(6).
42 Companies Act 2006 s 162(6). For these purposes, a shadow director is treated as an officer of the company: s 162(6). As to the meaning of 'shadow director' see PARA 512. As to the meaning of 'officer who is in default' see PARA 316; and as to the meaning of 'officer' generally see PARA 679.

A person guilty of such an offence is liable on summary conviction to a fine and for continued contravention to a daily default fine not exceeding one-tenth of the greater of £5,000 or level 4 on the standard scale: see the Companies Act 2006 s 162(7) (amended by SI 2015/664). In the case of liability on summary conviction the fine is one not exceeding level 5 on the standard scale: see the Companies Act 2006 s 162(7) (as so amended). By virtue of the Legal Aid, Sentencing and Punishment of Offenders Act 2012 s 85, however, where the offence is committed on or after 12 March 2015, it is punishable by a fine of an unlimited amount. As to the standard scale and the powers of magistrates' courts to issue fines on summary conviction see SENTENCING vol 92 (2015) PARA 176. As to the meaning of 'daily default fine' see PARA 1816.
43 As to the meaning of 'the court' see PARA 160 note 12.
44 Companies Act 2006 s 162(8). See also PARA 350 note 30. As to the procedure for making claims and applications to the court under companies legislation see PARA 306.
45 Ie the Companies Act 2006 ss 167A–167E (not yet in force): see PARA 551 et seq.
46 Companies Act 2006 s 161A (added by the Small Business, Enterprise and Employment Act 2015 Sch 5 Pt 1 paras 5, 6). As to the power to extend the alternative method of record-keeping to public companies see s 167F; and PARA 551. As to the meanings of 'private company' and 'public company' see PARA 95.

(B) Register of Directors' Residential Addresses

536. The register of directors' residential addresses. Every company[1] must keep a register of directors' residential addresses[2].

The register must state the usual residential address of each of the company's directors[3].

If default is made in complying with this requirement to keep such a register[4], an offence is committed by the company, and by every officer of the company who is in default[5].

The above provisions must be read with the provisions of the Companies Act 2006[6] which allow for an alternative method of record-keeping in the case of private companies[7].

1 As to the meaning of 'company' under the Companies Acts see PARA 21; and as to the meaning of the 'Companies Acts' see PARA 13.

2 Companies Act 2006 s 165(1). The provisions of s 165 apply only to directors who are individuals, not where the director is a body corporate or a firm that is a legal person under the law by which it is governed: s 165(6). As to the prospective prohibition on the appointment of corporate directors see PARA 526. As to the meaning of 'director' under the Companies Acts see PARA 512. As to the meaning of 'body corporate' see PARA 1 note 5. As to the meaning of 'firm' see PARA 105 note 15. As to the requirement for a company to keep a register of directors see PARA 535.

The Secretary of State may make provision by regulations amending the Companies Act 2006 s 165, so as to add to or remove items from the particulars required to be contained in a company's register of directors' residential addresses: s 166(1). As to the Secretary of State see PARA 6. As to the making of regulations under the Companies Act 2006 generally see ss 1288–1292. Regulations under s 166 are subject to affirmative resolution procedure (ie the regulations must not be made unless a draft of the statutory instrument containing them has been laid before Parliament and approved by a resolution of each House of Parliament): see ss 166(2), 1290. At the date at which this volume states the law, no such regulations had been made.

The provisions of the Companies Act 2006 ss 165–166 apply to unregistered companies by virtue of the Unregistered Companies Regulations 2009, SI 2009/2436, Sch 1 para 6(1): see PARA 1857. As to the meaning of 'unregistered company' see PARA 1856.

3 Companies Act 2006 s 165(2). If a director's usual residential address is the same as his service address (as stated in the company's register of directors), the register of directors' residential addresses need only contain an entry to that effect: s 165(3). However, this does not apply if his service address is stated to be 'The company's registered office': s 165(3). See also note 2. As to addresses on the register that are not to be made available by the registrar for public inspection see s 1088; and PARA 150 et seq. As to requirements relating to service addresses generally see PARA 745.

4 Ie in complying with the Companies Act 2006 s 165 (see the text and notes 1–3): see s 165(4).

5 Companies Act 2006 s 165(4). For these purposes, a shadow director is treated as an officer of the company: s 165(4). See also note 2. As to the meaning of 'shadow director' see PARA 512. As to the meaning of 'officer who is in default' see PARA 316. As to the meaning of 'officer' generally see PARA 679.

A person guilty of such an offence is liable on summary conviction to a fine and for continued contravention to a daily default fine not exceeding one-tenth of the greater of £5,000 or level 4 on the standard scale: Companies Act 2006 s 165(5) (amended by SI 2015/664). In the case of liability on summary conviction the fine is one not exceeding level 5 on the standard scale: see the Companies Act 2006 s 165(5) (as so amended). By virtue of the Legal Aid, Sentencing and Punishment of Offenders Act 2012 s 85, however, where the offence is committed on or after 12 March 2015, it is punishable by a fine of an unlimited amount. As to the standard scale and the powers of magistrates' courts to issue fines on summary conviction see SENTENCING vol 92 (2015) PARA 176. As to the meaning of 'daily default fine' see PARA 1816. See also note 2.

6 Ie the Companies Act 2006 ss 167A–167E (not yet in force): see PARA 551 et seq.

7 Companies Act 2006 s 161A (added by the Small Business, Enterprise and Employment Act 2015 Sch 5 Pt 1 paras 5, 6). As to the power to extend the alternative method of record-keeping to public companies see s 167F; and PARA 551. As to the meanings of 'private company' and 'public company' see PARA 95.

537. Protection from disclosure of information about director's residential address: meaning of 'protected information'. Provision is made[1] for protecting, in the case of a company director[2] who is an individual[3], information as to his usual residential address[4], and the information that his service address[5] is his usual residential address[6]. That information is referred to for these purposes[7] as 'protected information'[8]. Information does not cease to be protected information on the individual ceasing to be a director of the company[9].

1 Ie in the Companies Act 2006 Pt 10 Ch 8 (ss 240–246) (see also PARA 537 et seq): see s 240(1). Where regulations under s 1046 require an overseas company to register particulars of an individual's usual residential address, they must contain provision corresponding to that made by Pt 10 Ch 8: see s 1055; and PARA 2015. As to the meaning of 'overseas company' see PARA 2013.
The provisions of the Companies Act 2006 s 240 apply to unregistered companies by virtue of the Unregistered Companies Regulations 2009, SI 2009/2436, Sch 1 para 7(1): see PARA 1857. As to the meaning of 'unregistered company' see PARA 1856.
2 As to the meaning of 'company' under the Companies Acts see PARA 21; and as to the meaning of 'director' under the Companies Acts see PARA 512. As to the meaning of the 'Companies Acts' see PARA 13.
3 See the Companies Act 2006 s 240(1).
4 Companies Act 2006 s 240(1)(a). As to the circumstances in which the registrar of companies may put a director's usual residential address on the public record see PARA 549.
5 As to requirements relating to service addresses generally see PARA 745; and see PARA 535 note 8.
6 Companies Act 2006 s 240(1)(b).
7 Ie in the Companies Act 2006 Pt 10 Ch 8 (see also PARA 537 et seq): see s 240(2).
8 Companies Act 2006 s 240(2). As to the use or disclosure of protected information see PARA 538 et seq. The Companies Act 2006 s 240 also applies to information within s 790ZF(2) (see PARA 491): see s 790ZF(1); and PARA 491.
Where a director's usual residential address appears as a service address in the company's register of directors by virtue of the Companies Act 2006 (Commencement No 8, Transitional Provisions and Savings) Order 2008, SI 2008/2860, Sch 2 para 27 (see PARA 535 note 8), or in the register of companies by virtue of Sch 2 para 32 (see PARA 535 note 8), that address is not protected information for the purposes of the Companies Act 2006 Pt 10 Ch 8 (see also PARA 537 et seq): see the Companies Act 2006 (Commencement No 8, Transitional Provisions and Savings) Order 2008, SI 2008/2860, Sch 2 para 33. As to the registrar of companies see PARA 142 et seq.
9 Companies Act 2006 s 240(3). References in Pt 10 Ch 8 (see also PARA 537 et seq) to a director include, to that extent, a former director: s 240(3).

538. Restrictions on use or disclosure of protected information about directors. A company[1] must not use or disclose protected information[2] about any of its directors[3], except:

(1) for communicating with the director concerned[4];
(2) in order to comply with any requirement of the Companies Acts as to particulars to be sent to the registrar of companies[5]; or
(3) in accordance with the provisions governing the disclosure of such information under court order[6].

The registrar must omit protected information from the material on the register[7] that is available for inspection[8] both where it is contained in a document delivered to him in which such information is required to be stated[9] and, in the case of a document having more than one part, where it is contained in a part of the document in which such information is required to be stated[10]. However, the registrar is not obliged to check other documents or, as the case may be, other parts of the document to ensure the absence of protected information[11], or to omit from the material that is available for public inspection anything registered before the protected information provisions[12] came into force[13].

The registrar himself must not use or disclose protected information except as permitted[14] or in accordance with the provisions governing the disclosure of such information under court order[15].

1 As to the meaning of 'company' under the Companies Acts see PARA 21; and as to the meaning of the 'Companies Acts' see PARA 13.
2 As to the meaning of 'protected information' for these purposes see PARA 537. The Companies Act 2006 ss 241, 242 also apply to information within s 790ZF(2) (see PARA 491): see s 790ZF(1); and PARA 491.

3 Companies Act 2006 s 241(1). The provisions of s 241(1) do not prohibit any use or disclosure of protected information with the consent of the director concerned: s 241(2). As to the meaning of 'director' under the Companies Acts see PARA 512. Where regulations under s 1046 require an overseas company to register particulars of an individual's usual residential address, they must contain provision corresponding to that made by Pt 10 Ch 8 (ss 240–246): see s 1055; and PARA 2015. As to the meaning of 'overseas company' see PARA 2013.
The provisions of the Companies Act 2006 ss 241, 242 apply to unregistered companies by virtue of the Unregistered Companies Regulations 2009, SI 2009/2436, Sch 1 para 7(1): see PARA 1857. As to the meaning of 'unregistered company' see PARA 1856.
4 Companies Act 2006 s 241(1)(a).
5 Companies Act 2006 s 241(1)(b). As to the meaning of 'registrar of companies' see PARA 126 note 2.
6 Companies Act 2006 s 241(1)(c). Head (3) in the text refers to the use or disclosure of protected information in accordance with s 244 (see PARA 548): see s 241(1)(c).
7 As to the meaning of the 'register' see PARA 142.
8 Companies Act 2006 s 242(1). Protected information within s 242(1) must not be made available by the registrar of companies for public inspection: see s 1087(1)(b); and PARA 146. As to the circumstances in which the registrar of companies may put a director's usual residential address on the public record see PARA 549.
9 Companies Act 2006 s 242(1)(a). See also note 8.
10 Companies Act 2006 s 242(1)(b). See also note 8.
11 Companies Act 2006 s 242(2)(a).
12 Ie the Companies Act 2006 Pt 10 Ch 8 (see also PARA 537 et seq): see s 242(2)(b).
13 Companies Act 2006 s 242(2)(b). The provisions of Pt 10 Ch 8 came into force on 1 October 2009: see the Companies Act 2006 (Commencement No 8, Transitional Provisions and Savings) Order 2008, SI 2008/2860, art 3(i).
14 Ie as permitted by the Companies Act 2006 s 243 (see PARA 539): see s 242(3).
15 Companies Act 2006 s 242(3). The text refers to the use or disclosure of protected information in accordance with s 244 (see PARA 548): see s 242(3).

539. Permitted use or disclosure of protected information about directors by the registrar. The registrar of companies[1] may use protected information[2] for communicating with the director[3] in question[4].

The registrar may disclose protected information to a public authority[5] specified for these purposes[6] by regulations made by the Secretary of State[7], or to a credit reference agency[8].

The Secretary of State may make provision by regulations:

(1) specifying conditions for the disclosure of protected information[9], and providing for the charging of fees[10]; or
(2) requiring the registrar, on application, to refrain from disclosing protected information relating to a director to a credit reference agency[11].

1 As to the meaning of 'registrar of companies' see PARA 126 note 2.
2 As to the meaning of 'protected information' for these purposes see PARA 537. The Companies Act 2006 s 243 also applies to information within s 790ZF(2) (see PARA 491): see s 790ZF(1); and PARA 491.
3 As to the meaning of 'director' under the Companies Acts see PARA 512; and as to the meaning of the 'Companies Acts' see PARA 13.
4 Companies Act 2006 s 243(1). The registrar must not use or disclose protected information except as permitted by s 243 or in accordance with s 244 (see PARA 548): see s 242(3); and PARA 538. As to the circumstances in which the registrar of companies may put a director's usual residential address on the public record see PARA 549. Where regulations under s 1046 require an overseas company to register particulars of an individual's usual residential address, they must contain provision corresponding to that made by Pt 10 Ch 8 (ss 240–246): see s 1055; and PARA 2015. As to the meaning of 'overseas company' see PARA 2013.
The provisions of the Companies Act 2006 s 243 apply to unregistered companies by virtue of the Unregistered Companies Regulations 2009, SI 2009/2436, reg 3, Sch 1 para 7(1), (2), but with the Companies Act 2006 s 243 as modified thereby: see PARA 1857. As to the meaning of 'unregistered company' see PARA 1856.
5 For these purposes, 'public authority' includes any person or body having functions of a public nature: see the Companies Act 2006 s 243(7).

6 Ie specified for the purposes of the Companies Act 2006 s 243: see s 243(2)(a). The public authorities specified for the purposes of s 243(2) are set out in the Companies (Disclosure of Address) Regulations 2009, SI 2009/214, Sch 1: see PARA 540. The public authorities specified for the purposes of the Companies Act 2006 s 243 as applied by s 790ZF (see PARA 491) are listed in the Register of People with Significant Control Regulations 2016, SI 2016/339, Sch 3: reg 22(1).

7 Companies Act 2006 s 243(2)(a). See also notes 4, 6. As to the Secretary of State see PARA 6. As to the making of regulations under the Companies Act 2006 generally see ss 1288–1292. Regulations under s 243 are subject to negative resolution procedure (ie the statutory instrument containing the regulations is subject to annulment in pursuance of a resolution of either House of Parliament): see ss 243(8), 1289. In exercise of the power conferred by s 243(2)–(6) (see also the text and notes 8–11), the Secretary of State has made the Companies (Disclosure of Address) Regulations 2009, SI 2009/214: see PARA 540 et seq.

8 Companies Act 2006 s 243(2)(b). For these purposes, 'credit reference agency' means a person carrying on a business comprising the furnishing of information relevant to the financial standing of individuals, being information collected by the agency for that purpose: see s 243(7). See also notes 4, 7.

9 Ie in accordance with the Companies Act 2006 s 243: see s 243(3). See also notes 4, 7.

10 Companies Act 2006 s 243(3). See also notes 4, 7. Partly in exercise of the powers conferred by s 243(3), the Secretary of State has made the Registrar of Companies (Fees) (Companies, Overseas Companies and Limited Liability Partnerships) Regulations 2012, SI 2012/1907. Accordingly, in respect of the performance of the registrar's functions in relation to the inspection of the register and the provision of copies of material on the register, where that material is protected information to which the Companies Act 2006 s 242(1) applies (see PARA 538), the fees so payable are those specified in the Registrar of Companies (Fees) (Companies, Overseas Companies and Limited Liability Partnerships) Regulations 2012, SI 2012/1907, Sch 3 (substituted with effect from 30 June 2016 by SI 2016/621).

11 Companies Act 2006 s 243(4). Regulations under s 243(4) may make provision as to:

(1) who may make an application (s 243(5)(a));
(2) the grounds on which an application may be made (s 243(5)(b));
(3) the information to be included in and documents to accompany an application (s 243(5)(c)); and
(4) how an application is to be determined (s 243(5)(d)).

Provision under head (4) above may in particular confer a discretion on the registrar or provide for a question to be referred to a person other than the registrar for the purposes of determining the application: s 243(6). See also notes 4, 7.

540. Permitted disclosure by registrar to specified public authorities of protected information about directors. The registrar of companies[1] may disclose protected information[2] to a specified public authority[3] where the following conditions[4] are satisfied[5]:

(1) the specified public authority has delivered to the registrar of companies a statement that it intends to use the protected information only for the purpose of facilitating the carrying out by that specified public authority of a public function[6] (the 'permitted purpose')[7];
(2) the specified public authority ('the authority') has delivered to the registrar a statement that it will, where it supplies a copy of the protected information to a processor[8] for the purpose of processing the information for use in respect of the permitted purpose[9]:
    (a) ensure that the processor is one who carries on business in the European Economic Area[10];
    (b) require that the information is not transmitted outside the European Economic Area by the processor[11]; and
    (c) require that the processor does not disclose the information except to the authority or an employee of the authority[12].

A specified public authority must deliver to the registrar such information or evidence as he may direct for the purpose of enabling him to determine[13] whether to disclose protected information[14]; and the registrar may require such information or evidence to be verified in such manner as he may direct[15].

The specified public authority must inform the registrar immediately of any change in respect of any statement so delivered to the registrar[16] or information or evidence provided for the purpose of enabling him to determine whether to disclose protected information[17].

1 As to the registrar of companies see PARA 126 et seq.
2 As to the meaning of 'protected information' for the purposes of the Companies Act 2006 Pt 10 Ch 8 (ss 240–246) (see PARAS 537 et seq, 548–549), under which the Companies (Disclosure of Address) Regulations 2009, SI 2009/214, have been made, see PARA 537.
3 For these purposes, 'specified public authority' means any public authority specified in the Companies (Disclosure of Address) Regulations 2009, SI 2009/214, Sch 1 (amended by virtue of the Crime and Courts Act 2013 Sch 8 Pt 4 para 190; and by SI 2010/2156; SI 2011/2085; SI 2012/700; SI 2013/472; SI 2014/469; SI 2014/549; SI 2014/631; SI 2015/842; SI 2016/339), which sets out the public authorities that are specified for the purposes of the Companies Act 2006 s 243(2) (see PARA 539): see the Companies (Disclosure of Address) Regulations 2009, SI 2009/214, regs 1(2), 2(5).
4 Ie the conditions specified in the Companies (Disclosure of Address) Regulations 2009, SI 2009/214, Sch 2 paras 2, 3 (see heads (1)–(2) in the text): see reg 2(1). The provisions of Sch 2 paras 2, 3 set out the conditions specified for the disclosure of protected information by the registrar to a specified public authority: Sch 2 para 1.
5 Companies (Disclosure of Address) Regulations 2009, SI 2009/214, reg 2(1). As to the fee payable by a specified public authority for an application under reg 2 see the Registrar of Companies (Fees) (Companies, Overseas Companies and Limited Liability Partnerships) Regulations 2012, SI 2012/1907, Sch 3 (substituted with effect from 30 June 2016 by SI 2016/621).
6 For these purposes:
   (1) 'public function' includes any function conferred by or in accordance with any provision contained in any enactment, any function conferred by or in accordance with any provision contained in the EU Treaties or any EU instrument, any similar function conferred on persons by or under provisions having effect as part of the law of a country or territory outside the United Kingdom, and any function exercisable in relation to the investigation of any criminal offence or for the purpose of any criminal proceedings (see the Companies (Disclosure of Address) Regulations 2009, SI 2009/214, Sch 2 para 11(1) (amended by SI 2011/1043));
   (2) any reference to the disclosure for the purpose of facilitating the carrying out of a public function includes disclosure in relation to, and for the purpose of, any proceedings whether civil, criminal or disciplinary in which the specified public authority engages while carrying out its public functions (Companies (Disclosure of Address) Regulations 2009, SI 2009/214, Sch 2 para 11(2)(b)).
7 Companies (Disclosure of Address) Regulations 2009, SI 2009/214, Sch 2 para 2. As to the meaning of 'registrar of companies' see PARA 126 note 2. As to the delivery of documents to the registrar see PARA 136; and as to the requirements generally for the proper delivery of documents to the registrar see PARA 137.
8 For these purposes, 'processor' means any person who provides a service which consists of putting information into data form or processing information in data form and any reference to a processor includes a reference to his employees: see the Companies (Disclosure of Address) Regulations 2009, SI 2009/214, Sch 2 para 11(1). In Sch 2, any reference to an employee of any person who has access to protected information is deemed to include any person working or providing services for the purposes of that person or employed by or on behalf of, or working for, any person who is so working or who is supplying such a service: see Sch 2 para 11(2)(a).
9 Companies (Disclosure of Address) Regulations 2009, SI 2009/214, Sch 2 para 3. The provisions of Sch 2 para 3 are subject to the provisions of Sch 2 para 4: see Sch 2 para 3. Accordingly, Sch 2 para 3 does not apply where the specified public authority is the National Crime Agency, Secret Intelligence Service, Security Service or Government Communications Headquarters: Sch 2 para 4 (amended by SI 2016/339). As to the National Crime Agency see POLICE AND INVESTIGATORY POWERS vol 84 (2013) PARA 424 et seq; as to the Government Communications Headquarters see CONSTITUTIONAL AND ADMINISTRATIVE LAW vol 20 (2014) PARA 245; as to the Secret Intelligence Service see CONSTITUTIONAL AND ADMINISTRATIVE LAW vol 20 (2014) PARA 244; and as to the Security Service see CONSTITUTIONAL AND ADMINISTRATIVE LAW vol 20 (2014) PARA 243.
10 Companies (Disclosure of Address) Regulations 2009, SI 2009/214, Sch 2 para 3(a). See also note 9.

11 Companies (Disclosure of Address) Regulations 2009, SI 2009/214, Sch 2 para 3(b). See also note 9.
12 Companies (Disclosure of Address) Regulations 2009, SI 2009/214, Sch 2 para 3(c). See also note 9.
13 Ie in accordance with the Companies (Disclosure of Address) Regulations 2009, SI 2009/214: see reg 2(2).
14 Companies (Disclosure of Address) Regulations 2009, SI 2009/214, reg 2(2).
15 Companies (Disclosure of Address) Regulations 2009, SI 2009/214, reg 2(3).
16 Ie delivered pursuant to the Companies (Disclosure of Address) Regulations 2009, SI 2009/214, Sch 2 (see the text and notes 4–12): see reg 2(4).
17 Companies (Disclosure of Address) Regulations 2009, SI 2009/214, reg 2(4).

541. Permitted disclosure by registrar to credit reference agencies. The registrar of companies[1] must refrain from disclosing protected information[2] to a credit reference agency[3] if such information relates to a section 243 beneficiary[4] or a section 243 applicant[5].

However, subject to this restriction, the registrar may disclose protected information to a credit reference agency where the following conditions[6] are satisfied[7]:

(1) the credit reference agency:
   (a) is carrying on in the United Kingdom[8] or in another EEA state a business comprising the furnishing of information relevant to the financial standing of individuals, being information collected by the agency for that purpose[9];
   (b) maintains appropriate procedures to ensure that an independent person can investigate and audit the measures maintained by the agency for the purposes of ensuring the security of any protected information disclosed to that agency[10], and for the purposes of ensuring that it complies with its obligations under the Data Protection Act 1998[11] or, where the agency carries on business in a EEA state other than the United Kingdom, with its obligations under legislation implementing[12] the Data Protection Directive[13];
   (c) has not been found guilty of an offence under the Companies Act 2006 provisions which prohibit the making of false statements to the registrar[14] or under the false representation provisions of the Fraud Act 2006[15] or under the provisions of the Data Protection Act 1998 which govern a failure to comply with an enforcement notice, an information notice or a special information notice[16] in circumstances where it has used the protected information for purposes other than those described in heads (2)(a) to (2)(e) below[17];
(2) the credit reference agency has delivered to the registrar a statement that it intends to use the protected information only for the purposes of[18]:
   (a) providing an assessment of the financial standing of a person[19];
   (b) meeting any obligations contained in money laundering rules[20] or in any legislation of another EEA state implementing[21] the Directive concerning money laundering and terrorist financing[22];
   (c) conducting conflict of interest checks required or made necessary by any enactment[23];
   (d) the provision of protected information to either a specified public authority[24] or to a credit reference agency[25] which has satisfied the relevant requirements[26] necessary before the registrar can disclose protected information to it[27]; or

(e) conducting checks for the prevention and detection of crime and fraud[28];

(3) the credit reference agency has delivered to the registrar a statement that it intends to take delivery of and to use the protected information only in the United Kingdom or in another EEA state[29];

(4) the credit reference agency has delivered to the registrar a statement that it will, where it supplies a copy of the protected information to a processor[30] for the purpose of processing the information for use in respect of the purposes referred to in head (2) above[31]:

(a) ensure that the processor is one who carries on business in the European Economic Area[32];

(b) require that the information is not transmitted outside the European Economic Area by the processor[33]; and

(c) require that the processor does not disclose the information except to the credit reference agency or an employee of the credit reference agency[34]; and

(5) the credit reference agency has delivered to the registrar a statement that it meets the conditions set out in head (1) above[35].

A credit reference agency must[36] deliver to the registrar such information or evidence, in addition to the statement required by head (5) above, as he may direct for the purpose of enabling him to determine[37] whether to disclose protected information[38]; and the registrar may require such information or evidence to be verified in such manner as he may direct[39].

The credit reference agency must inform the registrar immediately of any change in respect of any statement so delivered to the registrar[40] or information or evidence provided for the purpose of enabling the registrar to determine whether to disclose protected information[41].

1 As to the registrar of companies see PARA 126 et seq.
2 As to the meaning of 'protected information' for the purposes of the Companies Act 2006 Pt 10 Ch 8 (ss 240–246) (see PARAS 537 et seq, 548–549), under which the Companies (Disclosure of Address) Regulations 2009, SI 2009/214, have been made, see PARA 537.
3 As to the meaning of 'credit reference agency' for the purposes of the Companies Act 2006 Pt 10 Ch 8 see PARA 539 note 8.
4 As to the meaning of 'section 243 beneficiary' see PARA 151 head (3).
5 Companies (Disclosure of Address) Regulations 2009, SI 2009/214, reg 4. For these purposes, 'section 243 applicant' means an individual by whom or in respect of whom a section 243 application has been made but in respect of which application the registrar either has not made a determination, or has made a determination, not being a section 243 decision, and any appeal to the court in respect of that application under reg 14 (see PARA 547) has not been determined by the court: see reg 1(2). As to the meanings of 'section 243 application' and 'section 243 decision' see PARA 151 head (3).
6 Ie the conditions specified in the Companies (Disclosure of Address) Regulations 2009, SI 2009/214, Sch 2 paras 6–10 (see heads (1)–(5) in the text): see reg 3(1). The provisions of Sch 2 paras 6–10 set out the conditions specified for the disclosure of protected information by the registrar to a credit reference agency: Sch 2 para 5.
7 Companies (Disclosure of Address) Regulations 2009, SI 2009/214, reg 3(1). As to the fee payable by a credit reference agency for an application under reg 3 see the Registrar of Companies (Fees) (Companies, Overseas Companies and Limited Liability Partnerships) Regulations 2012, SI 2012/1907, Sch 3 (substituted with effect from 30 June 2016 by SI 2016/621).
8 As to the meaning of 'United Kingdom' see PARA 1 note 5.
9 Companies (Disclosure of Address) Regulations 2009, SI 2009/214, Sch 2 para 6(a).
10 Companies (Disclosure of Address) Regulations 2009, SI 2009/214, Sch 2 para 6(b)(i).
11 As to a person's obligations under the Data Protection Act 1998 generally see CONFIDENCE AND INFORMATIONAL PRIVACY vol 19 (2011) PARA 95 et seq.
12 Ie legislation implementing Council Directive (EC) 95/46 (OJ L281, 23.11.95, p 31) on the protection of individuals with regard to the processing of personal data and on the free movement

of such data (as to which see CONFIDENCE AND INFORMATIONAL PRIVACY vol 19 (2011) PARA 95 et seq): see the Companies (Disclosure of Address) Regulations 2009, SI 2009/214, Sch 2 para 6(b)(ii).

13 Companies (Disclosure of Address) Regulations 2009, SI 2009/214, Sch 2 para 6(b)(ii).

14 Ie the Companies Act 2006 s 1112 (general offence of making false statements to registrar) (see PARA 132): see the Companies (Disclosure of Address) Regulations 2009, SI 2009/214, Sch 2 para 6(c)(i).

15 Companies (Disclosure of Address) Regulations 2009, SI 2009/214, Sch 2 para 6(c)(i). The text refers to an offence under the Fraud Act 2006 s 2 (fraud by false representation) (see CRIMINAL LAW vol 25 (2016) PARA 346): see the Companies (Disclosure of Address) Regulations 2009, SI 2009/214, Sch 2 para 6(c)(i).

16 Ie under the Data Protection Act 1998 s 47 (see CONFIDENCE AND INFORMATIONAL PRIVACY vol 19 (2011) PARA 166): see the Companies (Disclosure of Address) Regulations 2009, SI 2009/214, Sch 2 para 6(c)(ii). As to enforcement notices see CONFIDENCE AND INFORMATIONAL PRIVACY vol 19 (2011) PARA 152; as to information notices see CONFIDENCE AND INFORMATIONAL PRIVACY vol 19 (2011) PARA 158; and as to special information notices see CONFIDENCE AND INFORMATIONAL PRIVACY vol 19 (2011) PARA 159.

17 Companies (Disclosure of Address) Regulations 2009, SI 2009/214, Sch 2 para 6(c)(ii).

18 Companies (Disclosure of Address) Regulations 2009, SI 2009/214, Sch 2 para 7. As to the delivery of documents to the registrar see PARA 136; and as to the requirements generally for the proper delivery of documents to the registrar see PARA 137.

19 Companies (Disclosure of Address) Regulations 2009, SI 2009/214, Sch 2 para 7(a).

20 Ie obligations contained in the Money Laundering Regulations 2007, SI 2007/2157 (see FINANCIAL SERVICES REGULATION vol 50A (2016) PARA 759 et seq), or any rules made pursuant to the Financial Services and Markets Act 2000 s 137A which relate to the prevention and detection of money laundering in connection with the carrying on of regulated activities by authorised persons (see FINANCIAL SERVICES REGULATION vol 50 (2015) PARA 59): see the Companies (Disclosure of Address) Regulations 2009, SI 2009/214, Sch 2 para 7(b) (amended by SI 2013/472).

21 Ie legislation implementing European Parliament and Council Directive (EC) 2005/60 (OJ L309, 25.11.2005, p 15) on the prevention of the use of the financial system for the purpose of money laundering and terrorist financing (now repealed and replaced by European Parliament and Council Directive (EU) 2015/849 (OJ L141, 5.6.2015, p 73)) (see FINANCIAL SERVICES REGULATION vol 50A (2016) PARA 759 et seq): see the Companies (Disclosure of Address) Regulations 2009, SI 2009/214, Sch 2 para 7(b). Member states must bring into force the laws, regulations and administrative provisions necessary to comply with European Parliament and Council Directive (EU) 2015/849 (OJ L141, 5.6.2015, p 73) by 26 June 2017: art 67(1).

22 Companies (Disclosure of Address) Regulations 2009, SI 2009/214, Sch 2 para 7(b) (as amended: see note 20).

23 Companies (Disclosure of Address) Regulations 2009, SI 2009/214, Sch 2 para 7(c).

24 Ie a public authority specified in the Companies (Disclosure of Address) Regulations 2009, SI 2009/214, Sch 1 (see PARA 540 note 3): see Sch 2 para 7(d)(i).

25 See the Companies (Disclosure of Address) Regulations 2009, SI 2009/214, Sch 2 para 7(d)(ii).

26 Ie, in relation to a specified public authority, satisfied the requirements of the Companies (Disclosure of Address) Regulations 2009, SI 2009/214, Sch 2 paras 2, 3 (see PARA 540) and, in relation to a credit reference agency, satisfied the requirements of Sch 2 Pt 2 (paras 5–10) (see the text and notes 6–35): see Sch 2 para 7(d)(i), (ii).

27 Companies (Disclosure of Address) Regulations 2009, SI 2009/214, Sch 2 para 7(d)(i), (ii).

28 Companies (Disclosure of Address) Regulations 2009, SI 2009/214, Sch 2 para 7(e).

29 Companies (Disclosure of Address) Regulations 2009, SI 2009/214, Sch 2 para 8.

30 As to the meaning of 'processor' for these purposes see PARA 540 note 8.

31 Companies (Disclosure of Address) Regulations 2009, SI 2009/214, Sch 2 para 9.

32 Companies (Disclosure of Address) Regulations 2009, SI 2009/214, Sch 2 para 9(a).

33 Companies (Disclosure of Address) Regulations 2009, SI 2009/214, Sch 2 para 9(b).

34 Companies (Disclosure of Address) Regulations 2009, SI 2009/214, Sch 2 para 9(c). As to the meaning of references to 'employee' for these purposes see PARA 540 note 8.

35 Companies (Disclosure of Address) Regulations 2009, SI 2009/214, Sch 2 para 10. The registrar may rely on a statement delivered to him by a credit reference agency under Sch 2 para 10 as sufficient evidence of the matters stated in it: reg 3(2).

36 Ie notwithstanding the Companies (Disclosure of Address) Regulations 2009, SI 2009/214, reg 3(2) (see note 35): see reg 3(3).

37 Ie in accordance with the Companies (Disclosure of Address) Regulations 2009, SI 2009/214: see reg 3(3).

38 Companies (Disclosure of Address) Regulations 2009, SI 2009/214, reg 3(3).
39 Companies (Disclosure of Address) Regulations 2009, SI 2009/214, reg 3(4).
40 Ie delivered pursuant to the Companies (Disclosure of Address) Regulations 2009, SI 2009/214, Sch 2 (see the text and notes 8–35): see reg 3(5).
41 Companies (Disclosure of Address) Regulations 2009, SI 2009/214, reg 3(5).

542. Application by individual to withhold protected information relating to a director. A section 243 application[1] may be made to the registrar of companies[2] by an individual who is, or proposes to become, a director[3]. The grounds on which such an application may be made are that the individual making the application[4]:

(1) reasonably believes that there is a serious risk that he, or a person who lives with him, will be subjected to violence or intimidation as a result of the activities of at least one of[5]:
   (a) the companies of which he is, or proposes to become, a director[6];
   (b) the companies of which he was a director[7];
   (c) the companies of which that individual is, or proposes to become, a registrable person[8];
   (d) the companies of which that individual used to be a registrable person[9];
   (e) the overseas companies[10] of which he is or has been a director, secretary or permanent representative[11]; or
   (f) the limited liability partnerships[12] of which he is or has been a member[13];
(2) is or has been employed by a relevant organisation[14]; or
(3) is the subject of an application to protect usual residential address information[15] which has been determined by the registrar in favour of the applicant and that determination has not ceased[16] to have effect[17].

The application must contain:

(i) a statement of the grounds on which the application is made[18];
(ii) the name and any former name of the applicant[19];
(iii) the date of birth of the applicant[20];
(iv) the usual residential address of the applicant[21];
(v) the e-mail address of the applicant, if any[22];
(vi) where the registrar has allocated a unique identifier to the applicant, that unique identifier[23];
(vii) the name and registered number of each company of which the applicant is, or proposes to become, a director[24];
(viii) the name and registered number of each company of which the applicant is, or proposes to become, a registrable person[25];
(ix) where the grounds of the application are those described in head (1)(b), head (1)(c), head (1)(d), head (1)(e) or head (1)(f) above, the name and registered number of the company, overseas company or limited liability partnership[26];
(x) where the grounds of the application are those described in head (3) above, the name and registered number of the company in relation to which the determination was made, unless the determination relates to a proposed company which was never incorporated[27].

Where the grounds of the application are those described in head (1) or head (2) above, the application must be accompanied by evidence which supports the applicant's statement of the grounds on which the application is made[28]. The registrar may direct that additional information or evidence should be delivered to him, what such information or evidence should be and how it should be verified[29].

The registrar may refer to a relevant body any question relating to an assessment of, where the grounds of the application are those described in head (1) above, the nature and extent of any risk of violence or intimidation considered by the applicant to arise in relation to himself, or to a person who lives with him[30] or, where the grounds of the application are those described in head (2) above, whether the applicant is or has been employed by a relevant organisation[31].

The registrar must determine the application[32] and, within seven days beginning with the date that the determination is made, send to the applicant notice of the determination[33]. Where the application is unsuccessful, that notice must inform the applicant of the applicant's right to apply for permission to appeal against the determination within 28 days beginning with the date of the notice[34].

The registrar must not make available for public inspection any section 243 application[35] or any documents provided in support of that application[36].

1 As to the meaning of 'section 243 application' see PARA 151 head (3).

2 As to the registrar of companies see PARA 126 et seq.

3 Companies (Disclosure of Address) Regulations 2009, SI 2009/214, reg 5(1). As to a company's directors see PARA 512 et seq. As to the delivery of documents to the registrar see PARA 136; and as to the requirements generally for the proper delivery of documents to the registrar see PARA 137.

4 Companies (Disclosure of Address) Regulations 2009, SI 2009/214, reg 5(2).

5 Companies (Disclosure of Address) Regulations 2009, SI 2009/214, reg 5(2)(a) (amended by SI 2016/339).

6 Companies (Disclosure of Address) Regulations 2009, SI 2009/214, reg 5(2)(a)(i).

7 Companies (Disclosure of Address) Regulations 2009, SI 2009/214, reg 5(2)(a)(ii).

8 Companies (Disclosure of Address) Regulations 2009, SI 2009/214, reg 5(2)(a)(iia) (added by SI 2016/339). For these purposes, 'registrable person' means a registrable person under the Companies Act 2006 Pt 21A (ss 790A–790ZG) (see PARA 466 et seq): Companies (Disclosure of Address) Regulations 2009, SI 2009/214, reg 1(2) (definition added by SI 2016/339).

9 Companies (Disclosure of Address) Regulations 2009, SI 2009/214, reg 5(2)(a)(iib) (added by SI 2016/339).

10 As to overseas companies see PARAS 29, 2013 et seq.

11 Companies (Disclosure of Address) Regulations 2009, SI 2009/214, reg 5(2)(a)(iii). As to the meaning of 'permanent representative' for these purposes see PARA 151 note 11.

12 For these purposes, 'limited liability partnership' means a limited liability partnership incorporated under the Limited Liability Partnerships Act 2000 (see PARTNERSHIP vol 79 (2014) PARA 233 et seq): see the Companies (Disclosure of Address) Regulations 2009, SI 2009/214, reg 1(2).

13 Companies (Disclosure of Address) Regulations 2009, SI 2009/214, reg 5(2)(a)(iv).

14 Companies (Disclosure of Address) Regulations 2009, SI 2009/214, reg 5(2)(b) (amended by SI 2016/339). As to the meaning of 'relevant organisation' for these purposes see PARA 151 note 14.

15 Ie an application made under the Register of People with Significant Control Regulations 2016, SI 2016/339, reg 25 (see PARA 496), reg 26 (see PARA 497) or reg 27 (see PARA 498).

16 Ie under the Register of People with Significant Control Regulations 2016, SI 2016/339, reg 31: see PARA 499.

17 Companies (Disclosure of Address) Regulations 2009, SI 2009/214, reg 5(2)(c) (added by SI 2016/339).

18 Companies (Disclosure of Address) Regulations 2009, SI 2009/214, reg 5(3)(a)(i).

19 Companies (Disclosure of Address) Regulations 2009, SI 2009/214, reg 5(3)(a)(ii). As to the meanings of 'name' and 'former name' for these purposes see PARA 151 note 27.

20 Companies (Disclosure of Address) Regulations 2009, SI 2009/214, reg 5(3)(a)(iii).

21 Companies (Disclosure of Address) Regulations 2009, SI 2009/214, reg 5(3)(a)(iv).

22 Companies (Disclosure of Address) Regulations 2009, SI 2009/214, reg 5(3)(a)(iva) (added by SI 2016/339).

23 Companies (Disclosure of Address) Regulations 2009, SI 2009/214, reg 5(3)(a)(v). As to the allocation of unique identifiers see PARA 144.

24 Companies (Disclosure of Address) Regulations 2009, SI 2009/214, reg 5(3)(a)(vi). As to company names and trading names generally see PARA 195 et seq. As to a company's registered number see PARAS 134–135.

25 Companies (Disclosure of Address) Regulations 2009, SI 2009/214, reg 5(3)(a)(via) (added by SI 2016/339).
26 Companies (Disclosure of Address) Regulations 2009, SI 2009/214, reg 5(3)(a)(vii) (amended by SI 2016/339).
27 Companies (Disclosure of Address) Regulations 2009, SI 2009/214, reg 5(3)(a)(viii) (added by SI 2016/339).
28 Companies (Disclosure of Address) Regulations 2009, SI 2009/214, reg 5(3)(b) (substituted by SI 2016/339).
29 Companies (Disclosure of Address) Regulations 2009, SI 2009/214, reg 8(1).
30 Companies (Disclosure of Address) Regulations 2009, SI 2009/214, reg 5(4)(a). As to the meaning of 'relevant body' see PARA 151 note 41.
31 Companies (Disclosure of Address) Regulations 2009, SI 2009/214, reg 5(4)(b).
32 For the purpose of determining any section 243 application, the registrar may accept any answer to a question referred in accordance with the Companies (Disclosure of Address) Regulations 2009, SI 2009/214, reg 5(4) (see the text and notes 30–31) as providing sufficient evidence (where the grounds of the application are those described in head (1) in the text) of the nature and extent of any risk relevant to the applicant, or to persons who live with the applicant, or of whether an applicant is or has been employed by a relevant organisation: reg 8(3).
33 Companies (Disclosure of Address) Regulations 2009, SI 2009/214, reg 5(5) (substituted by SI 2016/339).
34 Companies (Disclosure of Address) Regulations 2009, SI 2009/214, reg 5(6) (added by SI 2016/339).
35 Companies (Disclosure of Address) Regulations 2009, SI 2009/214, reg 8(2)(a).
36 Companies (Disclosure of Address) Regulations 2009, SI 2009/214, reg 8(2)(b).

543. Application by company to withhold protected information relating to its directors. A company ('the applicant') may make a section 243 application[1] to the registrar of companies[2] relating to an individual ('D') who is, or proposes to become, a director[3] of the company[4]. A company may, however, only make such an application where D has given consent for the company to make the application on his behalf[5].

The grounds on which such an application may be made are that:

(1) the applicant reasonably believes that there is a serious risk that D, or a person who lives with D, will be subjected to violence or intimidation as a result of the applicant's activities; or
(2) D is the subject of an application to protect usual residential address information[6] which has been determined by the registrar in favour of the applicant and that determination has not ceased[7] to have effect[8].

Where the grounds of the application are those described in head (2) above, the application must only relate to one individual who is, or proposes to become, a director of the company[9].

The application must contain:

(a) a statement of the grounds on which the application is made[10];
(b) confirmation that D consents to the making of the application[11];
(c) the name and registered number[12] of the applicant[13];
(d) the address of the registered office[14] of the applicant[15];
(e) the e-mail address of the applicant, if any[16];
(f) the name and any former name of D[17];
(g) the date of birth of D[18];
(h) the usual residential address of D[19];
(i) the e-mail address of D, if any[20];
(j) where the registrar has allocated a unique identifier to D, that unique identifier[21];
(k) where D is a director of another company, the name and registered number of that company[22]; and

(l) where the grounds of the application are those described in head (2) above, the name and registered number of the company in relation to which the determination was made, unless the determination relates to a proposed company which was never incorporated[23].

Where the grounds of the application are those described in head (1) above, the application must be accompanied by evidence which supports the applicant's statement of the grounds on which the application is made[24]. The registrar may refer to a relevant body[25] any question relating to an assessment of the nature or extent of any risk of violence or intimidation[26].

The registrar must determine the application[27] and, within seven days beginning with the date that the determination is made, send to the applicant and to D notice of the determination[28]. Where the application is unsuccessful, that notice must inform the applicant of the applicant's right to apply for permission to appeal against the determination within 28 days beginning with the date of the notice[29].

The registrar must not make available for public inspection any section 243 application[30] or any documents provided in support of that application[31].

1 As to the meaning of 'section 243 application' see PARA 151.
2 As to the registrar of companies see PARA 126 et seq.
3 As to a company's directors see PARA 512 et seq. As to the prospective prohibition on the appointment of corporate directors see PARA 526. As to the delivery of documents to the registrar see PARA 136; and as to the requirements generally for the proper delivery of documents to the registrar see PARA 137.
4 Companies (Disclosure of Address) Regulations 2009, SI 2009/214, reg 6(1) (reg 6 substituted by SI 2016/339).
5 Companies (Disclosure of Address) Regulations 2009, SI 2009/214, reg 6(2) (as substituted: see note 4).
6 Ie an application made under the Register of People with Significant Control Regulations 2016, SI 2016/339, reg 25 (see PARA 496), reg 26 (see PARA 497) or reg 27 (see PARA 498).
7 Ie under the Register of People with Significant Control Regulations 2016, SI 2016/339, reg 31: see PARA 499.
8 Companies (Disclosure of Address) Regulations 2009, SI 2009/214, reg 6(3) (as substituted: see note 4).
9 Companies (Disclosure of Address) Regulations 2009, SI 2009/214, reg 6(4) (as substituted: see note 4).
10 Companies (Disclosure of Address) Regulations 2009, SI 2009/214, reg 6(5)(a) (as substituted: see note 4).
11 Companies (Disclosure of Address) Regulations 2009, SI 2009/214, reg 6(5)(b) (as substituted: see note 4).
12 As to company names and trading names generally see PARA 195 et seq. As to a company's registered number see PARAS 134–135.
13 Companies (Disclosure of Address) Regulations 2009, SI 2009/214, reg 6(5)(c) (as substituted: see note 4).
14 As to a company's registered office see PARA 124.
15 Companies (Disclosure of Address) Regulations 2009, SI 2009/214, reg 6(5)(d) (as substituted: see note 4).
16 Companies (Disclosure of Address) Regulations 2009, SI 2009/214, reg 6(5)(e) (as substituted: see note 4).
17 Companies (Disclosure of Address) Regulations 2009, SI 2009/214, reg 6(5)(f) (as substituted: see note 4). As to the meanings of 'name' and 'former name' for these purposes see PARA 151 note 27.
18 Companies (Disclosure of Address) Regulations 2009, SI 2009/214, reg 6(5)(g) (as substituted: see note 4).
19 Companies (Disclosure of Address) Regulations 2009, SI 2009/214, reg 6(5)(h) (as substituted: see note 4).
20 Companies (Disclosure of Address) Regulations 2009, SI 2009/214, reg 6(5)(i) (as substituted: see note 4).

21 Companies (Disclosure of Address) Regulations 2009, SI 2009/214, reg 6(5)(j) (as substituted: see note 4). As to the allocation of unique identifiers see PARA 144.
22 Companies (Disclosure of Address) Regulations 2009, SI 2009/214, reg 6(5)(k) (as substituted: see note 4).
23 Companies (Disclosure of Address) Regulations 2009, SI 2009/214, reg 6(5)(l) (as substituted: see note 4).
24 Companies (Disclosure of Address) Regulations 2009, SI 2009/214, reg 6(6) (as substituted: see note 4).
25 As to the meaning of 'relevant body' for these purposes see PARA 151 note 41.
26 Companies (Disclosure of Address) Regulations 2009, SI 2009/214, reg 6(7) (as substituted: see note 4).
27 For the purpose of determining any section 243 application, the registrar may accept any answer to a question referred in accordance with the Companies (Disclosure of Address) Regulations 2009, SI 2009/214, reg 6(7) (see the text and notes 25–26) as providing sufficient evidence (where the grounds of the application are those described in reg 6(3(a)) (see head (1) in the text)) of the nature and extent of any risk relevant to the directors on behalf of whom the application is made, or to persons who live with any such director: reg 8(3) (amended by SI 2016/339).
28 Companies (Disclosure of Address) Regulations 2009, SI 2009/214, reg 6(8) (as substituted: see note 4).
29 Companies (Disclosure of Address) Regulations 2009, SI 2009/214, reg 6(9) (as substituted: see note 4).
30 Companies (Disclosure of Address) Regulations 2009, SI 2009/214, reg 8(2)(a).
31 Companies (Disclosure of Address) Regulations 2009, SI 2009/214, reg 8(2)(b).

544. Application on behalf of proposed directors by subscriber to memorandum of association to withhold protected information. A subscriber to a memorandum of association[1] ('the applicant') may make a section 243 application[2] to the registrar of companies[3] relating to an individual ('D') who proposes to become, on or after the formation of the company to which the memorandum relates, a director[4] of the company[5]. A subscriber to a memorandum of association may only, however, make such an application where D has given consent for the subscriber to make the application on his behalf[6].

The grounds on which such an application may be made are that:

(1) the applicant reasonably believes that there is a serious risk that D, or a person who lives D, will be subjected to violence or intimidation as a result of the proposed activities of the proposed company to which the memorandum relates; or
(2) D is the subject of an application to protect usual residential address information[7] which has been determined by the registrar in favour of the applicant and that determination has not ceased[8] to have effect[9].

Where the grounds of the application are those described in head (2) above, the application must only relate to one individual who proposes to become a director in relation to the proposed company[10].

The application must contain:

(a) a statement of the grounds on which the application is made[11];
(b) confirmation that D consents to the making of the application[12];
(c) the name and any former name of the applicant[13];
(d) the usual residential address of the applicant[14];
(e) the e-mail address of the applicant, if any[15];
(f) the name of the proposed company to which the memorandum relates[16];
(g) the name and any former name of D[17];
(h) the date of birth of D[18];
(i) the usual residential address of D[19];
(j) the e-mail address of D, if any[20];
(k) where the registrar has allocated a unique identifier to D, that unique identifier[21];

(l) where D is a director of another company, the name and registered number of that company[22]; and

(m) where the grounds of the application are those described in head (2) above, the name and registered number of the company in relation to which the determination was made, unless the determination relates to a proposed company which was never incorporated[23].

Where the grounds of the application are those described in head (1) above, the application must be accompanied by evidence which supports the applicant's statement of the grounds on which the application is made[24]. The registrar may refer to a relevant body[25] any question relating to an assessment of the nature or extent of any risk of violence or intimidation[26].

The registrar must determine the application[27] and, within seven days beginning with the date that the determination is made, send to the applicant and to D notice of the determination[28]. Where the application is unsuccessful, that notice must inform the applicant of the applicant's right to apply for permission to appeal against the determination within 28 days beginning with the date of the notice[29].

The registrar must not make available for public inspection any section 243 application[30] or any documents provided in support of that application[31].

1 As to a company's memorandum of association and its subscribers see PARA 97 et seq.
2 As to the meaning of 'section 243 application' see PARA 151 head (3).
3 As to the registrar of companies see PARA 126 et seq.
4 As to the prospective prohibition on the appointment of corporate directors see PARA 526. As to company formation and registration under the Companies Act 2006 see PARA 95 et seq. As to the delivery of documents to the registrar see PARA 136; and as to the requirements generally for the proper delivery of documents to the registrar see PARA 137.
5 Companies (Disclosure of Address) Regulations 2009, SI 2009/214, reg 7(1) (reg 7 substituted by SI 2016/339).
6 Companies (Disclosure of Address) Regulations 2009, SI 2009/214, reg 7(2) (as substituted: see note 5).
7 Ie an application made under the Register of People with Significant Control Regulations 2016, SI 2016/339, reg 25 (see PARA 496), reg 26 (see PARA 497) or reg 27 (see PARA 498).
8 Ie under the Register of People with Significant Control Regulations 2016, SI 2016/339, reg 31: see PARA 499.
9 Companies (Disclosure of Address) Regulations 2009, SI 2009/214, reg 7(3) (as substituted: see note 5).
10 Companies (Disclosure of Address) Regulations 2009, SI 2009/214, reg 7(4) (as substituted: see note 5).
11 Companies (Disclosure of Address) Regulations 2009, SI 2009/214, reg 7(5)(a) (as substituted: see note 5).
12 Companies (Disclosure of Address) Regulations 2009, SI 2009/214, reg 7(5)(b) (as substituted: see note 5).
13 Companies (Disclosure of Address) Regulations 2009, SI 2009/214, reg 7(5)(c) (as substituted: see note 5). As to the meanings of 'name' and 'former name' for these purposes see PARA 151 note 27.
14 Companies (Disclosure of Address) Regulations 2009, SI 2009/214, reg 7(5)(d) (as substituted: see note 5).
15 Companies (Disclosure of Address) Regulations 2009, SI 2009/214, reg 7(5)(e) (as substituted: see note 5).
16 Companies (Disclosure of Address) Regulations 2009, SI 2009/214, reg 7(5)(f) (as substituted: see note 5).
17 Companies (Disclosure of Address) Regulations 2009, SI 2009/214, reg 7(5)(g) (as substituted: see note 5).
18 Companies (Disclosure of Address) Regulations 2009, SI 2009/214, reg 7(5)(h) (as substituted: see note 5).
19 Companies (Disclosure of Address) Regulations 2009, SI 2009/214, reg 7(5)(i) (as substituted: see note 5).

20 Companies (Disclosure of Address) Regulations 2009, SI 2009/214, reg 7(5)(j) (as substituted: see note 5).
21 Companies (Disclosure of Address) Regulations 2009, SI 2009/214, reg 7(5)(k) (as substituted: see note 5). As to the allocation of unique identifiers see PARA 144.
22 Companies (Disclosure of Address) Regulations 2009, SI 2009/214, reg 7(5)(l) (as substituted: see note 5).
23 Companies (Disclosure of Address) Regulations 2009, SI 2009/214, reg 7(5)(m) (as substituted: see note 5).
24 Companies (Disclosure of Address) Regulations 2009, SI 2009/214, reg 7(6) (as substituted: see note 5).
25 As to the meaning of 'relevant body' for these purposes see PARA 151 note 41.
26 Companies (Disclosure of Address) Regulations 2009, SI 2009/214, reg 7(7) (as substituted: see note 5).
27 For the purpose of determining any section 243 application, the registrar may accept any answer to a question referred in accordance with the Companies (Disclosure of Address) Regulations 2009, SI 2009/214, reg 7(7) (see the text and notes 25–26) as providing sufficient evidence (where the grounds of the application are those described in reg 7(3)(a)) (see head (1) in the text) of the nature and extent of any risk relevant to the proposed directors on behalf of whom the application is made, or to persons who live with any such proposed director: reg 8(3) (amended by SI 2016/339).
28 Companies (Disclosure of Address) Regulations 2009, SI 2009/214, reg 7(8) (as substituted: see note 5).
29 Companies (Disclosure of Address) Regulations 2009, SI 2009/214, reg 7(9) (as substituted: see note 5).
30 Companies (Disclosure of Address) Regulations 2009, SI 2009/214, reg 8(2)(a).
31 Companies (Disclosure of Address) Regulations 2009, SI 2009/214, reg 8(2)(b).

545. Duration of successful decision to withhold protected information about directors. A section 243 decision[1] continues to have effect until[2]:

(1) either the section 243 beneficiary[3], or his personal representative[4], has notified the registrar of companies[5] in writing that he wishes the section 243 decision to cease to apply[6]; or

(2) the registrar has made a revocation decision[7] in relation to that beneficiary[8],

whichever first occurs[9].

1 As to the meaning of 'section 243 decision' see PARA 151 head (3).
2 Companies (Disclosure of Address) Regulations 2009, SI 2009/214, reg 15(1).
3 Companies (Disclosure of Address) Regulations 2009, SI 2009/214, reg 15(1)(a)(i). As to the meaning of 'section 243 beneficiary' see PARA 151.
4 Companies (Disclosure of Address) Regulations 2009, SI 2009/214, reg 15(1)(a)(ii). For these purposes, 'personal representative' means the executor, original or by representation, or administrator for the time being of a deceased person: reg 15(3). See further WILLS AND INTESTACY vol 103 (2010) PARA 608.
5 As to the registrar of companies see PARA 126 et seq. As to the delivery of documents to the registrar see PARA 136; and as to the requirements generally for the proper delivery of documents to the registrar see PARA 137.
6 Companies (Disclosure of Address) Regulations 2009, SI 2009/214, reg 15(1)(a).
7 For these purposes, 'revocation decision' in relation to a section 243 decision means a determination by the registrar to revoke that decision in accordance with the Companies (Disclosure of Address) Regulations 2009, SI 2009/214, reg 16 (see PARA 546): see reg 15(3).
8 Companies (Disclosure of Address) Regulations 2009, SI 2009/214, reg 15(1)(b).
9 Companies (Disclosure of Address) Regulations 2009, SI 2009/214, reg 15(1).

546. Revocation of decision to withhold protected information about directors. The registrar of companies[1] may revoke a section 243 decision[2] at any time if he is satisfied that the section 243 beneficiary[3] or any other person, in purported compliance with any provision of the Disclosure of Address Regulations[4], is found guilty of an offence of making false statements to the registrar[5] (a 'revocation decision')[6].

If the registrar proposes to make a revocation decision, he must send the beneficiary notice of his intention[7]. The notice must:

(1) inform the beneficiary that he may, within the period of 28 days beginning with the date of the notice, deliver representations in writing to the registrar[8]; and

(2) state that, if representations are not received by the registrar within that period, the revocation decision will be made at the expiry of that period[9].

If, within the period so specified[10], the beneficiary delivers representations as to why the revocation decision should not be made, the registrar must have regard to the representations in determining whether to make the revocation decision, and must, within five working days of making his decision, send notice of it to the beneficiary[11].

Any communication by the registrar in respect of a revocation decision or proposed revocation decision must be sent to the beneficiary[12]:

(a) in the case of an individual, to his usual residential address[13];

(b) in the case of a company, to its registered office[14]; or

(c) in the case of a partnership[15], to the address specified in its section 243 application[16].

1 As to the registrar of companies see PARA 126 et seq.

2 As to the meaning of 'section 243 decision' see PARA 151 head (3).

3 For these purposes, 'section 243 beneficiary' includes where the section 243 decision was made following an application under the Companies (Disclosure of Address) Regulations 2009, SI 2009/214, reg 6 (see PARA 543) or reg 7 (see PARA 544), the applicant: reg 16(6). As to the meaning of 'section 243 beneficiary' generally see PARA 151.

4 Ie in purported compliance with any provision of the Companies (Disclosure of Address) Regulations 2009, SI 2009/214 (see PARA 540 et seq): see reg 16(1).

5 Ie under the Companies Act 2006 s 1112 (false statements made to registrar) (see PARA 132): see the Companies (Disclosure of Address) Regulations 2009, SI 2009/214, reg 16(1).

6 Companies (Disclosure of Address) Regulations 2009, SI 2009/214, reg 16(1).

7 Companies (Disclosure of Address) Regulations 2009, SI 2009/214, reg 16(2). As to the service of documents on a company generally see PARA 743 et seq; and as to the provision made for the sending or supplying of documents or information to or from a company (the 'company communications provisions') see PARA 750 et seq.

8 Companies (Disclosure of Address) Regulations 2009, SI 2009/214, reg 16(3)(a). As to the delivery of documents to the registrar see PARA 136; and as to the requirements generally for the proper delivery of documents to the registrar see PARA 137.

9 Companies (Disclosure of Address) Regulations 2009, SI 2009/214, reg 16(3)(b).

10 Ie within the period specified in the Companies (Disclosure of Address) Regulations 2009, SI 2009/214, reg 16(3) (see the text and notes 8–9): see reg 16(4).

11 Companies (Disclosure of Address) Regulations 2009, SI 2009/214, reg 16(4). As to the meaning of 'working day' for these purposes see PARA 151 note 47.

12 Companies (Disclosure of Address) Regulations 2009, SI 2009/214, reg 16(5).

13 Companies (Disclosure of Address) Regulations 2009, SI 2009/214, reg 16(5)(a).

14 Companies (Disclosure of Address) Regulations 2009, SI 2009/214, reg 16(5)(b). As to a company's registered office see PARA 124.

15 As to the meaning of 'partnership' for these purposes see PARA 156 note 15.

16 Companies (Disclosure of Address) Regulations 2009, SI 2009/214, reg 16(5)(c). As to the meaning of 'section 243 application' see PARA 151 head (3).

547. Appeal against decision that application to withhold protected information about directors has been unsuccessful. An applicant who has received notice[1] that his section 243 application[2] has been unsuccessful may appeal to the High Court on the grounds that the decision is unlawful[3], is irrational or unreasonable[4], or has been made on the basis of a procedural impropriety or otherwise contravenes the rules of natural justice[5]. No such appeal may be brought, however, unless the permission of the court has been obtained[6]. No application for such permission may be made after 28 days beginning with the date of the notice of determination[7] unless the court is satisfied that there was good reason for the failure of the applicant to seek permission before the end of that period[8]. An applicant who seeks permission to appeal must serve written notice of the application on the registrar within seven days beginning with the date on which the application for permission was issued[9].

The court determining an appeal may either dismiss the appeal[10] or quash the decision[11]. Where the court quashes a decision, it may refer the matter to the registrar of companies[12] with a direction to reconsider it and make a determination in accordance with the findings of the court[13].

1 Ie under the Companies (Disclosure of Address) Regulations 2009, SI 2009/214, reg 5(5) (see PARA 542), reg 6(8) (see PARA 543) or reg 7(8) (see PARA 544): see reg 14(1) (amended by SI 2016/339).
2 As to the meaning of 'section 243 application' see PARA 151 head (3).
3 Companies (Disclosure of Address) Regulations 2009, SI 2009/214, reg 14(1)(a).
4 Companies (Disclosure of Address) Regulations 2009, SI 2009/214, reg 14(1)(b).
5 Companies (Disclosure of Address) Regulations 2009, SI 2009/214, reg 14(1)(c). As to procedural fairness and the rules of natural justice see JUDICIAL REVIEW vol 61 (2010) PARAS 625 et seq, 629 et seq.
6 Companies (Disclosure of Address) Regulations 2009, SI 2009/214, reg 14(2) (amended by SI 2016/339).
7 Ie the notice under the Companies (Disclosure of Address) Regulations 2009, SI 2009/214, reg 5(5) (see PARA 542), reg 6(8) (see PARA 543) or reg 7(8) (see PARA 544).
8 Companies (Disclosure of Address) Regulations 2009, SI 2009/214, reg 14(3) (substituted by SI 2016/339).
9 Companies (Disclosure of Address) Regulations 2009, SI 2009/214, reg 14(3A) (added by SI 2016/339).
10 Companies (Disclosure of Address) Regulations 2009, SI 2009/214, reg 14(4)(a).
11 Companies (Disclosure of Address) Regulations 2009, SI 2009/214, reg 14(4)(b).
12 As to the registrar of companies see PARA 126 et seq.
13 Companies (Disclosure of Address) Regulations 2009, SI 2009/214, reg 14(4).

548. Disclosure of protected information about directors under court order. The court[1] may make an order for the disclosure of protected information[2] by the company[3] or by the registrar of companies[4], if:

(1) there is evidence that service of documents at a service address other than the director's usual residential address[5] is not effective to bring them to the notice of the director[6]; or

(2) it is necessary or expedient for the information to be provided in connection with the enforcement of an order or decree of the court[7],

and the court is otherwise satisfied that it is appropriate to make the order[8].

An order for disclosure by the registrar is to be made only if the company does not have the director's usual residential address, or has been dissolved[9].

The order may be made on the application of a liquidator[10], creditor or member of the company[11], or any other person appearing to the court to have a sufficient interest[12].

The order must specify the persons to whom, and purposes for which, disclosure is authorised[13].

1 As to the meaning of 'the court' see PARA 160 note 12.
2 As to the meaning of 'protected information' for these purposes see PARA 537. The Companies Act 2006 s 244 also applies to information within s 790ZF(2) (see PARA 491): see s 790ZF(1); and PARA 491. Section 244 does not, however, apply to information relating to a person if an application under regulations made under s 790ZG (see PARA 492) has been granted with respect to that information and has not been revoked: see s 790ZF(3); and PARA 491. As to such applications see PARA 495 et seq.
3 As to the meaning of 'company' under the Companies Acts see PARA 21; and as to the meaning of the 'Companies Acts' see PARA 13.

4 Companies Act 2006 s 244(1). The registrar must not use or disclose protected information except as permitted by s 243 (see PARA 539) or in accordance with s 244: see s 242(3); and PARA 538. As to the meaning of 'registrar of companies' see PARA 126 note 2. Where regulations under s 1046 require an overseas company to register particulars of an individual's usual residential address, they must contain provision corresponding to that made by Pt 10 Ch 8 (ss 240–246): see s 1055; and PARA 2015. As to the meaning of 'overseas company' see PARA 2013.

The provisions of the Companies Act 2006 s 244 apply to unregistered companies by virtue of the Unregistered Companies Regulations 2009, SI 2009/2436, Sch 1 para 7(1): see PARA 1857. As to the meaning of 'unregistered company' see PARA 1856.

5 As to requirements relating to service addresses generally see PARA 745; and see PARA 535 note 8. As to the meaning of 'director' under the Companies Acts see PARA 512.

6 Companies Act 2006 s 244(1)(a).

7 Companies Act 2006 s 244(1)(b).

8 Companies Act 2006 s 244(1).

9 Companies Act 2006 s 244(2). As to the dissolution of a company see PARA 1703 et seq.

10 As to the appointment of liquidators generally see COMPANY AND PARTNERSHIP INSOLVENCY vol 17 (2011) PARA 909 et seq.

11 As to the meaning of 'member of the company' see PARA 323.

12 Companies Act 2006 s 244(3). Cf the wording in s 1029(2) ('any other person appearing to the court to have an interest in the matter') (regarding applications to the court for restoration to the register): see PARA 1718. In relation to an application for an order under s 244, the claimant must notify the director concerned of the application: CPR PD 49A—*Applications Under the Companies Acts and Related Legislation* para 9.

13 Companies Act 2006 s 244(4).

549. Circumstances in which registrar may put director's address on the public record. The registrar of companies[1] may put a director's's[2] usual residential address on the public record[3], if:

(1) communications sent by the registrar to the director and requiring a response within a specified period remain unanswered[4]; or

(2) there is evidence that service of documents at a service address provided in place of the director's usual residential address is not effective to bring them to the notice of the director[5].

The registrar must give notice of the proposal to the director[6], and to every company[7] of which the registrar has been notified that the individual is a director[8]. The notice must state the grounds on which it is proposed to put the director's usual residential address on the public record[9], and specify a period within which representations may be made before that is done[10]. It must be sent to the director at his usual residential address, unless it appears to the registrar that service at that address may be ineffective to bring it to the individual's notice, in which case it may be sent to any service address provided in place of that address[11].

The registrar must take account of any representations received within the specified period[12].

The registrar, on so deciding[13] that a director's usual residential address is to be put on the public record, must proceed as if notice of a change of registered particulars had been given[14], stating that address as the director's service address[15], and stating that the director's usual residential address is the same as his service address[16]. The registrar must give notice of having done so to the director[17], and to the company[18].

On receipt of the notice, the company must enter the director's usual residential address in its register of directors[19] as his service address[20], and state in its register of directors' residential addresses[21] that his usual residential address is the same as his service address[22]. If the company has been notified by the director in question of a more recent address as his usual residential address, it must enter that address in its register of directors as the director's service address[23], and give notice to the registrar as on a change of registered particulars[24]. Alternatively, if an election to keep information about directors on the central register[25] is in force in respect of the company's register of directors[26], the company must, in place of making such an entry and giving such notice[27], deliver the required particulars[28] to the registrar[29].

If a company fails to comply with the above requirements[30], an offence is committed by the company, and by every officer of the company who is in default[31].

A director whose usual residential address has been put on the public record by the registrar in this way[32] may not register a service address other than his usual residential address for a period of five years from the date of the registrar's decision[33].

1 As to the meaning of 'registrar of companies' see PARA 126 note 2.
2 As to the meaning of 'director' under the Companies Acts see PARA 512; and as to the meaning of the 'Companies Acts' see PARA 13.
3 Companies Act 2006 s 245(1). What is meant by putting the address on the public record is explained in s 246 (see the text and notes 13–36): s 245(6). A director's usual residential address is included in the definition of 'protected information' which the registrar must not otherwise use or disclose except as permitted by s 243 (see PARA 539) or in accordance with s 244 (see PARA 548): see s 242(3); and PARA 538. Where regulations under s 1046 require an overseas company to register particulars of an individual's usual residential address, they must contain provision corresponding to that made by Pt 10 Ch 8 (ss 240–246): see s 1055; and PARA 2015. As to the meaning of 'overseas company' see PARA 2013.
The provisions of the Companies Act 2006 ss 245, 246 apply to unregistered companies by virtue of the Unregistered Companies Regulations 2009, SI 2009/2436, Sch 1 para 7(1): see PARA 1857. As to the meaning of 'unregistered company' see PARA 1856.
4 Companies Act 2006 s 245(1)(a).
5 Companies Act 2006 s 245(1)(b). As to requirements relating to service addresses generally see PARA 745; and see PARA 535 note 8.
6 Companies Act 2006 s 245(2)(a).
7 As to the meaning of 'company' under the Companies Acts see PARA 21.
8 Companies Act 2006 s 245(2)(b).
9 Companies Act 2006 s 245(3)(a).
10 Companies Act 2006 s 245(3)(b).
11 Companies Act 2006 s 245(4).
12 Companies Act 2006 s 245(5).
13 Ie in accordance with the Companies Act 2006 s 245 (see the text and notes 1–12): see s 246(1).
14 Companies Act 2006 s 246(1). As to the notice to be given of a change of registered particulars see PARA 550.
15 Companies Act 2006 s 246(1)(a).
16 Companies Act 2006 s 246(1)(b).
17 Companies Act 2006 s 246(2)(a).
18 Companies Act 2006 s 246(2)(b).
19 As to the requirement for a company to keep a register of directors see PARA 535; and as to the option to keep information about directors on the central register see PARA 551 et seq.
20 Companies Act 2006 s 246(3)(a). This does not, however, apply if an election under the Companies Act 2006 s 167A (see PARA 551) is in force in respect of the company's register of directors: s 246(3A)(a) (s 246(3A), (4A) added by the Small Business, Enterprise and Employment Act 2015 Sch 5 Pt 2 paras 11, 15(a), (b)).
21 As to the register of directors' residential addresses see PARA 536 et seq; and as to the option to keep information about directors on the central register see PARA 551 et seq.
22 Companies Act 2006 s 246(3)(b). This does not, however, apply if an election under the Companies Act 2006 s 167A (see PARA 551) is in force in respect of the company's register of directors' residential addresses: s 246(3A)(b) (as added: see note 20).
23 Companies Act 2006 s 246(4)(a).
24 Companies Act 2006 s 246(4)(b).
25 As to the central register see PARA 142.
26 Ie an election under the Companies Act 2006 s 167A (see PARA 551).
27 Ie in place of doing the things mentioned in the Companies Act 2006 s 246(4)(a), (b) (see the text and notes 23–24).
28 Ie deliver the particulars in accordance with the Companies Act 2006 s 167D (see PARA 553).

29 Companies Act 2006 s 246(4A) (as added: see note 20).
30 Ie fails to comply with the Companies Act 2006 s 246(3) or s 246(4) (see the text and notes 19–24), or with s 246(3), s 264(4) or s 264(4A) (see the text and notes 19–29): see s 246(5) (amended by the Small Business, Enterprise and Employment Act 2015 Small Business, Enterprise and Employment Act 2015 Sch 5 Pt 2 paras 11, 15(c)).
31 Companies Act 2006 s 246(5) (as amended: see note 30). As to the meaning of 'officer who is in default' see PARA 316. As to the meaning of 'officer' generally see PARA 679.
A person guilty of such an offence is liable on summary conviction to a fine and for continued contravention to a daily default fine not exceeding one-tenth of the greater of £5,000 or level 4 on the standard scale: Companies Act 2006 s 246(6) (amended by SI 2015/664). In the case of liability on summary conviction the fine is one not exceeding level 5 on the standard scale: see the Companies Act 2006 s 246(6) (as so amended). By virtue of the Legal Aid, Sentencing and Punishment of Offenders Act 2012 s 85, however, where the offence is committed on or after 12 March 2015, it is punishable by a fine of an unlimited amount. As to the standard scale and the powers of magistrates' courts to issue fines on summary conviction see SENTENCING vol 92 (2015) PARA 176. As to the meaning of 'daily default fine' see PARA 1816.
32 Ie under the Companies Act 2006 s 246 (see the text and notes 13–34): see s 246(7).
33 Companies Act 2006 s 246(7).

(C) Changes to Registers relating to Directors

550. Company's duty to notify registrar of changes relating to directors or particulars. A company[1] must, within the period of 14 days from[2]:

(1) a person becoming or ceasing to be a director[3]; or
(2) the occurrence of any change in the particulars contained in its register of directors[4] or its register of directors' residential addresses[5],

give notice to the registrar of companies[6] of the change and of the date on which it occurred[7].

Notice of a person having become a director of the company must contain a statement of the particulars of the new director that are required to be included in the company's register of directors and its register of directors' residential addresses[8], and must be accompanied by a statement by the company that the person has consented to act in that capacity[9].

Where a company gives notice of a change of a director's service address[10] as stated in the company's register of directors[11], and where the notice is not accompanied by notice of any resulting change in the particulars contained in the company's register of directors' residential addresses[12], the notice must be accompanied by a statement that no such change is required[13].

If default is made in complying with these requirements[14], an offence is committed by the company, and by every officer of the company who is in default[15].

Whenever the registrar registers notice under the above provisions[16] of a person having become a director of a company, as soon as reasonably practicable after registering the document, he must notify the person or each person named in the document as having become a director of the company[17]. The notice must state that the person is named in the document as a director of the company, and include such information relating to the office and duties of a director, or such details of where information of that sort can be found, as the Secretary of State may from time to time direct the registrar to include[18].

The above provisions must be read with the provisions of the Companies Act 2006[19] which allow for an alternative method of record-keeping in the case of private companies[20].

1 As to the meaning of 'company' under the Companies Acts see PARA 21; and as to the meaning of the 'Companies Acts' see PARA 13.
2 Companies Act 2006 s 167(1).

The provisions of the Companies Act 2006 s 167 apply to unregistered companies by virtue of the Unregistered Companies Regulations 2009, SI 2009/2436, Sch 1 para 6(1): see PARA 1857. As to the meaning of 'unregistered company' see PARA 1856.

3 Companies Act 2006 s 167(1)(a). As to the meaning of 'director' under the Companies Acts see PARA 512.

4 As to the requirement for a company to keep a register of directors see PARA 535; and as to the option to keep information about directors on the central register see PARA 551 et seq.

5 Companies Act 2006 s 167(1)(b). As to the register of directors' residential addresses see PARA 536 et seq; and as to the option to keep information about directors on the central register see PARA 551 et seq.

6 As to the meaning of 'registrar of companies' see PARA 126 note 2. As to the delivery of documents to the registrar see PARA 136; and as to the requirements for the proper delivery of documents to the registrar see PARA 137.

7 Companies Act 2006 s 167(1). Notifications of any change among the company's directors, or of any change in the particulars of directors required to be delivered to the registrar, are subject to the 'Directive disclosure requirements' and public notice by the registrar must be given of the receipt of such documents: see PARA 139.

8 Companies Act 2006 s 167(2)(a). The Secretary of State may make provision by regulations requiring a statement or notice sent to the registrar of companies under s 167(2) that relates (wholly or partly) to a person disqualified under Pt 40 (ss 1182–1191) (see PARA 1812) or a person who is subject to a disqualification order or disqualification undertaking under the Company Directors Disqualification Act 1986 (see PARA 1762 et seq) to be accompanied by an additional statement stating that the person has obtained permission from a court to act in the capacity in question: see the Companies Act 2006 s 1189; and PARA 1815.

9 Companies Act 2006 s 167(2)(b) (substituted by the Small Business, Enterprise and Employment Act 2015 s 100(1), (4)). For transitional provisions see s 100(6).

10 As to requirements relating to service addresses generally see PARA 745; and see PARA 535 note 8.

11 Companies Act 2006 s 167(3)(a). As to the statement of a director's service address see s 163(1)(b); and PARA 535.

12 Companies Act 2006 s 167(3)(b).

13 Companies Act 2006 s 167(3).

14 Ie in complying with the Companies Act 2006 s 167 (see the text and notes 1–13): see s 167(4).

15 Companies Act 2006 s 167(4). For these purposes, a shadow director is treated as an officer of the company: s 167(4). As to the meaning of 'shadow director' see PARA 512. As to the meaning of 'officer who is in default' see PARA 316; and as to the meaning of 'officer' generally see PARA 679.

A person guilty of such an offence is liable on summary conviction to a fine and for continued contravention to a daily default fine not exceeding one-tenth of the greater of £5,000 or level 4 on the standard scale: Companies Act 2006 s 167(5) (amended by SI 2015/664). In the case of liability on summary conviction the fine is one not exceeding level 5 on the standard scale': see the Companies Act 2006 s 167(5) (as so amended). By virtue of the Legal Aid, Sentencing and Punishment of Offenders Act 2012 s 85, however, where the offence is committed on or after 12 March 2015, it is punishable by a fine of an unlimited amount. As to the standard scale and the powers of magistrates' courts to issue fines on summary conviction see SENTENCING vol 92 (2015) PARA 176. As to the meaning of 'daily default fine' see PARA 1816.

16 Ie notice under the Companies Act 2006 s 167: see the text and notes 1–15.

17 Companies Act 2006 s 1079B(1)(b), (2)(b) (s 1079B added by the Small Business, Enterprise and Employment Act 2015 s 101(1)). For transitional provisions see s 101(2). The notice may be sent in hard copy or electronic form to any address for the person that the registrar has received from either the subscribers or the company: Companies Act 2006 s 1079B(4) (as so added).

The provisions of the Companies Act 2006 s 1079B apply to unregistered companies in cases where the document registered by the registrar is a notice under s 167 of a person having become a director of a company: see the Unregistered Companies Regulations 2009, SI 2009/2436, Sch 1 para 19A (added by SI 2015/1695); and PARA 1857. As to the meaning of 'unregistered company' see PARA 1856.

18 Companies Act 2006 s 1079B(3) (as added: see note 17).

19 Ie the Companies Act 2006 ss 167A–167E: see PARA 551 et seq.

20 Companies Act 2006 s 161A (added by the Small Business, Enterprise and Employment Act 2015 Sch 5 Pt 1 paras 5, 6). As to the power to extend the alternative method of record-keeping to public companies see s 167F; and PARA 551. As to the meanings of 'private company' and 'public company' see PARA 95.

E. OPTION TO KEEP INFORMATION ABOUT DIRECTORS ON CENTRAL REGISTER

551. Right to make an election to keep information about directors on the central register. As from 30 June 2016[1], the following provisions have effect.

An election may be made[2] in respect of a register of directors[3] or a register of directors' residential addresses[4], or both[5]. The election may be made:

(1) by the subscribers wishing to form a private company[6] under the Companies Act 2006[7]; or

(2) by the private company itself once it is formed and registered[8].

The election is made by giving notice of election to the registrar of companies[9]. If the notice is given by subscribers wishing to form a private company, it must be given when the documents required to be delivered[10] are delivered to the registrar[11].

An election so made takes effect when the notice of election is registered by the registrar[12]. The election remains in force until either the company ceases to be a private company, or a notice of withdrawal sent by the company[13] is registered by the registrar, whichever occurs first[14].

The Secretary of State[15] may by regulations[16] amend the Companies Act 2006 to extend the provisions regarding the option to keep information about directors on the central register[17], with or without modification, to public companies[18] or public companies of a class specified in the regulations, and to make such other amendments as the Secretary of State thinks fit in consequence of that extension[19].

1 See the Small Business, Enterprise and Employment Act 2015 (Commencement No 4, Transitional and Savings Provisions) Regulations 2016, SI 2016/321, reg 6(c).
2 Ie under the Companies Act 2006 s 167A: see the text and notes 3–11.
3 As to the register of directors see PARA 535.
4 As to the register of directors' residential addresses see PARA 536 et seq.
5 Companies Act 2006 s 167A(1) (ss 167A, 167B, 167F added by the Small Business, Enterprise and Employment Act 2015 Sch 5 Pt 1 paras 5, 7). The text of the Companies Act 2006 s 167A does not specify the nature of the election which may be made in respect of the registers referred to in notes 3–4, but the Small Business, Enterprise and Employment Act 2015 Sch 5 Pt 1 para 7 adds before the Companies Act 2006 ss 167A–167F the heading 'Option to keep information on the central register'. As to the central register see PARA 142 et seq.
6 As to the meaning of 'private company' see PARA 95. As to the Secretary of State's power to extend the right to make such an election to public companies see the text and notes 14–18.
7 Companies Act 2006 s 167A(2)(a) (as added: see note 5). As to the formation of a company under the Companies Act 2006 see PARA 95 et seq.
8 Companies Act 2006 s 167A(2)(b) (as added: see note 5).
9 Companies Act 2006 s 167A(3) (as added: see note 5). As to the meaning of 'registrar of companies' see PARA 126 note 2. As to the meaning of 'company' under the Companies Acts see PARA 21.
10 Ie the documents required to be delivered under the Companies Act 2006 s 9: see PARA 104.
11 Companies Act 2006 s 167A(4) (as added: see note 5).
12 Companies Act 2006 s 167B(1) (as added: see note 5).
13 Ie under the Companies Act 2006 s 167E: see PARA 554.
14 Companies Act 2006 s 167B(2) (as added: see note 5).
15 As to the Secretary of State see PARA 6.
16 Regulations under the Companies Act 2006 s 167F are subject to affirmative resolution procedure (ie the regulations must not be made unless a draft of the statutory instrument containing them has been laid before Parliament and approved by a resolution of each House of Parliament): see s 167F(2) (as added: see note 5), s 1290. As to the making of regulations under the Companies Act 2006 generally see ss 1288–1292.
17 Ie the Companies Act 2006 ss 167A–167E: see the text and notes 2–14; and PARAS 552–554.
18 As to the meaning of 'public company' see PARA 95.
19 Companies Act 2006 s 167F(1) (as added: see note 5).

552. Effect of election to keep directors' information on central register on statutory obligations regarding registers of directors and of directors' residential addresses. As from 30 June 2016[1], the following provisions have effect.

If an election to keep directors' information on the central register is in force[2] with respect to a company[3], the company's statutory obligations[4] to keep and maintain a register of the relevant kind[5], and to notify the registrar of companies[6] of changes to it, do not apply with respect to the period when the election is in force[7].

1 See the Small Business, Enterprise and Employment Act 2015 (Commencement No 4, Transitional and Savings Provisions) Regulations 2016, SI 2016/321, reg 6(c).
2 Ie an election under the Companies Act 2006 s 167A: see PARA 551. As to the central register see PARA 142 et seq.
3 As to the meaning of 'company' under the Companies Acts see PARA 21; and as to the meaning of the 'Companies Acts' see PARA 13.
4 Ie its obligations under the Companies Act 2006 ss 162–167: see PARAS 535–536, 550.
5 The reference in the text to a register 'of the relevant kind' is to a register (whether a register of directors or a register of directors' residential addresses) of the kind in respect of which the election is made: Companies Act 2006 s 167C(2) (s 167C added by the Small Business, Enterprise and Employment Act 2015 Sch 5 Pt 1 paras 5, 7). As to the register of directors see PARA 535; and as to the register of directors' residential addresses see PARA 536 et seq.
6 As to the meaning of 'registrar of companies' see PARA 126 note 2.
7 Companies Act 2006 s 167C(1) (as added: see note 5).

553. Duty to notify registrar of changes in directors' information during period when election to keep such information on central register is in force. As from 30 June 2016[1], the following provisions have effect.

During the period when an election to keep directors' information on the central register[2] is in force[3], the following duty applies[4]. The company[5] must deliver to the registrar of companies[6]:

(1) any information of which the company would during that period have been obliged to give notice[7], had the election not been in force; and
(2) any statement that would have had to accompany such a notice[8].

The information, and any accompanying statement, must be delivered as soon as reasonably practicable after the company becomes aware of the information and, in any event, no later than the time by which the company would have been required[9] to give notice of the information[10]. If default is made in complying with this duty, an offence is committed by the company, and by every officer of the company who is in default[11].

Whenever the registrar registers notice under the above provisions[12] of a person having become a director of a company, as soon as reasonably practicable after registering the document, he must notify the person or each person named in the document as having become a director of the company[13]. The notice must state that the person is named in the document as a director of the company, and include such information relating to the office and duties of a director, or such details of where information of that sort can be found, as the Secretary of State may from time to time direct the registrar to include[14].

1 See the Small Business, Enterprise and Employment Act 2015 (Commencement No 4, Transitional and Savings Provisions) Regulations 2016, SI 2016/321, reg 6(c).
2 Ie an election under the Companies Act 2006 s 167A: see PARA 551. As to the central register see PARA 142 et seq.
3 As to when such an election is in force see PARA 551.
4 Companies Act 2006 s 167D(1) (s 167D added by the Small Business, Enterprise and Employment Act 2015 Sch 5 Pt 1 paras 5, 7).
5 As to the meaning of 'company' under the Companies Acts see PARA 21; and as to the meaning of the 'Companies Acts' see PARA 13.
6 As to the meaning of 'registrar of companies' see PARA 126 note 2. As to the delivery of documents to the registrar see PARA 136; and as to the requirements generally for the proper delivery of documents to the registrar see PARA 137.
7 Ie under the Companies Act 2006 s 167: see PARA 550.

8 Companies Act 2006 s 167D(2) (as added: see note 4).
9 See note 7.
10 Companies Act 2006 s 167D(3) (as added: see note 4).
11 Companies Act 2006 s 167D(4) (as added: see note 4). For this purpose a shadow director is treated as an officer of the company: s 167D(4) (as so added). As to shadow directors see PARA 513. As to the meaning of 'officer who is in default' see PARA 316; and as to the meaning of 'officer' generally see PARA 679.

A person guilty of such an offence is liable on summary conviction, in England and Wales, to a fine and, for continued contravention, a daily default fine not exceeding the greater of £500 and one-tenth of level 4 on the standard scale: s 167D(5)(a) (as so added). As to the standard scale and the powers of magistrates' courts to issue fines on summary conviction see SENTENCING vol 92 (2015) PARA 176.
12 Ie notice under the Companies Act 2006 s 167D: see the text and notes 1–11.
13 Companies Act 2006 s 1079B(1)(b), (2)(b) (s 1079B added by the Small Business, Enterprise and Employment Act 2015 s 101(1)). For transitional provisions see s 101(2). The notice may be sent in hard copy or electronic form to any address for the person that the registrar has received from either the subscribers or the company: Companies Act 2006 s 1079B(4) (as so added). Note that s 1079B was brought into force on 10 October 2015: see the Small Business, Enterprise and Employment Act 2015 (Commencement No 2 and Transitional Provisions) Regulations 2015, SI 2015/1689, reg 4(b).
14 Companies Act 2006 s 1079B(3) (as added: see note 13).

554. Withdrawing the election to keep directors' information on the central register. As from 30 June 2016[1], the following provisions have effect.

A company[2] may withdraw an election to keep directors' information on the central register[3] made[4] by or in respect of it[5]. Withdrawal is achieved by giving notice of withdrawal to the registrar of companies[6] and the withdrawal takes effect when the notice is registered by the registrar[7].

The effect of withdrawal is that the company's statutory obligation to keep and maintain a register of directors[8] or a register of directors' residential addresses[9] ('a register of the relevant kind') and its statutory obligation[10] to notify the registrar of changes to that register, apply from then on with respect to the period going forward[11]. This means that, when the withdrawal takes effect:

(1) the company must enter in that register all the information that is required to be contained in that register in respect of matters that are current as at that time[12]; but
(2) the company is not required to enter in its register information relating to the period when the election was in force that is no longer current[13].

1 See the Small Business, Enterprise and Employment Act 2015 (Commencement No 4, Transitional and Savings Provisions) Regulations 2016, SI 2016/321, reg 6(c).
2 As to the meaning of 'company' under the Companies Acts see PARA 21; and as to the meaning of the 'Companies Acts' see PARA 13.
3 Ie an election under the Companies Act 2006 s 167A: see PARA 551. As to the central register see PARA 142 et seq.
4 Ie made under the Companies Act 2006 s 167A: see PARA 551.
5 Companies Act 2006 s 167E(1) (s 167 added by the Small Business, Enterprise and Employment Act 2015 Sch 5 Pt 1 paras 5, 7).
6 Companies Act 2006 s 167E(2) (as added: see note 5). As to the meaning of 'registrar of companies' see PARA 126 note 2. As to the delivery of documents to the registrar see PARA 136; and as to the requirements generally for the proper delivery of documents to the registrar see PARA 137.
7 Companies Act 2006 s 167E(3) (as added: see note 5).
8 Ie its obligation under the Companies Act 2006 s 162: see PARA 535.
9 Ie its obligation under the Companies Act 2006 s 165: see PARA 536.
10 Ie its obligation under the Companies Act 2006 s 167: see PARA 550.
11 Companies Act 2006 s 167E(4) (as added: see note 5).
12 Companies Act 2006 s 167E(5)(a) (as added: see note 5).
13 Companies Act 2006 s 167E(5)(b) (as added: see note 5).

F. RETIREMENT AND REMOVAL OF DIRECTORS

555. Provision in articles as to termination of a director's appointment etc. A company's articles of association[1] usually contain full provisions as to the termination of a director's appointment[2]. Provision is usually made for vacation of office by a director in all or some of the following cases[3], that is to say if he:

(1) fails to acquire or ceases to hold his qualification shares[4]; or
(2) becomes bankrupt[5] or insolvent[6]; or
(3) becomes physically or mentally incapable for a period of time[7]; or
(4) is concerned or participates in the profits of any contract with the company[8]; or
(5) continually absents himself for more than the prescribed period from the meetings of the board without leave[9]; or
(6) is convicted of an indictable offence[10]; or
(7) resigns his office[11]; or
(8) reaches an age limit, where the imposition of such a limit is a proportionate means of achieving a legitimate aim[12].

The articles may also provide for vacation of office by any director who holds any other office of profit under the company except that of managing director or manager[13].

The wording of the articles is usually such that the office is automatically vacated by any of the acts specified, and the board of directors cannot waive the vacation[14]; but each case depends upon the true construction of the articles.

If the articles provide for the director to vacate office if he is so requested by all his co-directors, although the power of removal is fiduciary, the office will be vacated immediately if the director receives a notice in writing signed by all the other directors, even if one or more of them had acted for ulterior reasons[15].

If, as the result of the operation of any such articles, there are no directors of the company acting as such, no valid decisions may be taken which are required by the articles to be taken by the directors[16], but where a person continues to act as a director, though he has vacated office under the articles, the statutory presumption as to validity applies, notwithstanding that he has ceased to hold office[17].

Provision may be made in the articles for the retirement of directors by rotation[18].

Where the statutes of a company provide for the removal of directors for reasonable cause, the criterion of reasonableness is that which is reasonable in the eyes of a meeting of the company[19].

1 As to a company's articles of association see PARA 227 et seq. As to model articles of association prescribed for the purposes of the Companies Act 2006, and their application generally, see PARA 227 et seq. Different versions of model articles have been so prescribed for use by private companies limited by shares (see the Companies (Model Articles) Regulations 2008, SI 2008/3229, reg 2, Sch 1), private companies limited by guarantee (see reg 3, Sch 2), and public companies (see reg 4, Sch 3). As to the meanings of 'company limited by guarantee', 'company limited by shares', 'limited company', 'private company' and 'public company' see PARA 95. The default articles prescribed for the purposes of the Companies Act 1985 ('legacy articles'), ie the Companies (Tables A to F) Regulations 1985, SI 1985/805, have not been revoked and may, in their amended form, continue to be used by companies after the commencement of the Companies Act 2006: see PARA 229.

2 The Companies (Model Articles) Regulations 2008, SI 2008/3229, Sch 1 art 18, Sch 2 art 18, Sch 3 art 22 (each amended by the Mental Health (Discrimination) Act 2013 s 3(1)) provide that a person ceases to be a director as soon as:

(1) that person ceases to be a director by virtue of any provision of the Companies Act 2006 or is prohibited from being a director by law (eg under the Company Directors Disqualification Act 1986 (see PARA 1762 et seq));

(2) a bankruptcy order is made against that person;
(3) a composition is made with that person's creditors generally in satisfaction of that person's debts;
(4) a registered medical practitioner who is treating that person gives a written opinion to the company stating that that person has become physically or mentally incapable of acting as a director and may remain so for more than three months;
(5) notification is received by the company from the director that the director is resigning from office, and such resignation has taken effect in accordance with its terms.

As to bankruptcy orders generally see BANKRUPTCY AND INDIVIDUAL INSOLVENCY vol 5 (2013) PARA 198 et seq. As to compositions generally see BANKRUPTCY AND INDIVIDUAL INSOLVENCY vol 5 (2013) PARA 43 et seq. As to a company's directors generally see PARA 512 et seq.

The Companies (Tables A to F) Regulations 1985, SI 1985/805, Schedule Table A art 81 makes very similar provision but with the inclusion of an additional ground, namely where the director is absent for more than six consecutive months without permission of the directors from meetings of directors held during that period and the directors resolve that his office be vacated (see also head (5) in the text). The Companies (Tables A to F) Regulations 1985, SI 1985/805, Schedule Table A provides regulations for the management of a company limited by shares but art 81 is applied by Table C (regulations for the management of a company limited by guarantee and not having a share capital), Table D Pt III (regulations for the management of a company limited by guarantee and having a share capital), and Table E (an unlimited company having a share capital). As to the meaning of 'unlimited company' see PARA 95. As to the meanings of 'company having a share capital' and 'share capital' see PARA 1231.

3 These examples may expand upon or supplement the provision made by the model articles cited in note 2.

4 See PARA 531. Where the article declared the office of director vacated 'if he cease to hold the due qualification', it was held that the article did not apply to a case in which the qualification had never been held (*Salton v New Beeston Cycle Co* [1899] 1 Ch 775; *Dent's Case, Forbes's Case* (1873) 8 Ch App 768 at 775 per Lord Selborne LC); but it was otherwise if the words were 'if he does not acquire etc'. Where the amount of qualification is increased, an existing director does not thereby cease to hold the requisite qualification, but must obtain the larger qualification within a reasonable time: *Molineaux v London, Birmingham and Manchester Insurance Co Ltd* [1902] 2 KB 589, CA.

5 Being already a bankrupt is not becoming bankrupt: *Dawson v African Consolidated Land and Trading Co* [1898] 1 Ch 6, CA. See also note 2. As to undischarged bankrupts, persons subject to bankruptcy restrictions orders and persons subject to bankruptcy restrictions undertakings acting as directors see PARA 529.

6 A director is 'insolvent' where his creditors pass a resolution accepting a composition of their claims (*Harold Sissons & Co Ltd v Sissons* (1910) 54 Sol Jo 802), or where he makes offers of a composition to them (*James v Rockwood Colliery Co* (1912) 106 LT 128), or where there are a number of bankruptcy petitions which are withdrawn in order to give the director time to pay (*London and Counties Assets Co Ltd v Brighton Grand Concert Hall and Picture Palace Ltd* [1915] 2 KB 493, CA). See also note 2.

7 See also note 2.

8 See also PARAS 569, 598.

9 As to the meaning of 'absents himself' see *McConnell's Claim* [1901] 1 Ch 728; *Re London and Northern Bank, Mack's Claim* [1900] WN 114 (both these cases showing that the absence must be voluntary and not accidental). See also *Willsmore v Willsmore and Tibbenham Ltd* (1965) 109 Sol Jo 699 (injunction granted on balance of convenience to restrain directors from treating plaintiff as having vacated office, it being alleged that the absences of the plaintiff, who owned half the shares, were in part involuntary and in part with the informal consent of the other directors). The absence dates from the first meeting which the director fails to attend: *McConnell's Claim* [1901] 1 Ch 728; *Re London and Northern Bank, Mack's Claim* [1900] WN 114. See also note 2.

10 'Indictable offence' in such an article means an offence which is capable of being dealt with on indictment: *Hastings and Folkestone Glassworks Ltd v Kalson* [1949] 1 KB 214, [1948] 2 All ER 1013, CA.

11 As to resignation see PARA 556 et seq.

12 The imposition of an age limit used to be obligatory, in relation to public companies, under the Companies Act 1985 s 293 (repealed). However, a company which imposes age limits in its articles of association must now give effect to the Equality Act 2010 ss 13(2), 19(2)(d) (see DISCRIMINATION vol 33 (2013) PARAS 66, 72).

13 This provision is not included in any of the model articles (as to which see notes 1–2). The holding of the office of unpaid secretary is not holding another office of profit (*Iron Ship Coating Co v*

Blunt (1868) LR 3 CP 484); but the paid trusteeship of a debenture trust deed is a place of profit, although it is not, strictly speaking, held under the company (*Astley v New Tivoli Ltd* [1899] 1 Ch 151). A solicitor does not hold an office of profit (*Re Harper's Ticket Issuing and Recording Machine Ltd* [1912] WN 263), unless he has a fixed salary and certain obligations (*Re Liberator Permanent Benefit Building Society* (1894) 71 LT 406, DC). As to the secretary and manager and other officers see PARA 679 et seq.

14 *Re Bodega Co Ltd* [1904] 1 Ch 276. As to the statutory presumption validating any act by any person acting as director notwithstanding disqualification or defect in appointment see the Companies Act 2006 s 161; and PARA 520.

15 *Samuel Tak Lee v Chou Wen Hsien* [1984] 1 WLR 1202, [1985] BCLC 45, PC.

16 *Re Zinotty Properties Ltd* [1984] 3 All ER 754, [1984] 1 WLR 1249.

17 See the Companies Act 2006 s 161; and PARA 520.

18 See the Companies (Model Articles) Regulations 2008, SI 2008/3229, Sch 3 art 21 (applying to public companies only: see note 1), which provides that, at the first annual general meeting all the directors must retire from office (see Sch 3 art 21(1)); and that, at every subsequent annual general meeting, any directors who have been appointed by the directors since the last annual general meeting, or who were not appointed or re-appointed at one of the preceding two annual general meetings, must retire from office and may offer themselves for re-appointment by the members (see Sch 3 art 21(2)). As to the requirement to hold an annual general meeting see PARA 702. As to membership of a company generally see PARA 323 et seq.

Similar, but more prescriptive, provision for retirement is made by the Companies (Tables A to F) Regulations 1985, SI 1985/805, Schedule Table A arts 73–75, 80 (arts 73–75, 80 revoked, in relation to a private company limited by shares, by SI 2007/2541, affecting companies registered after 1 October 2007). The Companies (Tables A to F) Regulations 1985, SI 1985/805, Schedule Table A provides regulations for the management of a company limited by shares but arts 73–75, 80 are applied by Table C (regulations for the management of a company limited by guarantee and not having a share capital), Table D Pt III (regulations for the management of a company limited by guarantee and having a share capital), and Table E (an unlimited company having a share capital). The Companies (Tables A to F) Regulations 1985, SI 1985/805, Schedule Table A art 73 does not apply to an extraordinary meeting (*Lord Claud Hamilton's Case* (1873) 8 Ch App 548), or to signatories of the memorandum or to de facto directors (*John Morley Building Co v Barras* [1891] 2 Ch 386). As to the meaning of 'extraordinary meeting' see PARA 1983. As to a company's memorandum of association and its subscribers see PARA 97 et seq. As to the Companies (Tables A to F) Regulations 1985, SI 1985/805, Schedule Table A art 73 see also *Walker v Kenns Ltd* [1937] 1 All ER 566, CA (effect of vacation of office on service agreement providing for ipso facto determination); *Re David Moseley & Sons Ltd* [1939] Ch 719, [1939] 2 All ER 791 (article providing number 'nearest to but not exceeding one-third' inapplicable when only two directors). Under a special Act, it was held that directors had no power to retire until the first ordinary meeting: see *Re South London Fish Market Co* (1888) 39 ChD 324, CA. As to the Companies (Tables A to F) Regulations 1985, SI 1985/805, Schedule Table A art 74 see *Eyre v Milton Pty Ltd* [1936] Ch 244, CA (use of 'by lot' or 'by ballot'). The Companies (Tables A to F) Regulations 1985, SI 1985/805, Schedule Table A art 75 (if the company, at the meeting at which a director retires by rotation, does not fill the vacancy) was designed in part to avoid the position arising in *Grundt v Great Boulder Pty Gold Mines Ltd* [1948] Ch 145, [1948] 1 All ER 21 (approving *Holt v Catterall* (1931) 47 TLR 332, and disapproving *Robert Batcheller & Sons Ltd v Batcheller* [1945] Ch 169, [1945] 1 All ER 522), where provisions for automatic re-election were held to apply even though the director had in fact been refused such re-election. See also *Re Great Northern Salt and Chemical Works, ex p Kennedy* (1890) 44 ChD 472. The Companies (Tables A to F) Regulations 1985, SI 1985/805, Schedule Table A art 75 does not apply if at an adjourned meeting the place is filled: *Spencer v Kennedy* [1926] Ch 125. Nor does the article apply to signatories of the memorandum: *John Morley Building Co v Barras* [1891] 2 Ch 386. See also *Bennett Bros (Birmingham) Ltd v Lewis* (1903) 20 TLR 1, CA.

19 *Inderwick v Snell* (1850) 2 Mac & G 216. Where a company in regular meeting has resolved on the removal of directors, the court will not, in the absence of fraud, review the considerations which might have affected the passing of the resolution: *Inderwick v Snell* (1850) 2 Mac & G 216. For a case where the validity of a non-fiduciary power vested in life directors to remove other directors was upheld see *Bersel Manufacturing Co Ltd v Berry* [1968] 2 All ER 552, HL. As to the retirement and removal of directors see also PARA 555 et seq. As to the obligation of a company which has obtained admission to the official list of the UK Listing Authority to notify a Regulatory Information Service ('RIS') of board changes see PARA 517 note 7.

556. Resignation of director. Where, by the articles of association[1], a director[2] has power to resign at any time[3], his resignation takes effect independently of acceptance by the other directors or the company[4]. Where the articles of association of a company provide that the office of a director is to be vacated by that mere fact if by notice in writing to the company a director resigns office, an oral resignation, if accepted by the company, is valid[5].

1 As to a company's articles of association see PARA 227 et seq.
2 As to a company's directors generally see PARA 512 et seq.
3 Ie as allowed for under the model articles of association prescribed for the purposes of the Companies Act 2006, namely the Companies (Model Articles) Regulations 2008, SI 2008/3229, reg 2, Sch 1 art 18, reg 3, Sch 2 art 18, reg 4, Sch 3 art 22, and under the default articles prescribed for the purposes of the Companies Act 1985 ('legacy articles'), which have not been revoked and may, in their amended form, continue to be used by companies after the commencement of the Companies Act 2006, namely the Companies (Tables A to F) Regulations 1985, SI 1985/805, Schedule Table A art 81 (as to which see PARA 555 note 2). As to the model articles of association prescribed for the purposes of the Companies Act 2006, and their application generally, see PARA 227 et seq; and as to the 'legacy articles' see PARA 229.
4 *Glossop v Glossop* [1907] 2 Ch 370; *Transport Ltd v Schonberg* (1905) 21 TLR 305 (where it was also held that the other directors accepted the resignation); *Re Montrotier Asphalte Co, Perry's Case* (1876) 34 LT 716. Cf *Municipal Freehold Land Co v Pollington* (1890) 59 LJ Ch 734. Where the resignation of a director has been concealed from the shareholders, the director is not liable for statements made in the report with his name on it if he has not taken part in the concealment: see *Re National Bank of Wales Ltd* [1899] 2 Ch 629 at 667, CA, per Lindley MR.
5 *Latchford Premier Cinema Ltd v Ennion* [1931] 2 Ch 409.

557. **Removal from office; director's right to protest.** A company[1] may by ordinary resolution at a meeting[2] remove a director[3] before the expiration of his period of office[4], notwithstanding anything in any agreement between it and him[5]. Special notice is required[6] of such a resolution to remove a director, or to appoint somebody instead of a director so removed at the meeting at which he is removed[7]. On receipt of notice of an intended resolution so to remove a director[8], the company must forthwith send a copy of it to the director concerned[9]; and the director is entitled to be heard on the resolution at the meeting, whether or not he is a member of the company[10]. Where notice is given of any such intended resolution to remove a director[11], and the director concerned makes with respect to it representations in writing, not exceeding a reasonable length[12], to the company and requests their notification to members of the company, the company must, unless the representations are received by it too late for it to do so[13]:

(1) in any notice of the resolution given to members of the company, state the fact of the representations having been made[14]; and
(2) send a copy of such representations to every member of the company to whom notice of the meeting is sent, whether before or after receipt of the representations by the company[15].

If a copy of the representations is not sent as required[16] because it was received too late, or because of the company's default, the director may, without prejudice to his right to be heard orally, require that the representations be read out at the meeting[17].

Copies of the representations need not be sent out, however, nor need the representations be read out at the meeting if, on the application either of the company or of any other person who claims to be aggrieved, the court[18] is satisfied that the director's right to protest[19] is being abused[20]. The court may order the company's costs on such an application to be paid in whole or in part by the director, notwithstanding that he is not a party to the application[21].

Where directors attempt to avoid removal under the statutory provisions by failing to call a meeting and then omitting to attend a requisitioned general meeting, so as to avoid the presence of a quorum, the court will convene a meeting in exercise of its statutory powers[22].

A vacancy created by the removal of a director under the statutory powers[23], if not filled at the meeting at which he is removed, may be filled as a casual vacancy[24]; and a person appointed director in place of a person so removed is treated, for the purpose of determining the time at which he or any other director is to retire, as if he had become director on the day on which the person in whose place he is appointed was last appointed a director[25].

The administrator[26] of a company has power to remove any director of the company and to appoint any person to be a director of it, whether to fill a vacancy or otherwise[27].

1 As to the meaning of 'company' under the Companies Acts see PARA 21; and as to the meaning of the 'Companies Acts' see PARA 13.

2 As to resolutions of the company see PARA 689 et seq. As to the meaning of 'ordinary resolution' see PARA 685.

3 As to the meaning of 'director' under the Companies Acts see PARA 512.

4 As to the appointment of directors see PARA 518 et seq.

5 Companies Act 2006 s 168(1). A resolution under s 168 removing a director before the expiration of his period of office may not be passed as a written resolution: see s 288(2); and PARA 695. In addition to the statutory right of removal, provision as to the termination of a director's appointment may be made in the company's articles of association: see PARA 555.

By a suitable loading of voting rights in favour of a director threatened with removal, the statutory provisions governing removal may be effectively nullified: *Bushell v Faith* [1970] AC 1099, [1970] 1 All ER 53, HL. Before 1948, it was impossible to remove directors who had been appointed for a definite period, unless the original articles, or the articles as altered by special resolution, gave power to do so (*Re Imperial Hydropathic Hotel Co, Blackpool v Hampson* (1882) 23 ChD 1, CA); nor could they resign (*Re South London Fish Market Co* (1888) 39 ChD 324, CA); but an alteration of the articles made in good faith for the benefit of the company which enabled a permanent director to be removed was (and still would be) valid (*Shuttleworth v Cox Bros & Co (Maidenhead) Ltd* [1927] 2 KB 9, CA; and see *Southern Foundries (1926) Ltd v Shirlaw* [1940] AC 701, [1940] 2 All ER 445, HL). The court would not have enforced an agreement that a director should be irremovable; and, if the company had in general meeting resolved that a director must retire, the court would not have compelled it to allow him to act (*Bainbridge v Smith* (1889) 41 ChD 462, CA; *Harben v Phillips* (1883) 23 ChD 14, CA; *Browne v La Trinidad* (1887) 37 ChD 1, CA), even if there had been irregularities of procedure, provided that the final result was not in doubt (*Bentley-Stevens v Jones* [1974] 2 All ER 653, [1974] 1 WLR 638; cf *Hall v British Essence Co Ltd* (1946) 62 TLR 542). See also the text and note 22. As to a company's articles of association generally see PARA 227 et seq.

The provision made by the Companies Act 2006 s 168 is not to be taken as depriving a person removed under it of compensation or damages payable to him in respect of the termination of his appointment as director (or of any appointment terminating with that as director), or as derogating from any power to remove a director that may exist apart from s 168: s 168(5). A director appointed for a fixed term who was removed from office before the termination of his period of office under a power introduced by a change of the articles after his appointment was held in *Southern Foundries (1926) Ltd v Shirlaw* [1940] AC 701, [1940] 2 All ER 445, HL to be entitled to damages for breach of contract. Exactly similar principles would be applicable to removal under the Companies Act 2006 s 168. Conditions of appointment of a director may, however, authorise his removal without the giving of reasonable notice: see *Read v Astoria Garage (Streatham) Ltd* [1952] Ch 637, [1952] 2 All ER 292, CA; and PARA 578. While a company may have a statutory right conferred on it by the Companies Act 2006 to remove a director, exercise of that right may result, in an appropriate case, in the dismissed director petitioning for relief on the grounds that his removal from office amounted to conduct unfairly prejudicial to his interests as a member: see PARA 661.

6 As to the special notice required see PARA 689.

7 Companies Act 2006 s 168(2). See also note 5.

8 Ie an intended resolution so to remove a director under the Companies Act 2006 s 168 (see the text and notes 1–7): see s 169(1). As to the service of documents on a company generally see PARA 743 et seq.

9 Companies Act 2006 s 169(1). As to the provision made for the sending or supplying of documents or information to or from a company (the 'company communications provisions') see PARA 750 et seq.

10 Companies Act 2006 s 169(2). As to the meaning of 'member of a company' see PARA 323. There is no necessity for a director to be a shareholder: see PARA 525 et seq. Neither the model articles of association prescribed for the purposes of the Companies Act 2006 (ie the Companies (Model Articles) Regulations 2008, SI 2008/3229: see PARA 227 et seq) nor the default articles prescribed

for the purposes of the Companies Act 1985 ('legacy articles') (ie the Companies (Tables A to F) Regulations 1985, SI 1985/805, Schedule: see PARA 229) contain such a requirement, but they do provide that a director, whether or not he is not a member, is entitled to attend and speak at any general meeting: see the Companies (Model Articles) Regulations 2008, SI 2008/3229, Sch 1 art 40, Sch 2 art 26, Sch 3 art 32, the Companies (Tables A to F) Regulations 1985, SI 1985/805, Schedule Table A art 44; and see PARA 717. As to shareholders and membership of companies generally see PARA 323 et seq.

11 Ie under the Companies Act 2006 s 168 (see the text and notes 1–7): see s 169(3).

12 Presumably 1,000 words would be reasonable in a normal case: cf the Companies Act 2006 s 314(1) (cited in PARA 714).

13 Companies Act 2006 s 169(3).

14 Companies Act 2006 s 169(3)(a).

15 Companies Act 2006 s 169(3)(b).

16 Ie as required by the Companies Act 2006 s 169(3) (see the text and notes 11–15): see s 169(4).

17 Companies Act 2006 s 169(4).

18 As to the meaning of 'the court' see PARA 160 note 12.

19 Ie the rights conferred by the Companies Act 2006 s 169 (see the text and notes 8–17): see s 169(5).

20 Companies Act 2006 s 169(5). In relation to an application for an order under s 169(5), the claimant must notify the director concerned of the application: CPR PD 49A—*Applications under the Companies Acts and Related Legislation* para 8. As to the procedure that applies to applications etc made under companies legislation generally see PARA 306.

21 Companies Act 2006 s 169(6).

22 *Re Whitchurch Insurance Consultants Ltd* [1993] BCLC 1359, [1994] BCC 51; *Re Opera Photographic Ltd* [1989] 1 WLR 634, [1989] BCLC 763; *Re El Sombrero Ltd* [1958] Ch 900, [1958] 3 All ER 1. However, the court will not convene a meeting where to do so would override class rights: *Harman v BML Group Ltd* [1994] 1 WLR 893, [1994] 2 BCLC 674, CA (class rights designed to protect a member from removal as director). Nor will a meeting be convened to resolve a deadlock where a potential deadlock was a matter which must be taken to have been agreed on with the consent and for the protection of each of the parties: *Ross v Telford* [1998] 1 BCLC 82, CA; *Alvona Developments Ltd v Manhattan Loft Corporation (AC) Ltd* [2005] EWHC 1567 (Ch), [2005] All ER (D) 252 (Jul), [2006] BCC 119. As to the court's power to convene meetings see PARA 711. As to the quorum required for a meeting of directors see PARA 569.

23 Ie under the Companies Act 2006 s 168 (see the text and notes 1–7): see s 168(3).

24 Companies Act 2006 s 168(3). See also note 5. As to casual vacancies see PARA 521.

25 Companies Act 2006 s 168(4). See also note 5.

26 As to administrators see COMPANY AND PARTNERSHIP INSOLVENCY vol 16 (2011) PARA 158 et seq.

27 See the Insolvency Act 1986 Sch B1 para 61 (added by the Enterprise Act 2002 Sch 16). See also COMPANY AND PARTNERSHIP INSOLVENCY vol 16 (2011) PARA 260; COMPANY AND PARTNERSHIP INSOLVENCY vol 17 (2011) PARA 1246.

(iii) Remuneration of Directors

A. DIRECTORS' REMUNERATION: IN GENERAL

558. Whether directors have right to remuneration. In the absence of provision in a company's constitution[1] providing for their being paid for their services, a company's directors[2] are not entitled to be paid any remuneration[3], nor may they recover anything on a quantum meruit basis[4]. A person whose appointment as a director turns out to be a nullity may, however, recover on a quantum meruit for services rendered and accepted after the date of his purported appointment[5]. Where a company's articles of association[6] provide that the remuneration of a managing director is to be determined by the board of directors, and where no such determination is made, a managing director who claims remuneration on a quantum meruit basis will be unsuccessful[7]. The right to remuneration is based on an inference of law imposed on the parties where work has been done or goods have been delivered under what purports to be a binding contract, but is not so in fact[8]. Provided that there has been a genuine exercise of the company's power to award remuneration, the court will be reluctant to hold that the payments have been improper, but payments made where no services have in fact been rendered cannot properly be classified as remuneration[9]. Sums improperly received as remuneration may be recovered[10]. As the remuneration of a director is a payment for services rendered, the fact that a director holds his qualification shares as a trustee does not make him accountable for this remuneration to the beneficiary[11], unless the opportunity to gain that remuneration was gained as a result of a discretion vested in the director as a trustee[12]. Even if that opportunity was so gained, the terms of the trust instrument may render the trustees not accountable for their remuneration as directors[13].

The right to remuneration may be waived[14]; but a mere promise by the directors to forgo their remuneration, even if made in open meeting, is not enforceable[15]. Where there is an agreement not to claim remuneration which is supported by consideration, the agreement may be enforced by any party to it and would bar any claim by a director to remuneration[16]. Breach of an understanding between shareholders in a quasi-partnership that remuneration would not be paid to the directors constitutes grounds for a petition alleging unfairly prejudicial conduct[17].

A company owning shares in a second company, which are transferred to one of its own directors in order to qualify him as director of the second company to represent the interests of the first company, is not entitled to claim from the director his remuneration as director of the second company[18].

1 As to the meaning of references to a company's constitution for the purposes of the Companies Act 2006 Pt 10 (ss 154–259) (see PARA 512 et seq) see PARA 580 note 4.

2 As to a company's directors generally see PARA 512 et seq.

3 *Dunston v Imperial Gas Light Co* (1831) 3 B & Ad 125; *Young v Naval, Military and Civil Service Co-operative Society of South Africa* [1905] 1 KB 687 (where travelling and hotel expenses were disallowed); *Re French Protestant Hospital* [1951] Ch 567, [1951] 1 All ER 938 (body corporate incorporated by royal charter; improper for directors to alter byelaws to enable payment to be made to them where constitution did not give right to remuneration). See *York and North Midland Rly Co v Hudson* (1853) 16 Beav 485; but see also *Marmor Ltd v Alexander* 1908 SC 78, Ct of Sess; *Re Whitehall Court Ltd* (1887) 3 TLR 402; *Re Liverpool Household Stores Association* (1890) 59 LJ Ch 616; *Kerr v Marine Products Ltd* (1928) 44 TLR 292 (where the remuneration was under the articles to be determined by the company; and, no remuneration having been fixed, it was held that the directors were not entitled to pay a salary to a man appointed as overseas director under an article empowering the directors to appoint officers abroad and to fix their salary). Remuneration need not take the form of direct payments constituting a regular wage, salary cheque or credit but may take the form of payments made to third parties or commissions, fees or bonuses: *Currencies Direct v Ellis* [2002] EWCA Civ 779, [2002] 2 BCLC 482. As to provision that may be made in a company's constitution for the remuneration of directors to be fixed see PARA 559.

4 *Hutton v West Cork Rly Co* (1883) 23 ChD 654 at 671, CA, per Bowen LJ; *Re George Newman & Co* [1895] 1 Ch 674, CA; *Re Bodega Co Ltd* [1904] 1 Ch 276 (where a director continued to act as such after his office was vacated); *Re Consolidated Nickel Mines Ltd* [1914] 1 Ch 883 (where directors failed to convene the annual meeting at which they would have vacated office and they were held not entitled to remuneration after the date on which it should have been convened). See also *Guinness plc v Saunders* [1990] 2 AC 663, [1990] 1 All ER 652, HL (in the absence of a binding contract, the appellant-director was not entitled to claim reasonable remuneration on a quantum meruit based on an implied contract). As to quantum meruit see RESTITUTION vol 88 (2012) PARAS 407, 513 et seq.

5 *Craven-Ellis v Canons Ltd* [1936] 2 KB 403, [1936] 2 All ER 1066, CA. Cf *Brown and Green Ltd v Hays* (1920) 36 TLR 330.

6 As to a company's articles of association generally see PARA 227 et seq.

7 *Re Richmond Gate Property Co Ltd* [1964] 3 All ER 936, [1965] 1 WLR 335 (where there was a valid contract and no room for an implied contract or a contract imposed by law; and it appears from the judgment that there was an understanding that no remuneration should be paid to the

managing director until the company got on its feet, which it never did), distinguishing *Craven-Ellis v Canons Ltd* [1936] 2 KB 403, [1936] 2 All ER 1066, CA.

8 *Craven-Ellis v Canons Ltd* [1936] 2 KB 403 at 410, [1936] 2 All ER 1066 at 1072, CA, per Greer LJ.

9 *Re Halt Garage (1964) Ltd* [1982] 3 All ER 1016.

10 *Re George Newman & Co* [1895] 1 Ch 674, CA; *Re Bodega Co Ltd* [1904] 1 Ch 276; *Re Oxford Benefit Building and Investment Society* (1886) 35 ChD 502; *Brown and Green Ltd v Hays* (1920) 36 TLR 330; *Re Halt Garage (1964) Ltd* [1982] 3 All ER 1016 (sums paid to wife of main shareholder who took no part in the business recoverable). They will be ordered jointly and severally to repay with interest as on a breach of trust: *Re Oxford Benefit Building and Investment Society* (1886) 35 ChD 502; *Leeds Estate Building and Investment Co v Shepherd* (1887) 36 ChD 787 (where remuneration was payable only if a dividend had been paid). Cf *Re Whitehall Court Ltd* (1887) 56 LT 280 at 281 per Kay J. As to recovery, in a winding up, by misfeasance proceedings see COMPANY AND PARTNERSHIP INSOLVENCY vol 17 (2011) PARA 646 et seq.

11 *Re Dover Coalfield Extension Ltd* [1908] 1 Ch 65, CA; explained, and dictum of Warrington J (as reported at first instance in [1907] 2 Ch 76 at 83) criticised, in *Re Gee, Wood v Staples* [1948] Ch 284, [1948] 1 All ER 498. See also *Re Lewis, Lewis v Lewis* (1910) 103 LT 495.

12 *Re Macadam, Dallow and Moscrop v Codd* [1946] Ch 73, [1945] 2 All ER 664. See also *Williams v Barton* [1927] 2 Ch 9.

13 *Re Llewellin's Will Trusts, Griffiths v Wilcox* [1949] Ch 225, [1949] 1 All ER 487.

14 *Re Arigna Iron Mining Co* (1853) 1 Eq Rep 269.

15 *Lambert v Northern Railway of Buenos Ayres Co Ltd* (1869) 18 WR 180 (no evidence that shares had been purchased on the strength of the promise).

16 *West Yorkshire Darracq Agency v Coleridge* [1911] 2 KB 326 (agreement to which liquidator representing the company was party; consideration found in mutual forbearance to sue); *Re William Porter & Co Ltd* [1937] 2 All ER 361 (resolution of directors forgoing fees intended to be acted on by company).

17 *Fisher v Cadman* [2005] EWHC 377 (Ch), [2006] 1 BCLC 499. As to the protection of a company's members against unfair prejudice see PARA 657 et seq.

18 *Re Dover Coalfield Extension Ltd* [1908] 1 Ch 65, CA. Cf *Re Macadam, Dallow v Codd* [1946] Ch 73, [1945] 2 All ER 664. See also PARA 596.

559. How company directors' remuneration may be fixed. The remuneration of directors of a quoted company must be approved by resolution of the members of that company[1]. Subject to that, the remuneration of a company's directors[2] may be fixed by the company's articles of association[3] or the articles may provide that the remuneration is to be fixed by the company in some manner[4]. If fixed by the articles, it is subject to alteration by special resolution[5]. If dependent on a resolution of the company, it may be altered and the company may by ordinary resolution discriminate between the directors as to the amount of their remuneration[6]. If, under the company's articles, remuneration for the directors must be authorised by the company, and there is no such authorisation, any payments made to the directors are void and not merely voidable[7].

When a share qualification is required, the date when remuneration commences depends on whether the director was empowered to act before acquiring the qualification[8]. When once fixed by authorisation, the remuneration runs from that time, unless the resolution is otherwise expressed; a reference in the subsequent balance sheet to a sum charged from an earlier date will not bind the company[9]. The fact that the duties of directors are diminished as the result of a sale of the undertaking and assets of the company does not disentitle them from receiving the same remuneration as before[10].

Where articles provide that the board of directors may fix the remuneration of the directors, and may in addition grant special remuneration to any director who serves on any committee or who devotes special attention to the business of the company or who otherwise performs special services, it is only the board as a whole which can fix or grant the remuneration; and this is so even where there is an article which defines the board as the directors of the company for the time being (or a quorum of such directors assembled at a meeting of directors duly convened) or any committee authorised by the board to act on its behalf[11].

The UK Corporate Governance Code sets out as a main principle that there should be a formal and transparent procedure for developing policy on executive remuneration and for fixing the remuneration packages of individual directors and that no director should be involved in deciding his own remuneration[12]. It also states as a main principle that executive directors' remuneration should be designed to promote the long-term success of the company and that performance-related elements should be transparent, stretching and rigorously applied[13].

1 See the Companies Act 2006 s 226B; and PARA 604.

2 As to a company's directors generally see PARA 512 et seq.

3 The company cannot refuse to pay on the ground that the fees stated in the articles are excessive: *Re Anglo-Greek Steam Co* (1866) LR 2 Eq 1. See also *Re George Newman & Co* [1895] 1 Ch 674, CA (where all the shareholders agreed, but not at a meeting). The articles may be looked at to see the terms of the contract of service, though not forming the actual contract: *Re Peruvian Guano Co, ex p Kemp* [1894] 3 Ch 690 at 701 per Wright J. See also PARA 244. As to a company's articles of association generally see PARA 227 et seq. As to model articles of association prescribed for the purposes of the Companies Act 2006, and their application generally, see PARA 227 et seq. Different versions of model articles have been so prescribed for use by private companies limited by shares (see the Companies (Model Articles) Regulations 2008, SI 2008/3229, reg 2, Sch 1), private companies limited by guarantee (see reg 3, Sch 2), and public companies (see reg 4, Sch 3). As to the meanings of 'company limited by guarantee', 'company limited by shares', 'limited company', 'private company' and 'public company' see PARA 95. The default articles prescribed for the purposes of the Companies Act 1985 ('legacy articles'), ie the Companies (Tables A to F) Regulations 1985, SI 1985/805, have not been revoked and may, in their amended form, continue to be used by companies after the commencement of the Companies Act 2006: see PARA 229.

4 The Companies (Model Articles) Regulations 2008, SI 2008/3229, provide that directors may undertake any services for the company that the directors decide (see Sch 1 art 19(1), Sch 2 art 19(1), Sch 3 art 23(1)); and that directors are entitled to such remuneration as the directors determine both for their services to the company as directors, and for any other service which they undertake for the company (see Sch 1 art 19(2), Sch 2 art 19(2), Sch 3 art 23(2)). Unless the directors decide otherwise, directors are not accountable to the company for any remuneration which they receive as directors or other officers or employees of the company's subsidiaries or of any other body corporate in which the company is interested: see Sch 1 art 19(5), Sch 2 art 19(5), Sch 3 art 23(5).

The Companies (Tables A to F) Regulations 1985, SI 1985/805, Schedule Table A art 82 provides merely that the directors are entitled to such remuneration as the company may by ordinary resolution determine. As to the meaning of 'ordinary resolution' see PARA 685. The Companies (Tables A to F) Regulations 1985, SI 1985/805, Schedule Table A provides regulations for the management of a company limited by shares but art 82 is applied by Table C (regulations for the management of a company limited by guarantee and not having a share capital), Table D Pt III (regulations for the management of a company limited by guarantee and having a share capital), and Table E (an unlimited company having a share capital). As to the meaning of 'unlimited company' see PARA 95. As to the meanings of 'company having a share capital' and 'share capital' see PARA 1231.

5 *Boschoek Pty Co Ltd v Fuke* [1906] 1 Ch 148. As to the meaning of 'special resolution' see PARA 686.

6 *Foster v Foster* [1916] 1 Ch 532.

7 *Clark v Cutland* [2003] EWCA Civ 810, [2003] 4 All ER 733, [2004] 1 WLR 783; *Guinness plc v Saunders* [1990] 2 AC 663, [1990] 1 All ER 652, HL. If the shareholders are asked to sanction any extra remuneration, the notice of the meeting must point out the matter very clearly to them: *Normandy v Ind, Coope & Co Ltd* [1908] 1 Ch 84. A statement in a balance sheet of remuneration paid is not sufficient ratification: *Re London Gigantic Wheel Co Ltd* (1908) 24 TLR 618, CA. See also *Baillie v Oriental Telephone and Electric Co Ltd* [1915] 1 Ch 503, CA. The absence of a formal resolution for approval will not, however, be fatal, if the shareholders have applied their minds to the question: *Re Duomatic Ltd* [1969] 2 Ch 365, [1969] 1 All ER 161, applying *Parker & Cooper Ltd v Reading* [1926] Ch 975. See also PARA 738.

As to special remuneration and expenses etc see PARA 562.

8 *Re International Cable Co Ltd, ex p Official Liquidator* (1892) 66 LT 253; *Salton v New Beeston Cycle Co* [1899] 1 Ch 775; *Ex p European Central Rly Co, Walford's Case* (1869) 20 LT 74.
9 *Re London Gigantic Wheel Co Ltd* (1908) 24 TLR 618, CA.
10 *Re Consolidated Nickel Mines Ltd* [1914] 1 Ch 883.
11 *Guinness plc v Saunders* [1990] 2 AC 663, [1990] 1 All ER 652, HL. See also *Currencies Direct Ltd v Ellis* [2002] EWCA Civ 779, [2002] 2 BCLC 482 (no requirement for a specific agreement as to amount or form of remuneration). As to the quorum required for a meeting of directors see PARA 569.
12 See the UK Corporate Governance Code (Financial Reporting Council, September 2014) Section D.2.
13 See the UK Corporate Governance Code (Financial Reporting Council, September 2014) Section D.1.

560. How director's remuneration is payable. A company's articles of association[1] may make provision as to how a director's[2] remuneration is payable[3].

Unless otherwise stated, the remuneration is payable although no profits are made[4]. A fixed remuneration may be sued for, or proved for in a winding up, although there is no resolution of the board that it should be paid[5]. A statement in a balance sheet signed by the directors that a sum is due to those directors as remuneration is not effective as an acknowledgment[6] so as to prevent a claim in respect of that remuneration being barred by lapse of time[7].

Subject to any contrary express agreement of the parties, salary payable to a director is subject to apportionment, so that service for less than a whole year will entitle a director to a proportionate part[8]; it is apportionable if the remuneration is payable 'at the rate of' a fixed sum per annum[9].

Directors who are remunerated by a percentage of the net profits[10] or by commission on the sum available for distribution[11] are entitled to compute their remuneration on the profits before corporation tax is deducted[12].

Where the remuneration of the directors is a lump sum to be divided as they think fit, no director may sue for remuneration until a division has taken place[13], unless it is in addition provided that in default of agreement the remuneration should be equally divided, and there has been no agreement[14]. A director cannot obtain a mandatory injunction to compel the remaining directors to fix his remuneration[15]. Where directors are given a discretion to determine the time for payment of a director's remuneration, no claim will lie until they have so determined[16].

A special resolution of the company[17] altering directors' remuneration cannot alter the contractual rights of the directors[18] as regards remuneration actually earned.

1 As to a company's articles of association generally see PARA 227 et seq. As to model articles of association prescribed for the purposes of the Companies Act 2006, and their application generally, see PARA 227 et seq. Different versions of model articles have been so prescribed for use by private companies limited by shares (see the Companies (Model Articles) Regulations 2008, SI 2008/3229, reg 2, Sch 1), private companies limited by guarantee (see reg 3, Sch 2), and public companies (see reg 4, Sch 3). As to the meanings of 'company limited by guarantee', 'company limited by shares', 'limited company', 'private company' and 'public company' see PARA 95. The default articles prescribed for the purposes of the Companies Act 1985 ('legacy articles'), ie the Companies (Tables A to F) Regulations 1985, SI 1985/805, have not been revoked and may, in their amended form, continue to be used by companies after the commencement of the Companies Act 2006: see PARA 229.
2 As to a company's directors generally see PARA 512 et seq.
3 The Companies (Model Articles) Regulations 2008, SI 2008/3229, provide that, subject to the articles, a director's remuneration may take any form (see Sch 1 art 19(3), Sch 2 art 19(3), Sch 3 art 23(3)); and that, unless the directors decide otherwise, directors' remuneration accrues from day to day (see Sch 1 art 19(4), Sch 2 art 19(4), Sch 3 art 23(4)). The Companies (Tables A to F) Regulations 1985, SI 1985/805, Schedule Table A art 82 merely provides that, unless the ordinary resolution which determines directors' remuneration (as to which see PARA 559 note 4) provides otherwise, such remuneration will be deemed to accrue from day to day. As to the meaning of

'ordinary resolution' see PARA 685. The Companies (Tables A to F) Regulations 1985, SI 1985/805, Schedule Table A provides regulations for the management of a company limited by shares but art 82 is applied by Table C (regulations for the management of a company limited by guarantee and not having a share capital), Table D Pt III (regulations for the management of a company limited by guarantee and having a share capital), and Table E (an unlimited company having a share capital). As to the meaning of 'unlimited company' see PARA 95. As to the meanings of 'company having a share capital' and 'share capital' see PARA 1231.

As to how company directors' remuneration may be fixed see PARA 559.

4 *Re Lundy Granite Co Ltd, Lewis's Case* (1872) 26 LT 673. There is no general presumption to the contrary: *Nell v Atlanta Gold and Silver Consolidated Mines* (1895) 11 TLR 407, CA.

5 *Re New British Iron Co, ex p Beckwith* [1898] 1 Ch 324; *Nell v Atlanta Gold and Silver Consolidated Mines* (1895) 11 TLR 407, CA. As to proof in winding up see PARA 561; and COMPANY AND PARTNERSHIP INSOLVENCY vol 17 (2011) PARA 707 et seq.

6 Ie within the meaning of the Limitation Act 1980 s 30 (see LIMITATION PERIODS vol 68 (2008) PARA 1185).

7 *Re Coliseum (Barrow) Ltd* [1930] 2 Ch 44; *Re Transplanters (Holding Co) Ltd* [1958] 2 All ER 711, [1958] 1 WLR 822. As to the limitation period see the Limitation Act 1980 ss 5, 8; and LIMITATION PERIODS vol 68 (2008) PARA 956 et seq.

8 *Item Software (UK) Ltd v Fassihi* [2004] EWCA Civ 1244, [2005] 2 BCLC 91; and see the Companies (Tables A to F) Regulations 1985, SI 1985/805, Schedule Table A art 82; and the Companies (Model Articles) Regulations 2008, SI 2008/3229, Sch 1 art 19(3), (4), Sch 2 art 19(3), (4), Sch 3 art 23(3), (4) (cited in note 3).

Remuneration at a fixed sum per annum or for each year had been held not to be apportionable: see *McConnell's Claim* [1901] 1 Ch 728; *Inman v Ackroyd & Best Ltd* [1901] 1 KB 613, CA; *Salton v New Beeston Cycle Co* [1899] 1 Ch 775; and see the text and note 9. In *Moriarty v Regent's Garage Co* [1921] 1 KB 423, these decisions were strongly criticised and stated to be good law on the basis only that the payment to the directors in the two last-named cases was in the form of a lump sum, and that until a decision as to the division of the lump sum had been made no claim would lie, and it was held that the remuneration of a director was apportionable under the Apportionment Act 1870. Although *Moriarty v Regent's Garage Co* [1921] 1 KB 423 was overruled in the Court of Appeal (see [1921] 2 KB 766), the appeal was not decided on the applicability of the Apportionment Act 1870, the court holding that this question could not then be raised as it had not been raised in the county court. Cf *Boschoek Pty Co Ltd v Fuke* [1906] 1 Ch 148; *Re Central De Kaap Gold Mines* (1899) 69 LJ Ch 18; *Kempf v Offin River Gold Estates Ltd* (1908) Times, 10 April; *Swabey v Port Darwin Gold Mining Co* (1889) 1 Meg 385, CA; *Re Shaws, Bryant & Co* (1901) 45 Sol Jo 580. A term that the remuneration is apportionable was implied in *Swabey v Port Darwin Gold Mining Co*; but cf *Inman v Ackroyd & Best Ltd* [1901] 1 KB 613, CA; *Moriarty v Regent's Garage Co* [1921] 1 KB 423. Where it is provided that the directors are entitled to a share in profits by way of additional remuneration and that in default of agreement it should be divided equally, then, in the event of there being no agreement, a director who ceased to hold office during the year is entitled to a proportionate part: *Diamond v English Sewing Cotton Co Ltd* [1922] WN 237, CA.

9 *Gilman v Gülcher Electric Light Co* (1886) 3 TLR 133, CA; *Re AM Wood's Ships' Woodite Protection Co* (1890) 62 LT 760; *Swabey v Port Darwin Gold Mining Co* (1889) 1 Meg 385, CA. See also PERSONAL AND OCCUPATIONAL PENSIONS vol 80 (2013) PARA 201.

10 *Johnston v Chestergate Hat Manufacturing Co Ltd* [1915] 2 Ch 338.

11 *Edwards v Saunton Hotel Co Ltd* [1943] 1 All ER 176.

12 As to corporation tax see INCOME TAXATION vol 58A (2014) PARA 1018 et seq.

13 *Morrell v Oxford Portland Cement Co Ltd* (1910) 26 TLR 682; *Joseph v Sonora (Mexico) Land and Timber Co Ltd* (1918) 34 TLR 220. Continuing directors with power to divide remuneration among the directors may thus entirely deprive a retiring director of remuneration: *Gilman v Gülcher Electric Light Co* (1886) 3 TLR 133, CA. See also *Moriarty v Regent's Garage Co* [1921] 1 KB 423 (on appeal [1921] 2 KB 766, CA).

14 *Diamond v English Sewing Cotton Co Ltd* [1922] WN 237, CA (where the remuneration sued for was additional remuneration by way of a share in profits at a fixed rate).

15 *Dashwood v Cornish* (1897) 13 TLR 337, CA. As to mandatory orders see JUDICIAL REVIEW vol 61 (2010) PARA 703 et seq.

16 *Caridad Copper Mining Co v Swallow* [1902] 2 KB 44, CA.

17 As to the meaning of 'special resolution' see PARA 686.

18 *Swabey v Port Darwin Gold Mining Co* (1889) 1 Meg 385, CA.

561. Proof of directors' remuneration in winding up; execution. Remuneration is not due to the director in his character of a member of the company[1]. It may, therefore, be proved as a debt on winding up in competition with ordinary creditors[2]; and this will be in addition to remuneration earned in any other capacity, such as receiver and manager in a debenture holders' claim[3].

Directors who are paid by a percentage of the amount paid by way of dividend may prove for this in the winding up after creditors have been paid, if it was not unreasonable at the time to propose such dividend[4]. If, however, they are paid by a percentage on 'net profits', this refers to the company as a going concern and does not entitle them to a proportion of its assets on a sale of the undertaking[5]; and similarly, where the only contract between the director and the company is contained in the articles, his employment ceases automatically upon the winding up of the company[6].

A receiver by way of equitable execution will not be appointed in respect of directors' fees[7].

1 As to the director's right to remuneration see PARA 558 et seq. As to membership of a company see PARA 323 et seq.

2 *Re New British Iron Co, ex p Beckwith* [1898] 1 Ch 324; *Re Dale and Plant Ltd* (1889) 43 ChD 255; *Re Commercial and General Life Assurance etc Association, ex p Johnson* (1857) 27 LJ Ch 803; *Re Lundy Granite Co Ltd, Lewis's Case* (1872) 26 LT 673; *Re A1 Biscuit Co* (1899) 43 Sol Jo 657. Since it was expressly disapproved in Northern Ireland (see *Re Cinnamond Park & Co Ltd* [1930] NI 47), *Re Leicester Club and County Racecourse Co, ex p Cannon* (1885) 30 ChD 629 cannot now be regarded as good law. Remuneration which has been waived by a director cannot be recovered if the company gave consideration (such as deciding to continue its business) for the waiver: *Re William Porter & Co Ltd* [1937] 2 All ER 361. As to proof of debts in winding up generally see COMPANY AND PARTNERSHIP INSOLVENCY vol 17 (2011) PARA 707 et seq.

3 *Re South Western of Venezuela (Barquisimeto) Rly Co* [1902] 1 Ch 701. A debenture often gives power to appoint a receiver or manager on the occurrence of specified events: see PARA 1521. As to the meaning of 'debenture' see PARA 1482. As to the construction of references to receivers and managers for these purposes see PARA 1518.

4 *Re Peruvian Guano Co, ex p Kemp* [1894] 3 Ch 690; *Re Mercantile Trading Co, Stringer's Case* (1869) 4 Ch App 475.

5 *Frames v Bultfontein Mining Co* [1891] 1 Ch 140.

6 *Re TN Farrer Ltd* [1937] Ch 352, [1937] 2 All ER 505 (as employment was conditional upon the continued existence of the company, there was no compensation for loss of office on winding up).

7 *Hamilton v Brogden* [1891] WN 36. Such an appointment would probably destroy the security. Past fees not paid may be attached: *Hamilton v Brogden*. As to the appointment of a receiver by way of equitable execution see CIVIL PROCEDURE vol 12A (2015) PARA 1493 et seq.

562. Special remuneration and expenses of directors; director's pension. Apart from special provision in the company's articles of association[1], directors[2] are not entitled to claim travelling or other expenses[3]; and, where they have power to pay a co-director for extra services, the latter must prove the services and the agreement to pay for them[4]. As a matter of account the payment must not be attributed to capital expenditure[5].

Where a power of altering remuneration is reserved to the company, it may not grant a 'pension' to a managing director who retires as manager but not as director[6]. It was formerly not competent for a company which had ceased to carry on business to vote gratuitous remuneration to its officers and employees[7], but there is now an express statutory power to do so[8].

The special provisions for taxation of expenses, allowances and benefits in kind in relation to directors are discussed elsewhere in this work[9].

1 As to a company's articles of association generally see PARA 227 et seq. As to model articles of association prescribed for the purposes of the Companies Act 2006, and their application generally, see PARA 227 et seq. Different versions of model articles have been so prescribed for use by private companies limited by shares (see the Companies (Model Articles) Regulations 2008, SI 2008/3229, reg 2, Sch 1), private companies limited by guarantee (see reg 3, Sch 2), and public companies (see reg 4, Sch 3). As to the meanings of 'company limited by guarantee', 'company

limited by shares', 'limited company', 'private company' and 'public company' see PARA 95. The default articles prescribed for the purposes of the Companies Act 1985 ('legacy articles'), ie the Companies (Tables A to F) Regulations 1985, SI 1985/805, have not been revoked and may, in their amended form, continue to be used by companies after the commencement of the Companies Act 2006: see PARA 229.

2 As to a company's directors generally see PARA 512 et seq.

3 *Young v Naval, Military and Civil Service Co-operative Society of South Africa* [1905] 1 KB 687; *Marmor Ltd v Alexander* 1908 SC 78, Ct of Sess. As to the director's right to remuneration generally see PARA 558 et seq.

The Companies (Model Articles) Regulations 2008, SI 2008/3229, provide that the company may pay any reasonable expenses which the directors properly incur in connection with their attendance at meetings of directors or committees of directors, general meetings, or (except in the case of a private company limited by guarantee) separate meetings of the holders of any class of shares or (in all cases) separate meetings of the holders of debentures of the company, or otherwise in connection with the exercise of their powers and the discharge of their responsibilities in relation to the company: Sch 1 art 20, Sch 2 art 20, Sch 3 art 24. As to the meaning of 'debenture' see PARA 1482. As to shareholders generally see PARA 323 et seq. As to meetings of the company generally see PARA 701 et seq. As to meetings of directors see PARA 568 et seq. As to the extent to which directors may delegate powers, including to committees, see PARA 577.

The Companies (Tables A to F) Regulations 1985, SI 1985/805, Schedule Table A art 83 provides that directors may be paid all travelling, hotel, and other expenses properly incurred by them in connection with their attendance at meetings of directors or committees of directors or general meetings or separate meetings of the holders of any class of shares or of debentures of the company or otherwise in connection with the discharge of their duties. The Companies (Tables A to F) Regulations 1985, SI 1985/805, Schedule Table A provides regulations for the management of a company limited by shares but art 83 is applied by Table C (regulations for the management of a company limited by guarantee and not having a share capital), Table D Pt III (regulations for the management of a company limited by guarantee and having a share capital), and Table E (an unlimited company having a share capital). However, Table C modifies Table A art 83 to the extent that the words 'of any class of shares or' are omitted: see Table C art 9. As to the meaning of 'unlimited company' see PARA 95. As to the meanings of 'company having a share capital' and 'share capital' see PARA 1231.

4 *Lockhart v Moldacot Pocket Sewing Machine Co Ltd* (1889) 5 TLR 307. See also *Boschoek Pty Co Ltd v Fuke* [1906] 1 Ch 148 at 163 per Swinfen Eady J. Where a director's expense claims are made in a manner proper at the time and settled, it would be oppressive to make an order for account on the grounds that a subsequent retroactive memorandum requires such claims to be strictly documented: *Nelberg v Woking Shipping Co Ltd and Konnel Steamship Co Ltd* [1958] 2 Lloyd's Rep 560; *Guinness plc v Saunders* [1990] 2 AC 663, [1990] 1 All ER 652, HL.

5 *Ashton & Co Ltd v Honey* (1907) 23 TLR 253.

6 *Normandy v Ind, Coope & Co Ltd* [1908] 1 Ch 84. As to compensation for loss of office see PARA 621 et seq.

The Companies (Model Articles) Regulations 2008, SI 2008/3229, provide that, subject to the articles, a director's remuneration may include any arrangements in connection with the payment of a pension, allowance or gratuity, or any death, sickness or disability benefits, to or in respect of that director: see Sch 1 art 19(3), Sch 2 art 19(3), Sch 3 art 23(3).

Under the Companies (Tables A to F) Regulations 1985, SI 1985/805, Schedule Table A art 87, directors may provide benefits, whether by the payment of gratuities or pensions or by insurance or otherwise, for any director who has held but no longer holds any executive office or employment with the company or with any body corporate which is or has been a subsidiary of the company or a predecessor in business of the company or of any such subsidiary, and for any member of his family (including a spouse and a former spouse) or any person who is or was dependent on him, and may (as well before as after he ceases to hold such office or employment) contribute to any fund and pay premiums for the purchase or provision of any such benefit. Table A art 87 is applied by Table C (regulations for the management of a company limited by guarantee and not having a share capital), Table D Pt III (regulations for the management of a company limited by guarantee and having a share capital), and Table E (an unlimited company having a share capital).

7 *Stroud v Royal Aquarium and Summer and Winter Garden Society* (1903) 89 LT 243, following *Hutton v West Cork Rly Co* (1883) 23 ChD 654, CA; *Parke v Daily News Ltd* [1962] Ch 927, [1962] 2 All ER 929. Cf *Cowan v Seymour (Inspector of Taxes)* [1920] 1 KB 500, CA (where the payments were made by the shareholders).

8 See the Companies Act 2006 s 247; and PARA 586.

9 See the Income Tax (Earnings and Pensions) Act 2003; and INCOME TAXATION vol 58 (2014) PARA 730 et seq.

563. Particulars of directors' remuneration to be given in accounts, reports etc. The following information about directors' remuneration[1] must be given in notes to a company's annual accounts[2]:

(1) gains made by directors on the exercise of share options[3];
(2) benefits received or receivable by directors under long-term incentive schemes[4];
(3) payments for loss of office[5];
(4) benefits receivable, and contributions for the purpose of providing benefits, in respect of past services of a person as director or in any other capacity while director[6];
(5) consideration paid to or receivable by third parties for making available the services of a person as director or in any other capacity while director[7].

Details of advances and credits granted by a company to its directors, and of guarantees of any kind entered into by the company on behalf of its directors, also must be shown in the notes to its individual accounts[8].

The directors of a quoted company[9] must prepare a directors' remuneration report for each financial year of the company[10]. The members must by resolution approve the directors' remuneration report for the financial year[11], although no director's entitlement to remuneration is made conditional on the resolution being passed by reason only of the provision so made[12].

1 As to a company's directors generally see PARA 512 et seq. As to the directors' right to remuneration generally see PARA 558 et seq.
2 See the Companies Act 2006 s 412(1); and PARA 845. As to a company's annual accounts see PARA 788 et seq.
3 See the Companies Act 2006 s 412(2)(a); and PARA 845.
4 See the Companies Act 2006 s 412(2)(b); and PARA 845.
5 See the Companies Act 2006 s 412(2)(c); and PARA 845.
6 See the Companies Act 2006 s 412(2)(d); and PARA 845.
7 See the Companies Act 2006 s 412(2)(e); and PARA 845.
8 See the Companies Act 2006 s 413; and PARA 851.
9 As to the meaning of 'quoted company' in the Companies Act 2006 see PARA 70.
10 See the Companies Act 2006 s 420; and PARA 909 et seq.
11 See the Companies Act 2006 s 439; and PARA 934.
12 See the Companies Act 2006 s 439(5); and PARA 934. The remuneration of directors of a quoted company does, however, require the approval of the company's members under s 226B: see PARA 604.

B. DIRECTORS' SERVICE CONTRACTS

564. Directors' long-term service contracts. In relation to any provision under which the guaranteed term of a director's employment with the company of which he is a director[1], or (where he is the director of a holding company[2]) within the group consisting of that company and its subsidiaries[3], is, or may be, longer than two years[4], the company may not agree to such provision unless it has been approved[5]:

(1) by resolution[6] of the members of the company[7]; and
(2) in the case of a director of a holding company, by resolution of the members of that company[8].

1 As to the guaranteed term of a director's employment see PARA 603 note 1. As to the meaning of 'company' under the Companies Acts see PARA 21; as to the meaning of 'director' under the Companies Acts see PARA 512; and as to the meaning of the 'Companies Acts' see PARA 13.
2 As to the meaning of 'holding company' see PARA 22.

3 As to the meaning of 'subsidiary' see PARA 22.
4 See the Companies Act 2006 s 188(1); and PARA 603.
5 See the Companies Act 2006 s 188(2); and PARA 603. As to exceptions see s 188(6); and PARA 603.
6 As to resolutions and meetings of members see PARA 701 et seq. As to voting at meetings see PARA 724 et seq.
7 See the Companies Act 2006 s 188(2)(a); and PARA 603. As to the meaning of 'member of a company' see PARA 323.
8 See the Companies Act 2006 s 188(2)(b); and PARA 603.

565. Duty to keep directors' service contracts available for inspection. A company[1] must keep available for inspection[2]:

(1) a copy of every director's[3] service contract[4] with the company or with a subsidiary of the company[5]; or

(2) if the contract is not in writing, a written memorandum setting out the terms of the contract[6].

All the copies and memoranda must be kept available for inspection either at the company's registered office[7], or at a place specified in regulations[8].

The copies and memoranda must be retained by the company for at least one year from the date of termination or expiry of the contract and must be kept available for inspection during that time[9].

The company must give notice to the registrar of companies[10] of the place at which the copies and memoranda are kept available for inspection[11] and of any change in that place[12], unless they have at all times been kept at the company's registered office[13].

If default is made in complying with any of the requirements so to keep directors' service contracts etc available for inspection[14], or to keep them available in the proper place[15], or to retain them for the proper length of time[16], or if default is made for 14 days in complying with the requirement to give notice to the registrar of companies[17], an offence is committed by every officer of the company who is in default[18].

1 As to the meaning of 'company' under the Companies Acts see PARA 21; and as to the meaning of the 'Companies Acts' see PARA 13.
2 Companies Act 2006 s 228(1). See also notes 3–5. The provisions of s 1138 (duty to take precautions against falsification) do not apply to the documents required to be kept under s 228: see PARA 747.

Where the registrar changes the address of a company's registered office under the Companies Act 2006 s 1097A(7) or the Companies (Address of Registered Office) Regulations 2016, SI 2016/423 (see PARA 160), the company's duties under the Companies Act 2006 s 228 are suspended for a period of 28 days beginning on the day the address was changed: see the Companies (Address of Registered Office) Regulations 2016, SI 2016/423, reg 11; and PARA 160.
3 As to the meaning of 'director' under the Companies Acts see PARA 512. A shadow director is treated as a director for the purposes of the provisions of the Companies Act 2006 Pt 10 Ch 5 (ss 227–230) (see also PARA 566): s 230. As to the meaning of 'shadow director' see PARA 513.
4 For the purposes of the Companies Act 2006 Pt 10 (ss 154–259) (see PARA 512 et seq, 566 et seq) a director's 'service contract', in relation to a company, means a contract under which:

(1) a director of the company undertakes personally to perform services (as director or otherwise) for the company, or for a subsidiary of the company (s 227(1)(a)); or

(2) services (as director or otherwise) that a director of the company undertakes personally to perform are made available by a third party to the company, or to a subsidiary of the company (s 227(1)(b)).

The provisions of Pt 10 relating to directors' service contracts apply to the terms of a person's appointment as a director of a company (and are not restricted to contracts for the performance of services outside the scope of the ordinary duties of a director): see s 227(2). As to the meaning of 'subsidiary' see PARA 22. As to the requirement of members' approval for directors' long-term service contracts see PARA 603.

5 Companies Act 2006 s 228(1)(a). See also notes 3–4. The provisions of s 228 apply to a variation of a director's service contract as they apply to the original contract: s 228(7). As to the right of a member to inspect and request a copy of any director's service contracts etc see PARA 566.
6 Companies Act 2006 s 228(1)(b). See also notes 3–5.
7 Companies Act 2006 s 228(2)(a). See also notes 3–5. As to a company's registered office see PARA 124.
8 Companies Act 2006 s 228(2)(b). The text refers to a place specified in regulations made under s 1136 (see PARA 748): see s 228(2)(b). See also notes 3–5.
9 Companies Act 2006 s 228(3). See also notes 3–5.
10 Companies Act 2006 s 228(4). See also notes 3–5. As to the meaning of 'registrar of companies' see PARA 126 note 2. As to the delivery of documents to the registrar see PARA 136; and as to the requirements for the proper delivery of documents to the registrar see PARA 137.
11 Companies Act 2006 s 228(4)(a). See also notes 3–5.
12 Companies Act 2006 s 228(4)(b). See also notes 3–5.
13 Companies Act 2006 s 228(4). See also notes 3–5.
14 Ie in complying with the Companies Act 2006 s 228(1) (see the text and notes 1–6): see s 228(5).
15 Ie in complying with the Companies Act 2006 s 228(2) (see the text and notes 7–8): see s 228(5).
16 Ie in complying with the Companies Act 2006 s 228(3) (see the text and note 9): see s 228(5).
17 Ie in complying with the Companies Act 2006 s 228(4) (see the text and notes 10–13): see s 228(5).
18 Companies Act 2006 s 228(5). See also notes 3–5. As to the meaning of 'officer who is in default' see PARA 316. As to the meaning of 'officer' generally see PARA 679.

A person guilty of such an offence is liable on summary conviction to a fine not exceeding level 3 on the standard scale and for continued contravention to a daily default fine not exceeding one-tenth of level 3 on the standard scale: s 228(6). As to the standard scale and the powers of magistrates' courts to issue fines on summary conviction see SENTENCING vol 92 (2015) PARA 176; and as to the meaning of 'daily default fine' see PARA 1816.

566. Members' right to inspect and request copy of directors' service contracts. Every copy or memorandum that is required to be kept pursuant to a company's[1] duty to keep directors'[2] service contracts[3] available for inspection[4] must be open to inspection by any member of the company[5] without charge[6].

Any member of the company is entitled also, on request and on payment of such fee as may be prescribed[7], to be provided with a copy of any such copy or memorandum[8]. The copy must be provided within seven days after the request is received by the company[9].

If an inspection so required by a member of a company[10] is refused, or if default is made in so providing a member with such a copy or memorandum[11], an offence is committed by every officer of the company who is in default[12]. A person guilty of such an offence is liable on summary conviction to a fine not exceeding level 3 on the standard scale[13] and for continued contravention to a daily default fine[14] not exceeding one-tenth of level 3 on the standard scale[15].

In the case of any such refusal or default, the court[16] may by order compel an immediate inspection or, as the case may be, direct that the copy required be sent to the person requiring it[17].

1 As to the meaning of 'company' under the Companies Acts see PARA 21; and as to the meaning of the 'Companies Acts' see PARA 13.
2 As to the meaning of 'director' under the Companies Acts generally see PARA 512; and see PARA 565 note 3.
3 As to the meaning of a director's 'service contract', in relation to a company, for the purposes of the Companies Act 2006 Pt 10 (ss 154–259) (see PARA 512 et seq, 570 et seq) see PARA 565 note 4.
4 Ie under the Companies Act 2006 s 228 (see PARA 565): see s 229(1).
5 As to the meaning of 'member of the company' see PARA 323.
6 Companies Act 2006 s 229(1).
7 In the Companies Acts, 'prescribed' means prescribed (by order or by regulations) by the Secretary of State: Companies Act 2006 s 1167. As to the making of regulations under the Companies Act 2006 generally see ss 1288–1292. As to the Secretary of State see PARA 6. Partly in exercise of the

powers conferred by s 229(2), the Secretary of State has made the Companies (Fees for Inspection and Copying of Company Records) Regulations 2007, SI 2007/2612. See further note 8.

8 Companies Act 2006 s 229(2). For the prescribed fee see the Companies (Fees for Inspection and Copying of Company Records) Regulations 2007, SI 2007/2612, reg 4. As to the provisions made for company communications generally see PARA 750 et seq.

9 Companies Act 2006 s 229(2).

10 Ie under the Companies Act 2006 s 229(1) (see the text and notes 1–6): see s 229(3).

11 Ie in complying with the Companies Act 2006 s 229(2) (see the text and notes 7–9): see s 229(3).

12 Companies Act 2006 s 229(3). As to the meaning of 'officer who is in default' see PARA 316. As to the meaning of 'officer' generally see PARA 679.

13 As to the standard scale and the powers of magistrates' courts to issue fines on summary conviction see SENTENCING vol 92 (2015) PARA 176.

14 As to the meaning of 'daily default fine' see PARA 1816.

15 Companies Act 2006 s 229(4).

16 As to the meaning of 'the court' see PARA 160 note 12.

17 Companies Act 2006 s 229(5). As to the procedure for making claims and applications to the court under companies legislation see PARA 306. See also PARA 350 note 30.

(iv) Meetings of Directors

567. Decision-making by directors. A company's articles of association[1] usually contain provisions as to the way in which directors[2] at their meetings[3] may conduct business and make decisions, including allowance for decisions to be taken instead by way of directors' written resolutions[4]. Directors may validly act only when assembled at a board meeting[5], unless the articles otherwise provide[6], and subject to the qualification that the directors, provided they are unanimous, may determine matters within their jurisdiction by informal means[7]. The model articles of association[8] provide that any decision of the directors of a private company must be taken either by a majority decision at a meeting or by a decision taken unanimously[9]; and that decisions of the directors of a public company may be taken either at a directors' meeting, or in the form of a directors' written resolution[10]. In any case, under the articles, if the numbers of votes for and against a proposal at any directors' meeting are equal, the chairman or other director chairing the meeting has a casting vote, unless, in accordance with the articles, the chairman or other director is not to be counted as participating in the decision-making process for quorum or voting purposes[11]. Subject to the articles, the directors may make any rule which they think fit about how they take decisions, and about how such rules are to be recorded or communicated to directors[12].

At properly convened meetings of a company's directors, at which there is the prescribed quorum[13], directors may transact all business within their powers though no notice has been given to the members of the board that any special business is to be transacted[14]. They may take the items of business in such order as they think proper, and not necessarily in the order on the agenda paper[15].

If a power is given to directors by an article of association, the decision of the directors to exercise it should, it seems, be unanimous unless on the true construction of the article of association a majority decision is enough[16], as is the case under the model articles[17]. A subsequent meeting may ratify the business done at an informal meeting[18], and may ratify an unauthorised act of an agent of the company[19].

1 As to a company's articles of association generally see PARA 227 et seq. As to model articles of association prescribed for the purposes of the Companies Act 2006, and their application generally, see PARA 227 et seq. Different versions of model articles have been so prescribed for use by private companies limited by shares (see the Companies (Model Articles) Regulations 2008, SI 2008/3229, reg 2, Sch 1), private companies limited by guarantee (see reg 3, Sch 2), and public companies (see reg 4, Sch 3). As to the meanings of 'company limited by guarantee', 'company

limited by shares', 'limited company', 'private company' and 'public company' see PARA 95. The default articles prescribed for the purposes of the Companies Act 1985 ('legacy articles'), ie the Companies (Tables A to F) Regulations 1985, SI 1985/805, have not been revoked and may, in their amended form, continue to be used by companies after the commencement of the Companies Act 2006: see PARA 229.

2 As to a company's directors see PARA 512 et seq.

3 As to meetings of a company's directors see PARA 568 et seq.

4 Under the Companies (Model Articles) Regulations 2008, SI 2008/3229, a decision of the directors of a private company may be taken in accordance with Sch 1 art 8 or Sch 2 art 8, as the case may be, when all eligible directors (ie directors who would have been entitled to vote on the matter had it been proposed as a resolution at a directors' meeting) indicate to each other by any means that they share a common view on a matter: Sch 1 art 8(1), (3), Sch 2 art 8(1), (3). Such a decision may take the form of a resolution in writing, copies of which have been signed by each eligible director or to which each eligible director has otherwise indicated agreement in writing: Sch 1 art 8(2), Sch 2 art 8(2). However, a decision may not be taken in accordance with Sch 1 art 8 or Sch 2 art 8 (as the case may be) if the eligible directors would not have formed a quorum at such a meeting: Sch 1 art 8(4), Sch 2 art 8(4).

Any director of a public company may propose a directors' written resolution (Sch 3 art 17(1)); and the company secretary must propose a directors' written resolution if a director so requests (Sch 3 art 17(2)). A directors' written resolution is proposed by giving notice of the proposed resolution to the directors: Sch 3 art 17(3). Such notice must indicate the proposed resolution and the time by which it is proposed that the directors should adopt it (Sch 3 art 17(4)); and it must be given in writing to each director (Sch 3 art 17(5)). Any decision which a person giving notice of a proposed directors' written resolution takes regarding the process of adopting that resolution must be taken reasonably in good faith: Sch 3 art 17(6). A proposed directors' written resolution is adopted when all the directors who would have been entitled to vote on the resolution at a directors' meeting have signed one or more copies of it, provided that those directors would have formed a quorum at such a meeting: Sch 3 art 18(1). It is immaterial whether any director signs the resolution before or after the time by which the notice proposed that it should be adopted: Sch 3 art 18(2). Once a directors' written resolution has been adopted, it must be treated as if it had been a decision taken at a directors' meeting in accordance with the articles: Sch 3 art 18(3). As to the company secretary see PARA 669 et seq; and as to the requirement to keep records of resolutions etc see PARA 570.

Under the Companies (Tables A to F) Regulations 1985, SI 1985/805, Schedule Table A art 93, a resolution in writing signed by all the directors entitled to receive notice of a meeting of directors or of a committee of directors will be as valid and effectual as if it has been passed at a meeting of directors or (as the case may be) a committee of directors duly convened and held and may consist of several documents in the like form each signed by one or more directors; but a resolution signed by an alternate director need not also be signed by his appointor and, if it is signed by a director who has appointed an alternate director, it need not be signed by the alternate director in that capacity. As to the extent to which directors may delegate powers, including to committees, see PARA 577. The written resolution procedure is intended to facilitate the transaction of business but not to make fundamental changes to quorum requirements; hence a written resolution, passed in accordance with art 93 but signed by only one director, where the quorum fixed under art 89 (see PARA 569) for the transaction of any business is two directors, is invalid notwithstanding that the sole co-director is absent from the United Kingdom and not entitled to notice of a directors' meeting by virtue of art 88 (see note 8): *Hood Sailmakers Ltd v Axford* [1996] 4 All ER 830, [1997] 1 WLR 625, which was decided under equivalent provisions of the Companies Act 1948 Sch 1, Table A (see PARA 14). As to the meaning of 'United Kingdom' see PARA 1 note 5. Under the Companies (Tables A to F) Regulations 1985, SI 1985/805, Schedule Table A art 96, the company may by ordinary resolution suspend or relax to any extent, either generally or in respect of any particular matter, any provision of the articles prohibiting a director from voting at a meeting of directors or of a committee of directors; and Table A art 98 provides that, if a question arises at a meeting of directors or of a committee of directors as to the right of a director to vote, the question may, before the conclusion of the meeting, be referred to the chairman of the meeting and his ruling in relation to any director other than himself is final and conclusive. Schedule Table A art 97 provides that where proposals are under consideration concerning the appointment of two or more directors to offices or employments with the company or any body corporate in which the company is interested, the proposals may be divided and considered in relation to each director separately and (provided he is not for another reason precluded from voting) each of the directors concerned is entitled to vote and be counted in the quorum in respect of each resolution except that concerning his own appointment. The Companies (Tables A to F) Regulations 1985, SI 1985/805, Schedule Table A arts 93, 96–98 are applied by Table C, Table D Pt III, and Table E.

5 *Re Athenaeum Life Assurance Society, ex p Eagle Insurance Co* (1858) 4 K & J 549 at 558–559 per Page Wood V-C; *D'Arcy v Tamar, Kit Hill and Callington Rly Co* (1867) LR 2 Exch 158;

Bosanquet v Shortridge (1850) 4 Exch 699; *Re Haycraft Gold Reduction and Mining Co* [1900] 2 Ch 230. Cf *Re Liverpool Household Stores Association Ltd* (1890) 59 LJ Ch 616.

6 See the text and notes 8–12.

7 *Runciman v Walter Runciman plc* [1992] BCLC 1084 at 1092, [1993] BCC 223 at 230 per Simon Brown J; *Municipal Mutual Insurance Ltd v Harrop* [1998] 2 BCLC 540 at 551 per Rimer J; *Re Bonelli's Telegraph Co, Collie's Claim* (1871) LR 12 Eq 246 at 258–259 per Bacon V-C. See also PARA 255 et seq. As to the position of persons dealing with the company without notice of any defects in procedure see PARAS 265, 571.

8 Ie the model articles of association prescribed for the purposes of the Companies Act 2006 (see note 1). Under the Companies (Tables A to F) Regulations 1985, SI 1985/805, Schedule Table A art 88, questions arising at a meeting must be decided by a majority of votes and, in the case of an equality of votes, the chairman has a second or casting vote. A director who is also an alternate director is entitled, in the absence of his appointor, to a separate vote on behalf of his appointor in addition to his own vote: see Table A art 88. The Companies (Tables A to F) Regulations 1985, SI 1985/805, Schedule Table A provides regulations for the management of a company limited by shares but art 88 is applied by Table C (regulations for the management of a company limited by guarantee and not having a share capital), Table D Pt III (regulations for the management of a company limited by guarantee and having a share capital), and Table E (an unlimited company having a share capital). As to the meaning of 'unlimited company' see PARA 95. As to the meanings of 'company having a share capital' and 'share capital' see PARA 1231.

9 See the Companies (Model Articles) Regulations 2008, SI 2008/3229, Sch 1 art 7(1), Sch 2 art 7(1). Any such unanimous decision must be taken in accordance with Sch 1 art 8 or Sch 2 art 8, as the case may be: see note 4. If the company only has one director, and no provision of the articles requires it to have more than one director, the general rule does not apply, and the director may take decisions without regard to any of the provisions of the articles relating to directors' decision-making: Sch 1 art 7(2), Sch 2 art 7(2).

10 See the Companies (Model Articles) Regulations 2008, SI 2008/3229, Sch 3 art 7. Any such decision in the form of a written resolution must be taken in accordance with Sch 3 arts 17, 18: see note 4. Subject to the articles:

(1) a decision is taken at such a directors' meeting by a majority of the votes of the participating directors (Sch 3 art 13(1));
(2) each director participating in a directors' meeting has one vote (Sch 3 art 13(2)); and
(3) if a director has an interest in an actual or proposed transaction or arrangement with the company, that director and that director's alternate may not vote on any proposal relating to it (Sch 3 art 13(3)(a)), but this does not preclude the alternate from voting in relation to that transaction or arrangement on behalf of another appointor who does not have such an interest (Sch 3 art 13(3)(b)).

A director who is also an alternate director has an additional vote on behalf of each appointor who is not participating in a directors' meeting, and who would have been entitled to vote if he were participating in it: Sch 3 art 15. As to alternate directors see PARA 523.

11 See the Companies (Model Articles) Regulations 2008, SI 2008/3229, Sch 1 art 13(1), (2), Sch 2 art 13(1), (2), Sch 3 art 14(1), (2). As to chairing a directors' meeting see PARA 568. As to the quorum required for a meeting of directors see PARA 569; and see note 4.

A director's participation in a meeting for voting or quorum purposes may be restricted in relation to a resolution on which he is not entitled to vote: see PARA 595.

Subject to the articles, any notice or document to be sent or supplied to a director in connection with the taking of decisions by directors may also be sent or supplied by the means by which that director has asked to be sent or supplied with such notices or documents for the time being: Sch 1 art 48(2), Sch 2 art 34(2), Sch 3 art 79(2). A director may agree with the company that notices or documents sent to that director in a particular way are to be deemed to have been received within a specified time of their being sent, and for the specified time to be less than 48 hours: Sch 1 art 48(3), Sch 2 art 34(3), Sch 3 art 79(3). As to the provisions made for company communications generally see PARA 750 et seq.

12 See the Companies (Model Articles) Regulations 2008, SI 2008/3229, Sch 1 art 16, Sch 2 art 16, Sch 3 art 19.

13 As to the quorum see PARA 569. See, however, *Re Peruvian Rlys Co, ex p International Contract Co* (1868) 19 LT 803 (on appeal (1869) 4 Ch App 322); *Southern Counties Deposit Bank Ltd v Rider and Kirkwood* (1895) 73 LT 374, CA (where the court refused to declare a resolution invalid, which was passed at a meeting of the company called by less than a quorum of directors, the number having been the acting quorum for six years); *Boschoek Pty Co Ltd v Fuke* [1906] 1 Ch 148 at 162 per Swinfen Eady J (where a meeting called by de facto directors was held to be well called and the confirmation there passed was sufficient). As to de facto directors, and the duties which they owe, see PARA 512 note 8. An informal meeting

may not be sufficient to bind members (*Bottomley's Case* (1880) 16 ChD 681; *Re Scottish Petroleum Co* (1883) 23 ChD 413, CA) apart from such an article as the Companies (Tables A to F) Regulations 1985, SI 1985/805, Schedule Table A art 93 (cited in note 4). See also PARA 568.

14 *Compagnie de Mayville v Whitley* [1896] 1 Ch 788, CA; *A-G v Davy* (1741) 2 Atk 212.

15 *Re Cawley & Co* (1889) 42 ChD 209, CA.

16 *Perrott and Perrott Ltd v Stephenson* [1934] Ch 171 (where Bennett J considered that the rule of corporation law that, when a duty is delegated to a body of persons, those persons may act by a majority, has no application to companies incorporated under the Companies Acts, but applies to cases where a corporation is entrusted with a duty of a public nature).

17 See the Companies (Model Articles) Regulations 2008, SI 2008/3229, Sch 1 art 7, Sch 2 art 7, Sch 3 art 13, or the Companies (Tables A to F) Regulations 1985, SI 1985/805, Schedule Table A art 88 (cited in the note 8).

18 *Re Portuguese Consolidated Copper Mines Ltd, ex p Badman, ex p Bosanquet* (1890) 45 ChD 16, CA (allotment); *Re Phosphate of Lime Co, Austin's Case* (1871) 24 LT 932; cf *Briton Medical, General and Life Association v Jones (2)* (1889) 61 LT 384; *Hooper v Kerr, Stuart & Co Ltd* (1900) 83 LT 729; *Re Kinward Holdings* (1962) Guardian, 28 February (resolution to present petition for winding up of debtor company); *Municipal Mutual Insurance Ltd v Harrop* [1998] 2 BCLC 540 (signing of minutes of invalid meeting at later validly convened board meeting ratified resolutions passed at earlier meeting).

19 *Molineaux v London, Birmingham and Manchester Insurance Co Ltd* [1902] 2 KB 589, CA. As to companies and agency see PARA 268 et seq.

568. Meetings of directors. A company's articles of association[1] usually contain provisions as to meetings of directors[2], which may cover such matters as the proper calling of, and participation in, such a meeting[3], and the chairing of such a meeting[4].

A meeting of directors is not duly convened unless due notice has been given to all the directors entitled to receive it[5]. At a meeting not duly convened, proceedings are irregular and invalid[6], although the court will decline to interfere where the irregularity could be cured at any moment by going through the proper process[7].

Whether or not there was a regular board meeting is immaterial for purposes of binding the company if all the shareholders consent to what is done[8]. It is not necessary to give notice of an adjourned meeting[9]. If no fixed period of notice is required by the articles, the notice must be fair and reasonable[10].

Where the only two directors of a company meet casually, one director cannot treat the meeting as a board meeting against the wishes of the other[11].

1 As to a company's articles of association generally see PARA 227 et seq. As to the model articles of association that have been prescribed for the purposes of the Companies Act 2006, and their application generally, see PARA 227 et seq. Different versions of model articles have been so prescribed for use by private companies limited by shares (see the Companies (Model Articles) Regulations 2008, SI 2008/3229, reg 2, Sch 1), private companies limited by guarantee (see reg 3, Sch 2), and public companies (see reg 4, Sch 3). As to the meanings of 'company limited by guarantee', 'company limited by shares', 'limited company', 'private company' and 'public company' see PARA 95. The default articles prescribed for the purposes of the Companies Act 1985 ('legacy articles'), ie the Companies (Tables A to F) Regulations 1985, SI 1985/805, have not been revoked and may, in their amended form, continue to be used by companies after the commencement of the Companies Act 2006: see PARA 229.

2 See eg the Companies (Model Articles) Regulations 2008, SI 2008/3229, Sch 1 Pt 2 arts 7–16, Sch 2 Pt 2 arts 7–16, Sch 3 Pt 2 arts 7–19; the Companies (Tables A to F) Regulations 1985, SI 1985/805, Schedule Table A arts 88–98; and see also PARA 569 et seq. As to the extent to which directors may delegate powers, including to committees, see PARA 577; and as to the validity of acts notwithstanding defects in appointment see PARA 520.

3 Accordingly, under the Companies (Model Articles) Regulations 2008, SI 2008/3229, any director may call a directors' meeting by giving notice of the meeting to the directors: Sch 1 art 9(1), Sch 2 art 9(1), Sch 3 art 8(1), (3). Such a meeting may be called alternatively by authorising the company secretary (if any) to give such notice (see Sch 1 art 9(1), Sch 2 art 9(1)) or, in the case of a public company only, by a director requesting the company secretary to do so, and thereby obliging the secretary to call such a meeting (see Sch 3 art 8(2)). Notice of any directors' meeting must indicate its proposed date and time, where it is to take place and (if it is anticipated that directors participating in the meeting will not be in the same place) how it is proposed that they should

communicate with each other during the meeting: Sch 1 art 9(2), Sch 2 art 9(2), Sch 3 art 8(4). Notice of a directors' meeting must be given to each director: Sch 1 art 9(3), Sch 2 art 9(3), Sch 3 art 8(5). However, such notice need not be in writing (Sch 1 art 9(3), Sch 2 art 9(3), Sch 3 art 8(5)); and need not be given to directors who waive their entitlement to notice of that meeting, by giving notice to that effect to the company not more than seven days after the date on which the meeting is held (Sch 1 art 9(4), Sch 2 art 9(4), Sch 3 art 8(6)). Where such notice is given after the meeting has been held, that does not affect the validity of the meeting, or of any business conducted at it: see Sch 1 art 9(4), Sch 2 art 9(4), Sch 3 art 8(6). As to the company secretary see PARA 669 et seq.

Subject to the articles, anything sent or supplied by or to the company under the articles may be sent or supplied in any way in which the Companies Act 2006 provides for documents or information which are authorised or required by any provision of that Act to be sent or supplied by or to the company (as to which see PARA 750 et seq): Companies (Model Articles) Regulations 2008, SI 2008/3229, Sch 1 art 48(1), Sch 2 art 34(1), Sch 3 art 79(1). A director may agree with the company that notices or documents sent to that director in a particular way are to be deemed to have been received within a specified time of their being sent, and for the specified time to be less than 48 hours: Sch 1 art 48(3), Sch 2 art 34(3), Sch 3 art 79(3). Subject to the articles, directors participate in a directors' meeting, or part of a directors' meeting, when the meeting has been called and takes place in accordance with the articles, and they can each communicate to the others any information or opinions they have on any particular item of the business of the meeting: Sch 1 art 10(1), Sch 2 art 10(1), Sch 3 art 9(1). In determining whether directors are participating in a directors' meeting, it is irrelevant where any director is or how they communicate with each other: Sch 1 art 10(2), Sch 2 art 10(2), Sch 3 art 9(2). If all the directors participating in a meeting are not in the same place, they may decide that the meeting is to be treated as taking place wherever any of them is: Sch 1 art 10(3), Sch 2 art 10(3), Sch 3 art 9(3).

Under the Companies (Tables A to F) Regulations 1985, SI 1985/805, Schedule Table A art 88, subject to the provisions of the articles, the directors may regulate their proceedings as they think fit; and a director may (and the secretary, at the request of a director, must) call a meeting of the directors: Table A art 88. It is not necessary to give notice of a meeting to a director who is absent from the United Kingdom: Table A art 88. The Companies (Tables A to F) Regulations 1985, SI 1985/805, Schedule Table A provides regulations for the management of a company limited by shares but art 88 is applied by Table C (regulations for the management of a company limited by guarantee and not having a share capital), Table D Pt III (regulations for the management of a company limited by guarantee and having a share capital), and Table E (an unlimited company having a share capital). As to the meaning of 'unlimited company' see PARA 95. As to the meanings of 'company having a share capital' and 'share capital' see PARA 1231. As to the meaning of 'United Kingdom' see PARA 1 note 5.

See also the text and notes 8–12. As to the quorum required for a meeting of directors see PARA 569. A director's participation in a meeting may be restricted in relation to a resolution on which he is not entitled to vote: see PARA 595.

4 Under the Companies (Model Articles) Regulations 2008, SI 2008/3229, the directors may appoint a director to chair their meetings (Sch 1 art 12(1), Sch 2 art 12(1), Sch 3 art 12(1)); and the person so appointed for the time being is known as the chairman (Sch 1 art 12(2), Sch 2 art 12(2), Sch 3 art 12(2)). The directors may terminate the chairman's appointment at any time: Sch 1 art 12(3), Sch 2 art 12(3), Sch 3 art 12(4). If the chairman is not participating in a directors' meeting within ten minutes of the time at which it was to start, the participating directors must appoint one of themselves to chair it: Sch 1 art 12(4), Sch 2 art 12(4), Sch 3 art 12(5). In the case of a public company, the directors may appoint other directors as deputy or assistant chairmen to chair directors' meetings in the chairman's absence: Sch 3 art 12(3). Accordingly, the directors may terminate the appointment of the deputy or assistant chairman at any time (see Sch 3 art 12(4)); and Sch 3 art 12(5) applies if neither the chairman nor any director appointed generally to chair directors' meetings in the chairman's absence is participating in a meeting within ten minutes of the time at which it was to start (see Sch 3 art 12(5)).

The Companies (Tables A to F) Regulations 1985, SI 1985/805, Schedule Table A art 91 provides that the directors may appoint one of their number to be the chairman of the board of directors and may at any time remove him from that office; and, unless he is unwilling to do so, the director so appointed will preside at every meeting of directors at which he is present; but, if there is no director holding that office, or if the director holding it is unwilling to preside or is not present within five minutes after the time appointed for the meeting, the directors present may appoint one of their number to be chairman of the meeting. The Companies (Tables A to F) Regulations 1985, SI 1985/805, Schedule Table A art 91 is applied by Table C, Table D Pt III, and Table E. Where a chairman is elected for an unspecified period, he is not entitled to remain chairman so long as he is a director: see *Foster v Foster* [1916] 1 Ch 532. Where a director is appointed chairman irregularly, it has been held that acquiescence for a long period does not regularise his appointment: see *Clark v Workman* [1920] 1 IR 107.

A chairman's participation in a meeting may be restricted in relation to a resolution on which he is not entitled to vote: see PARA 595.

5 *Young v Ladies' Imperial Club* [1920] 2 KB 523, CA; *Re Portuguese Consolidated Copper Mines Ltd* (1889) 42 ChD 160, CA; *Moore v Hammond* (1827) 6 B & C 456; cf *Smyth v Darley* (1849) 2 HL Cas 789. The question whether a meeting has been duly convened if notice is dispatched to a director but not received, where the articles are silent on the point, is undecided: *Leary v National Union of Vehicle Builders* [1971] Ch 34 at 53, [1970] 2 All ER 713 at 723–724 per Megarry J. In the absence of special circumstances, every director who is within reach ought to have notice; residence abroad may amount to special circumstances; a director who is travelling about with no known address may be out of reach: see *Halifax Sugar Refining Co v Francklyn* (1890) 59 LJ Ch 591. See also note 3.

6 *Re Homer District Consolidated Gold Mines, ex p Smith* (1888) 39 ChD 546.

7 *Browne v La Trinidad* (1887) 37 ChD 1 at 17, CA; *Bentley-Stevens v Jones* [1974] 2 All ER 653, [1974] 1 WLR 638.

8 *Re Express Engineering Works Ltd* [1920] 1 Ch 466, CA. See also PARA 571. As to shareholders and membership of companies generally see PARA 323 et seq. As to company meetings see PARA 701 et seq.

9 *Wills v Murray* (1850) 4 Exch 843.

10 *Re Homer District Consolidated Gold Mines, ex p Smith* (1888) 39 ChD 546. Cf *Browne v La Trinidad* (1887) 37 ChD 1, CA.

11 *Barron v Potter* [1914] 1 Ch 895.

569. Quorum for directors' meetings. A quorum for a meeting of a company's directors[1] means the minimum number of directors who are authorised to act as a board[2] at a duly convened board meeting[3]. Each director of the quorum must be qualified to act, and, if by the withdrawal of those directors who are disqualified from voting on the ground of interest or otherwise there would be no quorum, no business may be transacted[4]. Where some of the directors are interested in a contract and are not permitted by the company's articles of association to be counted for quorum or for voting purposes[5], a reduction in the quorum for the purpose of authorising the contract is invalid[6]; and, where a transaction is really one transaction, the necessary quorum cannot be obtained by dividing the transaction into two[7]. Where no quorum is specified in the articles, the number who usually act will constitute a quorum[8]. Although one director cannot constitute a 'meeting'[9], the articles may permit one director to constitute a quorum[10]. Unless so provided by the articles, there cannot be a quorum competent to act where the number of directors is not filled up to the minimum number[11].

Even though a quorum is specified in the articles, the court may refuse to declare illegal resolutions passed by a number of directors less than that required to constitute the quorum, if that lesser number has been acting as a quorum for a number of years[12].

1 As to meetings of a company's directors see PARA 567 et seq. As to a company's directors see PARA 512 et seq.

2 As to the conduct of business at such meetings see PARA 567 et seq.

3 As to the calling of meetings of directors see PARA 568. As to a company's articles of association generally see PARA 227 et seq. As to model articles of association prescribed for the purposes of the Companies Act 2006, and their application generally, see PARA 227 et seq. Different versions of model articles have been so prescribed for use by private companies limited by shares (see the Companies (Model Articles) Regulations 2008, SI 2008/3229, reg 2, Sch 1), private companies limited by guarantee (see reg 3, Sch 2), and public companies (see reg 4, Sch 3). As to the meanings of 'company limited by guarantee', 'company limited by shares', 'limited company', 'private company' and 'public company' see PARA 95. The default articles prescribed for the purposes of the Companies Act 1985 ('legacy articles'), ie the Companies (Tables A to F) Regulations 1985, SI 1985/805, have not been revoked and may, in their amended form, continue to be used by companies after the commencement of the Companies Act 2006: see PARA 229.

Under the Companies (Model Articles) Regulations 2008, SI 2008/3229, the quorum for directors' meetings may be fixed from time to time by a decision of the directors, but it must never be less than two and, unless otherwise fixed, it is two: Sch 1 art 11(2), Sch 2 art 11(2), Sch 3 art 10(2). At a directors' meeting, unless a quorum is participating, no proposal is to be voted on, except a proposal to call another meeting: Sch 1 art 11(1), Sch 2 art 11(1), Sch 3 art 10(1). If the total number of directors for the time being is less than the quorum required, then:

(1) in the case of a private company, the directors must not take any decision other than a decision either to appoint further directors, or to call a general meeting so as to enable the shareholders (or, in the case of a company limited by guarantee, to enable its members) to appoint further directors (Sch 1 art 11(3), Sch 2 art 11(3)); and

(2) in the case of a public company:

  (a) if there is only one director, that director may appoint sufficient directors to make up a quorum or call a general meeting to do so (Sch 3 art 11(1), (2)); or

  (b) if there is more than one director, a directors' meeting may take place, if it is called in accordance with the articles and at least two directors participate in it, with a view to appointing sufficient directors to make up a quorum or calling a general meeting to do so (Sch 3 art 11(1), (3)(a)); and if a directors' meeting is called but only one director attends at the appointed date and time to participate in it, that director may appoint sufficient directors to make up a quorum or call a general meeting to do so (Sch 3 art 11(1), (3)(b)).

Further to head (2) above, if a public company has fewer than two directors, and the director (if any) is unable or unwilling to appoint sufficient directors to make up a quorum or to call a general meeting to do so, then two or more members may call a general meeting (or instruct the company secretary to do so) for the purpose of appointing one or more directors: see Sch 3 art 28; and PARA 713. As to shareholders and membership of companies generally see PARA 323 et seq.

The Companies (Tables A to F) Regulations 1985, SI 1985/805, Schedule Table A art 89 provides that the quorum necessary for the transaction of the business of the directors may be fixed by the directors and, unless so fixed at any other number, will be two. A person who holds office only as an alternate director is, if his appointor is not present, to be counted in the quorum: see Table A art 89. The continuing directors or a sole continuing director may act notwithstanding any vacancies in their number, but, if the number of directors is less than the number fixed as the quorum, the continuing director or directors may act only for the purpose of filling vacancies or of calling a general meeting: Table A art 90. As to alternate directors see PARA 523. The Companies (Tables A to F) Regulations 1985, SI 1985/805, Schedule Table A provides regulations for the management of a company limited by shares but arts 89, 90 are applied by Table C (regulations for the management of a company limited by guarantee and not having a share capital), Table D Pt III (regulations for the management of a company limited by guarantee and having a share capital), and Table E (an unlimited company having a share capital). As to the meaning of 'unlimited company' see PARA 95. As to the meanings of 'company having a share capital' and 'share capital' see PARA 1231.

See also the text and notes 4–12.

A director's participation in a meeting may be restricted for voting or quorum purposes in relation to a resolution on which he is not entitled to vote: see PARA 595.

4 *Re Greymouth-Point Elizabeth Railway and Coal Co Ltd, Yuill v Greymouth-Point Elizabeth Railway and Coal Co Ltd* [1904] 1 Ch 32; *Cox v Dublin City Distillery (No 2)* [1915] 1 IR 345, CA; *Re Olderfleet Shipbuilding and Engineering Co Ltd* [1922] 1 IR 26. Where a director who is an essential constituent of the quorum of a board meeting is shown in retrospect to have acted in breach of his fiduciary duty in voting on a resolution, he should be treated as having been incapable of voting on the business before the board and therefore should not be taken into account for the purpose of ascertaining whether a quorum of directors was present: see *Colin Gwyer & Associates Ltd v London Wharf (Limehouse) Ltd, Eaton Bray Ltd v Palmer* [2002] EWHC 2748 (Ch), [2003] 2 BCLC 153 (per curiam). The court will, however, rectify the register of a company by registering a transferee of shares if one of two directors refuses to attend a board meeting to pass the transfer and so prevents it being effected: *Re Copal Varnish Co Ltd* [1917] 2 Ch 349. Cf *Lubin v Draeger* (1918) 144 LT Jo 274. As to provision made for the conduct of business at directors' meetings see PARA 567.

5 See eg the Companies (Model Articles) Regulations 2008, SI 2008/3229, Sch 1 art 14, Sch 2 art 14, Sch 3 art 16; the Companies (Tables A to F) Regulations 1985, SI 1985/805, Schedule Table A arts 85–86, 94–95; and PARAS 590, 595, 598. However, the articles may provide that, in the case of certain contracts or arrangements, a director may be permitted to participate for quorum or for voting purposes notwithstanding the fact that otherwise he would have been disqualified on grounds of conflicts of interest: see eg the Companies (Model Articles) Regulations 2008, SI 2008/3229, Sch 1 art 14, Sch 2 art 14, Sch 3 art 16; the Companies (Tables A to F) Regulations 1985, SI 1985/805, Schedule Table A arts 85, 94; and PARAS 590, 595, 598. For a

case where a director was entitled to vote if he declared his interest but failed to do so and so was not entitled to vote see *Rolled Steel Products (Holdings) Ltd v British Steel Corpn* [1986] Ch 246, [1985] 3 All ER 52, CA. As to directors' interests in contracts generally see PARAS 598, 600 et seq.

6 *Re North Eastern Insurance Co* [1919] 1 Ch 198.

7 See note 6.

8 *Lyster's Case* (1867) LR 4 Eq 233 (where a forfeiture was good although ordered by a meeting of two out of six directors). See also *Re English etc Rolling Stock Co, Lyon's Case* (1866) 35 Beav 646 (allotment); *Re Regent's Canal Iron Co* [1867] WN 79; *Re Portuguese Consolidated Copper Mines Ltd* (1889) 42 ChD 160, CA; *York Tramways Co v Willows* (1882) 8 QBD 685 at 698, CA, per Brett LJ.

9 Cf *Sharp v Dawes* (1876) 2 QBD 26, CA; and *Re London Flats Ltd* [1969] 2 All ER 744, [1969] 1 WLR 711. However, see also *Re Fireproof Doors Ltd* [1916] 2 Ch 142.

10 *Re Fireproof Doors Ltd* [1916] 2 Ch 142. See also PARA 718.

11 *Re Scottish Petroleum Co* (1883) 23 ChD 413 at 431, CA, per Baggallay LJ; *Re Sly, Spink & Co Ltd* [1911] 2 Ch 430; *Faure Electric Accumulator Co v Phillipart* (1888) 58 LT 525; *Bottomley's Case* (1880) 16 ChD 681; *Kirk v Bell* (1851) 16 QB 290. However, see also *Thames-Haven Dock and Rly Co v Rose* (1842) 4 Man & G 552. Cf *Owen and Ashworth's Claim, Whitworth's Claim* [1901] 1 Ch 115, CA.

12 See the cases cited in note 8; and see PARA 567.

570. Records of directors' decisions. Every company[1] must cause minutes of all proceedings at meetings of its directors[2] to be recorded[3]; and the records must be kept for at least ten years from the date of the meeting[4]. If a company fails so to comply[5], an offence is committed by every officer of the company who is in default[6]. A person guilty of such an offence is liable on summary conviction to a fine not exceeding level 3 on the standard scale[7] and for continued contravention to a daily default fine[8] not exceeding one-tenth of level 3 on the standard scale[9].

Minutes recorded in accordance with these requirements[10], if purporting to be authenticated by the chairman of the meeting or by the chairman of the next directors' meeting[11], are evidence of the proceedings at the meeting[12]; and, where minutes have been so made[13] of the proceedings of a meeting of directors, then, until the contrary is proved, the meeting is deemed duly held and convened[14], all proceedings at the meeting are deemed to have duly taken place[15], and all appointments at the meeting are deemed valid[16].

The signature by the chairman of an entry in the record of a resolution accepting an agreement is a sufficient signature for the purposes of a memorandum required by the Statute of Frauds[17]. It is not necessary to prove that the person signing as chairman was in fact the chairman[18]. An entry of an allotment of shares to a director then present, who signed the minutes at the next meeting, is sufficient evidence of his agreement to take shares[19], but not where he was not present at either meeting and denies all knowledge[20].

In the absence of a minute other evidence may be given[21]; and, if the books of a company show a record of a transaction, as, for example, the forfeiture of shares, which would not be valid without a resolution of the directors, the court will, in the absence of other evidence, presume that such a resolution has been passed[22].

A company's articles of association[23] usually make provision for records to be kept and retained of directors' decisions[24] and of their written resolutions[25].

1 As to the meaning of 'company' under the Companies Acts see PARA 21; and as to the meaning of the 'Companies Acts' see PARA 13.

2 As to the meaning of 'director' under the Companies Acts see PARA 512. As to meetings of a company's directors see PARA 568 et seq.

3 Companies Act 2006 s 248(1). See also the text and notes 23–25. As to general provisions relating to company records see PARA 746 et seq.

4 Companies Act 2006 s 248(2). See also the text and notes 23–25.

5 Ie fails to comply with the Companies Act 2006 s 248 (see the text and notes 1–4): see s 248(3).

6 Companies Act 2006 s 248(3). As to the meaning of 'officer who is in default' see PARA 316. As to the meaning of 'officer' generally see PARA 679.
7 As to the standard scale and the powers of magistrates' courts to issue fines on summary conviction see SENTENCING vol 92 (2015) PARA 176.
8 As to the meaning of 'daily default fine' see PARA 1816.
9 Companies Act 2006 s 248(4).
10 Ie in accordance with the Companies Act 2006 s 248 (see the text and notes 1–4): see s 249(1).
11 As to the chairing of a directors' meeting see PARA 568.
12 Companies Act 2006 s 249(1). It is, however, only prima facie evidence: *Re Indian Zoedone Co* (1884) 26 ChD 70, CA; *Re Pyle Works (No 2)* [1891] 1 Ch 173 at 184 per Stirling J; *Re Leicester Mortgage Co Ltd* (1894) 38 Sol Jo 531, 564.
13 Ie made in accordance with the Companies Act 2006 s 248 (see the text and notes 1–4): see s 249(2).
14 Companies Act 2006 s 249(2)(a). As to the calling of, and participation in, meetings of a company's directors see PARA 568.
15 Companies Act 2006 s 249(2)(b). As to provision made for the conduct of business at a directors' meeting see PARA 567.
16 Companies Act 2006 s 249(2)(c). As to the invalidity etc of appointments made of directors see PARA 571.
17 Ie the Statute of Frauds (1677) s 4 (which now relates only to contracts of guarantee) (see FINANCIAL INSTRUMENTS AND TRANSACTIONS vol 49 (2015) PARA 677 et seq); and see *Jones v Victoria Graving Dock Co* (1877) 2 QBD 314, CA.
18 *Sheffield, Ashton-under-Lyne and Manchester Rly Co v Woodcock* (1841) 7 M & W 574.
19 *Re Llanharry Hematite Iron Ore Co Ltd, Roney's Case, Stock's Case* (1864) 4 De GJ & Sm 426.
20 *Tothill's Case* (1865) 1 Ch App 85.
21 *Re Pyle Works (No 2)* [1891] 1 Ch 173.
22 *Knight's Case* (1867) 2 Ch App 321; *Re Fireproof Doors Ltd* [1916] 2 Ch 142.
23 As to a company's articles of association generally see PARA 227 et seq. As to model articles of association prescribed for the purposes of the Companies Act 2006, and their application generally, see PARA 227 et seq. Different versions of model articles have been so prescribed for use by private companies limited by shares (see the Companies (Model Articles) Regulations 2008, SI 2008/3229, reg 2, Sch 1), private companies limited by guarantee (see reg 3, Sch 2), and public companies (see reg 4, Sch 3). As to the meanings of 'company limited by guarantee', 'company limited by shares', 'limited company', 'private company' and 'public company' see PARA 95. The default articles prescribed for the purposes of the Companies Act 1985 ('legacy articles'), ie the Companies (Tables A to F) Regulations 1985, SI 1985/805, have not been revoked and may, in their amended form, continue to be used by companies after the commencement of the Companies Act 2006: see PARA 229.
24 Under the Companies (Model Articles) Regulations 2008, SI 2008/3229, the directors of a private company must ensure that the company keeps a record, in writing, for at least ten years from the date of the decision recorded, of every unanimous or majority decision taken by the directors (ie whether taken at a meeting or otherwise): Sch 1 art 15, Sch 2 art 15. Under the Companies (Tables A to F) Regulations 1985, SI 1985/805, Schedule Table A art 100, the directors must cause minutes to be made in books kept for the purpose of all appointments of officers made by the directors, and of all proceedings at meetings of the company, of the holders of any class of shares in the company, and of the directors, and of committees of directors, including the names of the directors present at each such meeting. The Companies (Tables A to F) Regulations 1985, SI 1985/805, Schedule Table A provides regulations for the management of a company limited by shares but art 100 is applied by Table C (regulations for the management of a company limited by guarantee and not having a share capital), Table D Pt III (regulations for the management of a company limited by guarantee and having a share capital), and Table E (an unlimited company having a share capital). However, Table C modifies Table A art 100 by causing the words 'of the holders of any class of shares in the company' to be omitted: see Table C art 11. As to the meaning of 'unlimited company' see PARA 95. As to the meanings of 'company having a share capital' and 'share capital' see PARA 1231.

Where, under the articles, a contract can stand only if a minute of the directors approving it is entered in the record, the entry must be made within a reasonable time: *Toms v Cinema Trust Ltd* [1915] WN 29. The right of the beneficiaries of trust shares held by directors on their behalf to inspect a company's documents is not greater than the right conferred on shareholders by statute or by the articles: see *Butt v Kelson* [1952] Ch 197, sub nom *Re Butt, Butt v Kelson* [1952] 1 All ER 167, CA; and TRUSTS AND POWERS vol 98 (2013) PARA 402. As to shareholders and membership of companies generally see PARA 323 et seq.

25 Under the Companies (Model Articles) Regulations 2008, SI 2008/3229, the secretary of a public company must ensure that the company keeps a record, in writing, of all directors' written resolutions for at least ten years from the date of their adoption: Sch 3 art 18(4). As to the company secretary see PARA 669 et seq.

571. Invalidity of director's appointment and irregularity. The acts of a person acting as a director are valid notwithstanding that it is afterwards discovered[1]:

(1) that there was a defect in his appointment[2];
(2) that he was disqualified from holding office[3];
(3) that he had ceased to hold office[4];
(4) that he was not entitled to vote on the matter in question[5].

In the case of irregularity or informality in the proceedings of directors, where a shareholder has changed his position in reliance upon the acts of the directors being regular, the company cannot set up the irregularity of the proceedings to his detriment[6]; nor may it rely on the absence of a required authority given by general meeting[7]. Persons dealing with the company are, however, protected at common law from the consequences of any internal irregularities if they have acted without notice[8], and are protected more broadly, by statute, where a transaction is ultra vires the company or beyond the authority of the directors[9].

1 See the Companies Act 2006 s 161(1); and PARA 520.
2 See the Companies Act 2006 s 161(1)(a); and PARA 520.
3 See the Companies Act 2006 s 161(1)(b); and PARA 520. As to company directors' disqualification generally see PARA 1759 et seq.
4 See the Companies Act 2006 s 161(1)(c); and PARA 520. As to the retirement or removal of directors see PARA 555 et seq.
5 See the Companies Act 2006 s 161(1)(d); and PARA 520.
6 *Bargate v Shortridge* (1855) 5 HL Cas 297. Cf *Morris v Kanssen* [1946] AC 459, [1946] 1 All ER 586, HL (where this doctrine did not assist the invalidly appointed director himself).
7 *Re British Provident Life and Fire Assurance Society, Grady's Case* (1863) 1 De GJ & Sm 488 (where shares had been transferred and registered). As to meetings of the company see PARA 701 et seq.
8 See *Royal British Bank v Turquand* (1856) 6 E & B 327; and PARA 265.
9 As to the protection afforded persons dealing with the company in good faith under the Companies Act 2006 ss 39–42, which modify the common law 'ultra vires' rule, see PARAS 255, 263–264. As to the meaning of 'ultra vires' for these purposes see PARA 258.

(v) General Duties of Directors

A. DIRECTORS' DUTIES: INTRODUCTION

572. Scope and nature of directors' general duties. The Companies Act 2006 specifies[1] the general duties that are owed by a director[2] of a company[3] to the company[4]. Except as otherwise provided, more than one of the general duties may apply in any given case[5].

The general duties are based on certain common law rules and equitable principles as they apply in relation to directors and have effect in place of those rules and principles as regards the duties owed to a company by a director[6]. The general duties must be interpreted and applied in the same way as common law rules or equitable principles, and regard must be had to the corresponding common law rules and equitable principles in interpreting and applying the general duties[7]. The principles and rules which govern directors' fiduciary duties may be regarded as straightforward applications of ordinary principles of equity concerning fiduciary duties[8].

1 Ie in the Companies Act 2006 ss 171–177 (see PARA 580 et seq): see s 170(1).
2 As to the meaning of 'director' under the Companies Acts see PARA 512; and as to the meaning of the 'Companies Acts' see PARA 13. The general duties apply to a shadow director of a company

where and to the extent that they are capable of so applying: Companies Act 2006 s 170(5) (substituted by the Small Business, Enterprise and Employment Act 2015 s 89(1)). See further PARA 573. As to shadow directors see PARA 513.

3 As to the meaning of 'company' under the Companies Acts see PARA 21.

4 Companies Act 2006 s 170(1). As to the application and effect of the general duties see PARA 573. Although s 170(1) restates the common law formula that directors' duties are owed to the company (see PARA 574 et seq), remedies for their breach (or threatened breach) have not been codified under the Companies Act 2006. However, s 178 provides that the consequences of breach (or threatened breach) of ss 171–177 (see PARA 580 et seq) are the same as would apply if the corresponding common law rule or equitable principle applied; and those duties, except for s 174, which reflects the common law duty of care and skill (see PARA 588 et seq), are, accordingly, enforceable in the same way as any other fiduciary duty owed to a company by its directors: see PARA 599. The three main ways in which a company can take legal action against a director (or a former director) for breach of duty are:

(1) if the board of directors decides to commence proceedings (see PARA 581 et seq);
(2) through a derivative claim brought by one or more members to enforce a right which is vested in the company (see PARA 646 et seq); or
(3) if a liquidator or administrator (following the commencement of a formal insolvency procedure such as liquidation or administration) decides to commence proceedings (see COMPANY AND PARTNERSHIP INSOLVENCY). See also PARA 573.

5 Companies Act 2006 s 179.

6 Companies Act 2006 s 170(3). See note 7.

7 Companies Act 2006 s 170(4). When discussing this provision, and its interaction with s 170(3) (see the text and note 6), at the Bill stage, Lord Goldsmith (Attorney-General) stated (678 HL Official Report (5th series), 6 Feb 2006, GC cols 243–244) that:

(1) the court should be left to interpret the words that Parliament passes;
(2) the wording of [the Companies Act 2006] s 170(3) is intended to explain the origins of the general duties later set out . . . so that, once the Act is passed, one will go to the statutory statement of duties to identify the duty that the director owed; and
(3) the wording of s 170(4) deals with the interpretation of those duties . . . [and it does] two things. It would point the courts towards existing case law on those common law rules and equitable principles [ie that are now replaced by the statutory duties]. It will also allow the law to develop so that relevant case law after the duties come into force should also be taken into account [especially in having regard to the development in common law rules and equitable principles as they apply to other relationships, such as trustees and agents].

8 See *Shepherds Investments Ltd v Walters* [2006] EWHC 836 (Ch) at [132], [2007] 2 BCLC 202 at [132] per Etherton J. 'Fiduciary' is defined generally in *Bristol and West Building Society v Mothew(t/a Stapley & Co)* [1998] Ch 1 at 18, [1996] 4 All ER 698 at 711, CA, per Millett LJ ('a fiduciary is someone who has undertaken to act for or on behalf of another in a particular matter in circumstances which give rise to a relationship of trust and confidence'). See also *Henderson v Merrett Syndicates* [1995] 2 AC 145 at 206, [1994] 3 All ER 506 at 543, HL, per Lord Browne-Wilkinson (no single set of fiduciary duties applicable to all); and EQUITABLE JURISDICTION vol 47 (2014) PARA 231; *Premier Waste Management Ltd v Towers* [2011] EWCA Civ 923, [2012] IRLR 73, [2012] 1 BCLC 67; and EQUITABLE JURISDICTION vol 47 (2014) para 233.

573. Application and effect of directors' general duties. The general duties that the Companies Act 2006 sets out[1] as being owed by a director[2] of a company[3] to the company[4]:

(1) have effect subject to any rule of law enabling the company to give authority, specifically or generally, for anything to be done (or omitted) by the directors, or any of them, that would otherwise be a breach of duty[5]; and
(2) where the company's articles contain provisions for dealing with conflicts of interest[6], are not infringed by anything done (or omitted) by the directors, or any of them, in accordance with those provisions[7].

Otherwise, the general duties have effect, except as otherwise provided or the context otherwise requires, notwithstanding any enactment[8] or rule of law[9].

The application of the general duties is not affected by the fact that the case also falls within the provisions that govern transactions requiring the approval of members[10]; and compliance with the general duties does not remove the need for approval under any provision that is so applicable in relation to such transactions[11].

The general duties apply to a shadow director[12] of a company where and to the extent that they are capable of so applying[13]. The Secretary of State[14] may by regulations[15] make provision about the application of the general duties of directors to shadow directors[16]. The regulations may, in particular, make provision:

(a) for prescribed[17] general duties of directors to apply to shadow directors with such adaptations as may be prescribed;

(b) for prescribed general duties of directors not to apply to shadow directors[18].

A person who ceases to be a director[19] continues to be subject:

(i) to the duty to avoid conflicts of interest[20] as regards the exploitation of any property, information or opportunity of which he became aware at a time when he was a director[21]; and

(ii) to the duty not to accept benefits from third parties[22] as regards things done or omitted by him before he ceased to be a director[23];

and, to that extent, those duties apply to a former director as to a director, subject to any necessary adaptations[24].

In their application to a company that is a charity, the Companies Act 2006 provisions that set out the general duties of directors and the provisions supplementary thereto[25] have effect with modifications[26].

1 Ie in the Companies Act 2006 ss 171–177: see also PARA 580 et seq. As to the scope and nature of the directors' general duties see PARA 572.
2 As to the meaning of 'director' under the Companies Acts see PARA 512, and as to the meaning of the 'Companies Acts' see PARA 13. As to the application of the general rules to shadow directors see the text and notes 12–18.
3 As to the meaning of 'company' under the Companies Acts see PARA 21.
4 Companies Act 2006 s 180(4).
5 Companies Act 2006 s 180(4)(a).
6 As to the general duty to avoid conflicts of interest see PARA 590 et seq.
7 Companies Act 2006 s 180(4)(b). This provision should be read in conjunction with s 232(4) (which provides that nothing in s 232 prevents a company's articles from making such provision as has previously been lawful for dealing with conflicts of interest) (see PARA 639).
8 As to the meaning of 'enactment' see PARA 13 note 16.
9 Companies Act 2006 s 180(5).
10 See the Companies Act 2006 s 180(2); and PARA 602. The text refers to the provisions of Pt 10 Ch 4 (ss 188–225) or Pt 10 Ch 4A (ss 226A–226F) (transactions with directors requiring approval of members) (see PARA 601 et seq) except that where either Pt 10 Ch 4 or Pt 10 Ch 4A applies and approval is given under Pt 10 Ch 4 or Pt 10 Ch 4A, or where the matter is one as to which it is provided that approval is not needed, it is not necessary also to comply with s 175 (duty to avoid conflicts of interest) (see PARA 590 et seq) or s 176 (duty not to accept benefits from third parties) (see PARA 593 et seq): see s 180(2); and PARA 602. As to the meaning of 'member' see PARA 323.
11 See the Companies Act 2006 s 180(3); and PARA 602. The text refers to the need for approval under any applicable provision of Pt 10 Ch 4 or Pt 10 Ch 4A: see s 180(3); and PARA 602.
12 As to the meaning of 'shadow director' see PARA 513.
13 Companies Act 2006 s 170(5) (substituted by the Small Business, Enterprise and Employment Act 2015 s 89(1)).
14 As to the Secretary of State see PARA 6.
15 Such regulations are subject to affirmative resolution procedure (ie the regulations may not be made unless a draft of the statutory instrument containing them has been laid before Parliament and approved by a resolution of each House of Parliament): Small Business, Enterprise and Employment Act 2015 ss 89(5), 161(4). As to the making of regulations generally see s 161(1), (2).
16 Small Business, Enterprise and Employment Act 2015 s 89(2). At the date at which this volume states the law, no such regulations had been made.

17 'Prescribed' means prescribed in regulations: Small Business, Enterprise and Employment Act 2015 s 89(4).
18 Small Business, Enterprise and Employment Act 2015 s 89(3).
19 As to the retirement and re-appointment of directors see PARA 555 et seq.
20 Ie the duty in the Companies Act 2006 s 175 (see PARA 590 et seq): see s 170(2)(a).
21 Companies Act 2006 s 170(2)(a).
22 Ie the duty in the Companies Act 2006 s 176 (see PARA 593 et seq): see s 170(2)(b).
23 Companies Act 2006 s 170(2)(b).
24 Companies Act 2006 s 170(2).
25 Ie the Companies Act 2006 Pt 10 Ch 2 (ss 170–181) (see PARA 580 et seq): see s 181(1).
26 See the Companies Act 2006 s 181(1). The main modifications involve the substitution of s 175(3), (5) (see PARAS 590–591), and modifying the application of the Companies Act 2006 s 180(2)(b) (see PARA 602): see s 181(2), (3).

574. Directors' duties are generally owed to the company. In general, directors do not, solely by virtue of the office of director, owe fiduciary duties to shareholders[1], either collectively or individually[2]; directors owe their duties to the company[3]. However, duties owed by directors to shareholders may arise if there is a special factual relationship between the directors and the shareholders in the particular case capable of generating fiduciary obligations[4]. Likewise, directors do not owe fiduciary duties to the company's creditors, collectively or individually[5].

1 As to shareholders and membership of companies generally see PARA 323 et seq.
2 As to the role of nominee directors and their duties, if any, to their appointor see PARA 514.
3 This position is restated in the Companies Act 2006 s 170: see PARA 572. See also *Percival v Wright* [1902] 2 Ch 421; *Peskin v Anderson* [2001] 1 BCLC 372, CA; *Ross River Ltd v Waveley Commercial Ltd* [2013] EWCA Civ 910, [2014] 1 BCLC 545, [2013] All ER (D) 354 (Jul). If the company in turn owes fiduciary duties to a client, it is possible for a director of the company also to owe fiduciary duties to that client: see *Satnam Investments Ltd v Dunlop Heywood & Co Ltd* [1999] 3 All ER 652, [1999] 1 BCLC 385, CA (fiduciary duty owed by way of contractual and equitable obligations; duty breached when information offered to a third party); and *JD Wetherspoon plc v Van de Berg & Co Ltd* [2007] EWHC 1044 (Ch), [2007] All ER (D) 82 (May).
4 *Peskin v Anderson* [2001] 1 BCLC 372, CA. See also *Coleman v Myers* [1977] 2 NZLR 225. This might include a duty of disclosure where directors are purchasing shares in the company from shareholders: *Re Chez Nico (Restaurants) Ltd* [1992] BCLC 192 at 208 per Browne-Wilkinson V-C. See also *Platt v Platt* [1999] 2 BCLC 745 (where a director acquired shares from two shareholders who were his brothers on the basis of misrepresentation and in breach of the fiduciary relationship owed to them); affd on the basis of misrepresentation only [2001] 1 BCLC 698, CA. Cf *Sharp v Blank* [2015] EWHC 3220 (Ch), [2015] All ER (D) 171 (Nov) (directors of Lloyd's Bank recommending acquisition of HBOS and recapitalisation of Lloyd's through participation in a recapitalisation scheme, which they advised were in the best interests of shareholders and should be approved; Lloyd's directors had the benefit of detailed disclosure by HBOS and 'vastly superior knowledge' to that of the shareholders but that was not enough to establish a 'special relationship' between the directors and the shareholders such as would give rise to a fiduciary duty beyond the 'sufficient information' duty).
5 *Multinational Gas and Petrochemical Co v Multinational Gas and Petrochemical Services Ltd* [1983] Ch 258 at 288, [1983] 2 All ER 563 at 585, CA, per Dillon LJ; *Yukong Lines Ltd of Korea v Rendsburg Investments Corpn of Liberia, The Rialto (No 2)* [1998] 4 All ER 82 at 99, [1998] 1 WLR 294 at 312 per Toulson J. A director has an obligation, however, to have regard to creditors' interests in certain circumstances: see PARA 585.

575. Powers of directors to manage the business. The true position of directors[1] is that of agents for the company[2]. As such, they are clothed with the powers and duties of carrying on the whole of its business[3], subject, however, to the restrictions imposed by statute and by the company's constitution[4]. The intention of the company may be established by its directors, even if acting informally, depending upon the nature of the matter under consideration, the relative positions of the directors in the company, and generally all the circumstances of the case[5].

Articles of association[6] generally give directors very wide powers as to the control and management of the company and its affairs[7]; the powers given by the default or model articles[8] are sometimes amplified by special articles which enumerate the powers of the directors.

Where powers are delegated by the company to the directors[9], and the directors owing to dissensions and quarrels between them are unwilling or unable to act, the powers may be exercised by the company[10]. If, owing to disputes amongst the directors, they are unable to act and the affairs of the company cannot be carried on, the court will interfere by injunction and by the appointment of a receiver and manager of the undertaking and assets of the company until the management of the company is restored to a proper footing[11]. The court may also order a meeting of the company so that additional directors may be appointed[12].

The question of the limitation of the powers of directors has often arisen in connection with powers of borrowing and mortgaging[13]. Where the directors have a power to mortgage[14], they may exercise it to secure a past debt[15], provided that this does not constitute a preference, or to secure sums owing upon a bill of exchange given by directors for a debt of the company[16], or to secure a guarantee or by way of indemnity[17]. They may issue debentures to satisfy the creditors of a purchased business or in payment of the vendor[18]. Special rights may by suitable language be conferred on individual directors for their own personal benefits, in which case they may be used as they think fit[19].

Any power conferred on the company, or its officers, whether by the Companies Acts, or the Insolvency Act 1986, or by its constitution, which could be exercised in such a way as to interfere with the exercise by an administrator of his powers is not exercisable except with the consent of the administrator, which may be given either generally or in relation to particular cases[20].

1 As to a company's directors see PARA 512 et seq.

2 *Re Faure Electric Accumulator Co* (1888) 40 ChD 141. As to the liability of the company for the acts of its agents see PARA 268 et seq. Directors are not ipso facto agents for the shareholders: *Gramophone and Typewriter Ltd v Stanley* [1908] 2 KB 89 at 106, CA, per Buckley LJ; *Charitable Corpn v Sutton* (1742) 2 Atk 400; *Salmon v Quin & Axtens Ltd* [1909] 1 Ch 311 at 319, CA, per Farwell LJ (affd sub nom *Quin & Axtens Ltd v Salmon* [1909] AC 442, HL); *Re Olderfleet Shipbuilding and Engineering Co Ltd* [1922] 1 IR 26. Cf *Briess v Woolley* [1954] AC 333, [1954] 1 All ER 909, HL (when there was an agency in fact). They have also been called 'servants' (*Smith v Anderson* (1880) 15 ChD 247 at 276, CA) and 'managing partners' (*Re Forest of Dean Coal Mining Co* (1878) 10 ChD 450 at 451 per Jessel MR; *York and North-Midland Rly Co v Hudson* (1853) 16 Beav 485; *London Financial Association v Kelk* (1884) 26 ChD 107 at 143 per Bacon V-C; *Re Lands Allotment Co* [1894] 1 Ch 616 at 637, CA, per Kay LJ; *Automatic Self-Cleansing Filter Syndicate Co Ltd v Cunninghame* [1906] 2 Ch 34 at 45, CA, per Cozens-Hardy LJ). Cf *Sputz v Broadway Engineering Co Ltd* (1944) 171 LT 50. Such expressions indicate useful points of view, but are not exhaustive: *Re Imperial Hydropathic Hotel Co, Blackpool v Hampson* (1882) 23 ChD 1 at 12–13, CA, per Bowen LJ. They have also been called 'the directing mind and will of the company': *HL Bolton (Engineering) Co Ltd v TJ Graham & Sons Ltd* [1957] 1 QB 159 at 172, [1956] 3 All ER 624 at 630, CA, per Denning LJ. See also PARA 313.

3 Directors may bring a claim in the name of the company (*Compagnie de Mayville v Whitley* [1896] 1 Ch 788 at 803, CA, per Lindley LJ); they may petition in bankruptcy (*Re JG Tomkins & Co* [1901] 1 KB 476, CA); they may give gratuities to the employees (*Hampson v Price's Patent Candle Co* (1876) 45 LJ Ch 437); without interference by a meeting of the company itself, they may issue negotiable instruments, if the company has that power (*Peruvian Rlys Co v Thames and Mersey Marine Insurance Co, Re Peruvian Rlys Co* (1867) 2 Ch App 617); if they are directors of an insurance company, they may pay losses beyond those insured against (*Taunton v Royal Insurance Co* (1864) 2 Hem & M 135); they may grant pensions to the family of a manager (*Henderson v Bank of Australasia* (1888) 40 ChD 170; but cf *Re Lee, Behrens & Co Ltd* [1932] 2 Ch 46, where a grant of a pension to the widow of a managing director was held ultra vires; *Re W & M Roith Ltd* [1967] 1 All ER 427, [1967] 1 WLR 432, where a service agreement providing for a similar pension to a widow was held invalid as not having been entered into bona fide for

the benefit of and to promote the prosperity of the company (but as to the authority of these latter two cases see further PARA 260)) or to old retired employees or officers (*Cyclists' Touring Club v Hopkinson* [1910] 1 Ch 179); they may borrow and give security (*Gibbs and West's Case* (1870) LR 10 Eq 312; *Re Pyle Works (No 2)* [1891] 1 Ch 173 at 186 per Stirling J; *General Auction Estate and Monetary Co v Smith* [1891] 3 Ch 432); they may issue debentures at a discount (*Re Anglo-Danubian Steam Navigation and Colliery Co* (1875) LR 20 Eq 339 at 341 per Jessel MR); and without special authorisation, and subject to any reservation contained in the articles, they may make calls (*Ambergate, Nottingham and Boston and Eastern Junction Rly Co v Mitchell* (1849) 4 Exch 540) or enter into a compromise (*Bath's Case* (1878) 8 ChD 334, CA). Directors may pay reasonable brokerage on the issue of shares: *Metropolitan Coal Consumers' Association v Scrimgeour* [1895] 2 QB 604, CA. As to paying promotion expenses see PARA 56. Directors with very extensive powers were held justified in acquiring an estate for another company to build the Alexandra Palace and in promoting a subsidiary company (*London Financial Association v Kelk* (1884) 26 ChD 107), and in advancing on speculative building etc (*Sheffield and South Yorkshire Permanent Building Society v Aizlewood* (1889) 44 ChD 412; and see *Butler v Northern Territories Mines of Australia Ltd* (1906) 96 LT 41).

4 As to the meaning of references to a company's constitution for the purposes of the Companies Act 2006 Pt 10 (ss 154–259) (see PARA 512 et seq) see PARA 580 note 4. As to the ceasing of powers of directors in a compulsory winding up see COMPANY AND PARTNERSHIP INSOLVENCY vol 16 (2011) PARA 440; and as to the ceasing of their powers in a voluntary winding up see COMPANY AND PARTNERSHIP INSOLVENCY vol 17 (2011) PARA 959.

5 *HL Bolton (Engineering) Co Ltd v TJ Graham & Sons Ltd* [1957] 1 QB 159, [1956] 3 All ER 624, CA (determination of company's intention for purposes of the Landlord and Tenant Act 1954 s 30 (see LANDLORD AND TENANT vol 63 (2012) PARA 851 et seq)). Where a company gave an undertaking to the court to act in a way which required the consent of the company in general meeting, the court held that the directors were bound to convene a meeting and issue a circular inviting a favourable response, but that they had the same unrestricted right of voting at the meeting as they would have done if they were not directors: *Northern Counties Securities Ltd v Jackson & Steeple Ltd* [1974] 2 All ER 625, [1974] 1 WLR 1133.

6 As to a company's articles of association generally see PARA 227 et seq.

7 As to the powers of management that are usually conferred by articles of association see PARA 581.

8 See PARA 581 note 5. As to model articles of association prescribed for the purposes of the Companies Act 2006, and their application generally, see PARA 227 et seq. The default articles prescribed for the purposes of the Companies Act 1985 ('legacy articles'), ie the Companies (Tables A to F) Regulations 1985, SI 1985/805, have not been revoked and may, in their amended form, continue to be used by companies after the commencement of the Companies Act 2006: see PARA 229.

9 As to the extent to which directors may delegate powers, including to committees, see PARA 577.

10 *Barron v Potter* [1914] 1 Ch 895 (appointment of additional directors); *Foster v Foster* [1916] 1 Ch 532 (appointment of a managing director). As to resolutions of the company generally see PARA 689 et seq.

11 *Featherstone v Cooke* (1873) LR 16 Eq 298; *Trade Auxiliary Co v Vickers* (1873) LR 16 Eq 303; *Stanfield v Gibbon* [1925] WN 11.

12 See PARA 522. The power of the court referred to in the text is exercised under the Companies Act 2006 s 306 (see PARA 711).

13 The delegation of borrowing powers to the directors does not restrict the general power of the company to borrow, and it may exercise this power through agents so long as this is not prohibited by the memorandum or articles: *Mercantile Bank of India Ltd v Chartered Bank of India, Australia and China and Strauss & Co Ltd* [1937] 1 All ER 231. As to the directors' exercise of a company's powers for a proper purpose see PARA 583.

14 For companies formed under the Companies Act 1985 and its predecessor legislation (as to which see PARA 13 et seq), directors' powers were limited by the objects expressed in the company' s memorandum (see PARA 239 note 3). For companies formed under the Companies Act 2006, unless the articles specifically restrict the objects of a company, its objects are unrestricted (see s 31; and PARA 239) and, accordingly, the directors' powers, including the power to borrow and mortgage, are unrestricted, unless they are restricted by the constitution.

15 *Shears v Jacob* (1866) LR 1 CP 513; *Re Inns of Court Hotel Co* (1868) LR 6 Eq 82; *Re Patent File Co, ex p Birmingham Banking Co* (1870) 6 Ch App 83; *Australian Auxiliary Steam Clipper Co v Mounsey* (1858) 4 K & J 733.

16 *Scott v Colburn* (1858) 26 Beav 276.

17 *Re Pyle Works (No 2)* [1891] 1 Ch 173 at 186 per Stirling J.

18 *Salomon v A Salomon & Co Ltd* [1897] AC 22 at 39, HL, per Lord Watson.

19 *Bersel Manufacturing Co Ltd v Berry* [1968] 2 All ER 552, HL (power in life directors to remove other directors).

20 See the Insolvency Act 1986 Sch B1 para 64 (added by the Enterprise Act 2002 Sch 16). See also COMPANY AND PARTNERSHIP INSOLVENCY vol 16 (2011) PARA 261. As to administrators see COMPANY AND PARTNERSHIP INSOLVENCY vol 16 (2011) PARA 158 et seq.

576. Directors' right of indemnity for expenditure incurred. A company's directors[1] are entitled to be indemnified by the company for all debts, expenses, and liabilities incurred in the ordinary course of business, and for money borrowed and applied for those purposes[2], together, in the case of an actual expenditure, with simple interest[3]. If they guarantee a secured loan, they have, on paying off the loan, the usual right of a surety to subrogation[4].

The right to indemnity is limited to expenditure which has been incurred or an obligation adopted by directors on behalf of the company and in subjection to the special purposes of the company in accordance with its constitution[5]. Accordingly, directors may not use the funds of the company in payment of their own costs of legal proceedings, although these would not have been incurred if they had not been directors, unless incurred on behalf of the company or for its benefit[6].

In the absence of special provision to the contrary, the directors are not entitled to their expenses in travelling to and from board meetings[7].

If directors are holders on behalf of the company of unpaid shares which it has power to hold, they are entitled to be indemnified[8]. If, however, there is no such power, as where, for example, the shares are in the same company, they are liable for calls without any right of indemnity, even when all the shareholders have consented to the purchase[9]; but they are not liable in a winding up as contributories in respect of the amounts unpaid on shares transferred to them as trustees by way of security on the terms that the transfer is to be registered only with their consent, if they have given no consent to its registration[10].

If, although acting in the ordinary course of business, the directors exceed their borrowing powers, they cannot claim an indemnity from the company unless the borrowing is within the powers of the company and is ratified[11].

1 As to a company's directors see PARA 512 et seq.

2 As eg in respect of holding as lessees (*Re Pooley Hall Colliery Co* (1869) 21 LT 690); or as shareholders in other companies (see the text and notes 8–10); or in respect of contracts for the benefit of the company (*Gleadow v Hull Glass Co* (1849) 19 LJ Ch 44; *Poole, Jackson and Whyte's Case* (1878) 9 ChD 322, CA; *Gray v Seckham* (1872) 7 Ch App 680); or money advanced (*Re International Life Assurance Society, ex p Certain Directors* (1870) 39 LJ Ch 271; *Re Court Grange Silver-Lead Mining Co, ex p Sedgwick* (1856) 2 Jur NS 949; *Lowndes v Garnett and Moseley Gold Mining Co of America Ltd* (1864) 33 LJ Ch 418; *Baker's Case* (1860) 1 Drew & Sm 55). See also *Re German Mining Co, ex p Chippendale* (1853) 4 De GM & G 19; *Re Norwich Yarn Co, ex p Bignold* (1856) 22 Beav 143; *Troup's Case* (1860) 29 Beav 353; *Re Electric Telegraph Co of Ireland, Hoare's Case* (1861) 30 Beav 225. As to dividends paid out of capital with the knowledge of the shareholders and the directors' right of indemnity against them in such a case see PARA 1580.

3 *Re Norwich Yarn Co, ex p Bignold* (1856) 22 Beav 143 (the rate then allowed was 5% per annum). As to interest see generally FINANCIAL INSTRUMENTS AND TRANSACTIONS vol 49 (2015) PARA 90 et seq.

4 *Gibbs and West's Case* (1870) LR 10 Eq 312. Cf *Owen and Ashworth's Claim, Whitworth's Claim* [1901] 1 Ch 115, CA. It is a proper proceeding to give a charge on future calls in order to indemnify directors: *Re Pyle Works (No 2)* [1891] 1 Ch 173. As to subrogation see generally EQUITABLE JURISDICTION vol 47 (2014) PARA 207 et seq; FINANCIAL INSTRUMENTS AND TRANSACTIONS vol 49 (2015) PARA 763; INSURANCE vol 60 (2011) PARA 216.

5 *Pickering v Stephenson* (1872) LR 14 Eq 322 at 340 per Sir John Wickens V-C.

6 *Pickering v Stephenson* (1872) LR 14 Eq 322 (costs of prosecution for libel on themselves); *Studdert v Grosvenor* (1886) 33 ChD 528. Cf *Tomlinson v Scottish Amalgamated Silks Ltd (Liquidators)* 1935 SC (HL) 1. These costs they must repay (*Cullerne v London and Suburban General Permanent Building Society* (1890) 25 QBD 485 at 490, CA, per Lindley LJ, effectively overruling *Pickering v Stephenson* 1872) LR 14 Eq 322 on this point; *Re Liverpool*

Household Stores Association (1890) 59 LJ Ch 616); but costs of a prosecution for libel on the company itself, if properly incurred, must be paid by the company (*Studdert v Grosvenor* (1886) 33 ChD 538; but see *Kernaghan v Williams* (1868) LR 6 Eq 228). Directors cannot charge the company with the costs of an unsuccessful petition to wind up, presented by themselves, or of an unsuccessful appeal (*Smith v Duke of Manchester* (1883) 24 ChD 611) although authorised by the articles to take proceedings etc. If the directors are to be indemnified under a provision in the articles, it must be established that the provision has been incorporated in the contract between the company and a director; and relatively little may be required to incorporate the articles by implication: *Globalink Telecommunications Ltd v Wilmbury Ltd* [2002] EWHC 1988 (QB), [2003] 1 BCLC 145; *John v Price Waterhouse (t/a PricewaterhouseCoopers)* [2002] 1 WLR 953 at 960, [2001] All ER (D) 145 (Jul) per Ferris J. See also *Re Crossmore Electrical and Civil Engineering Ltd* [1989] BCLC 137; *Re a Company (No 004502 of 1988), ex p Johnson* [1992] BCLC 701. As to the right of an auditor to have costs that were incurred on behalf of the company assessed on an indemnity basis see *John v Price Waterhouse (t/a PricewaterhouseCoopers)* [2002] 1 WLR 953, [2001] All ER (D) 145 (Jul).

Nevertheless, a company may provide a director of the company or of its holding company with funds to meet expenditure incurred or to be incurred by him in defending himself either in an investigation by a regulatory authority, or against action proposed to be taken by a regulatory authority, in connection with any alleged negligence, default, breach of duty or breach of trust by him in relation to the company or an associated company, or to enable any such director to avoid incurring such expenditure: see the Companies Act 2006 s 206; and PARA 615.

7 *Young v Naval, Military and Civil Service Co-operative Society of South Africa* [1905] 1 KB 687; *Marmor Ltd v Alexander* 1908 SC 78, Ct of Sess; *Steel v Northern Co-operative Society Ltd* 1962 SLT 50. Cf the provision made for payment of reasonable expenses properly incurred in the course of such business in the Companies (Model Articles) Regulations 2008, SI 2008/3229, Sch 1 art 20 (private company limited by shares), Sch 2 art 20 (private company limited by guarantee), Sch 3 art 24 (public company), and in the 'legacy articles', ie the Companies (Tables A to F) Regulations 1985, SI 1985/805, which may, in their amended form, be used by companies after the commencement of the Companies Act 2006 (see the Companies (Tables A to F) Regulations 1985, SI 1985/805, Schedule Table A art 83).

8 *Re Financial Corpn, Goodson's Claim* (1880) 28 WR 760. See also *Re Waterloo Life etc Assurance Co, Saunders' Case* (1864) 2 De GJ & Sm 101 (where the shares were held as qualification shares); and PARA 344.

9 *Cree v Somervail* (1879) 4 App Cas 648, HL.

10 *Gray's Case* (1876) 1 ChD 664. As to the meaning of 'contributory' see COMPANY AND PARTNERSHIP INSOLVENCY vol 17 (2011) PARA 661.

11 *Re Worcester Corn Exchange Co* (1853) 3 De GM & G 180; *Re German Mining Co, ex p Chippendale* (1853) 4 De GM & G 19. The ratification may be in general meeting (*Irvine v Union Bank of Australia* (1877) 2 App Cas 366, PC), without special resolution (*Grant v United Kingdom Switchback Rlys Co* (1888) 40 ChD 135, CA); or it may be inferred (*Re Magdalena Steam Navigation Co* (1860) John 690). See also PARA 1443. As to the powers of companies see PARA 120. The ratification by a company of conduct by a director amounting to negligence, default, breach of duty or breach of trust in relation to the company, for the purpose of relieving the director of any liability for such conduct, is subject to statutory constraints: see the Companies Act 2006 s 239; and PARA 638.

577. Delegation of directors' powers. Without express authority to do so, a company's directors[1] cannot delegate their duties or powers[2].

However, a company's articles of association[3] generally confer such authority on the directors to delegate their powers to committees or local boards[4] or to managing directors[5]; and, where they have sufficient powers of delegation, the directors may delegate any of their powers to committees, or even to a single director[6].

Where any specific powers are properly delegated, the directors are absolved from liability for the exercise of those powers by the delegates[7]; but whilst directors are entitled (subject to the articles of association of the company) to delegate particular functions to those below them in the management chain, and to trust their competence and integrity to a reasonable extent, the exercise of the power of delegation does not absolve a director from the duty to supervise the discharge of the delegated functions[8]. Powers of delegation must be used bona fide and directors cannot form a committee to deal with the affairs of the company in order to exclude one or more of their number from acting[9].

Where powers are delegated to a committee and there is no provision for a quorum, the whole of a committee must meet and then act by a majority, and the committee has no power to add to its number or fill a vacancy[10]. An excessive exercise of the committee's powers may be ratified by the directors[11], who do not by delegation divest themselves of their powers[12], or, if need be, by the company[13]. Business informally transacted may, generally speaking, be ratified by a subsequent formal meeting[14].

A private company need not have more than one director[15], in which case it is proper for the whole of the directors' powers to be vested in him.

1 As to a company's directors see PARA 512 et seq.

2 *Howard's Case* (1866) 1 Ch App 561 (allotment of shares); *Southampton Dock Co v Richards* (1840) 1 Man & G 448 (making call). See also *Horn v Henry Faulder & Co* (1908) 99 LT 524 (delegation of control to departmental manager). As to the extent to which a stranger contracting with the company is protected where there is a power but it has not been properly exercised see PARAS 265–267. As to delegated power to bring proceedings in the name of the company see PARA 303.

3 As to a company's articles of association generally see PARA 227 et seq. As to model articles of association prescribed for the purposes of the Companies Act 2006, and their application generally, see PARA 227 et seq. Different versions of model articles have been so prescribed for use by private companies limited by shares (see the Companies (Model Articles) Regulations 2008, SI 2008/3229, reg 2, Sch 1), private companies limited by guarantee (see reg 3, Sch 2), and public companies (see reg 4, Sch 3). As to the meanings of 'company limited by guarantee', 'company limited by shares', 'limited company', 'private company' and 'public company' see PARA 95. The default articles prescribed for the purposes of the Companies Act 1985 ('legacy articles'), ie the Companies (Tables A to F) Regulations 1985, SI 1985/805, have not been revoked and may, in their amended form, continue to be used by companies after the commencement of the Companies Act 2006: see PARA 229.

4 Under the Companies (Model Articles) Regulations 2008, SI 2008/3229, subject to the articles, the directors may delegate any of the powers which are conferred on them under the articles to such person or committee, by such means (including by power of attorney), to such an extent, in relation to such matters or territories and on such terms and conditions, as they think fit: Sch 1 art 5(1), Sch 2 art 5(1), Sch 3 art 5(1). If the directors so specify, any such delegation may authorise further delegation of the directors' powers by any person to whom they are delegated (Sch 1 art 5(2), Sch 2 art 5(2), Sch 3 art 5(2)); and the directors may revoke any delegation in whole or part, or alter its terms and conditions (Sch 1 art 5(3), Sch 2 art 5(3), Sch 3 art 5(3)). Committees to which the directors delegate any of their powers must follow procedures which are based as far as they are applicable on those provisions of the articles which govern the taking of decisions by directors: Sch 1 art 6(1), Sch 2 art 6(1), Sch 3 art 6(1). The directors may make rules of procedure for all or any committees, which prevail over rules derived from the articles if they are not consistent with them: Sch 1 art 6(2), Sch 2 art 6(2), Sch 3 art 6(2). As to provision made for decision-making by directors at meetings see PARA 567.

The Companies (Tables A to F) Regulations 1985, SI 1985/805, Schedule Table A art 72 provides that the directors may delegate any of their powers to any committee consisting of one or more directors; and that they may also delegate to any managing director or any director holding any other executive office such of their powers as they consider desirable to be exercised by him. Any such delegation may be made subject to any conditions the directors may impose, and either collaterally with or to the exclusion of their own powers, and may be revoked or altered: Table A art 72. Subject to any such conditions, the proceedings of a committee with two or more members must be governed by the articles regulating the proceedings of directors so far as they are capable of applying: Table A art 72. See *Mitchell & Hobbs (UK) Ltd v Mill* [1996] 2 BCLC 102 (actual delegation required if a director is to claim powers of management separate from the collective board of directors). The directors may also, by power of attorney or otherwise, appoint any person to be the agent of the company for such purposes and on such conditions as they determine, including authority for the agent to delegate all or any of his powers: Companies (Tables A to F) Regulations 1985, SI 1985/805, Schedule Table A art 71. The Companies (Tables A to F) Regulations 1985, SI 1985/805, Schedule Table A provides regulations for the management of a company limited by shares but arts 71, 72 are applied by Table C (regulations for the management of a company limited by guarantee and not having a share capital), Table D Pt III (regulations for the management of a company limited by guarantee and having a share capital), and Table E (an unlimited company having a share capital). As to the meaning of 'unlimited company' see PARA 95. As to the meanings of 'company having a share capital' and 'share capital' see PARA 1231.

5 As to the appointment of managing directors see PARA 578.

6 *Re Fireproof Doors Ltd* [1916] 2 Ch 142; *Re Taurine Co* (1883) 25 ChD 118, CA; *Re Scottish Petroleum Co, Maclagan's Case* (1882) 51 LJ Ch 841; *Harris' Case* (1872) 7 Ch App 587 (committee for allotment).

7 *Weir v Bell* (1878) 3 ExD 238, CA.

8 *Re Barings plc (No 5), Secretary of State for Trade and Industry v Baker (No 5)* [1999] 1 BCLC 433 at 489 per Jonathan Parker J; approved [2000] 1 BCLC 523, CA. See *Re Westmid Packing Services Ltd, Secretary of State for Trade and Industry v Griffiths* [1998] 2 All ER 124 at 129–130, [1998] 2 BCLC 646 at 653, CA, per Lord Woolf MR; and see *Re City Equitable Fire Insurance Co Ltd* [1925] Ch 407. See also PARA 588.

9 *Kyshe v Alturas Gold Co* (1888) 4 TLR 331; *Bray v Smith* (1908) 124 LT Jo 293.

10 *Re Liverpool Household Stores Association* (1890) 59 LJ Ch 616. As to the quorum required for a meeting of directors see PARA 569.

11 *Bolton Partners v Lambert* (1889) 41 ChD 295, CA; *Re Portuguese Consolidated Copper Mines Ltd, ex p Badman, ex p Bosanquet* (1890) 45 ChD 16; *Hooper v Kerr, Stuart & Co Ltd* (1900) 83 LT 729; *Re City Equitable Fire Insurance Co Ltd* [1925] Ch 407.

12 *Huth v Clarke* (1890) 25 QBD 391.

13 See also the Companies Act 2006 s 180(4)(a) (cited in PARA 573); and PARAS 567, 583.

14 *Re Phosphate of Lime Co, Austin's Case* (1871) 24 LT 932.

15 See the Companies Act 2006 s 154(1); and PARA 517.

578. Position of managing directors. A managing director may be either merely a director[1] with additional functions and additional remuneration[2], or else he may be a person holding two distinct positions, that of a director and that of a manager[3]. The directors have no general right to appoint a managing director[4], nor, it seems, to remunerate him under a power to remunerate employees[5], nor to delegate to him powers which they themselves would not possess unless expressly given to them[6]. Where such a power of appointment is conferred upon the directors by the company's articles of association[7], the company cannot take it away by means of an ordinary resolution[8]; but if, owing to internal dissensions, the directors cannot make the appointment, the company may do so[9].

The appointment of a director as managing director without any specified time limit does not entitle him to hold office as managing director so long as he remains a director, nor does an article which forbids a director from voting on a contract in which he is interested prevent him from voting for his own appointment as managing director, if the appointment carries no special remuneration; but it is otherwise if it does[10]. The appointment will usually terminate if for any reason the managing director ceases to be a director[11]. If, however, he ceases to be a director before the period for which he was appointed has expired as the result of the exercise of a power introduced into the articles after his appointment, he will be entitled to damages for breach of contract[12]; but he will not be so entitled if the power existed in the articles at the date of his appointment[13].

If invalidly appointed, a director may sue for services rendered upon a quantum meruit basis[14].

1 As to a company's directors see PARA 512 et seq.

2 *Re Newspaper Pty Syndicate Ltd, Hopkinson v Newspaper Pty Syndicate Ltd* [1900] 2 Ch 349 at 350 per Cozens-Hardy J. It is obviously beyond the powers of the directors to purport to appoint a non-director to this position: see *Craven-Ellis v Canons Ltd* [1936] 2 KB 403, [1936] 2 All ER 1066, CA. A managing director's duties may be strictly controlled by contract: *Harold Holdsworth & Co (Wakefield) Ltd v Caddies* [1955] 1 All ER 725, [1955] 1 WLR 352, HL.

3 *Goodwin v Brewster (Inspector of Taxes)* (1951) 32 TC 80, CA. The statement in the text was approved in *Harold Holdsworth & Co (Wakefield) Ltd v Caddies* [1955] 1 All ER 725 at 729, [1955] 1 WLR 352 at 357, HL, per Viscount Kilmuir LC. As to presuming delegation see PARA 271 et seq. As to the duty of a managing director to exploit every opening for the

company's business even if it involves an alteration of the objects see *Fine Industrial Commodities Ltd v Powling* (1954) 71 RPC 253.

4 *Boschoek Pty Co Ltd v Fuke* [1906] 1 Ch 148 at 159 per Swinfen Eady J.

5 *Normandy v Ind, Coope & Co Ltd* [1908] 1 Ch 84; *Re Lee, Behrens & Co Ltd* [1932] 2 Ch 46 (as to the status of this case see PARA 260); *Kerr v Walker* 1933 SC 458, Ct of Sess. See also *Sputz v Broadway Engineering Co Ltd* (1944) 171 LT 50. However, it was stated in *Anderson v James Sutherland (Peterhead) Ltd* 1941 SC 230, Ct of Sess that the functions of a managing director and a director were not the same, and that in the former capacity he was within the category of members of the company 'employed by the company in any capacity'. As to payment by a percentage of profits see PARAS 560–561.

6 *Cartmell's Case* (1874) 9 Ch App 691. Cf *Gibson v Barton* (1875) LR 10 QB 329 at 336 per Blackburn J.

7 As to a company's articles of association generally see PARA 227 et seq.

The Companies (Model Articles) Regulations 2008, SI 2008/3229, provide that directors may undertake any services for the company that the directors decide: see Sch 1 art 19(1), Sch 2 art 19(1), Sch 3 art 23(1); and PARA 559. As to the model articles of association that have been prescribed for the purposes of the Companies Act 2006, and their application generally, see PARA 227 et seq.

The default articles prescribed for the purposes of the Companies Act 1985 ('legacy articles'), ie the Companies (Tables A to F) Regulations 1985, SI 1985/805, have not been revoked and may, in their amended form, continue to be used by companies after the commencement of the Companies Act 2006: see PARA 229. Accordingly, the Companies (Tables A to F) Regulations 1985, SI 1985/805, Schedule Table A makes provision for directors' appointments. Subject to the provisions of the Companies Acts, the directors may appoint one or more of their number to the office of managing director or to any other executive office of the company and may enter into an agreement or arrangement with any director for his employment by the company or for the provision by him of any services outside the scope of the ordinary duties of a director: Table A art 84. Any such appointment, agreement or arrangement may be made upon such terms as the directors determine and they may remunerate any such director for his services as they think fit; and any appointment of a director to an executive office will terminate if he ceases to be a director but without prejudice to any claim to damages for breach of the contract of service between the director and the company: Table A art 84. A managing director and a director holding any other executive office are not to be subject to retirement by rotation: Table A art 84. Cf *Read v Astoria Garage (Streatham) Ltd* [1952] Ch 637, [1952] 2 All ER 292, CA. See also *Harben v Phillips* (1883) 23 ChD 14 at 39, CA, per Cotton LJ; and cf *Bainbridge v Smith* (1889) 41 ChD 462 at 474, CA, per Cotton LJ; *Horn v Henry Faulder & Co Ltd* (1908) 99 LT 524.

The Companies (Tables A to F) Regulations 1985, SI 1985/805, Schedule Table A provides regulations for the management of a company limited by shares but art 84 is applied by Table C (regulations for the management of a company limited by guarantee and not having a share capital), Table D Pt III (regulations for the management of a company limited by guarantee and having a share capital), and Table E (an unlimited company having a share capital). As to the meaning of 'unlimited company' see PARA 95. As to the meanings of 'company having a share capital' and 'share capital' see PARA 1231.

8 *Thomas Logan Ltd v Davis* (1911) 104 LT 914; affd (1912) 105 LT 419, CA. As to ordinary resolutions see PARA 685.

9 *Foster v Foster* [1916] 1 Ch 532.

10 See note 9. As to the appointment of directors see PARA 517 et seq. As to directors' interests in contracts generally see PARAS 598, 600 et seq.

11 *Bluett v Stutchbury's Ltd* (1908) 24 TLR 469, CA; *Re Alexander's Timber Co* (1901) 70 LJ Ch 767. See also note 7. As to the retirement and re-appointment of directors see PARA 555.

12 *Nelson v James Nelson & Sons Ltd* [1914] 2 KB 770, CA; *Southern Foundries (1926) Ltd v Shirlaw* [1940] AC 701, [1940] 2 All ER 445, HL. See also note 7; and PARA 557.

13 *Read v Astoria Garage (Streatham) Ltd* [1952] Ch 637, [1952] 2 All ER 292, CA. Cf *Shindler v Northern Raincoat Co Ltd* [1960] 2 All ER 239, [1960] 1 WLR 1038, where *Read v Astoria Garage (Streatham) Ltd* [1952] Ch 637, [1952] 2 All ER 292, CA was not followed because the terms of the managing director's contract were inconsistent with powers in the articles which were held to be restricted by the contract, whereas there was no such inconsistency in *Read v Astoria Garage (Streatham) Ltd*. See PARA 557.

14 *Craven-Ellis v Canons Ltd* [1936] 2 KB 403, [1936] 2 All ER 1066, CA. See also PARA 558. As to quantum meruit see RESTITUTION vol 88 (2012) PARAS 407, 513 et seq.

579. Directors' position as trustees of the company's property. A company's directors[1] are trustees of the property of the company that is in their hands or under their control[2]; but they are not trustees for individual shareholders[3] or the creditors[4] of the company, nor are they in the same position as trustees of a will or settlement[5]. A director must account to the company for all of the company's property in his control[6].

Unless so directed by the articles, the directors are not bound to invest the funds (such as, for example, reserve funds of the company) only in securities which a trustee may invest in, but they may purchase such securities as they consider to be most beneficial for the company[7]. They may invest in the name of a sole trustee[8], and lend on securities of a speculative nature[9], but they are liable in respect of an investment made contrary to a resolution of the company effectively[10] directing a different investment[11]. Except in so far as they have properly delegated the duty of investing the funds of the company, and attending to the securities in which they are invested, directors are bound to see that the funds are in a proper state of investment[12]; and in order to ascertain the financial position of the company with a view to paying a dividend the directors should at least have before them a list of the investments[13].

1 As to a company's directors see PARA 512 et seq.

2 *Re Forest of Dean Coal Mining Co* (1878) 10 ChD 450; *Re Lands Allotment Co* [1894] 1 Ch 616, CA; *Re Faure Electric Accumulator Co* (1888) 40 ChD 141; *Flitcroft's Case* (1882) 21 ChD 519, CA; *Re Sharpe, Re Bennett, Masonic and General Life Assurance Co v Sharpe* [1892] 1 Ch 154, CA; *Re Oxford Benefit Building and Investment Society* (1886) 35 ChD 502 at 509 per Kay J; *Great Eastern Rly Co v Turner* (1872) 8 Ch App 149 at 152 per Lord Selborne LC; *Lindgren v L & P Estates Ltd* [1968] Ch 572, [1968] 1 All ER 917, CA (specific performance of contract ordered); *Selangor United Rubber Estates Ltd v Cradock (a bankrupt) (No 3)* [1968] 2 All ER 1073, [1968] 1 WLR 1555 (money in company's bank account); *International Sales and Agencies Ltd v Marcus* [1982] 3 All ER 551. See also *Regal (Hastings) Ltd v Gulliver* (1942) [1967] 2 AC 134n, [1942] 1 All ER 378; *Boardman v Phipps* [1967] 2 AC 46, [1966] 3 All ER 721, HL; *Canadian Aero Service Ltd v O'Malley* (1973) 40 DLR (3d) 371, Can SC; *Weber Feeds Ltd v Weber* (1979) 24 OR (2d) 754, Ont CA; *Belmont Finance Corpn Ltd v Williams Furniture Ltd (No 2)* [1980] 1 All ER 393, CA; *Rolled Steel Products (Holdings) Ltd v British Steel Corpn* [1986] Ch 246, [1985] 3 All ER 52, CA; *JJ Harrison (Properties) Ltd v Harrison* [2001] EWCA Civ 1467, [2002] 1 BCLC 162; *Bhullar v Bhullar* [2003] EWCA Civ 424, [2003] 2 BCLC 241. Consequently a change in the shareholders will not diminish their obligation to account: *Abbey Glen Property Corpn v Stumborg* (1978) 85 DLR (3d) 35, Alta SC. As to the general fiduciary position of directors see PARA 575. As to the duties of directors to safeguard the assets of the company and for that purpose to take reasonable steps to prevent and detect fraud and other irregularities see *Re Westmid Packing Services Ltd, Secretary of State for Trade and Industry v Griffiths* [1998] 2 All ER 124, [1998] 2 BCLC 646; and *Re Barings plc, Secretary of State for Trade and Industry v Baker (No 5)* [1999] 1 BCLC 433 (affd [2000] 1 BCLC 523) (both cases cited in PARA 589).

By the Companies Act 2006 s 222(2), a director is deemed to be trustee for the company of illegal payments made to him by way of compensation etc: see PARAS 620–625. As to joint and several liability see PARA 630 et seq.

3 They may, therefore, purchase shares in the company without disclosing to the vendors advantageous prospects of the company: *Percival v Wright* [1902] 2 Ch 421 (a case now regarded as of doubtful authority). Cf *Allen v Hyatt* (1914) 30 TLR 444, PC. For an example of a director being deemed to be trustee for individual shareholders or ex-shareholders see PARA 622. See also *Peskin v Anderson* [2001] 1 BCLC 372, CA (fiduciary duties owed by directors to shareholders arise in certain circumstances only); and PARA 575. As to shareholders and membership of companies generally see PARA 323 et seq.

4 See PARA 635.

5 *Owen and Ashworth's Claim, Whitworth's Claim* [1901] 1 Ch 115, CA (where a director took a transfer of a security irregularly issued to a creditor who had no notice of the irregularity).

6 *Cramer v Bird* (1868) LR 6 Eq 143 (defunct company; surplus assets); *Re Forest of Dean Coal Mining Co* (1878) 10 ChD 450 (omission to get in a debt; not liable for non-feasance in absence of fraud or dishonesty); *Re Lands Allotment Co* [1894] 1 Ch 616 at 631, CA, per Lindley LJ; *Selangor United Rubber Estates Ltd v Cradock (a bankrupt) (No 3)* [1968] 2 All ER 1073, [1968] 1 WLR 1555 (directors accountable for money of the company); *Re Duckwari plc* [1999] Ch 253, sub nom *Re Duckwari plc (No 2), Duckwari plc v Offerventure Ltd (No 2)* [1998] 2 BCLC 315, CA; *Bairstow v Queens Moat Houses plc* [2001] EWCA Civ 712, [2001] 2 BCLC 531; *CMS Dolphin Ltd v Simonet* [2001] 2 BCLC 704; *JJ Harrison (Properties) Ltd v Harrison* [2001] EWCA Civ 1467, [2002] 1 BCLC 162 (obligations of a director to deal with company property

as a trustee arise out of pre-existing duties as a director, not out of the circumstances in which the property was conveyed, and a claim based on the breach of such duties is proprietary in nature); *Re Loquitur Ltd, IRC v Richmond* [2003] EWHC 999 (Ch), [2003] 2 BCLC 442. As to a director's personal liability see PARA 633; and as to the liability of persons sharing in a breach of trust see PARA 632. As to relief against breach of trust or negligence see PARA 645.

7 *Burland v Earle* [1902] AC 83 at 97, PC.

8 See note 7.

9 Cf *Sheffield and South Yorkshire Permanent Building Society v Aizlewood* (1889) 44 ChD 412.

10 As to the extent to which shareholders can control directors' powers see PARA 581.

11 *Re British Guardian Life Assurance Co* (1880) 14 ChD 335.

12 *Re City Equitable Fire Insurance Co Ltd* [1925] Ch 407 at 501, CA, per Pollock MR. A finance committee is not entitled to leave even temporary investment of the company's funds under the entire control of one member: *Re City Equitable Fire Insurance Co Ltd* [1925] Ch 407, CA.

13 *Re City Equitable Fire Insurance Co Ltd* [1925] Ch 407 at 501, CA, per Pollock MR.

B. THE GENERAL DUTIES OF DIRECTORS

(A) Directors Acting within Powers

580. Directors' duty to act within powers. The Companies Act 2006, in setting out general duties[1] that are owed to the company[2], provides that a director[3] of a company must act in accordance with the company's constitution[4] and only exercise powers for the purposes for which they are conferred[5].

Generally, a company's directors may do whatever is fairly incidental to the exercise of their powers in carrying out the objects of the company[6].

1 Ie in the Companies Act 2006 ss 171–177: see also PARA 584 et seq. As to the scope and nature of the directors' general duties see PARA 572; and as to the application and effect of the general duties see PARA 573. As to the relevance of case law on those common law rules and equitable principles that are now replaced by the statutory duties see PARA 572 note 7; and see PARA 581 et seq.

2 As to the meaning of 'company' under the Companies Acts see PARA 21; and as to the meaning of the 'Companies Acts' see PARA 13.

3 As to the meaning of 'director' under the Companies Acts see PARA 512. The general duties apply also to a shadow director of a company where and to the extent that they are capable of so applying: see the Companies Act 2006 s 170(5); and PARA 573. As to shadow directors see PARA 513.

4 Companies Act 2006 s 171(a). See also PARA 581. References in Pt 10 (ss 154–259) (see PARA 512 et seq) to a company's constitution include any resolution or other decision come to in accordance with the constitution, and any decision by the members of the company (or a class of members) that is treated by virtue of any enactment or rule of law as equivalent to a decision by the company: s 257(1). This is in addition to the matters mentioned in s 17 (general provision as to matters contained in company's constitution) (see PARA 226): s 257(2). As to the meaning of 'enactment' see PARA 13 note 16; and as to the meaning of 'member of the company' see PARA 323. As to resolutions and decisions of the company generally see PARA 701 et seq. As to classes of share, and the rights attached to classes of share generally, see PARA 1246 et seq.

5 Companies Act 2006 s 171(b). See also PARA 583.

As to whether the rule in s 171(b) ('the proper purpose rule') applies for the purposes of Pt 22 (ss 791–828: see PARA 447 et seq) see *Eclairs Group Ltd v JKX Oil & Gas plc, Glengary Overseas Ltd v JKX Oil & Gas plc* [2015] UKSC 71, [2016] 1 BCLC 1, [2015] All ER (D) 20 (Dec).

As to the extent of a director's authority and powers etc see PARA 580 et seq. As to the liability of the company for the acts of its agents see PARA 268 et seq; and as to a director's position as a company's agent see PARA 270.

6 *Hutton v West Cork Rly Co* (1883) 23 ChD 654, CA; *Re Horsley & Weight Ltd* [1982] Ch 442 at 448, [1982] 3 All ER 1045 at 1050, CA, per Buckley LJ. However, in *Parke v Daily News Ltd* [1962] Ch 927, [1962] 2 All ER 929, it was held that directors were not entitled to treat dismissed employees generously beyond all entitlement (but see now the Companies Act 2006 s 247; and PARA 586). It is a breach of the duties owed by directors to the company (or alternatively an act which is ultra vires the company) to enter into an arrangement which sought to achieve a distribution of assets, as if on a winding up, without making proper provision for creditors: *MacPherson v European Strategic Bureau Ltd* [2000] 2 BCLC 683, CA. As to the meaning of 'ultra vires' for these purposes see PARA 258; and see PARA 582 et seq.

581. Directors' duty to act in accordance with constitution. The extent of the directors' authority to act[1] is a matter for the company's constitution[2], but is also a matter of agency law[3].

A company's articles of association[4] usually contain provisions as to the directors' general powers and responsibilities[5]. If, as is usual, the general management of the company's affairs is entrusted to the directors by the company's articles, a numerical majority of the shareholders insufficient to alter the articles cannot, in the absence of any provision in the articles reserving appropriate power, impose its will on the directors as regards matters so entrusted to them[6]. If the articles provide that regulations may be made by extraordinary resolution, an ordinary resolution is not sufficient to make a regulation which will control the directors[7]. If no power is reserved to the company to control the directors when acting within the powers conferred on them by the articles, the articles must be altered by special resolution, if it is desired to give the company such power[8]. Where, under the articles, the business of the company is to be managed by the directors and the articles confer on them the full powers of the company subject to such regulations, not inconsistent with the articles, as may be prescribed by the company, the shareholders are not enabled by resolution passed at a general meeting, without altering the articles, to give effective directions to the directors as to how the company's affairs are to be managed, nor are they able to overrule any decision reached by the directors in the conduct of company business[9]. An agreement made by the company which is inconsistent with the powers of management of the directors under the articles, as, for example, an agreement purporting to confer authority upon the manager of a department to act without interference by the directors, is ultra vires the articles[10].

1 As to a company's directors see PARA 512 et seq.

2 As to the meaning of references to a company's constitution under the Companies Act 2006 see PARA 226; and see PARA 580 note 4.

3 As to the directors' position as company's agents see PARA 270. As to notice of a company's constitution being assumed see PARA 265.

4 As to a company's articles of association generally see PARA 227 et seq. As to model articles of association prescribed for the purposes of the Companies Act 2006, and their application generally, see PARA 227 et seq. Different versions of model articles have been so prescribed for use by private companies limited by shares (see the Companies (Model Articles) Regulations 2008, SI 2008/3229, reg 2, Sch 1), private companies limited by guarantee (see reg 3, Sch 2), and public companies (see reg 4, Sch 3). As to the meanings of 'company limited by guarantee', 'company limited by shares', 'limited company', 'private company' and 'public company' see PARA 95. The default articles prescribed for the purposes of the Companies Act 1985 ('legacy articles'), ie the Companies (Tables A to F) Regulations 1985, SI 1985/805, have not been revoked and may, in their amended form, continue to be used by companies after the commencement of the Companies Act 2006: see PARA 229.

5 Under the Companies (Model Articles) Regulations 2008, SI 2008/3229, subject to the articles, the directors are responsible for the management of the company's business, for which purpose they may exercise all the powers of the company: Sch 1 art 3, Sch 2 art 3, Sch 3 art 3. The members or shareholders, as the case may be, may, by special resolution, direct the directors to take, or refrain from taking, specified action (Sch 1 art 4(1), Sch 2 art 4(1), Sch 3 art 4(1)); but no such special resolution invalidates anything which the directors have done before the passing of the resolution (Sch 1 art 4(2), Sch 2 art 4(2), Sch 3 art 4(2)). As to meetings of directors and their role in the management of a company see PARA 568 et seq; and as to the extent to which directors may delegate powers, including to committees, see PARA 577. As to presuming delegation see PARA 271 et seq. As to special resolutions see PARA 686. As to shareholders and the membership of companies generally see PARA 323 et seq.

The Companies (Tables A to F) Regulations 1985, SI 1985/805, Schedule Table A art 70 provides that, subject to the provisions of the Companies Acts, the memorandum and the articles, and to any directions given by special resolution, the business of the company must be managed by the directors who may exercise all the powers of the company. No alteration of the memorandum or articles and no such direction will invalidate any prior act of the directors which would have been valid if that alteration had not been made or that direction had not been given. The powers given by Table A art 70 may not be limited by any special power given to the directors by the articles and a meeting of directors at which a quorum is present may exercise all powers exercisable by the directors: Table A art 70. As to a company's memorandum of association (the role of which has been altered fundamentally under the Companies Act 2006) see PARA 97. As to the procedure for altering a company's constitutional documents generally see PARA 231 et seq. As to the quorum required for a meeting of directors see PARA 569. Under Table A art 70, the entire management of the company, including its financial direction, rests solely in the hands of the directors, and accordingly resolutions by the company purporting to interfere with this management are invalid: see *Scott v Scott* [1943] 1 All ER 582 (resolutions to make advance payments to shareholders pending declaration of dividends). As to resolutions of the company see PARA 701 et seq. The Companies (Tables A to F) Regulations 1985, SI 1985/805, Schedule Table A provides regulations for the management of a company limited by shares but art 70 is applied by Table C (regulations for the management of a company limited by guarantee and not having a share capital), Table D Pt III (regulations for the management of a company limited by guarantee and having a share capital), and Table E (an unlimited company having a share capital). As to the meaning of 'unlimited company' see PARA 95. As to the meanings of 'company having a share capital' and 'share capital' see PARA 1231.

6 See *Gramophone and Typewriter Ltd v Stanley* [1908] 2 KB 89 at 105–106, CA, per Buckley LJ; *Grundt v Great Boulder Pty Gold Mines Ltd* [1948] Ch 145 at 157, [1948] 1 All ER 21 at 29, CA, per Cohen LJ. As to the power of a majority to remove the directors under the Companies Act 2006 s 168 see PARA 557.

7 *Automatic Self-Cleansing Filter Syndicate Co Ltd v Cuninghame* [1906] 2 Ch 34, CA; *Thomas Logan Ltd v Davis* (1911) 104 LT 914 (affd (1912) 105 LT 419, CA). See also *Re Olderfleet Shipbuilding and Engineering Co Ltd* [1922] 1 IR 26; and see note 5.

8 *Quin & Axtens Ltd v Salmon* [1909] AC 442, HL.

9 See *John Shaw & Sons (Salford) Ltd v Shaw* [1935] 2 KB 113 at 134, CA, per Greer LJ; *Scott v Scott* [1943] 1 All ER 582; *Breckland Group Holdings Ltd v London & Suffolk Properties Ltd* [1989] BCLC 100. See also the cases cited in notes 6–7. Cf *Marshall's Valve Gear Co Ltd v Manning, Wardle & Co Ltd* [1909] 1 Ch 267. As to resolutions and meetings of the company generally see PARA 701 et seq.

10 *Horn v Henry Faulder & Co Ltd* (1908) 99 LT 524. As to the meaning of 'ultra vires' for these purposes see PARA 258; and see PARA 582 et seq.

582. Acts beyond the directors' authority. The validity of an act done by a company[1] may not be called into question on the ground of lack of capacity by reason of anything in the company's constitution[2].

In favour of a person dealing with the company in good faith, the power of the directors[3] to bind the company, or to authorise others to do so, is deemed to be free of any limitation under the company's constitution[4].

These provisions largely abolish the effect of the old ultra vires doctrine on relations between a company and third parties[5] and confer protection on such parties, unless they have acted in bad faith, in respect of acts beyond the authority of the directors[6].

1 As to the meaning of 'company' under the Companies Acts see PARA 21; and as to the meaning of the 'Companies Acts' see PARA 13.

2 See the Companies Act 2006 s 39(1); and PARAS 255, 264 et seq. As to the meaning of references to a company's constitution see PARA 226.

3 As to a company's directors see PARA 512 et seq.

4 See the Companies Act 2006 s 40(1); and PARA 262. The Companies Act 2006 s 40 has effect subject to s 41 (transactions with directors or their associates) (see PARA 263) and s 42 (application to acts of a company that is a charity) (see PARA 264): see s 40(6); and PARA 262.

5 See PARA 264.

6 See PARAS 262–263.

583. Directors' duty to exercise company's powers for purpose conferred. Directors in the exercise of their powers are fiduciary agents[1] for the company[2].

Save in relation to the special case of providing for employees on cessation or transfer of business[3], directors cannot in any case lawfully use their powers except for the benefit, or intended benefit, of the company[4]. The proper approach to an exercise of the directors' powers is to start with a consideration of the power itself then for the court to examine the substantial purpose for which it was exercised and to conclude whether that exercise was proper or not[5]. Their powers of making calls and forfeiting shares and so on must not be used to favour themselves above other shareholders[6], or to favour particular classes of shareholders[7]. It is unconstitutional for directors to enter into a management agreement which would frustrate the powers of management by directors at a time when, to the directors' knowledge, shareholders intend to appoint new directors, even though the directors so acting believe this to be in the best interests of the company[8].

The law relating to a company's proper purposes does not require a claimant to prove that a director[9] was dishonest, or that the director knew that he was pursuing a collateral purpose, and, in that sense, the test is an objective one[10].

When a dispute arises whether the directors of a company made a particular decision for one purpose or for another, or whether there being more than one purpose, one or another purpose was the substantial or primary purpose, the court is entitled to look at the situation objectively in order to estimate how critical or pressing or substantial an alleged requirement may have been[11].

Where directors exercise their powers improperly this may give rise to a claim by the company against them based on breach of duty[12]. However, a bona fide breach of duty may be ratified by an ordinary resolution after full and frank disclosure by the directors to the shareholders[13]. Acting fraudulently or in the furtherance of the director's own interests nullifies his actual authority, but not his apparent authority[14]. Where the other party to a transaction is on notice, however, that the transaction was entered into by the directors for purposes other than the purposes of the company in breach of their fiduciary duties, he cannot rely on the ostensible authority of the directors and, on ordinary principles of agency, cannot hold the company to the transaction[15].

The exercise by the directors of discretionary powers will not be interfered with unless it is proved that they have acted from some improper motive or arbitrarily and capriciously[16].

1 See PARA 270.
2 The directors are trustees of the property of the company in their hands or under their control: see PARA 579.
3 See PARA 586.
4 Directors may not approve transfers in order to compromise proceedings against themselves (*Bennett's Case* (1854) 5 De GM & G 284; *Re Mitre Assurance Co, Eyre's Case* (1862) 31 Beav 177), nor postpone a call for that purpose, nor cancel shares to release a shareholder from liability (*Richmond's Case, Painter's Case* (1858) 4 K & J 305), nor arrange with an applicant that he shall pay for shares only out of his emoluments as an officer of the company (*National House Property Investment Co v Watson* 1908 SC 888, following *Pellatt's Case* (1867) 2 Ch App 527; cf *Power v Hoey* (1871) 19 WR 916); they may not issue shares for an indirect purpose, such as to create votes (*Fraser v Whalley* (1864) 2 Hem & M 10; *Punt v Symons & Co Ltd* [1903] 2 Ch 506; *Piercy v S Mills & Co* [1920] 1 Ch 77; *Hogg v Cramphorn Ltd* [1967] Ch 254, [1966] 3 All ER 420; cf *Abbotsford Hotel Co Ltd and Bell v Kingham and Mann* (1910) 102 LT 118, CA; and see *Teck Corpn Ltd v Millar* (1972) 33 DLR (3d) 288, BC SC); nor may they draw bills for other purposes (*Balfour v Ernest* (1859) 5 CBNS 601); they may not summon a company meeting at such a date as to prevent shareholders voting (*Cannon v Trask* (1875) LR 20 Eq 669), or on a misleading notice (*Alexander v Simpson* (1889) 43 ChD 139, CA; *Jackson v Munster Bank* (1884) 13 LR Ir 118); nor may they prevent a properly elected director acting (*Pulbrook v Richmond Consolidated Mining Co* (1878) 9 ChD 610; *Munster v Cammell Co* (1882) 21 ChD 183; *Kyshe v Alturas Gold Co* (1888) 36 WR 496; *Harben v Phillips* (1883) 23 ChD 14, CA; *Grimwade v BPS Syndicate Ltd* (1915) 31 TLR 531).
5 *Howard Smith Ltd v Ampol Petroleum Ltd* [1974] AC 821, [1974] 1 All ER 1126, PC. See also *Extrasure Travel Insurances Ltd v Scattergood* [2002] EWHC 3093 (Ch), [2003] 1 BCLC 598; *CAS (Nominees) Ltd v Nottingham Forest FC plc* [2002] 1 BCLC 613.
6 *Alexander v Automatic Telephone Co* [1900] 2 Ch 56, CA; *Harris v North Devon Rly Co* (1855) 20 Beav 384 (forfeiture); *Bennett's Case* (1854) 5 De GM & G 284 at 297 (where shareholders

surrendered shares to nominees of the company and paid a considerable sum to the company out of which a debt due to a director was liquidated); *Gilbert's Case* (1870) 5 Ch App 559 (where a call was deferred to enable a director to transfer his shares). The onus is on the party who impeaches a call to show improper motive: *Odessa Tramways Co v Mendel* (1878) 8 ChD 235, CA. As to shareholders and membership of companies generally see PARA 323 et seq.

7 *Kerry v Maori Dream Gold Mines Ltd* (1898) 14 TLR 402, CA; *Howard Smith Ltd v Ampol Petroleum Ltd* [1974] AC 821, [1974] 1 All ER 1126, PC (power to issue and allot shares was improperly exercised where the sole object was to dilute the voting power of the majority shareholders so as to enable the minority shareholders to sell their shares more advantageously); *Re BSB Holdings Ltd (No 2)* [1996] 1 BCLC 155; *Mutual Life Insurance Co of New York v Rank Organisation Ltd* [1985] BCLC 11. See also PARA 584.

8 *Lee Panavision Ltd v Lee Lighting Ltd* [1992] BCLC 22, CA.

9 As to a company's directors see PARA 512 et seq.

10 *Extrasure Travel Insurances Ltd v Scattergood* [2002] EWHC 3093 (Ch) at [92], [2003] 1 BCLC 598 at [92] per Jonathan Crow.

11 *Howard Smith Ltd v Ampol Petroleum Ltd* [1974] AC 821, [1974] 1 All ER 1126, PC.

12 As to a director's duty to promote the success of a company see PARA 584 et seq; and as to remedies for breach see PARA 599 et seq. A claim for breach of duty will not lie at the suit of a creditor: *Western Finance Co Ltd v Tasker Enterprises Ltd* (1979) 106 DLR (3d) 81, Man CA.

13 *Bamford v Bamford* [1970] Ch 212, [1969] 1 All ER 969, CA (improper allotment of shares validated), applying dicta of Lord Russell of Killowen in *Regal (Hastings) Ltd v Gulliver* (1942) [1967] 2 AC 134n at 150, [1942] 1 All ER 378 at 380, HL, and of Sir Richard Baggallay in *North-West Transportation Co Ltd and Beatty v Beatty* (1887) 12 App Cas 589 at 593–594, PC, per Sir Richard Baggalay. As to *North-West Transportation Co Ltd and Beatty v Beatty* (1887) 12 App Cas 589 at 593–594, PC, per Sir Richard Baggalay, describing the circumstances in which a company cannot ratify breaches of duty by its directors, see *Franbar Holdings Ltd v Patel* [2008] EWHC 1534 (Ch) at [44]–[45], [2009] 1 BCLC 1, [2008] BCC 885 per William Trower QC; and see PARA 638. See also the Companies Act 2006 s 180; and PARA 573.

As to the knowledge required of a principal for ratification of an agent's act to be effective, and as to what constitutes ratificatory conduct, in the situation where one agent represented that another agent had authority to act on a principal's behalf, see *ING Re (UK) Ltd v R&V Versicherung AG* [2006] EWHC 1544 (Comm), [2006] 2 All ER (Comm) 870, [2007] 1 BCLC 108 (in order that a person might be heard to have ratified an act done without his authority, it was necessary that, at the time of the ratification, he should have full knowledge of all the material circumstances in which the act was done, unless he intended to ratify the act and take the risk whatever the circumstances might have been). The ratification, for the purpose of relieving the director of any liability for his conduct, by a company of conduct by a director amounting to negligence, default, breach of duty or breach of trust in relation to the company, as opposed to ratification in the sense of affirming or authorising the improper act, is subject to statutory constraints: see the Companies Act 2006 s 239; and PARA 638.

14 *Hopkins v TL Dallas Group Ltd* [2004] EWHC 1379 (Ch), [2005] 1 BCLC 543. See also *Criterion Properties plc v Stratford UK Properties LLC* [2004] UKHL 28 at [31], [2004] 1 WLR 1846, [2006] 1 BCLC 729 per Lord Scott of Foscote (apparent authority can only be relied on by someone who does not know that the agent has no actual authority, and if a person dealing with an agent knows or has reason to believe that the contract or transaction is contrary to the commercial interests of the agent's principal, it is likely to be very difficult for the person to assert with any credibility that he believed the agent did have actual authority; lack of such a belief would be fatal to a claim that the agent had apparent authority).

15 *Rolled Steel Products (Holdings) Ltd v British Steel Corp* [1986] Ch 246 at 296, [1985] 3 All ER 52 at 86, CA, per Slade LJ. See also *Criterion Properties plc v Stratford UK Properties LLC* [2004] UKHL 28 at [31], [2004] 1 WLR 1846, [2006] 1 BCLC 729 per Lord Scott of Foscote (cited in note 14); and *Wrexham Association Football Club Ltd v Crucialmove Ltd* [2006] EWCA Civ 237, [2008] 1 BCLC 508.

16 *Cannon v Trask* (1875) LR 20 Eq 669; *Robinson v Chartered Bank of India* (1865) LR 1 Eq 32. Even in such a case the order will not be made at the instance of some only of the members of the company: *Pergamon Press Ltd v Maxwell* [1970] 2 All ER 809, [1970] 1 WLR 1167; and see further PARA 655. In the absence of evidence to the contrary, the court will take it for granted that the directors have acted reasonably and in good faith: *Re Gresham Life Assurance Society, ex p Penney* (1872) 8 Ch App 446; *Gaiman v National Association for Mental Health* [1971] Ch 317, [1970] 2 All ER 362 (power of expulsion of members). See also *Mutual Life Insurance Co of New York v Rank Organisation Ltd* [1985] BCLC 11 (for good reasons, directors discriminated between shareholders when allotting shares to be offered for sale; since the power was exercised in good faith for the benefit of the company, and was exercised fairly as between the different

shareholders, which did not require identical treatment, the exercise was valid); and see now the Companies Act 2006 s 561 et seq; and PARA 1287 et seq. As to the exercise by directors of their discretion with regard to transfers of shares see PARA 404.

The court will not be ready to grant an injunction at the suit of a minority of the directors to control the activities of the majority: *Duncan Sandys v House of Fraser plc* 1984 SC 63,1985 SLT 200, Ct of Sess.

(B) Directors Promoting Success of the Company

584. Directors' duty to promote the success of the company. The Companies Act 2006, in setting out general duties[1] that are owed to the company[2], provides that a director[3] of a company must act in the way he considers, in good faith, would be most likely to promote the success of the company for the benefit of its members as a whole[4]. In doing so, he must have regard (amongst other matters) to:

(1) the likely consequences of any decision in the long term[5];
(2) the interests of the company's employees[6];
(3) the need to foster the company's business relationships with suppliers, customers and others[7];
(4) the impact of the company's operations on the community and the environment[8];
(5) the desirability of the company maintaining a reputation for high standards of business conduct[9]; and
(6) the need to act fairly as between members of the company[10].

Where the company is part of a group and has its own separate legal identity and its own separate creditors, the directors must continue to act in the interests of the company rather than the group[11]. In the absence of evidence of actual separate consideration of the interests of the company, the proper test is whether an intelligent and honest man in the position of a director of the company concerned could, in the whole of the existing circumstances, have reasonably believed that the transaction was for the benefit of the company[12]. Where a proposal affects the rights of different groups of shareholders as against each other, then the directors must not only exercise their powers in good faith in the interests of the company but they must also be exercised fairly as between the different classes or groups of shareholders[13]. Accordingly, the directors' powers of making calls and forfeiting shares and so on must not be used to favour themselves above other shareholders[14], or to favour particular classes of shareholders[15].

Where or to the extent that the purposes of the company consist of or include purposes other than the benefit of its members, the statutory duty[16] has effect as if the reference to promoting the success of the company for the benefit of its members were to achieving those purposes[17].

The duty so imposed[18] has effect subject to any enactment[19] or rule of law requiring directors, in certain circumstances, to consider or act in the interests of creditors of the company[20].

1 Ie in the Companies Act 2006 ss 171–177: see also PARAS 580 et seq, 587 et seq. As to the scope and nature of the directors' general duties see PARA 572; and as to the application and effect of the general duties see PARA 573. As to the relevance of case law on those common law rules and equitable principles that are now replaced by the statutory duties see PARA 572 note 7; and see PARA 580 et seq.

2 As to the meaning of 'company' under the Companies Acts see PARA 21; and as to the meaning of the 'Companies Acts' see PARA 13.

3 As to the meaning of 'director' under the Companies Acts see PARA 512. The general duties apply also to a shadow director of a company where and to the extent that they are capable of so applying: see the Companies Act 2006 s 170(5); and PARA 573. As to shadow directors see PARA 513.

4 Companies Act 2006 s 172(1). As to the meaning of 'member' see PARA 323.

This duty may require a director to disclose his own misconduct to his principal (or, more generally, information of relevance and concern to his principal) in order for the duty to be satisfied: *Item Software (UK) Ltd v Fassihi* [2004] EWCA Civ 1244, [2005] 2 BCLC 91 (director obliged to disclose secret approach to client). A director, for example, has a duty to communicate to the company information which he has acquired as director and which is relevant for the company to know and would be of interest to it: *Bhullar v Bhullar* [2003] EWCA Civ 424 at [41], [2003] 2 BCLC 241 per Jonathan Parker LJ; *British Midland Tool Ltd v Midland International Tooling Ltd* [2003] EWHC 466 (Ch), [2003] 2 BCLC 523. As part of the duty to communicate information of interest to the company, a director may have to report any knowledge he has acquired concerning competition activity involving both himself and others, whether or not the activity in itself would constitute a breach by anyone of any relevant duty owed to the company: *British Midland Tool Ltd v Midland International Tooling Ltd* [2003] EWHC 466 (Ch) at [81]–[91], [2003] 2 BCLC 523; *Crown Dilmun v Sutton* [2004] EWHC 52 (Ch) at [179]–[181], [2004] 1 BCLC 468. Cf *Horcal Ltd v Gatland* [1984] BCLC 549, CA. There is, however, no separate and independent duty of disclosure; the single and overriding touchstone is the fundamental duty of a director to act in what he considers in good faith to be in the best interests of the company: *Shepherds Investments Ltd v Walters* [2006] EWHC 836 (Ch) at [132], [2007] 2 BCLC 202 per Etherton J. See also *GHLM Trading Ltd v Maroo* [2012] EWHC 61 (Ch), [2012] 2 BCLC 369, [2012] 07 LS Gaz R 18. As to disclosure in the context of a director's general duty to avoid conflicts of interest see PARA 590 et seq.

The duty under the Companies Act 2006 s 172 was previously expressed (ie prior to directors' duties being set out in the Companies Act 2006) in terms of a duty to act bona fide in what the directors considered to be the interests of the company (and not for any collateral purpose): see *Re Smith & Fawcett Ltd* [1942] Ch 304, [1942] 1 All ER 542, CA; *Runciman v Walter Runciman plc* [1992] BCLC 1084, [1993] BCC 223; *Bishopsgate Investment Management Ltd (in liquidation) v Maxwell (No 2)* [1994] 1 All ER 261, [1993] BCLC 1282, CA; *Re DSD Holdings Ltd (No 2)* [1996] 1 BCLC 155; *Popely v Planarrive Ltd* [1997] 1 BCLC 8; *Knight v Frost* [1999] 1 BCLC 364; *CAS (Nominees) Ltd v Nottingham Forest FC plc* [2002] 1 BCLC 613; *Extrasure Travel Insurances Ltd v Scattergood* [2002] EWHC 3093 (Ch), [2003] 1 BCLC 598. See also *Howard Smith Ltd v Ampol Petroleum Ltd* [1974] AC 821, [1974] 1 All ER 1126, PC. The test was subjective, being directed at the director's state of mind (*Regentcrest plc v Cohen* [2001] 2 BCLC 80 (the question is whether the director honestly believed that his act or omission was in the interests of the company)); and this remains the case under the Companies Act 2006 s 172 (*Birdi v Specsavers Optical Group Ltd* [2015] EWHC 2870 (Ch) at [61], [2015] All ER (D) 144 (Oct)).

5 Companies Act 2006 s 172(1)(a).

6 Companies Act 2006 s 172(1)(b). By virtue of s 247, the powers of the directors of a company include (if they would not otherwise do so) power to make provision for the benefit of persons employed or formerly employed by the company, or any of its subsidiaries, in connection with the cessation or the transfer to any person of the whole or part of the undertaking of the company or that subsidiary; and this power is exercisable notwithstanding the general duty imposed by s 172: see PARA 586.

7 Companies Act 2006 s 172(1)(c).

8 Companies Act 2006 s 172(1)(d).

9 Companies Act 2006 s 172(1)(e).

10 Companies Act 2006 s 172(1)(f). See also the text and notes 18–20.

11 *Re Polly Peck International plc (in administration)* [1996] 2 All ER 433 at 444, [1996] 1 BCLC 428 at 440 per Robert Walker J; *Facia Footwear Ltd (in administration) v Hinchcliffe* [1998] 1 BCLC 218; *Secretary of State for Trade and Industry v Goldberg* [2003] EWHC 2843 (Ch), [2004] 1 BCLC 597; *Re Genosyis Technology Management Ltd, Wallach v Secretary of State for Trade and Industry* [2006] EWHC 989 (Ch), [2007] 1 BCLC 208 (a case under the Company Directors Disqualification Act 1986); *Re Mea Corporation, Secretary of State for Trade and Industry v Aviss* [2007] 1 BCLC 618 (a case under the Company Directors Disqualification Act 1986).

12 *Charterbridge Corpn Ltd v Lloyds Bank Ltd* [1970] Ch 62 at 74, [1969] 2 All ER 1185 at 1194, obiter per Pennycuik J; *Colin Gwyer & Associates Ltd v London Wharf (Limehouse) Ltd, Eaton Bray Ltd v Palmer* [2002] EWHC 2748 (Ch) at [73], [2003] 2 BCLC 153 per Leslie Kosmin QC;

Extrasure Travel Insurances Ltd v Scattergood [2002] EWHC 3093 (Ch) at [138], [2003] 1 BCLC 598 per Jonathan Crow. See also *Official Receiver v Stern* [2001] EWCA Civ 1787, [2002] 1 BCLC 119.

13 *Mutual Life Insurance Co of New York v Rank Organisation Ltd* [1985] BCLC 11; *Re BSB Holdings Ltd (No 2)* [1996] 1 BCLC 155.

14 *Alexander v Automatic Telephone Co* [1900] 2 Ch 56, CA; *Harris v North Devon Rly Co* (1855) 20 Beav 384 (forfeiture); *Bennett's Case* (1854) 5 De GM & G 284 at 297 (where shareholders surrendered shares to nominees of the company and paid a considerable sum to the company out of which a debt due to a director was liquidated); *Gilbert's Case* (1870) 5 Ch App 559 (where a call was deferred to enable a director to transfer his shares). The onus is on the party who impeaches a call to show improper motive: *Odessa Tramways Co v Mendel* (1878) 8 ChD 235, CA.

In *Hunter v Senate Support Services Ltd* [2004] EWHC 1085 (Ch), [2005] 1 BCLC 175, the court held that the decision of the directors to forfeit the claimant's shares for non-payment of a call was not made in bad faith but nevertheless was flawed (because the directors had proceeded on the mistaken basis that the only course available to them was forfeiture of the shares) and that the appropriate legal consequence of a relevant failure by directors to take into account a material consideration was voidability.

15 *Kerry v Maori Dream Gold Mines Ltd* (1898) 14 TLR 402, CA; *Howard Smith Ltd v Ampol Petroleum Ltd* [1974] AC 821, [1974] 1 All ER 1126, PC (power to issue and allot shares was improperly exercised where the sole object was to dilute the voting power of the majority shareholders so as to enable the minority shareholders to sell their shares more advantageously); *Re BSB Holdings Ltd (No 2)* [1996] 1 BCLC 155; *Mutual Life Insurance Co of New York v Rank Organisation Ltd* [1985] BCLC 11.

16 Ie the Companies Act 2006 s 172(1) (see the text and notes 1–10): see s 172(2).

17 Companies Act 2006 s 172(2).

18 Ie by the Companies Act 2006 s 172 (see the text and notes 1–10, 16–17): see s 172(3).

19 As to the meaning of 'enactment' see PARA 13 note16.

20 See the Companies Act 2006 s 172(3); and PARA 585.

585. Director's obligation to consider or act in the creditors' interests. The duty imposed on a director[1] by the Companies Act 2006[2], to act in the way he considers, in good faith, would be most likely to promote the success of the company[3] for the benefit of its members[4] as a whole, has effect subject to any enactment[5] or rule of law requiring directors, in certain circumstances, to consider or act in the interests of creditors of the company[6]. The obligation to have regard to the interests of the creditors, in addition to those of the shareholders or members[7], applies generally when the company, whether technically insolvent or not, is in financial difficulties such that the creditors' money is at risk[8].

A breach of this obligation may be challenged by a liquidator under the Insolvency Act 1986 as a misfeasance[9] or as a basis for a claim for wrongful trading[10]. The directors of an insolvent company cannot escape responsibility for breach of their fiduciary duty in relation to the interests of the creditors by raising a defence of illegality to an action brought by the liquidators to recover, for the benefit of those creditors, the loss caused to the company by their breach of fiduciary duty[11].

1 As to the meaning of 'director' under the Companies Acts see PARA 512; and as to the meaning of the 'Companies Acts' see PARA 13.

2 Ie by the Companies Act 2006 s 172 (see PARA 584): see s 172(3).

3 As to the meaning of 'company' under the Companies Acts see PARA 21.

4 As to the meaning of 'member' see PARA 323.

5 As to the meaning of 'enactment' see PARA 13 note 16.

6 Companies Act 2006 s 172(3). A director is otherwise not liable generally to creditors: see PARA 635.

7 As to shareholders and membership of companies generally see PARA 323 et seq.

8 *Re MDA Investment Management Ltd, Whalley v Doney* [2003] EWHC 2277 (Ch) at [70], [2004] 1 BCLC 217 at [70] per Park J. See also *West Mercia Safetywear Ltd v Dodd* [1988] BCLC 250, 4 BCC 30, CA (approving *Kinsela v Russell Kinsela Pty Ltd (in liquidation)* (1986) 4 NSWLR 722 at 730, NSW CA, per Street CJ); followed in *Re Micra Contracts Ltd (in*

liquidation) [2015] All ER (D) 24 (Aug). See *Facia Footwear Ltd (in administration) v Hinchcliffe* [1998] 1 BCLC 218; *Yukong Lines Ltd of Korea v Rendsburg Investments Corpn of Liberia, The Rialto (No 2)* [1998] 4 All ER 82, [1998] 1 WLR 294; *Re Pantone 485 Ltd, Miller v Bain* [2002] 1 BCLC 266; *Colin Gwyer & Associates Ltd v London Wharf (Limehouse) Ltd, Eaton Bray Ltd v Palmer* [2002] EWHC 2748 (Ch) at [74], [2003] 2 BCLC 153 per Leslie Kosmin QC; *Roberts v Frohlich* [2011] EWHC 257 (Ch), [2011] 2 BCLC 625, [2012] BCC 407; *Hedger (Liquidator of Pro4Sport Ltd) v Adams* [2015] EWHC 2540 (Ch), sub nom *Re Pro4Sport Ltd (in liquidation)* [2015] All ER (D) 12 (Sep). See also *Official Receiver v Stern* [2001] EWCA Civ 1787 at [31]–[32], [2002] 1 BCLC 119 per Morritt V-C. A failure to have regard to creditors' interests when obliged to do so merits disqualification: see *Re Genosyis Technology Management Ltd, Wallach v Secretary of State for Trade and Industry* [2006] EWHC 989 (Ch), [2007] 1 BCLC 208 (a case under the Company Directors Disqualification Act 1986); and *Re Mea Corporation, Secretary of State for Trade and Industry v Aviss* [2006] EWHC 1846 (Ch), [2007] 1 BCLC 618 (another case under the Company Directors Disqualification Act 1986 (s 6: see PARA 1769), where directors were found to be responsible for the failure of their companies to satisfy creditors and, in so doing, had failed to respect the fundamental principle that the director of a company owed a duty to exercise his powers in the best interests of the company).

A director to whom a debt is owing by the company is not in such a good position as an outside creditor; thus, where he is aware that the company is insolvent, he cannot by pressure obtain a valid security for his debt: *Gaslight Improvement Co v Terrell* (1870) LR 10 Eq 168. As to transactions at an undervalue and preferences in a winding up see COMPANY AND PARTNERSHIP INSOLVENCY vol 17 (2011) PARA 801 et seq.

9 Redress for individual creditors may lie through misfeasance proceedings by liquidators under the Insolvency Act 1986 s 212 (as to which see COMPANY AND PARTNERSHIP INSOLVENCY vol 17 (2011) PARA 646 et seq).

10 Ie, if the conditions are met, under the Insolvency Act 1986 s 214 (as to which see COMPANY AND PARTNERSHIP INSOLVENCY vol 17 (2011) PARA 872). The wording of the Insolvency Act 1986 s 214(4) is adopted in the Companies Act 2006 s 174(2) as a gloss on the duty of a director under s 174(1) to exercise reasonable care, skill and diligence: see PARA 588.

11 See J *Bilta (UK) Ltd (in liquidation) v Nazir* [2015] UKSC 23 at [130], [2015] 2 All ER 1083, [2015] 2 All ER (Comm) 281, sub nom *Jetivia SA v Bilta (UK) Ltd* [2015] 2 Lloyd's Rep 61 (creditors' interests within the scope of the fiduciary duty of the directors of an insolvent company towards the company is so that the directors should not be off the hook if they act in disregard of the creditors' interests. It would be contradictory, and contrary to the public interest, if in such circumstances their control of the company should provide a means for them to be let off the hook on the ground that their illegality tainted the liquidators' claim').

586. Directors' power to provide for employees on cessation or transfer of business. The powers of the directors[1] of a company[2] include, if they would not otherwise do so, power to make provision for the benefit of persons employed or formerly employed by the company, or any of its subsidiaries[3], in connection with the cessation or the transfer to any person of the whole or part of the undertaking[4] of the company or that subsidiary[5].

This power is exercisable notwithstanding the general duty imposed on a director by the Companies Act 2006[6], to act in the way he considers, in good faith, would be most likely to promote the success of the company for the benefit of its members[7] as a whole[8]. In the case of a company that is a charity[9], the power is exercisable notwithstanding any restrictions on the directors' powers, or the company's capacity, flowing from the objects of the company[10].

The power may only be exercised if sanctioned by a resolution of the company[11], or by a resolution of the directors[12], and only if such a resolution of the directors is authorised by the company's articles of association[13] and only if any other requirements of the company's articles as to the exercise of the power so conferred[14] are complied with[15].

Any payment made pursuant to this power[16] must be made before the commencement of any winding up of the company[17], and only out of profits of the company that are available for dividend[18]. A resolution of the directors that purports to exercise this power[19] is not sufficient sanction for payments to or for the benefit of directors, former directors or shadow directors[20].

1 As to the meaning of 'director' under the Companies Acts see PARA 512; and as to the meaning of the 'Companies Acts' see PARA 13.
2 As to the meaning of 'company' under the Companies Acts see PARA 21.
3 As to the meaning of 'subsidiary' see PARA 22.
4 As to the meaning of 'undertaking' see PARA 23 note 2.
5 Companies Act 2006 s 247(1). See also note 15. This provision negatives the effect of the decisions in *Hutton v West Cork Rly Co* (1883) 23 ChD 654, CA (a company carrying on business has power to expend its funds in gratuities to servants or directors, provided such grants are made for the purpose of advancing the interests of the company, and provided that the case is not one where the company has transferred its undertaking to another company and is being wound up); *Stroud v Royal Aquarium and Summer and Winter Garden Society Ltd* (1903) 89 LT 243; *Warren v Lambeth Waterworks* (1905) 21 TLR 685; *Parke v Daily News Ltd* [1962] Ch 927, [1962] 2 All ER 929.

As to the general duty of directors to have regard to the interests of the company's employees see the Companies Act 2006 s 172; and PARA 584.
6 Ie by the Companies Act 2006 s 172 (see PARA 584).
7 As to the meaning of 'member' see PARA 323.
8 Companies Act 2006 s 247(2).
9 In their application to a company that is a charity, the Companies Act 2006 Pt 10 Ch 2 (ss 170–181) (see PARA 573 et seq), which sets out the general duties of directors, has effect with modifications: see s 181(1); and PARA 573.
10 Companies Act 2006 s 247(3).
11 Companies Act 2006 s 247(4)(a). As to company resolutions generally see PARA 685 et seq.
12 Companies Act 2006 s 247(4)(b). As to directors' resolutions, and the provision made generally for the conduct of business at directors' meetings, see PARA 567.
13 Companies Act 2006 s 247(4), (5)(a). As to the meaning of references to a company's 'articles' see PARA 227 note 2. As to a company's articles of association generally see PARA 227 et seq. As to model articles of association prescribed for the purposes of the Companies Act 2006, and their application generally, see PARA 227 et seq. Different versions of model articles have been so prescribed for use by private companies limited by shares (see the Companies (Model Articles) Regulations 2008, SI 2008/3229, reg 2, Sch 1), private companies limited by guarantee (see reg 3, Sch 2), and public companies (see reg 4, Sch 3). As to the meanings of 'company limited by guarantee', 'company limited by shares', 'limited company', 'private company' and 'public company' see PARA 95. The default articles prescribed for the purposes of the Companies Act 1985 ('legacy articles'), ie the Companies (Tables A to F) Regulations 1985, SI 1985/805, have not been revoked and may, in their amended form, continue to be used by companies after the commencement of the Companies Act 2006: see PARA 229. See also note 15.
14 Ie by the Companies Act 2006 s 247: see s 247(6).
15 Companies Act 2006 s 247(4), (6).

Under the Companies (Model Articles) Regulations 2008, SI 2008/3229, the directors may decide to make provision for the benefit of persons employed or formerly employed by the company or any of its subsidiaries (other than a director or former director or shadow director) in connection with the cessation or transfer to any person of the whole or part of the undertaking of the company or that subsidiary: Sch 1 art 51, Sch 2 art 37, Sch 3 art 84.
16 Ie under the Companies Act 2006 s 247: see s 247(7).
17 Companies Act 2006 s 247(4), (7)(a). As to the effect of the commencement of winding up generally see COMPANY AND PARTNERSHIP INSOLVENCY vol 16 (2011) PARAS 439–440.
18 Companies Act 2006 s 247(4), (7)(b). As to distributions and dividends generally see PARA 1562 et seq.
19 Ie a resolution that is required by the Companies Act 2006 s 247(4) (see the text and notes 11–12): see s 247(5)(b).
20 Companies Act 2006 s 247(4), (5)(b). As to the meaning of 'shadow director' see PARA 513.

(C) *Directors' Exercise of Independent Judgment*

587. Director's duty to exercise independent judgment. The Companies Act 2006, in setting out general duties[1] that are owed to the company[2], provides that a director[3] of a company must exercise independent judgment[4]. This duty is not infringed by his acting either in accordance with an agreement duly entered into by the company that restricts the future exercise of discretion by its directors[5], or in a way authorised by the company's constitution[6].

Under the common law rules and equitable principles that apply in relation to this duty, directors in the exercise of their powers are fiduciary agents[7] for the company[8] and they owe a duty to the company to exercise an independent judgment accordingly[9]. Directors must not fetter their powers by contracts with or promises to other persons[10], but it does not follow that directors can never make a contract by which they bind themselves to the future exercise of their powers in a particular manner[11].

1 Ie in the Companies Act 2006 ss 171–177: see also PARA 580 et seq. As to the scope and nature of the directors' general duties see PARA 572; and as to the application and effect of the general duties see PARA 573. As to the relevance of case law on those common law rules and equitable principles that are now replaced by the statutory duties see PARA 572 note 7; and see the text and notes 7–11.

2 As to the meaning of 'company' under the Companies Acts see PARA 21; and as to the meaning of the 'Companies Acts' see PARA 13.

3 As to the meaning of 'director' under the Companies Acts see PARA 512. The general duties apply also to a shadow director of a company where and to the extent that they are capable of so applying: see the Companies Act 2006 s 170(5); and PARA 573. As to shadow directors see PARA 513.

4 Companies Act 2006 s 173(1). As to the delegation of directors' powers (by which the exercise of those powers may be affected by the will and judgment of others) see PARA 577.

5 Companies Act 2006 s 173(2)(a).

6 Companies Act 2006 s 173(2)(b). As to the meaning of references to a company's constitution for the purposes of Pt 10 (ss 154–259) (see PARA 512 et seq) see PARA 580 note 4. The provisions of s 173(2)(b) may have some relevance to the position of a nominee director who may find himself representing competing interests: see PARA 514; and see *Hawkes v Cuddy, Re Neath Rugby Ltd* [2009] EWCA Civ 291, [2009] 2 BCLC 427, [2010] BCC 597 (in which a nomination arrangement was subject to an informal agreement regarding its operation). See also the text and notes 10–11.

7 See PARA 270; and as to the position of directors generally see PARA 575.

8 The directors are trustees of the property of the company in their hands or under their control: see PARA 579.

9 See also *Fulham Football Club Ltd v Cabra Estates plc* [1994] 1 BCLC 363, CA; *Thorby v Goldberg* (1964) 112 CLR 597, Aust HC. As to the directors' responsibilities in a take-over see PARA 1683 et seq.

10 *Clark v Workman* [1920] 1 IR 107. See also *Horn v Henry Faulder & Co Ltd* (1908) 99 LT 524 (where an agreement giving a manager exclusive powers in a department contrary to an article giving the directors supreme control in the management of the company was held ultra vires the articles); and see the text and notes 5–6.

11 *Fulham Football Club Ltd v Cabra Estates plc* [1994] 1 BCLC 363 at 392, CA, per Neill LJ; *Thorby v Goldberg* (1964) 112 CLR 597, Aust HC. In so far as the cases of *Rackham v Peek Foods Ltd (1977)* [1990] BCLC 895 and *John Crowther Group plc v Carpets International plc* [1990] BCLC 460 (in neither of which was *Thorby v Goldberg* (1964) 112 CLR 597, Aust HC cited) can be read as laying down a general proposition that directors can never bind themselves as to the future exercise of their fiduciary powers, they would be wrong: *Fulham Football Club Ltd v Cabra Estates plc* [1994] 1 BCLC 363 at 393 per Neill LJ. See also the text and notes 5–6.

(D) Directors' Exercise of Care, Skill and Diligence

588. Director's duty to exercise reasonable care, skill and diligence. The Companies Act 2006, in setting out general duties[1] that are owed to the company[2], provides that a director[3] of a company must exercise reasonable care, skill and diligence[4]. This means the care, skill and diligence that would be exercised by a reasonably diligent person with:

(1) the general knowledge, skill and experience that may reasonably be expected of a person carrying out the functions carried out by the director in relation to the company[5]; and

(2) the general knowledge, skill and experience that the director has[6].

The wording that appears under heads (1) and (2) above is identical in its terms to the provisions of the Insolvency Act 1986 which deal with wrongful trading[7], in relation to the facts which a director of a company ought to know or ascertain, the conclusions which he ought to reach and the steps which he ought to take, being those which would be known or ascertained, or reached or taken, by a reasonably diligent person[8].

The court will assess the competence of the director in the context of and by reference to how a particular company's business is organised and the part which the director could reasonably have been expected to play, given the role in the management chain of the company which was in fact assigned to him, or which he in fact assumed, and by reference to his duties and responsibilities in that role[9]. There must be sufficient causal link between the breach of duty by the director and the loss suffered by the company[10].

Facts which may show imprudence in the exercise of powers clearly conferred upon directors will not subject them to personal responsibility unless the imprudence amounts to negligence, which must be distinctly charged[11]. If they act within their powers, they are not liable for loss to the company occasioned by mere imprudence or error of judgment[12], and, in making investments, they are only bound to act in the same manner as business persons of ordinary prudence[13].

Despite being obliged to exercise his own independent judgment[14], the fact that a director has acted in reliance on professional advice may be an important factor in determining if he was in breach of his duty to exercise reasonable care[15].

1 Ie in the Companies Act 2006 ss 171–177: see also PARA 580 et seq. As to the scope and nature of the directors' general duties see PARA 572; and as to the application and effect of the general duties see PARA 573. As to the relevance of case law on those common law rules and equitable principles that are now replaced by the statutory duties see PARA 572 note 7; and see PARA 581 et seq.

2 As to the meaning of 'company' under the Companies Acts see PARA 21; and as to the meaning of the 'Companies Acts' see PARA 13.

3 As to the meaning of 'director' under the Companies Acts see PARA 512. The general duties apply also to a shadow director of a company where and to the extent that they are capable of so applying: see the Companies Act 2006 s 170(5); and PARA 573. As to shadow directors see PARA 513.

4 Companies Act 2006 s 174(1).

It is, in any case, an implied term of a contract of service that a person will perform his duties with proper care and skill: see *Lister v Romford Ice and Cold Storage Co Ltd* [1957] AC 555 at 572–573, [1957] 1 All ER 125 at 130, HL, per Viscount Simonds; and EMPLOYMENT vol 39 (2014) PARA 65. See further PARA 589. However, the provisions of the Supply of Goods and Services Act 1982 s 13 (which state that, in a relevant contract for the supply of a service where the supplier is acting in the course of a business, there is an implied term that the supplier will carry out the service with reasonable care and skill) (see SALE OF GOODS AND SUPPLY OF SERVICES vol 91 (2012) PARA 330) do not apply to services rendered to a company by a director in his capacity as such: Supply of Services (Exclusion of Implied Terms) Order 1982, SI 1982/1771, art 2(2).

5 Companies Act 2006 s 174(2)(a).

6 Companies Act 2006 s 174(2)(b).

7 Ie the Insolvency Act 1986 s 214 (declaration of liability for wrongful trading) (see COMPANY AND PARTNERSHIP INSOLVENCY vol 17 (2011) PARA 872).

8 See the Insolvency Act 1986 s 214(4); and COMPANY AND PARTNERSHIP INSOLVENCY vol 17 (2011) PARA 872. In proceedings under the Insolvency Act 1986 s 214, the standard has been described as an objective minimum, although one which may be raised by the particular attributes of the director in question: see *Re Brian D Pierson (Contractors) Ltd* [2001] 1 BCLC 275 (no suggestion that any higher standard than the objective minimum applied in that case).

Prior to the enactment of the Companies Act 2006 s 174, the wording of the Insolvency Act 1986 s 214(4) (see note 7) was recognised judicially as being a useful exposition of the standard of care required of a director generally under company law: see *Norman v Theodore Goddard (a firm), (Quirk, third party)* [1991] BCLC 1028; *Re D'Jan of London Ltd* [1994] 1 BCLC 561 at 563 per Hoffmann LJ; *Re Landhurst Leasing plc, Secretary of State for Trade and Industry v Ball*

[1999] 1 BCLC 286 at 344 per Hart J; *Cohen v Selby* [2001] 1 BCLC 176 at 183, CA, per Chadwick LJ; *Re Loquitur Ltd, IRC v Richmond* [2003] EWHC 999 (Ch) at [241], [2003] 2 BCLC 442 per Etherton J. The statutory statement contained in the Insolvency Act 1986 s 214(4) was thought to reflect modern standards more accurately than the formulation, which had been much cited in this context, given in *Re City Equitable Fire Insurance Co Ltd* [1925] Ch 407 at 427–430 per Romer J (a director need not exhibit in the performance of his duties a greater degree of skill than may reasonably be expected from a person of his knowledge and experience). See also *Equitable Life Assurance Society v Bowley* [2003] EWHC 2263 (Comm) at [41], [2004] 1 BCLC 180.

9 *Bishopsgate Investment Management Ltd (in liquidation) v Maxwell (No 2)* [1994] 1 All ER 261 at 264, [1993] BCLC 1282 at 1285, CA, per Hoffmann LJ. It is arguable that a company may reasonably at least look to non-executive directors for independence of judgment and supervision of the executive management: see *Equitable Life Assurance Society v Bowley* [2003] EWHC 2263 (Comm) at [41], [2004] 1 BCLC 180 per Langley J. See also eg *Re Finelist Group Ltd, Secretary of State for Trade and Industry v Swan (No 2)* [2005] EWHC 603 (Ch), [2005] BCC 596, [2005] All ER (D) 102 (Apr) (manner in which very experienced, senior non-executive director dealt with serious 'whistle blowing' was wholly inappropriate, unsatisfactory and inadequate) (case decided under the Company Directors Disqualification Act 1986).

In *Bishopsgate Investment Management Ltd (in liquidation) v Maxwell (No 2)* [1994] 1 All ER 261 at 264, [1993] BCLC 1282 at 1285, CA, Hoffmann LJ acknowledged that, in the older cases, the duty of a director to participate in the management of a company is stated in very undemanding terms and that the law may be evolving in response to changes in public attitudes to corporate governance, as shown by the enactment of the provisions consolidated in the Company Directors Disqualification Act 1986. The directors' duty to exercise reasonable care, skill and diligence has often been discussed in the context of proceedings under the Company Directors Disqualification Act 1986 (as to which generally see PARA 1759 et seq) and a summary of the principles that govern this particular directors' duty is incomplete without reference also to matters, for example, which have been considered when determining the unfitness of directors under that Act (see PARA 1762 et seq). Accordingly, see also *Re Polly Peck International plc (No 2)* [1994] 1 BCLC 574 at 594 per Lindsay J; *Re Barings plc, Secretary of State for Trade and Industry v Baker (No 5)* [1999] 1 BCLC 433 at 489 per Jonathan Parker J (affd [2000] 1 BCLC 523, CA); *Re Vintage Hallmark plc, Secretary of State for Trade and Industry v Grove* [2006] EWHC 2761 (Ch), [2007] 1 BCLC 788, [2006] All ER (D) 196 (Nov) (all cases decided under the Company Directors Disqualification Act 1986).

10 *Cohen v Selby* [2001] 1 BCLC 176, CA. Where the alleged breach consists of an omission, it must be proved that compliance with the duty would have prevented the loss: *Bishopsgate Investment Management Ltd (in liquidation) v Maxwell (No 2)* [1994] 1 All ER 261 at 264, [1993] BCLC 1282 at 1285, CA, per Hoffmann LJ. The duty of care must be owed in respect of the type of loss that has occurred: *Re Continental Assurance Co of London plc (No 4), Singer v Beckett* [2007] 2 BCLC 287 at [405]–[407], [2001] BPIR 733 per Park J (a case decided under the Insolvency Act 1986 s 214 (declaration of liability for wrongful trading) (see COMPANY AND PARTNERSHIP INSOLVENCY vol 17 (2011) PARA 872)); and see *Lexi Holdings (in administration) v Luqman* [2009] EWCA Civ 117, [2009] 2 BCLC 1, [2009] BCC 716 (had the directors in question acted, losses would have been prevented; their failure to act meant that they were liable); *Weavering Capital (UK) Ltd (in liquidation) v Dabhia* [2013] EWCA Civ 71, sub nom *Weavering Capital (UK) Ltd (in liquidation) v Peterson* [2013] All ER (D) 169 (Feb) (directors negligently enabling fraudulent investment business to continue). As to a director's personal liability see PARA 633; and as to the liability of persons sharing in a breach of trust see PARA 632.

11 *Overend, Gurney & Co v Gibb and Gibb* (1872) LR 5 HL 480 at 487, 495 per Lord Hatherley LC; *Lagunas Nitrate Co v Lagunas Syndicate* [1899] 2 Ch 392 at 435, CA, per Lindley MR; *Re National Bank of Wales Ltd* [1899] 2 Ch 629, CA; *Re Brazilian Rubber Plantations and Estates Ltd* [1911] 1 Ch 425.

12 Eg by making loans to customers or others on insufficient security (*Dovey v Cory* [1901] AC 477, HL; *Re New Mashonaland Exploration Co* [1892] 3 Ch 577; *Rainford v James Keith and Blackman Co Ltd* [1905] 2 Ch 147, CA; *Turquand v Marshall* (1869) 4 Ch App 376; *Grimwade v Mutual Society* (1884) 52 LT 409); by approving transfer of partly paid shares (*Re Faure Electric Accumulator Co* (1888) 40 ChD 141; but see *Re Hoylake Rly Co, ex p Littledale* (1874) 9 Ch App 257, where calls were due); by including bad debts as good in balance sheet (*Re Railway and General Light Improvement Co, Marzetti's Case* (1880) 42 LT 206, CA); by allowing calls to remain unpaid (*Re Liverpool Household Stores Association* (1890) 59 LJ Ch 616 at 625 per Kekewich J); or by not suing for a debt (*Re Forest of Dean Coal Mining Co* (1878) 10 ChD 450; and see *London Financial Association v Kelk* (1884) 26 ChD 107). As to improper payment of dividends see PARAS 1580, 1585.

In *Re Continental Assurance Co of London plc (No 4), Singer v Beckett* [2007] 2 BCLC 287, [2001] BPIR 733, [2001] All ER (D) 229 (Apr), a case decided under the Insolvency Act 1986 s 214 (declaration of liability for wrongful trading) (see COMPANY AND PARTNERSHIP INSOLVENCY vol 17 (2011) PARA 872), liability was not established because the directors had made a genuine attempt to grapple with the company's real financial position and, after careful thought, they had decided (wrongly, as it turned out) that the company should trade on. Similarly, in *Re Uno plc and World of Leather plc, Secretary of State for Trade and Industry v Gill* [2004] EWHC 933 (Ch), [2006] BCC 725, a case decided under the Company Directors Disqualification Act 1986 (see note 9), it was held that continuing to accept customer deposits and using these to fund ongoing trading did not necessarily amount to unfitness, given that at all material times there was a reasonable prospect of avoiding insolvency thereby. See also *ARB International Ltd v Baillie* [2013] EWHC 2060 (Comm), [2014] Lloyd's Rep IR 10, [2013] All ER (D) 161 (Jul).

13 *Sheffield and South Yorkshire Permanent Building Society v Aizlewood* (1889) 44 ChD 412 at 454, 459 per Stirling J.

14 See the Companies Act 2006 s 173; and PARA 587.

15 See *Hedger (Liquidator of Pro4Sport Ltd) v Adams* [2015] EWHC 2540 (Ch) at [45]–[47], sub nom *Re Pro4Sport Ltd (in liquidation)* [2015] All ER (D) 12 (Sep) per Behrens J.

589. Directors' obligation to acquire knowledge and understanding and to exercise supervision. Directors, collectively and individually, have a continuing duty to acquire and maintain a sufficient knowledge and understanding of the company's business to enable them properly to discharge their duties as directors[1]. Whilst directors are entitled, subject to the articles of association of the company[2], to delegate particular functions to those below them in the management chain[3], and to trust their competence and integrity to a reasonable extent, the exercise of the power of delegation does not absolve a director from the duty to supervise the discharge of the delegated functions[4]. No rule of universal application can be formulated as to the duty to supervise, and the extent of the duty, and the question whether it has been discharged must depend on the facts of each particular case, including the director's role in the management of the company[5].

Directors are not guilty of negligence if they fail to supervise acts of co-directors whom they have no reason to distrust[6] or act in reliance on the officers of the company whom they are entitled to trust and whose reports and statements have misled them[7]; nor are they bound to know the contents of the company's books[8].

A director is not liable for the misapplication of a cheque properly drawn[9], but, before a director signs a cheque, he should satisfy himself that a resolution of the directors or of a committee of the directors has authorised the payment[10]. A director is not liable for omitting to claim a debt to the company, or to enforce a liability incurred before he joined the board[11].

1 See the following cases decided under the Company Directors Disqualification Act 1986 (see PARA 588 note 9): *Re Barings plc, Secretary of State for Trade and Industry v Baker (No 5)* [1999] 1 BCLC 433 at 489 per Jonathan Parker J (affd [2000] 1 BCLC 523 at 535–536, CA, per Morritt LJ); *Re Westmid Packing Services Ltd, Secretary of State for Trade and Industry v Griffiths* [1998] 2 All ER 124 at 130, [1998] 2 BCLC 646 at 653, CA, per Lord Woolf MR; *Re Landhurst Leasing plc, Secretary of State for Trade and Industry v Ball* [1999] 1 BCLC 286 at 346 per Hart J; *Official Receiver v Vass* [1999] BCC 516; *Re Kaytech International plc, Secretary of State for Trade and Industry v Kaczer* [1999] 2 BCLC 351 at 425, CA, per Robert Walker LJ; *Re Park House Properties Ltd* [1997] 2 BCLC 530 (company directors who were husband, wife, son and daughter all disqualified); *Re Galeforce Pleating Co Ltd* [1999] 2 BCLC 704; *Re Vintage Hallmark plc, Secretary of State for Trade and Industry v Grove* [2006] EWHC 2761 (Ch), [2007] 1 BCLC 788, [2006] All ER (D) 196 (Nov). A knowledge of the company's affairs includes an obligation on a director to be informed as to the financial affairs of the company: *Re Galeforce Pleating Co Ltd* [1999] 2 BCLC 704 at 716.

See also *Daniels v Anderson* (1995) 37 NSWLR 438, 16 ACSR 607, NSW CA; *Re Continental Assurance Co of London plc (No 4), Singer v Beckett* [2007] 2 BCLC 287, [2001] BPIR 733.

2 As to a company's articles of association generally see PARA 227 et seq.

3 As to the delegation of directors' powers generally see PARA 577.

4 See the following cases decided under the Company Directors Disqualification Act 1986 (see PARA 588 note 9): *Re Barings plc, Secretary of State for Trade and Industry v Baker (No 5)* [1999] 1 BCLC 433 at 489 per Jonathan Parker J (affd [2000] 1 BCLC 523 at 535–536, CA, per Morritt LJ); *Re Westmid Packing Services Ltd, Secretary of State for Trade and Industry v*

Griffiths [1998] 2 All ER 124 at 130, [1998] 2 BCLC 646 at 653, CA, per Lord Woolf MR (directors failed to resist colleague who dominated the company); *Re Landhurst Leasing plc, Secretary of State for Trade and Industry v Ball* [1999] 1 BCLC 286 at 346 per Hart J; *Re Stephenson Cobbold Ltd, Secretary of State for Trade and Industry v Stephenson* [2000] 2 BCLC 614 (director entitled to rely on advice of company's auditors); *Re Bradcrown Ltd, Official Receiver v Ireland* [2001] 1 BCLC 547 (director abdicated all responsibility to financial advisers); *Re Vintage Hallmark plc, Secretary of State for Trade and Industry v Grove* [2006] EWHC 2761 (Ch), [2007] 1 BCLC 788, [2006] All ER (D) 196 (Nov). A consistent theme in the cases decided under the Company Directors Disqualification Act 1986 is that, while the court had to consider the extent of a director's responsibility, a director could not avoid his responsibility by leaving the management to another or others: *Secretary of State for Business Enterprise and Regulatory Reform v Sullman* [2008] EWHC 3179 (Ch) at [2], [2009] 1 BCLC 397; *Secretary of State for Trade and Industry v Thornbury* [2007] EWHC 3202 (Ch), [2008] 1 BCLC 139 (it is no defence to say that the matter was left to others, unless and except to the extent that it was reasonable to do so). Accordingly, a director who has abdicated his responsibility to participate with fellow directors may be deemed to have acquiesced in misconduct (*Re AG (Manchester) Ltd (in liquidation), Official Receiver v Watson* [2008] EWHC 64 (Ch), [2008] 1 BCLC 321, [2008] All ER (D) 188 (Jan) (director who objected to malpractices was deemed nevertheless to be in dereliction of duty over her failure to resign on the matter)); and the duty to act cannot be excused by lack of curiosity or lack of action (*Lexi Holdings (in administration) v Luqman* [2009] EWCA Civ 117, [2009] 2 BCLC 1, [2009] All ER (D) 269 (Feb)).

See also *Re Continental Assurance Co of London plc (No 4), Singer v Beckett* [2007] 2 BCLC 287 at 445, [2001] BPIR 733; *Re City Equitable Fire Insurance Co Ltd* [1925] Ch 407; *Dovey v Cory* [1901] AC 477, HL.If it is pleaded that delegation was made to a person who was unsuitable to be entrusted with the powers, it must be established that the person was unsuitable and that the directors knew or ought to have known that or that they failed to consider the question at all: *Cohen v Selby* [2001] 1 BCLC 176 at 185, CA, per Chadwick LJ. The extent to which a non-executive director may reasonably rely on the executive directors and other professionals to perform their duties is one in which the law can fairly be said to be developing and is plainly 'fact sensitive': *Equitable Life Assurance Society v Bowley* [2003] EWHC 2263 (Comm) at [41], [2004] 1 BCLC 180 per Langley J.

5 *Re Barings plc, Secretary of State for Trade and Industry v Baker (No 5)* [1999] 1 BCLC 433 at 489 per Jonathan Parker J; affd [2000] 1 BCLC 523 at 535–536, CA, per Morritt LJ (case decided under the Company Directors Disqualification Act 1986 (see PARA 588 note 9)). The cogency of the evidence required also may vary according to the seriousness of the allegation: *Re Finelist Group Ltd, Secretary of State for Trade and Industry v Swan (No 2)* [2005] EWHC 603 (Ch), [2005] BCC 596, [2005] All ER (D) 102 (Apr) (case also decided under the Company Directors Disqualification Act 1986).

6 *Huckerby v Elliott* [1970] 1 All ER 189, DC (director failed to make specific inquiry whether a gaming licence had been obtained by a co-director). A director with grounds for suspecting the honesty of a fellow director will be liable if he or she fails to act on those suspicions: *Lexi Holdings (in administration) v Luqman* [2009] EWCA Civ 117, [2009] 2 BCLC 1, [2009] BCC 716. Older authorities must now be read in the light of the modern developments noted in PARA 588 notes 8–9.

7 *Dovey v Cory* [1901] AC 477, HL (affg *Re National Bank of Wales Ltd* [1899] 2 Ch 629, CA); *Prefontaine v Grenier* [1907] AC 101, PC; *Re City Equitable Fire Insurance Co Ltd* [1925] Ch 407, CA; *Ammonia Soda Co v Chamberlain* [1918] 1 Ch 266, CA.

8 *Hallmark's Case* (1878) 9 ChD 329, CA (where there was no obligation on the director to take shares, and knowledge that his name was on the share register was not imputed to him); *Re Printing Telegraph and Construction Co of the Agence Havas, ex p Cammell* [1894] 1 Ch 528 (affd [1894] 2 Ch 392, CA) (where the director retired upon being asked to apply for shares); *Dovey v Cory* [1901] AC 477 at 492, HL, per Lord Davey, following *Re Denham & Co* (1883) 25 ChD 752; *Cartmell's Case* (1874) 9 Ch App 691 (knowledge of the contents of the share register and entries in other books showing purchase of company's shares). See also *Turquand v Marshall* (1869) 4 Ch App 376; *Re British Provident Life and Fire Assurance Society, Lane's Case* (1863) 1 De GJ & Sm 504; *Re City Equitable Fire Insurance Co Ltd* [1925] Ch 407, CA. See also *Re Queen's Moat Houses plc, Secretary of State for Trade and Industry v Bairstow* [2004] EWHC 1730 (Ch), [2005] 1 BCLC 136 (defendant was not under a duty to verify the execution of tasks delegated to the finance director which were properly within the expertise of an accountant and which the defendant had no reason to doubt were being properly performed) (decided under the Company Directors Disqualification Act 1986 (see PARA 588 note 9)). As to statutory liability for failing to take reasonable steps to secure that proper accounts are kept see PARA 782.

9 *Re Montrotier Asphalte Co, Perry's Case* (1876) 34 LT 716.

10 *Re City Equitable Fire Insurance Co Ltd* [1925] Ch 407 (in which is also discussed at 460 how far precautions should be taken when the resolution which is acted on is one for payment of

cheques up to an aggregate amount); *Joint Stock Discount Co v Brown* (1869) LR 8 Eq 381 at 404 per Sir WM James V-C. Cf *Ramskill v Edwards* (1885) 31 ChD 100. See also *Dorchester Finance Co Ltd v Stebbing* (1977) [1989] BCLC 498 (directors negligent in signing blank cheques); *Re Finelist Group Ltd, Secretary of State for Trade and Industry v Swan (No 2)* [2005] EWHC 603 (Ch), [2005] BCC 596, [2005] All ER (D) 102 (Apr) (size of cheques should have put directors on inquiry). As to the extent to which directors may delegate powers, including to committees, see PARA 577.

11 *Re Forest of Dean Coal Mining Co* (1878) 10 ChD 450.

(E) Directors' Duty as to Conflicts of Interest

590. Director's duty to avoid conflicts of interest. The Companies Act 2006, in setting out general duties[1] that are owed to the company[2], provides that a director[3] of a company must avoid a situation in which he has, or can have, a direct or indirect interest that conflicts, or possibly may conflict, with the interests of the company[4]. This duty applies in particular to the exploitation of any property, information or opportunity, and it is immaterial whether the company could take advantage of the property, information or opportunity[5]. The duty is not, however, infringed if the matter is authorised by the directors[6], or by the shareholders[7], or by the articles[8].

The test is whether reasonable persons looking at the facts would think there was a real possibility of conflict[9].

A director must account to the company for any unauthorised profits made by him when in a position of conflict[10]. This rule is absolute and independent of any question of fraud or absence of good faith[11], and it matters not that the company itself could not have made the profits, or the quantum of profits, which the director made[12]. If, however, the company renounces its interest in a particular venture, with full knowledge of the circumstances, which is then taken up by the director, he will no longer be liable to account[13]. Equally, a company with full knowledge of the circumstances of a director's interest in a proposed transaction with the company may approve or acquiesce in his profiting[14].

If directors use their position as directors to obtain for themselves the property of the company, as, for example, by means of securing a beneficial contract, they cannot by using their voting power as shareholders in general meeting prevent the company from claiming the benefit of it[15]. A director continues to be subject to the duty to avoid conflicts of interest, as regards the exploitation of any property, even when he ceases to be a director[16], especially if he resigns with a view to taking advantage of current business opportunities available to the company[17].

The statutory duty to avoid conflicts of interest[18] does not apply to a conflict of interest arising in relation to a transaction or arrangement with the company[19]; and the duty is not infringed if the situation cannot reasonably be regarded as likely to give rise to a conflict of interest[20], or if the matter has been authorised by the directors[21].

Directors who make what they believe to be a beneficial contract for the company are not chargeable with breach of trust merely because in promoting the interests of the company they were promoting their own interests by enabling themselves to sell their shares at a profit[22].

1 Ie in the Companies Act 2006 ss 171–177: see also PARA 580 et seq. As to the scope and nature of the directors' general duties see PARA 572; and as to the application and effect of the general duties see PARA 573. As to the relevance of case law on those common law rules and equitable principles that are now replaced by the statutory duties see PARA 572 note 7.

2 As to the meaning of 'company' under the Companies Acts see PARA 21; and as to the meaning of the 'Companies Acts' see PARA 13.

3 As to the meaning of 'director' under the Companies Acts see PARA 512. The general duties apply also to a shadow director of a company where and to the extent that they are capable of so applying: see the Companies Act 2006 s 170(5); and PARA 573. As to shadow directors see PARA 513.

4 Companies Act 2006 s 175(1). Any reference in s 175 to a conflict of interest includes a conflict of interest and duty and a conflict of duties: s 175(7). See the text and notes 10–17. The duty to avoid conflicts has an obvious bearing on interests in proposed or existing transactions or agreements involving the company and special provision is made in relation to those: see the text and notes 18–19; and PARA 595 et seq.

At common law, the general rule is that no fiduciary is allowed to enter into engagements in which he has, or can have, a personal interest conflicting, or which may possibly conflict, with the interests of those whom he is bound to protect: *Aberdeen Rly Co v Blaikie Bros* (1854) 1 Macq 461 at 471 per Lord Cranworth LC (rule described as 'of universal application'); *Bray v Ford* [1896] AC 44 at 51, HL, per Lord Herschell (rule described as 'inflexible'); *Bhullar v Bhullar* [2003] EWCA Civ 424, [2003] 2 BCLC 241. As to the general fiduciary position of directors see PARA 572 et seq.

Directors cannot in the absence of express contract be restrained from acting as directors of a competing company: *London and Mashonaland Exploration Co Ltd v New Mashonaland Exploration Co Ltd* [1891] WN 165, approved in *Bell v Lever Bros Ltd* [1932] AC 161 at 195, HL, per Lord Blanesburgh. However, the principle established in *London and Mashonaland Exploration Co Ltd v New Mashonaland Exploration Co Ltd* [1891] WN 165 may be restricted to its very individual facts and (accordingly) limited in its application: see *In Plus Group Ltd v Pyke* [2002] EWCA Civ 370 at [84], [2002] 2 BCLC 201 per Sedley LJ; *British Midland Tool Ltd v Midland International Tooling Ltd* [2003] EWHC 466 (Ch) at [82], [2003] 2 BCLC 523 per Hart J; *Foster Bryant Surveying Ltd v Bryant* [2007] EWCA Civ 200 at [70], [2007] 2 BCLC 239 per Rix LJ. See also PARA 572. Where a director had been effectively excluded from the first company, it was not a breach of fiduciary duty for him to work for a competing company where, when entering into business with this company, he had not made use of the first company's property or of confidential information which had come to him as director of that company: *In Plus Group Ltd v Pyke* [2002] EWCA Civ 370, [2002] 2 BCLC 201.

5 Companies Act 2006 s 175(2). See the text and notes 10–17. As to a director's position at common law as trustee of the company's property see PARA 579.

6 See PARA 591.

7 See the Companies Act 2006 s 180(4)(a); and PARA 573. But see also the text and note 15. As to shareholders and membership of companies generally see PARA 323 et seq.

8 Ie but only to the extent permitted by the Companies Act 2006 s 180(4)(a) (see PARA 573), which must be read in conjunction with s 232(4) (providing that nothing in s 232 prevents a company's articles from making such provision as has previously been lawful for dealing with conflicts of interest) (see PARA 639). As to a company's articles of association generally see PARA 227 et seq.

The model articles of association that have been prescribed for the purposes of the Companies Act 2006 (ie the Companies (Model Articles) Regulations 2008, SI 2008/3229) (as to which see PARA 227 et seq) do not make any provision explicitly in relation to a director's interests but they do make provision (as do the Companies (Tables A to F) Regulations 1985, SI 1985/805, Schedule Table A arts 85–86 otherwise) for conflicts that may arise from any interests a director may have in an actual or proposed transaction or arrangement with the company: see PARA 595. See also PARA 598 note 4.

The Companies (Tables A to F) Regulations 1985, SI 1985/805, which constitute model articles that were prescribed for the purposes of the Companies Act 1985, have not been revoked and may, in their amended form, continue to be used by companies after the commencement of the Companies Act 2006: see PARA 229. Accordingly, the Companies (Tables A to F) Regulations 1985, SI 1985/805, Schedule Table A provides that, subject to the provisions of the Companies Act 2006, and provided that he has disclosed to the directors the nature and extent of any material interest of his, a director notwithstanding his office, may be a director or other officer of, or employed by, or otherwise interested in, any body corporate promoted by the company or in which the company is otherwise interested, and is not, by reason of his office, accountable to the company for any benefit which he derives from any such office or employment or from any interest in any such body corporate: see Table A art 85. For these purposes, an interest of which a director has no knowledge and of which it is unreasonable to expect him to have knowledge is not treated as an interest of his: see Table A art 86. Special provision is made by Table A arts 85–86 also in relation to interests in proposed or existing transactions or agreements involving the company: see PARA 595. The Companies (Tables A to F) Regulations 1985, SI 1985/805, Schedule Table A provides regulations for the management of a company limited by shares but arts 85–86 are applied by Table C (regulations for the management of a company limited by guarantee and not having a share capital), Table D Pt III (regulations for the management of a company limited by guarantee and having a share capital), and Table E (an unlimited company having a share capital). As to the meaning of 'unlimited company' see PARA 95. As to the meanings of 'company having a share capital' and 'share capital' see PARA 1231.

9 *Boardman v Phipps* [1967] 2 AC 46 at 124, [1966] 3 All ER 721 at 756, HL, per Lord Upjohn; *Bhullar v Bhullar* [2003] EWCA Civ 424, [2003] 2 BCLC 241. See also *Aberdeen Rly Co v Blaikie Bros* (1854) 1 Macq 461.

Where two directors became involved personally in a company transaction which was in danger of collapsing, but changed its terms so that the company did not receive a proper reward for brokering the substitute deal, the directors were in breach of the 'no conflicts' rule; and the subsequent redress they made to a third director for the wrong suffered did not retrospectively affect that breach: *Re Allied Business and Financial Consultants Ltd, O'Donnell v Shanahan* [2009] EWCA Civ 751, [2009] 2 BCLC 666, [2009] BCC 822 (revsg [2008] EWHC 1973 (Ch), sub nom *Re Allied Business and Financial Consultants Ltd* [2009] 1 BCLC 328).

10 *Bhullar v Bhullar* [2003] EWCA Civ 424, [2003] 2 BCLC 241; *Re Quarter Master UK Ltd, Quarter Master UK v Pyke* [2004] EWHC 1815 (Ch) at [54], [2005] 1 BCLC 245 per Paul Morgan QC. See also *Parker v McKenna* (1874) 10 Ch App 96 (where directors had to account for profits made in dealings with new capital); *Regal (Hastings) Ltd v Gulliver* (1942) [1967] 2 AC 134n, [1942] 1 All ER 378; *Cockburn v Newbridge Sanitary Steam Laundry Co Ltd and Llewellyn* [1915] 1 IR 237, CA. The 'no profits' rule applies to a person who has agreed to become a director (*Henderson v Huntington Copper and Sulphur Co* (1878) 5 R 1, HL; *Albion Steel and Wire Co v Martin* (1875) 1 ChD 580), and to persons entering into contracts on behalf of an intended company (*Phosphate Sewage Co v Hartmont* (1877) 5 ChD 394, CA), as well as to a de facto director. If necessary, the court will lift the corporate veil where a company is used by a director to receive, in breach of his fiduciary duty, profits or corporate property for which he is accountable: *Gencor ACP Ltd v Dalby* [2000] 2 BCLC 734; *Trustor AB v Smallbone (No 2)* [2001] 3 All ER 987, [2001] 1 WLR 1177 (relevant person had to have control of the company for the corporate veil to be pierced). As to de facto directors, and the duties which they owe, see PARA 512 note 8. See further *Re Imperial Land Co of Marseilles, ex p Larking* (1877) 4 ChD 566, CA (where the directors were not allowed to make a profit out of a fraudulent transaction); and PARA 594. See also the cases cited in note 11; and *Chan v Zacharia* (1984) 154 CLR 178 (cited with approval in *Don King Productions Inc v Warren* [2000] Ch 291 at 340–341, [1999] 2 All ER 218 at 238–239, CA, per Morritt LJ) regarding the interplay between the 'no-profits' rule and the 'no-conflict' rule, although it is clear from the Companies Act 2006 s 175(1) (see the text and notes 1–4) that the overriding rule is the 'no-conflict' rule.

The liability to account under the 'no profits' rule is not to be qualified by reference to whether the impugned transaction was (in the case of an alleged breach by a director) within or without the scope of the company's business: *Re Allied Business and Financial Consultants Ltd, O'Donnell v Shanahan* [2009] EWCA Civ 751, [2009] 2 BCLC 666, [2009] BCC 822. Accordingly, *Aas v Benham* [1891] 2 Ch 244, CA (see also PARTNERSHIP vol 79 (2014) PARA 106) is of no relevance in considering the extent and application of the 'no profit' and 'no conflict' rules so far as they apply to fiduciaries such as trustees and directors: *Re Allied Business and Financial Consultants Ltd, O'Donnell v Shanahan* [2009] EWCA Civ 751 at [61]–[69], [2009] 2 BCLC 666, [2009] BCC 822 per Rimer LJ. As to the duty to account in relation to partnerships see PARTNERSHIP vol 79 (2014) PARA 106.

As to the related question of whether an equitable allowance might be made in respect of services rendered by a director in earning any profits which are at issue see *Phipps v Boardman* [1964] 2 All ER 187 at 208, [1964] 1 WLR 993 at 1018 per Wilberforce J (affd sub nom *Boardman v Phipps* [1967] 2 AC 46, [1966] 3 All ER 721, HL) (allowance made to trustee for work performed for benefit of trust, even though outside terms of trust deed); *Guinness plc v Saunders* [1990] 2 AC 663 at 701, [1990] 1 All ER 652 at 667, HL, per Lord Goff of Chieveley; and *Crown Dilmun v Sutton* [2004] EWHC 52 (Ch) at [211]–[213], [2004] 1 BCLC 468 (where dishonesty is found, that will militate against making any allowances but it should not be excluded as a possibility). In *Re Quarter Master UK Ltd, Quarter Master UK v Pyke* [2004] EWHC 1815 (Ch), [2005] 1 BCLC 245, no allowance was made, applying the approach of *Guinness plc v Saunders* [1990] 2 AC 663 at 701, [1990] 1 All ER 652 at 667, HL, per Lord Goff of Chieveley, that the exercise of the jurisdiction is restricted to those cases where it cannot have the effect of encouraging trustees (or directors) in any way to put themselves in a position where their interests conflict with their duties as trustees (or directors). As to quantum meruit see RESTITUTION vol 88 (2012) PARAS 407, 513 et seq.

A director cannot avoid accountability for secret profits by the simple expedient of resigning: *News International plc v Clinger* [1998] All ER (D) 592. See also the Companies Act 2006 s 170(2) (a person who ceases to be a director continues to be subject to the duty in s 175); and PARA 573.

11 *Regal (Hastings) Ltd v Gulliver* (1942) [1967] 2 AC 134n, [1942] 1 All ER 378. See *Boardman v Phipps* [1967] 2 AC 46, [1966] 3 All ER 721, HL; *Industrial Development Consultants Ltd*

v Cooley [1972] 2 All ER 162, [1972] 1 WLR 443 (where there was an element of bad faith). See also *Parker v McKenna* (1874) 10 Ch App 96; *Island Export Finance Ltd v Umunna* [1986] BCLC 460; *Gencor ACP Ltd v Dalby* [2000] 2 BCLC 734; *Bhullar v Bhullar* [2003] EWCA Civ 424, [2003] 2 BCLC 241; *Gwembe Valley Development Co Ltd v Koshy (No 3)* [2003] EWCA Civ 1048, [2004] 1 BCLC 131; *Crown Dilmun v Sutton* [2004] EWHC 52 (Ch), [2004] 1 BCLC 468; *Murad v Al-Saraj* [2005] EWCA Civ 959, [2005] 32 LS Gaz R 31, [2005] All ER (D) 503 (Jul).

12 *Regal (Hastings) Ltd v Gulliver* (1942) [1967] 2 AC 134n, [1942] 1 All ER 378; *Industrial Development Consultants Ltd v Cooley* [1972] 2 All ER 162, [1972] 1 WLR 443; *Gencor ACP Ltd v Dalby* [2000] 2 BCLC 734 (a director's strict liability to account could not be answered by a claim that the company could not or would not have taken up the business opportunity or that the profit accrued because of the use of his own skill or property); *Bhullar v Bhullar* [2003] EWCA Civ 424, [2003] 2 BCLC 241; *Crown Dilmun v Sutton* [2004] EWHC 52 (Ch), [2004] 1 BCLC 468; *Re Quarter Master UK Ltd, Quarter Master UK v Pyke* [2004] EWHC 1815 (Ch), [2005] 1 BCLC 245; *Murad v Al-Saraj* [2005] EWCA Civ 959, [2005] 32 LS Gaz R 31, [2005] All ER (D) 503 (Jul) (the purpose of the rule is to act as a deterrent to discourage fiduciaries from placing themselves in a conflict of interest, or exploiting profit opportunities, and to encourage adherence to the no-profit rule).

13 See *Queensland Mines Ltd v Hudson* (1978) 52 ALJR 399, PC; *Furs Ltd v Tomkies* (1936) 54 CLR 583. However, the wrongdoer is not absolved by establishing that, in the absence of his wrongdoing, he could have secured the consent of the person, to whom the fiduciary duty was owed, to allow him to retain any profit: *Murad v Al-Saraj* [2005] EWCA Civ 959, [2005] 32 LS Gaz R 31, [2005] All ER (D) 503 (Jul) (person owed fiduciary duties to two others in relation to a joint venture, and made a secret profit which he concealed by fraudulent misrepresentation to those other parties; first party held accountable for full amount of secret profit because what would have happened if the truth had been told was irrelevant).

14 *Gwembe Valley Development Co Ltd v Koshy (No 3)* [2003] EWCA Civ 1048 at [65], [2004] 1 BCLC 131 per Mummery LJ; *Gencor ACP Ltd v Dalby* [2000] 2 BCLC 734 at 741 per Rimer J; *Crown Dilmun v Sutton* [2004] EWHC 52 (Ch) at [179], [2004] 1 BCLC 468 per Peter Smith J. See also *Parker v McKenna* (1874) 10 Ch App 96 at 124 per James LJ. In *Re Allied Business and Financial Consultants Ltd, O'Donnell v Shanahan* [2009] EWCA Civ 751, [2009] 2 BCLC 666, [2009] BCC 822, two directors obtained information while acting as directors in the course of setting up a property transaction for the company, but they made use of that information in order to take up the opportunity for their own benefit once the original transaction fell through; it was held that, as they did not offer the renewed opportunity to the company, but took it up personally, they engaged in a transaction that rendered them liable to account under the 'no profit' rule.

Requirements for disclosure are not confined to the nature of the director's interest: they extend to disclosure of its extent, including the source and scale of the profit made from his position, so as to ensure that the shareholders are 'fully informed of the real state of things': *Gwembe Valley Development Co Ltd v Koshy (No 3)* [2003] EWCA Civ 1048 at [65], [2004] 1 BCLC 13 per Mummery LJ, citing *Gray v New Augarita Porcupine Mines Ltd* [1952] 3 DLR 1 at 14, PC.

15 *Cook v Deeks* [1916] 1 AC 554, PC; *Burland v Earle* [1902] AC 83, PC; cf *EBM Co Ltd v Dominion Bank* [1937] 3 All ER 555, PC (transaction unenforceable where the company purported to apply its property for the benefit of certain directors). As to the ratification by a company of conduct by a director amounting to negligence, default, breach of duty or breach of trust in relation to the company, and as to the statutory limitation on such ratification that applies, see the Companies Act 2006 s 239; and PARA 638.

16 See the Companies Act 2006 s 170(2); and PARA 573. This provides that a person who ceases to be a director continues to be subject to the duty in s 175(2) (see the text and note 5), ie the 'no conflict' rule in s 175(1) (see the text and notes 1–4) falls away, but the 'no profit' duty in s 175(2) continues to apply to the extent dictated by s 170(2): see *Ultraframe (UK) Ltd v Fielding, Northstar Systems Ltd v Fielding* [2005] EWHC 1638 (Ch) at [1309]–[1310], [2005] All ER (D) 397 (Jul) per Lewison J; and *Wilkinson v West Coast Capital* [2005] EWHC 3009 (Ch) at [251], [2005] All ER (D) 346 (Dec) per Warren J.

17 *Island Export Finance Ltd v Umunna* [1986] BCLC 460; *CMS Dolphin Ltd v Simonet* [2001] 2 BCLC 704. The underlying basis of liability of a director who resigns and then exploits a maturing business opportunity of his former company is that the opportunity is to be treated as if it were property of the company in relation to which the director had fiduciary duties; and by seeking to exploit the opportunity after resignation he is appropriating for himself that property and he becomes constructive trustee of the fruits of his abuse of the company's property, which he has acquired in circumstances where he knowingly had a conflict of interest: *CMS Dolphin Ltd v Simonet* [2001] 2 BCLC 704. See also *Industrial Development Consultants Ltd v Cooley* [1972]

2 All ER 162, [1972] 1 WLR 443; *Shepherds Investments Ltd v Walters* [2006] EWHC 836 (Ch), [2007] 2 BCLC 202; and *Kingsley IT Consulting v McIntosh* [2006] EWHC 1288 (Ch), [2006] BCC 875.

Prior to resigning, a director must take care not to place himself in a position of conflict; however, the precise point at which preparations for the establishment of a competing business by a director become unlawful will turn on the actual facts of any particular case; the touchstone for what, on the one hand, is permissible, and what, on the other hand, is impermissible unless consent is obtained from the company or employer after full disclosure, is what, in the case of a director, will be in breach of the fiduciary duties: see *Shepherds Investments Ltd v Walters* [2006] EWHC 836 (Ch) at [108], [2007] 2 BCLC 202 per Etherton J; and see *Simtel Communications Ltd v Rebak* [2006] EWHC 572 (QB), [2006] 2 BCLC 571. A director is entitled to organise a state of affairs in anticipation of setting up a business after resigning from his former company, and to conduct that business in competition with his former company's business, provided that before his resignation he does not cross the line from legitimate preparation for future competition to breach of his fiduciary duty by performing more than mere preparatory acts and undertaking illegitimate activity such as working for a competitor, personally competing while still a director, concealing or diverting matured or maturing business opportunities, misusing the company's property, including confidential information and assets, or taking the steps necessary to establish a competing business so that it is up and running or ready to go as soon as the director resigns: see *Berryland Books Ltd v BK Books Ltd* [2009] EWHC 1877 (Ch), [2009] 2 BCLC 709 (revsd in part, without affecting this statement of principles, sub nom *Berryland Books v Baldwin* [2010] EWCA Civ 1440, [2010] All ER (D) 209 (Dec)). As to the fiduciary's duty to disclose his own misconduct to his principal see PARA 584.

18 See the Companies Act 2006 s 175(1); and the text and notes 1–4.

19 Companies Act 2006 s 175(3). For the purposes of Pt 10 (ss 154–259) (see PARA 512 et seq) it is immaterial whether the law that (apart from the Companies Act 2006) governs an arrangement or transaction is the law of the United Kingdom, or a part of it, or not: s 259. As to the meaning of 'United Kingdom' see PARA 1 note 5.

In relation to companies which are charities, it is provided, instead of the wording given in s 175(3), that the duty does not apply to a conflict of interest arising in relation to a transaction or arrangement with the company if or to the extent that the company's articles allow that duty to be so disapplied, which they may do only in relation to descriptions of transaction or arrangement specified in the company's articles: see s 175(3) (substituted by s 181(2)(a)). See also PARA 573. As to the meaning of references to a company's 'articles' see PARA 227 note 2.

20 Companies Act 2006 s 175(4)(a). See also the cases cited in note 8.

21 Companies Act 2006 s 175(4)(b). As to the authorisation that is so required see PARA 591.

22 *Hirsche v Sims* [1894] AC 654 at 660, PC. The court has power to sanction a sale by a trustee in bankruptcy to a company of which he and the committee of inspection are to be directors: see *Re Spink, ex p Slater* (1913) 108 LT 572; and BANKRUPTCY AND INDIVIDUAL INSOLVENCY vol 5 (2013) PARA 477.

591. Authorisation by directors regarding potential conflicts of interest. The statutory duty to avoid conflicts of interest[1] is not infringed if the matter has been authorised by the directors[2]. Such authorisation may be given by the directors[3]:

(1) where the company is a private company[4], and nothing in the company's constitution invalidates such authorisation, by the matter being proposed to and authorised by the directors[5]; or

(2) where the company is a public company[6], and its constitution includes provision[7] enabling the directors to authorise the matter, by the matter being proposed to and authorised by them in accordance with the constitution[8].

However, the authorisation is effective only if:

(a) any requirement as to the quorum at the meeting at which the matter is considered is met without counting the director in question or any other interested director[9]; and

(b) the matter was agreed to without their voting or would have been agreed to if their votes had not been counted[10].

In a case where the provisions which require conflicts of interest to be avoided[11] are complied with by directors' authorisation[12], the transaction or arrangement is not liable to be set aside by virtue of any common law rule or equitable principle requiring the consent or approval of the members of the company[13]. This is without prejudice to any enactment[14], or provision of the company's constitution, requiring such consent or approval[15].

1 See the Companies Act 2006 s 175; and PARA 590. As to the scope and nature of the directors' general duties see PARA 572; and as to the application and effect of the general duties see PARA 573. As to the relevance of case law on those common law rules and equitable principles that are now replaced by the statutory duties see PARA 572 note 7.
2 See the Companies Act 2006 s 175(4)(b); and PARA 590. As to the meaning of 'director' under the Companies Acts see PARA 512; and as to the meaning of the 'Companies Acts' see PARA 13.
3 In relation to companies which are charities, heads (1)–(2) in the text do not apply and it is provided instead that authorisation may be given by the directors where the company's constitution includes provision enabling them to authorise the matter, by the matter being proposed to and authorised by them in accordance with the constitution: see the Companies Act 2006 s 175(5) (substituted for these purposes by s 181(2)(b)). See PARA 573. As to the meaning of references to a company's constitution for the purposes of Pt 10 (ss 154–259) (see PARA 512 et seq) see PARA 580 note 4. As to the meaning of 'company' under the Companies Acts see PARA 21.
4 As to the meaning of 'private company' see PARA 95.
5 Companies Act 2006 s 175(5)(a). As to provision made for decision-making by directors at meetings see PARA 567. For transitional provisions see the Companies Act 2006 (Commencement No 5, Transitional Provisions and Savings) Order 2007, SI 2007/3495, Sch 4 para 47.
6 As to the meaning of 'public company' see PARA 95.
7 The model articles of association do not make any such provision: see PARA 227 et seq.
8 Companies Act 2006 s 175(5)(b).
9 Companies Act 2006 s 175(6)(a).
10 Companies Act 2006 s 175(6)(b).
11 Ie the Companies Act 2006 s 175 (see also PARA 590): see s 180(1).
12 Ie in accordance with the Companies Act 2006 s 175(5), (6) (see the text and notes 1–10).
13 Companies Act 2006 s 180(1). As to the meaning of 'member' see PARA 323.
14 As to the meaning of 'enactment' see PARA 13 note 16.
15 Companies Act 2006 s 180(1).

Where the Companies Act 2006 Pt 10 Ch 4 (ss 188–225) or Pt 10 Ch 4A (ss 226A–226F) (transactions with directors requiring approval of members) (see PARA 601 et seq) applies, and approval is given under Pt 10 Ch 4, or where the matter is one as to which it is provided that approval is not needed, it is not necessary also to comply with s 175: see s 180(2); and PARA 602.

592. Authorisation of conflicts by the articles. The general duties that are specified by the Companies Act 2006[1] as being owed by a director[2] of a company[3] to the company are not infringed, where the company's articles contain provisions for dealing with conflicts of interest[4], by anything done, or omitted, by the directors, or any of them, in accordance with those provisions[5].

In a case where the provisions requiring conflicts of interest to be avoided[6] are complied with by directors' authorisation[7], the transaction or arrangement is not liable to be set aside by virtue of any common law rule or equitable principle requiring the consent or approval of the members of the company[8]. This is without prejudice to any enactment[9], or provision of the company's constitution, requiring such consent or approval[10].

1 Ie in the Companies Act 2006 ss 171–177: see also PARA 580 et seq. As to the scope and nature of the directors' general duties see PARA 572.
2 As to the meaning of 'director' under the Companies Acts see PARA 512; and as to the meaning of the 'Companies Acts' see PARA 13. The general duties apply also to a shadow director of a company where and to the extent that they are capable of so applying: see the Companies Act 2006 s 170(5); and PARA 573. As to shadow directors see PARA 513.
3 As to the meaning of 'company' under the Companies Acts see PARA 21.
4 As to the general duty to avoid conflicts of interest see PARA 590 et seq.
5 See the Companies Act 2006 s 180(4)(b); and PARA 573. This provision should be read in conjunction with s 232(4) (which provides that nothing in s 232 prevents a company's articles from making such provision as has previously been lawful for dealing with conflicts of interest) (see PARA 639).

6 Ie the Companies Act 2006 s 175 (see also PARA 590): see s 180(1); and PARA 591.
7 Ie in accordance with the Companies Act 2006 s 175(5), (6) (see PARA 591).
8 See the Companies Act 2006 s 180(1); and PARA 591. As to the meaning of 'member' see PARA 323.
9 As to the meaning of 'enactment' see PARA 13 note 16.
10 See the Companies Act 2006 s 180(1); and PARA 591. As to the meaning of references to a company's constitution for the purposes of Pt 10 (ss 154–259) (see PARA 512 et seq) see PARA 580 note 4.

Where the Companies Act 2006 Pt 10 Ch 4 (ss 188–225) or Pt 10 Ch 4A (ss 226A–226F) (transactions with directors requiring approval of members) (see PARA 601 et seq) applies, and approval is given under Pt 10 Ch 4, or where the matter is one as to which it is provided that approval is not needed, it is not necessary also to comply with s 175: see s 180(2); and PARA 602.

(F) Benefits to Directors from Third Parties

593. Director's duty not to accept benefits from third parties. The Companies Act 2006, in setting out general duties[1] that are owed to the company[2], provides that a director[3] of a company must not accept a benefit from a third party[4] conferred by reason of either his being a director[5], or his doing, or not doing, anything as director[6].

This duty is not infringed if the acceptance of the benefit cannot reasonably be regarded as likely to give rise to a conflict of interest[7]; and the general duties that are so specified by the Companies Act 2006 as being owed by a director to the company:

(1) have effect subject to any rule of law enabling the company to give authority, specifically or generally, for anything to be done, or omitted, by the directors, or any of them, that would otherwise be a breach of duty[8]; and

(2) where the company's articles contain provisions for dealing with conflicts of interest, are not infringed by anything done, or omitted, by the directors, or any of them, in accordance with those provisions[9].

1 Ie in the Companies Act 2006 ss 171–177: see also PARA 580 et seq. As to the scope and nature of the directors' general duties see PARA 572; and as to the application and effect of the general duties see PARA 573. As to the relevance of case law on those common law rules and equitable principles that are now replaced by the statutory duties see PARA 572 note 7.
2 As to the meaning of 'company' under the Companies Acts see PARA 21; and as to the meaning of the 'Companies Acts' see PARA 13.
3 As to the meaning of 'director' under the Companies Acts see PARA 512. The general duties apply also to a shadow director of a company where and to the extent that they are capable of so applying: see the Companies Act 2006 s 170(5); and PARA 573. As to shadow directors see PARA 513.
4 For these purposes, a 'third party' means a person other than the company, an associated body corporate or a person acting on behalf of the company or an associated body corporate: Companies Act 2006 s 176(2). For the purposes of Pt 10 (ss 154–259) (see PARA 512 et seq), bodies corporate are 'associated' if one is a subsidiary of the other or both are subsidiaries of the same body corporate: s 256(a). As to the meaning of 'body corporate' for the purposes of the Companies Acts see PARA 1 note 5; and as to the meaning of 'subsidiary' see PARA 22.

As to bribes see PARA 594.
5 Companies Act 2006 s 176(1)(a).
6 Companies Act 2006 s 176(1)(b). Benefits received by a director from a person by whom his services (as a director or otherwise) are provided to the company are not regarded as conferred by a third party: s 176(3).
7 Companies Act 2006 s 176(4). Any reference in s 176 to a conflict of interest includes a conflict of interest and duty and a conflict of duties: s 176(5). As to the general duty to avoid conflicts of interest see PARA 590; and see especially the cases cited in PARA 590 note 9.

Where the Companies Act 2006 Pt 10 Ch 4 (ss 188–225) or Pt 10 Ch 4A (ss 226A–226F) (transactions with directors requiring approval of members) (see PARA 601 et seq) applies, and approval is given under Pt 10 Ch 4 or Pt 10 Ch 4A, or where the matter is one as to which it is provided that approval is not needed, it is not necessary also to comply with s 176: see s 180(2); and PARA 602.

8 See the Companies Act 2006 s 180(4)(a); and PARA 573. Head (1) in the text still would not, however, sanction receipt of a benefit amounting to a bribe (as to which see PARA 594).

9 See the Companies Act 2006 s 180(4)(b); and PARA 573. The provisions referred to in head (2) in the text may, of course, provide legitimately for directors' benefits. Head (2) in the text should be read in conjunction with s 232(4) (which provides that nothing in s 232 prevents a company's articles from making such provision as has previously been lawful for dealing with conflicts of interest) (see PARA 639).

594. Bribes received by a director. Whenever a company director[1] becomes entitled to a sum of money[2] by way of a bribe from a vendor to the company, the company may recover, from the person giving the bribe, a sum equal to the amount of the bribe, on the basis that the person who gave it, the vendor, received from the company more than he was entitled to, measured by the amount of the bribe, the excess being money received by the vendor to the company's use[3]. If property representing the bribe increases in value or if a cash bribe is invested advantageously, the false fiduciary is accountable not only for the original amount or value of the bribe but also for the increased value of the property representing the bribe[4]. The fact that the director has agreed subsequently with the person giving the bribe to accept a smaller sum in prompt settlement and that this has been recovered from the director in full satisfaction of all claims against him is no defence to the person giving the bribe in a claim by the company for the balance[5]. The company may also recover against the person who gives the bribe damages for any loss sustained through entering a disadvantageous contract[6], or it may rescind the contract[7]. A contract may be enforced by the company against the director if he has contracted as principal, deducting the amount of any secret profit which might accrue to him[8].

The criminal offences of bribing another person[9], being bribed[10], or bribing a foreign public official[11], and the possible liability of a director for such an offence, are discussed in an earlier part of this title[12].

1 As to a company's directors see PARA 512 et seq.

2 As to an offer of employment alleged to be in the nature of a bribe, but which did not lead to any conflict of interest, see *Amalgamated Industrials Ltd v Johnson & Firth Brown Ltd* (1981) Times, 15 April.

3 *Grant v Gold Exploration and Development Syndicate* [1900] 1 QB 233 at 249, CA, per Collins LJ. The principle that a person in a fiduciary position must not make secret profits is not based on actual fraud, but on motives of public policy: see *Bray v Ford* [1896] AC 44 at 51, HL, per Lord Herschell; *Harrington v Victoria Graving Dock Co* (1878) 3 QBD 549 (where it was held that, although the person to whom the bribe is payable has not in fact been perverted, he cannot recover the bribe in a claim). Cf *Kregor v Hollins* (1913) 109 LT 225, CA. As to bribery of agents generally see AGENCY vol 1 (2008) PARA 91 et seq.

4 *FHR European Ventures LLP v Mankarious* [2014] UKSC 45, [2015] AC 250, [2014] 4 All ER 79, applying *A-G for Hong Kong v Reid* [1994] 1 AC 324, [1994] 1 All ER 1, PC. See also *Daraydan Holdings Ltd v Solland International Ltd* [2004] EWHC 622 (Ch) at [75]–[86], [2005] Ch 119, [2005] 4 All ER 73 per Lawrence Collins J.

The Companies Act 2006 s 176 (duty not to accept benefits from third parties) (see PARA 593), which, together with s 178(2) (the duties, with the exception of the duty to exercise reasonable care, skill and diligence, are enforceable in the same way as any other fiduciary duty owed to a company by its directors) (see PARA 599), means that benefits accepted in breach of that duty (and, a fortiori, bribes) are held on trust for the company. As to the joint and several nature of the liability where more than one director is concerned see PARA 631.

5 See note 4.

6 *Salford Corpn v Lever* [1891] 1 QB 168, CA. See also *Grant v Gold Exploration and Development Syndicate* [1900] 1 QB 233 at 244, CA, per Smith LJ.

7 *Panama and South Pacific Telegraph Co v India Rubber, Gutta Percha and Telegraph Works Co* (1875) 10 Ch App 515.

8 *Whaley Bridge Calico Printing Co v Green* (1879) 5 QBD 109.

9 Ie an offence under the Bribery Act 2010 s 1: see CRIMINAL LAW vol 26 (2016) PARA 369.

10 Ie an offence under the Bribery Act 2010 s 2: see CRIMINAL LAW vol 26 (2016) PARA 369.

11 Ie an offence under the Bribery Act 2010 s 6: see CRIMINAL LAW vol 26 (2016) PARA 370.
12 See PARA 318.

(G) Directors' Duty to Declare Interest in Proposed Transactions etc

595. Director's duty to declare interest in proposed transaction or arrangement with the company. The Companies Act 2006, in setting out general duties[1] that are owed to the company[2], provides that if a director[3] of a company is in any way, directly or indirectly, interested in a proposed transaction or arrangement with the company, he must declare the nature and extent of that interest to the other directors[4].

The declaration may, but need not, be made either at a meeting of the directors[5], or by notice to the directors[6]. If such a declaration of interest[7] proves to be, or becomes, inaccurate or incomplete, a further declaration must be made[8]. Any declaration so required[9] must be made before the company enters into the transaction or arrangement[10].

This restriction[11] does not require a declaration of an interest of which the director is not aware or where the director is not aware of the transaction or arrangement in question[12]; and a director need not declare an interest:

(1) if it cannot reasonably be regarded as likely to give rise to a conflict of interest[13];
(2) if, or to the extent that, the other directors are already aware of it (and for this purpose the other directors are treated as aware of anything of which they ought reasonably to be aware)[14]; or
(3) if, or to the extent that, it concerns terms of his service contract[15] that have been or are to be considered either by a meeting of the directors[16], or by a committee of the directors appointed for the purpose under the company's constitution[17].

In a case where the provisions as the need to declare any interest in a proposed transaction or arrangement[18] are complied with, the transaction or arrangement is not liable to be set aside by virtue of any common law rule or equitable principle requiring the consent or approval of the members of the company[19]. This is without prejudice to any enactment[20], or provision of the company's constitution, requiring such consent or approval[21].

The strict common law doctrine against self-dealing by directors was commonly relaxed by means of a provision in the company's articles of association to this effect[22]. Accordingly, if a proposed decision of the directors is concerned with an actual or proposed transaction or arrangement with the company in which a director is interested, that director is not to be counted as participating in the decision-making process for quorum or voting purposes[23].

1 Ie in the Companies Act 2006 ss 171–177: see also PARA 580 et seq. As to the scope and nature of the directors' general duties see PARA 572; and as to the application and effect of the general duties see PARA 573. As to the relevance of case law on those common law rules and equitable principles that are now replaced by the statutory duties see PARA 572 note 7; and see PARA 596 et seq.

2 As to the meaning of 'company' under the Companies Acts see PARA 21; and as to the meaning of the 'Companies Acts' see PARA 13.

3 As to the meaning of 'director' under the Companies Acts see PARA 512. The general duties apply also to a shadow director of a company where and to the extent that they are capable of so applying: see the Companies Act 2006 s 170(5); and PARA 573. As to shadow directors see PARA 513.

4 Companies Act 2006 s 177(1). As to the requirement to declare an interest in an existing transaction or arrangement that has been entered into by the company see Pt 10 Ch 3 (ss 182–187); and PARA 600. As to the general duty to avoid conflicts of interest see PARA 590. In *Newgate Stud Co v Penfold* [2004] EWHC 2993 (Ch), [2008] 1 BCLC 46, where a director

bought a horse from his company via public auction, it was held that the self-dealing rule does and should apply to purchases at public auction because the inherent conflict in the fiduciary's position remains and there are many ways in which both the seller's agent and a bidder can influence the outcome of an auction both before the sale and during the bidding.

5 Companies Act 2006 s 177(2)(a). As to meetings of directors generally see PARA 568 et seq.

6 Companies Act 2006 s 177(2)(b). The text refers to notice that may be given to the directors in accordance with either s 184 or s 185: see s 177(2)(b). As to the application of Pt 10 Ch 3 (ss 182–187) to shadow directors see PARA 600.

Under the provisions of s 184, which apply to a declaration of interest made by notice in writing (s 184(1)), the director must send the notice to the other directors (s 184(2)). The notice may be sent in hard copy form (or, if the recipient has agreed to receive it in electronic form, in an agreed electronic form) (s 184(3)); and may be sent by hand or by post (or, if the recipient has agreed to receive it by electronic means, by agreed electronic means) (s 184(4)). Where a director declares an interest by notice in writing in accordance with s 184, the making of the declaration is deemed to form part of the proceedings at the next meeting of the directors after the notice is given (s 184(5)(a)); and the provisions of s 248 (minutes of meetings of directors) (see PARA 570) apply as if the declaration had been made at that meeting (s 184(5)(b)). As to directors' communications see PARA 568 note 3. As to documents or information sent or supplied in hard copy form see PARA 750; and as to documents or information sent or supplied in electronic form (or by electronic means) see PARA 751. As to the construction of references to service by post see STATUTES AND LEGISLATIVE PROCESS vol 96 (2012) PARA 1219.

General notice in accordance with s 185 is a sufficient declaration of interest in relation to the matters to which it relates: s 185(1). General notice is notice given to the directors of a company to the effect that the director either has an interest (as member, officer, employee or otherwise) in a specified body corporate or firm and is to be regarded as interested in any transaction or arrangement that may, after the date of the notice, be made with that body corporate or firm (s 185(2)(a)), or is connected with a specified person (other than a body corporate or firm) and is to be regarded as interested in any transaction or arrangement that may, after the date of the notice, be made with that person (s 185(2)(b)). The notice must state the nature and extent of the director's interest in the body corporate or firm or, as the case may be, the nature of his connection with the person: s 185(3). General notice is not effective, however, unless it is given at a meeting of the directors (s 185(4)(a)), or the director takes reasonable steps to secure that it is brought up and read at the next meeting of the directors after it is given (s 185(4)(b)). As to the meaning of 'member' see PARA 323; as to the meaning of 'officer' generally see PARA 679; as to the meaning of 'body corporate' for the purposes of the Companies Acts see PARA 1 note 5; and as to the meaning of 'firm' see PARA 105 note 15. As to the meaning of references to a director being 'connected' with a person see PARA 515.

See also the text and notes 22–23.

7 Ie under the Companies Act 2006 s 177: see s 177(3).

8 Companies Act 2006 s 177(3).

9 Ie required by the Companies Act 2006 s 177: see s 177(4).

10 Companies Act 2006 s 177(4).

11 Ie contained in the provisions of the Companies Act 2006 s 177: see s 177(5).

12 Companies Act 2006 s 177(5). For this purpose, a director is treated as being aware of matters of which he ought reasonably to be aware: s 177(5).

13 Companies Act 2006 s 177(6)(a).

14 Companies Act 2006 s 177(6)(b).

15 As to the meaning of a director's 'service contract', in relation to a company, for the purposes of the Companies Act 2006 Pt 10 (ss 154–259) (see PARA 512 et seq) see PARA 565 note 4.

16 Companies Act 2006 s 177(6)(c)(i).

17 Companies Act 2006 s 177(6)(c)(ii). As to the meaning of references to a company's constitution for the purposes of Pt 10 see PARA 580 note 4. As to the extent to which directors may delegate powers, including to committees, see PARA 577.

18 Ie the Companies Act 2006 s 177 (see the text and notes 1–17): see s 180(1).

19 Companies Act 2006 s 180(1). See also *Aberdeen Rly Co v Blaikie Bros* (1854) 1 Macq 461.

20 As to the meaning of 'enactment' see PARA 13 note 16.

21 Companies Act 2006 s 180(1).

22 As to a company's articles of association generally see PARA 227 et seq. As to model articles of association prescribed for the purposes of the Companies Act 2006, and their application generally, see PARA 227 et seq. Different versions of model articles have been so prescribed for use by private companies limited by shares (see the Companies (Model Articles) Regulations 2008, SI 2008/3229, reg 2, Sch 1), private companies limited by guarantee (see reg 3, Sch 2), and public companies (see reg 4, Sch 3). As to the meanings of 'company limited by guarantee', 'company limited by shares', 'limited company', 'private company' and 'public company' see PARA 95. The

default articles prescribed for the purposes of the Companies Act 1985 ('legacy articles'), ie the Companies (Tables A to F) Regulations 1985, SI 1985/805, have not been revoked and may, in their amended form, continue to be used by companies after the commencement of the Companies Act 2006: see PARA 229.

23 Companies (Model Articles) Regulations 2008, SI 2008/3229, Sch 1 art 14(1), Sch 2 art 14(1), Sch 3 art 16(1). However, when the company by ordinary resolution disapplies the provision of the articles which would otherwise prevent a director from being counted as participating in the decision-making process, or when the director's interest cannot reasonably be regarded as likely to give rise to a conflict of interest, or when the director's conflict of interest arises from a permitted cause, a director who is interested in an actual or proposed transaction or arrangement with the company is to be counted as participating in the decision-making process for quorum and voting purposes: Sch 1 art 14(2), (3), Sch 2 art 14(2), (3), Sch 3 art 16(2), (3). For these purposes, the following are permitted causes (Sch 1 art 14(4), Sch 2 art 14(4), Sch 3 art 16(4)), ie:

(1) a guarantee given, or to be given, by or to a director in respect of an obligation incurred by or on behalf of the company or any of its subsidiaries;

(2) subscription, or an agreement to subscribe, for shares or other securities of the company or any of its subsidiaries, or to underwrite, sub-underwrite, or guarantee subscription for any such shares or securities; and

(3) arrangements pursuant to which benefits are made available to employees and directors or former employees and directors of the company or any of its subsidiaries which do not provide special benefits for directors or former directors.

References to proposed decisions and decision-making processes include any directors' meeting or part of a directors' meeting: see Sch 1 art 14(5), Sch 2 art 14(5), Sch 3 art 16(1), (2). If a question arises at a meeting of directors or of a committee of directors as to the right of a director to participate in the meeting (or part of the meeting) for voting or quorum purposes, the question may, before the conclusion of the meeting, be referred to the chairman whose ruling in relation to any director other than the chairman is to be final and conclusive: Sch 1 art 14(6), Sch 2 art 14(6), Sch 3 art 16(5). However, if any question as to the right to participate in the meeting (or part of the meeting) should arise in respect of the chairman, the question is to be decided by a decision of the directors at that meeting, for which purpose the chairman is not to be counted as participating in the meeting (or that part of the meeting) for voting or quorum purposes: Sch 1 art 14(7), Sch 2 art 14(7), Sch 3 art 16(6). As to the meaning of 'ordinary resolution' see PARA 685. As to chairing a directors' meeting see PARA 568; and as to the quorum required for such a meeting see PARA 569.

The Companies (Tables A to F) Regulations 1985, SI 1985/805, Schedule Table A art 94 (amended by virtue of the Commissioners for Revenue and Customs Act 2005 s 50(1), (7)) provides that, save as otherwise provided by the articles, a director must not vote at a meeting of directors or of a committee of directors on any resolution concerning a matter in which he has, directly or indirectly, an interest or duty which is material and which conflicts or may conflict with the interests of the company unless his interest or duty arises only because the case falls within one or more of the following cases:

(a) the resolution relates to the giving to him of a guarantee, security, or indemnity in respect of money lent to, or an obligation incurred by him for the benefit of, the company or any of its subsidiaries;

(b) the resolution relates to the giving to a third party of a guarantee, security, or indemnity in respect of an obligation of the company or any of its subsidiaries for which the director has assumed responsibility in whole or part and whether alone or jointly with others under a guarantee or indemnity or by the giving of security;

(c) his interest arises by virtue of his subscribing or agreeing to subscribe for any shares, debentures, or other securities of the company or any of its subsidiaries, or by virtue of his being, or intending to become, a participant in the underwriting or sub-underwriting of an offer of any such shares, debentures, or other securities by the company or any of its subsidiaries for subscription, purchase or exchange;

(d) the resolution relates in any way to a retirement benefits scheme which has been approved, or is conditional upon approval, by the Commissioners for Revenue and Customs for taxation purposes.

For these purposes, an interest of a person who is, for any purpose of the Companies Act 2006 (excluding any statutory modification thereof not in force when this article becomes binding on the company), connected with a director must be treated as an interest of the director and, in relation to an alternate director, an interest of his appointor must be treated as an interest of the alternate director without prejudice to any interest which the alternate director has otherwise: see Table A art 94. A director is not to be counted in the quorum present at a meeting in relation to a resolution on which he is not entitled to vote: Table A art 95. As to alternate directors see PARA 523. As to the extent to which directors may delegate powers, including to committees, see PARA 577. As to the Commissioners for Revenue and Customs see INCOME TAXATION vol 58 (2014) PARA 33. The Companies (Tables A to F) Regulations 1985, SI 1985/805, Schedule Table A art 85 further provides that, subject to the provisions of the Companies Act 2006, and provided that he has disclosed to the directors the nature and extent of any material interest of his, a director notwithstanding his office:

(i) may be a party to, or otherwise interested in, any transaction or arrangement with the company or in which the company is otherwise interested;
(ii) may be a party to any transaction or arrangement with (or otherwise interested in) any body corporate promoted by the company or in which the company is otherwise interested; and
(iii) is not, by reason of his office, accountable to the company for any benefit which he derives from any such transaction or arrangement or from any interest in any such body corporate and no such transaction or arrangement is liable to be avoided on the ground of any such interest or benefit.

As to the avoidance of contracts see PARA 600 et seq. For these purposes, a general notice given to the directors that a director is to be regarded as having an interest of the nature and extent specified in the notice in any transaction or arrangement in which a specified person or class of persons is interested is deemed to be a disclosure that the director has an interest in any such transaction of the nature and extent so specified; and an interest of which a director has no knowledge and of which it is unreasonable to expect him to have knowledge is not treated as an interest of his: see Table A art 86. Table A arts 85–86 also make provision in relation to the avoidance of more general conflicts of interest which may arise from the position a director (or other officer) may hold within a company: see PARA 590. See also PARA 598 note 4. The Companies (Tables A to F) Regulations 1985, SI 1985/805, Schedule Table A provides regulations for the management of a company limited by shares but arts 85–86, 94–95 are applied by Table C (regulations for the management of a company limited by guarantee and not having a share capital), Table D Pt III (regulations for the management of a company limited by guarantee and having a share capital), and Table E (an unlimited company having a share capital). However, Table C modifies Table A art 94 to the extent that the words 'shares, debentures, or other securities' (see head (c) above) are omitted: see Table C art 10. As to the meaning of 'unlimited company' see PARA 95. As to the meanings of 'company having a share capital' and 'share capital' see PARA 1231.

As to the director's duty to declare any other interests see note 4.

596. Director's failure to make the required declaration of interest. In the event of a failure on the part of a director to comply with the duty to declare his interest in a contract between a company and a director[1] or his firm[2], or a company in which he is interested as a director or shareholder even though only a trustee of the shares[3], the director is liable to account for any profit made by him[4]. Further, the contract is voidable at the instance of the company[5]. If the statutory provisions[6] are not complied with, the contract, being voidable and not void[7], may be affirmed by the company when in possession of full information[8].

If the duty to make a declaration is not complied with and the company objects, it is immaterial that the terms are advantageous to it[9], or that as between the interested director and his co-directors the whole matter was above board[10].

Such a contract will not be specifically enforced[11], and the director cannot retain the profits[12]. This rule does not apply to contracts made before the company was formed with persons whose business is acquired by the company on formation, but it may apply to situations where a director causes his company to enter into a transaction with a close relation, or a spouse or other partner, on the ground that the potential for abuse existed in any case where an element of common financial interest could be discerned[13].

Although a director may be precluded by the articles from voting as a director in respect of his contract with the company[14], he may vote as a shareholder at a general meeting[15], but only to affirm the transaction, not to ratify his own breach of duty[16].

1 As to a company's directors see PARA 512 et seq.

2 *Flanagan v Great Western Rly Co* (1868) LR 7 Eq 116. The restriction applies to all contracts in which a director is interested and which are made in the execution of the company's business, such as the appointment of a managing director at a salary (*Foster v Foster* [1916] 1 Ch 532); the

allotment of debentures (*Cox v Dublin City Distillery (No 2)* [1915] 1 IR 345, CA; *Re North Eastern Insurance* Co [1919] 1 Ch 198); the issue of debentures as security for an overdraft guaranteed by the directors (*Victors Ltd v Lingard* [1927] 1 Ch 323); the allotment of shares (*Quinn v Robb* (1916) 141 LT Jo 6; *Neal v Quinn* [1916] WN 223). It also applies to a contract entered into with a business of which the director is a mortgagee in possession: *Star Steam Laundry Co v Dukas* (1913) 108 LT 367. See also *Holden v Southwark Corpn* [1921] 1 Ch 550; *Lapish v Braithwaite* [1926] AC 275, HL. The bankers of the company may still be its directors (*Sheffield, Ashton-under-Lyne and Manchester Rly Co v Woodcock* (1841) 7 M & W 574); and a director may lend money to his company at a profit (*Bluck v Mallalue* (1859) 27 Beav 398; *Re Cardiff Preserved Coal and Coke Co Ltd, Hill's Case* (1862) 32 LJ Ch 154), if it is without an unusual profit, such as a bonus.

3 *Transvaal Lands Co v New Belgium (Transvaal) Land and Development* Co [1914] 2 Ch 488, CA (rescission ordered after completion; the other company had notice of the irregularity; rescission possible). Cf *Regal (Hastings) Ltd v Gulliver* (1942) [1967] 2 AC 134n at 152n, [1942] 1 All ER 378 at 390–391, HL, per Lord Russell of Killowen. As to shareholders and membership of companies generally see PARA 323 et seq.

4 *Aberdeen Rly Co v Blaikie Bros* (1854) 2 Eq Rep 1281, HL; *Costa Rica Rly Co Ltd v Forwood* [1900] 1 Ch 756 (affd [1901] 1 Ch 746, CA); *Albion Steel and Wire Co v Martin* (1875) 1 ChD 580; *Redekop v Robco Construction Ltd* (1978) 89 DLR (3d) 507, BC SC. Cf *Re Republic of Bolivia Exploration Syndicate Ltd* [1914] 1 Ch 139. See generally *Hely-Hutchinson v Brayhead Ltd* [1968] 1 QB 549 at 571, [1967] 2 All ER 14 at 28 per Roskill J (affd [1968] 1 QB 573, [1967] 3 All ER 98, CA). As to the fiduciary position of the director generally see PARA 575.

5 *Aberdeen Rly Co v Blaikie Bros* (1854) 2 Eq Rep 1281, HL; *Ernest v Nicholls* (1857) 6 HL Cas 401; *Ridley v Plymouth Grinding and Baking Co* (1848) 2 Exch 711; *Albion Steel and Wire Co v Martin* (1875) 1 ChD 580. A contract is made with a director if made with a person who is elected an honorary director until completion and an ordinary director afterwards: *Stears v South Essex Gas-Light and Coke Co* (1860) 9 CBNS 180. When the articles provide that the interest of a director must be disclosed in the minutes, the contract is invalid unless the entry is made within a reasonable time: *Toms v Cinema Trust Co Ltd* [1915] WN 29; and see *Re British America Corpn* (1903) 19 TLR 662; *Exploring Land and Minerals Co Ltd v Kolckmann* (1905) 94 LT 234, CA.

6 As to the statutory duty of a director to disclose his interest see PARA 595.

7 *Aberdeen Rly Co v Blaikie Bros* (1854) 2 Eq Rep 1281, HL; *Movitex Ltd v Bulfield* [1988] BCLC 104.

8 *North-West Transportation Co Ltd and Beatty v Beatty* (1887) 12 App Cas 589, PC; *Grant v United Kingdom Switchback Rlys Co* (1888) 40 ChD 135, CA; *Murray's Executors' Case* (1854) 5 De GM & G 746. See also *Cook v Deeks* [1916] 1 AC 554, PC; *Jacobus Marler Estates Ltd v Jacobus Marler* (1913) 85 LJPC 167n. As to affirmation see *Re Marini Ltd* [2003] EWHC 334 (Ch), [2004] BCC 172; and *Ultraframe (UK) Ltd v Fielding, Northstar Systems Ltd v Fielding* [2005] EWHC 1638 (Ch) at [1441], [1449], [2005] All ER (D) 397 (Jul).

9 *Aberdeen Rly Co v Blaikie Bros* (1854) 2 Eq Rep 1281, HL.

10 *Albion Steel and Wire Co v Martin* (1875) 1 ChD 580. Cf *Bray v Ford* [1896] AC 44, HL.

11 *Flanagan v Great Western Rly Co* (1868) LR 7 Eq 116; *Imperial Mercantile Credit Association (Liquidators) v Coleman* (1873) LR 6 HL 189.

12 See the text and note 4.

13 See *Newgate Stud Co v Penfold* [2004] EWHC 2993 (Ch), [2008] 1 BCLC 46.

14 See eg PARA 595 note 23.

15 *North-West Transportation Co Ltd and Beatty v Beatty* (1887) 12 App Cas 589, PC. See also the cases cited in PARA 725.

16 See the Companies Act 2006 s 239(4); and PARA 638.

597. Effect of director's failure to disclose interest in proposed transaction on sales to the company. In order that the director[1] may retain a profit which he has made on a contract with the company, it is not enough that he should reveal to the shareholders the existence of his interest without specifying exactly what it is[2]. No ratification may take place in the absence of full disclosure[3]; but if full disclosure is contained in the notice convening the meeting, the company may by ordinary resolution confirm the contract[4]. It is unnecessary to hold a meeting if all the shareholders acquiesce[5].

Formerly, where a director sold property to his company, without disclosing his interest, the company might, on discovery, either rescind the sale, if that was still practicable, or affirm the sale and sue for damages[6], in which case it had to prove a breach of duty by the director amounting to negligence or misfeasance and resulting in pecuniary loss to the company[7]. Now, non-compliance with the duty to declare an interest[8] is a head of duty which requires the director to account for any profit regardless of rescission by the company[9].

If the director, while employed as a director to purchase property, buys on his own account and sells to the company without disclosure, he must account for the profit made by him[10].

1 As to a company's directors see PARA 512 et seq.
2 *Gwembe Valley Development Co Ltd (in receivership) v Koshy (No 3)* [2003] EWCA Civ 1048, [2004] 1 BCLC 131.
3 *Imperial Mercantile Credit Association (Liquidators) v Coleman* (1873) LR 6 HL 189 (where the articles required the director to vacate his seat if he did not 'declare his interest' in any contract) (cited also in PARA 598). See also *Dunne v English* (1874) LR 18 Eq 524. The issue of disclosure is very closely related to conflicts of interest and, more generally, to the fiduciary position of directors: see PARA 595.
4 See *Kaye v Croydon Tramways Co* [1898] 1 Ch 358, CA; *Bamford v Bamford* [1970] Ch 212, [1969] 1 All ER 969, CA. See also the Companies Act 2006 s 180(4)(a); and PARA 573. As to resolutions and meetings of the company generally see PARA 701 et seq.
5 *Parker & Cooper Ltd v Reading* [1926] Ch 975.
6 *Benson v Heathorn* (1842) 1 Y & C Ch Cas 326; *Jacobus Marler Estates Ltd v Marler* (1913) 85 LJPC 167n. See also *Re Cape Breton Co* (1885) 29 ChD 795, CA (affd on other grounds sub nom *Cavendish Bentinck v Fenn* (1887) 12 App Cas 652, HL); *Ladywell Mining Co v Brookes* (1887) 35 ChD 400, CA; *Re VGM Holdings Ltd* [1942] Ch 235, [1942] 1 All ER 224, CA.
7 *Cavendish Bentinck v Fenn* (1887) 12 App Cas 652 at 662, HL, per Lord Herschell.
8 Ie as required by the Companies Act 2006 s 177 (see PARA 595).
9 This follows from the fiduciary duty imposed by the Companies Act 2006 s 177 (see PARA 595) (see s 178(2); and PARA 599), as liability to account on a head of fiduciary duty is not dependent on the company rescinding the transaction; see s 195(3) (cited in PARA 608), s 213(3) (cited in PARA 618).
10 *Cavendish Bentinck v Fenn* (1887) 12 App Cas 652, HL.

598. Provision in articles for vacation of position where director interested in contract. If a company's articles of association[1] provide for a director[2] being disqualified by being in any way interested in a bargain or contract with the company, his office is vacated by his being a shareholder[3] in another company with which the contract is made[4].

If the articles provide for the vacation of his seat if he enters into a contract with the company without declaring his interest, it is not sufficient for him to intimate that he has an interest without declaring its specific nature[5].

1 As to a company's articles of association generally see PARA 227 et seq.
2 As to a company's directors see PARA 512 et seq.
3 As to shareholders and membership of companies generally see PARA 323 et seq.
4 *Todd v Robinson* (1884) 14 QBD 739, CA. The Companies (Tables A to F) Regulations 1985, SI 1985/805, reg 2, Schedule Table A arts 85, 86, 94, 95 assume full disclosure of the director's interest in accordance with the Companies Act 2006 and, with some exceptions, forbid him to vote and to be counted in the quorum in respect of such a contract, but provide no further sanction: see PARAS 590, 595. As to the quorum in company directors' meetings see PARA 569.
5 *Imperial Mercantile Credit Association (Liquidators) v Coleman* (1873) LR 6 HL 189. Cf *Turnbull v West Riding Athletic Club Leeds Ltd* (1894) 70 LT 92. As to whether, in the absence of contractual restraints or the disclosure of confidential information, the court will restrain a director of one company from joining the board of another competing company see PARA 590.

C. CIVIL CONSEQUENCES OF BREACH OF GENERAL DUTIES OF DIRECTORS

599. Civil consequences of breach of directors' general duties. The consequences of breach, or threatened breach, of the general duties that are specified in the Companies Act 2006[1] as being owed to the company[2] by a director[3] are the same as would apply if the corresponding common law rule or equitable principle applied[4].

Those duties[5], with the exception of the duty to exercise reasonable care, skill and diligence[6], are, accordingly, enforceable in the same way as any other fiduciary duty owed to a company by its directors[7].

1 Ie specified in the Companies Act 2006 ss 171–177: see PARA 580 et seq. As to the scope and nature of the directors' general duties see PARA 572; and as to the application and effect of the general duties see PARA 573. As to the relevance of case law on those common law rules and equitable principles that are now replaced by the statutory duties see PARA 572 note 7; and see PARA 630 et seq.

2 As to the meaning of 'company' under the Companies Acts see PARA 21; and as to the meaning of the 'Companies Acts' see PARA 13.

3 As to the meaning of 'director' under the Companies Acts see PARA 512. The general duties apply also to a shadow director of a company where and to the extent that they are capable of so applying: see the Companies Act 2006 s 170(5); and PARA 573. As to shadow directors see PARA 513.

4 Companies Act 2006 s 178(1). As to a director's liability at common law generally see PARA 630 et seq.

5 Ie the duties in the Companies Act 2006 ss 171–177: see PARA 580 et seq.

6 Ie except for the Companies Act 2006 s 174 (as to which see PARA 588): see s 178(2).

7 Companies Act 2006 s 178(2).

When considering the application of the Limitation Act 1980 to claims against fiduciaries, a six-year limitation period would apply under one or other provision of the Limitation Act 1980, applied directly or by analogy, unless it was specifically excluded by the Act or established case law; personal claims against fiduciaries would normally be subject to limits by analogy with claims in tort or contract: *Gwembe Valley Development Co Ltd v Koshy (No 3)* [2003] EWCA Civ 1048, [2004] 1 BCLC 131. Claims for breach of fiduciary duty by directors would normally be covered by the Limitation Act 1980 s 21 (time limit for actions in respect of trust property) (see LIMITATION PERIODS vol 68 (2008) PARA 1140 et seq) and the six-year time limit under the Limitation Act 1980 s 21(3) would apply, directly or by analogy, unless excluded by s 21(1)(a) or (b): *Gwembe Valley Development Co Ltd v Koshy (No 3)* [2003] EWCA Civ 1048, [2004] 1 BCLC 131. If a claim is a claim for, or is treated for limitation purposes as analogous to a claim for, 'fraud or fraudulent breach of trust' within the Limitation Act 1980 s 21(1)(a), no limitation period applies: see *Gwembe Valley Development Co Ltd v Koshy (No 3)* [2003] EWCA Civ 1048, [2004] 1 BCLC 131 (director's liability to account for secret profits made by him arose not out of simple non-disclosure but from a deliberate and dishonest concealment of his profits; in such circumstances, the claim was held to be a claim for fraudulent breach of trust and was not statute-barred). Likewise, where the claim against a director is a claim, or is treated for limitation purposes as analogous to a claim, 'to recover trust property or the proceeds of trust property in the possession of the trustee' within the Limitation Act 1980 s 21(1)(b), no limitation period applies: see *JJ Harrison (Properties) Ltd v Harrison* [2001] EWCA Civ 1467, [2002] 1 BCLC 162 (where a director purchased company property in breach of his duties to the company, his obligations to deal with the property as a trustee arose out of his pre-existing duties as a director and not out of the circumstances in which the property was conveyed to him). See also *Statek Corpn v Alford* [2008] EWHC 32 (Ch), [2008] BCC 266, [2008] All ER (D) 52 (Jan) (defendant had been a de facto director of the claimant company and, therefore, a trustee or fiduciary of its assets; the Limitation Act 1980 s 21(1) applied to the breach of fiduciary duty occasioned by his dishonest rendering of assistance to carry out the transactions complained of); *Burnden Holdings (UK) Ltd (in liquidation) v Fielding* [2016] EWCA Civ 557, [2016] All ER (D) 111 (Jun). As to the liability of directors generally see PARA 630 et seq. As to de facto directors, and the duties which they owe, see PARA 512 note 8.

For a case where equitable compensation was being claimed on behalf of a company and a defence of unconscionable delay ('laches') was raised see *Re Palmier plc (in liquidation), Sandhu v Sidhu* [2009] EWHC 983 (Ch), [2009] All ER (D) 93 (May).

(vi) Duty to Declare Interest in Existing Transaction or Arrangement

600. Directors' duty to declare interest in existing transaction or arrangement. Where a director[1] of a company[2] is in any way, whether directly or indirectly, interested in a transaction or arrangement that has been entered into by the company[3], he must declare the nature and extent of the interest to the other directors[4].

The declaration must be made:

(1) at a meeting of the directors[5]; or
(2) by notice in writing[6]; or
(3) by general notice[7].

If such a declaration of interest[8] proves to be, or becomes, inaccurate or incomplete, a further declaration must be made[9]. Any declaration so required[10] must be made as soon as is reasonably practicable[11].

This restriction[12] does not require a declaration of an interest of which the director is not aware or where the director is not aware of the transaction or arrangement in question[13]; and a director need not declare an interest:

(a) if it cannot reasonably be regarded as likely to give rise to a conflict of interest[14];
(b) if, or to the extent that, the other directors are already aware of it (and for this purpose the other directors are treated as aware of anything of which they ought reasonably to be aware)[15]; or
(c) if, or to the extent that, it concerns terms of his service contract[16] that have been or are to be considered either by a meeting of the directors[17], or by a committee of the directors appointed for the purpose under the company's constitution[18].

A director who fails to comply with these requirements[19] commits an offence[20]; and a person guilty of such an offence is liable on conviction on indictment or on summary conviction to a fine[21]. However, failure to comply with the statute does not give a separate right of action to the company for damages against a director as such liability must depend upon a breach of the director's fiduciary obligations[22].

The provisions which relate to a director's duty to declare any interest in an existing transaction or arrangement[23] apply to a shadow director[24] as they apply to a director[25], except that a shadow director must declare his interest, not at a meeting of the directors[26], but only by general notice, which is not effective when given by a shadow director for these purposes unless it is given by notice in writing sent to the other directors[27] and, where a general notice is treated as sufficient declaration[28], the requirement for the notice to be given at a meeting of the directors, or for the director to take reasonable steps to secure that it is brought up and read at the next meeting of the directors after it is given[29], does not apply[30].

1 As to the meaning of 'director' under the Companies Acts see PARA 512; and as to the meaning of the 'Companies Acts' see PARA 13.

2 As to the meaning of 'company' under the Companies Acts see PARA 21.

3 A realistic appraisal is required of the nature of the interest to see whether it is real and substantial or merely theoretical and insubstantial: *Re Dominion International Group plc (No 2)* [1996] 1 BCLC 572 (the Companies Act 2006 s 182 is not an appropriate place for the drawing of technical distinctions between vested and contingent interests and mere hopes or expectations) (decided under the Companies Act 1985 s 317 (repealed and replaced)).

4 Companies Act 2006 s 182(1). For the purposes of Pt 10 (ss 154–259) (see PARA 512 et seq) it is immaterial whether the law that (apart from the Companies Act 2006) governs an arrangement or transaction is the law of the United Kingdom, or a part of it, or not: s 259. As to the meaning of 'United Kingdom' see PARA 1 note 5. The Companies Act 2006 s 182 does not apply if or to the extent that the interest has been declared under s 177 (duty to declare interest in proposed transaction or arrangement) (see PARA 595): see s 182(1). As to the general duty to avoid conflicts of interest see PARA 590. As to the register of directors' interests that must be disclosed in relation to shares etc see PARA 463 et seq.

The requirement is for the director to declare the nature and extent of the interest to the other directors in accordance with s 182 (see the text and notes 5–18): see s 182(1). Informal disclosure made piecemeal, or proof of the knowledge of individual board members, does not comply with the formal requirements of disclosure to the board, which would involve an opportunity for consideration of the matter by the board as a body: *Gwembe Valley Development Co Ltd v Koshy (No 3)* [2003] EWCA Civ 1048 at [59], [2004] 1 BCLC 131 per Mummery LJ. See also *Guinness plc v Saunders* [1988] 2 All ER 940 at 944–945, [1988] 1 WLR 863 at 868–869, CA, per Fox LJ (on appeal but not affected on this point [1990] 2 AC 663, [1990] 1 All ER 652, HL); *Neptune (Vehicle Washing Equipment) Ltd v Fitzgerald* [1996] Ch 274 at 282–284, [1995] 3 All ER 811 at 817–819 per Lightman J; *Re MDA Investment Management Ltd, Whalley v Doney* [2003] EWHC 2277 (Ch), [2004] 1 BCLC 217. Cf *Lee Panavision Ltd v Lee Lighting Ltd* [1992] BCLC 22, CA (where the court hesitated to find that the failure formally to declare at a board meeting an interest common to all members and ex hypothesi already known to all of the members of the board, was a breach of the Companies Act 1985 s 317 (repealed: see now the Companies Act 2006 s 182)); and see the Companies Act 2006 s 177(6)(b) (a director need not declare an interest if, or to the extent that, the other directors are already aware of it); and PARA 595. See also *Runciman v Walter Runciman plc* [1992] BCLC 1084 at 1093; *MacPherson v European Strategic Bureau Ltd* [1999] 2 BCLC 203 at 219 per Ferris J (revsd but not on this point [2000] 2 BCLC 683, CA); *Re Marini Ltd* [2003] EWHC 334 (Ch) at [59]–[64], [2004] BCC 172 per Judge Richard Seymour QC.

Prior to statutory provision being made, it was held that a company might by apt words in its articles waive its right to full disclosure: *Imperial Mercantile Credit Association v Coleman* (1871) 6 Ch App 558 (revsd without affecting this point (1873) LR 6 HL 189); *Costa Rica Rly Co Ltd v Forwood* [1901] 1 Ch 746 at 760, CA, per Vaughan Williams LJ. It would appear that the Companies Act 2006 s 182 prevents a company from so waiving its right to disclosure as to sanction a contravention of that right.

Where a declaration of interest under s 182 is required of a sole director of a company that is required to have more than one director, the declaration must be recorded in writing, the making of the declaration is deemed to form part of the proceedings at the next meeting of the directors after the notice is given, and the provisions of s 248 (minutes of meetings of directors) (see PARA 570) apply as if the declaration had been made at that meeting: s 186(1). However, nothing in s 186 affects the operation of s 231 (terms of contract with sole member who is also a director must be set out in writing or recorded in minutes) (see PARA 629): s 186(2). As to a case which predated this statutory provision see *Neptune (Vehicle Washing Equipment) Ltd v Fitzgerald* [1996] Ch 274 at 282–284, [1995] 3 All ER 811 at 816–819 (sole director cannot evade compliance with duty of disclosure but the required meeting may be held by the director alone or with another).

5 Companies Act 2006 s 182(2)(a).

6 Companies Act 2006 s 182(2)(b). Head (2) in the text refers to notice in writing made in accordance with s 184: see s 182(2)(b). Under the provisions of s 184, which apply to a declaration of interest made by notice in writing (s 184(1)), the director must send the notice to the other directors (s 184(2)). The notice may be sent in hard copy form (or, if the recipient has agreed to receive it in electronic form, in an agreed electronic form) (s 184(3)); and may be sent by hand or by post (or, if the recipient has agreed to receive it by electronic means, by agreed electronic means) (s 184(4)). Where a director declares an interest by notice in writing in accordance with s 184, the making of the declaration is deemed to form part of the proceedings at the next meeting of the directors after the notice is given (s 184(5)(a)); and the provisions of s 248 (minutes of meetings of directors) (see PARA 570) apply as if the declaration had been made at that meeting (s 184(5)(b)). As to directors' communications see PARA 568 note 3. As to documents or information sent or supplied in hard copy form see PARA 750; and as to documents or information sent or supplied in electronic form (or by electronic means) see PARA 751. As to the construction of references to service by post see STATUTES AND LEGISLATIVE PROCESS vol 96 (2012) PARA 1219.

7 Companies Act 2006 s 182(2)(c). Head (3) in the text refers to general notice made in accordance with s 185: see s 182(2)(c). General notice in accordance with s 185 is a sufficient declaration of interest in relation to the matters to which it relates: s 185(1). General notice is notice given to the directors of a company to the effect that the director has an interest (as member, officer, employee or otherwise) in a specified body corporate or firm and is to be regarded as interested in any transaction or arrangement that may, after the date of the notice, be made with that body corporate or firm (s 185(2)(a)), or is connected with a specified person (other than a body corporate or firm) and is to be regarded as interested in any transaction or arrangement that may, after the date of the notice, be made with that person (s 185(2)(b)). The notice must state the nature and extent of the director's interest in the body corporate or firm or, as the case may be, the nature of his connection with the person: s 185(3). General notice is not effective, however,

unless it is given at a meeting of the directors (s 185(4)(a)), or the director takes reasonable steps to secure that it is brought up and read at the next meeting of the directors after it is given (s 185(4)(b)). Cf the text and notes 23–30. As to the meaning of 'member' see PARA 323. As to the meaning of 'officer' generally see PARA 679. As to the meaning of 'body corporate' for the purposes of the Companies Acts see PARA 1 note 5; as to the meaning of 'firm' see PARA 105 note 15; and as to the meaning of references to a director being 'connected' with a person see PARA 515.

8 Ie made under the Companies Act 2006 s 182: see s 182(3).

9 Companies Act 2006 s 182(3).

10 Ie required by the Companies Act 2006 s 182: see s 182(4).

11 Companies Act 2006 s 182(4). Failure to comply with this requirement does not affect the underlying duty to make the declaration: s 182(4).

12 Ie the restriction contained in the provisions of the Companies Act 2006 s 182: see s 182(5).

13 Companies Act 2006 s 182(5). For this purpose, a director is treated as being aware of matters of which he ought reasonably to be aware: s 182(5).

14 Companies Act 2006 s 182(6)(a).

15 Companies Act 2006 s 182(6)(b).

16 As to the meaning of a director's 'service contract', in relation to a company, for the purposes of the Companies Act 2006 Pt 10 (see PARA 512 et seq) see PARA 565 note 4.

17 Companies Act 2006 s 182(6)(c)(i).

18 Companies Act 2006 s 182(6)(c)(ii). As to the meaning of references to a company's constitution for the purposes of Pt 10 (see PARA 512 et seq) see PARA 580 note 4. As to the extent to which directors may delegate powers, including to committees, see PARA 577.

19 Ie with the requirements of the Companies Act 2006 s 182: see s 183(1).

20 Companies Act 2006 s 183(1). As to the possible vacation of position where a director is interested in a contract see PARA 598. As to the effect of a failure to disclose on sales to the company see PARA 597.

21 Companies Act 2006 s 183(2). In the case of liability on summary conviction the fine is one not exceeding the statutory maximum: see s 183(2). By virtue of the Legal Aid, Sentencing and Punishment of Offenders Act 2012 s 85, however, where the offence is committed on or after 12 March 2015, it is punishable by a fine of an unlimited amount. As to the statutory maximum and the powers of magistrates' courts to issue fines on summary conviction see SENTENCING vol 92 (2015) PARA 176.

22 *Coleman Taymar Ltd v Oakes* [2001] 2 BCLC 749. See also PARA 597. As to the general fiduciary position of directors see PARA 587.

23 Ie the Companies Act 2006 Pt 10 Ch 3 (ss 182–187): see s 187(1).

24 As to the meaning of 'shadow director' see PARA 513.

25 Companies Act 2006 s 187(1).

26 Ie because the Companies Act 2006 s 182(2)(a) (see the head (1) in the text) does not apply: s 187(2).

27 Ie general notice by a shadow director is not effective unless given by notice in writing in accordance with the Companies Act 2006 s 184 (see note 6): s 187(4).

28 Ie in the Companies Act 2006 s 185 (see note 7): see s 187(3).

29 Ie the provision made in the Companies Act 2006 s 185(4) (see note 7): see s 187(3).

30 Companies Act 2006 s 187(3).

(vii) Transactions with Directors Requiring Approval of Members

A. DIRECTORS' TRANSACTIONS REQUIRING APPROVAL: IN GENERAL

601. Transactions with directors requiring members' approval: in general. The Companies Act 2006 specifies[1] that certain transactions involving the directors of a company[2] (namely, directors' long-term service contracts[3], remuneration payments to directors of quoted companies[4], substantial property transactions[5], loan and similar financial transactions[6], and payments for loss of office[7]) require approval by resolution of the members, either by means of a resolution taken at a meeting of the company or, in the case of a private company, by means of a written resolution[8]. Shareholder approval is not required, however, in respect of certain of these transactions where the company is not a UK-registered company[9] or where the company is a wholly-owned subsidiary of another body corporate[10].

Approval may be required under more than one provision[11]. Where this is so, the requirements of each applicable provision must be met[12], although this does not require a separate resolution for the purposes of each provision[13]. In the case of approval of remuneration payments or payments for loss of office to directors of quoted companies[14], however, where the making of such a payment requires approval by a resolution of the members of the company concerned under another applicable provision[15], then approval so obtained[16] is to be treated as satisfying the specific requirements[17] relating to quoted companies[18].

1 Ie in the Companies Act 2006 Pt 10 Ch 4 (ss 188–225) and Pt 10 Ch 4A (ss 226A–226F): see also PARA 603 et seq.

2 As to the meaning of 'director' under the Companies Acts see PARA 512; and as to the meaning of 'company' under the Companies Acts see PARA 21. As to the meaning of the 'Companies Acts' see PARA 13. For the purposes of the Companies Act 2006 Pt 10 (ss 154–259) (see PARA 512 et seq), it is immaterial whether the law that (apart from the Companies Act 2006) governs an arrangement or transaction is the law of the United Kingdom, or a part of it, or not: s 259. As to the meaning of 'United Kingdom' see PARA 1 note 5.

3 See the Companies Act 2006 ss 188, 189; and PARA 603. For the purposes of ss 188, 189, a shadow director is treated as a director: s 223(1)(a). See also note 7. As to the meaning of 'shadow director' see PARA 513. As to directors' service contracts generally see PARA 564 et seq.

4 See the Companies Act 2006 ss 226A, 226B, 226D, 226E; and PARAS 604–605. For these purposes, 'quoted company' has the same meaning as in Pt 15 (ss 380–474) (see PARA 70): s 226A(1) (s 226A added by the Enterprise and Regulatory Reform Act 2013 s 80). References in the Companies Act 2006 Pt 10 Ch 4A to a director include a shadow director but references to loss of office as a director do not include loss of a person's status as a shadow director: s 226A(9) (as so added).

5 See the Companies Act 2006 ss 190–196; and PARA 606 et seq. For the purposes of ss 190–196, a shadow director is treated as a director: s 223(1)(b). See also note 7.

6 See the Companies Act 2006 ss 197–214; and PARA 610 et seq. For the purposes of ss 197–214, a shadow director is treated as a director: s 223(1)(c). See also note 7.

7 See the Companies Act 2006 ss 215–222, 226C–226E; and PARA 620 et seq. For the purposes of ss 215–222, a shadow director is treated as a director: s 223(1)(d). See also note 4. Any reference in ss 188–222 to loss of office as a director does not apply in relation to loss of a person's status as a shadow director: s 223(2).

8 As to the meaning of 'written resolution' see PARA 695. Where approval under Pt 10 Ch 4 is required by way of a written resolution, a memorandum setting out particulars of the proposed arrangement must be circulated to the members eligible to vote on the resolution at or before the time at which the proposed resolution is sent to the members: see eg the Companies Act 2006 s 188(5) (cited in PARA 603), s 197(3) (cited in PARA 610), s 198(4) (cited in PARA 611), s 200(4) (cited in PARA 612), s 203(3) (cited in PARA 614), s 217(3) (cited in PARA 621), s 218(3) (cited in PARA 622), s 219(3) (cited in PARA 623). Where approval under Pt 10 Ch 4 (see also PARA 603 et seq) is sought by written resolution, and a memorandum is required under Pt 10 Ch 4 to be sent or submitted to every eligible member before the resolution is passed, any accidental failure to send or submit the memorandum to one or more members must be disregarded for the purpose of determining whether the requirement has been met: s 224(1). This has effect subject to any provision of the company's articles: s 224(2). As to the meaning of references to a company's 'articles' under the Companies Act 2006 see PARA 227 note 2. As to membership of companies generally see PARA 323 et seq. As to approval given by resolutions in meetings of the company generally see PARA 701 et seq. As to eligible members in relation to a resolution proposed as a written resolution of a private company see PARA 695.

Under Pt 10 Ch 4A, a resolution approving a payment for the purposes of s 226B(1)(b) or 226C(1)(b) must not be passed unless a memorandum setting out particulars of the proposed payment (including its amount) is made available for inspection by the members of the company: see s 226D(1); and PARAS 604, 621.

9 As to the meaning of 'UK-registered company' see PARA 21.

10 See eg the Companies Act 2006 s 188(6) (cited in PARA 603), s 190(4) (cited in PARA 607), s 197(5) (cited in PARA 610), s 200(6) (cited in PARA 612), s 201(6) (cited in PARA 613), s 217(4) (cited in PARA 621), s 218(4) (cited in PARA 622), s 219(6) (cited in PARA 623). As to the meaning of 'body corporate' for the purposes of the Companies Acts see PARA 1 note 5. As to the meanings of 'subsidiary' and 'wholly-owned subsidiary' see PARA 22.

11 Companies Act 2006 s 225(1). The text refers to more than one provision of Pt 10 Ch 4 (see also PARA 603 et seq): see s 225(1).
12 Companies Act 2006 s 225(2).
13 Companies Act 2006 s 225(3).
14 Ie payments to which the Companies Act 2006 s 226B or 226C applies: see PARAS 604, 621.
15 Ie under the Companies Act 2006 Pt 10 Ch 4.
16 Ie approval obtained for the purposes of the Companies Act 2006 Pt 10 Ch 4.
17 Ie the requirements of the Companies Act 2006 s 226B(1)(b) or, as the case may be, s 226C(1)(b) (see PARAS 604, 621).
18 See the Companies Act 2006 s 226F(2) (s 226F added by the Enterprise and Regulatory Reform Act 2013 s 80). The Companies Act 2006 Pt 10 Ch 4A does not affect any requirement for approval by a resolution of the members of a company which applies in relation to the company under Pt 10 Ch 4: s 226F(1) (as so added).

602. Interaction of provisions governing transactions requiring members' approval with directors' general duties. The application of the general duties to which the directors of a company[1] are subject[2] is not affected by the fact that the case also falls within the provisions which govern transactions requiring the approval of members[3], except that where those provisions[4] apply[5], and:

(1) approval is duly given[6]; or

(2) the matter is one as to which it is provided that approval is not needed[7],

it is not necessary also to comply with the duty to avoid conflicts of interest[8] or the duty[9] not to accept benefits from third parties[10].

Compliance with the general duties does not remove the need for approval under any of the provisions[11] which apply to transactions requiring the approval of members[12].

1 As to the meaning of 'director' under the Companies Acts see PARA 512; and as to the meaning of 'company' under the Companies Acts see PARA 21. As to the meaning of the 'Companies Acts' see PARA 13.
2 Ie the duties specified in the Companies Act 2006 ss 171–177: see PARA 580 et seq. As to the scope and nature of the directors' general duties see PARA 572; and as to the application and effect of the general duties see PARA 573.
3 Ie within the Companies Act 2006 Pt 10 Ch 4 (ss 188–225) or Pt 10 Ch 4A (ss 226A–226F) (see PARAS 601, 603 et seq): see s 180(2) (s 180(2), (3) amended by the Enterprise and Regulatory Reform Act 2013 s 81(1), (2)). As to the meaning of 'member' see PARA 323.
4 Ie the Companies Act 2006 Pt 10 Ch 4 or Pt 10 Ch 4A (see PARAS 601, 603 et seq): see s 180(2) (as amended: see note 3).
5 Companies Act 2006 s 180(2) (as amended: see note 3).
6 Companies Act 2006 s 180(2)(a) (as amended: see note 3). Head (1) in the text refers to approval given under Pt 10 Ch 4 or Pt 10 Ch 4A (see PARAS 601, 603 et seq), whichever is concerned: see s 180(2)(a) (as so amended).
7 Companies Act 2006 s 180(2)(b). Head (2) in the text (which disapplies certain duties under Pt 10 Ch 4 in relation to cases excepted from the requirement to obtain approval by members under Pt 10 Ch 4) applies to charitable companies only if or to the extent that the company's articles allow those duties to be so disapplied, which they may do only in relation to descriptions of transaction or arrangement specified in the company's articles: s 181(3). See PARA 573. As to the meaning of references to a company's 'articles' under the Companies Act 2006 see PARA 227 note 2.
8 Ie the duty in the Companies Act 2006 s 175 (see PARA 590): see s 180(2).
9 Ie the duty in the Companies Act 2006 s 176 (see PARA 593): see s 180(2).
10 Companies Act 2006 s 180(2).
11 Ie in the Companies Act 2006 Pt 10 Ch 4 or Pt 10 Ch 4A (see PARAS 601, 603 et seq): see s 180(3) (as amended: see note 3).
12 Companies Act 2006 s 180(3) (as amended: see note 3).

B. DIRECTORS' SERVICE CONTRACTS

603. Requirement of members' approval for directors' long-term service contracts. In relation to any provision under which the guaranteed term of a director's employment[1] with the company of which he is a director, or, where he is the director of a holding company[2], within the group consisting of that company and its subsidiaries[3], is, or may be, longer than two years[4], the company may not agree to such provision unless it has been approved[5]:

(1) by resolution[6] of the members of the company[7]; and
(2) in the case of a director of a holding company, by resolution of the members of that company[8].

If, more than six months before the end of the guaranteed term of a director's employment, the company enters into a further service contract, otherwise than in pursuance of a right conferred, by or under the original contract, on the other party to it, this restriction[9] applies as if there were added to the guaranteed term of the new contract the unexpired period of the guaranteed term of the original contract[10].

A resolution approving provision to which this restriction[11] applies must not be passed unless a memorandum setting out the proposed contract incorporating the provision is made available to members[12]:

(a) in the case of a written resolution[13], by being sent or submitted to every eligible member[14] at or before the time at which the proposed resolution is sent or submitted to him[15];
(b) in the case of a resolution at a meeting, by being made available for inspection by members of the company both:
    (i) at the company's registered office[16] for not less than 15 days ending with the date of the meeting[17]; and
    (ii) at the meeting itself[18].

No such approval is, however, required[19] on the part of the members of a body corporate[20] that either is not a UK-registered company[21], or is a wholly-owned subsidiary[22] of another body corporate[23].

If a company agrees to provision in contravention of this restriction[24], the provision is void, to the extent of the contravention[25], and the contract is deemed to contain a term entitling the company to terminate it at any time by the giving of reasonable notice[26].

1 The guaranteed term of a director's employment is:
(1) the period (if any) during which the director's employment is to continue, or may be continued otherwise than at the instance of the company (whether under the original agreement or under a new agreement entered into in pursuance of it), and cannot be terminated by the company by notice, or can be so terminated only in specified circumstances (Companies Act 2006 s 188(3)(a)); or
(2) in the case of employment terminable by the company by notice, the period of notice required to be given (s 188(3)(b)); or
(3) in the case of employment having both a period within head (1) above and a period within head (2) above) the aggregate of those periods (s 188(3)).

For these purposes, 'employment' means any employment under a director's service contract: s 188(7). As to the meaning of a director's 'service contract', in relation to a company, for the purposes of Pt 10 (ss 154–259) see PARA 565 note 4. As to the meaning of 'company' under the Companies Acts see PARA 21; and to the meaning of the 'Companies Acts' see PARA 13. For the purposes of ss 188, 189 (see the text and notes 2–26), a shadow director is treated as a director: s 223(1)(a). As to the meaning of 'director' in the Companies Act 2006 generally see PARA 512; and as to shadow directors see PARA 513.

As to the general application of the Companies Act 2006 Pt 10 Ch 4 (ss 188–225) see PARA 601; and as to how those provisions interact with the directors' general duties see PARA 602.

2 As to the meaning of 'holding company' see PARA 22.
3 As to the meaning of 'subsidiary' see PARA 22.
4 Companies Act 2006 s 188(1).
5 Companies Act 2006 s 188(2). In accordance with the principle set out in *Re Duomatic Ltd* [1969] 2 Ch 365, [1969] 1 All ER 161 (see PARA 738), the procedural steps set out in the Companies Act 2006 s 188 can be bypassed by the unanimous informal consent of the shareholders: *Wright v Atlas Wright (Europe) Ltd* [1999] 2 BCLC 301, CA.

6 As to resolutions and meetings of members see PARA 701 et seq. As to voting at meetings see PARA 725 et seq.
7 Companies Act 2006 s 188(2)(a). As to the meaning of 'member of a company' see PARA 323.
8 Companies Act 2006 s 188(2)(b).
9 Ie the Companies Act 2006 s 188: see s 188(4).
10 Companies Act 2006 s 188(4).
11 Ie the Companies Act 2006 s 188: see s 188(5).
12 Companies Act 2006 s 188(5).
13 As to the meaning of 'written resolution' see PARA 695.
14 As to eligible members in relation to a resolution proposed as a written resolution of a private company see PARA 695. As to the provision made for the sending or supplying of documents or information to or from a company (the 'company communications provisions') see PARA 750 et seq.
15 Companies Act 2006 s 188(5)(a). Where approval under Pt 10 Ch 4 is sought by written resolution, and a memorandum is required under Pt 10 Ch 4 to be sent or submitted to every eligible member before the resolution is passed, provision is made for accidental failure to send or submit the memorandum to one or more members: see s 224; and PARA 601 note 8.
16 As to the company's registered office see PARA 124.
17 Companies Act 2006 s 188(5)(b)(i).
18 Companies Act 2006 s 188(5)(b)(ii).
19 Ie under the Companies Act 2006 s 188: see s 188(6).
20 As to the meaning of 'body corporate' for the purposes of the Companies Acts see PARA 1 note 5.
21 Companies Act 2006 s 188(6)(a). As to the meaning of 'UK-registered company' see PARA 21.
22 As to the meaning of 'wholly-owned subsidiary' see PARA 22.
23 Companies Act 2006 s 188(6)(b).
24 Ie in contravention of the Companies Act 2006 s 188: see s 189.
25 Companies Act 2006 s 189(a).
26 Companies Act 2006 s 189(b).

C. REMUNERATION PAYMENTS TO DIRECTORS OF QUOTED COMPANIES

604. Restrictions relating to remuneration payments to directors of quoted companies. A quoted company[1] may not make a remuneration payment[2] to a person who is, or is to be or has been, a director of the company[3] unless[4]:

(1) the payment is consistent with the approved directors' remuneration policy[5], namely the most recent remuneration policy to have been approved by a resolution passed by the members of the company in general meeting[6]; or
(2) the payment is approved by resolution of the members of the company[7].

A resolution approving a payment for the purposes of head (2) above must not be passed unless a memorandum setting out particulars of the proposed payment, including its amount, is made available for inspection by the members of the company:

(a) at the company's registered office[8] for not less than 15 days ending with the date of the meeting at which the resolution is to be considered; and
(b) at that meeting itself[9].

The memorandum must explain the ways in which the payment is inconsistent with the approved directors' remuneration policy[10]. The company must ensure that the memorandum is made available on the company's website[11] from the first day on which the memorandum is made available for inspection[12] until its next accounts meeting[13]; but failure to comply with this requirement does not affect the validity of the meeting at which a resolution is passed approving a payment to which the memorandum relates or the validity of anything done at the meeting[14].

Nothing in heads (1) and (2) above:

(i) authorises the making of a remuneration payment in contravention of the articles[15] of the company concerned[16];

(ii) applies in relation to a remuneration payment made to a person who is, or is to be or has been, a director of a quoted company before the earlier of:
   (A) the end of the first financial year of the company to begin on or after the day on which it becomes a quoted company; and
   (B) the date from which the company's first directors' remuneration policy to be approved[17] takes effect[18].

1 As to the meaning of 'quoted company' for these purposes see PARA 601 note 4; and see PARA 70.
2 For these purposes, 'remuneration payment' means any form of payment or other benefit (other than a payment for loss of office) made to or otherwise conferred on a person as consideration for the person:
   (1) holding, agreeing to hold or having held office as director of a company (Companies Act 2006 s 226A(1)(a) (ss 226A, 226B, 226D, s 226F added by the Enterprise and Regulatory Reform Act 2013 s 80)); or
   (2) holding, agreeing to hold or having held, during a period when the person is or was such a director, any other office or employment in connection with the management of the affairs of the company, or any office, as director or otherwise, or employment in connection with the management of the affairs of any subsidiary undertaking of the company (Companies Act 2006 s 226A(1)(b) (as so added)).

   References in Pt 10 Ch 4A (ss 226A–226F) to the making of a remuneration payment are to be read in accordance with s 226A (s 226A(5) (as so added)); and references therein to a payment by a company include a payment by another person at the direction of, or on behalf of, the company (s 226A(6) (as so added)).
3 References in the Companies Act 2006 Pt 10 Ch 4A to a payment to a person ('B') who is, has been or is to be a director of a company include a payment to a person connected with B, or a payment to a person at the direction of, or for the benefit of, B or a person connected with B: s 226A(7) (as added: see note 2). Section 252 (see PARA 515) applies for the purposes of determining whether a person is connected with a person who has been, or is to be, a director of a company as it applies for the purposes of determining whether a person is connected with a director: s 226A(8) (as so added). As to the meaning of references to a 'director' for these purposes see PARA 601 note 4.
4 Companies Act 2006 s 226B(1) (as added: see note 2).
5 Companies Act 2006 s 226B(1)(a) (as added: see note 2). 'Directors' remuneration policy' means the policy of a quoted company with respect to the making of remuneration payments and payments for loss of office: s 226A(1) (as so added). As to the meaning of 'payment for loss of office' see PARA 620 (definition applied by s 226A(1) (as so added)).
6 See the Companies Act 2006 s 226B(2) (as added: see note 2). As to resolutions and meetings of members see PARA 701 et seq. As to voting at meetings see PARA 725 et seq. As to the meaning of 'member of a company' see PARA 323.
7 Companies Act 2006 s 226B(1)(b) (as added: see note 2). Where, however, the making of a payment to which s 226B applies requires approval by a resolution of the members of the company concerned under Pt 10 Ch 4 (ss 188–225) (see PARAS 601 et seq, 606 et seq), approval obtained for the purposes of Pt 10 Ch 4 is to be treated as satisfying the requirements of s 226B(1)(b): s 226F(2) (as added: see note 2). The Companies Act 2006 Pt 10 Ch 4A does not affect any requirement for approval by a resolution of the members of a company which applies in relation to the company under Pt 10 Ch 4: s 226F(1) (as so added).
8 As to the company's registered office see PARA 124.
9 Companies Act 2006 s 226D(1) (as added: see note 2).
10 Companies Act 2006 s 226D(2) (as added: see note 2).
11 For these purposes, the 'company's website' is the website on which the company makes material available under the Companies Act 2006 s 430 (see PARA 945): s 226D(7) (as added: see note 2).
12 Ie under the Companies Act 2006 s 226D(1): see the text and notes 8–10.
13 Companies Act 2006 s 226D(3) (as added: see note 2). As to the meaning of 'accounts meeting' see PARA 946 note 4.
14 Companies Act 2006 s 226D(4) (as added: see note 2).
15 As to the meaning of references to a company's 'articles' under the Companies Act 2006 see PARA 227 note 2.
16 Companies Act 2006 s 226D(5) (as added: see note 2).
17 Ie under the Companies Act 2006 s 439A: see PARA 934.
18 Companies Act 2006 s 226D(6) (as added: see note 2).

605. Civil consequences of remuneration payments made without approval. An obligation, however arising, to make a payment which would be in contravention of the statutory restrictions on remuneration payments to directors of quoted companies[1] has no effect[2].

If a payment is made in contravention of those restrictions[3]:

(1) it is held by the recipient on trust for the company[4] or other person making the payment; and

(2) in the case of a payment by a company[5], any director[6] who authorised the payment is jointly and severally liable to indemnify the company that made the payment for any loss resulting from it[7].

If, however, in proceedings against a director for the enforcement of a liability under head (2) above, the director shows that he has acted honestly and reasonably, and the court considers that, having regard to all the circumstances of the case, the director ought to be relieved of liability, the court[8] may relieve the director, either wholly or in part, from liability on such terms as the court thinks fit[9].

1 Ie in contravention of the Companies Act 2006 s 226B: see PARA 604.
2 Companies Act 2006 s 226E(1) (s 226E added by the Enterprise and Regulatory Reform Act 2013 s 80).
3 See note 1.
4 As to the meaning of 'company' under the Companies Acts see PARA 21; and as to the meaning of the 'Companies Acts' see PARA 13.
5 As to the meaning of references to 'a payment by a company' see PARA 604 note 2.
6 As to the meaning of references to a 'director' for these purposes see PARA 601 note 4.
7 Companies Act 2006 s 226E(2) (as added: see note 2).
8 As to the meaning of 'the court' see PARA 160 note 12.
9 Companies Act 2006 s 226E(5) (as added: see note 2).

D. SUBSTANTIAL PROPERTY TRANSACTIONS WITH DIRECTORS

606. Requirement of members' approval for substantial property transactions with directors. A company[1] may not enter into an arrangement under which[2]:

(1) a director[3] of the company or of its holding company[4], or a person connected with such a director[5], acquires or is to acquire[6] from the company, whether directly or indirectly, a substantial non-cash asset[7]; or

(2) the company acquires or is to acquire a substantial non-cash asset, whether directly or indirectly, from such a director or a person so connected[8],

unless the arrangement has been approved by a resolution[9] of the members of the company or is conditional on such approval being obtained[10]. If the director or connected person is a director of the company's holding company or a person connected with such a director, the arrangement must also have been approved by a resolution of the members of the holding company or be conditional on such approval being obtained[11].

However, a company is not subject to any liability by reason of a failure to obtain any approval so required[12].

1 As to the meaning of 'company' under the Companies Acts see PARA 21; and as to the meaning of the 'Companies Acts' see PARA 13.
2 Companies Act 2006 s 190(1).

As to the general application of the Companies Act 2006 Pt 10 Ch 4 (ss 188–225) see PARA 601; and as to how those provisions interact with the directors' general duties see PARA 602.

3 For the purposes of the Companies Act 2006 ss 190–196 (see the text and notes 1–2, 4–12; and PARAS 607–609), a shadow director is treated as a director: s 223(1)(b). As to the meaning of 'director' under the Companies Acts generally see PARA 512; and as to shadow directors see

PARA 513. As to an application of the Companies Act 2006 s 190 to a shadow director see *Ultraframe (UK) Ltd v Fielding; Northstar Systems Ltd v Fielding* [2005] EWHC 1638 (Ch), [2005] All ER (D) 397 (Jul).

4 As to the meaning of 'holding company' see PARA 22.

5 As to the meaning of references to a person being 'connected' with a director see PARA 515. As to the validity generally of transactions involving a director or a person connected with a director see PARA 263.

6 There is no basis for interpreting the words 'is to acquire' in the Companies Act 2006 s 190(1) as 'may acquire'; s 190(1) requires a high degree of certainty at the time when the arrangement is entered into that the asset will be acquired: *Smithton Ltd v Naggar* [2014] EWCA Civ 939, [2015] 1 WLR 189, [2015] 2 BCLC 22. A beneficiary's right to compel the trustee to comply with its obligations under the trust is a personal right and not an interest in or right over property, but the beneficiary of a bare trust, who could compel the trustee to wind up the trust and hand over the trust property, might be said to have a right over property: *Granada Group Ltd v The Law Debenture Pension Trust Corpn plc* [2015] EWHC 1499 (Ch), [2015] 2 BCLC 604.

7 Companies Act 2006 s 190(1)(a). In the Companies Acts, 'non-cash asset' means any property or interest in property, other than cash; and, for this purpose, 'cash' includes foreign currency: s 1163(1). A reference to the transfer or acquisition of a non-cash asset includes the creation or extinction of an estate or interest in, or a right over, any property, and the discharge of a liability of any person, other than a liability for a liquidated sum: s 1163(2). An exclusive licence of design rights is a non-cash asset for this purpose as the ability of the licensee to exercise rights which would otherwise be exercisable by the design right owner is a right over property: *Ultraframe (UK) Ltd v Fielding; Northstar Systems Ltd v Fielding* [2005] EWHC 1638 (Ch), [2005] All ER (D) 397 (Jul).

The meaning of a 'substantial non-cash asset' for the purposes of the Companies Act 2006 s 190 is given in s 191: see ss 190(1), 191(1). Accordingly, an asset is a 'substantial' asset in relation to a company if its value exceeds 10% of the company's asset value and is more than £5,000, or if its value exceeds £100,000: s 191(2). For this purpose, a company's 'asset value' at any time is either the value of the company's net assets determined by reference to its most recent statutory accounts or (if no statutory accounts have been prepared) the amount of the company's called-up share capital: s 191(3). A company's 'statutory accounts' means its annual accounts prepared in accordance with Pt 15 (ss 380–474) (see PARA 765 et seq), and its 'most recent' statutory accounts means those in relation to which the time for sending them out to members (see s 424; and PARA 936) is most recent: s 191(4). Whether an asset is a substantial asset is to be determined as at the time the arrangement is entered into: s 191(5). For the purposes of s 190, an arrangement involving more than one non-cash asset, or an arrangement that is one of a series involving non-cash assets, must be treated as if they involved a non-cash asset of a value equal to the aggregate value of all the non-cash assets involved in the arrangement or, as the case may be, the series: s 190(5). As to the meanings of 'share' and 'share capital' see PARA 1231; and as to the meaning of 'called-up share capital' see PARA 1237. As to the meaning of 'member' see PARA 323. The onus is on the person alleging a contravention of this provision to prove that the value of the non-cash asset exceeds the requisite value: *Niltan Carson Ltd (joint receivers and managers) v Hawthorne* [1988] BCLC 298. As to the criteria that ought to be applied when calculating the value of a non-cash asset see *Micro Leisure Ltd v County Properties and Developments Ltd (No 2)* 1999 SLT 1428 (value must be determined in the context of the particular transaction).

The Secretary of State may by order substitute for any sum of money specified in the Companies Act 2006 Pt 10 (ss 154–259) a larger sum specified in the order: s 258(1). An order does not have effect in relation to anything done or not done before it comes into force; and, accordingly, proceedings in respect of any liability incurred before that time may be continued or instituted as if the order had not been made: s 258(3). An order under s 258 is subject to negative resolution procedure (ie the statutory instrument containing the order is subject to annulment in pursuance of a resolution of either House of Parliament): ss 258(2), 1289. As to the Secretary of State see PARA 6. At the date at which this volume states the law, no such order has been made. As to the making of orders under the Companies Act 2006 generally see ss 1288–1292.

8 Companies Act 2006 s 190(1)(b).

9 As to resolutions and meetings of members see PARA 701 et seq. As to voting at meetings see PARA 725 et seq.

10 Companies Act 2006 s 190(1). This requirement does not apply to a transaction so far as it relates to anything to which a director of a company is entitled under his service contract, or to payment for loss of office as defined in s 215 (payments to which the requirements of Pt 10 Ch 4 (ss 188–225) or Pt 10 Ch 4A (ss 226A–226F) apply) (see PARA 620): s 190(6) (amended by the Enterprise and Regulatory Reform Act 2013 s 81(1), (3)). As to the meaning of a director's 'service contract', in relation to a company, for the purposes of the Companies Act 2006 Pt 10 see

PARA 565 note 4. As to other exceptions to this requirement see PARA 607; as to liabilities arising from any contravention of this requirement see PARA 608; and as to the effect of subsequent affirmation see PARA 609.

It is appropriate to construe the statutory provisions purposively to protect shareholders: *Micro Leisure Ltd v County Properties and Developments Ltd* 1999 SLT 1307, Ct of Sess. See also *British Racing Drivers' Club Ltd v Hextall Erskine & Co (a firm)* [1996] 3 All ER 667, [1997] 1 BCLC 182 (purpose of shareholders' approval is to allow members to check on potential abuse of position by directors and to ensure an objective approach). Where a meeting was attended by all those entitled to attend a general meeting and a decision was made, it could not be said that there was breach of the statutory provisions simply because the minutes of the meeting categorised it as a board meeting instead of a general meeting: *Re Conegrade Ltd* [2002] EWHC 2411 (Ch), [2003] BPIR 358, [2002] All ER (D) 19 (Nov). In accordance with the principle set out in *Re Duomatic Ltd* [1969] 2 Ch 365, [1969] 1 All ER 161 (see PARA 738), the procedural steps set out in the Companies Act 2006 s 190 can be bypassed by the unanimous informal consent of the shareholders: *NBH Ltd v Hoare* [2006] EWHC 73 (Ch), [2006] 2 BCLC 649 (decided under the Companies Act 1985 s 320(1)).

11 Companies Act 2006 s 190(2). See also *British Racing Drivers' Club Ltd v Hextall Erskine & Co (a firm)* [1996] 3 All ER 667, [1997] 1 BCLC 182.

12 Companies Act 2006 s 190(3). The text refers to approval required by s 190: see s 190(3).

607. Exceptions to requirement for approval of substantial property transactions with directors. Approval is not required[1] for substantial property transactions involving a director[2] of the company[3] or of its holding company[4], or a person connected with such a director[5], in the following cases:

(1) on the part of the members of a body corporate[6] that either is not a UK-registered company[7], or is a wholly-owned subsidiary[8] of another body corporate[9];

(2) for a transaction between a company and a person in his character as a member of that company[10], or for a transaction between a holding company and its wholly-owned subsidiary[11], or between two wholly-owned subsidiaries of the same holding company[12];

(3) on the part of the members of a company that is being wound up (unless the winding up is a members' voluntary winding up)[13], or that is in administration[14], or for an arrangement entered into by such a company[15].

(4) for a transaction on a recognised investment exchange[16] effected by a director, or a person connected with him, through the agency of a person who in relation to the transaction acts as an independent broker[17].

1 Ie under the Companies Act 2006 s 190: see PARA 606. As to liabilities arising from any contravention of s 190 see PARA 608; and as to the effect of subsequent affirmation see PARA 609.

As to the general application of the Companies Act 2006 Pt 10 Ch 4 (ss 188–225) see PARA 601; and as to how those provisions interact with the directors' general duties see PARA 602.

2 As to the meaning of 'director' for these purposes see PARA 606 note 3.

3 As to the meaning of 'company' under the Companies Acts see PARA 21.

4 As to the meaning of 'holding company' see PARA 22.

5 As to the meaning of references to a person being 'connected' with a director see PARA 515. As to the validity generally of transactions involving a director or a person connected with a director see PARA 263.

6 As to the meaning of 'body corporate' for the purposes of the Companies Acts see PARA 1 note 5.

7 Companies Act 2006 s 190(4)(a). As to the meaning of 'UK-registered company' see PARA 21.

8 As to the meaning of 'wholly-owned subsidiary' see PARA 22.

9 Companies Act 2006 s 190(4)(b).

10 Companies Act 2006 s 192(a). As to the meaning of 'member of a company' see PARA 323. When discussing this provision at the Bill stage, Lord Sainsbury of Turville stated: 'it is intended to cover transactions such as the payment of the dividend in specie as well as the distribution of assets to a member of a company during the winding-up of the company and in satisfaction of his rights qua member in the liquidation. Likewise a duly sanctioned return of capital in the form of non-cash assets would fall within this exception. It is also intended to put beyond doubt that the

issue of shares or other rights to a member does not require approval under the rules for substantial property transactions': 678 HL Official Report (5th series), 9 Feb 2006, GC col 347.

11 Companies Act 2006 s 192(b)(i).

12 Companies Act 2006 s 192(b)(ii).

13 Companies Act 2006 s 193(1)(a), (2)(a). As to winding up in general see COMPANY AND PARTNERSHIP INSOLVENCY vol 16 (2011) PARA 380 et seq. As to members' voluntary winding up see COMPANY AND PARTNERSHIP INSOLVENCY vol 17 (2011) PARA 898 et seq.

14 Companies Act 2006 s 193(1)(b), (2)(a). For these purposes, a company is 'in administration' while the appointment of an administrator of the company has effect: see the Insolvency Act 1986 Sch B1 para 1(2)(a) (added by the Enterprise Act 2002 Sch 16); and COMPANY AND PARTNERSHIP INSOLVENCY vol 16 (2011) PARA 161 (definition applied by the Companies Act 2006 s 193(1)(b)). Prior to the enactment of the Companies Act 2006, the exemption to which head (3) in the text relates was available only to a liquidator and not to an administrator or receiver: see eg *Demite Ltd v Protec Health Ltd* [1998] BCC 638.

15 Companies Act 2006 s 193(2)(b).

16 For these purposes, 'recognised investment exchange' has the same meaning as in the Financial Services and Markets Act 2000 Pt XVIII (ss 285–313) (see FINANCIAL SERVICES REGULATION vol 50A (2016) PARA 939 et seq): Companies Act 2006 s 194(2)(b).

17 Companies Act 2006 s 194(1). For these purposes, 'independent broker' means a person who, independently of the director or any person connected with him, selects the person with whom the transaction is to be effected: s 194(2)(a).

608. Civil consequences of contravening restrictions on substantial property transactions with directors. Where a company[1] enters into an arrangement in contravention of the statutory provisions[2] which require approval for substantial property transactions involving a director[3] of the company or of its holding company[4], or a person connected with such a director[5], that arrangement, and any transaction entered into in pursuance of the arrangement, whether by the company or any other person, is voidable at the instance of the company[6], unless:

(1) restitution of any money or other asset that was the subject matter of the arrangement or transaction is no longer possible[7]; or

(2) the company has been indemnified[8] by any other person for the loss or damage suffered by it[9]; or

(3) rights acquired in good faith, for value and without actual notice of the contravention by any person who is not a party to the arrangement or transaction would be affected by its avoidance[10].

Whether or not the arrangement or any such transaction has been avoided, each of the following persons[11], namely:

(a) any director of the company or of its holding company with whom the company entered into the arrangement in contravention of the statutory provisions[12];

(b) any person with whom the company entered into the arrangement in like contravention[13] who is connected with a director of the company or of its holding company[14];

(c) the director of the company or of its holding company with whom any such person is connected[15]; and

(d) any other director of the company who authorised the arrangement or any transaction entered into in pursuance of such an arrangement[16],

is liable[17] to account to the company for any gain that he has made directly or indirectly by the arrangement or transaction[18] and, jointly and severally with any other person so liable[19], to indemnify the company for any loss or damage resulting from the arrangement or transaction[20]. However, in the case of an arrangement entered into by a company in contravention of the statutory provisions[21] with a person connected with a director of the company or of its holding company, that director is not liable by virtue of head (c) above if he shows that he took all reasonable steps to secure the company's compliance[22].

Furthermore, in any case, a person so connected is not liable by virtue of head (b) above[23], and a director is not liable by virtue of head (d) above[24], if he shows that, at the time the arrangement was entered into, he did not know the relevant circumstances constituting the contravention[25].

Nothing in the provisions governing civil liability[26] is to be read as excluding the operation of any other enactment[27] or rule of law by virtue of which the arrangement or transaction may be called in question or any liability to the company may arise[28].

1 As to the meaning of 'company' under the Companies Acts see PARA 21; and as to the meaning of the 'Companies Acts' see PARA 13.

2 Ie in contravention of the Companies Act 2006 s 190 (see PARA 606): see s 195(1).
As to the general application of the Companies Act 2006 Pt 10 Ch 4 (ss 188–225) see PARA 601; and as to how those provisions interact with the directors' general duties see PARA 602.

3 As to the meaning of 'director' for these purposes see PARA 606 note 3.

4 As to the meaning of 'holding company' see PARA 22.

5 Companies Act 2006 s 195(1). As to the meaning of references to a person being 'connected' with a director see PARA 515. As to the validity generally of transactions involving a director or a person connected with a director see PARA 263.

6 Companies Act 2006 s 195(2). As to the effect of subsequent affirmation see PARA 609.

7 Companies Act 2006 s 195(2)(a).

8 Ie in pursuance of the Companies Act 2006 s 195: see s 195(2)(b).

9 Companies Act 2006 s 195(2)(b).

10 Companies Act 2006 s 195(2)(c).

11 Companies Act 2006 s 195(3). The provisions of s 195(3), (4) are subject to the provisions of s 195(6), (7) (see the text and notes 21–25): s 195(5).

12 Companies Act 2006 s 195(4)(a). The text refers to contravention of s 190 (see PARA 606): see s 195(4)(a). See also note 11.

13 Ie in contravention of the Companies Act 2006 s 190 (see PARA 606): see s 195(4)(b).

14 Companies Act 2006 s 195(4)(b). See also note 11.

15 Companies Act 2006 s 195(4)(c). See also note 11.

16 Companies Act 2006 s 195(4)(d). See also note 11.

17 Companies Act 2006 s 195(3). See also note 11. See *Lexi Holdings (in administration) v Luqman* [2008] EWHC 1639 (Ch) at [176]–[178], [2008] 2 BCLC 725 (revsd on other grounds [2009] EWCA Civ 117, [2009] 2 BCLC 1, [2009] BCC 716); *Neville v Krikorian* [2006] EWCA Civ 943, [2007] 1 BCLC 1.

18 Companies Act 2006 s 195(3)(a). See also note 11. It is for the person liable to account to provide information so that his gain might be assessed: *Micro Leisure Ltd v County Properties and Developments Ltd* 1999 SLT 1307, Ct of Sess. Where a director or person connected with him has sold assets to a company at an overvalue and no loss was made by the company on a resale of those assets, it does not follow that the director is liable to account to the company for the extra profit the company might have made when it sold the assets on, since although the court would take account of movements of value after the purchase if the asset fell in value, if the company did not make a loss after the purchase, any change in the value of the asset in the period when it was owned by the vendor before the sale to the company is irrelevant: *NBH Ltd v Hoare* [2006] EWHC 73 (Ch), [2006] 2 BCLC 649, applying *Re Duckwari plc* [1999] Ch 253 at 260–261, sub nom *Re Duckwari plc (No 2), Duckwari plc v Offerventure Ltd (No 2)* [1998] 2 BCLC 315 at 320, CA, per Nourse LJ (cited also in note 20).

19 Ie liable under the Companies Act 2006 s 195: see s 195(3)(b).

20 Companies Act 2006 s 195(3)(b). See also note 11. The liability to indemnify the company is intended to place the company in a position equivalent to that in which it would have been had rescission been ordered: *Re Duckwari plc* [1999] Ch 253, sub nom *Re Duckwari plc (No 2), Duckwari plc v Offerventure Ltd (No 2)* [1998] 2 BCLC 315, CA (the loss suffered by the company which had acquired a non-cash asset from a person connected with one of its directors was the difference between the value of the property at acquisition and realisation). This liability reflects the general liability of trustees to make good any misapplication of trust moneys: *Re Duckwari plc* [1999] Ch 253 at 262–265, sub nom *Re Duckwari plc (No 2), Duckwari plc v Offerventure Ltd (No 2)* [1998] 2 BCLC 315 at 321–322, 324, CA, per Nourse LJ. The extent of relief is limited to the loss or damage resulting from the acquisition of property and does not extend to the borrowing costs incurred in the acquisition: *Re Duckwari plc (No 2)* [1999] Ch 268, sub nom *Re Duckwari plc (No 3), Duckwari plc v Offerventure Ltd (No 3)* [1999] 1 BCLC 168, CA. See also note 18.

21 Ie in contravention of the Companies Act 2006 s 190 (see PARA 606): see s 195(6).
22 Companies Act 2006 s 195(6). The text refers to compliance with s 190 (see PARA 606): see s 195(6). See also note 11.
23 Companies Act 2006 s 195(7)(a). See also note 11.
24 Companies Act 2006 s 195(7)(b). See also note 11.
25 Companies Act 2006 s 195(7). See also note 11.
26 Ie nothing in the Companies Act 2006 s 195: see s 195(8).
27 As to the meaning of 'enactment' see PARA 13 note 16.
28 Companies Act 2006 s 195(8).

609. Effect of substantial property transaction or arrangement with director being subsequently affirmed. Where a transaction or arrangement is entered into by a company[1] in contravention of the statutory provisions[2] which require approval for substantial property transactions involving a director[3] of the company or of its holding company[4], or a person connected with such a director[5], but where, within a reasonable period, it is affirmed[6]:

(1) in a case where approval was required by way of a resolution of the members of the company[7] or where the arrangement was conditional on such approval being obtained[8], by resolution of the members of the company[9]; and

(2) in a case where the director or connected person is a director of the company's holding company or a person connected with such a director, and the arrangement must also have been approved by a resolution of the members of the holding company or be conditional on such approval being obtained[10], by resolution of the members of the holding company[11],

the transaction or arrangement may no longer be avoided[12].

1 As to the meaning of 'company' under the Companies Acts see PARA 21; and as to the meaning of the 'Companies Acts' see PARA 13.
2 Ie in contravention of the Companies Act 2006 s 190 (see PARA 606): see s 196.
As to the general application of the Companies Act 2006 Pt 10 Ch 4 (ss 188–225) see PARA 601; and as to how those provisions interact with the directors' general duties see PARA 602.
3 As to the meaning of 'director' for these purposes see PARA 606 note 3.
4 As to the meaning of 'holding company' see PARA 22.
5 As to the meaning of references to a person being 'connected' with a director see PARA 515. As to the validity generally of transactions involving a director or a person connected with a director see PARA 263.
6 Companies Act 2006 s 196.
7 As to the meaning of 'member of the company' see PARA 323. As to resolutions and meetings of members see PARA 701 et seq. As to voting at meetings see PARA 725 et seq.
8 Ie in the case of a contravention of the Companies Act 2006 s 190(1) (see PARA 606): see s 196(a).
9 Companies Act 2006 s 196(a).
10 Ie in the case of a contravention of the Companies Act 2006 s 190(2) (see PARA 606): see s 196(b).
11 Companies Act 2006 s 196(b).
12 Companies Act 2006 s 196. The text refers to avoidance of the transaction or arrangement under s 195 (see PARA 608): see s 196.

E. LOANS, QUASI-LOANS AND CREDIT TRANSACTIONS INVOLVING DIRECTORS

(A) Requirements of Members' Approval for Loans etc to Directors

610. Requirement of members' approval for loans and guarantees etc to directors. A company[1] may not either make a loan to a director[2] of the company or of its holding company[3], or give a guarantee or provide security in connection with a loan made by any person to such a director[4], unless the transaction has been approved by a resolution of the members of the company[5]. If the director is a director of the company's holding company, the transaction must also have been approved by a resolution of the members of the holding company[6].

A resolution approving such a transaction[7] must not be passed unless a memorandum setting out the matters mentioned in heads (i) to (iii) below is made available to members[8]:

(1) in the case of a written resolution[9], by being sent or submitted to every eligible member[10] at or before the time at which the proposed resolution is sent or submitted to him[11]; or

(2) in the case of a resolution at a meeting, by being made available for inspection by members of the company both:

(a) at the company's registered office[12] for not less than 15 days ending with the date of the meeting[13]; and

(b) at the meeting itself[14].

The matters to be disclosed for these purposes are:

(i) the nature of the transaction[15];

(ii) the amount of the loan and the purpose for which it is required[16]; and

(iii) the extent of the company's liability under any transaction connected with the loan[17].

No such approval is, however, required[18] on the part of the members of a body corporate[19] that either is not a UK-registered company[20], or is a wholly-owned subsidiary[21] of another body corporate[22].

1 As to the meaning of 'company' under the Companies Acts see PARA 21; and as to the meaning of the 'Companies Acts' see PARA 13.

2 For the purposes of the Companies Act 2006 ss 197–214 (see the text and notes 3–22; and PARA 611 et seq), a shadow director is treated as a director: s 223(1)(c). As to the meaning of 'director' generally see PARA 512; and as to shadow directors see PARA 513. A transaction which is described as a loan to a director may in fact be a misappropriation of the company's assets: *Bracken Partners Ltd v Gutteridge* [2003] EWHC 1064 (Ch) at [33]–[35], [2003] 2 BCLC 84 per Peter Leaver QC; affd on different grounds [2003] EWCA Civ 1875, [2004] 1 BCLC 377. Equally, 'advance dividends' paid to directors of a company prior to its liquidation may be regarded as loans in breach of the statutory provisions and not remuneration or a dividend properly paid: see *First Global Media Group Ltd v Larkin* [2003] EWCA Civ 1765, [2003] All ER (D) 293 (Nov). However, where a director has done work for or rendered services to the company and has received consideration from it in respect of that work or services, the sums may not be repayable to the company as loans: *Currencies Direct Ltd v Ellis* [2002] EWCA Civ 779, [2002] 2 BCLC 482. As to the approval required for quasi-loans and credit transactions etc see PARA 611 et seq.

3 Companies Act 2006 s 197(1)(a). As to the meaning of 'holding company' see PARA 22.

As to the general application of the Companies Act 2006 Pt 10 Ch 4 (ss 188–225) see PARA 601; and as to how those provisions interact with the directors' general duties see PARA 602.

4 Companies Act 2006 s 197(1)(b).

5 Companies Act 2006 s 197(1). As to the meaning of 'member of the company' see PARA 323. As to resolutions and meetings of members see PARA 701 et seq. As to voting at meetings see PARA 725 et seq.

As to the need for approval of loans to persons connected with a director see PARA 612; and as to the need for approval of related arrangements see PARA 614. As to general exceptions to the requirement for approval under s 197 see PARA 615 et seq; as to liabilities arising from any contravention of this requirement see PARA 618; and as to the effect of subsequent affirmation see PARA 619.

6 Companies Act 2006 s 197(2).

7 Ie a transaction to which the Companies Act 2006 s 197 applies: see s 197(3).

8 Companies Act 2006 s 197(3).

9 As to the meaning of 'written resolution' see PARA 695.

10 As to eligible members in relation to a resolution proposed as a written resolution of a private company see PARA 695. As to the provision made for the sending or supplying of documents or information to or from a company (the 'company communications provisions') see PARA 750 et seq.

11 Companies Act 2006 s 197(3)(a). Where approval under Pt 10 Ch 4 is sought by written resolution, and a memorandum is required under Pt 10 Ch 4 to be sent or submitted to every eligible member before the resolution is passed, provision is made for accidental failure to send or submit the memorandum to one or more members: see s 224; and PARA 601 note 8.

12 As to the company's registered office see PARA 124.

13 Companies Act 2006 s 197(3)(b)(i). See also note 11.
14 Companies Act 2006 s 197(3)(b)(ii). See also note 11.
15 Companies Act 2006 s 197(4)(a).
16 Companies Act 2006 s 197(4)(b). For the purposes of s 197, the value of a transaction or arrangement is determined as follows, and the value of any other relevant transaction or arrangement is taken to be the value so determined reduced by any amount by which the liabilities of the person for whom the transaction or arrangement was made have been reduced: s 211(1). The value of a loan is the amount of its principal (s 211(2)); and the value of a guarantee or security is the amount guaranteed or secured (s 211(5)). If the value of a transaction or arrangement is not capable of being expressed as a specific sum of money, whether because the amount of any liability arising under the transaction or arrangement is unascertainable, or for any other reason, and whether or not any liability under the transaction or arrangement has been reduced, its value is deemed to exceed £50,000: s 211(7). For these purposes, the person for whom a transaction or arrangement is entered into is, in the case of a loan, the person to whom it is made (s 212(a)); and, in the case of a guarantee or security, the person for whom the transaction is made in connection with which the guarantee or security is entered into (s 212(c)). As to the Secretary of State's power by order to substitute for any sum of money specified in the Companies Act 2006 Pt 10 (ss 154–259) (see PARA 512 et seq) a larger sum specified in the order see PARA 606 note 7.
17 Companies Act 2006 s 197(4)(c).
18 Ie under the Companies Act 2006 s 197: see s 197(5).
19 As to the meaning of 'body corporate' for the purposes of the Companies Acts see PARA 1 note 5.
20 Companies Act 2006 s 197(5)(a). As to the meaning of 'UK-registered company' see PARA 21.
21 As to the meaning of 'wholly-owned subsidiary' see PARA 22.
22 Companies Act 2006 s 197(5)(b).

611. Requirement of members' approval for quasi-loans to directors. A company[1], which is either a public company[2] or a company associated with a public company[3], may not either make a quasi-loan to a director[4] of the company or of its holding company[5], or give a guarantee or provide security in connection with a quasi-loan made by any person to such a director[6], unless the transaction has been approved by a resolution of the members of the company[7]. If the director is a director of the company's holding company, the transaction must also have been approved by a resolution of the members of the holding company[8].

A resolution approving such a transaction[9] must not be passed unless a memorandum setting out the matters mentioned in heads (i) to (iii) below is made available to members[10]:

(1) in the case of a written resolution[11], by being sent or submitted to every eligible member[12] at or before the time at which the proposed resolution is sent or submitted to him[13]; or
(2) in the case of a resolution at a meeting, by being made available for inspection by members of the company both:
    (a) at the company's registered office[14] for not less than 15 days ending with the date of the meeting[15]; and
    (b) at the meeting itself[16].

The matters to be disclosed for these purposes are:

(i) the nature of the transaction[17];
(ii) the amount of the quasi-loan and the purpose for which it is required[18]; and
(iii) the extent of the company's liability under any transaction connected with the quasi-loan[19].

No such approval is, however, required[20] on the part of the members of a body corporate that either is not a UK-registered company[21], or is a wholly-owned subsidiary[22] of another body corporate[23].

1 As to the meaning of 'company' under the Companies Acts see PARA 21; and as to the meaning of the 'Companies Acts' see PARA 13.

2 As to the meaning of 'public company' see PARA 95.

3 See the Companies Act 2006 s 198(1). For the purposes of Pt 10 (ss 154–259) (see PARA 512 et seq), companies are 'associated' if one is a subsidiary of the other or both are subsidiaries of the same body corporate: s 256(b). As to the meaning of 'body corporate' for the purposes of the Companies Acts see PARA 1 note 5; and as to the meaning of 'subsidiary' see PARA 22.

As to the general application of the Companies Act 2006 Pt 10 Ch 4 (ss 188–225) see PARA 601; and as to how those provisions interact with the directors' general duties see PARA 602.

4 As to the meaning of 'director' for these purposes see PARA 610 note 2. A 'quasi-loan' is a transaction under which one party (the 'creditor') agrees to pay, or pays otherwise than in pursuance of an agreement, a sum for another (the 'borrower') or agrees to reimburse, or reimburses otherwise than in pursuance of an agreement, expenditure incurred by another party for another (the 'borrower) on terms that the borrower, or a person on his behalf, will reimburse the creditor, or in circumstances giving rise to a liability on the borrower to reimburse the creditor: Companies Act 2006 s 199(1). Any reference to the 'person to whom a quasi-loan is made' is a reference to the borrower: s 199(2). The 'liabilities of the borrower under a quasi-loan' include the liabilities of any person who has agreed to reimburse the creditor on behalf of the borrower: s 199(3).

5 Companies Act 2006 s 198(2)(a). As to the meaning of 'holding company' see PARA 22.

6 Companies Act 2006 s 198(2)(b).

7 Companies Act 2006 s 198(2). As to the meaning of 'member of the company' see PARA 323. As to resolutions and meetings of members see PARA 701 et seq. As to voting at meetings see PARA 725 et seq.

As to the need for approval of quasi-loans to persons connected with a director see PARA 612; and as to the need for approval of related arrangements see PARA 614. As to general exceptions to the requirement for approval under s 198 see PARA 615 et seq; as to liabilities arising from any contravention of this requirement see PARA 618; and as to the effect of subsequent affirmation see PARA 619.

8 Companies Act 2006 s 198(3).

9 Ie a transaction to which the Companies Act 2006 s 198 applies: see s 198(4).

10 Companies Act 2006 s 198(4).

11 As to the meaning of 'written resolution' see PARA 695.

12 As to eligible members in relation to a resolution proposed as a written resolution of a private company see PARA 695. As to the provision made for the sending or supplying of documents or information to or from a company (the 'company communications provisions') see PARA 750 et seq.

13 Companies Act 2006 s 198(4)(a). Where approval under Pt 10 Ch 4 is sought by written resolution, and a memorandum is required under Pt 10 Ch 4 to be sent or submitted to every eligible member before the resolution is passed, provision is made for accidental failure to send or submit the memorandum to one or more members: see s 224; and PARA 601 note 8.

14 As to the company's registered office see PARA 124.

15 Companies Act 2006 s 198(4)(b)(i). See also note 13.

16 Companies Act 2006 s 198(4)(b)(ii). See also note 13.

17 Companies Act 2006 s 198(5)(a).

18 Companies Act 2006 s 198(5)(b). For the purposes of ss 198, 199, the value of a transaction or arrangement is determined as follows, and the value of any other relevant transaction or arrangement is taken to be the value so determined reduced by any amount by which the liabilities of the person for whom the transaction or arrangement was made have been reduced: s 211(1). The value of a quasi-loan is the amount, or maximum amount, that the person to whom the quasi-loan is made is liable to reimburse the creditor (s 211(3)); and the value of a guarantee or security is the amount guaranteed or secured (s 211(5)). If the value of a transaction or arrangement is not capable of being expressed as a specific sum of money, whether because the amount of any liability arising under the transaction or arrangement is unascertainable, or for any other reason, and whether or not any liability under the transaction or arrangement has been reduced, its value is deemed to exceed £50,000: s 211(7). For these purposes, the person for whom a transaction or arrangement is entered into is, in the case of a quasi-loan, the person to whom it is made (s 212(a)); and, in the case of a guarantee or security, the person for whom the transaction is made in connection with which the guarantee or security is entered into (s 212(c)). As to the Secretary of State's power by order to substitute for any sum of money specified in the Companies Act 2006 Pt 10 (ss 154–259) (see PARA 512 et seq) a larger sum specified in the order see PARA 606 note 8.

19 Companies Act 2006 s 198(5)(c).

20 Ie under the Companies Act 2006 s 198: see s 198(6).

21 Companies Act 2006 s 198(6)(a). As to the meaning of 'UK-registered company' see PARA 21.

22 As to the meaning of 'wholly-owned subsidiary' see PARA 22.
23 Companies Act 2006 s 198(6)(b).

612. Requirement of members' approval for loans and quasi-loans to persons connected with director. A company[1], which is either a public company[2] or a company associated with a public company[3], may not either make a loan or quasi-loan[4] to a person connected with a director[5] of the company or of its holding company[6], or give a guarantee or provide security in connection with a loan or quasi-loan made by any person to a person connected with such a director[7], unless the transaction has been approved by a resolution of the members of the company[8]. If the connected person is a person connected with a director of the company's holding company, the transaction must also have been approved by a resolution of the members of the holding company[9].

A resolution approving such a transaction[10] must not be passed unless a memorandum setting out the matters mentioned in heads (i) to (iii) below is made available to members[11]:

(1) in the case of a written resolution[12], by being sent or submitted to every eligible member[13] at or before the time at which the proposed resolution is sent or submitted to him[14]; or
(2) in the case of a resolution at a meeting, by being made available for inspection by members of the company both:
  (a) at the company's registered office[15] for not less than 15 days ending with the date of the meeting[16]; and
  (b) at the meeting itself[17].

The matters to be disclosed for these purposes are:

(i) the nature of the transaction[18];
(ii) the amount of the loan or quasi-loan and the purpose for which it is required[19]; and
(iii) the extent of the company's liability under any transaction connected with the loan or quasi-loan[20].

However, no such approval is required[21] on the part of the members of a body corporate[22] that either is not a UK-registered company[23], or is a wholly-owned subsidiary[24] of another body corporate[25].

1 As to the meaning of 'company' under the Companies Acts see PARA 21; and as to the meaning of the 'Companies Acts' see PARA 13.
2 As to the meaning of 'public company' see PARA 95.
3 See the Companies Act 2006 s 200(1). As to the meaning of companies which are 'associated' for the purposes of Pt 10 (ss 154–259) (see PARA 512 et seq) see PARA 611 note 3.
As to the general application of the Companies Act 2006 Pt 10 Ch 4 (ss 188–225) see PARA 601; and as to how those provisions interact with the directors' general duties see PARA 602.
4 As to the meaning of 'quasi-loan' for these purposes see PARA 611 note 4.
5 As to the meaning of the 'person to whom a quasi-loan is made' see PARA 611 note 4. As to the meaning of references to a person being 'connected' with a director see PARA 515; and as to the meaning of 'director' for these purposes see PARA 610 note 2. As to the validity generally of transactions involving a director or a person connected with a director see PARA 263.
6 Companies Act 2006 s 200(2)(a). As to the meaning of 'holding company' see PARA 22.
7 Companies Act 2006 s 200(2)(b).
8 Companies Act 2006 s 200(2). As to the meaning of 'member of the company' see PARA 323. As to resolutions and meetings of members see PARA 701 et seq. As to voting at meetings see PARA 725 et seq.
As to the need for approval of related arrangements see PARA 614. As to general exceptions to the requirement for approval under s 200 see PARA 615 et seq; as to liabilities arising from any contravention of this requirement see PARA 618; and as to the effect of subsequent affirmation see PARA 619.
9 Companies Act 2006 s 200(3).
10 Ie a transaction to which the Companies Act 2006 s 200 applies: see s 200(4).

11 Companies Act 2006 s 200(4).
12 As to the meaning of 'written resolution' see PARA 695.
13 As to eligible members in relation to a resolution proposed as a written resolution of a private company see PARA 695. As to the provision made for the sending or supplying of documents or information to or from a company (the 'company communications provisions') see PARA 750 et seq.
14 Companies Act 2006 s 200(4)(a). Where approval under Pt 10 Ch 4 is sought by written resolution, and a memorandum is required under Pt 10 Ch 4 to be sent or submitted to every eligible member before the resolution is passed, provision is made for accidental failure to send or submit the memorandum to one or more members: see s 224; and PARA 601 note 8.
15 As to the company's registered office see PARA 124.
16 Companies Act 2006 s 200(4)(b)(i). See also note 13.
17 Companies Act 2006 s 200(4)(b)(ii). See also note 13.
18 Companies Act 2006 s 200(5)(a).
19 Companies Act 2006 s 200(5)(b). As to determining the value of such a transaction or arrangement, and the person for whom such a transaction or arrangement is entered into, in the case of loans, see PARA 610 note 16; and, the case of quasi-loans, see PARA 611 note 18.
20 Companies Act 2006 s 200(5)(c). As to the meaning of the 'liabilities of the borrower under a quasi-loan' see PARA 611 note 4.
21 Ie under the Companies Act 2006 s 200: see s 200(6).
22 As to the meaning of 'body corporate' for the purposes of the Companies Acts see PARA 1 note 5.
23 Companies Act 2006 s 200(6)(a). As to the meaning of 'UK-registered company' see PARA 21.
24 As to the meaning of 'wholly-owned subsidiary' see PARA 22.
25 Companies Act 2006 s 200(6)(b).

613. Requirement of members' approval for credit transactions for benefit of directors. A company[1], which is either a public company[2] or a company associated with a public company[3], may not either enter into a credit transaction as creditor for the benefit of a director[4] of the company or of its holding company[5], or a person connected with such a director[6], or give a guarantee or provide security in connection with a credit transaction entered into by any person for the benefit of such a director, or a person connected with such a director[7], unless the transaction (that is, the credit transaction, the giving of the guarantee or the provision of security, as the case may be) has been approved by a resolution of the members of the company[8]. If the director or connected person is a director of the company's holding company or a person connected with such a director, the transaction must also have been approved by a resolution of the members of the holding company[9].

A resolution approving such a transaction[10] must not be passed unless a memorandum setting out the matters mentioned in heads (i) to (iii) below is made available to members[11]:

(1) in the case of a written resolution[12], by being sent or submitted to every eligible member[13] at or before the time at which the proposed resolution is sent or submitted to him[14]; or
(2) in the case of a resolution at a meeting, by being made available for inspection by members of the company both:
    (a) at the company's registered office[15] for not less than 15 days ending with the date of the meeting[16]; and
    (b) at the meeting itself[17].

The matters to be disclosed for these purposes are:

(i) the nature of the transaction[18];
(ii) the value of the credit transaction and the purpose for which the land, goods or services sold or otherwise disposed of, leased, hired or supplied under the credit transaction are required[19]; and
(iii) the extent of the company's liability under any transaction connected with the credit transaction[20].

No such approval is, however, required[21] on the part of the members of a body corporate[22] that either is not a UK-registered company[23], or is a wholly-owned subsidiary[24] of another body corporate[25].

1 As to the meaning of 'company' under the Companies Acts see PARA 21; and as to the meaning of the 'Companies Acts' see PARA 13.
2 As to the meaning of 'public company' see PARA 95.
3 See the Companies Act 2006 s 201(1). As to the meaning of companies which are 'associated' for the purposes of Pt 10 (ss 154–259) (see PARA 512 et seq) see PARA 611 note 3.

As to the general application of the Companies Act 2006 Pt 10 Ch 4 (ss 188–225) see PARA 601; and as to how those provisions interact with the directors' general duties see PARA 602.

4 As to the meaning of 'director' for these purposes see PARA 610 note 2. For these purposes, a 'credit transaction' is a transaction under which one party (the 'creditor') supplies any goods or sells any land under a hire-purchase agreement or a conditional sale agreement, leases or hires any land or goods in return for periodical payments, or otherwise disposes of land or supplies goods or services on the understanding that payment (whether in a lump sum or instalments or by way of periodical payments or otherwise) is to be deferred: Companies Act 2006 s 202(1). Any reference to the 'person for whose benefit a credit transaction is entered into' is to the person to whom goods, land or services are supplied, sold, leased, hired or otherwise disposed of under the transaction: s 202(2). For these purposes, 'conditional sale agreement' has the same meaning as in the Consumer Credit Act 1974 (see CONSUMER CREDIT vol 21 (2011) PARA 64); and 'services' means anything other than goods or land: Companies Act 2006 s 202(3). In the Companies Acts, 'hire-purchase agreement' has the same meaning as in the Consumer Credit Act 1974 (see CONSUMER CREDIT vol 21 (2011) PARA 66): Companies Act 2006 s 1173(1).
5 As to the meaning of 'holding company' see PARA 22.
6 Companies Act 2006 s 201(2)(a). As to the meaning of references to a person being 'connected' with a director see PARA 515. As to the validity generally of transactions involving a director or a person connected with a director see PARA 263.
7 Companies Act 2006 s 201(2)(b).
8 Companies Act 2006 s 201(2). As to the meaning of 'member of the company' see PARA 323. As to resolutions and meetings of members see PARA 701 et seq. As to voting at meetings see PARA 725 et seq.

As to the need for approval of related arrangements see PARA 614. As to general exceptions to the requirement for approval under s 201 see PARA 615 et seq; as to liabilities arising from any contravention of this requirement see PARA 618; and as to the effect of subsequent affirmation see PARA 619.

9 Companies Act 2006 s 201(3).
10 Ie a transaction to which the Companies Act 2006 s 201 applies: see s 201(4).
11 Companies Act 2006 s 201(4).
12 As to the meaning of 'written resolution' see PARA 695.
13 As to eligible members in relation to a resolution proposed as a written resolution of a private company see PARA 695. As to the provision made for the sending or supplying of documents or information to or from a company (the 'company communications provisions') see PARA 750 et seq.
14 Companies Act 2006 s 201(4)(a). Where approval under Pt 10 Ch 4 is sought by written resolution, and a memorandum is required under Pt 10 Ch 4 to be sent or submitted to every eligible member before the resolution is passed, provision is made for accidental failure to send or submit the memorandum to one or more members: see s 224; and PARA 601 note 8.
15 As to the company's registered office see PARA 124.
16 Companies Act 2006 s 201(4)(b)(i). See also note 14.
17 Companies Act 2006 s 201(4)(b)(ii). See also note 14.
18 Companies Act 2006 s 201(5)(a).
19 Companies Act 2006 s 201(5)(b). For the purposes of ss 201, 202, the value of a transaction or arrangement is determined as follows, and the value of any other relevant transaction or arrangement is taken to be the value so determined reduced by any amount by which the liabilities of the person for whom the transaction or arrangement was made have been reduced: s 211(1). The value of a credit transaction is the price that it is reasonable to expect could be obtained for the goods, services or land to which the transaction relates if they had been supplied (at the time the transaction is entered into) in the ordinary course of business and on the same terms (apart from price) as they have been supplied, or are to be supplied, under the transaction in question (s 211(4)); and the value of a guarantee or security is the amount guaranteed or secured (s 211(5)). If the value of a transaction or arrangement is not capable of being expressed as a specific sum of money, whether because the amount of any liability arising under the transaction or arrangement is unascertainable, or for any other reason, and whether or not any liability under the transaction

or arrangement has been reduced, its value is deemed to exceed £50,000: s 211(7). For these purposes, the person for whom a transaction or arrangement is entered into is, in the case of a credit transaction, the person to whom goods, land or services are supplied, sold, hired, leased or otherwise disposed of under the transaction (s 212(b)); and, in the case of a guarantee or security, the person for whom the transaction is made in connection with which the guarantee or security is entered into (s 212(c)). As to the Secretary of State's power by order to substitute for any sum of money specified in the Companies Act 2006 Pt 10 (ss 154–259) (see PARA 512 et seq) a larger sum specified in the order see PARA 606 note 7.

20 Companies Act 2006 s 201(5)(c).

21 Ie under the Companies Act 2006 s 201: see s 201(6).

22 As to the meaning of 'body corporate' for the purposes of the Companies Acts see PARA 1 note 5.

23 Companies Act 2006 s 201(6)(a). As to the meaning of 'UK-registered company' see PARA 21.

24 As to the meaning of 'wholly-owned subsidiary' see PARA 22.

25 Companies Act 2006 s 201(6)(b).

614. Requirement of members' approval for related arrangements involving directors. A company[1] may not

(1) take part in an arrangement under which another person enters into a transaction that, if it had been entered into by the company, would have required approval[2] by members of the company[3], and that person, in pursuance of the arrangement, obtains a benefit from the company or a body corporate[4] associated with it[5]; or

(2) arrange for the assignment to it, or assumption by it, of any rights, obligations or liabilities under a transaction that, if it had been entered into by the company, would have required such approval[6],

unless the arrangement in question has been approved by a resolution of the members of the company[7]. If the director or connected person for whom the transaction is entered into is a director of the company's holding company or a person connected with such a director, the arrangement must also have been approved by a resolution of the members of the holding company[8].

A resolution approving such an arrangement[9] must not be passed unless a memorandum setting out the matters mentioned in heads (A) to (C) below is made available to members[10]:

(a) in the case of a written resolution[11], by being sent or submitted to every eligible member[12] at or before the time at which the proposed resolution is sent or submitted to him[13]; or

(b) in the case of a resolution at a meeting, by being made available for inspection by members of the company both:

  (i) at the company's registered office[14] for not less than 15 days ending with the date of the meeting[15]; and

  (ii) at the meeting itself[16].

The matters to be disclosed for these purposes are:

(A) the matters that would have to be disclosed if the company were seeking approval of the transaction to which the arrangement relates[17];

(B) the nature of the arrangement[18]; and

(C) the extent of the company's liability under the arrangement or any transaction connected with it[19].

No such approval is, however, required[20] on the part of the members of a body corporate that either is not a UK-registered company[21], or is a wholly-owned subsidiary[22] of another body corporate[23].

1 As to the meaning of 'company' under the Companies Acts see PARA 21; and as to the meaning of the 'Companies Acts' see PARA 13.

2 Ie, in the case of loans made to a director of the company or of its holding company, or a guarantee given or security provided in connection with a loan made by any person to such a

director, under the Companies Act 2006 s 197 (see PARA 610), in the case of quasi-loans made to a director of the company or of its holding company, or a guarantee given or security provided in connection with a quasi-loan made by any person to such a director, under s 198 (see PARA 611), in the case of loans or quasi-loans made to a person connected with a director of the company or of its holding company, or a guarantee given or security provided in connection with a loan or quasi-loan made by any person to a person connected with such a director, under s 200 (see PARA 612), or in the case of credit transactions entered into by a company as creditor for the benefit of a director of the company or of its holding company (or a person connected with such a director) or a guarantee given or security provided in connection with a credit transaction entered into by any person for the benefit of such a director (or a person connected with such a director), under s 201 (see PARA 613): see s 203(1)(a)(i). In determining for the purposes of s 203 whether a transaction is one that would have required approval under s 197, s 198, s 200 or s 201 if it had been entered into by the company, the transaction is to be treated as having been entered into on the date of the arrangement: s 203(6). As to the meaning of 'director' for these purposes see PARA 610 note 2; as to the meaning of 'credit transaction' for these purposes see PARA 613 note 4; as to the meaning of 'holding company' see PARA 22; and as to the meaning of 'quasi-loan' for these purposes see PARA 611 note 4. As to the meaning of references to a person being 'connected' with a director see PARA 515. As to the validity generally of transactions involving a director or a person connected with a director see PARA 263.

As to the general application of the Companies Act 2006 Pt 10 Ch 4 (ss 188–225) see PARA 601; and as to how those provisions interact with the directors' general duties see PARA 602.

3 Companies Act 2006 s 203(1)(a)(i). As to the meaning of 'member of the company' see PARA 323. As to resolutions and meetings of members see PARA 701 et seq. As to voting at meetings see PARA 725 et seq.

As to liabilities arising from any contravention of this requirement see PARA 618; and as to the effect of subsequent affirmation see PARA 619.

4 As to the meaning of 'body corporate' for the purposes of the Companies Acts see PARA 1 note 5.

5 Companies Act 2006 s 203(1)(a)(ii). As to the meaning of companies which are 'associated' for the purposes of Pt 10 (ss 154–259) (see PARA 512 et seq) see PARA 611 note 3; and as to the meaning of bodies corporate which are 'associated' for the purposes of Pt 10 see PARA 593 note 4.

6 Companies Act 2006 s 203(1)(b).

7 Companies Act 2006 s 203(1).

8 Companies Act 2006 s 203(2).

9 Ie an arrangement to which the Companies Act 2006 s 203 applies: see s 203(3).

10 Companies Act 2006 s 203(3).

11 As to the meaning of 'written resolution' see PARA 695.

12 As to eligible members in relation to a resolution proposed as a written resolution of a private company see PARA 695. As to the provision made for the sending or supplying of documents or information to or from a company (the 'company communications provisions') see PARA 750 et seq.

13 Companies Act 2006 s 203(3)(a). Where approval under Pt 10 Ch 4 is sought by written resolution, and a memorandum is required under Pt 10 Ch 4 to be sent or submitted to every eligible member before the resolution is passed, provision is made for accidental failure to send or submit the memorandum to one or more members: see s 224; and PARA 601 note 8.

14 As to the company's registered office see PARA 124.

15 Companies Act 2006 s 203(3)(b)(i). See also note 13.

16 Companies Act 2006 s 203(3)(b)(ii). See also note 13.

17 Companies Act 2006 s 203(4)(a). The value of an arrangement to which s 203 applies is the value of the transaction to which the arrangement relates (s 211(6)); and the person for whom a transaction or arrangement is entered into is, in the case of an arrangement within s 203, the person for whom the transaction is made to which the arrangement relates (s 212(d)). See also note 2.

18 Companies Act 2006 s 203(4)(b).

19 Companies Act 2006 s 203(4)(c).

20 Ie under the Companies Act 2006 s 203: see s 203(5).

21 Companies Act 2006 s 203(5)(a). As to the meaning of 'UK-registered company' see PARA 21.

22 As to the meaning of 'wholly-owned subsidiary' see PARA 22.

23 Companies Act 2006 s 203(5)(b).

(B) General Exceptions to Requirements of Members' Approval for Loans etc to Directors

615. Exceptions to requirement for approval of loans, quasi-loans and credit transactions. Approval is not required in relation to loans, quasi-loans and credit transactions[1] for anything done by a company[2]:

(1) to provide a director of the company or of its holding company, or a person connected with any such director, with funds to meet expenditure incurred or to be incurred by him[3] for the purposes of the company[4], or for the purpose of enabling him properly to perform his duties as an officer of the company[5], or to enable any such person to avoid incurring such expenditure[6];

(2) to provide a director of the company or of its holding company with funds to meet expenditure incurred or to be incurred by him[7] in defending any criminal or civil proceedings in connection with any alleged negligence, default, breach of duty or breach of trust by him in relation to the company or an associated company[8], or in connection with a specified application for relief[9], or to enable any such director to avoid incurring such expenditure[10], if it is done on the following terms[11]:

 (a) that the loan is to be repaid, or (as the case may be) any liability of the company incurred under any transaction connected with the thing done is to be discharged[12], in the event of the director being convicted in the proceedings[13], in the event of judgment being given against him in the proceedings[14], or in the event of the court refusing to grant him relief on the application[15]; and

 (b) that it is to be so repaid or discharged not later than the date when the conviction becomes final[16], the date when the judgment becomes final[17], or the date when the refusal of relief becomes final[18];

(3) to provide a director of the company or of its holding company with funds to meet expenditure incurred or to be incurred by him in defending himself either in an investigation by a regulatory authority[19], or against action proposed to be taken by a regulatory authority[20], in connection with any alleged negligence, default, breach of duty or breach of trust by him in relation to the company or an associated company[21]; or to enable any such director to avoid incurring such expenditure[22].

1 Ie, in the case of loans made to a director of the company or of its holding company, or a guarantee given or security provided in connection with a loan made by any person to such a director, under the Companies Act 2006 s 197 (see PARA 610), in the case of quasi-loans made to a director of the company or of its holding company, or a guarantee given or security provided in connection with a quasi-loan made by any person to such a director, under s 198 (see PARA 611), in the case of loans or quasi-loans made to a person connected with a director of the company or of its holding company, or a guarantee given or security provided in connection with a loan or quasi-loan made by any person to a person connected with such a director, under s 200 (see PARA 612), or in the case of credit transactions entered into by a company as creditor for the benefit of a director of the company or of its holding company (or a person connected with such a director) or a guarantee given or security provided in connection with a credit transaction entered into by any person for the benefit of such a director (or a person connected with such a director), under s 201 (see PARA 613): see ss 204(1), 205(1), 206(1). As to the meaning of 'company' under the Companies Acts see PARA 21; as to the meaning of 'director' for these purposes see PARA 610 note 2; and as to the meaning of the 'Companies Acts' see PARA 13. As to the meaning of 'credit transaction' for these purposes see PARA 613 note 4; as to the meaning of 'holding company' see PARA 22; and as to the meaning of 'quasi-loan' for these purposes see

PARA 611 note 4. As to the meaning of references to a person being 'connected' with a director see PARA 515. As to the validity generally of transactions involving a director or a person connected with a director see PARA 263.

As to the general application of the Companies Act 2006 Pt 10 Ch 4 (ss 188–225) see PARA 601; and as to how those provisions interact with the directors' general duties see PARA 602.

2 As to exceptions to the requirement for approval that apply to loans and quasi-loans but not to credit transactions see PARA 616; and as to exceptions to the requirement for approval that apply to credit transactions but not to loans and quasi-loans see PARA 617.

3 Companies Act 2006 s 204(1)(a). The provisions of s 204 do not authorise a company to enter into a transaction if the aggregate of the value of the transaction in question, and the value of any other relevant transactions or arrangements, exceeds £50,000: s 204(2). As to the Secretary of State's power by order to substitute for any sum of money specified in Pt 10 (ss 154–259) (see PARA 512 et seq) a larger sum specified in the order see PARA 606 note 7. The provisions of s 210 have effect for determining what are 'other relevant transactions or arrangements' for the purposes of any exception to s 197 (see PARA 610), s 198 (see PARA 611), s 200 (see PARA 612) or s 201 (see PARA 613); and, for these purposes, the 'relevant exception' means the exception for the purposes of which that falls to be determined: s 210(1). Accordingly, other relevant transactions or arrangements are those previously entered into, or entered into at the same time as the transaction or arrangement in question in relation to which the following conditions are met (s 210(2)):

(1) where the transaction or arrangement in question is entered into either for a director of the company entering into it, or for a person connected with such a director, the conditions are that the transaction or arrangement was, or is, entered into for that director, or a person connected with him, by virtue of the relevant exception by that company or by any of its subsidiaries (s 210(3));

(2) where the transaction or arrangement in question is entered into either for a director of the holding company of the company entering into it, or for a person connected with such a director, the conditions are that the transaction or arrangement was, or is, entered into for that director, or a person connected with him, by virtue of the relevant exception by the holding company or by any of its subsidiaries (s 210(4)).

A transaction or arrangement entered into by a company that, at the time it was entered into, either was a subsidiary of the company entering into the transaction or arrangement in question, or was a subsidiary of that company's holding company, is not a relevant transaction or arrangement if, at the time the question arises whether the transaction or arrangement in question falls within a relevant exception, it is no longer such a subsidiary: s 210(5). As to the meaning of 'subsidiary' see PARA 22. As to determining the value of transactions and other relevant transactions or arrangements generally, and as to determining the person for whom a transaction or arrangement is entered into, see PARAS 610 note 16, 611 note 18, 613 note 19.

4 Companies Act 2006 s 204(1)(a)(i). See also note 3.

5 Companies Act 2006 s 204(1)(a)(ii). As to the meaning of 'officer' see PARA 679. See also note 3.

6 Companies Act 2006 s 204(1)(b). See also note 3.

7 Companies Act 2006 s 205(1)(a).

8 Companies Act 2006 s 205(1)(a)(i). As to the meaning of companies which are 'associated' for the purposes of Pt 10 (ss 154–259) (see PARA 512 et seq) see PARA 611 note 3. The Companies Act 2006 contains for the first time a statutory statement of directors' duties: see Pt 10 Ch 2 (ss 170–181); and PARA 572 et seq. As to directors' fiduciary duties owed to the company see PARA 584 et seq.

9 Companies Act 2006 s 205(1)(a)(ii). The reference in s 205(1)(a)(ii) to an application for relief is to an application for relief under s 661(3) or s 661(4) (power of court to grant relief in case of acquisition of shares by innocent nominee) (see PARA 1386), or under s 1157 (general power of court to grant relief in case of honest and reasonable conduct) (see PARA 645): s 205(5).

10 Companies Act 2006 s 205(1)(b).

11 Companies Act 2006 s 205(1).

12 Companies Act 2006 s 205(2)(a).

13 Companies Act 2006 s 205(2)(a)(i).

14 Companies Act 2006 s 205(2)(a)(ii).

15 Companies Act 2006 s 205(2)(a)(iii).

16 Companies Act 2006 s 205(2)(b)(i). For this purpose, a conviction, judgment or refusal of relief becomes final (if not appealed against) at the end of the period for bringing an appeal or (if appealed against) when the appeal (or any further appeal) is disposed of (s 205(3)); and an appeal is disposed of if it is determined and the period for bringing any further appeal has ended, or if it is abandoned or otherwise ceases to have effect (s 205(4)).

17 Companies Act 2006 s 205(2)(b)(ii). See also note 16.

18 Companies Act 2006 s 205(2)(b)(iii). See also note 16.

19 Companies Act 2006 s 206(a)(i).

20 Companies Act 2006 s 206(a)(ii).
21 Companies Act 2006 s 206(a).
22 Companies Act 2006 s 206(b). Note that the terms set out in relation to head (2) in the text (see heads (2)(a)–(2)(b) in the text) have not been applied for the purposes of head (3) in the text.

616. Exceptions to requirement for approval applicable to loans and quasi-loans to directors but not to credit transactions for their benefit. Approval is not required under the provisions which govern the making of loans or quasi-loans[1]:

(1) for a company to make a loan or quasi-loan, or to give a guarantee or provide security in connection with a loan or quasi-loan, if the aggregate of the value of the transaction[2], and the value of any other relevant transactions or arrangements[3], does not exceed £10,000[4];
(2) for the making of a loan or quasi-loan to an associated body corporate[5], or for the giving of a guarantee or provision of security in connection with a loan or quasi-loan made to an associated body corporate[6];
(3) for the making of a loan or quasi-loan, or the giving of a guarantee or provision of security in connection with a loan or quasi-loan, by a money-lending company[7] if:
    (a) the transaction (that is, the loan, quasi-loan, guarantee or security) is entered into by the company in the ordinary course of the company's business[8]; and
    (b) the value of the transaction is not greater, and its terms are not more favourable, than it is reasonable to expect the company would have offered to a person of the same financial standing but unconnected with the company[9].

1 Ie, in the case of loans made to a director of the company or of its holding company, or a guarantee given or security provided in connection with a loan made by any person to such a director, under the Companies Act 2006 s 197 (see PARA 610), in the case of quasi-loans made to a director of the company or of its holding company, or a guarantee given or security provided in connection with a quasi-loan made by any person to such a director, under s 198 (see PARA 611) or, in the case of loans or quasi-loans made to a person connected with a director of the company or of its holding company, or a guarantee given or security provided in connection with a loan or quasi-loan made by any person to a person connected with such a director, under s 200 (see PARA 612): see ss 207(1), 208(1), 209(1). As to the meaning of 'company' under the Companies Acts see PARA 21; as to the meaning of 'director' for these purposes see PARA 610 note 2; and as to the meaning of the 'Companies Acts' see PARA 13. As to the meaning of 'holding company' see PARA 22; and as to the meaning of 'quasi-loan' for these purposes see PARA 611 note 4. As to the meaning of references to a person being 'connected' with a director see PARA 515. As to the validity generally of transactions involving a director or a person connected with a director see PARA 263. As to exceptions to the requirement for approval that apply to loans and quasi-loans and to credit transactions alike see PARA 615; and as to exceptions to the requirement for approval that apply to credit transactions but not to loans and quasi-loans see PARA 617. As to the meaning of 'credit transaction' for these purposes see PARA 613 note 4.

As to the general application of the Companies Act 2006 Pt 10 Ch 4 (ss 188–225) see PARA 601; and as to how those provisions interact with the directors' general duties see PARA 602.
2 Companies Act 2006 s 207(1)(a).
3 Companies Act 2006 s 207(1)(b). The provisions of s 210 have effect for determining what are 'other relevant transactions or arrangements' for the purposes of any exception to s 197 (see PARA 610), s 198 (see PARA 611) or s 200 (see PARA 612): see PARA 615 note 3. As to determining the value of transactions and other relevant transactions or arrangements generally, and as to determining the person for whom a transaction or arrangement is entered into, see PARAS 610 note 16, 611 note 18, 613 note 19.
4 Companies Act 2006 s 207(1). As to the Secretary of State's power by order to substitute for any sum of money specified in Pt 10 (ss 154–259) (see PARA 512 et seq) a larger sum specified in the order see PARA 606 note 7.
5 Companies Act 2006 s 208(1)(a). As to the meaning of bodies corporate which are 'associated' for the purposes of Pt 10 (ss 154–259) (see PARA 512 et seq) see PARA 593 note 4.
6 Companies Act 2006 s 208(1)(b).

7 Companies Act 2006 s 209(1). For these purposes, a 'money-lending company' means a company whose ordinary business includes the making of loans or quasi-loans, or the giving of guarantees or provision of security in connection with loans or quasi-loans: s 209(2).
8 Companies Act 2006 s 209(1)(a).
9 Companies Act 2006 s 209(1)(b). The condition specified in head (3)(b) in the text does not of itself prevent a company from making a home loan either to a director of the company (or of its holding company), or to an employee of the company, if loans of that description are ordinarily made by the company to its employees and the terms of the loan in question are no more favourable than those on which such loans are ordinarily made: s 209(3). For this purpose, a 'home loan' means a loan:
(1) for the purpose of facilitating the purchase, for use as the only or main residence of the person to whom the loan is made, of the whole or part of any dwelling-house together with any land to be occupied and enjoyed with it (s 209(4)(a));
(2) for the purpose of improving a dwelling house or part of a dwelling house so used or any land occupied and enjoyed with it (s 209(4)(b)); or
(3) in substitution for any loan made by any person and falling within head (1) or head (2) above (s 209(4)(c)).

617. Exceptions to requirement for approval applicable to credit transactions for the benefit of directors but not to loans and quasi-loans to them. Approval is not required[1] for a company[2] to enter into a credit transaction[3], or to give a guarantee or provide security in connection with a credit transaction, if:

(1) the aggregate of the value of the transaction (that is, of the credit transaction, guarantee or security)[4], and the value of any other relevant transactions or arrangements[5], does not exceed £15,000[6];
(2) the transaction is entered into by the company in the ordinary course of the company's business[7], and the value of the transaction is not greater, and the terms on which it is entered into are not more favourable, than it is reasonable to expect the company would have offered to, or in respect of, a person of the same financial standing but unconnected with the company[8].

Nor is such approval required[9]:

(a) to enter into a credit transaction as creditor for the benefit of an associated body corporate[10]; or
(b) to give a guarantee or provide security in connection with a credit transaction entered into by any person for the benefit of an associated body corporate[11].

1 Ie under the Companies Act 2006 s 201 (see PARA 613): see s 207(2), (3).
As to the general application of the Companies Act 2006 Pt 10 Ch 4 (ss 188–225) see PARA 601; and as to how those provisions interact with the directors' general duties see PARA 602.
2 As to the meaning of 'company' under the Companies Acts see PARA 21; and as to the meaning of the 'Companies Acts' see PARA 13.
3 As to the meaning of 'credit transaction' for these purposes see PARA 613 note 4.
4 Companies Act 2006 s 207(2)(a).
5 Companies Act 2006 s 207(2)(b). The provisions of s 210 have effect for determining what are 'other relevant transactions or arrangements' for the purposes of any exception to s 201 (see PARA 613): see PARA 615 note 3. As to determining the value of transactions and other relevant transactions or arrangements generally, and as to determining the person for whom a transaction or arrangement is entered into, see PARAS 610 note 16, 611 note 18, 613 note 19.
6 Companies Act 2006 s 207(2). As to the Secretary of State's power by order to substitute for any sum of money specified in Pt 10 (ss 154–259) (see PARA 512 et seq) a larger sum specified in the order see PARA 606 note 7.
7 Companies Act 2006 s 207(3)(a).
8 Companies Act 2006 s 207(3)(b).
9 Ie under the Companies Act 2006 s 201 (see PARA 613): see s 208(2).
10 Companies Act 2006 s 208(2)(a). As to the meaning of bodies corporate which are 'associated' for the purposes of Pt 10 see PARA 593 note 4.
11 Companies Act 2006 s 208(2)(b).

(C) Contravention of Requirements of Members' Approval for Loans etc to Directors

618. Civil consequences for breach of prohibition on loans etc to directors. Where a company[1] enters into a transaction or arrangement in contravention of the statutory provisions which require approval[2] for loans, quasi-loans, credit transactions and related arrangements[3], the transaction or arrangement is voidable at the instance of the company[4], unless:

(1) restitution of any money or other asset that was the subject matter of the transaction or arrangement is no longer possible[5]; or

(2) the company has been indemnified for any loss or damage resulting from the transaction or arrangement[6]; or

(3) rights acquired in good faith, for value and without actual notice of the contravention by any person who is not a party to the transaction or arrangement would be affected by its avoidance[7].

Whether or not the transaction or arrangement has been avoided, each of the following persons[8], namely:

(a) any director of the company or of its holding company with whom the company entered into the transaction or arrangement in contravention of the statutory provisions[9];

(b) any person with whom the company entered into the transaction or arrangement in like contravention[10] who is connected with a director of the company or of its holding company[11];

(c) the director of the company or of its holding company with whom any such person is connected[12]; and

(d) any other director of the company who authorised the transaction or arrangement[13],

is liable[14] to account to the company for any gain that he has made directly or indirectly by the transaction or arrangement[15], and, jointly and severally with any other person so liable[16], to indemnify the company for any loss or damage resulting from the transaction or arrangement[17]. However, in the case of a transaction or arrangement entered into by a company in contravention of the statutory provisions[18] governing credit transactions, certain loans and quasi-loans and related arrangements, and made with a person connected with a director of the company or of its holding company, that director is not liable by virtue of head (c) above if he shows that he took all reasonable steps to secure the company's compliance[19]. Furthermore, in any case, a person so connected is not liable by virtue of head (b) above[20], and a director is not liable by virtue of head (d) above[21], if he shows that, at the time the arrangement was entered into, he did not know the relevant circumstances constituting the contravention[22].

Nothing in the provisions governing civil liability[23] is to be read as excluding the operation of any other enactment[24] or rule of law by virtue of which the transaction or arrangement may be called in question or any liability to the company may arise[25].

1 As to the meaning of 'company' under the Companies Acts see PARA 21; and as to the meaning of the 'Companies Acts' see PARA 13.

2 Ie, in the case of loans made to a director of the company or of its holding company, or a guarantee given or security provided in connection with a loan made by any person to such a director, under the Companies Act 2006 s 197 (see PARA 610), in the case of quasi-loans made to a director of the company or of its holding company, or a guarantee given or security provided in connection with a quasi-loan made by any person to such a director, under s 198 (see PARA 611), in the case of loans or quasi-loans made to a person connected with a director of the company or of its holding company, or a guarantee given or security provided in connection with a loan or quasi-loan made by any person to a person connected with such a director, under s 200

(see PARA 612), in the case of credit transactions entered into by a company as creditor for the benefit of a director of the company or of its holding company (or a person connected with such a director) or a guarantee given or security provided in connection with a credit transaction entered into by any person for the benefit of such a director (or a person connected with such a director), under s 201 (see PARA 613) or, in the case of an arrangement under which another person enters into a transaction that, if it had been entered into by the company, would have required approval under s 197, s 198, s 200 or s 201, and that person, in pursuance of the arrangement, obtains a benefit from the company or a body corporate associated with it, or where a company arranges for the assignment to it, or assumption by it, of any rights, obligations or liabilities under a transaction that, if it had been entered into by the company, would have required such approval, under s 203 (see PARA 614): see s 213(1). As to the meaning of 'director' for these purposes see PARA 610 note 2. As to the meaning of 'credit transaction' for these purposes see PARA 613 note 4; as to the meaning of 'holding company' see PARA 22; and as to the meaning of 'quasi-loan' for these purposes see PARA 611 note 4. As to the meaning of references to a person being 'connected' with a director see PARA 515. As to the validity generally of transactions involving a director or a person connected with a director see PARA 263.

As to the general application of the Companies Act 2006 Pt 10 Ch 4 (ss 188–225) see PARA 601; and as to how those provisions interact with the directors' general duties see PARA 602.

3 See the Companies Act 2006 s 213(1).

4 Companies Act 2006 s 213(2). Moneys paid under the transaction or arrangement in question are recoverable by the company in this way irrespective of the terms on which the transaction or arrangement was made: *Tait Consibee (Oxford) Ltd v Tait* [1997] 2 BCLC 349, CA; *Currencies Direct Ltd v Ellis* [2002] 1 BCLC 193 (affd on different grounds [2002] EWCA Civ 779, [2002] 2 BCLC 482). However, a company may seek to recover without recourse to the statutory provision: *Currencies Direct Ltd v Ellis* [2002] 1 BCLC 193 (affd on different grounds [2002] EWCA Civ 779, [2002] 2 BCLC 482). As to the effect of subsequent affirmation see PARA 609.

Because a voidable loan stands until avoided, the statutory provision for avoidance is inimical to the concept of a constructive trusteeship or any form of tracing claim, at least in the absence of special circumstances: *Re Ciro Citterio Menswear plc (in administration), Ciro Citterio Menswear plc v Thakrar* [2002] EWHC 293 (Ch), [2002] 2 All ER 717, [2002] 1 WLR 2217 (distinguished in *Baker v Potter* [2004] EWHC 1422 (Ch) at [109], [2004] All ER (D) 174 (Jun)). Cf *Re Duckwari plc* [1999] Ch 253, sub nom *Re Duckwari plc (No 2), Duckwari plc v Offerventure Ltd (No 2)* [1998] 2 BCLC 315, CA (cited in PARA 608); and see *Re Lands Allotment Co* [1894] 1 Ch 616 at 631, CA, per Lindley LJ. Set-off under the Insolvency Rules 1986, SI 1986/1925, r 4.90 (see COMPANY AND PARTNERSHIP INSOLVENCY vol 17 (2011) PARA 746) could not be invoked by a director whose liability to the company arose out of an unlawful loan: *Re a Company (No 1641 of 2003)* [2003] EWHC 2652 (Ch), [2004] 1 BCLC 210.

5 Companies Act 2006 s 213(2)(a).

6 Companies Act 2006 s 213(2)(b).

7 Companies Act 2006 s 213(2)(c).

8 Companies Act 2006 s 213(3). The provisions of s 213(3), (4) are subject to the provisions of s 213(6), (7) (see the text and notes 18–22): s 213(5).

9 Companies Act 2006 s 213(4)(a). The text refers to contravention of the Companies Act 2006 s 197 (see PARA 610), s 198 (see PARA 611), s 201 (see PARA 613) or s 203 (see PARA 614): see s 213(4)(a). See also note 8.

10 Ie in contravention of any of the Companies Act 2006 s 197 (see PARA 610), s 198 (see PARA 611), s 201 (see PARA 613) or s 203 (see PARA 614): see s 213(4)(b).

11 Companies Act 2006 s 213(4)(b). See also note 8.

12 Companies Act 2006 s 213(4)(c). See also note 8.

13 Companies Act 2006 s 213(4)(d). See also note 8.

14 See the Companies Act 2006 s 213(3). See also note 8. A director who knowingly allowed a practice to continue under which lending by the company to his co-director was treated as acceptable had authorised the individual payments which were made in accordance with that practice notwithstanding that he did not have actual knowledge of each individual payment at the time that it was made: *Neville v Krikorian* [2006] EWCA Civ 943, [2007] 1 BCLC 1. See also *Queensway Systems Ltd (in liquidation) v Walker* [2006] EWHC 2496 (Ch), [2007] 2 BCLC 577 (directors who took funds from their company in the form of interest-free loans and, at the end of each financial year, declared dividends which were then used to extinguish their liability to the company were jointly and severally liable for the repayment of the outstanding loans when they were unable to establish that a dividend had been properly declared).

15 Companies Act 2006 s 213(3)(a). See also note 8.

16 Ie liable under the Companies Act 2006 s 213: see s 213(3)(b).

17 Companies Act 2006 s 213(3)(b). See also note 8.

18 Ie in contravention of the Companies Act 2006 s 200 (see PARA 612), s 201 (see PARA 613) or s 203 (see PARA 614): see s 213(6).
19 Companies Act 2006 s 213(6). The text refers to securing compliance with s 200 (see PARA 612), s 201 (see PARA 613) or s 203 (see PARA 614), as the case may be: see s 213(6). See also note 8.
20 Companies Act 2006 s 213(7)(a). See also note 8.
21 Companies Act 2006 s 213(7)(b). See also note 8.
22 Companies Act 2006 s 213(7). See also note 8.
23 Ie nothing in the Companies Act 2006 s 213: see s 213(8).
24 As to the meaning of 'enactment' see PARA 13 note 16.
25 Companies Act 2006 s 213(8). See also *Baker v Potter* [2004] EWHC 1422 (Ch), [2004] All ER (D) 174 (Jun); *Queensway Systems Ltd (in liquidation) v Walker* [2006] EWHC 2496 (Ch), [2007] 2 BCLC 577.

619. Effect of transaction or arrangement being subsequently affirmed. Where a transaction or arrangement is entered into by a company[1] in contravention of the statutory provisions which require approval[2] for loans, quasi-loans, credit transactions and related arrangements, but where, within a reasonable period, it is affirmed[3]:

(1) in the case of a contravention of the requirement for a resolution of the members of the company[4], by a resolution of the members of the company[5]; and
(2) in the case of a contravention of the requirement for a resolution of the members of the company's holding company, by a resolution of the members of the holding company[6],

the transaction or arrangement may no longer be avoided[7].

1 As to the meaning of 'company' under the Companies Acts see PARA 21; and as to the meaning of the 'Companies Acts' see PARA 13.
2 Ie, in the case of loans made to a director of the company or of its holding company, or a guarantee given or security provided in connection with a loan made by any person to such a director, under the Companies Act 2006 s 197 (see PARA 610), in the case of quasi-loans made to a director of the company or of its holding company, or a guarantee given or security provided in connection with a quasi-loan made by any person to such a director, under s 198 (see PARA 611), in the case of loans or quasi-loans made to a person connected with a director of the company or of its holding company, or a guarantee given or security provided in connection with a loan or quasi-loan made by any person to a person connected with such a director, under s 200 (see PARA 612), in the case of credit transactions entered into by a company as creditor for the benefit of a director of the company or of its holding company (or a person connected with such a director) or a guarantee given or security provided in connection with a credit transaction entered into by any person for the benefit of such a director (or a person connected with such a director), under s 201 (see PARA 613) or, in the case of an arrangement under which another person enters into a transaction that, if it had been entered into by the company, would have required approval under s 197, s 198, s 200 or s 201, and that person, in pursuance of the arrangement, obtains a benefit from the company or a body corporate associated with it, or where a company arranges for the assignment to it, or assumption by it, of any rights, obligations or liabilities under a transaction that, if it had been entered into by the company, would have required such approval, under s 203 (see PARA 614): see s 214. As to the meaning of 'director' for these purposes see PARA 610 note 2. As to the meaning of 'credit transaction' for these purposes see PARA 613 note 4; as to the meaning of 'holding company' see PARA 22; and as to the meaning of 'quasi-loan' for these purposes see PARA 611 note 4. As to the meaning of references to a person being 'connected' with a director see PARA 515. As to the validity generally of transactions involving a director or a person connected with a director see PARA 263.

As to the general application of the Companies Act 2006 Pt 10 Ch 4 (ss 188–225) see PARA 601; and as to how those provisions interact with the directors' general duties see PARA 602.
3 Companies Act 2006 s 214.
4 As to the meaning of 'member of the company' see PARA 323. As to resolutions and meetings of members see PARA 701 et seq. As to voting at meetings see PARA 725 et seq.
5 Companies Act 2006 s 214(a).
6 Companies Act 2006 s 214(b).
7 Companies Act 2006 s 214. The text refers to avoidance of the transaction or arrangement under s 213 (see PARA 618): see s 214.

F. PAYMENT TO DIRECTORS FOR LOSS OF OFFICE

(A) *Meaning of 'Payment for Loss of Office'*

620. Meaning of 'payment for loss of office' in relation to directors. For the purposes of the provisions which govern transactions with directors[1] requiring the approval of members[2], 'payment for loss of office' means a payment made to a director or past director of a company[3]:

(1) by way of compensation[4] for loss of office as director of the company[5];

(2) by way of compensation for loss, while director of the company or in connection with his ceasing to be a director of it, of[6]:

(a) any other office or employment in connection with the management of the affairs of the company[7]; or

(b) any office, as director or otherwise, or employment in connection with the management of the affairs of any subsidiary undertaking[8] of the company[9];

(3) as consideration for or in connection with his retirement from his office as director of the company[10]; or

(4) as consideration for or in connection with his retirement, while director of the company or in connection with his ceasing to be a director of it, from[11]:

(a) any other office or employment in connection with the management of the affairs of the company[12]; or

(b) any office, as director or otherwise, or employment in connection with the management of the affairs of any subsidiary undertaking of the company[13].

For the purposes of the provisions which govern payments for loss of office requiring members' approval[14], payment to a person connected with a director[15], or payment to any person at the direction of, or for the benefit of, a director or a person connected with him[16], is treated as payment to the director[17].

1 For the purposes of the Companies Act 2006 ss 215–222 (see PARA 601 et seq), a shadow director is treated as a director: s 223(1)(d); but see note 5. As to the meaning of 'director' under the Companies Acts see PARA 512; and as to the meaning of the 'Companies Acts' see PARA 13. As to shadow directors see PARA 513.

2 Ie in the Companies Act 2006 Pt 10 Ch 4 (ss 188–225) or Pt 10 Ch 4A (ss 226A–226F) (see PARA 601 et seq): see ss 215(1), 226A(1), (5) (s 226A added by the Enterprise and Regulatory Reform Act 2013 s 80). As to the meaning of 'member of the company' see PARA 323.

As to the general application of the Companies Act 2006 Pt 10 Ch 4 see PARA 601; and as to how those provisions interact with the directors' general duties see PARA 602.

3 Companies Act 2006 s 215(1). The definition of 'payment for loss of office' in s 215 is applied for the purposes of Pt 10 Ch 4A (special provision as to directors of quoted companies): see s 226A(1), (5) (as added: see note 2). As to the meaning of 'company' under the Companies Acts see PARA 21.

The information required to be provided by s 412 (information about directors' emoluments and other benefits) may include payments for loss of office: see PARA 845. The requirements imposed by s 190 (substantial property transactions) do not apply to a transaction so far as it relates to payment for loss of office as defined in s 215: see s 190(6); and PARA 606.

4 The references to compensation and consideration include benefits otherwise than in cash and references in the Companies Act 2006 Pt 10 Ch 4 (see PARA 601 et seq) to payment have a corresponding meaning: s 215(2). See also note 3. As to the meaning of 'cash' see PARA 606 note 7. See also *Mercer v Heart of Midlothian plc* 2001 SLT 945, Ct of Sess (where it was not proved that the claimant's enjoyment of benefits had been of any cost to the defendant).

5 Companies Act 2006 s 215(1)(a). As to the retirement or removal of directors see PARA 555 et seq. References in ss 215–222 (see the text and notes 1–4, 6–17; and PARA 621 et seq) and in Pt 10 Ch 4A (see PARA 626 et seq) to loss of office as a director do not include loss of a person's status as a shadow director: ss 223(2), 226A(9) (s 226A(9) as added: see note 2).

6 Companies Act 2006 s 215(1)(b). See also note 3.

7 Companies Act 2006 s 215(1)(b)(i). See also note 3. This provision closes the loophole discussed in *Taupo Totara Timber Co Ltd v Rowe* [1978] AC 537 at 545–546, [1977] 3 All ER 123 at 127–128, PC (sum contractually payable on retirement in connection, not simply with the office of director, but also with some employment held by director).

8 As to the meaning of 'subsidiary undertaking' see PARA 23.

9 Companies Act 2006 s 215(1)(b)(ii). See also note 3.

10 Companies Act 2006 s 215(1)(c). See also note 3.

11 Companies Act 2006 s 215(1)(d). See also note 3.

12 Companies Act 2006 s 215(1)(d)(i). See also note 3.

13 Companies Act 2006 s 215(1)(d)(ii). See also note 3.

14 Ie the Companies Act 2006 ss 217–221 (see PARA 621 et seq): see s 215(3). References in ss 217–221 to payment by a person include payment by another person at the direction of, or on behalf of, the person referred to: s 215(4). Nothing in s 215 (other than the definition of 'payment for loss of office', as to the application of which see note 3) or in ss 216–222 applies in relation to a payment for loss of office to a director of a quoted company other than a payment to which s 226C (see PARA 626) does not apply by virtue of s 226D(6) (see PARA 626): see s 215(5) (added by the Enterprise and Regulatory Reform Act 2013 s 81(1), (4)). As to the meaning of 'quoted company' in the Companies Act 2006 see PARA 70; and see PARA 601 note 4.

15 Companies Act 2006 s 215(3)(a). See also note 14. As to the meaning of references to a person being 'connected' with a director see PARA 515. As to the validity generally of transactions involving a director or a person connected with a director see PARA 263.

16 Companies Act 2006 s 215(3)(b). See also note 14.

17 Companies Act 2006 s 215(3). See also note 14.

(B) Payment to Directors for Loss of Office where Company is not Quoted Company

621. Requirement of members' approval for payment by company for loss of office. A company[1] may not make a payment for loss of office[2] to a director[3] of the company unless the payment has been approved by a resolution of the members of the company[4]; and a company may not make such a payment to a director of its holding company[5] unless the payment has been approved by a resolution of the members of each of those companies[6].

A resolution approving such a payment[7] must not be passed unless a memorandum setting out particulars of the proposed payment, including its amount, is made available to the members of the company whose approval is sought[8]:

(1) in the case of a written resolution[9], by being sent or submitted to every eligible member[10] at or before the time at which the proposed resolution is sent or submitted to him[11]; or
(2) in the case of a resolution at a meeting, by being made available for inspection by members of the company both:
    (a) at the company's registered office[12] for not less than 15 days ending with the date of the meeting[13]; and
    (b) at the meeting itself[14].

If the proposal is not so approved, the directors responsible for authorising the payment are guilty of misfeasance[15].

No such approval is, however, required[16] on the part of the members of a body corporate[17] that either is not a UK-registered company[18], or is a wholly-owned subsidiary[19] of another body corporate[20].

Special provision is made with regard to payments for loss of office where the company is a quoted company[21].

1 As to the meaning of 'company' under the Companies Acts see PARA 21; and as to the meaning of the 'Companies Acts' see PARA 13.

2 As to the meaning of 'payment for loss of office' see PARA 620.

3 As to the meaning of 'director' for these purposes see PARA 620 note 1. See also PARA 620 note 5.

4 Companies Act 2006 s 217(1). As to the meaning of 'member of the company' see PARA 323. As to resolutions and meetings of members see PARA 701 et seq. As to voting at meetings see PARA 725 et seq.

As to exceptions to the requirement to obtain members' approval for payments to a director for loss of office see PARA 624; and as to civil consequences that may arise from any contravention of the requirement see PARA 625. As to the general application of the Companies Act 2006 Pt 10 Ch 4 (ss 188–225) see PARA 601; and as to how those provisions interact with the directors' general duties see PARA 602. See also the text and note 21.

5 As to the meaning of 'holding company' see PARA 22.

6 Companies Act 2006 s 217(2).

7 Ie a payment to which the Companies Act 2006 s 217 applies: see s 217(3).

8 Companies Act 2006 s 217(3).

9 As to the meaning of 'written resolution' see PARA 695.

10 As to eligible members in relation to a resolution proposed as a written resolution of a private company see PARA 695. As to the provision made for the sending or supplying of documents or information to or from a company (the 'company communications provisions') see PARA 750 et seq.

11 Companies Act 2006 s 217(3)(a). Where approval under Pt 10 Ch 4 is sought by written resolution, and a memorandum is required under Pt 10 Ch 4 to be sent or submitted to every eligible member before the resolution is passed, provision is made for accidental failure to send or submit the memorandum to one or more members: see s 224; and PARA 601 note 8.

12 As to the company's registered office see PARA 124.

13 Companies Act 2006 s 217(3)(b)(i). See also note 11.

14 Companies Act 2006 s 217(3)(b)(ii). See also note 11.

15 *Re Duomatic Ltd* [1969] 2 Ch 365, [1969] 1 All ER 161. As to the power of the court to grant relief from liability in certain cases see PARA 645.

16 Ie under the Companies Act 2006 s 217: see s 217(4).

17 As to the meaning of 'body corporate' for the purposes of the Companies Acts see PARA 1 note 5.

18 Companies Act 2006 s 217(4)(a). As to the meaning of 'UK-registered company' see PARA 21.

19 As to the meaning of 'wholly-owned subsidiary' see PARA 22.

20 Companies Act 2006 s 217(4)(b).

21 See PARA 626 et seq. Nothing in s 217 applies in relation to a payment for loss of office to a director of a quoted company other than a payment to which s 226C (see PARA 626) does not apply by virtue of s 226D(6) (see PARA 626): see s 215(5) (added by the Enterprise and Regulatory Reform Act 2013 s 81(1), (4)). As to the meaning of 'quoted company' in the Companies Act 2006 see PARA 70; and see PARA 601 note 4.

622. Requirement of members' approval for payment for loss of office on a transfer of undertaking or property. No payment for loss of office[1] may be made by any person to a director[2] of a company[3] in connection with the transfer of the whole or any part of the undertaking[4] or property of the company unless the payment has been approved by a resolution of the members of the company[5]; and no such payment may be made by any person to a director of a company in connection with the transfer of the whole or any part of the undertaking or property of a subsidiary[6] of the company unless the payment has been approved by a resolution of the members of each of the companies[7].

Where in connection with any such transfer[8]:

(1) a director of the company either is to cease to hold office[9], or is to cease to be the holder of any other office or employment in connection with the management of the affairs of the company[10], or any office, as director or otherwise, or employment in connection with the management of the affairs of any subsidiary undertaking of the company[11]; and

(2) the price to be paid to the director for any shares[12] in the company held by him is in excess of the price which could at the time have been obtained by other holders of like shares[13], or if any valuable consideration is given to the director by a person other than the company[14],

the excess or, as the case may be, the money value of the consideration is taken[15] to have been a payment for loss of office[16].

A resolution approving any payment for loss of office on a transfer of undertaking[17] must not be passed unless a memorandum setting out particulars of the proposed payment, including its amount, is made available to the members of the company whose approval is sought[18]:

(a) in the case of a written resolution[19], by being sent or submitted to every eligible member[20] at or before the time at which the proposed resolution is sent or submitted to him[21]; or

(b) in the case of a resolution at a meeting, by being made available for inspection by members of the company both:

  (i) at the company's registered office[22] for not less than 15 days ending with the date of the meeting[23]; and

  (ii) at the meeting itself[24].

No such approval is, however, required[25] on the part of the members of a body corporate[26] that either is not a UK-registered company[27], or is a wholly-owned subsidiary[28] of another body corporate[29].

Special provision is made with regard to payments for loss of office where the company is a quoted company[30].

1 As to the meaning of 'payment for loss of office' see PARA 620.
2 As to the meaning of 'director' for these purposes see PARA 620 note 1. See also PARA 620 note 5.
3 As to the meaning of 'company' under the Companies Acts see PARA 21.
4 As to the meaning of 'undertaking' in the Companies Acts see PARA 23 note 2.
5 Companies Act 2006 s 218(1). As to the meaning of 'member of the company' see PARA 323. As to resolutions and meetings of members see PARA 701 et seq. As to voting at meetings see PARA 725 et seq. A payment made in pursuance of an arrangement entered into as part of the agreement for the transfer in question (or within one year before or two years after that agreement) and to which the company whose undertaking or property is transferred (or any person to whom the transfer is made) is privy, is presumed, except in so far as the contrary is shown, to be a payment to which s 218 applies: s 218(5).

As to exceptions to the requirement to obtain members' approval for payments to a director for loss of office see PARA 624; and as to civil consequences that may arise from any contravention of the requirement see PARA 625. As to the general application of the Companies Act 2006 Pt 10 Ch 4 (ss 188–225) see PARA 601; and as to how those provisions interact with the directors' general duties see PARA 602. See also the text and note 30.
6 As to the meaning of 'subsidiary' see PARA 22.
7 Companies Act 2006 s 218(2). See also note 5.
8 Ie as is mentioned in the Companies Act 2006 s 218: see s 216(1), (2).
9 Companies Act 2006 s 216(1)(a).
10 Companies Act 2006 s 216(1)(b)(i).
11 Companies Act 2006 s 216(1)(b)(ii). As to the meaning of 'subsidiary undertaking' see PARA 23.
12 As to the meaning of 'share' see PARA 1231.
13 Companies Act 2006 s 216(2)(a).
14 Companies Act 2006 s 216(2)(b).
15 Ie for the purposes of the Companies Act 2006 s 218: see s 216(2).
16 Companies Act 2006 s 216(2).
17 Ie a payment to which the Companies Act 2006 s 218 applies: see s 218(3).
18 Companies Act 2006 s 218(3).
19 As to the meaning of 'written resolution' see PARA 695.
20 As to eligible members in relation to a resolution proposed as a written resolution of a private company see PARA 695. As to the provision made for the sending or supplying of documents or information to or from a company (the 'company communications provisions') see PARA 750 et seq.
21 Companies Act 2006 s 218(3)(a). Where approval under Pt 10 Ch 4 is sought by written resolution, and a memorandum is required under Pt 10 Ch 4 to be sent or submitted to every eligible member before the resolution is passed, provision is made for accidental failure to send or submit the memorandum to one or more members: see s 224; and PARA 601 note 8.

22 As to the company's registered office see PARA 124.
23 Companies Act 2006 s 218(3)(b)(i). See also note 21.
24 Companies Act 2006 s 218(3)(b)(ii). See also note 21.
25 Ie under the Companies Act 2006 s 218: see s 218(4).
26 As to the meaning of 'body corporate' for the purposes of the Companies Acts see PARA 1 note 5.
27 Companies Act 2006 s 218(4)(a). As to the meaning of 'UK-registered company' see PARA 21.
28 As to the meaning of 'wholly-owned subsidiary' see PARA 22.
29 Companies Act 2006 s 218(4)(b).
30 See PARA 626 et seq. Nothing in ss 216, 218 applies in relation to a payment for loss of office to a director of a quoted company other than a payment to which s 226C (see PARA 626) does not apply by virtue of s 226D(6) (see PARA 626): see s 215(5) (added by the Enterprise and Regulatory Reform Act 2013 s 81(1), (4)). As to the meaning of 'quoted company' in the Companies Act 2006 see PARA 70; and see PARA 601 note 4.

623. Requirement of shareholders' approval for payment for loss of office in connection with share transfer. No payment for loss of office[1] may be made by any person to a director[2] of a company[3] in connection with a transfer of shares[4] in the company, or in a subsidiary[5] of the company, resulting from a takeover bid[6] unless the payment has been approved by a resolution of the relevant shareholders[7].

Where in connection with any such transfer[8]:

(1) a director of the company either is to cease to hold office[9], or is to cease to be the holder of any other office or employment in connection with the management of the affairs of the company[10], or any office (as director or otherwise) or employment in connection with the management of the affairs of any subsidiary undertaking of the company[11]; and

(2) the price to be paid to the director for any shares in the company held by him is in excess of the price which could at the time have been obtained by other holders of like shares[12], or if any valuable consideration is given to the director by a person other than the company[13],

the excess or, as the case may be, the money value of the consideration is taken[14] to have been a payment for loss of office[15].

A resolution approving a payment for loss of office in connection with a transfer of shares[16] must not be passed unless a memorandum setting out particulars of the proposed payment, including its amount, is made available to the members of the company whose approval is sought[17]:

(a) in the case of a written resolution[18], by being sent or submitted to every eligible member[19] at or before the time at which the proposed resolution is sent or submitted to him[20]; or

(b) in the case of a resolution at a meeting, by being made available for inspection by members of the company both:

 (i) at the company's registered office[21] for not less than 15 days ending with the date of the meeting[22]; and

 (ii) at the meeting itself[23].

Neither the person making the offer, nor any associate of his[24], is entitled to vote on the resolution[25]. Where, however, the resolution is proposed as a written resolution, they are entitled, if they would otherwise be so entitled, to be sent a copy of it[26], and at any meeting to consider the resolution they are entitled, if they would otherwise be so entitled, to be given notice of the meeting, to attend and speak and if present, in person or by proxy, to count towards the quorum[27].

If at a meeting to consider the resolution a quorum is not present, and after the meeting has been adjourned to a later date a quorum is again not present, the payment is[28] deemed to have been approved[29].

No approval is required[30] on the part of shareholders in a body corporate[31] that either is not a UK-registered company[32], or is a wholly-owned subsidiary[33] of another body corporate[34].

Special provision is made with regard to payments for loss of office where the company is a quoted company[35].

1 As to the meaning of 'payment for loss of office' see PARA 620.
2 As to the meaning of 'director' for these purposes see PARA 620 note 1. See also PARA 620 note 5.
3 As to the meaning of 'company' under the Companies Acts see PARA 21.
4 As to the meaning of 'share' see PARA 1231.
5 As to the meaning of 'subsidiary' see PARA 22.
6 As to takeover offers generally see PARA 1662 et seq.
7 Companies Act 2006 s 219(1). For these purposes, the relevant shareholders are the holders of the shares to which the bid relates and any holders of shares of the same class as any of those shares: s 219(2). As to the meaning of 'class of shares' see PARA 1246. As to shareholders and the membership of companies generally see PARA 323 et seq. As to resolutions and meetings of members see PARA 701 et seq; and as to voting at meetings see PARA 725 et seq. A payment made in pursuance of an arrangement entered into as part of the agreement for the transfer in question (or within one year before or two years after that agreement) and to which the company whose shares are the subject of the bid (or any person to whom the transfer is made) is privy, is presumed, except in so far as the contrary is shown, to be a payment to which s 219 applies: s 219(7).

As to exceptions to the requirement to obtain members' approval for payments to a director for loss of office see PARA 624; and as to civil consequences that may arise from any contravention of the requirement see PARA 625. As to the general application of the Companies Act 2006 Pt 10 Ch 4 (ss 188–225) see PARA 601; and as to how those provisions interact with the directors' general duties see PARA 602. See also the text and note 35.
8 Ie as is mentioned in the Companies Act 2006 s 219: see s 216(1), (2).
9 Companies Act 2006 s 216(1)(a).
10 Companies Act 2006 s 216(1)(b)(i).
11 Companies Act 2006 s 216(1)(b)(ii). As to the meaning of 'subsidiary undertaking' see PARA 23.
12 Companies Act 2006 s 216(2)(a).
13 Companies Act 2006 s 216(2)(b).
14 Ie for the purposes of the Companies Act 2006 s 219: see s 216(2).
15 Companies Act 2006 s 216(2).
16 Ie a payment to which the Companies Act 2006 s 219 applies: see s 219(3).
17 Companies Act 2006 s 219(3).
18 As to the meaning of 'written resolution' see PARA 695.
19 As to eligible members in relation to a resolution proposed as a written resolution of a private company see PARA 695. As to the provision made for the sending or supplying of documents or information to or from a company (the 'company communications provisions') see PARA 750 et seq.
20 Companies Act 2006 s 219(3)(a). Where approval under Pt 10 Ch 4 is sought by written resolution, and a memorandum is required under Pt 10 Ch 4 to be sent or submitted to every eligible member before the resolution is passed, provision is made for accidental failure to send or submit the memorandum to one or more members: see s 224; and PARA 601 note 8.
21 As to the company's registered office see PARA 124.
22 Companies Act 2006 s 219(3)(b)(i). See also note 20.
23 Companies Act 2006 s 219(3)(b)(ii). See also note 20.
24 Ie as defined in the Companies Act 2006 s 988 (see PARA 1694): see s 219(4).
25 Companies Act 2006 s 219(4).
26 Companies Act 2006 s 219(4)(a).
27 Companies Act 2006 s 219(4)(b).
28 Ie for the purposes of the Companies Act 2006 s 219: see s 219(5).
29 Companies Act 2006 s 219(5).
30 Ie under the Companies Act 2006 s 219: see s 219(6).
31 As to the meaning of 'body corporate' for the purposes of the Companies Acts see PARA 1 note 5.
32 Companies Act 2006 s 219(6)(a). As to the meaning of 'UK-registered company' see PARA 21.
33 As to the meaning of 'wholly-owned subsidiary' see PARA 22.
34 Companies Act 2006 s 219(6)(b).
35 See PARA 626 et seq. Nothing in ss 216, 219 applies in relation to a payment for loss of office to a director of a quoted company other than a payment to which s 226C (see PARA 626) does not

apply by virtue of s 226D(6) (see PARA 626): see s 215(5) (added by the Enterprise and Regulatory Reform Act 2013 s 81(1), (4)). As to the meaning of 'quoted company' in the Companies Act 2006 see PARA 70; and see PARA 601 note 4.

624. Exceptions to requirement for approval for payment for loss of office. Approval is not required under the provisions[1] that govern payments made to the director[2] of a company for loss of office for a payment made in good faith[3]:

(1) in discharge of an existing legal obligation[4];
(2) by way of damages for breach of such an obligation[5];
(3) by way of settlement or compromise of any claim arising in connection with the termination of a person's office or employment[6]; or
(4) by way of pension in respect of past services[7].

A payment part of which falls within one or more of these categories[8] and part of which does not is treated as if the parts were separate payments[9].

Nor is such approval required[10] if:

(a) the payment in question is made by the company or any of its subsidiaries[11]; and
(b) the amount or value of the payment, together with the amount or value of any other relevant payments[12], does not exceed £200[13].

Special provision is made with regard to payments for loss of office where the company is a quoted company[14].

1 Ie, in relation to the requirement of members' approval for payment for loss of office made by the company, under the Companies Act 2006 s 217 (see PARA 621) and, in relation to such payments on a transfer of undertaking or property, under s 218 (see PARA 622) and, in relation to the requirement of shareholders' approval for such payments in connection with a share transfer, under s 219 (see PARA 623): see s 220(1). As to the meaning of 'payment for loss of office' see PARA 620. As to the meaning of 'company' under the Companies Acts see PARA 21; and as to the meaning of the 'Companies Acts' see PARA 13.

2 As to the meaning of 'director' for these purposes see PARA 620 note 1. See also PARA 620 note 5.

3 Companies Act 2006 s 220(1).

4 Companies Act 2006 s 220(1)(a). Head (1) in the text may apply, for example, to contractual payments due under service agreements between the company and its managing director: see *Taupo Totara Timber Co Ltd v Rowe* [1978] AC 537, [1977] 3 All ER 123, PC (sum contractually payable on retirement).

In relation to a payment within the Companies Act 2006 s 217 (payment by company) (see PARA 621), an existing legal obligation means an obligation of the company, or any body corporate associated with it, that was not entered into in connection with, or in consequence of, the event giving rise to the payment for loss of office: s 220(2). As to the meaning of 'body corporate' for the purposes of the Companies Acts see PARA 1 note 5; and as to the meaning of bodies corporate which are 'associated' for the purposes of the Companies Act 2006 Pt 10 (ss 154–259) (see PARA 512 et seq) see PARA 593 note 4.

In relation to a payment within s 218 (payment in connection with transfer of undertaking or property) (see PARA 622) or s 219 (payment in connection with transfer of shares) (see PARA 623) an existing legal obligation means an obligation of the person making the payment that was not entered into for the purposes of, in connection with or in consequence of, the transfer in question: s 220(3).

In the case of a payment within both s 217 and s 218, or within both s 217 and s 219, s 220(2) applies and not s 220(3): s 220(4).

5 Companies Act 2006 s 220(1)(b). See also note 4. If the director's service agreement contains inflation-proofing of his salary, this may be taken into account in arriving at any damages: *Re Crowther & Nicholson Ltd* (1981) 125 Sol Jo 529. As to directors' service contracts under the Companies Act 2006 see PARA 564 et seq.

6 Companies Act 2006 s 220(1)(c). Where the sum paid as compensation is payable under the terms of the service agreement upon the company electing to terminate it in accordance with its terms, the sum is a profit from the employment and taxable as such: *Dale v De Soissons* [1950] 2 All ER 460, CA.

7 Companies Act 2006 s 220(1)(d). This does not cover a lump sum payment made by directors who have no other power to pay pensions on the eve of liquidation: *Gibson's Executor v Gibson* 1980

SLT 2, Ct of Sess. Cf provision that may be made in a company's articles of association for special remuneration and expenses and pensions (cited in PARA 562).

8 Ie part of which falls within the Companies Act 2006 s 220(1): see s 220(5).

9 Companies Act 2006 s 220(5).

10 Ie, in relation to the requirement of members' approval for payment for loss of office made by the company, under the Companies Act 2006 s 217 (see PARA 621) and, in relation to such payments on a transfer of undertaking or property, under s 218 (see PARA 622) and, in relation to the requirement of shareholders' approval for such payments in connection with a share transfer, under s 219 (see PARA 623): see s 221(1).

11 Companies Act 2006 s 221(1)(a). As to the meaning of 'subsidiary' see PARA 22.

12 For this purpose, 'other relevant payments' are payments for loss of office in relation to which the following conditions are met (Companies Act 2006 s 221(2)):

(1) where the payment in question is one to which s 217 (payment by company) (see PARA 621) applies, the conditions are that the other payment was or is paid:
  (a) by the company making the payment in question or any of its subsidiaries (s 221(3)(a));
  (b) to the director to whom that payment is made (s 221(3)(b)); and
  (c) in connection with the same event (s 221(3)(c));

(2) where the payment in question is one to which s 218 (payment in connection with transfer of undertaking or property) (see PARA 622) or s 219 (payment in connection with transfer of shares) (see PARA 623) applies, the conditions are that the other payment was (or is) paid in connection with the same transfer:
  (a) to the director to whom the payment in question was made (s 221(4)(a)); and
  (b) by the company making the payment or any of its subsidiaries (s 221(4)(b)).

13 Companies Act 2006 s 221(1)(b). As to the Secretary of State's power by order to substitute for any sum of money specified in Pt 10 (see PARA 512 et seq) a larger sum specified in the order see PARA 606 note 7.

14 See PARA 626 et seq. Nothing in ss 216–221 applies in relation to a payment for loss of office to a director of a quoted company other than a payment to which s 226C (see PARA 626) does not apply by virtue of s 226D(6) (see PARA 626): see s 215(5) (added by the Enterprise and Regulatory Reform Act 2013 s 81(1), (4)). As to the meaning of 'quoted company' in the Companies Act 2006 see PARA 70; and see PARA 601 note 4.

625. Civil consequences of payments for loss of office made without required approval. If a payment for loss of office[1] is made in contravention of the restriction imposed on such payments being made by a company[2] without members' approval[3], it is held by the recipient on trust for the company making the payment[4], and any director[5] who authorised the payment is jointly and severally liable to indemnify the company that made the payment for any loss resulting from it[6].

If a payment is made in contravention of the restriction imposed on such payments being made on a transfer of undertaking or property without members' approval[7], it is held by the recipient on trust for the company whose undertaking or property is or is proposed to be transferred[8].

If a payment is made in contravention of the restriction imposed on such payments being made in connection with a share[9] transfer without shareholders' approval[10], it is held by the recipient on trust for persons who have sold their shares as a result of the offer made[11], and the expenses incurred by the recipient in distributing that sum amongst those persons must be borne by him and not retained out of that sum[12].

Special provision is made with regard to payments for loss of office where the company is a quoted company[13].

1 As to the meaning of 'payment for loss of office' see PARA 620.

2 As to the meaning of 'company' under the Companies Acts see PARA 21; and as to the meaning of the 'Companies Acts' see PARA 13.

3 Ie in contravention of the Companies Act 2006 s 217 (see PARA 621): see s 222(1). If a payment is in contravention of both s 217 and s 218 (see PARA 622), s 222(2) (see the text and notes 7–8) applies rather than s 222(1): s 222(4). If a payment is in contravention of s 217 and s 219 (see PARA 623), s 222(3) (see the text and notes 9–12) applies rather than s 222(1), unless the court directs otherwise: s 222(5). As to the meaning of 'the court' see PARA 160 note 12.

4 Companies Act 2006 s 222(1)(a). These statutory provisions give effect to and somewhat expand a principle of law already well recognised: see *Southall v British Mutual Life Assurance Society* (1871) 6 Ch App 614; *Gaskell v Chambers* (1858) 28 LJ Ch 385; *Kaye v Croydon Tramways Co* [1898] 1 Ch 358, CA; *Tiessen v Henderson* [1899] 1 Ch 861. As to the company's power to sell property see PARAS 322, 1620. See further *Clarkson v Davies* [1923] AC 100, PC. As to the fiduciary position of directors in respect of company property under their control see PARAS 579, 587.

5 As to the meaning of 'director' for these purposes see PARA 620 note 1. See also PARA 620 note 5.

6 Companies Act 2006 s 222(1)(b).

7 Ie in contravention of the Companies Act 2006 s 218 (see PARA 622): see s 222(2). See also note 3.

8 Companies Act 2006 s 222(2). See further *Clarkson v Davies* [1923] AC 100, PC (in a claim to recover sums improperly paid to a director by way of compensation on the transfer of a business from one company to another, the transferor company is a necessary party). See also notes 3–4.

9 As to the meaning of 'share' see PARA 1231.

10 Ie in contravention of the Companies Act 2006 s 219 (see PARA 623): see s 222(3).

11 Companies Act 2006 s 222(3)(a). See also notes 3–4.

12 Companies Act 2006 s 222(3)(b). See also notes 3–4.

13 See PARA 626 et seq. Nothing in ss 217–222 applies in relation to a payment for loss of office to a director of a quoted company other than a payment to which s 226C (see PARA 626) does not apply by virtue of s 226D(6) (see PARA 626): see s 215(5) (added by the Enterprise and Regulatory Reform Act 2013 s 81(1), (4)). As to the meaning of 'quoted company' in the Companies Act 2006 see PARA 70; and see PARA 601 note 4.

(C) Payment to Directors for Loss of Office where Company is Quoted Company

626. Restrictions relating to payments for loss of office to directors of quoted companies. No payment for loss of office[1] may be made by any person to a person who is, or has been, a director[2] of a quoted company[3] unless[4]:

(1) the payment is consistent with the approved directors' remuneration policy[5], namely the most recent remuneration policy to have been approved by a resolution passed by the members of the company in general meeting[6]; or

(2) the payment is approved by resolution of the members of the company[7].

A resolution approving a payment for the purposes of head (2) above must not be passed unless a memorandum setting out particulars of the proposed payment, including its amount, is made available for inspection by the members of the company:

(a) at the company's registered office[8] for not less than 15 days ending with the date of the meeting at which the resolution is to be considered; and

(b) at that meeting itself[9].

The memorandum must explain the ways in which the payment is inconsistent with the approved directors' remuneration policy[10]. The company must ensure that the memorandum is made available on the company's website[11] from the first day on which the memorandum is made available for inspection[12] until its next accounts meeting[13]; but failure to comply with this requirement does not affect the validity of the meeting at which a resolution is passed approving a payment to which the memorandum relates or the validity of anything done at the meeting[14].

Nothing in heads (1) and (2) above:

(i) authorises the making of payment for loss of office in contravention of the articles[15] of the company concerned[16];

(ii) applies in relation to a payment for loss of office made to a person who is, or is to be or has been, a director of a quoted company before the earlier of:

(A) the end of the first financial year of the company to begin on or after the day on which it becomes a quoted company; and

(B) the date from which the company's first directors' remuneration policy to be approved[17] takes effect[18].

1 As to the meaning of 'payment for loss of office' see PARA 620.
2 As to the meaning of references to a 'director' for these purposes see PARA 601 note 4; and as to the meaning of references to a payment to a person who is, has been or is to be a director of a company see PARA 604 note 3.
3 As to the meaning of 'quoted company' for these purposes see PARA 601 note 4; and see PARA 70.
4 Companies Act 2006 s 226C(1) (ss 226C, 226D, 226F added by the Enterprise and Regulatory Reform Act 2013 s 80).
5 Companies Act 2006 s 226C(1)(a) (as added: see note 4). As to the meaning of 'directors' remuneration policy' see PARA 604 note 5.
6 See the Companies Act 2006 s 226C(2) (as added: see note 4). As to resolutions and meetings of members see PARA 701 et seq. As to voting at meetings see PARA 725 et seq. As to the meaning of 'member of a company' see PARA 323.
7 Companies Act 2006 s 226C(1)(b) (as added: see note 4). Where, however, the making of a payment to which s 226C applies requires approval by a resolution of the members of the company concerned under Pt 10 Ch 4 (ss 188–225) (see PARA 601 et seq, 606 et seq), approval obtained for the purposes of Pt 10 Ch 4 is to be treated as satisfying the requirements of s 226C(1)(b): s 226F(2) (as added: see note 2). The Companies Act 2006 Pt 10 Ch 4A does not affect any requirement for approval by a resolution of the members of a company which applies in relation to the company under Pt 10 Ch 4: s 226F(1) (as so added).
8 As to the company's registered office see PARA 124.
9 Companies Act 2006 s 226D(1) (as added: see note 2).
10 Companies Act 2006 s 226D(2) (as added: see note 2).
11 For these purposes, the 'company's website' is the website on which the company makes material available under the Companies Act 2006 s 430 (see PARA 945): s 226D(7) (as added: see note 2).
12 Ie under the Companies Act 2006 s 226D(1): see the text and notes 8–10.
13 Companies Act 2006 s 226D(3) (as added: see note 2). As to the meaning of 'accounts meeting' see PARA 946 note 4.
14 Companies Act 2006 s 226D(4) (as added: see note 2).
15 As to the meaning of references to a company's 'articles' under the Companies Act 2006 see PARA 227 note 2.
16 Companies Act 2006 s 226D(5) (as added: see note 2).
17 Ie under the Companies Act 2006 s 439A: see PARA 934.
18 Companies Act 2006 s 226D(6) (as added: see note 2).

627. Payments to director of quoted company in connection with share transfer or transfer of undertaking or property to be treated as payments for loss of office. Where, in connection with a relevant transfer[1], a director[2] of a quoted company[3] is to cease to hold office as director, or to cease to be the holder of:

(1) any other office or employment in connection with the management of the affairs of the company; or

(2) any office, as director or otherwise, or employment in connection with the management of the affairs of any subsidiary undertaking[4] of the company[5],

then if in connection with the transfer:

(a) the price to be paid to the director for any shares[6] in the company held by the director is in excess of the price which could at the time have been obtained by other holders of like shares; or

(b) any valuable consideration is given to the director by a person other than the company,

the excess or, as the case may be, the money value of the consideration is taken[7] to have been a payment for loss of office[8]. As such, it must either:

(i) be consistent with the approved directors' remuneration policy[9]; or

(ii) be approved by resolution of the members of the company[10];

but nothing in heads (i) and (ii) above authorises the making of payment for loss of office in contravention of the articles[11] of the company concerned[12], or applies in relation to a payment for loss of office made to a person who is, or is to be or has been, a director of a quoted company before the earlier of:

(A) the end of the first financial year of the company to begin on or after the day on which it becomes a quoted company; and

(B) the date from which the company's first directors' remuneration policy to be approved[13] takes effect[14].

1 For these purposes, 'relevant transfer' means the following (Companies Act 2006 s 226A(4) (ss 226A, 226D, 226F added by the Enterprise and Regulatory Reform Act 2013 s 80)), ie:
   (1) a transfer of the whole or any part of the undertaking or property of the company or a subsidiary of the company;
   (2) a transfer of shares in the company, or in a subsidiary of the company, resulting from a takeover bid.
2 As to the meaning of references to a 'director' for these purposes see PARA 601 note 4.
3 As to the meaning of 'quoted company' for these purposes see PARA 601 note 4; and see PARA 70.
4 As to the meaning of 'subsidiary undertaking' see PARA 23.
5 Companies Act 2006 s 226A(2) (as added: see note 1).
6 As to the meaning of 'share' see PARA 1231. As to share capital generally see PARA 1231 et seq.
7 Ie for the purposes of the Companies Act 2006 s 226C: see PARA 626.
8 Companies Act 2006 s 226A(3) (as added: see note 1). As to the meaning of 'payment for loss of office' see PARA 620.
9 See the Companies Act 226A(1)(a); and PARA 626 head (1). As to the meaning of 'directors' remuneration policy' see PARA 604 note 5.
10 See the Companies Act 226A(1)(b); and PARA 626 head (2). Where, however, the making of such a payment requires approval by a resolution of the members of the company concerned under Pt 10 Ch 4 (ss 188–225) (see PARAS 601 et seq, 606 et seq), approval obtained for the purposes of Pt 10 Ch 4 is to be treated as satisfying the requirements of s 226C(1)(b): s 226F(2) (as added: see note 2). The Companies Act 2006 Pt 10 Ch 4A does not affect any requirement for approval by a resolution of the members of a company which applies in relation to the company under Pt 10 Ch 4: s 226F(1) (as so added).
11 As to the meaning of references to a company's 'articles' under the Companies Act 2006 see PARA 227 note 2.
12 See the Companies Act 2006 s 226D(5) (as added: see note 1).
13 Ie under the Companies Act 2006 s 439A: see PARA 934.
14 See the Companies Act 2006 s 226D(6) (as added: see note 1).

628. Civil consequences of payments for loss of office made without approval. An obligation, however arising, to make a payment which would be in contravention of the statutory restrictions on payments for loss of office to directors of quoted companies[1] has no effect[2].

If a payment is made in contravention of those restrictions[3]:

(1) it is held by the recipient on trust for the company[4] or other person making the payment; and

(2) in the case of a payment by a company[5], any director[6] who authorised the payment is jointly and severally liable to indemnify the company that made the payment for any loss resulting from it[7].

If, however, in proceedings against a director for the enforcement of a liability under head (2) above, the director shows that he has acted honestly and reasonably, and the court considers that, having regard to all the circumstances of the case, the director ought to be relieved of liability, the court[8] may relieve the director, either wholly or in part, from liability on such terms as the court thinks fit[9].

If a payment for loss of office is made in contravention of the statutory restrictions[10] to a director of a quoted company:

(a) in connection with the transfer of the whole or any part of the undertaking[11] or property of the company or a subsidiary[12] of the company, head (2) above does not apply, and the payment is held by the recipient on trust for the company whose undertaking or property is or is proposed to be transferred[13];

(b) in connection with a transfer of shares[14] in the company, or in a subsidiary of the company, resulting from a takeover bid:
   (i) head (2) above does not apply;
   (ii) the payment is held by the recipient on trust for persons who have sold their shares as a result of the offer made; and
   (iii) the expenses incurred by the recipient in distributing that sum amongst those persons is to be borne by the recipient and not retained out of that sum[15].

1 Ie in contravention of the Companies Act 2006 s 226C: see PARAS 626–627. As to the meaning of 'quoted company' for these purposes see PARA 601 note 4; and see PARA 70; and as to the meaning of 'payment for loss of office' see PARA 620.
2 Companies Act 2006 s 226E(1) (s 226E added by the Enterprise and Regulatory Reform Act 2013 s 80).
3 See note 1.
4 As to the meaning of 'company' under the Companies Acts see PARA 21; and as to the meaning of the 'Companies Acts' see PARA 13.
5 As to the meaning of references to a payment by a company see PARA 604 note 2.
6 As to the meaning of references to a 'director' for these purposes see PARA 601 note 4.
7 Companies Act 2006 s 226E(2) (as added: see note 2).
8 As to the meaning of 'the court' see PARA 160 note 12.
9 Companies Act 2006 s 226E(5) (as added: see note 2).
10 See note 1.
11 As to the meaning of 'undertaking' see PARA 23 note 2.
12 As to the meaning of 'subsidiary' see PARA 22.
13 Companies Act 2006 s 226E(3) (as added: see note 2).
14 As to the meaning of 'share' see PARA 1231. As to share capital generally see PARA 1231 et seq.
15 Companies Act 2006 s 226E(4) (as added: see note 2).

(viii) Contracts involving Limited Company with Sole Member

629. Contracts with a sole member who is also a director. Where a limited company[1] having only one member[2] enters into a contract with the sole member of the company[3], and the sole member is also a director of the company[4], and where the contract is not entered into in the ordinary course of the company's business[5], the company must, unless the contract is in writing, ensure that the terms of the contract are either set out in a written memorandum[6] or recorded in the minutes of the first meeting of the directors of the company[7] following the making of the contract[8].

If a company fails to comply with this restriction[9], an offence is committed by every officer of the company who is in default[10], and a person guilty of such an offence is liable on summary conviction to a fine[11].

Nothing in the provisions which set out this restriction[12] is to be read as excluding the operation of any other enactment[13] or rule of law applying to contracts between a company and a director of that company[14]. Failure to comply with this restriction[15] in relation to a contract does not, however, affect the validity of that contract[16].

1 As to the meaning of 'limited company' see PARA 95. As to the meaning of 'company' under the Companies Acts see PARA 21; and as to the meaning of the 'Companies Acts' see PARA 13.
2 As to the meaning of 'member' see PARA 323.
3 Companies Act 2006 s 231(1)(a).

4 Companies Act 2006 s 231(1)(b). As to the meaning of 'director' under the Companies Acts see PARA 512. For these purposes, a shadow director is treated as a director: s 231(5). As to the meaning of 'shadow director' see PARA 513.
5 Companies Act 2006 s 231(1)(c). As to the meaning of 'business' generally see PARA 1 note 1.
6 Companies Act 2006 s 231(2)(a).
7 As to meetings of directors generally see PARA 568 et seq.
8 Companies Act 2006 s 231(2)(b).
9 Ie fails to comply with the Companies Act 2006 s 231: see s 231(3).
10 Companies Act 2006 s 231(3). As to the meaning of 'officer who is in default' see PARA 316. As to the meaning of 'officer' generally see PARA 679.
11 Companies Act 2006 s 231(4). In the case of liability on summary conviction the fine is one not exceeding level 5 on the standard scale: see s 231(4). By virtue of the Legal Aid, Sentencing and Punishment of Offenders Act 2012 s 85, however, where the offence is committed on or after 12 March 2015, it is punishable by a fine of an unlimited amount. As to the standard scale and the powers of magistrates' courts to issue fines on summary conviction see SENTENCING vol 92 (2015) PARA 176.
12 Ie nothing in the Companies Act 2006 s 231: see s 231(7).
13 As to the meaning of 'enactment' see PARA 13 note 16.
14 Companies Act 2006 s 231(7).
15 Ie failure to comply with the Companies Act 2006 s 231: see s 231(6).
16 Companies Act 2006 s 231(6).

(ix) Directors' Liabilities for Breach of Duty

A. LIABILITIES OF DIRECTORS

630. Directors' liability to company. A company's directors[1], acting as such within their powers[2] and within the powers of the company[3] and without fraud, negligence or breach of fiduciary duty, incur no personal liability[4]. Where, however, they expend the property of the company in a manner which is outside their powers, as, for example, in paying a dividend out of capital[5], or returning capital without legal reduction of capital[6], or making unauthorised investments[7], there is a liability on them to recoup any loss, and, if they occasion damage to the company by negligence, they may be liable to the extent of the damage caused[8]. If they dispose of the company's assets in breach of their fiduciary duties they may be treated as having committed a breach of trust and a director who is himself the recipient of assets holds them upon a trust for the company[9].

A director who signed various stock transfers whereby shares held by the company as trustee for a number of pension funds were transferred to another company of which he was also a director, without the authority of the board of directors, and as a result of the transfer the company suffered loss, was in breach of duty and liable to the company for the loss as he was exercising his powers for an improper purpose[10]. If a company is the victim of a conspiracy by its directors who force it to do something illegal, it is not to be regarded as a party thereto by reason of the directors' knowledge, but may sue them in conspiracy for any loss it suffers[11]. The claim may be brought by the company, but, where the cause of action arises from an actual or proposed act or omission involving negligence, default, breach of duty or breach of trust by a director of the company, any member of the company may take action, with the permission of the court[12]. It may be possible for the company to ratify conduct by a director amounting to a breach of duty, in which case no liability arises[13].

Proceedings may be taken in the winding up of a company against the directors for negligence, default, breach of duty, and breach of trust[14].

A claim may be made by the company or on behalf of the company, for example, by a liquidator, but, if the company has been dissolved, the liability of the directors is extinguished by that dissolution, unless the dissolution is set aside by the court[15].

1 As to a company's directors see PARA 512 et seq.
2 As to the powers of directors see PARA 584 et seq.
3 As to the powers of companies see PARA 251 et seq. As to acts which are beyond the board of directors' authority see PARA 582.
4 As to the general duties of directors see PARA 572 et seq.
5 *Re Sharpe, Re Bennett, Masonic and General Life Assurance Co v Sharpe* [1892] 1 Ch 154 at 165–166, CA, per Lindley LJ. See also *Flitcroft's Case* (1882) 21 ChD 519 at 535–536, CA, per Cotton LJ; *Bairstow v Queens Moat Houses plc* [2001] EWCA Civ 712, [2001] 2 BCLC 531; *Re Loquitur Ltd, IRC v Richmond* [2003] EWHC 999 (Ch) at [135]–[137], [2003] 2 BCLC 442 per Etherton J. See also PARA 1563.

Directors who took funds from their company in the form of interest-free loans and, at the end of each financial year, declared dividends which were then used to extinguish their liability to the company were jointly and severally liable for the repayment of the outstanding loans when they were unable to establish that a dividend had been properly declared: *Queensway Systems Ltd (in liquidation) v Walker* [2006] EWHC 2496 (Ch), [2007] 2 BCLC 577.

6 See *Moxham v Grant* [1900] 1 QB 88, CA (claim for repayment enforceable against directors or shareholders; directors entitled to indemnity); *Holmes v Newcastle-upon-Tyne Freehold Abattoir Co* (1875) 1 ChD 682 (all shareholders and persons who took part in the transaction being before the court, repayment ordered). The doing of ultra vires acts may also be restrained: *Smith v Duke of Manchester* (1883) 24 ChD 611. See also PARA 582.
7 *Re Lands Allotment Co* [1894] 1 Ch 616, CA.
8 As to a director's duty to exercise reasonable care, skill and diligence see PARA 588 et seq.
9 As to a director's liability for breach of trust see PARA 631.
10 *Bishopsgate Investment Management Ltd (in liquidation) v Maxwell (No 2)* [1994] 1 All ER 261 at 265, CA, per Hoffmann LJ. As to the common law principles which govern the exercise of a company's powers for an improper purpose see PARA 583.
11 *Belmont Finance Corpn Ltd v Williams Furniture Ltd* [1979] Ch 250, [1979] 1 All ER 118, CA (financial aid by company for purchase of its own shares).
12 See the Companies Act 2006 Pt 11 Ch 1 (ss 260–264) (derivative claims in England and Wales or Northern Ireland); and PARA 646 et seq.
13 See PARA 638.
14 See COMPANY AND PARTNERSHIP INSOLVENCY vol 17 (2011) PARA 646 et seq. See also eg *City of London Group plc v Lothbury Financial Services Ltd* [2012] EWHC 3148 (Ch), [2012] All ER (D) 188 (Nov) (director did not breach fiduciary duty to company by transferring business as he had not embarked on strategy with company's administration in mind).
15 *Coxon v Gorst* [1891] 2 Ch 73. As to the power of the court to declare a dissolution void see COMPANY AND PARTNERSHIP INSOLVENCY vol 17 (2011) PARA 896.

631. Breach of trust by directors. Although the directors of a company[1] are not properly speaking trustees, they have always been considered and treated as trustees of company money or property which comes into their hands or which is under their control[2]. A director who has misapplied or retained or become liable or accountable for any money or property of the company is treated as having committed a breach of trust and must make good the money or property so misapplied and account for any gains made by him[3].

Where the loss arises from the unauthorised application of the company's property, the measure of compensation is the value of the company's property which has been misapplied and the director may be held liable even though he has not himself received any of the misapplied property[4]. If improper dividends are paid, on the basis that either statute or common law has been breached, the entire amount is recoverable from the directors[5]. If, on the other hand, a dividend could lawfully be declared, and the directors declare an excessive dividend, the directors are liable only for the excess, being the unlawful part[6]. If a director is the recipient of company assets obtained in breach of his fiduciary duties, he holds those assets on trust for the company as a result of his pre-existing trustee-like responsibilities to the company[7]. In this way, the underlying basis of the liability of a director who exploits, after his resignation, a maturing business opportunity of the company is that the opportunity is to be treated as if it were the property of the company in relation to which the director had fiduciary duties; by seeking to exploit the opportunity after resignation, he is appropriating to himself that property, and he is just as accountable as a trustee who retires without properly accounting for trust property[8].

Where the director's breach of fiduciary duty does not involve any use of the company's assets or property, so that the question is not one of a specific fund or asset being returned to the company, his liability is a personal liability in equity to account to the company for unauthorised profits made by him which are treated as taken for and on behalf of the company[9].

A director may also be liable to pay equitable compensation to a company where, as a result of a breach of fiduciary duty on his part, the company has suffered loss[10].

Where the money of the company has been applied for purposes which the company cannot sanction, the directors must replace it, however honestly they may have acted[11].

A director is liable for the acts of his co-directors, if, knowing that they intend to commit a breach of trust, he does not, by applying for an injunction or otherwise[12], take steps to prevent it. A managing director is equally responsible although required 'to act under the orders and directions of the board'[13]. However, a director is not so liable where he does not know of the breach of trust before or at its occurrence, for example, by his absence from a board meeting, and does not expressly or tacitly concur in its continuance[14]. If he is in fact acting on the instructions of a third party, he will be fixed with that person's knowledge of the transaction[15]. Merely attending a director's meeting which confirms the illegal acts of a past meeting is not necessarily sufficient to fix responsibility[16]. The liability of directors participating in breaches of trust and in respect of secret profits is joint and several[17].

The estate of a deceased director has always been liable for his breaches of trust[18]; and, since 25 July 1934[19], all causes of action subsisting against a deceased person at his death generally survive against his estate[20].

1 As to a company's directors see PARA 512 et seq.

2 *Re Lands Allotment Co* [1894] 1 Ch 616, CA; *Re Forest of Dean Coal Mining Co* (1878) 10 ChD 450 at 453 per Jessel MR; *Re Sharpe, Re Bennett, Masonic and General Life Assurance Co v Sharpe* [1892] 1 Ch 154 at 165, CA, per Lindley LJ; *Belmont Finance Corpn Ltd v Williams Furniture Ltd (No 2)* [1980] 1 All ER 393 at 404, CA, per Buckley LJ; *Re Duckwari plc* [1999] Ch 253, sub nom *Re Duckwari plc (No 2), Duckwari plc v Offerventure Ltd (No 2)* [1998] 2 BCLC 315, CA; *JJ Harrison(Properties) Ltd v Harrison* [2001] EWCA Civ 1467, [2002] 1 BCLC 162; *Re Loquitur Ltd, IRC v Richmond* [2003] EWHC 999 (Ch) at [135], [2003] 2 BCLC 442 per Etherton J; *Gwembe Valley Development Co Ltd v Koshy (No 3)* [2003] EWCA Civ 1048, [2004] 1 BCLC 131. As to the directors' position at common law as trustees of the company's property see PARA 579 et seq.

3 *Flitcroft's Case* (1882) 21 ChD 519 at 535–536, CA, per Cotton LJ; *Bairstow v Queens Moat Houses plc* [2001] EWCA Civ 712, [2001] 2 BCLC 531; *JJ Harrison(Properties) Ltd v Harrison* [2001] EWCA Civ 1467, [2002] 1 BCLC 162; *Re Duckwari plc* [1999] Ch 253, sub nom *Re Duckwari plc (No 2), Duckwari plc v Offerventure Ltd (No 2)* [1998] 2 BCLC 315, CA; *Re Loquitur Ltd, IRC v Richmond* [2003] EWHC 999 (Ch) at [135]–[137], [2003] 2 BCLC 442 per Etherton J; *Re MDA Investment Management Ltd, Whalley v Doney* [2004] EWHC 42 (Ch), [2004] All ER (D) 165 (Jan). See also the cases cited in note 2; and *Land Credit Co of Ireland v Lord Fermoy* (1870) 5 Ch App 763 (company's money used for purchasing its shares); *Joint Stock Discount Co v Brown* (1869) LR 8 Eq 381 (buying shares in another company); *Imperial Mercantile Credit Association v Chapman* (1871) 19 WR 379 (loans to brokers for losses incurred in 'bulling' the market); *Selangor United Rubber Estates Ltd v Cradock (a bankrupt) (No 3)*

[1968] 2 All ER 1073, [1968] 1 WLR 1555 (company's money utilised for acquisition of its own shares). See also *Access Bank plc v Akingbola* [2012] EWHC 2148 (Comm), [2012] All ER (D) 02 (Aug).

As to the duty to account see further *CMS Dolphin Ltd v Simonet* [2001] 2 BCLC 704 (profits from subsequent contracts); *Re Quarter Master UK Ltd, Quarter Master UK v Pyke* [2004] EWHC 1815 (Ch), [2005] 1 BCLC 245 (liability of director and company through which his profits are channelled); *Murad v Al-Saraj* [2005] EWCA Civ 959 at [56], [77], [108], [2005] All ER (D) 503 (Jul) (purpose of accounting and burden of proof); *Kingsley IT Consulting Ltd v McIntosh* [2006] EWHC 1288 (Ch), [2006] All ER (D) 237 (Feb) (profits from subsequent contracts); *Foster Bryant Surveying Ltd v Bryant* [2007] EWCA Civ 200 at [88], [101], [2007] 2 BCLC 239 (purpose of accounting).

Proceedings for misfeasance are generally taken in the winding up of the company: see COMPANY AND PARTNERSHIP INSOLVENCY vol 17 (2011) PARA 646.

4 *Gwembe Valley Development Co Ltd v Koshy (No 3)* [2003] EWCA Civ 1048 at [142], [2004] 1 BCLC 131 per Mummery LJ.

5 *Re Lands Allotment Co* [1894] 1 Ch 616, CA; *Bairstow v Queens Moat Houses plc* [2001] EWCA Civ 712, [2001] 2 BCLC 531, distinguishing *Target Holdings Ltd v Redferns (a firm)* [1996] AC 421, [1995] 3 All ER 785, HL. See also *Inn Spirit Ltd v Burns* [2002] EWHC 1731 (Ch), [2002] 2 BCLC 780; *Allied Carpets Group plc v Nethercott* [2001] BCC 81. Quaere whether directors might be excused under the Companies Act 2006 s 1157 (see PARA 645) from repaying more than is necessary to enable creditors to be paid in full: *Inn Spirit Ltd v Burns* [2002] EWHC 1731 (Ch) at [30], [2002] 2 BCLC 780 per Rimer J.

6 See *Re Marini Ltd* [2003] EWHC 334 (Ch), [2004] BCC 172.

7 *JJ Harrison(Properties) Ltd v Harrison* [2001] EWCA Civ 1467, [2002] 1 BCLC 162. See also *Allied Carpets Group plc v Nethercott* [2001] BCC 81; *Clark v Cutland* [2003] EWCA Civ 810, [2003] 4 All ER 733, [2004] 1 WLR 783 (company entitled to proprietary remedy where unauthorised payments to pension fund trustees were received by them as innocent volunteers); *Bracken Partners Ltd v Gutteridge* [2003] EWCA Civ 1875, [2004] 1 BCLC 377; *Primlake Ltd v Matthew Associates* [2006] EWHC 1227 (Ch), [2007] 1 BCLC 666; and the cases cited in notes 5–6.

8 See *CMS Dolphin Ltd v Simonet* [2001] 2 BCLC 704; approved in *Foster Bryant Surveying Ltd v Bryant* [2007] EWCA Civ 200 at [8]–[10], [2007] 2 BCLC 239 per Rix LJ.

9 *Gwembe Valley Development Co Ltd v Koshy (No 3)* [2003] EWCA Civ 1048 at [118], [2004] 1 BCLC 131 per Mummery LJ; and see also this case at first instance, sub nom *DEG-Deutsche Investitions und Entwicklungsgesellschaft mbH v Koshy (No 2), Gwembe Valley Development Co Ltd v Koshy (No 3)* [2002] 1 BCLC 478 at 561 per Rimer J. The court will impose a constructive trust on such profits for the company's benefit, such trust being a class 2 trust within the classification given in *Paragon Finance plc v DB Thakerar & Co* [1999] 1 All ER 400 at 408–409, CA, per Millett LJ, ie a trust obligation arising directly out of an unlawful transaction which gave rise to the profits and which is impeached by the claimant: *Gwembe Valley Development Co Ltd v Koshy (No 3)* [2003] EWCA Civ 1048 at [119], [2004] 1 BCLC 131 per Mummery LJ. See also *Premier Waste Management Ltd v Towers* [2011] EWCA Civ 923, [2012] IRLR 73, [2012] 1 BCLC 67 (director required to account for secret profit from unapproved loan of equipment by supplier where no evidence of loss to company or value to him).

10 *Swindle v Harrison* [1997] 4 All ER 705, CA; *Target Holdings Ltd v Redferns (a firm)* [1996] AC 421, [1995] 3 All ER 785, HL. Quaere whether the remedy of equitable compensation is available, as distinct from the remedies of rescission and account of profits, where there is a mere failure by a director to disclose his interest in a transaction with a company: *Gwembe Valley Development Co Ltd v Koshy (No 3)* [2003] EWCA Civ 1048 at [143], [2004] 1 BCLC 131 per Mummery LJ. See also *Extrasure Travel Insurances Ltd v Scattergood* [2002] EWHC 3093 (Ch), [2003] 1 BCLC 598; and *Shepherds Investments Ltd v Walters* [2006] EWHC 836 (Ch), [2007] 2 BCLC 202.

11 *Re Sharpe, Re Bennett, Masonic and General Life Assurance Co v Sharpe* [1892] 1 Ch 154 at 165–166, CA, per Lindley LJ; *Cullerne v London and Suburban General Permanent Building Society* (1890) 25 QBD 485 at 490, CA, per Lindley LJ, overruling *Pickering v Stephenson* (1872) LR 14 Eq 322. See also *Peel v London and North Western Rly Co* [1907] 1 Ch 5 at 20, CA, per Buckley LJ; *London Trust Co Ltd v Mackenzie* (1893) 62 LJ Ch 870; contra *Re Kingston Cotton Mill Co (No 2)* [1896] 1 Ch 331 at 346 per Vaughan Williams J (revsd on one point [1896] 2 Ch 279, CA). Where money paid to a company for a particular purpose has been misapplied by the sole shareholders and directors, they may be personally liable to account for the company's breach of trust to the persons paying the money: *Brenes & Co v Downie* 1914 SC 97, Ct of Sess.

12 *Re Lands Allotment Co* [1894] 1 Ch 616, CA; *Neville v Krikorian* [2006] EWCA Civ 943, [2007] 1 BCLC 1. Cf *J & P Coats Ltd v Crossland* (1904) 20 TLR 800; *British Midland Tool Ltd*

v Midland International Tooling Ltd [2003] EWHC 466 (Ch), [2003] 2 BCLC 523. A protest is not sufficient (*Jackson v Munster Bank* (1885) 15 LR Ir 356; *Joint Stock Discount Co v Brown* (1869) LR 8 Eq 381). See also *Ramskill v Edwards* (1885) 31 ChD 100 at 111 per Pearson J; *Land Credit Co of Ireland v Lord Fermoy* (1870) 5 Ch App 763; *London Trust Co Ltd v Mackenzie* (1893) 62 LJ Ch 870. Acquiescence is not to be too readily inferred: *Ashhurst v Mason* (1875) LR 20 Eq 225. As to ratification by acquiescence see AGENCY vol 1 (2008) PARA 68.

13 *Ramskill v Edwards* (1885) 31 ChD 100.

14 *Cargill v Bower* (1878) 10 ChD 502; *Caledonian Heritable Security Co (liquidator) v Curror's Trustee* (1882) 9 R 1115 (loan without security); *Re Denham & Co* (1883) 25 ChD 752 (dividends paid out of capital); *Marquis of Bute's Case* [1892] 2 Ch 100.

15 *Selangor United Rubber Estates Ltd v Cradock (No 3)* [1968] 2 All ER 1073, [1968] 1 WLR 1555. See also PARA 632.

16 *Re Montrotier Asphalte Co, Perry's Case* (1876) 34 LT 716; *Ashhurst v Mason* (1875) LR 20 Eq 225.

17 *Re Carriage Co-operative Supply Association* (1884) 27 ChD 322; *Re Englefield Colliery Co* (1878) 8 ChD 388, CA; *Re Oxford Benefit Building and Investment Society* (1886) 35 ChD 502; *Leeds Estate Building and Investment Co v Shepherd* (1887) 36 ChD 787; *Re Faure Electric Accumulator Co* (1888) 40 ChD 141 at 158 per Kay J. Cf *General Exchange Bank v Horner* (1870) LR 9 Eq 480; *Gluckstein v Barnes* [1900] AC 240 at 255, HL, per Lord Macnaghten; *Re Duckwari plc* [1999] Ch 253 at 262, sub nom *Re Duckwari plc (No 2), Duckwari plc v Offerventure Ltd (No 2)* [1998] 2 BCLC 315 at 322, CA, per Nourse LJ. See also *Benson v Heathorn* (1842) 1 Y & C Ch Cas 326.

18 *Re Sharpe, Re Bennett, Masonic and General Life Assurance Co v Sharpe* [1892] 1 Ch 154, CA; *Joint Stock Discount Co v Brown* (1869) LR 8 Eq 381; *Ramskill v Edwards* (1885) 31 ChD 100. Cf *Shepheard v Bray* [1906] 2 Ch 235 (revsd by consent, and doubted [1907] 2 Ch 571, CA).

19 Ie the date on which the Law Reform (Miscellaneous Provisions) Act 1934 came into force.

20 See the Law Reform (Miscellaneous Provisions) Act 1934 s 1; and WILLS AND INTESTACY vol 103 (2010) PARA 1280 et seq. There are certain immaterial exceptions: see s 1(1); and WILLS AND INTESTACY vol 103 (2010) PARA 1280.

632. Liability of persons sharing in breach of trust by directors. All persons dealing with a director[1], knowing that he is committing a breach of trust in the transaction, must repay the loss to the company with interest[2].

In a claim based on knowing receipt of trust funds, the test for knowledge in such a claim is simply whether the defendant's knowledge makes it unconscionable for him to retain the benefit of the receipt[3]. A third party who dishonestly procures or assists the directors in a breach of their fiduciary duties is liable; and for the most part dishonesty is to be equated with conscious impropriety[4]. A fraudulent breach of trust is established in such cases where a person is proved to have acted in a way that was contrary to normally acceptable standards of honest conduct, and was conscious of, or deliberately turned a blind eye to, those elements of the transaction in question that made his participation fall below those standards; but it is not necessary to establish that the person in question knew or gave any thought to what amounted to normally acceptable standards of conduct[5].

A director who is in partnership is liable as regards his separate estate for the property of a company which has come into the hands of his firm and which is misappropriated by his firm with his concurrence[6].

1 As to a company's directors see PARA 512 et seq.

2 *Gray v Lewis* (1869) LR 8 Eq 526 at 544 per Sir R Malins V-C (revsd on the facts (1873) 8 Ch App 1035). Cf *Lund v Blanshard* (1844) 4 Hare 9; *Bryson v Warwick and Birmingham Canal Co* (1853) 4 De GM & G 711. As to the rate of interest see TRUSTS AND POWERS vol 98 (2013) PARA 692.

3 *Bank of Credit and Commerce International (Overseas) Ltd (in liquidation) v Akindele* [2001] Ch 437, [2000] 4 All ER 221, CA. See also *Crown Dilmun v Sutton* [2004] EWHC 52 (Ch) at [200], [2004] 1 BCLC 468 per Peter Smith J; and TRUSTS AND POWERS vol 98 (2013) PARA 131.

4 *Royal Brunei Airlines Sdn Bhd v Tan* [1995] 2 AC 378, [1995] 3 All ER 97, PC. See also *Twinsectra Ltd v Yardley* [2002] UKHL 12 at [36], [2002] 2 AC 164, [2002] 2 All ER 377 per Lord Hutton (dishonesty requires knowledge by the defendant that what he was doing would be

regarded as dishonest by honest people, although he should not escape a finding of dishonesty because he sets his own standards of honesty and does not regard as dishonest what he knows would offend the normally accepted standards of honest conduct). See also *Crown Dilmun v Sutton* [2004] EWHC 52 (Ch) at [204], [2004] 1 BCLC 468 per Peter Smith J; *Bracken Partners Ltd v Gutteridge* [2003] EWCA Civ 1875, [2004] 1 BCLC 377; *Barlow Clowes International Ltd (in Liquidation) v Eurotrust International Ltd* [2005] UKPC 37, [2006] 1 All ER 333, [2006] 1 WLR 1476; *Abou-Ramah v Abacha* [2006] EWCA Civ 1492, [2007] 1 All ER (Comm) 827; *Mullarkey v Broad* [2007] EWHC 3400 (Ch), [2008] 1 BCLC 638; *Statek Corpn v Alford* [2008] EWHC 32 (Ch), [2008] BCC 266, [2008] All ER (D) 52 (Jan); *Novoship (UK) Ltd v Nikitin* [2014] EWCA Civ 908, [2015] QB 499, [2014] All ER (D) 63 (Jul) (dishonest solicitation and receipt of bribes). Accessory liability for dishonest assistance in a breach of trust is discussed fully in TRUSTS AND POWERS vol 98 (2013) PARA 131; but see also the text and note 5.

As to the duties of directors to safeguard the assets of the company, and for that purpose to take reasonable steps to prevent and detect fraud and other irregularities, see eg *Re Barings (No 5)* [1999] 1 BCLC 433; *Re Westmid Packing Services Ltd* [1988] 2 BCLC 646, CA; *Lexi Holdings (in administration) v Luqman* [2009] EWCA Civ 117, [2009] 2 BCLC 1, [2009] BCC 716; and see PARA 589.

5 See *Mullarkey v Broad* [2007] EWHC 3400 (Ch) at [36]–[38], [2008] 1 BCLC 638 per Lewison J, following *Abou-Ramah v Abacha* [2006] EWCA Civ 1492 at [69], [2007] 1 All ER (Comm) 827 per Arden LJ, in stating that the meaning of dishonesty in this respect is as laid down in *Twinsectra Ltd v Yardley* [2002] UKHL 12, [2002] 2 AC 164, [2002] 2 All ER 377, as interpreted in *Barlow Clowes International Ltd (in Liquidation) v Eurotrust International Ltd* [2005] UKPC 37, [2006] 1 All ER 333.

6 *Re Macfadyen, ex p Vizianagaram Mining Co Ltd* [1908] 2 KB 817, CA. The proof is for a debt and not for damages: *Re Macfadyen, ex p Vizianagaram Mining Co Ltd*; *Re Collie, ex p Adamson* (1878) 8 ChD 807 at 819, CA, per James LJ and Baggallay LJ.

633. Directors' liability for breach of duty in tort. A company's directors[1] are not liable for the company's torts unless they themselves committed or authorised[2], directed or procured the commission of the tortious act[3]; the mere fact that its directors are the sole directors and shareholders will not automatically render them liable for torts committed by the company[4]. Nor is a governing or managing director automatically so liable[5]. Such liability is not automatic; if the tort involved required some particular state of mind or knowledge on the part of the tortfeasor, the director could not be made liable without proof that he himself had that state of mind or knowledge[6]. However, the suggestion that he must, to be liable, in every case act deliberately or recklessly is not justified[7].

A director is not liable as joint tortfeasor with the company, on the basis that he authorised, directed or procured the wrongful act, if he does no more than carry out his constitutional role in the governance of the company[8].

A director cannot escape liability for deceit on the ground that his act was committed on behalf of the company[9]; but he will not be liable for negligent misstatement where the claimant cannot establish any assumption of responsibility on the part of the director on which the claimant could reasonably rely[10].

Where the director is liable personally for the commission of a tort, his liability depends upon the usual principles and does not derive from his status as director, regardless of the fact that others, such as a company, may be liable also for the same tort, depending on the circumstances[11].

1 As to a company's directors see PARA 512 et seq.

2 See note 11.

3 *Rainham Chemical Works v Belvedere Fish Guano Co* [1921] 2 AC 465 at 475–476, HL, per Lord Buckmaster; *Performing Right Society Ltd v Ciryl Theatrical Syndicate Ltd* [1924] 1 KB 1 at 14–15, CA, per Atkin LJ; *British Thomson-Houston Co Ltd v Sterling Accessories Ltd* [1924] 2 Ch 33; *Mancetter Developments Ltd v Garmanson Ltd* [1986] QB 1212, [1986] 1 All ER 449, CA. See also *Wah Tat Bank Ltd v Chan Cheng Kum* [1975] AC 507, [1975] 2 All ER 257, PC; *C Evans & Sons Ltd v Spritebrand Ltd* [1985] 2 All ER 415, [1985] 1 WLR 317, CA; *Trevor*

Ivory Ltd v Anderson [1992] 2 NZLR 517, NZCA; *MCA Records Inc v Charly Records Ltd* [2001] EWCA Civ 1441, [2002] FSR 401, [2003] 1 BCLC 93.

4 *British Thomson-Houston Co Ltd v Sterling Accessories Ltd* [1924] 2 Ch 33. See also *Societa Esplosivi Industriali SpA v Ordnance Technologies Ltd* [2007] EWHC 2875 (Ch), [2008] 2 All ER 622, [2008] 2 BCLC 428 (defendant, as the only director and shareholder in the defendant company, had personal liability for breaching, or allowing the breach of, the claimant's design right).

5 *Performing Right Society Ltd v Ciryl Theatrical Syndicate Ltd* [1924] 1 KB 1 at 14–15, CA, per Atkin LJ.

6 *C Evans & Sons Ltd v Spritebrand Ltd* [1985] 2 All ER 415 at 424, [1985] 1 WLR 317 at 329, CA, per Slade LJ.

7 *C Evans & Sons Ltd v Spritebrand Ltd* [1985] 2 All ER 415, [1985] 1 WLR 317, CA (disapproving *White Horse Distillers Ltd v Gregson Associates Ltd* [1984] RPC 61 and dictum of Whitford J in *Hoover plc v George Hulme (Stockport) Ltd* [1982] FSR 565 at 595–597; and doubting *Mentmore Manufacturing Co Ltd v National Merchandising Manufacturing Co Inc* (1978) 89 DLR (3d) 195).

8 *MCA Records Inc v Charly Records Ltd* [2001] EWCA Civ 1441, [2002] FSR 401, [2003] 1 BCLC 93 (intellectual property infringement); *Koninklijke Philips Electronics NV v Prico Digital Disc GmbH* [2003] EWHC 2588 (Ch), [2004] 2 BCLC 50 (patent infringement).

9 *Standard Chartered Bank v Pakistan National Shipping Corpn (No 2)* [2002] UKHL 43, [2003] 1 AC 959, [2003] 1 BCLC 244 (director liable not because he was a director but because he had committed a fraud); and see *GE Commercial Finance Ltd v Gee* [2005] EWHC 2056 (QB), [2006] 1 Lloyd's Rep 337 (intent to enter into conspiracy in order to benefit the group and to injure the claimant not shared by all directors).

10 *Williams v Natural Life Health Foods Ltd* [1998] 2 All ER 577, [1998] 1 BCLC 689, HL. See also *Partco Group Ltd v Wragg* [2002] EWCA Civ 594, [2002] 2 Lloyd's Rep 343, [2002] 2 BCLC 323. See also the Companies Act 2006 s 463 (liability for false or misleading statements in reports); and PARA 949.

11 *Standard Chartered Bank v Pakistan National Shipping Corpn (No 2)* [2003] 1 AC 959, [2003] 1 BCLC 244, HL (fraudulent misrepresentation). See also *Williams v Natural Life Health Foods Ltd* [1998] 2 All ER 577, [1998] 1 BCLC 689, HL (negligent misstatement); *Noel v Poland* [2001] 2 BCLC 645 (fraudulent misrepresentation); *Contex Drouzhba Ltd v Wiseman* [2007] EWCA Civ 1201, [2008] 1 BCLC 631; and MISREPRESENTATION vol 76 (2013) PARA 803.

634. Directors' liability for false statements etc in offer documents etc. Directors[1] may incur liability to persons who subscribe for shares or debentures of the company in reliance on offer documents which contain material misrepresentations of fact[2].

They may also incur liability by reason of false reports made by them to the company with the intention of attracting investors, and acted on by a subsequent investor to his damage[3].

A director is not liable for untrue representations made to the shareholders in the balance sheets of the company if he honestly believed the representations to be true, and acted without negligence[4]. Where a company is formed to take over an existing business which turns out to be ruinous, the directors will not be responsible for making the purchase unless the ruinous nature of the business must have been obvious to any person acting with an ordinary degree of prudence, on the same principle that protects an agent purchasing by authority of his principal[5]. Shareholders will be liable in damages to persons to whom they have sold their shares on the faith of fraudulent statements made on their behalf by a director authorised to negotiate on their behalf[6].

A director who has in fact retired is not liable for subsequent statements or acts, although he may know that his name is appearing on a report which is impugned[7].

1 As to a company's directors see PARA 512 et seq.

2 As to statutory liability for misstatements see PARA 1259 et seq. As to claims in deceit see PARA 1270 et seq.

3 *Scott v Dixon* (1859) 29 LJ Ex 62n. See further PARA 1087.

4 *Dovey v Cory* [1901] AC 477, HL.

5 *Overend, Gurney & Co v Gibb and Gibb* (1872) LR 5 HL 480 at 487, 495 per Lord Hatherley LC. See AGENCY vol 1 (2008) PARA 74 et seq.
6 *Briess v Woolley* [1954] AC 333, [1954] 1 All ER 909, HL.
7 *Re National Bank of Wales Ltd* [1899] 2 Ch 629, CA; affd on other grounds sub nom *Dovey v Cory* [1901] AC 477, HL.

635. Directors' liability to creditors. A company's directors[1] are not trustees for the creditors, present[2] or future[3], of the company, even as regards one to whom the company stands in a fiduciary relationship[4]. The creditors, therefore, except as holders of security on any property of the company, and for the purpose of realising their security, have no right of interference with the company or its affairs, and have no remedy against a director for negligence in the conduct of its business[5] or for breach of contract by the company[6]. A creditor cannot obtain an injunction against either the company or its directors in respect of ultra vires acts[7]. However, the rule making the directors liable for ultra vires acts operates to preserve the capital of the company and make it available for payment of creditors[8].

Directors may, however, be liable to third persons for breach of warranty of authority to act on behalf of the company[9]; and they are also jointly and severally liable, if a public company of which they are directors enters into transactions before the company has been issued by the registrar with a certificate that it may do business and exercise borrowing powers[10] and then fails to comply with its obligations in that connection within 21 days from being called upon to do so, to indemnify the other party to the transaction in respect of any loss or damage suffered by him by reason of such failure by the company[11].

Directors are not liable in negligence to the company's creditors unless particular circumstances exist, for example, by way of agreement or a contractual guarantee[12].

1 As to a company's directors see PARA 512 et seq.
2 *Poole, Jackson and Whyte's Case* (1878) 9 ChD 322, CA (where directors paid up their shares in full, whereby a creditor was preferred in obtaining payment and they themselves were relieved from liability as guarantors); *Re AM Wood's Ships' Woodite Protection Co Ltd* (1890) 62 LT 760 (where directors, in good faith, paid themselves remuneration in advance which they applied in payment of amounts unpaid on their shares).
3 *Multinational Gas and Petrochemical Co v Multinational Gas and Petrochemical Services Ltd* [1983] Ch 258 at 288, [1983] 2 All ER 563 at 585, CA, per Dillon LJ. See also *Kuwait Asia Bank EC v National Mutual Life Nominees Ltd* [1991] 1 AC 187, [1990] 3 All ER 404, PC (in circumstances where a bank held a beneficial interest in a company and appointed two directors of that company as its nominees, it was decided that a shareholder or other person who has powers to appoint a director, without fraud or bad faith, owes no duty to creditors of the company to make sure that any director so appointed discharges his duties appropriately); *Yukong Lines Ltd of Korea v Rendsburg Investments Corpn of Liberia, The Rialto (No 2)* [1998] 4 All ER 82, [1998] 1 WLR 294 (the director of an insolvent company did not owe a direct fiduciary duty towards an individual creditor nor was an individual creditor entitled to sue for breach of the fiduciary duty owed by the director to the company). See also PARA 585.
4 *Bath v Standard Land Co Ltd* [1911] 1 Ch 618, CA. A director does, however, have a duty in some circumstances to consider or act in the interests of creditors: see PARA 585.
5 *Wilson v Lord Bury* (1880) 5 QBD 518, CA.
6 *Ferguson v Wilson* (1866) 2 Ch App 77 (where an action was founded on a resolution of the board to allot shares to the plaintiff).
7 *Mills v Northern Rly of Buenos Ayres Co* (1870) 5 Ch App 621; and see *Lawrence v West Somerset Mineral Rly Co* [1918] 2 Ch 250 at 256–257 per Eve J.
8 As to acts which are beyond the board of directors' authority see PARA 582. Redress for individual creditors may lie through misfeasance proceedings by liquidators under the Insolvency Act 1986 s 212 (as to which see COMPANY AND PARTNERSHIP INSOLVENCY vol 17 (2011) PARA 646 et seq) or, if the conditions are met, through liability for fraudulent or wrongful trading under the Insolvency Act 1986 ss 213, 214 (as to which see COMPANY AND PARTNERSHIP INSOLVENCY vol 17 (2011) PARAS 869, 872) or, if conditions are met, from the adjustment of prior

transactions under s 238 (as to which see COMPANY AND PARTNERSHIP INSOLVENCY vol 17 (2011) PARA 801 et seq), or arising from breach by a director of the company name requirements under s 216 (see s 217; and COMPANY AND PARTNERSHIP INSOLVENCY vol 17 (2011) PARA 874 et seq) or as a result of acting while disqualified (see the Company Directors Disqualification Act 1986 s 15(1)(a); and PARA 1808).

9 *Firbank's Executors v Humphreys* (1886) 18 QBD 54, CA; *Elkington & Co v Hurter* [1892] 2 Ch 452; *West London Commercial Bank v Kitson* (1884) 13 QBD 360, CA (acceptance of bills). See also PARA 462. If the misrepresentation is as to law, they will not be liable: *Rashdall v Ford* (1866) LR 2 Eq 750; *Beattie v Lord Ebury* (1874) LR 7 HL 102. See AGENCY vol 1 (2008) PARA 160.

10 See the Companies Act 2006 s 761(1); and PARA 67.

11 See the Companies Act 2006 s 767(3); and PARA 69.

12 See *Nordic Oil Services Ltd v Berman* 1993 SLT 1164, Ct of Sess.

636. Termination of directors' liability. A director who is charged with breach of trust may plead the Limitation Act 1980 except where the claim is founded upon any fraud or fraudulent breach of trust to which he was a party or privy[1], or is to recover trust property or its proceeds[2] still, at the time of the proceedings brought[3], retained by him or previously received by him and converted to his use[4].

If money wrongfully paid has been replaced before litigation either specifically or by contra accounts, the directors cannot be made liable in misfeasance proceedings[5].

An order of discharge in bankruptcy releases a director from any liability for a breach of trust, unless it is a fraudulent breach of trust[6].

1 *Gwembe Valley Development Co Ltd v Koshy (No 3)* [2003] EWCA Civ 1048, [2004] 1 BCLC 131. See also *Mullarkey v Broad* [2007] EWHC 3400 (Ch), [2008] 1 BCLC 638; and PARA 632.

2 *JJ Harrison (Properties) Ltd v Harrison* [2001] EWCA Civ 1467, [2002 1 BCLC 162.

3 *Thorne v Heard and Marsh* [1894] 1 Ch 599, CA.

4 See the Limitation Act 1980 s 21; *Gwembe Valley Development Co Ltd v Koshy (No 3)* [2003] EWCA Civ 1048, [2004] 1 BCLC 131; *JJ Harrison (Properties) Ltd v Harrison* [2001] EWCA Civ 1467, [2002] 1 BCLC 162; *Eurocruit Europe Ltd (in liquidation), Goldfarb v Poppleton* [2007] EWHC 1433 (Ch), [2007] 2 BCLC 598 (claim under the Insolvency Act 1986 s 212 (as to which see COMPANY AND PARTNERSHIP INSOLVENCY vol 17 (2011) PARA 646 et seq) did not have a limitation period distinct from the limitation period applicable to the underlying claim); *Statek Corpn v Alford* [2008] EWHC 32 (Ch), [2008] BCC 266, [2008] All ER (D) 52 (Jan); and see *Re Lands Allotment Co* [1894] 1 Ch 616, CA; *Re Sharpe, Re Bennett, Masonic and General Life Assurance Co v Sharpe* [1892] 1 Ch 154, CA. See further PARA 579; and LIMITATION PERIODS vol 68 (2008) PARA 1140 et seq. As to claims in respect of the statutory liability with regard to offer documents see PARA 1259.

5 *Re David Ireland & Co* [1905] 1 IR 133, CA.

6 See generally BANKRUPTCY AND INDIVIDUAL INSOLVENCY vol 5 (2013) PARA 649 et seq. As to a company's directors see PARA 512 et seq.

637. Directors' right to contribution. A director[1] is entitled to contribution from such of his co-directors as have concurred in an ultra vires transaction in respect of which money has been recovered from him[2]. This is an equitable right quite apart from contract[3], and is available against the estate of a deceased director who was liable to contribute[4].

Shareholders who receive illegal payments knowingly, being constructive trustees for the company, must indemnify directors who are called upon to repay, or must themselves repay, if sued directly[5]. A director who has had the sole benefit of the breach of trust may not claim contribution against his co-directors[6].

In a claim for contribution the defendant is not estopped from disputing the validity of the judgment in the claim against the claimant[7].

Directors who have concurred in the cancellation of the shares of a co-director in pursuance of an transaction agreement, although they may be liable to the company, are not liable to their co-director for contribution towards his liability for costs[8].

1 As to a company's directors see PARA 512 et seq.

2 *Ashhurst v Mason* (1875) LR 20 Eq 225 (where he was transferee of unpaid shares to relieve an ex-director); *Ramskill v Edwards* (1885) 31 ChD 100 (where he had afterwards concurred in an unauthorised loan); and see *Queensway Systems Ltd (in liquidation) v Walker* [2006] EWHC 2496 (Ch) at [75], [2007] 2 BCLC 577 per Paul Girolami QC (causative responsibility is only one, albeit important, factor in determining what contribution it is just and equitable to order). As to acts which are ultra vires the company or beyond the board of directors' authority see PARA 582.

3 *Jackson v Dickinson* [1903] 1 Ch 947; *Ramskill v Edwards* (1885) 31 ChD 100 (where the defendant died after the action was brought); *Shepheard v Bray* [1906] 2 Ch 235 (compromised on appeal [1907] 2 Ch 571, CA); *Wolmershausen v Gullick* [1893] 2 Ch 514. As to contribution in respect of statutory liability with regard to offer documents see PARA 1259.

4 See note 3.

5 *Moxham v Grant* [1900] 1 QB 88, CA; *Re National Funds Assurance Co* (1878) 10 ChD 118 at 129 per Jessel MR (cases of dividends paid out of capital).

6 *Walsh v Bardsley* (1931) 47 TLR 564.

7 See *Parker v Lewis* (1873) 8 Ch App 1056; *Shepheard v Bray* [1906] 2 Ch 235 (compromised on appeal [1907] 2 Ch 571, CA). Cf *Printing, Telegraph and Construction Co of the Agence Havas v Drucker* [1894] 2 QB 801, CA; *Furness, Withy & Co Ltd v Pickering* [1908] 2 Ch 224; *Wye Valley Rly Co v Hawes* (1880) 16 ChD 489, CA.

8 *Walkers' Case* (1856) 8 De GM & G 607.

638. Ratification of acts giving rise to liability. Under the Companies Act 2006[1], a company[2] may ratify conduct[3] by a director[4] amounting to negligence, default, breach of duty or breach of trust[5] in relation to the company[6]. However, any conduct so authorised must be bona fide and honest and not likely to jeopardise the company's solvency or cause loss to its creditors[7].

The decision of the company to ratify such conduct must be made by resolution of the members of the company[8]. Where the resolution is proposed as a written resolution[9] neither the director (if a member of the company) nor any member connected with him[10] is an eligible member[11]. Where the resolution is proposed at a meeting, it is passed only if the necessary majority is obtained disregarding votes in favour of the resolution by the director (if a member of the company) and any member connected with him[12].

Nothing in these provisions[13] affects the validity of a decision taken by unanimous consent of the members of the company[14], or any power of the directors to agree not to sue, or to settle or release a claim made by them on behalf of the company[15].

Nor do these provisions[16] affect any other enactment[17] or rule of law imposing additional requirements for valid ratification or any rule of law as to acts that are incapable of being ratified by the company[18].

1 Ie by means of the Companies Act 2006 s 239, which applies: see s 239(1).

2 As to the meaning of 'company' under the Companies Acts see PARA 21; and as to the meaning of the 'Companies Acts' see PARA 13.

3 For these purposes, 'conduct' includes acts and omissions: Companies Act 2006 s 239(5)(a).

4 For these purposes, 'director' includes a former director; and a shadow director is treated as a director: Companies Act 2006 s 239(5)(c), (c). As to the meaning of 'director' under the Companies Acts see PARA 512; and as to the meaning of 'shadow director' see PARA 513.

5 The Companies Act 2006 contains for the first time a statutory statement of directors' duties: see Pt 10 Ch 2 (ss 170–181); and PARA 572 et seq. As to directors' fiduciary duties owed to the company see PARA 584 et seq.

6 Companies Act 2006 s 239(1).

7 *Bowthorpe Holdings Ltd v Hills* [2002] EWHC 2331 (Ch) at [51], [2003] 1 BCLC 226 per Morritt V-C, citing *Re Horsley & Weight Ltd* [1982] Ch 442 at 455, [1982] 3 All ER 1045 at 1055, CA, per Cumming-Bruce LJ, and at 456 and 1056 per Templeman LJ. See also *Rolled Steel Products (Holdings) Ltd v British Steel Corp* [1986] Ch 246 at 296, [1985] 3 All ER 52 at 86–87, CA, per Slade LJ; *West Mercia Safetywear Ltd v Dodd* [1988] BCLC 250 at 252, CA, per Dillon LJ; *Official Receiver v Stern* [2001] EWCA Civ 1787 at [31]–[33], [2002] 1 BCLC 119 per Morritt V-C. As to ratification in the context of an application to continue a claim under the derivative action provisions see PARA 654 et seq. See also PARA 277.

8 Companies Act 2006 s 239(2). As to the meaning of 'member of the company' see PARA 323. As to resolutions and meetings of members see PARA 701 et seq. As to voting at meetings see PARA 725 et seq.
9 As to the meaning of 'written resolution' see PARA 695.
10 As to the meaning of references to a director being 'connected' with a person see PARA 515. For these purposes, in the Companies Act 2006 s 252 (meaning of 'connected person') (see PARA 515), s 252(3) does not apply (exclusion of person who is himself a director): s 239(5)(d). The 'connected person' provisions in s 239(3), (4) impose additional requirements for effective ratification.
11 Companies Act 2006 s 239(3). As to eligible members in relation to a resolution proposed as a written resolution of a private company see PARA 695. See also note 10.
12 Companies Act 2006 s 239(4). This provision does not prevent the director or any such member from attending, being counted towards the quorum and taking part in the proceedings at any meeting at which the decision is considered: s 239(4). See also note 10. As to the quorum at company meetings see PARA 718.
13 Ie nothing in the Companies Act 2006 s 239: see s 239(6).
14 Companies Act 2006 s 239(6)(a). See PARA 738.
15 Companies Act 2006 s 239(6)(b).
16 Ie the Companies Act 2006 s 239: see s 239(7).
17 As to the meaning of 'enactment' see PARA 13 note 16.
18 Companies Act 2006 s 239(7).

B. DIRECTORS' STATUTORY PROTECTION FROM CERTAIN LIABILITIES

639. Avoidance of exemptions from directors' liability. Any provision[1] that purports to exempt a director[2] of a company, to any extent, from any liability that would otherwise attach to him in connection with any negligence, default[3], breach of duty or breach of trust[4] in relation to the company is void[5].

Any provision by which a company, directly or indirectly, provides an indemnity, to any extent, for a director of the company, or of an associated company[6], against any liability attaching to him in connection with any negligence, default, breach of duty or breach of trust in relation to the company of which he is a director, is also void[7], except as permitted by the provisions which allow a company to provide insurance against any such liability[8], or to provide qualifying third party indemnity[9], or to provide qualifying pension scheme indemnity[10].

1 The Companies Act 2006 s 232 applies to any provision, whether contained in a company's articles or in any contract with the company or otherwise: s 232(3). The words 'or otherwise' must be construed ejusdem generis with the preceding words, the genus being any arrangement between the company and its officers: *Burgoine v Waltham Forest London Borough Council* [1997] 2 BCLC 612 (decided under the Companies Act 1985 s 310 (repealed; see now the Companies Act 2006 ss 232, 532, 533; and see also PARAS 1052–1053). Nothing in the Companies Act 2006 s 232 prevents a company's articles from making such provision as has previously been lawful for dealing with conflicts of interest: s 232(4). As to the meaning of 'company' under the Companies Acts see PARA 21; and as to the meaning of the 'Companies Acts' see PARA 13. As to the meaning of references to a company's 'articles' see PARA 227 note 2. As to model articles of association prescribed for the purposes of the Companies Act 2006, and their application generally, see PARA 227 et seq. Different versions of model articles have been so prescribed for use by private companies limited by shares (see the Companies (Model Articles) Regulations 2008, SI 2008/3229, reg 2, Sch 1), private companies limited by guarantee (see reg 3, Sch 2), and public companies (see reg 4, Sch 3). As to the meanings of 'company limited by guarantee', 'company limited by shares', 'limited company', 'private company' and 'public company' see PARA 95. The default articles prescribed for the purposes of the Companies Act 1985 ('legacy articles'), ie the Companies (Tables A to F) Regulations 1985, SI 1985/805, have not been revoked and may, in their amended form, continue to be used by companies after the commencement of the Companies Act 2006: see PARA 229. As to conflicts of interest see PARA 590 et seq.
2 As to the meaning of 'director' under the Companies Acts see PARA 512.
3 *Customs and Excise Comrs v Hedon Alpha Ltd* [1981] QB 818, [1981] 2 All ER 697, CA (the word 'default' signified misconduct by an officer or auditor of the company in that capacity). See also *Re Duckwari plc* [1999] Ch 253 at 265–266, sub nom *Re Duckwari plc (No 2), Duckwari plc*

v Offerventure Ltd (No 2) [1998] 2 BCLC 315 at 325, CA; and *Queensway Systems Ltd (in liquidation) v Walker* [2006] EWHC 2496 (Ch) at [66]–[68], [2007] 2 BCLC 577.

4 The Companies Act 2006 contains for the first time a statutory statement of directors' duties (see Pt 10 Ch 2 (ss 170–181); and PARA 572 et seq); and the extent to which these general duties may be modified is limited to modifications permitted by the relevant duty (see eg s 173(2)(b) (conduct authorised by the company's constitution); and PARA 587) and by s 180 (which provides that, where the need to avoid conflicts of interest is complied with by directors' authorisation, the transaction or arrangement is not liable to be set aside by virtue of any common law rule or equitable principle requiring the consent or approval of the members of the company, subject to any enactment, or provision of the company's constitution, requiring such consent or approval: see PARA 591). *Movitex Ltd v Bulfield* [1988] BCLC 104 (which considered the scope available under the then-existing statutory provisions to modify directors' obligations) needs to be considered now in the light of the statutory framework provided by the Companies Act 2006. As to directors' fiduciary duties owed to the company generally see PARA 584 et seq.

5 Companies Act 2006 s 232(1). See also note 1. As to provision made for the ratification of acts giving rise to liability see PARA 638. As to the statutory provisions that are intended to protect auditors from liability see ss 532, 533; and PARAS 1052–1053. See also *Mutual Reinsurance Co Ltd v Peat Marwick Mitchell & Co* [1997] 1 Lloyd's Rep 253, [1997] 1 BCLC 1, CA (auditors).

The repeal of the Companies Act 1985 ss 306, 307 and of the Insolvency Act 1986 s 75 (provisions relating to unlimited liability of directors and others) does not affect the operation of those provisions in relation to liabilities arising before 1 October 2009 or in connection with the holding of an office to which a person was appointed before that date on the understanding that their liability would be unlimited: see the Companies Act 2006 (Consequential Amendments, Transitional Provisions and Savings) Order 2009, SI 2009/1941, art 9.

6 As to the meaning of companies which are 'associated' for the purposes of the Companies Act 2006 Pt 10 (ss 154–259) (see PARA 512 et seq) see PARA 611 note 3.

7 Companies Act 2006 s 232(2). See also note 1. Under the Companies Act 1985 s 310 (repealed; see now the Companies Act 2006 s 232; and see also PARAS 1052–1053), the prohibition was held to apply only to indemnities given by the company concerned and not to indemnities given by third parties (see *Burgoine v Waltham Forest London Borough Council* [1997] 2 BCLC 612); but that loophole has now been closed by the Companies Act 2006 s 232(2).

The Companies (Model Articles) Regulations 2008, SI 2008/3229, provide that a relevant director of the company or an associated company may be indemnified out of the company's assets against:

(1) any liability incurred by that director in connection with any negligence, default, breach of duty or breach of trust in relation to the company or an associated company (Sch 1 art 52(1)(a), Sch 2 art 38(1)(a), Sch 3 art 85(1)(a));
(2) any liability incurred by that director in connection with the activities of the company or an associated company in its capacity as a trustee of an occupational pension scheme as defined in the Companies Act 2006 s 235(6) (see PARA 641) (Companies (Model Articles) Regulations 2008, SI 2008/3229, Sch 1 art 52(1)(b), Sch 2 art 38(1)(b), Sch 3 art 85(1)(b));
(3) any other liability incurred by that director as an officer of the company or an associated company (Sch 1 art 52(1)(c), Sch 2 art 38(1)(c), Sch 3 art 85(1)(c)).

However, these provisions do not authorise any indemnity which would be prohibited or rendered void by any provision of the Companies Acts or by any other provision of law: Sch 1 art 52(2), Sch 2 art 38(2), Sch 3 art 85(2). For these purposes, companies are 'associated' if one is a subsidiary of the other or both are subsidiaries of the same body corporate; and a 'relevant director' means any director or former director of the company or an associated company: Sch 1 art 52(3), Sch 2 art 38(3), Sch 3 art 85(3). There is no equivalent provision made in the Companies (Tables A to F) Regulations 1985, SI 1985/805, but Schedule Table A art 118 provides for every director or other officer or auditor of the company to be indemnified against any liability incurred by him in defending any proceedings, whether civil or criminal, in which judgment is given in his favour or in which he is acquitted or in connection with any application in which relief is granted to him by the court from liability for negligence, default, breach of duty or breach of trust in relation to the affairs of the company: see PARA 641.

8 Companies Act 2006 s 232(2)(a). The text refers to the provision which is allowed by s 233 (see PARA 640): see s 232(2)(a). See also note 1.

9 Companies Act 2006 s 232(2)(b). The text refers to the provision which is allowed by s 234 (see PARA 641): see s 232(2)(b). See also note 1.

10 Companies Act 2006 s 232(2)(c). The text refers to the provision which is allowed by s 235 (see PARA 641): see s 232(2)(c). See also note 1.

640. Exception for provision of insurance against directors' liability. The statutory prohibition[1] on a company[2], either directly or indirectly, providing an indemnity, to any extent, for a director[3] of the company, or of an associated company[4], against any liability attaching to him in connection with any negligence, default, breach of duty or breach of trust in relation to the company of which he is a director, is subject to the proviso that this provision[5] does not prevent a company from purchasing and maintaining for a director of the company, or of an associated company, insurance against any such liability[6].

1 Ie the prohibition contained in the Companies Act 2006 s 232(2) (see PARA 639): see s 233.
2 As to the meaning of 'company' under the Companies Acts see PARA 21; and as to the meaning of the 'Companies Acts' see PARA 13.
3 As to the meaning of 'director' under the Companies Acts see PARA 512.
4 As to the meaning of companies which are 'associated' for the purposes of the Companies Act 2006 Pt 10 (ss 154–259) (see PARA 512 et seq) see PARA 611 note 3.
5 Ie the Companies Act 2006 s 232(2) (see PARA 639): see s 233.
6 Companies Act 2006 s 233. The text refers to any such liability as is mentioned in s 232(2) (see PARA 639): see s 233.

The model articles of association that have been prescribed for the purposes of the Companies Act 2006 (ie the Companies (Model Articles) Regulations 2008, SI 2008/3229: see PARA 227 et seq) provide that directors may decide to purchase and maintain insurance, at the expense of the company, for the benefit of any relevant director in respect of any relevant loss: Sch 1 art 53(1), Sch 2 art 39(1), Sch 3 art 86(1). For these purposes, a 'relevant director' means any director or former director of the company or an associated company; a 'relevant loss' means any loss or liability which has been or may be incurred by a relevant director in connection with that director's duties or powers in relation to the company, any associated company or any pension fund or employees' share scheme of the company or associated company; and companies are 'associated' if one is a subsidiary of the other or both are subsidiaries of the same body corporate: Sch 1 art 53(2), Sch 2 art 39(2), Sch 3 art 86(2). Different versions of model articles have been so prescribed for use by private companies limited by shares (see the Companies (Model Articles) Regulations 2008, SI 2008/3229, reg 2, Sch 1), private companies limited by guarantee (see reg 3, Sch 2), and public companies (see reg 4, Sch 3). As to the meanings of 'company limited by guarantee', 'company limited by shares', 'limited company', 'private company' and 'public company' see PARA 95. The default articles prescribed for the purposes of the Companies Act 1985 ('legacy articles'), ie the Companies (Tables A to F) Regulations 1985, SI 1985/805, have not been revoked and may, in their amended form, continue to be used by companies after the commencement of the Companies Act 2006: see PARA 229. No provision is made therein which is equivalent exactly to that made in the Companies (Model Articles) Regulations 2008, SI 2008/3229, but see PARAS 639 note 7, 641 note 10.

641. Exception for provision of qualifying indemnities. The statutory prohibition[1] on a company[2], either directly or indirectly, providing an indemnity, to any extent, for a director[3] of the company, or of an associated company[4], against any liability attaching to him in connection with any negligence, default, breach of duty or breach of trust in relation to the company of which he is a director, is subject to the proviso that this provision[5] does not apply to:

(1) qualifying third party indemnity provision[6]; or
(2) qualifying pension scheme indemnity provision[7].

For the purposes of head (1) above, 'third party indemnity provision' means provision for indemnity against liability incurred by the director to a person other than the company or an associated company[8]; and such provision is 'qualifying third party indemnity provision' if the following requirements are met[9], namely that the provision must not provide any indemnity against[10]:

(a) any liability of the director to pay a fine imposed in criminal proceedings[11], or a sum payable to a regulatory authority by way of a penalty in respect of non-compliance with any requirement of a regulatory nature, however arising[12]; or

(b) any liability incurred by the director in defending criminal proceedings in which he is convicted[13], or in defending civil proceedings brought by the company, or an associated company, in which judgment is given against him[14], or in connection with an application for relief[15] in which the court refuses to grant him relief[16].

For the purposes of head (2) above, 'pension scheme indemnity provision' means a provision indemnifying a director of a company that is a trustee of an occupational pension scheme[17] against liability incurred in connection with the company's activities as trustee of the scheme[18]; and such provision is a 'qualifying pension scheme indemnity provision' if the following requirements are met[19], namely that the provision must not provide any indemnity against[20]:

(i) any liability of the director to pay a fine imposed in criminal proceedings[21], or a sum payable to a regulatory authority by way of a penalty in respect of non-compliance with any requirement of a regulatory nature, however arising[22]; or

(ii) any liability incurred by the director in defending criminal proceedings in which he is convicted[23].

A qualifying indemnity provision[24] must be disclosed in the directors' report[25].

1 Ie the prohibition contained in the Companies Act 2006 s 232(2) (see PARA 639): see ss 234(1), 235(1).
2 As to the meaning of 'company' under the Companies Acts see PARA 21; and as to the meaning of the 'Companies Acts' see PARA 13.
3 As to the meaning of 'director' under the Companies Acts see PARA 512.
4 As to the meaning of companies which are 'associated' for the purposes of the Companies Act 2006 Pt 10 (ss 154–259) (see PARA 512 et seq) see PARA 611 note 3.
5 Ie the Companies Act 2006 s 232(2) (see PARA 639): see ss 234(1), 235(1).
6 Companies Act 2006 s 234(1).
7 Companies Act 2006 s 235(1).
8 Companies Act 2006 s 234(2).
9 See note 8.
10 Companies Act 2006 s 234(3).

Cf the Companies (Tables A to F) Regulations 1985, SI 1985/805, reg 2, Schedule Table A art 118, which provides that, subject to the provisions of the Companies Acts, but without prejudice to any indemnity to which a director may otherwise be entitled, every director or other officer or auditor of the company must be indemnified out of the assets of the company against any liability incurred by him in defending any proceedings, whether civil or criminal, in which judgment is given in his favour or in which he is acquitted or in connection with any application in which relief is granted to him by the court from liability for negligence, default, breach of duty or breach of trust in relation to the affairs of the company. This article may be so framed as to cover proceedings for liability for ultra vires acts: *Viscount of the Royal Court of Jersey v Shelton* [1986] 1 WLR 985, PC (disapproving dictum of Lindley LJ in *Cullerne v London and Suburban General Permanent Building Society* (1890) 25 QBD 485 at 488, CA, and applying *Re Claridge's Patent Asphalte Co Ltd* [1921] 1 Ch 543). A director's expenses of defending himself against an allegation that he did something which he did not in fact do and which it was not his duty to do are not incurred by him as such and are therefore not recoverable under an indemnity covering 'any act done by him as director', or under the general law: *Tomlinson v Scottish Amalgamated Silks Ltd (liquidators)* 1935 SC (HL) 1. As to the statutory provisions that are intended to protect auditors from liability see PARAS 1052–1053. The default articles prescribed for the purposes of the Companies Act 1985 ('legacy articles'), ie the Companies (Tables A to F) Regulations 1985, SI 1985/805, have not been revoked and may, in their amended form, continue to be used by companies after the commencement of the Companies Act 2006: see PARA 229. The Companies (Tables A to F) Regulations 1985, SI 1985/805, Schedule Table A provides regulations for the management of a company limited by shares but Table A art 118 is applied by Table C (regulations for the management of a company limited by guarantee and not having a share capital), Table D Pt III (regulations for the management of a company limited by guarantee and having a share capital), and Table E (an unlimited company having a share capital). As to the meanings of 'company limited by guarantee', 'company limited by shares', 'limited company', 'public company' and 'unlimited company' see PARA 95. As to the meanings of 'company having a share capital' and 'share capital' see PARA 1231. As to the general provision that is made in similar vein by the Companies (Model Articles) Regulations 2008, SI 2008/3229, see PARA 639 note 7.

11 Companies Act 2006 s 234(3)(a)(i).
12 Companies Act 2006 s 234(3)(a)(ii).
13 Companies Act 2006 s 234(3)(b)(i). The references in s 234(3)(b) to a conviction, judgment or refusal of relief are to the final decision in the proceedings: s 234(4). For this purpose, a conviction, judgment or refusal of relief becomes final (if not appealed against) at the end of the period for bringing an appeal or (if appealed against) when the appeal (or any further appeal) is disposed of (s 234(5)(a)); and an appeal is disposed of if it is determined and the period for bringing any further appeal has ended, or if it is abandoned or otherwise ceases to have effect (s 234(5)(b)). See also note 10.
14 Companies Act 2006 s 234(3)(b)(ii). See also note 13.
15 The reference in the Companies Act 2006 s 234(3)(b)(iii) to an application for relief is to an application for relief under s 661(3) or s 661(4) (power of court to grant relief in case of acquisition of shares by innocent nominee) (see PARA 1386), or under s 1157 (general power of court to grant relief in case of honest and reasonable conduct) (see PARA 645): s 234(6).
16 Companies Act 2006 s 234(3)(b)(iii). See also note 13. As to the meaning of 'the court' see PARA 160 note 12.
17 For this purpose, 'occupational pension scheme' means a pension scheme as defined in the Finance Act 2004 s 150(5) (ie a pension scheme established by an employer or employers and having (or capable of having) effect so as to provide benefits to or in respect of any or all of the employees of that employer or those employers, or any other employer (whether or not it also has or is capable of having effect so as to provide benefits to or in respect of other persons)) that is established under a trust: Companies Act 2006 s 235(6).
18 Companies Act 2006 s 235(2).
19 See note 18.
20 Companies Act 2006 s 235(3).
21 Companies Act 2006 s 235(3)(a)(i).
22 Companies Act 2006 s 235(3)(a)(ii).
23 Companies Act 2006 s 235(3)(b). The reference in s 235(3)(b) to a conviction is to the final decision in the proceedings: s 235(4). For this purpose, a conviction becomes final (if not appealed against) at the end of the period for bringing an appeal or (if appealed against) when the appeal (or any further appeal) is disposed of (s 235(5)(a)); and an appeal is disposed of if it is determined and the period for bringing any further appeal has ended, or if it is abandoned or otherwise ceases to have effect (s 235(5)(b)).
24 Ie a qualifying third party indemnity provision or a qualifying pension scheme indemnity provision: see the Companies Act 2006 s 236(1); and PARA 642.
25 See the Companies Act 2006 s 236(1); and PARA 642.

642. Required disclosure in directors' report of qualifying indemnity provision. The Companies Act 2006[1] requires disclosure in the directors' report[2] of any qualifying third party indemnity provision[3], and any qualifying pension scheme indemnity provision[4]. Such provision is referred for these purposes as 'qualifying indemnity provision'[5].

If, when a directors' report is approved[6], any qualifying indemnity provision, whether made by the company or otherwise, is in force for the benefit of one or more directors of the company, the report must state that such provision is in force[7]; and if at any time during the financial year to which a directors' report relates any such provision was in force for the benefit of one or more persons who were then directors of the company, the report must state that such provision was in force[8].

If when a directors' report is approved qualifying indemnity provision made by the company is in force for the benefit of one or more directors of an associated company[9], the report must state that such provision is in force[10]; and if at any time during the financial year to which a directors' report relates any such provision was in force for the benefit of one or more persons who were then directors of an associated company, the report must state that such provision was in force[11].

1 Ie the Companies Act 2006 s 236: see s 236(1).

2 As to the duty imposed on the directors of a company to prepare a directors' report for each financial year of the company see PARA 894 et seq. As to the meaning of 'company' under the Companies Acts see PARA 21; and as to the meaning of 'director' under the Companies Acts see PARA 512. As to the meaning of the 'Companies Acts' see PARA 13. As to the meaning of 'financial year' see PARA 785.
3 As to qualifying third party indemnity provision see the Companies Act 2006 s 234; and PARA 641.
4 Companies Act 2006 s 236(1). As to qualifying pension scheme indemnity provision see s 235; and PARA 641.
5 Companies Act 2006 s 236(1).
6 As to the approval of directors' reports see PARA 906 et seq.
7 Companies Act 2006 s 236(2).
8 Companies Act 2006 s 236(3).
9 As to the meaning of companies which are 'associated' for the purposes of the Companies Act 2006 Pt 10 (ss 154–259) (see PARA 512 et seq) see PARA 611 note 3.
10 Companies Act 2006 s 236(4).
11 Companies Act 2006 s 236(5).

643. Copy of qualifying indemnity provision must be available for inspection. Where qualifying indemnity provision[1] is made for a director[2] of a company[3], then the company of which he is a director, whether the provision is made by that company or an associated company[4], and, where the provision is made by an associated company, that company, or, as the case may be, each of those companies, must keep available for inspection[5]:

(1) a copy of the qualifying indemnity provision[6]; or
(2) if the provision is not in writing, a written memorandum setting out its terms[7].

The copy or memorandum must be kept available for inspection either at the company's registered office[8], or at a place specified in regulations[9]. The copy or memorandum must be retained by the company for at least one year from the date of termination or expiry of the provision and must be kept available for inspection during that time[10].

The company must give notice to the registrar of companies[11]:

(a) of the place at which the copy or memorandum is kept available for inspection[12]; and
(b) of any change in that place[12],

unless it has at all times been kept at the company's registered office[14].

If default is made in complying with any of the requirements so to keep any qualifying indemnity provision available for inspection[15], or to keep it available in the proper place[16], or to retain it for the proper length of time[17], or if default is made for 14 days in complying with the requirement to give notice to the registrar of companies[18], an offence is committed by every officer of the company who is in default[19].

1 For these purposes, 'qualifying indemnity provision' means qualifying third party indemnity provision and qualifying pension scheme indemnity provision: Companies Act 2006 s 237(9). As to qualifying third party indemnity provision and qualifying pension scheme indemnity provision see PARA 641.
2 As to the meaning of 'director' under the Companies Acts see PARA 512. As to the meaning of the 'Companies Acts' see PARA 13.
3 As to the meaning of 'company' under the Companies Acts see PARA 21
4 As to the meaning of companies which are 'associated' for the purposes of the Companies Act 2006 Pt 10 (ss 154–259) (see PARA 512 et seq) see PARA 611 note 3.
5 See the Companies Act 2006 s 237(1), (2). The provisions of s 1138 (duty to take precautions against falsification) do not apply to the documents required to be kept under s 237: see PARA 747. As to a members' right to inspect and request a copy of any qualifying indemnity provision see PARA 644.

Where the registrar changes the address of a company's registered office under the Companies Act 2006 s 1097A(7) or the Companies (Address of Registered Office) Regulations 2016, SI 2016/423 (see PARA 160), the company's duties under the Companies Act 2006 s 237 are suspended for a period of 28 days beginning on the day the address was changed: see the Companies (Address of Registered Office) Regulations 2016, SI 2016/423, reg 11; and PARA 160.

6 Companies Act 2006 s 237(2)(a). The provisions of s 237 apply to a variation of a qualifying indemnity provision as they apply to the original provision: s 237(8).

7 Companies Act 2006 s 237(2)(b).

8 Companies Act 2006 s 237(3)(a). As to a company's registered office see PARA 124.

9 Companies Act 2006 s 237(3)(b). The text refers to a place specified in regulations made under s 1136 (see PARA 748): see s 237(3)(b).

10 Companies Act 2006 s 237(4).

11 Companies Act 2006 s 237(5). As to the meaning of 'registrar of companies' see PARA 126 note 2. As to the delivery of documents to the registrar see PARA 136; and as to the requirements for the proper delivery of documents to the registrar see PARA 137.

12 Companies Act 2006 s 237(5)(a).

12 Companies Act 2006 s 237(5)(a).

14 Companies Act 2006 s 237(5).

15 Ie in complying with the Companies Act 2006 s 237(2) (see the text and notes 5–7): see s 237(6).

16 Ie in complying with the Companies Act 2006 s 237(3) (see the text and notes 8–9): see s 237(6).

17 Ie in complying with the Companies Act 2006 s 237(4) (see the text and note 10): see s 237(6).

18 Ie in complying with the Companies Act 2006 s 237(5) (see the text and notes 11–14): see s 237(6).

19 Companies Act 2006 s 237(6). As to the meaning of 'officer who is in default' see PARA 316. As to the meaning of 'officer' generally see PARA 679.

A person guilty of such an offence is liable on summary conviction to a fine not exceeding level 3 on the standard scale and for continued contravention to a daily default fine not exceeding one-tenth of level 3 on the standard scale: s 237(7). As to the standard scale and the powers of magistrates' courts to issue fines on summary conviction see SENTENCING vol 92 (2015) PARA 176; and as to the meaning of 'daily default fine' see PARA 1816.

644. Members' right to inspect and request copy of qualifying indemnity provision. Every copy or memorandum that is required to be kept pursuant to the duty of a company[1] to keep any qualifying indemnity provision[2] available for inspection[3] must be open to inspection by any member of the company[4] without charge[5].

Any member of the company is entitled also, on request and on payment of such fee as may be prescribed[6], to be provided with a copy of any such copy or memorandum[7]. The copy must be provided within seven days after the request is received by the company[8].

If an inspection so required by a member of a company[9] is refused, or if default is made in so providing a member with a copy or memorandum[10], an offence is committed by every officer of the company who is in default[11]. A person guilty of such an offence is liable on summary conviction to a fine not exceeding level 3 on the standard scale[12] and for continued contravention to a daily default fine[13] not exceeding one-tenth of level 3 on the standard scale[14].

In the case of any such refusal or default, the court[15] may by order compel an immediate inspection or, as the case may be, direct that the copy required be sent to the person requiring it[16].

1 As to the meaning of 'company' under the Companies Acts see PARA 21; and as to the meaning of the 'Companies Acts' see PARA 13.

2 Ie any qualifying third party indemnity provision or qualifying pension scheme indemnity provision: see PARA 641.

3 Ie under the Companies Act 2006 s 237 (see PARA 643): see s 238(1).

4 As to the meaning of 'member of the company' see PARA 323.

5 Companies Act 2006 s 238(1).

6 In the Companies Acts, 'prescribed' means prescribed (by order or by regulations) by the Secretary of State: Companies Act 2006 s 1167. As to the making of regulations under the Companies Act

2006 generally see ss 1288–1292. As to the Secretary of State see PARA 6. Partly in exercise of the powers conferred by s 238(2), the Secretary of State has made the Companies (Fees for Inspection and Copying of Company Records) Regulations 2007, SI 2007/2612. See further note 7.

7 Companies Act 2006 s 238(2). For the prescribed fee see the Companies (Fees for Inspection and Copying of Company Records) Regulations 2007, SI 2007/2612, reg 4. As to the provision made for the sending of documents or information from a company (the 'company communications provisions') see PARA 750 et seq.

8 Companies Act 2006 s 238(2).

9 Ie under the Companies Act 2006 s 238(1) (see the text and notes 1–5): see s 238(3).

10 Ie in complying with the Companies Act 2006 s 238(2) (see the text and notes 6–8): see s 238(3).

11 Companies Act 2006 s 238(3). As to the meaning of 'officer who is in default' see PARA 316. As to the meaning of 'officer' generally see PARA 679.

12 As to the standard scale and the powers of magistrates' courts to issue fines on summary conviction see SENTENCING vol 92 (2015) PARA 176.

13 As to the meaning of 'daily default fine' see PARA 1816.

14 Companies Act 2006 s 238(4).

15 As to the meaning of 'the court' see PARA 160 note 12.

16 Companies Act 2006 s 238(5). As to the procedure for making claims and applications to the court under companies legislation see PARA 306. See also PARA 535 note 47.

645. Power of court to give relief against liability of directors etc. If, in proceedings for negligence, default, breach of duty or breach of trust[1] against:

(1) an officer of a company[2]; or

(2) a person employed by a company as auditor[3] (whether or not he is an officer of the company)[4],

it appears to the court[5] hearing the case that the officer or person is or may be liable, but that he acted honestly and reasonably[6] and that, having regard to all the circumstances of the case[7], including those connected with his appointment, he ought fairly to be excused, the court may relieve him, either wholly or in part, from his liability on such terms as the court thinks fit[8]. The power to grant relief does not extend to relief against claims by third parties[9], being limited to proceedings the essential nature of which is to enforce, at the suit of, or on behalf of, the company, the duties that a director or other person owes to the company[10].

Where such a case is being tried by a judge with a jury, the judge may, after hearing the evidence and if he is satisfied that the defendant ought[11] to be relieved either in whole or in part from the liability sought to be enforced against him, withdraw the case from the jury and forthwith direct judgment to be entered for the defendant on such terms as to costs or otherwise as the judge may think proper[12].

If any such officer or person as is mentioned in head (1) or head (2) above has reason to apprehend that a claim will or might be made against him in respect of negligence, default, breach of duty or breach of trust[13], then he may apply to the court for relief[14]; and the court on any such application has the same power to relieve him as it would have had if it had been a court before which proceedings against him for negligence, default, breach of duty or breach of trust had been brought[15].

Under the provisions described above, a director may be relieved against liability in respect of a transaction that is wholly ultra vires[16] or where he has acted without obtaining[17] or after ceasing to hold[18] his qualification shares[19].

1 The Companies Act 2006 contains for the first time a statutory statement of directors' duties: see Pt 10 Ch 2 (ss 170–181); and PARA 572 et seq. As to directors' fiduciary duties owed to the company see PARA 584 et seq.

2 Companies Act 2006 s 1157(1)(a). As to the meaning of 'officer' (which includes a director) see PARA 679. As to the meaning of 'company' under the Companies Acts see PARA 21; and as to the meaning of the 'Companies Acts' see PARA 13. As an officer of the company, an administrator could be protected under the Companies Act 2006 s 1157: *Re Home Treat Ltd* [1991] BCLC 705 (court protected the administrators by an order relieving them of any future claim against them)

(case decided under the Companies Act 1985 s 727). As to administrators see COMPANY AND PARTNERSHIP INSOLVENCY vol 16 (2011) PARA 158 et seq. However, given that the statutory definition of 'shadow director', which is specified for the purposes of the Companies Act (see PARA 513), is not incorporated by reference into the definition of 'officer' for those same purposes, it must follow that a shadow director cannot be relieved from liability under the statutory provisions: see *Ultraframe (UK) Ltd v Fielding, Northstar Systems Ltd v Fielding* [2005] EWHC 1638 (Ch) at [1452], [2005] All ER (D) 397 (Jul) per Lewison J.

3 As to the persons qualified to act as auditors see PARA 1060 et seq.

4 Companies Act 2006 s 1157(1)(b).

5 As to the meaning of 'the court' see PARA 160 note 12.

6 Failure to seek legal advice was held to be acting unreasonably in *Re Duomatic Ltd* [1969] 2 Ch 365, [1969] 1 All ER 161; as was the making of a payment which the directors had no power to make in *Gibson's Executor v Gibson* 1980 SLT 2, Ct of Sess. Questions of reasonableness may depend to some extent on past practice of the company: *Re Duomatic Ltd* [1969] 2 Ch 365 at 375, [1969] 1 All ER 161 at 170 per Buckley J.

The test of reasonableness is not subjective and it is questionable whether the test is subjective as regards honesty: *Bairstow v Queens Moat Houses plc* [2001] EWCA Civ 712 at [58], [2001] 2 BCLC 531 per Robert Walker LJ; cf *Coleman Taymar Ltd v Oakes* [2001] 2 BCLC 749 at 770 per Reid J; *Re Produce Marketing Consortium Ltd* [1989] 3 All ER 1 at 5–6, [1989] 1 WLR 745 at 749–751 per Knox J. See also *Re D'Jan of London Ltd* [1994] 1 BCLC 561 at 564 per Hoffmann LJ (conduct may be reasonable for this purpose despite falling short of the standard of reasonable care at common law); *Queensway Systems Ltd (in liquidation) v Walker* [2006] EWHC 2496 (Ch), [2007] 2 BCLC 577. It is not reasonable to improperly transfer company funds without regard to the interests of the company (*Extrasure Travel Insurances Ltd v Scattergood* [2002] EWHC 3093 (Ch), [2003] 1 BCLC 598; *Re In a Flap Envelope Co Ltd, Willmott v Jenkin* [2003] EWHC 3047 (Ch) at [63], [2004] 1 BCLC 64 per Jonathan Crow (sitting as a deputy judge of the High Court)); or to have the company enter into a one-sided agreement (*Re Duckwari plc* [1999] Ch 253, sub nom *Re Duckwari plc (No 2), Duckwari plc v Offerventure Ltd (No 2)* [1998] 2 BCLC 315, CA); or to make dividend payments without making provision for a possible tax liability (*Re Loquitur Ltd, IRC v Richmond* [2003] EWHC 999 (Ch) at [141], [2003] 2 BCLC 442 per Etherton J).

The burden of proving honesty and reasonableness is on those seeking relief: *Bairstow v Queens Moat Houses plc* [2001] EWCA Civ 712 at [58], [2001] 2 BCLC 531 per Robert Walker LJ; *Re Loquitur Ltd, IRC v Richmond* [2003] EWHC 999 (Ch) at [228], [2003] 2 BCLC 442 per Etherton J; *Re In a Flap Envelope Co Ltd, Willmott v Jenkin* [2003] EWHC 3047 (Ch) at [59], [2004] 1 BCLC 64 per Jonathan Crow (sitting as a deputy judge of the High Court). The requirements of honesty and reasonableness are not alternatives: *PNC Telecom plc v Thomas (No 2)* [2007] EWHC 2157 (Ch), [2008] 2 BCLC 95.

7 The test is whether the director had acted with the reasonable care and circumspection which could reasonably be expected of him in the circumstances: *PNC Telecom plc v Thomas (No 2)* [2007] EWHC 2157 (Ch), [2008] 2 BCLC 95. See also *Re J Franklin & Son Ltd* [1937] 4 All ER 43 (relief refused); *Selangor United Rubber Estates Ltd v Cradock (a bankrupt) (No 3)* [1968] 2 All ER 1073, [1968] 1 WLR 1555 (relief refused where directors acted blindly at the behest of a third party). In general, the wishes of the members (or, if the company is insolvent, its creditors) must be taken into account: *Re Barry and Staines Linoleum Ltd* [1934] Ch 227.

8 Companies Act 2006 s 1157(1). For these purposes, 'liability' includes liability to account for profits: *Coleman Taymar Ltd v Oakes* [2001] 2 BCLC 749; and see *First Global Media Group Ltd v Larkin* [2003] EWCA Civ 1765, [2003] All ER (D) 293 (Nov); *Queensway Systems Ltd (in liquidation) v Walker* [2006] EWHC 2496 (Ch), [2007] 2 BCLC 577 (director authorised arrangements or transactions such that she was liable even for those sums paid to or for the benefit of others rather than herself). Relief may be so granted only by the court in which the pending proceedings are taken (*Re Gilt Edge Safety Glass Ltd* [1940] Ch 495, [1940] 2 All ER 237); and it would require an exceptional case for a court to conclude on an interim application that it was appropriate to grant relief (*Equitable Life Assurance Society v Bowley* [2003] EWHC 2263 (Comm), [2004] 1 BCLC 180). The court is reluctant to exercise its discretion at the expense of the company's creditors: *Re Marini Ltd* [2003] EWHC 334 (Ch), [2004] BCC 172; *Inn Spirit Ltd v Burns* [2002] EWHC 1731 (Ch) at [30], [2002] 2 BCLC 780 per Rimer J; and see *Re Simmon Box (Diamonds) Ltd* [2000] BCC 275 at 288 (revsd on other grounds *Cohen v Selby* [2001] 1 BCLC 176, sub nom *Re Simmon Box (Diamonds) Ltd* [2002] BCC 82, CA). There can be no question of relief where a director holds company funds as a constructive trustee (*Guinness plc v Saunders* [1990] 2 AC 663, [1990] 1 All ER 652, HL); or where he has been found guilty of dishonestly preparing false accounts (*Bairstow v Queens Moat Houses plc* [2001] EWCA Civ 712 at [63], [2001] 2 BCLC 531 per Robert Walker LJ); and it would require an extremely

powerful case to persuade the court to exercise its discretion to relieve a director from liability if he has obtained a material personal benefit through a breach of duty (see *Re In a Flap Envelope Co Ltd, Willmott v Jenkin* [2003] EWHC 3047 (Ch) at [64], [2004] 1 BCLC 64 per Jonathan Crow (sitting as a deputy judge of the High Court). Relief is not available to a director against whom a liquidator has sought a contribution in the insolvent liquidation of the company under the Insolvency Act 1986 s 214 (see COMPANY AND PARTNERSHIP INSOLVENCY vol 17 (2011) PARA 872): *Re Produce Marketing Consortium Ltd* [1989] 3 All ER 1, [1989] 1 WLR 745; *Re Brian D Pierson (Contractors) Ltd* [2001] 1 BCLC 275 at 308–309 per Hazel Williamson QC. Where, as is usually the case, a director is paid for his services, the court is less disposed to give him relief than it would be to give it to a person acting gratuitously: *National Trustees Co of Australasia v General Finance Co of Australasia* [1905] AC 373 at 381, PC. See also *Re Welfab Engineers Ltd* [1990] BCLC 833 (directors who were alleged to have breached their duty by selling company's assets at an undervalue were held not to have acted in breach of that duty and, even if they had, it was a case where, having acted honestly and reasonably, they ought to be excused under the Companies Act 2006 s 1157) (case decided under the Companies Act 1985 s 727 (repealed)).

9 *Customs and Excise Comrs v Hedon Alpha Ltd* [1981] QB 818, [1981] 2 All ER 697, CA. See also *First Independent Factors & Finance v Mountford* [2008] EWHC 835 (Ch), [2008] 2 BCLC 297 (director, who was held personally liable for debts of phoenix company, could not seek relief under the Companies Act 2006 s 1157 as that provision does not apply to claims against directors brought by strangers (in this case, creditors)) (case decided under the Companies Act 1985 s 727 (repealed)). See also *IRC v McEntaggart* [2004] EWHC 3431 (Ch), [2006] 1 BCLC 476 (provisions for relief inapplicable to proceedings under the Company Directors Disqualification Act 1986 s 15 (see PARA 1808)).

10 See *IRC v McEntaggart* [2004] EWHC 3431 (Ch), [2006] 1 BCLC 476 (cited in note 9).

11 Ie in pursuance of the Companies Act 2006 s 1157(1) (see the text and notes 1–8): see s 1157(3).

12 Companies Act 2006 s 1157(3). The statutory provision need not be pleaded: see *Singlehurst v Tapscott Steamship Co Ltd* [1899] WN 133, CA; *Re Kirbys Coaches Ltd* [1991] BCLC 414. If, however, they are pleaded, no particulars of the plea can be ordered, since the plea could, with leave, be deleted and such leave would, on a proper exercise of discretion, be given; but the right to claim relief would continue, even if the plea were deleted: *Re Kirbys Coaches Ltd* [1991] BCLC 414

13 Companies Act 2006 s 1157(2). This provision is directed only to future proceedings and does not apply to proceedings which have been commenced and are pending before another court: *Re Gilt Edge Safety Glass Ltd* [1940] Ch 495, [1940] 2 All ER 237.

14 Companies Act 2006 s 1157(2)(a). As to applications made to the court under the Companies Act 2006 see generally PARA 306.

Approval is not required under s 197 (see PARA 610), s 198 (see PARA 611), s 200 (see PARA 612), or s 201 (see PARA 613) for anything done by a company to provide a director of the company or of its holding company with funds to meet expenditure incurred or to be incurred by him in connection with an application for relief under s 1157: see s 205; and PARA 615.

The statutory prohibition on a company, either directly or indirectly, providing third party indemnity (to any extent) for a director of the company, or of an associated company, against any liability attaching to him in connection with any negligence, default, breach of duty or breach of trust in relation to the company of which he is a director applies to an application for relief under s 1157 in which the court refuses to grant him relief: see s 234; and PARA 641. Section 532 (voidness of provisions protecting auditors from liability) (see PARA 1052) does not prevent a company from indemnifying an auditor against any liability incurred by him in connection with an application under s 1157 in which relief is granted to him by the court: see s 533; and PARA 1053.

15 Companies Act 2006 s 1157(2)(b).

16 *Re Claridge's Patent Asphalte Co Ltd* [1921] 1 Ch 543.

17 *Re Barry and Staines Linoleum Ltd* [1934] Ch 227.

18 *Re Gilt Edge Safety Glass Ltd* [1940] Ch 495, [1940] 2 All ER 237.

19 As to qualification shares see PARA 531 et seq.

INDEX

Companies

References are to paragraph numbers; superior figures refer to notes

Words and Phrases

Words in parentheses indicate the context in which the word or phrase is used

References are to paragraph numbers; superior figures refer to notes